THE LEGAL
AND REGULATORY
ENVIRONMENT
OF BUSINESS

THE LEGAL AND REGULATORY ENVIRONMENT OF BUSINESS

Henry R. Cheeseman
University of Southern California

MACMILLAN PUBLISHING COMPANY
New York

COLLIER MACMILLAN PUBLISHERS
London

Macmillan Publishing Company
866 Third Avenue, New York, New York 10022

Collier Macmillan Canada, Inc.

Library of Congress Cataloging in Publication Data

Cheeseman, Henry R.
  The legal and regulatory environment of business.

  Includes index.
  1. Industrial laws and legislation—United States.
2. Trade regulation—United States.   I. Title.
KF1600.C45 1985   343.73'07   84–17113
ISBN 0-02-322260-3   347.3037

Printing: 1 2 3 4 5 6 7 8   Year: 5 6 7 8 9 0 1 2 3

ISBN 0-02-322260-3

Love is measured by the freedom
accorded its participants

PREFACE

This book has been written primarily for Legal Environment courses in a Business School curriculum. Its main focus is on the government's attempt to regulate business through *public law.* The title of this book, *The Legal and Regulatory Environment of Business,* describes its coverage and reflects the importance of administrative agency regulations on business decisions and activities. This book leaves for traditional business law courses coverage of *private law* topics such as contracts and the Uniform Commercial Code. Of course, where public law and private law overlap (e.g., in corporation law), and where the public law aspects of an area outweigh its private law aspects, that area has been included in this book.

The study of law, particularly public law and government regulation, is as much a study of social responsibility, ethics, policy, and economics as it is a study of legal rules. All public law is enacted to serve a stated social policy—for example, to prevent discrimination or to protect consumers. Some public laws are enacted to force business to meet its social responsibility (e.g., environmental protection laws), while other public laws are passed to outlaw unethical conduct (e.g., laws prohibiting white-collar crime). All public laws and regulations cause certain economic consequences, some detrimental to the profitability of business, such as the prohibition against price fixing, and some beneficial to American business, such as tariffs.

AACSB Accreditation Standards. The American Assembly of Collegiate Schools of Business (AACSB) has established accreditation standards for business schools which require that policy, ethics, economics, and the social responsibility of business be integrated into business school curriculums. AACSB Standard IV(b) provides that a Business School curriculum should include

a background of the economic and legal environment as it pertains to profit and/or nonprofit organizations along with ethical considerations and social and political influences as they affect such organizations . . .

It would be difficult to integrate these issues in many traditional and specialized courses in the business school curriculum (e.g., statistics, accounting, finance courses). However, these issues may best be integrated into a business school curriculum in a Legal Environment course, where actual legal cases in which businesses have found themselves embroiled are examined, many of which involve breaches of the legal, ethical, and social responsibilities of business.

Coverage of Social Responsibility, Ethics, Policy, and Economics Issues in this Book.   A few legal environment textbooks have attempted to cover social responsibility and ethics issues, but usually only by attaching a chapter to the end of the book, or a few paragraphs at the end of a chapter. A few of these books also attempt to cover policy issues but usually in the same fashion, and no legal environment book currently covers the economic consequences of public law and regulation. I feel this fragmentary coverage is insufficient to meet the needs of students or the charge of the AACSB. In this book I have presented what I believe to be the most extensive and *integrated* coverage of social responsibility, ethics, policy, and economic issues of any legal environment book currently available.

First, "The Social Responsibility of Business" is presented as the *second* chapter in this book. Its placement at this juncture of the book is deliberate— to provide a setting for the study of social responsibility and ethics throughout the remainder of the book. Unlike most social responsibility chapters in legal environment books, which present a few quotations on ethics or social responsibility in isolation without any application to actual cases, this chapter presents actual cases on some of the most important legal issues presently facing American business. For example, *Silkwood v. Kerr-McGee Corporation* examines the involvement of business in the major social issue of the 1980s, nuclear power. *Sindell v. Abbott Laboratories* examines the market share liability of the manufacturers of the drug DES, for the effects of the drug upon the daughters of women who took it during their pregnancies 30 years earlier. Also covered are the Johns-Manville Corporation petition to reorganize under the protection of the Bankruptcy Court in order to avoid liability for all the injuries caused by asbestosis contracted from the products it manufactured and the Dalkon Shield case, which caused severe injury, infertility, and abortions to women who used the product.

Second, an *eight-chapter sequence* has been written, in two parts, primarily emphasizing the social responsibility and ethical considerations of business. Part IV, "The Social Responsibility of Business," is a four-chapter section that covers such topics as environmental protection, regulation of the safety of foods, drugs, and cosmetics, the civil liability of manufacturers and distributors for defective products under the doctrine of strict liability in tort, debtor–creditor relations and debt collection practices, and bankruptcy liquidations and reorganizations. Part V, "Ethical Considerations in Business," is another four-chapter sequence that covers deceptive and unfair advertising by business, infringement of trademarks, copyrights and patents, misappropriation of trade secrets and ideas, product disparagement, unfair competition and other business torts, and state and federal white-collar crimes.

Third, social responsibility, ethics, policy, and economics issues are wholly integrated in this book, in that *every* case is followed by case questions that will stimulate discussion of the factual and legal issues of the case, and also by separate *policy issue, economics issue, ethics issue,* and *social responsibility* questions. These questions are relevant to class discussions of the particular case and are not left for an isolated discussion at the end of the chapter or book. No other legal environment text so thoroughly integrates these important issues throughout the book.

Trend of the Law. A legal environment course should not only present the law as it is and has been but also provide its students with a feeling of where the law is headed in the future. For this reason the book includes a separate section entitled "Trend of the Law" as the final topic in each chapter. No other legal environment book currently contains a similar section. Like any estimate or projection, the "Trend of the Law" sections in this book obviously reflect my own experiences, biases, and opinions. However, these sections meet their important goals of stimulating student thinking and class discussion. Each professor should present his or her own view of what the future of the law holds for the area being covered.

Subjects Covered. This book is organized according to the subject areas of public law that regulate the activities of business. It is divided into six main parts, each of which contains several related chapters. Each chapter is organized with an Introduction, which discusses the business setting and history of the area of the law covered, followed by text and cases applying the legal principles of the chapter. Chapters usually contain six to eight cases carefully selected and edited to present modern applications of the legal issues covered. As previously discussed, each case is followed by relevant policy, economics, ethics, and social responsibility questions, and each chapter contains a final section on the "Trend of the Law." Following each chapter are approximately ten Review Questions, which give the facts of actual cases decided by the courts in the area of the law discussed and require short essays as answers.

This book contains several chapters on areas not covered in many other legal environment books but that are expanding and modern areas of business law which are important for many business students to know. These chapters are Franchising (Chapter 12), Proxy Contests and Tender Offers (Chapter 15), Commodities Regulation (Chapter 16), Bankruptcy (Chapter 20), Trademarks, Copyrights, and Patents (Chapter 22), and Business Crimes (Chapter 24).

Use of These Materials in Diverse Teaching Formats. With the view that a short book designed to be taught straight through would be unsatisfactory for many users, I have written the most comprehensive and diverse legal environment and regulation book available, believing that each professor will design a course that best serves his or her interests, the curriculum requirements of the school, and the needs of his or her students. All the materials in this book can be covered in a two-quarter or two-semester course. In designing a one-quarter or one-semester course, the professor is provided the flexibility to emphasize traditional legal environment subjects, or to design courses that emphasize social responsibility and ethical considerations of business, regulation, finance, accounting, marketing, or management topics. The majority of the subjects covered in this book also are tested on the C.P.A. examination. Several chapters contain special sections entitled "Accountant's Liability" to highlight materials pertinent to C.P.A. students.

The materials in this book have particularly been designed to stimulate class discussions through the use of the Socratic method of teaching. Naturally, because of the breadth and depth of coverage, this book is also extremely effective for a lecture format course. A glossary of important legal terms and the Table of Cases appear before the general index at the back of the book.

Package.   This text is accompanied by an Instructor's Manual that includes answers to the end-of-chapter Review Questions, and an extensive test bank. A Student Guide is available to assist students in the mastering of the material presented in the text.

Acknowledgments.   I wish to express my appreciation to the following persons: Lawrence VandenBos, who has prepared the *Student Guide* to accompany this book; the professionals of Macmillan Publishing Company with whom it has been a pleasure writing this book, including: David Forgione, whose enthusiasm originally persuaded me to choose Macmillan; Chip Price, who smoothed over many rough edges; Jack Repcheck, my current editor at Macmillan, whose encouragement was necessary; Hurd Hutchins, who shepherded the manuscript through production and design; Camilla Hewitt, the copy editor, almost all of whose excellent suggestions I accepted.

I also thank the following institutions and places: the University of Southern California, where I have taught graduate and undergraduate Legal Environment courses since 1978, and its students; the law libraries of Los Angeles, namely those of the U.S.C., UCLA, and Whittier Schools of Law; and Sun Valley, Idaho, under whose clear skies most of the text of this book was written. I also thank Molly and McKay for their companionship.

I would also like to thank those who reviewed this text in manuscript form. The conscientious comments of the following instructors helped to refine the focus of the final product: Marianne Jennings of Arizona State University, Kurtis Klumb of the University of Wisconsin-Milwaukee, Donald Hall of California State University-Los Angeles, Sandra Hurd of Syracuse University, William Clarritt of Rutgers University-Newark, Harold Hotelling of the University of Kentucky, Ralph Quinones of the University of Wisconsin-Oshkosh, S. Jay Sklar of Temple University, Howard Ward of the University of Detroit, Daphyne Saunders of James Madison University, Ronald Singer of the University of Wisconsin-Parkside, J. Fred Hamblen of East Carolina University, Frank Land of the University of North Carolina at Greensboro, Jan Henkel of the University of Georgia, and Jeffrey Cross of Montclair State College.

At the writing of this Preface I have spent over two thousand hours preparing this manuscript. I loved every minute, and the knowledge gained has been sufficient reward for the endeavor. I hope this book will serve you well.

H.R.C.

BRIEF CONTENTS

DETAILED CONTENTS

II ANTITRUST LAW 161

III   SECURITIES REGULATION   303

IV THE SOCIAL RESPONSIBILITY OF BUSINESS   423

INTRODUCTION FOR THE STUDENT

The study of law differs considerably from the study of many other business topics. First, there are no numbers, no equations, no formulas. Therefore there are no precise answers. For some students this may be a blessing, for others a curse. Second, unlike many other academic subjects, the study of law is "relevant." The cases in this book are actual fact situations and lawsuits in which real business executives have found themselves embroiled. Generally, in each case one of the parties wins and the other loses, often large sums of money, and occasionally fines or imprisonment are imposed.

Third, business does not operate in a vacuum. Unlike many theory courses, the study of law involves the study of emotions, sociology, penology, economics, policy, ethics, and social responsibility. The cases and materials in this book are designed to present the substantive rules of public law, and to promote discussion of the policies, economics, ethics, and social responsibility of business underlying legal disputes.

This book is written for you, the student. Learning should be enjoyable as well as rewarding. In this book I have attempted to present to you the most important legal issues and cases facing a business executive today. The cases and materials are meant to be analyzed, discussed, even argued if necessary. If your professor merely requires you to memorize the Black Letter rules of the law, without discussion of the legal issues and cases, you are being demeaned as nothing more than a large parrot. To get the most out of this course, argue with your professor and fellow students. It may be the most rewarding experience of your academic life.

KEY TERMS

Before you embark upon the study of law, you should know the following key legal terms.

Plaintiff. The "plaintiff" is the party who originally brought the lawsuit.

Defendant. The "defendant" is the party against who the lawsuit has been brought.

Petitioner or Appellant. The "petitioner," often also referred to as the "appellant," is the party who has appealed the decision of the trial court or lower court. The petitioner may be either the plaintiff or defendant, depending on who lost the case at the trial court or lower court level.

Respondent or Appellee.   The "respondent," often referred to as the "appellee," is the party who must answer the petitioner's appeal. The respondent may be either the plaintiff or defendant, depending upon which party is the petitioner. In some cases, both the plaintiff *and* the defendant may disagree with the trial court or lower court's decision, and both parties may appeal the decision.

Name of the Case on Appeal.   The name of the case is set forth in bold letters above the text of each case presented in this book. The case name usually contains the names of the parties to the lawsuit. However, where there are multiple plaintiffs or defendants, some of the names of the parties may be omitted from the case name. Abbreviations are also often used in case names. The sequence of names in a case name does not necessarily reflect the plaintiff and defendant, or petitioner and respondent, in any set order. Appellate courts differ as to whether they leave the case name with the plaintiff's name first, or whether on appeal the petitioner's name (i.e., the former defendant's name) appears first. The text of the case should be referred to in order to properly determine the status of the parties in the case.

Case Citation.   The case *citation* consists of a number such as "104 S.Ct. 774" as set forth below the case names in this book. The case citation identifies the book in the law library in which the case may be found. For example, the case in the above citation may be found in Volume 104 of the *Supreme Court Reporter* at page 774. The year and the name of the court that decided the case are presented below the case name for each case presented in this book.

Affirm.   A higher court may *affirm* the decision of the lower court. Where the reviewing court affirms the lower court's decision, it agrees with the decision issued by the lower court. The winning party at the lower court level remains the winning party in the decision of the reviewing court.

Reverse.   A higher court may *reverse* the decision of the lower court. Where the reviewing court reverses the decision of the lower court, it disagrees with the decision reached by the lower court. Where the reviewing court reverses the lower court's decision, the losing party at the lower court level becomes the winning party at the higher court level, and *vice versa*.

Remand.   Often on appeal the higher court, when it announces its decision, will *remand* the case back to the trial court for further proceedings consistent with the opinion issued by the reviewing court. For example, where the lower court makes an error in interpreting a law, the reviewing court may issue an opinion that corrects the error in interpretation and remand the case back to the trial court for a new trial based on the correct interpretation of the law.

BRIEFING A CASE

The court decisions presented in this book are usually those made by appellate or supreme courts. Trial court decisions are hardly ever presented. The reason for this is that it is the appellate courts and supreme courts of this country which are charged with interpreting the law. Their decisions usually become precedent for lower courts to use when deciding individual legal disputes in the future. Since actual decisions of the courts may be long, often over 50 pages, the cases presented in this book have been highly edited. The editing was done with a goal of succinctly presenting the most important legal issue of each case for review by the student.

It is often helpful for a student to "brief" a case in order to clarify the legal issues involved and to gain a better understanding of the case. Briefing a case generally consists of making a summary of each of the following items of the case.

Facts. The important facts of a case should be stated briefly. Extraneous facts and facts of minor importance should be omitted from the brief. The facts of the case are usually set forth at the beginning of the case, but not necessarily. Important facts may be found throughout the case. Diagrams are often helpful to keep the parties of the lawsuit straight.

Issue. It is crucial in the briefing of a case to identify the *issue* presented to the court to decide. The issue on appeal is most often a legal question, although questions of fact are sometimes the subject of an appeal. The issue presented in each case is usually quite specific, and should be asked in a question form. For example, the issue statement, "Is Mary liable?" is too broad. A more proper statement of the issue would be, "Is Mary liable to Joe for breach of the contract made between them based on her refusal to make the payment due on September 30 as agreed in the contract?"

Lower Court Decision. In order to properly understand a case, the student should know the decision of the lower court—for example, which party won and why. Most of the cases in this book set forth the decision of the lower court. Some cases do not set forth the trial or lower court decision where it is unnecessary for the understanding of the issue on appeal.

Appellate Court Decision (if applicable). Often, the decision of the trial court may have already been appealed to an intermediate appellate court. If there has been such an appeal, the student should know the decision of the intermediate appellate court, which is now being appealed to a higher court.

Holding. The "holding" is the decision reached by the present court. The holding should state which party won and what remedy the court has awarded.

Reasoning. When an appellate court or supreme court issues a decision, which is often called an "opinion," the court will normally state the reasoning it used in reaching its decision. The rationale for the decision may be based on the specific facts of the case, public policy, prior law, and other matters.

The reasoning of the court may appear anywhere in the case, but often appears towards the end of the decision.

If these items are contained in a student's brief of a case, he or she should have a sufficient understanding of the case to discuss it thoroughly in class.

The following case, *Sony Corporation of America v. Universal City Studios,* is presented as an illustrative judicial decision. A sample brief of this decision is presented following the case.

SAMPLE JUDICIAL DECISION

SONY CORPORATION OF AMERICA *et al.* v. UNIVERSAL CITY STUDIOS, INC. *et al.*

104 S.Ct. 774 (1984)
UNITED STATES SUPREME COURT

Justice Stevens delivered the opinion of the Court.

The two respondents in this action, Universal Studios, Inc. and Walt Disney Productions, produce and hold the copyrights on a substantial number of motion pictures and other audiovisual works. In the current marketplace, they can exploit their rights in these works in a number of ways: by authorizing theatrical exhibitions, by licensing limited showings on cable and network television, by selling syndication rights for repeated airings on local television stations, and by marketing programs on prerecorded videotapes or videodiscs. Some works are suitable for exploitation through all of these avenues, while the market for other works is more limited.

Petitioner Sony manufactures millions of Betamax video tape recorders [VTR's] and markets these devices through numerous retail establishments, some of which are also petitioners in this action.

THE DISTRICT COURT'S DECISION

The District Court concluded that noncommercial home use recording of material broadcast over the public airwaves was a fair use of copyrighted works and did not constitute copyright infringement. It emphasized the fact that the material was broadcast free to the public at large, the noncommercial character of the use, and the private character of the activity conducted entirely within the home.

The District Court assumed that Sony had con-structive knowledge of the probability that the Beta-max machine would be used to record copyrighted programs, but found that Sony merely sold a "product capable of a variety of uses, some of them allegedly infringing." It reasoned:

> Selling a staple article of commerce—*e.g.,* a typewriter, a recorder, a camera, a photocopying machine—technically contributes to any infringing use subsequently made thereof, but this kind of 'contribution,' if deemed sufficient as a basis for liability, would expand the theory beyond precedent and arguably beyond judicial management.
>
> Commerce would indeed be hampered if manufacturers of staple items were held liable as contributory infringers whenever they 'constructively' knew that some purchasers on some occasions would use their product for a purpose which a court later deemed, as a matter of first impression, to be an infringement.

THE COURT OF APPEALS' DECISION

The Court of Appeals reversed the District Court's judgment on respondents' copyright claim. It did not set aside any of the District Court's findings of fact. Rather, it concluded as a matter of law that the home use of a VTR was not a fair use because it was not a "productive use."

On the issue of contributory infringement, the Court of Appeals first rejected the analogy to staple articles of commerce such as tape recorders or photocopying machines. . . . VTR's, however, are sold "for the primary purpose of reproducing television programming" and "virtually all" such programming is copyrighted material. The Court of Appeals concluded, therefore, that VTR's were not suitable for any substantial noninfringing use even if some copyright owners elect not to enforce their rights.

[*THE U. S. SUPREME COURT'S DECISION*]

Article I, Sec. 8 of the Constitution provides that:

> The Congress shall have Power . . . to Promote the Progress of Science and useful Arts, by securing for limited Times to Authors and Inventors the exclusive Right to their respective Writings and Discoveries.

It is intended to motivate the creative activity of authors and inventors by the provision of a special reward, and to allow the public access to the products of their genius after the limited period of exclusive control has expired.

Respondents argue . . . for the proposition that supplying the "means" to accomplish an infringing activity and encouraging that activity through advertisement are sufficient to establish liability for copyright infringement. This argument rests on a gross generalization that cannot withstand scrutiny. . . . Petitioners in the instant case do not supply Betamax consumers with respondents' works; respondents do. Petitioners supply a piece of equipment that is generally capable of copying the entire range of programs that may be televised: those that are uncopyrighted, those that are copyrighted but may be copied without objection from the copyright holder, and those that the copyright holder would prefer not to have copied. The Betamax can be used to make authorized or unauthorized uses of copyrighted works, . . .

The only contact between Sony and the users of the Betamax that is disclosed by this record occurred at the moment of sale. . . . Accordingly, the sale of copying equipment, like the sale of other articles of commerce, does not constitute contributory infringement if the product is widely used for legitimate, unobjectionable purposes. Indeed, it need merely be capable of substantial noninfringing uses.

When these factors are all weighed in the "equitable rule of reason" balance, we must conclude that this record amply supports the District Court's conclusion that home time-shifting is fair use. In light of the findings of the District Court regarding the state of the empirical data, it is clear that the Court of Appeals erred in holding that the statute as presently written bars such conduct.

One may search the Copyright Act in vain for any sign that the elected representatives of the millions of people who watch television every day have made it unlawful to copy a program for later viewing at home, or have enacted a flat prohibition against the sale of machines that make such copying possible.

It may well be that Congress will take a fresh look at this new technology, just as it so often has examined other innovations in the past. But it is not our job to apply laws that have not yet been written. Applying the copyright statute, as it now reads, to the facts as they have been developed in this case, the judgment of the Court of Appeals must be reversed.

Justice Blackmun, with whom **Justice Marshall, Justice Powell,** and **Justice Rehnquist** join, dissenting.

It may be tempting, as, in my view, the Court today is tempted, to stretch the doctrine of fair use so as to permit unfettered use of this new technology in order to increase access to television programming. But such an extension risks eroding the very basis of copyright law, by depriving authors of control over their works and consequently of their incentive to create. . . . Like so many other problems created by the interaction of copyright law with a new technology, "[t]here can be no really satisfactory solution to the problem presented here, until Congress acts."

Case Brief: *Sony Corp. v. Universal City Studios, Inc.*

1. Citation: 104 S.Ct. 774
   Year: 1984
   Court: U.S. Supreme Court
2. Plaintiffs: Universal City Studios, Walt Disney Productions, and other producers of copyrighted television programs.

3. Defendants: Sony Corporation of America and other manufacturers of video tape recorders.

4. Facts: The defendants produce and distribute Betamax and other video tape recorders, which are purchased and used by consumers to tape copyrighted television programs. Consumers most often tape copyrighted television programs for time-shifting purposes, although some taping of the programs is for commercial purposes. The plaintiffs produce copyrighted television programs that are copied by consumers and others on the defendants' video recorders.

5. Issue: Did the defendants engage in contributory infringement in violation of federal copyright law?

6. Lower Court: The trial court, the Federal District Court, held for the defendants.

7. Appellate Court: The intermediate appellate court, the Federal Court of Appeals, reversed, holding for the plaintiffs.

8. Holding: In a 5–4 decision the U.S. Supreme Court reversed, and affirmed the original decision of the Federal District Court, holding that the defendants were not liable for contributory copyright infringement.

9. Reasoning: The defendants manufactured and distributed a product that could be used to copy uncopyrighted material, and for both the authorized and unauthorized copying of copyrighted materials. The majority of the purchasers of the defendants' video tape recorders used the equipment to copy copyrighted materials for "time-shifting" purposes. This use qualified for the "fair use" exception for copying copyrighted material. Therefore, if the users of the defendants' products are not liable for copyright infringement under the "fair use" doctrine, then the defendants are not liable for contributory copyright infringement for selling the video tape recorders to such users.

THE LEGAL FRAMEWORK OF BUSINESS

1 THE NATURE OF LAW

INTRODUCTION

In order to facilitate the peaceful coexistence of individuals and the orderly development of commerce, each society, no matter how simple or complex, must develop and enforce certain rules to govern the conduct of the individuals and organizations within it. Such rules become the "law" of the society. Originally, rules of law were only informal traditions of society or "gentlemen's agreements" between private parties. Eventually, these informal rules were formalized either by judicial decisions or by legislative pronouncements.

Although the laws of different societies may vary considerably (e.g., socialist societies, communist societes, democracies), without law, and its equal enforcement, the structure of any society would break down into utter chaos. Judge Learned Hand, in *The Spirit of Liberty*, said:

Without it [law] we cannot live; only with it can we insure the future which by right is ours. The best of men's hopes are enmeshed in its success; when it [law] fails it [men's hopes] fail; the measure in which it can reconcile our passions, our wills, our conflicts, is the measure of our opportunity to find ourselves.

In order to function within a society, a person should have a firm grasp of the specific "laws" which regulate his conduct, both in his personal life and in his business transactions. *Ignorantia juris quod quisque tenetur scire, neminem excusat*—ignorance of the law excuses no man! If ignorance of the law excused a person for breaking the law, would you be taking this course?

9

THE NATURE OF LAW

"Law" is a very broad concept for which a precise definition is difficult to state. *Black's Law Dictionary* (fifth ed.) provides these two definitions:

1. Law, in its generic sense, is a body of rules of action or conduct prescribed by controlling authority, and having binding legal force.
2. That which must be obeyed and followed by citizens subject to sanctions or legal consequences is a law.

In many legal disputes there is no "right" or "wrong" side. Both parties to the lawsuit may have valid legal rights that they are attempting to assert or defend. The function of the court is to balance these competing legal rights and reach a decision in the individual case before it. Judge Joseph Sedita discussed competing legal rights in *Kramer v. Kramer,* 444 N.Y.S.2d 991 (1981):

. . . Each person has a duty in society to avoid breaches of other persons' zones of personal freedom and power, which we refer to as their "rights." A unique problem arises, however, in that bubbling cauldron of social interactions which we call society. The problem arises when individual zones of freedom and power (rights) overlap. In these cases the law must determine who had the "superior" right. A person whose lesser right is infringed by a superior right ordinarily has no claim for damages . . . because the superior right creates a corresponding duty to observe that superior right. The person exercising the superior right has not acted beyond his or her zone of personal freedom and is therefore not liable for a breach of duty to another. Upon these basic principles, the law seeks to adjust rights and fairly compensate those whose rights have been breached by a failure to observe the duties imposed by life in society. . . .

The process of "sorting out" hierarchies of competing rights is many times a difficult and complex enterprise within the framework of our adversarial system.

CLASSIFICATIONS OF THE LAW

The study of law requires that students learn to properly "classify" the law. Such classification makes the study of law much more manageable. The major classifications of law are:

Public Law and Private Law. *Public law* affects the relationship between an individual or a business and the *government.* Most public law regulates and sets limits on the activities of natural persons and fictitious legal persons (corporations) in society. Constitutional law, antitrust law, securities regulation, consumer protection law, environmental protection law, and other regulatory and administrative law are examples of public law. This book concentrates on the study of public law.

Private law consists of those laws that affect dealings between *individuals* in society. Contract law, property law, agency and partnership law, the law of sales and negotiable instruments, etc., are examples of private law. Private law allocates rights and duties by voluntary agreement between individuals. Traditional business law textbooks emphasize the study of private law.

Some laws are considered both public and private law, for example corporate law. Corporations are created by a grant from the government and are regulated by the government, but they also order and allocate individual rights among the members of society.

Criminal Law and Civil Law. One of the major classification of law is between *criminal law* and *civil law*. Criminal law is usually defined by the legislature, and concerns wrongs committed against society as a whole, e.g., murder or burglary. Under criminal law, the state seeks redress against a criminal for violating the public trust, and seeks a penalty (e.g., fine, imprisonment) for the commission of the criminal act.

Civil law is generally defined as "that law whereby an individual sues another individual for some alleged wrong committed against him." Civil suits may be for a breach of contract, for negligence in running into someone with an automobile, for libel or slander, and so forth. In a civil lawsuit, the complaining party is seeking some sort of remedy, usually an award of money damages, for the injury he has been caused by the other party's actions.

Substantive Law and Procedural Law. *Substantive law* consists of the court decisions, statutes, rules, and regulations that set forth and create legal *rights* and *obligations* in society. Laws against murder, decisions allowing persons to freely contract together, and statutes prohibiting price-fixing are all examples of substantive law. Substantive law can be subclassified into categories affecting specific subject matters, e.g., law of contracts, corporation law, partnership law, antitrust law, criminal law.

Procedural law consists of establishing the *methods* for enforcing the rights created by substantive law. Procedural law covers how to initiate a lawsuit, determining the proper court, what documents should be filed and when, how to call witnesses, etc. In *Kramer v. Kramer*, cited above, Judge Sedita discussed the importance of procedural law, stating:

. . . We arm each combatant with certain procedural rights which may be exercised (so as long as they are not abused) under judicial supervision. When properly utilized, they may be temporarily superior to a substantive right tentatively asserted at the inception and during the pendency of litigation.

Other classifications of law are possible. Each student is encouraged to make his own classifications and subclassifications ("pigeonholes") for an organized and efficient study of the law.

THEORIES OF THE LAW

A *theory* is a specific set of principles that explains (predicts) the occurrence of a certain phenomenon. Several theories of law have been advanced, including the following.

1. *Moral theory:* the law developed based on what was "correct." St. Thomas Aquinas asserted that such morality-based law came from a divine source. Other philosophers have believed that the ultimate morality, and thus law, developed from the nature of human beings.
2. *Historical theory:* the law is really an aggregation of the traditions and customs of our society as they have developed over the ages.
3. *Command theory:* the law is merely a set of rules as developed and communicated by the ruling political entity or system, for violation of which penalties are provided.
4. *Sociological theory:* the law is really a means of social control, whereby the competing classes and values of society are balanced.
5. *Economic:* as the world developed into a complex commercial and industrial society, laws developed to protect, limit, or promote the economic interests of persons within a society.

Although no single theory seems to explain the past development of law, a combination of theories, or the use of different theories at different times or under different political systems, may help to predict the development of the law in the future. It is generally believed that the law becomes fairer and more consistent over time, as unfair laws are continually being challenged and replaced by more just laws.

In *The Queen v. Dudley and Stephens* the English court used the morality theory of the law to justify its decision.

MORALITY AND THE LAW

THE QUEEN v. DUDLEY AND STEPHENS

14 Q.B.D. 273 (1884)
QUEEN'S BENCH DIVISION

Indictment for the murder of Richard Parker on the high seas within the jurisdiction of the Admiralty.

At the trial before **Huddleston, B.,** at the Devon and Cornwall Winter Assizes, November 7, 1884, the jury, at the suggestion of the learned judge, found the facts of the case in a special verdict which stated "that on July 5, 1884, the prisoners, Thomas Dudley and Edward Stephens, with one Brooks, all able-bodied English seamen, and the deceased also an English boy, between seventeen and eighteen years of age, the crew of an English yacht, a registered English vessel, were cast away in a storm on the high seas 1600 miles from the Cape of Good Hope, and were compelled to put into an open boat belonging to the said yacht. That in this boat they had no supply of water and no supply of food, except two 1lb. tins of turnips, and for three days they had nothing else to subsist upon. That

on the fourth day they caught a small turtle, upon which they subsisted for a few days, . . . That on the twelfth day the remains of the turtle were entirely consumed, and for the next eight days they had nothing to eat. That they had no fresh water, except such rain as they from time to time caught in their oilskin capes. That the boat was drifting on the ocean, and was probably more than 1000 miles away from land.

That . . . [on the twentieth day], no vessel appearing, Dudley told Brooks that he had better go and have a sleep, and made signs to Stephens and Brooks that the boy had better be killed. The prisoner Stephens agreed to the act, but Brooks dissented from it. That the boy was then lying at the bottom of the boat quite helpless, and extremely weakened by famine and by drinking sea water, and unable to make any resistance, nor did he ever assent to his being killed. The prisoner Dudley offered a prayer asking forgiveness for them all if either of them should be tempted to commit a rash act, and that their souls might be saved. That Dudley, with the assent of Stephens, went to the boy, and telling him that his time was come, put a knife into his throat and killed him then and there; that the three men fed upon the body and blood of the boy for four days; that on the fourth day after the act had been committed the boat was picked up by a passing vessel, and the prisoners were rescued, still alive, but in the lowest state of prostration.

With regard to the substantial question in the case—whether the prisoners in killing Parker were guilty of murder—the law is that where a private person acting upon his own judgment takes the life of a fellow creature, his act can only be justified on the ground of self-defence—self-defence against the acts of the person whose life is taken. This principle has been extended to include the case of a man killing another to prevent him from committing some great crime upon a third person. But the principle has no application to this case, for the prisoners were not protecting themselves against any act of Parker.

Though law and morality are not the same, and many things may be immoral which are not necessarily illegal, yet the absolute divorce of law from morality would be of fatal consequence; and such divorce would follow if the temptation to murder in this case were to be held by law an absolute defence of it. It is not so. To preserve one's life is generally speaking a duty, but it may be the plainest and the highest duty to sacrifice it. War is full of instances in which it is a man's duty not to live, but to die. The duty, in case of shipwreck, of a captain to his crew, of the crew to the passengers, of soldiers to women and children, as in the noble case of the *Birkenhead;* these duties impose on men the moral necessity, not of the preservation, but of the sacrifice of their lives for others, from which in no country, least of all, it is to be hoped, in England, will men ever shrink, as indeed, they have not shrunk. It is not correct, therefore, to say that there is any absolute or unqualified necessity to preserve one's life. . . .

We are often compelled to set up standards we cannot reach ourselves, and to lay down rules which we could not ourselves satisfy. But a man has no right to declare temptation to be an excuse, though he might himself have yielded to it, nor allow compassion for the criminal to change or weaken in any manner the legal definition of the crime. It is therefore our duty to declare that the prisoners' act in this case was wilful murder, that the facts as stated in the verdict are no legal justification of the homicide; and to say that in our unanimous opinion the prisoners are upon this special verdict *guilty* of murder. . . .

The Court then proceeded to pass sentence of death upon the prisoners.

CASE QUESTIONS

1. Did Dudley and Stephens have a right to live? Did Parker have a right to live? Who had the "superior" right? The "inferior" right?
2. Was this case an instance of the application of:
   a. substantive law or procedural law?
   b. public law or private law?
   c. criminal law or civil law?
3. Which theory(ies) of law applied in this case?
   a. Moral theory
   b. Historical theory
   c. Command theory
   d. Sociological theory
   e. Economic theory
   If more than one theory applied, which was the dominant theory?
4. Why wasn't Brooks charged with the murder of Parker in this case? Did Brooks eat the boy to stay alive? Should this have been a crime?

Policy Issue. Should society establish legal standards that mortal men cannot meet?

Ethics Issue. If you were Dudley or Stephens, what would you have done? Would this have been ethical? Legal?

Social Responsibility.
a. Should one man give his life so that two others may live?
b. Would the decision in this case have been different if the persons in the boat had drawn lots to see who should be killed?

NOTE: The Queen commuted the death sentence of the defendants to six months in prison.

FUNCTIONS OF THE LAW

It is often appropriate to define the law by its functions within a society. These functions generally are:

1. *Keeping the peace:* preventing chaotic and violent disturbances (e.g., crime, revolution) by which innocent persons or their property may be injured or destroyed.
2. *Shaping and enforcing moral standards of conduct:* helping to initiate and facilitate social development, for example by discouraging drug use.
3. *Promoting social justice:* using the force of law and government to promote and guarantee equal access to social, political, and economic opportunities and benefits to all (e.g., by prohibiting discrimination).
4. *Maintaining the status quo:* the enforcement of the law tends to promote and maintain the existing status quo of society.
5. *Facilitating orderly change:* in a society that is continuously changing to meet new social problems, technological developments, and so on, the law provides a means to initiate changes in the rules of society in an orderly manner.
6. *Facilitating planning:* by having a well developed set of rules, the law provides the basis for individuals and businesses to plan their activities in a lawful manner.
7. *Providing the basis for compromise:* the law encourages the peaceful compromise and settlement of disputes and provides an objective forum (the court system) to hear and decide disputes.
8. *Maximizing individual freedom:* a rational and well-established but not overly restrictive set of laws enables individuals to pursue their personal and business interests free from unlawful interference from others.

The case *W. C. Ritchie & Co. v. Wayman* illustrates a *public* law where the government regulated the ability of an employee and an employer to freely contract regarding employment.

FUNCTION OF THE LAW

W. C. RITCHIE & CO. v. WAYMAN, ATTORNEY FOR COOK COUNTY, ILL.

91 N.E. 695 (1910)
SUPREME COURT OF ILLINOIS

Hand, J.

The object of this litigation is to test the constitutionality of the act of 1909, which is generally referred to as the "Woman's Ten-Hour Law." It is first contended that the act of 1909, known as the "Woman's Ten-Hour Law," is in conflict with section 2 of article 2 of the Constitution of 1870, which provides that "no person shall be deprived of life, liberty or property, without due process of law."

If, therefore, the public interest requires that the time which women shall be permitted to work in any mechanical establishment or factory or laundry should be limited to ten hours in any one day, we are unable to see why this statute is not constitutional. If this statute can be sustained, it must be sustained, we think, as an exercise of the police power.

The police power is a very broad power, and may be applied to the regulation of every property right so far as it may be reasonably necessary for the state to exercise such power to guard the health, morals, and general welfare of the public. It is known to all men (and what we know as men we cannot profess to be ignorant of as judges) that woman's physical structure and the performance of maternal functions place her at a great disadvantage in the battle of life; that while a man can work for more than ten hours a day without injury to himself, a woman, especially when the burdens of motherhood are upon her, cannot; that while a man can work standing upon his feet for more than ten hours a day, day after day, without injury to himself, a woman cannot, and that to require a woman to stand upon her feet for more than ten hours in any one day and perform severe manual labor while thus standing, day after day, has the effect to impair her health, and that as weakly and sickly women cannot be the mothers of vigorous children.

We think the general consensus of opinion, not only in this country but in the civilized countries of Europe, is, that a working day of not more than ten hours for women is justified for the following reasons: (1) The physical organization of woman; (2) her maternal functions; (3) the rearing and education of children; (4) the maintenance of the home; and these conditions are so far matters of general knowledge that the courts will take judicial cognizance of their existence. Surrounded as women are by the changing conditions of society, and the evolution of employment which environs them, we agree fully with what is said by the Supreme Court of Washington in the *Buchanan Case:* "Law is, or ought to be, a progressive science."

We are of the opinion the act of 1909 is constitutional in all of its particulars and as an entirety.

CASE QUESTIONS

1. Who enacted the statute in this case? What did the statute provide?
2. What evidence did the court cite to support its decision? What do you think of the court's statement, "What we know as men we cannot profess to be ignorant of as judges"?
3. What *function* of the law was advanced in this case?

Policy Issue. Is the law, as the court stated, a "progressive science"? Is the law really a "science"? How would this case be decided today?

Economics Issue. Why did the plaintiff company bring this action?

Ethics Issue. Was it ethical for the plaintiff business to expect its employees to work longer than ten-hour days?

Social Responsibility. Does the government have the responsibility to protect its citizens from entering into certain contracts? Or should people be allowed to enter into any contracts they wish to, as long as it doesn't harm third parties?

NOTE: Fifteen years earlier (1895) the same court held that a statute which prohibited women from working more than eight hours in a day was *unconstitutional.* How do you reconcile this earlier case and the case just presented?

FLEXIBILITY OF THE LAW

It is impossible to foresee the hundreds of millions of decisions and transactions that take place in society daily (e.g., persons driving automobiles that could hit other persons, persons and businesses entering into contracts). It is also impossible to draft laws that will fit every possible situation in the future. Therefore, the law provides *general standards of conduct* applicable to members of society as they conduct their activities. Each individual's actions are then measured against these standards. The courts apply these general legal standards to the specific situations and disputes that are presented to them.

A criticism often voiced by beginning students of the law is that the law is "too uncertain," that there is "too much discretion" given the judges, and that "you never know where you stand." In a democratic society, it is this flexibility of the law that provides its greatest value, because it allows the law to grow with the changing norms of society.

In the excerpt from his book *Law and the Modern Mind* that follows, Judge Jerome Frank discusses the flexibility of the law.

FLEXIBILITY OF THE LAW

LAW AND THE MODERN MIND

JUDGE JEROME FRANK
N.Y.: BRENTANO'S, INC., 1930

The law always has been, is now, and will ever continue to be, largely vague and variable. And how could this be otherwise? The law deals with human relations in their most complicated aspects. The whole confused, shifting helter-skelter of life parades before it—more confused than ever, in our kaleidoscopic age.

Even in a relatively static society, men have never been able to construct a comprehensive, eternized set of rules anticipating all possible legal disputes and formulating in advance the rules which would apply to them. Even in such a social order no one can foresee all the future permutations and combinations of events; situations are bound to occur which were never contemplated when the original rules were made. How much less is such a frozen legal system possible in modern times. New instruments of production, new modes of travel and of dwelling, new credit and ownership devices, new concentrations of capital, new social customs, habits, aims and ideals—all these factors of innovation make vain the hope that definitive legal rules can be drafted that will forever solve all legal problems. When human relationships are transforming daily, legal relationships cannot be expressed in enduring form. The constant development of unprecedented problems requires a legal system capable of fluidity and pliancy. Our society would be strait-jacketed were not the courts, with the able assistance of the lawyers, constantly overhauling the law and adapting it to the realities of ever-changing social, industrial, and political conditions; although changes cannot be made lightly, yet rules of law must be more or less impermanent, experimental and therefore not nicely calculable. *Much of the uncertainty of law is not an unfortunate accident; it is of immense social value.*

FAIRNESS OF THE LAW

The law and its application is not one hundred percent fair or just. There are misuses and oversights in the legal system, abuses of discretion by judges, unequal applications of the law, and procedural mishaps that allow some guilty parties to go free. Further, there is generally a "lag" between changes in the underlying norms of society and when the law finally reflects these changes.

On the whole, however, the American legal system is the most comprehensive and democratic system of laws ever enacted and enforced in the history of the world. The American system of law reflects as closely as possible the attitudes of the citizenry of the United States and provides individuals and businesses with both substantial protection and freedom in conducting their daily affairs.

This U.S. Supreme Court case, *Rostker v. Goldberg*, examines the fairness of a federal law that required males, but not females, to register for the draft.

FAIRNESS OF THE LAW

ROSTKER, DIRECTOR OF THE SELECTIVE SERVICE v. GOLDBERG

453 U.S. 57 (1981)
UNITED STATES SUPREME COURT

Justice Rehnquist delivered the opinion of the Court.

Registration for the draft . . . was discontinued in 1975. In early 1980, President Carter determined that it was necessary to reactivate the draft registration process. The immediate impetus for this decision was the Soviet armed invasion of Afghanistan.

Congress agreed that it was necessary to reactivate the registration process, and allocated funds for that purpose in a joint resolution. . . . The resolution did not allocate all the funds originally requested by the President, but only those necessary to register males.

These events of last year breathed new life into a lawsuit which had been essentially dormant in the lower courts for nearly a decade. It began in 1971 when several men subject to registration for the draft and subsequent induction into the Armed Services filed a complaint in the United States District Court for the Eastern District of Pennsylvania challenging the [Military Selective Service Act] on several grounds.

The question of registering women for the draft not only received considerable national attention and was the subject of wide-ranging public debate, but also was extensively considered by Congress in hearings, floor debate, and in committee. The foregoing clearly establishes that the decision to exempt women from registration was not the "accidental byproduct of a traditional way of thinking about women."

Women as a group, however, unlike men as a group, are not eligible for combat. The restrictions on the participation of women in combat in the Navy and Air Force are statutory. The Army and Marine Corps preclude the use of women in combat as a matter of established policy.

This is not a case of Congress arbitrarily choosing to burden one of two similarly situated groups, such as would be the case with an all-black or all-white, or an all-Catholic or all-Lutheran, or an all-Republican or all-Democratic registration. Men and women, because of the combat restrictions on women, are simply not similarly situated for purposes of a draft or registration for a draft.

In light of the foregoing, we conclude that Congress acted well within its constitutional authority when it authorized the registration of men, and not women, under the Military Selective Service Act. The decision of the District Court holding otherwise is accordingly *reversed*.

Justice **Marshall,** with whom Justice **Brennan** joins, dissenting.

The Court today places its imprimatur on one of the most potent remaining public expressions of "ancient canards about the proper role of women," It upholds a statute that requires males but not females to register for the draft, and which thereby categorically excludes women from a fundamental civic obligation. Because I believe the Court's decision is inconsistent with the Constitution's guarantee of equal protection of the laws, I dissent.

CASE QUESTIONS

1. Who were the plaintiffs in this case? Women who wanted to register for the draft?

2. Was the "combat" distinction used by the court in this case valid? Or was it "bootstrapping"?
3. Did the court avoid the real issue in this case? Should women have been exempted from combat duty?
4. Has the law, as a "progressive science," changed much since the *Ritchie* case?

Policy Issue. Is it "fair" to require males, but not females, to register for the draft?

Ethics Issue. Is it ethical for one-half of the population to accept the benefits of our democratic form of government without being subject to registration for the draft?

Economics Issue. What is the economic effect on a person who is drafted? Does *he* benefit economically by being drafted?

Social Responsibility. Do females owe a duty of social responsibility to defend the country?

NOTE: Nine out of every ten positions in the military are *non*combat positions. Should women be subject to registration for these positions?

Trend of the Law

The law is a dynamic process that is continually changing over time. As the norms of society change, the law will change. A substantial increase in the volume of laws passed and cases decided is concerned with regulating the activities of business. The legal regulation of business is projected to continue and to escalate in the future. The law must, therefore, remain flexible in order to apply to a changing business environment.

The law is generally quite logical and usually fair, although in any individual lawsuit at least one party, or both parties if the court has reached a compromise solution, will believe the law to be unfair.

REVIEW QUESTIONS

1. What is the definition(s) of "law"?
2. Can a society exist without laws?
3. Should ignorance of the law be an excuse for violating the law?
4. a. What are legal "rights"?
   b. "Superior" legal rights?
   c. "Inferior" legal rights?
   d. Why can't all legal rights be equal?
5. Compare and contrast the following:
   a. public law and private law
   b. criminal law and civil law
   c. substantive law and procedural law
6. Explain the following theories of law:
   a. moral theory
   b. historical theory
   c. command theory

    d. sociological theory

    e. economic theory

7. Should law and morality be the same?
8. Describe the following functions of the law and their benefits to business:

    a. keeping the peace

    b. shaping and enforcing moral standards

    c. promoting social justice

    d. maintaining the status quo

    e. facilitating orderly change

    f. facilitating planning

    g. providing a basis for compromise

    h. maximizing individual freedom

9. Should the law be flexible? Why or why not?
10. Is the law "fair"? Can it be?
11. From the late 1800s onward, it was common in many states to provide separate schools for white and black children. Black students were denied access to all white schools. The laws that mandated separate schools were based upon an 1896 decision of the U.S. Supreme Court, *Plessey v. Ferguson*. In *Plessey*, the court held that it was constitutionally permissible for a state to provide "separate but equal" facilities in public transportation systems. The *Plessey* court held:

> [The Constitution] could not have been intended to abolish distinctions based upon color, or to enforce social, as distinguished from political equality. . . . Laws [requiring] their separation in places . . . do not necessarily imply the inferiority of either race to the other. . . . The most common instance of this is connected with the establishment of separate schools for white and colored children . . . the constitutionality of which does not seem to have been questioned.

In the early 1950s, a number of black schoolchildren who were denied access to white public schools sued in the federal court system. These suits alleged that segregated public schools were not "equal" and they could not be made "equal" and hence the black school children were deprived of equal protection of the laws in violation of the Fourteenth Amendment. Morally, how should the courts have decided these cases? If you believe that these laws should have been declared unconstitutional, how could the court overturn a previous decision that allowed "separate but equal" facilities? Why do you believe that the *Plessey* court originally allowed "separate but equal" facilities?

2 THE SOCIAL RESPONSIBILITY OF BUSINESS

INTRODUCTION

Business does not operate in a vacuum. Decisions made by business executives have far-reaching effects on employees, shareholders, bondholders, competition, consumers, and the public at large. Often in the past business decisions were made based only on a cost-benefit analysis and the effect on the "bottom line."

However, with the increased awareness and aggressiveness of consumers, and the expanding regulation of business by the government, many business decisions today must also take into consideration the effects of such decisions on society. Society, which has granted rights to fictitious legal "persons," the corporations, now demands that these "persons" consider their corporate social responsibility when decisions are made by their stewards, the corporate managers and directors. In his current book Michael Novak discusses corporate ethics and social responsibility.

THE SOCIAL RESPONSIBILITY OF BUSINESS

TOWARD A THEOLOGY OF THE CORPORATION

MICHAEL NOVAK
AMERICAN ENTERPRISE INSTITUTE, 1981

The corporation is an invention of democratic capitalism, or, to put it another way, the corporation is an invention of law that made democratic capitalism possible. Neither participatory democracy nor capitalism could exist without the corporation. The existence and practice of the corporation, further-more, give the lie to all theories of democracy and capitalism that focus exclusively on the individual to the neglect of human sociality. The corporation is an expression of the social nature of humans. Moreover, it offers a metaphor for the ecclesial community that is in some ways more illuminating than metaphors based on the human body ("the mystical body") or on the family, the clan, the tribe, or the chosen people.

Not all corporations are economic, of course. Political parties are incorporated, as are labor unions, universities, foundations, many charitable organizations, and many institutions of research, invention, science, and the arts. The development of corporate law opened human history to the action of social institutions freely entered into. Where they appear, these "mediating structures," which are larger than the individual but smaller than the state, make possible the flowering of human initiative, cooperation, and accountability.

In order not to think of corporations in a merely mythical way, exaggerating their nature, scope, and relative position in society, it is important to grasp a picture of the factual context. Some of the numbers may be surprising to some readers. How many corporations are there in the United States? Some 2 million economic corporations now report to the Internal Revenue Service. According to the Small Business Administration, there are an additional 13 million unincorporated small businesses. (Since the active labor force in the United States numbers nearly 100 million persons, there is, on average, one business corporation for every six or seven workers.) Defined by the number of laborers employed by each enterprise, by the total assets of the enterprise, and by the annual sales volume of the enterprise, there are approximately 15 million small businesses in the United States and about 700,000 large businesses.

In recent years, the level of employment in industrial corporations has remained relatively static, or even declined, while the number of jobs in the service sector and in government employment has been growing rapidly. From 1969 to 1976, for example, nearly all the 9 million new jobs added to the economy were added in government employment (3 million) and in small businesses mostly in the service sector (6 million). Employment in large businesses has been relatively static; the Small Business Administration claims that 87 percent of all new jobs in the private sector are created by small businesses. Many of these small businesses, from rock groups to boutiques, spring up among young adults.

Of the approximately 100 million Americans who

work, some 16 million civilians work for federal, state, and local governments. Another 4 million work under contract to the government. In addition, all those on unemployment compensation, social security, and welfare depend on the state for income. Some 46 million of the workers in the private sector work for small businesses such as taxi fleets, local dairies and bakeries, retail stores, auto dealers, and restaurants. The remainder, about 38 million, work for the estimated 700,000 large corporations, which thus employ on average 54 persons each. The New York Stock Exchange, the American Stock Exchange, and the Over-the-Counter market together list some 5,250 corporations whose shares are owned by the public and publicly traded. All these corporations rank as large businesses, although many of them employ only a few hundred workers.

Each year *Fortune* magazine lists the 500 largest industrial corporations in America. Over the years, corporations disappear and rankings change as new technologies spawn new giants and old technologies and methods of operation result in the decline or bankruptcy of others. For example, the tenth largest corporation, Chrysler, appears to some to be in its death throes. Within the *Fortune* 500, the top hundred are truly giants; the fifth hundred rank dramatically lower in net worth, annual gross sales, and numbers of employees. Altogether, the top 500 corporations employ about 16 million Americans, about as many as those employed by the state, 4 million more than those who attend American colleges and universities as graduate students and undergraduates. The average work force of the top 500 corporations is 28,000, approximately the number of students enrolled on the campuses of some major universities.

It is a common mistake to believe that almost anyone can manage a large corporation and to underestimate the relative scarcity of high talent. Literary intellectuals (including theologians) tend to value a type of intelligence, important for its own sake but not necessarily adequate to the demands of economic management. Indeed, the sort of work intellectuals value most highly is often unlikely to be successful in the market. Their way of thinking, then, has a natural affinity to aristocratic rather than to commercial ideals. In much of our work we reject the standards of the market in preference for judgments made in the light of intrinsic values of traditional weight. We tend to think that persons of industry and commerce exercise vulgar judgment. Yet creative practical intelligence must also go against the market; it claims to change the market. An economic system like ours rewards such dissent, anticipation, and innovation. It also penalizes mistaken strategic decisions, which can threaten to bankrupt even the tenth largest company, Chrysler. At the time when corporate decisions must be made, it is not at all certain which of competing decisions will be the correct one. Practical intelligence of a high order is often obliged to fight its way through legions of doubters who "know" from the conventional wisdom that novel proposals cannot work.

Moreover, folklore is full of "robber barons," "fat cats," "tycoons," and images of hereditary wealth and financial control, dating from an era prior to the managerial revolution. Corporate executives normally do not own the corporations they manage. They are hired professionals, often of uncommon talent, and relatively mobile. The average length of service of a chief executive officer is about that of a professional football player: six years. The pay—in the *Fortune* 500 it averages $400,000 per year—is about commensurate with that of top professionals in sports, entertainment, television journalism, or writers of best-sellers. It is rarely as dramatic as that of some television and movie producers, inventors, and others.

The imagery surrounding corporate leaders is mainly negative; it seems to be inspired ideologically (and even ethnically). Few people write or talk about "fat cat" professors or journalists, athletes or actors, surgeons or lawyers, whose incomes are comparable or higher. In *The View from Sunset Boulevard,* Ben Stein has reproduced interviews that dramatize quite starkly the antibusiness attitudes of the makers of television and the ideological distortions of their perceptions.

In their useful little casebook, *Full Value,* Oliver F. Williams and John W. Houck give two categories of moral flaw often cited by a public that is losing confidence in the moral integrity of business: "1. numerous violations of legal codes that have come to the attention of the public, such as price fixing, tax law violations, and bribery. 2. breaches of the professional code of ethics by business persons, such as deceptive advertising, selling company secrets, and dishonesty in expense accounts." These problems are immemorial; no system will ever eliminate them. They are encountered, analogously, in politics, government service, the academy, and other professions.

In this respect the debate about the social responsibility of business has been badly drawn. Though not designed to be either political institutions or moral-cultural institutions, business enterprises are, as it were, plants that cannot flourish independently of the trebly differentiated roots from which they have sprung. Their responsibility to themselves entails sophisticated attention to the political and moral-cultural requirements of their own existence. Such are the fact of life of democratic capitalism.

CORPORATE SOCIAL RESPONSIBILITY IN THE NUCLEAR AGE

Corporations owe a duty of social responsibility not to harm human beings or the environment in the course of their business activities. A breach of this duty is actionable by an injured party. However, in the present nuclear age, where corporations have become large institutions that rival the size of many governments, and where corporations have substantial resources, power, and influence, corporations may not only owe a duty to refrain from causing harm but arguably owe a duty to take positive action to advance the welfare of society.

Because the government is often slow to act, and sometimes fails to act, business may owe a duty to voluntarily initiate changes that will benefit society without waiting for the enactment of a law by the government that forces the change. For example, in the area of employment, business should advance the equal employment opportunity of all minority classes by eliminating discrimination in employment against all classes, whether presently protected by law or not. In the area of environmental protection, factories could voluntarily install the most advanced pollution control equipment rather than merely the equipment that meets government standards. The examples of voluntary action that business could take to advance the welfare of society are almost endless. The following editorial excerpt discusses the social responsibility of business in the modern nuclear age.

CORPORATIONS HAVE A SPECIAL RESPONSIBILITY IN NUCLEAR AGE

HAROLD WILLENS
LOS ANGELES TIMES, MARCH 11, 1984

Like most things in life, corporate responsibility must respond to the requirements of new conditions or run the risk of becoming irrelevant.

There is ample precedent for a definition of "corporate responsibility" that depicts it as change-directed and dynamic rather than static. The concept of social responsibility on the part of business entities was born as nothing more than a means of responding to public pressure. From this completely reactive and largely cosmetic beginning, there evolved a process that changed the concept to serious efforts in civic participation and action directed toward betterment of community and country.

This evolution reached a point at which the influential Business Roundtable could describe the social obligation of the business community as a responsibility "which rises above the bottom line to consider the impact of its actions on all, from shareholders to the society at large." However, too many corporate "leaders" continue to cling to a parochial perspective, seeing social responsibility as no more than a necessary and minimal response to situations that threaten a company's welfare through aroused public opinion.

That view is too skimpy to meet the challenge of a nuclear age, in which business is endangered by much more than militant neighbors or irritated consumers. What endangers the business community today is nothing less than the growing threat of total extinction.

This new era to which a new kind of corporate responsibility must respond began on July 16, 1945, when the first nuclear explosion turned sand into glass in the New Mexico desert. Twenty-one days later, the world learned the stunning news that with a single new bomb the United States had leveled an entire Japanese city. Three days after that another city was destroyed. Obscured by the relief that at last World War II had ended was the faint recognition that something else—perhaps something terrible—had begun.

Because businesspeople do possess inordinate power and influence in our society, policy makers are particularly receptive and responsive to them. The combination of pragmatism and political influence is unique to the business sector and places business leaders in a position to be change-agents at a time when redirection of national policy is desperately needed.

To meet this challenge, out of enlightened self-interest, corporate responsibility in this nuclear age requires recognizing that there is nothing partisan, political—or even ideological—about efforts to stop and reverse the nuclear arms race through a series of sensible steps that can in no way jeopardize our national security. And it requires recognizing that failure to participate in such efforts would be the ultimate form of corporate irresponsibility.

The following two cases demonstrate the difficult issues of social responsibility and ethics facing corporations and business executives today. Issues of corporate social responsibility and the ethics of business executives arise in the majority of the legal cases covered in this book. Questions regarding *policy, ethics* and *social responsibility* follow each case.

NUCLEAR CONTAMINATION

BILL M. SILKWOOD, ADMINISTRATOR OF THE ESTATE OF KAREN G. SILKWOOD, DECEASED v. KERR-McGEE CORPORATION

104 S.Ct. 615 (1984)
UNITED STATES SUPREME COURT

Justice White delivered the opinion of the Court.

Karen Silkwood was a laboratory analyst for Kerr-McGee at its Cimmaron plant near Crescent, Oklahoma. The plant fabricated plutonium fuel pins for use as reactor fuel in nuclear power plants. Accordingly, the plant was subject to licensing and regulation by the Nuclear Regulatory Commission (NRC) pursuant to the Atomic Energy Act. . . .

During a three-day period of November 1974, Silkwood was contaminated by plutonium from the Cimmaron plant. On November 5, Silkwood was grinding and polishing plutonium samples, utilizing glove boxes designed for that purpose. In accordance with established procedures, she checked her hands for contamination when she withdrew them from the glove box. When some contamination was detected, a more extensive check was performed. A monitoring device revealed contamination on Silkwood's left hand, right wrist, upper arm, neck, hair, and nostrils. She was immediately decontaminated, and at the end of her shift, the monitors detected no contamination. However, she was given urine and fecal kits and was instructed to collect samples in order to check for plutonium discharge.

The next day, Silkwood arrived at the plant and began doing paperwork in the laboratory. Upon leaving the laboratory, Silkwood monitored herself and again discovered surface contamination. Once again, she was decontaminated.

On the third day, November 7, Silkwood was monitored upon her arrival at the plant. High levels of contamination were detected. Four urine sam-

ples and one fecal sample submitted that morning were also highly contaminated. Suspecting that the contamination had spread to areas outside the plant, the company directed a decontamination squad to accompany Silkwood to her apartment. Silkwood's roommate, who was also an employee at the plant, was awakened and monitored. She was also contaminated, although to a lesser degree than Silkwood. The squad then monitored the apartment, finding contamination in several rooms, with especially high levels in the bathroom, the kitchen, and Silkwood's bedroom.

The contamination level in Silkwood's apartment was such that many of her personal belongings had to be destroyed. Silkwood herself was sent to the Los Alamos Scientific Laboratory to determine the extent of contamination in her vital body organs. She returned to work on November 13. That night, she was killed in an unrelated automobile accident.

Bill Silkwood, Karen's father, brought the present diversity action in his capacity as administrator of her estate. The action was based on common law tort principles under Oklahoma law and was designed to recover for the contamination injuries to Karen's person and property. Kerr-McGee stipulated that the plutonium which caused the contamination came from its plant, and the jury expressly rejected Kerr-McGee's allegation that Silkwood had intentionally removed the plutonium from the plant in an effort to embarrass the company.

During the course of the trial, evidence was presented which tended to show that Kerr-McGee did not always comply with NRC regulations. One Kerr-McGee witness conceded that the amount of plutonium which was unaccounted for during the period in question exceeded permissible limits.

[T]he court submitted the claims to the jury on alternative theories of strict liability and negligence. . . . The court also instructed the jury with respect to punitive damages, explaining the standard by which Kerr-McGee's conduct was to be evaluated in determining whether such damages should be awarded:

> [T]he jury may give damages for the sake of example and by way of punishment, if the jury finds the defendant or defendants have been guilty of oppression, fraud, or malice, actual or presumed. . . .
>
> Exemplary damages are not limited to cases where there is direct evidence of fraud, malice or gross negligence. They may be allowed when there is evidence of such recklessness and wanton disregard of another's rights that malice and evil intent will be inferred. If a defendant is grossly and wantonly reckless in exposing others to dangers, the law holds him to have intended the natural consequences of his acts, and treats him as guilty of a willful wrong.

. . . The jury returned a verdict in favor of Silkwood, finding actual damages of $505,000 ($500,000 for personal injuries and $5,000 for property damage) and punitive damages of $10,000,000. The trial court entered judgment against Kerr-McGee in that amount.

Kerr-McGee renewed its contentions with greater success before the Court of Appeals for the Tenth Circuit. That court. . . . held that because of the federal statutes regulating the Kerr-McGee plant, "punitive damages may not be awarded in this case."

In reaching its conclusion with respect to the punitive damages award, the Court of Appeals adopted a broad preemption analysis. It concluded that "any state action that competes substantially with the AEC (NRC) in its regulation of radiation hazards associated with plants handling nuclear material" was impermissible.

[I]nsofar as damages for radiation injuries are concerned, preemption should not be judged on the basis that the federal government has so completely occupied the field of safety that state remedies are foreclosed but on whether there is an irreconcilable conflict between the federal and state standards or whether the imposition of a state standard in a damages action would frustrate the objectives of the federal law. We perceive no such conflict or frustration in the circumstances of this case.

We also reject Kerr-McGee's submission that the punitive damages award in this case conflicts with Congress' express intent to preclude dual regulation of radiation hazards. [C]ongress did not believe that it was inconsistent to vest the NRC with exclusive regulatory authority over the safety aspects of nuclear development while at the same time allowing plaintiffs like Silkwood to recover for injuries caused by nuclear hazards.

We conclude that the award of punitive damages in this case is not preempted by federal law. . . . The judgment of the Court of Appeals with respect to punitive damages is therefore *reversed,* and the case is *remanded* to the Court of Appeals for proceedings consistent with this opinion.

Justice Blackmun, with whom **Justice Marshall** joins, dissenting.

The $10 million fine that the jury imposed is 100 times greater than the maximum fine that may be imposed by the Nuclear Regulatory Commission for a single violation of federal standards. The fine apparently is more than 10 times greater than the largest single fine that the Commission has ever imposed. The complete federal occupation of safety regulation compels the conclusion that such an award is preempted.

Justice Powell, with whom **The Chief Justice** and **Justice Blackmun** join, dissenting.

Punitive damages, unrelated to compensation for any injury or damage sustained by a plaintiff, are "regulatory" in nature rather than compensatory.

The facts are instructive. During a three-day period in November 1974, petitioner Silkwood was contaminated by plutonium from one of respondent Kerr-McGee's plants that had been built and was operated pursuant to federal law and subject to extensive regulation by the AEC. Silkwood was absent from her job for only a week—from November 7 until she returned to work on November 13. That night she was killed—as the Court states—"in an unrelated automobile accident."

There is no evidence that Silkwood suffered any specific injury, temporary or permanent, other than mental distress for a short period.

Today, the Court opens a wide and inviting door to indirect regulation by juries authorized to impose damages to punish and deter on the basis of inferences even when a plant has taken the utmost precautions provided by law. Not only is this unfair; it also could discourage investment needed to further the acknowledged national need for this alternate source of energy. I would affirm the judgment of the Court of Appeals.

CASE QUESTIONS

1. What job did Karen Silkwood perform for the Kerr-McGee Corporation? Was she exposed to any health dangers on the job?
2. Who was the plaintiff in this case? Why wasn't Karen Silkwood the defendant?
3. What was the jury award in this case? What are punitive damages?

Policy Issue. Why are punitive damages awarded? Should jurors be given the authority to award damages to "punish and deter"? Are punitive damages "regulatory" in nature?

Economics Issue. Will the investment in nuclear energy be "discouraged" by the *Silkwood* decision? Explain.

Ethics Issue. What was Kerr-McGee's *legal* argument on appeal? Was it ethical for Kerr-McKee to try to get out from paying the jurors' award of damages?

Social Responsibility. Did Kerr-McGee owe a duty of social responsibility to protect Karen Silkwood from plutonium contamination? To Karen's roommate? To society? Did Kerr-McKee breach its duty of social responsibility in this case?

* * *

NOTE: The Karen Silkwood story was the basis of the movie "Silkwood," which was released in 1983. It was nominated for "best picture of the year."

UNSAFE PRODUCTS

SINDELL v. ABBOTT LABORATORIES

26 C.3d 588 (1980)
SUPREME COURT OF CALIFORNIA

Mosk, Justice.

This case involves a complex problem both timely and significant: may a plaintiff, injured as the result of a drug administered to her mother during pregnancy, who knows the type of drug involved but cannot identify the manufacturer of the precise product, hold liable for her injuries a maker of a drug produced from an identical formula?

Plaintiff Judith Sindell brought an action against eleven drug companies and Does 1 through 100, on behalf of herself and other women similarly situated. The complaint alleges as follows:

Between 1941 and 1971, defendants were engaged in the business of manufacturing, promoting, and marketing diethylstilbesterol (DES), a drug which is a synthetic compound of the female hormone estrogen. The drug was administered to plaintiff's mother and the mothers of the class she represents, for the purpose of preventing miscarriage. In 1947, the Food and Drug Administration authorized the marketing of DES as a miscarriage preventative, but only on an experimental basis, with a requirement that the drug contain a warning label to that effect.

DES may cause cancerous vaginal and cervical growths in the daughters exposed to it before birth, because their mothers took the drug during pregnancy. The form of cancer from which these daughters suffer is known as adenocarcinoma, and it manifests itself after a minimum latent period of 10 or

12 years. It is a fast-spreading and deadly disease, and radical surgery is required to prevent it from spreading. DES also causes adenosis, precancerous vaginal and cervical growths which may spread to other areas of the body. The treatment for adenosis is cauterization, surgery, or cryosurgery. Women who suffer from this condition must be monitored by biopsy or colposcopic examination twice a year, a painful and expensive procedure. Thousands of women whose mothers received DES during pregnancy are unaware of the effects of the drug.

In 1971, the Food and Drug Administration ordered defendants to cease marketing and promoting DES for the purpose of preventing miscarriages, and to warn physicians and the public that the drug should not be used by pregnant women because of the danger to their unborn children.

Because of defendants' advertised assurances that DES was safe and effective to prevent miscarriage, plaintiff was exposed to the drug prior to her birth. She became aware of the danger from such exposure within one year of the time she filed her complaint. As a result of the DES ingested by her mother, plaintiff developed a malignant bladder tumor which was removed by surgery. She suffers from adenosis and must constantly be monitored by biopsy or colposcopy to insure early warning of further malignancy.

Plaintiff seeks compensatory damages of $1 million and punitive damages of $10 million for herself. For the members of her class, she prays for equitable relief in the form of an order that defendants warn physicians and others of the danger of DES and the necessity of performing certain tests to determine the presence of disease caused by the drug, and that they establish free clinics in California to perform such tests. . . . [T]he court dismissed the action.

This case is but one of a number filed throughout the country seeking to hold drug manufacturers liable for injuries allegedly resulting from DES prescribed to the plaintiffs' mothers since 1947. According to a note in the Fordham Law Review, estimates of the number of women who took the drug during pregnancy range from 1½ million to 3 million. Hundreds, perhaps thousands, of the daughters of these women suffer from adenocarcinoma, and the incidence of vaginal adenosis among them is 30 to 90 percent.

We begin with the proposition that, as a general rule, the imposition of liability depends upon a showing by the plaintiff that his or her injuries were caused by the act of the defendant or by an instrumentality under the defendant's control.

In our contemporary complex industrialized society, advances in science and technology create fungible goods which may harm consumers and which cannot be traced to any specific producer. . . . [W]e acknowledge that some adaptation of the rules of causation and liability may be appropriate in these recurring circumstances.

From a broader policy standpoint, defendants are better able to bear the cost of injury resulting from the manufacture of a defective product. As was said by Justice Traynor in *Escola v. Coca Cola Bottling Company,* "[t]he cost of an injury and the loss of time or health may be an overwhelming misfortune to the person injured, and a needless one, for the risk of injury can be insured by the manufacturer and distributed among the public as a cost of doing business." The manufacturer is in the best position to discover and guard against defects in its products and to warn of harmful effects; thus, holding it liable for defects and failure to warn of harmful effects will provide an incentive to product safety.

[W]e hold it to be reasonable in the present context to measure the likelihood that any of the defendants supplied the product which allegedly injured plaintiff by the percentage which the DES sold by each of them for the purpose of preventing miscarriage bears to the entire production of the drug sold by all for that purpose. Plaintiff asserts in her briefs that Eli Lilly and Company and five or six other companies produced 90 percent of the DES marketed.

If plaintiff joins in the action the manufacturers of a substantial share of the DES which her mother might have taken, the injustice of shifting the burden of proof to defendants to demonstrate that they could not have made the substance which injured plaintiff is significantly diminished. While 75 to 80 percent of the market is suggested as the requirement by the Fordham Comment (at p. 996), we hold only that a substantial percentage is required.

The presence in the action of a substantial share of the appropriate market also provides a ready means to apportion damages among the defendants. Each defendant will be held liable for the proportion of the judgment represented by its share of that market unless it demonstrates that it could not have made the product which caused plaintiff's injuries. In the present case, as we have see, one DES manufacturer was dismissed from the action upon filing a declaration that it had not manufactured DES until after plaintiff was born. Once plaintiff has met her burden of joining the required defendants, they in turn may cross-complaint against other DES manufacturers, not joined in the action, which they can allege might have supplied the injury-causing product.

Under this approach, each manufacturer's liability would approximate its responsibility for the injuries caused by its own products. Some minor discrepancy in the correlation between market share and liability is inevitable; therefore, a defendant may be held liable for a somewhat different percentage of the damage than its share of the appropriate market would justify. It is probably impossible, with the passage of time, to determine market share with mathematical exactitude.

[U]nder the rule we adopt, each manufacturer's liability for an injury would be approximately equivalent to the damages caused by the DES it manufactured.

The judgments are *reversed*.

* * *

Richardson, Justice, dissenting.

I respectfully dissent. In these consolidated cases the majority adopts a wholly new theory which contains these ingredients: The plaintiffs were not alive at the time of the commission of the tortious acts. They sue a generation later. They are permitted to receive substantial damages from multiple defendants without any proof that any defendant caused or even probably caused plaintiffs' injuries.

Although the majority purports to change only the required burden of proof by shifting it from plaintiffs to defendants, the effect of its holding is to guarantee that plaintiffs will prevail on the causation issue because defendants are no more capable of disproving factual causation than plaintiffs are of proving it. "Market share" liability thus represents a new high water mark in tort law.

The "market share" thesis may be paraphrased. Plaintiffs have been hurt by *someone* who made DES. Because of the lapse of time no one can

prove who made it. Perhaps it was not the named defendants who made it, but they did make some. Although DES was apparently safe at the time it was used, it was subsequently proven unsafe as to some daughters of some users. Plaintiffs have suffered injury and defendants are wealthy. There should be a remedy. Strict products liability is unavailable because the element of causation is lacking. Strike that requirement and label what remains "alternative" liability, "industry-wide" liability, or "market share" liability, proving thereby that if you hit the square peg hard and often enough the round holes will really become square, although you may splinter the board in the process.

Respectfully, I think this is unreasonable overreaction for the purpose of achieving what is perceived to be a socially satisfying result.

CASE QUESTIONS

1. In what year did the plaintiff's mother take DES? In what year did the plaintiff bring the lawsuit against the defendants?
2. What injuries did the plaintiff suffer? How long did it take for the injuries to manifest themselves in this case?
3. Did the plaintiff name the specific manufacturer who produced the DES her mother took as the *sole* defendant in this case? Why or why not?
4. Who did the plaintiff name as defendants? How were the defendants selected?
5. What does the "market share" liability test of the majority opinion provide? Does this test eliminate the traditional element of "causation" required in most lawsuits?

Policy Issue. Should a manufacturer be held liable to persons injured by a product it made? Should a manufacturer be held liable to a person injured by another manufacturer's product?

Economic Issue. How many women took DES during their pregnancies? What would you estimate the potential money liability of DES manufacturers to be under the following tests?

a. Without the doctrine of "market share" liability?
b. If the "market share" liability" test is adopted by all states?

Ethics Issue. Was it ethical for the defendant manufacturers to argue that each one individually should not be held liable to the plaintiff if she could not prove which one of the defendants actually produced the DES taken by her mother?

Social Responsibility. Did the manufacturers owe a duty of social responsibility to the mothers who took DES? To the daughters who may have been injured by the DES? Even though it was not foreseeable that the injuries would occur?

Did the executives and board of directors owe a social responsibility to their employees, shareholders, and bondholders to defend the *Sindell* case?

If you were the president or a member of the board of directors of one of the defendants, what would you have done?

Trend of the Law

The social responsibility of business and the ethics of business executives will receive increased attention in the future. As corporations become even larger and more influential, they will be expected to shoulder a greater degree of social responsibility in society. Corporations will be called upon to share their wealth and assist in supporting civic organizations such as the opera, contribute to charitable causes such as the United Way, and to support higher education through scholarships and financial contributions to colleges and universities. It is anticipated that if business does not voluntarily meet its social responsibility in the future, the government will enact laws requiring business to do so.

REVIEW QUESTIONS

1. Do corporations owe a duty of social responsibility to society? If so, does this duty conflict with its duties to shareholders?
2. Do corporations owe a *positive* duty to advance the welfare of society?
3. Do business executives owe a duty to act ethically in their business dealings?
4. Is the folklore of "robber barons," "fat cats," and business "tycoons" a proper image for modern business executives?
5. What is the social responsibility of corporations in the Nuclear Age? Is it any different from the duty owed in the 1890s? The 1940s? The 1970s?
6. Can society be injured as much from the negligence of business executives as from the fraud or intentional acts of executives? Explain.
7. *The Dalkon Shield Case.* Businesses are being sued for breaching their duty of social responsibility, particularly where such breaches cause injury to individual members of society. For example, thousands of lawsuits have been brought against the manufacturer of the Dalkon Shield, an intrauterine device (IUD) for contraception, which allegedly caused women such problems as infection, pelvic inflammatory disease, infertility, spontaneous abortion, and birth defects in their children. In approving a $4.6 million settle-

ment by the manufacturer of the Dalkon Shield with seven plaintiffs, U.S. District Court Judge Miles Lord (Minneapolis) called the Dalkon Shield an "instrument of death, mutilation, and disease" and chastised the executives of the company for violating "every ethical precept" of the Hippocratic oath, the medical profession's promise to save lives. Judge Lord stated:

> Your company in the face of overwhelming evidence denies its guilt and continues its monstrous mischief. . . . You have taken the bottom line as your guiding beacon and the low road as your route. This is corporate irresponsibility at its meanest.

The Dalkon Shield was used by more than 2 million women in the early 1970s, and was taken off the market in 1974.
   a. What has been the cost to society?
   b. Can it ever be recompensed?
   c. What is the potential money liability of the manufacturer?
   d. Did the manufacturer of the Dalkon Shield meet its duty of social responsibility in this case?

8. *The Johns-Manville Corporation Bankruptcy.* The Johns-Manville Corporation was a profitable company with valuable natural resources when it declared bankruptcy in 1983. Why did it declare bankruptcy? Because the company was a major producer of asbestos, which was used, among other things, as insulation for buildings. Excessive exposure to asbestos can cause asbestosis, a fatal lung disease. Persons who contracted asbestosis, and families of such persons, brought thousands of lawsuits against the Johns-Manville Corporation. Lawsuits were being filed at the rate of approximately 400 per week when the corporation declared bankruptcy.

   As a response, the Johns-Manville Corporation filed for bankruptcy with the argument that if it did not, a viable company that provided thousands of jobs and served a useful purpose in this country would be destroyed, and that without the declaration of bankruptcy, a few of the plaintiffs who first filed their lawsuits would win awards of millions of dollars, leaving nothing for the remainder of the plaintiffs. Under the bankruptcy court's protection, the company can be restructured to survive, and all of the plaintiffs will receive some monetary payment for their injuries.
   a. Did the Johns-Manville Corporation meet its duty of social responsibility in this case?
   b. Should the corporation be held liable for injuries that no one knew asbestos caused?
   c. If you were the president or a member of the board of directors of the Johns-Manville Corporation, what would you have done?
   d. What is the morality of bankruptcy?

9. *The Cigarette Manufacturers Case.* Business often has the power to sway public opinion. In around 1980 the voters of California were presented with a ballot proposition that separate smoking and nonsmoking areas should be established in public buildings and business establishments, including places of employment. The cigarette manufacturers spent approximately $8 million on a successful advertising campaign to defeat the proposition. The opposing side spent only a fraction of that amount.

   The theme of the advertising campaign by the cigarette manufacturers was that the proposed law was an unwarranted intrusion and regulation of an individual's right to choose where and whether to smoke. The advertisements did not mention the harmful effects of smoking, or the nonsmokers' right to breathe clean air.

a. Do you think that the advertising campaign had any effect on the election?
b. Did the advertising campaign by the cigarette manufacturers advance the welfare of society?
c. Do smokers have the right to smoke?
d. Do nonsmokers have the right to breathe clean air?
e. Do these rights conflict?
f. Which right should the law protect?

3 THE AMERICAN COURT SYSTEM

INTRODUCTION

In many early societies, controversies were settled by duelling, war, or some other form of physical combat. Although the physically strongest party usually won, he was not necessarily the party who had the "right" on his side. In the United States there has developed a highly detailed and democratic legal system where disputing parties present their case to an appropriate forum (the courts) and have it decided peacefully by their fellow citizens (the jury). The process of bringing, maintaining, and defending a lawsuit in court is called *litigation.*

THE HISTORY OF AMERICAN LAW

English Common Law. Prior to the Norman conquest of England in 1066, each locality in England was subject to local laws as developed by the chieftain in control of each area. There was no uniform system of law for the land. William the Conqueror and his successors attempted to replace the various local laws with one uniform system of law. In order to acomplish this, the

King appointed his followers judges in all local areas to administer the law in a uniform manner everywhere. The body of rules developed by these judges in settling actual disputes became known as the *common law*. The common law was then used as precedent by other judges in solving subsequent and similar disputes.

At common law, form was often emphasized over substance, and only money damages could be awarded. Many disputes arose which would be unfairly decided at common law, or for which common law courts could not assign a proper remedy. Therefore, parallel to the common law of England there also developed another branch of law known as *equity*. The law of equity was administered by a separate set of courts known as the Courts of Chancery, under the authority of the Lord Chancellor. After first presenting and having his case decided by the common law court, an aggrieved party could petition the Lord Chancellor, the most powerful executive officer of the King, for a more equitable remedy.

The Court of Chancery gradually developed a set of rules and remedies that were not limited to money damages, and which could be applied more flexibly to solve legal disputes equitably and fairly. Grants of specific performance of a contract and issuance of injunctions to prevent parties from injuring others' rights are examples of equitable remedies developed in the Courts of Chancery. The Chancery Court inquired into the merits of a case, rather than emphasizing procedure. Equitable decrees of the Court of Chancery overruled the decisions of the common law courts.

As trade developed in the Middle Ages, the merchants and traders throughout England and much of Europe established their own courts to administer a special set of rules in legal disputes involving commercial situations. Common trade practices and usage became the precedent for subsequent judicial decisions. The merchant courts were absorbed into the regular common law court system of England in the early 1900s.

Roman Law.   One of the earliest civilized societies, ancient Rome, developed a detailed body of law dating from its earliest time and persisting to the eventual fall of the Roman empire. Commonly referred to as *Roman law*, or *civil law*, it was based more on the explicit statements of the law as set forth in statutes and ordinances than on common law as developed through judicial decisions. Roman law forms the basis of the modern legal systems of several European countries, including Germany, France, and Spain.

Systems of jurisprudence different from both the English *common law* and the Roman *civil law* have developed throughout the world. Legal systems range from those based on ukases as announced by a central government (e.g., Soviet law) to those based on a few major ethical standards (countries in the Orient). Still other legal systems are based on religious teachings (countries in the Middle East).

Adoption of English Common Law in America.   The decisions of the common law courts, Chancery courts and merchant courts made up the majority of the law of England. Statutory law constituted a small portion of the English law. When the colonies in the United States were first settled, the

English system of law was conveniently adopted as the major system of jurisprudence in the new world. Most of the states of the Union and the provinces of Canada adopted the English common law system. Much of the English common law has since been codified by statute in many states. In this excerpt from *Penny v. Little*, 4 Ill. 301 (1841), Justice Douglas eloquently describes the common law.

The common law is a beautiful system; containing the wisdom and experience of ages. Like the people it ruled and protected, it was simple and crude in the infancy, and became enlarged, improved, and polished, as the nation advanced in civilization, virtue, and intelligence. Adopting itself to the conditions and circumstances of the people, and relying upon them for its administration, it necessarily improved as the condition of the people was elevated. . . .

The inhabitants of this country always claimed the common law as their birthright, and at an early period established it as the basis of their jurisprudence.

Mexico and the province of Quebec in Canada, because of their French and Spanish heritage, adopted Roman civil law as the basis of their systems of jurisprudence. One U.S. state, Louisiana, originally a French colony, also bases its legal system on Roman civil law. Roman law has also influenced the developed of the laws of several other states, particularly California and Texas.

SOURCES OF AMERICAN LAW

There are several sources of law in America, including:

1. the U.S. Constitution
2. treaties
3. state constitutions
4. statutes
5. court decisions
6. executive orders
7. ordinances
8. administrative regulations.

The U.S. Constitution.   The Constitution of the United States is the basic source of law in the United States. It was purposely written by its framers in broad and general language to withstand the test of time. The Constitution of the United States is the "supreme law of the land," taking precedence over any state or federal law that comes into conflict with it.

The federal Constitution includes 26 amendments. The first ten amendments are collectively referred to as the *Bill of Rights.* They were adopted immediately following the ratification of the Constitution. The Bill of Rights provides certain basic personal rights (e.g., freedom of speech, press, religion). Additional amendments have since been adopted that guarantee voting rights to certain classes of persons, prohibit discrimination, etc. One amendment, which provided for the prohibition of alcoholic beverages, has since been repealed.

Treaties. The U.S. Constitution provides that treaties may be made by the President with the heads of foreign governments. Treaties must be ratified by the United States Senate. Treaties also become part of the "supreme law of the land." Treaties have not traditionally had much impact on domestic law or business relations. However, with increasing international economic relations, treaties may have more of an impact on business in the future.

State Constitutions. States also have their own constitutions. Although often patterned after the federal Constitution, many state constitutions are more detailed than the federal document. Unless in conflict with federal law, state constitutions provide the supreme law for the citizens of the states.

Statutes. The Congress of the United States and state legislatures are the source of much new law that affects business. After appropriate hearings and committee reviews, legislatures pass (*enact*) *statutes.* Unlike a court decision, which generally settles an individual dispute between two parties, a statute applies prospectively to everyone, unless specific classes of people are exempted from its reach. Under its legislative powers, Congress has passed such statutes as the Internal Revenue Code, securities laws, antitrust laws, and a myriad of other statutory systems. State legislatures have similar power to enact statutes, which typically include corporation laws, consumer protection laws, environmental laws, etc. Because legislators are elected, the statutes that they enact are considered to closely represent the desires and norms of society.

After a decade of work, and with the assistance of hundreds of lawyers, businessmen and other professionals, the National Conference of Commissioners on Uniform State Laws and the American Law Institute published a finished draft of the *Uniform Commercial Code* in 1952. The UCC, by statute, clarifies and liberalizes many of the rules and basic principles underlying commercial transactions. The Code also makes more definite the terms and legal relationships between parties involved in commercial transactions. Forty-nine states, the District of Columbia, and the Virgin Islands have adopted the Uniform Commercial Code. Louisiana has adopted only certain Articles of the Code.

Judicial Decisions. A lawsuit commonly involves two or more parties interested in the resolution of a particular problem, which they have presented to the court. The court's decision in an individual case usually applies only to the parties to that lawsuit. However, in arriving at its decision, the court usually reviews, analyzes, and applies prior legal decisions to the facts of the case. In the course of its opinion, the court may define certain terms or words, interpret the language of a statute, refine an established legal doctrine, or announce a new legal principle.

The equitable doctrines developed by the English Courts of Chancery have been merged with the common law in the United States. Therefore, in most American jurisdictions a court may either issue a decision based upon the law or issue an equitable decree.

Executive Orders. The President of the United States, governors of states, and mayors of cities are often empowered by the legislature or other appropriate body to issue *executive orders* to further the purpose of a statute or ordinance. These executive orders have the force of law. Executive orders form but a small portion of the law of the United States.

Ordinances.   The state, by statute, may delegate a number of functions to other governmental bodies. These may consist of counties, townships, or municipalities (i.e., cities), or other governmental bodies with limited or specialized functions (e.g., school districts, water districts). Within the established limits and powers granted them by the legislature, these government bodies may issue *ordinances* to regulate the activities of persons subject to their jurisdiction. Such ordinances (e.g., zoning laws, building codes, parking regulations) have the force of law.

Administrative Regulations.   As society and commerce became more complex, the Congress and state legislatures exercised their power to delegate their responsibilities and created a large number of administrative agencies. Such agencies are generally established with the goal of creating a body of professionals who are experts in regulating a certain portion of commerce. In addition to creating these administrative agencies, the Congress and legislatures have also delegated to agencies the power to issue rules and regulations to further the purpose of the statutes that they were empowered to administer. Regulations issued by administrative agencies carry the force of law.

THE COURT SYSTEMS OF THE UNITED STATES

There are two major court systems in the United States charged with interpreting these laws and applying them to individual disputes. They are (1) the state court system and (2) the federal court system.

State Court Systems   There are fifty separate state court systems in the United States. Although state court systems may differ somewhat, they usually consist of several trial courts and at least one appellate court. The courts that make up a typical state court system are:

1. small claims court
2. inferior trial court
3. trial court of general jurisdiction
4. intermediate appellate court
5. supreme court

Lesser populated states may have only one trial court, and possibly only one appellate court, the supreme court.

Small Claims Court.   Most states have created a special court of limited jurisdiction known as the *small claims court.* Small claims courts are generally restricted to hearing cases that are under a certain dollar amount, such as $1,500.00. Parties usually appear in small claims court without the aid of a lawyer. In many jurisdictions, lawyers are forbidden to appear on behalf of a claimant or defendant in small claims court. The evidentiary rules in small claims court are much less restrictive than in other court proceedings. The popular television series, "The People's Court" with retired California Judge Wapner presiding, is based on actual disputes that qualify to be presented in a California small claims court.

Businesses are increasingly involved in disputes before small claims courts. The purchase price of most consumer goods falls within the dollar-amount jurisdiction of small claims courts. Therefore, when a consumer has a problem with a defective product or poor service, he can sue the company that provided it in small claims court. On the other hand, businesses often use small claims courts to sue their customers in order to collect unpaid accounts.

Inferior Trial Courts.   Inferior trial courts include those established to hear limited or specialized matters, such as traffic court, courts for divorce and family law matters, probate courts, and justice-of-the-peace courts. Small dollar-amount claims of a general nature are usually heard by inferior trial courts, often referred to as municipal courts. The maximum dollar-amount limit of inferior trial courts varies from state to state (e.g., under $15,000). A decision of an inferior trial court can usually be appealed to the trial court of general jurisdiction, which then acts as an appellate court.

Trial Courts of General Jurisdiction.   Each state has a trial court, which hears the majority of cases brought in the state court system. Negligence cases, breach of contract cases, corporate law cases, and criminal law cases are brought and maintained in these trial courts. Most states refer to the trial courts of general jurisdiction as "superior courts." Other states have different names for their general-jurisdiction trial courts.

Each county of a state usually has a general-jurisdiction trial court, and populous counties generally have more than one general-jurisdiction trial court, to handle the heavy demand. Some states further divide their general-jurisdiction trial courts into two divisions, one to hear civil suits (an individual suing an individual), and one to hear criminal cases (the state suing an individual). General-jurisdiction courts are often referred to as *courts of record* because the testimony given at trial is recorded by a court stenographer. The written or demonstrative evidence presented at trial is also kept on file.

Intermediate Appellate Court.   Most states have an intermediate *appellate* court to which decisions of the state's trial courts may be appealed. The intermediate appellate court reviews the record of the trial court to determine if there has been any prejudicial error committed at the trial court level. The record of the trial court is usually copied and sent to the appellate court. Some states do not have an intermediate appellate court. In these states appeals are taken directly to the State Supreme Court.

State Supreme Court.   Each state has a supreme court, which is the highest court in the state court system. It hears appeals from the intermediate appellate courts and, under appropriate circumstances, directly from trial courts. The supreme court examines the record of the trial court and, if applicable, the decision of the intermediate appellate court, to determine if there has been

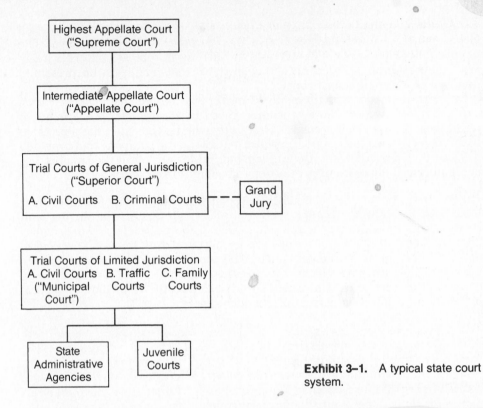

Exhibit 3–1.   A typical state court system.

any prejudicial error committed by the lower court. The decision of a state supreme court is final, unless, of course, a question of federal law is involved that can be appealed to the United States Supreme Court.

Exhibit 3–1 shows a typical state court system.

The Federal Court System.   Article III of the Constitution establishes a federal Supreme Court, enumerates those cases that may be brought in federal courts, and authorizes Congress to establish additional federal courts. The judges and justices of the federal court system are appointed by the President for life. A federal judge can only be removed by an impeachment proceeding. Pursuant to Article III, Congress has created the following courts:

1. special courts
2. District Courts
3. Courts of Appeals

Special Courts.   Congress has exercised its constitutional power and created several special federal courts that have jurisdiction over particular subject matters. These include:

1. a Tax Court to hear certain cases concerning federal tax laws
2. a Court of Claims to hear claims against the United States

3. a Customs Court to hear appeals of decisions of customs officers
4. a Court of Custom and Patent Appeals to review decisions of the Patent and Trademark Office and the Customs Court.

Most recently the Congress has established the Bankruptcy Court as an adjunct court to the federal district courts to hear matters relating to the bankruptcy laws.

District Courts.   The District Court is the trial court of the federal court system. Each state has at least one District Court, and the more populous states contain several District Courts. Once the federal District Court in the Canal Zone is phased out, there will be 94 federal District Courts. Each District Court serves as the federal trial court for a designated geographical area. The majority of federal cases originate in these federal District Courts.

Courts of Appeals.   In addition to the specialized courts and federal trial courts (District Courts), Congress has also established a federal intermediate appellate court known as the Court of Appeals. The country is divided into 12 geographical "circuits," with a Court of Appeals located in each circuit and one in Washington, D.C. The primary purpose of a Court of Appeals is to hear appeals from the district courts located within its circuit. Generally, no witnesses or evidence are heard by the Courts of Appeals. The function of the three-judge panel of the Courts of Appeals is to review the record of the trial court and determine whether some prejudicial error occurred at the lower court.

Exhibit 3–2 shows the geographical circuits and the locations of the federal Courts of Appeals.

Jurisdiction of the Federal Courts.   Questions often arise as to whether a case should be brought in the federal or state court system. Generally, federal courts have jurisdiction to hear only cases provided for in the Constitution. The state courts have jurisdiction to hear all other matters. There are some matters that *must* be presented to federal court. Federal courts have *exclusive jurisdiction* (i.e., state courts cannot hear cases) in matters involving federal crimes, bankruptcy, patents and copyrights, in suits against the United States, and in some areas of admiralty law.

Federal courts have jurisdiction to hear any case involving a "federal question." A *federal question* exists where a case requires an interpretation of the U.S. Constitution or of a treaty, federal statute, or federal regulation. The majority of the federal court cases in this book involve federal question jurisdiction.

In addition to the "federal question" jurisdiction of federal courts, federal courts have jurisdiction where there is "diversity of citizenship." This category includes cases involving citizens of different states, citizens of a state and citizens or subjects of a foreign country, and citizens of a state where a foreign government is the plaintiff. The rationale behind the *diversity-of-citizenship* rule is that a state court might be biased when a citizen of the state is involved in a controversy with a citizen of another state. The majority of the cases filed in federal courts are based on diversity of citizenship. State courts have

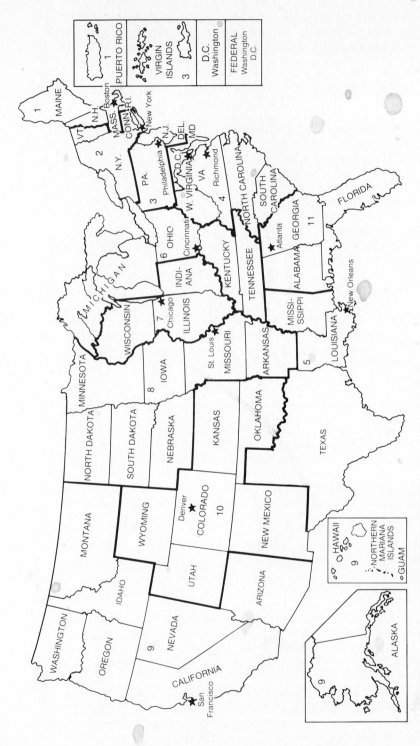

Exhibit 3-2. The 13 federal judicial circuits and courts of appeal.

concurrent jurisdiction with federal courts to hear federal-question and diversity-of-citizenship cases. However, where such a case has been brought in a state court, the other party can demand that the case be transferred to the proper federal court.

In cases involving a federal question or diversity of citizenship, the amount in question must exceed $10,000 before the federal district court has jurisdiction. If the amount is less than $10,000, the suit must be brought in state court. However, there is no minimum dollar requirement where the federal courts have exclusive jurisdiction over the matter in controversy. The $10,000 jurisdictional minimum also does not apply where a suit is brought against the federal government or against one of its employees.

The U.S. Supreme Court. The highest court of the land is the U.S. Supreme Court, located in Washington, D.C. It consists of nine justices, one of whom is appointed Chief Justice by the President, and eight Associate Justices, also appointed by the President. The Supreme Court's primary function is to hear appeals from federal Courts of Appeals and, under the proper circumstances, appeals from the highest state courts and other courts.

Appeal by Right. The Supreme Court *must* hear certain cases where there is an appeal by right because a "federal question" is involved. The following situations provide for *appeal by right* to the United States Supreme Court:

1. When a federal Court of Appeals declares a state statute to be in violation of federal law, including the U.S. Constitution, treaties, or other laws of the United States;
2. When a federal court holds an act of Congress to be unconstitutional, and the federal government or one of its employees is a party;
3. when the highest state court of appeals declares a federal law to be invalid, or upholds the validity of a state statute that has been challenged as in violation of the U.S. Constitution, or of treaties or other laws of the United States;
4. when a District Court has decided a hearing for an injunction in a civil (not criminal) action as required by Congress.

Although in theory the Supreme Court must hear any case that falls in one of these four categories, it has substantial discretion as to the scope of the review it will give to such cases. For example, the Supreme Court will allow full consideration (written briefs from all parties' lawyers and oral argument) of an appeal only if four of the nine justices vote to do so. If such a vote is not obtained, then the case is "dismissed." A dismissal may in essence serve to affirm the decision of the lower court, or be given because a "substantial federal question" is lacking, or for some procedural reason.

Writ of Certiorari. Where there is no appeal by right, the parties may still request the United States Supreme Court to hear their appeal. This is done by petitioning the Supreme Court to issue a writ of *certiorari.* The Supreme Court will not issue a *writ of certiorari* unless four of the justices approve it (the "rule of four"). The majority of petitions for writs of *certiorari* are denied.

If the writ is denied, the court refuses to hear the appeal and, in effect, the judgment of the lower court stands. When the writ is denied, the decision of the lower court has no value as precedent for the Supreme Court.

Decisions of the Supreme Court.   Often, the justices of the U.S. Supreme Court will agree on the decision and rationale for deciding a case. If all nine justices of the Court agree both as to the decision of the case and the reasoning that should be used to decide the case, then they will issue a *unanimous* decision. However on many occasions, particularly with the current makeup of the Supreme Court, the justices will not agree as to the outcome of a case or the reasoning that should support the decision of a case.

If five or more, but less than nine, of the justices agree as to a decision and the rationale for the decision, the opinion they issue is called a *majority* opinion. Any interpretation of law announced in a majority opinion becomes precedent and must be followed by all courts in the United States.

If five or more of the justices agree as to the outcome of a case, but less than five justices can agree as to the interpretation of the law that should support the case, none of the opinions announced by any of the justices become precedent for future court decisions. In this type of case justices often issue *concurring* opinions, which state their individual views of the case. Where a majority opinion cannot be reached, the decision reached by the Court is only binding on the parties to the specific dispute.

If a justice disagrees with a decision reached in a majority opinion or concurring opinions, he or she can *dissent.* A justice usually prepares and issues a *dissenting opinion* in which he or she explains the interpretation of the law that should be used to decide the case. Concurring and dissenting opinions are published following the majority opinion of the U.S. Supreme Court on each case. Where relevant, pertinent parts of concurring and dissenting opinions are included in some of the cases in this book.

Exhibit 3–3 is a diagram of the federal court system. The unbroken lines refer to appeals by right. Broken lines refer to cases reviewable at the discretion of the appellate court. The jurisdictional requirements for each court are noted.

☆ THE DOCTRINE OF *STARE DECISIS*

Legal principles and rules announced by an appellate or supreme court become *precedent* for the lower courts located in the jurisdiction of the higher court when they face similar issues in the future. That is, a lower court located in the jurisdiction of a higher court is bound to follow the opinions of the higher court in its own decisions. For example, decisions of the U.S. Supreme Court are precedent for all courts in the United States. Decisions of a state supreme court are precedent for all courts in that state. Adherence to precedent is known as the doctrine of *stare decisis* ("to stand by the decision").

A legal principle announced in one jurisdiction (e.g., in one state) is not precedent in another jurisdiction (e.g., in another state). However decisions from other jurisdictions are often referred to for guidance, particularly where

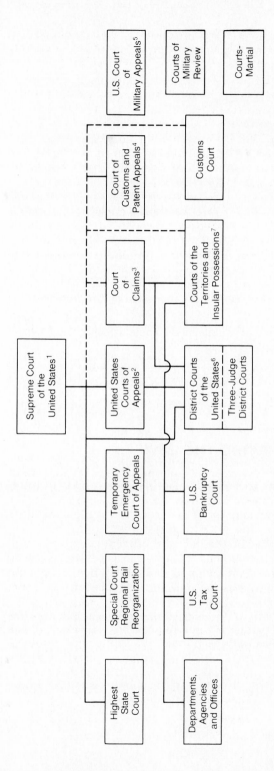

Diagram boxes:
- Supreme Court of the United States[1]
- Highest State Court
- Special Court Regional Rail Reorganization
- Temporary Emergency Court of Appeals
- United States Courts of Appeals[2]
- Court of Claims[3]
- Court of Customs and Patent Appeals[4]
- U.S. Court of Military Appeals[5]
- Departments, Agencies and Offices
- U.S. Tax Court
- U.S. Bankruptcy Court
- District Courts of the United States[6]
- Three-Judge District Courts
- Courts of the Territories and Insular Possessions[7]
- Customs Court
- Courts of Military Review
- Courts-Martial

1. Original jurisdiction in cases where a state, ambassador, public minister or consul is a party. Appellate jurisdiction for: (1) Cases where the highest court of appeal of a state holds a federal law invalid or upholds a state law that has been challenged as violating the United States Constitution or other federal law or treaty; (2) Cases from any federal court where an act of Congress has been held to be unconstitutional in a civil action where the federal government or one of its employees is a party; (3) Cases from a federal Court of Appeals in which a state statute has been held to be invalid because it violates federal law; (4) Cases based on a *writ of certiorari* involving a federal question; and (5) Appeals from certain orders of three-judge courts.

2. Appellate jurisdiction for: (1) Appeals from decisions of any District Court except where a direct review may be had by the Supreme Court; and (2) Review of decisions and enforcement of orders of federal administrative agencies.

3. Original jurisdiction of claims against the United States government, except for tort claims. Appellate jurisdiction from District Court judgments involving tort claims where the appellees consent.

4. Appellate jurisdiction for: (1) Appeals from the Customs Court, except where direct review may be had by the Supreme Court; and (2) Appeals from the Patent and Trademark Office, the Tariff Commission, and certain findings of the Secretaries of Commerce and Agriculture.

5. Appellate jurisdiction for all cases in which a sentence affects a general or flag officer or extends to death, for cases sent by the Judge Advocate General, and cases in which review is granted. Appeal to a higher federal court is permitted solely on defendant's petition for a *writ of habeus corpus*.

6. Original jurisdiction for: (1) "Federal questions" cases where the Constitution, laws or treaties of the United States is involved, and where the amount in controversy exceeds $10,000; (2) Diversity of citizenship cases where the amount in controversy exceeds $10,000; (3) Other federal questions where Congress has placed no limit on the amount in controversy; (4) Federal crimes and criminal proceedings against federal officers; (5) Admiralty and maritime cases; and (6) Judicial review of actions of federal administrative agencies. Appellate jurisdiction for cases appealed from the Bankruptcy Court unless the Circuit Court has created a three-judge bankruptcy panel to handle appeals, or unless both parties consent to take the appeal directly to the Circuit Court.

7. Mixed local and federal jurisdiction. Includes Puerto Rico, Guam, Virgin Islands, and Northern Marianas.

Exhibit 3-3. The federal court system.

the issue faced by the court is one of "first impression," that is, one faced for the first time by that particular court.

Reversal.   A court is not bound to follow a legal rule that it has itself announced in a prior court decision. For example, if a court considers a previously announced legal principle to be incorrect, the court may later *reverse* itself as to that rule of law. The court must wait until an actual controversy is presented before it can reverse a previously announced rule of law. A reversal does *not* retroactively reverse prior cases. The original decision in which the old rule of law was announced, and any subsequent decisions that were based on that rule of law, are allowed to stand. The new rule of law becomes precedent for all *future* cases subject to the jurisdiction of the reversing court. It is important to note that a lower court cannot reverse a decision of a higher court.

In *Flagiello v. Pennsylvania,* 208 A.2d 193 (1965), Justice Musmanno succinctly described the doctrine of *stare decisis* and the ability of a court to reverse itself.

Without *stare decisis,* there would be no stability in our system of jurisprudence.

Stare decisis channels the law. It erects lighthouses and flies the signals of safety. The ships of jurisprudence must follow that well-defined channel which, over the years, has been proved to be secure and trustworthy. . . .

[However,] when a rule offends against reason, when it is at odds with every precept of natural justice, and when it cannot be defended on its own merits, but has to depend on a discredited genealogy, courts not only possess the inherent power to repudiate, but, indeed, it is required, by the very nature of judicial function, to abolish such a rule.

INTERPRETING THE LAW

The judicial branch of government is charged with the responsibility of interpreting the law. The law being interpreted may be a statute passed by the legislative branch of government, an activity of the executive branch in administering the law, or a decision or ruling of an administrative agency.

After substantial early conflict between the different branches of government as to the *reviewing authority* of the judicial branch, the issue was resolved in the landmark case of *Marbury v. Madison* 5 U.S. (1 Cranch) (1803). In that case, Chief Justice Marshall wrote as the opinion of the court:

It is emphatically the province and duty of the judicial department to say what the law is. Those who apply the rule to particular cases, must of necessity expound and interpret that rule. If two laws conflict with each other, the courts must decide on the operation of each.

The courts can generally use any one or combination of four recognized standards for interpreting enacted law. These four standards are:

1. literal interpretation
2. precedent-based interpretation

3. purposive-based interpretation
4. policy-based interpretation.

Literal Interpretation.   The most obvious standard to use to interpret enacted law is to interpret the words of a statute *literally*. Under a literal interpretation, ordinary words are given their ordinary meaning, and technical words are given their technical meaning. To the layman, this seems like the only standard that should be applied by the courts when interpreting enacted law. However, the literal interpretation of enacted law is the mode of interpretation least used by the courts.

Precedent-Based Interpretation.   Under a precedent-based standard of interpretation, the court looks at *past* court decisions to determine if, and if so how, the courts have previously interpreted the statute or words of the statute being reviewed. Courts are generally reluctant to adopt an interpretation that differs from previously decided cases. A lower court is bound to follow a precedent established by a higher court within its jurisdiction.

Purposive-Based Interpretation.   The reviewing court may base its interpretation of a statute on what it determines Congress or the state legislature *intended* when the statute was enacted. In order to support a purposive-based interpretation of a statute, the court often reviews and cites legislative history (e.g., floor debates in Congress) during the time period preceding the enactedment of the statute.

Policy-Based Interpretation.   The broadest standard available to the courts for interpreting a statute is the *policy*-based standard of interpretation. Under this standard, the court ignores the literal meaning and legislative history of a statute, and interprets it to advance the policy which the court believes underlies the statute. Antidiscrimination laws are often interpreted using the policy-based standard.

In *Steelworkers v. Weber,* the Supreme Court had to choose from the standards of interpretation in order to decide whether a training program quota system which favored minorities over more qualified whites constituted "reverse discrimination" in violation of Title VII of the Civil Rights Act of 1964.

INTERPRETING ENACTED LAW

STEELWORKERS v. WEBER

443 U.S. 193 (1979)
UNITED STATES SUPREME COURT

Mr. Justice Brennan delivered the opinion of the Court.

In 1974, petitioner United Steelworkers of America (USWA) and petitioner Kaiser Aluminum & Chemical Corp. (Kaiser) entered into a master collective-bargaining agreement covering terms and conditions of employment at 15 Kaiser plants. The agreement contained, *inter alia,* an affirmative action plan designed to eliminate conspicuous racial imbalances in Kaiser's then almost exclusively white craftwork forces. Black craft-hiring goals were set for each Kaiser plant equal to the percentage of blacks in the respective local labor forces. To enable plants to meet these goals, on-the-job training programs were established to teach unskilled production workers—black and white—the skills necessary to become craft-workers. The plan reserved for black employees 50% of the openings in these newly created in-plant training programs.

Pursuant to the national agreement Kaiser altered its craft-hiring practice in the Gramercy plant. Rather than hiring already trained outsiders, Kaiser established a training program to train its production workers to fill craft openings. . . .

During 1974, the first year of the operation of the Kaiser-USWA affirmative action plan, 13 craft trainees were selected from Gramercy's production work force. Of these, seven were black and six white. The most senior black selected into the program had less seniority than several white production workers whose bids for admission were rejected. Thereafter one of those white production workers, respondent Brian Weber (hereafter respondent), instituted this class action in the United States District Court for the Eastern District of Louisiana.

The complaint alleged . . . [discrimination] against respondent and other similarly situated white employees in violation of sections 703(a) and (d) of Title VII [of the Civil Rights Act of 1964, as amended]. . . . Those sections make it unlawful to "discriminate . . . because of . . . race" in hiring and in the selection of apprentices for training programs.

Respondent's argument is not without force. But it overlooks the significance of the fact that the Kaiser-USWA plan is an affirmative action plan voluntarily adopted by private parties to eliminate traditional patterns of racial segregation. In this context respondent's reliance upon a literal construction of §§ 703 (a) and (d) . . . is misplaced.

Congress' primary concern in enacting the prohibition against racial discrimination in Title VII of the Civil Rights Act of 1964 was with "the plight of the Negro in our economy." 110 Cong. Rec. 6548

(1964) (remarks of Sen. Humphrey). . . . These remarks echoed President Kennedy's original message to Congress upon the introduction of the Civil Rights Act in 1963.

> There is little value in a Negro's obtaining the right to be admitted to hotels and restaurants if he has no cash in his pocket and no job. (109 Cong. Rec. 11159)

Given this legislative history, we cannot agree with respondent that Congress intended to prohibit the private sector from taking effective steps to accomplish the goal that Congress designed Title VII to achieve. It would be ironic indeed if a law triggered by a Nation's concern over centuries of racial injustice and intended to improve the lot of those who had "been excluded from the American dream for so long," 110 Cong. Rec. 6552 (1964) (remarks of Sen. Humphrey), constituted the first legislative prohibition of all voluntary, private, race-conscious efforts to abolish traditional patterns of racial segregation and hierarchy.

We therefore hold that Title VII's prohibition in §§ 703 (a) and (d) against racial discrimination does not condemn all private, voluntary, race-conscious affirmative action plans. . . . At the same time, the plan does not unnecessarily trammel the interests of the white employees. Moreover, the plan is a temporary measure; it is not intended to maintain racial balance, but simply to eliminate a manifest racial imbalance.

Accordingly, the judgment of the Court of Appeals for the Fifth Circuit is *reversed.*

Mr. Chief Justice Burger, dissenting.

The Court reaches a result I would be inclined to vote for were I a Member of Congress considering a proposed amendment of Title VII. I cannot join the Court's judgment, however, because it is contrary to the explicit language of the statute and arrived at by means wholly incompatible with long-established principles of separation of powers. Under the guise of statutory "construction," the Court effectively rewrites Title VII to achieve what it regards as a desirable result. It "amends" the statute to do precisely what both its sponsors and its opponents agreed the statute was *not* intended to do.

CASE QUESTIONS

1. Who were the plaintiffs? What "class" did they represent? What did the contract between the USWA and Kaiser provide?
2. What does the specific language of Title VII provide?
3. Did the court apply a *literal* standard of interpretation to the statute? If it had, how would the case have been decided?
4. Which of the following standards did the U.S. Supreme Court use in interpreting the statute?
   a. precedent-based standard
   b. purposive-based standard
   c. policy-based standard
5. Did the fact that the contract between the USWA and Kaiser was *voluntarily* entered into have any bearing on the decision in this case? Had Weber implicitly agreed to the quota system? Explain.

Policy Issue. Should the courts be permitted to ignore the literal meaning of a statute?

Was the Supreme Court guilty of "judicial legislation" as alleged by Chief Justice Burger in the dissent?

Economics Issue. What are the economic implications of the use of quotas? On whom?

Ethics Issue. Is it ethical for a minority to accept a position under a quota system? Is it ethical for a white worker to complain about quota systems?

Social Responsibility. Do corporations and unions owe a duty of social responsibility to provide special employment opportunities to minority applicants?

CONFLICTS OF THE LAW

Often, the activities leading up to a lawsuit (e.g., breach of contract, tortious conduct) may occur in many states. The question then arises as to which state's law applies in the case. Plaintiffs often attempt to go "forum shopping" to find the state whose law is most favorable to their lawsuits. Defendants also engage in forum shopping by trying to remove the lawsuit to a state whose laws are most favorable to the defendant's case. Courts must decide which state's law applies to a lawsuit.

If the laws of both states are the same regarding the legal issue involved, there is no conflict of law and it does not matter which state's law is applied to the case. However, where the states' laws differ, and both states have an "interest" in having their law applied to the case, the courts must apply the "comparative impairment" test to resolve the conflict between the states. Under the comparative impairment test, the court will apply the law of the state whose interest would be *more* impaired if its law were *not* applied. Conflict of laws is a complex subject. It is usually a separate course in most law school curriculums.

Federal Courts and State Law.   There is no federal "common law" (e.g., contract law, tort law). Where the U.S. Constitution or other federal law is not at issue, but the parties are before a federal court (e.g., diversity of citizenship jurisdiction), the federal courts are bound to apply the proper state law to the case.

Where no state law exists regarding a legal issue presented to a federal court in a diversity of citizenship case or other case not involving a federal law, the federal court may invoke the doctrine of "abstention." Under this doctrine, the federal court may hold the case in abeyance and direct the parties to litigate the case in state court. Federal courts may also invoke the doctrine of abstention when mixed questions of federal and state law are involved in a case. The parties may then appeal the decision of the state court regarding the federal law questions to the federal courts.

In the following excerpt from the landmark *Erie Railroad v. Tompkins* (1938) 304 U.S. 64, Justice Brandeis discussed the role of the federal courts in applying state law.

. . . *Swift v. Tyson,* 16 Pet. 1, 18, 10 L.Ed. 865, held that federal courts exercising jurisdiction on the ground of diversity of citizenship need not, in matters of general jurisprudence, apply the unwritten law of the state as declared by its highest court; that they are free to exercise an independent judgment as to what the common law of the state is—or should be. . . .

The mischievous results of the doctrine had become apparent. Diversity of citizenship jurisdiction was conferred in order to prevent apprehended discrimination in state courts against those not citizens of the state. *Swift v. Tyson* introduced grave discrimination by noncitizens against citizens. It made rights enjoyed under the unwritten "general law" vary according to whether enforcement was sought in the state or in the federal court; and the privilege of selecting the court in which the right should be determined was conferred upon the noncitizen. Thus, the doctrine rendered impossible equal protection of the law. In attempting to promote uniformity of law throughout the United States, the doctrine had prevented uniformity in the administration of the law of the state. . . .

Except in matters governed by the Federal Constitution or by acts of Congress, the law to be applied in any case is the law of the state. And whether the law of the state shall be declared by its Legislature in a statute or by its highest court in a decision is not a matter of federal concern. There is no federal general common law. Congress has no power to declare substantive rules of common law applicable in a state whether they be local in their nature or "general," whether they be commercial law or a part of the law of torts. And there is no clause in the Constitution that purports to confer such a power upon the federal courts. . . .

The majority of the cases in this book involve the application and interpretation of *federal* laws and regulations, and have therefore been decided by federal courts. Because of the importance of many of the topics covered, the majority of the cases covered in this book are decisions of the U.S. Supreme Court.

Trend of the Law

One of the most important issues that will face the courts in the future is the degree to which the courts will engage in what has commonly been referred to a "judicial legislation." In the 1950s and 1960s, the U.S. Supreme Court tended to interpret enacted law broadly in order to advance social issues such as antidiscrimination laws and individual rights of criminals. There is presently a growing conservative influence in this country to curtail this broad interpretation of law by judges and justices. The most recent appointments to the U.S. Supreme Court have been "strict constructionalists," who are generally less inclined to interpret statutes broadly. The trend in the future will be for the U.S. Supreme Court to apply more literal and purposive-based interpretations to enacted law.

REVIEW QUESTIONS

1. What is the "common law"?
2. What are the sources of American law?
3. What courts make up a typical state court system? Draw a diagram showing these courts, and their relation to one another.
4. What courts make up the federal court system? Draw a diagram showing these courts and their relation to one another.
5. With regards to the jurisdiction of federal courts, what do the following terms mean?
   a. "federal question" jurisdiction
   b. diversity-of-citizenship jurisdiction
   c. exclusive jurisdiction
   d. dollar-amount jurisdiction
6. With regard to the activities of the U.S. Supreme Court, what do the following terms mean?
   a. appeal by right
   b. writ of *certiorari*
   c. unanimous decision
   d. majority opinion
   e. concurring opinion
   f. dissenting opinion
7. Describe the following standards of interpretation:
   a. literal interpretation
   b. precedent-based interpretation
   c. purposive-based interpretation
   d. policy-based interpretation
8. What does the doctrine of *stare decisis* provide? What courts are bound by a precedent?
9. When does a conflict of law arise? What standard is used to determine which law applies in a conflict-of-laws problem?
10. Is there a federal "common law"? What law must a federal court apply when it is faced with a state law question?
11. What does the term "judicial legislation" mean? Do you think that there will be more or less judicial legislation in the future? Why or why not?

4 THE LITIGATION PROCESS

INTRODUCTION

There are two general types of lawsuits in which a person or business can become involved. The first type is a *civil* lawsuit, where one party sues another party for breach of contract, negligence, etc. The prayer (request) for relief is usually for an award of dollar damages to compensate the plaintiff for losses suffered. In a civil lawsuit, both plaintiff and defendant must pay for their own legal representation. The government does not provide lawyers to the parties in a civil lawsuit.

The second type of lawsuit is a *criminal* suit, where the plaintiff is the government. In a criminal suit, the government is usually seeking a jail sentence or fine against the defendant. In a criminal lawsuit the government employs the lawyers who prosecute the case against the defendant. These government lawyers, commonly called *prosecuting attorneys,* are full-time employees of the government. Generally, a defendant in a criminal case is responsible for paying for his or her own legal defense, including hiring a defense lawyer. If a criminal defendant cannot afford a lawyer, the U.S. Constitution provides that the government must provide a lawyer to the defendant

50

without charge. These lawyers, commonly called *defense attorneys,* are often full-time employees of the government, or they may be private attorneys appointed by the court and paid by the government to represent the accused.

A person involved in a lawsuit need not be represented by a lawyer. A person may appear in court *in propria persona* ("in one's own proper person") without a lawyer. This practice is not favored by the courts, on the theory that a person untrained in the law will not be able to represent himself adequately, and that the time and cost of the court will be substantially increased when a person unfamiliar with court procedure acts as his own lawyer. Because of the complexities of the law, and particularly legal procedure, most persons who sue (plaintiffs), or who are sued (defendants), hire lawyers to represent them in legal proceedings.

LEGAL REPRESENTATION

The most visible type of lawyer, the type most often portrayed in the media, is the trial lawyer. In this capacity the lawyer is a *litigator,* an adversary whose function is to serve and protect his client's interests. An ethical question often asked of criminal lawyers is, "How can you represent someone whom you know is guilty?" The usual answer of attorneys is that in our democratic society *every* person deserves legal representation, and the lawyer is merely performing an adversarial function without making an ethical decision regarding the guilt or innocence of his client.

The majority of lawyers are not litigators. A substantial amount of the work of lawyers, particularly of those representing business, consists of nontrial activities, including the formation of corporations, advising businesses, drafting contracts, negotiating labor settlements, dealing with regulatory agencies, negotiating deals on behalf of clients, etc.

When a person needs a lawyer, the most common method of selecting one is to ask a friend or acquaintance for a recommendation and referral. Most lawyers are listed in the classified telephone directory, and many lawyers now advertise in newspapers and other media. The majority of lawyers tend to specialize or emphasize practice in certain types of law. Generally, a client should select a lawyer who practices in the area of law in which the client's case or matter falls.

Lawyers' Fees. Lawyers generally charge clients by two different methods: either by the hour or on a contingency fee basis. Hourly charges of lawyers in urban areas generally range from approximately $75 to $200 per hour. In rural areas the hourly fees tend to be somewhat lower. Lawyers for defendants in lawsuits and most corporate lawyers charge by the hour.

Contingency fee arrangements are most prevalent by plaintiff's lawyers in personal injury cases. A lawyer representing a plaintiff who sues a defendant who negligently caused injury to the plaintiff generally receives 25 percent to 35 percent of the amount received by the plaintiff if the matter is "settled" before trial, and 35 percent to 45 percent of the award if the case goes to trial. If the lawyer's client loses at trial, the lawyer receives nothing for his work under a contingency fee arrangement. Over 80 percent of all lawsuits are settled before trial.

In addition to lawyers' fees, the parties to a lawsuit often have to pay other costs involved in the litigation, including filing fees, jury fees, expert witness fees, copying costs, etc. These costs can be substantial in many lawsuits.

Cost-Benefit Analysis of a Lawsuit.   As a potential plaintiff, or as a defendant in a lawsuit, a business person must make a rational economic decision whether to prosecute, defend, or settle a lawsuit. The items to include in a cost-benefit analysis of a lawsuit are:

1. probability of winning or losing
2. the amount to be won or lost
3. cost of lawyers
4. costs of discovery, filing fees, etc.
5. lost time of management and other personnel that will be consumed by the lawsuit
6. loss of the use of money held in escrow for the years while the lawsuit is pending
7. low rate of legal interest paid by the courts (7% in many states)
8. the effect on long-term relationships between the parties
9. the effect on the parties' reputation in the industry
10. aggravation and psychological problems associated with lawsuits
11. other factors.

Although the lay person may have a preconceived notion that the legal system is objective and fair, judges and justices are merely human beings like ourselves. They have biases, prejudices, and interests that may affect their decisions. They also make mistakes. Jurors are selected from members of the public. They are called upon to weigh the evidence, consider the credibility of witnesses, and to decide the facts of a case. They may also may be biased or make mistakes. As can be seen, the system of justice in this country is not perfect, nor is it a science. The unpredictability of the legal system must be factored into the cost-benefit analysis of a lawsuit.

STANDING TO SUE

The courts only hear specific cases that involve *actual disputes* or *controversies* between two or more parties. Courts will generally refuse to hear these types of cases:

1. hypothetical questions
2. minor disputes (e.g., social insults, internal family disputes)
3. questions that are *moot* (i.e., an issue no longer disputed because it has been settled).

In order to institute and prosecute a lawsuit, the plaintiff must have *standing to sue*. That is, the plaintiff must have some interest or stake in the outcome of the case to justify bringing the lawsuit. The court will *dismiss* a lawsuit where the plaintiff is found not to have standing to sue. For example, taxpayers are generally not considered to have sufficient standing to bring a lawsuit against the government for how tax dollars are spent.

In *Valley Forge Christian College v. Americans United for Separation of Church and State,* the U.S. Supreme Court found that the plaintiffs did not have standing as either "taxpayers" or "citizens" to maintain the lawsuit.

STANDING TO SUE

VALLEY FORGE CHRISTIAN COLLEGE v. AMERICANS UNITED FOR SEPARATION OF CHURCH AND STATE, INC.

454 U.S. 464 (1982)
UNITED STATES SUPREME COURT

Justice Rehnquist delivered the opinion of the Court.

The property which spawned this litigation was acquired by the Department of the Army in 1942. . . . The Army built on that land the Valley Forge General Hospital, and for 30 years thereafter, that hospital provided medical care for members of the Armed Forces. In April 1973, as part of a plan to reduce the number of military installations in the United States, the Secretary of Defense proposed to close the hospital, and the General Services Administration declared it to be "surplus property."

The Department of Health, Education, and Welfare (HEW) eventually assumed responsibility for disposing of portions of the property, and in August 1976, it conveyed a 77-acre tract to petitioner, the Valley Forge Christian College. The appraised value of the property at the time of conveyance was $577,500. This appraised value was discounted, however, by the Secretary's computation of a 100 percent public benefit allowance, which permitted petitioner to acquire the property without making any financial payment for it.

Petitioner is a nonprofit educational institution operating under the supervision of a religious order known as the Assemblies of God. By its own description, petitioner's purpose is "to offer systematic training on the collegiate level to men and women for Christian service as either ministers or laymen."

In September 1976, respondents Americans United for Separation of Church and State, Inc. (Americans United), and four of its employees, learned of the conveyance through a news release. Two months later, they brought suit in the United States District Court for the Eastern District of Pennsylvania to challenge the conveyance on the ground that it violated the Establishment Clause of the First Amendment. In its amended complaint, Americans United described itself as a nonprofit organization composed of 90,000 "taxpayer members." The complaint asserted that each member "would be deprived of the fair and constitutional use of his (her) tax dollar for constitutional purposes in violation of his (her) rights [of Freedom of Religion] under the First Amendment of the United States Constitution."

[The doctrine of standing] tends to assure that the legal questions presented to the court will be resolved, not in the rarified atmosphere of a debating society, but in a concrete factual context conducive to a realistic appreciation of the consequences of judicial action. . . . Those who do not possess . . . standing may not litigate as suitors in the courts of the United States.

Respondents, therefore, are plainly without standing to sue as taxpayers [or citizens]. . . . Their claim that the government has violated the Establishment Clause does not provide a special license to roam the country in search of governmental wrongdoing and to reveal their discoveries in federal court. The federal courts were simply not constituted as ombudsmen of the general welfare.

CASE QUESTIONS

1. What does the doctrine of "standing" require?
2. Who were the plaintiffs in this case? Does "taxpayer" status or "citizen" status alone constitute standing to sue?

Policy Issue. Should taxpayer status or citizen status be a sufficient ground to provide standing to sue? Or should some "injury in fact" be required to be shown?

Economics Issue. If taxpayer status alone constituted standing to sue, would the number and cost of lawsuits increase or decrease?

Ethics Issue.

a. Was it ethical for the plaintiffs to seek recission of the grant of property to the Christian College?
b. Was it ethical for the Christian College to accept the property free of charge?

Social Responsibility.

a. Does the government owe a duty of social responsibility to spend taxpayers money in a reasonable and conservative manner?
b. If taxpayers were given standing to sue, would government spending be more or less frivolous than it now is?

☆ JURISDICTION

In order for a court to hear a case, it must have *jurisdiction* to do so. The plaintiff must demonstrate:

1. *in personam* jurisdiction
2. subject matter jurisdiction
3. venue

In Personam Jurisdiction. When a person files a lawsuit in a court, that court automatically obtains personal jurisdiction over the plaintiff. This rule is based on the theory that the plaintiff has voluntarily submitted himself to the jurisdiction of the court. Jurisdiction over the defendant is usually obtained by personally serving a summons on the defendant when and if he is located within the state issuing the summons. Alternative forms of service (e.g., publication of notice, leaving the summons at a residence or office address, mailing the summons) are recognized by most states.

In this excerpt from the landmark *International Shoe Co. v. Washington,* 326 U.S. 310 (1945) Justice Stone announced the "minimum contacts" standard for finding personal jurisdiction over a defendant corporation.

Historically the jurisdiction of courts to render judgment *in personam* is grounded on their de facto power over the defendant's person. Hence his presence within the territorial jurisdiction of a court was prerequisite to its rendition of a judgment personally binding him. But now that the *capias ad respondendum* [writ] has given way to personal service of summons or other form of notice, due process requires only that in order to subject a defendant to a judgment *in personam,* if he be not present within the territory of the forum, he must have certain minimum contacts with it such that the maintenance of the suit does not offend "traditional notions of fair play and substantial justice. . . ."

Since the corporate personality is a fiction, although a fiction intended to be acted upon as though it were a fact, it is clear that unlike an individual its "presence" without, as well as within, the state of its origin can be manifested only by activities carried on in its behalf by those who are authorized to act for it. . . . The terms "present" or "presence" are used merely to symbolize those activities of the corporation's agent within the state which courts will deem to be sufficient to satisfy the demands of due process. Those demands may be met by such contacts of the corporation with the state of the forum as make it reasonable, in the context of our federal system of government, to require the corporation to defend the particular suit which is brought there. An "estimate of the inconveniences" which would result to the corporation from a trial away from its "home" or principal place of business is relevant in this connection.

"Presence" in the state in this sense has never been doubted when the activities of the corporation there have not only been continuous and systematic, but also give rise to the liabilities sued on, even though no consent to be sued or authorization to an agent to accept service of process has been given. . . . Conversely it has been generally recognized that the casual presence of the corporate agent or even his conduct of single or isolated items of activities in a state in the corporation's behalf are not enough to subject it to suit on causes of action unconnected with the activities there. . . . To require the corporation in such circumstances to defend the suit away from its home or other jurisdiction where it carries on more substantial activities has been thought to lay too great and unreasonable a burden on the corporation to comport with due process. . . .

Subject-Matter Jurisdiction.   Subject-matter jurisdiction is generally not a problem for courts of general jurisdiction. However, for state courts of limited jurisdiction, only certain types of cases may be heard, e.g., family law matters or cases of up to a certain dollar amount. Where a plaintiff wants to bring his case in federal court, specific subject matter requirements must be met, such as "federal question," or diversity of citizenship. Where a court has neither *in personam* nor subject-matter jurisdiction, the case cannot be heard by that court.

Venue.   A lawsuit must also be brought in the proper venue. *Venue* pertains to the specific geographical location where the lawsuit is filed in the proper jurisdiction. Most states provide by statute that the proper venue is the county where the defendant resides. However, other factors, such as location of witnesses or evidence, where the contract is executed or the accident occurred, the residence of the plaintiff, and hardships of travel, will be considered in establishing the proper venue.

In many cases the determination of jurisdiction and venue is an important first issue to be addressed by the parties and decided by the court. "Forum shopping" by the parties is not favored by the courts.

"Long Arm" Statutes.   Originally, summonses were not valid if they were served beyond the border of the state issuing the summons. However, most states have adopted "long arm" statutes, which allow for service of summons across state lines. Long arm statutes make the defendant subject to the personal jurisdiction of the issuing state as long as the defendant has had constitutionally recognized "minimum contacts" with the issuing state. Most states provide that out-of-state defendants are subject to process under their long arm statute if: (1) the defendant enters into the state to conduct business that is the subject matter of the lawsuit or commits a tort in the issuing state (*in personam* jurisdiction); or (2) the defendant owns property in the issuing state that is the subject matter of the lawsuit (*in rem* jurisdiction).

In *World-Wide Volkswagen Corp. v. Woodson, District Judge of Creek County, Oklahoma,* the Supreme Court held that a defendant was not subject to a state's long arm statute merely because a product that defendant sold in another state was involved in an accident in the state seeking jurisdiction.

IN PERSONAM JURISDICTION, "LONG ARM" STATUTE

WORLD-WIDE VOLKSWAGEN CORP. v. WOODSON, DISTRICT JUDGE OF CREEK COUNTY, OKLAHOMA

444 U.S. 286 (1980)
UNITED STATES SUPREME COURT

Mr. Justice White delivered the opinion of the Court.

Respondents Harry and Kay Robinson purchased a new Audi automobile from petitioner Seaway Volkswagen, Inc. (Seaway) in Massena, N.Y., in 1976. The following year the Robinson family, who resided in New York, left that State for a new home in Arizona. As they passed through the State of Oklahoma, another car struck their Audi in the rear, causing a fire which severely burned Kay Robinson and her two children.

The Robinsons subsequently brought a products liability action in the District Court for Creek County, Okla., claiming that their injuries resulted from defective design and placement of the Audi's gas tank and fuel system. They joined as defendants the automobile's manufacturer, Audi NSU Auto Union Aktiengesellschaft (Audi); its importer, Volkswagen of America, Inc. (Volkswagen); its regional distributor, petitioner World-Wide Volkswagen Corporation (World-Wide); and its retail dealer, petitioner Seaway. Seaway and World-Wide entered special appearances, claiming that Oklahoma's exercise of jurisdiction over them would offend the limitations on the State's jurisdiction imposed by the Due Process Clause of the Fourteenth Amendment.

The facts presented to the District Court showed that World-Wide is incorporated and has its business office in New York. It distributes vehicles, parts and accessories, under contract with Volkswagen, to retail dealers in New York, New Jersey, and Connecticut. Seaway, one of these retail dealers, is incorporated and has its place of business in New York. Insofar as the record reveals, Seaway and World-Wide are fully independent corporations whose relations with each other and with Volkswagen and Audi are contractual only.

The Supreme Court of Oklahoma . . . held that personal jurisdiction over petitioners was authorized by Oklahoma's "Long-Arm" Statute. . . .

As has long been settled, and as we reaffirm today, a state court may exercise personal jurisdiction over a nonresident defendant only so long as there exist "minimum contacts" between the defendant and the forum State. *International Shoe Co. v. Washington.* . . .

Applying these principles to the case at hand, we find in the record before us a total absence of those affiliating circumstances that are a necessary predicate to any exercise of state-court jurisdiction. Petitioners carry on no activity whatsoever in Oklahoma. They close no sales and perform no services there. They avail themselves of none of the privileges and benefits of Oklahoma law. They solicit no business there either through salespersons or through advertising reasonably calculated to reach the State. Nor does the record show that they regularly sell cars at wholesale or retail to Oklahoma customers or residents or that they indirectly, through others, serve or seek to serve the Oklahoma market. In short, respondents seek to base jurisdiction on one, isolated occurrence and whatever inferences can be drawn therefrom: the fortuitous circumstance that a single Audi automobile, sold in New York to New York residents, happened to suffer an accident while passing through Oklahoma.

It is argued, however, that because an automobile is mobile by its very design and purpose it was "foreseeable" that the Robinsons' Audi would cause injury in Oklahoma. . . . If foreseeability were the criterion, a local California tire retailer could be forced to defend in Pennsylvania when a blowout occurs there, a Wisconsin seller of a defective automobile jack could be haled before a distant court for damage caused in New Jersey, or a Florida soft drink concessionaire could be summoned to Alaska to account for injuries happening there. . . . Every seller of chattels would in effect appoint the chattel his agent for service of process. His amenability to suit would travel with the chattel.

In our view, whatever marginal revenues petitioners may receive by virtue of the fact that their products are capable of use in Oklahoma is far too attenuated a contact to justify that State's exercise of *in personam* jurisdiction over them.

Reversed.

Case Questions

1. What is *in personam* jurisdiction?
2. What does a state "long arm" statute provide? Must a state meet the "minimum contacts" test of *International Shoe* before it can envoke its long arm statute?
3. What state were the plaintiffs residents of? Coming from? Going to? What state were the defendants residents of? Where was the lawsuit brought? Why?

Policy Issue. Should courts require *in personam* jurisdiction over the parties to a lawsuit prior to making the state's court system available to the parties? Or should the lawsuit follow the product?

Economics Issue. Why do you think the plaintiffs sued in Oklahoma rather than in New York or Arizona?

Ethics Issue. Is it ethical for plaintiffs to go "forum shopping"?

Social Responsibility. Do states owe a duty of social responsibility to make its courts open to any person that wants to sue in that state? If not, to whom do states owe a duty of social responsibility to provide a court system?

THE LITIGATION PROCESS

In order to file and maintain a lawsuit, or to defend a lawsuit, a party must follow established legal procedures. The bringing, maintaining, and defending of a lawsuit is known as "litigation." The litigation process consists of several phases, including:

1. Pleadings
2. Discovery
3. Motions prior to trial or pretrial motions
4. Selecting a jury
5. Trial
6. Appeal

The following materials describe the legal procedures of the litigation process in a typical court system. The legal procedures of some state or federal courts may differ slightly from the procedures discussed.

Pleadings   In order to place a case properly before the court, the parties must prepare and serve the necessary written documents on the opposing party and file such documents with the court. The legal documents that properly place a lawsuit before the court are generally known as the "pleadings." The major forms of *pleadings* are: (1) the complaint; and (2) the answer.

Complaint.   The first step in bringing a lawsuit is for a party to prepare and file with the court a document which is known as a *complaint.* The complaint, usually prepared by a party's lawyer, states the name of the party filing the lawsuit (the plaintiff), the name of the party being sued (the defendant), and in general terms sets forth the ultimate facts of the dispute (e.g., the making and alleged breach of a contract), the theory of law under which the plaintiff believes he is entitled to recover (e.g., contract versus tort), and the damages or other remedy the plaintiff is seeking from the defendant ("prayer for relief").

The complaint must be accompanied by a *summons.* While the complaint notifies the defendant what the allegations against him are, the summons orders the defendant to appear in court to respond to the allegations made by the plaintiff. The complaint and summons must usually both be served on the defendant. Although personal service is generally required, other types of service (e.g., mail) may be permitted.

Answer.   Once a defendant has been properly served with a summons and complaint, he must formally respond to the complaint by filing an *answer.* The answer is a document filed with the court and served on the plaintiff. Usually certain items alleged in the complaint are admitted in the answer, such as names, addresses, dates, etc. If the defendant disagrees with information alleged in the complaint, he can either deny the complaint generally (general denial), or deny each allegation separately (specific denial). The defendant may believe that he has a defense to the plaintiff's charge (e.g., self-defense), and may plead this as an *affirmative defense* in his answer.

If the defendant believes that he has a cause of action against the plaintiff, he may file a *cross-complaint* against the plaintiff. Thus, the defendant becomes the "cross-complaint" and the plaintiff becomes the "cross-defendant" on the cross-complaint. If a party fails to answer a complaint or cross-complaint, the other party may take a *default judgment* against him. A default judgment has the same effect as if the parties had gone through trial and the defaulting party had lost.

Intervention and Consolidation.   If other parties have an interest in the lawsuit between the plaintiff and defendant, they can request that the court allow them to *intervene* as additional parties to the lawsuit. Intervention in a lawsuit by a third party will be permitted by the court only upon a showing that the proposed intervenor has a legitimate interest in the outcome of the lawsuit (e.g., defendant's insurance company).

If several parties have separately sued the same defendant (as in an airplane crash case with multiple plaintiffs), the court on proper motion by any party may *consolidate* all the actions in one trial. Upon a proper showing that the lawsuits have arisen out of the same fact situation and that none of the parties will be unduly prejudiced, the court will consolidate actions in order to save the time and expense of multiple trials.

Discovery   The purpose of *discovery* is to allow each party to thoroughly prepare for trial, to prevent surprise, to save expensive court time at trial, and to allow all parties to examine the strengths and weaknesses of their case to enhance the possibility of settlement prior to trial. There are several types of discovery, including (1) depositions, (2) interrogatories, (3) request for admissions, and (4) production of documents.

Depositions.   The most common form of discovery is through taking *depositions.* A deposition is *oral* testimony, usually given at the office of one of the lawyers. It is generally recorded in writing (*transcribed*) by a court reporter. The person giving the testimony (the *deponent*) is under oath just as if he were giving the testimony in court. The deponent may be one of the parties to the lawsuit, a witness to the accident or dispute, or anyone who has information concerning the dispute. Because the purpose of depositions is to discover all the facts surrounding a dispute, more leniency is allowed in asking questions than would be permitted at trial.

The scope of examination at a deposition is much broader than allowed by the formal rules of evidence at trial. Generally, all questions that appear "reasonably calculated to lead to the discovery of admissible evidence" are allowed in depositions. The rationale for this more liberal rule is that free questioning during depositions will lead to the discovery of the complete facts surrounding a dispute prior to trial. Worthless cases are more apt to be dismissed and other cases settled with liberal discovery. This excerpt sets forth Section 26(b) of the Federal Rules of Civil Procedure regarding the scope of discovery allowed in depositions taken in federal court actions.

Scope of Examination . . . the deponent may be examined regarding any matter, not privileged, which is relevant to the subject matter involved in the pending action, whether it relates to the claim or defense of the examining party or to the claim or defense of any other party, including the existence, description, nature, custody, condition and location of any books, documents, or other tangible things and the identity and location of persons having knowledge of relevant facts. It is not ground for objection that the testimony will be inadmissible at the trial if the testimony sought appears reasonably calculated to lead to the discovery of admissible evidence. . . .

If a deponent dies or becomes incapacitated between the date of his deposition and trial, his deposition may be used as evidence at trial. A deposition may also be used at trial to *impeach* a witness' credibility if his testimony at trial differs from that given in a prior deposition.

Interrogatories.   Further discovery may be taken in the form of *interrogatories.* Interrogatories are *written* questions submitted by one party to a lawsuit to the other party to a lawsuit. The interrogatories usually ask questions as to what happened, who was involved, who are witnesses to the accident, and so forth. Interrogatories must be answered in writing.

Request for Admissions.   A party may also make a *request for admission* from the other party. A request for admission is in writing, and *requests* the other party to *admit* that he was at a specific place at a specific time, that he drove at 55 miles per hour, etc. If the requests are admitted to, then such facts will not have to be proven at trial.

Production of Documents.   In many cases, e.g., contract disputes, or antitrust cases, a substantial portion of the lawsuit may be based on what is contained in specific documents, memoranda, and correspondence between the parties and with others. Each party is allowed to request a *production of documents* from the other side. Such production of documents may be requested in conjunction with a deposition or submission of interrogatories, or may be made separately. If the documents are too voluminous to be moved, are in permanent storage, or their removal would disrupt the business of the party from whom the request is made, the requesting party may be required to go to the other party's place of business to review the documents.

Pretrial Motions.   At any time after pleadings have been filed and prior to trial, either party may make a number of pretrial motions to the court. Pretrial motions are allowed on the rationale that certain cases can be disposed of, either for lack of merit or failure to follow proper procedure, prior to reaching trial. Pretrial motions are based on documents filed by the parties and brief hearing (a few minutes to a few hours) before the court. The main pretrial motions are: (1) motion to dismiss; (2) motion for judgment on the pleadings; and (3) motion for summary judgment.

Motion to Dismiss.   Instead of filing an answer, the defendant may file a motion to dismiss (sometimes called a "demurrer") to the court. A motion to dismiss alleges that even if all the facts contained in the plaintiff's complaint are true, the plaintiff still cannot prevail in the lawsuit. For example, if the plaintiff's complaint alleges facts which patently show that the defendant was not negligent, then the complaint will be dismissed.

Motion for Judgment on the Pleadings.   After all the pleadings are filed (complaint, answer, cross-complaint, etc.), either party can make a *motion for a judgment on the pleadings.* This motion alleges that the case can be decided by looking at the pleadings filed, and that no *factual* evidence need be considered in deciding the case. A judgment on the pleadings will be granted, for example, if the complaint is insufficient to state a cause of action (e.g., improperly drafted), if a remedy is not available as requested in the complaint, or if defendant has admitted the allegations of the complaint in his answer.

If a *demurrer* is granted solely because the plaintiff's or defendant's pleadings are insufficient or improperly drafted, the court may grant the losing party an opportunity to correct the error by filing proper pleadings. Filing of a motion for judgment on the pleadings is considered a *demurrer* to the complaint.

Motion for Summary Judgment.   The major pretrial motion is the *motion for summary judgment.* When both parties agree that the facts of a case are not in dispute, or one party believes that the other party does not have any facts which can dispute the facts of his case, and allegedly there is only a dispute as to the relevant *law* that is applicable to the case, either party may file a motion for summary judgment with the court. This motion is usually based on written affidavits and a brief hearing before the court. In this excerpt from *Talley v. MFA Mutual Insurance Co.*, 620 S.W.2d 260 (Arkansas, 1981), the court explained the requirements for granting a summary judgment motion.

It is well settled that a summary judgment is an extreme remedy and is only proper whenever the pleadings and proof show that no genuine issue exists as to a material fact, and the moving party is entitled to a judgment as a matter of law. Any proof submitted with the motion must be viewed in the light most favorable to the party resisting the motion with all doubts and inferences being resolved against the moving party.

If the court finds that there actually is a dispute as to the facts, it will deny the motion for summary judgment and let that factual issue be decided at trial. If the court finds there is no dispute as to the facts, it will apply the law to the facts of the case and either grant or deny the motion for summary judgment. A grant of summary judgment in many cases ends a lawsuit or portions of a lawsuit.

SELECTING A JURY

Once discovery and pretrial motions are completed, each party must certify to the court that he is ready to proceed to trial. In most jurisdictions, the court will order the parties to appear at a mandatory settlement conference prior to trial. If a settlement is not reached at that time, a trial date is set. In many urban areas such as Los Angeles and New York, civil cases may take from three to five years to get to trial. The Sixth Amendment to the Constitution guarantees the right to a speedy trial in criminal matters. Criminal trials have priority in all jurisdictions, with most being held within ninety days of arrest. Continuances (postponements) of trials for legitimate reasons such as illness are often granted in both civil and criminal trials.

Generally, each party has the right to request a jury trial, and if either party does so, a jury must be selected. If both parties waive their right to a jury, the judge will hear and decide the case without the aid of a jury. In most jurisdictions, a jury of twelve persons is selected to hear the case. Juries of a lesser number (i.e., six jurors) have been held to be constitutional. The pool of potential jurors is usually selected from the adult population from voting registration or automobile registration lists. In this excerpt from *Press-Enterprise Co. v. Superior Court of California*, 104 S.Ct. 819 (1984), Chief Justice Burger discussed the history of open jury trials.

The roots of open trials reach back to the days before the Norman Conquest when cases in England were brought before "moots" a town meeting kind of body such as the local court of the hundred or the county court. Attendance was virtually compulsory on the part of the freemen of the community, who represented the "patria," or the "country," in rendering judgment. The public aspect thus was "almost a necessary incident of jury trials, since the presence of a jury . . . already insured the presence of a large part of the public."

As the jury system evolved in the years after the Norman Conquest, and the jury came to be but a small segment representing the community, the obligation of all freeman to attend criminal trials was relaxed; however, the public character of the proceedings, including jury selection, remained unchanged. Later, during the fourteenth and fifteenth centuries, the jury became an impartial trier of facts, owing in large part to a development in that period, allowing challenges.

The presumptive openness of the jury selection process in England, not surprisingly, carried over into proceedings in colonial America. . . . Public jury selection thus was the common practice in America when the Constitution was adopted. . . . This openness has what is sometimes described as a "community therapeutic value."

Voir Dire.   Jurors are selected through a process called *voir dire* ("to speak the truth"), whereby each party and the judge has the right to question each prospective juror to determine if he or she has a bias that would excuse him or her from sitting as a juror in the case before the court. Challenges "for cause" (e.g., prospective juror is related to either party, has a financial or other interest in the case, or has formed some previous bias that would affect his impartiality as a juror) are unlimited. Most jurisdictions usually allow each party a certain number of *peremptory* challenges (often six), whereby a juror can be excused without cause. Once a panel of twelve jury members (or fewer if allowed by the jurisdiction) is agreed upon, they are *impanelled* to hear and decide the facts of the case.

This case, *Ham v. South Carolina,* is an example of the use of *voir dire* examination of prospective jurors at trial.

VOIR DIRE

HAM v. SOUTH CAROLINA

409 U.S. 524 (1973)
UNITED STATES SUPREME COURT

Mr. Justice Rehnquist delivered the opinion of the Court.

Petitioner was convicted in the South Carolina trial court of the possession of marihuana in violation of state law. He was sentenced to 18 months' confinement, and on appeal his conviction was affirmed by a divided South Carolina Supreme Court. Petitioner is a young, bearded Negro who has lived most of his life in Florence County, South Carolina.

Prior to the trial judge's *voir dire* examination of prospective jurors, petitioner's counsel requested the judge to ask jurors four questions relating to possible prejudice against petitioner. The first two questions sought to elicit any possible racial prejudice against Negroes; the third question related to possible prejudice against beards; and the fourth dealt with pretrial publicity relating to the drug problem. The trial judge, while putting to the prospective jurors three general questions as to bias, prejudice, or partiality that are specified in the South Carolina statutes, declined to ask any of the four questions posed by petitioner.

We think that the Fourteenth Amendment required the judge in this case to interrogate the jurors upon the subject of racial prejudice. South Carolina law permits challenges for cause, and authorizes the trial judge to conduct *voir dire* examination of potential jurors. The State having created this statutory framework for the selection of juries, the essential fairness required by the Due Process Clause of the Fourteenth Amendment requires that under the facts shown by this record the petitioner be permitted to have the jurors interrogated on the issue of racial bias.

The inquiry as to racial prejudice derives its constitutional stature from the firmly established precedent of *Aldridge* and the numerous state cases upon which it relied, and from a principal purpose as well as from the language of those who adopted the Fourteenth Amendment. The trial judge's refusal to inquire as to particular bias against beards, after his inquiries as to bias in general, does not reach the level of a constitutional violation.

Petitioner's final question related to allegedly prejudicial pretrial publicity. But the record before us contains neither the newspaper articles nor any description of the television program in question. Because of this lack of material in the record substantiating any pretrial publicity prejudicial to this petitioner, we have no occasion to determine the merits of his request to have this question posed on *voir dire*.

Because of the trial court's refusal to make any inquiry as to racial bias of the prospective jurors after petitioner's timely request therefor, the judgment of the Supreme Court of South Carolina is *reversed*.

Case Questions

1. What is *voir dire*?
2. Which of the following issues was (were) a proper subject for *voir dire*?
   a. Racial bias
   b. Bias against beards
   Were these issues treated differently by the court? Why? If a juror hated people with beards, could it affect the outcome of the case?
3. Is pretrial publicity (e.g., newspaper articles) a proper subject for *voir dire*? Should it be?

Policy Issue. Should members of the public sit as jurors? Are they qualified? Who usually sits as jurors? Should paid professional jurors replace public jurors? Why or Why not?

Economics Issue. Is the present court system and judicial process too expensive? Should the litigation process be streamlined? If so, how?

Ethics Issue. Is it ethical for a lawyer to try to "pack" the jury?

Social Responsibility. Do citizens owe a duty of social responsibility to sit as jurors? If you wanted to get out of jury duty, what would you do?

Know

The Trial. In *McDonough Power Equipment, Inc. v. Greenwood,* 104 S.Ct. 845 (1984), Justice Rehnquist stated:

This Court has long held that " '[a litigant] is entitled to a fair trial but not a perfect one,' for there are no perfect trials."

Trials are costly, not only for the parties, but also for the jurors performing their civic duty and for society, which pays the judges and support personnel who manage the trials. It seems doubtful that our judicial system would have the resources to provide litigants with perfect trials, were they possible, and still keep abreast of its constantly increasing case load. Even this straightforward products liability suit extended over a three-week period.

The typical trial must be held pursuant to complex, and often restrictive, procedures. If a case proceeds to trial, the sequence of events at a typical trial is:

1. Opening statements
2. Plaintiff's case
3. Motion for nonsuit
4. Defendant's case
5. Closing statements
6. Jury instructions
7. Jury deliberation and verdict
8. Motion for judgment N.O.V.
9. Judgment

Opening Statements.   Each party's attorney is usually allowed to make an *opening statement* to the jury. Normally, the plaintiff's attorney proceeds first, followed by the defendant's attorney. In an opening statement, each lawyer summarizes what he believes to be the main factual and legal issues of the case in order to inform the jury what the lawsuit is about and why his client's position or claim is valid. Information given in an opening statement is not evidence, and is subject to limitations of time and relevancy as determined by the judge. A party may waive (give up) his opportunity to make an opening statement.

one who brought the lawsuit

Plaintiff's Case.   Once the opening statements are concluded, the plaintiff usually must proceed to put his case on. The plaintiff bears the "burden of proof" to persuade the trier of fact on the merits of his case. In a criminal case, the prosecution has the burden of proving the guilt of the accused criminal "beyond a reasonable doubt." In a civil case, the plaintiff must generally prove the allegations of the complaint by a "preponderance of the evidence." Under this balancing test, the trier of fact must find that there is a greater weight of evidence in support of the allegations then against them. If a plaintiff fails to prove his allegations, he loses the lawsuit.

Witnesses are called to testify at court by serving upon them a *subpoena.* A subpoena is a document issued by the court on the request of one of the parties or the court which commands a person to appear and give testimony at trial. Failure to obey a subpoena subjects a person to *contempt of court* proceedings and possible fine or imprisonment. Witnesses may also volunteer to give testimony without the issuance of a subpoena. The parties (i.e., plaintiff or defendant) may be called as witnesses without the service of a subpoena.

Parties may also call *expert witnesses* (e.g., engineers, doctors, psychiatrists, economists) to give testimony. Expert witnesses are persons who are not actual witnesses to an accident or dispute, but who are experts in some relevant area and whose testimony may help a jury to decide a case. Expert witnesses are paid a fee for their services by the party who calls them to testify.

Usually, the trial proceeds with the plaintiff's attorney "calling" his first witness to the witness stand. After the witness is "sworn in," the plaintiff's attorney questions the witness on *direct examination.* Questions are oral and may either ask for oral responses or for the witness to identify documents.

Demonstrative evidence such as maps, charts, or medical models may be used. After the plaintiff's attorney has completed his direct examination of a witness, the defendant's attorney may *cross-examine* the witness. The defendant's attorney may not at this time go into any area of questions other than on the subjects inquired into by the plaintiff's attorney.

Each witness may be asked further questions on *redirect* and *recross*-examination until the attorneys have completed their questioning of the witness. The witness is then excused, but the court may reserve the right to call the witness back at a later time in the trial.

Motion for Nonsuit. Once the plaintiff has completed setting forth his evidence, and has "rested" his case, the defendant can make a motion to the court for a judgment for *nonsuit*. A motion for nonsuit requests the court to award judgment for the defendant based on the assertion that the plaintiff, who has been given his chance to prove his case, has not done so based on the evidence he has presented, and it therefore will be unnecessary for the defendant to have to call his witnesses and put on his evidence. Motions for nonsuits are rarely granted.

Defendant's Case. If a motion for nonsuit has not been made or has been denied, the defendant must then give his evidence and testimony to rebut the plaintiff's allegations, or to prove affirmative defenses or allegations made in a cross-complaint if either are a part of the pleadings. The procedure of direct examination by defendant's attorney and cross-examination by plaintiff's attorney of each witness called by the defendant continues until the defendant has put forth all of his evidence. The court has wide discretion in allowing parties to put forth additional evidence throughout the trial.

Closing Statements. At the conclusion of the evidence, after both parties have "rested," each party's attorney is allowed to make a *closing argument* to the jury. In the closing arguments each attorney, sometimes passionately, summarizes the factual and legal issues, points out the strengths of his case and the weaknesses of the other side's case, and tries to convince the jury to render a judgment for his client. Anything said in closing arguments is not considered evidence.

Jury Instructions. After closing arguments are completed, the judge will read *jury instructions* to the jury. Jury instructions are statements by the judge of what the *law* is that the jury is to apply to the case. For example, if the case before the court is a negligence matter involving an automobile accident, the judge will instruct the jury as to what the law of negligence is in that state.

Jury Deliberation and Verdict. After the instructions are given to the jury, the jury retires to the jury room to deliberate its findings. This may take from a few minutes to many months. In most cases where the jury deliberation takes more than one day, the jurors are allowed to go home at night, but are admonished by the judge not to discuss the case with anyone. In some unusual and important cases the jury is actually *sequestered* (separated or isolated), from the public during deliberation, usually spending evenings at a hotel and under the supervision of court personnel until a decision in the case is reached.

In most civil cases (e.g., negligence, breach of contract) at least nine of the twelve jurors must decide in favor of plaintiff in order for him to win the lawsuit. In a criminal case the jury must be unanimous in order to arrive at a decision for conviction or acquittal. Where a jury has not reached the requisite vote for either the plaintiff or defendant, it is a "hung" jury. The plaintiff may then sue the defendant again until a decision is reached.

Motion for Judgment N.O.V.   A motion for *judgment N.O.V.* ("not withstanding the verdict") may be made to the trial court by the losing party. It asks the court to overturn the jury verdict and enter judgment for the requesting party. For such a motion to be granted, the petitioning party must show that there was no evidence presented at trial that would support the verdict of the jury. A judgment N.O.V. is rarely granted.

Judgment.   Once a jury has returned its verdict, the court will enter its decision in the form of a *judgment* for the winning party. The trial court may also issue a written memorandum of its decision, containing a statement of the *questions of law* and *questions of fact* as found by the court and the jury. The written memorandum, together with the documents presented during trial and the recorded testimony of witnesses, constitute a permanent record of the trial proceedings, which is usually kept on file at the trial court or archives.

Double Jeopardy and *Res Judicata*.   The "double jeopardy" clause of the Fifth Amendment means that no person, whether natural or artificial (i.e., a corporation) can be tried for the same crime by the same jurisdiction more than once. If the jury finds a person innocent of the crime charged, he can never be tried again for that crime in that jurisdiction. But if the jury returns a hung verdict, that is, could not agree as to a verdict, than the state may prosecute the accused again.

The same act may, however, be a crime in several jurisdictions. For example, kidnapping a person and bringing him across a state line would be a crime in both states as well as a federal crime. Three jurisdictions, two states and the federal government, could each bring criminal charges against the accused without violating the double jeopardy clause.

A decision in favor of the defendant in a civil lawsuit is *res judicata* ("a matter adjudged"), which bars the plaintiff from suing the defendant again on the same issue. The losing plaintiff may appeal the decision of the trial court to the proper appellate court.

PRIVILEGE AGAINST SELF-INCRIMINATION

The Fifth Amendment to the U.S. Constitution provides that no person shall be compelled to be a witness against himself. This principle is based on the axiom that the government bears the burden of proving the accused guilty of the crime charged, and that, unlike the inquisitions of past times, the accused does not have to assist in his own criminal prosecution. If a person declines to testify against himself (popularly known as "taking the Fifth"), he may still be found criminally liable based upon other evidence.

A person may plead the Fifth Amendment right against self-incrimination whether or not he is presently charged with a crime. For example, if someone has been apprehended while in the commission of a crime, that person does not have to testify against himself at his own trial. If a person is called as a witness to testify to some other matter, whether criminal or civil, that person does not have to testify and may plead the Fifth Amendment if in testifying he or she would incriminate himself or herself as to some criminal activity that he or she has participated in, whether related to the matter at hand or not. The Fifth Amendment privilege against self-incrimination has been extended to custodial interrogation (e.g., questioning by police on the street). as well as to testimony given in court or during the course of any other official investigation.

Other Privileges.   Generally, a person may consult a lawyer and disclose to the lawyer all facts regarding the past commission of a crime without fear that the lawyer will testify against him. This confidentiality is the well-known *attorney-client privilege*. For it to apply, the information must be told to the lawyer in his capacity as a lawyer. The privilege may be asserted by the accused to prevent his lawyer from testifying, or the lawyer may assert the privilege himself. Other such privileges exist for the doctor-patient relation, the psychiatrist-patient relation and the priest or minister-client relation. A spouse may choose not to testify against his or her spouse, based on the argument that to compel a spouse to do so would wreck the family relationship. The rule has recently been extended so that a spouse may prevent his or her spouse from testifying against him or her. There is no federal accountant-client privilege.

REVIEW ON APPEAL

Once a decision is made by a trial court, either side may appeal the decision. Requesting an appeal consists of filing the appropriate *notice* and *petition* of appeal within a specified period of time after a decision is rendered by the trial court (e.g., 60 days). The *petitioner* on appeal or *appellant* may have been either the plaintiff or the defendant at trial. The party answering an appeal is the *respondent* or *appellee*. Occasionally both parties appeal the same decision.

The appellate court does not hear new testimony, but only reviews the record of the lower court to see if there has been prejudicial error by the trial court. The petitioner or respondent may request the appellate court to review the entire trial court record or only relevant portions thereof. Both questions of fact and questions of law may be appealed.

Questions of Fact. The jury decides *questions of fact.* The jury answers such questions as, "Was plaintiff driving the automobile that struck defendant? Was plaintiff negligent in doing so?" "Was plaintiff intoxicated at the time of the accident?" etc. Questions of fact are very difficult to appeal. As long as the appellate court can find *some* evidence in the trial court record to support the finding of fact, it will not overrule the finding of fact as made by the trier of fact (the jury, or if there is no jury, then the judge) at the trial.

Questions of Law. Errors with regard to *questions of law* are more apt to be reversed on appeal. For example, if the trial court judge makes an error in instructing the jury as to the law that is applicable to the case, or in an interpretation of a statute, or makes other errors in deciding questions of law throughout a trial (e.g., allows evidence secured in an unlawful search and seizure), the appellate court is more likely to reverse the decision of the lower court, or reverse and remand the case for a new trial.

The appellant must file an *opening brief* with the appellate court that sets forth legal research and cites relevant evidence from the trial court record to support his contended position on appeal. The appellee then files a *respondent's brief* answering appellant's position. The appellant may then file a final *rebuttal brief.* After the briefs and record are reviewed by the appellate court, the court will set the case for hearing. At such a hearing each party's lawyer is allowed a limited (e.g., one-hour) oral presentation. The justices often use the hearing to ask questions of the lawyers to help clarify important or uncertain issues in the case.

Appellate Court Decision. Some time after oral argument the appellate court will deliver its opinion in the case. The appellate court may:

1. *affirm* the decision of the lower court and allow the decision and judgment of the lower court to stand;
2. *reverse* the lower court, thus making the losing party at the lower court the winning party on appeal, or vice versa;
3. *reverse and remand,* which means that it is reversing the decision or some portion of the decision of the lower court but is sending the case back for a new trial on all or part of the issues of the case;
4. if faced with several issues, *affirm in part* and *reverse in part* the decision of the lower court.

Decisions of state and federal appellate and supreme courts are "reported," that is, they are published in formal volumes (reporters) that are available in law libraries. Most states have a separate reporter that publishes the cases decided by the appellate and supreme courts of the state. There are also reporters that collect and report cases of states in a specific geographical region (e.g., *Pacific Reporter, Southern Reporter*), A separate reporter reports federal appellate court cases. Several reporters collect and report the cases decided by the United States Supreme Court. Many specialized areas have a separate reporter that collects all decisions relevant to that specialty (e.g., Bankruptcy Reporter). The majority of trial court cases are not reported, except decisions of federal district courts.

ARBITRATION

Rather than have a dispute resolved by the courts, many private parties agree to have their dispute decided through *arbitration.* Arbitration is a nonjudicial means of settling controversies. Generally, the parties select an arbitrator or panel of arbitrators to hear the dispute. The parties present their case to the arbitrator, usually under less restrictive rules of evidence than those applied by the courts. The arbitrator will make a decision, generally called an "award." The award of the arbitrator, usually by prior agreement of the parties, is not appellable or is restricted to a limited judicial review. Many contracts, labor agreements, etc., contain mandatory arbitration clauses.

Trend of the Law

The court system is often criticized for being inefficient, costly, and unfair in its decisions. In many instances, complex legal procedures seem to overwhelm the determination of the merits of a case. Lawyers often use discovery and pretrial motions to hinder, delay, and harass opponents, as well as to increase the hours billable to their clients. The court system is presently entering a period of self-examination. Some courts have taken steps to prevent harassment by limiting the number of times a person's deposition may be taken, the number of interrogatories that can be served on an opposing party, etc. However, much needs to be done in the area of court reform in order to eliminate the misuse of legal procedures.

America is a litigious society. Only Israel has more lawsuits per capita than the United States. As the courts become more crowded and the cost of legal representation increases, more parties will turn to *nonjudicial* means of settling disputes in the future. The process of arbitration will be used to settle an increasing number of contract disputes. Private profit-oriented court systems will be developed to provide less costly and faster methods of dispute resolution than government-supported court systems currently offer.

REVIEW QUESTIONS

1. What is the function of:
   a. prosecuting attorneys?
   b. defense attorneys?
2. Must a party have a lawyer represent him in a lawsuit? What does *"in propria persona"* mean?
3. What does the legal doctrine of "standing" require? Explain.
4. Explain the following terms:
   a. *in personam* jurisdiction

b. subject matter jurisdiction
c. venue
5. What does a "long-arm" statute provide? What does the "minimum contacts" test require?
6. Describe the following:
    a. complaint
    b. answer
    c. summons
    d. intervention
    e. consolidation
7. Describe the following types of discovery:
    a. deposition
    b. interrogatories
    c. request for admissions
    d. production of documents
8. Describe the following pretrial motions:
    a. motion to dismiss
    b. motion for judgment on the pleadings
    c. motion for summary judgment
9. What is *voir dire?* Describe the following:
    a. peremptory challenges
    b. "for cause" challenges
10. Describe what happens at the following phases of a typical trial:
    a. opening statements
    b. plaintiff's case
    c. motion for nonsuit
    d. defendant's case
    e. closing statements
    f. jury instructions
    g. jury deliberation and verdict
    h. motion for judgment N.O.V.
    i. judgment
11. What do the following terms mean?
    a. direct examination
    b. cross examination
    c. sequester
12. What does the Fifth Amendment right against self-incrimination provide? What other privileges against testifying are there?
13. What do the following terms mean?
    a. double jeopardy
    b. *res judicata*
14. Describe the following. Which one is more apt to be appealed? Why?
    a. questions of fact
    b. questions of law
15. What is arbitration? Will it be used more or less in the future? Why?

ADMINISTRATIVE AGENCIES

INTRODUCTION

In today's modern economic environment, among the most important constraints on the operation of a business are the thousands of regulations and rules adopted by hundreds of state and federal administrative agencies. Regulations issued by administrative agencies carry the force of law. Because of their numbers and importance, administrative agencies are often referred to as the "fourth branch of government."

Businesses are required to prepare and file numerous reports to administrative agencies. Reporting to administrative agencies costs business millions of dollars per year. Business is also subject to inspection by certain administrative agencies, and to the assessment of fines and other penalties for violation of administrative law. A further cost to business is the length of time required before an administrative agency acts (e.g., to issue a license). The lost time caused by excessive bureaucracy, commonly referred to as "red tape," also costs business millions of dollars per year.

Regulation by administrative agencies is sometimes positive for business. For example, direct subsidies to agriculture benefit that industry. Other benefits to business may be indirect. For example, many industries are "protected" from competition by administrative regulations that require a new entrant in the industry to be licensed by an administrative agency. Refusal by the agency to grant new licenses protects, and often creates, monopoly power in the existing companies in that industry. Regulatory agencies may be given authority to set prices or rates for products and services sold by industry members. Studies have shown that often these rates are higher than competitive rates would have been.

One industry may benefit and another suffer from the same regulation. For example, if the Interstate Commerce Commission sets higher rates for trucking firms, freight business may transfer to railroads. Industries like banking and transportation have enjoyed the protection of regulation for decades. Economists argue that some industries (e.g., railroads) have been so regulated that the regulation has caused their collapse. The modern trend is for government to deregulate many of the presently regulated industries. For example, airline fares currently reflect deregulation.

This chapter emphasizes the *procedural* aspects of administrative law. Most of the remaining chapters in this book focus on the study of substantive administrative law.

THE NATURE OF REGULATION

Regulations passed by administrative agencies often cause economic loss to business. For example, the enactment of a regulation setting limits on pollution increases the cost of doing business: pollution control equipment must be purchased, production curtailed, etc. Generally, a person or business that is caused a loss by regulation, or even driven out of business by regulation, has *no* cause of action against the government for damages.

Regulation Versus "Taking." If the government "takes" property from an individual or business, the Due Process and Just Compensation Clauses of the Fifth Amendment require that the government compensate the owner of the property and any other injured party (e.g., lessee). A substantive question often arises as to whether a rule enacted by an administrative agency is "regulation," for which no payment has to be made by the government for losses incurred, or is a "taking" of property, where due process requires the government to pay for the property taken. The Supreme Court has held that the mere *regulation* of property is not a compensable "taking" within the meaning of the Fifth Amendment.

In *Loretto v. Teleprompter Manhattan CATV Corp.*, the U.S. Supreme Court held that a New York law which required landlords to allow a private company to hook up a cable television line to residental apartment buildings was not regulation, but was a "taking" of property covered by the Fifth Amendment.

REGULATION VERSUS "TAKING"

JEAN LORETTO, ON BEHALF OF HERSELF AND ALL OTHERS SIMILARLY SITUATED v. TELEPROMPTER MANHATTAN CATV CORP. *ET AL.*

458 U.S. 419 (1982)
UNITED STATES SUPREME COURT

Justice Marshall delivered the opinion of the court.

New York law provides that a landlord must permit a cable television company to install its cable facilities upon his property. N.Y. Exec. Law § 828 (1) (McKinney Supp. 1982). In this case, the cable installation occupied portions of appellant's roof and the side of her building.

The New York Court of Appeals ruled that this appropriation does not amount to a taking. The Court of Appeals ruled that the law serves a legitimate police power purpose—eliminating landlord fees and conditions that inhibit the development of CATV, which has important educational and community benefits. Rejecting the argument that a physical occupation authorized by government is necessarily a taking, the court stated that the regulation does not have an excessive economic impact upon appellant when measured against her aggregate property rights, and that it does not interfere with any reasonable investment-backed expectations. Accordingly, the court held that Section 828 does not work a taking of appellant's property.

We conclude that a permanent physical occupation authorized by government is a taking without regard to the public interests that it may serve.

In *United States v. Pewee Coal Co.,* the Court unanimously held that the Government's seizure and direction of operation of a coal mine to prevent a national strike of coal miners constituted a taking, . . . The plurality had little difficulty concluding that because there had been an "actual taking of possession and control," the taking was as clear as if the Government held full title and ownership. . . . In *United States v. Central Eureka Mining Co.,* by contrast, the Court found no taking where the Government had issued a war-time order requiring nonessential gold mines to cease operations for the purpose of conserving equipment and man-

power for use in mines more essential to the war effort. . . . The Court reasoned that "the Government did not occupy, use, or in any manner take physical possession of the gold mines or the equipment connected with them."

The historical rule that a permanent physical occupation of another's property is a taking has more than tradition to commend it. Such an appropriation is perhaps the most serious form of invasion of an owner's property interests. To borrow a metaphor, *cf. Andrus v. Allard,* the government does not simply take a single "strand" from the "bundle" of property rights: it chops through the bundle, taking a slice of every strand.

This Court has consistently affirmed that States have broad power to regulate housing conditions in general and the landlord-tenant relationship in particular without paying compensation for all economic injuries that such regulation entails. In none of these cases, however, did the government authorize the permanent occupation of the landlord's property by a third party. Consequently, our holding today in no way alters the analysis governing the State's power to require landlords to comply with building codes and provide utility connections, mailboxes, smoke detectors, fire extinguishers, and the like in the common area of a building. So long as these regulations do not require the landlord to suffer the physical occupation of a portion of his building by a third party, they will be analyzed under the multi-factor inquiry generally applicable to non-possessory governmental activity.

Our holding today is very narrow. We affirm the traditional rule that a permanent physical occupation of property is a taking. In such a case, the property owner entertains an historically-rooted expectation of compensation, and the character of the invasion is qualitatively more intrusive than perhaps any other category of property regulation.

The issue of the amount of compensation that is due, on which we express no opinion, is a matter for the state courts to consider on remand. . . . The judgment of the New York Court of Appeals is *reversed* and the case is *remanded* for further proceedings not inconsistent with this opinion.

Justice Blackmun, with whom **Justice Brennan** and **Justice White** join, dissenting.

Before examining the Court's new takings rule, it is worth reviewing what was "taken" in this case. At issue are about 36 feet of cable one-half inch in diameter and two 4″ × 4″ × 4″ metal boxes. Jointly, the cable and boxes occupy only about one-eighth of a cubic foot of space on the roof of appellant's Manhattan apartment building.

The Court's recent Takings Clause decisions teach that *nonphysical* government intrusions on private property, such as zoning ordinances and other land-use restrictions, have become the rule rather than the exception. Modern government regulation exudes intangible "externalities" that may diminish the value of private property far more than minor physical touchings. Nevertheless, as the Court recognizes, it has "often upheld substantial regulation of an owner's use of his own property where deemed necessary to promote the public interest."

In the end, what troubles me most about today's decision is that it represents an archaic judicial response to a modern social problem. Cable television is a new and growing, but somewhat controversial, communications medium. . . . The New York legislature not only recognized, but responded to, this technological advance by enacting a statute that sought carefully to balance the interests of all private parties. New York's courts in this litigation, with only one jurist in dissent, unanimously upheld the constitutionality of that considered legislative judgment.

CASE QUESTIONS

1. What was the plaintiff's legal theory on appeal to the Supreme Court?
2. What is the economic significance of finding a "taking" versus economic "regulation"?
3. **a.** Was the court's decision based on a deep-seated view in America of protecting *tangible* property?
   b. Should *intangible* property be accorded the same protection?
4. Explain the "bundle of rights" ("strands") argument of the court. Does this make sense? Will a person be as harmed by the government taking 10 percent of all strands as by taking one of ten strands?
5. How did the court avoid equating the CATV hookup with the mailbox? Was this a valid distinction?

Policy issue. If all government regulation was considered a compensable "taking" of property, would there be any government regulation?

Economics issue.
a. Would rent control cause a greater or lesser economic loss to the landlord than the CATV hookup?
b. Would the rent control statute be treated the same as the CATV hookup by the Supreme Court? Does the distinction make sense?

Ethics Issue. Was it ethical for Mrs. Loretto to contest the New York law?

Social Responsibility.
a. Does the owner of property owe a duty of social responsibility to allow the CATV hookup to his property?
b. What social welfare is advanced by CATV?

ADMINISTRATIVE AGENCIES

Administrative agencies, also called *regulatory agencies,* have proliferated in this century, particularly since World War II. Administrative agencies are generally established with the goal of creating a body of professionals who are "experts" in regulating a certain portion of national commerce. Administrative agencies may be created by local, state, and federal governments, and range from local zoning commissions to large and complex federal agencies. The detailed study of local and state administrative agencies is beyond the scope of this book. The majority of the materials in this book cover federal administrative agencies and their regulations.

There are generally two types of federal administrative agencies: agencies within the *executive* branch of government, and "independent" agencies created by the *legislative* branch of government. The majority of administrative agencies are in the executive branch of government. The independent agencies created by Congress—the legislative branch—have broader regulatory powers over key areas of the national economy, including land and air transportation, gas and electric power, communications, labor relations, investment markets, and trade regulations. There are over 50 independent administrative agencies of the federal government. Attention is usually focused on the "Big Seven," which include (date of establishment in parentheses):

Civil Aeronautics Board (1938)
Federal Communications Commission (1934)
Federal Power Commission (1930)
Federal Trade Commission (1914)
Interstate Commerce Commission (1887)
National Labor Relations Board (1935)
Securities and Exchange Commission (1934)

The organizational charts for two federal agencies are set forth on the following pages. Exhibit 5–1 is the organizational chart of the Nuclear Regulatory Commission, an *independent* agency created by Congress. Exhibit 5–2 is the organization chart of the Department of Agriculture, which is part of the *executive* branch of government.

Administrative Procedure Act. Administrative law is composed of a mix of *substantive* and *procedural* law. Each administrative agency is generally empowered to administer a particular body of "substantive" law, e.g., antitrust law, securities laws. However, in doing so, agencies must follow prescribed administrative procedural law. The Administrative Procedure Act ("APA") was enacted by Congress in 1946. The APA does not address any particular administrative law subject, such as antitrust law, securities regulation, etc. Instead, the APA establishes *procedures* for the operation of administrative agencies, including rule-making. Most states have statutes somewhat similar to the APA to govern the activities of their state administrative agencies.

THE DELEGATION DOCTRINE

Under the Constitution, each branch of the government is given certain powers. The legislative branch is given the power to make the law, the judicial branch the power to interpret the law, and the executive branch the power to enforce the law. Under the doctrine of "separation of powers," one branch of the government cannot perform the functions of the others.

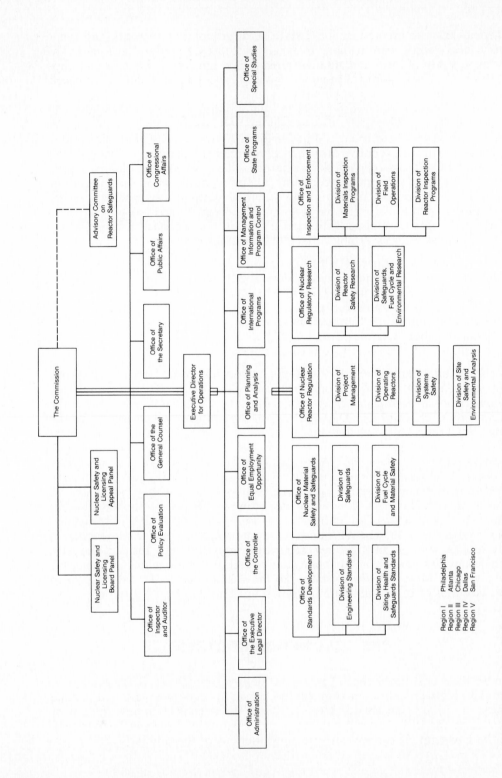

Exhibit 5-1. Organizational chart of the Nuclear Regulatory Commission.

76

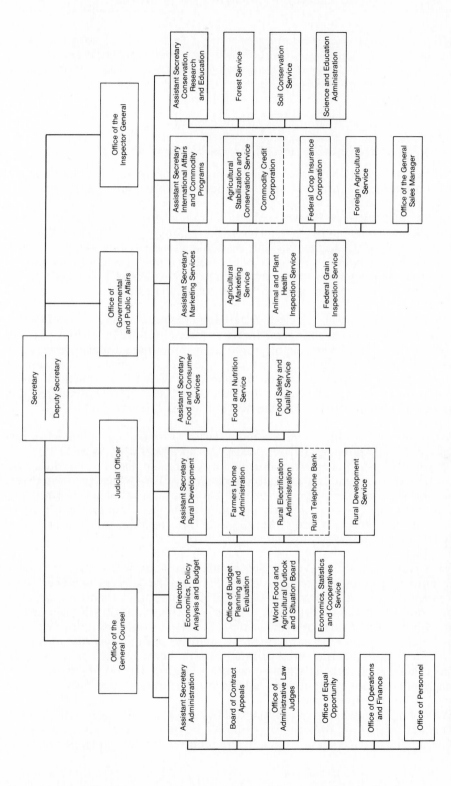

Exhibit 5–2. Organizational chart of the Department of Agriculture.

Administrative agencies do not constitute a formal branch of the government. In order to function, administrative agencies have to be created and given powers by the branches of government. Generally, most administrative agencies possess some powers of all three branches of government, including the powers to:

1. adopt rules and regulations (legislative power)
2. adjudicate controversies (judicial powers)
3. investigate, prosecute and advise (executive power).

Courts have generally glossed over the problem of the separation of powers when examining the functions and activities of administrative agencies.

Delegation of Legislative Powers.   When Congress creates an administrative agency, it usually delegates certain rule-making powers to the agency. Without a delegation of power from Congress, administrative agencies could not make law by adopting *regulations*. The concept of delegation of Congressional power to administrative agencies has gone through three distinct phases of review by the United States Supreme Court. The three phases are:

Phase One: Pre-1930s.   Originally, the issue of whether Congress could delegate its power at all was addressed by the Supreme Court. In a series of cases beginning in the late 1800s, the Supreme Court held that administrative agencies could exercise legislative powers if the powers were limited to: (1) ascertaining facts, (2) filling in details, or (3) complying with a fixed standard. Thus, although they were given some powers, under these narrow standards the authority of administrative agencies was substantially curtailed.

Phase Two: NIRA Cases.   In the 1930s, the Supreme Court invalidated numerous delegations of legislative powers to administrative agencies and to the executive branch of government. In a most notable decision, the Supreme Court held the National Industrial Recovery Act (NIRA), which gave the President substantial economic powers to help the country out of the Depression, unconstitutional. The court found that many of the acts adopted by Congress did not provide sufficient *standards* to guide the President in adopting codes or regulations to implement the acts.

Phase Three: Post-NIRA Cases.   Subsequent decisions by the Supreme Court have upheld the delegation of broad powers by Congress to the President, and particularly to administrative agencies. Although most modern case decisions require that Congress set "standards" for the administrative agency to follow when making rules or decisions, the Supreme Court has upheld delegation of legislative power to administrative agencies under somewhat meaningless standards (i.e., that they must promote "public convenience" or "interest"). It has upheld such delegation even where Congress has set *no* standard to guide the decision-making of administrative agencies (e.g., that they may "apportion water in time of shortage").

Even though Congress delegates broad powers to an administrative agency, the agency cannot act outside the scope of the delegated power. Any action by the administrative agency outside the scope of its delegated power is an unconstitutional *ultra vires* (act beyond the scope of lawful power). The courts generally construe the statutes delegating legislative power narrowly, thus avoiding many constitutional issues regarding the delegation doctrine.

Congress may not lawfully delegate power to *private* parties. Any such delegation is *void*. The rationale for this rule is to prevent any possible "favoritism" that may develop if Congress could delegate its power to private parties. The U.S. Supreme Court has held that the power to *tax* may *not* be delegated by Congress to administrative agencies or other branches of government.

Because Congress seems to have been given the authority to validly delegate extremely broad powers to administrative agencies, the doctrine of *non*delegation of legislative power is usually not an issue in modern administrative law cases.

RULE-MAKING BY ADMINISTRATIVE AGENCIES

Based on the delegation of legislative powers to them, administrative agencies are usually authorized to adopt rules and regulations to further the purposes of the statutes that they are empowered to administer. Federal statutes generally provide broad rule-making powers. Rule-making includes the process of formulating, amending, and appealing rules and regulations. The characteristics of a "rule," as opposed to an agency decision or order, are:

1. a rule generally applies to *future* situations
2. a rule usually addresses a *class* of persons rather than a specific party
3. a rule often requires future adjudication to develop its specifics.

When a federal administrative agency proposes to adopt a rule, it must follow the procedures outlined in the APA (5 U.S.C. § 533). The agency must publish a general notice of the proposed rule-making in the *Federal Register*. The *Federal Register* is generally read by the lobbyists and other interested parties who "track" legislation that will affect their particular industries or other constituents. In place of a general published notice, the agency may name and personally serve the interested parties. This second method of notice is seldom used by agencies.

An agency notice of proposed rule-making must include:

1. a statement of the time, place, and nature of the public rule-making proceedings
2. reference to the legal authority under which the rule is proposed
3. either the terms or substance of the proposed rule, or a description of the subjects and issues involved.

Public Participation in Rule-Making. After giving the required notice of proposed rule-making, the administrative agency must give interested persons the opportunity to participate in the rule-making procedure. This is generally accomplished by accepting the submission of written data, opinions, views, and arguments from interested persons. The agency may, and frequently does, provide for oral presentation of information from interested parties.

The notice and public participation in rule-making requirements as specified in the APA do not apply to the adoption of "interpretative" rules, general statements of policy, or rules of agency organization, procedure, or practice. The agency also does not have to adhere to the notice and public participation requirements if the agency for "good cause" finds that the notice and public comment procedure is "impracticable, unnecessary, or contrary to public interest." This latter exception is seldom used by administrative agencies.

After the comments from interested persons are reviewed, the agency usually announces its *final rule-making* in the matter. The agency must incorporate in the final rule a concise general statement of the basis and purpose for the final rule-making. The agency usually comments on the most relevant suggestions received from interested parties regarding the rule.

Set forth here is the notice of proposed rule-making of the Department of the Interior, Bureau of Land Management, regarding its proposed rules for the Outer Continental Shelf Mineral Leasing program.

PROPOSED RULE-MAKING

OUTER CONTINENTAL SHELF LEASING, GENERAL

43 CFR PART 3300
DEPARTMENT OF THE INTERIOR, BUREAU OF LAND MANAGEMENT

Agency.

Bureau of Land Management, Interior.

Action.

Proposed rulemaking.

Summary.

This proposed rule-making implements the changes mandated in the Outer Continental Shelf Mineral Leasing program administered by the Secretary of the Interior by the passage of the Outer Continental Shelf Lands Act Amendments of 1978. The proposed rule-making also contains changes to make Part 3300 more readable as directed by Executive Order 12044. The subparts have also been rearranged to make the part easier to follow and understand.

Date.

Comments by April 2, 1979.

Address.

Send comments to: Director (210), Bureau of Land Management, 1800 C. Street, N.W., Washington, D.C. 20240.

Comments will be available for public review in room 5555 of the above address during regular business hours (7:45 A.M.–4:15 P.M.) Monday through Friday.

For further information contact:

William Quinn (202) 334–8457, or
Abigail B. Miller (202) 343–6264, or
Robert B. Bruce (202) 343–8735.

Supplementary Information.

The passage of the Outer Continental Shelf Lands Act Amendments of 1978 (43 U.S.C. 1331 *et seq.*), mandated a number of changes in the Outer Continental Shelf programs, with special emphasis on the leasing program that is the responsibility of the Department of the Interior. This proposed rulemaking incorporates those mandated changes in Part 3300 of Title 43 of the Code of Federal Regulations.

Most of the changes that are being made in the proposed rulemaking are minor and are in compliance with the requirement of the provisions of the Outer Continental Shelf Lands Act Amendments of 1978. Some of the changes that the proposed rules include are the mechanism for the employment of new bidding systems for mineral leases when they are developed; the requirement for greater cooperation by Federal agencies in the OCS program; and the enhancement of the roles of State and local governments in the OCS program, to name a few. Some of these matters are covered in existing regulations but the proposed rulemaking consolidates them into one document.

There are several specific changes made by the proposed rulemaking. Two changes that are considered important are the incorporating of new provisions of the Outer Continental Shelf Lands Act Amendments which allow the offering of leases for terms longer than five years and allow lease areas larger than the 5760-acre maximum set by the law prior to the amendments.

Statements of Policy. Rule-making can be distinguished from general "statements of policy" that are issued by administrative agencies. General *statements of policy* merely announce a proposed course of action that an agency intends to follow in the future. Statements of policy are analogous to the "press releases" issued by businesses. The adoption of a statement of policy by an administrative agency does not require notice and the participation of the public. In this excerpt from *Pacific Gas and Electric Co. v. Federal Power Commission,* 506 P.2d 33 (1974), Judge MacKinnon discusses the differences between rule-making and general statements of policy of an administrative agency.

Professor Davis has described the distinction between substantive rules and general statements of policy as a "fuzzy product." Unfortunately the issues in this case compel us to attempt to define the fuzzy perimeters of a general statement of policy.

The critical distinction between a substantive rule and a general statement of policy is the different practical effect that these two types of pronouncements have in subsequent administrative proceedings. A properly adopted substantive rule establishes a standard of conduct which has the force of law. In subsequent administrative proceedings involving a substantive rule, the issues are whether the adjudicated facts conform to the rule and whether the rule should be waived or applied in that particular instance. The underlying policy embodied in the rule is not generally subject to challenge before the agency.

A general statement of policy, on the other hand, does not establish a "binding norm." It is not finally determinative of the issues or rights to which it is addressed. The agency cannot apply or rely upon a general statement of policy as law because a general statement of policy only announces what the agency seeks to establish as policy. A policy statement announces the agency's tentative intentions for the future. When the agency applies the policy in a particular situation, it must be prepared to support the policy just as if the policy statement had never been issued. An agency cannot escape its responsibility to present evidence and reasoning supporting its substantive rules by announcing binding precedent in the form of a general statement of policy.

Judicial Review of Administrative Rules. *Rule-making* by administrative agencies is subject to judicial review. The scope of the review depends on whether the rule is a "legislative" rule, or an "interpretive" rule.

A *legislative (substantive) rule* is one that *fills a gap* in a statute. An administrative agency may be expressly empowered by statute to fill the gaps in a statute (for example, by statutory language such as, "defined by the agency"). Where not expressly provided, the authority of an administrative agency to fill the gaps in a statute may be inferred from the general grant of rule-making power from the legislature. Because legislative rules fill the gaps in a statute, they have the *force of law.* Legislative rules are generally presumed to be valid. A reviewing court will usually invalidate a legislative rule only if the agency has made an *error* regarding a question of law. Some courts have applied the "substantial evidence test" in reviewing legislative rules. This, however, is the minority rule.

An *interpretive rule* is a rule adopted by an administrative agency that merely *interprets* a statute or prior adopted legislative rule. Because the interpretation of a statute or legislative rule is a question of law, the reviewing court may substitute its own *independent judgment* for that of the administrative agency. However, courts often defer to the expertise of the administrative agency.

ADJUDICATIVE POWER OF ADMINISTRATIVE AGENCIES

Judicial power can be delegated to administrative agencies. Under this power, administrative agencies act like courts: they hold hearings, take evidence, render decisions, and award damages. The officer at the administrative agency who hears and decides cases is called an *Administrative Law Judge* (ALJ).

An administrative agency can impose a *civil* penalty (i.e., a fine) without a jury trial as long as a "public right" is created and is being enforced under a statute enacted by the legislature. Administrative agencies may not impose imprisonment as a remedy except in extreme circumstances, such as temporary confinement of aliens or quarantine of persons to prevent the spread of an infectious disease. Although an administrative agency cannot *define* crimes (a function of the legislative branch), it may adopt a regulation that it is a crime to violate. However, the courts, not the agency, must prosecute the violation.

In adjudicating matters, an administrative agency must comply with procedural due process as guaranteed by the U.S. Constitution and most state constitutions. Under procedural due process, a party to an administrative action must be given adequate *notice* of the allegations or charges against him, and be provided an opportunity to present evidence on the matter. Many matters require a *hearing* before the administrative agency. In this excerpt from *Atlas Roofing Co., Inc. v. OSHA*, 430 U.S. 441 (1977), Justice White held that a defendant in an administrative agency adjudicative action does *not* have a right to a jury trial.

The Seventh Amendment provides that "[i]n Suits at common law, where the value in controversy shall exceed twenty dollars, the right of trial by jury shall be preserved . . . ."

Petitioners claim that to permit Congress to assign the function of adjudicating the Government's rights to civil penalties for violation of the statute to a different forum—an administrative agency in which no jury is available—would be to permit Congress to deprive a defendant of his Seventh Amendment jury right. We disagree. At least in cases in which "public rights" are being litigated—e.g., cases in which the Government sues in its sovereign capacity to enforce public rights created by statutes within the power of Congress to enact—the Seventh Amendment does not prohibit Congress from assigning the factfinding function and initial adjudication to an administrative forum with which the jury would be incompatible. . . .

[*T*]*he Seventh Amendment is generally inapplicable in administrative proceedings, where jury trials would be incompatible with the whole concept of administrative adjudication. . . .*

Congress is not required by the Seventh Amendment to choke the already crowded federal courts with new types of litigation or prevented from committing some new types of litigation to administrative agencies with special competence in the relevant field. This is the case even if the Seventh Amendment would have required a jury where the adjudication of those rights is assigned to a federal court of law instead of an administrative agency.

Pursuant to APA section 555(b), any party or witness required to appear before an administrative agency investigative hearing is entitled to have an attorney appear and represent him or her.

Judicial Review of Administrative Agency Adjudication.

Decisions of Administrative Law Judges are generally appealable to the proper federal Court of Appeals. A question arises as to the *scope* of the review that the court may make of the agency decision. The scope of the review often rests on whether the finding of the administrative agency was: (1) a question of *law,* or (2) a question of *fact.*

Questions of Law. Where an administrative agency has decided a "question of law," courts are free to apply a broad standard of review and to *substitute their own judgment* for that of the administrative agency. For example, the statutory interpretation of a word (e.g., *employee*) is a question of law which the reviewing court can render its own independent definition of. Based on the ability of a reviewing court to substitute its independent judgment regarding questions of law, administrative agency findings of law are more often appealed than findings of fact.

Questions of Fact. Judicial review of the *fact* finding of an administrative agency is limited. A court will not generally set aside a fact finding by an agency unless the agency's finding is *unsupported* by "substantial evidence" on the "whole evidence." "Substantial evidence" is relevant evidence that "a reasonable mind might accept as adequate to support a conclusion." The phrase, "whole evidence," requires the reviewing court to look at the record produced by both sides, not just the evidence that supports the agency's decision. The "substantial evidence test" has not been applied consistently by the courts. Generally, the courts *defer* to the fact findings of an administrative agency. Deference is based on the "expertise" of the agency, the ability of the agency's administrative law judge to examine the demeanor of the witness, and the technical and scientific facts involved in many administrative agency determinations.

Often an administrative agency makes a finding that involves a *mixed* question of law and fact. On review, the court has to determine if the finding is more a "question of law," for which it can substitute its own independent judgment, or more a "question of fact," to which the narrower substantial evidence test is applied. The determining factor is often whether the agency's expertise was required to reach the finding. If it is, the court is more apt to conclude the mixed question was actually a question of fact to which the narrower standard of review will be applied.

JUDICIAL REVIEW OF ADMINISTRATIVE AGENCY ACTIONS

Many federal statutes expressly provide for judicial review of an administrative agency decision. If there is no specific statutory grant of review, Section 702 of the APA generally applies. Section 702 provides:

A person suffering legal wrong because of federal agency action, or adversely affected or aggrieved by agency action within the meaning of a relevant statute, is entitled to judicial review thereof.

In order to have standing to sue, a plaintiff must also show that he falls within the "zone of interest" that is regulated or protected by the relevant statute. A plaintiff must satisfy four conditions in order to show that the court is a proper forum to review an action by an administrative agency. The conditions are:

1. the plaintiff has "exhausted" all available administrative remedies
2. the agency does not have "primary jurisdiction" over the matter
3. the plaintiff's claim is "ripe"
4. the ruling or decision of the agency is final.

Exhaustion of Administrative Remedies. A plaintiff must exhaust all administrative remedies before judicial review of his complaint is available. That is, a plaintiff may not seek judicial review of an agency action if additional administrative remedies are available, such as ability to seek the review of a decision of an Administrative Law Judge by an entire Commission.

In this excerpt from *McKart v. United States*, 395 U.S. 520 (1968), Justice Thurgood Marshall explains the public policy underlying the doctrine of exhaustion of administrative remedies.

The doctrine of exhaustion of administrative remedies is well established in the jurisprudence of administrative law. . . . A primary purpose is, of course, the avoidance of premature interruption of the administrative process. The agency, like a trial court, is created for the purpose of applying a statute in the first instance. Accordingly, it is normally desirable to let the agency develop the necessary factual background upon which decisions should be based. And since agency decisions are frequently of a discretionary nature or frequently require expertise, the agency should be given the first chance to exercise that discretion or to apply that expertise. And of course it is generally more efficient for the administrative process to go forward without interruption than it is to permit the parties to seek aid from the courts at various intermediate stages. The very same reasons lie behind judicial rules sharply limiting interlocutory appeals.

Closely related to the above reasons is a notion peculiar to administrative law. The administrative agency is created as a separate entity and invested with certain powers and duties. The courts ordinarily should not interfere with an agency until it has completed its action, or else has clearly exceeded its jurisdiction. As Professor Jaffe puts it, "[t]he exhaustion doctrine is, therefore, an expression of executive and administrative autonomy." This reason is particularly pertinent where the function of the agency and the particular decision sought to be reviewed involve exercise of discretionary powers granted the agency by Congress, or require application of special expertise.

The doctrine of exhaustion of administrative remedies is subject to several exceptions, the most important of which are:

1. if the administrative agency is deadlocked and cannot reach a decision
2. if the administrative action is not authorized by the relevant statute
3. if the administrative procedure violates the Constitution
4. if it is futile to proceed any further at the administrative level (i.e., agency announces it will not reverse its policy or decision)
5. if the administrative agency is "plainly" wrong and irreparable harm (e.g., substantial increase in costs) will be caused to the plaintiff if the plaintiff has to comply with the agency procedure.

Where one of the preceding exceptions is available, the agency action is subject to immediate judicial review.

Doctrine of "Primary Jurisdiction."   Many statutes expressly grant administrative agencies jurisdiction to conduct initial trials of cases challenging regulations, rules, or policies that they have adopted to enforce the statute. Where no express jurisdiction is provided, the administrative agency may be given jurisdiction to conduct the initial trial under the doctrine of *primary jurisdiction*. Where "primary jurisdiction" of the administrative agency is found, the plaintiff must seek adjudication by the administrative agency prior to seeking judicial review.

Condition that militate *against* the finding of "primary jurisdiction" of administrative agencies, and where the court will be more lenient in granting immediate judicial review, are:

1. if a question of law is at issue (versus a question of fact)
2. if the issue is nontechnical in nature (i.e., the expertise of the agency is not required)
3. if the plaintiff is unable to initiate agency action
4. if an administrative agency has become protective of the industry it is supposed to regulate and therefore may not render an objective decision
5. if the issue to be resolved is traditionally a judicial issue.

"Ripeness" of Claim.   The court will deny a plaintiff review of his claim if the case is not "ripe." *Ripeness* requires that the administrative rule or policy being challenged has been specifically applied by the plaintiff to the present action. For example, a plaintiff could not sue to overturn an agency regulation that does not apply to the activities of the plaintiff, or would only apply to the plaintiff at some later date (e.g., when plaintiff plans to enter the industry, at some future date). The ripeness doctrine serves to prevent the litigation of abstract policies that may never cause any harm to the plaintiff.

Recently the courts have tended to more liberally construe the ripeness doctrine and to allow immediate review of administrative agency rules or actions.

Final Order Rule.   Judicial review of decisions of administrative agencies is not available until the ruling of the agency is *final*. Under the "final order rule," preliminary, intermediate or procedural action by the agency during the course of its decision-making or rule-making is not appealable to the judicial branch until the agency issues its *final order* in the matter. The purpose of the rule is to prevent the disruption of agency action until the agency has actually decided a case or issued a rule. Courts make an exception to the final order rule and will hear a case if the plaintiff would incur "irreparable injury" or "economic hardship" if it had to wait for the final order of the administrative agency before seeking judicial review—for example, if an administrative rule would drive a company out of business while the agency heard the matter.

Once a court determines that a decision by an administrative agency is reviewable, the court may *stay*—that is, halt—the disputed agency action while the case is being reviewed by the court. A stay is usually issued to postpone the effective date of an administrative rule until after the court has issued its decision.

Abuse of Discretion.   Many types of administrative decisions specifically lie within the *discretion* of an administrative agency (e.g., rulemaking, licensing). The APA permits a court to hold unlawful and set aside a discretionary agency action, finding, or conclusion which is found to be "arbitrary, capricious or an abuse of discretion." Since all three terms essentially mean the same thing, the test is generally referred to as the "abuse of discretion" standard.

In order to find an abuse of discretion, the court must engage in a "substantial inquiry" of the agency decision. The court is generally limited to reviewing the record made by the agency, and can take no new evidence on the matter. The courts will find an "abuse of discretion" where the administrative agency:

1. failed to consider appropriate factors
2. considered inappropriate factors
3. made a clear error in judgment.

It is rare for the courts to overturn an agency's discretionary action based on the "abuse of discretion" standard.

Where an administrative agency has made a discretionary decision regarding a matter, but has failed to sufficiently describe its reasons for the decision, the court may order the agency to submit a detailed statement of the reasons underlying the agency's decision. Certain types of agency discretionary action are totally *exempt* from normal judicial review. Examples of exempt areas are:

1. decisions of the military regarding personnel (e.g., leaves);
2. admission of aliens (the attorney general can waive requirements for admission); and
3. agency decisions involving economic consideration (such as rate making).

LICENSING POWER OF ADMINISTRATIVE AGENCIES

One of the major functions of many administrative agencies is the granting (or refusal to grant) *licenses* to applicants to enter particular industries, expand service, and to practice certain professions. Licenses from administrative agencies are generally required to enter such industries as banking, transportation (e.g., trucking, airlines) communications (e.g., television and radio stations), and many professions, such as lawyers, doctors, architects, accountants, contractors. Owing to the deference the courts give to the expertise of administrative agencies, licensing decisions are seldom overturned by the courts.

In *Bowman Transportation, Inc. v. Arkansas-Best Freight System, Inc.* the Supreme Court applied the "abuse of discretion" standard and upheld a discretionary licensing decision of the Interstate Commerce Commission in granting a trucking license to three applicants.

JUDICIAL REVIEW OF LICENSING DECISION

BOWMAN TRANSPORTATION, INC. v. ARKANSAS-BEST FREIGHT SYSTEM, INC.

419 U.S. 281 (1974)
UNITED STATES SUPREME COURT

Mr. Justice Douglas delivered the opinion of the Court.

Ten applications of motor carriers to conduct general commodities operations between points in the Southwest and Southeast were consolidated in one proceeding. . . . The hearing examiners, after extensive hearings, rejected each application. The [Interstate Commerce] Commission granted three of the applications of appellant carriers. Appellees, competing carriers, brought an action in the District Court, to suspend, enjoin, and annul that portion of the order of the Commission that authorizes issuance of certificates of public convenience and necessity to Red Ball, Bowman, and Johnson. The District Court refused to enforce the

Commission's order because its findings and conclusions were arbitrary, capricious, and without rational basis within the meaning of the Administrative Procedure Act. . . .

The Motor Carrier provisions of the Interstate Commerce Act, 49 Stat. 551, 49 U.S.C. Section 307, empower the Commission to grant an application for a certificate if it finds (1) that the applicant is "fit, willing, and able properly to perform the service proposed"; and (2) that the service proposed "is or will be required by the present or future public convenience and necessity." The Commission made both findings. . . .

Under the "arbitrary and capricious" standard the scope of review is a narrow one. . . . The court is not empowered to substitute its judgment for that of the agency." The agency must articulate a "rational connection between the facts found and the choice made."

EVIDENCE AS TO EXISTING SERVICE

The applicant carriers presented exhibits showing the time in transit of selected shipments that had been consigned to appellee carriers by particular shippers during a designated study period. . . . The appellee carriers offered studies of their own. . . . The issue before the Commission was not whether the appellees' service met some absolute standard of performance but whether the "public convenience and necessity" would be served by the entry of new carriers into the markets served by appellees. . . . Certainly the Commission was entitled . . . to conclude that service would be improved by granting the applications.

EVIDENCE OF APPLICANTS' FITNESS

The applicants supported their service proposals with exhibits showing transit times over comparable distances on other routes. . . . A general assumption that competition would force new entrants to exceed the pre-existing quality of service in an effort to attract business might have to yield in the face of an applicant whose shortcomings elsewhere were many and flagrant. But no such evidence was offered here, and none of the applicants was so characterized. Indeed the examiners found that "in the main the carriers participating in these proceedings are substantial and responsible carriers," and no party has disputed this finding. We do not find the Commission's treatment of the evidence arbitrary.

Having found that the admission of the applicant carriers to the routes they sought would produce benefits to the consumers served, the Commission proceeded to consider the effect of new entry upon the appellees. While the Commission acknowledged that competition from new entrants might cause at least short-run business losses for existing carriers, it found that, with the exception of one carrier, none would be "seriously adversely affected." Further, the Commission concluded that in any event, "the gains to be derived by the shipping public in general far outweigh any adverse effect this carrier or any other protestant may experience."

The Commission stated in its opinion that "grants of authority will subject some of protestants' traffic to the possibility of diversion," but went on to make findings that there would be no "serious adverse impact.". . . It was rational for the Commission so to conclude that the new entrant may be expected not to swallow up existing carriers, especially if the latter make efforts to attract business. . . . [T]he Commission granted only three of the 10 pending applications, . . . We cannot say that the balance it struck was arbitrary or contrary to law.

Hearings on the applications in these cases began in 1966 and concluded in 1967. Thereafter, the parties prepared extensive briefs for the examiners, who rendered their decision in November 1969. The decision of the Commission was handed down on December 30, 1971. Thus, the evidentiary material pertained to service conditions which were dated by five years at the time the Commission rendered its decision. . . . More than 900 witnesses testified in the original hearings, which consumed 150 days. . . . [W]e conclude that there is sound basis for adhering to our practice of declining to require reopening of the record, except in the most extraordinary circumstances.

A policy in favor of competition embodied in the laws has application in a variety of economic affairs. Even where Congress has chosen Government regulation as the primary device for protecting the public interest, a policy of facilitating competitive market structure and performance is entitled to consideration. The Commission, of course, is entitled to conclude that preservation of a competitive structure in a given case is overridden by other interests, but where, as here, the Commission concludes that competition "aids in the attainment of the objectives of the national transportation policy," we have no basis for disturbing the Commission's accommodation.

Reversed and remanded.

CASE QUESTIONS

1. How many applicants for trucking licenses were there? How many licenses were granted?
2. What was the decision of:
   a. the hearing officer [ALJ]?
   b. the Interstate Commerce Commission?
   c. the District Court?

3. What test is applied by courts in reviewing discretionary decisions by administrative agencies? Explain. Is the test too harsh?
4. Were the following statutory requirements met in this case?
   a. Applicants were "fit, willing, and able" to perform the services.
   b. The "public convenience and necessity" would be served by the entry of additional trucking firms.
5. How long did the administrative procedure and lawsuit take? Is this an example of bureaucratic "red tape"?

Policy Issue.
a. Should administrative agencies be granted broad discretionary powers to approve or disapprove applications for licenses to enter industries?

b. Should free entry to all industries be allowed?

Economics Issue.
a. Why did the plaintiff-appellee trucking firms try to prevent the applicant trucking firms from being granted licenses?
b. Do you think that the trucking licenses in this case were very valuable? Explain.

Ethics Issue. Was it ethical for the existing trucking firms to bring a lawsuit to prevent competition from entering the trucking industry?

Social Responsibility. Does the government owe a duty of social responsibility to protect consumers by enacting licensing procedures for admitting companies to an industry?

ADMINISTRATIVE AGENCY SEARCHES

In order to fulfill its rule-making, policy-making, and adjudicative functions, an administrative agency must be able to obtain information from the businesses that the agency regulates. An agency has a number of different methods of obtaining information, including:

1. voluntary submission of information by companies
2. use of subpoena power
3. physical inspection of business premises
4. administrative hearings
5. required reports.

Subpoena Power. An administrative agency may issue a *subpoena* to obtain information from a business. The party to whom the subpoena is issued may comply with the subpoena or resist it. If the party resists the subpoena, the administrative agency may seek judicial enforcement of the subpoena. In order to obtain a court order to enforce a subpoena, an agency must state its purpose for seeking the information, and show that it has reasonable grounds to "believe" that the document requested will prove a violation of the law. "Fishing expeditions" by administrative agencies are prohibited. If the party ignores a judicial order that enforces an agency subpoena, the court may hold the resisting party in contempt of court. Section 555(d) of the Administrative Procedure Act, which follows, explains the procedure for seeking and enforcing an administrative agency subpoena.

Agency subpoenas authorized by law shall be issued to a party on request and, when required by rules of procedure, on a statement or showing of general relevance and reasonable scope of the evidence sought. On contest, the court shall sustain the subpoena or similar process or demand to the extent that it is found to be in accordance with law. In a proceeding for enforcement, the court shall issue an order requiring the appearance of the witness or the production of the evidence or data within a reasonable time under penalty of punishment for contempt in case of contumacious failure to comply.

Unreasonable Search and Seizure.

An administrative agency may seek to gather information through the physical inspection of business premises. Most inspections by administrative agencies are considered "searches" subject to the protection of the Fourth Amendment to the U.S. Constitution. The Fourth Amendment provides:

The right of the people to be secure in their persons, houses, papers, and effects, against unreasonable searches and seizures, shall not be violated, and no Warrants shall issue, but upon probable cause, supported by Oath or affirmation, and particularly describing the place to be searched, and the persons or things to be seized.

The purpose of the Fourth Amendment to the Constitution is to protect persons from overzealous governmental investigative activities. The Fourth Amendment protects persons against "unreasonable" searches and seizures of information. The Fourth Amendment seeks to balance the individual's right to personal privacy with the government's need to know information in order to administer laws. The Fourth Amendment only protects persons and businesses against *unreasonable* search and seizures. *Reasonable* search and seizures are valid under the Fourth Amendment. Searches by administrative agencies are generally considered reasonable within the meaning of the Fourth Amendment where:

1. the party voluntarily agrees to the search
2. the search is conducted pursuant to a validly issued search warrant
3. a warrantless search is conducted in an emergency situation (e.g., search incident to an arrest, "pat-down" search)
4. the business is part of a special industry where warrantless searches are automatically considered valid (e.g., liquor, firearms)
5. the business is part of a hazardous industry (e.g., coal mine) and a statute expressly provides for nonarbitrary warrantless searches.

Where police, law enforcement officers, administrative or other government investigative personnel conduct a search that does not meet one of the previously enumerated exceptions, the search is "unreasonable" and violates the Fourth Amendment. Evidence derived from an unreasonable search and seizure is generally considered to be tainted evidence ("fruit of a tainted tree"). Tainted evidence is generally inadmissible as evidence at a trial or administrative hearing against the person searched. However, the evidence is admissible against other persons. The courts are becoming somewhat more lenient in allowing the admissibility of tainted evidence against any defendant.

In *Donovan v. Dewey*, the Supreme Court held that a warrantless search of a quarry by an administrative agency, pursuant to the Federal Mine and Safety Act, was a reasonable search under the Fourth Amendment.

K Now

ADMINISTRATIVE AGENCY SEARCH

DONOVAN, SECRETARY OF LABOR, v. DEWEY

452 U.S. 594 (1981)
UNITED STATES SUPREME COURT

Justice Marshall delivered the opinion of the Court.

The Federal Mine Safety and Health Act of 1977 requires the Secretary of Labor to develop detailed mandatory health and safety standards to govern the operation of the Nation's mines. Section 103 (a) of the Act provides that federal mine inspectors are to inspect underground mines at least four times per year and surface mines at least twice a year to insure compliance with these standards, and to make followup inspections to determine whether previously discovered violations have been corrected. This section also grants mine inspectors "a right of entry to, upon, or through any coal or other mine" and states that "no advance notice of an inspection shall be provided to any person."

In July 1978, a federal mine inspector attempted to inspect quarries owned by appellee Waukesha Lime and Stone Co. in order to determine whether all 25 safety and health violations uncovered during a prior inspection had been corrected. After the inspector had been on the site for about an hour, Waukesha's president, appellee Douglas Dewey, refused to allow the inspection to continue unless the inspector first obtain a search warrant. The inspector issued a citation to Waukesha for terminating the inspection, and the Secretary subsequently filed this civil action in the District Court for the Eastern District of Wisconsin seeking to enjoin appellees from refusing to permit warrantless searches of the Waukesha facility.

The District Court granted summary judgment in favor of appellees on the ground that the Fourth Amendment prohibited the warrantless searches of stone quarries authorized by Section 103(a) of the Act.

[T]he Fourth Amendment protects the interest of the owner of property in being free from *unreasonable* intrusions onto his property by agents of the government. Inspections of commercial property may be unreasonable if they are not authorized by law or are unnecessary for the furtherance of federal interests. Similarly, warrantless inspections of commercial property may be constitutionally objectionable if their occurrence is so random, infrequent, or unpredictable that the owner, for all practical purposes, has no real expectation that his property will from time to time be inspected by government officials.

However, the assurance of regularity provided by a warrant may be unnecessary under certain inspection schemes. Thus, in *Colonnade Corp. v. United States,* we recognized that because the alcoholic beverage industry had long been "subject to close supervision and inspection," Congress enjoyed "broad power to design such powers of inspection . . . as it deems necessary to meet the evils at hand." Similarly, in *United States v. Biswell,* this Court concluded that the Gun Control Act of 1968 provided a sufficiently comprehensive and predictable inspection scheme that the warrantless inspections mandated under the statute did not violate the Fourth Amendment.

We re-emphasized this exception to the warrant *had to have a warrant* requirement most recently in *Marshall v. Barlow's, Inc.* In that case, we held that absent consent a warrant was constitutionally required in order to conduct administrative inspections under . . . the Occupational Safety and Health Act of 1970. That statute imposes health and safety standards on all businesses engaged in or affecting interstate commerce that have employees, and authorized representatives of the Secretary to conduct inspections to ensure compliance with the Act. However, the Act fails to tailor the scope and frequency of such administrative inspections to the particular health and safety concerns posed by the numerous and varied businesses regulated by the statute. . . . Similarly, the Act does not provide any standards to guide inspectors either in their selection of establishments to be searched or in the exercise of their authority to search. . . . Accordingly, we concluded that a warrant was constitutionally required. . . . However, we expressly limited our holding to the inspection provisions of the Occupational Safety and Health Act, noting that the "reasonableness of a warrantless search . . . will depend upon the specific enforcement needs and privacy guarantees of each statute"

Applying this analysis to the case before us, we conclude that the warrantless inspections required by the Mine Safety and Health Act do not offend the Fourth Amendment. As an initial matter, it is undisputed that there is a substantial federal interest in improving the health and safety conditions in the Nation's underground and surface mines. In enacting the statute, Congress was plainly aware that the mining industry is among the most hazardous in the country and that the poor health and safety record of this industry has significant deleterious effects on interstate commerce. . . . In designing an inspection program, Congress expressly recognized that a warrant requirement could significantly frustrate effective enforcement of the Act. Thus, it provided in § 103 (a) of the Act that "no advance notice of an inspection shall be provided to any person." In explaining this provision, the Senate Report notes:

> [I]n [light] of the notorious ease with which many safety or health hazards may be concealed if advance warning of inspection is obtained, a warrant requirement would seriously undercut this Act's objectives.

Unlike the statute at issue in *Barlow's,* the Mine Safety and Health Act applies to industrial activity with a notorious history of serious accidents and unhealthful working conditions. The Act is specifically tailored to address those concerns, and the regulation of mines it imposes is sufficiently pervasive and defined that the owner of such a facility cannot help but be aware that he "will be subject to effective inspection." First, the Act requires inspection of *all* mines and specifically defines the frequency of inspection. . . . Second, the standards with which a mine operator is required to comply are all specifically set forth in the Act or in Title 30 of the Code of Federal Regulations.

Under these circumstances, it is difficult to see what additional protection a warrant requirement would provide. . . . Accordingly, we conclude that the general program of warrantless inspections au-

thorized by Section 103 (a) of the Act does not violate the Fourth Amendment.

The judgment of the District Court is *reversed,* and the case is *remanded* for further proceedings consistent with this opinion.

Justice Stewart, dissenting.

As I read today's opinion, Congress is left free to avoid the Fourth Amendment industry by industry. . . . Congress after today can define any industry as dangerous, regulate it substantially, and provide for warrantless inspections of its members. But, because I do not believe that Congress can, by legislative fiat, rob the members of any industry of their constitutional protection, I dissent from the opinion and judgment of the Court.

CASE QUESTIONS

1. Are all searches illegal under the Fourth Amendment? If not, what searches are illegal? Lawful?
2. Does the Warrant Clause of the Fourth Amendment protect businesses as well as individuals from *unreasonable* search and seizures?
3. What was the decision of the court as to the reasonableness of the warrantless searches in the following cases?
   a. *Colonnade Corp. v. U.S.*
   b. *U.S. v. Biswell*
   c. *Marshall v. Barlow's Inc.*

How do you reconcile the decision reached in these cases with the decision reached in *Donovan v. Dewey?*

Policy Issue. Should an administrative agency be granted greater powers to search businesses subject to its jurisdiction than that given to police on the street to search criminal suspects?

Economics Issue. Why may it be cheaper in the long run to let an agency inspector inspect business premises without a search warrant?

Ethics Issue. Was it ethical for Mr. Dewey to refuse the mine inspector's request to search the quarries? If you were Mr. Dewey, what would you have done?

Social Responsibility. Does a business owe a duty of social responsibility to make its business premises open for inspection by administrative agency personnel?

Immunity of Agency Employees. The Supreme Court, in *Butz v. Economou,* 438 U.S. 478 (1978), has held that—like judges, legislators, and others involved in the judicial process—administrative law judges, agency attorneys, and other agency executives and personnel are *immune* from lawsuits based on actions and decisions made by them while performing agency duties. In this excerpt from *Butz v. Economou,* cited above, Justice White states the argument for granting absolute immunity from prosecution to agency personnel.

[T]here is a serious danger that the decision to authorize proceedings will provoke a retaliatory response. An individual targeted by an administrative proceeding will react angrily and may seek vengeance in the courts. A corporation will muster all of its financial and legal resources in an effort to prevent administrative sanctions. "When millions may turn on regulatory decisions, there is a strong incentive to counter-attack."

We believe that agency officials must make the decision to move forward with an administrative proceeding free from intimidation or harassment. . . .

PUBLIC DISCLOSURE OF AGENCY ACTIONS

Public and Congressional concern over the secrecy of administrative agency actions led Congress to enact several statutes to promote public disclosure of agency activities and to help protect private persons from unwarranted administrative agency actions. These statutes include:

1. the Freedom of Information Act
2. the Government in the Sunshine Act
3. the Equal Access to Justice Act.

The Freedom of Information Act. The Freedom of Information Act, as contained in APA Section 52, amended 1974, requires federal administrative agencies to make public, upon request, certain agency documents. The Act provides for the publication of certain agency information (e.g., agency procedures, rules and interpretations) in the *Federal Register,* and the publication of quarterly indexes to certain documents. It specifies time limits and fees for the copying of documents and provides for disciplinary action against agency employees who arbitrarily refuse to honor proper requests for agency documents under the Act.

Certain documents are statutorily exempt from public disclosures under the Freedom of Information Act, including:

1. documents that are classified in the interests of national security by the President
2. documents where statutes specifically prohibit disclosure
3. law enforcement records where disclosure would interfere with law enforcement proceedings
4. documents that describe agency personnel practices
5. intra- and interagency memoranda
6. medical, personnel, and similar files

7. documents that contain "trade secrets" or other confidential or privileged information
8. documents pertaining to the operations of financial institutions and
9. geological and geophysical data and maps.

Decisions by administrative agencies not to publicly disclose documents under the Freedom of Information Act are subject to judicial review by the proper Federal District Court. The court may award attorney fees to a successful petitioner under the Act.

The Government in the Sunshine Act.   In 1976, Congress enacted the Government in the Sunshine Act. Under this Act, meetings of administrative agencies that are headed by two or more persons appointed by the President must be open to the public unless the meeting qualifies for one of the specified exemptions, and the agency by majority vote closes the meeting to the public. "Meetings" subject to the Act include deliberations of agency members where official agency business is conducted or decided. Day-to-day operations of agency personnel are not subject to the Act.

The agency meetings that are exempt from the Government in the Sunshine Act parallel those situations where documents are exempt from public disclosure under the Freedom of Information Act (see preceding list). Also exempt are agency meetings that:

1. accuse any person of a crime
2. concern the agency's issuance of a subpoena
3. significantly frustrate the implementation of a proposed agency action

Decisions by administrative agencies to close their meetings are subject to judicial review by the proper Federal District Court.

The Equal Access to Justice Act.   In 1980, Congress enacted the Equal Access to Justice Act. Under the Act, a private party to an administrative agency action can recover attorney's fees and other costs of litigation where the agency position was *not* "substantially justified." The courts have generally held that an administrative agency action must be extremely outrageous before an award will be made to a private party under the Equal Access to Justice Act.

Trend of the Law

Administrative agencies will continue to play an important and increasing role in the regulation of business in the future. Certain established administrative agencies will be called upon in the future to apply well-developed statutory and regulatory schemes to an ever-changing business environment. Other newly created administrative agencies (e.g., the Nuclear Regulatory Commission) will increase in importance as they develop regulations to apply to previously unregulated or underregulated business environments.

Many of the well-established administrative agencies and regulatory schemes are *industry-specific* in nature, that is, the statutes were passed and regulatory agencies created to regulate individual industries (e.g., the Interstate Commerce Commission was created to regulate railroads, and eventually trucking). However, many other administrative agencies were created to regulate the entire American economy. For example, the Occupational Safety and Health Administration was created to regulate the safety of the work environment in almost all industries and businesses in the United States. The Environmental Protection Agency was created to enforce environmental laws against all covered businesses regardless of type. A substantial amount of the regulation of business in the future will come from these non-industry-specific administrative agencies.

In conclusion, administrative agencies will be the most important source of new laws to regulate business in the future. The remainder of this book covers the specific regulatory schemes (e.g., antitrust laws, securities regulation, environmental law, labor law) and the agencies empowered to enforce these statutes and regulations, including the Federal Trade Commission, the Securities and Exchange Commission, the Environmental Protection Agency, and the National Labor Relations Board.

REVIEW QUESTIONS

1. Section 4.1 of an Illinois statute empowered the Illinois Human Relations Commission to define real estate "areas." Individuals who did not wish to sell their property or be solicited were permitted to notify the Commission, which would then bar realtors within that area from soliciting any sales from that individual. The Commission would send a list of these property owners to realtors and others "known or believed by the Commission to be soliciting" sales in the area. The Illinois Criminal Code made it a misdemeanor to solicit sales from an individual named in a list received from the Commission. Tibbits attempted to solicit sales from individuals on the list. He was subsequently charged with violating the Criminal Code. At trial, his defense counsel asserted that the statute permitting the Commission to define areas was unconstitutional because it was an unlawful delegation of power from the legislature to the Commission. Was this defense successful?

2. The Nebraska Grade A Milk Control Act required the Director of the Department of Agriculture and Inspection to adopt regulations prescribing minimum sanitary and quality standards for milk production. Any producer who violated these standards was guilty of a misdemeanor, punishable by a fine of $25.00 to $100.00. The Act provided little guidance to the Director; its only directive was that the Director should adopt standards in compliance with the Milk Ordinance and Code which had been promulgated by the United States Department of Health, Education and Welfare.

This code was not a law, but rather a set of recommendations, advisory in nature, which was never formally published by the Department. Lincoln Dairy Company filed suit in the Nebraska state court asking the court to declare the law unconstitutional. Will the dairy prevail?

3. The Colorado Tax Commission and the Colorado State Board of Equalization ordered a blanket 41 percent increase in the valuation of all taxable property in Denver, Colorado. Bi-Metallic Investment Company, a large Denver land holder, sued to attempt to stop enforcement of the order. The company argued that it had not been allowed an opportunity to be heard in opposition to the order. Bi-Metallic claimed that it was being effectively deprived of its property without due process of the law. Was Bi-Metallic entitled to a direct opportunity to be heard?

4. During the oil and gas shortage in 1973 and 1974, the Federal Power Commission issued an administrative order concerning natural gas supplies. Titled "Statement of Policy," the order expressed the Commission's policy that the national interests would best be served by assigning curtailment priorities on the basis of end use rather than on the basis of prior contractual commitments. The order further stated that the Commission intended to follow this type of priority schedule unless a particular pipeline company demonstrated that a different curtailment plan was more in the public interest. A number of commercial gas users filed suit in Federal District Court. Primarily, they contended that the order was really a substantive rule, not a policy statement, and therefore rule-making procedures that had not been followed by the Commission should have been followed. Since the procedures were not followed, the users contended that the order should be declared invalid. Will the users be successful?

5. The Occupational Safety and Health Act gives inspectors the discretionary power to impose civil penalties up to $10,000 upon employers who fail to maintain safe and sanitary working conditions. Any employer can challenge the penalty in a proceeding before an administrative law judge. The judge's decision is then adopted as the position of the Occupational Safety and Health Review Commission unless a commissioner requests a full hearing before the Commission. All Commission findings are reviewable by the federal appeal courts, which are bound to the Commission's factual findings under the standard of "supported by substantial evidence on the record when considered as a whole. . . ." Once all appeals are exhausted, if the defendant does not pay the outstanding fine, the Commission can sue in Federal District Court. A number of employers who were fined by the Commission formed a class action suit. They contended that these statutory procedures were unconstitutional because they eliminated the employers' right to a jury trial as guaranteed by the Seventh Amendment. What was the result of this class action suit?

6. The Wisconsin State Board of Medical Examiners investigated Dr. Larkin to determine whether his medical license should be revoked. After finishing the investigation, the Board gave notice that an adversary hearing would be held to determine if his license should be revoked. Prior to the hearing, Larkin filed an action in District Court requesting the Court to issue an injunction to restrain the hearing. Larkin alleged that when

an agency first investigates and then adjudicates the same case, there is a constitutional risk of bias. Does Larkin's argument have any merit?

7. Universal Camera Corporation appealed from an order of the National Labor Relations Board ordering the reinstatement of a firm employee who had been discharged because he gave testimony under the Wagner Act. Universal was also ordered to cease and desist from discriminating against other employees who testified or filed charges under the Wagner Act. On appeal, the Court of Appeals held that the NRLB's order was supported by substantial evidence. The Court found substantial support in the evidence that was most favorable to the NRLB's decision. Universal appealed this decision to the U.S. Supreme Court, claiming that the appellate court had used the wrong standard on review. What is the standard that appellate courts are required to apply when reviewing agency orders? Did the Court of Appeals apply the correct standard in this case?

8. Under the Department of Transportation Act of 1966, the Secretary of Transportation may not authorize federal highway construction funds for projects that pass through public parks if a feasible and prudent alternate route exists. If no such route exists, the Secretary can only approve funds if there has been "all possible planning to minimize harm" to the park. Paul Volpe, the Secretary, announced that the Department of Transportation had agreed with local Memphis officials who planned to construct a six-lane highway through a public park. The announcement, which authorized federal highway funds for the project, was not accompanied by any factual findings.

   The Citizens to Protect Overton Park sued Volpe, claiming that he failed to state factual findings upon which he based his decision. The complaint also alleged that Volpe failed to explain why no other prudent route existed and to show that all possible steps had been taken to minimize harm to the park. Volpe gave affidavits to the District Court stating the reasons why the Department approved the project. Based on these affidavits the District Court granted Volpe's motion for a summary judgment. The citizens appealed, asking the Circuit Court for a *de novo* review of the Secretary's decision. Should the Circuit Court conduct a *de novo* review?

9. The National Labor Relations Act empowers the National Labor Relations Board to hold hearings on complaints filed against employers. The Board has the discretion to make an initial determination of whether or not hearings are appropriate. The Board's conclusions can not be implemented until they have been affirmed by the Court of Appeals. Bethlehem Ship Building Company was charged with violating portions of the National Labor Relations Act. Before any hearings were held by the NLRB, Bethlehem filed suit in District Court requesting that the Court stop the Board from holding any hearings. Bethlehem argued that the hearings were unwarranted since the plant under investigation was not manufacturing goods involved in interstate commerce (a prerequisite for NLRB jurisdiction). Bethlehem also claimed that the holding of hearings would result in irreparable damage in the form of costs, loss of time, and impairment of employee good will. Can the District Court grant an injunction to enjoin the NLRB from holding hearings?

10. The Far East Conference, an association of steamship companies, established a two-tiered pricing system where shippers who contracted to deal only with conference shippers received a lower price. A higher price was charged to those who did not join in this exclusivity agreement. The U.S. Government filed suit in District Court seeking to enjoin the shippers from this two-tiered pricing practice. The government argued that this pricing arrangement violated the antitrust provisions of the Sherman Act. Far East admitted that they engaged in this pricing system but argued that the case should be dismissed because the Federal Maritime Board, an administrative agency, had primary jurisdiction to consider the issues, which required expert and technical knowledge to resolve. Should the District Court have dismissed the case?

11. The Federal Food, Drug, and Cosmetic Act required manufacturers of prescription drugs to print the "established" or "generic" name of each drug sold on its label. This designation was required to be printed in type at least half as large as the type used on its "proprietary" or trade name. The Commissioner of Food and Drugs, under authority derived from the Act, promulgated a regulation requiring that the drug's established name accompany each reference to its proprietary name. Interested parties were allowed to comment at public hearings about the proposed regulation before the Commissioner finally decided to adopt it. The regulation became effective immediately upon publication and the agency planned no further hearings prior to enforcement.

    Individual drug manufacturers formed an association comprised of the manufacturers of more than 90 percent of the nation's supply of prescription drugs. The association sued to enjoin enforcement of the regulation and to have it declared invalid. The association claimed that the Commissioner exceeded his authority by issuing the challenged regulation and that they were faced with an unacceptable dilemma since they were forced either to incur the expenses of a costly label changeover or to bear the penalties which would result from noncompliance. The government argued that since the regulation had not been applied, the case should be dismissed because it was not ripe for review. Can the District Court review the validity of the regulation?

12. The Federal Trade Commission filed a complaint against Standard Oil Company alleging that the FTC had "reason to believe" that Standard Oil was engaging in an unfair method of competition and was therefore violating the Federal Trade Commission Act. While the case was still pending before an administrative law judge, Standard sued the FTC in District Court claiming that the complaint issued by the FTC was unlawful because the FTC did not have any reason to believe that Standard Oil and seven other oil companies had violated the law. Standard Oil claimed that the FTC complaint resulted from public pressure exerted during the 1973 gasoline shortage. Can the District Court review the Federal Trade Commission's actions?

13. Section 8 of the Occupational Safety and Health Act (OSHA) allows agents of the Labor Department to search the work area of any employment facility within the Act's jurisdiction. The purpose of the search is to inspect for violations of the OSHA regulations. No search warrant is required.

An OSHA inspector attempted to search the nonpublic area of Barlows, Inc., a plumbing and electrical installation business. No complaint had been filed against the firm; it simply turned up in the agency's selection process. Barlows refused to admit the inspector after it was determined that he did not have a search warrant. Marshall, the OSHA Secretary, petitioned the District Court to issue an order compelling Barlows to admit the inspector. The order was issued but Barlows refused to admit the inspector. Barlows then petitioned the District Court to enjoin OSHA from conducting warrantless searches. Should the District Court grant Barlows' request?

14. West Publishing Company and the United States Air Force conducted negotiations over a period of time. The Air Force was attempting to purchase West's Keynote System, which is utilized in legal reporting, for use in the Air Force's own electronic legal reporting system. During the negotiations the Air Force generated a number of documents dealing with the potential deal. After West concluded the deal, Mead Data Central, Inc., a competitor with West, filed a request for certain Air Force documents under the Freedom of Information Act. The Air Force released a large number of the documents but chose to retain seven of them which the Air Force claimed to be exempt. These documents consisted of:

a. legal opinions concerning the deal that were a part of a professional attorney-client relationship

b. a document that basically reviewed the background of the negotiations with West, including offers and counteroffers made to the firm

c. internal memos dealing with the proposed transaction.

Mead sued the Air Force in District Court, asking the Court to grant an order requiring the Air Force to release the documents. In general, what type of information must be released under the Freedom of Information Act and why? If one document contains both information that should be disclosed and material that is protected, can the Court force the Air Force to make this material public? As to each type of document, discribe the circumstances under which the Air Force would be required to disclose the material.

6 THE CONSTITUTION AND BUSINESS

INTRODUCTION

Prior to the American Revolution, each of the 13 original colonies operated as a separate sovereignty under the English rule. Representatives of the colonies first met as a Continental Congress in September, 1774. After hostilities with Great Britain started, the Continental Congress declared independence in 1776. The Continental Congress adopted the *Articles of Confederation* in 1778. The Articles of Confederation created a federal Congress composed of representatives of the 13 new states.

The Articles of Confederation was a very weak document. It did not provide Congress with the power to levy and collect taxes, to regulate foreign commerce, or to regulate interstate commerce. Unanimous approval by the States was needed to amend the Articles of Confederation. Congress could only enact federal legislation with the concurrence of at least nine state legislatures.

The Constitutional Convention was held in Philadelphia in May, 1787. The primary purpose of the Convention was to remedy the weakness of the federal government, which was caused by the limitations contained in the Articles of Confederation. After substantial debate, the delegates drafted the new United States Constitution. In September, 1787, the new Constitution was reported to Congress. State ratification of the Constitution was completed in 1788.

THE CONSTITUTION OF THE UNITED STATES

Following its famous *Preamble*, which sets forth the purposes of the Constitution ("We the people. . . .), the Constitution of the United States contains seven *Articles* which establish the basic "rules" for the operation of the country. Drafted in general language adaptable to changing conditions, the major provisions of the seven articles are as follows.

Article I.   Article I establishes the *legislative* branch of government, defines limits the powers of the House of Representatives and Senate, sets forth the manner of electing and removing members of Congress, and establishes the power of Congress to levy and collect taxes, regulate commerce (the "Commerce Clause"), coin money, and raise and support armies.

Article II.   Article II vests *executive* power in the President, defines the qualifications for the executive office, specifies the term of office, establishes the manner of election of the President, makes the President the Commander in Chief of the Army, Navy, and Militia, and authorizes the President to enter into treaties upon the advice and consent of the Senate.

Article III.   Article III creates the *judicial* branch of government, establishes the Supreme Court, extends judicial power to all cases in law and equity, defines the original jurisdiction of the Supreme Court, authorizes Congress to establish other inferior federal courts, and defines and establishes punishments for treason.

Article IV.   Article IV, the "states' relations article," establishes the relationship among the states, and contains the "full faith and credit" clause and the "privileges and immunities" clause.

Article V.   Article V establishes the methods for amending the Constitution. Twenty-six amendments have been added to the Constitution to date.

Article VI.   Article VI contains the Supremacy Clause, which makes all federal laws and treaties the "supreme law of the land."

Article VII.   Article VII provided for the ratification of the Constitution by the original colonial states.

Amendments to the Constitution.   Article V of the U.S. Constitution provides methods for adding amendments to the Constitution. In 1778, upon the recommendations of the states of Massachusetts, New Hampshire and New York, the ten amendments known as the "Bill of Rights" were added to the U.S. Constitution. Since that time, sixteen additional amendments have been added to our Constitution. The original seven articles and 26 amendments presently make up the Constitution of the United States. This chapter covers the major provisions of the original seven Articles. Chapter 7 covers the amendments to the Constitution. The full text of the Constitution may be found in Appendix A of this book.

Federal Regulation of Business.   To the extend that the federal government may regulate business, it must look to the United States Constitution for the grant of such power. Generally, the federal government's power to regulate business derives from the Commerce Clause of Article I of the U.S. Constitution. The other provisions of the Constitution and the 26 amendments to the Constitution also give additional powers to the federal government over the affairs of business.

Since the federal government is only given those powers *enumerated* in the U. S. Constitution, all residual powers not explicitly granted to the federal government are "reserved" to the states. The powers of state and local governments to regulate business are derived from these residual powers. Each state has enacted a state Constitution, some provisions of which are applicable to business. In the following excerpt from *Martin v. Hunter's Lessee*, 14 U.S. (1 Wheat) 304 (1B16), Justice Story explains the concept of the division of power between the federal and state governments as provided in the U.S. Constitution.

The constitution of the United States was ordained and established, not by the states in their sovereign capacities, but emphatically, as the preamble of the constitution declares, by "the people of the United States." There can be no doubt that it was competent to the people to invest the general government with all the powers which they might deem proper and necessary; to extend or restrain these powers according to their own good pleasure, and to give them a paramount and supreme authority.

As little doubt can there be, that the people had a right to prohibit to the states the exercise of any powers which were, in their judgment, incompatible with the objects of the general compact; to make the powers of the state governments, in given cases, subordinate to those of the nation, or to reserve to themselves those sovereign authorities which they might not choose to delegate to either.

These deductions do not rest upon general reasoning, plain and obvious as they seem to be. They have been positively recognised by one of the articles in amendment of the constitution, which declares, that "the powers not delegated to the United States by the constitution, nor prohibited by it to the states, are reserved to the *states* respectively, or *to the people.*"

THE DOCTRINE OF SEPARATION OF POWERS

✳ The doctrine of separation of powers is one of the most important constitutional law concepts. The doctrine is based on a theory that each branch of government (legislative, executive, and judicial) has specific governmental functions to perform. Generally, the functions of the three branches of government are:

1. the legislative branch is charged with *making* law by the enactment of statutes
2. the executive branch is charged with *administering* the law
3. the judicial branch has the responsibility for *interpreting* and applying the law to individual disputes as these are presented to the courts.

Checks and Balances. The doctrine of separation of powers is also based on a theory of "checks and balances," whereby each branch of government is given some capacity by the Constitution to limit the performance or power of the other two branches of government. For example, the judicial branch reviews the constitutionality of the activities of the executive and the legislative branches. The legislative branch limits the power of the executive and establishes the jurisdiction of the federal courts. And the executive appoints the judiciary with the advice and consent of the Senate.

The stability of our democracy is built upon the fine tuning of the interrelated exercise of the independent powers of each branch of government.

 THE SUPREMACY CLAUSE

Article VI of the U.S. Constitution contains the Supremacy Clause. The Supremacy Clause provides, "This Constitution, and the Laws of the United States which shall be made in Pursuance thereof . . . shall be the supreme law of the land." Laws made pursuant to the Constitution include federal statutes, treaties with foreign nations, and regulations of federal administrative agencies.

The Preemption Doctrine. Issues involving the Supremacy Clause of the U.S. Constitution often arise when a state or local law comes in *conflict* with federal law. Under the "preemption doctrine," state or local law that conflicts with valid federal law is *preempted* by the federal law. The conflicting state or local law is null and *void* to the extent of the conflict. On many occasions, when the federal legislature enacts a statute, it will expressly provide that the statute either does or does not preempt any state regulation of the area. Often, however, the federal law will be silent on the point, placing the burden on the courts to determine whether the state or local law is impliedly preempted by the federal law.

Under present Supreme Court policy, the conflict between the state and federal law must be *direct* and *substantial* in order for federal law to preempt state law. State law that merely supports or supplements federal law, but does not directly conflict with it, is generally held to be valid unless the federal government has decreed itself to be the exclusive regulator of the area of interest. In determining whether the preemption doctrine applies, the court will consider such factors as:

1. legislative history regarding the passage of the federal law
2. the completeness of the federal regulatory scheme in the area
3. the federal interest in dominating the regulation of the area
4. the similarity of federal and state law and the directness of the conflict
5. other relevant factors.

If the state and federal laws cannot be reconciled, the federal law predominates under the preemption doctrine.

Ray v. Atlantic Richfield Co. is a recent illustration of the Supreme Court's approach in applying the Supremacy Clause and the preemption doctrine in a business situation.

THE SUPREMACY CLAUSE

RAY, GOVERNOR OF WASHINGTON v. ATLANTIC RICHFIELD CO.

435 U.S. 151 (1978)
UNITED STATES SUPREME COURT

Mr. Justice White delivered the opinion of the Court.

Pursuant to the Ports and Waterways Safety Act of 1972 (PWSA), navigation in Puget Sound, a body of inland water lying along the northwest coast of the State of Washington, is controlled in major respects by federal law. The PWSA also subjects to federal rule the design and operating characteristics of oil tankers.

This case arose when Chapter 125, Laws of Washington, 1975, First Extraordinary Session, Wash.Rev.Code section 88.16.170 *et seq.* (Tanker Law), was adopted with the aim of regulating in particular respects the design, size, and movement of oil tankers in Puget Sound. In response to the constitutional challenge to the law brought by the appellees herein [ARCO and other oil companies], the District Court held that under the Supremacy Clause, Art. VI, cl. 2 of the Constitution, which declares that the federal law "shall be the supreme Law of the Land," the Tanker Law could not coexist with the PWSA and was totally invalid.

Located adjacent to Puget Sound are six oil refineries having a total combined processing capacity of 359,500 barrels of oil per day. In 1971, appellee Atlantic Richfield Company (ARCO) began operating an oil refinery at Cherry Point, situated in the northern part of the Sound. Since then, the crude oil processed at that refinery has been delivered principally by . . . tankers from the Persian Gulf; tankers will also be used to transport oil there from the terminus of the Trans-Alaska Pipeline at Valdez, Alaska.

On the day the Tanker Law became effective, ARCO brought suit in the United States District Court for the Western District of Washington, seeking a judgment declaring the statute unconstitutional and enjoining its enforcement. . . . The complaint alleged that the statute was pre-empted by federal law, in particular the PWSA, and that it was thus invalid under the Supremacy Clause. . . .

Under the relevant cases, one of the legitimate inquiries is whether Congress has either explicitly or implicitly declared that the States are prohibited from regulating the various aspects of oil-tanker operations and design with which the Tanker Law is concerned. As the Court noted in. . . . [*Rice v. Santa Fe Elevator Corp.*]:

> [The congressional] purpose may be evidenced in several ways. The scheme of federal regulation may be so pervasive as to make reasonable the inference that Congress left no room for the States to supplement it. Or the Act of Congress may touch a field in which the federal interest is so dominant that the

federal system will be assumed to preclude enforcement of state laws of the same subject. Likewise, the object sought to be obtained by the federal law and the character of obligations imposed by it may reveal the same purpose.

Even if Congress has not completely foreclosed state legislation in a particular area, a state statute is void to the extent that it actually conflicts with a valid federal statute. A conflict will be found "where compliance with both federal and state regulations is a physical impossibility . . .," or where the state "law stands as an obstacle to the accomplishment and execution of the full purposes and objectives of Congress."

This statutory pattern shows that Congress, insofar as design characteristics are concerned, has entrusted to the Secretary [of Transportation] the duty of determining which oil tankers are sufficiently safe to be allowed to proceed in the navigable waters of the United States. This indicates to us that Congress intended uniform national standards for design and construction of tankers that would foreclose the imposition of different or more stringent state requirements.

Refusing to accept the federal judgment, however, the State now seeks to exclude from Puget Sound vessels certified by the Secretary as having acceptable design characteristics, unless they satisfy the different and higher design requirements imposed by the state law. The Supremacy Clause dictates that the federal judgment that a vessel is safe to navigate United States waters prevail over the contrary state judgment.

That the Nation was to speak with one voice with respect to tanker design standards is supported by the legislative history of Title II, particularly as it reveals a decided congressional preference for arriving at international standards for building tank vessels. . . .

Congress expressed a preference for international action and expressly anticipated that foreign vessels would or could be considered sufficiently safe for certification by the Secretary if they satisfied the requirements arrived at by treaty or convention; it is therefore clear that Title II leaves no room for the States to impose different or stricter design requirements than those which Congress has en-

acted with the hope of having them internationally adopted or has accepted as the result of international accord. A state law in this area, such as the first part of § 88.16.190(2), would frustrate the congressional desire of achieving uniform, international standards. . . .

[W]e conclude that Washington is *precluded* from enforcing the size limitation contained in the Tanker Law.

CASE QUESTIONS

1. What does the Supremacy Clause of the U.S. Constitution provide?
2. What federal statute was involved in this case? Did the statute *explicitly* declare that federal law preempted navigation in Puget Sound?
3. What state statute was involved in this case? Did the state statute directly conflict with the federal statute? If so, how?
4. What factors did the U.S. Supreme Court consider in finding the state statute unconstitutional? Explain.

Policy Issue.
a. Should the U.S. Constitution be the "supreme law of the land"? If not, what law, if any, should be? Could be?
b. Did the Framers of the Constitution anticipate the present substantial involvement of the federal government in regulating the economy?

Economics Issue. Who would have been helped economically by the state law? Harmed economically by the state law?

Ethics Issue. Was it ethical for ARCO and the other oil companies to to sue to have the state law voided?

Social Responsibility.
a. Does the federal government owe a duty of social responsibility to the citizens of this country to enforce uniform national laws?
b. Do states owe a duty of social responsibility to enact laws to protect the welfare of its residents? Do these two duties often conflict?

THE COMMERCE CLAUSE

The power of the *federal* government to regulate business activity is found in Section 8 of Article I of the U.S. Constitution (the "Commerce Clause"). The Commerce Clause states:

The Congress shall have power . . . to regulate Commerce with foreign Nations, and among the several States, and with the Indian Tribes. . . .

Although not a further subject of this chapter, the regulation of commerce with Indian tribes is currently receiving increased attention owing to the location of substantial natural resources on Indian reservations, and as Native Americans assert rights claimed under old treaties. The Commerce Clause regulates two major types of modern commerce, *foreign* commerce and *interstate* commerce. The language of the Commerce Clause has been broadly and liberally construed by the courts in giving the federal government power to regulate business activity.

Federal Regulation of Foreign Commerce. The power to regulate foreign commerce has been held to be *exclusively* vested in the federal government. Direct or indirect action by state or local governments that interferes with the federal regulation of commerce with foreign nations is invalid as a violation of the Commerce Clause. For example, states may not prohibit goods from being imported into them, or otherwise interfere with federal regulation of commerce with foreign nations. However, state or local laws that do not discriminate against foreign commerce (e.g., inventory taxes) do not violate the Commerce Clause.

Federal Regulation of Interstate Commerce. In *Gibbons v. Ogden,* 22 U.S. (9 Wheat) (1824), the Supreme Court held that in order for Congress to have the power to regulate commerce "among the several states" *interstate commerce* must be involved. Purely *intra*state commerce generally is not covered by the Commerce Clause and is therefore not subject to regulation by the federal government. In this excerpt from *Gibbons,* Chief Justice Marshall noted the difference between interstate and intrastate commerce.

The subject to which the power is . . . applied, is to commerce "among the several states." The word "among" means intermingled with. . . .

Comprehensive as the word "among" is, it may be properly restricted to that commerce which concerns more states than one. . . . The genius and character of the whole government seem to be, that its action is to be applied to all the external concerns of the nation, and to those internal concerns which affect the states generally; but not to those which are completely within a particular state, which do not affect other states, and with which it is not necessary to interfere, for the purpose of executing some of the general powers of the government. The completely internal commerce of a state, then, may be considered as reserved for the state itself.

Prior to the adoption of the Interstate Commerce Act in 1887 (affecting commerce *between states*) and the Sherman Antitrust Act in 1890, Congress barely utilized its powers under the Commerce Clause.

The United States Supreme Court originally applied a narrow view of the power of Congress to regulate business under the Commerce Clause. In *Hammer v. Dagenhart,* 247 U.S. 251 (1918), (a child labor case) the Supreme Court held a federal statute prohibiting the interstate transportation of goods made by children in factories to be an unconstitutional use of the Commerce Clause. This restrictive view was continued in *Schechter Poultry Corp. v. United States,* 295 U.S. 495 (1935), the "Sick Chicken Case," where industry codes for poultry slaughterhouses adopted pursuant to the federal Industrial Recovery Act of 1933 were held to be unconstitutional.

In 1937, after a change of membership on the Supreme Court, the court upheld the constitutionality of the Depression-era National Labor Relations Act. In *United States v. Darby,* 312 U.S. 100 (1941), the Supreme Court specifically overruled *Hammer v. Dagenhart* and held that minimum-wage and maximum-hour provisions of the Federal Labor Standards Act were constitutional under the Commerce Clause. Federal government regulation of commerce "among the several states" has burgeoned since the *Darby* decision.

Defining "Interstate Commerce." In *Gibbons v. Ogden,* cited above, the Supreme Court held that in order for Congress to have the power to regulate commerce "among the several states," *interstate* commerce must be involved. Originally, the courts required the affected activity to be *"in"* interstate commerce. The Supreme Court has expanded the definition of "interstate commerce" to generally include *intra*state activities that have a substantial *"effect"* on interstate commerce as falling within the Commerce Clause. Thus, the activity itself does not have to be involved in interstate commerce. Any local activity that has an *effect* on interstate commerce may be regulated by the federal government under this interpretation of the Commerce Clause. In this excerpt from *Perez v. United States,* 402 U.S. 146 (1971) the U.S. Supreme Court explained the modern coverage of the Commerce Clause:

The Commerce Clause reaches in the main three categories of problems. First, the use of channels of interstate or foreign commerce which Congress deems are being misused, as for example, the shipment of stolen goods or of persons who have been kidnapped. Second, protection of the instrumentalities of interstate commerce, as for example, the destruction of an aircraft, or persons or things in commerce, as for example, thefts from interstate shipments. Third, those activities affecting commerce. It is with this last category that we are here concerned.

Parties who are accused of violating federal law often argue that they are not engaged in "interstate commerce" and therefore federal law does not apply to their activities. However, under the modern broad definition of interstate commerce, it is highly likely that most of the business activity in America is subject to federal regulation under the Commerce Clause.

In *McLain v. Real Estate Board of New Orleans,* the Supreme Court applied the modern definition of "interstate commerce" and held that activities of real estate brokers in Louisiana were subject to regulation under *federal* antitrust laws.

INTERSTATE COMMERCE

MCLAIN v. REAL ESTATE BOARD OF NEW ORLEANS

444 U.S. 232 (1980)
UNITED STATES SUPREME COURT

Mr. Chief Justice Burger delivered the opinion of the Court.

The complaint in this private antitrust action, filed in the Eastern District of Louisiana in 1975, alleges that real estate brokers in the Greater New Orleans area have engaged in a price-fixing conspiracy in violation of Section 1 of the Sherman Act. No trial has as yet been had on the merits of the claims since the complaint was dismissed for failure to establish the interstate commerce component of Sherman Act jurisdiction.

The complaint asserts a claim individually and on behalf of that class of persons who employed the services of a respondent real estate broker in the purchase or sale of residential property in the Louisiana parishes of Jefferson or Orleans (the Greater New Orleans area) during the four years preceding the filing of the complaint.

Respondents contended that the activities of respondent real estate brokers were purely local in nature; . . . and that the conclusory assertion in the complaint that respondents' activities "are within the flow of interstate commerce and have an effect upon that commerce" was insufficient by itself to establish federal jurisdiction.

The broad authority of Congress under the Commerce Clause has, of course, long been interpreted to extend beyond activities actually *in* interstate commerce to reach other activities that, while wholly local in nature, nevertheless substantially *affect* interstate commerce. . . . This Court has often noted the correspondingly broad reach of the Sherman Act.

To establish the jurisdictional element of a Sherman Act violation it would be sufficient for petitioners to demonstrate a substantial effect on interstate commerce generated by respondents' brokerage activity.

On the record thus far made, it cannot be said that there is an insufficient basis for petitioners to proceed at trial to establish Sherman Act jurisdiction. It is clear that an appreciable amount of commerce is involved in the financing of residential property in the Greater New Orleans area and in the insuring of titles to such property. The presidents of two of the many leading institutions in the area stated in their deposition testimony that those institutions committed hundreds of millions of dollars to residential financing during the period covered by the complaint. The testimony further demonstrates that this appreciable commercial activity has occurred in interstate commerce. Funds were raised from out-of-state investors and from interbank loans obtained from interstate financial institutions. Multistate lending institutions took mortgages insured under federal programs which entailed interstate transfers of premiums and settlements. Mortgage obligations physically and constructively were traded as financial instruments in the interstate secondary mortgage market. Before making a mortgage loan in the Greater New Orleans area, lending institutions usually, if not always, required title insurance, which was furnished by interstate corporations. Reading the pleadings, as supplemented, most favorably to petitioners, for present purposes we take these facts as established.

Here, what was submitted to the District Court shows a sufficient basis for satisfying the Act's jurisdictional requirements under the effect-on-commerce theory so as to entitle the petitioners to go forward. We therefore conclude that it was error to dismiss the complaint at this stage of the proceedings. The judgment of the Court of Appeals is *vacated,* and the case is *remanded* for further proceedings consistent with this opinion.

CASE QUESTIONS

1. What law were the defendants alleged to have violated? Was it a state or federal law? Why would have mattered in this case?
2. What does the "effects test" of interstate commerce provide?

3. Would the mere sale of of real property in Louisiana to out-of-state purchasers have been sufficient to constitute interstate commerce under the "effects test"?

Policy Issue. Should the federal government be permitted to regulate the majority of commerce in this country under the broad "effects test" interpretation of the Commerce Clause?

Economics Issue. Would the real estate brokers have benefited economically if they had per-

suaded the Supreme Court that only *intrastate* commerce was involved in this case?

Ethics Issue. Did the real estate brokers in Louisiana act ethically in this case?

Social Responsibility. Did the plaintiffs in this case owe a duty of social responsibility to society to bring this lawsuit? Do you think this duty was the underlying reason why the plaintiffs brought this lawsuit? What is a "class action" lawsuit?

UNDUE BURDEN ON INTERSTATE COMMERCE

In addition to authorizing the federal government to regulate interstate commerce through the adoption and enforcement of federal statutes such as the antitrust laws and the securities laws, the Commerce Clause also prohibits state and local governments from substantially interfering with interstate commerce. The purpose of protecting "interstate commerce" from certain state or local regulation is to prevent state and local governments from impeding national commerce in order to advance conflicting state or regional interests. In striking down an Oklahoma statutory scheme that completely prohibited the out-of-state shipment of natural gas found within the state, in *Oklahoma v. Kansas Natural Gas Co.*, 221 U.S. 229 (1911), the Supreme Court stated:

If the States have such power [to regulate interstate commerce] a singular situation might result. Pennsylvania might keep its coal, the Northwest its timber, the mining States their minerals. And why may not the products of the field be brought within the principle? . . . To what consequences does such power tend? If one State has it, all States have it; embargo may be retaliated by embargo, and commerce will be halted at state lines.

State "Police Power." State and local governments may regulate business under an inherent *police power* reserved to the states under the U.S. Constitution. The police power authorizes state and local governments to enact laws to protect the "public health and safety" and to promote the "public welfare." State or local regulation of business cannot impose an "undue burden" on interstate commerce.

If the federal government has elected to exclusively regulate an area, no state or local regulation under the police power is permitted. However, where the federal government has not elected to regulate an area, or where federal regulation of an area is not exclusive and comprehensive, state and local governments may regulate its interstate business activity under their police powers if they do not violate the Commerce Clause. Where a state or local regulation *unduly* burdens interstate commerce, the regulation is unconstitutional as a violation of the Commerce Clause.

In *Kassel v. Consolidated Freightways Corporation* the U.S. Supreme Court held that an Iowa state law limiting the length of commercial trucks permitted to pass within the boundaries of that state was a "substantial interference" on interstate commerce and therefore was unconstitutional under the Commerce Clause.

STATE ACTION IN VIOLATION OF THE COMMERCE CLAUSE

KASSEL v. CONSOLIDATED FREIGHTWAYS CORPORATION

450 U.S. 662 (1981)
UNITED STATES SUPREME COURT

Justice Powell announced the judgment of the Court and delivered an opinion in which **Justice White, Justice Blackmun,** and **Justice Stevens** joined.

Respondent Consolidated Freightways Corporation of Delaware (Consolidated) is one of the largest common carriers in the country. It offers service in 48 states under a certificate of public convenience and necessity issued by the Interstate Commerce Commission. Among other routes, Consolidated carries commodities through Iowa on Interstate 80, the principal east-west route linking New York, Chicago, and the west coast, and on Interstate 35, a major north-south route.

Consolidated mainly uses two kinds of trucks. One consists of a three-axle tractor pulling a 40-foot two-axle trailer. This unit, commonly called a single, or "semi," is 55 feet in length overall. Such trucks have long been used on the Nation's highways. Consolidated also uses a two-axle tractor pulling a single-axle trailer which, in turn, pulls a single-axle dolly and a second single-axle trailer. This combination, known as a double, or twin, is 65 feet long overall. Many trucking companies, including Consolidated, increasingly prefer to use doubles to ship certain kinds of commodities. Doubles have larger capacities, and the trailers can be detached and routed separately if necessary. Consolidated would like to use 65-foot doubles on many of its trips through Iowa.

The State of Iowa, however, by statute restricts the length of vehicles that may use its highways. Unlike all other States in the West and Midwest, Iowa generally prohibits the use of 65-foot doubles

within its borders. Instead, most truck combinations are restricted to 55 feet in length.

Because of Iowa's statutory scheme, Consolidated cannot use its 65-foot doubles to move commodities through the State. Instead, the company must do one of four things: (i) use 55-foot singles; (ii) use 60-foot doubles; (iii) detach the trailers of a a 65-foot double and shuttle each through the State separately; or (iv) divert 65-foot doubles around Iowa.

Dissatisfied with these options, Consolidated filed this suit in the District Court averring that Iowa's statutory scheme unconstitutionally burdens interstate commerce. Iowa defended the law as a reasonable safety measure enacted pursuant to its police power. The State asserted that 65-foot doubles are more dangerous than 55-foot singles and, in any event, that the law promotes safety and reduces road wear within the State by diverting much truck traffic to other States.

In a 14-day trial, both sides adduced evidence on safety, and on the burden on interstate commerce imposed by Iowa's law. On the question of safety, the District Court found that the "evidence clearly establishes that the twin is as safe as the semi."

In light of these findings, the District Court applied the standard we enunciated in *Raymond Motor Transportation, Inc. v. Rice,* and concluded that the state law impermissibly burdened interstate commerce:

[T]he balance here must be struck in favor of the federal interests. The *total effect* of the law as a safety measure in reducing accidents and casualties is so slight and problematical that it does not outweigh the national interest in keeping interstate commerce free from interferences that seriously impede it. (emphasis in original).

The Court of Appeals for the Eighth Circuit affirmed. . . . Iowa appealed, and we noted probable jurisdiction. . . .

The Commerce Clause does not, of course, invalidate all state restrictions on commerce. It has long been recognized that, "in the absence of conflicting legislation by Congress, there is a residuum of power in the state to make laws governing matters of local concern which nevertheless in some measure affect interstate commerce or even, to some extent, regulate it." *Southern Pacific Co. v. Arizona.* The extent of permissible state regulation is not always easy to measure. It may be said with confidence, however, that a State's power to regulate commerce is never greater than in matters traditionally of local concern. For example, regulations that touch upon safety—especially highway safety—are those that "the Court has been reluctant to invalidate." *Raymond.*

But the incantation of a purpose to promote the public health or safety does not insulate a state law from Commerce Clause attack. Regulations designed for that salutary purpose nevertheless may further the purpose so marginally, and interfere with commerce so substantially, as to be invalid under the Commerce Clause.

Moreover, Iowa's law is now out of step with the laws of all other Midwestern and Western States. Iowa thus substantially burdens the interstate flow of goods by truck. In the absence of congressional action to set uniform standards, some burdens associated with state safety regulations must be tolerated. But where, as here, the State's safety interest has been found to be illusory, and its regulations impair signficantly the federal interest in efficient and safe interstate transportation, the state law cannot be harmonized with the Commerce Clause.

Consolidated, meanwhile, demonstrated that Iowa's law substantially burdens interstate commerce. Trucking companies that wish to continue to use 65-foot doubles must route them around Iowa or detach the trailers of the doubles and ship them through separately. Alternatively, trucking companies must use the smaller 55-foot singles or 60-foot doubles permitted under Iowa law. Each of these options engenders inefficiency and added expense. The record shows that Iowa's law added about $12.6 million each year to the costs of trucking companies. Consolidated alone incurred about $2 million per year in increased costs.

In addition to increasing the costs of the trucking companies (and, indirectly, of the service to consumers), Iowa's law may aggravate, rather than ameliorate, the problem of highway accidents. Fifty-five foot singles carry less freight than 65-foot doubles. Either more small trucks must be used to carry the same quantity of goods through Iowa, or the same number of larger trucks must drive longer distances to bypass Iowa. In either case, as the District Court noted, the restriction requires more highway miles to be driven to transport the same quantity of goods. Other things being equal, accidents are proportional to distance traveled. Thus, if 65-foot doubles are as safe as 55-foot singles, Iowa's law tends to *increase* the number of accidents, and to shift the incidence of them from Iowa to other states.

It is thus far from clear that Iowa was motivated primarily by a judgment that 65-foot doubles are less safe than 55-foot singles. Rather, Iowa seems to have hoped to limit the use of its highways by deflecting some through traffic. In the District Court and Court of Appeals, the State explicitly attempted to justify the law by its claimed interest in keeping trucks out of Iowa. The Court of Appeals correctly concluded that a State cannot constitutionally promote its own parochial interests by requiring safe vehicles to detour around it.

Because Iowa has imposed this burden without any significant countervailing safety interest, its statute violates the Commerce Clause. The judgment of the Court of Appeals is *affirmed*.

CASE QUESTIONS

1. What did the Iowa statute provide? Did the Iowa statute affect the plaintiff's business activities?
2. Does the Commerce Clause of the Constitution invalidate *all* state restrictions on interstate commerce? Explain.
3. What does state "police power" provide? What

did Iowa assert it was protecting under its state police power?

4. What rationale (evidence) did the Supreme Court cite to justify its decision in this case? Was the rationale strong or weak?

Policy Issue. Should a state be able to place the welfare of its residents above the welfare of the nation in enacting protectionistic laws?

Economics Issue. Who economically benefited from the decision in this case?

Ethics Issue. Was it ethical for Iowa to divert traffic around the state?

Social Responsibility. Does a state owe a duty of social responsibility to other states not to hinder the flow of commerce to other states?

THE TAXING POWER

The power of taxation is *exclusively* vested in the legislative branch of our government. Article I, Section B of the U.S. Constitution gives Congress the power "to levy and collect Taxes, Duties, Imports, and Excise." The Sixteenth Amendment to the Constitution further provides, "The Congress shall have the power to levy and collect taxes on incomes, from whatever source derived, without apportionment among the several states, and without regard to any census or enumeration." State constitutions and local government charters also provide the power for these government bodies to levy and collect taxes to raise revenues for government services.

The theory underlying the power of taxation is that certain government functions are necessary (e.g., defense, public roads) and must be supported by the public. The taxing power gives government the authority, and force, to enact and collect taxes to support public functions. The U.S. Supreme Court has upheld the government's ability to levy and collect taxes. Few questions are currently raised regarding the constitutionality of federal taxes.

The Commerce Clause and Taxation. Interstate commerce is not exempt from state and local property taxes, income taxes, and sales or use taxes, and other taxes. However, certain constitutional limits are placed upon state and local governments' ability to tax interstate commerce.

In order for a state or local government to validly tax interstate commerce, there must be a showing that:

1. there is a sufficient *nexus* between the activity being taxed and the imposition of the tax
2. the tax does not discriminate against interstate commerce
3. the tax does not impose an "undue burden" on interstate commerce
4. the tax is fairly apportioned.

The Commerce Clause requires states to use reasonable apportionment formulate to prevent the multiple taxation of the same property. That is, each of several states cannot tax the entire net income of a corporation that does business in many states.

The interrelationship of two Constitutional provisions, the commerce clause and the taxing power, is demonstrated in *Commonwealth Edison Co. v. Mon-*

tana where the Supreme Court held that a state's tax on the severance of minerals located in the state was constitutional.

TAXATION AND THE COMMERCE CLAUSE

COMMONWEALTH EDISON CO. v. MONTANA

453 U.S. (1981)
UNITED STATES SUPREME COURT

Justice Marshall delivered the opinion of the Court.

Montana, like many other States, imposes a severance tax on mineral production in the State. In this appeal, we consider whether the tax Montana levies on each ton of coal mined in the State, Mont.Code § 15–35–101 *et seq.* (1979), violates the Commerce and Supremacy Clauses of the United States Constitution.

Buried beneath Montana are large deposits of low sulfur coal, most of it on federal land. Since 1921, Montana has imposed a severance tax on the output of Montana coal mines, including coal mined on federal land. . . . [I]n 1975, the Montana Legislature enacted the tax schedule at issue in this case. Mont.Code section 15–35–103 (1979). The tax is levied at varying rates depending on the value, energy content, and method of extraction of the coal, and may equal at a maximum 30% of the "contract sales price."

Appellants, 4 Montana coal producers and 11 of their out-of-state utility company customers, filed these suits in Montana state court in 1978. They sought refunds of over $5.4 million in severance taxes paid under protest, a declaration that the tax is invalid under the Supremacy and Commerce Clauses, and an injunction against further collection of the tax. Without receiving any evidence, the court upheld the tax and dismissed the complaints.

On appeal, the Montana Supreme Court affirmed the judgment of the trial court. The supreme court held that the tax is not subject to scrutiny under the Commerce Clause because it is imposed on the severance of coal, which the court characterized as an intrastate activity preceding entry of the coal into interstate commerce. In this regard, the Montana court relied on this Court's decisions in

Heisler v. Thomas Colliery Co., . . . As an alternative basis for its resolution of the Commerce Clause issue, the Montana court held, as a matter of law, that the tax survives scrutiny under the four-part test articulated by this Court in *Complete Auto Transit, Inc. v. Brady.*

We . . . hold that a state severance tax is not immunized from Commerce Clause scrutiny by a claim that the tax is imposed on goods prior to their entry into the stream of interstate commerce. . . . We agree with appellants that the Montana tax must be evaluated under *Complete Auto Transit's* four-part test. Under that test, a state tax does not offend the Commerce Clause if it "is applied to an activity with a substantial nexus with the taxing State, is fairly apportioned, does not discriminate against interstate commerce, and is fairly related to services provided by the State."

Appellants do not dispute that the Montana tax satisfies the first two prongs of *Complete Auto Transit* test. As the Montana Supreme Court noted, "there can be no argument here that a substantial, in fact, the only nexus of the severance of coal is established in Montana." Nor is there any question here regarding apportionment or potential multiple taxation, for as the state court observed, "the severance can occur in no other state" and "no other state can tax the severance." Appellants do contend, however, that the Montana tax is invalid under the third and fourth prongs of the *Complete Auto Transit* test.

[T]he gravamen of appellants' claim is that a state tax must be considered discriminatory for purposes of the Commerce Clause if the tax burden is borne primarily by out-of-state consumers.

[A]ppellants' assertion that Montana may not "exploit" its "monopoly" position by exporting tax burdens to other States cannot rest on a claim that there is need to protect the out-of-state consumers of Montana coal from discriminatory tax treatment. . . . [T]here is no real discrimination in this case; the tax burden is borne according to the amount of coal consumed and not according to any distinction between in-state and out-of-state consumers. Rather, appellants assume that the Commerce Clause gives residents of one State a right of access at "reasonable" prices to resources located in another State that is richly endowed with such resources, without regard to whether and on what terms residents of the resource-rich State have access to the resources. We are not convinced that the Commerce Clause, of its own force, gives the residents of one State the right to control in this fashion the terms of resource development and depletion in a sister State.

Furthermore, there can be no question that Montana may constitutionally raise general revenue by imposing a severance tax on coal mined in the State. The entire value of the coal, before transportation, originates in the State, and mining of the coal depletes the resource base and wealth of the State, thereby diminishing a future source of taxes and economic activity.

Appellants argue, however, that the fourth prong of the *Complete Auto Transit* test must be construed as requiring a factual inquiry into the relationship between the revenues generated by a tax and costs incurred on account of the taxed activity, in order to provide a mechanism for judicial disapproval under the Commerce Clause of state taxes that are excessive. This assertion reveals that appellants labor under a misconception about a court's role in cases such as this. The simple fact is that the appropriate level or rate of taxation is essentially a matter for legislative, and not judicial, resolution. . . . In essence, appellants ask this Court to prescribe a test for the validity of state taxes that would require state and federal courts, as a matter of federal constitutional law, to calculate acceptable rates or levels of taxation of activities that are conceded to be legitimate subjects of taxation. This we decline to do.

We are satisfied that the Montana tax, assessed under a formula that relates the tax liability to the value of appellant coal producers' activities within the State, comports with the requirements of the *Complete Auto Transit* test.

Justice Blackmun, with whom **Justice Powell** and **Justice Stevens** join, dissenting.

The State of Montana has approximately 25% of all known United States coal reserves, and more than 50% of the Nation's low-sulfur coal reserves. . . . Approximately 70–75% of Montana's coal lies under land owned by the Federal Government in the State. . . . The great bulk of the coal mined in Montana—indeed, allegedly as much as 90%— is exported to other States pursuant to long-term purchase contracts with out-of-state utilities. . . .

As the Montana Legislature foresaw, the imposition of this severance tax has generated enormous revenues for the State. Montana collected $33.6 million in severance taxes in fiscal year 1978 and appellants alleged that it would collect not less than $40 million in fiscal year 1979. It has been suggested that by the year 2010, Montana will have collected more than $20 billion through the implementation of this tax.

CASE QUESTIONS

1. What is a severance tax? Is it a federal or state tax? What was the severance tax applied to in this case?
2. Did the Supreme Court find that there was *intra*state or *inter*state commerce involved in this case?
3. What does the four-part *Complete Auto Transit* test provide? If the four parts are met, is the state tax on the interstate commerce valid?

Policy Issue. Should a resource-rich state be able to charge (tax) consumers in other states for use of its resources?

Economics Issue. Why did the appellants sue in this case? What states will be economically harmed by this decision? Benefited by the decision?

Ethics Issue. Is what Montana did in this case ethical?

Social Responsibility. Does a state owe a duty of social responsibility to share its natural resources with the other states of the Union?

Taxation as Regulation. Government taxation not only imposes a financial burden or business, but often works as a *regulation* of business. For example, depreciation allowances are provided as an incentive for businesses to invest in plant and equipment. A deduction for interest payments on borrowed funds is provided as an incentive for businesses to expand operations through debt. Gasoline taxes are used to equalize competition between different modes of transportation, as well as to reduce energy consumption.

The regulatory impact of taxation cannot be ignored or underestimated. Every new tax or change in existing tax law affects the ability of business to compete. The regulatory effect of a tax may be negative, or positive, on certain segments of business. Even taxes that are not levied on business itself may affect business; for example, increase in individual income taxes or social security taxes decreases consumer purchasing power.

A taxpayer generally does not have standing to sue the government regarding how tax revenues are spent by the government. This rule is based on the theory that all persons enjoy the protection and services provided by the government without any relation to the tax they pay. Further, the fact that a tax may destroy the value of the property or destroy a business or a person's employment does not provide a basis for an action against the government to determine whether the tax is constitutional. As the Supreme Court stated in *Carmichael v. Southern Coal & Coke Co.*, 301 U.S. 495 (1936):

[T]he only benefit to which it [the taxpayer] is constitutionally entitled . . . [is] that derived from his enjoyment of the privileges of living in an organized society, established and safeguarded by the devotion of taxes to public purposes.

THE IMPORT-EXPORT CLAUSE

Article I, Section 9 of the U.S. Constitution is known as the Import-Export Clause. The Import-Export Clause (1) prohibits states from taxing *imports and exports;* and (2) prohibits the federal government from directly taxing *exports.* The original purpose of the Import-Export Clause was to prevent seaboard states from taxing imports which were "in transit" to inland states. The Supreme Court explained the purpose of the Import-Export Clause in this excerpt from *Michelin Tire Corp. v. Wages*, 423, U.S. 276 (1976):

One of the major defects of the Articles of Confederation, and a compelling reason for the calling of the Constitutional Convention of 1787, was the fact that the Articles essentially left the individual States free to burden commerce both among themselves and with foreign countries very much as they pleased. Before 1787 it was commonplace for seaboard States to derive revenue to defray the costs of state and local governments by imposing taxes on imported goods destined for customers in inland States. At the same time, there was no secure source of revenue for the central government. . . .

The Framers of the Constitution thus sought to alleviate three main concerns by committing sole power to lay imposts and duties on imports in the Federal Government, with no concurrent state power: the Federal Government must speak with one voice when regulating commercial relations with foreign governments, and tariffs, which might affect foreign relations, could not be implemented by the States consistently with that exclusive power; import revenues were to be the major source of revenue of the Federal Government and should not be diverted to the States; and harmony among the States might be disturbed unless seaboard States, with their crucial ports of entry, were prohibited from levying taxes on citizens of other States by taxing goods merely flowing through their ports to the inland States not situated as favorably geographically.

The Import-Export Clause has been given a narrow interpretation by the courts. The majority of questions today concern deciding when property *ceases* to be an import or export, and therefore when it is no longer subject to the Import-Export Clause. Once property is no longer considered an import or export, and no longer subject to the Import-Export Clause, it may be taxed by state and local governments. For example, inventory and sales taxes on imports once they are no longer "in transit" do not violate the Import-Export Clause.

THE STATES' RELATIONS ARTICLE

Article IV of the Constitution is often referred to as the "states' relations article." In addition to providing for the addition of new states and making rules for governing territories and properties of the United States, Article IV also contains the Full Faith and Credit clause and the Privilege and Immunities Clause.

The Full Faith and Credit Clause.   Article IV of the U.S. Constitution contains the Full Faith and Credit Clause, which provides,

Full Faith and Credit shall be given in each State to the public Acts, Records, and judicial proceedings of every other State. . . .

The Full Faith and Credit Clause provides that *final* decisions or judgments rendered in individual disputes by the courts or agencies of one state shall be enforced against an original party to the lawsuit or proceeding who is located in another state. Thus, the Full Faith and Credit Clause serves to prevent persons from fleeing to one state to avoid liability on a judgment rendered in another state. The Full Faith and Credit Clause does not make judicial decisions of the courts of one state precedent in another state.

The States' Relations Article also provides for the *extradition* of persons accused of crimes from the state they are located in to the state that has accused them of the crime. Proper procedure and judicial proceedings must be followed before extradition will be ordered.

The Privileges and Immunities Clause.   Article IV, Section 2 of the Constitution contains the "privileges and immunities" clause. This clause states,

the citizens of each State shall be entitled to all Privileges and Immunities of Citizens in the several States.

The purpose of the Privileges and Immunities Clause is to promote the unity of the peoples of the United States by preventing discrimination by a state in favor of its own citizens over citizens of other states. The Fourteenth Amendment also contains a Privileges and Immunities Clause applicable to the states. Examples of state regulations that are *void* as violations of the Privileges and Immunities Clause are:

1. restrictions by a state regarding the ownership of property within the state by citizens of other states
2. state regulations on citizens of other states regarding ingress or egress to and from the state, or transportation within the state
3. laws passed by states to either promote or protect business located in the state from competition of businesses located in other states (e.g., tariffs).

Certain distinctions between the rights of citizens of a state and nonresidents are valid under the Privileges and Immunities Clause. For example, limited residency voting requirements, resident versus higher out-of-state student tuition at universities, and state licensing of professionals such as lawyers, doctors, etc., do not violate the Privilege and Immunities Clause of the Constitution.

The case of *Hicklin v. Orbeck* illustrates a state law regarding employment that was held to be unconstitutional under the Privileges and Immunities Clause.

PRIVILEGES AND IMMUNITIES CLAUSE

HICKLIN v. ORBECK, COMMISSIONER OF THE DEPARTMENT OF LABOR OF ALASKA

vol. *series of books where it can be found*
437 U.S. 518 (1978) } *where the entire opinion can*
UNITED STATES SUPREME COURT) *be found*

Mr. Justice Brennan delivered the opinion of the Court.

In 1972, professedly for the purpose of reducing unemployment in the State, the Alaska Legislature passed an Act entitled "Local Hire Under State Leases." Alaska Stat.Ann. Section 38.40.010 to 38.40.090 (1977). The key provision of "Alaska Hire," as the Act has come to be known, is the requirement that "all oil and gas leases, easements or right-of-way permits for oil or gas pipeline purposes, unitization agreements, or any renegotiation of any of the preceding to which the state is a party" contain a provision "requiring the employment of qualified Alaska residents" in preference to nonresidents. Alaska Stat. Ann. Section 38.40.030 (a)

(1977). This employment preference is administered by providing persons meeting the statutory requirements for Alaskan residency with certificates of residence—"resident cards"—that can be presented to an employer covered by the Act as proof of residency.

Although enacted in 1972, Alaska Hire was not seriously enforced until 1975, when construction on the Trans-Alaska Pipeline was reaching its peak.

At the time the suit was filed, the provision setting forth the qualifications for Alaskan residency for purposes of Alaska Hire . . . included a one-year durational residency requirement. By a vote of 3 to 2, . . ., the . . . [Alaska Supreme Court] held that the Act's general preference for Alaska residents was constitutionally permissible. Appellants appealed the State Supreme Court's judgments. . . .

Appellants' principal challenge to Alaska Hire is made under the Privileges and Immunities Clause of Art. IV, § 2: "The Citizens of each State shall be entitled to all Privileges and Immunities of Citizens in the several States.". . . The purpose of the Clause, as described in *Paul v. Virginia,* is

> to place the citizens of each State upon the same footing with citizens of other States, so far as the advantages resulting from citizenship in those States are concerned. It relieves them from the disabilities of alienage in other States; it inhibits discriminating legislation against them by other States; it gives them the right of free ingress into other States, and egress from them; it insures to them in other States the same freedom possessed by the citizens of those States in the acquisition and enjoyment of property and in the pursuit of happiness; and it secures to them in other States the equal protecton of their laws. It has been justly said that no provision in the Constitution has tended so strongly to constitute the citizens of the United States one people as this.

[In *Toomer v. Witsell*] the Court reasoned that although the Privileges and Immunities Clause "does not preclude disparity of treatment in the many situations where there are perfectly valid independent reasons for it, . . . [i]t does bar discrimination against citizens of other States where there is no substantial reason for the discrimination beyond the mere fact that they are citizens of other States." A "substantial reason for the discrimination" would not exist, the Court explained, "unless there is something to indicate that noncitizens constitute a peculiar source of the evil at which the [discriminatory] statute is aimed." Moreover, even where the presence or activity of nonresidents causes or exacerbates the problem the State seeks to remedy, there must be a "reasonable relationship between the danger represented by noncitizens, as a class, and the . . . discrimination practiced upon them."

[A]laska Hire's discrimination against nonresidents cannot withstand scrutiny under the Privileges and Immunities Clause. . . . [c]ertainly no showing was made on this record that nonresidents were "a peculiar source of the evil" Alaska Hire was enacted to remedy, namely, Alaska's "uniquely

high unemployment.". . . What evidence the record does contain indicates that the major cause of Alaska's high unemployment was not the influx of nonresidents seeking employment, but rather the fact that a substantial number of Alaska's jobless residents—especially the unemployed Eskimo and Indian residents—were unable to secure employment either because of their lack of education and job training or because of their geographical remoteness from job opportunities. . . .

Moreover, even if the State's showing is accepted as sufficient to indicate that nonresidents were "a peculiar source of evil," *Toomer . . .* [compels] the conclusion that Alaska Hire nevertheless fails to pass constitutional muster. For the discrimination the Act works against nonresidents does not bear a substantial relationship to the particular "evil" they are said to present. Alaska Hire simply grants all Alaskans, regardless of their employment status, education, or training, a flat employment preference for all jobs covered by the Act. A highly skilled and educated resident who has never been unemployed is entitled to precisely the same preferential treatment as the unskilled, habitually unemployed Arctic Eskimo enrolled in a job-training program. . . . Even if a statute granting an employment preference to unemployed residents or to residents enrolled in job-training programs might be permissible, Alaska Hire's across-the-board grant of a job preference to all Alaskan residents clearly is not.

[T]he breadth of the discrimination mandated by Alaska Hire goes far beyond the degree of resident bias Alaska's ownership of the oil and gas can justifiably support. The confluence of these realities points to but one conclusion: Alaska Hire cannot withstand constitutional scrutiny. As Mr. Justice Cardozo observed in *Baldwin v. G. A. F. Seelig, Inc.,* the Constitution "was framed upon the theory that the peoples of the several states must sink or swim together, and that in the long run prosperity and salvation are in union and not division."

Reversed. ← holding

CASE QUESTIONS

1. **a.** What does the Privileges and Immunities Clause of the U.S. Constitution provide?
   b. Why was this clause included in the Constitution?

2. Does the Privileges and Immunities Clause bar *all* discrimination by a state against *non*residents? Explain.
3. What "evil" did the Alaska Hire Statute purport to address? Was the evil a reality in this case?
4. Assuming that the evil did exist, did the scope of the Alaska Hire Statute bear a "substantial relationship" to the evil? Explain.

Policy Issue. If Alaska had won this case, do you think other states would have retaliated with similar legislation?

Economics Issue. What would have been the economic consequences had the court decided the case in favor of Alaska?

Ethics Issue. Was it ethical for Alaska to attempt to protect employment opportunities in the state from competition from outsiders?

Social Responsibility. Does a state owe a duty of social responsibility to make its job opportunities available to all job applicants, whether residents or nonresidents?

THE CONTRACT CLAUSE

Section 10 of Article I of the U.S. Constitution contains what is commonly referred to as the Contract Clause. This clause provides,

No State shall . . . pass any . . . Law impairing the Obligation of Contracts.

Thus, where a state enacts legislation that changes *vested* contract rights, the state statute is unconstitutional. States may enact legislation that affects the *prospective* rights of parties to contract as long as such laws meet the Constitutional test of due process. The Contract Clause has not been interpreted literally, thus allowing states to enact laws that affect vested contract rights in emergency situations. For example, a state may temporarily confiscate boats, automobiles, and other goods that are under private contract—that is, privately owned—for use in helping to save persons and property in natural disasters such as floods or earthquakes.

The Contract Clause does *not* apply to the *federal* government. Therefore, the federal government *may* enact laws that impair existing contracts. For example, a federally-ordered grain embargo or blockade of trade that affects existing contracts between foreign countries and American farmers is not covered by the Contract Clause.

THE DOCTRINE OF EXECUTIVE SOVEREIGNTY

Article II, Section 2 of the Constitution gives the President the power to make treaties with the advice and consent of the Senate. Treaties entered into by the President become part of the "supreme law of the land" under the Supremacy Clause, and have the same force and effect as the Constitution and Laws enacted by Congress.

In addition to the treaty power explicitly enumerated in the Constitution, the Supreme Court has held that the executive branch has discretion and freedom in *international* relations which it does not possess in domestic affairs. This investment of the executive branch with powers over external sovereignty is not enumerated in the Constitution, but was *implied* to flow directly from the Crown to the federal government when the Union was formed over 200 years ago. Under this implied power, the President may enter into *executive agreements* with foreign nations. In *U.S. v. Curtis-Wright Corp.*, 299 U.S. 304 (1936) the Supreme Court discussed the doctrine of external sovereignty.

[T]he primary purpose of the Constitution was to carve from the general mass of legislative powers *then possessed by the states* such portions as it was thought desirable to vest in the federal government, leaving those not included in the enumeration still in the states. . . . [S]ince the states severally never possessed international powers, such powers could not have been carved from the mass of state powers but obviously were transmitted to the United States from some other source. . . .

[T]he investment of the federal government with the powers of external sovereignty did not depend upon the affirmative grants of the Constitution. The powers to declare and wage war, to conclude peace, to make treaties, to maintain diplomatic relations with other sovereignties, if they had never been mentioned in the Constitution, would have vested in the federal government as necessary concomitants of nationality. . . . As a member of the family of nations, the right and power of the United States in that field are equal to the right and power of the other members of the international family. Otherwise, the United States is not completely sovereign.

When, therefore, the external sovereignty of Great Britain in respect of the colonies ceased, it immediately passed to the Union.

The Executive and Domestic Affairs.   The President may issue executive orders under power granted by Congress or enumerated in the Constitution that affect *domestic* actions of business. However, under the doctrine of separation of powers, the executive can only *administer* laws, not make law. Any exercise of executive power by the President is subject to review by the judicial branch of government for its compliance with the Constitution. The recent trend has been for the Supreme Court to limit the executive power of the President in the regulation of business.

Youngstown Co. v. Sawyer demonstrates the application of the doctrine of the "separation of powers" by the Supreme Court in holding unconstitutional a Presidential executive order that attempted to regulate business and union activity.

EXECUTIVE SOVEREIGNTY

YOUNGSTOWN CO. v. SAWYER, SECRETARY OF COMMERCE

343 U.S. 579 (1952)
UNITED STATES SUPREME COURT

Mr. Justice Black delivered the opinion of the Court.

In the latter part of 1951, a dispute arose between the steel companies and their employees over terms and conditions that should be included in new collective bargaining agreements. . . . On April

4, 1952, the Union gave notice of a nation-wide strike called to begin at 12:01 A.M. April 9. The indispensability of steel as a component of substantially all weapons and other war materials led the President to believe that the proposed work stoppage would immediately jeopardize our national defense and that governmental seizure of the steel mills was necessary in order to assure the continued availability of steel. Reciting these considerations for his action, the President, a few hours before the strike was to begin, issued Executive Order 10340, . . . The order directed the Secretary of Commerce to take possession of most of the steel mills and keep them running.

Obeying the Secretary's orders under protest, the companies brought proceedings against him in the District Court. Their complaints charged that the seizure was not authorized by an act of Congress or by any constitutional provisions. . . .

It is clear that if the President had authority to issue the order he did, it must be found in some provision of the Constitution. And it is not claimed that express constitutional language grants this power to the President. The contention is that presidential power should be implied from the aggregate of his powers under the Constitution. Particular reliance is placed on provisions in Article II which say that "The executive Power shall be vested in a President . . ."; that "he shall take Care that the Laws be faithfully executed"; and that he "shall be Commander in Chief of the Army and Navy of the United States."

The order cannot properly be sustained as an exercise of the President's military power as Commander in Chief of the Armed Forces. Even though "theater of war" be an expanding concept, we cannot with faithfulness to our constitutional system hold that the Commander in Chief of the Armed Forces has the ultimate power as such to take possession of private property in order to keep labor disputes from stopping production. This is a job for the Nation's lawmakers, not for its military authorities.

Nor can the seizure order be sustained because of the several constitutional provisions that grant executive power to the President. In the framework of our Constitution, the President's power to see that the laws are faithfully executed refutes the idea that he is to be a lawmaker. The Constitution limits his functions in the lawmaking process to the recommending of laws he thinks wise and the vetoing of laws he thinks bad.

The Founders of this Nation entrusted the lawmaking power to the Congress alone in both good and bad times. It would do no good to recall the historical events, the fears of power and the hopes for freedom that lay behind their choice. Such a review would but confirm our holding that this seizure order cannot stand.

The judgment of the District Court is *affirmed.*

would have had to ask congress to pass a law.

CASE QUESTIONS

1. **a.** What does the doctrine of "separation of powers" provide?
   b. What is the function of the executive branch of government?
   c. Of the U.S. Supreme Court?
2. What military action was the United States involved in at the time this case arose (1952)?
3. What provisions of the Constitution did President Truman assert gave him the power to take control of the steel mills? How did the Supreme Court decide these claims? Explain.

Policy Issue. Should the President be given the power to take over businesses in emergency situations? In time of war? Do you agree with the decision in this case?

Economics Issue. If the Executive Order had been upheld, what would have been the economic consequences to the steel companies? To the union?

Ethics Issue. Was it ethical for the union members to go on strike when they did? Do you think they were trying to take advantage of the situation?

Social Responsibility. Do employers and unions owe a duty of social responsibility not to stop the production of needed materials in time of war?

Trend of the Law

The constitutional doctrines discussed in this chapter will continue to be addressed by the courts in the future, particularly by the U.S. Supreme Court. While the 1950s, 1960s and 1970s saw the Supreme Court address important issues of individual rights (e.g., discrimination cases, search and seizure cases), the 1980s have witnessed an increasing workload for the Supreme Court of cases involving the application of Constitutional law issues to business. Particularly, the courts will be faced with an increasing number of situations that will require an interpretation of the Commerce Clause and other provisions of the Constitution in a rapidly changing business environment.

REVIEW QUESTIONS

1. What is the source of the powers of the federal government?
2. What powers are "reserved" to the states? Explain.
3. Should the U.S. Constitution have been drafted in more specific language? What would have been the benefits? The detriments?
4. Define the following constitutional law concepts and terms:
   a. Separation of powers
   b. The Supremacy Clause
   c. The preemption doctrine
   d. Interstate commerce
   e. Intrastate commerce
   f. Police power
   g. The Import-Export Clause
   h. The Full Faith and Credit Clause
   i. The Privileges and Immunities Clause
   j. The Contracts Clause
   k. The doctrine of executive sovereignty
5. Perez, who was involved in an automobile accident which resulted in a damage judgment against him, filed for bankruptcy to have the judgment discharged. An Arizona statute provided that when a judgment for personal injuries is unsatisfied the state may suspend that person's driver's license. Perez filed an action to prevent the suspension of his driver's license on the ground that the Arizona law was unconstitutional under the Supremacy Clause, since the state statute was in conflict with the federal law of bankruptcy. Will Perez prevail on his claim?
6. The city of Burbank, California, adopted an ordinance that prohibited jet aircraft from taking off or landing at the Hollywood-Burbank airport, located in Burbank, between the hours of 11:00 in the evening and 7:00 the next morning. Lockheed Air Terminal, Inc., the owner of the airport, brought an action against the city seeking an injunction against the enforce-

ment of the ordinance on the grounds that the city ordinance conflicted with federal law (the Federal Aviation Act and Federal Noise Control Act) in violation of the Commerce and Supremacy Clauses of the U.S. Constitution. The Noise Control Act did not expressly preempt the regulation of air traffic. Will the court issue the injunction? Y

7. The defendant, a member of organized crime, used extortion to collect illegal rates of interest from borrowers. He was convicted of "loan sharking" in violation of the Federal Consumer Credit Protection Act. The defendant challenged the constitutionality of the federal statute, arguing that Congress had no power to control and regulate a local activity such as loan sharking. Is the federal statute constitutional?

8. Pursuant to the Agricultural Adjustment Act enacted by Congress in 1938, the Secretary of Agriculture set acreage allotments for each state, which then apportioned the allotment to individual farms throughout the state. Filburn, a farmer, was allotted a 1941 quota of 11.1 acres for the planting of wheat. Filburn instead sowed and harvested 23 acres of wheat, all for home consumption. The Secretary of Agriculture assessed a $117.11 penalty against Filburn. Can Filburn's activity be regulated by federal law under the Commerce Clause? Y

9. Exxon Corporation produced and refined petroleum products nationwide and also operated retail service stations in many states, including Maryland. Maryland enacted a statute that made it unlawful for a producer or refiner of petroleum products to also operate retail service stations in the state, and provided for divestiture of such stations by such producers and refiners. Exxon sued the State of Maryland. Does the state statute violate the Commerce Clause of the U.S. Constitution?

10. The National Geographic Society (Society), a nonprofit scientific and educational corporation in Washington, D.C., maintained two offices in California from which employees solicited mail order business for items sold by the Society. The California offices only took orders; all mail orders were filled and billed from offices in Washington, D.C. and elsewhere. Employees in the California offices also solicited $1 million of advertising during the year. Pursuant to a statute, the State of California assessed a "use tax" liability against the Society of $85,596 for taxes that the Society should have collected under the law from its customers. The Society argued that there was not the proper "nexus" between the Society and the state as required by the Commerce Clause for the imposition of tax collection liability. Who wins?

11. Michelin Tire Corporation operated a warehouse located in the State of Georgia from which the corporation supplied franchise dealers in six southeastern states. All of the tires were brought into the United States from Nova Scotia, Canada and from France. The State of Georgia imposed a nondiscriminatory *ad valorem* property (inventory) tax on the tires in Michelin's Georgia warehouse. Is the tax assessment unconstitutional under the Import-Export Clause of the U.S. Constitution?

12. In 1963, Allied Structural Steel Corporation adopted a pension plan for its employees where the employer, and not the employees, made contributions to the plan. Under the contract, the employer reserved the right to terminate the pension plan at any time for any reason. Allied closed

a part of its business in Minnesota and terminated the pension plan of its employees. In 1974 the State of Minnesota enacted a statute that assessed a charge on any employer who terminated a pension plan. Allied was assessed a charge of $185,000 by the state. Is the assessment valid?

13. A joint resolution of Congress in 1934 authorized the President to embargo the sale of arms to the countries fighting in the Gran Chaco War (Bolivia and Paraguay). President Roosevelt immediately proclaimed an embargo in accordance with the resolution. Curtiss-Wright, an arms manufacturer, was indicted for conspiracy to sell arms to Bolivia. During the trial, the firm argued that the Joint Resolution attempted to unconstitutionally delegate legislative power to the President. Does Curtiss-Wright's argument have merit or was this embargo a valid exercise of executive power? Why does the Constitution vest power over external affairs in the executive branch of government?

14. Nebraska Mining Company owned a piece of property situated on the Missouri River. The Missouri River forms the state boundary between Nebraska and Missouri; Nebraska Mining's property was on the Nebraska side of the river. Missouri Mining Company owned land that was on the opposite bank. Over a period of years, the Missouri River's course changed dramatically, greatly expanding Nebraska Mining's property holdings and greatly reducing Missouri Mining's property. Neither firm had been concerned about these changes since no valuable minerals had been discovered on either side of the river. Early last year Nebraska Mining discovered a large vein of iron on property that had changed hands as a result of the shift in the river. Missouri Mining sued in Nebraska state court to obtain title to the disputed property. Ownership of the property depended upon whether the shift in the river had been caused by either accretion or avulsion. Both sides fully litigated the issue in the Nebraska courts, which found that the land was in Nebraska and therefore the Nebraska Mining Company was the proper owner. Missouri Mining then decided to sue in the Missouri state court system, claiming that the land was actually in Missouri, so the Nebraska court could not properly decide the case. The case was transferred to the federal court system to decide if Missouri Mining had a right to sue again over the same issue. Can Missouri Mining sue in Missouri? If so, how should the Missouri courts treat the findings of the prior litigation in Nebraska?

15. South Carolina enacted a law that attempted to regulate the commercial shrimp fishing industry in the three-mile maritime belt off the coast of the state. The law imposed license fees on shrimp boats: $25 on those owned by residents and $2,500 on those belonging to nonresidents. The law effectively precluded nonresident fishermen from following the shrimp in their migration pattern down the coast to Florida when the shrimp entered South Carolina waters. There was no evidence to indicate that the nonresidents used larger boats or different fishing methods. A group of nonresident fishermen challenged the law, claiming that the purpose and effect of the law was "not to conserve shrimp, but to exclude nonresidents and thereby create a commercial monopoly for South Carolina residents." Is the law constitutional?

7 THE BILL OF RIGHTS AND BUSINESS

INTRODUCTION

In 1791, four years after the Constitution was ratified, the Bill of Rights was adopted. The Bill of Rights contains ten amendments to the Constitution, which guarantees certain basic rights, liberties, and freedoms (e.g., freedom of speech, religion, press). The Bill of Rights is usually thought to apply to *personal* rights of individuals. However, on many occasions the activities of business and corporations either fall under the protection of, or violate the rights guaranteed by, the Bill of Rights.

Since the original ten amendments of the Bill of Rights were adopted over 200 years ago, 16 additional amendments have been added to the Constitution. These amendments include voting rights, prohibition against slavery, prohibition against discrimination, and authorization of an income tax. The Eighteenth Amendment, which prohibited the manufacture, sale, or transportation of intoxicating liquors, has been repealed.

This chapter covers the provisions of the Bill of Rights and other amendments to the Constitution, particularly the First and Fourteenth Amendments. The amendments to the Constitution are set forth in Appendix A to this book.

THE FIRST AMENDMENT

The First Amendment to the Constitution establishes the basic freedoms of (1) speech, (2) religion, (3) association, and (4) the press. The First Amendment provides:

Congress shall make no law respecting an establishment of religion, or prohibiting the free exercise thereof; or abridging the freedom of speech, or of the press; or the rights of the people peaceably to assemble, and to petition the Government for a redress of grievances.

The First Amendment broadly advances the view of the Framers as to the intrinsic value of speech for individual members of the nation. The First Amendment guarantees the free flow of ideas, which is necessary to support the democratic political process and the free enterprise economic system of this country. Any *government* action that hinders or impedes on these freedoms is unconstitutional.

Standards of Review. The Supreme Court has generally adopted three different standards for reviewing First Amendment cases, which are:

1. the strict scrutiny test
2. the intermediate scrutiny test
3. the balancing test.

Strict Scrutiny Test. The Supreme Court applies the strict scrutiny test to any government activity or regulation that somehow treats persons differently because of their *race* or *sex*. Hardly any government action that does so can withstand the strict scrutiny test. Government action that cannot be justified under the strict scrutiny test is unconstitutional. Most government actions examined under the strict scrutiny test are found to be unconstitutional.

Intermediate Scrutiny Test. The Supreme Court has adopted a middle approach, the *intermediate* scrutiny test, to examine government action which regulates persons based on *protected classes* other than race or sex, such as age classification or alienage. If it can be shown that a legitimate government interest is served by the classification, the state action or regulation will be held to be valid. For example, a mandatory retirement age of 50 for policemen and firemen has been held to be valid based on safety reasons. If a government regulation or action does not meet the intermediate scrutiny test, it is unconstitutional. Cases examined under the intermediate scrutiny test are approximately equally split between being found to be valid or unconstitutional.

Balancing Test. A *balancing* test is applied by the Supreme Court to all government regulation and action that does not involve a protected class such as race, sex, or age. Most government *economic* regulation of business falls in this category. Generally, most economic regulation by the government is held to be constitutional under this balancing test, often referred to as the *rational basis test.*

FREEDOM OF SPEECH

The most honored freedom guaranteed by the Bill of Rights is the First Amendment *freedom of speech.* Many of the other freedoms guaranteed by the Constitution and amendments thereto, such as freedom of the press, freedom of religion, etc., would be meaningless without the freedom of speech.

The First Amendment only protects *speech,* not *conduct.* For example, punching someone in the face to show that person that you dislike him is conduct, which is unprotected by the First Amendment. The First Amendment protects both oral and written speech.

Symbolic Speech.   The First Amendment also protects "symbolic" speech. For example, the Supreme Court held that a person who wore a jacket which read "Fuck the Draft" to protest the Vietnam War was symbolic speech, and was protected by the First Amendment. In *Schad v. Mount Ephram,* 452 U.S. 61 (1981), the Supreme Court held that live nude dancing was a form of entertainment, and was protected *speech* under the First Amendment.

In *First National Bank of Boston v. Bellotti,* the U.S. Supreme Court held that the First Amendment guarantee of freedom of speech applies not only to individuals, but also to corporations.

THE CORPORATION AND FREEDOM OF SPEECH

FIRST NATIONAL BANK OF BOSTON v. BELLOTTI, ATTORNEY GENERAL OF MASSACHUSETTS

435 U.S. 765 (1978)
UNITED STATES SUPREME COURT

Mr. Justice Powell delivered the opinion of the Court.

The statute at issue, Massachusetts General Laws ch. 55, Section 8, prohibits appellants, two national banking associations and three business corporations, from making contributions or expenditures "for the purpose of . . . influencing or affecting the vote on any question submitted to the voters, other than one materially affecting any of the property, business or assets of the corporation." The statute further specifies that "[n]o question submitted to the voters solely concerning the taxation of the income, property or transactions of individuals shall be deemed materially to affect the property, business or assets of the corporation." A corporation that violates Section 8 may receive a maximum fine of $50,000; a corporate officer, director, or agent who violates the section may receive a maximum fine of $10,000 or imprisonment for up to one year, or both.

Appellants wanted to spend money to publicize their views on a proposed constitutional amendment that was to be submitted to the voters as a ballot question at a general election on November 2, 1976. The amendment would have permitted the legislature to impose a graduated tax on the income of individuals. After appellee, the Attorney General of Massachusetts, informed appellants that he intended to enforce Section 8 against them, they brought this action seeking to have the statute declared unconstitutional. . . .

The court below . . . held that corporate speech is protected by the First Amendment only when it pertains directly to the corporation's business interests. . . . The question in this case, simply put, is whether the corporate identity of the speaker deprives this proposed speech of what otherwise would be its clear entitlement to protection. We turn now to that question.

In the realm of protected speech, the legislature is constitutionally disqualified from dictating the subjects about which persons may speak and the speakers who may address a public issue. If a legislature may direct business corporations to "stick to business," it also may limit other corporations—religious, charitable, or civic—to their respective "business" when addressing the public. Such power in government to channel the expression of views is unacceptable under the First Amendment.

According to appellee, corporations are wealthy and powerful and their views may drown out other points of view. . . . But there has been no showing that the relative voice of corporations has been overwhelming or even significant in influencing referenda in Massachusetts, or that there has been any threat to the confidence of the citizenry in government.

The under-inclusiveness of the statute is self-evident. Corporate expenditures with respect to a referendum are prohibited, while corporate activity with respect to the passage or defeat of legislation is permitted, . . . The fact that a particular kind of ballot question has been singled out for special treatment undermines the likelihood of a genuine state interest in protecting shareholders. It suggests instead that the legislature may have been concerned with silencing corporations on a particular subject.

Nor is the fact that Section 8 is limited to banks and business corporations without relevance. Excluded from its provisions and criminal sanctions are [other] entities or organized groups. . . . [T]he exclusion of Massachusetts business trusts, real estate investment trusts, labor unions, and other associations undermines the plausibility of the State's purported concern for the persons who happen to be shareholders in the banks and corporations covered by Section 8.

Because that portion of Section 8 challenged by appellants prohibits protected speech in a manner unjustified by a compelling state interest, it must be invalidated. The judgment of the Supreme Judicial Court is *reversed.*

CASE QUESTIONS

1. What did the Massachusetts statute in question provide? What were the penalties for violating the statute?
2. Did the statute apply to *all* corporate speech? To *all* corporations?
3. What did the "stick to business" theory of the lower court provide?

Policy Issue. Do large corporations have an advantage over individuals in public debates that will affect business (e.g., the passage of bottle laws, nonsmoking laws)? If so, should this advantage be curtailed? If so, how?

Economics Issue. How would the passage of the graduated income tax on individuals have affected the State of Massachusetts? The First National Bank of Boston?

Ethics Issue. Was it ethical for the State of Massachusetts to try to silence opposition to the proposed constitutional amendment that would have permitted the legislature to impose a graduated income tax on individuals?

Social Responsibility. Do corporations owe a duty of social responsibility to speak out on political issues? Or should they remain neutral?

Unprotected Speech. It is important to note that the freedom of speech guarantee of the First Amendment is *not* absolute. There is certain speech the *content* of which is not protected. Exceptions to the speech protection of the First Amendment are:

1. dangerous speech
2. "fighting words,"
3. subversive incitement speech
4. obscene words.

Dangerous Words Exception. Speech that unnecessarily creates dangerous conditions is not protected by the First Amendment. For example, yelling "Fire!" in a crowded theater, when there is no fire, is not protected speech.

"Fighting Words" Exception. Speech that is likely to provoke a hostile or violent audience response is not protected by the First Amendment. For example, in *Chaplinshy v. New Hampshire*, 315 U. S. 568 (1942), the Supreme Court unanimously upheld a conviction of a defendant who had gotten into a fight after calling a marshal a "damned Fascist." The test is whether the words are "likely to provoke an average person to retaliation." In *Terminiello v. Chicago*, 337 U.S. 1 (1949), the Supreme Court reversed the breach-of-the-peace conviction of a defendant who denounced various racial and political groups as "slimy scum" and used other derogatory language. The same speech may be protected speech to one audience and unprotected "fighting words" to another audience.

Subversive Incitement Exception. The First Amendment does not protect speech that incites subversive activities. For example, a speech that incites the violent or revolutionary overthrow of the government of the United States is not protected. In *Noto v. United States*, 367 U.S. 290 (1961), the Supreme Court announced the following test: "The mere abstract teaching [of] the moral propriety or even moral necessity for a resort to force and violence, is not the same as preparing a group for violent action and steeling it to such action." In *Brandenburg v. Ohio*, 395 U.S. 444 (1969), the Supreme Court held that a meeting of the Ku Klux Klan was protected advocacy, and not incitement of lawless action.

Obscenity Exception. The U.S. Supreme Court has held that obscenity is not protected by the First Amendment. One of the most difficult tasks for the courts is to define speech that is "obscene." Prior to 1973, when it decided *Miller v. California* (below), the Supreme Court had trouble agreeing on a definition of obscenity. As one Supreme Court Justice stated, "I know it when I see it." Currently, the general standards of *Miller* must be applied on a case-by-case basis.

FREEDOM OF SPEECH
FREEDOM OF THE PRESS

MILLER v. CALIFORNIA

413 U.S. 15 (1973)
UNITED STATES SUPREME COURT

Mr. Chief Justice Burger delivered the opinion of the Court.

Appellant conducted a mass mailing campaign to advertise the sale of illustrated books, euphemistically called "adult" material. After a jury trial, he was convicted of violating California Penal Code Section 311.2(a), a misdemeanor, by knowingly distributing obscene matter, and the Appellate Department, Superior Court of California, County of Orange, summarily affirmed the judgment without opinion. Appellant's conviction was specifically based on his conduct in causing five unsolicited advertising brochures to be sent through the mail in an envelope addressed to a restaurant in Newport Beach, California. The envelope was opened by the manager of the restaurant and his mother. They had not requested the brochures; they complained to the police.

The brochures advertise four books entitled "Intercourse," "Man-Woman," "Sex Orgies Illustrated," and "An Illustrated History of Pornography," and a film entitled "Marital Intercourse." While the brochures contain some descriptive printed material, primarily they consist of pictures and drawings very explicitly depicting men and women in groups of two or more engaging in a variety of sexual activities, with genitals often prominently displayed.

It is in this context that we are called on to define the standards which must be used to identify obscene material that a State may regulate without infringing on the First Amendment as applicable to the States through the Fourteenth Amendment.

This much has been categorically settled by the Court, that obscene material is unprotected by the First Amendment. *Roth v. United States*: "The First and Fourteenth Amendments have never been treated as absolutes." We acknowledge, however, the inherent dangers of undertaking to regulate any form of expression. State statutes designed to regulate obscene materials must be carefully limited.

The basic guidelines for the trier of fact must be: (a) whether "the average person, applying contemporary community standards" would find that the work, taken as a whole, appeals to the prurient interest; (b) whether the work depicts or describes, in a patently offensive way, sexual conduct specifically defined by the applicable state law; and (c) whether the work, taken as a whole, lacks serious literary, artistic, political, or scientific value. We do not adopt as a constitutional standard the *"utterly without redeeming social value"* test of *Memoirs v. Massachusetts* (1966); that concept has never commanded the adherence of more than three Justices at one time.

We emphasize that it is not our function to propose regulatory schemes for the States. That must await their concrete legislative efforts. It is possible, however, to give a few plain examples of what a state statute could define for regulation under part (b) of the standard announced in this opinion, *supra:*

(a) Patently offensive representations or descriptions of ultimate sexual acts, normal or perverted, actual or simulated.

(b) Patently offensive representations or descriptions of masturbation, excretory functions, and lewd exhibition of the genitals.

Sex and nudity may not be exploited without limit by films or pictures exhibited or sold in places of public accommodation any more than live sex and nudity can be exhibited or sold without limit in such public places. At a minimum, prurient, patently offensive depiction or description of sexual conduct must have serious literary, artistic, political, or scientific value to merit First Amendment protection.

This may not be an easy road, free from difficulty. But no amount of "fatigue" should lead us to adopt a convenient "institutional" rationale—an absolutist, "anything goes" view of the First Amendment—because it will lighten our burdens.

Under a National Constitution, fundamental First Amendment limitations on the powers of the States do not vary from community to community, but this does not mean that there are, or should or can be, fixed, uniform national standards of precisely what appeals to the "prurient interest" or is "patently offensive." . . . To require a State to structure obscenity proceedings around evidence of a *national* "community standard" would be an exercise in futility.

It is neither realistic nor constitutionally sound to read the First Amendment as requiring that the people of Maine or Mississippi accept public depiction of conduct found tolerable in Las Vegas, or New York City. . . . We hold that the requirement that the jury evaluate the materials with reference to "contemporary standards of the State of California" serves this protective purpose and is constitutionally adequate.

In sum, we (a) reaffirm the *Roth* holding that obscene material is not protected by the First Amendment; (b) hold that such material can be regulated by the States, subject to the specific safeguards enunciated above, without a showing that the material is *"utterly* without redeeming social value"; and (c) hold that obscenity is to be determined by applying "contemporary community standards," not "national standards." The judgment of the Appellate Department of the Superior Court, Orange County, California, is *vacated* and the case *remanded* to that court for further proceedings not inconsistent with the First Amendment standards established by this opinion.

Mr. Justice Douglas, dissenting.

Today we leave open the way for California to send a man to prison for distributing brochures that advertise books and a movie under freshly written standards defining obscenity which until today's decision were never the part of any law.

The Court has worked hard to define obscenity and concededly has failed. . . . My Brother **Stewart** in *Jacobellis* [*v. Ohio*] commented that the difficulty of the Court in giving content to obscenity was that it was "faced with the task of trying to define what may be indefinable."

The difficulty is that we do not deal with constitutional terms, since "obscenity" is not mentioned in the Constitution or Bill of Rights. So there are no constitutional guidelines for deciding what is and what is not "obscene." The Court is at large be-

cause we deal with tastes and standards of literature. What shocks me may be sustenance for my neighbor. What causes one person to boil up in rage over one pamphlet or movie may reflect only his neurosis, not shared by others. We deal here with a regime of censorship which, if adopted, should be done by constitutional amendment after full debate by the people.

The idea that the First Amendment permits government to ban publications that are "offensive" to some people puts an ominous gloss on freedom of the press. That test would make it possible to ban any paper or any journal or magazine in some benighted place. . . . As is intimated by the Court's opinion, the materials before us may be garbage. But so is much of what is said in political campaigns, in the daily press, on TV, or over the radio.

CASE QUESTIONS

1. What materials were sent through the mails by the defendant? Did the persons who received the materials request them? What did the materials depict?
2. Is *all* speech protected by the First Amendment? Is *obscenity* protected?
3. Describe the three-part *Miller* test. Is this test easy to apply? Explain.
4. Why did the Supreme Court announce guidelines to be followed by states in drafting legislation to regulate obscene materials?
5. Did the Supreme Court announce a *national* standard for determining if materials are "obscene"? If not, what geographical standard applies? Explain.
6. Did the court decide this case? If not, how would you decide this case based on the new obscenity standard adopted by the Supreme Court?
7. What did Justice Douglas argue in his dissent? Do you agree?

Policy Issue. Should there be an obscenity exception to the First Amendment's protection of freedom of speech? Why or why not?

Economics Issue. Does the obscenity exception to freedom of speech protection have any economic consequences? If so, to who? Explain.

Ethics Issue. Under the *Miller* test, might an item (e.g., a book) be protected free speech in one part of the country but not in another? Is it ethical for the majority of a community to impose their definition of obscenity on the other members of the community?

Social Responsibility. Do distributors of highly sensitive sexual materials owe a duty of social responsibility not to send such items through the mails to nonrequesting parties?

COMMERCIAL FREE SPEECH

Historically, it has been largely undecided whether pure "commercial" speech is accorded First Amendment protection. In the landmark case, *Virginia State Board of Pharmacy v. Virginia Citizens Consumer Council, Inc.*, 425 U.S. 748 (1976), the U.S. Supreme Court held that *commercial* speech is protected under the First Amendment. In that case, where the Supreme Court held as unconstitutional a state statute providing that a pharmacist was guilty of unprofessional conduct if he advertised the price, discount, or credit terms of prescription drugs, the Court supported its decision with the following reasoning:

Freedom of speech presupposes a willing speaker. But where a speaker exists, as is the case here, the protection afforded is to the communication, to its source and to its recipients both. . . . [T]his Court has referred to a First Amendment right to "receive information and ideas," and that freedom of speech " 'necessarily protects the right to receive' " . . . If there is a right to advertise, there is a reciprocal right to receive the advertising, and it may be asserted by these appellees.

The appellants contend that the advertisement of prescription drug prices is outside the protection of the First Amendment because it is "commercial speech." There can be no question that in past decisions the Court has given some indication that commercial speech is unprotected.

Here . . . the question whether there is a First Amendment exception for "commercial speech" is squarely before us. Our pharmacist does not wish to editorialize on any subject, cultural, philosophical, or political. He does not wish to report any particularly newsworthy fact, or to make generalized observations even about commercial matters. The "idea" he wishes to communicate is simply this: "I will sell you the X prescription drug at the Y price." Our question, then, is whether this communication is wholly outside the protection of the First Amendment.

We begin with several propositions that already are settled or beyond serious dispute. It is clear, for example, that speech does not lose its First Amendment protection because money is spent to project it, as in a paid advertisement of one form or another, *Buckley v. Valeo.* Speech likewise is protected even though it is carried in a form that is "sold" for profit, *Smith v. California.*

Focusing first on the individual parties to the transaction that is proposed in the commercial advertisement, we may assume that the advertiser's interest is a purely economic one. That hardly disqualifies him for protection under the First Amendment. . . . As to the particular consumer's interest in the free flow of commercial information, that interest may be as keen, if not keener by far, than his interest in the day's most urgent political debate. Appellees' case in this respect is a convincing one. Those whom the suppression of prescription drug price information hits the hardest are the poor, the sick, and particularly the aged. A disproportionate amount of their income tends to be spent on prescription drugs; yet they are the least able to learn, by shopping from pharmacist to pharmacist, where their scarce dollars are best spent. When drug prices vary as strikingly as they do, information as to who is charging what becomes more than a convenience. It could mean the alleviation of physical pain or the enjoyment of basic necessities.

Generalizing, society also may have a strong interest in the free flow of commercial information. Even an individual advertisement, though entirely "commercial," may be of general public interest. . . . Our pharmacist, for example, could cast himself as a commentator on store-to-store disparities in drug prices, giving his own and those of a competitor as proof.

Advertising, however tasteless and excessive it sometimes may seem, is nonetheless dissemination of information as to who is producing and selling what product for what reason, and at what price. So long as we preserve a predominantly free enterprise economy, the allocation of our resources in large measure will be made through numerous private economic decisions. It is a matter of public interest that those decisions, in the aggregate, be intelligent and well informed. To this end, the free flow of commercial information is indispensable.

Reasonable Time, Place, and Manner Restrictions.   Although certain speech may be accorded First Amendment protection and therefore cannot be totally suppressed, the U.S. Supreme Court has held that even some forms of protected speech may be subject to reasonable "time, place, and manner" restrictions. For example, in *Young v. American Mini Theatres*, 427 U.S. 50 (1976), the Supreme Court upheld a zoning ordinance of the City of Detroit that prohibited "adult" theaters and bookstores within 500 feet of residential areas. The court reasoned that this was a reasonable time, place, and manner restriction on otherwise protected speech.

Time, place, and manner restrictions must protect a legitimate state interest, and be no broader than necessary to protect such interest. For example, if the zoning ordinance in *Young v. American Mini Theatres* had prohibited adult theaters and bookstores in the entire city of Detroit, the ordinance would have been struck down as being overly broad to protect an otherwise legitimate state interest. Commercial speech is subject to reasonable time, place, and manner restrictions. In *Virginia State Board of Pharmacy*, discussed previously, the Supreme Court stated:

In concluding that commercial speech, like other varieties, is protected, we of course do not hold that it can never be regulated in any way. Some forms of commercial speech regulation are surely permissible. . . . There is no claim, for example, that the prohibition on prescription drug price advertising is a mere time, place, and manner restriction. . . .

In *Metromedia, Inc. v. City of San Diego* the U.S. Supreme Court held that a zoning ordinance which limited the use of billboards in a city was a proper "time, place, and manner" restriction on commercial speech, but *voided* the ordinance because it also unconstitutionally limited the use of billboards for *non*commercial speech.

COMMERCIAL FREE SPEECH

METROMEDIA, INC. v. CITY OF SAN DIEGO

453 U.S. 490 (1981)
UNITED STATES SUPREME COURT

Justice White announced the judgment of the Court and delivered an opinion in which **Justice Stewart, Justice Marshall** and **Justice Powell** join.

Stating that its purpose was "to eliminate hazards to pedestrians and motorists brought about by distracting sign displays" and "to preserve and improve the appearance of the City," San Diego enacted an ordinance to prohibit "outdoor advertising display signs."

The ordinance provides two kinds of exceptions to the general prohibition: on-site signs and signs falling within 12 specified categories. . . . The specific categories exempted from the prohibition include: government signs; signs located at public bus stops; signs manufactured, transported or stored within the city, if not used for advertising purposes; commemorative historical plaques; religious symbols; signs within shopping malls; for-sale and for-lease signs; signs on public and commercial vehicles; signs depicting time, temperature, and news; approved temporary, off-premises, subdivision directional signs; and "temporary political campaign signs." Under this scheme, on-site commercial advertising is permitted, but other commercial advertising and noncommercial communications using fixed-structure signs are everywhere forbidden unless permitted by one of the specified exceptions.

Appellants are companies that were engaged in the outdoor advertising business in San Diego at the time the ordinance was passed. Each owns a substantial number of outdoor advertising displays (approximately 500 to 800) within the city. These signs are all located in areas zoned for commercial and industrial purposes, most of them on property leased by the owners to appellants for the purpose of maintaining billboards.

Billboards, . . . like other media of communication, combine communicative and noncommunicative aspects. As with other media, the government has legitimate interests in controlling the noncommunicative aspects of the medium, . . . but the First and Fourteenth Amendments foreclose a similar interest in controlling the communicative aspects.

The extension of First Amendment protections to purely commercial speech is a relatively recent development in First Amendment jurisprudence.

[I]n *Central Hudson v. Public Service Comm'n,* 447 U.S. 557 (1980), we held that: "The Constitution . . . accords a lesser protection to commercial speech than to other constitutionally guaranteed expression. The protection available for a particular commercial expression turns on the nature both of the expression and of the governmental interests served by its regulation." We then adopted a four-part test for determining the validity of government restrictions on commercial speech as distinguished from more fully protected speech. (1) The First Amendment protects commercial speech only if that speech concerns lawful activity and is not misleading. A restriction on otherwise protected commercial speech is valid only if it (2) seeks to implement a substantial governmental interest, (3) directly advances that interest, and (4) reaches no farther than necessary to accomplish the given objective.

There can be little controversy over the application of the first, second, and fourth criteria. There is no suggestion that the commercial advertising at issue here involves unlawful activity or is misleading. Nor can there be substantial doubt that the twin goals that the ordinance seeks to further—traffic safety and the appearance of the city—are substantial governmental goals. . . . Similarly, we reject appellants' claim that the ordinance is broader than necessary and, therefore, fails the fourth part of the *Central Hudson* test. If the city has a sufficient basis for believing that billboards are traffic hazards and are unattractive, then obviously the most direct and perhaps the only effective approach to solving the problems they create is to prohibit them. The city has gone no farther than necessary in seeking to meet its ends. Indeed, it has stopped short of fully accomplishing its ends: It has not prohibited all billboards, but allows on-site advertising and some other specifically exempted signs.

The more serious question, then, concerns the third of the *Central Hudson* criteria: Does the ordinance "directly advance" governmental interests in traffic safety and in the appearance of the city? It is asserted that the record is inadequate to show any connection between billboards and traffic safety. The California Supreme Court noted the meager record on this point but held "as a matter of law that an ordinance which eliminates billboards designed to be viewed from the streets and highways reasonably relates to traffic safety." Noting that "billboards are intended to, and undoubtedly do, divert a driver's attention from the roadway," and that whether the "distracting effect contributes to traffic accidents invokes an issue of continuing controversy," the California Supreme Court agreed with many other courts that a legislative judgment that billboards are traffic hazards is not manifestly unreasonable and should not be set aside. We likewise hesitate to disagree with the accumulated, common-sense judgments of local lawmakers and of the many reviewing courts that billboards are real and substantial hazards to traffic safety. There is nothing here to suggest that these judgments are unreasonable.

We reach a similar result with respect to the second asserted justification for the ordinance—advancement of the city's esthetic interests. It is not speculative to recognize that billboards by their very nature, wherever located and however constructed, can be perceived an "esthetic harm."

In sum, insofar as it regulates commercial speech the San Diego ordinance meets the constitutional requirements of *Central Hudson*. . . . It does not follow, however, that San Diego's general ban on signs carrying noncommercial advertising is also valid under the First and Fourteenth Amendments. . . . Because the San Diego ordinance reaches too far into the realm of protected speech, we conclude that it is unconstitutional on its face. The judgment of the California Supreme Court is *reversed* and the case *remanded* to that court.

CASE QUESTIONS

1. What did the San Diego ordinance provide? Were there any exemptions to the ordinance?
2. Do billboards have *communicative* aspects? *Noncommunicative* aspects? Which does the First Amendment protect?
3. Is commercial speech protected by the First Amendment? Is this protection *absolute?* Or may commercial speech be regulated?
4. What does the four-part *Central Hudson* test for regulating commercial speech provide? Explain.
5. Was the four-part *Central Hudson* test met by the "time, place, and manner" restriction in this case?
6. Do you agree with the court's finding that there is a connection between billboards and traffic safety? Between billboards and esthetic harm?
7. Why was the San Diego ordinance found unconstitutional in this case?

Policy Issue. Should commercial speech such as advertisements be protected under the First Amendment? Do you think this was the intent of the Framers when they drafted the Bill of Rights?

Economics Issue. What were the economic effects of the ordinance? After this decision, do you think San Diego would again attempt to regulate billboards?

Ethics Issue. Was it ethical for San Diego to argue traffic safety and esthetic harm to support the ordinance when some forms of billboards and signs were exempted from the coverage of the ordinance?

Social Responsibility. Does a city owe a duty of social responsibility to protect its citizens from "esthetic harm"?

FREEDOM OF THE PRESS

The First Amendment provides a separate clause which protects the freedom "of the press." It is the only form of business given explicit constitutional protection. The freedom of the press is closely interwoven with the freedom of speech. In most cases involving the freedom of the press, the freedom of speech provision of the First Amendment is also usually raised as an issue. The freedom of the press, like the freedom of speech, is not an *absolute* right, but may, in proper circumstances, be regulated by the government. As Chief Justice Burger noted in his concurring opinion in the *Bellotti* case, previously presented,

> The court has not yet squarely resolved whether the Press Clause confers upon the "institutional press" any freedom from government restraints not enjoyed by all others.

The Press Clause of the First Amendment has been raised in a variety of situations, including cases involving a newsman's desire to keep informants and information confidential, the government's attempts to restrain the publication of certain information by the press, unequal taxation of the press, and search and seizure of the media.

Freedom of Speech and the Press.   Generally, the government may not enact regulation which impairs the freedom of the press to publish what it feels it should in order to keep the public informed. In *Near v. Minnesota*, 283 U.S. 697 (1931), the U.S. Supreme Court reversed a lower court decision that had upheld a state's right, under a statute, to abate the publication of any "malicious, scandalous or defamatory newspaper." In that case Justice Hughes' opinion for the court stated:

> If we cut through mere details of procedure, the operation and effect of the statute in substance is that public authorities may bring the owner or publisher of a newspaper or periodical before a judge upon a charge of conducting a business of publishing scandalous and defamatory matter—in particular that the matter consists of charges against public officers of official dereliction—and unless the owner or publisher is able and disposed to bring competent evidence to satisfy the judge that the charges are true and are published with good motives and for justifiable ends, his newspaper or periodical is suppressed and further publication is made punishable as a contempt. This is of the essence of censorship.

> The question is whether a statute authorizing such proceedings in restraint of publication is consistent with the conception of the liberty of the press as historically conceived and guaranteed. In determining the extent of the constitutional protection, it has been generally, if not universally, considered that it is the chief purpose of the guaranty to prevent previous restraints upon publication. The struggle in England, directed against the legislative power of the licenser, resulted in renunciation of the censorship of the press. The liberty deemed to be established was thus described by Blackstone: "The liberty of the press is indeed essential to the nature of a free state; . . ."

Prior Restraints.   The U.S. Supreme Court is particularly sensitive to prohibiting government censorship in the form of prior restraints on speech. A *prior restraint* is where the government attempts in advance to prohibit the media from publishing or showing certain materials. Most prior restraints are held to be unconstitutional. As Justice O'Connor of the Supreme Court has stated,

A free society prefers to punish the few who abuse rights of speech *after* they break the law than to throttle them and all others beforehand.

Under this theory, it is the preference of the courts to allow material to be published, speeches to be made, or movies or television programs to be shown, and then *subsequently* to examine whether the content of the material was protected free speech or whether it fell within one of the several unprotected excepted classes, such as obscene materials.

The First Amendment does not place an absolute ban on prior restraints. There are certain narrowly drawn exceptions where a prior restraint may be valid. For example, in *U.S. v. Progressive, Inc.*, 467 F.Supp. 990 (1979), a Federal District Court in Wisconsin issued an order enjoining *The Progressive*, a monthly magazine, from publishing an article entitled "The H-Bomb Secret: How We Got It, Why We're Telling It," which described technically how to make a hydrogen bomb. However, in *New York Times Co. v. U.S.*, 403 U.S. 713 (1971), the Supreme Court held, based on several concurring opinions, that the government did not meet its burden of justifying a prior restraint against the publication of the "Pentagon Papers," which were alleged by the government to contain classified military information regarding the Vietnam War which was said to be vital to the national security.

A brief prior restraint may be valid if certain procedural safeguards are followed. In *Southeastern Promotions v. Conrad*, 420 U.S. 546 (1975), the Supreme Court held that the directors of the publicly-owned Chattanooga Metropolitan Auditorium had violated the constitutional prohibition against unreasonable prior restraints when it refused to allow performance of the live musical "Hair." The directors made their decision without ever viewing a performance of the musical. In that case, however, Justice Blackmun of the Supreme Court announced the standards for validly applying a prior restraint:

Labeling respondents' action a prior restraint does not end the inquiry. Prior restraints are not unconstitutional *per se*. We have rejected the contention that the First Amendment's protection "includes complete and absolute freedom to exhibit, at least once, any and every kind of motion picture . . . even if this film contains the basest type of pornography, or incitement to riot, or forceful overthrow of orderly government. . . ."

The settled rule is that a system of prior restraint "avoids constitutional infirmity only if it takes place under procedural safeguards designed to obviate the dangers of a censorship system." *Freedman v. Maryland.* We held in *Freedman*, and we reaffirm here, that a system of prior restraint runs afoul of the First Amendment if it lacks certain safeguards: *First*, the burden of instituting judicial proceedings, and of proving that the material is unprotected, must rest on the censor. *Second*, any restraint prior to judicial review can be imposed only for a specified brief period and only for the purpose of preserving the status quo. *Third*, a prompt final judicial determination must be assured.

Procedural safeguards were lacking here in several respects. The board's system did not provide a procedure for prompt judicial review. . . . Effective review on the merits was not obtained until more than five months later. Throughout, it was petitioner, not the board, that bore the burden of obtaining judicial review. Petitioner was forced to forego the initial dates planned for the engagement and to seek to schedule the performance at a later date. The delay and uncertainty inevitably discouraged use of the forum.

Taxation of the Press.   The Press Clause of the First Amendment prohibits the government from levying special taxes on the press. If the government were allowed to do so, it could effectively stifle the freedom of the press in this country. In *Minneapolis Star & Tribune Co. v. Minnesota Commissioner of Revenue,* 103 S.Ct. 1365 (1983), the Supreme Court held that a "use" tax on the cost of paper and ink products was unconstitutional under the freedom of press where the first $100,000 worth of products were exempted from the tax, which thereby only applied to eleven newspapers statewide, with just one paper, the appellant, paying roughly two thirds of the revenues collected under the tax. Justice O'Connor stated in her opinion for the court:

Clearly, the First Amendment does not prohibit all regulation of the press. It is beyond dispute that the States and the Federal Government can subject newspapers to generally applicable economic regulations without creating constitutional problems.

There is substantial evidence that differential taxation of the press would have troubled the Framers of the First Amendment. The role of the press in mobilizing sentiment in favor of independence was critical to the Revolution. When the Constitution was proposed without an explicit guarantee of freedom of the press, the Antifederalists objected. . . . The concerns voiced by the Antifederalists led to the adoption of the Bill of Rights.

The fears of the Antifederalists were well-founded. A power to tax differentially, as opposed to a power to tax generally, gives a government a powerful weapon against the taxpayer selected. When the State imposes a generally applicable tax, there is little cause for concern. We need not fear that a government will destroy a selected group of taxpayers by burdensome taxation if it must impose the same burden on the rest of its constituency. When the State singles out the press, though, the political constraints that prevent a legislature from passing crippling taxes of general applicability are weakened, and the threat of burdensome taxes becomes acute. That threat can operate as effectively as a censor to check critical comment by the press, undercutting the basic assumption of our political system that the press will often serve as an important restraint on government. "[A]n untrammeled press [is] a vital source of public information," *Grosjean,* and an informed public is the essence of working democracy.

Minnesota's ink and paper tax violates the First Amendment not only because it singles out the press, but also because it targets a small group of newspapers. . . . Whatever the motive of the legislature in this case, we think that recognizing a power in the State not only to single out the press but also to tailor the tax so that it singles out a few members of the press presents such a potential for abuse that no interest suggested by Minnesota can justify the scheme.

Defamation.   Members of the press and others are not protected from private tort liability for *defamation.* Defamation is generally defined as publishing to a third party an untrue fact about a person. Businesses and corporations may be defamed if it can be proven that a property right has been damaged by the defamation. Defamation by the oral word is *slander*. Defamation by the printed word or other visual means (e.g., statute) is *libel*. Because of its permanent nature, defamation in television broadcasts is considered libel.

Where a "public figure" (e.g., a politician or sports figure) is the plaintiff in a a defamation lawsuit, he or she must prove that the press had *actual malice* in publishing the untrue statement before the press will be held liable for libel. The reason for requiring the additional element of malice is to reach a balance between the public's right to know and the public figure's desire to protect himself from defamatory statements. Proof of actual malice usually requires a showing that the press had knowledge of the falsity of the statement, or "reckless disregard" for the truth or falsity of the statement, at the time the untrue statement was made.

The U.S. Supreme Court has held that a journalist-defendant in a civil defamation case does *not* have a First Amendment right to protect his opinion, judgments or convictions ("state of mind") developed while writing a story. However, a plaintiff seeking to prove the actual malice necessary for a case of defamation against a journalist-defendant is allowed to inquire into the "state of mind" of the defendant-journalist in discovery procedures.

Informants.   The press has no constitutional privilege to protect the identity of informants or the information received from informants. In *Branzburg v. Hayes*, 408 U.S. 665 (1972), the U.S. Supreme Court held that requiring a newsman to appear and testify before state or federal grand juries and reveal the source of information used in a newspaper story did not abridge the freedoms of speech and press of the First Amendment.

The press is not accorded any special treatment with regard to searches of newsrooms and the seizure of documents located there. In *Zurcher v. Stanford Daily*, 436 U.S. 547 (1978), the Supreme Court upheld a warrant authorizing the search of a campus newspaper for photographs of violent demonstrations on campus.

THE BROADCAST MEDIA AND THE FIRST AMENDMENT

The broadcast media are often subject to government regulation. For example, both radio and television broadcast companies are subject to regulation by the Federal Communications Commission (FCC). The FCC has authority to grant licenses, to renew licenses, and to regulate the content of the broadcasts. The majority of the First Amendment cases involving the broadcast media consist of freedom of speech challenges, usually involving the alleged censorship of the FCC. The use of offensive words by the broadcast media causes particular problems for the courts to decide.

Offensive Speech and the Media.   Certain speech may be *offensive* but not *obscene*. A total ban against *offensive* speech is unconstitutional. Offensive speech, however, is subject to reasonable "time, place, and manner" restrictions, particularly when transmitted over the media (e.g., radio, television). The offensive speech must be a substantial intrusion on the privacy of others before regulation of the speech is considered reasonable. Further, an alternative forum must be available for the speech before it can be restricted. For example, nude dancing may generally be prevented from appearing on prime-time television, but could not be prevented as a live performance at a local theatre.

The government must have a legitimate interest in regulating obscene speech, such as protecting unwilling viewers or listeners, particularly children. However, in this area the law is unclear. In *Erznoznik v. Jacksonville,* 422 U.S. 205 (1975), the U.S. Supreme Court held a city ordinance unconstitutional which prohibited the showing of films containing nudity where "the human male or female bare buttocks, human female bare breasts, or human pubic areas" were visible from public streets. Justice Powell's majority opinion stated:

The plain, if at times disquieting, truth is that in our pluralistic society, constantly proliferating new and ingenious forms of expression, we are inescapably captive audiences for many purposes. Much that we encounter offends our esthetic, if not our political and moral, sensibilities. Nevertheless, the Constitution does not permit government to decide which types of otherwise protected speech are sufficiently offensive to require protection for the unwilling listener or viewer. Rather, absent the narrow circumstances described above, the burden normally falls upon the viewer to avoid further bombardment of [his] sensibilities simply by averting [his] eyes.

In *FCC v. Pacifica Foundation* the U.S. Supreme Court was faced with deciding whether certain "offensive" words should be allowed to be transmitted over the radio. [Caution: this case contains language that may be offensive to some readers.]

THE FIRST AMENDMENT AND THE MEDIA

FEDERAL COMMUNICATIONS COMMISSION v. PACIFICA FOUNDATION

438 U.S. 726 (1978)
UNITED STATES SUPREME COURT

Mr. Justice Stevens delivered the opinion of the Court.

A satiric humorist named George Carlin recorded a 12-minute monologue entitled "Filthy Words" before a live audience in a California theater. He began by referring to his thoughts about "the words you couldn't say on the public, ah, airwaves, um, the ones you definitely wouldn't say, ever." He proceeded to list those words and repeat them over and over again in a variety of colloquialisms. The transcript of the recording, which is appended to

this opinion, indicates frequent laughter from the audience.

At about 2 o'clock in the afternoon on Tuesday, October 30, 1973, a New York radio station, owned by respondent Pacifica Foundation, broadcast the "Filthy Words" monologue. A few weeks later a man, who stated that he had heard the broadcast while driving with his young son, wrote a letter complaining to the Commission. He stated that, although he could perhaps understand the "record's being sold for private use, I certainly cannot understand the broadcast of same over the air that, supposedly, you control." . . . Pacifica characterized George Carlin as "a significant social satirist" who

like Twain and Sahl before him, examines the language of ordinary people. . . . Carlin is not mouthing obscenities, he is merely using words to satirize as harmless and essentially silly our attitudes towards those words.

Pacifica stated that it was not aware of any other complaints about the broadcast.

On February 21, 1975, the [Federal Communications] Commission issued a declaratory order granting the complaint and holding that Pacifica "could have been the subject of administrative sanctions." [T]he Commission found a power to regulate indecent broadcasting in 18 . . . U.S.C. Section 1464 (1976 ed.), which forbids the use of "any obscene, indecent, or profane language by means of radio communications," . . .

The Commission characterized the language used in the Carlin monologue as "patently offensive," though not necessarily obscene, and expressed the opinion that it should be regulated by principles analogous to those found in the law of nuisance where the "law generally speaks to *channeling* behavior more than actually prohibiting it. . . . In summary, the Commission stated: "We therefore hold that the language as broadcast was indecent and prohibited by 18 U.S.C. Section 1464."

The United States Court of Appeals for the District of Columbia Circuit reversed, with each of the three judges on the panel writing separately.

We have long recognized that each medium of expression presents special First Amendment problems. And of all forms of communication, it is broadcasting that has received the most limited First Amendment protection. Thus, although other speakers cannot be licensed except under laws that carefully define and narrow official discretion, a broadcaster may be deprived of his license and his forum if the Commission decides that such an action would serve "the public interest, convenience, and necessity." Similarly, although the First Amendment protects newspaper publishers from being required to print the replies of those whom they criticize, *Miami Herald Publishing Co. v. Tornillo,* it affords no such protection to broadcasters;

on the contrary, they must give free time to the victims of their criticism. *Red Lion Broadcasting Co. v. FCC.*

The reasons for these distinctions are complex, but two have relevance to the present case. First, the broadcast media have established a uniquely pervasive presence in the lives of all Americans. Patently offensive, indecent material presented over the airwaves confronts the citizen, not only in public, but also in the privacy of the home, where the individual's right to be left alone plainly outweighs the First Amendment rights of an intruder. Because the broadcast audience is constantly tuning in and out, prior warnings cannot completely protect the listener or viewer from unexpected program content. To say that one may avoid further offense by turning off the radio when he hears indecent language is like saying that the remedy for an assault is to run away after the first blow. One may hang up on an indecent phone call, but that option does not give the caller a constitutional immunity or avoid a harm that has already taken place.

Second, broadcasting is uniquely accessible to children, even those too young to read. Although Cohen's written message might have been incomprehensible to a first grader, Pacifica's broadcast could have enlarged a child's vocabulary in an instant. Other forms of offensive expression may be withheld from the young without restricting the expression at its source. Bookstores and motion picture theaters, for example, may be prohibited from making indecent material available to children. We held in *Ginsberg v. New York,* that the government's interest in the "well-being of its youth" and in supporting "parents' claim to authority in their own household" justified the regulation of otherwise protected expression. The ease with which children may obtain access to broadcast material, coupled with the concerns recognized in *Ginsberg,* amply justify special treatment of indecent broadcasting.

It is appropriate, in conclusion, to emphasize the narrowness of our holding. This case does not involve a two-way radio conversation between a cab driver and a dispatcher, or a telecast of an Elizabethan comedy. We have not decided that an occasional expletive in either setting would justify any sanction or, indeed, that this broadcast would justify a criminal prosecution. The Commission's decision rested entirely on a nuisance rationale under which context is all-important. . . . As Mr. Justice Sutherland wrote, a "nuisance may be merely a right thing in the wrong place,—like a pig in the parlor instead of the barnyard." We simply hold that when the Commission finds that a pig has entered the parlor, the exercise of its regulatory power does not depend on proof that the pig is obscene.

The judgment of the Court of Appeals is *reversed.*

APPENDIX TO OPINION OF THE COURT

The following is a verbatim transcript of "Filthy Words" prepared by the Federal Communications Commission.

> Okay, I was thinking one night about the words you couldn't say on the public, ah, airwaves, um, the ones you definitely wouldn't say, ever, . . . The original seven words were, shit, piss, fuck, cunt, cocksucker, motherfucker, and tits. Those are the ones that will curve your spine, grow hair on your hands and (laughter) maybe, even bring us, God help us, peace without honor (laughter) um, and a bourbon. (laughter) . . .
>
> The word shit, uh, is an interesting kind of word in that the middle class has never really accepted it and approved it. . . . At work you can say it like crazy. Mostly figuratively, Get that shit out of here, will ya? I don't want to see that shit anymore. I can't *cut* that shit, buddy. I've had that shit up to here. I think you're full of shit myself. (laughter) He don't know shit from Shinola. (laughter) You know that? (laughter) Always wondered how the Shinola people felt about that (laughter) . . . Oh, *the* shit is going to hit *de* fan. (laughter) Built like a brick shit-house. (laughter) Up, he's up shit's creek. (laughter) He's had it. (laughter) He hit me, I'm sorry. (laughter) Hot shit, holy shit, tough shit, eat shit. (laughter) shit-eating grin. . . . Wow! Shit-fit. Whew! Glad I wasn't there. (murmur, laughter) All the animals—Bull shit, horse-shit, cow shit, rat shit, bat shit. (laughter) First time I heard bat shit, I really came apart. . . . Get your shit together. Shit or get off the pot. (laughter) I got a shit-load full of them. (laughter) I got a shit-pot full, all right. Shit-head, shit-heel, shit in your heart, shit for brains, (laughter) shit-face, heh (laughter) I always try to think how that could have originated; . . .
>
> The big one, the word fuck that's the one that hangs them up the most. [']Cause in a lot of cases that's the very act that hangs them up the most. So, it's natural that the word would, uh, have the same effect. . . . It's a heavy. It's one that you have toward the end of the argument. (laughter) Right? (laughter) You finally can't make out. Oh, fuck you man. I said, fuck you. (laughter, murmur) Stupid fuck. (laughter) Fuck

> you and everybody that looks like you. (laughter) man. . . . Fuck the ump, fuck the ump, fuck the ump, fuck the ump, fuck the ump. Easy on the clutch Bill, you'll fuck that engine again. (laughter) The other shit one was, I don't give a shit. Like it's worth something, you know? (laughter) I don't give a shit. Hey, well, I don't take no shit, (laughter) you know what I mean? . . . You wouldn't shit me, would you? (laughter) . . .
>
> I found three more words that had to be put on the list of words you could never say on television, and they were fart, turd and twat, those three. (laughter) Fart, we talked about, it's harmless. It's like tits, it's a cutie word, no problem. Turd, you can't say but who wants to, you know? (laughter) . . . Now the word twat is an interesting word. Twat! Yeh, right in the twat. (laughter) Twat is an interesting word because it's the only one I know of, the only slang word applying to the, a part of the sexual anatomy that doesn't have another meaning to it. Like, ah, snatch, box and pussy all have other meanings, man. Even in a Walt Disney movie, you can say, We're going to snatch that pussy and put him in a box and bring him on the airplane. (murmer, laughter) Everybody loves it. The twat stands alone, man, as it should. And two-way words. Ah, ass is okay providing you're riding into town on a religious feast day. (laughter) You can't say, up your *ass*. (laughter) You can say, stuff it! (murmur) There are certain things you can say its weird but you can just come so close. Before I cut, I, uh, want to, ah, thank you for listening to my words, man, fellow, uh space travelers. Thank you man for tonight and thank you also. (clapping whistling)

Mr. Justice Brennan, with whom **Mr. Justice Marshall** joins, dissenting.

This majority apparently believes that the FCC's disapproval of Pacifica's afternoon broadcast of Carlin's "Dirty Words" recording is a permissible time, place, and manner regulation.

However, I believe that an individual's actions in switching on and listening to communications transmitted over the public airways and directed to the public at large do not implicate fundamental privacy interests, even when engaged in within the home.

[U]nlike other intrusive modes of communication, such as sound tracks, "[t]he radio can be turned off,"—and with a minimum of effort. As Chief Judge Bazelon aptly observed below, "having elected to receive public air waives, the scanner who stumbles onto an offensive program is in the same position as the unsuspecting passers-by in *Cohen* . . . ; Whatever the minimal discomfort suffered by a listener who inadvertently tunes into a program he finds offensive during the brief interval before he can simply extend his arm and switch stations or flick the "off" button, it is surely worth the candle to preserve the broadcaster's right to send, and the right of those interested to receive, a message entitled to full First Amendment protection. To reach a contrary balance, as does the Court, is clearly to follow Mr. Justice Stevens' reliance on animal metaphors, "to burn the house to roast the pig."

The opinion of my Brother Powell acknowledges that there lurks in today's decision a potential for " 'reduc[ing] the adult population . . . to [hearing] only what is fit for children,' " but expresses faith that the FCC will vigilantly prevent this potential from ever becoming a reality. I am far less certain than my Brother Powell that such faith in the Commission is warranted, . . .

[T]he opinions of my Brother Powell, and my Brother Stevens, both stress the time-honored right of a parent to raise his child as he sees fit—a right this Court has consistently been vigilant to protect. Yet this principle supports a result directly contrary to that reached by the Court. *Yoder* and *Pierce* hold that parents, *not* the government, have the right to make certain decisions regarding the upbringing of their children. As surprising as it may be to individual Members of this Court, some parents may actually find Mr. Carlin's unabashed attitude towards the seven "dirty words" healthy, and deem it desirable to expose their children to the manner in which Mr. Carlin defuses the taboo surrounding the words. Such parents may constitute a minority of the American public, but the absence of great numbers willing to exercise the right to raise their children in this fashion does not alter the right's nature or its existence. Only the Court's regrettable decision does that.

As demonstrated above, neither of the factors . . . —the intrusive nature of radio and the presence of children in the listening audience—can, when taken on its own terms, support the FCC's disapproval of the Carlin monologue. . . . The rationales could justify the banning from radio of a myriad of literary works, novels, poems, and plays by the likes of Shakespeare, Joyce, Hemingway, Ben Jonson, Henry Fielding, Robert Burns, and Chaucer; they could support the suppression of a good deal of political speech, such as the Nixon tapes; and they could even provide the basis for imposing sanctions for the broadcast of certain portions of the Bible. See, e.g.,

> I Samuel 25:22: "So and more also do God unto the enemies of David, if I leave of all that *pertain* to him by the morning light any that pisseth against the wall"; II Kings 18:27 and Isaiah 36:12: "[H]ath *he* not *sent me* to the men which sit on the wall, that they may eat their own dung, and drink their own piss with you?"; Ezekiel 23:3: "And they committed whoredoms in Egypt; they committed whoredoms in their youth; there were their breasts pressed, and there they bruised the teats of their virginity."; Ezekiel 23:21: "Thus thou calledst to remembrance the lewdnes of thy youth, in bruising thy teats by the Egyptians for the paps of thy youth." [The Holy Bible, King James Version, Oxford, 1897]

Today's decision will thus have its greatest impact on broadcasters desiring to reach, and listening audiences composed of, persons who do not share the Court's view as to which words or expressions are acceptable and who, for a variety of reasons, including a conscious desire to flout majoritarian conventions, express themselves using words that may be regarded as offensive by those from different socio-economic backgrounds. In this context, the Court's decision may be seen for what, in the broader perspective, it really is: another of the dominant culture's inevitable efforts to force those groups who do not share its mores to conform to its way of thinking, acting, and speaking.

CASE QUESTIONS

1. Are the broadcast media subject to government regulation? If so, what federal agency is responsible for regulating the broadcast media?
2. Over what medium was the Carlin monologue broadcast? At what time of the day?
3. Did the Supreme Court find that the Carlin monologue was *obscene?* If the broadcast had been found to be obscene, would this have ended the case? Why or why not?
4. Is *offensive* language protected by the First Amendment? If so, is any regulation of offen-

sive language tolerated by the First Amendment? Explain.

5. Did the Supreme Court find that the regulation of the broadcast of the Carlin monologue was a proper "time, place, and manner" restriction of otherwise protected speech?

6. Do you think that the Carlin monologue could have "enlarged a child's vocabulary" as the Court asserted?

7. Was Carlin's monologue a "pig in the parlor"? Does Carlin rank with Mark Twain and Mort Sahl as a significant social satirist?

8. In order to protect the right of a minority in society to hear Carlin's monologue, should the listeners of public radio be required to endure the "minimal discomfort" of flicking the "off" button on the radio, as Justice Brennan asserted in his dissent?

9. Do you think the Court's opinion in this case contributes to reducing the adult population to hearing on the radio only what is fit for children?

10. Should the Bible be treated the same as Carlin's monologue because it contains "filthy words"? Why or why not?

11. Do persons of some socioeconomic backgrounds use the words of Carlin's monologue in everyday speech? Do you?

Policy Issue. Should an Elizabethan comedy that contains "filthy words" be treated any differently from Carlin's monologue? Why or why not?

Economics Issue. Should the broadcast media provide special "adults only" channels for the broadcast of such materials as the Carlin monologue? Would it make economic sense to do so? Would adults patronize such stations?

Ethics Issue. Is it ethical for one segment of society (e.g., parents) to dictate what other persons can hear or see on the broadcast media?

Social Responsibility. Does the broadcasting industry owe a special duty of social responsibility to society? If so, why? To what segment of society does the broadcasting industry owe such a duty?

FREEDOM TO ASSEMBLE

The First Amendment guarantees the right of persons to *assemble.* The freedom to assemble or meet or gather is based on a belief that persons, in order to promote their right of freedom of speech, must be allowed to assemble to exchange their beliefs, and to organize in order to collectively present their beliefs to the government. As Justice Harlan wrote for the Supreme Court in *NAACP v. Alabama,* 357 U.S. 449:

Effective advocacy of both public and private points of view, particularly controversial ones, is undeniably enhanced by group association, as this Court has more than once recognized by remarking upon the close nexus between the freedoms of speech and assembly.

A further purpose served by the First Amendment right to assemble is to prevent "guilt by association." The Founding Fathers were particularly sensitive to the "chilling effect" that guilt by association has on freedom of speech, and therefore incorporated the right to freely assemble in the First Amendment of the Bill of Rights.

Right to Petition the Government. The First Amendment also provides the right of persons to petition the government for a redress of grievances. Under this right, a person may not be hindered in an attempt to bring a case before a court or administrative agency, or in lobbying the legislative and executive branches of government. The right to petition is closely related to the First Amendment right to assemble.

A major Supreme Court case that applied the Freedom to Assemble Clause of the First Amendment is *NAACP v. Claiborne Hardware Co.*, where members of a local branch of the National Association for the Advancement of Colored People (NAACP) boycotted white merchants in Mississippi.

FREEDOM TO ASSEMBLE

NAACP v. CLAIBORNE HARDWARE CO.

458 U.S. 886 (1982)
UNITED STATES SUPREME COURT

Justice Stevens delivered the opinion of the Court.

The boycott of white merchants in Claiborne County, Mississippi, that gave rise to this litigation . . . included elements of criminality and elements of majesty. Evidence that fear of reprisals caused some black citizens to withhold their patronage from respondents' businesses convinced the Supreme Court of Mississippi that the entire boycott was unlawful and that each of the 92 petitioners was liable for all of its economic consequences.

The boycott of white merchants at issue in this case took many forms. The boycott was launched at a meeting of a local branch of the NAACP attended by several hundred persons. Its acknowledged purpose was to secure compliance by both civic and business leaders with a lengthy list of demands for equality and racial justice. The boycott was supported by speeches and nonviolent picketing. Participants repeatedly encouraged others to join in its cause.

As we so recently acknowledged in *Citizens Against Rent Control v. Berkeley,* "the practice of persons sharing common views banding together to achieve a common end is deeply embedded in the American political process." We recognized that "by collective effort individuals can make their views known, when, individually, their voices would be faint or lost."

The right to associate does not lose all constitu-

tional protection merely because some members of the group may have participated in conduct or advocated doctrine that itself is not protected.

In sum, the boycott clearly involved constitutionally protected activity. The established elements of speech, assembly, association and petition, "though not identical, are inseparable." *Thomas v. Collins.* Through exercise of these First Amendment rights, petitioners sought to bring about political, social, and economic change. Through speech, assembly, and petition—rather than through riot or revolution—petitioners sought to change a social order that had consistently treated them as second-class citizens.

The First Amendment does not protect violence. "Certainly violence has no sanctuary in the First Amendment, and the use of weapons, gunpowder, and gasoline may not constitutionally masquerade under the guise of 'advocacy.'" *Samuels v. Mackell.*

Civil liability may not be imposed merely because an individual belonged to a group, some members of which committed acts of violence. For liability to be imposed by reason of association alone, it is necessary to establish that the group itself possessed unlawful goals and that the individual held a specific intent to further those illegal aims.

The chancellor awarded respondents damages for all business losses that were sustained during a seven-year period beginning in 1966 and ending

December 31, 1972. With the exception of Aaron Henry, all defendants were held jointly and severally liable for these losses.

The taint of violence colored the conduct of some of the petitioners. They, of course, may be held liable for the consequences of their violent deeds. The burden of demonstrating that it colored the entire collective effort, however, is not satisfied by evidence that violence occurred or even that violence contributed to the success of the boycott. A massive and prolonged effort to change the social, political, and economic structure of a local environment cannot be characterized as a violent conspiracy simply by reference to the ephemeral consequences of relatively few violent acts.

The judgment is *reversed*. The case is *remanded* for further proceedings not inconsistent with this opinion.

CASE QUESTIONS

1. What does the Freedom to Assemble Clause of the First Amendment provide?

2. What was the purpose of the boycott? Was it successful?
3. Does the First Amendment protect speech that is accompanied by violence?
4. Did the defendants engage in violence in this case? Was it sufficient to lose First Amendment protection?

Policy Issue. What damages did the lower court award? If this decision was left to stand, would it hinder a person's interest in joining a boycott?

Economics Issue. What effect did the boycott have on business?

Ethics Issue. Was it ethical for the merchants to sue the consumers for not shopping at their stores? For causing damages to their property?

Social Responsibility. Do consumers owe a duty of social responsibility to boycott merchants who are not obeying the law? Who are acting discriminatorily?

FREEDOM OF RELIGION

The First Amendment contains two clauses regarding the protection of religion, namely the Establishment Clause and the Freedom of Expression Clause.

The Establishment Clause, which prohibits laws "respecting the establishment of religion," generally is concerned with problems regarding the separation of church and state. The U.S. Supreme Court has held that the use of tax funds to support both parochial schools and prayer in public schools violates the Establishment Clause. However, in 1984 the Supreme Court held by an aggregation of concurring opinions that a municipality did not violate the Establishment Clause of the First Amendment where it displayed a representation of the Nativity scene at Christmas. The majority of Establishment Clause cases arise in nonbusiness settings.

The Free Exercise Clause of the First Amendment forbids laws "prohibiting the free exercise" of religion. The Free Exercise Clause may at times conflict with laws that affect modern business practices, particularly in employment situations.

Sunday "Blue Laws."   The First Amendment freedom of religion traditionally affected business with regard to Sunday "blue laws." Under such laws, states and local communities often prohibit or limit certain business activities on Sundays. Blue laws range from absolute prohibition of the operation of certain businesses on Sunday (e.g., liquor stores, retail stores) to appropriate "time, place, and manner" restrictions (e.g., only beer and wine may be sold on Sunday). Sunday blue laws that regulate the conduct of business have been held to be constitutional.

The case of *Thomas v. Review Board of the Indiana Employment Security Division* is one of the most recent cases in which the U.S. Supreme Court discussed freedom of religion in an employment setting.

FREEDOM OF RELIGION

THOMAS v. REVIEW BOARD OF THE INDIANA EMPLOYMENT SECURITY DIVISION

450 U.S. 707 (1981)
UNITED STATES SUPREME COURT

Chief Justice Burger delivered the opinion of the Court.

Thomas, a Jehovah's Witness, was hired initially to work in the roll foundry at Blaw-Knox. The function of that department was to fabricate sheet steel for a variety of industrial uses. On his application form, he listed his membership in the Jehovah's Witnesses, and noted that his hobbies were Bible study and Bible reading. However, he placed no conditions on his employment; and he did not describe his religious tenets in any detail on the form.

Approximately a year later, the roll foundry closed, and Blaw-Knox transferred Thomas to a department that fabricated turrets for military tanks. On his first day at this new job, Thomas realized that the work he was doing was weapons related. He checked the bulletin board where in-plant openings were listed, and discovered that all of the remaining departments at Blaw-Knox were engaged directly in the production of weapons [turrets for military tanks]. Since no transfer to another department would resolve his problem, he asked for a layoff. When that request was denied, he quit, asserting that he could not work on weapons without violating the principles of his religion. The record does not show that he was offered any non-weapons work by his employer, or that any such work was available.

Upon leaving Blaw-Knox, Thomas applied for unemployment compensation benefits under the Indiana Employment Security Act. At an administrative

hearing where he was not represented by counsel, he testified that he believed that contributing to the production of arms violated his religion. He said that when he realized that his work on the tank turret line involved producing weapons for war, he consulted another Blaw-Knox employee—a friend and fellow Jehovah's Witness. The friend advised him that working on weapons parts at Blaw-Knox was not "unscriptural." Thomas was not able to "rest with" this view, however. He concluded that his friend's view was based upon a less strict reading of Witness' principles than his own.

The Review Board adopted the referee's findings and conclusions, and affirmed the denial of [unemployment] benefits. The Supreme Court of Indiana, dividing 3-2, . . . denied Thomas benefits. The court held that Thomas had quit voluntarily for personal reasons, and therefore did not qualify for benefits.

Only beliefs rooted in religion are protected by the Free Exercise Clause, which, by its terms, gives special protection to the exercise of religion. *Sherbert v. Verner.* The determination of what is a "religious" belief or practice is more often than not a difficult and delicate task, as the division in the Indiana Supreme Court attests. However, the resolution of that question is not to turn upon a judicial perception of the particular belief or practice in question; religious beliefs need not be acceptable, logical, consistent, or comprehensible to others in order to merit First Amendment protection.

The Indiana Supreme Court . . . concluded that "although the claimant's reasons for quitting were described as religious, it was unclear what his belief was, and what the religious basis of his belief was." In that court's view, Thomas had made a merely "personal philosophical choice rather than a religious choice."

The Indiana court also appears to have given significant weight to the fact that another Jehovah's Witness had no scruples about working on tank turrets; for that other Witness, at least, such work was "scripturally" acceptable. Intrafaith differences of that kind are not uncommon among followers of a particular creed, and the judicial process is singularly ill equipped to resolve such differences in relation to the Religion Clauses. One can, of course, imagine an asserted claim so bizarre, so clearly nonreligious in motivation, as not to be entitled to protection under the Free Exercise Clause; but that is not the case here, and the guarantee of free exercise is not limited to beliefs which are shared by all of the members of a religious sect. Particularly in this sensitive area, it is not within the judicial function and judicial competence to inquire whether the petitioner or his fellow worker more correctly perceived the commands of their common faith. Courts are not arbiters of scriptural interpretation.

On this record, it is clear that Thomas terminated his employment for religious reasons.

The mere fact that the petitioner's religious practice is burdened by a governmental program does not mean that an exemption accommodating his practice must be granted. The state may justify an inroad on religious liberty by showing that it is the least restrictive means of achieving some compelling state interest.

The purposes urged to sustain the disqualifying provision of the Indiana unemployment compensation scheme are two-fold: (1) to avoid the widespread unemployment and the consequent burden on the fund resulting if people were permitted to leave jobs for "personal" reasons; and (2) to avoid a detailed probing by employers into job applicants' religious beliefs. These are by no means unimportant considerations. When the focus of the inquiry is properly narrowed, however, we must conclude that the interests advanced by the State do not justify the burden placed on free exercise of religion.

There is no evidence in the record to indicate that the number of people who find themselves in the predicament of choosing between benefits and religious beliefs is large enough to create "widespread unemployment," or even to seriously affect unemployment—and no such claim was advanced by the Review Board. Similarly, although detailed inquiry by employers into applicants' religious beliefs is undesirable, there is no evidence in the record to indicate that such inquiries will occur in Indiana, or that they have occurred in any of the states that extend benefits to people in the petitioner's position. Nor is there any reason to believe that the number of people terminating employment for religious reasons will be so great as to motivate employers to make such inquiries.

Neither of the interests advanced is sufficiently compelling to justify the burden upon Thomas' religious liberty. Accordingly, Thomas is entitled to receive benefits. . . .

Reversed.

CASE QUESTIONS

1. Which of the following provisions of the First Amendment was raised as an issue in this case? What does each clause provide?
   a. Establishment Clause
   b. Free Exercise Clause
2. What job was the plaintiff assigned? What religion did he practice? Is it a majority religion?
3. Why did the plaintiff quit his job? What benefits were denied him? Why?
4. What is the difference between a *philosophy* and a *religion*? Which is covered by the First Amendment? Why isn't the other covered?
5. Do religious beliefs exempt practitioners from all conflicting business regulation?

Policy Issue. Would the Supreme Court's decision have been different if the belief held by Thomas had been held by all: (a) Catholics, (b) Jews, (c) Protestants, or, (d) Hare Krishnas?

Economics Issue. Does the decision of this case have any major economic consequences for employers?

Ethics Issue. Was it ethical for Thomas to argue that he could not work on tank turrets when other members of his faith claimed otherwise? How did the Supreme Court reconcile this intra-faith difference?

Social Responsibility. Does business owe a duty of social responsibility to take into consideration an employee's religion when assigning job tasks or hours?

THE FOURTEENTH AMENDMENT

The Fourteenth Amendment was originally adopted in 1868 to guarantee rights to all persons born or naturalized in the United States, particularly to the recently freed slaves. Since that time, the provisions of the Fourteenth Amendment have been applied to thousands of modern-day situations, often involving business. Section 1 of the Fourteenth Amendment provides in pertinent part:

No State shall make or enforce any law which shall abridge the privileges or immunities of citizens of the United States; nor shall any State deprive any person of life, liberty or property, without due process of law, nor deny to any person within its jurisdiction the equal protection of the laws.

The Privileges and Immunities Clause of the Fourteenth Amendment, which applies to *state* action, is similar to the Privileges and Immunities Clause of Article IV of the Constitution, which applies to *federal* action. The Privileges and Immunities Clause was covered in the previous chapter. The other two clauses of the Fourteenth Amendment, the Due Process Clause and Equal Protection Clause, are covered in this section.

The Due Process Clause. The Due Process Clause is contained in two amendments to the U.S. Constitution. The Fifth Amendment provides, "No person shall . . . be deprived of life, liberty, or property without due process of the law." The Fifth Amendment Due Process Clause is used to invalidate *federal* law. The Due Process Clause of the Fourteenth Amendment, quoted previously, is used to invalidate *state* and *local* law that violates the U.S. Constitution. Most state constitutions also contain a due process clause.

The Due Process Clauses of the Fifth and Fourteenth Amendments only apply to *government* action. Private action of individuals, no matter how unfair, wrong, or discriminatory, does not violate due process. However, private action may give rise to civil lawsuits for breach of contract, fraud, and other wrongful actions.

Due process protects citizens from arbitrary, capricious, unreasonable, or unfair action by the government. The Fifth and Fourteenth Amendments do not prohibit the government from *taking* a person's "life, liberty, or property." These clauses only guarantee that *due process is followed before* the government takes a person's life, liberty, or property. There are generally two categories of due process cases: "procedural" due process, and "substantive" due process.

"Procedural" Due Process.   Procedural due process requires that before the government deprives a person of life, liberty, or property, that person must be given proper *notice* and a *hearing* at which to present his position on the matter. For example, if the government wishes to take a person's home under the doctrine of "eminent domain" in order to build a freeway, the government must give the homeowner sufficient notice of its intent, and provide a hearing at which the homeowner may present his arguments against such taking.

"Substantive" Due Process.   Substantive due process provides that any statute or ordinance enacted by government which affects a person's property, liberty, or individual rights must be *clear* on its face. Statutes or regulations that do not meet the "clearness" criterion are held "void for vagueness." The test to determine whether a law is void for vagueness is whether a "reasonable person" would understand the law in order to be able to clearly determine if he or she is in violation of the law. For example, a city ordinance that made it illegal for persons to wear "clothes of the opposite sex" was held *void* by the courts as violating substantive due process. Substantive due process is often raised by business to try to defeat government statutes or ordinances that are believed to be vague, ambiguous, or contradictory.

In *City of Chicago v. Scandia Books, Inc.*, which follows, the Appellate Court of Illinois upheld a zoning ordinance that restricted "adult" bookstores to certain areas of the city against a charge of vagueness under substantive due process.

SUBSTANTIVE DUE PROCESS

CITY OF CHICAGO v. SCANDIA BOOKS, INC.

430 N.E.2D 14 (1981)
APPELLATE COURT OF ILLINOIS

Justice Johnson:

On September 24, 1979, the City of Chicago (City) filed a complaint for injunctive and other relief against defendants. The complaint alleged that Scandia Books, Inc., doing business as Broadway Book Shop, located at 3120–22 North Broadway, was doing business as an adult bookstore within the definitions of Sections 3A, 3E, and 3F of the Ordinance. The City prayed for a preliminary injunction and permanent injunction to enjoin defendants from operating and maintaining an adult bookstore in any zoning district other than a C–2 zoning district. (Municipal Code of the City of Chicago 1977, Ch. 194C, Section 4.1(4).)

Robert Eggert testified that he is a police officer of the city of Chicago, and that he was sent to investigate the bookstore in question in June 1980. The store was divided into two parts by a swinging door and a counter. The front area of the store has racks containing magazines such as *Time* and *Life,* and Bibles and paperback books. In the back area, there were rubber paraphernalia, magazines and books pertaining to sexual acts between members of the same sex and the opposite sex. On June 13, 1980, Officer Eggert returned to the bookstore to have an evidence technician take pictures of the interior of the store.

The photos showed the different booths which contained adult films, the south wall with books on lesbianism, and the area where rubber products are displayed. The trial court ruled that the regulated uses of the Ordinance had been violated and enjoined further use of the premises as an adult bookstore.

Defendants contend the Ordinance (Municipal Code of the City of Chicago 1977, Ch. 194C, Section 3A) is so vague and indefinite as to violate the due process clause of both the U.S. Constitution and the Illinois Constitution. . . . Section 3A of the Ordinance provides:

> *Adult Book Stores.* An establishment having as a substantial or significant portion of its stock in trade, books, magazines, films for sale or viewing on premises by use of Motion Picture devices or any other coin-operated means, and other periodicals which are distinguished or characterized by their emphasis on matter depicting, describing or relating to 'Specified Sexual Activities,' or 'Specified Anatomical Areas,' or an establishment with a segment or section devoted to the sale or display of such material.

[T]he Ordinance in question was enacted by the City to deter the decrease in property values, increase in crime, neighborhood decline, and the adverse effect on business and residential districts caused by the influx of adult bookstore businesses. The primary control or regulation of the Ordinance is the prevention of concentration of these kinds of uses (adult) in any one area. Chicago has provided that no adult use shall be located within 1000 feet of any zoning district which is zoned for residential use. Thus, the restriction on First Amendment freedoms is no greater than is necessary to further Chicago's interest in the protection of its citizenry and neighborhoods.

In support of their claim that the provision of the Ordinance which defines adult bookstores is vague, defendants point to the words, "substantial or significant" as being unconstitutionally vague. We find defendants' argument without merit. The word, "substantial" as used in the definition of adult bookstores is not so indefinite as to render the Ordinance void and unenforceable. That term has been construed as having an ascertainable meaning in nu-

merous statutory schemes. Additionally, the definition of an adult bookstore in the Ordinance includes an establishment with a segment or section devoted to the sale or display of adult material. Clearly, the record shows that defendants' bookstore contained a section devoted to the sale or display of adult material.

We cannot say that the Ordinance is so vague as to violate the due process clause of the Illinois or the United States constitutions. The language in question gave defendants a sufficiently definite warning and fair notice as to the forbidden conduct regulated by the Ordinance. Accordingly, the issuance of the permanent injunction is upheld.

For the foregoing reasons, the judgment of the circuit court of Cook County is *affirmed.*

CASE QUESTIONS

1. What did the Chicago zoning ordinance provide? How did it effect the defendant?
2. What is "procedural" due process? "Substantive" due process? Which was involved in this case?
3. Did the zoning ordinance in this case violate the Due Process Clause?

Policy Issue. Does the Due Process Clause "void for vagueness" overbreadth test hinder the government in its regulation of the economy?

Economics Issue. Who was economically harmed by the zoning ordinance? Benefited by the ordinance?

Ethics Issue. Do you think the defendant knew he was meant to be covered by the ordinance? Did the defendant act ethically when he raised the Due Process Clause as a challenge to the ordinance?

Social Responsibility. Do the owners of "adult" bookstores owe a duty of social responsibility *not* to locate near residential areas? Why or why not?

The Equal Protection Clause. The Equal Protection Clause of the Fourteenth Amendment prevents states from enacting and enforcing legislation that treats persons differently based on a classification unrelated to the objective of a statute or law. The Equal Protection Clause does not make all classifications of persons unlawful, but is designed to prevent "invidious" discrimination.

A classification involving a *suspect* class (e.g., race, sex) will be struck down unless some "compelling state interest" is promoted by the law. When no suspect class is negatively affected by a state law, the courts apply the "rational basis" test to determine if the statute meets the Equal Protection Clause. If the classification is *rationally related* to the state's objective in passing the legislation, the classification will be upheld.

In *Zobel v. Williams* the U.S. Supreme Court applied the rational basis test and held that a state statute which discriminated between residents and nonresidents, and among residents, violated the Equal Protection Clause.

EQUAL PROTECTION CLAUSE

ZOBEL v. WILLIAMS, COMMISSIONER of Revenue of Alaska

457 U.S. 55 (1982)
UNITED STATES SUPREME COURT

Chief Justice Burger delivered the opinion of the Court.

The 1967 discovery of large oil reserves on state-owned land in the Prudhoe Bay area of Alaska resulted in a windfall to the State. The State, which had a total budget of $124 million in 1969, before the oil revenues began to flow into the state coffers, received $3.7 billion in petroleum revenues during the 1981 fiscal year. This income will continue, and most likely grow for some years in the future. Recognizing that its mineral reserves, although large, are finite and that the resulting income will not continue in perpetuity, the State took steps to assure that its current good fortune will bring long range benefits. To accomplish this Alaska in 1976 adopted a constitutional amendment establishing the Permanent Fund into which the State must deposit at least 25% of its mineral income each year. Alaska Const., Art. IX, Section 15. The amendment prohibits the legislature from appropriating any of the principal of the fund but permits use of the fund's earnings for general governmental purposes.

In 1980, the legislature enacted a dividend program to distribute annually a portion of the Fund's earnings directly to the State's adult residents. Under the plan, each citizen 18 years of age or older receives one dividend unit for each year of resi-

dency subsequent to 1959, the first year of statehood. The statute fixed the value of each dividend unit at $50 for the 1979 fiscal year; a one-year resident thus would receive one unit, or $50, while a resident of Alaska since it became a State in 1959 would receive 21 units, or $1,050. The value of a dividend unit will vary each year depending on the income of the Permanent Fund and the amount of that income the State allocates for other purposes. The State now estimates that the 1985 fiscal year dividend will be nearly four times as large as that for 1979.

Appellants, residents of Alaska since 1978, brought this suit in 1980 challenging the dividend distribution plan as violative of their right to equal protection guarantees and their constitutional right to migrate to Alaska, to establish residency there and thereafter to enjoy the full rights of Alaska citizenship on the same terms as all other citizens of the State.

Appellants established residence in Alaska two years before the dividend law was passed. The distinction they complain of is not one which the State makes between those who arrived in Alaska after the enactment of the dividend distribution law and those who were residents prior to its enactment. Appellants instead challenge the distinctions made within the class of persons who were residents when the dividend scheme was enacted in 1980. The distinctions appellants attack include the preference given to persons who were residents when Alaska became a State in 1959 over all those who have arrived since then, as well as the distinctions made between all *bona fide* residents who settled in Alaska at different times during the 1959 to 1980 period.

When a State distributes benefits unequally, the distinctions it makes are subject to scrutiny under the Equal Protection Clause of the Fourteenth Amendment. Generally, a law will survive that scrutiny if the distinction it makes rationally furthers a legitimate state purpose. Some particularly invidious distinctions are subject to more rigorous scrutiny.

The State advanced and the Alaska Supreme Court accepted three purposes justifying the distinctions made by the dividend program: (a) creation of a financial incentive for individuals to establish and maintain residence in Alaska; (b) encouragement of prudent management of the Permanent Fund; and (c) apportionment of benefits in recognition of undefined "contributions of various kinds, both tangible and intangible, which residents have made during their years of residency."

As the Alaska Supreme Court apparently realized, the first two state objectives—creating a financial incentive for individuals to establish and maintain Alaska residence, and assuring prudent management of the Permanent Fund and the State's natural and mineral resources—are not rationally related to the distinctions Alaska seeks to make between newer residents and those who have been in the State since 1959.

The last of the State's objectives—to reward citizens for past contributions—alone was relied upon by the Alaska Supreme Court to support the retrospective application of the law to 1959. However, that objective is not a legitimate state purpose.

If the States can make the amount of a cash dividend depend on length of residence, what would preclude varying university tuition on a sliding scale based on years of residence—or even limiting access to finite public facilities, eligibility for student loans, for civil service jobs, or for government contracts by length of domicile? Could States impose different taxes based on length of residence? Alaska's reasoning could open the door to state apportionment of other rights, benefits and services according to length of residency. It would permit the states to divide citizens into expanding numbers of permanent classes. Such a result would be clearly impermissible.

We hold that the Alaska dividend distribution plan violates the guarantees of the Equal Protection Clause of the Fourteenth Amendment. Accordingly, the judgment of the Alaska Supreme Court is reversed and the case is remanded for further proceedings not inconsistent with this opinion.

Reversed and remanded.

CASE QUESTIONS

1. What does the "strict scrutiny" test provide? Was a suspect class involved in this case?
2. What does the "rational basis" test provide? Was it applied in this case?
3. What did Alaska's dividend program provide? What was the source of the money of the Alaska Permanent Fund?
4. Did the plaintiffs qualify to receive payments from the fund? If so, would they have received more or less than other Alaska residents? Than nonresidents?

Policy Issue. What is the purpose of the Equal Protection Clause? If there was no Equal Protection Clause in the U.S. Constitution, could the country survive as a nation? Explain.

Economics Issue. Should nonresidents be able to participate in the natural resource benefits of a state by merely moving to that state? Will the decision in this case increase or decrease the migration to the State of Alaska?

Ethics Issue. Was it ethical for the plaintiffs to want payment of as much money from the fund as would be received by long-time residents of Alaska?

Social Responsibility. Does a state owe a duty of social responsibility to treat its residents with preference over nonresidents? Or to treat all citizens of the country equally?

The Incorporation Doctrine.   The Fourteenth Amendment not only contains substantive provisions (e.g., the Due Process Clause, the Equal Protection Clause), but has also been interpreted to *incorporate* other amendments of the U.S. Constitution so as to make them applicable to *state* action. Since 1925, the U.S. Supreme Court has interpreted the Fourteenth Amendment as *incorporating* the majority of the provisions of the Bill of Rights to apply to activities of state and local governments. Only a few of the provisions of the first eight amendments of the Bill of Rights have not been "absorbed" piecemeal through the Fourteenth Amendment to apply to nonfederal government action.

Trend of the Law

The provisions of the Bill of Rights, particularly the First Amendment freedoms of speech, assembly, and religion, will increase in importance in the future as they are applied by the courts to business situations. The courts will also be faced with a growing number of cases involving "time, place, and manner" restrictions on commercial free speech as states and municipalities become even more aggressive in trying to protect the safety, welfare, and esthetics of their communities. Commercial free speech will be further defined in the future as the Supreme Court is presented with various attempts by governments to censor communications, particularly broadcasts over radio and television. Local governments will have to be careful to follow the strict procedural guidelines for applying prior restraints on the showing of moving pictures, live theater presentations, and other drama.

The courts will also be faced with a growing number of cases brought by business to overturn statutes on an overbreadth, "void for vagueness" argument under the Due Process Clause. Equal Protection Clause cases will most likely arise where government action somehow treats two classes of persons differently, particularly protected classes such as races and sexes.

Amendment XXVI, which gave all citizens over the age of 18 the right to vote, was the last amendment added to the U.S. Constitution (1971). The most recent attempt to add an amendment to the U.S. Constitution concerned the controversial proposed 27th amendment, the "Equal Rights Amendment" (ERA). The ERA provided: "Equality of rights under the law shall not be denied or abridged by the United States or by any state on account of sex." Critics of the ERA argued that the rights of the proposed amendment were already guaranteed to women under other laws of the land (e.g., Title VII of the Civil Rights Act of 1964). After years of struggle by the proponents of ERA, the amendment received the endorsement of 35 states, three short of the number required for ratification.

Although other amendments to the Constitution have been suggested in recent years (e.g., to balance the budget, to permit prayer in school), it is doubtful that any new amendments will be added to the U.S. Constitution within the near future.

REVIEW QUESTIONS

1. In December 1965, Tinker, a high school student in Des Moines, Iowa, decided along with two other students to wear a black armband to school to publicize his objections to the Vietnam War and his support for a truce. The students were asked to remove their armbands and they refused. In accordance with a policy adopted by the school authorities two days earlier in anticipation of such a protest, all three students were immediately sent home and suspended from school until they would return without their armbands. They did not return until their specified period of protest was over. Tinker and his parents sued in District Court seeking injunctive relief against the disciplinary action. Were Tinker's actions protected by the First Amendment?

2. Jenkins was a movie theatre owner in Albany, Georgia. Jenkins was convicted by a jury of the crime of distributing obscene material, for showing the film *"Carnal Knowledge"* in his theatre. The film depicted two young men who met in college and followed them through their lifelong friendship. Both these characters were preoccupied with their sex lives and the movie portrayed this preoccupation. There were scenes in which sexual conduct, including sexual intercourse, was to be understood to be taking place but the camera did not focus on the bodies of the actors at such times. There was no exhibition whatsoever of the actors' genitals, lewd or otherwise, during these scenes. Jenkins appeals this conviction alleging that the film is not obscene and is therefore protected by the First Amendment. Will Jenkins' conviction be overturned?

3. In December 1973, the Public Service Commission ordered all electric utilities in New York State to cease all advertising that "promot(es) the use of electricity." The order was based upon the Commission's finding that the utilities did not have enough fuel to supply customer demands. Three years later, when the oil shortage was over, the Commission reviewed the ban and decided to extend it. The Commission divided all advertising into two types, "promotional—advertising intended to stimulate the purchase of utility services—and institutional and informational, a broad category inclusive of all advertising not clearly intended to promote sales." The Commission declared all promotional advertising contrary to the national policy of conserving energy. A large utility company challenged the ban, arguing that the Commission had restrained commercial speech in violation of the First and Fourteenth Amendments. Is the allegation valid?

4. The Borough of Mount Ephraim, New Jersey enacted a zoning ordinance

that prohibited all live entertainment in any establishment within the Borough. Schad operated an adult bookstore within the Borough. The store originally sold books and magazines and it operated coin devices which allowed a customer to sit in a booth and watch an adult film. Three years later the store installed an additional coin-operated machine permitting the customer to watch a live dancer, usually nude, performing behind a glass panel. Schad was convicted for violating the zoning ordinance and fined. He appealed this conviction, claiming that the ordinance prohibiting all live entertainment violated his right of free expression guaranteed by the First Amendment. On appeal Mount Ephraim argued that it had a legitimate interest in prohibiting live entertainment since it created parking and police protection problems. Is live nude dancing considered "speech"? Assuming that it is, what type of speech is Mount Ephraim trying to regulate and is this regulation constitutional?

5. The City of Jacksonville has an ordinance that prohibits the showing of films containing nudity ("female buttocks and bare breasts") on drive-in movie theatre screens which are visible from a public place. Erznoznik, the manager of the University Drive-In Theatre, was charged with violating the statute. Erznoznik challenged the validity of the ordinance, claiming that it unconstitutionally infringed on his free speech rights. The city of Jacksonville argued that the statute (1) protected citizens against unwilling exposure to materials which may be offensive; (2) was within the city's police power to protect children; and (3) prevented nudity on drive-in movie theatre screens from distracting passing motorists, which increased the likelihood of accidents. The city conceded that the ordinance swept far beyond the permissible restraints on obscenity under the Miller test, but it argued that the content-based regulation was a reasonable time, place, and manner restriction. Is the city's argument persuasive?

6. A Minnesota statute provided that any person who published or circulated a malicious, scandalous, and defamatory news periodical was guilty of a nuisance. The person found to be guilty of the nuisance could be enjoined perpetually from committing or maintaining the nuisance. The only defense that could be asserted was that the material was true and was published with good motives. Near was the publisher of the *Saturday Press*. The Press published a series of articles that made charges of extensive corruption and dereliction of duty against several city and county officials, including one member of the grand jury. In essence, the articles charged that a Jewish gangster was in control of gambling, bootlegging, and racketeering in Minneapolis and that law enforcement officers and agencies were not attempting to stop this activity. Near was perpetually enjoined by the Minnesota courts from publishing the *Saturday Press* since the courts found that the periodical was a public nuisance. Near appeals to the Supreme Court. What should the court decide and why?

7. Branzburg was a Louisville *Courier-Journal* reporter who wrote a news article based on his observation of two persons who synthesized hashish from marijuana, a violation of local law. Branzburg was called before a local grand jury but he refused to identify the persons involved. Pappas was a television newsman-photographer who went to a Black Panther conference and gained entrance to the Panther headquarters. He did not

report on any information that he discovered. He was called before a grand jury that was investigating civil disorders but he refused to testify about anything he heard while within the Panther headquarters. Caldwell was a *New York Times* reporter who also covered the Black Panthers. He wrote several articles and then was called to testify before a federal grand jury that was investigating possible threats and conspiracies to assassinate the President. He refused to testify. The reporters were all held in contempt of court for failure to testify. All three appealed to the United States Supreme Court, arguing that their information was privileged under Freedom of the Press guarantees. Legally and ethically what should the court decide?

8. In an effort to correct past injustices, a large group of black citizens in Claiborne County, Mississippi submitted a large list of demands (including desegregation of public facilities, hiring black policemen, ending verbal abuse by the police, and the hiring of more blacks by local stores) to local county officials. After the officials rejected the demands, the local NAACP chapter organized a black boycott of white merchants in the area. The boycott commenced in 1966 and was conducted by largely peaceful means, but it included some incidents of violence as well. Some blacks complained that blacks who were not sympathetic to the cause were coerced into joining the boycott. Citing these activities, the local merchants sued in Mississippi state court, alleging that the boycott was illegal. Since the boycott was allegedly illegal, the merchants sought damages from 92 named defendants for their economic losses accruing from the boycott. There was no evidence to show that any of these defendants had individually participated in violent activities. Should the court have recognized the merchants' claims and allowed damages?

9. The NAACP conducted activity in Alabama through unincorporated affiliates and therefore considered itself to be exempt from the requirement that foreign corporations register with the State before doing business. In 1956 the Alabama Attorney General brought suit in state court to enjoin the NAACP from engaging in further activities. Alabama alleged that the NAACP had recruited members, solicited contributions, opened a regional office in the state, assisted black students seeking admission to the state college, and had supported the black boycott of the Montgomery bus lines. A state court issued an order restraining the NAACP from engaging in these activities until it qualified for an exemption from registration in the pending hearing. Prior to the hearing, Alabama requested a number of documents pursuant to the case, including the names and addresses of all of the NAACP's "members" and "agents." The NAACP produced a large number of the documents but refused to supply the membership lists. The court fined the NAACP and prevented it from obtaining a hearing on the merits of its exemption claim until it produced the records. Was the court order constitutional?

10. The University of Missouri at Kansas City had a policy that permitted the use of its facilities by all registered student groups. Cornerstone was one such group that had used the facilities for several years. In 1977, the University barred Cornerstone from using school facilities for its meetings because of their religious content. The school prohibited the use of

its facilities "for purposes of religious worship or religious teaching" because it believed that permitting the continuance of such meetings would violate the Establishment Clause. Cornerstone sued in District Court, claiming that their rights of free speech and free exercise of religion were violated. May the University close its facilities to groups that hold religious activities?

11. Sherbert, a member of the Seventh Day Adventist Church, was discharged by her South Carolina employer for refusing to work on Saturday, the Sabbath Day in her denomination. Sherbert made a good-faith effort to obtain new work but was unsuccessful because her religious beliefs forced her to refuse to work on Saturdays. She filed a claim for unemployment benefits under the South Carolina Unemployment Compensation Act. The Act had a provision whereby the Employment Security Commission could refuse benefits to workers who fail, without good cause, to accept "suitable work when offered . . . by the employment office or the employer. . . ." The Act also provided that no employee should be required to work on Sunday. Sherbert sued the Commission seeking to obtain benefits. Was the denial constitutional?

12. Irvis, a black, was invited by a member of the Harrisburg, Pennsylvania branch of the Moose Lodge to dine in the private dining room of the Lodge. The Lodge refused to serve Irvis solely because of his race. Irvis sued in District Court, claiming that because the Pennsylvania Liquor Authority had issued the Moose Lodge a private club license which authorized sale of alcoholic beverages on its premises, the refusal of service to him was "state action" for purposes of the Equal Protection clause of the Fourteenth Amendment. Irvis named both the Moose Lodge and the Pennsylvania Liquor Authority as defendants, and he sought injunctive relief that would have required the liquor board to revoke the Lodge's license so long as it continued its discriminatory practices. Was Irvis's claim valid?

13. California Penal Code Section 261.5 prohibits sex with a female under the age of 18 but does not prohibit sex with males under 18. In July 1978 Michael M., a 17½-year-old male, was charged with having sexual intercourse with a 16½-year-old female. The Sonoma County Municipal Court found that Michael did engage in the activity. Michael sought to have the complaint set aside on the grounds that the exclusion of males from the protection of the statute violated the Equal Protection clause. Does Michael's claim have merit and how would the court analyse this case?

14. The Mississippi University for Women, created by the Mississippi legislature in 1884, has traditionally barred males from enrolling. Hogan applied to the Nursing School but was turned down because of his gender. He was allowed to audit any classes that he desired but he was not allowed to take any classes for credit. Hogan sued in District Court, contending that the females-only policy of the University violated the Equal Protection Clause of the Fourteenth Amendment. In defense, the University argued that (1) the all-female requirement was necessary to compensate for past discriminatory practices against women; and (2) admitting men would tend

to adversely affect the women of the school. What type of analysis should
the court apply in this case? Under that analysis, will Hogan be successful?

15. Texas Education Code Section 21.031 prohibited the use of state funds
for the education of any children not legally admitted to the United States.
In a class action suit, a group of parents with children who were denied
an education sued Texas, claiming that the statute violated the Equal Protection Clause of the Fourteenth Amendment. At trial, Texas argued that
the law was not unduly discriminatory and was, in fact, justified for three
reasons: (1) it was designed to protect the state from an influx of illegal
aliens; (2) it would relieve some of the special burdens that educating
undocumented immigrants imposes on the educational system; and (3) it
would relieve the state of the burden of educating children who are less
likely to remain in the state and contribute than other children. How
should the court decide this issue? What type of analysis should be applied?

ANTITRUST LAW

8 MONOPOLIZATION

INTRODUCTION

Early English common law held that all contracts in "restraint of trade" were void *per se*. Modern American common law, although generally hostile toward contracts in restraint of trade, upholds reasonable restraints (e.g., covenants not to compete).

During the latter half of the nineteenth century, the American economy rapidly changed from a rural, agricultural economy to an industrialized, urban economy. Wealth and economic power became concentrated in the hands of a few individuals and corporations through the use of predatory practices, mergers, and attempts to monopolize basic industries. The common law was largely ineffective in dealing with these abuses. In order to prevent collusive, monopolizing, and unfair business practices, Congress enacted a series of *anti-trust* laws in the late 1800s and early 1900s.

FEDERAL ANTITRUST LAWS

Congress enacted federal antitrust laws pursuant to the power granted by the Commerce Clause of the U.S. Constitution. Antitrust law is one of the most comprehensive and pervasive bodies of law that regulates the conduct of American business. Unlike much regulation that is *industry specific* (e.g., regulation of financial institutions, airlines, public utilities), the antitrust laws have a general application to most industries, businesses and professions in the United States. The major federal antitrust statutes and their dates of passage are:

Sherman Act (1890)
Clayton Act (1914)
Federal Trade Commission Act (1914)
Robinson-Patman Act (1936)
Hart-Scott-Rodino Antitrust Improvement Act (1976)

Including subsequent amendments, these statutes provide the basic antitrust law of the United States today. In *United States v. Topco Associates, Inc.*, 405 U.S. 596 (1972), Justice Marshall eloquently stated the purpose of the federal antitrust laws.

Antitrust laws in general, and the Sherman Act in particular, are the Magna Carta of free enterprise. They are as important to the preservation of economic freedom and our free-enterprise system as the Bill of Rights is to the protection of our fundamental personal freedoms. And the freedom guaranteed each and every business, no matter how small, is the freedom to compete—to assert with vigor, imagination, devotion, and ingenuity whatever economic muscle it can muster.

DEFENDANTS IN ANTITRUST ACTIONS

Generally, all businesses, except those exempt from antitrust laws, may be held liable as defendants in antitrust actions.

Exemptions from Antitrust Law. Certain industries and businesses are *expressly* exempted from antitrust laws by statute, including agricultural organizations and cooperatives; fishing; fish processing and fish marketing cooperatives; motor, rail, and ship common carriers; export trade associations; insurance; and bank mergers. These statutory exemptions exist because there is a government agency charged with regulating each exempted industry, and that agency will make decisions in the "public interest," including a concern for possible antitrust problems.

Other exemptions from federal antitrust laws have been *implied* by the courts, including exemption for air carriers, stock exchanges, labor unions, and professional baseball. No other professional sport is exempt from antitrust laws. Often a defendant will argue that his occupation or business is not a "trade or commerce" that is covered by antitrust laws. There is an implied "state action" exemption from federal antitrust law where state law is clearly designed to displace federal antitrust law, as in the case of state licensing requirements, state regulation of prices, etc.

Interstate Commerce. In order for federal antitrust laws to apply to an individual fact situation, "interstate commerce" must be found. For most antitrust violations, and unless otherwise indicated in these antitrust materials, the activities in the case must only have to have an *affect* on interstate commerce in order for federal antitrust law to apply. If solely *intrastate* commerce is found, federal antitrust law does not apply. The Sherman Act does not apply if the interstate commerce involved is negligibly small (*de minimis*). Many states have enacted state antitrust laws that apply to intrastate activity. Most state statutes are patterned after the federal antitrust laws.

Section 3 of the Sherman Act specifically covers restraints of trade and monopolies in "trade or commerce in any territory of the United States," or between such a territory and a state or foreign nation. The Sherman Act has been held to cover *extraterritorial* activities where the intent of the parties is to affect commerce with the United States, and the conduct actually does cause effects in the United States. Where the defendant's foreign activity is required by foreign law, the activity is held not to violate American antitrust law.

In *Goldfarb v. Virginia State Bar* the United States Supreme Court found interstate commerce and rejected the asserted "learned professions" exemption from antitrust laws, holding that professionals (e.g., lawyers) are covered by antitrust laws.

price-fixing is against anti-trust laws   *lawyers are in business to make a profit ∴ they are succeptible to regulation by Antitrust laws*

EXEMPTIONS FROM ANTITRUST LAW

GOLDFARB v. VIRGINIA STATE BAR

421 U.S. 773 (1975)
UNITED STATES SUPREME COURT

Mr. Chief Justice Burger delivered the opinion of the Court.

In 1971 petitioners, husband and wife, contracted to buy a home in Fairfax County, Va. The financing agency required them to secure title insurance; this required a title examination, and only a member of the Virginia State Bar could legally perform that service. Petitioners therefore contacted a lawyer, who quoted them the precise fee suggested in a minimum-fee schedule published by respondent Fairfax County Bar Association; the lawyer told them that it was his policy to keep his charges in line with the minimum-fee schedule, which provided for a fee of 1 percent of the value of the property involved. Petitioners then tried to find a lawyer who would examine the title for less than the fee fixed by the schedule. They sent letters to 36 other Fairfax County lawyers requesting their fees. Nineteen replied, and none indicated that he would charge less than the rate fixed by the schedule; several stated that they knew of no attorney who would do so. . . . The fee schedule the lawyers referred to is a list of recommended minimum prices for common legal services.

After a trial solely on the issue of liability the District Court held that the minimum-fee schedule violated the Sherman Act. . . . [I]t rejected the County Bar's contention that as a "learned profession" the practice of law is exempt from the Sherman Act.

The Court of Appeals reversed as to liability. . . . [T]he Court of Appeals held . . . the County Bar immune because the practice of law is not "trade or commerce" under the Sherman Act. . . .

INTERSTATE COMMERCE

The County Bar argues, as the Court of Appeals held, that any effect on interstate commerce caused by the fee schedule's restraint on legal services was incidental and remote.

As the District Court found, "a significant portion of funds furnished for the purchasing of homes in Fairfax County comes from without the State of Virginia," and "significant amounts of loans on Fairfax County real estate are guaranteed by the United States Veterans Administration and Department of Housing and Urban Development, both headquartered in the District of Columbia." Thus in this class action the transactions which create the need for the particular legal services in question frequently are interstate transactions.

Given the substantial volume of commerce involved, and the inseparability of this particular legal service from the interstate aspects of real estate transactions, we conclude that interstate commerce has been sufficiently affected.

LEARNED PROFESSION

The County Bar argues that Congress never intended to include the learned professions within the terms "trade or commerce" in Section 1 of the Sherman Act, and therefore the sale of professional services is exempt from the Act. No explicit exemption or legislative history is provided to support this contention; rather, the existence of state regulation seems to be its primary basis. Also, the County Bar maintains that competition is inconsistent with the practice of a profession because enhancing profit is not the goal of professional activities; the goal is to provide services necessary to the community.

In arguing that learned professions are not "trade or commerce" the County Bar seeks a total exclusion from antitrust regulation. Whether state regulation is active or dormant, real or theoretical, lawyers would be able to adopt anticompetitive practices with impunity. We cannot find support for the proposition that Congress intended any such sweeping exclusion. The nature of an occupation, standing alone, does not provide sanctuary from the Sherman Act . . . nor is the public-service aspect of professional practice controlling in determining whether Section 1 includes professions. Congress

intended to strike as broadly as it could in Section 1 of the Sherman Act, and to read into it so wide an exemption as that urged on us would be at odds with that purpose.

The language of Section 1 of the Sherman Act, of course, contains no exception. "Language more comprehensive is difficult to conceive." And our cases have repeatedly established that there is a heavy presumption against implicit exemptions.

The judgment of the Court of Appeals is *reversed* and the case is *remanded* to that court with orders to remand to the District Court for further proceedings consistent with this opinion.

CASE QUESTIONS

1. Did the Supreme Court find "interstate" commerce in this case? If it had not, could federal antitrust laws have been applied to the activities of the defendants?
2. Did the minimum-fee schedule in this case constitute price-fixing? Is this a violation of antitrust law?
3. Does the Sherman Act contain an *express* exemption for the "learned professions"?
4. Did the Supreme Court find that the profession of law was a "trade or commerce" within the meaning of federal antitrust law?
5. How did the Court answer the argument of the defendants that there is an *implied* "learned professions" exemption from antitrust law?
6. Should there be any exemptions from antitrust law? Should unions be exempt? Why is professional baseball exempt?

Policy Issue. Should professional services be covered by antitrust law? Or should there be an *implied* exemption for the learned professions?

Economics Issue. Would legal fees be higher or lower under a minimum-fee schedule? Explain.

Ethics Issue. Was it ethical for the lawyers in this case to argue that they were exempt from the laws which they drafted and which they enforce against other businesses in society?

Social Responsibility. Do you believe that the primary goal of the legal profession is to "provide services necessary to the community" and that "enhancing profit is not a goal of professional activities"? Ask your professor if he will represent you free of charge.

PLAINTIFFS IN ANTITRUST ACTIONS

The government of the United States and private parties may initiate and maintain actions against defendants for violating the antitrust laws. The Justice Department is authorized to bring actions to enforce the provisions of the Sherman Act. The Federal Trade Commission (FTC) is empowered to bring actions to enforce the Federal Trade Commission Act. The Justice Department and the FTC are both authorized to bring and maintain legal actions to enforce the provisions of the Clayton Act, including the Robinson-Patman Act.

The government may seek either criminal or civil remedies against defendants in antitrust actions. Private parties may bring *civil* actions against defendants for violating any of the antitrust laws.

Civil Actions for Treble Damages.   Section 4 of the Clayton Act provides:

Any person who shall be injured in his business *or property* by reason of *anything* forbidden in the antitrust laws may sue therefor in any district court of the United States . . . without respect to the amount in controversy, and shall recover threefold the damages by him sustained, and the cost of suit, including a reasonable attorney's fee.

Under Section 4, a plaintiff may sue for treble damages for the violation of *any* antitrust law, including violations of the Sherman Act, Federal Trade Commission Act, Robinson-Patman Act, and Clayton Act. Section 4 was enacted to provide an incentive for private parties to bring actions to enforce the antitrust laws, thereby supplementing limited government resources. The incentive seems to have worked, in that the majority of antitrust actions are brought by private plaintiffs seeking treble damages in civil lawsuits. A plaintiff in a private civil antitrust action may recover threefold:

1. "lost profits" that could have been earned in a freely competitive market
2. "increased costs" of business from actual purchases made or business transacted
3. the "decrease in value" of an investment in tangible or intangible property.

Although damages may sometimes be difficult to determine in antitrust actions with precise accuracy, the courts only require the plaintiff prove a "just and reasonable estimate of the damages based upon relevant data." The rationale for this rule is that it is fairer to place the risk of uncertainty on the wrongdoer than on the complaining party. The purpose of allowing an award for costs and reasonable attorneys' fees is to protect the plaintiff from having his antitrust damage claim diluted by the costs of instituting and maintaining the successful litigation.

my concern?

Section 4 has been criticized for prompting plaintiffs to bring frivolous lawsuits with the hope of obtaining a large award of treble damages.

Either the government or private parties may seek *injunctive* relief under the equitable power of the federal courts. For further equitable relief, the federal courts may order that particular acts or conduct of the defendant be restrained, order the division of a company's assets to form a competing company, compel a company to license its patents to others on a reasonable royalty basis, cancel contracts, etc. The government can also seek the divestiture of subsidiaries of the defendant.

Effect of Government Judgment.   If the government obtains a final court *judgment* that a person has violated the antitrust laws, the judgment is *prima facie* evidence against the defendant in subsequent private civil treble damage actions. The government and the defendant may enter into a "consent decree" stipulating to some specified remedy to settle the government's action, such as an injunction, a licensing of patent, etc. Such a consent decree may *not* be used by a private party to establish an antitrust violation. The rationale is that a consent decree does not acknowledge the guilt of the defendant, but only consists of a determination of a remedy.

Where the government has brought an action against a defendant, a private party is usually *not* allowed to "intervene" in the government antitrust action, because the "public interest" which the government represents and the "private interest" of the private litigant may not be the same.

Statute of Limitations.   There is a four-year Statute of Limitations on private antitrust suits. The period runs from the date of the injury, not from the date on which the anticompetitive conduct took place. If the defendant has "fraudulently concealed" the violation, the Statute of Limitation period runs from the time when the plaintiff discovered, or should have discovered with reasonable diligence, that his rights have been invaded. The Statute of Limitations is "tolled" (does not run) during a suit by the government or during a Federal Trade Commission proceeding.

"interesting" ******   If a plaintiff sues with "unclean hands" after having participated in the antitrust violation with the defendant, this does not prevent the plaintiff from suing the defendant for treble damages. The rationale is that the "ever-present threat" of suit, particularly from accomplices, will deter antitrust violations.

Plaintiffs: Consumers.   Generally, any person who is injured in his or her "business or property" may bring a treble damage action against a defendant under Section 4 of the Clayton Act. It is obvious that a business which deals with another business and is injured in its "business or property" by an antitrust violation of the other company is such a "person." Questions have often arisen as to whether consumers are injured in their "business or property" by antitrust violations within the meaning of Section 4 of the Clayton Act.

**   In *Reiter v. Sonotone Corp.* the Supreme Court held that consumers are considered to be injured in their "property" by antitrust violations, and may therefore bring and maintain actions for treble damages against defendants under Section 4 of the Clayton Act.

TREBLE DAMAGE ACTION
REITER v. SONOTONE CORP.

442 U.S. 330 (1979)
UNITED STATES SUPREME COURT

Mr. Chief Justice Burger delivered the opinion of the Court.

Petitioner brought a class action on behalf of herself and all persons in the United States who purchased hearing aids manufactured by five corporations, respondents here. Her complaint alleges that respondents have committed a variety of antitrust violations, including vertical and horizontal price fixing. Because of these violations, the complaint alleges, petitioner and the class of persons she seeks to represent have been forced to pay illegally fixed higher prices for the hearing aids and related services they purchased from respondents' retail dealers. Treble damages and injunctive relief are sought under Section 4 . . . of the Clayton Act, as amended.

The Court of Appeals reversed [the District Court and held] that retail purchasers of consumer goods and services who allege no injury of a commercial or business nature are not injured in their "business or property" within the meaning of Section 4. We granted *certiorari.*

The argument of respondents is straightforward: the phrase "business or property" means "business activity or property related to one's business." Brief for Respondents 11 n. 7.

When a commercial enterprise suffers a loss of money it suffers an injury in both its "business" and its "property." But neither term is rendered redundant by recognizing that a consumer not engaged in a "business" enterprise, but rather acquiring goods or services for personal use, is injured in "property" when the price of those goods or services is artificially inflated by reason of the anticompetitive conduct complained of. The phrase "business or property" also retains restrictive significance. It would, for example, exclude personal injuries suffered [e.g., emotional distress]. . . .

We simply give the word "property" the independent significance to which it is entitled in this context. A consumer whose money has been diminished by reason of an antitrust violation has been injured "in his . . . property" within the meaning of Section 4.

Nor does her [Reiter] status as a "consumer" change the nature of the injury she suffered or the intrinsic meaning of "property" in Section 4. . . . [W]e have often referred to "consumers" as parties entitled to seek damages under Section 4 without intimating that consumers of goods and services purchased for personal rather than commercial use were in any way foreclosed by the statutory language from asserting an injury in their "property."

Respondents also argue that allowing class actions to be brought by retail consumers like the petitioner here will add a significant burden to the already crowded dockets of the federal courts. That may well be true but cannot be a controlling consideration here. We must take the statute as we find it. Congress created the treble-damages remedy of Section 4 precisely for the purpose of encouraging *private* challenges to antitrust violations. These private suits provide a significant supplement to the limited resources available to the Department of Justice for enforcing the antitrust laws and deterring violations. Indeed, nearly 20 times as many private antitrust actions are currently pending in the federal courts as actions filed by the Department of Justice. To be sure, these private suits impose a heavy litigation burden on the federal courts; it is the clear responsibility of Congress to provide the judicial resources necessary to execute its mandates.

The judgment of the Court of Appeals is *reversed,* and the case is *remanded* for further proceedings consistent with this opinion.

Mr. Justice Rehnquist, concurring.

I think that the Court's observation, that "the treble-damages remedy of Section 4 took on new practical significance for consumers with the advent of . . . [class actions]" is a miracle of understatement; and in the absence of any jurisdictional limit, there is considerable doubt in my mind whether this type of action is indeed ultimately of primary benefit to consumers themselves, who may recover virtually no monetary damages, as opposed to the attorneys for the class, who stand to obtain handsome rewards for their services. Be that as it may, the problem, if there is one, is for Congress and not for the courts.

CASE QUESTIONS

1. What does Section 4 of the Clayton Act provide?
2. Did the Supreme Court accept the argument that the plaintiffs were not injured in their "business or property" within the meaning of Section 4? Explain.
3. Can consumers be plaintiffs in antitrust actions?
4. Do attorneys benefit most from class action tre-

ble damage antitrust lawsuits, as Justice Rehnquist argues?

Policy Issue. Should private parties be allowed to be plaintiffs in antitrust actions? Why or why not?

Economics Issue. Does the award of treble damages provide an incentive for plaintiffs to bring private *civil* antitrust actions? Explain.

Ethics Issue. Was it ethical for the defendants to argue that the antitrust laws should not protect consumers from collusive business practices?

Social Responsibility. Do corporations owe a duty of social responsibility not to harm consumers through collusive business practices? Do corporations owe a duty to shareholders to defend against all lawsuits, even in actions like this case?

The *Illinois Brick* Rule. Often, plaintiffs do not buy a product directly from the originator of the antitrust violation. For example, if a group of manufacturers engage in a price-fixing scheme, and then sell the products to wholesalers, who sell to retailers, who sell to consumers, can the consumer who bought the final product sue the original antitrust violator under federal antitrust law? The answer to this question seemed to be "yes" until the U.S. Supreme Court decided *Illinois Brick Co. v. Illinois* in 1977.

  In that case, the Supreme Court held that in order for a plaintiff to bring an antitrust action against a defendant the plaintiff must have purchased the product of service *directly* from the defendant. In essence, the Supreme Court has eliminated the "passing-on" offense doctrine, whereby a plaintiff would argue that the effect of the original antitrust violation (e.g., overcharging) was "passed on" to the plaintiff through the chain of distribution, thereby injuring the plaintiff in his "business or property" as required under Section 4. As a result of the *Illinois Brick* decision, an *indirect* purchaser can no longer maintain an antitrust action against a defendant with whom the plaintiff has not directly dealt. The reasons given by the Court for the adoption of the *Illinois Brick* decision are:

1. that it is too difficult for the courts to analyze the economic effects of antitrust violations so far down the distributional chain
2. that the rule will protect defendants from multiple liability if plaintiffs at different distributional levels sue the same defendant for the same violation in different actions
3. that the rule will simplify litigation in antitrust actions.

The *Illinois Brick* rule has received substantial criticism from the plaintiffs' antitrust bar and from the academic community for prohibiting many consumers from bringing private antitrust actions against antitrust violators. The chilling effect of *Illinois Brick* is predicted to substantially lessen the importance of private antitrust lawsuits in advancing antitrust laws.

The *Illinois Brick* case follows.

*[handwritten margin notes: KNOW; * must bring about lawsuits : subcontractors must file; → discourages litigation; can't use passing-on defense; ∴ to be consistent say it can be used offensively]*

DIRECT PURCHASERS AS PLAINTIFFS

ILLINOIS BRICK CO. v. ILLINOIS

431 U.S. 720 (1977)
UNITED STATES SUPREME COURT

Mr. Justice White delivered the opinion of the Court.

*[handwritten: * is passed along further in the chain]*

Hanover Shoe, Inc. v. United Shoe Machinery Corp., 392 U.S. 481 (1968), involved an antitrust treble-damages action brought under Section 4 of the Clayton Act against a manufacturer of shoe machinery by one of its customers, a manufacturer of shoes. In defense, the shoe machinery manufacturer sought to show that the plaintiff had not been injured in its business as required by Section 4 because it had passed on the claimed illegal overcharge to those who bought shoes from it. Under the defendant's theory, the illegal overcharge was absorbed by the plaintiff's customers—indirect purchasers of the defendant's shoe machinery—who were the persons actually injured by the antitrust violation. . . . In *Hanover Shoe* this Court rejected as a matter of law this defense that indirect rather than direct purchasers were the parties injured by the antitrust violation.

[Defendant-petitioners] manufacture and distribute concrete block in the Greater Chicago area. They sell the block primarily to masonry contractors, who submit bids to general contractors for the masonry portions of construction projects. The general contractors in turn submit bids for these projects to customers such as the respondents in this case, the State of Illinois and 700 local governmental entities in the Greater Chicago area, including counties, municipalities, housing authorities, and school districts. Respondents are thus indirect purchasers of concrete block, which passes through two separate levels in the chain of distribution before reaching respondents. The block is purchased directly from petitioners by masonry contractors and

used by them to build masonry structures; those structures are incorporated into entire buildings by general contractors and sold to respondents.

Respondent State of Illinois, on behalf of itself and respondent local governmental entities, brought this antitrust treble-damages action under Section 4 of the Clayton Act, alleging that petitioners had engaged in a combination and conspiracy to fix the prices of concrete block in violation of Section 1 of the Sherman Act. The complaint alleged that the amounts paid by respondents for concrete block were more than $3 million higher by reason of this price-fixing conspiracy. The only way in which the antitrust violation alleged could have injured respondents is if all or part of the overcharge was passed on by the masonry and general contractors to respondents, rather than being absorbed at the first two levels of distribution.

The District Court granted petitioners' motion [for partial summary judgment], but the Court of Appeals reversed, holding that indirect purchasers such as respondents in this case can recover treble damages for an illegal overcharge if they can prove that the overcharge was passed on to them through intervening links in the distribution chain. . . . We granted *certiorari,* to resolve a conflict among the Courts of Appeals.

[W]e conclude that whatever rule is to be adopted regarding pass-on in antitrust damages actions, it must apply equally to plaintiffs and defendants. We thus decline to construe Section 4 to permit offensive use of a pass-on theory against an alleged violator that could not use the same theory as a defense in an action by direct purchasers. In this case, respondents seek to demonstrate that masonry contractors, who incorporated petitioners' block into walls and other masonry structures, passed on the alleged overcharge on the block to general contractors, who incorporated the masonry structures into entire buildings, and that the general contractors in turn passed on the overcharge to respondents in the bids submitted for those buildings. We think it clear that under a fair reading of *Hanover Shoe* petitioners would be barred from asserting this theory in a suit by the masonry contractors.

We are left, then, with two alternatives: either we must overrule *Hanover Shoe* (or at least narrowly confine it to its facts), or we must preclude respondents from seeking to recover on their pass-on theory. We choose the latter course.

For the reasons stated, the judgment is *reversed,* and the case is *remanded* for further proceedings consistent with this opinion.

Mr. Justice Brennan, with whom **Mr. Justice Marshall** and **Mr. Justice Blackman** join, dissenting.

Today's decision flouts Congress' purpose and severely undermines the effectiveness of the private treble-damages action as an instrument of antitrust enforcement. . . . Injured consumers are precluded from recovering damages from manufacturers, and direct purchasers who act as middlemen have little incentive to sue suppliers so long as they may pass on the bulk of the illegal overcharges to the ultimate consumers.

CASE QUESTIONS

1. Who was the plaintiff in *Hanover Shoe?* The defendant? How did the Supreme Court decide the pass-on *defense* issue in that case? Explain.
2. Who was the plaintiff in *Illinois Brick?* The defendant? How did the Supreme Court decide the pass-on *offense* issue in *Illinois Brick?* Explain.
3. Did the Court only have the two choices that it cited in this case? Could it have let the *Hanover Shoe* decision stand yet still find that the pass-on offense did not prohibit consumers and other indirect purchasers from suing antitrust violators?
4. Do you agree with the Supreme Court's holding and reasoning in *Illinois Brick?*

Policy Issue. Will consumers be helped or hurt by the *Illinois Brick* decision? Are the concerns of Justice Brennan in the dissenting opinion well founded?

Economics Issue. Does the *Illinois Brick* decision help or hurt businesses? Only some businesses?

Ethics Issue. Was it ethical for the defendant to argue the pass-on offense doctrine as a defense to the charge of price fixing?

Social Responsibility. Do corporations owe a duty of social responsibility not to engage in antitrust violations even where the pass-on offense doctrine will shield them from most liability exposure?

Criminal Penalties for Antitrust Violations. Violations of either Section 1 ("restraints of trade") or Section 2 ("act of monopolizing") of the Sherman Act are criminal felonies. Corporations can be fined up to $1,000,000. Responsible individuals (e.g., officers, directors) can be fined up to $100,000, sentenced to up to three years in prison, or both. A criminal conviction under the antitrust laws requires proof of criminal intent. There are no criminal penalties for violating the Clayton Act, the Robinson-Patman Act, or the Federal Trade Commission Act.

An action for a criminal violation of the antitrust laws is brought by the Department of Justice. Once the Justice Department decides to seek a criminal prosecution, it usually convenes a grand jury and seeks the proper indictment. Transcripts of grand jury proceedings are generally secret. If an indictment is issued, the Department of Justice proceeds with the criminal litigation against the defendant. Under the Antitrust Civil Process Act, the Department of Justice may issue a *Civil Investigative Demand* to any person to obtain documents prior to commencing a formal proceeding.

MONOPOLIZATION

Section 2 of the Sherman Act prohibits the act of monopolizing by a *single* firm. Section 2 provides:

Every person who shall monopolize, or attempt to monopolize, or combine or conspire with any other person or persons to monopolize any part of the trade or commerce among the several states, or with foreign nations shall be deemed guilty of a misdemeanor. . . .

The rationale for outlawing the act of monopolizing is on the economic theory that a firm with monopoly power is able to reduce output and thereby raise prices for the goods or services it sells or provides. Monopoly prices and profits are higher than the competitive price and profit would be if there was not a monopoly market structure.

Section 2 of the Sherman Act does not outlaw monopolies but only forbids the *"act* of monopolizing." To prove the unlawful act of monopolization in violation of Section 2, the following elements must be shown:

1. defendant possesses monopoly power
2. in a relevant market
3. and the defendant has willfully acquired or maintained that power.

Monopoly Power.   In determining whether "monopoly power" exists, courts are faced with the task of deciding when the mere "market power" of a single firm becomes so great as to legally constitute monopoly power. "Market power" has generally been defined by the courts to be the power to "control prices" or "exclude competition."

The courts, being untrained in sophisticated economic theory and analysis, have chosen to define market power and monopoly power in terms of percentage of market share. The courts have held that market shares of 90 percent, 85 percent, 75 percent, and 71–76 percent are sufficient to constitute "monopoly power." A market share of 20 percent has been held to be insufficient to constitute monopoly power. The courts have been generally inconclusive in determining whether market shares in the intermediate range constitute monopoly power. Each case is approached on its individual facts and circumstances.

Relevant Product Market.   Defining the "relevant market" is normally one of the most disputed elements of a Section 2 action. The courts have defined the relevant market of Section 2 as the "area of effective competition" of the defendant. This determination consists of an analysis of (1) the relevant *product* market, and (2) the relevant *geographic* market.

The relevant product market is generally defined to include substitute products that are "reasonably interchangeable" by consumers for the same purpose. Although this product definition is broad, the courts have generally applied a narrow interpretation of this definition; they have held that professional championship boxing matches are a distinct market from professional boxing matches, gospel music is a distinct product market from music generally, etc.

The defendant will usually argue for a large relevant market so that its share of the market will look smaller than if a narrow relevant market definition were used. The plaintiff will generally argue for a narrow definition of the relevant market.

In *United States v. E. I. du Pont de Nemours & Co.* the Supreme Court was faced with the interrelated problem of determining "monopoly power" and defining the relevant *product* market under Section 2 of the Sherman Act in a charge of monopolization brought against du Pont by the Justice Department.

MONOPOLY POWER, RELEVANT PRODUCT MARKET

UNITED STATES v. E. I. du PONT de NEMOURS & CO.

351 U.S. 377 (1956)
UNITED STATES SUPREME COURT

Mr. Justice Reed delivered the opinion of the Court.

The United States brought this civil action under Section 4 of the Sherman Act against E. I. du Pont de Nemours and Company. The complaint, filed December 13, 1947, in the United States District Court. . . . , charged du Pont with monopolizing, attempting to monopolize and conspiracy to monopolize interstate commerce in cellophane and cellulosic caps and bands in violation of Section 2 of the Sherman Act. . . . After a lengthy trial, judgment was entered for du Pont on all issues.

During the period that is relevant to this action, du Pont produced almost 75 percent of the cellophane sold in the United States, and cellophane constituted less than 20 percent of all "flexible packaging material" sales. . . . The court below found that the "relevant market for determining the extent of du Pont's market control is the market for flexible packaging materials," and that competition from those other materials prevented du Pont from possessing monopoly powers in its sales of cellophane.

The Government asserts that cellophane and other wrapping materials are neither substantially fungible nor like priced. For these reasons, it argues that the market for other wrappings is distinct from the market for cellophane and that the competition afforded cellophane by other wrappings is not strong enough to be considered in determining whether du Pont has monopoly powers. Market delimitation is necessary under du Pont's theory to determine whether an alleged monopolist violates Section 2. The ultimate consideration in such a determination is whether the defendants control the price and competition in the market for such part of trade or commerce as they are charged with monopolizing. Every manufacturer is the sole producer of the particular commodity it makes but its control in the above sense of the relevant market depends upon the availability of alternative commodities for buyers: i.e., whether there is a cross-elasticity of demand between cellophane and the other wrappings. This interchangeability is largely gauged by the purchase of competing products for similar uses considering the price, characteristics and adaptability of the competing commodities.

Our cases determine that a party has monopoly

power if it has, over "any part of the trade or commerce among the several States," a power of controlling prices or unreasonably restricting competition.

If cellophane is the "market" that du Pont is found to dominate, it may be assumed it does have monopoly power over that "market." Monopoly power is the power to control prices or exclude competition. It seems apparent that du Pont's power to set the price of cellophane has been limited only by the competition afforded by other flexible packaging materials. Moreover, it may be practically impossible for anyone to commence manufacturing cellophane without full access to du Pont's technique. However, du Pont has no power to prevent competition from other wrapping materials. The trial court consequently had to determine whether competition from the other wrappings prevented du Pont from possessing monopoly power in violation of Section 2. Price and competition are so intimately entwined that any discussion of theory must treat them as one.

If a large number of buyers and sellers deal freely in a standardized product, such as salt or wheat, we have complete or pure competition. Patents, on the other hand, furnish the most familiar type of classic monopoly. As the producers of a standardized product bring about significant differentiations of quality, design, or packaging in the product that permit differences of use, competition becomes to a greater or less degree incomplete and the producer's power over price and competition greater over his article and its use, according to the differentiation he is able to create and maintain. A retail seller may have in one sense a monopoly on certain trade because of location, as an isolated country store or filling station, or because no one else makes a product of just the quality or attractiveness of his product, as for example in cigarettes. Thus one can theorize that we have monopolistic competition in every nonstandardized commodity with each manufacturer having power over the price and production of his own product. However, this power that, let us say, automobile or soft-drink manufacturers have over their trademarked products is not the power that makes an illegal monopoly. Illegal power must be appraised in terms of the competitive market for the product.

Determination of the competitive market for com-

modities depends on how different from one another are the offered commodities in character or use, how far buyers will go to substitute one commodity for another. For example, one can think of building materials as in commodity competition but one could hardly say that brick competed with steel or wood or cement or stone in the meaning of Sherman Act litigation; the products are too different. This is the interindustry competition emphasized by some economists. On the other hand, there are certain differences in the formulae for soft drinks but one can hardly say that each one is an illegal monopoly. Whatever the market may be, we hold that control of price or competition establishes the existence of monopoly power under Section 2.

The Relevant Market

When a product is controlled by one interest, without substitutes available in the market, there is monopoly power. . . . But where there are market alternatives that buyers may readily use for their purposes, illegal monopoly does not exist merely because the product said to be monopolized differs from others. If it were not so, only physically identical products would be a part of the market. To accept the Government's argument, we would have to conclude that the manufacturers of plain as well as moistureproof cellophane were monopolists, and so with films such as Pliofilm, foil, glassine, polyethylene, and Saran, for each of these wrapping materials is distinguishable.

An element for consideration as to cross-elasticity of demand between products is the responsiveness of the sales of one product to price changes of the other. If a slight decrease in the price of cellophane causes a considerable number of customers of other flexible wrappings to switch to cellophane, it would be an indication that a high cross-elasticity of demand exists between them; that the products compete in the same market. The court below held that the "[g]reat sensitivity of customers in the flexible packaging markets to price or quality changes" prevented du Pont from possessing monopoly control over price. The record sustains these findings.

We conclude that cellophane's interchangeability with the other materials mentioned suffices to make it a part of this flexible packaging material market.

On the findings of the District Court, its judgment is *affirmed*.

CASE QUESTIONS

1. What does Section 2 of the Sherman Act provide?
2. What was the government's definition of the relevant *product* market in this case? Du Pont's definition? Which definition did the Supreme Court adopt?
3. Does *product differentiation* (e.g., Coca-Cola versus Pepsi-Cola) create separate product markets for Section 2 purposes? Should it?
4. Do you agree with the Court's statement that bricks, steel, and wood are not part of the same product market? If only home building was involved, would they be competing products?

5. What does *cross-elasticity of demand* mean? Explain.

Policy Issue. Is the definition of the relevant product market important to a Section 2 action? Explain.

Economics Issue. Can a monopolist charge higher prices than would be paid in a competitive marketplace? Does a corporation's monopoly position help or hurt shareholders?

Ethics Issue. Do you think that du Pont acted unethically in making its cellophane a successful product? Is it ethical for the government to sue successful corporations under the antitrust laws?

Social Responsibility. Do corporations owe a duty of social responsibility to not be so successful as to create a monopoly?

Relevant Geographic Market. The relevant geographic market is generally defined as the area in which the defendant and its competitors (if any) sell the product. The relevant geographical market may be defined as a national, state, regional, or local area. The courts may define certain submarkets of a larger market as the proper relevant market (e.g., a multistate region) for the inquiry into a Section 2 violation. The cost of transportation is generally used by the courts in limiting the size of a relevant geographical market.

In the following case, *American Football League v. National Football League,* the Court of Appeals defined the relevant *geographic* market in a Sherman Act Section 2 monopolization action brought by the then new American Football League against the long-established National Football League.

[handwritten: Not as important as du Pont]

[handwritten: in this case the entire country]

RELEVANT GEOGRAPHIC MARKET

AMERICAN FOOTBALL LEAGUE v. NATIONAL FOOTBALL LEAGUE

323 F.2d 124 (1963)
UNITED STATES COURT OF APPEALS, FOURTH CIRCUIT

Haynsworth, Circuit Judge.

The American Football League and owners of its franchises are contending against the National Football League and the owners of its franchises for victory in the courts. The American Football League and the owners of its franchises lost in the Court below. . . .

The two football leagues, American and National, are unincorporated associations. In each instance, the team owners are corporations, each of which was the holder of a franchise to operate a professional football team in a designated city.

The National Football League was organized in 1920. For a number of years its existence was precarious. Until the last ten years, its membership was far from static. . . . In 1959, the National Football League operated with twelve teams located in eleven cities. There were two teams in Chicago and one each in Cleveland, New York, Philadelphia, Pittsburgh, Washington, Baltimore, Detroit, Los Angeles, San Francisco, and Green Bay, Wisconsin. In 1960, two additional franchises were placed, one in Dallas and one in Minneapolis-St. Paul. . . .

The American Football League was organized in 1959, and began with a full schedule of games in 1960. Affiliated with it were eight teams located in eight cities, Boston, Buffalo, Houston, New York, Dallas, Denver, Los Angeles and Oakland. After the 1960 season, the Los Angeles team was moved to San Diego.

In this Court, the plaintiffs contend that the relevant market is composed of those seventeen cities in which National now either has operating franchises, or which it seriously considered in connection with its expansion plans in 1959.

In very different contexts, the relevant market has been found to be a single city, a group of cities, a state, or several states. In considering an attempt to monopolize, it, of course, is appropriate to limit the relevant geographic market to the area which the defendant sought to appropriate to itself. . .

Though there may be in the nation no more than some thirty desirable sites for the location of professional football teams, those sites, scattered throughout the United States, do not constitute the relevant market. The relevant market is nationwide. . . .

[T]he fact that the American League was successfully launched, could stage a full schedule of games in 1960, has competed very successfully for outstanding players, and has obtained advantageous contracts for national television coverage strongly supports the District Court's finding that National did not have the power to prevent, or impede, the formation of the new league. Indeed, at the close of the 1960 season, representatives of

the American League declared that the League's success was unprecedented.

We conclude, therefore, that the District Court properly held that the plaintiffs have shown no monopolization by the National League, or its owners, of the relevant market, and no attempt or conspiracy by them, or any of them, to monopolize it or any part of it. No violation of the Sherman Act having been established, the judgment of the District Court is affirmed.

Affirmed.

CASE QUESTIONS

1. When was the NFL formed? How many teams did the NFL have in 1960? Where were they located?
2. When was the AFL formed? How many teams did the AFL have in 1960? Where were they located?
3. What did the plaintiff AFL assert as the relevant *geographic* market in this case? Was it a narrow or broad definition? Why?
4. What relevant geographical market did the Supreme Court find in this case? Was it a narrow or broad definition?

Policy Issue. Do you agree with the relevant geographical market found by the Supreme Court in this case? If not, what geographical market would you have chosen?

Economics Issue. Was the AFL successful as a football league? Was this an "insurance" lawsuit by the AFL in case it failed?

Ethics Issue. Was it ethical for the AFL to sue the NFL in this case? Why or why not?

Social Responsibility. Did the NFL owe a duty of social responsibility to give up certain of its cities to the AFL?

NOTE: The NFL and AFL subsequently merged into one football league.

Willful Act.   Monopoly power alone is not unlawful under Section 2 of the Sherman Act. The plaintiff must prove that the defendant has engaged in some *willful act* or conduct to obtain or maintain its monopoly power ("act of monopolizing".)

Any act that itself violates the antitrust laws (e.g., conduct constituting a restraint of trade under Sherman Act Section 1, or a merger in violation of Clayton Act Section 7) is sufficient to prove the purposeful act or conduct in violation of Sherman Act Section 2. *Lawful* acts coupled with monopoly power have been held to violate Section 2 where the defendant has "purposefully and intentionally acquired, maintained, or exercised" that power (e.g., pricing below average or marginal cost, leasing equipment without offering users the opportunity to purchase the equipment). A specific intent to monopolize is not required. Only a showing of deliberate or purposeful conduct is needed.

In *Greyhound Computer Corporation, Inc. v. International Business Machines Corporation* the Court of Appeals affirmed a trial court decision which held that certain changes by IBM in the terms of its sales of used computer equipment to leasing companies constituted an *act* of "monopolizing" in violation of Section 2 of the Sherman act.

ACT OF MONOPOLIZING

GREYHOUND COMPUTER CORPORATION, INC. v. INTERNATIONAL BUSINESS MACHINES CORPORATION

559 F.2d 488 (1977)
UNITED STATES COURT OF APPEALS, NINTH DISTRICT

Browning, Circuit Judge

Greyhound Computer Corporation brought this action against International Business Machines Corporation alleging IBM had monopolized or attempted to monopolize various markets in the electronic data processing industry in violation of Section 2 of the Sherman Act. After presentation of Greyhound's case the district court granted IBM's motion for a directed verdict. This appeal followed.

IBM manufactures entire computer systems, including mainframes and peripherals. It also provides software and support services to its customers. Like other manufacturers, IBM both leases and sells its computers.

Greyhound is a leasing company; it does not manufacture computers. It buys computers from others and leases them in competition with computer manufacturers and other leasing companies. . . . Greyhound is both a customer and competitor of IBM. Greyhound's antitrust claim is that IBM restricted sales of its computer equipment in order to monopolize the leasing market in which Greyhound competes.

THE RELEVANT MARKET

Greyhound's major contention is that IBM has monopolized or attempted to monopolize a submarket for leasing general purpose digital computers for commercial application.

Leases and sales serve different customer needs. Greyhound offered testimony that general purpose commercial computers are purchased by banks, insurance companies, and other businesses with predictable long-term data processing needs and the capacity to undertake long-term financial commitments. Computers are leased by customers that have variable business requirements and a need to keep abreast of advancing technology. . . . IBM argues that both leasing and buying are merely methods of financing the use of computer systems.

We conclude that the evidence was sufficient, though by no great margin, to permit the jury to find that the differences between leasing and selling general purpose computers were of sufficient significance to justify treatment of the two forms of distribution as distinct submarkets for competitive purposes.

POSSESSION OF MONOPOLY POWER

The evidence in this record permitted a calculation of IBM's share of revenues from leasing of general purpose computers at 82.5 percent in 1964, 75.1 percent in 1967, and 64.68 percent in 1970. The portion of the market not controlled by IBM was dispersed among many other companies, none accounting for more than 4 percent of total lease revenues.

Evidence other than IBM's predominant share of the market supported an inference of market dominance. About 80 percent in dollar value of the installed base of general purpose systems is IBM equipment. IBM's senior vice president testified that rental prices of some models could be increased without proportionate decreases in demand. Other evidence indicating IBM's ability to manage its prices with little regard to competition included testimony that IBM based its prices on a 30 percent profit objective, that it never set a price simply to meet competition, and that its prices were 5 to 15 percent above those of the best of its competition.

IBM responds that other evidence in the record indicates IBM did not possess monopoly power. None of this evidence compelled a ruling in IBM's favor as a matter of law.

WILLFUL ACQUISITION OR MAINTENANCE OF MONOPOLY POWER

There was ample evidence that IBM officials became concerned that the balance between sales and rental had turned too heavily toward sales, and deliberately set about to reverse the trend. Greyhound asserts that in pursuit of this goal IBM adopted certain practices that reflect "the willful acquisition or maintenance of [monopoly] power as distinguished from growth or development as a consequence of a superior product, business acumen, or historic accident." *United States v. Grinnell Corp.*

Until late 1963 IBM's technological discount on second generation equipment was 10 percent per year, up to a maximum of 75 percent. Thus, equipment on the market for several years could be purchased at 25 percent of original cost. Leasing companies made extensive use of the second generation discount. IBM's Management Review Committee observed in 1965 that one reason for the rapid growth of leasing companies was their

ability to purchase equipment at substantial discounts and return a profit in a short period of time.

In 1963 IBM reduced the annual discount from 10 to 5 percent per year and the cumulative maximum from 75 to 35 percent. In 1964, shortly after the announcement of System 360, the discount was changed to 12 percent after the first year with no further discounts in succeeding years. Thus, the lowest price at which a purchaser could obtain a third generation IBM computer was 88 percent of the original price.

These changes restricted the capacity of leasing companies to compete by inhibiting purchases late in the product cycle. Because reduction of the discount increased the price leasing companies had to pay for their equipment, growth of their inventory was curtailed.

There was evidence from which the jury could infer that these anticompetitive consequences were intended.

Judgment *affirmed*.

CASE QUESTIONS

1. What did plaintiff Greyhound Computer assert was the relevant *product* market in this case? What did IBM assert was the relevant product market? Which definition did the court adopt?
2. What is "monopoly power"? Is it a necessary element for a Section 2 action? Why or why not?
3. Is the possession of monopoly power in a relevant market sufficient to prove a violation of Section 2? If not, what else must be shown? Explain.
4. Did the court find that IBM had "willfully acquired or maintained" its monopoly power? What evidence did the court cite to support its decision in this matter?

Policy Issue. Should *monopolies* be outlawed by antitrust law? Or just the *act of monopolizing*, as currently provided in Section 2 of the Sherman Act?

Economics Issue. Was IBM's decision to increase its involvement in the leasing of computers a good corporate decision (e.g., for the "bottom line")?

Ethics Issue. Was it ethical for IBM to reduce the discounts to the companies that were engaged in purchasing used computers from IBM and leasing them to other businesses?

Social Responsibility. Does a corporation owe a duty of social responsibility not to take competitive actions that will harm smaller competitors? If a corporation followed such a practice, would consumers be helped or harmed?

Attempts and Conspiracies to Monopolize. Section 2 of the Sherman Act outlaws "attempts" and "conspiracies" to monopolize. A single firm may be found liable for an attempt to monopolize a relevant market. Proof of an attempt to monopolize requires the showing of a defendant's *specific intent* to exclude competitors and to gain monopoly power. The courts have defined an unlawful attempt to monopolize as

"the employment of methods, means and practices which would, if successful, accomplish monopolization, and which, though falling short, nevertheless approaches so close as to create a dangerous probability of it. . . ."

Section 2 makes it illegal for any person "to conspire with any other person or persons to monopolize. . . . " Two or more firms are required to find an unlawful conspiracy to monopolize. A conspiracy to monopolize charge is seldom brought since the necessary conduct also constitutes the easier-to-prove conspiracy in restraint of trade.

The act of monopolizing in violation of Sherman Act Section 2 has been held to apply to monopoly *buying* power of purchasers ("monopsony power").

Defenses to Monopolization. Courts have recognized two narrow *defenses* to a finding of an act of monopolization under Sherman Act Section 2. The two defenses are: (1) an "innocently acquired" monopoly, and (2) a "thrust upon" monopoly.

"Innocently Acquired" Monopoly. If a monopoly is innocently acquired due to "superior business acumen" or "superior skill, foresight or industry," it is not a violation of the Sherman Act, Section 2. The argument for the "innocently acquired" defense is that no *act* of monopolizing has occurred, and to punish superior business skill would be to condemn the very behavior that the antitrust laws wish to enhance through competition. If an innocently acquired monopoly is later exercised in a "ruthless, predatory, or exclusionary" manner, it will be held to be an act of monopolizing in violation of Section 2.

"Thrust-Upon" Monopoly. Where a monopoly has been "thrust upon" a defendant (i.e., it is natural monopoly such as a utility company) there is no violation of Sherman Act Section 2 because there is no (requisite) purposeful act or conduct. Where the population of an area is so small that it can only support one of a certain type of business (e.g., a small-town newspaper), the "thrust-upon monopoly" defense may be raised against a Section 2 action.

[handwritten notes at top: "read carefully", "#Know", "their monopoly is because they're better at what they do. Monopoly not intentional", "developed a new product wasn't a willfull acquisition of a monopoly"]

SUPERIOR BUSINESS ACUMEN

BERKEY PHOTO, INC. v. EASTMAN KODAK COMPANY

603 F.2d 263 (1979)
UNITED STATES COURT OF APPEALS, SECOND CIRCUIT

Irving R. Kaufman, Chief Judge.

To millions of Americans, the name Kodak is virtually synonymous with photography. Founded over a century ago by George Eastman, the Eastman Kodak Company has long been the preeminent firm in the amateur photographic industry. It provides products and services covering every step in the creation of an enduring photographic record from an evanescent image. Snapshots may be taken with a Kodak camera on Kodak film, developed by Kodak's Color Print and Processing Laboratories, and printed on Kodak photographic paper. The firm has rivals at each stage of this process, but in many of them it stands, and has long stood, dominant. It is one of the giants of American enterprise, with international sales of nearly $6 billion in 1977 and pretax profits in excess of $1.2 billion.

This action, one of the largest and most significant private antitrust suits in history, was brought by Berkey Photo, Inc., a far smaller but still prominent participant in the industry. Berkey competes with Kodak in providing photofinishing services—the conversion of exposed film into finished prints, slides, or movies. Until 1978, Berkey sold cameras as well. It does not manufacture film, but it does purchase Kodak film for resale to its customers, and it also buys photofinishing equipment and supplies, including color print paper, from Kodak.

The two firms thus stand in a complex, multifaceted relationship, for Kodak has been Berkey's competitor in some markets and its supplier in others. In this action, Berkey claims that every aspect of the association has been infected by Kodak's monopoly power in the film, color print paper, and camera markets, willfully acquired, maintained, and exercised in violation of Section 2 of the Sherman Act.

After more than four years of pretrial maneuvering, the trial got under way in July 1977 before Judge Marvin E. Frankel of the Southern District of New York. Despite the daunting complexity of

the case—the exhibits numbered in the thousands—Kodak demanded a jury. Accordingly, the trial was conducted in two parts, one to determine liability and the other to measure damages. It ran continuously, except for a one-month hiatus between the two segments, until the final verdict was rendered on March 22, 1978.

After deliberating for eight days on liability and five on damages, the jury found for Berkey on virtually every point, . . . Trebled and supplemented by attorneys' fees and costs pursuant to Section 4 of the Clayton Act, Berkey's judgment reached a grand total of $87,091,309.47, with interest, of course, continuing to accrue.

The principal markets relevant here, each nationwide in scope, are amateur conventional still cameras, conventional photographic film, photofinishing services, photofinishing equipment, and color print paper.

THE 110 SYSTEM

We commented earlier on the camera revolution sparked by Kodak's introduction of the 126 Instamatic in 1963. Ben Berkey, chairman of Berkey Photo, described the camera's cartridge-loading feature as "fool-proof" and remarked that the new simple system gave the industry "a great boost." Even before the 126 was introduced, however, Kodak had set its sights on a new, smaller line of Instamatic cameras.

Kodak proceeded with its plans for introduction of the 110 system, of which Kodacolor II had become an integral part. On March 16, 1972, amid great fanfare, the system was announced. Finally, said Kodak, there was a "little camera that takes big pictures." Kodacolor II was "a remarkable new film"—indeed, the best color negative film Kodak had ever manufactured.

As Kodak had hoped, the 110 system proved to be a dramatic success. In 1972—the system's first year—the company sold 2,984,000 Pocket Instamatics, more than 50% of its sales in the amateur conventional still camera market. The new camera thus accounted in large part for a sharp increase in total market sales, from 6.2 million units in 1971 to 8.2 million in 1972. Rival manufacturers hastened to market their own 110 cameras, but Kodak stood alone until Argus made its first shipment of the "Carefree 110" around Christmas 1972. The next year, although Kodak's competitors sold over 800,000 110 cameras, Kodak retained a firm lead with 5.1 million. Its share of 110 sales did not fall below 50 percent until 1976. Meanwhile, by 1973 the 110 had taken over most of the amateur market from the 126, and three years later it accounted for nearly four-fifths of all sales.

Berkey's Keystone division was a late entrant in the 110 sweepstakes, joining the competition only in late 1973. Moreover, because of hasty design, the original models suffered from latent defects, and sales that year were a paltry 42,000. With interest in the 126 dwindling, Keystone thus suffered a net decline of 118,000 unit sales in 1973. The following year, however, it recovered strongly, in large part because improvements in its pocket cameras helped it sell 406,000 units, 7 percent of all 110s sold that year.

Berkey contends that the introduction of the 110 system was both an attempt to monopolize and actual monopolization of the camera market. It also alleges that the marketing of the new camera constituted an impermissible leveraging of Kodak's film monopoly into the two photofinishing markets, services and equipment.

PREDISCLOSURE

Through the 1960s, Kodak followed a checkered pattern of predisclosing innovations to various segments of the industry. Its purpose on these occasions evidently was to ensure that the industry would be able to meet consumers' demand for the complementary goods and services they would need to enjoy the new Kodak products. But predisclosure would quite obviously also diminish Kodak's share of the auxiliary markets. It was therefore, in the words of Walter Fallon, Kodak's chief executive officer, "a matter of judgment on each and every occasion" whether predisclosure would be for or against Kodak's self-interest. Thus, well before the 1965 introduction of Super-8 movie films, Kodak,

which had a relatively small share of the movie camera market, provided sufficient information to companies such as Keystone and Bell & Howell to enable them to make cameras to use the new film. It also released processing information so that photofinishers could develop the film. But in 1963, when Kodak came out with Kodacolor X and the 126 Instamatic, it kept its own counsel until the date of introduction.

Withholding from others advance knowledge of one's new products, therefore, ordinarily constitutes valid competitive conduct. Because, as we have already indicated, a monopolist is permitted, and indeed encouraged, by Section 2 to compete aggressively on the merits, any success that it may achieve through "the process of invention and innovation" is clearly tolerated by the antitrust laws. *United Shoe Machinery Corp.*

We do not perceive, however, how Kodak's introduction of a new format was rendered an unlawful act of monopolization in the camera market because the firm also manufactured film to fit the cameras. The 110 system was in substantial part a camera development.

Clearly, then, the policy considerations militating against predisclosure requirements for monolithic monopolists are equally applicable here. The first firm, even a monopolist, to design a new camera format has a right to the lead time that follows from its success. The mere fact that Kodak manufactured film in the new format as well, so that its customers would not be offered worthless cameras, could not deprive it of that reward. Nor is this conclusion altered because Kodak not only participated in but dominated the film market. Kodak's ability to pioneer formats does not depend on it possessing a film monopoly.

SYSTEMS SELLING

Berkey's claims regarding the introduction of the 110 camera are not limited to its asserted right to predisclosure. The Pocket Instamatic not only initiated a new camera format, it was also promoted together with a new film. . . . Berkey contends that this program of selling was anticompetitive and therefore violated Section 2. We disagree.

[A]ny firm, even a monopolist, may generally bring its products to market whenever and however it chooses. Rather, Berkey's argument is more subtle. It claims that by marketing the Pocket Instamatics in a system with a widely advertised new film, Kodak gained camera sales at Berkey's expense.

Even a monopolist, however, must generally be responsive to the demands of customers, for if it persistently markets unappealing goods it will invite a loss of sales and an increase of competition. If a monopolist's products gain acceptance in the market, therefore, it is of no importance that a judge or jury may later regard them as inferior, so long as that success was not based on any form of coercion. Certainly the mere introduction of Kodacolor II along with the Pocket Instamatics did not coerce camera purchasers. Unless consumers desired to use the 110 camera for its own attractive qualities, they were not compelled to purchase Kodacolor II—especially since Kodak did not remove any other films from the market when it introduced the new one. If the availability of Kodacolor II spurred sales of the 110 camera, it did so because some consumers regarded it as superior, at least for the smaller format.

We conclude, therefore, that Kodak did not contravene the Sherman Act merely by introducing Kodacolor II simultaneously with the Pocket Instamatic and advertising the advantages of the new film for taking pictures with a small camera. . . . We, therefore, reverse so much of the judgment as awarded Berkey damages based on the introduction of the 110 camera.

ATTORNEYS' FEES

Under Section 4 of the Clayton Act, the successful plaintiff in a suit for treble damages may be awarded reasonable attorneys' fees. Judge Frankel awarded $5.3 million in counsel fees, calculated essentially on the hourly rate at which counsel agreed to bill their client. . . . But inasmuch as we have reversed the judgment for Berkey on its single most significant claim, and have remanded other claims for a new trial, it is plain that the award of attorneys' fees must be vacated for reconsideration by the district court.

CASE QUESTIONS

1. What was the business relationship between Berkey Photo and Kodak? Explain.
2. What was the 110 camera introduced by Kodak? Was Kodacolor II film an integral part of the camera? Were the camera and film successful?
3. What was the relevant *geographic* market? The relevant *product* markets?
4. Berkey argued that Kodak's failure to predisclose the development of the 110 camera was a willful act of monopolization in violation of Section 2 of the Sherman Act. Did the court agree? Why or why not?
5. Berkey argued that Kodak's "system selling" of the new camera *and* new film together as a system constituted a willful act of monopolization in violation of Section 2. Did the court agree? Why or why not?
6. What does the "superior business acumen" doctrine, also known as the "innocently acquired monopoly" doctrine, provide?

Policy Issue. Should a corporation be allowed to keep the fruits of its superior business acumen? Even if it leads to a monopoly position?

Economics Issue. Was this decision important economically to Kodak? To Berkey Photo? To Berkey's lawyers?

Ethics Issue. Did Berkey Photo act ethically when it sued Kodak in this case?

Social Responsibility. Does a corporation the size of Kodak owe a duty of social responsibility to *predisclose* the specifications of its new products so that smaller companies can produce competing or ancillary products to coincide with the introduction of the new product? Did IBM predisclose the introduction of its personal computer? Why or why not?

Trend of the Law

The economy of the United States has become increasingly more concentrated in recent years. This has particularly been the case during the 1980s, when the government permitted some of the largest mergers in history. Under current statutory language, monopolists who have not engaged in a willful act of monopolization are not considered to have violated Section 2 of the Sherman Act. In view of the intense international competition with American business from large foreign corporations that are often subsidized by their governments, it is highly unlikely that Congress will amend the antitrust laws to outlaw monopolies *per se* in the foreseeable future.

The courts in the future will have to wrestle with the difficult problem of defining those activities which constitute willful acts of *monopolization*. As in the past, the delineation of relevant geographical and product markets at the outset of a lawsuit will continue to be of utmost importance in all monopolization cases brought under Section 2 of the Sherman Act in the future.

REVIEW QUESTIONS

1. In 1961, Grinnell Corporation controlled 87 percent of the national accredited central-station protective-service business (automatic central alarm systems). Each central service station (CSPS) was physically independent from other such stations, operating in delineated spheres with a common radius of about 25 miles. The reason for this independence was twofold: (1) alerted CSPS employees had to be able to reach the scene of an alarm swiftly; and (2) transmitting electronic signals over great distances was expensive. Yet, with respect to its financing, selling, advertising, and overall planning, the enterprise was national in character.

   Grinnell's protective signalling systems were approved by insurance underwriters, which enabled subscribers to Grinnell's systems (and others similarly approved) to obtain premium discounts on fire and burglary insurance. Grinnell faced competition from 33 other approved CSPS companies: seven operated in cities with no CSPS competition, 23 operated in cities where they competed against Grinnell CSPS systems; and three operated in cities where there was CSPS competition, but not from Grinnell. In a suit by the United States against Grinnell Corporation for violation of Section 2 of the Sherman Act, what would the relevant market analysis look like? Is there a relevant product market? A relevant geographic market? What additional factors might the government look to?

2. The Aluminum Company of America (Alcoa), through the use of patents and exclusive licenses for smelting and other aluminum manufacturing processes, initially achieved a dominant position in the U.S. aluminum industry.

By the time these licenses had expired in the early 1900s, Alcoa controlled 66 percent of the domestic aluminum market. This control gradually increased; by 1938 Alcoa produced over 90 percent of the "virgin" ingots in the United States and only faced competition from foreign producers of "secondary" ingots. Alcoa could effectively deal with this foreign competition, however, both by fixing its prices and by restricting or expanding its production volume—by simply anticipating changes in ingot demand. At no time did Alcoa consciously attempt to exclude competitors from the aluminum market; it merely followed good business practices to continue the successes it had initially achieved as a result of its patents and licenses. Is Alcoa guilty of monopolization under Section 2 of the Sherman Act?

3. Four affiliated corporations had controlling interests in movie theatres in 85 towns in Oklahoma, Texas, and New Mexico. In 32 of the towns there were competing theaters; the remaining 53 towns were "closed" towns— towns without competing theaters. The corporations used their market dominance to exact exclusive privileges from film distributors who feared losing the bulk of their market outlets. The distributors had to lease films for the entire theater chain at a discount price. Furthermore, the agreements stipulated that the corporations' movie houses could play films out of the order of their release and could restrict the availability of first-run films to the towns with competing theater operators. Does the use of the corporations' market dominance to obtain these concessions from the film distributors violate Section 2 of the Sherman Act? In making your decision, how much of a factor is the "specific intent" of the corporations?

4. In the early 1950s, United Shoe Machinery Corporation was the primary producer of the machines required to produce shoes, controlling 75–85 percent of the domestic shoe machinery business. United Shoe obtained its position in an innocent fashion, simply by using good business practices: constantly improving its machinery, obtaining patents on these improvements, and providing machines with free repair service for every step of the shoemaking process. Gradually, however, United's business practices became geared toward protecting its market position. It leased its major machines for ten-year periods, giving favorable terms if the machines were kept until the end of the period or if they were replaced by United machines. Those machines that the company sold were offered on a sliding price scale, depending upon whether United faced competition in the manufacture of the individual product. (If it did, United's profit margin was low; if not it was high). Lastly, the firm offered free repair service on its machines, which effectively precluded the development of independent service organizations to repair United's complex machinery. Any other firms which wanted to enter the shoemaking business had to offer a free repair service, which was prohibitively expensive. In a suit by the Justice Department against United, will United be found guilty of monopolization despite the fact that it obtained its market power by legitimate practices?

5. Prior to 1948, the *Lorain Journal* was the only newspaper in Lorain, Ohio. As such, the newspaper was able to substantially monopolize the mass dissemination of news and advertising in Lorain. In 1948, WEOL, a radio station, was licensed to establish and operate in a town eight miles south of Lorain. Many of the local town merchants decided to supplement their

local newspaper advertising with local radio advertising. The *Journal* responded by denying advertising space to those who advertised on WEOL. Since local Lorain advertising was WEOL's greatest source of potential income, the *Journal's* actions threatened the radio station's existence. Did the *Lorain Journal's* actions violate the "attempt to monopolize" clause of Section 2 of the Sherman Act?

6. The *Haverhill Gazette* was the only newspaper in Haverhill, New Hampshire. The city was so small that it was not economically feasible to publish more than one newspaper. When the *Gazette* suffered labor difficulties, several local retailers asked the Union Leader Corporation, which published the only newspaper in nearby Manchester, New Hampshire, to have the *Gazette* publish a throwaway "shopper" containing advertisements. Instead, Union Leader began publishing a regular daily paper called the *Haverhill Journal.* In doing so, Union Leader refused to sell advertising in the *Journal* to those who advertised in the *Gazette.* Furthermore, the *Journal* gave "secret" preferential rates to some subscribers and made cash payments to certain Haverhill businessmen if they would help make the *Journal* become the only newspaper in Haverhill. The *Journal* attempted to buy the *Gazette* but was unsuccessful. The *Gazette* was later purchased by a consortium of New England publishers. Did Union Leader Corporation violate Section 2 of the Sherman Act? If so, why?

7. Eastman Kodak Co. was purchasing photo supply stores throughout the Southeastern United States. The firm offered to purchase Southern Photo Material's Atlanta store. When Southern Photo refused, Kodak immediately stopped doing business with the firm. Since Kodak controlled a large portion of the camera-supply and film-distribution business in the United States, Southern's business dropped appreciably. Southern sued in federal District Court, alleging that Kodak was attempting to monopolize the photo-supply business. Was Kodak's refusal to deal with Southern lawful?

8. Food Machinery and Chemical Corporation (FMCC) obtained a patent on a sewage treatment device known as a "knee action swing diffuser." FMCC subsequently brought a patent infringement action against Walker Process Equipment. As its defense, Walker claimed that FMCC obtained its patent by intentionally misrepresenting the facts of its invention to the Patent Office. Walker maintained that such conduct stripped FMCC of its exemption from the antitrust laws and rendered it liable for treble damages under Section 2 of the Sherman Act and Section 4 of the Clayton Act. Is the fraudulent procurement of a patent sufficient grounds for a private antitrust damage action?

9. Otter Tail Power Company had a natural monopoly on electric power. In the geographic area which it serviced, it "wheeled" electric power to 465 of 510 towns, or 91 percent of the market. When Otter Tail's franchises in four cities that it serviced—Elbow Lake, Minnesota; Hankinson, North Dakota; Colman, South Dakota; and Aurora, South Dakota—terminated, those cities voted to establish their own municipal distribution systems. Otter Tail responded by either refusing to sell energy at wholesale prices to the proposed municipal systems or by refusing to provide any power at all. Otter Tail also instituted litigation to delay municipal ownership and invoked provisions in its contracts with other power suppliers that denied

the municipal systems any access to those suppliers through Otter Tail's transmission systems. In a suit against Otter Tail for violation of the "attempt to monopolize" clause of Section 2 of the Sherman Act, how persuasive will Otter Tail's argument be that its actions were permissible in defense of its natural monopoly?

9 RESTRAINTS OF TRADE

INTRODUCTION

The Sherman Act of 1890 has been characterized by the Supreme Court in *Appalachian Coals, Inc. v. United States,* 288 U.S. 344 (1933), as "a charter of freedom." For almost 90 years it has provided an incentive for robust and free competition in the United States. The most frequently invoked section of the Act is Section 1, which provides:

[handwritten: at least 2 businesses + an agreement]

[handwritten: know]

Every contract, combination in the form of trust or otherwise, or conspiracy in restraint of trade or commerce among the several states, or with foreign nations is declared to be illegal.

Section 1 of the Sherman Act only applies to conduct by *two or more* parties. The concept of *agreement* is critical to a Section 1 cause of action. Generally, in order for there to be a violation of Sherman Act Section 1, at least *two* parties must enter into an agreement to restrain trade. In many situations the evidence of an agreement may be circumstantial. Lacking evidence of an express agreement, whether written or oral, the courts can infer an agreement from the action of the defendants.

[handwritten: (winter) Don't take this literally... still used Some essence of proof.]

Section 1 not only prohibits agreements in restraint of trade, but also prohibits conspiracies or combinations in restraint of trade. A conspiracy in violation of antitrust law usually consists of an agreement between or among two or more business entities. The courts have held that a parent and a subsidiary, or two or more subsidiaries, may conspire in violation of Section 1. The courts have recently given the concept of *combination* an expanded and independent definition different from the term *agreement*. The term *combination* brings within the ambit of the Section 1 fact situations where defendants merely knowingly acquiesce to an illegal restraint of trade.

When examining restraints of trade under Section 1 of the Sherman Act, it must be determined, first, whether the restraint being examined is a "horizontal" or "vertical" restraint, and second, whether the "rule of reason" or the *per se* standard should be applied in the analysis.

RESTRAINTS OF TRADE

There are two types of restraints of trade that are prohibited under Section 1 of the Sherman Act, (1) *horizontal* restraints of trade, and (2) *vertical* restraints of trade.

Horizontal Restraints of Trade. Horizontal restraints occur where two or more competitors at the same level of distribution enter into a contract, combination, or conspiracy to restrain trade. For example, where two or more manufacturers agree with each other to set the prices at which they will sell their similar products (e.g., automobiles) to wholesalers, there is an illegal *horizontal* restraint of trade because the agreeing manufacturers are all *competitors* at the same level of distribution.

Vertical Restraints of Trade. A vertical restraint of trade occurs where two or more parties at different levels of distribution enter into a contract, combination, or conspiracy to restrain trade. For example, where a manufacturer and a number of wholesalers agree to divide a market into separate geographical areas, assign a separate geographical territory to each wholesaler, and agree that no wholesaler can sell products to any customers located in another wholesaler's territory, there is an illegal *vertical* restraint of trade between the manufacturer and each wholesaler. This is because the illegal agreement was between parties who are not competitors, namely the manufacturer and each wholesaler. In this example, the wholesalers who have commonly agreed to the division of markets may also be guilty of a horizontal restraint of trade among themselves.

The Rule-of-Reason and *Per Se* Rules. In the landmark case *Standard Oil Co. v. United States*, 221 U.S. 1 (1911), the U.S. Supreme Court held that contracts or conspiracies were illegal under Section 1 of the Sherman Act only if the restraint was "unreasonable." Thus, any restraint that is found to be "reasonable" is lawful under Section 1. Two different standards have been developed by the courts to examine "restraints of trade" under Section 1 of the Sherman Act:

1. the "rule of reason"
2. the *per se* rule.

prove occurance + effect had an anti

The "Rule of Reason" Standard.   Under the "rule of reason" standard, the court must consider and balance the *procompetitive* and *anticompetitive* effects of the restraint. Obviously, courts want to encourage rather than discourage competition. In applying the "rule of reason" standard the court may consider such factors as the restraint's impact on competition, structure of the industry (competitive or concentrated), the firm's market power and position in the industry, the history and duration of the restraint, and the reasons for the adoption of the restraint. Not all effects or consequences of the restraint must be weighed by the court. The inquiry of the court must be sufficient to warrant the conclusion that the restraint is either *reasonable* and therefore lawful, or *unreasonable* and therefore illegal under Section 1 of the Sherman Act.

The U.S. Supreme Court has recently affirmed the "rule of reason" standard for examining antitrust violations of the Sherman Act. In *National Society of Professional Engineers v. United States*, 435 U.S. 679 (1978), Justice Stevens stated:

The test prescribed in *Standard Oil* is whether the challenged contracts or acts "were unreasonably restrictive of competitive conditions." Unreasonableness under that test could be based either (1) on the nature or character of the contracts, or (2) on surrounding circumstances giving rise to the inference or presumption that they were intended to restrain trade and enhance prices. Under either branch of the test, the inquiry is confined to a consideration of impact on competitive conditions.

In this respect the rule of reason has remained faithful to its origins. From Justice Brandeis' opinion for the Court in *Chicago Board of Trade*, to the Court opinion authored by Justice Powell in *Continental T.V., Inc.*, the Court has adhered to the position that the inquiry mandated by the rule of reason is whether the challenged agreement is one that promoted competition or one that suppresses competition. The true test of legality is whether the restraint imposed is such as merely regulates and perhaps thereby promote competition or whether it is such as may suppress or even destroy competition.

Plaintiff has to show certain activity "occurred" not that it has a detrimental affect

Easier to prove

The "Per Se" Rule.   In some circumstances the courts have determined that an activity is so unreasonable as a matter of *law* that it is held to be illegal *per se.* In these *per se* areas, the only problem is one of "characterization." Once the restraint has been found and characterized as a *per se* violation of Section 1, no justification or defense for the restraint is allowed. In *Northern Pacific R.R. Co. v. United States* 356 U.S. 1 (1958), Justice Clark explained the appropriateness and need for *per se* rules:

[T]here are certain agreements or practices which because of their pernicious effect on competition and lack of any redeeming virtue are conclusively presumed to be unreasonable and therefore illegal without elaborate inquiry as to the precise harm they have caused or the business excuse for their use. This principle of *per se* unreasonableness not only makes the type of restraints which are proscribed by the Sherman

Act more certain to the benefit of everyone concerned, but it also avoids the necessity for an incredibly complicated and prolonged economic investigation into the entire history of the industry involved, as well as related industries, in an effort to determine at large whether a particular restraint has been unreasonable—an inquiry so often wholly fruitless when undertaken.

In *Arizona v. Maricopa County Medical Society*, 457 U.S. 332 (1982), the U.S. Supreme Court recently affirmed the use of the *per se* rule to find certain activities illegal restraints of trade in violation of Section 1 of the Sherman Act. In that case Justice Stevens wrote in the opinion of the court:

The elaborate inquiry into the reasonableness of a challenged business practice entails significant costs. Litigation of the effect or purpose of a practice often is extensive and complex. Judges often lack the expert understanding of industrial market structures and behavior to determine with any confidence a practice's effect on competition. And the result of the process in any given case may provide little certainty or guidance about the legality of a practice in another context.

The costs of judging business practices under the rule of reason, however, have been reduced by the recognition of *per se* rules. Once experience with a particular kind of restraint enables the Court to predict with confidence that the rule of reason will condemn it, it has applied a conclusive presumption that the restraint is unreasonable. As in every rule of general application, the match between the presumed and the actual is imperfect. For the sake of business certainty and litigation efficiency, we have tolerated the invalidation of some agreements that a fullblown inquiry might have proved to be reasonable.

HORIZONTAL *PER SE* RESTRAINTS OF TRADE

The following three types of *horizontal* restraints are considered *per se* violations of the Sherman Act, Section 1:

1. price fixing
2. division of markets
3. group boycotts.

Price Fixing. Where competitors fix the prices of the goods or services they sell, thus eliminating price competition among themselves, it is an unreasonable horizontal restraint of trade and a *per se* violation of Section 1 of the Sherman Act. No defenses or justifications of any kind (e.g., the price is "reasonable," the fixing protects the parties from "ruinous competition") are recognized where price fixing is shown. The reasoning behind the *per se* rule against price fixing is that the actual or potential threat to the economic system of such agreements overshadows any justification for them. A party may be held liable for price fixing even if he does not have the power to influence price in the marketplace.

Price fixing has been defined as the "raising, depressing, fixing, pegging, or stabilizing" of the price of a commodity or service. The courts have applied an expansive definition of price fixing. This clearly includes setting *minimum* prices. The courts have also held that price fixing includes setting (maximum) prices, on the argument that maximum prices tend to "stabilize" prices and cause a distortion of the allocation of resources in society. Agreements to limit the quantity of a commodity or service to be produced have also been held to be price fixing, on the theory that a limitation of quantity tends to increase price. An agreement among *purchasers* to limit the price they will offer for a commodity or service is price fixing.

"List prices" and "suggested retail prices" have generally been held *not* to violate antitrust laws, in that such prices are usually negotiable. Government-regulated industries (e.g., railroads, banks) are generally permitted to fix prices and rates without violating Section 1 of the Sherman Act.

In *Arizona v. Maricopa County Medical Society* the U. S. Supreme Court characterized a maximum fee schedule as "price fixing," and held it to be a horizontal restraint of trade and *per se* violation of section 1 of the Sherman Act.

PRICE FIXING

ARIZONA v. MARICOPA COUNTY MEDICAL SOCIETY

U.S. 457 (1982) 332
UNITED STATES SUPREME COURT

Justice Stevens delivered the opinion of the Court.

The question presented is whether Section 1 of the Sherman Act has been violated by an agreement among competing physicians setting, by majority vote, the maximum fees that they may claim in full payment for health services provided to policyholders of specified insurance plans. The United States Court of Appeals for the Ninth Circuit held that the question could not be answered without [applying the Rule of Reason test and] evaluating the actual purpose and effect of the agreement at a full trial.

The Maricopa Foundation for Medical Care is a nonprofit Arizona corporation composed of licensed doctors of medicine, osteopathy, and podiatry engaged in private practice. Approximately 1,750 doctors, representing about 70 percent of the practitioners in Maricopa County, are members. . . . The foundation . . . establishes the schedule of maximum fees that participating doctors agree to accept as payment in full for services performed for patients insured under plans approved by the foundation. . . . [T]he foundation is considered an "insurance administrator" by the Director of the Arizona Department of Insurance. Its participating doctors, however, have no financial interest in the operation of the foundation.

The impact of the foundation fee schedules on medical fees and on insurance premiums is a matter of dispute. The State of Arizona contends that the periodic upward revisions of the maximum fee schedules have the effect of stabilizing and enhancing the level of actual charges by physicians, and that the increasing level of their fees in turn increases insurance premiums. The foundations, on the other hand, argue that the schedules impose a meaningful limit on physicians' charges, and that the advance agreement by the doctors to accept the maxima enables the insurance carriers to limit and to calculate more efficiently the risks they underwrite and therefore serves as an effective cost containment mechanism that has saved patients and insurers millions of dollars.

The respondents recognize that our decisions establish that price fixing agreements are unlawful on their face. But they argue that the *per se* rule does not govern this case because the agreements

→ still violates act just as bad as minimum prices

at issue are horizontal and fix maximum prices, are among members of a profession, are in an industry with which the judiciary has little antitrust experience, and are alleged to have procompetitive justifications.

We are . . . unpersuaded by the argument that we should not apply the *per se* rule in this case because the judiciary has little antitrust experience in the health care industry. In unequivocal terms, we stated that, ''[w]hatever may be its peculiar problems and characteristics, the Sherman Act, so far as price-fixing agreements are concerned, establishes one uniform rule applicable to all industries alike.'' *Socony-Vacuum.* We also stated that ''[t]he elimination of so-called competitive evils [in an industry] is no legal justification'' for price fixing agreements, yet the Court of Appeals refused to apply the *per se* rule in this case in part because the health care industry was so far removed from the competitive model. Consistent with our prediction in *Socony-Vacuum,* the result of this reasoning was the adoption by the Court of Appeals of a legal standard based on the reasonableness of the fixed prices, an inquiry we have so often condemned.

The respondents' principal argument is that the *per se* rule is inapplicable because their agreements are alleged to have procompetitive justifications. The argument indicates a misunderstanding of the *per se* concept. The anticompetitive potential inherent in all price-fixing agreements justifies their facial invalidation even if procompetitive justifications are offered for some. Those claims of enhanced competition are so unlikely to prove significant in any particular case that we adhere to the rule of law that is justified in its general application. Even when the respondents are given every benefit of the doubt, the limited record in this case is not inconsistent with the presumption that the respondents' agreements will not significantly enhance competition.

Our adherence to the *per se* rule is grounded not only on economic prediction, judicial convenience, and business certainty, but also on a recognition of the respective roles of the Judiciary and the Congress in regulating the economy. Given its generality, our enforcement of the Sherman Act has required the Court to provide much of its substantive content. By articulating the rules of law with

some clarity and by adhering to rules that are justified in their general application, however, we enhance the legislative prerogative to amend the law. The respondents' arguments against application of the *per se* rule in this case therefore are better directed to the legislature. Congress may consider the exception that we are not free to read into the statute.

[T]he fee agreements disclosed by the record in this case are among independent competing entrepreneurs. They fit squarely into the horizontal price-fixing mold.

The judgment of the Court of Appeals is *reversed.*

CASE QUESTIONS

1. What did the defendant's fee schedule provide? Who enforced the fee schedule?
2. What is the difference between the following tests? Which one did the Supreme Court apply in this case?
   a. rule of reason test
   b. *per se* test
3. What is *price fixing?* Are any defenses or justifications (e.g., procompetitive effects) allowed once an activity has been characterized as ''price fixing''?

Policy Issue. Were *per se* rules contemplated when Congress enacted the Sherman Act in 1890? Who developed *per se* rules? Do *per se* rules serve any useful purpose? Or do they merely help lazy judges?

Economics Issue. Why is the setting of *maximum* prices considered price fixing? Do maximum prices help or hurt consumers? Explain.

Ethics Issue. Was it ethical for the doctors to argue that the court should apply a rule of reason analysis because the judiciary has ''little antitrust experience''? Does this argument actually support the use of *per se* rules?

Social Responsibility. Do doctors owe a duty of social responsibility to engage in free competition in providing medical services to the public? Or does concerted action such as setting maximum prices help consumers?

Division of Markets. An agreement among competitors to *divide* a market and each exclusively serve a portion of the market is a horizontal restraint of trade in violation of Section 1 of the Sherman Act. Division of markets, also commonly known as "market sharing," may be of at least three types, with competitors dividing the relevant market by (1) geographical territories, (2) individual customers, or (3) the selling of specific products.

Market sharing is a *per se* violation of Section 1, based on the theory that when competitors agree to divide a market and not sell in each other's territory, they effectively create small "monopolies." The *per se* rule against "division of markets" applies to both direct and indirect market-sharing arrangements. No defenses or justifications for market sharing are recognized under the *per se* rule.

In *intra*brand competition, more than one party sells the same product in a market. In *inter*brand competition, several similar products are sold in the same market. Market-sharing agreements generally reduce the *intra*brand competition of a product. Criticism has been leveled at the *per se* rule against the division of markets because the courts fail to balance the loss of *intra*brand competition against the possible increase in *inter*brand competition that may be created through a market sharing agreement.

In the landmark antitrust case *United States v. Topco Associates, Inc.* the U.S. Supreme Court was called upon to apply the *per se* rule against market sharing, by both territories and customers, to a very difficult fact situation.

[handwritten: ✱ Classify cases as horizontal vs. vertical Per se. or rule of reason]

[handwritten: horizontal, division of market, (can't be justified) per se rule]

MARKET SHARING

UNITED STATES v. TOPCO ASSOCIATES, INC.

405 U.S. 596 (1972)
UNITED STATES SUPREME COURT

Mr. Justice Marshall delivered the opinion of the Court.

The United States brought this action for injunctive relief against alleged violation by Topco Associates, Inc. (Topco), of Section 1 of the Sherman Act, as amended. Following a trial on the merits, the United States District Court for the Northern District of Illinois entered judgment for Topco, and the United States appealed directly to this Court pursuant to Section 2 of the Expediting Act. We noted probable jurisdiction.

Topco is a cooperative association of approximately 25 small and medium-sized regional supermarket chains that operate stores in some 33 States. Each of the member chains operates independently; there is no pooling of earnings, profits, capital, management, or advertising resources. No grocery business is conducted under the Topco name. Its basic function is to serve as a purchasing agent for its members. In this capacity, it procures and distributes to the members more than 1,000 different food and related nonfood items, most of which are distributed under brand names owned by Topco. The association does not itself own any manufacturing, processing, or warehousing facilities, and the items that it procures for members are usually shipped directly from the packer or manufacturer to the members. Payment is made either to Topco or directly to the manufacturer. . . .

Topco was founded in the 1940s by a group of small, local grocery chains, independently owned and operated, that desired to cooperate to obtain high quality merchandise under private labels in order to compete more effectively with larger national and regional chains. . . . Although only 10 percent of the total goods sold by Topco members bear the association's brand names, the profit on these goods is substantial and their very existence has improved the competitive potential of Topco members with respect to other large and powerful chains.

Membership [in Topco] must first be approved by the board of directors, and thereafter by an affirmative vote of 75 percent of the association's members. . . . Following approval, each new member signs an agreement with Topco designating the territory in which that member may sell Topco-brand products. No member may sell these products outside the territory in which it is licensed. Most licenses are exclusive, and even those denominated "coextensive" or "nonexclusive" prove to be *de facto* exclusive. . . . When combined with each member's veto power over new members, provisions for exclusivity work effectively to insulate members from competition in Topco-brand goods. Should a member violate its license agreement and sell in areas other than those in which it is licensed, its membership can be terminated.

The Government maintains that this scheme of dividing markets violates the Sherman Act because it operates to prohibit competition in Topco-brand products among grocery chains engaged in retail operations.

Topco essentially maintains that it needs territorial divisions to compete with larger chains; that the association could not exist if the territorial divisions were anything but exclusive; and that by restricting competition in the sale of Topco-brand goods, the association actually increases competition by enabling its members to compete successfully with larger regional and national chains.

The District Court, considering all these things relevant to its decision, agreed with Topco. . . . The court held that Topco's practices were procompetitive and, therefore, consistent with the purposes of the antitrust laws. But we conclude that the District Court used an improper analysis in reaching its result.

While the Court has utilized the "rule of reason" in evaluating the legality of most restraints alleged to be violative of the Sherman Act, it has also devel-

oped the doctrine that certain business relationships are *per se* violations of the Act without regard to a consideration of their reasonableness.

It is only after considerable experience with certain business relationships that courts classify them as *per se* violations of the Sherman Act. One of the classic examples of a *per se* violation of Section 1 is an agreement between competitors at the same level of the market structure to allocate territories in order to minimize competition. Such concerted action is usually termed a "horizontal" restraint, in contradistinction to combinations of persons at different levels of the market structure, e.g., manufacturers and distributors, which are termed "vertical" restraints. This Court has reiterated time and time again that "[h]orizontal territorial limitations . . . are naked restraints of trade with no purpose except stifling of competition." *White Motor Co. v. United States.* Such limitations are *per se* violations of the Sherman Act.

We think that it is clear that the restraint in this case is a horizontal one, and, therefore, a *per se* violation of Section 1. Without territorial restrictions, Topco members may indeed "[cut] each other's throats." But, we have never found this possibility sufficient to warrant condoning horizontal restraints of trade.

We also strike down Topco's other restrictions. . . . These restrictions amount to regulation of the customers to whom members of Topco may sell Topco-brand goods. Like territorial restrictions, limitations on customers are intended to limit intrabrand competition. . . .

We *reverse* the judgment of the District Court and *remand* the case for entry of an appropriate decree.

CASE QUESTIONS

1. What is "market sharing"? Were Topco members granted exclusive *geographical* territories in this case?
2. Could Topco members sell Topco products outside their assigned geographical territory? If they could have, would this case have been decided differently? Explain.
3. Did the Supreme Court consider the alleged *procompetitive* effects of the Topco arrangement? Why or why not?

4. Was the *customer* assignment practiced by Topco a form of market sharing in violation of Section 1? Why or why not?

Policy Issue. If one large corporation were to buy all of the individual Topco members, could it then set a single price for each Topco product sold by its many outlets? Is this rule fair when it could not be accomplished by the many small firms in this case?

Economics Issue. Did the Topco arrangement have any *pro*competitive effects? If so, what were they? Will the Topco members "cut each other's throats" after this decision?

Ethics Issue. Was it ethical for the government to sue the many small "mom-and-pop" grocery stores in this case who were only trying to compete with large chain stores?

Social Responsibility. Does the government owe a duty of social responsibility to assist small businesses to compete with large corporations?

Group Boycotts. Where two or more competitors, as a group, agree not to deal with another firm, there is a combination or agreement in restraint of trade that violates Section 1 of the Sherman Act. For example, an express agreement among competitors not to deal with some other individual or firm is an obvious example of a prohibited group boycott. *Group boycotts,* also known as "refusals to deal," include agreements among competitors to deal with others only on certain terms (e.g., credit terms), and agreements among competitors to coerce other parties (suppliers or customers) not to deal with some third party.

A group boycott is an unreasonable restraint of trade and *per se* violation of Section 1 of the Sherman Act. Courts are more lenient in characterizing agreements as group boycotts. Therefore, the *per se* rule against group boycotts has been called a "soft" *per se* rule.

In *Fashion Originators' Guild of America, Inc. v. Federal Trade Commission* the Supreme Court characterized the activities of competing clothing designers and manufacturers as a "group boycott" against clothing retailers and a *per se* violation of Section 1 of the Sherman Act.

GROUP BOYCOTTS

**FASHION ORIGINATORS' GUILD OF AMERICA, INC.
v. FEDERAL TRADE COMMISSION**

*312 U.S. 457 (1941)
UNITED STATES SUPREME COURT*

Mr. Justice Black delivered the opinion of the Court.

Some of the members of the combination design, manufacture, sell and distribute women's garments—chiefly dresses. Others are manufacturers, converters, or dyers of textiles from which these garments are made. Fashion Originators' Guild of America (FOGA), an organization controlled by these groups. . . . The garment manufacturers claim to be creators of original and distinctive designs of fashionable clothes for women, and the textile manufacturers claim to be creators of similar original fabric designs. After these designs enter the channels of trade, other manufacturers systematically make and sell copies of them, the copies usually selling at prices lower than the garments copied. Petitioners call this practice of copying unethical and immoral, and give it the name of "style piracy."

[B]ecause of these alleged wrongs, petitioners, while continuing to compete with one another in many respects, combined among themselves to combat and, if possible, destroy all competition from the sale of garments which are copies of their "original creations." They admit that to destroy such competition they have in combination purposely boycotted and declined to sell their products to retailers who follow a policy of selling garments copied by other manufacturers from designs put out by Guild members. As a result of their efforts, approximately 12,000 retailers throughout the country have signed agreements to "cooperate" with the Guild's boycott program, but more than half of these signed the agreements only because constrained by threats that Guild members would not sell to retailers who failed to yield to their demands—threats that have been carried out by the Guild practice of placing on red cards the names of noncooperators (to whom no sales are to be made), placing on white cards the names of cooperators (to whom sales are to be made), and then distributing both sets of cards to the manufacturers.

The 176 manufacturers of women's garments who are members of the Guild occupy a commanding position in their line of business. In 1936, they sold in the United States more than 38 percent of all women's garments wholesaling at $6.75 and up, and more than 60 percent of those at $10.75 and above. The power of the combination is great; competition and the demand of the consuming public make it necessary for most retail dealers to stock some of the products of these manufacturers.

The Guild maintains a Design Registration Bureau for garments, and the Textile Federation maintains a similar Bureau for textiles. The Guild employs "shoppers" to visit the stores of both cooperating and noncooperating retailers, "for the purpose of examining their stocks, to determine and report as to whether they contain . . . copies of registered designs . . ." An elaborate system of trial and appellate tribunals exists, for the determination of whether a given garment is in fact a copy of a Guild member's design. In order to assure the success of its plan of registration and restraint, and to ascertain whether Guild regulations are being violated, the Guild audits its members' books. And if violations of Guild requirements are discovered, as, for example, sales to red-carded retailers, the violators are subject to heavy fines.

[T]he findings of the [Federal Trade] Commission bring petitioners' combination in its entirety well within the inhibition of the policies declared by [Section 1 of] the Sherman Act itself. . . .

[A]mong the many respects in which the Guild's plan runs contrary to the policy of the Sherman Act are these: it narrows the outlets to which garment and textile manufacturers can sell and the sources from which retailers can buy; subjects all retailers and manufacturers who decline to comply with the Guild's program to an organized boycott; takes away the freedom of action of members by requiring each to reveal to the Guild the intimate details of their individual affairs; and has both as its necessary tendency and as its purpose and effect the direct suppression of competition from the sale of unregistered textiles and copied designs. In addition to all this, the combination is in reality an extragovernmental agency, which prescribes rules for the regulation and restraint of interstate commerce, and provides extrajudicial tribunals for determination and punishment of violations, and thus "trenches upon the power of the national legislature and violates the statute."

But petitioners further argue that their boycott and restraint of interstate trade is not within the ban of the policies of the Sherman [Act] . . . because "the practices of FOGA were reasonable and necessary to protect the manufacturer, laborer, retailer and consumer against the devastating evils growing from the pirating of original designs and had in fact benefited all four." The Commission declined to hear much of the evidence that petitioners desired to offer on this subject. As we have pointed out, however, the aim of petitioners' combination was the intentional destruction of one type of manufacture and sale which competed with Guild members. The purpose and object of this combination, its potential power, its tendency to monopoly, the coercion it could and did practice upon a rival method of competition, all brought it within the policy of the prohibition declared by the Sherman [Act]. . . .

Under these circumstances it was not error to refuse to hear the evidence offered, for the reasonableness of the methods pursued by the combination to accomplish its unlawful object is no more material than would be the reasonableness of the prices fixed by unlawful combination. Nor can the unlawful combination be justified upon the argument that systematic copying of dress designs is itself tortious, or should now be declared so by us. In the first place, whether or not given conduct is tortious is a question of state law,. . . . In the second place, even if copying were an acknowledged tort under the law of every state, that situation would not justify petitioners in combining together to regulate and restrain interstate commerce in violation of federal law.

The decision below is accordingly *affirmed*.

CASE QUESTIONS

1. How did the boycott in this case work? What were the *horizontal* aspects of the boycott?

2. Who was being boycotted in this case? The style pirates? Or someone else?

3. How was the boycott policed? Would the boycott have worked without an effective system of policing?

4. Did the reason for the group boycott in this case matter to the Supreme Court? Why or why not?

Policy Issue. Should group boycotts be *per se* violations of Section 1 of the Sherman Act? Do you think the defendants were justified in using the group boycott in this case?

Economics Issue. What were the economic consequences of this decision on the FOGA members? On the style pirates? On consumers?

Ethics Issue. Did the style pirates act ethically in this case? Did the FOGA members act ethically in this case? Who acted more unethically?

Social Responsibility. Do innocent business persons owe a duty of social responsibility not to act illegally, even to combat illegal conduct by competitors? Are honest business persons at a disadvantage under our legal system?

HORIZONTAL RESTRAINTS OF TRADE AND THE "RULE OF REASON"

If a horizontal restraint cannot be characterized as one of the previously covered *per se* violations, then the restraint will be examined by the courts using the "rule-of-reason" test. Under the rule-of-reason test, the pro- and anticompetitive effects of the restraint will be analyzed and balanced by the courts to determine whether the restraint is "reasonable," and therefore lawful, or "unreasonable," and therefore illegal under Section 1 of the Sherman Act. Some of the types of restraints that are examined under the rule of reason test are most trade association activities, self-regulation by industries, and joint ventures.

Trade Association Activities. Most dissemination or exchange of information among competitors occurs under the auspices of a trade association. Trade associations are generally formed with the purpose of promoting a certain industry and its members. An important tool in accomplishing this goal is the dissemination and exchange of information among its members. Certain exchanges of information between competitors have been held to be restraints of trade in violation of Section 1 of the Sherman Act. Dissemination of information among competitors is examined by the use of the "rule of reason" test.

Exchange of information among competitors regarding *prices charged* is very suspect, and is usually held to violate Section 1. Where the price information exchanged consists of information regarding either current or future prices (as opposed to past prices), identifies actual buyers, or occurs in a highly concentrated or oligopolistic market structure, courts have generally held such exchange of price information to be unlawful. The rationale is that competition in price is a cornerstone of a purely competitive society, and that exchange of price information may have an anticompetitive effect.

When only average costs, freight rates, and terms of past transactions are exchanged, and there is no mention of individual purchasers, courts usually hold such dissemination of information to be lawful.

When information other than price (e.g., credit background of customers, quantity sold, advertising costs) is exchanged, courts are less likely to find a violation of Section 1 under the "rule of reason" test. If the exchange of *nonprice* information is found to lessen or suppress competition, to assist in policing a cartel, or to facilitate interrelated and interdependent pricing, then it is held to be a restraint of trade in violation of the Sherman Act, Section 1.

Self-Regulation. Trade associations and their members consistently try to regulate the activities of members by either self-imposed regulations or adherence to longstanding traditions. Almost all such "self-regulation" has some anticompetitive effect. Courts are generally hostile toward private lawmaking. Where self-regulation by trade associations "suppresses or destroys" competition, it is an unreasonable restraint of trade in violation of the Sherman Act, Section 1. Reasonable restraints caused by self-regulation are allowed under the "rule of reason" test.

Joint Ventures. In a joint venture, two or more separate business entities enter into an agreement to accomplish some joint purpose of limited scope and duration, such as a construction project or joint research. A joint venture is not a merger of the firms, but only a contractual arrangement. Although a joint venture is usually known by an individual name, each participant of the joint venture retains its identity, as either a shareholder or partner in the joint venture.

Joint ventures are usually examined for their antitrust effects by using the "rule of reason" test. The purpose and effect of the joint venture will be analyzed to see if the restraint on competition is necessary (i.e., the project is too large or complicated for one firm to complete alone), or whether some less restrictive alternative is available. The structure of the industry (oligopolistic versus competitive) and the size of the participants in the joint venture are important factors in analyzing a joint venture for possible violation of Sherman Act Section 1.

In *National Society of Professional Engineers v. United States* the "rule of reason" test was applied by the Supreme Court in finding a certain trade association activity of engineers to be a restraint of trade in violation of Section 1 of the Sherman Act.

THE "RULE OF REASON"

NATIONAL SOCIETY OF PROFESSIONAL ENGINEERS v. UNITED STATES

435 U.S. 679 (1978)
UNITED STATES SUPREME COURT

Mr. Justice Stevens delivered the opinion of the Court.

This is a civil antitrust case brought by the United States to nullify an association's canon of ethics prohibiting competitive bidding by its members. The question is whether the canon may be justified under the Sherman Act, Section 1, because it was adopted by members of a learned profession for the purpose of minimizing the risk that competition would produce inferior engineering work endangering the public safety. The District Court rejected this justification without making any findings on the likelihood that competition would produce the dire consequences foreseen by the association. The Court of Appeals affirmed.

Engineering is an important and learned profession. . . . Engineering fees, amounting to well over $2 billion each year, constitute about 5 percent of total construction costs. . . . The National Society of Professional Engineers (Society) was organized in 1935 to deal with the nontechnical aspects of engineering practice, including the promotion of the professional, social, and economic interests of its members. Its present membership of 69,000 resides throughout the United States and in some foreign countries.

The charges of a consulting engineer may be computed in different ways. He may charge the client a percentage of the cost of the project, may set his fee at his actual cost plus overhead plus a reasonable profit, may charge fixed rates per hour for different types of work, may perform an assignment for a specific sum, or he may combine one or more of these approaches. . . . This case . . . involves a charge that the members of the Society have unlawfully agreed to refuse to negotiate or even to discuss the question of fees until after a prospective client has selected the engineer for a particular project. Evidence of this agreement is found in . . . the Society's Code of Ethics, adopted in July 1964.

In . . . defense, the Society averred that the standard set out in the Code of Ethics was reasonable because competition among professional engineers was contrary to the public interest. It was averred that it would be cheaper and easier for an engineer "to design and specify inefficient and unnecessarily expensive structures and methods of construction." Accordingly, competitive pressure to offer engineering services at the lowest possible price would adversely affect the quality of engineering. Moreover, the practice of awarding engineering contracts to the lowest bidder, regardless of quality, would be dangerous to the public health, safety, and welfare. For these reasons, the Society claimed that its Code of Ethics was not an "unreasonable restraint of interstate trade or commerce."

THE RULE OF REASON

One problem presented by the language of Section 1 of the Sherman Act is that it cannot mean what it says. The statute says that "every" contract that restrains trade is unlawful. But, as Mr. Justice Brandeis perceptively noted, restraint is the very essence of every contract; read literally, Section 1 would outlaw the entire body of private contract law.

Congress, however, did not intend the text of the Sherman Act to delineate the full meaning of the statute or its application in concrete situations. The legislative history makes it perfectly clear that it expected the courts to give shape to the statute's broad mandate by drawing on common-law tradition. The Rule of Reason, with its origins in common-law precedents long antedating the Sherman Act, has served that purpose. It has been used to give the Act both flexibility and definition, and its central principle of antitrust analysis has remained constant. Contrary to its name, the Rule does not open the field of antitrust inquiry to any argument in favor of a challenged restraint that may fall within the realm of reason. Instead, it focuses directly on the challenged restraint's impact on competitive conditions.

In this case we are presented with an agreement among competitors to refuse to discuss prices with potential customers until after negotiations have resulted in the initial selection of an engineer. While this is not price fixing as such, no elaborate industry analysis is required to demonstrate the anticompetitive character of such an agreement. It operates as an absolute ban on competitive bidding, applying with equal force to both complicated and simple projects and to both inexperienced and sophisticated customers. As the District Court found, the ban "impedes the ordinary give and take of the market place," and substantially deprives the customer of "the ability to utilize and compare prices in selecting engineering services." On its face, this agreement restrains trade within the meaning of Section 1 of the Sherman Act.

The Society nonetheless invokes the Rule of Reason, arguing that its restraint on price competition ultimately inures to the public benefit by preventing the production of inferior work and by insuring ethical behavior. As the preceding discussion of the Rule of Reason reveals, this Court has never accepted such an argument.

Petitioner's ban on competitive bidding prevents all customers from making price comparisons in the initial selection of an engineer, and imposes the Society's views of the costs and benefits of competition on the entire marketplace. It is this restraint that must be justified under the Rule of Reason, and petitioner's attempt to do so on the basis of the potential threat that competition poses to the public safety and the ethics of its profession is nothing less than a frontal assault on the basic policy of the Sherman Act. . . . The Sherman Act reflects a legislative judgment that ultimately competition will produce not only lower prices, but also better goods and services. "The heart of our national economic policy long has been faith in the value of competition." *Standard Oil Co.* v. *FTC.*

The judgment entered by the District Court, as modified by the Court of Appeals, prohibits the Society from adopting any official opinion, policy statement, or guideline stating or implying that competitive bidding is unethical. . . . Having found the Society guilty of a violation of the Sherman Act,

the District Court was empowered to fashion appropriate restraints on the Society's future activities both to avoid a recurrence of the violation and to eliminate its consequences.

The judgment of the Court of Appeals is *affirmed.*

CASE QUESTIONS

1. What does the "rule-of-reason" test provide? Is it more difficult for a court to apply than a *per se* test?
2. Should Section 1 of the Sherman Act be read *literally*? Why or why not?
3. What did the canon of ethics at issue in this case provide? Explain.
4. Why couldn't the activities of the defendants in this case be characterized as "price fixing"? If they had been, would the rule of reason have applied?
5. What were the *pro*competitive effects of the canon of ethics? The *anti*competitive effects? Using the rule-of-reason balancing test, did the court find a lawful *reasonable* restraint? Or an *unreasonable* restraint in violation of Section 1?

Policy Issue. Should *all* restraints be subject to *per se* rules? If so, what would be the consequences? Should *all* restraints be subject to a rule-of-reason analysis? Or is the present use of both the *per se* and rule-of-reason tests efficient? Effective?

Economics Issue. What economic effect do you think the canon of ethics that prohibited competitive bidding by engineers had on the price of engineering services?

Ethics Issue. Was it ethical for professional engineers to agree not to talk price with clients prior to the client awarding the work to an engineer? Should engineers be treated any differently by the antitrust laws merely because they are "professionals"?

Social Responsibility. Do you think the engineers had the public "health, safety, and welfare" foremost in their minds when they adopted the canon of ethics prohibiting competitive bidding?

CONSCIOUS PARALLELISM

Where there is no showing of an "agreement," "combination," or "conspiracy," there is no violation of Section 1 of the Sherman Act. Mere "conscious parallelism" by many firms in an industry based on "independent business judgment" has been held not to violate Section 1. However, if the conscious parallelism is "interdependent," that is, if each defendant has knowledge of the other defendants' participation in the restraint of trade and will benefit only if all participate, the conduct *is* an unreasonable restraint of trade in violation of Sherman Act Section 1.

In the landmark case, *Theatre Enterprises, Inc. v. Paramount Films Distribution Corp.* (1954), the U.S. Supreme Court found that similar individual decisions of many film distribution companies not to deal with a certain movie theater constituted "conscious parallelism." The court held this *not* to be a restraint of trade in violation of Section 1 of the Sherman Act.

[handwritten margin note: Couldn't prove an agreement exists ∴ no violation]

CONSCIOUS PARALLELISM

THEATRE ENTERPRISES, INC. v. PARAMOUNT FILM DISTRIBUTION CORP.

346 U.S. 537 (1954)
UNITED STATES SUPREME COURT

Mr. Justice Clark delivered the opinion of the Court.

Petitioner brought this suit for treble damages and an injunction under Section 4 . . . of the Clayton Act, alleging that respondent motion picture producers and distributors had violated the antitrust laws by conspiring to restrict "first-run" pictures to downtown Baltimore theatres, thus confining its suburban theatre to subsequent runs and unreasonable "clearances." After hearing the evidence a jury returned a general verdict for respondents. The Court of Appeals for the Fourth Circuit affirmed the judgment based on the verdict. We granted *certiorari.*

The opinion of the Court of Appeals contains a complete summary of the evidence presented to the jury. We need not recite that evidence again. It is sufficient to note that petitioner owns and operates the Crest Theatre, located in a neighborhood shopping district some six miles from the downtown shopping center in Baltimore, Maryland. The Crest, possessing the most modern improvements and appointments, opened on February 26, 1949. Before and after the opening, petitioner, through its president, repeatedly sought to obtain first-run features for the theatre. Petitioner approached each respondent separately, initially requesting exclusive first-runs, later asking for first-runs on a "day and date" basis. But respondents uniformly rebuffed petitioner's efforts and adhered to an established policy of restricting first-runs in Baltimore to the eight downtown theatres. Admittedly there is no direct evidence of illegal agreement between the respondents and no conspiracy is charged as to the independent exhibitors in Baltimore, who account for 63 percent of first-run exhibitions. The various respondents advanced much the same reasons for denying petitioner's offers. Among other reasons, they asserted that day-and-date first-runs are normally granted only to noncompeting theatres. Since the Crest is in "substantial competition" with the downtown theatres, a day-and-date arrangement would be economically unfeasible. . . . [A]n exclusive license would be economically unsound because the Crest is a suburban theatre, located in a small shopping center, and served by limited public transportation facilities; and, with a drawing area of less than one-tenth that of a downtown theatre, it cannot compare with those easily accessible theatres in the power to draw patrons. Hence the downtown theatres offer far greater opportunities for the widespread advertisement and exploitation of newly released features, which is thought necessary to maximize the over-all return from subsequent runs as well as first-runs.

The crucial question is whether respondents' conduct toward petitioner stemmed from independent decision or from an agreement, tacit or express. To be sure, business behavior is admissible circumstantial evidence from which the fact finder may infer agreement. *Interstate Circuit, Inc.* v. *United States, United States* v. *Paramount Pictures, Inc.* But this Court has never held that proof of parallel business behavior conclusively establishes agreement or, phrased differently, that such behavior itself constitutes a Sherman Act offense. Circumstantial evidence of consciously parallel behavior may have made heavy inroads into the traditional judicial attitude toward conspiracy; but "conscious parallelism" has not yet read conspiracy out of the Sherman Act entirely.

Here each of the respondents had denied the existence of any collaboration and in addition had introduced evidence of the local conditions surrounding the Crest operation which, they contended, precluded it from being a successful first-run house. They also attacked the good faith of the guaranteed offers of the petitioner for first-run pictures and attributed uniform action to individual business judgment motivated by the desire for maximum revenue. This evidence, together with other testimony of an explanatory nature, raised fact issues requiring the trial judge to submit the issue of conspiracy to the jury.

Affirmed.

CASE QUESTIONS

1. Was there any *direct* evidence of a "contract, combination, or conspiracy" among the defendants in this case?
2. What is "circumstantial evidence"? Can it be used to prove a "contract, combination, or conspiracy" required to support a violation of Section 1?
3. What reason did each of the motion picture producers and distributors give for not showing "first-run" films at the plaintiff-petitioner's Crest Theatre?
4. What is "conscious parallelism"? Is it a horizontal restraint of trade in violation of Section 1 of the Sherman Act? Explain.

Policy Issue. Should conscious parallelism be a violation of Section 1? What about "price leadership," for example where one automobile manufacturer announces a price increase and all other manufacturers then follow?

Economics Issue. Did the petitioner suffer as much from the conscious parallelism in this case as he would have if the respondents had actually engaged in an illegal group boycott?

Ethics Issue. Was it ethical for the movie producers and distributors to only permit the showing of first-run films at large downtown theaters and not at small suburban theaters?

Social Responsibility. Do businesses owe a duty of social responsibility to sell their goods or services to whoever wants to purchase them? Is it legal to *refuse to deal* with another party?

VERTICAL RESTRAINTS OF TRADE

In addition to horizontal restraints of trade, Section 1 of the Sherman Act also prohibits certain *vertical* restraints of trade. "Vertical" restraints are agreements among firms at different levels of production (manufacturers with wholesalers, wholesalers with retailers, etc.) to restrain trade. Generally, there are two kinds of vertical restraints: (1) vertical *price* restraints ("resale price maintenance"), which are subject to a *per se* rule, and (2) vertical *nonprice* restraints, which are examined using the rule of reason.

RESALE PRICE MAINTENANCE

Resale price maintenance is a vertical restraint where a seller of a product (a manufacturer) requires that the buyer of the product (a wholesale or retailer) sell the product to a customer at a specified price. Intuitively, it would seem that a manufacturer would benefit when retailers compete in price to sell its products because a lower retail price should increase the volume of sales. An economic rationale often offered for resale price maintenance is for a manufacturer to protect the profit margin of retailers who provide a specialized service (e.g., furniture showrooms) or advice (e.g., camera sales) to consumers. An effective minimum resale price agreement would eliminate cut-rate sellers of the product.

Resale price maintenance is a vertical restraint of trade and is a *per se* violation of Section 1 Sherman Act. The rationale for the *per se* rule is that the setting of a maximum price, which logically should be in the consumers' best interests, may in fact be a tacit method of setting a fixed minimum price. This *per se* rule, however, applies to the setting of both *vertical* minimum and maximum prices.

The *per se* rule applies to both direct and indirect methods of attempting to maintain resale prices. Although generally both consignments and "suggested" retail prices are valid, in certain circumstances they may merely act as a sham for a disguised resale price maintenance scheme. If they can be "characterized" as resale price maintenance, both consignment agreements and suggested resale prices are illegal *per se*.

State "Fair Trade" Laws. The Miller-Tydings Amendment in 1937 and the McGuire Act of 1952 exempted certain types of resale price maintenance agreements from both the Sherman Act and the Federal Trade Commission Act if they were otherwise valid under state law. States were thus authorized to legalize resale price maintenance schemes by passing "fair trade" laws. In 1975, Congress repealed the power of states to authorize fair trade laws. The Automobile Information Disclosure Act requires automobile dealers to label new cars with a suggested retail price, and exempts automobile dealers from prosecution under the antitrust laws for using "sticker" prices.

In *Simpson v. Union Oil Co.* the U.S. Supreme Court held that a "consignment" arrangement was resale price maintenance, a restraint of trade, and a *per se* violation of Section 1 of the Sherman Act.

(one person owns the property but gives it to someone else to sell.)

Wasn't consignment - so it is a violation

RESALE PRICE MAINTENANCE

SIMPSON v. UNION OIL CO.

377 U.S. 13 (1964)
UNITED STATES SUPREME COURT

Mr. Justice Douglas delivered the opinion of the Court.

This is a suit for damages under Section 4 of the Clayton Act, for violation of Section 1 . . . of the Sherman Act, as amended. The complaint grows out of a so-called retail dealer "consignment" agreement which, it is alleged, Union Oil requires lessees of its retail outlets to sign, of which

Simpson was one. The "consignment" agreement is for one year and thereafter until canceled, is terminable by either party at the end of any year and, by its terms, ceases upon any termination of the lease. The lease is also for one year; and it is alleged that it is used to police the retail prices charged by the consignees, renewals not being made if the conditions prescribed by the company are not met. The company, pursuant to the "consignment" agreement, sets the prices at which the retailer sells the gasoline. While "title" to the consigned gasoline "shall remain in Consignor until sold by Consignee," and while the company pays all property taxes on all gasoline in possession of Simpson, he must carry personal liability and property damage insurance by reason of the "consigned" gasoline and is responsible for all losses of the "consigned" gasoline in his possession, save for specified acts of God. Simpson is compensated by a minimum commission and pays all the costs of operation in the familiar manner.

The retail price fixed by the company for the gasoline during the period in question was 29.9 cents per gallon; and Simpson, despite the company's demand that he adhere to the authorized price, sold it at 27.9 cents, allegedly to meet a competitive price. Solely because Simpson sold gasoline below the fixed price, Union Oil refused to renew the lease; termination of the "consignment" agreement ensued; and this suit was filed.

The District Court granted the company's motion [for summary judgment]. . . . The Court of Appeals affirmed. . . . The case is here on a writ of *certiorari*.

Consignments perform an important function in trade and commerce, and their integrity has been recognized by many courts, including this one. [However,] the interests of the Government also frequently override agreements that private parties make. Here we have an antitrust policy expressed in Acts of Congress. Accordingly, a consignment, no matter how lawful it might be as a matter of private contract law, must give way before the federal antitrust policy. Thus a consignment is not allowed to be used as a cloak to avoid [the antitrust laws]. . . .

Resale price maintenance of gasoline through the "consignment" device is increasing. The "consignment" device in the gasoline field is used for resale price maintenance. The theory and practice

of gasoline price fixing in vogue under the "consignment" agreement has been well exposed by Congress. . . . By reason of the lease and "consignment" agreement dealers are coercively laced into an arrangement under which their supplier is able to impose noncompetitive prices on thousands of persons whose prices otherwise might be competitive. The evil of this resale price maintenance program, like that of the requirements contracts held illegal by *Standard Oil Co. v. United States,* is its inexorable potentiality for and even certainty in destroying competition in retail sales of gasoline by these nominal "consignees" who are in reality small struggling competitors seeking retail gas customers.

As we have said, an owner of an article may send it to a dealer who may in turn undertake to sell it only at a price determined by the owner. There is nothing illegal about that arrangement. When, however, a "consignment" device is used to cover a vast gasoline distribution system, fixing prices through many retail outlets, the antitrust laws prevent calling the "consignment" an agency, for then [Section 1] . . . would be avoided merely by clever manipulation of words, not by differences in substance. The present, coercive "consignment" device, if successful against challenge under the antitrust laws, furnishes a wooden formula for administering prices on a vast scale.

To allow Union Oil to achieve price fixing in this vast distribution system through this "consignment" device would be to make legality for antitrust purposes turn on clever draftsmanship. We refuse to let a matter so vital to a competitive system rest on such easy manipulation. . . . Hence on the issue of resale price maintenance under the Sherman Act there is nothing left to try, for there was an agreement for resale price maintenance, coercively employed.

The case must be *remanded* for a hearing on . . . the damages, if any, suffered.

CASE QUESTIONS

1. What is a *vertical* restraint of trade? How does it differ from a *horizontal* restraint of trade?
2. What is "resale price maintenance"? Explain.
3. Why would a manufacturer impose a resale price

maintenance scheme on its retail dealers? What are the benefits to the manufacturer?

4. What is a "consignment"? How does it differ from a sale? Are they both subject to antitrust laws?

5. Was there a consignment or a sale in this case? Are all consignments illegal under Section 1 of the Sherman Act?

Policy Issue. Should a manufacturer be permitted to set the price at which retailers can sell its products? Should resale price maintenance be examined under the rule of reason rather than under the *per se* rule?

Economics Issue. Will this decision economically help or hurt manufacturers? Retailers? Consumers?

Ethics Issue. Was it ethical for Simpson to breach the consignment agreement and sell the gasoline for 27.9 cents per gallon? Was it ethical for Union Oil to terminate the consignment agreement with Simpson?

Social Responsibility. Do large corporations like Union Oil owe a duty of social responsibility not to use private contract law to coerce favorable agreements from less powerful parties such as Simpson?

NONPRICE VERTICAL RESTRAINTS OF TRADE

If a vertical restraint cannot be characterized as resale price maintenance, which is subject to the *per se* rule, then the restraint is a *nonprice* vertical restraint, which is subject to examination using the rule of reason. The court will apply the balancing test of the rule of reason to determine whether the restraint is a lawful reasonable restraint or an unreasonable restraint in violation of Section 1 of the Sherman Act. Common *nonprice* vertical restraints subject to analysis using the rule of reason are: (1) exclusive distributorships, (2) requirements contracts, and (3) customer and territorial restrictions.

Exclusive Distributorships. An agreement whereby a manufacturer appoints a certain distributor as his sole outlet in a given territory is examined under the "rule of reason" test to see if it violates the Sherman Act, Section 1. Generally, a manufacturer may choose his outlet in a given region. Exclusive distributorship agreements are usually only struck down as an "unreasonable" restraint of trade where there is no *inter*brand competition for the manufacturer's product, and *intra*brand competition is crucial to avoid a monopoly situation.

Requirements Contracts. In a "requirements" contract a buyer agrees to purchase all his needed goods from one supplier. Whether or not the requirements contract *forecloses* other sellers to such a degree as to be an unreasonable restraint of trade in violation of Sherman Act Section 1 is a question to be addressed by the courts on a case-by-case basis.

The U.S. Supreme Court has developed two separate tests for examining the lawfulness of requirements contracts, the "quantitative substantially" test and the "market share" test. Under the "quantitative substantially" test, the court focuses on the dollar amount foreclosed. (For example, a requirements contract was found illegal where only 6.9% of the market but $58 million of the business was foreclosed.) In a later decision, the Supreme Court focused on the size of the "market share" foreclosed by a requirements contracts. The "market share" test seems to be the better test in that it is more closely aligned with a full scale "rule of reason" inquiry of other Sherman Act Section 1 actions.

Customer and Territorial Restrictions. Often, a manufacturer or wholesaler will place a vertical customer or territorial restriction on its dealers or distributors. The U.S. Supreme Court has been presented the question of the legality of such nonprice vertical restraints on a number of occasions. The decisions of the Supreme Court in this area have been some of the most debated cases in the history of antitrust law.

In *United States v. Arnold Schwinn & Co.,* 388 U.S. 365, (1969), the United States Supreme Court held that all *nonprice* restrictions placed on retailers by manufacturers or wholesalers (e.g., assignment of customers or territories) were *per se* violations of the Sherman Act, Section 1. The same Court, however, held that if the goods were *consigned* by a manufacturer to a retailer, the "rule of reason" test would apply to determine if there was an unreasonable restraint of trade.

After substantial criticism of the *Schwinn* rule by attorneys and academics the Supreme Court, in *Continental TV, Inc. v. GTE Sylvania, Inc.,* 433 U.S. 36 (1977), overruled *Schwinn.* After the *Continental TV* case all *nonprice* vertical restraints (e.g., location, territory, customer) are examined using the "rule of reason" test. The reason for the change was the Court's recognition that certain nonprice vertical restrictions actually foster *inter*brand competition. Under the rule of reason test the court must examine all relevant factors (such as degree of interbrand competition, market power of manufacturer, etc.) in determining whether a nonprice vertical restrain violates the Sherman Act, Section 1.

The landmark antitrust case *Continental TV, Inc. v. GTE Sylvania, Inc.* is presented following.

NONPRICE VERTICAL RESTRAINTS

CONTINENTAL TV, INC. v. GTE SYLVANIA, INC.

433 U.S. 36 (1977)
UNITED STATES SUPREME COURT

Mr. Justice Powell delivered the opinion of the Court.

Respondent GTE Sylvania Inc. (Sylvania) manufactures and sells television sets through its Home Entertainment Products Division. Prior to 1962, like most other television manufacturers, Sylvania sold its televisions to independent or company-owned distributors, who in turn resold to a large and diverse group of retailers. Prompted by a decline in its market share to a relatively insignificant 1–2 percent of national television sales, Sylvania conducted an intensive reassessment of its marketing strategy, and in 1962 adopted the franchise plan challenged here. Sylvania phased out its wholesale distributors and began to sell its televisions directly to a smaller and more select group of franchised retailers. An acknowledged purpose of the change was to decrease the number of competing Sylvania retailers in the hope of attracting the more aggressive and competent retailers thought necessary to the improvement of the company's market position. To this end, Sylvania limited the number of franchises granted for any given area and required each franchisee to sell his Sylvania products only from the location or locations at which he was franchised. A franchise did not constitute an exclusive territory, and Sylvania retained sole discretion to increase the number of retailers in an area in light of the success or failure of existing retailers in developing their market. The revised marketing strategy appears to have been successful during the period at issue here, for by 1965 Sylvania's share of national television sales had increased to approximately 5 percent, and the company ranked as the Nation's eighth largest manufacturer of color television sets.

This suit is the result of the rupture of a franchiser-franchisee relationship that had previously prospered under the revised Sylvania plan. Dissatisfied with its sales in the city of San Francisco, Sylvania decided in the spring of 1965 to franchise Young Brothers, an established San Francisco retailer of televisions, as an additional San Francisco retailer. The proposed location of the new franchise was approximately a mile from a retail outlet operated by petitioner Continental TV, Inc. (Continental), one of the most successful Sylvania franchisees. Continental protested that the location of the new franchise violated Sylvania's marketing policy, but Sylvania persisted in its plans. Continental then canceled a large Sylvania order and placed a large order with Phillips, one of Sylvania's competitors.

During this same period, Continental expressed a desire to open a store in Sacramento, Cal., a desire Sylvania attributed at least in part to Continental's displeasure over the Young Brothers decision. Sylvania believed that the Sacramento market was adequately served by the existing Sylvania retailers and denied the request. In the face of this denial, Continental advised Sylvania in early September 1965, that it was in the process of moving Sylvania merchandise from its San Jose, Cal., warehouse to a new retail location that it had leased in Sacramento. Two weeks later, allegedly for unrelated reasons, Sylvania's credit department reduced Continental's credit line from $300,000 to $50,000. . . . Shortly thereafter, Sylvania terminated Continental's franchises. . . .

[T]he jury found that Sylvania had engaged "in a contract, combination or conspiracy in restraint of trade . . ." and assessed Continental's damages at $591,505, which was trebled to produce an award of $1,774,515.

We turn . . . to Continental's contention that Sylvania's restriction on retail locations is a *per se* violation of Section 1 of the Sherman Act as interpreted in *Schwinn* [*United States v. Arnold, Schwinn & Co.*]. Since the early years of this century a judicial gloss on the statutory language [of Section 1] has established the "rule of reason" as the prevailing standard of analysis. *Standard Oil Co. v. United States*. . . . *Per se* rules of illegality are appropriate only when they relate to conduct that is manifestly anticompetitive. *Northern Pac. R. Co. v. United States*.

The pivotal factor [in *Schwinn*] was the passage of title: all restrictions were held to be *per se* illegal where title had passed, and all were evaluated and sustained under the rule of reason where it had not. The location restriction at issue here would be subject to the same pattern of analysis under *Schwinn*.

It appears that this distinction between sale and nonsale transactions resulted from the Court's effort to accommodate the perceived intrabrand harm and interbrand benefit of vertical restrictions. The *per se* rule for sale transactions reflected the view that vertical restrictions are "so obviously destructive" of intrabrand competition that their use would "open the door to exclusivity of outlets and limitation of territory further than prudence permits." Conversely, the continued adherence to the traditional rule of reason for nonsale transactions reflected the view that the restrictions have too great a potential for the promotion of interbrand competition to justify complete prohibition. The Court's opinion provides no analytical support for these contrasting positions.

Vertical restrictions reduce intrabrand competition by limiting the number of sellers of a particular product competing for the business of a given group of buyers. Location restrictions have this effect because of practical constraints on the effective marketing area of retail outlets.

Vertical restrictions promote interbrand competition by allowing the manufacturer to achieve certain efficiencies in the distribution of his products. These "redeeming virtues" are implicit in every decision sustaining vertical restrictions under the rule of reason. Economists have identified a number of ways in which manufacturers can use such restrictions to compete more effectively against other manufacturers. For example, new manufacturers and manufacturers entering new markets can use the restrictions in order to induce competent and aggressive retailers to make the kind of investment of capital and labor that is often required in the distribution of products unknown to the consumer. Established manufacturers can use them to induce retailers to engage in promotional activities or to provide service and repair facilities necessary to the efficient marketing of their products. Service and repair are vital for many products, such as automobiles and major household appliances. The availability and quality of such services affect a manufacturer's goodwill and the competitiveness of his product. Because of market imperfections such as the so-called "free rider" effect, these services might not be provided by retailers in a purely competitive situation, despite the fact that each retailer's benefit would be greater if all provided the services than if none did.

We conclude that the distinction drawn in *Schwinn* between sale and nonsale transactions is not sufficient to justify the application of a *per se* rule in one situation and a rule of reason in the other. The question remains whether the *per se* rule stated in *Schwinn* should be expanded to include nonsale transactions or abandoned in favor of a return to the rule of reason. We have found no persuasive support for expanding the *per se* rule. As noted above, the *Schwinn* Court recognized the undesirability of "prohibit[ing] all vertical restrictions of territory and all franchising. . . ." . . . Accordingly, we conclude that the *per se* rule stated in *Schwinn* must be *overruled*.

In sum, we conclude that the appropriate decision is to return to the rule of reason that governed vertical restrictions prior to *Schwinn*. When anticompetitive effects are shown to result from particular vertical restrictions they can be adequately policed under the rule of reason, the standard traditionally applied for the majority of anticompetitive practices challenged under Section 1 of the Act. Accordingly, the decision of the Court of Appeals is *affirmed*.

CASE QUESTIONS

1. Under the *Schwinn* rule, did the *per se* test apply to *all* vertical restraints of trade? If not, to which vertical restraints did the *per se* rule apply? To which restraints did the rule of reason apply?
2. Did the title to the goods pass from Sylvania to Continental TV in this case? Was this a sale or a consignment? Under the *Schwinn* rule, was this transaction subject to the *per se* rule or the rule of reason?
3. What is an *exclusive* territory? Is it the same as "market sharing"? If not, what is the difference?
4. Did Sylvania assign an exclusive territory to its franchisees? Could Sylvania increase the number of franchisees in a territory? Did Sylvania grant another franchise in Continental TV's territory?
5. Did Continental TV seek another territory? Did Sylvania grant Continental a franchise in Sacramento? How did Continental respond? How did Sylvania respond?
6. What was the award of the trial court?
7. After *Continental TV v. Sylvania*, what test is used to analyze each of the following?
   a. resale price maintenance
   b. nonprice vertical restraints

Policy Issue. Did the sale versus consignment rule of the *Schwinn* case make sense? Does the price versus nonprice distinction of the *Sylvania* case make sense? Which is the better rule?

Economics Issue. Did the Supreme Court's opinion affect the lower court's decision in favor of Continental TV? Why did the Supreme Court hear this case?

Ethics Issue. Was it ethical for Continental TV to breach the franchise agreement and ship Sylvania TVs to Sacramento? Was it ethical for Sylvania to terminate Continental TV's Sylvania franchise in San Francisco?

Social Responsibility. Do justices owe a duty of social responsibility to correct and overrule previous decisions? Should judges and justices be liable for their negligence in deciding legal cases? Should past litigants be accorded the benefit of a new decision that would have changed the outcome of such prior cases?

THE *NOERR* DOCTRINE

Section 1 of the Sherman Act does not prevent competitors from joining in a concerted action to try to influence either the legislative or the executive branch of government to take some action (e.g., pass a law) which would have an anticompetitive effect, produce a restraint, or produce a monopoly. Commonly known as the *"Noerr* doctrine," and named after the case in which the doctrine was announced, *Eastern Railroad Presidents Conference v. Noerr Motor Freight, Inc.*, 365 U.S. 127 (1961), this constitutional right to petition the government has been extended to activities intended to influence decisions by administrative agencies and the courts. In this excerpt from that case, Justice Black discussed the policy underlying the adoption of the doctrine.

In a representative democracy such as this, these branches of government [legislature and executive] act on behalf of the people and, to a very large extent, the whole concept of representation depends upon the ability of the people to make their wishes known to their representatives. To hold that the government retains the power to act in this representative capacity and yet hold, at the same time, that the people cannot freely inform the government of their wishes would impute to the Sherman Act a purpose to regulate, not business activity, but political activity, a purpose which would have no basis whatever in the legislative history of that Act. Secondly, and of at least equal significance, such a construction of the Sherman Act would raise important constitutional questions. The right of petition is one of the freedoms protected by the Bill of Rights, and we cannot, of course, lightly impute to Congress an intent to invade these freedoms. Indeed, such an imputation would be particularly unjustified in this case in view of all the countervailing considerations enumerated above. For these reasons, we think it clear that the Sherman Act does not apply to the activities of the railroads at least insofar as those activities comprised mere solicitation of governmental action with respect to the passage and enforcement of laws.

The *Noerr* doctrine right to petition the government is not absolute. For example, if a concerted attempt by competitors to influence governmental action is a mere "sham," or is merely to harass competitors, the courts may find the activity to be a "combination" in restraint of trade in violation of Section 1 of the Sherman Act.

Trend of the Law

Because of the substantial number of restraint-of-trade cases that have been brought under Section 1 of the Sherman Act, it is the most developed area of federal antitrust law. Direct agreements to fix prices, engage in group boycotts, or to divide markets arise less frequently than in the past. This is because of the ease of characterizing these as *per se* violations of Section 1. The courts will be faced in the future with more sophisticated and indirect methods for restraining trade. Further, since the U.S. Supreme Court has held that "conscious parallelism" is not illegal as a restraint of trade, the courts will be faced in the future with the difficult problem of defining whether certain forms of tacit activity (e.g., following a price leader) constitutes the necessary "contract, combination, or conspiracy" in order to find a violation of Section 1 of the Sherman Act.

Since the Supreme Court decided the *Continental TV, Inc. v. Sylvania, Inc.* case in 1977, the courts have been faced with the additional burden of having to apply the more difficult rule-of-reason test to all nonprice vertical restraints of trade. In the horizontal restraint area, trade association activities will continue to pose a problem for the courts in applying the rule of reason standard. With a greater number of cases arising that require the application of the more complex rule-of-reason standard rather than the simpler *per se* rule, judges and justices will be forced to reach a greater understanding of economic principles in order to solve the complex antitrust problems that will arise in the future. Some universities are presently offering special economics courses for judges and justices to gain this knowledge.

REVIEW QUESTIONS

1. During the Depression in the early 1930s, oil was pumped out of the ground at a rate which far exceeded demand. The surplus drove the price of the oil so low that production costs were greater than the selling price. This situation was exacerbated by independent oil producers. These producers had no storage facilities and had to sell the oil as soon as it was pumped. They could not temporarily discontinue pumping because once the wells were discontinued, it was economically infeasible to open them. The major oil companies, which controlled most of the market, entered into an informal agreement in which each of them bought the surplus of these independent producers and stored it, thereby stabilizing the supply of oil. The oil companies did not attempt to set any arbitrary price. Did the oil companies' actions restrain trade in violation of Sherman Act Section 1? *Yes. Same as price fixing - stabalize supply ∴ affects price*

2. Seagram Corporation and Calvert Corporation, two subsidiaries of Joseph Seagram and Sons, Inc., sold liquor only to Indiana distributors who agreed not to sell the liquor for more than a maximum price set by the firms. Both firms instituted the policy in an effort to increase their market share and to protect consumers. The firms did not set a minimum price. Kieffer-Steward Co., an Indiana drug company that had a large wholesale liquor division, brought an antitrust action against Seagram and Calvert under Section 1 of the Sherman Act. The company asked for treble damages. When a combination sets a maximum sale price, has it violated the Sherman Act? *Yes*

3. Given the nature of the music industry, most individual composers and authors are not able to compete on their own. As a method of dealing with this problem, many artists banded together to form ASCAP and BMI,

both of which essentially market the artists' collective works. The artists grant these firms the collective rights to license their works in return for royalties, which are distributed according to type and use of the music. Both firms market the compositions primarily by issuing blanket licenses to users. The licenses allow the buyer to perform any and all the compositions owned by the members of the firm for a stated term. Fees for the licenses are either a percentage of total revenues or a flat dollar amount. Columbia Broadcasting Systems (CBS) filed a complaint alleging that AS-CAP and BMI, through the use of blanket licenses, were engaging in *per se* price fixing. Can the activity be *characterized* as price fixing? What approach should the courts use in deciding the case?

4. Several national film distributors agreed to impose price restrictions on local theatre owners who were showing subsequent-run films. The national distributors met with local distributors and convinced them to require a minimum admission charge of 25 cents. At the time, most theatres charged less than 25 cents. The United States charged these national distributors with price fixing. At trial, the government showed that after the alleged conspiracy had been entered into, all subsequent-run theatres raised their prices to 25 cents. At the trial there was no testimony offered stating that an explicit agreement had been reached. Does the existence of an agreement have to be definitely established to find a conspiracy in restraint of trade?

5. Ten film distributors that controlled 60 percent of the national film market joined together and required all theatre owners to sign standard contracts. After experimenting with different formulations for six years, the distributors wrote a contract requiring that all disputes must be submitted to arbitration (an unusual practice) or a $500 bond be posted. If any owner refused to comply, all ten distributors agreed to refuse to do business with him. Is the Sherman Act violated when competitors combine to require all of their customers to accept certain arbitrary provisions? What type of agreement is this commonly known as?

6. A large group of retail lumber dealers formed the Eastern States Retail Lumber Dealers' Association. All members entered into an informal agreement in which they would refuse to buy from wholesalers who were selling directly to the public. If a member learned that his wholesaler was dealing directly with the public, he was to stop purchasing goods from the firm and also report the activity to the Association. The Association regularly printed lists of these targeted wholesalers and distributed them to all retail members. There were many instances in which as soon as a wholesaler's name was published, the Association's members refused to buy from that wholesaler. Did this informal agreement violate the Sherman Act?

7. The United States government brought antitrust complaints against two trade associations for impermissible restraints of trade. The government charged cargo container manufacturers with illegal restraint of trade because they freely exchanged selling price information on request, with the expectation that there would be reciprocity in similar future situations. While these exchanges were sporadic, the container market was relatively inelastic. Price was the only major variable and manufacturers tended to meet the price of their competitors. The government also issued a

complaint against the Chicago Board of Trade. The Board restricted deals in Chicago grain to hours in which the Board was in operation. The policy was imposed to restrict price gouging, which had occurred at various times in the past. People who dealt in arriving grain, a small segment of the overall grain market, had to abide by the final call price of the day or wait until the next day when the market system would again determine a new price. Was either activity a violation of antitrust law? Why?

8. Dr. Miles Medical Company manufactured homemade medicine under a secret process. The firm sold the medicine to 400 wholesalers and 25,000 retailers under contracts that called for a minimum price schedule for the different medicines. John D. Park and Sons, a wholesale drug company, refused to enter into any contracts with Dr. Miles but was able to obtain quantities of the drugs from other sources. Park and Sons then sold these medicines for less than the minimum established price. Dr. Miles sued Park and Sons for interference in contractual relations and Park and Sons raised a restraint of trade argument as an affirmative defense. Could Dr. Miles legally dictate the prices that its wholesalers and retailers could charge? Why or why not? If not, what type of restraint was the firm engaging in?

9. The St. Louis *Herald* signed contracts with all of its distributors which set a ceiling on the price that could be charged for the newspapers. Albrecht, the distributor for Route 99, decided not to comply with the suggested retail price schedule and was told his distributorship would be cancelled if he did not comply. Under terms of their agreement with Albrecht, the *Herald* informed him that it was going to send letters to all his customers advising them that it would deliver the papers for the suggested retail price. Of Albrecht's 1,200 customers, 314 switched. Albrecht's distributorship was later cancelled and he sold it to a third party for a substantially lower price that he would have received had he transfered all 1,200 accounts. Albrecht then sued for an antitrust violation based upon price fixing. He sought to recover the damages that he suffered as a result of the lower sales price. Did the *Herald* violate the antitrust laws by competing with a nonconforming dealer?

10. The United States charged two major drug manufacturers, Parke-Davis and Colgate, with anticompetitive price fixing in violation of the antitrust laws. Colgate, which had no monopolistic control of its market, refused to sell its products to retailers who did not comply with the firm's price list. Even though there were numerous "like-kind" products in the marketplace, once Colgate discovered that a retailer had violated the terms of the price list, the firm refused to accept further orders. Parke-Davis also announced a policy of not dealing with wholesalers and retailers who refused to adhere to its announced price schedule. Since the firm also did not have any monopolistic control of its market, it enlisted the aid of cooperative wholesale buyers to ensure maximum compliance at the retail level. Did Colgate's and/or Parke-Davis' actions violate the antitrust laws?

11. Trucking Unlimited and California Motor Transport (CMT) were competing trucking firms that operated within, into, and out of California. Trucking Unlimited instituted numerous state and federal judicial and administrative proceedings against CMT and other competitors. The proceedings

attempted to resist and defeat applications by CMT to acquire operating rights, to transfer, or to register those rights. Evidence indicated that Trucking Unlimited's motivation was to secure a monopoly position in the trucking industry. Evidence also indicated that many of these proceedings were designed to injure and harass CMT. Are the activities of Trucking Unlimited permitted under the *Noerr* Doctrine? Is Trucking Unlimited's motive relevant?

10 MERGERS

INTRODUCTION

A company may expand by two general methods: internal growth and external growth. A firm expands through internal growth by entering new product or geographical markets *de novo* ("newly"). That is, the firm invests its capital, builds new plants or offices, and hires personnel to run the new operations.

The second method of expansion is through external growth, which is accomplished by *acquiring* existing firms in an industry. A firm may choose to grow externally, rather than internally, for a number of reasons, including:

1. to take advantage of economies of scale and other efficiencies of operations
2. to combine with a firm with complementary assets (for example, a cash-rich company and a capital-intensive company merge)
3. to take advantage of the low stock price of the acquired company
4. to diversify into other products in order to spread the risk and smooth out business product cycles
5. to consolidate financial statements and create a positive effect on earnings and other financial data (e.g., tax loss carrybacks)

6. to create market or monopoly power in a product or geographical area
7. to grow for growth's sake (i.e., to be "Number One").

Methods of External Growth.   There are several methods for a firm to grow
by external means, including:

1. consolidation
2. merger
3. purchase of assets
4. ownership of a subsidiary
5. joint venture.

①*Consolidation.*   A technical "consolidation" occurs where two corporations
join together and form a third corporation. The two original corporations dis-
solve, and the new corporation survives with the combined assets and liabilities
of the original corporations.

almost any
activities
include all above

②*Merger.*   A technical "merger" is where one corporation (the "acquiring"
corporation) acquires another corporation (the "acquired" corporation), the
acquired corporation is dissolved, and the acquiring corporation survives with
the assets and liabilities of both corporations.

③*Purchase of Assets.*   A technical "purchase and sale of assets" occurs where
one corporation (the "purchasing" corporation) purchases the *assets* of another
corporation (the "selling" corporation), the selling corporation dissolves, and
the purchasing corporation survives. The liabilities of the selling corporation
are also usually transferred to the purchasing corporation.

④*Subsidiary.*   One corporation may acquire an interest in another corporation by purchasing the *stock,* in whole or part, of the second corporation.
Generally, the purchasing corporation is known as the *parent* and the other
company is called a *subsidiary.* Both corporations keep their separate legal
status, although the parent corporation may control the operational policies
of its subsidiary.

⑤*Joint Venture.*   A joint venture is an agreement between two or more corporations to pool their assets to accomplish a limited purpose which, generally,
none of the corporations have the resources to complete on their own, such
as drilling for oil on the North Slope of Alaska. All corporations retain their
separate legal status, and often form a separate corporation, in which the
original corporations become the shareholders, to operate the joint venture.
Antitrust law applies to all of the above types of external expansion.

CLASSIFICATION OF MERGERS

Following the establishment of powerful cartels in the later 1800s by merger
and acquisition (such as Standard Oil, the Sugar Trusts, etc.), the federal government attempted to regulate merger activity. The policy behind the regulation

of mergers was to promote competition and prevent the concentration of economic power of the country in too few hands. Basically, the four federal statutes which Congress enacted that apply to and constrain mergers between corporations, are:

1. the Sherman Act, Section 1 (1890)
2. the Clayton Act, Section 7 (1914)
3. the Bank Merger Act (1966)
4. the Hart-Scott-Rodino Antitrust Act (1976).

Technical consolidations, mergers, and other acquisitions are referred to as "mergers" under antitrust law. There are generally four classifications of mergers for antitrust law purposes:

1. horizontal mergers
2. vertical mergers
3. market extension mergers
4. conglomerate mergers.

Horizontal Merger. A "horizontal merger" is a merger between two companies who are *competitors* in the same line of business in the same market. For example, the merger of two grocery stores serving the same geographical marketplace is a horizontal merger.

Vertical Merger. A "vertical merger" is a merger between a supplier and a customer that "integrates" the operations of the two firms. A merger of a producer of spark plugs with the producer of steel used in the sparks plugs, or with an automobile manufacturer who places spark plugs in its automobiles, are examples of a vertical merger.

Market Extension Merger. A "market extension merger" is a merger between two companies in the same field whose sales do not overlap. For example, a merger between two regional brewers who do not serve the same marketplace is a geographic market extension merger. A merger between a producer of metal containers and a producer of glass containers is a product market extension merger.

Conglomerate Merger. "Conglomerate mergers" are all those mergers that are not classified as horizontal, market extension, or vertical mergers. The most obvious example of a conglomerate merger is the consolidation of two companies from totally unrelated lines of business, such as a steel producer and a clothing retailer.

Premerger Notification. In 1976, Congress enacted the Hart-Scott-Rodino Antitrust Act. Pursuant to the Act, the Federal Trade Commission adopted certain *premerger notification* rules. These rules require certain firms that propose to merge to notify the Justice Department and the Federal Trade Commission in advance of the merger. Once a premerger notification is given, either the Justice Department or Federal Trade Commission may take legal action to prevent the merger. In order to be covered by the premerger notification rules, both a size of firm test and a transaction test must be met.

The premerger notification rules apply to mergers where (1) the acqui*ring* firm has net annual sales or total assets of $100 million or more, *and* (2) the acqui*red* firm is (a) involved in manufacturing and has annual net sales or total assets of $5 million or more, or (b) is not in manufacturing and has total assets (sales are irrelevant) of $5 million or more.

If the *size-of-the-firm* test is not met, the premerger notification rules apply to merger *transactions* where: (1) the value of the purchase exceeds $15 million, *and* (2) the acquiring firm acquires at least 15 percent of the fair market value of the assets or 15 percent of the current value of the securities of the acquired firm.

In order to cover "minnow swallowing the whale" mergers, the premerger notification rules apply *whenever* the acqui*ring* firm has annual sales of $10 million or more, *and* the acqui*red* firm has annual sales of $100 million or more.

Department of Justice "Merger Guidelines."   In order to assist the courts in their determination of what mergers may violate Section 7 of the Clayton Act, in 1968 the Department of Justice issued a set of "merger guidelines." The guidelines, although having no force of law and being only an advisory tool, have been adopted by many courts in analyzing mergers. The guidelines are different for horizontal, vertical, and conglomerate mergers.

In 1982, the Justice Department's merger guidelines were amended. The amended guidelines are less stringent than the prior guidelines and introduce the use of the Herfindahl index for determining concentration ratios. Under the Herfindahl index, the percent market share of each firm in the relevant market is squared and the squares are summed to reach one number which represents the concentration of that market. Premerger and postmerger Herfindahl indexes can be compared to see what increase in concentration will occur because of the merger.

Sherman Act, Section 1.   The federal government originally tried to address the problem of mergers through the use of Section 1 of the Sherman Act ("restraint of trade"). However, early merger decisions under the Sherman Act were extremely unsuccessful for the federal government. Section 7 of the Clayton Act, which will be discussed later, only applies to mergers "in" interstate commerce, while the Sherman Act applies to activities that "affect" interstate commerce; thus the Sherman Act may be applied to *intra*state mergers. Furthermore, because the Clayton Act does not provide for criminal penalties whereas the Sherman Act does, the Sherman Act may be used against mergers where criminal sanctions are sought by the government.

THE CLAYTON ACT, SECTION 7

In 1914 Congress enacted the Clayton Act, which contained Section 7 to regulate mergers. The original Section 7 only applied to mergers and acquisitions where the *stock* of another corporation was acquired. The purchase of the *assets* of one corporation by another corporation was not covered. Further, the original Section 7 only covered *horizontal* mergers. Vertical, market extension, and conglomerate mergers were not covered by the 1914 provision.

The Celler-Kefauver Act was passed by Congress in 1950. This Act amended Section 7 of the Clayton Act to cover both *asset* acquisitions and mergers other than horizontal mergers, i.e., vertical and conglomerate mergers. Section 7 presently makes unlawful the *acquisition* by any corporation subject to Federal Trade Commission jurisdiction of:

the stock or any part of the assets of another corporation also engaged in commerce where the effect of the acquisition may be to substantially lessen competition in any line of commerce in any section of the country.

In the following excerpt from *Brown Shoe Co., Inc. v. United States*, 370 U.S. 294 (1962), Chief Justice Warren summarized the purposes of Section 7 of the Clayton Act.

As enacted in 1914, Section 7 of the original Clayton Act prohibited the acquisition by one corporation of the *stock* of another corporation when such acquisition would result in a substantial lessening of competition *between the acquiring and the acquired* companies, or tend to create a monopoly in any line of commerce. The Act did not, by its explicit terms, or as construed by this Court, bar the acquisition by one corporation of the *assets* of another. Nor did it appear to preclude the acquisition of stock in any corporation other than a direct competitor.

The dominant theme pervading congressional consideration of the 1950 amendments was a fear of what was considered to be a rising tide of economic concentration in the American economy. . . . What were some of the factors, relevant to a judgment as to the validity of a given merger, specifically discussed by Congress in redrafting Section 7?

First, there is no doubt that Congress did wish to "plug the loophole" and to include within the coverage of the Act the acquisition of assets no less than the acquisition of stock.

Second, . . . it hoped to make plain that Section applied not only to mergers between actual competitors, but also to vertical and conglomerate mergers whose effect may tend to lessen competition in any line of commerce in any section of the country.

Third, it is apparent that a keystone in the erection of a barrier to what Congress saw was the rising tide of economic concentration, was its provision of authority for arresting mergers at a time when the trend to a lessening of competition in a line of commerce was still in its incipiency. Congress saw the process of concentration in American business as a dynamic force; it sought to assure the Federal Trade Commission and the courts the power to brake this force at its outset and before it gathered momentum.

In *FTC v. Procter & Gamble Co.*, 386 U.S. 568 (1967), Justice Douglas wrote for the Supreme Court:

Section 7 of the Clayton Act was intended to arrest the anticompetitive effects of market power in their incipiency. The core question is whether a merger may substantially lessen competition, and necessarily requires a prediction of the merger's impact on competition, present and future. . . . And there is certainly no requirement that the anticompetitive power manifest itself in anticompetitive action before Section 7 can be called into play. If the enforcement of Section 7 turned on the existence of actual anticompetitive practices, the congressional policy of thwarting such practices in their incipiency would be frustrated.

In applying Section 7 of the Clayton Act to mergers, the court's analysis in each case must consist of determining the meaning and application of the following three phrases of Section 7:

1. "line of commerce"
2. "section of the country"
3. "substantially lessen competition."

Line of Commerce.   Section 7 of the Clayton Act requires the determination of the relevant *line of commerce* before a merger can be analyzed. The determination of the relevant line of commerce is somewhat similar to the delineation of the relevant product market in monopolization actions brought under Section 2 of the Sherman Act. Generally, the courts emphasize the interchangeability of products in determining the relevant "line of commerce." Because of the *prophylactic* (preventative) nature of Section 7, the courts tend to require a lesser showing of interchangeability than required under Section 2 of the Sherman Act.

"Section of the Country."   Section 7 requires courts to define the relevant "section of the country." In doing so, courts generally follow the "relevant geographical market" analysis of Sherman Act Section 1 cases, that is, defining "the area where the effect of the merger on competition will both be immediate and direct."

Under a Section 7 action, the defendant usually argues for a narrow definition of "section of the country," whereas the opponent argues for a broader definition of this term. The trend has been to favor a more narrow, or local, definition of the relevant "section of the country" in Section 7 actions.

In *United States v. Connecticut National Bank*, the U.S. Supreme Court defined the relevant "line of commerce" and "section of the country" in a merger action brought under Section 7 of the Clayton Act.

LINE OF COMMERCE
SECTION OF THE COUNTRY

UNITED STATES v. CONNECTICUT NATIONAL BANK

418 U.S. 656 (1974)
UNITED STATES SUPREME COURT

Mr. Justice Powell delivered the opinion of the Court.

This case concerns the legality of a proposed consolidation of two nationally chartered commercial banks operating in adjoining regions of Connecticut. The United States brought a civil antitrust action challenging the consolidation under Section 7 of the Clayton Act. Following a lengthy trial and on the basis of extensive findings and conclusions, the United States District Court for the District of Connecticut dismissed the Government's complaint.

The banks desiring to consolidate, Connecticut National Bank (CNB) and First New Haven National Bank (FNH), have offices in contiguous areas in the southwestern portion of Connecticut. CNB maintains its headquarters in the town of Bridgeport, which is situated on the Long Island Sound approximately 60 miles from New York City. CNB is the fourth largest commercial bank in the State. At year-end 1972, it held 6.2 percent of the deposits in commercial banks in Connecticut. CNB operates 51 offices located in Bridgeport and nearby towns in the extreme southwest section of Connecticut.

FNH has its headquarters in the town of New Haven, approximately 19 miles to the northeast of Bridgeport along the Long Island Sound. FNH is the eighth largest commercial bank in Connecticut. At the end of 1972, it held 4.1 percent of commercial bank deposits in the State. FNH operates 22 bank offices in New Haven and surrounding towns.

We have . . . held that the legality of a market extension merger must be determined against the backdrop of properly defined product and geographic markets. In our view, the District Court erred in its definition of both concepts, and it is not possible to ascertain the degree, if any, to which those errors may have influenced its conclusions with regard to the Government's potential-competition arguments.

Line of Commerce

The District Court concluded that the appropriate "line of commerce" within the meaning of Section 7 included both commercial banks and savings banks. [W]e hold for several reasons that the District Court was mistaken in including both savings and commercial banks in the same product market for purposes of this case.

We believe that the District Court overestimated the degree of competitive overlap that in fact exists between savings banks and commercial banks in Connecticut. To be sure, there is a large measure of similarity between the services marketed by the two categories of banks. In our view, however, the overlap is not sufficient at this stage in the development of savings banks in Connecticut to treat them together with commercial banks in the instant case. . . . [C]ommercial banks in Connecticut offer a "cluster of products and services" that their savings bank counterparts do not.

The District Court concluded that "meaningful competition" existed between commercial and savings banks for commercial loans. This conclusion is not supported by the record. Commercial loans, generally speaking, are relatively short-term loans to business enterprises of all sizes, usually for purposes of inventory or working capital. At the end of 1971 commercial banks in Connecticut had outstanding $1.03 billion in commercial loans. Savings banks, by comparison, had $26 million in such loans at that time. The disparity in these figures demonstrates that the commercial bank-loan business in Connecticut is controlled almost exclusively by commercial banks. Moreover, commercial banks in the State offer credit-card plans, loans for securities purchases, trust services, investment services, computer and account services, and letters of credit. Savings banks do not.

Accordingly, on remand the District Court should treat commercial banking as the relevant product market.

Section of the Country

The District Court ruled that the relevant geographic market, or "section of the country," under Section 7, is the State as a whole.

The State cannot be the relevant geographic market, however, because CNB and FNH are not direct competitors on that basis (or for that matter on any other basis pertinent to this appeal). The two banks do not operate statewide, nor do their customers as a general rule utilize commercial banks on that basis. The offices of the two banks are restricted to adjoining sections of the southwest segment of Connecticut. . . . [T]he geographic market must be delineated in a way that takes into account the local nature of the demand for most bank services.

On remand the District Court must determine pursuant to the localized approach denoted above the geographic market in which CNB operates and to which the bulk of its customers may turn for alternative commercial bank services. It must do the same with regard to FNH, . . . We are not unaware of the difficulty of the assignment confronting the District Court. An element of "fuzziness would seem inherent in any attempt to delineate the relevant geographical market."

The judgment is *vacated* and the case is *remanded* for further consideration consistent with this opinion.

CASE QUESTIONS

1. What is a *market extension* merger? Explain.
2. What had the District Court defined as the relevant "line of commerce"? Did the Supreme Court agree? Explain.
3. With the current "development of savings banks," would the determination of the relevant line of commerce be the same *today?* What would it be today?

4. What had the District Court defined as the relevant "section of the country"? Did the Supreme Court agree? Explain.

Policy Issue. Does the determination of the relevant line of commerce and section of the country involve a degree of "fuzziness"? Does this pose a problem for firms that wish to merge?

Economics Issue. Do mergers harm or benefit the economy? Employees? Consumers?

Ethics Issue. Is it ethical for large firms to merge? Even if it increases concentration? Or creates a monopoly?

Social Responsibility. Do corporations owe a duty of social responsibility to expand *internally* rather than through merger?

"Substantially Lessen Competition." Section 7 was designed by Congress to have a *preventative*, rather than merely a corrective, effect. Section 7 is used to attack potentially anticompetitive mergers *before* they occur. Courts under Section 7 invalidate mergers where the merger would create a "tendency" toward a monopoly, or where there is a "reasonable likelihood" of a substantial lessening of competition.

Section 7 does not deal with mere possibilities, but with actual demonstrated estimates of "probabilities." An actual showing that competition would be substantially lessened is not required. Only a showing that there would be a *tendency* to the substantial lessening of competition or tendency to create a monopoly is needed to prove a Section 7 violation. In *Brown Shoe Co. v. United States* the Supreme Court described this test.

While providing no definite quantitative or qualitative tests by which enforcement agencies could gauge the effects of a given merger to determine whether it may "substantially" lessen competition or tend toward monopoly, Congress indicated plainly that a merger had to be functionally viewed, in the context of its particular industry. That is, whether the consolidation was to take place in an industry that was fragmented rather than concentrated, that had seen a recent trend toward domination by a few leaders or had remained fairly consistent in its distribution of market shares among the participating companies, that had experienced easy access to markets by suppliers and easy access to suppliers by buyers or had witnessed foreclosure of business, that had witnessed the ready entry of new competition or the erection of barriers to prospective entrants, all were aspects, varying in importance with the merger under consideration, which would properly be taken into account.

Congress used the words *"may be* substantially to lessen competition" (emphasis supplied), to indicate that its concern was with probabilities, not certainties. Statutes existed for dealing with clear-cut menaces to competition; no statute was sought for dealing with ephemeral possibilities. Mergers with a probable anticompetitive effect were to be proscribed by this Act.

In *United States v. E. I. du Pont de Nemours & Co.* Justice Brennan wrote a majority opinion in which the Supreme Court found that du Pont's ownership of 23 percent of the stock of General Motors, and the resulting business transactions between the two corporations, caused a substantial lessening of competition in violation of Section 7 of the Clayton Act.

"SUBSTANTIALLY LESSEN COMPETITION"

UNITED STATES v. E. I. DU PONT DE NEMOURS & CO.

353 U.S. 586 (1957)
UNITED STATES SUPREME COURT

Mr. Justice Brennan delivered the opinion of the Court.

This is a direct appeal under Section 2 of the Expediting Act from a judgment of the District Court for the Northern District of Illinois, dismissing the Government's action brought in 1949. . . . The complaint alleged a violation of Section 7 of the Act resulting from the purchase by E. I. du Pont de Nemours and Company in 1917–1919 of a 23 percent stock interest in General Motors Corporation.

The primary issue is whether du Pont's commanding position as General Motors' supplier of automotive finishes and fabrics was achieved on competitive merit alone, or because its acquisition of the General Motors' stock, and the consequent close intercompany relationship, led to the insulation of most of the General Motors' market from free competition, with the resultant likelihood, at the time of suit, of the creation of a monopoly of a line of commerce.

General Motors is the colossus of the giant automobile industry. It accounts annually for upwards of two-fifths of the total sales of automotive vehicles in the Nation. In 1955 General Motors ranked first in sales and second in assets among all United States industrial corporations and became the first corporation to earn over a billion dollars in annual net income. In 1947 General Motors' total purchases of all products from du Pont were $26,628,274, of which $18,938,229 (71 percent) repre-

sented purchases from du Pont's Finishes Division. . . . Expressed in percentages, du Pont supplied 67 percent of General Motors' requirements for finishes in 1946 and 68 percent in 1947. In fabrics du Pont supplied 52.3 percent of requirements in 1946, and 38.5 percent in 1947. Because General Motors accounts for almost one-half of the automobile industry's annual sales, its requirements for automotive finishes and fabrics must represent approximately one-half of the relevant market for these materials. Because the record clearly shows that quantitatively and percentagewise du Pont supplies the largest part of General Motors' requirements, we must conclude that du Pont has a substantial share of the relevant market.

[T]he Government may proceed at any time that an acquisition may be said with reasonable probability to contain a threat that it may lead to a restraint of commerce or tend to create a monopoly of a line of commerce.

The Company's interest in buying into General Motors was stimulated by Raskob and Pierre S. du Pont, then du Pont's president, who acquired personal holdings of General Motors stock in 1914. General Motors was organized six years earlier by William C. Durant to acquire previously independent automobile manufacturing companies—Buick, Cadillac, Oakland and Oldsmobile. Durant later brought in Chevrolet, organized by him when he was temporarily out of power, during 1910–1915, and a bankers' group controlled General Motors.

In 1915, when Durant and the bankers deadlocked on the choice of a Board of Directors, they resolved the deadlock by an agreement under which Pierre S. du Pont was named Chairman of the General Motors Board, and Pierre S. du Pont, Raskob and two nominees of Mr. du Pont were named neutral directors.

On December 19, 1917, Raskob submitted a Treasurer's Report to the du Pont Finance Committee recommending a purchase of General Motors stock in the amount of $25,000,000. That report makes clear that more than just a profitable investment was contemplated. A major consideration was that an expanding General Motors would provide a substantial market needed by the burgeoning du Pont organization. Raskob's summary of reasons in support of the purchase includes this statement: "Our interest in the General Motors Company will undoubtedly secure for us the entire Fabrikoid, Pyralin [celluloid], paint and varnish business of those companies, *which is a substantial factor."* (Emphasis added.)

This background of the acquisition, particularly the plain implications of the contemporaneous documents, destroys any basis for a conclusion that the purchase was made "solely for investment."

In less than four years, by August 1921, Lammot du Pont, then a du Pont vice-president and later Chairman of the Board of General Motors, in response to a query from Pierre S. du Pont, then Chairman of the Board of both du Pont and General Motors, "whether General Motors was taking its entire requirements of du Pont products from du Pont," was able to reply that four of General Motors' eight operating divisions bought from du Pont their entire requirements of paints and varnishes, five their entire requirements of Fabrikoid, four their entire requirements of rubber cloth, and seven their entire requirements of Pyralin and celluloid.

The fact that sticks out in this voluminous record is that the bulk of du Pont's production has always supplied the largest part of the requirements of the one customer in the automobile industry connected to du Pont by a stock interest. The inference is overwhelming that du Pont's commanding position was promoted by its stock interest and was not gained solely on competitive merit.

The statutory policy of fostering free competition is obviously furthered when no supplier has an ad-

vantage over his competitors from an acquisition of his customer's stock likely to have the effects condemned by the statute. We repeat that the test of a violation of Section 7 is whether, at the time of suit, there is a reasonable probability that the acquisition is likely to result in the condemned restraints. The conclusion upon this record is inescapable that such likelihood was proved as to this acquisition. The fire that was kindled in 1917 continues to smolder. It burned briskly to forge the ties that bind the General Motors market to du Pont, and if it has quieted down, it remains hot, and, from past performance, is likely at any time to blaze and make the fusion complete.

The judgment must therefore be *reversed* and the cause *remanded* to the District Court for a determination, after further hearing, of the equitable relief necessary and appropriate in the public interest to eliminate the effects of the acquisition offensive to the statute.

CASE QUESTIONS

1. When did du Pont purchase the stock in General Motors? When was this lawsuit brought? Did this time period matter to the maintaining of this Section 7 action?

2. Once the lawsuit was brought, how long did it take before it was decided by the Supreme Court? Did the Supreme Court's decision finally end the case?

3. Did du Pont purchase the GM stock for investment purposes?

4. Did the Supreme Court find a *probability* of a substantial lessening of competition in this case? What evidence did the Court cite? Explain.

5. Do you agree with the decision of the Supreme Court in this case? Why or why not?

Policy Issue. Should the government have been allowed to bring this antitrust action 40 years after du Pont had purchased the General Motors' stock?

Economics Issue. Did the ownership of the General Motors stock benefit du Pont economically? Who did it harm?

Ethics Issue. Was the purchase of the General Motors stock by du Pont ethical?

Social Responsibility. Do corporations owe a duty of social responsibility not to transact business with other corporations in which they have an ownership interest?

NOTE: Du Pont and affiliated persons had to divest themselves of the General Motors stock. Congress enacted special legislation to ease the tax burden of the divestiture.

HORIZONTAL MERGERS

Horizontal mergers, where competitive firms who serve the same market propose to merge, are subject to review under Section 7 of the Clayton Act. Before 1963, when the Supreme Court decided *United States v. Philadelphia National Bank,* horizontal mergers were analyzed by the use of market share data. No specific guidelines were available; each merger had to be reviewed on a case-by-case basis to determine whether it caused a substantial lessening of competition.

Presumptive Illegality Test.   In an attempt to lay down an objective guideline for analyzing when a horizontal merger may violate Section 7, the United States Supreme Court developed a "presumptive illegality" test in *United States v. Philadelphia National Bank.* In that case, the court held that where the *merged* firm would have 30 percent or more market share of the relevant market, *and* the merger would cause a 33 percent or more increase in concentration in such market, the merger would be presumed "illegal." After such showing, the burden switches to the defendant to prove that the merger would *not* tend to substantially lessen competition.

Mergers with smaller market share and concentration increases than *Philadelphia Bank* are not presumed illegal, but are tested on a case-by-case basis to see if Section 7 has been violated. Increases in market share and increases in concentration ratios smaller than those found in *Philadelphia Bank* have been held to violate Section 7. This case is presented next.

HORIZONTAL MERGER

UNITED STATES v. PHILADELPHIA NATIONAL BANK

374 U.S. 321 (1963)
UNITED STATES SUPREME COURT

Mr. Justice Brennan delivered the opinion of the Court.

The United States, appellant here, brought this civil action in the United States District Court to enjoin a proposed merger of The Philadelphia National Bank (PNB) and Girard Trust Corn Exchange Bank (Girard), appellees here. The complaint charged violation of . . . Section 7 of the Clayton Act. From a judgment for appellees after trial, the United States appealed to this Court under Section 2 of the Expediting Act. Probable jurisdiction was noted.

THE PROPOSED MERGER OF PNB AND GIRARD

The Philadelphia National Bank and Girard Trust Corn Exchange Bank are, respectively, the second and third largest of the 42 commercial banks with head offices in the Philadelphia metropolitan area, which consists of the City of Philadelphia and its three contiguous counties in Pennsylvania. The home county of both banks is the city itself; Pennsylvania law, however, permits branching into the counties contiguous to the home county, and both banks have offices throughout the four-county area. PNB, a national bank, has assets of over $1,000,000,000, making it (as of 1959) the twenty-first largest bank in the Nation. Girard, a state bank, is a member of the FRS and is insured by the FDIC; it has assets of about $750,000,000. Were the proposed merger to be consummated, the resulting bank would be the largest in the four-county area, with (approximately) 36 percent of the area banks' total assets, 36 percent of deposits, and 34 percent of net loans. It and the second largest (First Pennsylvania Bank and Trust Company, now the largest) would have between them 59 percent of the total assets, 58 percent of deposits, and 58 percent of the net loans, while after the merger the four largest banks in the area would have 78 percent of total assets, 77 percent of deposits, and 78 percent of net loans.

The present size of both PNB and Girard is in part the result of mergers. Indeed, the trend toward concentration is noticeable in the Philadelphia area generally, in which the number of commercial banks has declined from 108 in 1947 to the present 42. Since 1950, PNB has acquired nine formerly independent banks and Girard six; and these acquisitions have accounted for 59 percent and 85 percent of the respective banks' asset growth during the period, 63 percent and 91 percent of their deposit growth, and 12 percent and 37 percent of their loan growth. During this period, the seven largest banks in the area increased their combined share of the area's total commercial bank resources from about 61 percent to about 90 percent.

THE LAWFULNESS OF THE PROPOSED MERGER UNDER SECTION 7

We agree with the District Court that the cluster of products (various kinds of credit) and services (such as checking accounts and trust administration) denoted by the term "commercial banking" composes a distinct line of commerce. . . . [T]he four-country area in which appellees' offices are located would seem to be the relevant geographical market.

Having determined the relevant market, we come to the ultimate question under Section 7: whether the effect of the merger "may be substantially to lessen competition" in the relevant market. Clearly, this is not the kind of question which is susceptible of a ready and precise answer in most cases. It requires not merely an appraisal of the immediate impact of the merger upon competition, but a prediction of its impact upon competitive conditions in the future; this is what is meant when it is said that the amended Section 7 was intended to arrest anticompetitive tendencies in their "incipiency." . . . [U]nless businessmen can assess the legal consequences of a merger with some confidence, sound business planning is retarded. . . . And so in any case in which it is possible, without doing violence to the congressional objective embodied in Section 7, to simplify the test of illegality, the courts ought to do so in the interest of sound and practical judicial administration. This is such a case.

Specifically, we think that a merger which produces a firm controlling an undue percentage share of the relevant market, and results in a significant increase in the concentration of firms in that market, is so inherently likely to lessen competition substantially that it must be enjoined in the absence of evidence clearly showing that the merger is not likely to have such anticompetitive effects.

Such a test lightens the burden of proving illegality only with respect to mergers whose size makes them inherently suspect in light of Congress' design in Section 7 to prevent undue concentration.

The merger of appellees will result in a single bank's controlling at least 30 percent of the commercial banking business in the four-county Philadelphia metropolitan area. Without attempting to specify the smallest market share which would still be considered to threaten undue concentration, we are clear that 30 percent presents that threat. Further, whereas presently the two largest banks in the area (First Pennsylvania and PNB) control between them approximately 44 percent of the area's commercial banking business, the two largest after the merger (PNB-Girard and First Pennsylvania) will control 59 percent. Plainly, we think, this increase of more than 33 percent in concentration must be regarded as significant.

Our conclusion that these percentages raise an inference that the effect of the contemplated merger of appellees may be substantially to lessen competition is not an arbitrary one, although neither the terms of Section 7 nor the legislative history suggests that any particular percentage share was deemed critical.

[I]t is suggested that the increased lending limit of the resulting bank will enable it to compete with the large out-of-state banks, particularly the New York banks, for very large loans. We reject this application of the concept of "countervailing power." If anticompetitive effects in one market could be justified by procompetitive consequences in another, the logical upshot would be that every firm in an industry could, without violating Section 7, embark on a series of mergers that would make it in the end as large as the industry leader. For if all the commercial banks in the Philadelphia area merged into one, it would be smaller than the largest bank in New York City.

The judgment of the District Court is *reversed* and the case *remanded* with direction to enter judgment enjoining the proposed merger.

CASE QUESTIONS

1. What is a *horizontal* merger? Explain.
2. What was the relevant "line of commerce" in this case? The relevant "section of the country?"
3. What is "concentration" in an antitrust sense? Was the relevant market increasing or decreasing in concentration?
4. Where did the presumptive illegality test come from? The U.S. Constitution? Congress? The Supreme Court?
5. What is an *objective* test? Was the presumptive illegality test an objective test?
6. The presumptive illegality test for horizontal mergers contains two subtests, both of which must be met before the proposed merger is presumed to be illegal:
   a. *30 percent "market share" test.*
      (1) Would the merged firms, *after* the merger, control 30 percent or more of the market share of the relevant market?
   (2) Did PNB and Girard in this case?
   b. *33 percent increase in "concentration" test.*
      (1) Would the proposed merger cause an increase in concentration of 33 percent or more in the relevant market?
      (2) Did the PNB–Girard merger meet this test? Completing the following table may help you answer this question.

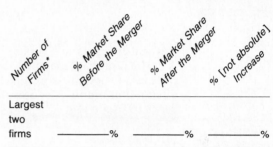

Number of Firms*	% Market Share Before the Merger	% Market Share After the Merger	% [not absolute] Increase
Largest two firms	———%	———%	———%

* The court may choose the number of firms it deems relevant.

7. If a proposed merger falls within the presumptive illegality test, is the merger absolutely prohibited under Section 7 of the Clayton Act? Explain.
8. If a proposed merger does not meet the presumptive illegality test, is it automatically lawful? If not, what test is used to review the lawfulness of the merger?

Policy Issue. Does the presumptive illegality test help businesses in assessing the legality of proposed mergers? Why or why not?

Economics Issue. Is the presumptive illegality test supported by economic theory? Or is it a shortcut for lazy judges and justices?

Ethics Issue. Is it ethical for businesses to attempt to merge even if the merger would violate the presumptive illegality test?

Social Responsibility. Do the courts owe a duty of social responsibility to adopt *objective* tests to help clarify an otherwise confusing area of the law?

The Bank Merger Act of 1966. Congress enacted the *Bank Merger Act of 1966* in reaction to the *Philadelphia National Bank* case. The Bank Merger Act of 1966 legalizes bank mergers that are not challenged by the Attorney General within 30 days of the appropriate banking agency's approval. If a proposed bank merger is challenged by the Attorney General, the courts are not bound by the agency's determination, but may make their own judgment as to whether or not the bank merger violates Section 7.

The presumptive illegality test announced by the Supreme Court in *Philadelphia National Bank* is still precedent for all horizontal mergers in the banking industry and in other industries.

VERTICAL MERGERS

Vertical mergers are subject to review under Section 7 of the Clayton Act. A vertical merger may be "forward" into a purchasing market (i.e., a supplier attempts to acquire a purchaser), or "backward" into a supplying market (i.e., a retailer attempts to acquire a supplier). As in all merger actions, the relevant geographical and product markets must be determined in analyzing the legality of a vertical merger. These definitions are hotly contested in most vertical merger cases.

The rationale cited by the legislature and courts for preventing vertical mergers between suppliers and customers is that such a merger has the potential of *foreclosing* or squeezing out competitors who are purchasers or sellers to one of the parties of the proposed merger. In vertical mergers where the foreclosure is more than *de minimis,* the court must consider any economic or historical factors that are specific to the case, such as barriers to entry, trend toward concentration, nature and purpose of the merger, etc. The United States Supreme Court has not announced a presumptive illegality standard for vertical mergers.

In *Brown Shoe Co., Inc. v. United States* the Supreme Court enjoined a vertical merger between a shoe manufacturer and a shoe retailer, finding that the merger would substantially lessen competition.

VERTICAL MERGER

BROWN SHOE CO., INC. v. UNITED STATES

370 U.S. 294 (1962)
UNITED STATES SUPREME COURT

Mr. Chief Justice Warren delivered the opinion of the Court.

This suit was initiated in November 1955 when the Government filed a civil action in the United States District Court for the Eastern District of Missouri alleging that a contemplated merger between the G. R. Kinney Company, Inc. (Kinney), and the Brown Shoe Company, Inc. (Brown), through an exchange of Kinney for Brown stock, would violate Section 7 of the Clayton Act.

A motion by the Government for a preliminary injunction *pendente lite* was denied, and the companies were permitted to merge provided, however, that their businesses be operated separately and that their assets be kept separately identifiable. The merger was then effected on May 1, 1956.

THE VERTICAL ASPECTS OF THE MERGER

Economic arrangements between companies standing in a supplier-customer relationship are characterized as "vertical." The primary vice of a vertical merger or other arrangement tying a customer to a supplier is that, by foreclosing the competitors of either party from a segment of the market otherwise open to them, the arrangement may act as a "clog on competition," *Standard Oil Co. of California v. United States,* which "deprive[s] . . . rivals of a fair opportunity to compete." Every extended vertical arrangement by its very nature, for at least a time, denies to competitors of the supplier the opportunity to compete for part or all of the trade of the customer-party to the vertical arrangement. However, the Clayton Act does not render unlawful all such vertical arrangements, but forbids only those whose effect "may be substantially to lessen competition, or to tend to create a monopoly" "in any line of commerce in any section of the country."

The Product Market

The outer boundaries of a product market are determined by the reasonable interchangeability of use or the cross-elasticity of demand between the product itself and substitutes for it. However, within this broad market, well-defined submarkets may exist which, in themselves, constitute product markets for antitrust purposes.

[W]e conclude that the record supports the District Court's finding that the relevant lines of commerce are men's, women's, and children's shoes. . . . Appellant, however, contends that the District Court's definitions fail to recognize sufficiently "price/quality" and "age/sex" distinctions in shoes. Brown argues that the predominantly medium-priced shoes which it manufactures occupy a product market different from the predominantly low-priced shoes which Kinney sells.

[W]e agree with the District Court that in this case a further division of product lines based on "price/quality" differences [or "age/sex" distinctions] would be "unrealistic." . . . Further division does not aid us in analyzing the effects of this merger.

The Geographic Market

We agree with the parties and the District Court that insofar as the vertical aspect of this merger is concerned, the relevant geographic market is the entire Nation. The relationships of product value, bulk, weight and consumer demand enable manufacturers to distribute their shoes on a nationwide basis, as Brown and Kinney, in fact, do. The anticompetitive effects of the merger are to be measured within this range of distribution.

The Probable Effect of the Merger

Once the area of effective competition affected by a vertical arrangement has been defined, an analysis must be made to determine if the effect of the arrangement "may be substantially to lessen competition, or to tend to create a monopoly" in this market.

[T]he diminution of the vigor of competition which may stem from a vertical arrangement results primarily from a foreclosure of a share of the market otherwise open to competitors, . . . If the share of the market foreclosed is so large that it approaches monopoly proportions, the Clayton Act will, of course, have been violated; but the arrangement will also have run afoul of the Sherman Act . . . On the other hand, foreclosure of a *de minimis* share of the market will not tend "substantially to lessen competition."

Between these extremes, in cases such as the one before us, in which the foreclosure is neither of monopoly nor *de minimis* proportions, the percentage of the market foreclosed by the vertical arrangement cannot itself be decisive. In such cases, it becomes necessary to undertake an examination of various economic and historical factors in order to determine whether the arrangement under review is of the type Congress sought to proscribe.

The present merger involved neither small companies nor failing companies. In 1955, the date of this merger, Brown was the fourth largest manufacturer in the shoe industry with sales of approximately 25 million pairs of shoes and assets of over $72,000,000 while Kinney had sales of about 8 million pairs of shoes and assets of about $18,000,000. Not only was Brown one of the leading manufacturers of men's, women's, and children's shoes, but Kinney, with over 350 retail outlets, owned and operated the largest independent chain of family shoe stores in the Nation. Thus, in this industry, no merger between a manufacturer and an independent retailer could involve a larger potential market foreclosure. Moreover, it is apparent both from past behavior of Brown and from the testimony of Brown's President, that Brown would use its ownership of Kinney to force Brown shoes into Kinney stores.

Another important factor to consider is the trend toward concentration in the industry. . . . Brown argues that the shoe industry is at present composed of a large number of manufacturers and retailers, and that the industry is dynamically competitive. But remaining vigor cannot immunize a merger if the trend in that industry is toward oligopoly. It is the probable effect of the merger upon the *future* as well as the present which the Clayton Act commands the courts and the Commission to examine.

The District Court's findings, and the record facts, convince us that the shoe industry is being subjected to just such a cumulative series of vertical mergers which, if left unchecked, will be likely "substantially to lessen competition." . . . We reach this conclusion because the trend toward vertical integration in the shoe industry, when combined with Brown's avowed policy of forcing its own shoes upon its retail subsidiaries, may foreclose competition from a substantial share of the markets for men's, women's, and children's shoes, without producing any countervailing competitive, economic, or social advantages.

We hold that the District Court was correct in concluding that this merger may tend to lessen competition substantially in the retail sale of men's, women's, and children's shoes in the overwhelming majority of those cities and their environs in which both Brown and Kinney sell through owned or controlled outlets.

The judgment is *affirmed.*

CASE QUESTIONS

1. What is a vertical merger? Was this a "forwards" or "backwards" vertical merger?
2. What were the relevant *lines of commerce* in this case? Why did Brown Shoe argue for a further division of product lines based on "price/quality" and "age/sex" distinctions? Explain.
3. Are *all* vertical mergers illegal under Section 7? Which of the following mergers are illegal?
   a. merger where foreclosure is *de minimis*
   b. merger where foreclosure approaches monopoly proportions
4. Did the merger in this case fall under either of the two above categories? If not, what standard was used to judge the legality of this vertical merger?
5. Was the relevant market increasing or decreasing in concentration? Did this matter to the Court's decision?

Policy Issue. Should a court be permitted to assess *probable* and *future* effects of a merger in determining its legality under Section 7? Or should a court be only allowed to consider *actual* and *present* effects of a merger?

Economics Issue. What does *foreclosure* mean? Who would be *foreclosed* by this merger? Competitors of Brown Shoe? Competitors of Kinney? Kinney? Draw a diagram and show the foreclosure in this case.

Ethics Issue. Why do firms merge vertically? Is this conduct ethical?

Social Responsibility. Do firms owe a duty of social responsibility not to engage in vertical mergers? Is society (e.g., consumers) helped or harmed by vertical mergers?

MARKET-EXTENSION AND CONGLOMERATE MERGERS

"Market-extension" mergers between firms whose markets do not overlap (i.e., firms that make the same product but serve different geographical areas, or firms that make somewhat complementary but not similar products), and "Conglomerate" mergers (all mergers that cannot be defined as horizontal, vertical, or market extension mergers), are subject to review under Section 7 of the Clayton Act. However, the typical analyses applied to horizontal and vertical mergers do not apply to market-extension or conglomerate mergers.

This is because the service areas of the firms do not overlap as they do in horizontal mergers, and there is no foreclosure of competition as there is in vertical mergers.

Fearing that the wealth and power of the country could be accumulated in a relatively few corporations if market extension and conglomerate mergers went unchecked, the Justice Department and the Federal Trade Commission have advanced several theories to deal with market extension and conglomerate mergers, including

1. the "unfair advantage" theory
2. the potential competition theory
3. the "toehold" theory
4. *de novo* theory
5. potential reciprocity theory

The courts have accepted some of these theories, and rejected others.

"Unfair Advantage" Theory. The courts have held that where a large firm acquires a firm in a small market, which would give the acquired firm some "unfair advantage" because of the name, finances, or expertise of the acquiring firm, the merger may be enjoined under Clayton Act Section 7. The stated rationale for the application of the "unfair advantage" theory to enjoining conglomerate mergers under Section 7 is that some firms have "deep pockets," and to allow them to enter any market through merger would be unfair to other smaller firms in the industry and to consumers.

In the landmark case, *FTC v. Procter & Gamble Co.*, the Supreme Court enjoined a merger between Procter & Gamble Co. and Clorox Chemical Co. based on the theory that Procter & Gamble Co., because of its size, "deep pocket," and marketing power, would have an "unfair advantage" if it were allowed to enter the bleach market by merger with the Clorox Chemical Company.

"UNFAIR ADVANTAGE" THEORY

FEDERAL TRADE COMMISSION v. PROCTER & GAMBLE CO.

386 U.S. 568 (1967)
UNITED STATES SUPREME COURT

Mr. Justice Douglas delivered the opinion of the Court.

This is a proceeding initiated by the Federal Trade Commission charging that respondent, Procter & Gamble Co., had acquired the assets of Clorox Chemical Co. in violation of Section 7 of the Clayton Act, as amended by the Celler-Kefauver Act. The charge was that Procter's acquisition of Clorox might substantially lessen competition or tend to create a monopoly in the production and sale of household liquid bleaches.

At the time of the merger, in 1957, Clorox was the leading manufacturer in the heavily concentrated household liquid bleach industry. It is agreed that household liquid bleach is the relevant line of commerce. The product is used in the home as a germicide and disinfectant, and, more importantly, as a whitening agent in washing clothes and fabrics. It is a distinctive product with no close substitutes. Liquid bleach is a low-price, high-turnover consumer product sold mainly through grocery stores and supermarkets. The relevant geographical market is the Nation and a series of regional markets. Because of high shipping costs and low sales price, it is not feasible to ship the product more than 300 miles from its point of manufacture. Most manufacturers are limited to competition within a single region since they have but one plant. Clorox is the only firm selling nationally; it has 13 plants distributed throughout the Nation. Purex, Clorox's closest competitor in size, does not distribute its bleach in the northeast or mid-Atlantic States; in 1957, Purex's bleach was available in less than 50 percent of the national market.

After . . . hearings, the [hearing] examiner . . . held the acquisition unlawful and ordered divestiture. The Commission affirmed the examiner and ordered divestiture. The Court of Appeals for the Sixth Circuit reversed and directed that the Commission's complaint be dismissed.

Since all liquid bleach is chemically identical, advertising and sales promotion are vital. In 1957 Clorox spent almost $3,700,000 on advertising, imprinting the value of its bleach in the mind of the consumer. In addition, it spent $1,700,000 for other promotional activities. The Commission found that these heavy expenditures went far to explain why Clorox maintained so high a market share despite the fact that its brand, though chemically indistinguishable from rival brands, retailed for a price equal to or, in many instances, higher than its competitors.

Procter is a large, diversified manufacturer of low-price, high-turnover household products sold through grocery, drug, and department stores. Prior to its acquisition of Clorox, it did not produce household liquid bleach. Its 1957 sales were in excess of $1,100,000,000 from which it realized profits of more than $67,000,000; its assets were over $500,000,000. Procter has been marked by rapid growth and diversification. It has successfully developed and introduced a number of new products. Its primary activity is in the general area of soaps, detergents, and cleansers; in 1957, of total domestic sales, more than one-half (over $500,000,000)

were in this field. Procter was the dominant factor in this area. It accounted for 54.4 percent of all packaged detergent sales. The industry is heavily concentrated—Procter and its nearest competitors, Colgate-Palmolive and Lever Brothers, account for 80 percent of the market.

In the marketing of soaps, detergents, and cleansers, as in the marketing of household liquid bleach, advertising and sales promotion are vital. In 1957, Procter was the Nation's largest advertiser, spending more than $80,000,000 on advertising and an additional $47,000,000 on sales promotion. Due to its tremendous volume, Procter receives substantial discounts from the media. As a multi-product producer Procter enjoys substantial advantages in advertising and sales promotion. Thus, it can and does feature several products in its promotions, reducing the printing, mailing, and other costs for each product. It also purchases network programs on behalf of several products, enabling it to give each product network exposure at a fraction of the cost per product that a firm with only one product to advertise would incur.

The Commission found that the acquisition might substantially lessen competition. The findings and reasoning of the Commission need be only briefly summarized. The Commission found that the substitution of Procter with its huge assets and advertising advantages for the already dominant Clorox would dissuade new entrants and discourage active competition from the firms already in the industry due to fear of retaliation by Procter. The Commission thought it relevant that retailers might be induced to give Clorox preferred shelf space since it would be manufactured by Procter, which also produced a number of other products marketed by the retailers. There was also the danger that Procter might underprice Clorox in order to drive out competition, and subsidize the underpricing with revenue from other products. The Commission carefully reviewed the effect of the acquisition on the structure of the industry, noting that "[t]he practical tendency of the . . . merger . . . is to transform the liquid bleach industry into an arena of big business competition only, with the few small firms that have not disappeared through merger eventually falling by the wayside, unable to compete with their giant rivals."

The Court of Appeals said that the Commission's

finding of illegality had been based on "treacherous conjecture," mere possibility and suspicion.

All mergers are within the reach of § 7, . . . As noted by the Commission, this merger is neither horizontal, vertical, nor conglomerate. Since the products of the acquired company are complementary to those of the acquiring company and may be produced with similar facilities, marketed through the same channels and in the same manner, and advertised by the same media, the Commission aptly called this acquisition a "product-extension merger."

The anticompetitive effects with which this product-extension merger is fraught can easily be seen: the substitution of the powerful acquiring firm for the smaller, but already dominant, firm may substantially reduce the competitive structure of the industry by raising entry barriers and by dissuading the smaller firms from aggressively competing; . . .

The acquisition may also have the tendency of raising the barriers to new entry. The major competitive weapon in the successful marketing of bleach is advertising. Clorox was limited in this area by its relatively small budget and its inability to obtain substantial discounts. By contrast, Procter's budget was much larger; and, although it would not devote its entire budget to advertising Clorox, it could divert a large portion to meet the short-term threat of a new entrant. Procter would be able to use its volume discounts to advantage in advertising Clorox. Thus, a new entrant would be much more reluctant to face the giant Procter than it would have been to face the smaller Clorox.

Possible economies cannot be used as a defense to illegality. Congress was aware that some mergers which lessen competition may also result in economies but it struck the balance in favor of protecting competition.

The judgment of the Court of Appeals is *reversed* and *remanded* with instructions to affirm and enforce the Commission's order.

CASE QUESTIONS

1. Was this a horizontal merger? Why or why not?
2. What is a *product extension* merger? Explain.
3. What was the relevant line of commerce in this case? The relevant section of the country?
4. What does the "unfair advantage" theory adopted by the Supreme Court in this case provide? Explain.
5. What were the fears of the Supreme Court regarding the following Procter and Gamble marketing advantages?
   a. multiproduct network advertising
   b. underpricing competitors
   c. preferred shelf space
   d. discounting
   e. dissuading new entrants

   Do you believe these fears were well founded or "treacherous conjecture" as held by the Court of Appeals?
6. When did the merger take place? When was this case decided by the Supreme Court? Was this a well-written *legal* opinion?

Policy Issue. Does this case hold that "bigness is bad"? Should it be? Do you agree with the "unfair advantage" theory as developed by the Supreme Court?

Economics Issue. Can the economic efficiency of a merger justify the merger? Why or why not?

Ethics Issue. Is it ethical for a giant corporation to enter a market by acquiring a small firm through merger?

Social Responsibility. Do corporations owe a duty of social responsibility not to transform certain industries into an "arena of big business"?

The Potential Competition ("Waiting in the Wings") Theory. The U.S. Supreme Court has recognized a *potential competition* ("waiting in the wings") theory for enjoining market extension and conglomerate mergers. Under this theory, a merger is held to violate Section 7 of the Clayton Act if it would eliminate the *acquiring* firm from a perceived position of "waiting in the wings" to enter the industry into which it is merging.

The rationale underlying the "wings" theory is that if the acquiring firm is viewed by firms *in* the industry as a *potential entrant* into that industry, such pressure will force firms already in the marketplace to act more competitively. The perceived potential entrant, and the competition it is considered to cause in the industry, would be eliminated if the potential entrant were allowed to enter the industry through a conglomerate merger.

The elements necessary to establish a *prima facie* "wings" effect case to enjoin a market extension or conglomerate merger are:

1. the existing firms in the market are influenced by the potential entry of the acquiring firms
2. the acquiring firm has the capacity and means to individually enter the industry or market
3. the number of potential entrants is so low that the elimination of the acquiring firm from the "wings" of the market through a conglomerate merger would more than likely cause a substantial lessening of competition.

"Toehold" Theory. The Justice Department has often asserted that a conglomerate merger should be enjoined where a smaller firm than the one proposed to be acquired is available for acquisition, thus providing the acquiring firm with a "toehold" in the market rather than allowing the acquisition of a major company in the market. Although mentioning the "toehold" theory in dicta and dissenting opinions, the U.S. Supreme Court has not yet sanctioned the doctrine for enjoining conglomerate mergers.

De Novo *Theory.* The Justice Department has asserted that a proposed market extension or conglomerate merger may be struck down where it is shown that the acquiring firm could have entered the market of the acquired firm *de novo.* This "future deconcentration" theory has not been accepted by the courts. What would happen to most mergers if the courts applied the *de novo* theory to all mergers?

In *United States v. Falstaff Brewing Corp.* the Supreme Court applied the potential competition ("wings effect") theory to enjoin a geographical market-extension merger between two regional brewers.

"POTENTIAL COMPETITION" THEORY

UNITED STATES v. FALSTAFF BREWING CORP.

410 U.S. 526 (1973)
UNITED STATES SUPREME COURT

Mr. Justice White delivered the opinion of the Court.

Alleging that Falstaff Brewing Corp.'s acquisition of the Narragansett Brewing Co. in 1965 violated Section 7 of the Clayton Act, as amended, the United States brought this antitrust suit under the theory that potential competition in the New En-

gland beer market may be substantially lessened by the acquisition. The District Court held to the contrary, and we noted probable jurisdiction to determine whether the trial court applied an erroneous legal standard in so deciding.

As stipulated by the parties, the relevant product market is the production and sale of beer, and the six New England States compose the geographic market.

Of the Nation's ten largest brewers in 1964, only Falstaff and two others did not sell beer in New England; Falstaff was the largest of the three and had the closest brewery. In relation to the New England market, Falstaff sold its product in western Ohio, to the west and in Washington, D.C., to the south.

The acquired firm, Narragansett, was the largest seller of beer in New England at the time of its acquisition, with approximately 20 percent of the market; had been the largest seller for the five preceding years; had constantly expanded its brewery capacity between 1960 and 1965; and had acquired either the assets or the trademarks of several smaller brewers in and around the geographic market.

The fourth largest producer of beer in the United States at the time of acquisition, Falstaff was a regional brewer with 5.9 percent of the Nation's production in 1964, having grown steadily since its beginning as a brewer in 1933 through acquisition and expansion of other breweries. As of January 1965, Falstaff sold beer in 32 States, but did not sell in the Northeast, an area composed of New England and States such as New York and New Jersey; the area being the highest beer consumption region in the United States.

Falstaff met increasingly strong competition in the 1960's from four brewers who sold in all of the significant markets. National brewers possess competitive advantages since they are able to advertise on a nationwide basis, their beers have greater prestige than regional or local beers, and they are less affected by the weather or labor problems in a particular region. Thus Falstaff concluded that it must convert from "regional" to "national" status, if it was to compete effectively with the national producers. For several years Falstaff publicly expressed its desire for national distribution and after making several efforts in the early 1960's to enter the Northeast by acquisition, agreed to acquire Narragansett in 1965.

Before the acquisition was accomplished, the United States brought suit alleging that the acquisition would violate Section 7 because its effect may be to substantially lessen competition in the production and sale of beer in the New England market.

This contention was based on two grounds: because Falstaff was a potential entrant and because the acquisition eliminated competition that would have existed had Falstaff entered the market *de novo* or by acquisition and expansion of a smaller firm, a so-called "toe-hold" acquisition. The acquisition was completed after the Government's motions for injunctive relief were denied, and Falstaff agreed to operate Narragansett as a separate subsidiary until otherwise ordered by the court.

POTENTIAL COMPETITION THEORY

Section 7 of the Clayton Act forbids mergers in any line of commerce where the effect may be substantially to lessen competition or tend to create a monopoly. The section proscribes many mergers between competitors in a market, . . . Suspect also is the acquisition by a company not competing in the market but so situated as to be a potential competitor and likely to exercise substantial influence on market behavior. Entry through merger by such a company, although its competitive conduct in the market may be the mirror image of that of the acquired company, may nevertheless violate Section 7 because the entry eliminates a potential competitor exercising present influence on the market. As the Court stated in *United States v. Penn-Olin Chemical Co.,*

> The existence of an aggressive, well equipped and well financed corporation engaged in the same or related lines of commerce waiting anxiously to enter an oligopolistic market would be a substantial incentive to competition which cannot be underestimated.

The District Court, however, relying heavily on testimony of Falstaff officers, concluded that the company had no intent to enter the New England market except through acquisition and that it therefore could not be considered a potential competitor in that market. . . . The District Court erred as a matter of law.

The specific question with respect to this phase of the case is not what Falstaff's internal company decisions were but whether, given its financial capabilities and conditions in the New England market, it would be reasonable to consider it a potential entrant into that market. . . . The District Court should therefore have appraised the economic facts about Falstaff and the New England market in order to determine whether in any realistic sense Falstaff could be said to be a potential competitor on the fringe of the market with likely influence on existing competition.

[W]e *remand* this case for the District Court to make the proper assessment of Falstaff as a potential competitor.

DE NOVO THEORY

We leave for another day the question of the applicability of Section 7 to a merger that will leave competition in the marketplace exactly as it was, neither hurt nor helped, and that is challengeable under Section 7 only on grounds that the company could, but did not, enter *de novo* or through "toe-hold" acquisition and that there is less competition than there would have been had entry been in such a manner.

Mr. Justice Rehnquist, with whom **Mr. Justice Stewart** concurs, dissenting.

For this Court to reverse and to remand for consideration of a possible factual basis for a theory never advanced by the plaintiff is a drastic and unwarranted departure from the most basic principles of civil litigation and appellate review.

CASE QUESTIONS

1. Was this a horizontal merger? Why or why not?
2. What is a *geographic extension* merger? Explain.
3. What was the relevant line of commerce in this case? The relevant section of the country?
4. What does the "potential competition" theory provide? Why is it also called the "waiting in the wings" theory? *Who* is waiting in the wings?
5. *Whose* perception is important in the waiting in the wings theory? That of the acquiring company? The acquired company? Competitors of the acquired company? Why is their perception important? Explain.
6. Did the Supreme Court decide this case as to whether Falstaff violated the potential competition theory? How would you decide this issue on remand?
7. What does the *de novo* theory provide? Did the Supreme Court adopt this as a valid theory to prevent mergers?

Policy Issue. Was the potential competition theory advanced by the plaintiff in this case? Should courts be allowed to develop theories without the issue being before them in the pleadings?

Economics Issue. Did Falstaff's decision to expand into the New England market through the acquisition of Narragansett make economic sense for the firm? Why or why not?

Ethics Issue. Is it ethical for a corporation to expand its markets through external geographic extension mergers?

Social Responsibility. Do corporations owe a duty of social responsibility to expand into new markets only through *de novo* internal expansion rather than through external mergers?

Potential Reciprocity Theory. A conglomerate merger may be enjoined under the Clayton Act, Section 7 where *potential reciprocity* is shown. For example in Exhibit 10–1, a large computer company that purchases large amounts of paper products acquires a paper mill that sells raw product to a paper manufacturer. In this case, the *potential* for the computer company to require its immediate supplier to buy its raw product from its newly acquired paper mill before the computer company will buy the finished product creates a potential reciprocity that may violate Section 7.

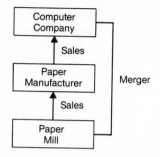

Exhibit 10–1. Diagram of potential reciprocity theory.

REMEDIES FOR VIOLATING SECTION 7

A Section 7 action may be brought by the Justice Department, Federal Trade Commission, or by any individual. The Justice Department will generally bring an action against a proposed merger and seek an *injunction* to prevent the merger. The Federal Trade Commission may seek to prevent a merger by issuing a *cease-and-desist* order. Where a merger has been consummated, the government may seek a *divestiture* of the merger. Criminal penalties are not available under the Clayton Act, but may be obtained if it is shown that the merger violates Section 1 of the Sherman Act ("restraint of trade").

An individual plaintiff may bring a private *civil* action for treble damages against a defendant for engaging in a merger in violation of Section 7 of the Clayton Act.

In *Brunswick Corp. v. Pueblo Bowl-O-Mat, Inc.* the Supreme Court held that a private plaintiff had failed to prove the requisite "antitrust injury" required to be successful in a Section 7 treble damage action.

ANTITRUST INJURY

BRUNSWICK CORP. v. PUEBLO BOWL-O-MAT, INC.

429 U.S. 477 (1977)
UNITED STATES SUPREME COURT

Mr. Justice Marshall delivered the opinion of the Court.

Petitioner is one of the two largest manufacturers of bowling equipment in the United States. Respondents are three of the 10 bowling centers owned by Treadway Companies, Inc. Since 1965, petitioner has acquired and operated a large number of bowling centers, including six in the markets in which respondents operate. Respondents instituted this action contending that these acquisitions violated various provisions of the antitrust laws.

In the late 1950s, the bowling industry expanded rapidly, and petitioner's sales of lanes, automatic pinsetters, and ancillary equipment rose accordingly. Since this equipment requires a major capital expenditure—$12,600 for each lane and pinsetter, —most of petitioner's sales were for secured credit.

In the early 1960s, the bowling industry went into a sharp decline. Petitioner's sales quickly dropped to preboom levels. Moreover, petitioner experienced great difficulty in collecting money owed it; by the end of 1964 over $100,000,000, or more than 25 percent, of petitioner's accounts were more than 90 days delinquent. Repossessions rose dramatically, but attempts to sell or lease the repossessed equipment met with only limited success. Because petitioner had borrowed close to $250,000,000 to finance its credit sales, it was, as the Court of Appeals concluded, "in serious financial difficulty."

To meet this difficulty, petitioner began acquiring and operating defaulting bowling centers when their equipment could not be resold and a positive cash flow could be expected from operating the centers. During the seven years preceding the trial in this case, petitioner acquired 222 centers, 54 of which it either disposed of or closed. These acquisitions made petitioner by far the largest operator of bowling centers, with over five times as many centers as its next largest competitor. Petitioner's net worth in 1965 was more than eight times greater, and its gross revenue more than seven times greater, than the total for the 11 next largest bowling chains. Nevertheless, petitioner controlled only 2 percent of the bowling centers in the United States.

Respondents initiated this action in June 1966, alleging, *inter alia,* that these acquisitions might substantially lessen competition or tend to create a monopoly in violation of Section 7 of the Clayton Act. Respondents sought damages, pursuant to Section 4 of the Act, for three times "the reasonably expectable profits to be made [by respondents] from the operation of their bowling centers."

Trial was held in the spring of 1973, following an initial mistrial due to a hung jury. . . . The jury returned a verdict in favor of respondents in the amount of $2,358,030, which represented the minimum estimate by respondents of the additional income they would have realized had the acquired centers been closed. As required by law, the District Court trebled the damages. It also awarded respondents costs and attorneys' fees totaling $446,-977.32, and, sitting as a court of equity, it ordered petitioner to divest itself of the centers involved here. Petitioner appealed.

Antitrust Injury

The issue for decision is a narrow one . . . , whether antitrust damages are available where the sole injury alleged is that competitors were contin-

ued in business, thereby denying respondents an anticipated increase in market shares.

Plainly, to recover damages respondents must prove more than that petitioner violated Section 7, since such proof establishes only that injury may result. Respondents contend that the only additional element they need demonstrate is that they are in a worse position than they would have been had petitioner not committed those acts. The Court of Appeals agreed.

Every merger of two existing entities into one, whether lawful or unlawful, has the potential for producing economic readjustments that adversely affect some persons. But Congress has not condemned mergers on that account; it has condemned them only when they may produce anticompetitive effects.

If the acquisitions here were unlawful, it is because they brought a "deep pocket" parent into a market of "pygmies." Yet respondents' injury—the loss of income that would have accrued had the acquired centers gone bankrupt—bears no relationship to the size of either the acquiring company or its competitors. Respondents would have suffered the identical "loss"—but no compensable injury—had the acquired centers instead obtained refinancing or been purchased by "shallow pocket" parents, . . . Thus, respondents' injury was not of "the type that the statute was intended to forestall."

[R]espondents complain that by acquiring the failing centers petitioner preserved competition, thereby depriving respondents of the benefits of increased concentration. The damages respondents obtained [at trial] are designed to provide them with the profits they would have realized had competition been reduced. The antitrust laws, however, were enacted for "the protection of *competition, not competitors.*" It is inimical to the purposes of . . . [antitrust] laws to award damages for the type of injury claimed here.

We therefore hold that for plaintiffs to recover treble damages on account of Section 7 violations, they must prove more than injury causally linked to an illegal presence in the market. Plaintiffs must prove *antitrust* injury, which is to say injury of the type the antitrust laws were intended to prevent and that flows from that which makes defendants' acts unlawful. The injury should reflect the anticompetitive effect either of the violation or of anticompetitive acts made possible by the violation.

Since respondents did not prove any cognizable damages and have not offered any justification for allowing respondents, after two trials and over 10 years of litigation, yet a third opportunity to do so, it follows that, petitioner is entitled . . . to judgment . . . notwithstanding the verdict [of the trial court].

CASE QUESTIONS

1. What type of "merger" occurred in this case? Was it a formal merger? Explain.
2. How did Brunswick finance the sale of the bowling alleys and equipment to bowling alley operators? Did Brunswick take a *secured* position in these alleys?
3. Did Brunswick have any other alternatives then to foreclose on the bowling alley and operate them? Did any of these alternatives make economic sense to Brunswick?
4. How much did the jury award the plaintiffs as damages? How were these damages calculated? Explain in detail.
5. Can there be a finding of a "substantial lessening of competition" as required by Section 7 without the defendant being liable for treble damages? Explain.

Policy Issue. If the Supreme Court had affirmed the award of the trial court, would it have advanced or hindered the purpose of the antitrust laws to foster competition?

Economics Issue. Do *all* mergers cause some economic injury? Explain. If so, should all mergers therefore be condemned? Why or why not?

Ethics Issue. Did Brunswick act unethically in this case? Did the plaintiff bowling alley operators act unethically?

Social Responsibility. Did Brunswick enter a market of "pygmies"? Did Brunswick owe a duty of social responsibility to keep the bowling alleys open? Or to close them?

Defenses to Section 7 Actions   One of the major ways for a defendant to defeat a charge under Clayton Act Section 7 is to show that the plaintiff has failed to prove one of the essential elements to a Section 7 action, for example by:

1. incorrect definition of the product market
2. incorrect definition of the relevant geographical market
3. showing no substantial lessening of competition
4. showing no injury caused by the antitrust violation.

In addition, a defendant can assert the following two defenses: the failing-company doctrine and the small-company doctrine.

"Failing Company" Doctrine.   Where a company is considered to be "failing," the courts have recognized an exception from Clayton Act Section 7 to allow a merger between the failing company and a competitor. The failing company exception has been narrowed recently to allow a merger of a failing company and a competitor, which would normally violate Section 7, only where there is no other alternative and no other purchaser could be interested. The burden of proof is on the party seeking to establish the "failing company" exception to Section 7.

"Small Company" Doctrine.   The courts have recognized, at least in *dicta*, that two or more small companies may be allowed to merge in order to compete

with large, dominant firms in the relevant market. The argument is that the "small company" doctrine promotes rather than hinders competition. One recent court decision seems to have rejected the small company doctrine; but its availability as an exception to a Clayton Act Section 7 action is currently suspect. In this excerpt from *Brown Shoe Co., Inc. v. United States*, Chief Justice Warren discussed both the "failing company" and the "small company" defense to a Clayton Act Section 7 charge.

[A]t the same time that it sought to create an effective tool for preventing all mergers having demonstrable anticompetitive effects, Congress recognized the stimulation to competition that might flow from particular mergers. When concern as to the Act's breadth was expressed, supporters of the amendments indicated that it would not impede, for example, a merger between two small companies to enable the combination to compete more effectively with larger corporations dominating the relevant market, nor a merger between a corporation which is financially healthy and a failing one which no longer can be a vital competitive factor in the market. . . . Taken as a whole, the legislative history illuminates congressional concern with the protection of *competition,* not *competitors,* and its desire to restrain mergers only to the extent that such combinations may tend to lessen competition.

 Increased economic efficiency has *never* been accepted by the legislature or the courts as a justification for a merger. The theory is that it is best to protect competition even if it means inefficiency in production. Congress has expressed a general preference that firms expand internally rather than seek efficiency of production through mergers.

Trend of the Law

The law regarding horizontal mergers is well established. In this area, the delineation of the relevant "line of commerce" and "section of the country" will remain the most important issues facing litigants and the courts in deciding horizontal merger cases under Section 7 of the Clayton Act. Other than the *Brown Shoe* case, the U.S. Supreme Court has not decided any major vertical merger cases. However, unlike the presumptive illegality test, which applies to horizontal mergers, there is no objective test to apply to help decide vertical merger cases. It is unlikely that such an objective standard can or will be delineated to measure the foreclosure that may be caused by vertical mergers.

The courts will continue to be faced in the future with the difficult task of applying the unfair competition and potential competition theories to market-extension and conglomerate mergers. It is unlikely that the Supreme Court will adopt either the toehold or *de novo* theories for preventing market-extension or conglomerate mergers.

The current trend in the law is for the government to challenge fewer companies attempting to merge. This trend was brought about by current Administration policy, as well as the substantial number of mergers caused by the recessionary times of the late 1970s and early 1980s. This trend toward the more liberalized application of the antitrust merger laws should continue for the foreseeable future.

REVIEW QUESTIONS

1. General Dynamics acquired Material Service Corporation, which owned United Electric Coal. Since General already controlled one strip mine, with the addition of United Electric's mine the firm became a substantial factor in the midwestern coal market. Although the total number of coal mines in the region had been declining up to the time of this purchase, most of the decline was due to a slackening in demand and the depletion of mineral resources rather than from mergers and acquisitions. In addition, United Electric had used up most of its coal reserves or already committed them to existing long-term contracts at the time of General's purchase. Further, for most uses, gasoline, oil, and nuclear power, which were in abundant supply, were all adequate substitutes for coal. The federal government brought an antitrust action against General Dynamics under Section 7 of the Clayton Act. The government argued that since there were fewer and fewer firms in the coal industry, the reduction of even a single competitor further centralized control. What is the relevant product market in this case? What would the government try to characterize as the relevant product market? What would be General Dynamic's characterization?

2. Alcoa was the leading producer of aluminum cable in the United States. Alcoa and Kaiser alone controlled over 50 percent of the market. Nine companies, including Rome Cable, which had a 1.3 percent market share, controlled 95.7 percent of the market. Alcoa purchased Rome Cable primarily because Rome manufactured copper cables, which would enable Alcoa to also compete in that market. Copper cable is used primarily to lay underground lines, whereas aluminum cable is used primarily above ground. Aluminum and copper are not readily interchangeable. The federal government sued Alcoa for an antitrust violation under Section 7 of the Clayton Act. The government argued that since the aluminum cable market was an oligopoly, the removal of any competitor, no matter how small, had an anticompetitive effect. Alcoa argued that the entire cable market is relevant and that in this market the acquisition of Rome would not violate Section 7. What was the relevant market in this case?

3. Bethlehem Steel was the second largest ingot producer in the U.S., with 15.4 percent of the market. Bethlehem and U.S. Steel together controlled nearly 45 percent of the market. Twelve companies controlled 83 percent of the market. Since the price of steel was relatively inelastic, both Bethlehem and U.S. Steel could affect the nationwide price of steel through their pricing and supply policies. Each firm had the ability to foreclose a potential source of supplies to buyers throughout the country. Bethlehem

acquired Youngstown, the fifth largest U.S. ingot producer with a 4.7 percent share of the market, in an effort to meet the competitive challenge of U.S. Steel and to expand its operations for the anticipated growth of the Chicago-area steel market. What type of merger is being attempted in this case? Does the merger violate Section 7 of the Clayton Act? What is the relevant analysis?

4. Von's Grocery Company proposed a merger with Shopping Bag Grocery Company. Von's was the third-largest food chain in the Los Angeles area and Shopping Bag was sixth. Their combined market share was 7.5 percent, which would make the merged firm the second largest grocer in Los Angeles. While both Von's and Shopping Bag had been expanding at a rapid rate for the previous eight years, the number of single-owner independent stores had declined by nearly 30 percent. During the same period, the number of grocery store chains had increased from 96 to 150 and nine of the top 20 chains had acquired 126 stores from their smaller competitors. Nevertheless, the Los Angeles market still had over 3,500 separate competitors. Does the combined market share of the merged firm violate Section 7 of the Clayton Act? *Yes, incipiency doctrine — "trend"*

5. Both Pennsalt Chemicals Co. and Olin Mathieson were diversified chemical companies. Both had considered expanding their business into the sale of sodium chlorate in the past but had dropped the idea. The two companies then decided to form a joint venture, Penn-Olin, to sell sodium chlorate. Within three years, Penn-Olin had a 27 percent market share in the southeastern United States. Are joint ventures subject to review under Section 7 of the Clayton Act? If so, what analysis will a court use?

6. National Bank of Commerce, the second-largest bank in Washington, had no branches in the Spokane area and was prohibited by state law from opening any. In order to expand, the firm acquired Washington Trust Bank, the largest bank in the Spokane area. The only other banks in the area were several small state banks. The federal government sued National for violation of the Clayton Act. What type of argument did the government make in this case? Does the merger violate Section 7?

7. Consolidated Foods, a large purchaser and distributor of processed foods, purchased Gentry, Inc, a manufacturer of dehydrated onion and garlic for use in food processing. Consolidated "suggested" to its suppliers that the firm would more readily do business with firms that used Gentry's products. However, Gentry's products were inferior to others available on the market. After the acquisition, Gentry's overall market share rose from 32 percent to 35 percent largely as a result of several new food-processing customers that the firm acquired; most of these new customers also were major suppliers to Consolidated. During the same period, however, Gentry's garlic sales dropped 12 percent. Did the merger violate Section 7 of the Clayton Act?

8. Grinnell is a diversified manufacturer with significant market shares in four industries: automatic sprinklers, sprinkler systems, power pipes, and pipe hangers. All of these markets, although relatively oligopolistic, have significant competition. There are no real entry barriers to any of these markets. Grinnell's market share does not exceed 25 percent in any of these markets and the firm cannot dictate price or foreclose competition.

International Telephone and Telegraph (ITT) is prepared to purchase Grinnell. ITT purchases less than 1 percent of the goods manufactured in any of these markets. ITT does not do business with many of Grinnell's customers and it has an antireciprocity policy that is widely known to all of its customers. Nevertheless, is the acquisition by a large conglomerate of a company having a major share of a given market a *per se* violation of the Clayton Act? Does ITT's proposed merger violate Section 7?

9. The *Star* and the *Citizen* were the only two local newspapers operating in Tucson, Arizona. Although both had made money in the past, the *Citizen* now began to slowly lose money (the *Star* was still profitable). Both newspapers agreed to form a new corporation, TNI, to jointly manage their financial interests. Although the *Citizen* had been losing money, it was not in danger of liquidation and had never been offered for sale prior to this merger. Is the merger legal under the failing-company doctrine? *No*

10. Ford Motor Company, the second-largest domestic automobile manufacturer, decided to enter the sparkplug market. The firm purchased a sparkplug plant, a battery plant, and extensive rights to a nationwide distribution system from Autolite, Inc, a major manufacturer of sparkplugs. Ford's purchase had an anticompetitive effect on the sparkplug industry because it removed a potential competitor ("waiting in the wings") and it foreclosed Ford as a major purchaser of sparkplugs. Ford's entry aggravated an already oligopolistic situation. The government sued Ford and the firm was found guilty of violating Section 7 of the Clayton Act. What remedy should the court provide?

11 PRICE DISCRIMINATION

INTRODUCTION

The American economy is comprised of a unique blend of large corporations and chain stores, intermediate size businesses, and thousands of "mom-and-pop" and boutique stores. Each must purchase supplies and sell goods at prices that allow them to make a profit in order to continue to stay in business. One method of achieving more sales, and thus larger profits, is to be able to purchase supplies at lower prices than the competitors, and thereby be able to undercut the competitors' prices and make larger profits. Sellers will often offer more favorable terms to preferred buyers (e.g., chain stores) than to other purchasers. This is commonly known as price discrimination.

Generally, price discrimination is defined as a vertical arrangement whereby a manufacturer or other distributor sells the same product to two or more different purchasers at different prices. Technically, price discrimination is the selling of the identical product to two different purchasers at prices that are in different ratios to the marginal cost of producing the products. The general definition is sufficient for the study of this chapter.

A seller's incentive to price discriminate is to obtain from each buyer individually or as a class the highest price that it will pay for a product. This can only be accomplished if the seller is able to charge different prices ("what each purchaser or market will bear") to different purchasers, rather than offering the same price to all purchasers equally. The incentive for a buyer to receive a price-discriminating price is the opportunity to purchase supplies more inexpensively than its competitors, and thereby either be able to sell the product at the same price as its competitors and make a larger profit, or to sell the product at a price lower than that of its competitors and make the same profit per item as its competitors on a consequently larger sales volume.

The Robinson-Patman Act. The coexistence of different-sized business organizations in the American economy is protected by the Clayton Act, which in general prohibits *price discrimination* that favors one buyer over another buyer. In 1936 Congress amended the Clayton Act; this amendment is known as the Robinson-Patman Act. This act was originally nicknamed the "chain store bill" because it was aimed at eliminating the preferential treatment accorded to chain stores by sellers of goods. Section 2(a) of the Robinson-Patman Act provides:

[I]t shall be unlawful for any person engaged in commerce . . . , either directly or indirectly, to discriminate in price between different purchasers of commodities of like grade and quality, . . . where the effect of such discrimination may be substantially to lessen competition or tend to create a monopoly in any line of commerce, or to injure, destroy, or prevent competition with any person who either grants or knowingly receives the benefit of such discrimination, or with customers of either of them: *Provided,* That nothing herein contained shall prevent differentials which make only due allowance for differences in the cost of manufacture, sale, or delivery resulting from the differing methods or quantities in which such commodities are to such purchasers sold or delivered . . .

PRICE DISCRIMINATION

There are numerous elements to a *prima facie* case of price discrimination. In summary, the elements are as follows.

1. A commodity of like grade and quality
2. is purchased by different purchasers
3. in two separate transactions contemporaneous in time
4. at different prices
5. where at least one transaction is across a state line
6. the effect of which "may be to substantially lessen competition . . . or tend to create a monopoly."

In order to price discriminate, a seller must also be able to identify and separate the buyers (i.e., by age, income, geography) and prevent the easy reselling of the product. Therefore, a firm must have "market power" to price discriminate. In a competitive market with homogeneous products, price discrimination by one seller would not be effective.

Commodities of Like Grade and Quality. The Robinson-Patman Act prohibits price discrimination in tangible "commodities." The provision of services (e.g., legal, medical), and the sale of intangibles (e.g., mutual fund shares, patents and copyrights, real estate leases), are not covered by the Robinson-Patman Act. "Mixed" sales, such as construction contracts where services and commodities are provided, are also not covered. Price discrimination in providing services or selling intangibles may be a "restraint of trade" in violation of Sherman Act Section 1, or an "unfair method of competition" in violation of the Federal Trade Commission Act Section 5.

Under the Robinson-Patman Act, the commodities must be of "like grade and quality." Products with *physical* differences that affect their purchase by consumers are not of "like grade and quality." Mere differences in labeling or brand name are generally held insufficient to justify price discrimination. As the court stated in *Hartley & Parker, Inc. v. Florida Beverage Corp.,* 307 U.S. 916 (1952), "Four Roses under any other name would still swill the same."

In *FTC v. Borden Co.,* the U.S. Supreme Court held that the sale of chemically similar products, one under an expensive brand name and the other under a less expensive private name, was a sale of commodities of "like grade and quality" and illegal as price discrimination under Section 2(a) of the Robinson-Patman Act.

COMMODITIES OF LIKE GRADE AND QUALITY

FEDERAL TRADE COMMISSION v. BORDEN CO.

383 U.S. 637 (1966)
UNITED STATES SUPREME COURT

Mr. Justice White delivered the opinion of the Court.

The Borden Company, respondent here, produces and sells evaporated milk under the Borden name, a nationally advertised brand. At the same time Borden packs and markets evaporated milk under various private brands owned by its customers. This milk is physically and chemically identical with the milk it distributes under its own brand but is sold at both the wholesale and retail level at prices regularly below those obtained for the Borden brand milk. The Federal Trade Commission found the milk sold under the Borden and the pri-

vate labels to be of like grade and quality as required for the applicability of Section 2(a) of the Robinson-Patman Act, held the price differential to be discriminatory within the meaning of the section, . . . The Court of Appeals set aside the Commission's order on the sole ground that as a matter of law, the customer label milk was not of the same grade and quality as the milk sold under the Borden brand.

The position of Borden and of the Court of Appeals is that the determination of like grade and quality, which is a threshold finding essential to the applicability of Section 2(a), may not be based solely on the physical properties of the products without regard to the brand names they bear and the relative public acceptance these brands enjoy— "consideration should be given to all commercially significant distinctions which affect market value, whether they be physical or promotional." Here, because the milk bearing the Borden brand regularly sold at a higher price than did the milk with a buyer's label, the court considered the products to be "commercially" different and hence of different "grade" for the purposes of Section 2(a), even though they were physically identical and of equal quality. Although a mere difference in brand would not in itself demonstrate a difference in grade, decided consumer preference for one brand over another, reflected in the willingness to pay a higher price for the well-known brand, was, in the view of the Court of Appeals, sufficient to differentiate chemically identical products and to place the price differential beyond the reach of Section 2(a). . . . We reject this construction of Section 2(a), . . .

During the 1936 hearings on the proposed amendments to Section 2 of the Clayton Act, . . . it was suggested that the proposed Section 2(a) be amended so as to apply only to sales of commodities of "like grade, quality and *brand.*" There was strong objection to the amendment and it was not adopted by the Committee.

If two products, physically identical but differently branded, are to be deemed of different grade because the seller regularly and successfully markets some quantity of both at different prices, the seller could, as far as Section 2(a) is concerned, make either product available to some customers and deny it to others, however discriminatory this might be and however damaging to competition. Those who were offered only one of the two products would be barred from competing for those customers who want or might buy the other. The retailer who was permitted to buy and sell only the more expensive brand would have no chance to sell to those who always buy the cheaper product or to convince others, by experience or otherwise, of the fact which he and all other dealers already know— that the cheaper product is actually identical with that carrying the more expensive label.

The seller, to escape the Act, would have only to succeed in selling some unspecified amount of each product to some unspecified portion of his customers, however large or small the price differential might be. The seller's pricing and branding policy, by being successful, would apparently validate itself by creating a difference in "grade" and thus taking itself beyond the purview of the Act.

The judgment of the Court of Appeals is *reversed* and the case is *remanded* for further proceedings consistent with this opinion.

Mr. Justice Stewart, with whom **Mr. Justice Harlan** joins, dissenting.

I cannot agree that mere physical or chemical identity between premium and private label brands is, without more, a sufficient basis for a finding of "like grade and quality" within the meaning of Section 2(a) of the Robinson-Patman Act. . . . By pursuing product comparison only so far as the result of laboratory analysis, the Court ignores a most relevant aspect of the inquiry into the question of "like grade and quality" under Section 2 (a): Whether the products are different in the eyes of the consumer.

CASE QUESTIONS

1. What is price discrimination? Is it legal?
2. What two products were manufactured and sold by defendant Borden Co.? Were the products sold at different prices?
3. How was Borden Co. able to distinguish the two products in the minds of consumers? What is "product differentiation"?
4. Did the courts find the two products to be of "like grade and quality"? Explain.

Policy Issue. Should price discrimination be prohibited by federal antitrust law? Does the law against price discrimination destroy the art of negotiating sales transactions?

Economics Issue. Who benefits from price discrimination? How? Are consumers harmed by price discrimination? Doesn't each consumer pay what he is *willing* to pay for the product?

Ethics Issue. Is it ethical for companies to convince the public, through advertising, that one brand of their product is better than another brand of their product when the products are physically identical?

Social Responsibility. Do corporations owe a duty of social responsibility to inform consumers that their named brand products do not differ physically from their private brand-label products?

DIRECT PRICE DISCRIMINATION

In order for there to be price discrimination in violation of the Robinson-Patman Act, there must be two separate transactions, at least one of which generates a discrimination "across a state line." The jurisdictional requirement of the Robinson-Patman Act is narrower than that of the Sherman Act ("affecting commerce"). The discrimination must occur in connection with a "purchase," i.e., a sales transaction. Leases and consignments are not covered by the Robinson-Patman Act.

There must be at least *two* purchases at different prices, and the purchases must be fairly contemporaneous. For example, a manufacturer may generally charge a different price to a wholesaler and a retailer. However, the mere use of a wholesaler's name, or creation of an unnecessary wholesaler in order to channel lower prices to a large retailer, is price discrimination under the Robinson-Patman Act.

Section 2(a) of the Clayton Act, as amended by the Robinson-Patman Act, only prohibits price discrimination whose *effect* may be "substantially to lessen competition." A price discrimination that is shown *not* to have this requisite effect is *not* unlawful. The plaintiff must prove that it was injured by the price discrimination.

Primary, Secondary and Tertiary Line Injury Price discrimination causes injury to many lines of competitors, purchasers, suppliers, and consumers. Traditionally, the courts have recognized three lines of injury from illegal price discrimination: primary-line injury, secondary-line injury, and tertiary-line injury.

Primary-Line Injury. The Robinson-Patman Act is specifically aimed at *primary*-line injury caused by price discrimination. Primary-line injury occurs to *competitors* of the price-discriminating seller. The usual case of primary-line injury occurs when a large competitor lowers its price in a local area while retaining its original price elsewhere, in order to drive a regional or local competitor out of business in the targeted area. If this practice were not regulated by the Robinson-Patman Act, large national companies could sustain a system of predatory price cutting in order to eliminate regional competitors.

A *prima facie* case of primary-line injury requires that the plaintiff prove a sustained (versus temporary) lowering of price by the defendant, that the price drop was "substantial," and that the defendant charged different prices to different purchasers with the knowledge and intent of destroying, injuring, or disciplining a competitor.

Secondary-Line Injury.   The majority of cases brought under the Robinson-Patman Act are for *secondary*-line injury. The usual secondary-line case occurs where a manufacturer charges different prices to two or more *wholesalers.* The wholesaler who is charged the higher price may sue the manufacturer for secondary-line injury suffered because of the price discrimination by the manufacturer.

A secondary-line injury case is not difficult to prove. Difference in price must be shown, but the competitive injury may be inferred from the price difference. However, if the price difference is only "temporary," there is no cause of action for secondary-line injury. Moreover, there is no illegal price discrimination if the "nonfavored" buyer could have purchased the goods from another source at the same price as that charged by the price-discriminating seller to the "favored buyer."

Tertiary Line Injury.   In the previous example, where the manufacturer price discriminated against two wholesalers, the customers of the "nonfavored" wholesaler may suffer a *tertiary* line injury, i.e., pay a higher price than a customer of the "favored" wholesaler. These customers may maintain an action against the manufacturer for such injury.

Exhibit 11–1 shows the primary, secondary, and tertiary line injury caused by price discrimination.

In *Perkins v. Standard Oil Co. of California,* which follows, the U.S. Supreme Court discussed the different lines of injury caused by price discrimination, finding that a private plaintiff at the "fourth line" of injury could collect *treble* damages from a price-discriminating defendant.

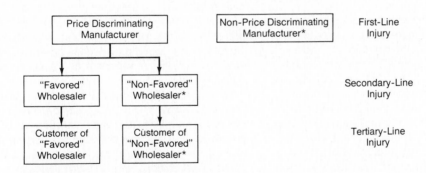

*Designates plaintiff at each line of injury

Exhibit 11–1.   Primary, secondary, and tertiary line injury from price discrimination.

LINE OF INJURY

PERKINS v. STANDARD OIL CO. OF CALIFORNIA

395 U.S. 642 (1969)
UNITED STATES SUPREME COURT

Mr. Justice Black delivered the opinion of the Court.

In 1959 petitioner, Clyde A. Perkins, brought this civil antitrust action against the Standard Oil Company of California seeking treble damages under Section 2 of the Clayton Act, as amended by the Robinson-Patman Act, for injuries alleged to have resulted from Standard's price discriminations in the sale of gasoline and oil during a period of over two years from 1955 to 1957. In 1963, after a lengthy and complicated trial, the jury returned a verdict for Perkins and assessed damages against Standard of $333,404.57, which, after trebling by the court and after the addition of attorney's fees, resulted in a total judgment against Standard of $1,298,213.71. On review, the Court of Appeals for the Ninth Circuit held that the assessment of damages included injuries to Perkins that were not recoverable under the Act and therefore ordered a new trial. We granted *certiorari*. . . .

Petitioner Perkins entered the oil and gasoline business in 1928 as the operator of a single service station in the State of Washington. By the mid-1950s he had become one of the largest independent distributors of gasoline and oil in both Washington and Oregon. He was both a wholesaler, operating storage plants and trucking equipment, and a retailer through his own Perkins stations. From 1945 until 1957, Perkins purchased substantially all of his gasoline requirements from Standard. From 1955 to 1957 Standard charged Perkins a higher price for its gasoline and oil than Standard charged to its own Branded Dealers, who competed with Perkins, and to Signal Oil & Gas Co., a wholesaler whose gas eventually reached the pumps of a major competitor of Perkins. Perkins contends that Standard's price and price-related discriminations against him seriously harmed his competitive position and forced him, in 1957, to sacrifice by sale what remained of his once independent business to one of the major companies in the gasoline business, Union Oil.

Standard admittedly sold gasoline to Signal at a lower price than it sold to Perkins. Signal sold this Standard gasoline to Western Hyway, which in turn sold the Standard gasoline to Regal Stations Co., Perkins' competitor. Perkins alleged that the lower price charged Signal by Standard was passed on to Signal's subsidiary Western Hyway, and then to Western's subsidiary, Regal. Regal's stations were thus able to undersell Perkins' stations and, according to Perkins, the resulting competitive harm, along with that he suffered at the hands of Standard's favored Branded Dealers, destroyed his ability to compete and eventually forced him to sell what was left of his business.

Here, Perkins' injuries resulted in part from impaired competition with a customer (Regal) of a customer (Western Hyway) of the favored purchaser (Signal). The Court of Appeals termed these injuries "fourth level" and held that they were not protected by the Robinson-Patman Act. We conclude that this limitation is wholly an artificial one and is completely unwarranted by the language or purpose of the Act.

Here, for example, Standard supplied gasoline and oil to Signal. Signal, allegedly because it furnished Standard with part of its vital supply of crude petroleum, was able to insist upon a discriminatorily lower price. Had Signal then sold its gas directly to the Regal stations, giving Regal stations a competitive advantage, there would be no question, even under the decision of the Court of Appeals in this case, that a clear violation of the Robinson-Patman Act had been committed. Instead of selling directly to the retailer Regal, however, Signal transferred the gasoline first to its subsidiary, Western Hyway, which in turn supplied the Regal stations. Signal owned 60 percent of the stock of Western Hyway; Western in turn owned 55 percent of the stock of the Regal stations. We find no basis in the language or purpose of the Act for immunizing Standard's price discriminations simply because the product in question passed through an additional formal exchange before reaching the level of Perkins' actual competitor. From Perkins' point of view, the competitive harm done him by Standard is certainly no less because of the presence of an additional link in this particular distribution chain from the producer to the retailer.

This evidence is sufficient to sustain the jury's award of damages under the Robinson-Patman Act. . . . The jury's verdict and judgment should be reinstated.

CASE QUESTIONS

1. Draw a diagram of the parties and levels of distribution involved in this case.
2. Did any of the following types of antitrust injury occur in this case?
   a. Primary line injury
   b. Secondary line injury
   c. Tertiary line injury
3. What line of injury was alleged to be covered by the Robinson-Patman Act in this case? How did the court decide this issue?
4. Why was Signal able to obtain a favorable discriminatory price from Standard Oil?

Policy Issue. Do you think that the U.S. Supreme Court would extend the prohibition against price discrimination to cover "fifth line" injury if the case presented itself?

Economics Issue. How much money was Perkins awarded as damages? How was this amount calculated? Is there an incentive not to price discriminate?

Ethics Issue. Was it ethical for Standard Oil to sell its products to Signal at lower prices than it sold to other parties?

Was it ethical for Standard Oil to raise as its defense the argument that "fourth line" injury should not be covered by Section 2(a) of the Clayton Act?

Social Responsibility. Do companies owe a duty of social responsibility not to treat certain customers "favorably"? Does such favorable treatment help or hurt business?

INDIRECT PRICE DISCRIMINATION

The Robinson-Patman Act also prohibits *indirect* price discrimination. Indirect price discrimination may arise from the use of preferential credit terms, different freight charges, or other preferential arrangements.

In one of the most prevalent types of *indirect* price discrimination, a seller adds a "phantom freight" charge to the cost of products purchased by certain disfavored customers. By charging for fictitious freight costs, the seller can discriminate in price between purchasers. "Base-point pricing" schemes, where all purchasers pay freight from a certain point no matter where they are located, and "zone-pricing" systems, where every purchase within a certain zone pays the same freight charge, are other examples of illegal indirect price discrimination.

In *Corn Products Refining Co. v. FTC* the U.S. Supreme Court found an *indirect* price discrimination in the form of a "base-point pricing" scheme in violation of Section 2(a) of the Robinson-Patman Act.

INDIRECT PRICE DISCRIMINATION
CORN PRODUCTS REFINING CO. v. FEDERAL TRADE COMMISSION

324 U.S. 726 (1945)
UNITED STATES SUPREME COURT

Mr. Chief Justice Stone delivered the opinion of the Court.

Petitioners, a parent corporation and its sales subsidiary, use a basing point system of pricing in their sales of glucose. They sell only at delivered prices, computed by adding to a base price at Chicago the published freight tariff from Chicago to the several points of delivery, even though deliveries are in fact made from their factory at Kansas City as well as from their Chicago factory. Consequently there is included in the delivered price on shipments from Kansas City an amount of "freight" which usually does not correspond to freight actually paid by petitioners.

The Federal Trade Commission instituted this proceeding . . . charging that petitioners' use of this single basing point system resulted in discriminations in price between different purchasers of the glucose, and violated Section 2(a) of the Act, as amended by . . . the Robinson-Patman Act. . . . After hearings, at which much of the evidence was stipulated, the Commission made its findings of fact. It concluded that petitioners had violated Section 2 of the Clayton Act, as amended, and ordered them to cease and desist from such violations. On petition to review the Commission's order, the Circuit Court of Appeals for the Seventh Circuit sustained the order. . . .

BASING POINT PRACTICES

The evidence as to petitioners' basing point system for the sale of glucose was stipulated. The Commission found from the evidence that petitioners have two plants for the manufacture of glucose or corn syrup, one at Argo, Illinois, within the Chicago switching district, and the other at Kansas City, Missouri. The Chicago plant has been in operation since 1910, and that at Kansas City since 1922. Petitioners' bulk sales of glucose are at delivered prices, which are computed, whether the shipments are from Chicago or Kansas City, at petitioners'

Chicago prices, plus the freight rate from Chicago to the place of delivery. Thus purchasers in all places other than Chicago pay a higher price than do Chicago purchasers. And in the case of all shipments from Kansas City to purchasers in cities having a lower freight rate from Kansas City than from Chicago, the delivered price includes unearned or "phantom" freight, to the extent of the difference in freight rates. Conversely, when the freight from Kansas City to the point of delivery is more than that from Chicago, petitioners must "absorb" freight upon shipments from Kansas City, to the extent of the difference in freight.

Petitioners' pricing system results inevitably in systematic price discriminations, since the prices they receive upon deliveries from Kansas City bear relation to factors other than actual costs of production or delivery.

We conclude that the discriminations involved in petitioners' pricing system are within the prohibition of the Act. We pass to the question whether these discriminations had the prescribed effect on competition [substantially to lessen competition].

Since petitioners' basing point system results in a Chicago delivered price which is always lower than any other, including that at Kansas City, a natural effect of the system is the creation of a favored price zone for the purchasers of glucose in Chicago and vicinity, which does not extend to other points of manufacture and shipment of glucose. Since the cost of glucose, a principal ingredient of low-priced candy, is less at Chicago, candy manufacturers there are in a better position to compete for business, and manufacturers of candy located near other factories producing glucose, distant from the basing point, as Kansas City, are in a less favorable position. The consequence is, as found by the Commission, that several manufacturers of candy, who were formerly located in Kansas City or other cities served from petitioners' Kansas City plant, have moved their factories to Chicago.

The Commission's conclusions are amply supported by its findings and the evidence, and the judgment is *affirmed.*

CASE QUESTIONS

1. What is a "base-point" pricing scheme? How was it used by defendant Corn Products in this case?
2. What is "phantom freight"? Is this case an example of direct or indirect price discrimination?
3. Would Corn Products have been able to engage in the price discrimination scheme in this case without market power? Explain.

Policy Issue. Should *indirect* methods of price discrimination be prohibited by the Robinson-Patman Act? Are the consequences of indirect price discrimination any different from those caused by direct price discrimination?

Economics Issue. How would Corn Products benefit economically from the base-point pricing scheme in this case? Who else benefited? Who was harmed?

Ethics Issue. Was it ethical for Corn Products to charge "phantom freight" to customers located outside the Chicago area?

Social Responsibility. Does a company owe a duty of social responsibility to sell its products at similar prices to all buyers?

BUYER'S RECEIPT OF A DISCRIMINATORY PRICE

Section 2(f) of the Robinson-Patman Act makes it unlawful for "any person . . . knowingly to induce or *receive* a discrimination in price that is prohibited under the Act. Therefore, a *buyer* may be held liable for damages when it knowingly "receives" a discriminatory price on a product. The plaintiff must show that the buyer *knew* that the price obtained was discriminatory. The requisite knowledge may be proved by showing the "trade experience" of the buyer.

DEFENSES TO PRICE DISCRIMINATION

Where a defendant has been charged with price discrimination in violation of the Robinson-Patman Act, the defendant may always assert that the plaintiff has failed to prove one of the necessary elements of a *prima facie* case of price discrimination—for example, that the alleged discriminatory purchase was not made contemporaneously with the plaintiff's purchase. In addition, a defendant may assert several *affirmative* defenses, including:

1. *de minimis* discrimination
2. changing conditions
3. meeting the competition
4. cost justification.

the effect on compet. is so slight

De Minimis Discrimination. If the charged discrimination has occurred, but the effect on the plaintiff's business is *de minimis,* the courts will dismiss the action upon the assertion of this defense by the defendant. The reasoning supporting the *de minimis* defense is that courts should not waste valuable court time addressing trivial charges of price discrimination when it has caused little, if any, injury to the plaintiff.

Changing Conditions. A defendant may assert "changing conditions" as a defense to a price discrimination charge. This defense is rarely accepted by the courts, and is generally limited to "temporary" situations, such as deterioration of perishable goods, distress sales pursuant to court order, discontinuance of a business, or obsolescence of seasonable goods.

Meeting the Competition. Section 2(b) of the Robinson-Patman Act expressly provides that a seller may lower his price "in good faith to meet an equally low price of a competitor." "Good faith" is the key to the successful assertion of the "meeting competition" defense. Where the seller in "good faith" lowers his price to meet his competition, his price can only "meet," and may not beat, the competitor's price.

A seller may not lower his price to meet a competitor's price if the seller knows that the competitor is engaging in price discrimination. Further, a seller may reduce his price only in response to an individual situation and not to compete with an intricate pricing system (i.e., a "base-point" price system) of competitors. The "meeting the competition" defense is rarely successful.

In *Great Atlantic & Pacific Tea Co., Inc. v. FTC*, which follows, the U.S. Supreme Court found that a *buyer* was not liable under Section 2(f) for receiving a discriminatory price on the grounds that the *seller* could have successfully asserted the meeting-the-competition defense if it had been charged with price discriminating.

BUYER'S RECEIPT OF A DISCRIMINATORY PRICE,
MEETING THE COMPETITION DEFENSE

GREAT ATLANTIC & PACIFIC TEA CO., INC. v. FEDERAL TRADE COMMISSION

440 U.S. 69 (1979)
UNITED STATES SUPREME COURT

Mr. Justice Stewart delivered the opinion of the Court.

The question presented in this case is whether the petitioner, the Great Atlantic & Pacific Tea Co. (A&P), violated Section 2(f) of the Clayton Act, as amended by the Robinson-Patman Act, by knowingly inducing or receiving illegal price discriminations from the Borden Co. (Borden).

The alleged violation was reflected in a 1965 agreement between A&P and Borden under which

Borden undertook to supply "private label" milk to more than 200 A&P stores in a Chicago area that included portions of Illinois and Indiana. This agreement resulted from an effort by A&P to achieve cost savings by switching from the sale of "brand label" milk (milk sold under the brand name of the supplying dairy) to the sale of "private label" milk (milk sold under the A&P label).

To implement this plan, A&P asked Borden, its longtime supplier, to submit an offer to supply under private label certain of A&P's milk and other dairy product requirements. After prolonged negotiations, Borden offered to grant A&P a discount for switching to private-label milk provided A&P would accept limited delivery service. Borden claimed that this offer would save A&P $410,000 a year compared to what it had been paying for its dairy products. A&P, however, was not satisfied with this offer and solicited offers from other dairies. A competitor of Borden, Bowman Dairy, then submitted an offer which was lower than Borden's.

At this point, A&P's Chicago buyer contacted Borden's chain store sales manager and stated: "I have a bid in my pocket. You [Borden] people are so far out of line it is not even funny. You are not even in the ball park." When the Borden representative asked for more details, he was told nothing except that a $50,000 improvement in Borden's bid "would not be a drop in the bucket."

Borden was thus faced with the problem of deciding whether to rebid. A&P at the time was one of Borden's largest customers in the Chicago area. Moreover, Borden had just invested more than $5 million in a new dairy facility in Illinois. The loss of the A&P account would result in underutilization of this new plant. Under these circumstances, Borden decided to submit a new bid which doubled the estimated annual savings to A&P, from $410,000 to $820,000. In presenting its offer, Borden emphasized to A&P that it needed to keep A&P's business and was making the new offer in order to meet Bowman's bid. A&P then accepted Borden's bid after concluding that it was substantially better than Bowman's.

Based on these facts, the Federal Trade Commission filed a three-count complaint against A&P. [The complaint] . . . charged that A&P had violated Section 2(f) of the Clayton Act, as amended by the Robinson-Patman Act, by knowingly inducing or receiving price discriminations from Borden.

An Administrative Law Judge found, after extended discovery and a hearing that lasted over 110 days, that A&P . . . had violated Section 2(f). . . . On review, the Commission held . . . that the . . . conduct on the part of A&P had violated Section 2 (f), finding that Borden had discriminated in price between A&P and its competitors, that the discrimination had been injurious to competition, and that A&P had known or should have known

that it was the beneficiary of unlawful price discrimination. The Commission rejected A&P's defenses that the Borden bid had been made to meet competition. . . .

The Robinson-Patman Act was passed in response to the problem perceived in the increased market power and coercive practices of chainstores and other big buyers that threatened the existence of small independent retailers. Notwithstanding this concern with buyers, however, the emphasis of the Act is in Section 2(a), which prohibits price discriminations by sellers. Indeed, the original Patman bill as reported by Committees of both Houses prohibited only seller activity, with no mention of buyer liability. Section 2(f), making buyers liable for inducing or receiving price discriminations by sellers, was the product of a belated floor amendment near the conclusion of the Senate debates. . . . As finally enacted, Section 2(f) provides:

> That it shall be unlawful for any person engaged in commerce, in the course of such commerce, knowingly to induce or receive a discrimination in price *which is prohibited by this section.* (Emphasis added.)

Liability under Section 2(f) thus is limited to situations where the price discrimination is one "which is prohibited by this section." While the phrase "this section" refers to the entire Section 2 of the Act, only subsections (a) and (b) dealing with seller liability involve discriminations in price. Under the plain meaning of Section 2(f), therefore, a buyer cannot be liable if a *prima facie* case could not be established against a seller or if the seller has an affirmative defense. In either situation, there is no price discrimination "prohibited by this section." The legislative history of Section 2(f) fully confirms the conclusion that buyer liability under Section 2(f) is dependent on seller liability under Section 2(a).

Because both the Commission and the Court of Appeals proceeded on the assumption that a buyer who accepts the lower of two competitive bids can be liable under Section 2(f) even if the seller has a meeting-competition defense, there was not a specific finding that Borden did in fact have such a defense. But it quite clearly did.

Borden was unable to ascertain the details of the Bowman bid. It requested more information about the bid from the petitioner, but this request was refused. It could not then attempt to verify the existence and terms of the competing offer from Bowman without risking Sherman Act liability. Faced with a substantial loss of business and unable to find out the precise details of the competing bid, Borden made another offer stating that it was doing so in order to meet competition. Under these circumstances, the conclusion is virtually inescapable that in making that offer Borden acted in a reasonable and good-faith effort to meet its competition, and therefore was entitled to a meeting-competition defense.

Since Borden had a meeting-competition defense and thus could not be liable under Section 2(b), the petitioner who did no more than accept that offer cannot be liable under Section 2(f).

Accordingly, the judgment is *reversed.*

CASE QUESTIONS

1. Who was sued in this case?
   a. Borden for *giving* a price-discriminating price to A&P
   b. A&P for *receiving* a price-discriminating price from Borden
2. What does the "meeting the competition" defense of Section 2(b) of the Robinson-Patman Act provide? Did Borden qualify for this defense?
3. Can a price discriminator "beat" the price of a competitor and still qualify for the meeting the competition defense? Do you think Borden met or beat the alleged bid by Bowman Dairy?
4. What does Section 2(f) of the Robinson-Patman Act provide? Did A&P *knowingly* receive a price discriminating price?
5. What was A&P's defense to the charge of violating Section 2(f)? Did the court accept this defense? Do you agree?

Policy Issue. Should there be any defenses to price discrimination? Should the following be permitted as defenses to price discrimination?
   a. *De minimis* discrimination
   b. Changing conditions
   c. Meeting the competition

Economics Issue. Did A&P benefit economically from using its leverage in this case? Was Borden taken advantage of?

Ethics Issue. Was it ethical for A&P to entice Borden to meet the Bowman bid? To use this fact as a defense to a charge of violating Section 2(f)? Was this an example of "bootstrapping"?

Social Responsibility. Does a corporation owe a duty of responsibility to shareholders to accept a price discriminating price? Does a company owe a duty of social responsibility not to?

Cost Justification. Section 2(a) of the Robinson-Patman Act provides a "cost justification" defense where the defendant shows that the discriminating price was based on a valid difference in the *cost* of manufacture, sale, or delivery of the product. Although an absolute defense to a charge of price discrimination, the "cost justification" defense (proper allocation of overhead and administrative costs, etc.) is difficult to prove and is restrictively interpreted by the courts. Cost differentials are allowed if a seller can properly classify its customers into reasonable categories based on the *average* cost of selling to each category. "Quantity discounts" may be justified if the defendant can prove (e.g., by detailed computations) that there is an *actual* cost saving based on the quantity sold.

In *FTC v. Morton Salt Co.* the Supreme Court held that the defendant had failed to prove the cost justification defense and was therefore liable for price discrimination.

COST JUSTIFICATION DEFENSE

FEDERAL TRADE COMMISSION v. MORTON SALT CO.

334 U.S. 37 (1948)
UNITED STATES SUPREME COURT

Mr. Justice Black delivered the opinion of the Court.

The Federal Trade Commission, after a hearing, found that the respondent, which manufactures and sells table salt in interstate commerce, had discriminated in price between different purchasers of like grades and qualities, and concluded that such discriminations were in violation of Section 2 of the Clayton Act, as amended by the Robinson-Patman Act. It accordingly issued a cease and desist order. Upon petition of the respondent the Circuit Court of Appeals . . . set aside the Commission's findings and order, directed the Commission to dismiss its complaint against respondent. . . .

Respondent manufactures several different brands of table salt and sells them directly to (1) wholesalers or jobbers, who in turn resell to the retail trade, and (2) large retailers, including chain store retailers. Respondent sells its finest brand of table salt, known as Blue Label, on what it terms a standard quantity discount system available to all customers. Under this system the purchasers pay a delivered price and the cost to both wholesale and retail purchasers of this brand differs according to the quantities bought. These prices are as follows, after making allowance for rebates and discounts:

	Per case
Less-than-carload purchases	$1.60
Carload purchases	1.50
5,000-case purchases in any consecutive 12 months	1.40
50,000-case purchases in any consecutive 12 months	1.35

Only five companies have ever bought sufficient quantities of respondent's salt to obtain the $1.35 per case price. These companies could buy in such quantities because they operate large chains of retail stores in various parts of the country. As a result of this low price these five companies have been able to sell Blue Label salt at retail cheaper than wholesale purchasers from respondent could reasonably sell the same brand of salt to independently operated retail stores, many of whom competed with the local outlets of the five chain stores.

Theoretically, these discounts are equally available to all, but functionally they are not. For as the record indicates (if reference to it on this point were necessary) no single independent retail grocery store, and probably no single wholesaler, bought as many as 50,000 cases or as much as $50,000 worth of table salt in one year. Furthermore, the record shows that, while certain purchasers were enjoying one or more of respondent's standard quantity discounts, some of their competitors made purchases in such small quantities that they could not qualify for any of respondent's discounts, even those based on carload shipments. The legislative history of the Robinson-Patman Act makes it abundantly clear that Congress considered it to be an evil that a large buyer could secure a competitive advantage over a small buyer solely because of the large buyer's quantity purchasing ability. The Robinson-Patman Act was passed to deprive a large buyer of such advantages except to the extent that a lower price could be justified by reason of a seller's diminished costs due to quantity manufacture, delivery or sale, or by reason of the seller's good faith effort to meet a competitor's equally low price.

Section 2(b) of the Act specifically imposes the burden of showing [cost] justification upon one who is shown to have discriminated in prices.

It is argued that the findings fail to show that respondent's discriminatory discounts had in fact caused injury to competition. There are specific findings that such injuries had resulted from respondent's discounts, although the statute does not require the Commission to find that injury has actually resulted. The statute requires no more than that the effect of the prohibited price discriminations "may be substantially to lessen competition . . . or to injure, destroy, or prevent competition.". . . Here the Commission found what would appear to be obvious, that the competitive opportunities of certain merchants were injured when they had to pay respondent substantially more for their goods than their competitors had to pay. The findings are adequate.

It is also argued that respondent's less-than-carload sales are very small in comparison with the total volume of its business and for that reason we should reject the Commission's finding. . . . To support this argument, reference is made to the fact that salt is a small item in most wholesale and retail businesses and in consumers' budgets. For several reasons we cannot accept this contention.

There are many articles in a grocery store that, considered separately, are comparatively small parts of a merchant's stock. Congress intended to protect a merchant from competitive injury attributable to discriminatory prices on any or all goods sold in interstate commerce, whether the particular goods constituted a major or minor portion of his stock. Since a grocery store consists of many comparatively small articles, there is no possible way effectively to protect a grocer from discriminatory prices except by applying the prohibitions of the Act to each individual article in the store.

Furthermore, in enacting the Robinson-Patman Act, Congress was especially concerned with protecting small businesses which were unable to buy in quantities, such as the merchants here who purchased in less-than-carload lots.

Apprehension is expressed in this Court that enforcement of the Commission's order against respondent's continued violations of the Robinson-Patman Act might lead respondent to raise table salt prices to its carload purchasers. Such a conceivable, though, we think, highly improbable, contingency, could afford us no reason for upsetting the Commission's findings and declining to direct compliance with a statute passed by Congress.

The judgment of the Circuit Court of Appeals is *reversed* and the proceedings are *remanded* to that court to be disposed of in conformity with this opinion.

CASE QUESTIONS

1. What did Morton Salt's pricing scheme provide? Was it made available to all purchasers? How many purchasers qualified under each price?
2. Were the following elements of price discrimination met in this case?
   a. Commodity
   b. Of "like grade and quality"
   c. Purchased in two separate transactions
   d. Contemporaneous in time
   e. At different prices
   f. Across a state line
   g. Which caused a substantial lessening of competition
3. Is a "cost justification" defense available to a charge of price discrimination? If so, is it an easy defense to prove? Why or why not?
4. Was Morton Salt held liable for price discrimination in this case? Do you think that Morton Salt could have proved a cost justification for its volume discounts in this case? Why do you think it was unsuccessful in convincing the court on this defense?

Policy Issue. Should a cost justification defense be allowed to a charge of price discrimination? Why or why not?

Should *small competitors* (*e.g.,* mom-and-pop stores) be protected by the antitrust laws?

Economics Issue. Who benefited economically from the Morton Salt pricing scheme in this case? Morton Salt? Chain stores? Mom-and-pop stores? Do volume sales make sense for a seller?

Ethics Issue. Was it ethical for Morton Salt to offer its pricing scheme to all purchasers when it knew that only large chain store purchasers could qualify for the best prices?

Social Responsibility. Does a manufacturer of a product owe a duty of social responsibility *not* to offer better prices to large chain stores than it does to other purchasers?

DISCRIMINATORY FEES, ALLOWANCES, AND SERVICES

In addition to prohibiting *price* discrimination under Section 2(a), Sections 2(c), 2(d), and 2(e) of the Robinson-Patman Act also prohibit *nonprice* discrimination between competitors wherever the seller pays fees or grants allowances or services to one purchaser and not to another.

Discriminatory Brokerage Fees. Section 2(c) of the Robinson-Patman Act makes it illegal for a seller to pay a buyer a "brokerage" fee or an "allowance in lieu of a brokerage fee" (i.e., a discount from the purchase price) where such a fee or allowance has not actually been earned by the buyer. The payment of unearned brokerage fees is indirect price discrimination and is *per se* illegal under Section 2(c). No competitive injury need be proven and no cost justification defense is permitted. Any payment by the seller to the buyer in connection with a sale of a commodity is suspect under Section 2(c) as an illegal "kickback."

Discriminatory Allowances and Services. Sections 2(d) and 2(e) of the Robinson-Patman Act prohibit sellers from paying allowances or furnishing services to customers unless they are "available on proportionately equal terms to all other customers competing in the distribution of such products . . ." The provision by a seller of discriminatory allowances or services to buyers is a *per se* violation of the Robinson-Patman Act. No competitive injury need be shown and no cost-justification defense is allowed. Buyers are also liable to prosecution for knowingly receiving discriminatory allowances and services.

The courts have interpreted Sections 2(d) and 2(e) to require that special services (such as product demonstrations), facilities, or allowances be "practically" available to all buyers. The Robinson-Patman Act allows a seller to reasonably determine schedules, time and scopes of demonstrations, etc., depending on the size, location, and volume of its customers. For example, a manufacturer of cookware may hold daily demonstrations for a month in a large urban department store, but only have one half-day demonstration in a rural general store, and still meet the "practically available" standard of Sections 2(d) and 2(e).

Only a Section 2(b) "meeting the competition" defense is permitted to a charge of nonprice discrimination under Section 2(c), (d) and (e) of the Robinson-Patman Act. No other defenses are permitted to these sections.

In *FTC v. Simplicity Pattern Co.*, the Supreme Court held that no defenses were available under Section 2(e) of the Robinson-Patman Act where the defendant has provided discriminatory allowances and services.

DISCRIMINATION IN SERVICES
FEDERAL TRADE COMMISSION v. SIMPLICITY PATTERN CO., INC.

360 U.S. 55 (1959)
UNITED STATES SUPREME COURT

Mr. Justice Clark delivered the opinion of the Court.

The Federal Trade Commission has found that Simplicity Pattern Co., Inc., one of the Nation's largest dress pattern manufacturers, discriminated in favor of its larger customers by furnishing to them services and facilities not accorded to competing smaller customers on proportionally equal terms.

Simplicity manufactures and sells tissue patterns which are used in the home for making women's and children's wearing apparel. Its volume of pattern sales, in terms of sales units, is greater than that resulting from the combined effort of all other major producers. The patterns are sold to some 12,300 retailers, with 17,200 outlets. For present purposes, these customers can be divided roughly into two categories. One, consisting largely of department and variety stores, comprises only 18 percent of the total number of customers, but accounts for 70 percent of the total sales volume. The remaining 82 percent of the customers are small stores whose primary business is the sale of yard-good fabrics.

The retail prices of Simplicity patterns are uniform at 25¢, 35¢, or 50¢. Similarly, Simplicity charges a uniform price, to all its customers, of 60 percent of the retail price. However, in the furnishing of certain services and facilities Simplicity does not follow this uniformity. It furnishes patterns to the variety stores on a consignment basis, requiring payment only as and when patterns are sold—thus affording them an investment-free inventory. The fabric stores are required to pay cash for their patterns in regular course. In addition, the cabinets and the catalogues are furnished to variety stores free while the fabric stores are charged therefor, the catalogues averaging from $2 to $3 each. Finally, all transportation costs in connection with its business with variety stores are paid by Simplicity but none is paid on fabric-store transactions.

The free services and facilities thus furnished variety store chains are substantial in value. As to four variety store chains, the catalogues which Simplicity furnished free in 1954 were valued at $128,904; the cabinets furnished free which those stores had on hand at the end of 1954 were valued at over $500,000; and their inventory of Simplicity's patterns at the end of 1954 was valued at more than $1,775,000, each of these values being based on Simplicity's usual sales price. Simplicity's president testified that it would cost over $2,000,000 annually to give its other customers the free transportation, free catalogues, and free cabinets furnished to variety stores.

[S]implicity not only takes advantage of the captive nature of the fabric stores in not granting them these advantages but compounds the damage by creating a sales outlet in the variety stores through the granting of these substantial incentives to engage in the pattern business. Without such partial subsidization the variety stores might not enter into the pattern trade at all.

Subsections (c), (d), and (e), on the other hand, unqualifiedly make unlawful certain business practices other than price discriminations. Subsection (c) applies to the payment or receipt of commissions or brokerage allowances "except for services rendered." Subsection (d) prohibits the payment by a seller to a customer for any services or facilities furnished by the latter, unless "such payment . . . is available on proportionally equal terms to all other [competing] customers." Subsection (e), which as noted is the provision applicable in this case, makes it unlawful for a seller

to discriminate in favor of one purchaser against another purchaser or purchasers of a commodity bought for resale . . . by . . . furnishing . . . any services or facilities connected with the processing, handling, sale, or offering for sale of such commodity so purchased upon terms not accorded to all purchasers on proportionally equal terms.

In terms, the proscriptions of these three subsections are absolute. Unlike Section 2(a), none of them requires, as proof of a *prima facie* violation, a showing that the illicit practice has had an injurious or destructive effect on competition. Similarly, none has any built-in defensive matter, as does Section 2(a).

Thus, a discrimination in prices may be rebutted by a showing under any of the Section 2(a) provisos, or under the Section 2(b) proviso—all of which by their terms apply to price discriminations. On the other hand, the only escape Congress has provided for discriminations in services or facilities is the permission to meet competition as found in the Section 2(b) proviso. We cannot supply what Congress has studiously omitted.

Simplicity's arguments to the contrary are based essentially on the ground that it would be "bad law and bad economics" to make discriminations unlawful even where they may be accounted for by cost differentials or where there is no competitive injury. Entirely aside from the fact that this Court is not in a position to review the economic wisdom of Congress, we cannot say that the legislative decision to treat price and other discriminations differently is without a rational basis.

We hold, therefore, that neither "cost-justification" nor an absence of competitive injury may constitute "justification" of a *prima facie* Section 2(e) violation. The judgment of the Court of Appeals must accordingly be reversed insofar as it set aside and remanded the Commission's order. . . .

CASE QUESTIONS

1. What were the two classes of customers served by Simplicity? Does a company always have to be able to *segregate* its customers in order to price discriminate? Explain.
2. Explain the price discrimination practiced by Simplicity in this case. Completing the following table may help you answer the question.

SIMPLICITY CASE

Item	Variety Stores	Fabric Stores
a. Clothes patterns (price)		
b. Means of Payment (cash/other)		
c. Cabinets (cost)		
d. Transportation (cost)		

3. Was this a case of *price* discrimination? If not, what section of the Robinson-Patman Act was alleged to have been violated by Simplicity? What does this section provide?
4. Are there any defenses to a charge of *nonprice* discrimination? Explain.

Policy Issue. Should the Robinson-Patman Act be expanded to prohibit price discrimination in the provision of *services* (e.g., prices charged by lawyers, doctors, accountants)?

Economics Issue. How did Simplicity benefit economically from the nonprice discrimination in this case? Will consumers be benefited or harmed by this decision?

Ethics Issue. Was it ethical for Simplicity to provide extra services to the larger variety stores and not to smaller fabric stores?

Social Responsibility. Do large corporations owe a duty of social responsibility not to drive small companies out of business through price and nonprice discrimination? Even if the small businesses are inefficient in distributing the product?

INTERLOCKING DIRECTORATES

Section 8 of the Clayton Act prohibits "interlocking directorates." Section 8 provides:

No person at the same time shall be a director in any two or more corporations, any one of which has capital, surplus, and undivided profits more than $1,000,000, engaged in whole or in part in commerce . . . if such corporations are or shall have been theretofore, by virtue of their business and location of operation, competitors, so that the elimination of competition by agreement between them would constitute a violation of any of the provisions of any of the antitrust laws.

The policy behind Section 8 is to protect against the obvious danger that an individual, as a director of two or more corporations, could coordinate the activities of these corporations in accomplishing activities illegal under the antitrust laws (e.g., price fixing, group boycott). Section 8 does not require a showing that the director actually engaged in an activity prohibited by the antitrust laws, but only that he occupies directorships at two competing corporations where such collusive activity is possible.

In the past, the Federal Trade Commission has usually challenged only directors serving on the boards of substantial competitors in direct competition with each other. The Justice Department, however, is currently pursuing a more rigorous program of enforcing the Clayton Act, Section 8 against directorates shared by firms engaged in "related businesses."

In *U.S. v. Sears, Roebuck & Co.* the court held that a director who sat on the Board of Directors of two competing corporations violated Section 8 of the Clayton Act, and ordered the director to resign from the board of at least one of the corporations.

INTERLOCKING DIRECTORATES

UNITED STATES v. SEARS, ROEBUCK & CO.

111 F.SUPP. 614 (1953)
UNITED STATES DISTRICT COURT, S.D. NEW YORK

Weinfeld, District Judge.

Plaintiff moves for summary judgment in an action seeking *inter alia* an order directing the resignation of the individual defendant as a director of one or both of the corporate defendants because he is alleged to be an interlocking director in violation of Section 8 of the Clayton Act.

The following facts are admitted by defendants: that Sears, Roebuck & Company (hereafter called Sears) and The B. F. Goodrich Company (hereafter called Goodrich) are New York corporations of the required size; that the defendant Sidney J. Weinberg (hereafter called Weinberg) has been for many years, and now is, a director of both Sears and Goodrich; that each corporation is engaged in commerce as the term is used in the Clayton Act; that they are competitors in the sale of the following

items at retail in commerce as the term is used in the Clayton Act: (1) refrigerators, washers, stoves, and other home appliances; (2) hardware; (3) automotive supplies; (4) sporting goods; (5) tires, tubes and recaps; (6) radios and television sets; (7) toys.

The basic issue presented for decision under the admitted facts is whether Sears and Goodrich are "competitors, so that the elimination of competition by agreement between them would constitute a violation of any of the provisions of any of the antitrust laws." If so, then Section 8 forbids Weinberg to be a director of both.

Defendants in substance contend that [Section 8] . . . requires a finding that a hypothetical merger between the two corporations would violate the antitrust laws before the same director is forbidden them; . . . In essence, the defendants would apply the merger test as spelled out in Section 7 of the Clayton Act.

The plaintiff urges to the contrary that "a violation of any of the provisions of any of the antitrust laws" is not limited to a merger or acquisition situation; that it includes agreements to fix prices or divide markets; that such agreements are illegal *per se;* and that, therefore, Sears and Goodrich may not retain in their service the same director since an agreement between them to fix prices or to divide territories would constitute a *per se* violation of Section 1 of the Sherman Act.

[T]he broad purposes of Congress are unmistakably clear. Congress had been aroused by the concentration of control by a few individuals or groups over many gigantic corporations which in the normal course of events should have been in active and unrestrained competition.

[T]he defendants' construction would denude of meaning the phrase *"any of the provisions of any of the antitrust laws."* (Emphasis supplied.) This language is broad enough to cover all methods of violating antitrust legislation. At the time of the passage of Section 8, price fixing and division of territory agreements were in common use to effect such violations. Merger or acquisition was not the sole means used to achieve this result. There is no logical basis upon which to infer that the all-inclusive language was intended to exclude the other known methods from the reach of Section 8.

The defendants have conceded that they are competitors in the sale of the seven categories of items at retail in commerce as the term is used in the Clayton Act. The sales of the seven items in the 97 communities amounted to $80,000,000 for 1951. The fact that this volume of sales may represent but a small percentage of either or both of the corporate defendants' annual sales, or a fraction of the annual retail sales volume of all distributors in the country of those commodities, does not militate against the undesirability of directorates common to both corporations.

The fact that [price fixing or other antitrust violations have] not happened up to the present does not mean that it may not happen hereafter.

Since Sears and Goodrich are competitors, since a price fixing or division of territory agreement would eliminate competition between them, and since such an agreement would *per se* violate at least one "of the provisions of . . . the antitrust laws," namely Section 1 of the Sherman Act, it follows that Section 8 forbids defendant Weinberg to be a director of both corporations.

The government's motion for summary judgment *is granted.*

CASE QUESTIONS

1. What does Section 8 of the Clayton Act provide?
2. Were the companies on whose board of directors Mr. Weinberg sat "competitors" within the meaning of Section 8? Explain.
3. Is a showing of an *actual* violation of antitrust laws (e.g., price fixing, group boycott) required in order to prove a Section 8 violation?

Policy Issue. Do you think that "interlocking directorates" pose as great a threat to competition as asserted by the court?

Economics Issue. Are directors paid for serving on boards of directors of corporations? If so, how much money?

Ethics Issue. Is there a conflict-of-interest problem when a person sits on the boards of directors of two or more competing corporations? Explain.

Social Responsibility. Does a director owe a duty when he makes a decision on behalf of a corporation to consider the effects of that decision on the bottom line? On society? Do these duties ever conflict?

THE FEDERAL TRADE COMMISSION ACT

Section 5 of the Federal Trade Commission Act prohibits "unfair methods of competition" and "unfair or deceptive acts or practices in or affecting commerce." The Federal Trade Commission has *exclusive* authority to enforce Section 5 of the Act.

The Federal Trade Commission Act has been interpreted broadly to include any violation of the Sherman Act. The Federal Trade Commission has concurrent authority with the Department of Justice in enforcing the Clayton Act. The power of the Federal Trade Commission in enforcing the Federal Trade Commission Act was stated by the United States Supreme Court in *FTC v. Motion Picture Adv. Co.*, 344 U.S. 392 (1953)

It is . . . clear that the Federal Trade Commission Act was designed to supplement and bolster the Sherman Act and the Clayton Act . . . to stop in their incipiency acts and practices which, when full blown, would violate those Acts . . . as well as to condemn as 'unfair methods of competition' existing violations of them.

Unfair Methods of Competition.   Section 5 of the Federal Trade Commission Act has been held to apply to:

1. actual violations of the Sherman or Clayton Acts, but also to:
2. conduct that violates the "spirit" of the acts
3. conduct that "fills in the gaps" of those acts
4. any other conduct deemed to be an "unfair method of competition" even though not in violation of the "letter" or "spirit" of the acts.

Where the conduct of the defendant does not otherwise violate the letter or spirit of the Sherman or Clayton Acts, the Federal Trade Commission uses a general test of "unfairness" in determining whether there has been an "unfair method of competition." The standard of unfairness applied by the Federal Trade Commission includes an inquiry into whether the questionable practice offends public policy, is immoral, oppressive, unscrupulous or unethical, or causes substantial injury to consumers or competitors.

In *Atlantic Refining Co. v. FTC*, the Supreme Court found an "unfair method of competition" in violation of Section 5 of the Federal Trade Commission Act.

THE FEDERAL TRADE COMMISSION ACT

ATLANTIC REFINING CO. v. FEDERAL TRADE COMMISSION

381 U.S. 357 (1965)
UNITED STATES SUPREME COURT

Mr. Justice Clark delivered the opinion of the Court.

The Federal Trade Commission has found that an agreement between the Atlantic Refining Company (Atlantic) and the Goodyear Tire & Rubber Company (Goodyear), under which the former "sponsors" the sale of the tires, batteries and accessory (TBA) products of the latter to its wholesale outlets and its retail service station dealers, is an unfair method of competition in violation of Section 5 of the Federal Trade Commission Act, as amended. Under the plan Atlantic sponsors the sale of Goodyear products to its wholesale and retail outlets on an overall commission basis. Goodyear is responsible for its sales and sells at its own price to Atlantic wholesalers and dealers for resale; it bears all of the cost of distribution through its warehouses, stores and other supply points and carries on a joint sales promotion program with Atlantic. The latter, however, is primarily responsible for promoting the sale of Goodyear products to its dealers and assisting them in their resale; for this it receives a commission on all sales made to its wholesalers and dealers.

The hearing examiner, with the approval of the Commission and the Court of Appeals, enjoined the use of direct methods of coercion on the part of Atlantic upon its dealers in the inauguration and promotion of the plan. It [the FTC] prohibited Atlantic from participating in any such commission arrangement. Similarly, it forbade Goodyear from continuing the arrangement with Atlantic or any other oil company. Goodyear and Atlantic filed separate appeals. The Court of Appeals approved the findings of the Commission and affirmed its order. . . .

Atlantic is a major producer, refiner and distributor of oil and its by-products. Its market is confined to portions of 17 States along the eastern seaboard. . . . In 1955 Atlantic had 2,493 lessee dealers, who purchased 39.1 percent of its gasoline sales, and 3,044 contract dealers, who bought 18.1 percent.

Goodyear is the largest manufacturer of rubber products in the United States with sales of over $1,000,000,000 in 1954. It distributes tires, tubes and accessories through 57 warehouses located throughout the country.

The Goodyear-Atlantic agreement required Atlantic to assist Goodyear "to the fullest practicable extent in perfecting sales, credit, and merchandising arrangements" with all of Atlantic's outlets. This included announcement to its dealers of its sponsorship of Goodyear products followed by a field representative's call to "suggest . . . the maintenance of adequate stocks of merchandise" and "maintenance of proper identification and advertising" of such merchandise. Atlantic was to instruct its salesmen to urge dealers to "vigorously" represent Goodyear, and to "cooperate with and assist" Goodyear in its "efforts to promote and increase the sale" by Atlantic dealers of Goodyear products. And it was to "maintain adequate dealer training

programs in the sale of tires, batteries, and accessories.". . . Its [Atlantic's] commission of 10 percent on sales to Atlantic dealers and 7.5 percent on sales to its wholesalers was paid on the basis of a master sheet prepared by Goodyear and furnished Atlantic each month.

The effectiveness of the program is evidenced by the results. Within seven months after the agreement Goodyear had signed up 96 percent and 98 percent, respectively, of Atlantic's dealers in two of the three areas assigned to it. In 1952 the sale of Goodyear products to Atlantic dealers was $4,175,890. . . .

Section 5 of the Federal Trade Commission Act declares "[u]nfair methods of competition in commerce, and unfair . . . acts or practices in commerce . . . unlawful."

Certainly there is "warrant in the record" for the findings of the Commission here. Substantial evidence supports the conclusion that notwithstanding Atlantic's contention that it and its dealers are mutually dependent upon each other, they simply do not bargain as equals. Among the sources of leverage in Atlantic's hands are its lease and equipment loan contracts with their cancellation and short-term provisions. . . . It must also be remembered that Atlantic controlled the supply of gasoline and oil to its wholesalers and dealers. This was an additional source of economic leverage, as was its extensive control of all advertising on the premises of its dealers. . . . Indeed, the Commission could properly have concluded that it was for this bundle of persuasion that Goodyear paid Atlantic its commission.

At the outset we must stress what we do not find present here. We recognize that the Goodyear-Atlantic contract is not a tying arrangement. Atlantic is not required to tie its sale of gasoline and other petroleum products to purchases of Goodyear tires, batteries and accessories. . . . It has long been recognized that there are many unfair methods of competition that do not assume the proportions of antitrust violations.

[T]he Commission . . . found that wholesalers and manufacturers of competing brands, and even Goodyear wholesalers who were not authorized supply points, were foreclosed from the Atlantic market. . . . It also found that the plight of Atlantic wholesalers and retailers was equally clear. They had to compete with other wholesalers and retailers who were free to stock several brands, but they were effectively foreclosed from selling brands other than Goodyear.

On this record we cannot say that the Commission's remedy is unreasonable and the judgments are therefore *affirmed*.

CASE QUESTIONS

1. What products did Goodyear make? What line of business was Atlantic engaged in?
2. Did Goodyear force Atlantic and its dealers to carry Goodyear products?
3. What did the agreement between Goodyear and Atlantic provide? What incentive did Atlantic have to promote Goodyear products?
4. What does Section 5 of the Federal Trade Commission Act provide? Does Section 5 require a violation of another antitrust law (e.g., Sherman Act, Clayton Act)? Explain.
5. Who was *foreclosed* by the Goodyear-Atlantic agreement? Explain.

Policy Issue. Is Section 5 of the FTC Act needed? Would the Goodyear-Atlantic agreement had been prohibited under antitrust law?

Economics Issue. Did the agreement benefit Goodyear? Atlantic? Atlantic dealers?

Ethics Issue. Will the "fairness" standard of Section 5 of the FTC Act promote more ethical conduct by business?

Social Responsibility. Did the Goodyear-Atlantic agreement have any detrimental effects on society? On consumers?

Trend of the Law

Price discrimination will remain one of the most complex and confusing areas of federal antitrust law. To the layman, it may seem that price discrimination exists almost everywhere in the economy of the country. However, much of the price discrimination in our society is in the area of charges for *services* (e.g., discriminatory prices for airplane seats), which are not covered by the Robinson-Patman Act. Further, even where there is price discrimination, the price discriminator may do so with a plan of asserting a proper defense to a change of price discrimination (e.g., cost justification).

Blatant direct price discrimination has been reduced considerably in this country. Much of the current price discrimination occurs through complex pricing strategies that are often difficult to detect. Other discrimination occurs in the providing of services. Uncovering and proving many of the complicated price discrimination schemes will be a constant problem for competitors and the courts in the future.

Academics and practitioners have criticized the Robinson-Patman Act as being too complex, and its application often not leading to efficient economic results. However, in *Jefferson County Pharmaceutical Assn. Inc. v. Abbott Laboratories,* 103 S.Ct. 1011 (1983) the Supreme Court reaffirmed its policy of applying the Robinson-Patman Act as drafted by the Congress, stating in part:

The Robinson-Patman Act has been widely criticized, both for its effects and for the policies that it seeks to promote. Although Congress is well aware of these criticisms, the Act has remained in effect for almost half a century. And it certainly is "not for [this Court] to indulge in the business of policy-making in the field of antitrust legislation. . . . Our function ends with the endeavor to ascertain from the words used, construed in the light of the relevant material, what was in fact the intent of Congress.

Criticism of the Robinson-Patman Act will continue in the future.

REVIEW QUESTIONS

1. In 1959, Utah Pie Company entered the rapidly growing frozen-pie business in Salt Lake City. Utah Pie had previously baked and sold pies in Salt Lake City for 30 years. Because its plant was located in Salt Lake City, Utah Pie could sell its pies cheaper than its competitors. In response, the competitors, Continental Baking Company, Carnation Company, and Pet Milk Company, began to sell their pies below cost for varying amounts of time. The firms subsidized their losses in the Salt Lake City market with gains in other markets. The net effect of these practices was a drastic reduction in the price of pies, from over $4.15 in 1958 to between $2.75 and $3.46 in 1961. In a suit by Utah Pie against its competitors, does the competitors' reduction in price violate Section 2(a) of the Clayton Act? *Yes, long-run lessens competition & promotes a monopoly "unfair method"*

2. A number of oil companies engaged in a gas war in Smyrna, Georgia. American Oil Company (Amoco), in order to allow its dealers in Smyrna to effectively compete, sold gasoline to its Smyrna dealers for as much as 11.5¢ less per gallon than its price to its dealers in neighboring Marietta, Georgia. The price war lasted only 17 days. In response, the FTC issued a cease-and-desist order, holding that Amoco's practices violated Section 2(a) of the Clayton Act. Was the FTC's order valid?

3. Anheuser-Busch sold its Budweiser brand beer in competition with four other national beers and in competition with many other regional beers. Budweiser and the other nationally marketed beers sold for a higher price than the regional beers. Anheuser-Busch decided to lower its price on Budweiser in St. Louis to meet the price of its regional competitors. As a result, over a two-year period Anheuser-Busch's market share increased by 5 percent. The FTC subsequently entered a cease-and-desist order against the beer company, arguing that since the price reduction took business away from competitors, it lessened competition in violation of Section 2(a) of the Robinson-Patman Act. Was the FTC's action proper?

4. The Sun Oil Corporation had 39 independent dealers in Jacksonville, Florida, selling its Sunoco brand gasoline. McLean was one of those dealers. Across the street from his service station, a Super-Test discount station opened. To help McLean meet Super-Test's cut-rate competition, Sun lowered the prices that it charged to McLean for a two-month period. Sun, however, did not reduce the price that it charged for Sunoco gasoline to any of the other 38 Sunoco retailers in Jacksonville. Additionally, the

Super-Test retailer did not receive any price supports from his wholesaler. In an action against Sun for price discrimination, will Sun be able to successfully claim as a defense that its actions were used solely to meet the competition?

5. In an attempt to attract new customers, Sunshine Biscuits, Inc., offered its products to certain buyers at a discount price. The FTC charged Sunshine with violating Section 2(a) of the Robinson-Patman Act. Sunshine defended itself by invoking the "meeting the competition" defense authorized by Section 2(b). The Commission concluded, however, that the Section 2(b) defense "is limited in its scope to those situations in which a seller is acting in self-defense against competitive price attacks and is not applicable where the seller makes discriminatory price reductions in order to obtain new customers. . . ." Was the Commission's finding consistent with current law? Why or why not?

6. Southgate Brokerage acted as a broker for various canning firms. Southgate would find various wholesale buyers for the canning firms and receive a commission on each sale. The firm also acted as a middleman. Southgate would purchase the canned foods directly from the canners and then resell the goods directly to the wholesalers for a profit. Southgate also received a commission on these sales. Can a broker making purchases for itself require brokerage commissions?

7. Canada Foods, Ltd., enlisted several brokers to sell its apple concentrate for $1.30 a gallon. The J. M. Smucker Co., a buyer, negotiated with Phipps and Henry Broch and Company, two of Canada Foods' brokers, to buy a 500-gallon order of the concentrate at $1.25 per gallon. Both brokers attempted to have Smucker buy at the higher price. Finally, to secure the order, Broch agreed to reduce its brokerage fee from 5 percent to 3 percent and to charge Smucker the equivalent of $1.25 per gallon. Broch made this concession to Smucker only. All other buyers were charged $1.30 per gallon and a 5 percent brokerage fee. Could Broch accept a lower commission in order to obtain a lower equivalent price for a customer?

8. Lever Brothers, a national soap products distributor, offered two types of promotional aids to its retail customers. Under the Cooperative Merchandising Agreement (CMA), Lever required the retailer to conduct at least nine feature sales of the company's products, promoted by newspaper, radio, or handbill advertising as well as by store displays. The company provided a variable amount of support depending upon the product involved, the quantity ordered, and the promotional medium chosen. Retailers using newspaper advertising received a subsidy between 12½¢ and 20¢ per case while radio and handbill advertisers received between 8¢ and 9¢ per case. The company also had a Cooperative Merchandising Plan (CMP). Under the CMP, small retailers who could not afford large advertising expenditures received a subsidy of 5¢ per case when they offered a feature sale supported by a store display. If the retailers also chose to advertise, they received the same price supports given under the CMA. Under Section 2(d) of the Clayton Act, may a supplier condition promotional aid payments upon the method of advertising used?

9. Fred Meyer, Inc., operated a chain of 13 supermarkets in the Portland,

Oregon area. Meyer used its buying power to purchase goods directly from suppliers rather than from traditional middlemen (wholesalers). Beginning in 1936, Meyer conducted an annual four-week promotional campaign in its stores, which focused on the distribution of coupon books to customers. Each page in the coupon book featured an advertisement for a manufacturer's product. For this advertising space, Meyer charged at least $350 to each manufacturer. Some suppliers further underwrote the promotion by providing Meyer with discount prices for purchases of the advertised items. The FTC concluded that this promotional scheme violated the Clayton Act in the following manners:

a. the $350 fee paid to Meyer violated Section 2(d) because it was a promotional allowance not made available on proportionately equal terms to competing retailers

b. the supplier's additional underwriting amounted to price discrimination under Section 2(a)

c. the inducement of suppliers to discriminate in price violated Section 2(f).

Meyer argued that it did not violate Section 2(d) of the Act. Meyer contended that as a retailer, it did not compete at the same functional level as wholesalers and therefore Meyer was not in competition with them. Secondly, Meyer argued that since other retailers dealt with wholesalers rather than suppliers, the retailers were not entitled to the aid that Meyer received from the suppliers. Do you find Meyer's arguments persuasive? Why or why not?

10. Two of Vanity Fair Paper Mills' customers approached the firm asking it to provide promotional aid honoring their anniversary sales. The customers gave Vanity Fair the option of buying promotional advertising space for as little as $56 or as much as $4,000. Vanity Fair did not indicate to any other customers that it would provide any promotional aid; however, no other customer had inquired about aid either. The FTC charged Vanity Fair with violating Section 2(d) and Section 2(e) of the Clayton Act. Were Vanity Fair's actions lawful?

11. Automatic Canteen Company was a large buyer of candy and other confectionery products for resale through its vending machines. The Company, through the use of its high-volume buying power, was able to obtain substantial cost savings, prices as much as 33 percent lower than those charged by sellers to its competitors. There was no indication that Automatic Canteen knew that it was receiving discriminatory prices. Automatic Canteen did not know, and did not try to find out, whether or not the savings that it received were justified by cost savings to the seller. The FTC issued a complaint against the firm for violation of Section 2(f) of the Robinson-Patman Act. Was the firm liable?

12. Manufacturers of automobile replacement parts give buyers a varying discount based upon the quantity of parts ordered. American Motors Specialties and a number of other automobile repair dealers formed a buying cooperative to take advantage of these discounts. All orders were placed by the cooperative but the shipments were sent directly to the ordering repair business. Did American and the other jobbers violate Section 2(f) of the Robinson-Patman Act?

12 FRANCHISING

INTRODUCTION

Franchising, as a form of distribution, has been in use in the American economy since the early 1900s. Franchising as a form of business was originally pioneered by the automobile and soft drink industries but recently has spread to almost all forms of business. In the following excerpt from *Principe v. McDonald's Corporation*, 631 F.2d 303 (1980), the court described the modern McDonald's franchise.

Far from merely licensing franchisees to sell products under its trade name, a modern franchisor such as McDonald's offers its franchisees a complete method of doing business. It takes people from all walks of life, sends them to its management school, and teaches them a variety of skills ranging from hamburger grilling to financial planning. It installs them in stores whose market has been researched and whose location has been selected by experts to maximize sales potential. It inspects every facet of every store several times a year and consults with each franchisee about his operation's strengths and weaknesses. Its regime pervades all facets of the business; from the design of the menu board to the amount of catsup on the hamburgers, nothing is left to chance. This pervasive franchisor supervision and control benefits the franchisee in turn. His business is identified with a network of stores whose very uniformity and predictability attracts customers. In short, the modern franchisee pays not only for the right to use a trademark but for the right to become a part of a system whose business methods virtually guarantee his success.

Currently, franchises account for over *one quarter* of all retail sales in the United States from over 600,000 outlets. Franchising is also making important inroads in the service industries, such as real estate brokerage and banking. In the future, franchising will continue to expand as one of the most dominant forms of business in the United States and the world.

THE NATURE OF FRANCHISING

In the franchise agreement, one party (the "franchis*or*") licenses another party (the "franchis*ee*") to use the franchisor's trademark, trade name, commercial symbol, or copyright in distributing or selling goods or services. The franchisor is the licensor, and the franchisee is the licensee. Usually, the franchisee is in charge of the day-to-day operation of the franchise, while the franchisor is responsible for setting quality control standards, advertising, promotion, and other strategies for the entire franchise system.

Although each franchise is legally independent of all other franchisees and of the franchisor, in aggregate the franchises form an integrated system for distributing the franchisor's goods throughout geographical regions or the entire country.

Advantages of the Franchise Form of Business.   The advantage of the franchise form of business to the franchisee is that he is given the opportunity to operate his own business independently, yet he has available the marketing strength and expertise of the franchisor to assist him. The advantage of franchising to the franchisor is that its products and services can be made available through franchise outlets to thousands of consumers who would not otherwise be offered the products through company-owned stores. Franchising can increase the sales volume and profit potential of the franchisor significantly beyond that which would be generated from company owned stores only. The advantage of franchising to consumers is that consumers are offered a greater number and variety of products and services than would otherwise be available.

Other economic advantages of the franchising form of business are:

1. there is usually a *production* advantage (i.e., economies of scale) to producing large quantities of similar products for regional or national distribution
2. there is an *advertising* cost advantage from the use of regional or national advertising, which benefits all franchise outlets in the designated region or throughout the country
3. there is usually a *marketing* advantage associated with promoting the uniformity of the franchise product or service by maintaining quality control standards. For example, you can generally expect that a "Big Mac" will be similar in taste and quality across the nation.

Definition of Franchising.   Most state laws are in accord with the California Franchise Investment Law of 1971, California Corporations Code Section 31005, which comprehensively defines "franchising" as:

(a) "Franchise" means a contract or agreement, either expressed or implied, whether oral or written, between two or more persons by which:

(1) A franchise is granted the right to engage in the business of offering, selling or distributing goods or services under a marketing plan or system prescribed in substantial part by a franchisor; and

(2) The operation of the franchisee's business pursuant to such plan or system is substantially associated with the franchisor's trademark, service mark, trade name, logotype, advertising or other commercial symbol designating the franchisor or its affiliate; and

(3) The franchisee is required to pay, directly or indirectly, a franchise fee.

Types of Franchises.   There are basically three types of franchises that fall under the above definition: distributorships, manufacturing or processing plants, and chain-style businesses. Some franchisors also grant "area" franchises. Most state franchise laws also include contracts, including leases between petroleum corporations and service station dealers, within their legal definition of *franchise.*

Distributorship.   In a "distributorship" form of franchising, generally a manufacturer (the franchisor) licenses a retail dealer (the franchisee) to distribute or sell a product manufactured by the franchisor. The retail dealer-franchisee is usually given an exclusive territory in which to sell the manufacturer-franchisor's product. In a common example of a distributorship form of franchise, an automobile manufacturer licenses a car dealership to sell its automobiles from a specific location.

Manufacturing or Processing Plant.   In a "manufacturing" or "processing plant" form of franchising a franchisor, pursuant to a franchise agreement, provides the essential parts, ingredients, or formula to the franchisee that enable him to make a particular product, and the franchisee manufactures or assembles the product. The franchisee produces and distributes the product, either at wholesale or retail, or both, depending on the terms of the franchise agreement. An example of the manufacturing or processing plant form of franchising is a soft drink company that licenses regional bottling companies to produce and distribute soft drinks under the secret formula provided by the soft drink corporation, e.g., Coca-Cola.

Chain Form of Franchising.   In a "chain" form of franchising, a franchisor licenses a franchisee to use the franchisor's trademark, trade name, or logo in distributing products and services. The products are *not* usually manufactured by the franchisor or franchisee, but are prepared by the franchisee at the franchise site. For example, McDonald's outlets for the distribution of hamburgers and other foods are an example of a chain form of franchise. The franchisor in a chain form of franchising generally sets quality control standards to which its franchisees must adhere in order to keep their franchises.

"Area" Franchise.   Often a franchisor will grant to a franchisee, for appropriate consideration, the right to sell or negotiate the sale of additional franchises on behalf of the franchisor in a specified geographical area. This type

of franchise is called an "area franchise," and the franchisee to whom the area franchise is awarded is called a "sub-franchisor." The sub-franchisor usually receives compensation based on the number of franchisees he recruits for the area, or a fixed percentage of the sales of all franchises located in the territory of the area franchise.

The Law and Franchising.   There is no uniform body of law that regulates franchising as a form of business. The law of franchising is drawn from contract law, corporation law, agency law, negligence, the Uniform Commercial Code, equity, and state and federal statutes. Since franchising is a relatively new form of doing business, there has not yet developed a large body of judicially made common law in the area. Many of the legal issues presented to the courts regarding franchising problems are issues of "first impression."

Many states have enacted special statutes that are applicable to the sale and operation of franchises. State franchising laws generally:

1. require the registration of the offer to sell franchises, which is usually registered at the state's Department of Corporations
2. require the disclosure of pertinent information by the franchisor to proposed franchisee in a "prospectus"
3. provide for civil liability of franchisors to franchisees and prospective franchisees for making misleading, fraudulent, or untrue statements
4. empower the state to issue cease-and-desist orders and obtain injunctions against franchisors and franchisees for prohibited acts.

The State of California has one of the most comprehensive state laws for the regulation of the sale and operation of franchises. The California legislature's statement of intent for enacting the California Franchise Investment Law follows.

The Legislature hereby finds and declares that the widespread sale of franchises is a relatively new form of business which has created numerous problems both from an investment and a business point of view in the State of California. Prior to the enactment of this division, the sale of franchises was regulated only to the limited extent to which the Corporate Securities Law of 1968 applied to such transactions. California franchisees have suffered substantial losses where the franchisor or his representative has not provided full and complete information regarding the franchisor-franchisee relationship, the details of the contract between franchisor and franchisee, and the prior business experience of the franchisor.

It is the intent of this law to provide each prospective franchisee with the information necessary to make an intelligent decision regarding franchises being offered. Further, it is the intent of this law to prohibit the sale of franchises where such sale would lead to fraud or a likelihood that the franchisor's promises would not be fulfilled, and to protect the franchisor by providing a better understanding of the relationship between the franchisor and franchisee with regard to their business relationship.

Other than Federal Trade Commission rules, which are covered in this chapter, there is no standard federal law of franchising. The Justice Department may bring an action against a franchisor or franchisee who violates any one of a number of federal laws applicable to all businesses, e.g., the antitrust laws, the antidiscrimination laws, the labor laws. It is often difficult to define a franchise as a "security" so as to apply the federal securities laws.

THE FRANCHISE AGREEMENT

After a prospective franchisee has investigated the different franchise opportunities available, and decided on a particular franchise, he usually files an application with the franchisor for a franchise. The application is often quite detailed, and usually requires the applicant to submit biographical and financial statements, personal references, credit references, etc. After an investigation of the applicant's qualifications, the franchisor will either deny or approve the applicant.

Once an applicant is approved by the franchisor, the franchisor and franchisee execute a *franchise agreement.* Many states permit a franchise agreement to be oral, implied, or written. Most states, however, have enacted a Statute of Frauds which requires that a franchise agreement be in writing before it is enforceable.

Even where there is a Statute of Frauds which would require a franchise agreement to be in writing, but the promise of the franchise agreement is oral, courts can apply the equitable doctrine of "promissory estoppel" and hold that the defendant is *estopped* (prevented) from raising the Statute of Frauds as a defense to the enforcement of the oral franchise agreement. The reason the courts apply the doctrine of estoppel is to prevent "unjust enrichment" or "unconscionable loss" to the parties.

Terms of a Franchise Agreement. The franchise agreement is usually a very long and complex document that contains all the terms and conditions applicable to the arrangement between the franchisor and franchisee. The franchise agreement is normally a standard form of contract prepared by the franchisor. There is usually little room for individual negotiation by the franchisee regarding the terms of the franchise agreement.

Common terms in a franchise agreement include a description of the business, capital requirements, record-keeping requirements, standards of operation, quality control standards, restrictions on the use of the franchisor's trade name or logo, requirements for training personnel, hours of operation, sign requirements, prohibitions as to the assignment of the franchise, provisions for terminating the franchise, and other terms pertinent to the franchise operation. In addition to specific terms, and in an effort to provide general standards of conduct, franchise agreements often contain provisions requiring the parties to act in "good faith," with "reasonableness," and to use their "best efforts" to accomplish the objectives of the franchise.

It is a common practice in franchise agreements for the franchisor to require its franchisees and their personnel to attend extensive training programs, either at the franchisor's training facilities or on-site at the franchise. Requirements for both initial franchisee training prior to opening a franchise and training of personnel throughout the duration of the franchise are commonly held to be lawful.

In order to protect its name and reputation, a franchisor may lawfully set and enforce *quality control* standards that must be adhered to by its franchisees. The franchisor is generally given the right in the franchise agreement to make periodic inspections of franchise premises to determine if its quality control standards are being met by its franchisees. Legal questions often arise as to whether the degree of control exercised by the franchisor exceeds that necessary to ensure compliance with quality control standards.

Covenant Not to Compete. Most franchise agreements contain a "covenant not to compete" provision. A covenant not to compete is an agreement by the franchisee that after termination of the franchise agreement he will not compete directly with the franchisor. The covenant usually specifies a particular scope, duration, and area limitation. For example, a covenant not to enter "any business" near the franchisor is too broad and will be held void. A time limitation of ten years is generally held to be void as being too long in duration, whereas three-year covenants not to compete have generally been held valid. A geographical limitation to a single city is usually valid, whereas a geographical limitation preventing competition within an entire state has generally been held void. Each case will be decided on the particular facts and circumstances.

Payment of Franchise Fees. In return for the use of the franchisor's trademark and other assistance, the franchisee is commonly charged certain fees by the franchisor. Franchise fees paid by the franchisee to the franchisor normally include:

1. an initial fee or lump sum payment for the privilege of being granted the franchise license
2. a stated percentage of annual sales
3. an assessment for the payment of a portion of the franchisor's advertising and administrative expenses, usually based on a fixed dollar amount per franchise or a percentage of gross sales
4. payment for products and supplies purchased from the franchisor.

In some franchise operations, the payment of the initial license fee by the franchisee is the main source of income to the franchisor. The practice of charging high initial license fees without providing continuing assistance is an area of concern and possible fraudulent activity in the franchise business. A "pyramid" scheme, where high initiation fees are charged and split with persons bringing in a new franchisee, particularly where few if any products are sold by the company, has generally been held to be a "security" that requires registration under the federal securities laws. Many such schemes have been held to be fraudulent, for which civil and criminal liability lies.

Breach of the Franchise Agreement. During the period of the franchise, each party to the franchise agreement expects the other party to adhere to, and perform under, the lawful terms and conditions of the franchise agreement. The franchise agreement is an enforceable contract between the franchisor and the franchisee. If a franchisee or franchisor breaches the franchise agreement, the nonbreaching party may generally rescind the franchise agreement and seek restitution, or affirm the agreement and sue the breaching party for damages, or take whatever other action is provided for in the franchise agreement.

Since the franchise agreement is based on the law of contracts, some courts have expanded the doctrine of the *implied* covenant of "good faith and fair dealing" to franchise agreements. This covenant, originally developed to prevent oppressive practices by insurance companies (as when an insurance company refuses to settle a lawsuit below policy limits, the case goes to trial, and the jury award substantially exceeds the policy limits, causing loss to the insured), holds that the parties to a contract owe an *implied* duty of good faith and fair dealing to one another to perform under the contract. A breach of this covenant is a *tort,* for which noncontract damages (e.g., pain and suffering, emotional distress, punitive damages) may lie, i.e., may be recovered under law. The doctrine is particularly applicable to the franchise area where large and powerful franchisors deal with relatively powerless franchisees.

In *Principe v. McDonald's Corporation,* which was mentioned previously, the court found in favor of franchisor McDonald's where a franchise had sued McDonald's charging a violation of antitrust laws. In its decision, the court carefully described the McDonald's franchise. This portion of the opinion is set forth following.

FRANCHISE AGREEMENT

PRINCIPE v. McDONALD'S CORPORATION

631 F.2d 303 (1980)
United States Court of Appeals, Fourth Circuit

Harry Phillips, Senior Circuit Judge.

At the time this suit was filed, McDonald's consisted of at least four separate corporate entities. McDonald's Systems, Inc. controlled franchise rights and licensed franchisees to sell hamburgers under the McDonald's name. Franchise Realty Interstate Corporation (Franchise Realty) acquires real estate, either by purchase or long-term lease, builds McDonald's hamburger restaurants, and leases them either to franchisees or to a third corporation, McOpCo. McOpCo, which is not a party to this suit, operates about one-fourth of the McDonald's restaurants in the United States as company stores. Straddling this triad is McDonald's Corporation, the parent, who owns all the stock of the other defendants. . . . [W]e shall refer to them collectively as McDonald's unless the context requires otherwise.

McDonald's is not primarily a fast food retailer. While it does operate over a thousand stores itself, the vast majority of the stores in its system are operated by franchisees. Nor does McDonald's sell equipment or supplies to its licensees. Instead its primary business is developing and collecting royalties from limited-menu fast food restaurants operated by independent business people.

McDonald's develops new restaurants according to master plans that originate at the regional level and must be approved by upper management.

After the specifics of each proposed new restaurant are approved, McDonald's decides whether the store will be company operated or franchised. If the decision is to franchise the store McDonald's begins the process of locating a franchisee. This involves offering the store either to an existing franchisee or to an applicant on the franchise waiting list. Applicants need not live near the store in order to be offered the franchise, and they need not accept the first franchise they are offered. . . . McDonald's often does not know who will operate a franchised store until it is nearly completed because a new restaurant may be offered to and rejected by several different applicants.

Meanwhile, Franchise Realty acquires the land, either by purchase or long-term lease, and constructs the store. Acquisition and development costs averaged over $450,000 per store in 1978. All McDonald's restaurants bear the same distinctive features with a few exceptions due to architectural restrictions: the golden arches motif, the brick and glass construction and the distinctive roofline. According to the defendants, these features identify the stores as a McDonald's even where zoning restrictions preclude other advertising or signs.

As constructed, McDonald's restaurants are finished shells; they contain no kitchen or dining room equipment. Furnishing store equipment is the responsibility of the operator, whether a franchisee or McOpCo. McDonald's does provide specifications such equipment must meet, but does not sell the equipment itself.

Having acquired the land, begun construction of the store and selected an operator, McDonald's enters into two contracts with the franchisee. Under the first, the franchise agreement, McDonald's grants the franchisee the rights to use McDonald's food preparation system and to sell food products under the McDonald's name. The franchise pays a $12,500 franchise fee and agrees to remit three per cent of his gross sales as a royalty in return. Under the second contract, the lease, McDonald's grants the franchisee the right to use the particular store premises to which his franchise pertains. In return, the franchisee pays a $15,000 refundable security deposit (as evidence of which he receives a twenty-year non-negotiable non-interest bearing note) and agrees to pay eight and one half per cent of his gross sales as rent. These payments under the franchise and lease agreements are McDonald's only sources of income from its franchised restaurants. The franchisee also assumes responsibility under the lease for building maintenance, improvements, property taxes and other costs associated with the premises. Both the franchise agreement and the lease generally have twenty-year durations, both provide that termination of one terminates the other, and neither is available separately.

We noted that "the very essence of a franchise is the purchase of several related products in a single competitively attractive package." *Phillips v. Crown Central Petroleum Corporation.*

McDonald's practice of developing a system of company-owned restaurants operated by franchisees has substantial advantages, both for the company and for franchisees. It is part of what makes a McDonald's franchise uniquely attractive to franchisees.

First, because it approaches the problem of restaurant site selection systematically, McDonald's is able to obtain better sites than franchisees could select. Armed with its demographic information, guided by its staff of experts and unencumbered by preferences of individual franchisees, McDonald's can wield its economic might to acquire sites where new restaurants will prosper without undercutting existing franchisees' business or limiting future expansion. Individual franchisees are unlikely to possess analytical expertise, undertake elaborate market research or approach the problem of site selection from an area-wide point of view. Individual franchisees benefit from the McDonald's approach because their stores are located in areas McDonald's has determined will produce substantial fast-food business and on sites where that business is most likely to be diverted to their stores. Because McDonald's purposefully locates new stores where they will not undercut existing franchisees' business, McDonald's franchisees do not have to compete with each other, a substantial advantage in the highly competitive fast-food industry.

Second, McDonald's policy of owning all of its own restaurants assures that the stores remain part of the McDonald's system. McDonald's franchise arrangements are not static: franchisees retire or die; occasionally they do not live up to their franchise obligations and must be replaced; even if no such contingency intervenes, the agreements normally expire by their own terms after twenty years. If franchisees owned their own stores, any of these events could disrupt McDonald's business and have a negative effect on the system's goodwill. Buildings whose architecture identified them as former McDonald's stores would sit idle or be used for other purposes. Replacement franchisees would have to acquire new and perhaps less desirable sites, a much more difficult and expensive process after the surrounding business area has matured.

By owning its own stores, McDonald's assures its continued presence on the site, maintains the store's patronage even during management changes and avoids the negative publicity of having former McDonald's stores used for other purposes. By preserving the goodwill of the system in established markets, company store ownership produces attendant benefits for franchisees.

Third, because McDonald's acquires the sites and builds the stores itself, it can select franchisees based on their management potential rather than their real estate expertise or wealth. Ability to emphasize management skills is important to McDonald's because it has built its reputation largely on the consistent quality of its operations rather than on the merits of its hamburgers. A store's quality is largely a function of its management. McDonald's policy of owning its own stores reduces a franchisee's initial investment, thereby broadening the applicant base and opening the door to persons who otherwise could not afford a McDonald's franchise. Accordingly, McDonald's is able to select franchisees primarily on the basis of their willingness to work for the success of their operations. Their ability to begin operating a McDonald's restaurant without having to search for a site, negotiate for the land, borrow hundreds of thousands of dollars and construct a store building is of substantial value to franchisees.

Finally, because both McDonald's and the franchisee have a substantial financial stake in the success of the restaurant, their relationship becomes a sort of partnership that might be impossible under other circumstances. McDonald's spends close to half a million dollars on each new store it establishes. Each franchisee invests over $100,000 to make the store operational. Neither can afford to ignore the other's problems, complaints or ideas. Because its investment is on the line, the Company cannot allow its franchisees to lose money. This being so, McDonald's works with its franchisees to build their business, occasionally financing improvements at favorable rates or even accepting reduced royalty payments in order to provide franchisees more working capital.

All of these factors contribute significantly to the overall success of the McDonald's system. The formula that produced systemwide success, the formula that promises to make each new McDonald's store successful, that formula is what McDonald's sells its franchisees. To characterize the franchise as an unnecessary aggregation of separate products tied to the McDonald's name is to miss the point entirely. Among would-be franchisees, the McDonald's name has come to stand for the formula, including all that it entails.

Affirmed.

CASE QUESTIONS

1. What functions did the following corporations serve in the McDonald's franchise operation?
   a. McDonald's Systems
   b. Franchise Realty
   c. McOpCo
   d. McDonald's Corporation
2. Which party builds the McDonald's restaurants, the franchisor or the franchisee? Who owns the land and premises?
3. What did each of the following two contracts entered into between McDonald's and its franchisees provide?
   a. the franchise agreement
   b. the lease
4. Does McDonald's require its franchisees to purchase their equipment and supplies from it?
5. What are the following charges and how are they calculated in a McDonald's franchise arrangement?
   a. franchise fee
   b. royalty payment
   c. rent payment
   Does McDonald's charge any other fees to its franchisees?
6. What benefits did the court find in the following elements of a McDonald's franchise arrangement?
   a. site selection
   b. ownership of land and premises
   c. selection of franchisees
   d. investment in the franchises

Policy Issue. Is franchising an important form of distribution? Does franchising help or hurt "mom-and-pop" stores?

Economics Issue. Is franchising an economically beneficial form of business to the franchisor? To the franchisees? Explain.

Ethics Issue. Is it ethical for McDonald's not to permit its franchisees to own the land and premises of their franchise?

Social Responsibility. Does the franchising form of business help or hurt society? Does it increase the availability of products and services? The quality of products and services?

FEDERAL TRADE COMMISSION DISCLOSURE RULES

Pursuant to the Federal Trade Commission Act, the Federal Trade Commission (FTC) is empowered to adopt rules and regulations, and to issue orders, regarding franchising arrangements. Under this authority, and to respond to the widespread frauds and other abuses that have occurred in the franchising area, the FTC has adopted rules governing the offer, sale, and operation of franchises. FTC rules particularly address the delineation of the rights between the franchisor and the franchisee, with the objective of placing the franchisee on a more equal standing with the franchisor in the negotiation and execution of the franchise agreement.

The FTC rules regarding franchising only apply to business relationships defined as a "franchise" by the FTC. The FTC Act provides two definitions of franchising, a traditional definition and a more expansive definition.

Traditional Definition.   The FTC's "traditional" definition of a franchise requires that a business arrangement meet three requirements:

1. The franchisee is required to pay a fee of at least $500 to the franchisor within the first six months of business.
2. The franchisor exercises "significant control" over the franchisee (e.g., management), *or* gives "significant assistance" to the franchisee in its methods of operation (e.g., develops business plan, provides promotional activities).
3. The goods or services distributed by the franchise bear the franchisor's trademark, trade name, or symbol, *or* the franchisee is required to meet quality standards as set by the franchisor.

McDonald's and Coca-Cola bottling franchises meet this traditional definition of "franchise."

Expansive Definition.   The second FTC definition of "franchise" is somewhat broader than the traditional definition, but also has three requirements:

1. The franchisee is obligated to pay the franchisor a fee of at least $500 during the first six months of business.
2. The franchisee sells or distributes goods or services supplied by the franchisor or other party with whom the franchisor requires the franchisee to deal.
3. The franchisor secures the sales area for the franchisee.

For example, vending machine supply contracts fall within this broader FTC definition of *franchise.*

The $500 floor of "required" payment for both definitions applies not only to payments for the use of the franchisor's trademark or trade name, but also to equipment, tools, and other goods or services provided by the franchisor. The initial inventory of the franchisee is not included in the $500 unless the required inventory is "unreasonable" in quantity or price. Any noninventory items that may be purchased from alternative sources are also excluded from the $500 floor amount.

If any one of the requirements of the two FTC definitions of a "franchise" is not met (e.g., the franchisor does not require the franchisee to pay at least $500 to the franchisor during the first six months of business), the business arrangement does not meet the required definition of *franchise* and is therefore not subject to the FTC franchising rules.

Disclosure Statement. Where a business arrangement falls within the FTC definition of a "franchise," the franchisor is required to disclose to the franchisee in a separate document the following information:

1. the franchisor's name and address
2. the names of the officers and directors of the franchisor
3. any felony convictions of the officers or directors for fraud, embezzlement, misappropriation or conversion of property, or restraint of trade
4. any civil litigation or administrative agency action against any officer or director for fraud, dishonesty, breach of a franchise agreement, or other civil action regarding a franchise relationship
5. any bankruptcy proceedings in which an officer or director has been involved
6. a description of the franchise, its form, products, and trademarks
7. the description of the market of the franchise
8. a listing of the competitors of the franchise
9. the material terms and requirements of the franchise agreement, including the initial payment, recurring payments, and obligations of the franchisee to purchase goods from the franchisor or its affiliated companies
10. requirements for personal participation of the franchisee in the franchise
11. a description of the training programs available to the franchisee
12. a description of the financing arrangements available to the franchisee
13. a disclosure of any restrictions on the franchisee's territories, site location, customers, etc.
14. the grounds for termination of the franchise
15. statistics showing the number of the franchisor's franchises which were terminated during the preceding year
16. the grounds for denying the renewal of the franchise
17. balance sheets and income statements of the franchisor for the preceding three years; these financial statements do not have to be certified under the FTC rules if they are prepared in accordance with generally accepted accounting standards and auditing procedures.

The franchisor's disclosure statement setting forth the above information does *not* have to be reviewed by the FTC prior to its use. The cover of the franchisor's required disclosure statement must contain the following language in at least 12-point boldface type:

**INFORMATION FOR PROSPECTIVE FRANCHISEES REQUIRED
BY FEDERAL TRADE COMMISSION**

* * * * *

To protect you, we've required your franchisor to give you this information. We haven't checked it, and don't know if it's correct. It should help you make up your mind. Study it carefully. While it includes some information about your contract, don't rely on it alone to understand your contract. Read all of your contract carefully. Buying a franchise is a complicated investment. Take your time to decide. If possible, show your contract and this information to an advisor, like a lawyer or an accountant. If you find anything you think may be wrong or anything important that's been left out, you should let us know about it. It may be against the law.

There may also be laws on franchising in your state. Ask your state agencies about them.

Earnings and Sales Projections. In the past, many franchisors made overly optimistic sales and earnings projections to entice prospective franchisees to open franchises. These projections were often made by hypothetical examples, or by presenting the actual results of only the most successful franchises in the chain. Where a franchisor uses *hypothetical* sales, income or profit projections, the FTC rules further require that the franchisor disclose to the prospective franchisee in a separate document:

1. the assumptions underlying the estimates
2. the number and percentage of its franchise outlets that have at least equalled the estimates
3. the following cautionary statement in at least 12-point boldface type:

CAUTION

These figures are only estimates of what we think you may earn. There is no assurance you'll do as well. If you rely upon our figures, you must accept the risk of not doing so well.

If instead of using hypothetical estimates, the franchisor presents to the prospective franchisee the actual sales, income, and profit figures from existing franchise outlets, the document that discloses this information must contain the following cautionary statement in at least 12-point boldface type:

CAUTION

Some outlets have (sold) (earned) this amount. There is no assurance you'll do as well. If you rely upon our figures, you must accept the risk of not doing so well.

Remedies for Violations of FTC Disclosure Rules. Where a franchisor violates FTC disclosure rules, the franchisor is subject to a number of actions, including:

1. an injunction against further franchise sales
2. civil fines of up to $10,000 per violation
3. an FTC action in federal District Court against the franchisor on behalf of the injured franchisee to recover damages suffered by the franchisee.

There are several exceptions to the FTC disclosure rules, including employment relationships, cooperative associations, and relationships among general partners. The FTC Act also exempts automobile dealerships and oil and gasoline franchises from its disclosure rules. The rationale for these exemptions is that most automobile dealerships are large and sophisticated organizations that do not require the protection of the FTC, and oil and gasoline franchises are usually subject to similar rules contained in the federal Petroleum Marketing Practices Act.

ANTITRUST LAW AND FRANCHISING

In order to create a successful franchise system with uniform quality of the product or service throughout the franchise network, the franchisor must be able to wield a certain degree of control over the operations of its franchisees. Such control is usually allocated by the terms of franchise agreement. The *type* and *degree* of control exercised by the franchisor over the franchisees will determine whether there is a lawful or unlawful practice under federal antitrust law.

Price Controls as Antitrust Violations.   Price controls in franchise agreements commonly violate the antitrust laws in at least three situations:

1. If a franchisor sets a retail price to which each franchisor is required to adhere when selling the product of service to the public, this constitutes "resale price maintenance," a vertical restraint of trade and *per se* violation of Section 1 of the Sherman Act. A franchisor may, however, "suggest" retail prices for franchisees; the franchisees do not have to adhere to such suggestions.
2. If the franchisor charges a different price to two or more of its franchisees for the same products or supplies, this constitutes "price discrimination," and is a violation of Section 2 of the Clayton Act (Robinson-Patman Act).
3. If the franchisees agree among themselves that they will all charge an agreed-upon price for their products or services, this constitutes "price fixing," a horizontal restraint of trade and *per se* of Section 1 of the Sherman Act.
4. If the franchisor sets quotas as to the quantity of products that may be sold by each franchisee, that constitutes "price fixing," a *per se* violation of Section 1 of the Sherman Act.

Nonprice Violations of Antitrust Laws.   Franchisors and franchisees are often found liable for *nonprice* violations of the antitrust laws, including:

1. agreeing with others not to deal with (i.e., to boycott) third parties; this is often done in an attempt to "punish" the boycotted franchisee for taking some action against the wishes of the franchisor
2. setting territorial restrictions that attempt to prevent franchisees from selling to customers located in another franchisee's market area, which is a form of division of markets

3. setting customer restrictions whereby each franchisee is limited to selling to certain identified customers, which is also a division of markets.

All of these activities have been held to be *per se* violations of Section 1 of the Sherman Act.

Tying Arrangements. A "tying" arrangement is a *vertical* restraint wherein a seller refuses to sell one product (the "tying" product) to a customer unless the customer purchases a second product (the "tied" product). The products may be used in fixed proportions (like nuts and bolts), be designed to be used together (like computers and computer discs), or be usable together (like beer and peanuts). A seller must have substantial market power in the tying product, otherwise the "tie" will not be successful.

Section 3 of the Clayton Act makes tying arrangements unlawful. Section 3 provides in pertinent part:

It shall be unlawful for any person . . . to lease or make a sale . . . of goods [or] commodities . . . or fix a price charged therefor . . . on the condition [or] agreement . . . that the leasee or purchaser thereof shall not use or deal in the goods [or] . . . commodities of a competitor . . . of the lessor or seller, where the effect . . . may be to substantially lessen competition or tend to create a monopoly in any line of commerce.

Tying arrangements also violate Section 1 of the Sherman Act as an unreasonable *restraint of trade*. In order to establish a cause of action for "tying," the plaintiff must:

1. show a *tie* of separate products
2. prove the market power of the manufacturer
3. show that more than a *de minimus* amount of commerce is affected.

Generally, tying arrangements are held to be illegal *per se*. The rationale the *per se* rule is that tying arrangements have as their purpose the limitation of competition. However, the *per se* rule of tying arrangements is not an *absolute* rule. The courts have recognized two limited defenses to an action for tying:

1. if the tie is "instituted by launching a new business with a highly uncertain future"
2. where the tie is necessary to protect the manufacturer's goodwill. The defense of the protection of goodwill hardly ever succeeds.

Franchising and Tying Arrangements. Some franchisors, for the professed reason of assuring quality control, *require* their franchisees to purchase supplies and materials used in the operation of the franchises directly from the franchisor. Under this arrangement, the franchisor is guaranteed a profit on the sale of products to its franchisees. The courts, however, have held that such a requirement in a franchise agreement is a "tying arrangement," which is a *per se* violation of Section 3 of the Clayton Act. The "tying" product is the franchise itself, and the "tied" product is the supplies and materials.

A franchisor may lawfully set quality control standards and *offer* to sell to its franchisees supplies and materials that meet these standards. However, the franchisees must have the legal right to purchase needed supplies and materials from any other alternative source as long as the supplies meet the quality control standards set by the franchisor.

In *Siegel v. Chicken Delight, Inc.* the court found an illegal tying arrangement where a franchisor required a franchisee to purchase all of its products from the franchisor, although comparable products could have been purchased from competitors of the franchisor.

Not o.k.

TYING ARRANGEMENT

SIEGEL v. CHICKEN DELIGHT, INC.

448 F.2d 43 (1971)
United States Court of Appeals, Ninth Circuit

Merrill, Circuit Judge.

This antitrust suit is a class action in which certain franchisees of Chicken Delight seek treble damages for injuries allegedly resulting from illegal restraints imposed by Chicken Delight's standard form franchise agreements.

FACTUAL BACKGROUND

Over its eighteen years existence, Chicken Delight has licensed several hundred franchisees to operate home delivery and pick-up food stores. It charged its franchisees no franchise fees or royalties. Instead, in exchange for the license granting the franchisees the right to assume its identity and adopt its business methods and to prepare and market certain food products under its trade-mark, Chicken Delight required its franchisees to purchase a specified number of cookers and fryers and to purchase certain packaging supplies and mixes exclusively from Chicken Delight. The prices fixed for these purchases were higher than, and included a percentage markup which exceeded that of, comparable products sold by competing suppliers.

THE EXISTENCE OF AN UNLAWFUL TYING ARRANGEMENT

The District Court ruled that the license to use the Chicken Delight name, trade-mark, and method of operations was "a tying item in the traditional sense," the tied items being the cookers and fryers, packaging products, and mixes.

Chicken Delight urges us to hold that its trademark and franchise licenses are not items separate and distinct from the packaging, mixes, and equipment, which it says are essential components of the franchise system. To treat the combined sale of all these items as a tie-in for antitrust purposes, Chicken Delight maintains, would be like applying the antitrust rules to the sale of a car with its tires or a left shoe with the right. Therefore, concludes Chicken Delight, the lawfulness of the arrangement should not be measured by the rules governing tie-ins. We disagree.

The historical conception of a trade-mark as a strict emblem of source of the product to which it attaches has largely been abandoned. The burgeoning business of franchising has made trademark licensing a widespread commercial practice and has resulted in the development of a new rationale for trade-marks as representations of product quality. This is particularly true in the case of a franchise system set up not to distribute the trade-marked goods of the franchisor, but, as here, to conduct a certain business under a common trademark or trade name. Under such a type of franchise, the trade-mark simply reflects the goodwill and quality standards of the enterprise which it identifies.

This being so, it is apparent that the goodwill

of the Chicken Delight trade-mark does not attach to the multitude of separate articles used in the operation of the licensed system or in the production of its end product. . . . Thus, sale of a franchise license, with the attendant rights to operate a business in the prescribed manner and to benefit from the goodwill of the trade name, in no way requires the forced sale by the franchisor of some or all of the component articles.

First, Chicken Delight contends that the arrangement was a reasonable device for measuring and collecting revenue. There is no authority for justifying a tying arrangement on this ground. Unquestionably, there exist feasible alternative methods of compensation for the franchise licenses, including royalties based on sales volume or fees computed per unit of time, which would neither involve tie-ins nor have undesirable anticompetitive consequences.

Second, Chicken Delight advances as justification the fact that when it first entered the fast food field in 1952 it was a new business and was then entitled to the protection afforded by *United States v. Jerrold Electronics Corp.*

We find no merit in this contention. Whatever claim Chicken Delight might have had to a new business defense in 1952—a question we need not decide—the defense cannot apply to the 1963–70 period.

The third justification Chicken Delight offers is the "marketing identity" purpose, the franchisor's preservation of the distinctiveness, uniformity and quality of its product.

In the case of a trade-mark this purpose cannot be lightly dismissed. Not only protection of the franchisor's goodwill is involved. The licensor owes an affirmative duty to the public to assure that in the hands of his licensee the trade-mark continues to represent that which it purports to represent. For a licensor, through relaxation of quality control, to permit inferior products to be presented to the public under his licensed mark might well constitute a misuse of the mark.

However, to recognize that such a duty exists is not to say that every means of meeting it is justified. Restraint of trade can be justified only in the absence of less restrictive alternatives. In cases such as this, where the alternative of specification is available, the language used in *Standard Oil Co.*

v. United States, in our view states the proper test, applicable in the case of trade-marks as well as in other cases:

> the protection of the good will of the manufacturer of the tying device—fails in the usual situation because specification of the type and quality of the product to be used in connection with the tying device is protection enough. . . . The only situation, indeed, in which the protection of good will may necessitate the use of tying clauses is where specifications for a substitute would be so detailed that they could not practicably be supplied.

We conclude that the District Court was not in error in holding as matter of law that Chicken Delight's contractual requirements constituted a tying arrangement in violation of [antitrust law]. Upon this aspect of the case, judgment is *affirmed*.

THE MEASURE OF DAMAGES

It is by no means clear that any of the parties to the tying arrangements understood that the tying items were to be given free of charge. Indeed, the more reasonable reading of the contracts and of Chicken Delight's representations is that they stated simply that the contract prices for the tied items were to be the full compensation asked by Chicken Delight for both those items and the franchise licenses.

Upon the issue of damages, judgment is *reversed* and the case *remanded* for limited new trial.

CASE QUESTIONS

1. Did Chicken Delight require its franchisees to purchase their equipment and supplies from it? How did this differ from the McDonald's franchise?
2. Did Chicken Delight charge any franchise fees or royalties to its franchisees? How did this differ from the McDonald's franchise?
3. What purposes does a trademark serve in a modern franchise arrangement? Explain.
4. What is a "tying arrangement"? Is it illegal under federal antitrust law?
5. In this case, what did the court find as the *tying* product? The *tied* product?
6. How did the court answer each of the following arguments, alleged by Chicken Delight to justify its tying arrangement?

a. device for measuring and collecting revenue
b. new business that needed protection
c. protect its marketing identity

Policy Issue. Should a franchisor be allowed to require its franchisees to purchase supplies from it? Why or why not?

Economics Issue. How would you decide the issue of damages on remand?

Ethics Issue. Was it ethical for Chicken Delight to charge higher prices to its franchisees for equipment and supplies than other suppliers charged for the same items?

Social Responsibility. Does a franchisor owe a duty of responsibility to deal fairly with its franchisees? Do the franchisees owe a duty of responsibility not to "bite the hand that feeds them"?

TRADEMARK LAW AND FRANCHISING

The essence of most successful franchises is the ability of the franchisor, with the assistance of all its franchisees, to increase the public's perception of the quality of the products associated with the franchisor's trademarks. For example, McDonald's Corporation spends a considerable amount of money promoting and advertising such trademarked registered products as the "Big Mac," "Egg McMuffin," and "Chicken McNuggets."

Because a trademark, trade name, or logo is a very important part of the success of a franchise operation, and is of considerable value to the franchisor, the typical franchise agreement contains provisions setting forth in detail the authorized uses of the trademark or trade name, prohibitions of unauthorized uses, and the terms for the discontinuance of the use of the trademark or trade name by the franchisee upon termination of the franchise.

A franchisor may bring an action for *trademark infringement* against any party for the unauthorized use of a trademark. A franchisor may also bring an action for trademark infringement against any franchisee who exceeds the scope of the authorized use of the franchisor's trademarks as granted in the franchise agreement. The franchisor's action in either case may be for an injunction to prevent any further unauthorized use, for damages, or both.

Unfair Competition. A franchisor may also bring a common law tort action against a third party or a franchisee for unfair competition. Most unfair competition actions in a franchise setting bear on someone stealing the "trade secrets" of the franchisor (e.g., Jack's "secret sauce," the Colonel's chicken batter recipe), the stealing of customer lists, and business espionage.

In *Kentucky Fried Chicken Corporation v. Diversified Container Corporation,* the court found the defendant liable for both statutory trademark infringement *and* common law "unfair competition" in that the defendant had produced boxes to hold Kentucky Fried Chicken that were inferior to the quality standards set by the plaintiff and that contained the unauthorized trademarks and commercial symbols of the plaintiff.

*[handwritten: * can specify quality of product]*

[handwritten: Not a tying arrangement only require prior approval]

[handwritten: KFC has a vested interest in container]

TRADEMARK INFRINGEMENT, UNFAIR COMPETITION

KENTUCKY FRIED CHICKEN CORPORATION v. DIVERSIFIED CONTAINER CORPORATION

549 F.2d 368 (1977)
UNITED STATES COURT OF APPEALS, FIFTH CIRCUIT

Goldberg, Circuit Judge.

This case presents us with something mundane, something novel, and something bizarre. The mundane includes commercial law issues now well delimited by precedent. The novel aspects of the case center on intriguing and difficult interrelationships between trademark and antitrust concepts. And the bizarre element is the facially implausible—some might say unappetizing—contention that the man whose chicken is "finger-lickin' good" has unclean hands.

Kentucky Fried Chicken Corporation, a franchisor of fast-food restaurants, brought this action claiming that defendants were infringing its trademarks and engaging in unfair competition by their manner of selling boxes and other supplies to Kentucky Fried franchisees. Defendants placed Kentucky Fried's trademarks on the supplies without Kentucky Fried's consent, and they allegedly misled franchisees with respect to the supplies' source and quality. Defendants counterclaimed, asserting that Kentucky Fried's franchise agreements, which required franchisees to buy supplies from approved sources, constituted an illegal tying arrangement. The district court, in a penetrating opinion . . . ruled in Kentucky Fried's favor on every issue and enjoined defendants' activities.

FACTS

Colonel Harland Sanders founded the Kentucky Fried Chicken business in the early 1950s. The Colonel prepared chicken in accordance with his own secret recipe, and among the Colonel's achievements has been to convince much of the American public that his product bears a close resemblance to the southern fried chicken that preceded peanuts as the south's most famous cuisine. The Colonel no longer owns the business, having transferred it in five different segments. The plaintiff, Kentucky Fried Chicken Corporation, now conducts the business in 47 states, and four unrelated entities conduct the business in the other three states.

Although Kentucky Fried owns some retail stores, its primary manner of conducting business, and the one of importance here, is franchising local outlets for its product. The franchise agreements require franchisees to purchase various supplies and equipment from Kentucky Fried or from sources it approves in writing. The agreements provide that such approval "shall not be unreasonably withheld." Before purchasing supplies from a source not previously approved, a franchisee must submit a written request for approval, and Kentucky Fried may require that samples from the supplier be submitted for testing. Of crucial importance is the fact that Kentucky Fried has never refused a request to approve a supplier.

The supplies that are subject to the approved-source requirement include those around which this litigation revolves: three sizes of carry-out chicken boxes, napkins, towelettes, and plastic eating utensils technically known as "sporks."

The specifications for these supplies require, among other things, that they bear various combinations of Kentucky Fried's trademarks. The marks, now widely known to the American public, include (1) "it's finger-lickin' good," (2) "Colonel Sanders' Recipe," (3) the portrait of Harland Sanders, (4) "Kentucky Fried Chicken," and (5) "Colonel Sanders' Recipe, Kentucky Fried Chicken."

Upon its formation in 1972, defendant Diversified Container Corporation (Container) began using Kentucky Fried's marks without its consent. Container used the marks on chicken cartons, napkins and towelettes that it advertised and sold to Kentucky Fried franchisees. Unlike other suppliers who sought and received approval, Container never requested that Kentucky Fried approve it as a source of these products, and in important respects Container's products failed to meet Kentucky Fried's specifications.

Container garnered buyers for its low-quality imitations of Kentucky Fried's supplies by making inaccurate and misleading statements. Container's advertisements invited franchisees to "buy direct and save" and represented that Container's products met "all standards." Container affixed Kentucky Fried's trademarks to the shipping boxes in which it delivered chicken cartons to franchisees. And when asked by franchisees whether Container was an "approved supplier" of cartons, Container employees evaded the question and said that Container sold "approved boxes."

ANTITRUST

The franchisor will succeed only by establishing a favorable reputation among the consuming public, and in building that reputation the franchisor must depend largely on the quality of the franchisee's performance. A franchisor will rarely have an opportunity to explain to a dissatisfied customer that the fault was only that of the particular franchisee.

With this background we turn to Container's claim that Kentucky Fried's arrangement constitutes a tie. Kentucky Fried does not expressly require franchisees to purchase from it the allegedly tied products. Instead, the franchise agreements permit franchisees to purchase the supplies from any source Kentucky Fried approves in writing. At the time of trial there were ten approved sources for cartons, only one of which was an affiliate of Kentucky Fried. Franchisees were free to recommend additional suppliers for approval, and the franchise agreement mandated that Kentucky Fried's approval "not be unreasonably withheld."

The difference between this arrangement and a traditional tie is readily apparent. Here the franchise agreement does not require franchisees to take the "tied" product (supplies) from Kentucky Fried in order to obtain the "tying" product (the franchise). Franchisees need not purchase a single unit of the supplies in question from Kentucky Fried; they can take their entire requirements from other sources.

Here, Kentucky Fried seeks to justify its approved-source requirement as a device for controlling quality. Kentucky Fried's argument possesses

a substantial measure of intuitive appeal. A customer dissatisfied with one Kentucky Fried outlet is unlikely to limit his or her adverse reaction to the particular outlet; instead, the adverse reaction will likely be directed to all Kentucky Fried stores. The quality of a franchisee's product thus undoubtedly affects Kentucky Fried's reputation and its future success. Moreover, this phenomenon is not limited to the quality of the chicken itself. Finger-lickin' good chicken alone does not a satisfied customer make. Kentucky Fried has a legitimate interest in whether cartons are so thin that the grease leaks through or heat readily escapes, in whether the packet of utensils given a carry-out customer contains everything it should and in whether the towelette contains a liquid that will adequately perform the Herculean task of removing Augean refuse from the customer's face and hands.

The district court correctly held for Kentucky Fried with respect to Container's antitrust counterclaim.

UNFAIR COMPETITION

The first theory upon which Kentucky Fried relies is unfair competition. Unfair competition is a common law tort that occurs when one business entity "palms off" its products as those of another. The determinative question is whether the tortfeasor's practices are likely to mislead customers into believing that the product emanates from or has been endorsed by the claimant. A claimant need not demonstrate that any customers have suffered actual confusion; the test is likelihood of confusion.

[C]ontainer's cartons do not have its own name printed on them, and Container's advertisements avoid any notice that its products are not approved by Kentucky Fried. Of even greater significance, Container ships its products in packing boxes that bear Kentucky Fried's trademarks. Use of the marks on packing boxes could have no purpose or effect other than to mislead customers. Any doubt on this score vanishes when Container's numbering system is considered. Container affixes a seven-digit number to each shipping case; the number has no purpose in Container's invoicing system; and remarkably enough the number contains exactly the same digits, albeit rearranged, as does one of Kentucky Fried's standard part numbers for cartons.

Kentucky Fried augmented this showing of Container's confusing tactics by producing evidence that Container had achieved its result. Franchisees were actually misled. An unfair competition plaintiff succeeds by establishing likelihood of confusion; actual confusion is not necessary. When there is evidence of actual confusion, however, it provides persuasive support for an inference that confusion is likely.

In sum, Kentucky Fried has produced overwhelming proof that Container's behavior was designed to create confusion, that it was likely to succeed, and that in some instances it actually succeeded. A more solid showing of unfair competition has rarely been assembled. One cannot read this record without concluding that Container poached on Kentucky Fried's chicken coop and did so overtly and avariciously. Container fell just short of costuming its sales force in the garb of the Colonel, goatee and all. We uphold the District Court's ruling on this issue.

TRADEMARK INFRINGEMENT

In the case at bar Container has concededly used Kentucky Fried's marks without Kentucky Fried's consent. . . . [However,] Kentucky Fried's marks, says Container, apply only to chicken, not to paper products. We reject this assertion.

[A]lthough Kentucky Fried's registration refers only to chicken (and other food products), we believe that closely related products are included as well. We deal here not with Kentucky Fried spaceships or Kentucky Fried writing pens, but with the paper products necessary to the operation of a store that sells Kentucky Fried *chicken*. As the district court noted, Kentucky Fried could hardly emboss its trademarks upon the chicken itself. There is a symbiotic relationship between Kentucky Fried chicken and its cartons and accoutrements. Under these circumstances we hold that the registration is sufficient to encompass the tangential supplies.

We therefore hold that Container infringed Kentucky Fried's trademarks.

CONCLUSION

[K]entucky Fried established its right to the district court's injunction. . . . The decision of the district court is *affirmed*.

CASE QUESTIONS

1. Who brought the action? Why? Did the defendant file a counterclaim? What for?
2. Did Kentucky Fried Chicken sell supplies to its franchisees? If so, were the franchisees *required* to purchase their supplies from Kentucky Fried Chicken? How did this differ from the Chicken Delight franchise agreement?
3. How did the court decide the tying arrangement issue? Explain.
4. Did Diversified Container Corporation apply to become an approved Kentucky Fried Chicken supplier? Was it approved to use the Kentucky Fried Chicken trademark?
5. What does the common law doctrine of "palming off" provide? Is it an actionable act of *unfair competition?* What evidence did the court cite in finding Diversified Container liable for unfair competition in this case?
6. What defense did Diversified Container raise to Kentucky Fried Chicken's charge of trademark infringement? Explain. Did the court accept this defense?

Policy Issue. Is a trademark a valuable property right? Should it be protected by law? Explain.

Economics Issue. What remedy did the court award Kentucky Fried Chicken? Why do you think Kentucky Fried Chicken didn't sue Diversified Container for damages?

Ethics Issue. Were the activities of Diversified Container ethical? Discuss.

Social Responsibility. Does a franchisor owe a duty of social responsibility to protect the quality of the products or services that its franchisees sell? Why or why not?

TORT LIABILITY OF FRANCHISEES AND FRANCHISORS

If properly organized and operated, the franchisee is an independent business entity that is legally separate from the franchisor. Usually, the franchisor and franchisee are two separately organized corporations with different shareholders, directors, and officers. Under this legal arrangement, a franchisee is generally considered an "independent contractor" in its dealings, purchases, and contracts with the franchisor. A franchisor and franchisee are always liable for their own torts and contracts.

Where separate legal status is properly maintained, and no special relationship is formed between the franchisor and the franchisee, the general rule is that a franchisor is *not* liable for contracts entered into or torts (negligence) committed by a franchisee. Problems of franchisor liability for actions of a franchisee usually arise where a franchisee is found to be an "agent" of the franchisor. An agency between a franchisor and a franchisee can be found where there is either (1) an actual agency or (2) an "apparent" agency.

Actual Agency.   A franchisor can *expressly* appoint a franchisee to act as its agent. An express agency can be either written or oral, except for those agencies that are required by the Statute of Frauds to be in writing, such as for the purchase of real estate. An "actual" agency can also be found where there is no express agency agreement, but where the franchisor exercises such excessive control over the operations of the franchisee that the franchise is no longer considered an independent business entity. The key element in finding an actual agency is the degree of "control" wielded by the franchisor over the franchisee. In an actual agency law situation, the franchisee is the "agent" and the franchisor is the "principal." Under the law of agency, a principal is generally liable for the contracts and negligent acts of the agent while the agent is acting "within the scope of his employment."

Apparent Agency.   Even where no express or actual agency is found, a franchisor may be found liable for the actions of a franchisee under the doctrine of *apparent agency.* In apparent agency, also commonly known as *ostensible agency,* the franchisor *leads* a third person to believe that the franchisee is an agent of the franchisor, when actually he is not. If a third person relies on this belief and suffers injury, the franchisor will be held liable as the principal for the actions of its franchisee, whom it has led the third party into believing was its agent. Apparent-agency problems often arise where the franchisor and franchisee market their goods or services under the same name, and make no effort to inform third parties of the separate legal status of the two organizations.

In *Orlando Executive Park, Inc. v. P.D.R.,* the court found that the Howard Johnson Company, as the franchisor, was liable as a principal under the doctrine of "apparent agency" for damages suffered by a third party that was caused by the negligence of a Howard Johnson franchisee.

Strictly deal w/

TORT LIABILITY

ORLANDO EXECUTIVE PARK, INC. v. P.D.R.

402 So.2d 442 (1981)
DISTRICT COURT OF APPEAL OF FLORIDA

Orfinger, Judge.

In an action for damages brought by appellee [P.D.R.] against the appellants, Orlando Executive Park, Inc. (OEP), and Howard Johnson Company (HJ), the jury returned a verdict for the appellee in the amount of $750,000 as compensatory damages against both defendants jointly, . . . The defendants have appealed the final judgment for compensatory damages.

The factual circumstances giving rise to this litigation, viewed in the light most favorable to the plaintiff, follow: Plaintiff, a 33-year-old married woman, and the mother of a small child, was employed as a supervisor for a restaurant chain. Her duties required that she travel occasionally to Orlando and because of the distance from her home, she stayed overnight in the Orlando area on those occasions.

On October 22, 1975, she was in Orlando performing the duties of her employment. She telephoned the Howard Johnson's Motor Lodge involved in this action at approximately 9:30 P.M. and made a room reservation. Approximately ten minutes later she left the restaurant and drove directly to the motor lodge. When she arrived, she signed the registration form which had already been filled out by the desk clerk and was directed to her room, which was located on the ground level in building "A," the first building behind the registration office. Plaintiff parked her car, went to her room, and left her suitcase there. She then went back to her car to get some papers and when starting back to her room, she noticed a man standing in a walkway behind the registration office. Having re-entered the building and while proceeding back along the interior hallway to her room, she was accosted by the man she had seen behind the registration office, who struck her very hard in the throat and on the back of her neck and then choked her until she became unconscious. When consciousness returned, plaintiff found herself lying on the floor of the hallway with her assailant sitting on top of her,

grabbing her throat. Plaintiff was physically unable to speak and lapsed into an unconscious or semiconscious state. Her assailant stripped her jewelry from her and then dragged her down the hallway to a place beneath a secluded stairwell, where he kicked her and brutally forced her to perform an unnatural sex act. He then disappeared in the night and has never been identified.

Plaintiff's action for damages was based on her claim that defendants owed her the legal duty to exercise reasonable care for her safety while she was a guest on the premises. And she alleged that this duty had been breached by, *inter alia,* allowing the building to remain open and available to anyone who cared to enter, by failing to have adequate security on the premises either on the night in question or prior thereto so as to deter criminal activity against guests which had occurred before and which could foreseeably occur again, failing to install TV monitoring equipment in the public areas of the motel to deter criminal activity, failing to establish and enforce standards of operation at the lodge which would protect guests from physical attack and theft of property, and failure to warn plaintiff that there had been prior criminal activity on the premises and that such activity would or might constitute a threat to her safety on the premises.

There was evidence submitted tending to show serious physical and psychological injury as a result of this assault, which was susceptible of the conclusion that within a year following the assault, plaintiff lost her job because of memory lapses, mental confusion, and inability to tolerate and communicate with people. There was evidence from which the jury could conclude that this injury was permanent and that she would require expensive, long-term medical and psychiatric treatment, and that she had suffered a great loss in her earning capacity.

The motor lodge is a part of a large complex known as "Howard Johnson's Plaza" located just off Interstate 4. The complex includes a Howard

Johnson's Restaurant, the Howard Johnson's Motor Lodge, a pub, an adult theater, and five office buildings. The motor lodge contains approximately three hundred guest rooms in six separate buildings, plus a registration office, and it was owned and operated by defendant Orlando Executive Park, Inc., under a license agreement with the parent company, Howard Johnson Company. The restaurant, the pub and the adult theater on the property were operated by the defendant, Howard Johnson Company. Approximately 75 percent of the Howard Johnson motor lodges throughout the country are owned and operated by licensees. The Howard Johnson Company never established any standards or procedures to be followed by licensees relating to the matter of guest security, although it has established such procedures for the lodges which it owns and operates. Each licensee handled that problem as it deemed best.

For the six-month period prior to the incident in question, management of the motor lodge was aware of approximately thirty criminal incidents occurring on the premises. While most of these involved burglary, some of them involved direct attacks upon the guests.

LIABILITY OF FRANCHISEE ORLANDO EXECUTIVE PARK, INC.

It seems clear in Florida registered guests in a hotel or motel are business invitees to whom the hotel or motel owes a duty of reasonable care for their safety.

Obviously, a six-unit, one building "Mom and Pop" motel will not have the same security problems as a large highrise thousand-room hotel, or of a three-hundred-room motor lodge spread out over six buildings. Each presents a peculiar security problem of its own. How the means necessary to fulfill the duty of care [are implemented] varies with the peculiar circumstances of each case. . . .

Plaintiff adduced evidence that reasonable measures were not taken. . . . Plaintiff . . . proved that the area under the stairwell where she was dragged was dark and secluded and was in itself a security hazard which should have been boarded up as had other similar stairwells in the motel. OEP management actively discouraged criminal investigations by sheriff's deputies, minimizing any deterrent effect they may have had. . . . It cannot be said that there

was a complete absence of probative facts to support the jury's conclusion.

LIABILITY OF FRANCHISOR HOWARD JOHNSON COMPANY

Appellee sought damages against HJ solely on the apparent agency doctrine, and the jury was so instructed. . . . The doctrine of apparent agency, sometimes referred to as agency by estoppel, consists of three primary elements:

1. a representation by the principal
2. reliance on that representation by a third person
3. a change of position by the third person in reliance upon such representation to his detriment.

[G]as station signs alone do not make a gas station operator a general agent of the oil company. *Cawthon v. Phillips Petroleum Co.* The reason for this is that it is common knowledge that gas station operators are independent contractors, and "these signs and emblems represent no more than notice to a motorist that a given company's products are being marketed at the station." Thus, the "representation" made by service station signs is only that a certain kind of gasoline is sold, not that the operator is an agent for the oil company with respect to any standard of service, car repair, or maintenance of premises.

While OEP might not be HJ's agent for all purposes, the signs, national advertising, uniformity of building design and color schemes allows the public to assume that this and other similar motor lodges are under the same ownership. A HJ official testified that it was the HJ marketing strategy to appear as a "chain that sells a product across the nation." Additionally, the license agreement between HJ and OEP clearly gives HJ the right to control the architectural design and the "standards of operation and service . . . and the licensee agrees at all times to conform to such standards."

Florida has adopted Section 267 of the *Restatement (Second) of Agency* (1958), which says:

> One who represents that another is his servant or other agent and thereby causes a third person justifiably to rely upon the skill of such apparent agent is subject to liability to the third person for harm caused by the lack of care or skill of one appearing to be a servant or other agent as if he were such.

There was sufficient evidence for the jury to reasonably conclude that HJ represented to the traveling public that it could expect a particular level of service at a Howard Johnson Motor Lodge. The uniformity of signs, design and color scheme easily leads the public to believe that each motor lodge is under common ownership or conforms to common standards, and the jury could find they are intended to do so.

On the question of reliance, the jury had a right to conclude that appellee believed exactly what appellant wanted her to believe, i.e., that she was dealing with Howard Johnson's, "a chain that sells a product across the nation." Appellee testified that . . . she was not aware that any of the HJ motels were individually owned, but assumed "they were Howard Johnson's".

The judgment appealed from is *affirmed*.

CASE QUESTIONS

1. What injuries did the plaintiff suffer? Where? Why wasn't the plaintiff identified in the case name?
2. Who owned the motel where the plaintiff was injured? Who was the franchisee? The franchisor?
3. Is the owner of a motel *absolutely liable* for any injury suffered by a guest on its premises? If not, when will a motel owner be held liable? Explain.
4. Under the *tort* doctrine of negligence, a defendant is not liable to the plaintiff unless it has breached a duty that it owed to the plaintiff. What duty did the *franchisee* owe and breach in this case? What evidence did the court cite to support this finding?
5. Is a *franchisor* always liable for the negligent conduct of its franchisees? Why or why not? Was the franchisor liable in *Cawthon v. Phillips Petroleum Co.?* Explain.
6. What does the doctrine of *apparent authority* provide? What evidence did the court cite to support its finding of Howard Johnson's liability in this case?

Policy Issue. Should the law be changed to hold a franchisor liable for *all* of the negligent conduct of its franchisees? Why or why not?

Economics Issue. Why did the plaintiff also name Howard Johnson's as a defendant in this lawsuit? If this had been a "mom-and-pop" motel, do you think the court would have decided the case differently? Explain.

Ethics Issue. Was it ethical for Howard Johnson's to argue it was not liable for the serious injuries suffered by the plaintiff at one of its franchisees?

Social Responsibility. Do franchisors owe a duty of social responsibility to establish and enforce standards of conduct on their franchisees? Had Howard Johnson's established such standards and procedures for its franchisees regarding guest safety?

TERMINATION OF THE FRANCHISE AGREEMENT

The franchisor, in an attempt to control its distribution outlets, usually tries to retain as much freedom as possible in terminating its franchises. The franchisor usually tries to achieve this by putting termination provisions in the franchise agreement. A substantial amount of litigation has arisen over the termination of franchises by franchisors. Lawsuits often turn on whether the franchisor is terminating the agreement "for cause," or does not have a valid cause for doing so, or is relying on the "at will" nature of most employment relationships to justify the termination.

Termination "For Cause." Most franchise agreements contain a provision that allows a franchisor to terminate the franchise agreement "for cause." Failure of a franchisee to adhere to quality control standards is usually "just cause" for terminating a franchise agreement. "For cause" termination provisions in franchise agreements are generally held to be lawful.

Unreasonably strict application of a "for cause" termination provision by a franchisor is often held by the courts to be a wrongful termination of the franchise. For example, where a franchisor attempts to terminate a franchise merely because the franchisee has failed to meet one of the franchise standards on an isolated occasion, the termination is usually not valid. The courts will particularly find a wrongful termination where a "for cause" standard is strictly invoked by the franchisor to terminate a franchise where it is shown that the franchisor has an ulterior motive for the termination, e.g., to make the franchise a company-owned outlet.

Termination "At Will."   Where a franchise agreement provides that it is terminable "at will" by the franchisor, most courts hold that the provision is *void* as "unconscionable." The argument for this rule is that normally the franchisee has invested time and money into promoting the "good will" of the franchise, particularly where the franchise has been successful, and to allow the franchisor to terminate the franchise at his pleasure to take advantage of this past success would be "unfair" and "oppressive."

In some franchised industries, notably automobile and gasoline-dealer franchises, excessive cancellation of franchise agreements by franchisors has led many states to enact statutes to protect franchisees against unreasonable, "bad faith," or wrongful termination of franchise agreements. At the federal level, the Automobile Dealers' Day in Court Act and the Petroleum Marketing Practices Act of 1979 now prohibit franchisors from terminating franchisees without "good cause."

Where a franchise agreement has been wrongfully terminated by a franchisor, the court may order any one of a number of remedies, including:

1. an award of damages
2. an equitable order directing the franchisor to specifically perform the franchise agreement
3. where applicable, an award of tort damages, e.g., where there is a breach of the implied covenant of good faith and fair dealing.

Where a franchise agreement is to be terminated, the law requires that the franchisor give proper notice of the proposed termination to the franchisee. State law differs as to the length of time which is considered sufficient legal notice. If improper notice is given, the termination is ineffective.

"Unconscionable" Contracts.   The courts have often used the theory of "unconscionable contract" to *void* provisions in franchise agreements that are overreaching, unfair, or oppressive to the franchisee. In order to prove the unconscionability of a contract or contract provision, the plaintiff must prove:

1. that the defendant had unequal bargaining power
2. that he unreasonably used this power
3. that the plaintiff had no other alternative but to enter into the agreement.

For example, although McDonald's Corporation is large and generally does not deviate from its franchise form contracts, McDonald's generally has not acted unconscionably, because the franchise applicant can also apply for other fast food franchises, e.g., Burger King or Wendy's. If all fast food franchisors used the exact same contract, then the third element above would be met, and the contracts would most likely be found to be unconscionable.

In *Shell Oil Co. v. Marinello* the court held that a provision in a franchise agreement which gave the franchisor the right to terminate the contract "at will" was *unconscionable* and *void,* and judicially modified the franchise agreement to provide for an implied legal existence of an indefinite duration.

"UNCONSCIONABLE" CONTRACT

SHELL OIL COMPANY v. MARINELLO

307 A.2d 598 (1973)
SUPREME COURT OF NEW JERSEY

Sullivan, J.

This case involves the interpretation of a lease and a dealer agreement entered into between Shell Oil Company (Shell) and Frank Marinello (Marinello), one of its service station operators, and a determination of the extent of Shell's right to terminate such lease and agreement.

Shell, a major oil company, is a supplier of motor vehicle fuels and automotive lubricants under the trade name "Shell." It also supplies tires, batteries and accessories (TBA) to its dealers for resale. Its products are sold in hundreds of Shell service stations throughout the State. Many of the service station locations are controlled by Shell through long-term leases. In the past, Shell's practice has been not to operate these stations itself, but to lease the station premises to an operator with whom it enters into a dealer or franchise agreement.

This is essentially the relationship before us for consideration. Shell controls a service station located at Route #5 and Anderson Avenue, Fort Lee, Bergen County. In 1959 it leased the station to Marinello, and at the same time entered into a written dealer agreement with the lessee. . . . The . . . lease is subject to termination by Marinello at any time by giving at least 90 days notice and by Shell at the end of the primary period or of any such subsequent year by giving at least 30 days notice. . . . The dealer agreement . . . is subject to termination at any time by giving at least 10 days notice.

By letter dated April 14, 1972, Shell notified Marinello that it was terminating the aforesaid lease and the dealer agreement effective May 31, 1972. Marinello immediately filed suit in the Superior Court, . . . After a nine-day trial a decision was rendered in favor of Marinello. . . . Shell appealed from the judgment. . . .

Shell argues that its lease of the service station premises to Marinello is independent of its dealer agreement with him, and that its legal rights as a landlord under the lease are absolute and cannot be restricted. This is pure sophistry. The two contractual documents are but part of an integrated business relationship. They were entered into simultaneously, have the same commencement and expiration dates, and expressly refer to the Route #5 service station premises.

These instruments, and the business relationship created thereby, cannot be viewed in the abstract. Shell is a major oil company. It not only controls the supply, but, in this case, the business site. The record shows that while the product itself and the location are prime factors in the profitability of a service station, the personality and efforts of the operator and the good will and clientele generated thereby are of major importance. The amount of fuel, lubricants and TBA a station will sell is directly related to courtesy, service, cleanliness and hours of operation, all dependent on the particular operator.

Marinello testified that when the station was offered to him in 1959 he was told by the Shell representative that the station was run down, but that a good operator could make money and that if he built up the business his future would be in the station.

Viewing the combined lease and franchise against the foregoing background, it becomes apparent that Shell is the dominant party and that the relationship lacks equality in the respective bargaining positions of the parties. For all practical purposes Shell can dictate its own terms. The dealer, particularly if he has been operating the station for a period of years and built up its business and clientele, when the time for renewal of the lease and dealer agreement comes around, cannot afford to risk confrontation with the oil company. He just signs on the dotted line.

Where there is grossly disproportionate bargaining power, the principle of freedom to contract is non-existent and unilateral terms result. In such a situation courts will not hesitate to declare void as against public policy grossly unfair contractual provisions which clearly tend to the injury of the public in some way. *Henningsen v. Bloomfield Motors, Inc.*

In *Ellsworth Dobbs, Inc. v. Johnson*, 50 N.J. 528, we said:

> Grossly unfair contractual obligations resulting from the use of such expertise or control by the one possessing it, which result in assumption by the other contracting party of a burden which is at odds with the common understanding of the ordinary and untrained member of the public, are considered unconscionable and therefore unenforceable.

Applying the foregoing to the case before us, it is clear that the provisions of the lease and dealer agreement giving Shell the right to terminate its business relationship with Marinello, almost at will, are the result of Shell's disproportionate bargaining position and are grossly unfair.

It is a fallacy to state that the right of termination is bilateral. The oil company can always get another person to operate the station. It is the incumbent dealer who has everything to lose since, even if he had another location to go to, the going business

and trade he built up would remain with the old station.

The relationship between Shell and Marinello is basically that of franchise. The lease is an integral part of that same relationship. Our Legislature, in enacting the Franchise Practices Act, has declared that distribution and sales through franchise arrangements in New Jersey vitally affect the general economy of the State, the public interest and the public welfare. The Act prohibits a franchisor from terminating, cancelling or failing to renew a franchise without good cause, which is defined as the failure by the franchisee to substantially comply with the requirements imposed on him by the franchise.

Marinello . . . produced proof that the appearance of his station was good and the volume of gasoline pumped over the past three years was excellent for a neighborhood station. He said that his hours of operation since 1959 had been 6:30 A.M. to midnight. He asserted that he tried keeping open for 24 hours for a short while, but neighbors complained and Shell told him to stop. He attributed his present difficulties with Shell to his refusal to accede to Shell's request that he lower his price from 3¢ to 5¢ a gallon during an area "gas war." (Marinello said he would have had to absorb a loss from 2¢ to 4¢ a gallon.) He also said that he was told by the assistant district manager for Shell that one of the reasons his lease was not being renewed was he did not buy enough TBA.

The trial court found that Marinello had substantially performed his obligations in a satisfactory manner and had not given Shell any just cause to terminate the lease and franchise. The record amply supports this finding and conclusion. We will not disturb it. . . . We hold:

1. that the lease and dealer agreement herein are integral parts of a single business relationship, basically that of a franchise
2. that the provision giving Shell the absolute right to terminate on 10 days notice is void as against the public policy of this State
3. that said public policy requires that there be read into the existing lease and dealer agreement, and all future lease and dealer agreements which may be negotiated in good faith between the parties, the restriction that Shell not have the unilateral right to terminate, cancel or fail to re-

new the franchise, including the lease, in absence of a showing that Marinello has failed to substantially perform his obligations under the lease and dealer agreement, i.e., for good cause, and

4. that good cause for termination has not been shown in this case.

Based on the foregoing, Marinello's franchise, including his lease, would have legal existence for an indefinite period, subject to his substantially performing his obligations thereunder.

The judgment of the trial court is *modified* so as to conform with this opinion, and, as modified, is *affirmed.*

CASE QUESTIONS

1. Was the relationship between Shell and Marinello a "franchise" under New Jersey law? Do you think the dealer agreement and lease termed themselves a "franchise"?
2. Why did Shell terminate Marinello's dealership? Was this action by Shell permitted by the *express* terms of the dealer agreement and lease?
3. What does the doctrine of *unconscionable contract* provide? Explain this doctrine.
4. Did the court find the termination provisions in this case to be unconscionable? What does the term *void* mean?
5. Under the contracts as the court modified them, can Shell ever terminate Marinello's franchise? If so, under what conditions?

Policy Issue. Should a court be allowed to *rewrite* a contract, as the court did in this case? Why or why not?

Economics Issue. What are the economic consequences of this case? On Shell? On Shell franchisees? Can this case be used as precedent to *void* the termination provision in all Shell dealer agreements and leases?

Ethics Issue. Was Shell's actions in this case ethical?

Social Responsibility. Does a franchisor owe a duty of social responsibility to consider the harm that will be caused to franchisees when it makes a corporate decision? Even if that decision makes economic sense to the franchisor?

UNFAIR METHODS OF COMPETITION AND FRANCHISING

Section 5 of the Federal Trade Commission Act empowers the FTC to hold that certain business practices, including transactions by and between franchisors and franchisees, are "unfair methods of competition." The term *unfair method of competition* includes any violation of the antitrust laws, or any other business practice that the FTC finds to be "deceptive, manipulative, or unfair." The FTC may issue cease-and-desist orders, seek injunctions, or file damage lawsuits for violations of the letter or spirit of FTC Act Section 5.

In *FTC v. Brown Shoe Co., Inc.* the Supreme Court held that a provision in a franchise agreement which gave special benefits to franchisees who agreed not to carry products of competitors of the franchisor was an "unfair method of competition" in violation of FTC Act Section 5.

UNFAIR METHOD OF COMPETITION

FEDERAL TRADE COMMISSION v. BROWN SHOE CO., INC.

384 U.S. 316 (1966)
UNITED STATES SUPREME COURT

Mr. Justice Black delivered the opinion of the Court.

Section 5 . . . of the Federal Trade Commission Act empowers and directs the Commission "to prevent persons, partnerships, or corporations . . . from using unfair methods of competition in commerce and unfair or deceptive acts or practices in commerce." Proceeding under the authority of Section 5, the Federal Trade Commission filed a complaint against the Brown Shoe Co., Inc., one of the world's largest manufacturers of shoes with total sales of $236,946,078 for the year ending October 31, 1957. The unfair practices charged against Brown revolve around the "Brown Franchise Stores' Program" through which Brown sells its shoes to some 650 retail stores. The complaint alleged that under this plan Brown, a corporation engaged in interstate commerce, had

> entered into contracts or franchises with a substantial number of its independent retail shoe store operator customers which require said customers to restrict their purchases of shoes for resale to the Brown lines and which prohibit them from purchasing, stocking or reselling shoes manufactured by competitors of Brown.

Brown's customers who entered into these restrictive franchise agreements, so the complaint charged, were given in return special treatment and valuable benefits which were not granted to Brown's customers who did not enter into the agreements [architectural plans, costly merchandising records, services of a Brown field representative, and a right to participate in group insurance at lower rates than the dealer could obtain individually].

In its answer to the Commission's complaint Brown admitted that approximately 259 of its retail customers had executed written franchise agreements and that over 400 others had entered into

its franchise program without execution of the franchise agreement.

[T]he Commission concluded that the restrictive contract program was an unfair method of competition within the meaning of Section 5 and ordered Brown to cease and desist from its use. On review the Court of Appeals set aside the Commission's order. In doing so the court said:

> By passage of the Federal Trade Commission Act, particularly Section 5 thereof, we do not believe that Congress meant to prohibit or limit sales programs such as Brown Shoe engaged in in this case. . . . The custom of giving free service to those who will buy their shoes is widespread, and we cannot agree with the Commission that it is an unfair method of competition in commerce.

[I]t is now recognized . . . that the Commission has broad powers to declare trade practices unfair. This broad power of the Commission is particularly well established with regard to trade practices which conflict with the basic policies of the Sherman and Clayton Acts even though such practices may not actually violate these laws. The record in this case shows beyond doubt that Brown, the country's second largest manufacturer of shoes, has a program, which requires shoe retailers, unless faithless to their contractual obligations with Brown, substantially to limit their trade with Brown's competitors. This program obviously conflicts with the central policy of both Section 1 of the Sherman Act and Section 3 of the Clayton Act against contracts which take away freedom of purchasers to buy in an open market.

Brown nevertheless contends that the Commission had no power to declare the franchise program unfair without proof that its effect "may be to substantially lessen competition or tend to create a monopoly" which of course would have to be proved if the Government were proceeding against Brown under Section 3 of the Clayton Act rather than Section 5 of the Federal Trade Commission Act. We reject the argument that proof of this Section 3 element must be made for as we pointed out above our cases hold that the Commission has power under Section 5 to arrest trade restraints in their incipiency without proof that they amount to an outright violation of Section 3 of the Clayton Act or other provisions of the antitrust laws.

We hold that the Commission acted well within its authority in declaring the Brown franchise program unfair. . . .

Reversed.

CASE QUESTIONS

1. What did the written Brown Shoe franchise agreement provide? Explain.
2. Did all Brown Shoe franchisees sign the written restrictive franchise agreement?
3. How did Brown Shoe treat its franchisees differently? Which group of franchisees were treated preferentially? How?
4. Did the FTC find that Brown Shoe's actions constituted an "unfair method of competition" under Section 5 of the FTC Act? Do you agree?
5. Do you think that the actions of Brown Shoe could have been found to have violated the following antitrust laws?
   a. an unreasonable restraint of trade under Section 1 of the Sherman Act
   b. a tying arrangement under Section 3 of the Clayton Act

Policy Issue. Is the provision of Section 5 of the FTC Act prohibiting "unfair methods of competition" too broad? Does it give the FTC too much discretion?

Economics Issue. Did the restrictive franchise agreement in this case benefit Brown Shoe economically? The franchisees? Explain.

Ethics Issue. Was it ethical for Brown Shoe, as a franchisor, to give preferential treatment to its franchisees who would agree not to carry competitors' shoes?

Social Responsibility. Do franchisors owe a duty of social responsibility to allow its franchisees to carry competitor's products? Are McDonald's franchisees allowed to sell Burger King products? Should they be?

Trend of the Law

Franchising as a form of business will continue to expand in the future. In addition to a predicted increase in the number of fast-food and similar franchises that distribute products, a substantial growth of franchising will occur in the service industries, such as real estate brokerage, employment and temporary help services, accounting and bookkeeping, banking, computer sales and software services, and a myriad of other services.

As franchising becomes more important, states will expand the laws that are applicable to the franchise relationship, with regard to both clarifying the rights between the parties to franchise agreement and clarifying the rights of third parties against franchisors and franchisees in tort and contract actions. It can be expected that the laws of many states will become more similar in the future as states adopt and refine their laws applicable to franchising.

REVIEW QUESTIONS

1. Jerrold Electronics Corporation was the first company to develop community television antennas. The firm sold entire systems, not separate parts. Jerrold only sold its system on the condition that the firm also installed and serviced the system. Most of the contracts forbid the installation of any additional equipment without Jerrold's approval. For many years Jerrold was the leader in this field, so it was not feasible to allow other firms to provide independent installation and servicing. However, over time, several new firms have entered the market and now offer comparable quality products and services. The United States brings suit against Jerrold. Does Jerrold have a service tie-in agreement that violates Section 3 of the Clayton Act?

2. Standard Oil Company of California (Chevron) controlled a substantial share of the gasoline sales market in the western United States. The company was the largest single manufacturer and retailer in the area, controlling 23 percent of the total market. As was standard practice in the industry, Chevron had exclusive dealership contracts with 5,937 independent stations, which accounted for 16 percent of the total number of retail gasoline stations in the market. The contracts required that these independent dealers must exclusively purchase all their gasoline as well as accessory supplies from Chevron. The United States government sued Chevron, claiming that since the firm controlled a substantial share of the market, these exclusive dealing contracts violated Section 3 of the Clayton Act. Did the government's suit have merit?

3. IBM and Remington were the only two manufacturers in the late 1930s manufacturing tabulating machines that made automatic computations and calculations using punch cards. Each firm leased its machines to customers with the express condition that the lease would terminate immediately if the lessor did not use the punch cards manufactured by the lessee company. IBM, which had 81 percent of the market, and Remington agreed not to sell the cards to each other's customers. The United States sued IBM, alleging that the firm's activities violated Section 3 of the Clayton Act. Was this a tying arrangement?

4. Congress granted Northern Pacific Railway Company approximately 40,000,000 acres of land shortly after the Civil War as an inducement to build a railroad network. The firm eventually sold or leased the majority of this land. In a large number of its sales contracts and most of its lease agreements Northern inserted "preferential routing" clauses requiring the grantee or lessee to ship all commodities on Northern's network if Northern met the price of its competitors and provided comparable service. Alternative means of transportation existed for a majority of these shipments. The federal government sued Northern, claiming that these contracts violated Section 3 of the Clayton Act. Is this a tying arrangement in violation of Section 3?

5. A large number of cement manufacturers banded together to form the Cement Institute. The Institute was arranged to establish a uniform pricing system. Under this system, all cement manufacturers charged a uniform price for delivered cement throughout the United States. The Institute's members controlled a majority of the cement market. Any member who

did not follow the Institute's pricing system had various sanctions imposed on it. Buyers who dealt with nonmembers or foreign companies were also boycotted. The Federal Trade Commission investigated the Cement Institute and conducted hearings. The Commission then issued a cease-and-desist order. Under FTC Act Section 5, was the Cement Institute engaging in an unfair method of competition? Assuming that the Institute was not violating any antitrust laws, could the FTC nevertheless have issued the cease-and-desist order?

6. American Cyanamid Company obtained a patent on the drug aureomycin in 1949, before the molecular structure of the drug was known. In 1952, the molecular structure was discovered and a Pfizer Company scientist was able to alter the structure slightly to produce a vastly superior drug, tetracycline. Both Cyanamid and Pfizer applied for a patent on the drug. The companies settled the dispute privately: Cyanamid withdrew its application in exchange for a free licensing agreement. Bristol then applied for a patent and the Patent Office found the drug unpatentable. Pfizer then submitted a knowingly false affidavit, which the Patent Office relied on to change its declaration and issue a patent to Pfizer. Cyanamid knew of the false affidavit and withheld this information from the Patent Office. Do both Cyanamid's and Pfizer's actions violate Section 5 of the FTC Act? If so, what remedy should the Commission provide?

7. Grand Union Company solicited and received promotional payments and advertising allowances from its suppliers. These benefits were not available on proportionately equal terms to Grand Union's competitors. The FTC successfully prosecuted the suppliers for these unfair payments under Section 2(d) of the Robinson-Patman Act. The FTC then brought an action against Grand Union, alleging that the firm had violated Section 5 of the Clayton Act. The Commission entered a cease-and-desist order and Grand Union appealed. Did Grand Union's actions constitute a violation of Section 5?

SECURITIES REGULATION

13 DISTRIBUTION OF SECURITIES

INTRODUCTION

Before 1933, the securities markets of the United States were not regulated by the federal government. There was substantial stock speculation during the 1920s in this country and abroad. People bought and sold large sums of securities "on margin," that is, they borrowed the money for their stock purchases from banks, brokers, and other lenders. As prices continued to rise, investors could sell the securities at a higher price than they had paid and use the profit to repay the loan, or take out a new loan to cover additional stock purchases. However, on "Black Friday" the stock prices on the New York Stock Exchange and other exchanges fell dramatically, and continued to fall. Banks and other lenders "called" the margin loans, and when investors could not repay the loans, the lenders foreclosed on other property of the borrowers. The Great Depression of the 1930s ensued.

Following the stock market "crash" of 1929, substantial public and government pressure was brought on Congress to enact legislation to help prevent the stock speculation of the 1920s, and create a more informed securities market in this country. After numerous hearings and debates, Congress enacted the Securities Act of 1933, which generally regulates the *original issuance* of securities, and the Securities Exchange Act of 1934, which generally regulates the *subsequent trading* in securities. The breadth of Congress's purpose in enacting this scheme of federal securities law is demonstrated by the following passage from the Senate Report preceding the enactment of the 1933 Act.

The purpose of this bill is to protect the investing public and honest business. . . . The aim is to prevent further exploitation of the public by the sale of unsound, fraudulent, and worthless securities through misrepresentation; to place adequate and true information before the investor; to protect honest enterprise, seeking capital by honest presentation, against the competition afforded by dishonest securities offered to the public through crooked promotion; to restore the confidence of the prospective investor in his ability to select sound securities; to bring into productive channels of industry and development capital which has grown timid to the point of hoarding; and to aid in providing employment and restoring buying and consuming power. [S. Rep. No. 47, 73d Cong., 1st Sess., 1 (1933).]

The federal securities laws are based upon the constitutional power of Congress to regulate interstate commerce. The courts have generally applied an expansive definition of *interstate commerce* for the purposes of the federal securities laws. For example, use of a "means" of interstate commerce (e.g., the telephone), even if wholly *intra*state, has been held to be sufficient to invoke federal securities laws.

State "Blue Sky" Laws.   Most states have enacted comprehensive securities laws that apply to securities transactions. State securities laws are generally referred to as *"blue sky" laws*. Where a securities transaction qualifies for an exemption from federal registration, the transaction usually has to be registered with the state securities agency *unless* the transaction also qualifies for an exemption from state securities law. Most states have attempted to coordinate their securities laws, including exemptions, with federal securities laws. Except in a few of the most populous states, state regulation of securities has generally been ineffective because of narrow state statutes and the inadequate budgets of state regulatory agencies. A coverage of state securities laws is beyond the scope of this book.

DISTRIBUTION OF SECURITIES

Most securities are issued by corporations. Corporations are legal entities which are created by a grant of authority by the state. Corporations are *fictitious persons* that can own and sell property, enter into contracts, sue and be sued, take most other legal actions available to natural persons, and issue securities (e.g., common and preferred stock, bonds). The "owners" of a corporation are the shareholders who own the stock of the corporation. The shareholders of a corporation have "limited liability": if a corporation is sued and the court awards a judgment against it, the shareholders are only liable up to the amount of their capital investment in the stock of the corporation. For example, if an award against a corporation is for $1,000,000, and there is only $400,000 of capital in the corporation, the plaintiff in the lawsuit can only collect the $400,000 from the corporation. The shareholders are not personally liable for the unpaid balance of $600,000. (By contrast, a partner in a general partnership and the owner of a sole proprietorship are both *personally* liable for the debts of their business enterprises.)

A small corporation may choose to issue only one class of stock, generally common stock. Larger and more complex corporations may choose to issue several *types* of stock (e.g., common stock and preferred stock), and several *classes* of each type of stock (e.g., class 1 common stock, class 2 common stock, class 1 preferred stock, and class 2 preferred stock). The holders of preferred stock are usually paid a stated fixed dividend on their stock (e.g., $1.00 per share every quarter). Preferred stock may also be accorded other preferences (e.g., paid prior to common stock upon the liquidation of the corporation).

Common stockholders are the "residual" owners of the corporation. For example, if the corporation makes a profit of $1 million for the year *after* administrative expenses, dividends on preferred stock, taxes, and other expenses have been paid, the board of directors of the corporation can, at their discretion, choose to pay a dividend to the common stockholders. In the alternative, the board of directors can elect to pay only part or none of the profits to the common stockholders as a dividend, retaining the unpaid amount for use by the corporation. The unpaid portion, known as *retained earnings,* is added to the capital account of the common stockholders of the corporation. Unless otherwise provided, preferred stockholders, once they have been paid the stated fixed dividend, cannot participate in the residual value of the corporation's earnings.

A corporation may legally borrow money from banks and other lenders, including the public, in order to operate and expand the business of the corporation. The large debts of corporations generally fall into two categories, bonds and debentures. A *bond* is a loan to the corporation from a lender, generally the public; the borrower pledges a specific piece of property (e.g., a machine, a parcel of real estate) as *security* for the loan. If the corporation fails to repay the loan, the lender may foreclose on (take over) the piece of property that was pledged as security for the loan. A *debenture* is where the corporation borrows money from a lender, again often the public, but does not pledge any property as security for the loan. The loan becomes a general obligation of the corporation, equal in status to its other general credit obligations, such as trade credit. If the lender fails to repay the loan, the bondholders must bring a legal action against the corporation to recover payment for the loan out of the general revenues and unsecured assets of the corporation.

The common stock, preferred stock, bonds, and debentures of corporations are its "securities." The corporation or other business entity that issues a security is known as the *issuer.*

Types of Underwriting.   Large, well-known corporations often sell securities directly to the public without the aid of securities professionals such as underwriters and brokers. Small, risky corporations also generally sell their securities directly to the public without the aid of securities professionals because it is often difficult to attract securities professionals to deal in these securities. Most issuers, however, do employ securities professionals to assist in the distribution of securities.

An "underwriter" is a securities company that enters into an underwriting contract with the issuer to assist in the distribution of the securities to be offered by the issuer. There may be several underwriters involved in a large distribution of securities. Underwriters typically contract with other securities companies to act as dealers in helping to sell the issuer's securities. There are generally three major types of underwriting agreements:

1. standby underwriting
2. firm-commitment underwriting
3. best-efforts underwriting.

Standby Underwriting. In a "standby" underwriting arrangement, the issuer sells its securities directly to the public, but pays a fee to an underwriter for the agreement that the underwriter will purchase the unsold portion of the offering from the issuer. The fee charged by an underwriter for a standby commitment is based on the status of the issuer, the probability that the public will purchase the securities, and other risk factors. Under a standby underwriting arrangement, the issuer is assured that it will sell *all* of the securities of the issue, either to the public or to the standby underwriter.

Firm-Commitment Underwriting. In a "firm-commitment" underwriting arrangement, an issuer sells its securities *directly* to the underwriter, and not to the public. The underwriter thereafter sells the securities to the public, hopefully at a higher price than it had to pay the issuer for the securities. In a firm-commitment underwriting arrangement, the underwriter recovers the "spread" (difference) between what it paid for the securities and what it receives as payment for them on the subsequent sale to the public. Under a firm-commitment underwriting, the issuer is assured of selling the entire issue to the firm-commitment underwriter.

Best-Efforts Underwriting. In a "best-efforts" underwriting arrangement, the underwriter contracts with the issuer to use its *best efforts* to distribute the securities of the issuer to the public. A best-efforts underwriter is paid a *commission* on the securities it sells on behalf of the issuer. The commission is agreed upon by the issuer and underwriter based on the risk factors of the offering; it is usually a percentage of the sales price of the securities. Under a best-efforts underwriting arrangement, the issuer is not assured that the entire issue will be sold, only that the underwriter will use its best efforts to do so.

Once securities have been originally issued by the corporation to stockholders and bondholders, the securities are generally freely transferable and may be sold like any other asset. A large *aftermarket* for the buying and selling of securities has developed in this country, as witnessed by the New York Stock Exchange, American Stock Exchange, and the over-the-counter market.

Definition of "Security." In order to be subject to federal securities laws, the instrument in question must be found to be a "security" within the meaning of federal securities laws. Federal securities law defines the following instruments and interests as *securities:*

1. interests or instruments that are commonly known as "securities" (e.g., common and preferred stocks, bonds, debentures, warrants)
2. interests or instruments specifically mentioned in the Act: preorganization subscriptions, fractional and undivided interests in oil, gas, or other mineral rights, collateral trust certificates, deposit receipts for foreign securities, equipment trust certificates, and certificates of interest in unincorporated investment trusts
3. "investment contracts" and "certificates of interest or participation in any profit-sharing agreement."

The* Howey *Test. The Securities and Exchange Commission, and the courts, have broadly defined the contracts and arrangements which are considered "investment contracts" and "profit-sharing" schemes subject to *registration* as a security under the 1933 Act. In *S.E.C. v. W. J. Howey Co.*, 328 U.S. 293 (1946), the U.S. Supreme Court defined an "investment certificate" as any contract or profit-making scheme whereby a person

1. invests his money
2. in a common enterprise, and
3. expects to make a profit solely from the efforts of a promoter or third party who is responsible for the management of the enterprise.

The courts have since refined the definition of an investment contract through a case-by-case application of the *Howey* test. Recent expansion of the definition has included interests in land, general and limited partnerships, franchises, pyramid sales schemes, club memberships, commodities investments, and other business arrangements. The court, in *Doran v. Petroleum Management Corp.*, 545 F.2d 893, (1977), stated that securities regulation

is often a matter of the hound chasing the hare as issuers devise new ways to issue their securities and the definition of a security itself expands.

In *International Brotherhood of Teamsters, Chauffeurs, Warehousemen & Helpers of America v. Daniel* the Supreme Court applied the *Howey* test, finding that the defendants were *not* subject to the federal securities laws because the union's noncontributory, compulsory pension plan did not constitute a "security."

DEFINITION OF "SECURITY"

INTERNATIONAL BROTHERHOOD OF TEAMSTERS, CHAUFFEURS, WAREHOUSEMEN & HELPERS OF AMERICA v. DANIEL

439 U.S. 551 (1979)
UNITED STATES SUPREME COURT

In 1954 multiemployer collective bargaining between Local 705 of the International Brotherhood of Teamsters, Chauffeurs, Warehousemen, and Helpers of America and Chicago trucking firms produced a pension plan for employees represented by the Local. The plan was compulsory and noncontributory. Employees had no choice as to participation in the plan, and did not have the option of demanding that the employer's contribution be paid directly to them as a substitute for pension eligibility. The employees paid nothing to the plan themselves.

At the time respondent brought suit, employers contributed $21.50 per employee man-week and pension payments ranged from $425 to $525 a month depending on age at retirement. In order to receive a pension an employee was required to have 20 years of continuous service, including time worked before the start of the plan.

The meaning of "continuous service" is at the center of this dispute. Respondent began working as a truckdriver in the Chicago area in 1950, and joined Local 705 the following year. . . . He retired in 1973 and applied to the plan's administrator for a pension. The administrator determined that respondent was ineligible because of a break in service between December 1960 and July 1961. Respondent appealed the decision to the trustees, who affirmed. Respondent then asked the trustees to waive the continuous-service rule as it applied to him. After the trustees refused to waive the rule, respondent brought suit in federal court against the International Union (Teamsters), Local 705 (Local), and Louis Peick, a trustee of the Fund.

Respondent's complaint alleged that the Teamsters, the Local, and Peick misrepresented and omitted to state material facts with respect to the value of a covered employee's interest in the pension plan. Count I of the complaint charged that these misstatements and omissions constituted a

fraud in connection with the sale of a security in violation of Section 10 (b) of the Securities Exchange Act of 1934, and the Securities and Exchange Commission's Rule. . . . Respondent sought to proceed on behalf of all prospective beneficiaries of Teamsters pension plans and against all Teamsters pension funds.

The District Court . . . held that respondent's interest in the Pension Fund constituted a security within the meaning of . . . an "investment contract" as that term had been interpreted in *SEC v. W. J. Howey Co.* . . . [T]he Court of Appeals for the Seventh Circuit affirmed.

INVESTMENT OF MONEY

An employee who participates in a noncontributory, compulsory pension plan by definition makes no payment into the pension fund. He only accepts employment, one of the conditions of which is eligibility for a possible benefit on retirement. Respondent contends, however, that he has "invested" in the Pension Fund by permitting part of his compensation from his employer to take the form of a deferred pension benefit.

Only in the most abstract sense may it be said that an employee "exchanges" some portion of his labor in return for these possible benefits. He surrenders his labor as a whole, and in return receives a compensation package that is substantially devoid of aspects resembling a security. His decision to accept and retain covered employment may have only an attenuated relationship, if any, to perceived investment possibilities of a future pension. Looking at the economic realities, it seems clear that an employee is selling his labor primarily to obtain a livelihood, not making an investment.

Respondent also argues that employer contributions on his behalf constituted his investment into the Fund. But it is inaccurate to describe these payments as having been "on behalf" of any employee.

The trust agreement used employee man-weeks as a convenient way to measure an employer's overall obligation to the Fund, not as a means of measuring the employer's obligation to any particular employee. . . . Again, it ignores the economic realities to equate employer contributions with an investment by the employee.

EXPECTATION OF PROFITS FROM A COMMON ENTERPRISE

The Court of Appeals believed that Daniel's expectation of profit derived from the Fund's successful management and investment of its assets. To the extent pension benefits exceeded employer contributions and depended on earnings from the assets, it was thought they contained a profit element. The Fund's trustees provided the managerial efforts which produced this profit element.

It is true that the Fund, like other holders of large assets, depends to some extent on earnings from its assets. In the case of a pension fund, however, a far larger portion of its income comes from employer contributions, a source in no way dependent on the efforts of the Fund's managers. The Local 705 Fund, for example, earned a total of $31 million through investment of its assets between February 1955 and January 1977. During this same period employer contributions totaled $153 million. Not only does the greater share of a pension plan's income ordinarily come from new contributions, but unlike most entrepreneurs who manage other people's money, a plan usually can count on increased employer contributions, over which the plan itself has no control, to cover shortfalls in earnings.

As we have demonstrated above, the type of pension plan at issue in this case bears no resemblance to the kind of financial interests the Securities Acts were designed to regulate.

ERISA

If any further evidence were needed to demonstrate that pension plans of the type involved are not subject to the Securities Acts, the enactment of ERISA in 1974, 88 Stat., 829, would put the matter to rest. Unlike the Securities Acts, ERISA deals expressly and in detail with pension plans. ERISA requires pension plans to disclose specified information to employees in a specified manner, in contrast to the indefinite and uncertain disclosure obligations imposed by the antifraud provisions of the Securities Acts.

The existence of this comprehensive legislation governing the use and terms of employee pension plans severely undercuts all arguments for extending the Securities Acts to noncontributory, compulsory pension plans.

We hold that the Securities Acts do not apply to a noncontributory, compulsory pension plan. Because the . . . counts of respondent's complaint do not provide grounds for relief in federal court, the District Court should have granted the motion to dismiss them. The judgment below is therefore *reversed.*

CASE QUESTIONS

1. What is a "compulsory noncontributory" pension plan? Why didn't the plaintiff qualify for a pension in this case?
2. What law did the plaintiff allege was violated in this case? Was it federal labor law?
3. What is a "security"? Must a security be found before federal securities laws apply to a situation?
4. What are the elements of the *Howey* test? Were these elements met in this case? Explain in detail.
5. Did the existance of the ERISA statute have any effect on the Supreme Court's decision? Explain.

Policy Issue. Should federal securities laws address all forms of unfairness in our economic system? Why or why not?

Economics Issue. What would have been the economic consequences if the Supreme Court had found a security in this case? Explain.

Ethics Issue. Why did the plaintiff sue under federal *securities* law instead of *labor* law?

Social Responsibility. Did the union and its pension administrator act responsibly in this case? Does a union owe a duty of social responsibility to its members beyond its contractual obligations? Should Daniel have been awarded his pension in this case?

THE SECURITIES ACT OF 1933

The Securities Act of 1933 regulates the *original* issuance of securities by a corporation or other business entity. It generally provides that securities must be *registered* with the SEC before they can be issued to the public. The Act also provides certain exemptions from this registration requirement and authorizes legal actions for violations of the provisions of the Act. The objectives of the Securities Act of 1933 are to promote *full disclosure* and to prevent *fraud* in the issuance of securities.

The Securities and Exchange Commission. In 1934, with the passage of the Securities Exchange Act, Congress created the Securities and Exchange Commission (SEC) to administer federal securities laws, including both the Securities Act of 1933 and the Securities Exchange Act of 1934. The SEC is composed of five members, who are appointed by the President to serve five-year terms. The terms are staggered, with no more than one member's term to expire each year. Vacancies caused by resignation or other reason may be filled immediately. No more than three members of the SEC may belong to the same political party.

Pursuant to authority granted by Congress, the SEC has the power to issue *rules* and *regulations* to further the purposes of the federal securities laws. Pursuant to this authority, the SEC has adopted a complex scheme of rules to regulate the distribution and trading of securities. The SEC is also empowered to bring lawsuits against defendants to enforce the provisions of the federal securities laws and the SEC rules adopted thereunder.

Registration of Securities. If an instrument or interest qualifies as a "security," Section 5(a) of the Securities Act of 1933 requires that the security be registered with the SEC before it can be distributed to investors. This is done by filing a *registration statement* with the SEC. Section 5(a) provides:

Unless a registration statement is in effect as to a security, it shall be unlawful for any person, directly or indirectly . . . to make use of any means or instruments of transportation or communication in interstate commerce or of the mails to sell . . . such security . . .

The registration requirement of Section 5 applies to all "persons" selling securities through the facilities of interstate commerce. "Persons" includes corporations and other business entities such as partnerships, limited partnerships, and business associations.

Registration Statement. A registration statement is a written document usually prepared by the lawyers for the issuer, with input from management and others involved in the registration process (e.g., accountants, underwriters). The registration statement discloses information about the issuer of the securities and other matters so that a prospective investor can make an informed decision as to whether to purchase the securities offered by the issuer. The SEC requires that the registration statement contain the following information:

1. name of the issuer
2. type of business in which the issuer is engaged
3. a balance sheet of issuer dated no more than ninety days prior to the date that the registration statement was filed
4. a year-to-date profit-and-loss statement of the issuer
5. profit-and-loss statements of the issuer for at least the past five years
6. a certification by an independent accountant

The SEC may require additional information to be disclosed in the registration statement, including facts that could affect the value of the securities (e.g., book value of shares, price at which securities are sold to officers and directors); factors used in determining the offering price of the securities; the use of the proceeds of the issue; "high risk" factors of the investment such as absence of operating history of the issuer; degree of competition in the industry; reliance on limited product line; pending or threatened litigation against the issuer; relevant governmental regulation; and personal dealings of the corporation with its management.

A registration statement becomes "effective," that is, the issuer can issue the proposed securities, on the twentieth day after it has been filed with the SEC *unless* the SEC takes any of the following actions.

First, if the registration does not contain the required information, or if the SEC wants to request additional information, the SEC can issue a *stop order*, which delays the effective date. Each amendment that the SEC requires pursuant to a stop order causes a new 20-day time period to begin toward the effective date. When all the information required by the SEC by amendment has been filed, the SEC generally waives the remainder of the 20-day period and allows the registration to become effective so that the issuer can immediately issue its securities.

Second, if when it is filed the registration statement is clearly inadequate on its face, the SEC may decline to accept it by issuing a *refusal order*. A refusal order must be issued by the SEC within ten days of the filing of the registration statement in order to be effective. If a refusal order is not issued, the SEC can still postpone the effective date by issuing a stop order and requiring amendments to be made to the registration statement by the issuer. An issuer may withdraw a registration statement if it obtains the permission of the SEC to do so.

The SEC does *not* pass upon the "merits" of the securities proposed to be offered, or as to the accuracy of the data supplied in the registration statement. The SEC only decides whether, in its judgment, the issuer has supplied *sufficient information* to allow a prospective investor to make an informed and rational decision regarding the purchase of the securities.

Disclosure of "Soft" Information. In the past, the SEC generally required that issuers only include verifiable facts ("hard" information) in their registration statements. The SEC has recently shifted its position, and presently allows and promotes the disclosure by the issuer of material "soft" information (e.g., earnings estimates, market value appraisals of assets) in a registration statement.

Management may include *soft* information in a registration statement without liability under the securities laws if the *estimates* and *projections* are made in "good faith," are presented in an "appropriate format," and are accompanied by information adequate to allow an investor to make a judgment as to the probable accuracy of the projection.

Prospectus. In order to sell securities to the public, an issuer must prepare a *prospectus* for distribution to investors. A prospectus is a written document, which generally contains relevant information from the registration statement filed with the SEC. A proposed prospectus is usually submitted to the SEC as part of the registration statement filing. The Securities Act of 1933 specifies the information which must be disclosed in a prospectus, which is similar to that which must be disclosed in the registration statement. Section 5(b) of the 1933 Act makes it unlawful for any person

(1) to make use of any means or instruments of transportation or communication in interstate commerce or of the mails to carry or transmit any prospectus relating to any security with respect to which a registration statement has been filed under this subchapter, unless such prospectus meets the requirements of . . . [this Act].

Shelf Registration. In March 1982, the SEC adopted Rule 415, which provides for "shelf registration" of securities. The rule permits an issuer to file a registration statement with the SEC that is valid for a two-year period. The issuer can make an immediate offering of securities at any time during this two-year period by merely placing a sticker on the prospectus included in its already-effective registration statement. Shelf registration is supported by large corporations that continually offer securities to the public. Investment banking firms and securities firms have generally opposed shelf registration because it allows issuers to distribute securities to the public without their assistance. Shelf registration saves preparing a new registration statement each time securities are proposed to be issued, and no 20-day waiting period for an effective date is required. The issuer must keep the registration statement up to date by filing post-effective amendments, or by incorporating by reference other documents filed by the issuer with the SEC.

THE THREE TIME PERIODS

There are three distinct time periods in the process of issuing securities. Each period has special rules which regulate the activities in which the issuer and its representatives may engage during that period. The three time periods are the prefiling period, the waiting period, and the post-effective period.

The Prefiling Period. The period of time when a company is contemplating the issuance of securities, but *before* the issuer actually files a registration statement with the SEC, is known as the "prefiling" period. Often, during this period of time, companies contemplating the issuance of securities attempt to take actions that set the securities up for a sale at a higher price. These often consist of a public relations and advertising campaign wherein the company promotes its successes, products, and future.

Conditioning the Market. Activities of a company to promote itself prior to issuing securities is known as "conditioning the market." Conditioning the market during the prefiling period usually violates Section 5(c) of the Securities Act of 1933. Section 5(c) makes it unlawful for any person to "offer to sell" or "offer to buy" any security *unless* a registration statement has been filed with the SEC regarding such security. Activities such as speeches by company officials, press releases, and advertisements that attempt to condition the market may be considered unlawful "offers to sell" or "offers to buy" securities in violation of Section 5(c) if a registration statement has not yet been filed with the SEC.

However, information about the normal operations of the company and information required to be disseminated by law (such as quarterly and annual reports) may be released by the company during the prefiling period without violating the Section 5(c) prohibition against conditioning the market.

The Waiting Period. The "waiting period" is the time period *after* the issuer has filed its registration statement with the SEC, but *prior* to the effective date of the registration. During the waiting period the issuer and its underwriter and dealers *may* "condition" the market for the future sale of the securities when the registration becomes effective. The SEC promotes the dissemination of information to the public during this period so that when the registration becomes effective the public will have had time to investigate the offering and to make an informed decision whether to purchase the securities being offered by the issuer.

The SEC, however, restricts the type and format of the information that may be provided by the issuer to the public during the waiting period. The issuer may provide information verbally to prospective investors (e.g., by telephone), and may submit and make *oral offers* during this period. The SEC also permits—but *only* permits—the following types of *written offers.*

Tombstone Advertisement. A tombstone advertisement is one that usually appears in financial newspapers announcing the securities offering. A tombstone ad generally contains minimal information, usually consisting of the name of the issuer, the type of security being offered (e.g., common stock), the offering price, the names of all the securities dealers who will execute orders for the purchase of the securities, and the address from which a prospectus can be obtained. A copy of a tombstone ad as it appeared in the *Wall Street Journal* is presented in Exhibit 13–1.

Preliminary Prospectus. A preliminary prospectus contains all the information that will be included in the final prospectus, except for information that will not be available until the registration becomes effective, such as the sale price. The use of a preliminary prospectus, which is the successor to the famous "red herring" type of prospectus permitted under prior law, must be discontinued once the registration is effective. The final prospectus must now be used.

This advertisement is neither an offer to sell nor a solicitation of offers to buy any of these securities. The offering is made only by the Prospectus.

NEW ISSUE

September 20, 1984

2,000,000 Shares

HUNTER MOUNTAIN WATER COMPANY

Common Stock

Price $5 per share

Copies of the Prospectus may be obtained from such of the underwriters as are registered dealers in securities in this State.

Montgomery Securities	*Sutro & Co.* Incorporated
Bear, Stearns & Co.	*Blyth Eastman Paine Webber* Incorporated
Alex, Brown & Sons Incorporated	*Donaldson, Lufkin & Jenrette* Securities Corporation
Drexel Burnham Lambert Incorporated	*Hambrecht & Quist* Incorporated
E. F. Hutton & Company Inc.	*Kidder, Peabody & Co.* Incorporated
Lazard Freres & Co.	*Prudential-Bache* Securities
L. F. Rothschild, Unterberg, Towbin	*Smith Barney, Harris Upham & Co.* Incorporated
Wertheim & Co., Inc. *Dean Witter Reynolds Inc.*	*Rotan Mosle Inc.*
Allen & Company Incorporated	*A. G. Edwards & Sons, Inc.*
Oppenheimer & Co., Inc.	*Robertson, Colman & Stephens*
Bateman Eichler, Hill Richards Incorporated	*Boettcher & Company, Inc.*
Cable, Howse & Ragen	*Seidler Amdec Securities Inc.*
Birr, Wilson & Co., Inc.	*Van Kasper & Company*
Pacific Securities, Inc.	*Henry F. Swift & Co.*

Wedbush, Noble, Cooke, Inc.

Exhibit 13–1. A tombstone ad.

Summary Prospectus Prepared by an Independent Organization. A summary prospectus may be distributed to prospective investors during the waiting period. A summary prospectus is just what its name implies, a *summary* of the information to be contained in the final prospectus. All issuers may use a summary prospectus that is prepared by an independent organization for use by the issuer. This type of summary prospectus must be discontinued once the registration is effective; now the final prospectus must be used.

Summary Prospectus Prepared by the Issuer. If an issuer has *either* (1) net assets of at least $5 million, *or* (2) an aggregate net income of $500,000 per year for the past three years, the issuer may prepare its own summary prospectus for use during the waiting period. The use of this type of summary prospectus does not have to be discontinued after the registration is effective provided that an investor is given a final prospectus before or at the time of purchasing the securities.

A prospectus used by an issuer and distributed by the issuer or its representatives must contain the following language in capital letters and in boldface type:

THESE SECURITIES HAVE NOT BEEN APPROVED OR DISAPPROVED BY THE SECURITIES AND EXCHANGE COMMISSION NOR HAS THE COMMISSION PASSED UPON THE ACCURACY OR ADEQUACY OF THIS PROSPECTUS. ANY REPRESENTATION TO THE CONTRARY IS A CRIMINAL OFFENSE.

Post-effective Period. The "post-effective" period begins once the registration becomes *effective.* Offers received by the issuer from prospective investors during the waiting period can be *accepted* by the issuer at this time.

However, any *written* offer made *by* the issuer or its representatives during the post-effective period is itself considered a "prospectus." Since such a writing would not meet the requirements of a formal prospectus, it would violate Section 5(b) of the 1933 Act, which provides that it is unlawful for any person

(2) to carry or cause to be carried through the mails or in interstate commerce any . . . security for the purpose of sale or for delivery after sale, unless accompanied or preceded by a prospectus that meets the requirements of [this Act]

In order for a written offer to be lawful during the post-effective period, the issuer or its representative must either send a final prospectus to the prospective investor *prior to* or *at the time* of making the written offer to that person. The final prospectus is often referred to as the "statutory prospectus." The offering period will remain open pursuant to the terms of the registration statement. When the stock is sold, or if the stock is not sold but the offering period has run, the offering is closed.

The following outline summarizes the activities in which the issuer and its representatives may engage during the three time periods relevant to a securities offering.

Prefiling, Waiting and Post-effective Periods

I. PreFiling Period:
    A. The issuer and its representatives *may not:*
        1. solicit or make offers to sell securities
        2. accept offers from investors to purchase securities
        3. "condition" the market
II. Waiting Period:
    A. The issuer and its representatives *may:*
        1. make oral offers
        2. make the following written offers:
            i. tombstone advertisement
            ii. preliminary prospectus
            iii. summary prospectus prepared by an independent organization
            iv. summary prospectus prepared by the issuer if qualified to do so
    B. The issuer and its representatives *may not:*
        1. make any written offer except those listed above
        2. accept any offer by an investor to purchase securities
III. Post-effective Period:
    A. The issuer and its representatives *may:*

1. solicit and make oral offers
2. make written offers if preceded or accompanied by a final prospectus
3. accept offers if preceded or accompanied by a final prospectus

Civil Liability Under Section 12(1).   Where an issuer, underwriter, or dealer sells unregistered securities, makes unlawful offers, or otherwise violates Section 5 of the Securities Act of 1933, an injured plaintiff may bring a private *civil* action against the defendant under Section 12(1) of the Act. In a Section 12(1) action, a successful plaintiff may either (1) collect damages against the defendant, or (2) rescind the stock purchase contract and receive back the consideration he paid for the securities.

In *Diskin v. Lomasney & Co.* the court permitted an investor to rescind a purchase of securities more than eight months after the securities were purchased because the broker-dealer who sold the securities to the investor made an *illegal offer* to the investor during the waiting period.

gives buyer of the stock a windfall

"WAITING" PERIOD

DISKIN v. LOMASNEY & CO.

452 F.2d 871 (1971)
UNITED STATES COURT OF APPEALS, SECOND CIRCUIT

Friendly, Chief Judge.

During the summer of 1968 plaintiff Diskin had conversations with defendant Lomasney, general partner of defendant Lomasney & Co., a broker-dealer, with respect to securities of two companies, Ski Park City West, S.I. and Continental Travel, Ltd. Lomasney & Co. had agreed to sell up to 60,000 common shares of the former on a "best efforts" basis and was the principal underwriter for the sale of 350,000 common shares of the latter. A preliminary registration statement with respect to the shares of Continental Travel had been filed with the Securities and Exchange Commission on August 28, 1968, but did not become effective until February 11, 1969. On September 17, 1968, Lomasney sent Diskin a final prospectus for the Ski Park City West, S.I., stock, along with a letter, the body of which read as follows:

I am enclosing herewith, a copy of the Prospectus on SKI PARK CITY WEST. This letter will also assure you that if you take 1,000 shares of SKI PARK CITY WEST at the issue price, we will commit to you the sale at the public offering price when, as and if issued, 5,000 shares of CONTINENTAL TRAVEL, LTD.

On the same day Diskin placed an order for the 1,000 shares of Ski Park City West and received a written confirmation. He later paid for these, and the validity of their offer and sale is unquestioned.

On February 12, 1969, Lomasney sent Diskin a confirmation of the sale of 5,000 shares of Continental Travel at $12 per share, apparently without any further communication. Diskin received from Lomasney a final prospectus and registration statement for these shares prior to February 28, 1969, when he paid the bill of $60,000, and received delivery. On November 19, 1969, Diskin demanded rescission. Having received no answer, he brought this action in the District Court for the Southern District of New York on January 6, 1970, claiming that the letter of September 17, 1968, insofar as it related to shares of Continental Travel, was a violation of Section 5(b)(1) of the Securities Act of 1933. This provision makes it unlawful for any person

to make use of any means or instruments of transportation or communication in interstate commerce or of the mails to carry or transmit any prospectus relating to any security with respect to which a registration statement has been filed under this subchapter, unless such prospectus meets the requirements of section 77j.

The parties submitted agreed findings of fact and stipulated that the case should be decided thereon. The district judge dismissed the complaint. . . .

Manifestly, Congress did not intend that a sale of a few shares of a registered security or in a transaction exempted by § 4 should enable a dealer to offer the purchaser the "right to subscribe" to thousands of shares of some gamy unregistered issue without conforming with the requirements of the statute—thereby opening not a mere hole but a large sluice in the protection the Securities Act was intended to afford.

[T]he mere filing of a registration statement does not ensure the legality of *any* written offer made during the post-filing, pre-effective period; to be lawful, such written offers must be made by way of a "prospectus" which meets the requirements of [the Act]. We perceive no basis for disagreeing with Professor Loss' summary of the law in this respect:

> In sum, there are five legal ways in which offers may be made during the waiting period even if the mails or interstate facilities are used: by means of (1) oral communication, (2) the "tombstone ad," . . . (3) the preliminary prospectus, . . . (4) the "buff card" type of summary prospectus independently prepared, . . . and (5) the summary prospectus filed as part of the registration statement. . . . [l. Loss, Securities Regulation 243 (2d ed. 1961).]

The letter of September 17, 1968, was none of these. Indeed, the confirmation of February 12, 1969, was a further violation unless a prospectus had been furnished, . . .

We pass therefore to the arguments which defendants made in their memorandum, which the District Court did not reach. These were (1) that the letter was not an "offer" but was a mere expression of willingness to sell; (2) that the violation was cured by Diskin's receipt of a prospectus prior to the actual purchase; . . . Although there is a paucity of authority on these issues, we think none constituted a valid defense.

The result here reached may appear to be harsh, since Diskin had an opportunity to read the final

prospectus before he paid for the shares. But the 1954 Congress quite obviously meant to allow rescission or damages in the case of illegal offers as well as of illegal sales. . . . In any event, it made altogether clear that an offeror of a security who had failed to follow one of the allowed paths could not achieve absolution simply by returning to the road of virtue before receiving payment.

The judgment dismissing the complaint is *reversed,* with instructions to enter judgment for the plaintiff that, upon delivery of 5,000 shares of Continental Travel, Ltd., he shall receive $60,000 with interest from February 28, 1969, and costs.

CASE QUESTIONS

1. *Ski Park City West (SPC):* Answer the following questions:
   a. What was the effective date of the registration statement?
   b. When was the offer letter sent by Lomasney & Co. to Diskin?
   c. Was the offer letter accompanied by a prospectus?
   d. Was Diskin's purchase of the SPC stock an issue in this case?
2. *Continental Travel, Inc.* (Continental): Answer the following questions:
   a. When was the registration statement filed with the SEC?
   b. When was the *offer letter* sent by Lomasney & Co. to Diskin?
   c. When was the effective date?
   d. When did Lomasney & Co. send Diskin a confirmation letter?
   e. When did Lomasney & Co. send Diskin a prospectus?
   f. When did Diskin pay for the Continental stock?
   g. When did Diskin demand rescission of the Continental stock purchase?
3. Did the September 17 letter fall within one of the lawful means of making an offer during the "waiting period"?

Policy Issue. Was the decision to allow Diskin to rescind the contract for the purchase of the Continental stock and get his money back a "harsh result"? Should Lomasney & Co. been allowed to have returned to the "road of virtue" because it sent Diskin a prospectus before Diskin had actually paid for the Continental stock? Why or why not?

Economics Issue. If the price of the Continental stock had gone up, do you think Diskin would have rescinded the stock purchase contract?

Ethics Issue. Did Lomasney & Co. act unethically in this case? Did Diskin act unethically when he rescinded the Continental stock purchase?

Social Responsibility. Do securities professionals owe a duty of social responsibility as to the performance of their functions?

EXEMPTIONS FROM REGISTRATION

Certain securities and transactions are *exempt* from registration. The major exemptions from registration are set out in the following list. The last three exemptions on the list are provided pursuant to Regulation D, which was adopted by the SEC in March, 1982. Regulation D replaced a number of SEC rules that provided similar, but more complex exemption from registration.

(a private exchange)

Exemptions From Registration

1. Transactions involving other than an "issuer, underwriter or dealer." [Section 4(1)].
2. Intrastate offering [Section 3(a) and Rule 147].
3. Private placement offering [Section 4(2) and Rule 506].
4. Small offering under $500,000 [Section 3(b) and Rule 504].
5. Small offering under $5,000,000 [Section 3(b) and Rule 505].

Transaction Not by an "Issuer, Underwriter or Dealer."   Persons who invest in stock may at a later date decide to sell the stock. In doing so, they would not want to have to register the stock with the Securities and Exchange Commission as usually required under Section 5(a) of the 1933 Act. Section 4(1) of the Securities Act of 1933 expressly exempts securities from registration if the securities are sold in a transaction *not* by an "issuer, underwriter or dealer." For example, a person who sells stock in a private transaction, either over an exchange or not, generally qualifies for the exemption under Section 4(1).

However, when a major shareholder sells a large block of stock, the transaction may be considered a "distribution," subject to registration under Section 5. This frequently happens when a large shareholder sells some of his stock simultaneously with the corporation's issuance of additional stock. The courts have interpreted Section 5 liability for failure to register to apply not only to the persons who actually "passed" the title to a security, but also to persons who participate and assist others in the distribution of unregistered securities.

In *United States v. Wolfson* the court held that certain major shareholders of a corporation had made a "distribution" of stock subject to registration under Section 5, and that the transaction did *not* qualify for a Section 4(1) exemption as being by someone other than an "issuer, underwriter, or dealer."

TRANSACTION NOT BY AN "ISSUER, UNDERWRITER OR DEALER"

UNITED STATES v. WOLFSON

405 F.2d 779 (1968)
UNITED STATES COURT OF APPEALS, SECOND CIRCUIT

Woodbury, Senior Circuit Judge.

It was stipulated at the trial that at all relevant times there were 2,510,000 shares of Continental Enterprises, Inc., issued and outstanding. The evidence is clear, indeed is not disputed, that of these the appellant Louis E. Wolfson himself with members of his immediate family and his right hand man and first lieutenant, the appellant Elkin B. Gerbert, owned 1,149,775 or in excess of 40 percent. The balance of the stock was in the hands of approximately 5,000 outside shareholders. The government's undisputed evidence at the trial was that between August 1, 1960, and January 31, 1962, Wolfson himself sold 404,150 shares of Continental through six brokerage houses, that Gerbert sold 53,000 shares through three brokerage houses and that members of the Wolfson family, including Wolfson's wife, two brothers, a sister, the Wolfson Family Foundation and four trusts for Wolfson's children sold 176,675 shares through six brokerage houses.

Gerbert was a director of Continental. Wolfson was not, nor was he an officer, but there is ample evidence that nevertheless as the largest individual shareholder he was Continental's guiding spirit in that the officers of the corporation were subject to his direction and control and that no corporate policy decisions were made without his knowledge and consent. Indeed Wolfson admitted as much on the stand. No registration statement was in effect as to Continental; its stock was traded over-the-counter.

The appellants do not dispute the foregoing basic facts. They took the position at the trial that they had no idea during the period of the alleged conspiracy, stipulated to be from January 1, 1960, to January 31, 1962, that there was any provision of law requiring registration of a security before its distribution by a controlling person to the public. On the stand in their defense they took the position that they operated at a level of corporate finance far above such "details" as the securities laws; as to

whether a particular stock must be registered. They asserted and their counsel argued to the jury that they were much too busy with large affairs to concern themselves with such minor matters and attributed the fault of failure to register to subordinates in the Wolfson organization and to failure of the brokers to give notice of the need.

Section 4 of the Act exempts certain transactions from the provisions of Section 5 including:

> (1) Transactions by any person other than an issuer, underwriter, or dealer.

The appellants argue that they come within this exemption for they are not issuers, underwriters or dealers. At first blush there would appear to be some merit in this argument. The immediate difficulty with it, however, is that Section 4(1) by its terms exempts only "transactions," not classes of persons, . . . and then goes on to provide:

> As used in this paragraph the term 'issuer' shall include, in addition to an issuer, any person directly or indirectly *controlling* or controlled by *the issuer,* or any person under direct or indirect common control with the 'issuer.'

In conclusion it will suffice to say that full consideration of the voluminous record in this rather technical case discloses no reversible error.

Affirmed.

CASE QUESTIONS

1. How many shares of Continental Enterprises, Inc. were outstanding? How much of that did the defendants own? Did they sell?
2. What does Section 5 of the Securities Act of 1933 provide? Did Wolfson *et al.* file a registration statement before selling the Continental stock?
3. What does Section 4(1) of the 1933 Act provide? Explain.
4. Was the stock sale by Wolfson *et al.* an ordinary

stock transaction? Or was it a "distribution"? Explain.

5. Did the transaction qualify for a Section 4(1) exemption from registration? Was Wolfson an "issuer"?

Policy Issue. Did it matter to the court that Wolfson operated "at a level of corporate finance far above such 'details' as securities laws"?

Economics Issue. Why would the Wolfsons not want to register the sale of the securities? Explain.

Ethics Issue. Was it ethical for the Wolfsons' attorney to argue that his clients were too busy to concern themselves with such "minor matters" as securities laws?

Social Responsibility. Should busy persons be responsible for knowing all the federal and state laws that affect their business operation? Is this possible? Is ignorance of the law an excuse?

Intrastate Offering Exemption. In order to facilitate the raising of capital for *local* purposes, Congress provided, in Section 3(a) of the Securities Act of 1933, an "intrastate" offering exemption from registration. The exemption provides:

Any security which is a part of an issue offered and sold only to persons resident within a single State or Territory, where the issuer of such security is a person resident and doing business within or, if a corporation, incorporated by and doing business within, such State or Territory.

In order to qualify for the intrastate offering exemption, the issuer must be a *resident* of the state in which the securities are to be offered and sold. A corporation can therefore only qualify for an intrastate offering exemption in one state—the state in which it is incorporated.

Section 3(a) further requires that the issuer be "doing business" in the state in order to qualify for an *intrastate* offering exemption. "Doing business" is usually judged in this context by whether the issuer does the majority of its business in the state. The SEC adopted Rule 147 to help clarify the "doing business" test. Under Rule 147, an issuer is *presumed* to be doing business in a state if the following objective criteria are met:

1. 80 percent of the issuer's consolidated gross *revenues* are derived from operations located in, or services provided in, the state.
2. 80 percent of the issuer's consolidated *assets* are located in the state.
3. 80 percent of the proceeds from the proposed securities offering will be used in the issuer's operations in the state.
4. The issuer's principal office is located in the state.

If any one of the above objective criteria is not met, the issuer cannot be presumed to be doing business in the state. The issuer may, however, try to qualify as "doing business" within the state under the broader standards of Section 3(a) of the 1933 Act.

In order to qualify for the intrastate exemption from registration, the entire issue of securities must be both *offered* and *sold* only to *residents* of that state. Residency is usually determined by a permanent-residence test. The issuer and others involved in the distribution of the securities must act with "good faith," use due care, and conduct a reasonable investigation to assure that the offerees and investors are residents of the state in which the intrastate offering is being made. This usually consists of verbally asking potential investors what their state of residency is prior to discussing the offering with them.

With regard to actual purchasers, Rule 147 requires that the issuer obtain a *written affidavit* from each investor stating that he or she is a resident of the state in which the intrastate offering is being made. As long as the issuer, underwriter, and dealers have acted in good faith, made a reasonable investigation, and obtained the requisite affidavit from the investors, the intrastate offering exemption will not be lost if a nonresident is found to have misrepresented his residence and purchased stock.

"Coming-to-Rest" Test. In order to preserve the intrastate offering exemption, the issuer, underwriter, and dealers involved are under a duty to restrict the *future* transfer of the securities to *nonresidents.* If the securities offered in an intrastate offering "come to rest" in the hands of nonresident purchasers within a certain time period after the offering, the intrastate offering exemption may be lost. If the intrastate offering exemption is lost, the issuer must register the securities with the SEC pursuant to Section 5 of the 1933 Act.

The SEC and the courts have generally held that if in-state resident purchasers either hold the securities for at least one year, or only transfer the securities to other state residents, then the "coming-to-rest" test of Section 3(a) is presumed to have been met. After one year, the resident purchasers may sell or otherwise transfer their stock to nonresident purchasers without affecting the status of the original intrastate offering exemption.

If the resident purchasers transfer their stock to nonresidents within 90 days of the offering, it is presumed under Section 3(a) that they had this intent when they purchased the stock. Section 3(a) is therefore presumed to be violated, and the intrastate offering exemption will be lost. This presumption can be *rebutted* by proper evidence. For example, if the resident purchaser sells his stock to a nonresident within 90 days of the offering in order to raise money for an emergency medical operation, the intrastate offering exemption would not be lost. Sales by resident purchasers to nonresidents during the *nonpresumption* period (between 90 days and one year of the offering), are judged on a case-by-case basis.

Rule 147 clarifies Section 3(a) by establishing an objective standard for meeting the "coming-to-rest" test. If there have been no sales by resident purchasers to nonresidents during the first *nine months* immediately following an intrastate offering of securities, the coming-to-rest test of Rule 147 is met. If there have been sales of securities by residents to nonresidents during the nine-month period immediately following the intrastate offering, the Rule 147 objective coming-to-rest test is not met, and the issuer must try to qualify for the coming-to-rest test under the Section 3(a) presumptive time periods, or register the security.

The following outline summarizes the tests which must be met in order for an issuer to qualify a transaction for an *intrastate offering exemption* from registration.

Intrastate Offering Exemption

I. *Residency* test of the *issuer*
   A. Incorporated or organized in the state
II. "Doing-business" test of *issuer:*
   A. Meet the objective tests of Rule 147:
      1. 80 percent of consolidated gross *revenues* derived from in-state operations
      2. 80 percent of consolidated *assets* located in-state
      3. 80 percent of the *proceeds* from the issue to be used in operations in-state
      4. principal office of the issuer located in-state, or
   B. Prove that the issuer is "doing business" in the state under the broad standard of Section 3(a)
III. *Original* purchase residency test of offerees and investors:
   A. All offerees and investors must be residents of the state, or
   B. If there are one or more nonresident purchasers
      1. issuer, underwriter and dealers used "good faith"
      2. made a reasonable investigation
      3. obtained affidavits of residency of all purchasers
IV. *Subsequent* purchase "coming to rest" test:
   A. Rule 147 nine-month objective test met, or
   B. Section 3(a) one-year holding test met, or
   C. Evidence introduced to rebut a presumption of illegality

In *SEC v. McDonald Investment Co.* the court found that a securities offering did not qualify for an intrastate offering exemption because the proceeds of the offering were going to be used out of state.

"INTRASTATE" OFFERING

SECURITIES AND EXCHANGE COMMISSION v. McDONALD INVESTMENT COMPANY

343 F.SUPP. 343 (1972)
UNITED STATES DISTRICT COURT, MINNESOTA

Neville, District Judge.

Plaintiff, the Securities and Exchange Commission, instituted this lawsuit pursuant to . . . the 1933 Securities Act. The defendants are McDonald Investment Company, a Minnesota corporation, and H. J. McDonald, the company's president, treasurer, and owner of all the company's outstanding common stock. Plaintiff requests that the defendants be permanently enjoined from offering for sale and selling securities without having complied with the registration requirements of Section 5 of the Act.

Plaintiff and defendants have stipulated to the following pertinent facts: The defendant company was organized and incorporated in the State of Minnesota on November 6, 1968. The principal and only business office from which the defendants conduct their operations is located in Rush City, Minnesota, and all books, correspondence, and other records of the company are kept there.

Sales of the installment notes, according to the amended prospectus of January 18, 1972, are to be made to Minnesota residents only.

No registration statement as to the installment notes described in McDonald Investment Company's amended prospectus is in effect with the United States Securities and Exchange Commission, nor has a registration statement been filed with the Commission.

[In the] instant case . . . the income-producing operations of the defendant, after completion of the offering, are to consist entirely of earning interest on its loans and receivables invested outside the state of Minnesota. While the defendant will not participate in any of the land developer's operations, nor will it own or control any of the operations, the fact is that the strength of the installment notes depends perhaps not legally, but practically, to a large degree on the success or failure of land developments located outside Minnesota, such land not being subject to the jurisdiction of the Minnesota court.

Defendant corporation . . . has been in business in Minnesota for some period of time, is not a "Johnny come lately" and is not part of any syndicate or similar enterprise; yet to relieve it of the federal registration requirements where none or very little of the money realized is to be invested in Minnesota, would seem to violate the spirit if not the letter of the Act.

Exemptions under the Act are strictly construed, with the burden of proof on the one seeking to establish the same. . . . [P]laintiff's request for a permanent injunction should be *granted*.

CASE QUESTIONS

1. What does Section 3(a) of the Securities Act of 1933 provide? Explain.
2. What does the "doing business" test of Rule 147 require? Did the defendant qualify under this test? Why or why not?

Policy Issue. What is the public purpose underlying the intrastate offering exemption?

Economics Issue. Why would an issuer want to qualify for an intrastate offering exemption? Explain.

Ethics Issue. Did the defendant deliberately attempt to evade the provisions of the securities laws?

Social Responsibility. Should an issuer of securities be allowed to raise funds from residents in-state and not have to register with the SEC? Don't residents of a single state need the same protection as investors nationwide?

Private-Placement Exemption.   Section 4(2) of the Securities Act of 1933 exempts from registration securities offerings by an issuer "not involving any public offering." Pursuant to Section 4(2), the SEC adopted Regulation D, which includes Rule 506. Rule 506 sets forth the requirements for qualifying for a *private-placement* offering exemption. The rationale for the private-placement exemption is that if an offering is made mostly to persons who are either wealthy or financially astute, the protections accorded to investors by the disclosure requirements of the registration process are not needed.

There is no dollar limit on the amount of securities that may be sold pursuant to a valid private-placement offering exemption, as long as the other criteria for the exemption are met. Generally, in order to qualify for a private placement exemption, the issuer should be concerned with determining which investors are "accredited investors" and unaccredited investors, and providing the required information to these investors.

"Accredited Investor."   A private placement can have any number of "accredited" investors. Rule 501 of Regulation D expressly defines an *accredited investor* as any party who meets one of the following objective standards:

1. any *person* (including corporations and business associations) who *purchases* at least $150,000 of the securities being offered where the total purchase price does not exceed 20 percent of the purchaser's *net worth*

2. any *natural person* who had an individual *income* in excess of $200,000 in each of the two most recent years and who reasonably expects an income in excess of $200,000 in the current year
3. any *natural person* whose individual *net worth,* or joint net worth with that of the spouse, at the time of purchase exceeds $1 million
4. directors, officers or general partners of the issuer, investment companies, employee benefit plans, and nonprofit organizations of a certain size (assets of $5 million or more).

Nonaccredited Investor. Any person or legal entity that does not qualify as an "accredited investor" under one of the categories specified in Rule 501 is a *nonaccredited* investor. The Rule 506 private placement exemption requires that there be no more than 35 nonaccredited investors. If there are more than 35 nonaccredited investors, the offering loses its private placement exemption.

With regard to nonaccredited investors, Rule 506 specifically requires that the issuer "reasonably believe" that each nonaccredited investor, either alone *or* with his representative (e.g., lawyer, accountant, financial consultant) has knowledge and experience in financial and business matters such that he is capable of evaluating the merits and risks of the private-placement investment. This "smart" test for nonaccredited investors does not apply to the small offering exemptions, which are discussed in the following section.

Required Disclosures. To qualify for a private placement exemption under Rule 506, the issuer must provide certain information to all accredited and nonaccredited investors. The issuer has a choice as to the form of the disclosure, including providing recent annual reports and definitive proxy statements to the investors, or alternatively providing investors with the information contained in its most recent Form 10-K, Form S-1 or Form 10 filed with the SEC. This information must be supplemented if any material change has occurred between the time when the information was prepared and the time that the offering is made.

The following outline summarizes the criteria which must be met in order for a securities offering to qualify under the private-placement exemption of Rule 506.

Private Placement Exemption [Rule 506]

I. Dollar amount of offering:
   A. No limit
II. Number of investors: → *based solely on financial status*
   A. "Accredited" investors: No limit
   B. Nonaccredited investors:
      1. Limited to 35
      2. Must be capable alone or with the assistance of a representative of evaluating the merits and risk of the investment
III. Disclosure of information:
   A. Must disclose information about the issuer and securities
   B. May be in the form of annual reports, proxy statements, and documents filed with the SEC

Small Offering Exemptions. Section 3(b) of the Securities Act of 1933 empowers the SEC to create exemptions for offerings that do not exceed a specific dollar amount as periodically authorized by Congress. Currently, the congressionally set limit is $5 million. Pursuant to this authority, the SEC has provided two "small offering" exemptions from the registration requirements of the Act, which are contained respectively in Rules 504 and 505 of Regulation D.

Rule 504 Exemption. Rule 504 of Regulation D provides an exemption from registration for securities offerings of less than $500,000, provided the other criteria of Rule 504 are met. Under Rule 504, there are no limits on the number of investors that may purchase securities pursuant to the exemption. There are no "suitability" tests (e.g., income, net worth, financial astuteness) for investors under Rule 504. Thus, an issuer can sell securities to a large number of unsophisticated and nonwealthy persons and not lose the Rule 504 exemption as long as less than $500,000 is raised by the offering.

Rule 504 does *not* require the issuer to provide the investors with any information regarding the issue. Generally, however, to prevent lawsuits under the antifraud provisions of the securities laws (such as Section 10(G) of the 1934 Act), issuers usually provide relevant information about its operations and the issue to investors. Rule 504 was primarily designed to provide a means for persons to raise a small amount of capital without having to go through the extensive and expensive registration process required under Section 5.

Rule 505 Exemption. Rule 505 provides an exemption from registration for securities offerings of less than $5,000,000, provided the other criteria of Rule 505 are met. Unlike Rule 504, Rule 505 makes a distinction between accredited and nonaccredited investors. Under the Rule 505 small-offering exemption, there is a limit of no more than 35 *nonaccredited* investors. There is no limit to the number of "accredited" investors as defined in Rule 501 and discussed previously.

Further, an issuer seeking a Rule 505 exemption must provide material information to all investors. This requirement is met if the issuer provides

Small Offering Exemptions [Rule 504 and Rule 505]

	Rule 504	*Rule 505*
1. Dollar limit	$500,000	$5,000,000
2. Number of investors		
a. nonaccredited	No limit	35
b. accredited	No limit	No limit
3. Disclosure of information	None required, advisable to disclose relevant information	Required to disclose material information, including past financial statements and summary of business operations

the investor with the financial statements of the issuer for the past three years, a brief statement outlining the business and products of the issuer, the competition, and the regulatory climate in which the issuer operates. The issuer usually provides at least this amount of information in order to avoid liability exposure under the antifraud provisions of the securities laws.

The table on page 327 summarizes the criteria that must be met to qualify for one of the small offering exemptions provided in Rules 504 and 505 of Regulation D.

INTEGRATION AND AGGREGATION

Businessmen often propose the idea that instead of registering one large offering of securities with the SEC they will stagger several offerings, each of which qualifies for an exemption from registration. The SEC prohibits this process under its *integration* and *aggregation* rules. If two otherwise exempt offerings are similar and made at the same time, they will be considered by the SEC as merely two phases of the same offering. The SEC will "integrate" the two offerings and consider them *one offering*, and "aggregate" the dollar amounts and number of nonaccredited investors to see if the claimed exemptions are lost and the offering should be registered under Section 5.

The SEC has adopted an objective "safe harbor" rule, which provides that any securities offerings made more than six months before or *six* months after the date of the present offering will not be integrated with the present offering. Therefore, there is a floating twelve-month period *outside* of which none of the securities offerings will be integrated by the SEC with the current offering. If the securities offerings do not qualify for the six-month safe harbor rule, they will be integrated and aggregated to see if the combined single issue qualifies for an exemption in itself. If not, the issue will have to be registered with the SEC.

Example of Integration and Aggregation. The following example demonstrates the applicability of the SEC's integration and aggregation rules. Assume that an issuer distributes similar securities (e.g., common stock) pursuant to the following three offerings, each which would individually qualify for an exemption from registration as listed.

Integration and Aggregation

Date of Offering	Terms of Offering	Exemption
January 1	$200,000 9 nonaccredited investors all in-state resident investors disclosure of material information	Rule 504 "small" offering

April 1	$4,000,000 20 nonaccredited investors all out-of-state investors disclosure of material information	Rule 505 "small" offering
August 1	$8,000,000 30 nonaccredited investors all in-state resident investors disclosure of material information	Section 3(a) and Rule 147 "intrastate" offering

January 1 Issue.   Standing alone, the January 1 issue qualifies for a Rule 504 "small offering" exemption because less than $500,000 is being raised by that offering.

April 1 Issue.   The April 1 issue, standing by itself, qualifies for a Rule 505 "small offering" exemption from registration. The offering was less than $5,000,000, was sold to fewer than 35 nonaccredited investors, and the material information was disclosed to the investors. However, the April 1 issue will be *integrated* with the January 1 issue because they are made within six months of each other and do not therefore qualify under the SEC's "safe harbor" rule. These two issues are integrated and aggregated to produce a *single* offering consisting of:

$4,200,000
29 nonaccredited investors
Proper disclosure under Rule 505

The integrated offering still qualifies for a Rule 505 exemption, because less than $5,000,000 of securities are issued to fewer than 35 unaccredited investors, and proper disclosure has been made to the investors.

August 1 Issue.   The August 1 issue itself qualifies for an intrastate offering exemption from registration in that all the securities of the offering were sold to residents of one state. However, the August 1 issue will be integrated with the April 1 issue because they are made within six months of each other and do not therefore qualify for the SEC's "safe harbor" rule. These two issues integrate and aggregate to produce a *single* offering consisting of:

$12,000,000
50 nonaccredited investors
20 out-of-state investors

The integrated offering does not qualify for a "small offering" exemption for either of two reasons, first, because over $5,000,000 of securities have been issued, and second, because there are over 35 nonaccredited investors. The integrated offering also does not qualify for an "intrastate offering" exemption because there are out-of-state investors involved in the offering. Therefore, under the integration and aggregation rules, these two offerings lose their exemptions from registration. The issuer must register the integrated offering with the SEC.

Note, however, that the January 1 issue is not integrated with the August 1 issue because it falls in the "safe harbor" period, having been issued over six months prior to the August 1 issue.

Resale Restrictions.   Securities issued pursuant to exemptions from registration are considered "restricted" securities and are subject to the *resale* prohibitions discussed previously. In order to assist in preventing the unlawful resale or transfer of exempt securities in the future, the issuer is generally required to take the following actions:

1. Advise investors that the securities they have purchased have not been registered with the SEC, are issued pursuant to an exemption from such registration, and disclose to the investors the resale restrictions applicable to their securities.
2. Obtain an "investment letter" from each investor stating his qualifications to purchase the securities (e.g., state of residency for an intrastate exemption), and an *affidavit* that he or she will abide by the resale restrictions of the securities.
3. Place a restrictive "legend" on each stock certificate or other instrument, stating that the security has been issued pursuant to an exemption from registration and is subject to certain resale restrictions.
4. Provide "stop transfer" instructions to the transfer agent, which is usually a bank, not to transfer ownership of the securities issued pursuant to an exemption unless the restrictions on transfer (e.g., the nine-month "coming-to-rest" test for transfer of securities issued pursuant to an intrastate offering to nonresidents) have been met.

Although securities may not have to be registered with the SEC because the transaction or securities qualify for one of the previously discussed exemptions from registration, all *exempted* transactions are still subject to the other provisions of the federal securities laws, particularly the antifraud provisions.

In *SEC v. Murphy* the court held found that multiple issues of securities should be integrated, and held that the integrated issue did not qualify for a private placement exemption from registration.

PRIVATE PLACEMENT EXEMPTION, INTEGRATION OF OFFERINGS

SECURITIES AND EXCHANGE COMMISSION v. MURPHY

626 F.2d 633 (1980)
UNITED STATES COURT OF APPEALS, NINTH CIRCUIT

Ferguson, Circuit Judge.

Stephen Murphy appeals from a district court decision permanently enjoining him from violating the registration and antifraud provisions of the securities laws and requiring him to mail copies of the court's order to present and future business associates and investors.

Stephen Murphy formed Intertie, a California

company that provided financing, construction, and management of cable television systems, in December, 1971, and he was its president and director until February, 1974, when he became vice-president, treasurer, and director. In May, 1975, he resigned from these positions after an unsuccessful proxy fight, but he regained control of the company in August, 1975, and became chairman of the board.

Intertie's business involved the promotion of approximately 30 limited partnerships to which it sold cable television systems. Most commonly, Intertie would buy a cable television system, making a cash down payment and financing the remainder, and then sell it to a partnership for a cash down payment and non-recourse promissory notes in favor of Intertie and lease it back from the partnership. Murphy was the architect of this financing scheme, by which Intertie took in approximately $7.5 million from 400 investors. Intertie engaged International Securities Corporation (ISC), a securities brokerage firm, to sell most of these partnership interests, and it agreed that ISC would receive a 10 percent sales commission. ISC's president, Jack Glassford, and ISC shared a 3 percent commission override. From this 3 percent, starting in the summer of 1974, Murphy received a one-half percent commission on the sales of partnership interests.

Under ISC's sales program, representatives contacted potential investors to interest them in purchasing limited partnership shares in cable television systems. An ISC sales representative was usually the general partner in the venture. Intertie and ISC did not register the limited partnership interests as securities but relied on the private offering exemption of Section 4(2) of the Securities Act, . . . which provides a "safe harbor" for private placements that meet certain specified conditions.

Intertie took no steps to assure that the offering and sale were directed only to a small number of sophisticated, informed investors; in fact, it did not even number its memoranda so that it could monitor the volume of offers made.

ISC's salesmen promoted sales of the partnership interests with offering memoranda describing Intertie as "the undisputed industry leader" and a company which could purchase, construct and operate cable television systems "better, faster, more profitabl[y] and with less invested capital than ever

before." The memoranda, the salesmen, and Intertie did not disclose that Intertie was losing money, had large short-term debt obligations in connection with the acquisition of the cable television facilities which it resold to the limited partnerships, and could not continue to meet obligations of existing partnerships without refinancing debts or obtaining capital from new partnerships. Nor did they disclose that Intertie was commingling the funds from the various partnerships.

Offering memoranda represented that Intertie had "only a limited history of operations" and did not reveal that Intertie had sold cable systems to at least eight or nine partnerships by January, 1974, and at least twenty by August, 1974.

Murphy did not make Intertie's financial statements available to the investors. In his deposition, he described Intertie's response to requests for financial information:

> [S]ome guys called up particularly early in '74 and said, "I have a potential investor and want to see Intertie's financial statement," and they were told, "if that is a condition, we are not going to furnish it."

By September, 1974, the company had a serious working capital deficiency and a negative net worth of over $600,000; its current assets were $2.3 million; its current liabilities were $6.4 million. Throughout 1974, Intertie used funds generated from new partnership offerings to meet Intertie's debt service obligations on prior systems. Included in those funds were investments from two limited partnerships for systems in New Mexico, which Intertie never built, although it prepared tax returns on behalf of the partnerships and took an investment tax credit and accelerated depreciation on the nonexistent facilities. In December, 1975, Murphy filed a petition for Chapter XI bankruptcy for Intertie, and Intertie is now a debtor in possession with Murphy as president.

SECURITY

Murphy argues on appeal that the shares in limited partnerships in the cable television systems were not securities. That argument is disingenuous. An investment contract is a security. . . . Under the test for an investment contract established in *SEC v. W. J. Howey Co.,* a limited partnership generally is a security, because, by definition, it involves investment in a common enterprise with profits to come solely from the efforts of others.

NOT EXEMPT FROM REGISTRATION

Murphy contends . . . that the limited partnership interests were exempt from registration under the private offering exemption in Section 4(2) of the 1933 Act. . . . The problem in this case, as the SEC conceded at oral argument, is that it is not clear who was the issuer of the securities at suit.

In a corporate offering, the issuer generally is the company whose stock is sold. Here there is no company issuing stock, but instead, a group of individuals investing funds in an enterprise for profit, and receiving in return an entitlement to a percentage of the proceeds of the enterprise.

In determining that a security qualifies as a private offering, then, we must make sure that the offerees are provided with or given access to the information that is material to their investment decision. . . . The information crucial to the investment decision would be that concerning the entity which was responsible for the success or failure of the enterprise.

Here, Murphy himself conceded that information about Intertie's finances was material to the decision whether to invest in a limited partnership that Intertie promoted. Given the realities of Intertie's financing scheme, that concession was unavoidable. Intertie developed the partnership offering plan and assumed a major role in engaging investors. It engineered and operated the systems from which the investors would receive their returns. It managed many of the partnerships and it prepared tax forms for most of them. Without generating new capital through continued partnership offerings, Intertie could not meet its obligations on the systems sold to previous investors.

For all these reasons, Intertie clearly held the key to success or failure of the partnerships. Accordingly, Intertie was the entity about which the investors needed information, and, therefore, it is properly considered the issuer of the securities for purposes of determining the availability of a private offering exemption.

We hold . . . that when a person organizes or sponsors the organization of limited partnerships and is primarily responsible for the success or failure of the venture for which the partnership is formed, he will be considered an issuer for purposes of determining the availability of the private offering exemption.

INTEGRATION OF OFFERINGS

In Securities Act Release No. 4552 (Nov. 6, 1962), 27 Fed.Reg. 11316, the Commission set out five factors to be used in determining whether to consider apparently separate offerings as one integrated offering. These factors guide our evaluation. The factors are: (a) whether the offerings are part of a single plan of financing; (b) whether the offerings involve issuance of the same class of securities; (c) whether the offerings are made at or about the same time; (d) whether the same kind of consideration is to be received; and (e) whether the offerings are made for the same general purposes.

Applying these factors to the undisputed facts, we conclude that the offerings of limited partnership interests must be considered integrated.

The Commission's evidence was more than adequate to support the injunction here. The above-listed factors militate strongly in favor of granting an injunction. The District Court's summary judgment ruling indicated that defendant had, at the least, acted recklessly in violating the registration provisions. As established through Murphy's own admissions, these violations occurred repeatedly, but Murphy nonetheless insisted that he had done nothing wrong. In addition, his new venture, Xanadex, provides ample opportunity for continued misconduct.

In the present proceeding, the totality of the circumstances strongly suggests the need for an injunction.

The judgment of the District Court is *affirmed*.

CASE QUESTIONS

1. What does the private placement offering provide? Explain.
2. Were the limited partnership interests in this case "securities" under the *Howey* test? Explain.
3. Who was the *issuer* in this case? If each of the limited partnerships had been considered a separate issuer, would each offering have qualified

for a private placement exemption from registration?

4. What does the doctrine of *integration* provide? Were the offerings by the limited partnerships integrated in this case?

Policy Issue. Was the penalty assessed against Murphy sufficient? Did it require him not to do anything that he wasn't already forbidden to do?

Economics Issue. How much money did the limited partners invest? What do you think happened to the money?

Ethics Issue. Did Murphy act ethically in this case?

Social Responsibility. Did the bankruptcy in this case cause any problems to society? Explain.

CIVIL LIABILITY UNDER THE 1933 ACT

Section 11 of the Securities Act of 1933 provides that an issuer or any other party who makes a misrepresentation or fails to disclose material facts with regards to a registration statement or prospectus may be held liable to a plaintiff in a private *civil* lawsuit. The following persons may be liable under Section 11 for "material" misrepresentations or omissions in a registration statement and prospectus:

1. every person who *signs* the registration statement, whether required to do so or not (the principal executive officer, chief financial officer, principal accounting officer, and a majority of the board of directors are required to sign the registration statement)
2. every person who was a *director* of the issuer, whether such person signed the registration statement or not
3. every "expert" who certifies preparation of the registration statement (e.g., certified public accountants, appraisers, consultants)
4. every underwriter involved in the distribution of the securities
5. every person who "controls" any person who is liable under Section 11.

In a Section 11 action, the misrepresentation or omission must be of a *material* fact. That misrepresentation, however, does not have to be the sole factor that influenced the plaintiff to deal in the security. In *Matter of Charles A. Howard,* 1 S.E.C. 6 (1934), the court defined a material fact as:

[A] fact which if it had been correctly stated or disclosed would have deterred or tended to deter the average prudent investor from purchasing [or selling] the securities in question.

The plaintiff does not have to have actually read the misrepresenting registration statement or prospectus, but may prove that he relied on secondary sources (such as a broker or dealer) who repeated the misrepresentation. *Privity of contract* between the plaintiff and defendant is not required to find a defendant liable under Section 11.

Due Diligence Defense. Signers, members of boards of directors, and other nonexperts are not absolutely liable for material misrepresentations or omissions in a registration statement or prospectus. Section 11(b) provides that a nonexpert may assert a "due diligence" defense to an allegation of liability under Section 11. Section 11(b) provides:

[N]o person, other than the issuer, shall be liable . . . who shall sustain the burden of proof . . . that . . .

[A]s regards any part of the registration statement not purporting to be made on the authority of an expert . . . he had, after reasonable investigation, reasonable ground to believe and did believe, at the time such part of the registration statement became effective, that the statements therein were true and that there was no omission to state a material fact required to be stated therein or necessary to make the statements therein not misleading; and

[A]s regards any part of the registration statement purporting to be made on the authority of an expert (other than himself) . . . he had no reasonable ground to believe and did not believe, at the time such part of the registration statement became effective, that the statements therein were untrue or that there was an omission to state a material fact required to be stated therein or necessary to make the statements therein not misleading. . . .

In determining what constitutes a reasonable investigation and reasonable belief, the courts apply the broad standard measured by the reasonable pains that a "prudent man" would take in the management of his own affairs.

Section 24 of the Securities Act of 1933 makes it a criminal act for any person to *willfully* make a material misrepresentation or deceptively omit a material fact in a registration statement.

ACCOUNTANT'S LIABILITY

Accountants, as "experts," may be held civilly liable under Section 11(a) of the 1933 Act for *misrepresentations* and *omissions* of material facts that occur in information they prepare that are included in registration statements and prospectuses (e.g., financial statements). Privity of contract with the third-party plaintiff, or reliance by the plaintiff on the misinformation, is not required to hold accountants and other experts liable under section 11(a). Accountants can also be held liable under Section 11(a) for their *negligence* in preparing accounting information contained in registration statements and prospectuses. The damages that may be awarded against accountants and other experts in a Section 11 action are the same as those that can be awarded against nonexperts.

Due Diligence Defense. Accountants, as well as other "experts," may prove a "due diligence" defense to a charge of liability under Section 11(a). With regards to accountants and other experts, Section 11(b) provides:

[N]o person . . . shall be liable . . . who shall sustain the burden of proof . . . that . . .

[A]s regards any part of the registration statement purporting to be made upon his authority as an expert . . . he had, after reasonable investigation, reasonable ground to believe and did believe, at the time such part of the registration statement became effective, that the statements therein were true and that there was no omission to state a material fact required to be stated therein or necessary to make the statements therein not misleading . . .

The following outline summarizes the elements necessary for nonexperts and experts to prove a due-diligence defense.

Due Diligence Defenses

I. Nonexperts:
  A. Nonexpertised portion of the registration statement
    1. reasonable investigation was conducted
    2. reasonable grounds to believe that the statements were true
    3. did actually believe that the statements were true
  B. Expertised portion of the registration statement
    1. no reasonable grounds to believe that the statements were untrue
    2. did not actually believe that the statements were untrue
II. Experts:
  A. Expertised portion
    1. the expert conducted a reasonable investigation
    2. had reasonable grounds to believe that the statements were true
    3. did actually believe that the statements were true

Damages. Damages in a private civil action under Section 11 are determined as follows:

1. If the securities were sold by the plaintiff prior to the filing of a civil action under Section 11, the plaintiff may recover the difference between the price he paid for the stock and the price at which he sold the securities prior to the lawsuit.
2. If the securities have not been sold prior to the suit, the purchaser may recover the difference between the price he paid and the value of the securities at the time of suit.
3. If the securities are sold after the suit is instituted, the plaintiff may recover the difference between the price he paid for the securities and the actual value of the securities at the time of suit, unless the damages are *less* because of this later sale, in which event the plaintiff would be limited to the lesser difference.

In order to arrive at a damage figure, the value of the securities may be determined from market value data and any other relevant factors. A plaintiff is not required to mitigate damages in a Section 11 action.

Escott v. BarChris Construction Corporation is the leading securities case in which the court found numerous persons in the registration process, including accountants, civilly liable for misrepresentations in a registration statement and prospectus in violation of Section 11(a) of the 1933 Act.

everyone must make an independent investigation (handwritten margin note)

McLean, District Judge.

This is an action by purchasers of 5½ percent convertible subordinated fifteen-year debentures of BarChris Construction Corporation (BarChris). Plaintiffs purport to sue on their own behalf and "on behalf of all other and present and former holders" of the debentures.

The action is brought under Section 11 of the Securities Act of 1933. Plaintiffs allege that the registration statement with respect to these debentures filed with the Securities and Exchange Commission, which became effective on May 16, 1961, contained material false statements and material omissions.

At the time relevant here, BarChris was engaged primarily in the construction of bowling alleys, somewhat euphemistically referred to as "bowling centers." These were rather elaborate affairs. They contained not only a number of alleys or "lanes," but also, in most cases, bar and restaurant facilities. . . . It is estimated that in 1960 BarChris installed approximately three per cent of all lanes built in the United States.

In general, BarChris's method of operation was to enter into a contract with a customer, receive from him at that time a comparatively small down payment on the purchase price, and proceed to construct and equip the bowling alley. When the work was finished and the building delivered, the customer paid the balance of the contract price in notes, payable in installments over a period of years. BarChris discounted these notes with a factor and received part of their face amount in cash. The factor held back part as a reserve.

The registration statement of the debentures, in preliminary form, was filed with the Securities and Exchange Commission on March 30, 1961. A first amendment was filed on May 11 and a second on May 16. The registration statement became effective on May 16. The closing of the financing took place on May 24. On that day BarChris received the net proceeds of the financing.

On October 29, 1962, it [BarChris] filed in this court a petition for an arrangement under Chapter XI of the Bankruptcy Act. BarChris defaulted in the payment of the interest due on November 1, 1962 on the debentures.

THE DEBENTURE REGISTRATION STATEMENT

The registration statement in its final form contained a prospectus as well as other information. Plaintiffs' claims of falsities and omissions pertain solely to the prospectus, not to the additional data.

The prospectus contained, among other things, . . . financial information. It included a consolidated balance sheet as of December 31, 1960, with elaborate explanatory notes. These figures had been audited by Peat, Marwick. It also contained unaudited figures . . . for the first quarter ended March 31, 1961, . . .

Plaintiffs challenge the accuracy of a number of these figures.

SUMMARY

For convenience, the various falsities and omissions . . . are recapitulated here. They were as follows:

1960 BALANCE SHEET

Current Assets	
As per prospectus	$4,524,021
Correct figure	3,914,332
Overstatement	$ 609,689

CONTINGENT LIABILITIES AS OF APRIL 30, 1961

As per prospectus	$ 825,000
Correct figure	1,443,853
Understatement	$ 618,853

Capitol Lanes should
have been shown as a
direct liability $ 314,166

EARNINGS FIGURES FOR QUARTER ENDING
MARCH 31, 1961

(a) *Sales*

As per prospectus	$2,138,455
Correct figure	1,618,645
Overstatement	$ 519,810

(b) *Gross Profit*

As per prospectus	$ 483,121
Correct figure	252,366
Overstatement	$ 230,755

Backlog as of March 31, 1961	
As per prospectus	$6,905,000
Correct figure	2,415,000
Overstatement	$4,490,000

Failure to disclose officers' loans out-standing and unpaid on May 16, 1961	$ 386,615

Failure to disclose use of proceeds in manner not revealed in prospectus	
Approximately	$1,160,000

Failure to disclose customer's delinquencies in May 1961 and BarChris's potential liability with respect thereto	
	Over $1,350,000

Failure to disclose the fact that BarChris
was already engaged, and was about to
be more heavily engaged, in the operation
of bowling alleys

[T]here is no doubt that many of the misstatements and omissions in this prospectus were material. This is true of all of them which relate to the state of affairs in 1961, . . . I also find that . . . the balance sheet errors [for 1960] were material within the meaning of Section 11.

THE "DUE DILIGENCE" DEFENSES

The defendants do not agree among themselves as to who the "experts" were or as to the parts of the registration statement which were expertised. . . . On the first view, only those portions of the registration statement purporting to be made on Peat, Marwick's authority were expertised portions. On the other view, everything in the registration statement was within this category, because the two law firms were responsible for the entire document.

The first view is the correct one. To say that the entire registration statement is expertised because some lawyer prepared it would be an unreasonable construction of the statute. Neither the lawyer for the company nor the lawyer for the underwriters is an expert within the meaning of Section 11.

I turn now to the question of whether defendants have proved their due diligence defenses. The position of each defendant will be separately considered.

RUSSO

Russo was, to all intents and purposes, the chief executive officer of BarChris. He was a member of the executive committee. He was familiar with all aspects of the business. He was personally in charge of dealings with the factors. . . . He was thoroughly aware of BarChris's stringent financial condition in May 1961.

In short, Russo knew all the relevant facts. He could not have believed that there were no untrue statements or material omissions in the prospectus. Russo has no due diligence defenses.

VITOLO AND PUGLIESE

They were the founders of the business who stuck with it to the end. Vitolo was president and Pugliese was vice president. . . . Vitolo and Pugliese are each men of limited education. It is not hard to believe that for them the prospectus was difficult reading, if indeed they read it at all.

But whether it was or not is irrelevant. The liability of a director who signs a registration statement does not depend upon whether or not he read it or, if he did, whether or not he understood what he was reading.

And in any case, there is nothing to show that they made any investigation of anything which they may not have known about or understood. They have not proved their due diligence defenses.

KIRCHER

Kircher was treasurer of BarChris and its chief financial officer. He is a certified public accountant and an intelligent man. He was thoroughly familiar with BarChris's financial affairs.

Kircher's contention is that he had never before dealt with a registration statement, that he did not know what it should contain, and that he relied wholly on Grant, Ballard and Peat, Marwick to guide him. He claims that it was their fault, not his, if there was anything wrong with it. He says that all the facts were recorded in BarChris's books where these "experts" could have seen them if they had looked.

Under these circumstances, he was not entitled to sit back and place the blame on the lawyers for not advising him about it. . . . Kircher has not proved his due diligence defenses.

TRILLING

Trilling's position is somewhat different from Kircher's. He was BarChris's controller. He signed the registration statement in that capacity, although he was not a director.

Trilling entered BarChris's employ in October 1960. He was Kircher's subordinate. . . . He was a comparatively minor figure in BarChris. The description of BarChris's "management" on page 9 of the prospectus does not mention him. He was not considered to be an executive officer.

Trilling may well have been unaware of several of the inaccuracies in the prospectus. But he must have known of some of them. As a financial officer, he was familiar with BarChris's finances and with its books of account.

[H]e still did not establish his due diligence defenses. He did not prove that as to the parts of the prospectus expertised by Peat, Marwick he had no reasonable ground to believe that it was untrue. He also failed to prove, as to the parts of the prospectus not expertised by Peat, Marwick, that he made a reasonable investigation which afforded him a reasonable ground to believe that it was true. As far as appears, he made no investigation. He

did what was asked of him and assumed that others would properly take care of supplying accurate data as to the other aspects of the company's business. This would have been well enough but for the fact that he signed the registration statement. As a signer, he could not avoid responsibility by leaving it up to others to make it accurate. Trilling did not sustain the burden of proving his due diligence defenses.

BIRNBAUM — *didn't sign the original registration statement*

Birnbaum was a young lawyer, admitted to the bar in 1957, who, after brief periods of employment by two different law firms and an equally brief period of practicing in his own firm, was employed by Bar-Chris as house counsel and assistant secretary in October 1960. Unfortunately for him, he became secretary and a director of BarChris on April 17, 1961, after the first version of the registration statement had been filed with the Securities and Exchange Commission. He signed the later amendments, thereby becoming responsible for the accuracy of the prospectus in its final form.

One of Birnbaum's more important duties, first as assistant secretary and later as full-fledged secretary, was to keep the corporate minutes of Bar-Chris and its subsidiaries. This necessarily informed him to a considerable extent about the company's affairs.

Unlike Trilling, he was entitled to rely upon Peat, Marwick for the 1960 figures, for as far as appears, he had no personal knowledge of the company's books of account or financial transactions. . . . As a lawyer, he should have known his obligations under the statute. He should have known that he was required to make a reasonable investigation of the truth of all the statements in the unexpertised portion of the document which he signed. Having failed to make such an investigation, he did not have reasonable ground to believe that all these statements were true. Birnbaum has not established his due diligence defenses except as to the audited 1960 figures.

AUSLANDER

Auslander was an "outside" director, i. e., one who was not an officer of BarChris. He was chairman of the board of Valley Stream National Bank in Valley Stream, Long Island. In February 1961 Vitolo asked him to become a director of BarChris. Vitolo gave him an enthusiastic account of BarChris's progress and prospects. As an inducement, Vitolo said that when BarChris received the proceeds of a forthcoming issue of securities, it would deposit $1,000,000 in Auslander's bank.

Auslander was elected a director on April 17, 1961. The registration statement in its original form had already been filed, of course without his signature. On May 10, 1961, he signed a signature page for the first amendment to the registration statement which was filed on May 11, 1961. This was a separate sheet without any document attached. Auslander did not know that it was a signature page for a registration statement. He vaguely understood that it was something "for the SEC.". . . Auslander never saw a copy of the registration statement in its final form.

In considering Auslander's due diligence defenses, a distinction is to be drawn between the expertised and nonexpertised portions of the prospectus. As to the former, Auslander knew that Peat, Marwick had audited the 1960 figures. He believed them to be correct because he had confidence in Peat, Marwick. He had no reasonable ground to believe otherwise.

As to the nonexpertised portions, however, Auslander is in a different position. . . . Auslander made no investigation of the accuracy of the prospectus. He relied on the assurance of Vitolo and Russo, . . .

Section 11 imposes liability in the first instance upon a director, no matter how new he is. He is presumed to know his responsibility when he becomes a director. He can escape liability only by using that reasonable care to investigate the facts which a prudent man would employ in the management of his own property. In my opinion, a prudent man would not act in an important matter without any knowledge of the relevant facts, in sole reliance upon representations of persons who are comparative strangers and upon general information which does not purport to cover the particular case. To say that such minimal conduct measures up to the statutory standard would, to all intents and purposes, absolve new directors from responsibility merely because they are new. This is not a sensible construction of Section 11, when one bears in mind

its fundamental purpose of requiring full and truthful disclosure for the protection of investors.

I find and conclude that Auslander has not established his due diligence defense with respect to the misstatements and omissions in those portions of the prospectus other than the audited 1960 figures.

GRANT

Grant became a director of BarChris in October 1960. His law firm was counsel to BarChris in matters pertaining to the registration of securities. Grant drafted the registration statement for the stock issue in 1959 and for the warrants in January 1961. He also drafted the registration statement for the debentures. . . . Grant is sued as a director and as a signer of the registration statement.

Much of this registration statement is a scissors and paste-pot job. Grant lifted large portions from the earlier prospectuses, modifying them in some instances to the extent that he considered necessary. But BarChris's affairs had changed for the worse by May 1961. Statements that were accurate in January were no longer accurate in May. Grant never discovered this. He accepted the assurances of Kircher and Russo that any change which might have occurred had been for the better, rather than the contrary.

It is claimed that a lawyer is entitled to rely on the statements of his client and that to require him to verify their accuracy would set an unreasonably high standard. This is too broad a generalization. It is all a matter of degree. To require an audit would obviously be unreasonable. . . . There were things which Grant could readily have checked which he did not check.

Grant was entitled to rely on Peat, Marwick for the 1960 figures. He had no reasonable ground to believe them to be inaccurate. But [as to] the matters which . . . were not within the expertised portion of the prospectus . . . Grant was obliged to make a reasonable investigation. I am forced to find that he did not make one. After making all due allowances for the fact that BarChris's officers misled him, there are too many instances in which Grant failed to make an inquiry which he could easily have made which, if pursued, would have put him on his guard. In my opinion, this finding on the evidence in this case does not establish an unreasonably high standard in other cases for company counsel who are also directors. Each case must rest on its own facts. I conclude that Grant has not established his due diligence defenses except as to the audited 1960 figures.

THE UNDERWRITERS AND COLEMAN

The underwriters other than Drexel made no investigation of the accuracy of the prospectus.

Drexel did make an investigation. The work was in charge of Coleman, a partner of the firm. . . . Drexel's attorneys acted as attorneys for the entire group of underwriters.

On April 17, 1961 Coleman became a director of BarChris. He signed the first amendment to the registration statement filed on May 11 and the second amendment, constituting the registration statement in its final form, filed on May 16. He thereby assumed a responsibility as a director and signer in addition to his responsibility as an underwriter.

The underwriters say that the prospectus is the company's prospectus, not theirs. Doubtless this is the way they customarily regard it. But the Securities Act makes no such distinction. The underwriters are just as responsible as the company if the prospectus is false. And prospective investors rely upon the reputation of the underwriters in deciding whether to purchase the securities.

The purpose of Section 11 is to protect investors. To that end the underwriters are made responsible for the truth of the prospectus. . . . To effectuate the statute's purpose, the phrase "reasonable investigation" must be construed to require more effort on the part of the underwriters than the mere accurate reporting in the prospectus of "data presented" to them by the company. . . .

On the evidence in this case, I find that the underwriters' counsel did not make a reasonable investigation of the truth of those portions of the prospectus which were not made on the authority of Peat, Marwick as an expert. Drexel is bound by their failure.

The other underwriters, who did nothing and relied solely on Drexel and on the lawyers, are also bound by it. It follows that although Drexel and the other underwriters believed that those portions of the prospectus were true, they had no reasonable ground for that belief, within the meaning of the statute. Hence, they have not established their due diligence defense, except as to the 1960 audited figures.

The same conclusions must apply to Coleman. . . . When it came to verification, he relied upon his counsel to do it for him. Since counsel failed to do it, Coleman is bound by that failure. Consequently, in his case also, he has not established his due diligence defense except as to the audited 1960 figures.

PEAT, MARWICK — *didn't ask enough questions*

Peat, Marwick's work was in general charge of a member of the firm, Cummings, and more immediately in charge of Peat, Marwick's manager, Logan. Most of the actual work was performed by a senior accountant, Berardi, who had junior assistants, one of whom was Kennedy.

Berardi was then about thirty years old. He was not yet a C.P.A. He had had no previous experience with the bowling industry. This was his first job as a senior accountant. He could hardly have been given a more difficult assignment.

First and foremost is Berardi's failure to discover that Capitol Lanes had not been sold. This error affected both the sales figure and the liability side of the balance sheet. Fundamentally, the error stemmed from the fact that Berardi never realized that Heavenly Lanes and Capitol were two different names for the same alley. . . . The vital question is whether he failed to make a reasonable investigation which, if he had made it, would have revealed the truth.

Although the question is a rather close one, I find that Peat, Marwick has not sustained that burden. Peat, Marwick has not proved that Berardi made a reasonable investigation as far as Capitol Lanes was concerned and that his ignorance of the true facts was justified.

Berardi erred in computing the contingent [liabilities]. . . . Berardi did not make a reasonable investigation in this instance.

The purpose of reviewing events subsequent to the date of a certified balance sheet (referred to as an S-1 review when made with reference to a registration statement) is to ascertain whether any material change has occurred in the company's financial position which should be disclosed in order to prevent the balance sheet figures from being misleading. The scope of such a review, under generally accepted auditing standards, is limited. It does not amount to a complete audit.

Berardi made the S-1 review in May 1961. He devoted a little over two days to it, a total of 20½ hours. He did not discover any of the errors or omissions pertaining to the state of affairs in 1961 which I have previously discussed at length, all of which were material. The question is whether, despite his failure to find out anything, his investigation was reasonable within the meaning of the statute.

He did not examine any "important financial records" other than the trial balance. As to minutes, he read only what minutes Birnbaum gave him, which consisted only of the board of directors' minutes of BarChris. He did not read such minutes as there were of the executive committee. He did not know that there was an executive committee, . . . He did not read the minutes of any subsidiary. . . . He asked questions, he got answers which he considered satisfactory, and he did nothing to verify them.

Berardi had no conception of how tight the cash position was. He did not discover that BarChris was holding up checks in substantial amounts because there was no money in the bank to cover them. He did not know . . . of the officers' loans. Since he never read the prospectus, he was not even aware that there had ever been any problem about loans from officers.

During the 1960 audit Berardi had obtained some information from factors, not sufficiently detailed even then, as to delinquent notes. He made no inquiry of factors about this in his S-1 review. . . . He was content with Trilling's assurance that no liability theretofore contingent had become direct.

Apparently the only BarChris officer with whom Berardi communicated was Trilling. He could not recall making any inquiries of Russo, Vitolo or Pugliese.

There had been a material change for the worse in BarChris's financial position. That change was sufficiently serious so that the failure to disclose it made the 1960 figures misleading. Berardi did not discover it. As far as results were concerned, his S-1 review was useless.

Accountants should not be held to a standard higher than that recognized in their profession. I do not do so here. Berardi's review did not come up to that standard. He did not take some of the

steps which Peat, Marwick's written program prescribed. He did not spend an adequate amount of time on a task of this magnitude. Most important of all, he was too easily satisfied with glib answers to his inquiries.

This is not to say that he should have made a complete audit. But there were enough danger signals in the materials which he did examine to require some further investigation on his part. Generally accepted accounting standards required such further investigation under these circumstances. It is not always sufficient merely to ask questions.

Here again, the burden of proof is on Peat, Marwick. I find that that burden has not been satisfied. I conclude that Peat, Marwick has not established its due diligence defense.

CASE QUESTIONS

1. What statute were the defendants alleged to have violated? Can a defendant be found *personally* liable under this statute?
2. Did the court find that the entire registration statement was "expertised" because it was drafted by lawyers? Explain.
3. What does the due diligence defense for *nonexperts* provide? Explain the elements.
4. Who were the following persons? What was each of their activities with regards to the preparation of the registration statement? Did any of these persons prove a due diligence defense? Explain.
   a. Russo
   b. Vitolo and Pugliese
   c. Kircher
   d. Trilling
   e. Birnbaum
   f. Auslander
   g. Grant
   h. the underwriters
   i. Coleman
5. What services did Peat, Marwick, Mitchell & Co. (PMM) provide to BarChris regarding the preparation of the registration statement? Was PMM an "expert"?
6. Was PMM alleged to have committed *fraud* or *negligence?* Are both covered by Section 11?
7. What activities was PMM alleged to have been

liable for under Section 11? Did PMM prove a due diligence defense?

Policy Issue. Should accountants be held liable for misrepresentations contained in a registration statement that they did not make? Or should liability of accountants be limited to their own fraudulent acts?

Economics Issue. Why are accountants named as defendants in so many civil actions, particularly those brought under federal securities laws?

Ethics Issue. Which of the following defendants do you think acted unethically in this case?

a. Russo
b. Vitolo and Pugliese
c. Kircher
d. Trilling
e. Birnbaum
f. Auslander
g. Grant
h. the underwriters
i. Coleman
j. Peat, Marwick, Mitchell & Co.

Social Responsibility. Do accountants owe a duty of social responsibility to report fraud of a client that they uncover during an audit?

brokers could recover against the investors

Protection of Securities Professionals.   Section 17(a)(1) of the 1933 Act makes it unlawful for any person to "employ any device, scheme, or artifice to defraud" in the offer or sale of securities. In *U.S. v. Naftalin,* 441 U.S. 768 (1979), an investor placed an order with several securities brokers whereby the investor sold shares "short," hoping that the price of the securities would go down so that when he had to "cover" his short sale, that is, deliver the actual securities to his buyers at a later date, he could then purchase the shares at a price lower than he had agreed to sell them for and keep the difference between the contract price and the purchase price as profit. Instead, the price of the securities increased, the investor did not cover, and the securities brokers, in order to protect their reputations, purchased the securities and delivered them to the buyers. The securities brokers then sued Naftalin, the investor, in a civil suit under section 17(a)(1). The U.S. Supreme Court was faced with deciding whether securities professionals are protected under federal securities laws. The opinion of the Court stated:

In this Court, Naftalin does not dispute that, by falsely representing that he owned the stock he sold, he defrauded the brokers who executed his sales. He contends, however, that the Court of Appeals correctly held that Section 17(a)(1) applies solely to frauds directed against investors, and not to those against brokers.

[N]either this Court nor Congress has ever suggested that investor protection was the *sole* purpose of the Securities Act. . . . While investor protection was a constant preoccupation of the legislators, the record is also replete with references to the desire to protect ethical businessmen. As Representative Chapman stated, "[t]his legislation is designed to protect not only the investing public but at the same time to protect honest corporate business." Respondent's assertion that Congress' concern was limited to investors is thus manifestly inconsistent with the legislative history.

Moreover, the welfare of investors and financial intermediaries are inextricably linked—frauds perpetrated upon either business or investors can redound to the detriment of the other and to the economy as a whole. Fraudulent short sales are no exception. . . . Losses suffered by brokers increase their cost of doing business, and in the long run investors pay at least part of this cost through higher brokerage fees. In addition, unchecked short-sale frauds against brokers would create a level of market uncertainty that could only work to the detriment of both investors and the market as a whole. Finally, while the investors here were shielded from direct injury, that may not always be the case. Had the brokers been insolvent or unable to borrow, the investors might well have failed to receive their promised shares.

The decision of the Court of Appeals for the Eighth Circuit is *reversed.*

OTHER FEDERAL SECURITIES LEGISLATION

In addition to the Securities Act of 1933 and the Securities Exchange Act of 1934, Congress has enacted the following legislation to further regulate securities, securities transactions, and securities professionals.

Public Utility Holding Company Act. In the early 1900s, public utility companies were highly unregulated. In this environment public utilities, particularly gas and electric companies, created complex holding companies with many tiers of subsidiary companies, some consisting of hundreds of related firms. The reason was to create and take advantage of excess *leverage,* wherein the pyramid of companies was actually supported by very little equity capital (i.e., common or preferred stock) but by huge amounts of debt securities raised from an uninformed public. A small increase in utility rates would cause extreme returns to the equity holders. Losses were mostly absorbed by the public debt holders. Congress enacted the Public Utility Holding Company Act of 1935 to curtail such abuses. The Act requires a public utility holding company to register with the SEC and to disclose the details of its operations, financial condition, and organizational structure to the SEC and its securities holders.

The Trust Indenture Act. The Trust Indenture Act of 1939 was enacted by Congress to regulate the sale of bonds and other *debt* securities where the issue exceeds $1 million. A *trust indenture* is an agreement between an issuer and its bondholders that provides the terms of a bond or debenture. The Act requires that the trust indenture provide for the appointment of an indenture *trustee,* which must be a corporation that meets certain minimum capital requirements. The trustee owes a fiduciary duty to safeguard the interests of the bondholders, to represent the bondholders in any dealings with the issuer (e.g., if issuer attempts to change the terms of the indenture agreement), and to prepare and submit periodic reports to the bondholders regarding their interests.

The Investment Company Act. An "investment company" is a firm that raises money by selling securities to the public, and then invests this money in the securities of other companies. An investment company does not produce any products or provide any services other than acting as a holding company for securities investments. Because of the potential for abuse, Congress enacted the Investment Company Act of 1940 to regulate the activities of investment companies. Under the Act, an investment company must register with the

Mark & Kathy

SEC, and must disclose its financial statements, investments and investment policies to its shareholders. An investment company cannot change its investment policy (e.g., change from investing in AAA bonds to speculative penny stocks) without the approval of its shareholders. The Act also gives the shareholders the right to approve all contracts between an investment company and its managers. An investment company is also subject to the provisions of both the 1933 and 1934 securities acts.

The Investment Advisors Act.   The Investment Company Act of 1940 was passed by Congress to regulate the activities of persons and firms that provide investment advice to clients regarding securities investments. The Act requires investment advisors to register with the SEC. Investment advisors must disclose any interests that conflict with those of their clients (e.g., if an advisor owns securities in a company whose securities he recommends he must disclose this). A client may bring a civil action against an investment advisor who violates the antifraud provisions of the Act. The SEC may suspend or revoke the license of investment advisors who violate provisions of the Act.

Securities Investor Protection Act.   In 1970 Congress enacted the Securities Investor Protection Act, which created the Securities Investor Protection Corporation. The Act authorizes this nonprofit corporation to assess fees against brokerage firms, to supervise the liquidation of bankrupt brokerage firms, and to reimburse investors for losses caused by the failure of such firms. A special chapter of the Bankruptcy Reform Act of 1978 covers the liquidation of securities firms.

Trend of the Law

The provisions of the Securities Act of 1933 and the rules adopted thereunder will continue to have a major impact on the regulation of the economy as more corporations are formed, and both new and existing corporations and other business entities (e.g., limited partnerships) seek to raise funds in the capital markets. The adoption of Regulation D and other *objective* standards by the SEC makes it less difficult than previously for businesses to determine whether a securities offering qualifies for an exemption from registration.

Cases brought in the future under the 1933 Act will require the courts to apply well-established law to individual fact situations. Fraud and negligence actions under Section 11 for material misrepresentations and omissions in registration statements and prospectuses will continue to constitute the majority of the cases brought under the 1933 Act. Accountants will remain a prime target in Section 11 actions.

The courts will continue to expand the definition of "security" in the future, thus bringing more transactions within the coverage of the Securities Act of 1933.

REVIEW QUESTIONS

1. Dare to be Great ("Dare") was a corporation organized to sell contracts to the public for what were characterized as self-improvement courses. Dare marketed a contract whereby a purchaser received a number of taped lessons, some written materials, and attended a few group meetings "aimed at improving self-motivation and sales ability." The purchaser also received the right to sell these courses to other purchasers in exchange for a commission on each sale. In order to receive the commission, the purchaser was required to recruit prospective purchasers to a sales meeting. Dare instructed the purchaser (now salesman) to maximize his chances of success by imparting an aura of affluence through the purchase of a new car, new clothes, etc. At the meeting itself, representatives from Dare, following a set script, attempted to convince prospective purchasers that Dare was a sure route to riches. Dare salesmen ran the meetings and closed the majority of the sales to the new purchasers. The SEC sued Dare, alleging that these contracts were "investment contracts" and therefore securities that needed to be registered under federal securities laws. Under the *Howey* test, is such a contract a security? Which element of the *Howey* test would have been the most difficult for the SEC to prove?

2. Fifty-seven plaintiffs sued a large corporate developer who built and now operates a large cooperative housing project in New York City. The plaintiffs, tenants in the housing project, allege that in the initial information bulletin, the developer promised to absorb future cost increases due to inflation, but in fact the corporation has not done so. The plaintiffs are suing under the antifraud provisions of the Securities Act of 1933.

   The defendant developer runs a nonprofit low-cost cooperative housing unit which is subsidized by the State of New York. The state provides large, low-interest mortgage loans and substantial tax exemptions to keep the cost of the housing low. All tenants are state-approved lessors who have incomes below a certain specified level. To acquire an apartment, the lessor must purchase 18 shares of co-op stock for each room desired at $25 per share. Additionally, each tenant then must pay a monthly maintenance fee for the apartment. Should the tenant decide to leave the co-op, he must sell the shares back to the co-op at the same price of $25 per share.

   The developer has asked the court to dismiss the complaint, claiming that even if fraud has occurred, the stock involved is not a security within the meaning of the Securities Act of 1933. Do the shares constitute a security?

3. Koscot International was formed by a group of investors to run a fraudulent sales operation. Potential investors were promised large returns in exchange for small initial investments. These profits were generated either by reselling cosmetics in retail markets or by bringing new investors into the company. The recruiting aspect was the primary focus of the business; investors in the company who were able to secure a new investor received 60 percent of that new person's investment (typically $600 of a $1,000 investment or $3,000 of a $5,000 investment). The company provided a very detailed guide to all investors who attempted to recruit new investors;

the guide went so far as to provide a script of exactly what to say when trying to "hook" a new investor and recommended replacing any individual who did not "present the program verbatim."

The SEC sued the company, claiming that the recruiting aspects (not the retail sales aspects) of the company involved the offer and sale of a security within federal securities laws. What type of operation is Koscot, in effect, operating? Is the selling scheme an "investment contract" subject to registration within the meaning of the Securities Act of 1933?

4. Datronics Engineers, Inc. was sued by the SEC, who alleged that the company violated the Securities Act of 1934 by using the mail to distribute unregistered stock that it owned in other corporations to its stockholders. In nine different instances, Datronics contacted small privately-owned corporations and then arranged a merger with itself which served no legitimate business purpose. Datronics usually organized a subsidiary corporation. The subsidiary would distribute a portion of its stock to the sellers as payment for the merger, a portion of its stock to Datronics as compensation for the merger, and the balance to Datronics shareholders. Datronics did not register this subsidiary stock with the SEC before it distributed the shares through the mail to each group. Did Datronics' actions constitute a sale of a security within the meaning of the Security Act of 1933? What policy arguments could be made supporting a finding that Datronics was selling securities? Assuming that it is such a sale, was Datronics required to register the security with the SEC?

5. Manor Nursing Centers attempted to sell an initial offering of common stock to the public. In the registration statement and prospectus filed with the SEC, the company stated that:

> the shares will be sold on an all-or-nothing basis, meaning that unless all shares are sold, the offer will terminate and the money will be returned; the subscribers' funds will be maintained in escrow and will not be available for other use; the shares will only be sold for cash; and, no special compensation will be paid for certain purchasers who agree to participate.

From the very outset, shares could not be sold. Manor did not sell the entire offering or refund the investors' money; it did not set up an escrow account; it did not sell all shares on a cash basis; it sold shares to different investors for different prices; and it gave special compensation to certain purchasers. Manor did not amend the prospectus subsequent to the effective date of the registration to reflect these changes, which made the prospectus inaccurate. Certain purchasers brought suit against Manor under Section 5(b) of the Securities Act of 1933. They alleged that the security was not properly registered since the prospectus did not contain required accurate information during the post-effective period. Should the investors be successful? State your reasons.

6. Plaintiffs were a group of investors who purchased a $75 million bond offering by Douglas Aircraft Co. In the prospectus filed by Douglas with the SEC, Douglas included a projected income statement that stated "it is very likely that net income, if any, for fiscal year 1966 will be nominal." Douglas did not disclose in the statements either the assumptions underly-

ing the forecast or the fact that all previous internal forecasts in 1966 had been completely inaccurate. (They predicted profits but Douglas sustained continuing losses.) In fact, a reasonably prudent bond purchaser, who had the facts available to Douglas management at the time that the prospectus was issued, would not have concluded that the forecast would probably be accurate. Douglas lost $52 million for the year in which the bonds were purchased. As a result, the plaintiffs suffered a substantial loss on the face value of the bonds. The plaintiffs sued Douglas, alleging that the projected income statement was misleading and that this was a material item since a reasonable bond investor would have considered the fact to be important when making his decision whether to invest. Was Douglas required to present the projected income statement in the prospectus? Since Douglas did include the statement, discuss whether Douglas is liable for the inaccurate forecast. Whether you find Douglas liable or not, what steps should Douglas take in the future to avoid potential liability?

7. Two brothers named Blue purchased a large tract of land in Colorado named Cherry Creek. The brothers intended to develop the property into a large residential area. Since they had little prior experience, the Blues included Andrews, a real estate expert, in the deal. Andrews agreed to contribute 10 percent of the purchase price and further agreed to supply his real estate expertise as a consultant for the enterprise. Andrews was not given the right to share in the management or in any decision to sell, mortgage or dispose of the property. Andrews received four shares or 20 percent of the stock of Cherry Creek Drive, Inc. The parties did not develop the property and the Blues informed Andrews of an impending merger of Cherry Creek Drive with Medic-Shield Nursing Centers, Inc. In the merger proxy statement to the shareholders of Medic-Shield, the Blues were listed as the sole owners. The merger was approved by the shareholders and 81,925 shares of the merged corporation, Colorado & Western, were issued to the Blues. The Blues distributed 16,385 shares to Andrews. The stock was not registered under the Securities Act of 1933. The Blues later sold the land for $1,050,000, yet the value of Andrews' shares was never greater than $70,000. Andrews sued, claiming that the stock should have been registered. In defense, the Blues argued that the stock need not have been registered since they were neither issuers nor underwriters under Section 4(1) of the 1933 Act. Was their defense valid?

8. Truckee Showboat, Inc. offered to sell its unregistered capital stock in an advertisement placed in the Los Angeles *Times*. The advertisement stated that Truckee was offering 4,080 shares at $1,000 per share, exclusively to bona fide residents of California. The proceeds from the sale, less a selling commission of 20 percent, were to be used to acquire, refurbish, and operate the El Cortez Hotel in Las Vegas, Nevada. Truckee was organized in California and kept its books and records within the State. The firm owned a wholesale pharmaceutical business in San Francisco, California; however, this business was not related to the primary business of the Corporation which was located outside California. All its directors and officers were residents of California. Truckee was charged by the SEC with attempting to sell unregistered and nonexempt securities.

Was Truckee's offer legal? If not, what aspects of the offer were illegal? What would Truckee need to do in order to make the offering legal?

9. Lawler, a trustee in bankruptcy for Mower, brought an action for damages against Gilliam and Cooke. Mower, through his attorney, invested money in what turned out to be a fraudulent scheme run by Johnson. Johnson promised investors a 30–100 percent return on notes given to his purported industrial wine importing business. In fact, Johnson did not import wine; instead he used money from some investors to pay off others who had previously invested. Johnson eventually went bankrupt.

Through Mower's dealings, he learned that Gilliam and Cooke were offering limited partnerships for investment in Johnson's business. Mower contacted Gilliam and asked if he would introduce Mower to Johnson directly. Gilliam refused. However, he offered to represent Mower directly in investing money with Johnson. Gilliam told Mower that he and Cooke could get Mower a return of greater than 50 percent. Mower did not have access to any other information. Mower invested $270,000 with Cooke, who delivered the funds to Johnson in return for a note in that amount. Johnson also contracted with Cooke to pay a return of not less than $166,500 on the note and gave him a personal guarantee of payment for the face amount of the note plus the promised return. Cooke endorsed the note to Mower. Johnson did not pay money on either note and when Johnson's fraud was discovered, Lawler brought this action against Gilliam and Cooke under the Securities Act of 1933, alleging that they sold unregistered securities. Are the notes securities? If so, do Gilliam and Cooke qualify for any exemption from registering the securities? If Lawler is successful, what damages can he recover?

10. Continental Tobacco Co. sold unregistered five-year 6 percent debentures. The securities were offered to a small group of investors at various private meetings. These small meetings involved high pressure sales tactics. The company presented unaudited financial statements as well as other written and oral information about the firm's marketing and sales strategy. The company claimed that it would provide any additional information that the investors may have required; however, most of the sales were consummated at the meetings themselves or shortly thereafter.

The SEC sued, seeking an injunction to stop Continental from making further sales. At trial, the SEC showed that Continental offered stock to 38 persons. Continental did not show that any of these potential investors had actual access to additional information. Further, in at least three instances, Continental admitted that certain buyers did not have the requisite expertise to evaluate the merits of the issue. Further, Continental introduced no evidence to show the net worth of any of the individuals. No individual purchased more than $38,000 in debentures. You are the trial judge. Is Continental required to register the securities? (Discuss legal as well as policy considerations.) How may Continental modify any future offerings of this nature to enable the firm to qualify for an exemption to registration?

11. Westland Minerals Corporation promoted a venture called the "Ohio Program" which was primarily designed as a tax write-off. Investors placed money in a partnership that used it in oil drilling ventures. Each investor

was able to write off twice his original investment in its first year because the partnership borrowed additional money from Caribbean banks. These loans allowed the investor to write off his loss on this borrowed money as well as on his own investment. Westland faced one problem, however, with the scheme since most banks were unwilling to loan money that would only be secured by an oil well. Higgins, a partner in Coopers & Lybrand, an accounting firm, proposed a solution. Under his proposal, Westland received paper loans for tax purposes without receiving the actual money. Then, as part of Westland's sales presentation, the firm presented a tax opinion letter from Coopers & Lybrand which confirmed that any investor could write off twice his investment. The IRS discovered this paper transaction and disallowed the double deductions. A group of investors sued Coopers & Lybrand under the Securities Acts, alleging that the firm had committed fraud. Could they recover?

14 TRADING IN SECURITIES

INTRODUCTION

Once issued, the majority of the securities of the largest companies in America are listed on one or more of the stock exchanges. Some stock exchanges are national in scope, for example the New York Stock Exchange and the American Stock Exchange. Other exchanges are regional in scope, for example the Pacific Stock Exchange. There is also an organized "over-the-counter" market for trading securities of medium-sized firms. The securities of most small "closely held" corporations are not listed on stock exchanges. Parties may, of course, sell securities in private transactions without the aid of stock exchanges. However, the exchanges facilitate the easy transfer of securities without the seller and buyer having to contact one another directly.

Each securities exchange has detailed rules regulating how companies become "listed" on the exchange, what transactions may take place on the exchange, and how securities professionals become licensed members of the exchange. The National Association of Securities Dealers (NASD) is the organization that examines, licenses and regulates securities brokers and dealers.

THE SECURITIES EXCHANGE ACT OF 1934

One of the most important concerns underlying the passage of the federal securities laws of the 1930s was to create a scheme of regulation which would help insure a fair and honest market not only in the issuance of securities, but also in the subsequent *trading* of securities. One year after the Securities Act of 1933 was passed, Congress enacted the Securities Exchange Act of 1934 to regulate the trading of securities.

The primary goal of the 1934 Act of promoting an honest aftermarket for securities trading is accomplished by two major principles contained in the provisions of the Act:

1. *full disclosure provisions,* whereby covered companies are required to register their securities with the SEC and also to file periodic reports with the SEC
2. *antifraud provisions,* whereby certain persons who are privy to nonpublic information are prohibited from engaging in "insider trading."

Reporting Requirements for Traded Securities.   Section 12 of the 1934 Securities Exchange Act requires that certain securities be "registered" with the Securities and Exchange Commission after their original issuance. The following companies must register their equity securities with the SEC:

1. companies whose securities are traded on a national securities exchange
2. companies which have assets of $1 million or more *and* a class of equity securities that is held by 500 or more persons.

Securities of investment companies (i.e., mutual funds), savings and loan associations, religious, charitable, and educational organizations are exempt from registration under the 1934 Act. The SEC has the power to exempt other securities where such an exemption would not endanger investors and would be in the "public interest." Companies which are required to register with the SEC under Section 12 are referred to as "registered" or "reporting" companies. Information required to be filed with the SEC by "registered" companies includes:

1. information regarding the company's operations and business
2. financial structure of the company
3. securities outstanding
4. names and remuneration of directors and officers
5. names of principal shareholders and underwriters
6. bonus and profit-sharing arrangements
7. options outstanding with respect to securities
8. material contracts
9. certified financial statements.

The remainder of this chapter will focus on the antifraud provisions of the 1934 Act, primarily the prohibition against "insider trading" of Section 10(b) and Rule 10b-5 adopted thereunder.

SECTION 10(b) AND RULE 10b-5

Section 10(b) of the 1934 Act is the basic antifraud provision applicable to the trading of previously issued securities. Section 10(b) of the 1934 Act prohibits the use

in connection with the purchase or sale of any security . . . [of] any manipulative or deceptive device or contrivance in contravention of such rules and regulations as the Commission may prescribe.

Pursuant to its rulemaking authority under Section 10(b), the SEC promulgated Rule 10b-5. This rule clarifies the types of activities that are prohibited under Section 10(b) of the 1934 Act. The scope of Rule 10b-5 is extremely broad. It applies to both *sellers* and *purchasers* of securities. Rule 10b-5 provides in pertinent part:

It shall be unlawful for any person, directly or indirectly, by use of any means or instrumentality of interstate commerce or of the mails, or of any facility of any national securities exchange,

  a. to employ any device, scheme, or artifice to defraud,
  b. to make any untrue statement of a material fact or to omit to state a material fact necessary in order to make the statements made, in light of the circumstances under which they were made, not misleading, or
  c. to engage in any act, practice, or course of business which operates or would operate as a fraud or deceit upon any person, in connection with the purchase or sale of any security.

The term "security" is broadly defined for the purposes of applying Rule 10b-5. *All* security transactions are covered by Rule 10b-5, whether made on a national exchange, on a regional exchange, on an over-the-counter exchange, or in a private transaction. In order for Section 10b or Rule 10b-5 to apply to a security transaction, some connection with "interstate commerce" must be shown. The misrepresentation itself does not have to be transmitted in interstate commerce. It is sufficient that only some part of the transaction involve interstate commerce (e.g., delivery of the securities) in order for the "in connection with" interstate commerce test to be met.

INSIDER TRADING

Although SEC Rule 10b-5 is applicable to a number of situations (transfer of securities in mergers, proxy solicitation, etc.), the main purpose of the rule is to prevent trading in securities by "insiders" using inside information that is not known to the public.

If an "insider" possesses material inside information which is not known by the public, he is under a duty to either *refrain* from trading in the securities of the company, or to *disclose* the information to those persons whose purchase or sale of the securities might be affected by the information. This is often referred to as the *"Cady, Roberts* duty" after the case in which the rule was announced, *Matter of Cady, Roberts & Co.,* 40 SEC 907 (1961). If the insider discloses the information, he is generally free to trade in the securities as soon as the information becomes "public."

Generally, an insider is not prohibited from trading in his corporation's securities *unless* he possesses material inside information. This is usually a question of fact to be determined from the facts and circumstances of each case. The information qualifies as "inside information" if it is *material,* and is *not public.* The court in *SEC v. Texas Gulf Sulphur Co.,* 401 F.2d 833 (1968), provided the following guideline:

An insider is not, of course, always foreclosed from investing in his own company merely because he may be more familiar with company operations than are outside investors. An insider's duty to disclose information or his duty to abstain from dealing in his company's securities arises only in 'those situations which are essentially extraordinary in nature and which are reasonably certain to have a substantial effect on the market price of the security if [the extraordinary situation is] disclosed.'

Nor is an insider obligated to confer upon outside investors the benefit of his superior financial or other expert analysis by disclosing his educated guesses or predictions.

Definition of "Insider." The term *insider* is broadly defined by the courts, and includes corporate officers, employees at all levels, and agents and representatives of the corporation (lawyers, accountants, consultants). The possession of "inside information" does not necessarily make a person an insider. Some *fiduciary relationship* between the corporation and the person possessing the inside information must be established before the person is considered an insider for the purposes of Rule 10b-5.

In the controversial case *Chiarella v. U.S.* the U.S. Supreme Court held that a "mark-up" man at a financial printer was not an "insider" under Section 10(b) and Rule 10b-5 when he made profits in transactions in the stock of target companies where the tendering company employed the printer to prepare the documents relating to tender offers on the target companies.

DEFINITION OF "INSIDER"

CHIARELLA v. UNITED STATES

445 U.S. 222 (1980)
UNITED STATES SUPREME COURT

Mr. Justice Powell delivered the opinion of the Court.

Petitioner is a printer by trade. In 1975 and 1976, he worked as a "markup man" in the New York composing room of Pandick Press, a financial printer. Among documents that petitioner handled were five announcements of corporate takeover bids. When these documents were delivered to the printer, the identities of the acquiring and target corporations were concealed by blank spaces or false names. The true names were sent to the printer on the night of the final printing.

The petitioner, however, was able to deduce the names of the target companies before the final printing from other information contained in the documents. Without disclosing his knowledge, petitioner purchased stock in the target companies and sold the shares immediately after the takeover attempts were made public. By this method, petitioner realized a gain of slightly more than $30,000 in the course of 14 months. Subsequently, the Securities and Exchange Commission (Commission or SEC) began an investigation of his trading activities. In May 1977, petitioner entered into a consent decree with the Commission in which he agreed to return his profits to the sellers of the shares. On the same day, he was discharged by Pandick Press.

In January 1978, petitioner was indicted on 17 counts of violating Section 10(b) of the Securities Exchange Act of 1934 (1934 Act) and SEC Rule 10b-5. After petitioner unsuccessfully moved to dismiss the indictment, he was brought to trial and convicted on all counts. . . . The Court of Appeals for the Second Circuit affirmed petitioner's conviction. We granted *certiorari*. . . .

In this case, the petitioner was convicted of violating Section 10(b) although he was not a corporate insider and he received no confidential information from the target company. Moreover, the "market information" upon which he relied did not concern the earning power or operations of the target company, but only the plans of the acquiring company. Petitioner's use of that information was not a fraud under Section 10(b) unless he was subject to an affirmative duty to disclose it before trading.

The Court of Appeals affirmed the conviction by holding that "[a]nyone—corporate insider or not— who regularly receives material nonpublic information may not use that information to trade in securities without incurring an affirmative duty to disclose." . . . The Court of Appeals, like the trial court, failed to identify a relationship between petitioner and the sellers that could give rise to a duty. Its decision thus rested solely upon its belief that the federal securities laws have "created a system providing equal access to information necessary for reasoned and intelligent investment decisions." The use by anyone of material information not generally available is fraudulent, this theory suggests,

because such information gives certain buyers or sellers an unfair advantage over less informed buyers and sellers.

This reasoning suffers from two defects. First, not every instance of financial unfairness constitutes fraudulent activity under Section 10(b). Second, the element required to make silence fraudulent—a duty to disclose—is absent in this case. No duty could arise from petitioner's relationship with the sellers of the target company's securities, for petitioner had no prior dealings with them. He was not their agent, he was not a fiduciary, he was not a person in whom the sellers had placed their trust and confidence. He was, in fact, a complete stranger who dealt with the sellers only through impersonal market transactions.

We cannot affirm petitioner's conviction without recognizing a general duty between all participants in market transactions to forgo actions based on material, nonpublic information. Formulation of such a broad duty, which departs radically from the established doctrine that duty arises from a specific relationship between two parties should not be undertaken absent some explicit evidence of congressional intent.

Section 10(b) is aptly described as a catchall provision, but what it catches must be fraud. When an allegation of fraud is based upon nondisclosure, there can be no fraud absent a duty to speak. We hold that a duty to disclose under Section 10(b) does not arise from the mere possession of nonpublic market information. The contrary result is without support in the legislative history of Section 10(b) and would be inconsistent with the careful plan that Congress has enacted for regulation of the securities markets.

In its brief to this Court, the United States offers an alternative theory to support petitioner's conviction. It argues that petitioner breached a duty to the acquiring corporation when he acted upon information that he obtained by virtue of his position as an employee of a printer employed by the corporation. The breach of this duty is said to support a conviction under Section 10(b) for fraud perpetrated upon both the acquiring corporation and the sellers. We need not decide whether this theory has merit, for it was not submitted to the jury.

The judgment of the Court of Appeals is *reversed*.

Mr. Chief Justice Burger, dissenting.

As a general rule, neither party to an arm's-length business transaction has an obligation to disclose information to the other unless the parties stand in some confidential or fiduciary relation. This rule permits a businessman to capitalize on his experience and skill in securing and evaluating relevant information; it provides incentive for hard work, careful analysis, and astute forecasting. But the policies that underlie the rule also should limit its scope. In particular, the rule should give way when an informational advantage is obtained, not by superior experience, foresight, or industry, but by some unlawful means.

I would read Section 10(b) and Rule 10b-5 to encompass and build on this principle: to mean that a person who has misappropriated nonpublic information has an absolute duty to disclose that information or to refrain from trading.

CASE QUESTIONS

1. Who was the defendant's employer? What job did the defendant perform?
2. What types of firms hired Pandick Press?
   a. tendering companies?
   b. target companies?
3. How did the defendant make $30,000 trading securities? Explain.
4. What is a *consent decree?* What were the terms of the consent decree entered into between Chiarella and the SEC? Did it mention criminal prosecution? Should it have?
5. Did the U.S. Supreme Court find that the mere *possession* of inside information was sufficient to find a violation of Section 10(b) and Rule 10b-5?
6. What is a *fiduciary* relationship? Did the Supreme Court find the necessary relationship between Chiarella and the *target* companies to find a violation of section 10(b)?
7. Did the Court address the question of whether Chiarella breached a fiduciary duty to the *tendering* companies? If not, why not? How would you decide this question?

Policy Issue. Should the possession and use of inside information be sufficient to base a violation of Section 10(b) and Rule 10b-5? Or should a fiduciary relationship between the trader and the corporation be required to be shown?

Economics Issue. Why do people trade on inside information? Can large sums of money be made by using inside information? Explain.

Ethics Issue. Were the actions of Chiarella ethical in this case?

Social Responsibility. Did Chiarella owe a duty of social responsibility not to trade on the inside information he possessed? If so, why? Did he breach his duty of *loyalty* to his employer?

Elements of an Insider Trading Case. A *prima facie* case for liability for "insider trading" under Section 10(b) and Rule 10b-5 requires a showing that:

1. the defendant made a misrepresentation or omission
2. such misrepresentation or omission was of a "material" fact
3. it was made in connection with a purchase or sale of securities
4. the plaintiff relied on such misrepresentation
5. the plaintiff was injured thereby

Misrepresentation or Deceptive Omission of Fact. Rule 10b-5 requires that there must be a "misrepresentation, omission, deception, or fraud" in connection with the purchase or sale of securities. The threshold question in most Rule 10b-5 cases is whether a "deceptive" or "manipulative" practice has been shown.

The misrepresentation or deceptive omission must be of a "fact." Although a distinction is drawn between a *fact* (actionable) and an *opinion* (not actionable), the distinction may no longer be clear. Under the SEC's current policy of promoting the disclosure of "soft" information, such as earnings projections and estimates of market value of assets, a knowing misrepresentation regarding such estimates may be considered a misrepresentation of "fact" for Rule 10b-5 purposes.

Materiality.   Rule 10b-5 requires that the misrepresentation or undisclosed fact be "material." The basic standard of materiality is the objective test of whether there is a "substantial likelihood" that a "reasonable shareholder" would consider the fact significant in making his decision to purchase or sell the securities in question.

"Purchase" or "Sale" Requirement.   SEC Rule 10b-5 is applicable to a deceptive transaction where there has been either a "purchase" *or* "sale" of a security by the plaintiff. The courts broadly define "purchase" and "sale"; subscription agreement to purchase stock, pledge of securities as collateral, etc., have been held to be covered. Something beyond an "offer" is required. The plaintiff must be either the *actual* purchaser or seller of the securities in order to have standing to maintain a Rule 10b-5 action.

Reliance and Causation.   A cause of action under Section 10(b) and Rule 10b-5 requires a showing of *reliance* by the plaintiff on defendant's material misrepresentation or omission. Although in most circumstances the courts require actual reliance, in many Section 10(b) and Rule 10b-5 actions the court will presume that the plaintiff relied on the defendant's misrepresentation. The misrepresentation does not have to be the sole factor leading the plaintiff into the transaction, but only a "substantial" factor. The plaintiff must prove that the defendant's wrongful conduct was the cause ("causation in fact") of plaintiff's economic loss. The test is whether defendant's deception was a "substantial" factor in causing plaintiff's loss.

Although the early view required the plaintiff to be in direct "privity of contract" with the defendant in order to maintain a Rule 10b-5 action against the defendant, the modern view has eliminated the privity requirement. The reason for the change is that most securities transactions now occur on impersonal securities exchanges where the buyer and seller do not know the identity of each other.

Civil Remedies.   Although Section 10(b) and Rule 10b-5 do not expressly allow a *private right* of action thereunder, the courts have *implied* such rights. Generally, a plaintiff in a Section 10(b) and Rule 10b-5 civil action may seek as remedies: (1) recission of the securities contract, and/or (2) damages.

The traditional measure of *damages* was to allow the plaintiff to recover from the defendant the difference between the value the plaintiff gave up and the value he received in the transaction. The modern rule of damages in a Section 10(b) and Rule 10b-5 action allows the plaintiff to recover the profits that the defendant made on the transaction. In order to protect defendants from unlimited liability, courts have generally limited the "disgorgement of profits" to the losses suffered by the plaintiff. Punitive damages are not allowed in Section 10(b) or Rule 10b-5 actions.

Where a violation of Section 10(b) or Rule 10b-5 has been found, as an alternative to suing for damages a plaintiff may *rescind* the securities contract and recover what he paid for the securities if he was the purchaser, or recover the securities if he was the seller.

Defenses to a Section 10(b) or Rule 10b-5 Action. A defendant may defend a Section 10(b) or Rule 10b-5 action on the merits by showing that full disclosure was made and the statements made were true, that the untrue statements were not "material," did not cause plaintiff's loss, or that defendant lacked actual knowledge or intent to defraud. A defendant may raise procedural defenses (e.g., the statute of limitations has run) against an alleged violation of Section 10(b) or Rule 10b-5. Since the federal securities laws do not provide a statute of limitations for a Section 10(b) violation, applicable state law applies.

A plaintiff's "unclean hands" is generally not allowed as a defense to a Section 10(b) action. The argument for this rule is that the defendant should not be relieved of his liability for fraud or deception merely because the plaintiff may have contributed to the deceit.

SEC v. Texas Gulf Sulphur Co. is one of the major insider trading cases brought under Section 10(b) or Rule 10b-5.

"INSIDER" TRADING

SECURITIES AND EXCHANGE COMMISSION v. TEXAS GULF SULPHUR CO.

401 F.2d 833 (1968)
UNITED STATES COURT OF APPEALS, SECOND CIRCUIT

Waterman, Circuit Judge.

This action derives from the exploratory activities of TGS [Texas Gulf Sulphur] begun in 1957 on the Canadian Shield in eastern Canada. In March of 1959, aerial geophysical surveys were conducted over more than 15,000 square miles of this area. . . . These operations resulted in the detection of numerous anomalies, i.e., extraordinary variations in the conductivity of rocks, one of which was on the Kidd 55 segment of land located near Timmins, Ontario.

On October 29 and 30, 1963, Clayton conducted a ground geophysical survey on the northeast portion of the Kidd 55 segment which confirmed the presence of an anomaly and indicated the necessity of diamond core drilling for further evaluation. Drilling of the initial hole, K-55-1, at the strongest part of the anomaly was commenced on November 8 and terminated on November 12 at a depth of 655 feet.

Meanwhile, the core of K-55-1 had been shipped to Utah for chemical assay which, when received in early December, revealed an average mineral content of 1.18 percent copper, 8.26 percent zinc, and 3.94 percent ounces of silver per ton over a length of 602 feet. These results were so remarkable that neither Clayton, an experienced geophysicist, nor four other TGS expert witnesses, had ever seen or heard of a comparable initial exploratory drill hole in a base metal deposit.

With the aid of . . . a public relation consultant, [TGS] . . . drafted a press release designed to quell the rumors, which release, after having been channeled through . . . a TGS attorney, was issued at

3:00 P.M. on Sunday, April 12, and which appeared in the morning newspapers of general circulation on Monday, April 13. It read in pertinent part as follows:

> The work done to date has not been sufficient to reach definite conclusions and any statement as to size and grade of ore would be premature and possibly misleading. When we have progressed to the point where reasonable and logical conclusions can be made, TGS will issue a definite statement to its stockholders and to the public in order to clarify the Timmins project.

THE INDIVIDUAL DEFENDANTS

Appellant Crawford, who ordered the purchase of TGS stock shortly before the TGS April 16 official announcement, and defendant Coates, who placed orders with and communicated the news to his broker immediately after the official announcement was read at the TGS-called press conference, concede that they were in possession of material information. They contend, however, that their purchases were not proscribed purchases for the news had already been effectively disclosed. We disagree.

Crawford telephoned his orders to his Chicago broker about midnight on April 15 and again at 8:30 in the morning of the 16th, with instructions to buy at the opening of the Midwest Stock Exchange that morning. The trial court's finding that "he sought to, and did, 'beat the news,' " is well documented by the record. . . . Before insiders may act upon material information, such information must have been effectively disclosed in a manner sufficient to insure its availibility to the investing public. Particularly here, where a formal announcement to the entire financial news media had been promised in a prior official release known to the media, all insider activity must await dissemination of the promised official announcement.

Coates was absolved by the court below because his telephone order was placed shortly before 10:20 A.M. on April 16, which was after the announcement had been made even though the news could not be considered already a matter of public information. . . . The reading of a news release, which prompted Coates into action, is merely the first step in the process of dissemination required for compli-

ance with the regulatory objective of providing all investors with an equal opportunity to make informed investment judgments. Assuming that the contents of the official release could instantaneously be acted upon, at the minimum Coates should have waited until the news could reasonably have been expected to appear over the media of widest circulation, the Dow Jones broad tape, rather than hastening to insure an advantage to himself and his broker son-in-law.

Contrary to the belief of the trial court that Kline had no duty to disclose his knowledge of the Kidd project before accepting the stock option offered him, we believe that he, a vice president, who had become the general counsel of TGS in January 1964, but who had been secretary of the corporation since January 1961, and was present in that capacity when the options were granted, and who was in charge of the mechanics of issuance and acceptance of the options, was a member of top management and under a duty before accepting his option to disclose any material information he may have possessed, and, as he did not disclose such information to the Option Committee, we direct rescission of the option he received.

THE CORPORATE DEFENDANT

At 3:00 P.M. on April 12, 1964, evidently believing it desirable to comment upon the rumors concerning the Timmins project, TGS issued the press release quoted in pertinent part in the text, . . . , *supra*. The SEC argued below and maintains on this appeal that this release painted a misleading and deceptive picture of the drilling progress at the time of its issuance, and hence violated Rule 10b-5(2).

While we certainly agree with the trial court that "in retrospect, the press release may appear gloomy or incomplete," we cannot, from the present record, by applying the standard Congress intended, definitively conclude that it was deceptive or misleading to the reasonable investor, or that he would have been misled by it.

[W]e must *remand* to the District Court to decide whether the release was misleading to the reasonable investor and if found to be misleading, whether the court in its discretion should issue the injunction the SEC seeks.

CASE QUESTIONS

1. Was the information regarding the mineral find by TGS in Canada "inside information"? Was it *material?*
2. Did defendant Crawford personally trade in TGS stock? If so, when? Did Crawford "beat the news"?
3. When did defendant Coates telephone his brother-in-law to purchase the TGS stock? Did Coates personally trade in TGS stock?
4. Did Coates wait long enough after the press conference to purchase the stock? Did the court announce how much time is necessary for information to become "public" once it has been announced by a company?
5. What position did defendant Kline hold at TGS? How did Kline obtain TGS stock during the relevant period? Was this held to be in violation of Section 10(b) or Rule 10b–5? Do you agree?
6. Can a corporation be held liable under Section 10(b) and Rule 10b-5 for providing false information in a press release?

7. Did the court answer the question as to whether the TGS press release of April 13 was deceptive or manipulative in violation of Section 10(b) and Rule 10b-5? How would you decide this question?

Policy Issue. Should part of the compensation package of executives be the opportunity to make profits from the use of inside information?

Economics Issue. Is there much money to be made from insider trading? What do you think the probability of getting caught is?

Ethics Issue. Were the actions of defendants Crawford, Coates and Kline ethical in this case?

Social Responsibility. Do corporate officers and other insiders owe a duty of social responsibility not to engage in insider trading? Does insider trading serve any social good?

TIPPER-TIPPEE LIABILITY

If an insider discloses inside information to another person, he is the "tipper" and the person receiving the information is the "tippee." If the *tippee* trades in the securities of the corporation, and knew or should have known from the circumstances that the information he received was inside information, the tippee is liable to other traders who did not possess the inside information. For example, if Son, the president of ABC Corporation, gives Mother a birthday present consisting of inside information that the earnings of ABC Corporation have doubled and that this will be announced at a press conference tomorrow, and Mother knows of her son's position and trades in the securities of the ABC Corporation, Mother is liable under Section 10(b) and Rule 10b-5 as a *trading* "tippee."

Where a tippee knowingly trades on inside information, the *tipper* is also liable for the profits made by the tippee. If the tippee does not trade on the inside information, neither the tippee or the tipper is liable under Section 10(b) or Rule 10b-5.

If the tippee "tips" other persons, even if the tipper has made him promise not to, both the tippee (who is now a tipper) and the original tipper are liable for the profits made by these *remote tippees* if they trade in the securities of the corporation. The remote tippees are personally liable under Section 10(b) and Rule 10b-5 if they knew or should have known that the information they received was inside information. The *original tipper* always remains liable for the profits he personally makes by the use of inside information in violation of his fiduciary duty to the corporation.

"Disgorgement-of-Profits" Measure of Damages.   There has been some confusion in the federal courts as to what damages should be awarded in a tipper-tippee liability situation under Section 10(b) and Rule 10b-5. Often, courts have held that the tipper and tippee were liable to *all* persons who traded in the securities of the corporation without the benefit of the inside information. Under this measure of damages, a tipper and tippee could be held liable for millions of dollars of damages to thousands of traders on the New York or other stock exchanges—and this when they may have only made a few hundreds or thousands of dollars of illegal profits. The modern rule is to limit the liability of tippers and tippees to the profits they made by the illegal use of the inside information. This is known as the "disgorgement-of-profits" measure of damages. Under this measure, if the claims for damages of plaintiffs exceed the profits made by the tipper and tippee, the plaintiffs must share *pro rata* in the damage award.

In *Elkind v. Liggett & Myers, Inc.* the court found tipper-tippee liability where a corporate officer divulged nonpublic earnings information to a financial analyst, who informed several of his clients, who in turn sold stock in the company based on the information.

"TIPPER-TIPPEE" LIABILITY

ELKIND v. LIGGETT & MYERS, INC.

635 F.2d 156 (1980)
UNITED STATES COURT OF APPEALS, SECOND CIRCUIT

Mansfield, Circuit Judge.

This case presents a number of issues arising out of what has become a form of corporate brinkmanship—nonpublic disclosure of business-related information to financial analysts. The action is a class suit by Arnold B. Elkind on behalf of certain purchasers of the stock of Liggett & Myers, Inc. (Liggett) against it.

Liggett is a diversified company, with traditional business in the tobacco industry supplemented by acquisitions in such industries as liquor (Paddington Corp., importer of J&B Scotch), pet food (Allen Products Co. and Perk Foods Co., manufacturer of Alpo dog food), cereal, watchbands, cleansers and rugs. Its common stock is listed on the New York Stock Exchange.

The . . . "tip" occurred on July 17, one day before the preliminary earnings figures for the first half [of 1972] were released. Analyst Robert Cummins of Loeb Rhoades & Co. questioned Ralph Moore, Liggett's chief financial officer, about the recent decline in price of Liggett's common stock, as well as performance of the various subsidiaries. According to Cummins' deposition, he asked Moore whether there was a good possibility that earnings would be down, and received an affirmative ("grudging") response. Moore added that this information was confidential. Cummins sent a wire to his firm, and spoke with a stockholder who promptly sold 1,800 shares of Liggett stock on behalf of his customers.

The district court held that . . . [the] tip of material information in violation of Rule 10b-5, rendering Liggett liable to all persons who bought the company's stock . . . without knowledge of the tipped information.

Management must navigate carefully between the "Scylla" of misleading stockholders and the public by implied approval of reviewed analyses and the "Charybdis" of tipping material inside information by correcting statements which it knows to be erroneous.

The corporate officer dealing with financial analysts inevitably finds himself in a precarious position, which we have analogized to "a fencing match conducted on a tightrope." A skilled analyst with knowledge of the company and the industry may piece seemingly inconsequential data together with public information into a mosaic which reveals material nonpublic information. Whenever managers and analysts meet elsewhere than in public, there is a risk that the analysts will emerge with knowledge of material information which is not publicly available.

The July 17 tip . . . was sufficiently directed to the matter of earnings to sustain the district court's finding of materiality. . . . [T]here are sufficient indicia of materiality to support the district court's conclusion. The request by Moore (Liggett's chief financial officer) that Cummins not repeat what he had been told added to the impression that the earnings were worse than those following the stock expected them to be. Moreover, 1,800 shares were sold by a stockbroker on behalf of his customers, after speaking with Cummins by telephone. The stockbroker was left with the impression that "the second quarter was going to be very poor," which he considered significant enough to prompt the sale. We therefore conclude that the July 17 tip was one of material inside information.

The tipping of material information is a violation of the fiduciary's duty but no injury occurs until the information is used by the tippee. The entry into the market of a tippee with superior knowledge poses the threat that if he trades on the basis of the inside information he may profit at the expense of investors who are disadvantaged by lack of the inside information. For this both the tipper and the tippee are liable.

The award of damages is *reversed* and the case is *remanded* for a determination of damages recoverable for tippee-trading based on the July 17, 1972, tip, to be measured in accordance with the foregoing [disgorgement measure of damages].

CASE QUESTIONS

1. Did the conversation between Moore and Cummins constitute a "tip" of *material* inside information? How extensive was the conversation? What was said?
2. Is a *tippee* liable for the profits he makes in knowingly trading on inside information? Explain.
3. Is a *tipper* liable for the profits made by a tippee who trades on the tipper's tip of inside information? Do you agree with this rule?
4. Who traded the stock in this case? The original tippee? Or remote tippees?
5. Can the parties who purchased the stock sold by the remote tippees be individually identified? What is the potential money liability of a tippee and tipper for illegal insider trading?

Policy Issue. Should *tippees* be held liable for trading on inside information? Or should liability be limited to strict *insiders?*

Is it fair to make *tippers* liable for the profits made by *tippees?* If the rule were otherwise, would there be any incentive for an insider not to tip inside information?

Economics Issue. What does the "disgorgement-of-profits" measure of damages provide? Are tippers and tippees helped by this measure of damages?

Ethics Issue. Did the tipper Moore act unethically in this case? The tippee analyst Cummins? The Loeb Rhoades & Co. stockbroker who sold shares of Liggett stock on behalf of his customers?

Social Responsibility. Do tippees owe a duty of social responsibility not to trade on inside information that comes into their possession?

Derivative Theory of Tippee Liability. In *Dirks v. SEC* the U.S. Supreme Court held that a *tippee* who traded on inside information was not liable under Section 10(b) and Rule 10b-5 *unless* the insider-*tipper* who disclosed the inside information to the tippee breached his fiduciary duty to the corporation whose securities were traded by the tippee. This "derivative theory" of tippee liability is an extension of the breach-of-fiduciary-duty test of Section 10(b) and Rule 10b-5 liability originally developed by the U.S. Supreme Court in the *Chiarella* case presented earlier in this chapter.

The *Dirks v. SEC* case follows.

DERIVATIVE THEORY OF TIPPEE LIABILITY

DIRKS v. SECURITIES AND EXCHANGE COMMISSION

103 S.Ct. 3255 (1983)
UNITED STATES SUPREME COURT

Justice Powell delivered the opinion of the Court.

In 1973, Dirks was an officer of a New York broker-dealer firm who specialized in providing investment analysis of insurance company securities to institutional investors. On March 6, Dirks received information from Ronald Secrist, a former officer of Equity Funding of America. Secrist alleged that the assets of Equity Funding, a diversified corporation primarily engaged in selling life insurance and mutual funds, were vastly overstated as the result of fraudulent corporate practices. Secrist also stated that various regulatory agencies had failed to act on similar charges made by Equity Funding employees. He urged Dirks to verify the fraud and disclose it publicly.

Dirks decided to investigate the allegations. He visited Equity Funding's headquarters in Los Angeles and interviewed several officers and employees of the corporation. The senior management denied any wrongdoing, but certain corporation employees corroborated the charges of fraud. Neither Dirks nor his firm owned or traded any Equity Funding stock, but throughout his investigation he openly discussed the information he had obtained with a number of clients and investors. Some of these persons sold their holdings of Equity Funding securities, including five investment advisers who liquidated holdings of more than $16 million.

While Dirks was in Los Angeles, he was in touch regularly with William Blundell, the *Wall Street Journal*'s Los Angeles bureau chief. Dirks urged Blundell to write a story on the fraud allegations. Blundell did not believe, however, that such a massive fraud could go undetected and declined to write the story. He feared that publishing such damaging hearsay might be libelous.

During the two-week period in which Dirks pursued his investigation and spread word of Secrist's charges, the price of Equity Funding stock fell from $26 per share to less than $15 per share. This led the New York Stock Exchange to halt trading on March 27. Shortly thereafter California insurance authorities impounded Equity Funding's records and uncovered evidence of the fraud. Only then did the Securities and Exchange Commission (SEC) file a complaint against Equity Funding and only then, on April 2, did the *Wall Street Journal* publish a front-page story based largely on information assembled by Dirks. Equity Funding immediately went into receivership.

The SEC began an investigation into Dirks' role in the exposure of the fraud. After a hearing by an administrative law judge, the SEC found that Dirks had aided and abetted violations of . . . Section 10(b) of the Securities Exchange Act of 1934, and SEC Rule 10b-5, (1982), by repeating the allegations of fraud to members of the investment community who later sold their Equity Funding stock. . . . Recognizing, however, that Dirks "played an important role in bringing [Equity Funding's] massive fraud to light," the SEC only censured him.

Dirks sought review in the Court of Appeals for the District of Columbia Circuit. The court entered judgment against Dirks "for the reasons stated by the Commission in its opinion."

In effect, the SEC's theory of tippee liability . . . appears rooted in the idea that the antifraud provisions require equal information among all traders. This conflicts with the principle set forth in *Chiarella* that only some persons, under some circumstances, will be barred from trading while in possession of material nonpublic information. Judge Wright correctly read our opinion in *Chiarella* as repudiating any notion that all traders must enjoy equal information before trading: "[T]he 'information' theory is rejected.". . . We reaffirm today that "[a] duty [to disclose] arises from the relationship between parties . . . and not merely from one's ability to acquire information because of his position in the market."

Thus, the tippee's duty to disclose or abstain is derivative from that of the insider's duty. As we noted in *Chiarella,* "[t]he tippee's obligation has been viewed as arising from his role as a participant after the fact in the insider's breach of a fiduciary duty."

[A] tippee assumes a fiduciary duty to the shareholders of a corporation not to trade on material nonpublic information only when the insider has breached his fiduciary duty to the shareholders by disclosing the information to the tippee and the tippee knows or should know that there has been a breach.

Thus, the test is whether the insider personally will benefit, directly or indirectly, from his disclosure. Absent some personal gain, there has been no breach of duty to stockholders. And absent a breach by the insider, there is no derivative breach. As Commissioner Smith stated in *Investors Management Co.:* "It is important in this type of case to focus on policing insiders and what they do . . . rather than on policing information *per se* and its possession. . . ."

Under the inside-trading and tipping rules set forth above, we find that there was no actionable violation by Dirks. It is undisputed that Dirks himself was a stranger to Equity Funding, with no pre-existing fiduciary duty to its shareholders. He took no action, directly or indirectly, that induced the shareholders or officers of Equity Funding to repose trust or confidence in him. There was no expectation by Dirks' sources that he would keep their information in confidence. Nor did Dirks misappropriate or illegally obtain the information about Equity Fund-

ing. Unless the insiders breached their *Cady, Roberts* duty to shareholders in disclosing the nonpublic information to Dirks, he breached no duty when he passed it on to investors as well as to the *Wall Street Journal.*

It is clear that neither Secrist nor the other Equity Funding employees violated their *Cady, Roberts* duty to the corporation's shareholders by providing information to Dirks. The tippers received no monetary or personal benefit for revealing Equity Funding's secrets, nor was their purpose to make a gift of valuable information to Dirks. As the facts of this case clearly indicate, the tippers were motivated by a desire to expose the fraud. In the absence of a breach of duty to shareholders by the insiders, there was no derivative breach by Dirks. Dirks therefore could not have been "a participant after the fact in [an] insider's breach of a fiduciary duty." (*Chiarella.*)

We conclude that Dirks, in the circumstances of this case, had no duty to abstain from use of the inside information that he obtained. The judgment of the Court of Appeals therefore is *reversed.*

CASE QUESTIONS

1. What was the "information theory" of tippee liability applied by the SEC in this case? Explain.
2. What was the "derivative theory" of tippee liability applied by the U.S. Supreme Court in this case? How does this differ from the information theory?
3. Who traded the securities in this case? Dirks? Or someone he tipped? Are remote tippees also relieved of liability under the derivative theory?
4. Which of the following elements are necessary to find a tippee liable under Section 10(b) and Rule 10b-5 for trading on inside information?
   a. The insider-tipper breached a fiduciary duty to the shareholders of the corporation by disclosing the material inside information.
   b. The insider-tipper benefited directly or indirectly from the disclosure.
   c. The tippee knew or should have known that he was receiving inside information.
5. Which of the following qualifies as the requisite "personal gain" by the insider-tipper in disclosing the information?

a. The insider sells the information to a stranger.
b. A client of the insider pays a bribe to the insider for the information.
c. The insider tells the inside information to his mother.
d. The insider tells the inside information to his girlfriend.
c. The insider tells the information to an investigative reporter to help uncover a fraud.

Policy Issue. Should a tippee be relieved of liability for trading on inside information merely because the insider-tipper did not breach a fiduciary duty by disclosing the information?

Economics Issue. Did Dirks benefit economically from the inside information he possessed? Who did?

Ethics Issue. Although Dirks' disclosure was not unlawful under Section 10(b) or Rule 10b-5, were his actions ethical? Were the actions of the clients and investors whom he told and who traded on the inside information lawful? Ethical?

Social Responsibility. Did Dirks meet his duty of social responsibility by assisting to uncover the Equity Funding fraud? Was society better or worse off because of Dirks' actions in this case?

SHORT-SWING PROFITS

Section 16 of the Securities Exchange Act of 1934 applies to all companies whose equity securities are registered with the SEC under Section 12 of the Act. Under Section 16(a) of the Act, any person who is an "officer" of "director" of a corporation, or who beneficially owns 10 percent or more of a class of registered securities, is defined as an "insider" for Section 16 purposes. Any person qualifying as a Section 16 insider must file specified information with the SEC at the time of attaining such status and also at the end of any month in which he purchases or sells securities of the covered corporation.

The courts are often faced with the difficult question of whether a corporate employee is an "officer" covered by Section 16(a). Generally, the courts ignore the corporate title of a person, and instead examine the duties and responsibilities of the defendant at the corporation. The courts generally also examine the defendant's opportunity to acquire material inside information in trying to determine whether the defendant qualifies as an officer covered by Section 16(a). The courts have refused to apply Section 16 to nonofficer employees of the corporation, such as secretaries or clerical workers. These nonofficer employees are, however, subject to the provisions of Section 10(b).

Section 16(b) and Section 16(c). Section 16(b) of the Securities Exchange Act of 1934 requires that any profit made by an "insider" in the purchase or sale of an equity security of a corporation within a six-month period belongs to the corporation.

To establish liability under Section 16(b), there must be a purchase and sale, or a sale and purchase, of an *equity* security by a qualified insider within less than a six-month period. A conversion of a debt security into or from an equity security has been held to be a "purchase" or "sale" covered by Section 16(b). The sale of equity stock within six months of obtaining the stock through the exercise of a stock option (considered a "purchase") has been held to violate Section 16(b).

Involuntary transactions, such as a forced redemption of securities by a corporation, or an exchange of securities in a bankruptcy proceeding, do not qualify as the requisite "purchase" or "sale" transaction for Section 16(b) purposes.

Section 16(b) is a "strict liability" provision. Generally, *no* defenses to a Section 16(b) action may be raised, such as no intent to make insider profits, forced sale for personal reasons, etc. The reasoning underlying the strict liability rule of Section 16(b) is that an insider trading in the equity securities of his corporation is *presumed* to have used inside information.

As we have seen, in a "short sale" a person sells shares he does not presently own (sells "short"), and promises to deliver the securities at a specified date in the future. The hoped-for gain occurs if the stock decreases in value between the time the "short" sale is made and the time when the securities have to be delivered. Section 16(c) of the 1934 Act makes it unlawful for Section 16 insiders to engage in "short sales" of their corporation's equity securities.

Damages Under Section 16(b).

The usual measure of damages in a Section 16(b) action is the profit realized from the matching prohibited transactions (the difference between the purchase price and sale price). Courts generally use the "profit maximization" rule when determining Section 16(b) damages. This rule ignores exact matching stock certificates in the calculation of damages. For example, if an insider under Section 16 purchases 1,000 shares of his corporations stock at $2 per share on June 1, and purchases another 1,000 shares at $4 per share on August 1, and on October 1 he sells 500 shares at $8, the recoverable profit under Section 16(b) is $6 per share, no matter which certificates he sells (sales price of $8 per share minus the June 1 purchase price of $2 per share).

Any transaction within the six-month period that produces a loss will be ignored. (No "offset" is permitted.) Generally, dividends paid on the securities during the six-month period may be awarded as part of the "profits" realized. Interest on the profit may be awarded at the discretion of the court.

The corporation may bring an action under Section 16(b) to recover "short-swing" profits. If the corporation refuses to bring an action to recover the short-swing profits, a shareholder of the corporation may bring a derivative action on behalf of the corporation to do so.

In *Merrill Lynch, Pierce, Fenner & Smith, Inc. v. Livingston*, where an employer sued an employee for allegedly making short-swing profits in violation of Section 16(b), the court found that the employee was not an "officer" as defined in Section 16(a).

SECTION 16(b)

MERRILL LYNCH, PIERCE, FENNER & SMITH, INC., v. LIVINGSTON

566 F.2d 1119 (1978)
UNITED STATES COURT OF APPEALS, NINTH CIRCUIT

Hufstedler, Circuit Judge.

Merrill Lynch, Pierce, Fenner & Smith, Inc. ("Mer-

rill Lynch") obtained judgment against its employee Livingston requiring him to pay Merrill Lynch

$14,836.37, which was the profit that he made on short-swing transactions in the securities of his employer in alleged violation of Section 16(b) of the Securities Exchange Act of 1934.

From 1951 to 1972, Livingston was employed by Merrill Lynch as a securities salesman with the title of "Account Executive." In January, 1972, Merrill Lynch began an "Account Executive Recognition Program" for its career Account Executives to reward outstanding sales records. As part of the program, Merrill Lynch awarded Livingston and 47 other Account Executives the title "Vice President." Livingston had exactly the same duties after he was awarded the title as he did before the recognition. Livingston never attended, nor was he invited or permitted to attend, meetings of the Board of Directors or the Executive Committee. He acquired no executive or policy making duties. Executive and managerial functions were performed by approximately 350 "Executive Vice Presidents."

In November and December, 1972, Livingston sold a total of 1,000 shares of Merrill Lynch stock. He repurchased 1,000 shares of Merrill Lynch stock in March, 1973, realizing the profit in question.

To achieve the beneficial purposes of the statute, the court must look behind the title of the purchaser or seller to ascertain that person's real duties. Thus, a person who does not have the title of an officer, may, in fact, have a relationship to the company which gives him the very access to insider information that the statute was designed to reach. . . . [I]n *Colby v. Klune* [t]he court defined "officer" as:

> a corporate employee performing important executive duties of such character that he would be likely, in discharging those duties, to obtain confidential information about the company's affairs that would aid him if he engaged in personal market transactions. It is immaterial how his functions are labeled or how defined in the by-laws, or that he does or does not act under the supervision of some other corporate representatives.

Job labels were no more significant to the Fourth Circuit in *Gold v. Sloan*. One of the defendants, Rumbel, had the title of Vice President. However, his title was purely " 'titular' and not real" . . .

The title "Vice President" does no more than raise an inference that the person who holds the title has the executive duties and the opportunities for confidential information that the title implies. The inference can be overcome by proof that the title was merely honorary and did not carry with it any of the executive responsibilities that might otherwise be assumed. The record in this case convincingly demonstrates that Livingston was simply a securities salesman who had none of the powers of an executive officer of Merrill Lynch.

Livingston did not have the job in fact which would have given him presumptive access to insider information. Information that is freely circulated among nonmanagement employees is not insider information within the meaning of Section 16(b), even if the general public does not have the same information.

Reversed.

CASE QUESTIONS

1. What does Section 16(b) provide? Explain.
2. Who is covered by Section 16(b)? What does Section 16(a) provide?
3. What was the defendant's title? His job function? Was he an "executive"?

Policy Issue. Should company employees be prohibited from owning securities of the corporations they work for?

Economics Issue. Under the "strict liability" test of Section 16(b), can an executive ever retain profits made on a six-month trade in his company's stock? Even if it was innocently made? Or if the sale was to obtain funds for an emergency?

Ethics Issue. Did the defendant act ethically in this case? Did Merrill Lynch?

Social Responsibility. Do corporate employees owe a duty of social responsibility not to trade in the securities of their corporation where they possess information that is not known by the general public?

ACCOUNTANT'S LIABILITY

Professionals, such as accountants and lawyers, may be held liable to clients and third parties for violations of federal securities laws. Often, the professional is the party with the "deep pocket" whom the plaintiff considers most important for recovery of damages in the action. Most securities lawsuits against accountants and other professionals are based on Section 10(b) and Rule 10b-5. Accountants and other professionals can be held both civilly and criminally liable for violating Section 10(b) or Rule 10b-5.

Civil Liability of Accountants.   Prior to 1976, accountants in many federal Court of Appeals circuits were found civilly liable under Section 10(b) and Rule 10b-5 for *negligent* conduct. Other federal circuits held that accountants and other defendants could only be held civilly liable under Section 10(b) and Rule 10b-5 for *intentional* conduct that caused injury to a plaintiff. As of 1976, accountants had been held liable for millions of dollars of damages under the negligence standard. In the important case *Ernst & Ernst v. Hochfelder* the U.S. Supreme Court resolved this disagreement between the federal circuits.

CIVIL LIABILITY OF ACCOUNTANTS

ERNST & ERNST v. HOCHFELDER

425 U.S. 185 (1976)
UNITED STATES SUPREME COURT

Mr. Justice Powell delivered the opinion of the Court.

Petitioner, Ernst & Ernst, is an accounting firm. From 1946 through 1967 it was retained by First Securities Company of Chicago (First Securities), a small brokerage firm and member of the Midwest Stock Exchange and of the National Association of Securities Dealers, to perform periodic audits of the firm's books and records. In connection with these audits Ernst & Ernst prepared for filing with the Securities and Exchange Commission (Commission) the annual reports required of First Securities under Section 17(a) of the 1934 Act. It also prepared for First Securities responses to the financial questionnaires of the Midwest Stock Exchange (Exchange).

Respondents were customers of First Securities who invested in a fraudulent securities scheme perpetrated by Leston B. Nay, president of the firm and owner of 92 percent of its stock. Nay induced the respondents to invest funds in "escrow" accounts that he represented would yield a high rate of return. Respondents did so from 1942 through 1966, with the majority of the transactions occurring in the 1950s. In fact, there were no escrow accounts as Nay converted respondents' funds to his own use immediately upon receipt. These transactions were not in the customary form of dealings between First Securities and its customers. The respondents drew their personal checks payable to Nay or a designated bank for his account. No such escrow accounts were reflected on the books and records of First Securities, and none was shown on its periodic accounting to respondents in connection with their other investments. Nor were they included in First Securities' filings with the Commission or the Exchange.

This fraud came to light in 1968 when Nay committed suicide, leaving a note that described First Securities as bankrupt and the escrow accounts as "spurious." Respondents subsequently filed this action for damages against Ernst & Ernst in the United States District Court for the Northern District of Illinois under Section 10(b) of the 1934 Act. The complaint charged that Nay's escrow scheme violated Section 10(b) and Commission Rule 10b-5, and that Ernst & Ernst had "aided and abetted" Nay's violations by its "failure" to conduct proper audits of First Securities. As revealed through discovery, respondents' cause of action rested on a theory of negligent nonfeasance. The premise was that Ernst & Ernst had failed to utilize "appropriate auditing procedures" in its audits of First Securities, thereby failing to discover internal practices of the firm said to prevent an effective audit. The practice principally relied on was Nay's rule that only he could open mail addressed to him at First Securities or addressed to First Securities to his attention, even if it arrived in his absence. Respondents contended that if Ernst & Ernst had conducted a proper audit, it would have discovered this "mail rule." The existence of the rule then would have been disclosed in reports to the Exchange and to the Commission by Ernst & Ernst as an irregular procedure that prevented an effective audit. This would have led to an investigation of Nay that would have revealed the fraudulent scheme. Respondents specifically disclaimed the existence of fraud or intentional misconduct on the part of Ernst & Ernst.

Section 10(b) makes unlawful the use or employment of "any manipulative or deceptive device or contrivance" in contravention of Commission rules. The words "manipulative or deceptive" used in conjunction with "device or contrivance" strongly suggest that Section 10(b) was intended to proscribe knowing or intentional misconduct.

In its *amicus curiae* brief, however, the Commission contends that nothing in the language "manipulative or deceptive device or contrivance" limits its operation to knowing or intentional practices. . . . The argument simply ignores the use of the words "manipulative," "device," and "contrivance"—terms that make unmistakable a congressional intent to proscribe a type of conduct quite different from negligence. Use of the word "manipulative" is especially significant. It is and was virtually a term of art when used in connection with securities markets. It connotes intentional or willful conduct designed to deceive or defraud investors by controlling or artificially affecting the price of securities.

Although the extensive legislative history of the 1934 Act is bereft of any explicit explanation of Congress' intent, we think the relevant portions of that history support our conclusion that Section 10(b) was addressed to practices that involve some element of *scienter* and cannot be read to impose liability for negligent conduct alone.

We have addressed, to this point, primarily the language and history of Section 10(b). The Commission contends, however, that Subsections (b) and (c) of Rule 10b-5 are cast in language which—if standing alone—could encompass both intentional and negligent behavior. . . . [R]ule 10b-5 was adopted pursuant to authority granted the Commission under Section 10(b). The rulemaking power granted to an administrative agency charged with the administration of a federal statute is not the power to make law. Rather, it is " 'the power to adopt regulations to carry into effect the will of Congress as expressed by the statute.' "

The judgment of the Court of Appeals is *reversed.*

Mr. Justice Blackmun, with whom **Mr. Justice Brennan** joins, dissenting.

Once again the Court interprets Section 10(b) of the Securities Exchange Act of 1934, and the Securities and Exchange Commission's Rule 10b-5, restrictively and narrowly and thereby stultifies recovery for the victim.

Perhaps the Court is right, but I doubt it. It seems to me, however, that an investor can be victimized just as much by negligent conduct as by positive deception, and that it is not logical to drive a wedge between the two, saying that Congress clearly intended the one but certainly not the other. . . .

"In our complex society the accountant's certificate and the lawyer's opinion can be instruments for inflicting pecuniary loss more potent than the chisel or the crowbar."

CASE QUESTIONS

1. What was Mr. Nay's "mail rule"? Describe the plaintiff's argument as to how Ernst and Ernst (E&E) was negligent.
2. What law did the plaintiff allege that E&E violated? Did the plaintiff allege that E&E was negligent or fraudulent?
3. Define *scienter*. Do you think that only intentional conduct was intended to be covered by Section 10(b) when Congress drafted the Securities Exchange Act of 1934?
4. The Supreme Court dismissed the plaintiff's action against E&E because the plaintiff only alleged neglience against E&E. If the case had gone to trial, do you think that the plaintiff could have proved that E&E acted with scienter?

Policy Issue. Should Section 10(b) be interpreted to include *negligent* conduct? Can investors "be victimized just as much by negligent conduct as by positive deception"?

Economics Issue. If the Supreme Court had held that actions based on negligence (malpractice) could be brought under Section 10(b), what would have been the economic implications for the accounting profession?

Ethics Issue. Were the actions of Mr. Nay unethical in this case?

Social Responsibility. Who do accountants owe a duty of social responsibility to? Their client? Shareholders? Bondholders? Consumers?

After the *Ernst & Ernst* case, accountants and other defendants can only be held liable for *intentional* conduct or gross negligence under Section 10(b) and Rule 10b-5. Negligent conduct is not a basis for a lawsuit under this section and rule. By contrast, accountants and other defendants may be held liable for *negligent* conduct under Section 11 of the Securities Act of 1933 where there has been a misrepresentation or omission of a material fact in a registration statement and prospectus. Further, accountants and other defendants can always be sued by injured plaintiffs in a state court civil *malpractice* action under the common-law theory of negligence.

Criminal Liability of Accountants. Accountants and other defendants may be found criminally liable for *willfully* violating Section 10(b) and Rule 10b-5. The criminal penalties for violating Section 10(b) are a fine of not more than $10,000 and/or imprisonment for not more than five years.

Accountants and other defendants can be held criminally liable under Section 32(a) of the Securities Exchange Act of 1934 for *willfully* making a false or misleading statement in any report required to be filed with the SEC. An accountant and other defendants can also be held criminally liable for violating an SEC injunction.

U.S. v. Natelli is the leading case in which an accountant was held criminally liable for violating the securities laws.

CRIMINAL LIABILITY OF ACCOUNTANTS
UNITED STATES v. NATELLI

527 F.2d 311 (1975)
UNITED STATES COURT OF APPEALS, SECOND CIRCUIT

Gurfein, Circuit Judge.

Anthony M. Natelli and Joseph Scansaroli appeal from judgments of conviction entered in the United States District Court for the Southern District of New York on December 27, 1974 after a four-week trial before the Hon. Harold R. Tyler and a jury. Judge Tyler imposed a one-year sentence and a $10,000 fine upon Natelli, suspending all but 60 days of imprisonment, and a one-year sentence and a $2,500 fine upon Scansaroli, suspending all but 10 days of the imprisonment.

Both appellants are certified public accountants. Natelli was the partner in charge of the Washington, D.C. office of Peat, Marwick, Mitchell & Co. ("Peat"), a large independent firm of auditors, and the engagement partner with respect to Peat's audit engagement for National Student Marketing Corporation ("Marketing"). Scansaroli was an employee of Peat, assigned as audit supervisor on that engagement.

Count Two of the indictment charged that, in violation of Section 32(a) of the Securities Exchange Act of 1934, four of Marketing's officers and the appellants, as independent auditors, "wilfully and knowingly made and caused to be made false and misleading statements with respect to material facts" in a proxy statement for Marketing dated September 27, 1969 and filed with the Securities and Exchange Commission (SEC) in accordance with Section 14 of the 1934 Act.

The proxy statement was issued by Marketing in connection with a special meeting of its stockholders to consider *inter alia* a charter amendment increasing its authorized capital stock and the merger of six companies, including Interstate National Corporation ("Interstate") into Marketing.

Marketing was formed in 1966 by Cortes W. Randell. It provided to major corporate accounts a diversified range of advertising, promotional and marketing services designed to reach the youth market.

In late September or early October 1968 (after the close of the fiscal year), Randell and Bernard Kurek, Marketing's Comptroller, met with both appellants and discussed the method of accounting that Marketing had been using with respect to fixed-fee programs. In the fixed-fee program, Marketing would develop overall marketing programs for the client to reach the youth market by utilizing a combination of the mailings, posters and other advertising services offered by Marketing.

The difficulty immediately encountered was that the [client] "commitments" had not been booked during the fiscal year, and were not in writing. The Marketing stock which had initially been sold at $6 per share was selling in the market by September 1968 for $80, an increase of $74 in five months. A refusal to book the oral "commitments" would have resulted in Marketing's showing a large loss for the fiscal year—according to Kurek's computations, a loss of $232,000.

Pursuant to Randell's urging, Scansaroli did not seek any written verifications. He accepted a schedule prepared by Kurek which showed about $1.7 million in purported "commitments."

On the basis of the above, Natelli decided not only to recognize income on a percentage-of-completion basis, but to permit adjustment to be made on the books after the close of the fiscal year in the amount of $1.7 million for such "unbilled accounts receivable." This adjustment turned the loss for the year into a handsome profit of $388,031, showing an apparent doubling of the profit of the prior year.

After the 1968 audit had been given a full certificate by the auditors on November 14, 1968, . . . things began to happen with respect to the $1.7 million of "sales" that had been recorded as income after fiscal year end. Within five months of publication of the annual report, by May 1969, Marketing had written off over $1 million of the $1.7 million in "sales" which the auditors had permitted to be booked.

[A]ppellants were asked to design the write-off. . . . Instead of reducing 1968 earnings commensurately, however, no such reduction was made. Appellants were informed by tax accountants in Peat's employ that a certain deferred tax item should be reversed, resulting in a tax credit that happened to be approximately the same amount as the profit to be written off. Scansaroli "netted" this extraordinary item (the tax credit) with an unrelated ordinary item (the write-off of sales and profits). By this procedure he helped to conceal on the books the actual write-off of profits, further using the device of rounding off the tax item to make it conform exactly to the write-off. The effect of the netting procedure was to bury the retroactive adjustment which should have shown a material decrease in earnings for the fiscal year ended August 31, 1968.

THE PROXY STATEMENT

As part of the proxy statement, appellants set about to draft a footnote purporting to reconcile the Company's prior reported net sales and earnings from the 1968 report with restated amounts resulting from pooled companies reflected retroactively. The earnings summary in the proxy statement included companies acquired after fiscal 1968 and their pooled earnings. The footnote was the only place in the proxy statement which would have permitted an interested investor to see what Marketing's performance had been in its preceding fiscal year 1968, as retroactively adjusted, separate from the earnings and sales of the companies it had acquired in fiscal 1969.

At Natelli's direction, Scansaroli subtracted the written-off Marketing sales from the 1968 sales figures for the seven later acquired pooled companies without showing any retroactive adjustment for Marketing's own fiscal 1968 figures. There was no disclosure in the footnote that over $1 million of previously reported 1968 sales of Marketing had been written off. All narrative disclosure in the footnote was stricken by Natelli. This was a violation of Accounting Principles Board Opinion Number 9, which requires disclosure of prior adjustments which affect the net income of prior periods.

The proxy statement also required an unaudited statement of nine months' earnings through May 31, 1969. This was prepared by the Company, with the assistance of Peat on the same percentage of completion basis as in the 1968 audited statement. A commitment from Pontiac Division of General Motors amounting to $1,200,000 was produced two months after the end of the fiscal period. It was dated April 28, 1969.

The proxy statement was to be printed at the Pandick Press in New York on August 15, 1969. At about 3 A.M. on that day, Natelli informed Randell that the "sale" to the Pontiac Division for more than $1 million could not be treated as a valid commitment because the letter from Pontiac was not a legally binding obligation. Randell responded at once that he had a "commitment from Eastern Airlines" in a somewhat comparable amount attributable to the nine months fiscal period (which had ended more than two months earlier). Kelly, a salesman for Marketing, arrived at the printing plant several hours later with a commitment letter from Eastern Airlines, dated August 14, 1969, purporting to confirm an $820,000 commitment ostensibly entered into on May 14, just before the end of the nine-month fiscal period of September 1, 1968 through May 31, 1969. When the proxy statement was printed in final form, the Pontiac "sale" had been deleted, but the Eastern "commitment" had been inserted in its place.

The proxy statement was filed with the SEC on September 30, 1969.

NATELLI—SUFFICIENCY OF EVIDENCE

It is hard to probe the intent of a defendant. Circumstantial evidence, particularly with proof of motive, where available, is often sufficient to convince a reasonable man of criminal intent beyond a reasonable doubt. When we deal with a defendant who is a professional accountant, it is even harder, at times, to distinguish between simple errors of judgment and errors made with sufficient criminal intent to support a conviction, especially when there is no financial gain to the accountant other than his legitimate fee.

The original action of Natelli in permitting the booking of unbilled sales after the close of the fiscal period in an amount sufficient to convert a loss into a profit was contrary to sound accounting practice, . . . When the uncollectibility, and indeed, the nonexistence of these large receivables was established in 1969, the revelation stood to cause Natelli severe criticism and possible liability. He had a motive, therefore, intentionally to conceal the write-offs that had to be made.

Whether or not the deferred tax item was properly converted to a tax credit, the jury had a right to infer that "netting" the extraordinary item against ordinary earnings on the books in a special journal entry was, in the circumstances, motivated by a desire to conceal.

Honesty should have impelled appellants to disclose in the footnote which annotated their own audited statement for fiscal 1968 that substantial write-offs had been taken, after year end, to reflect a loss for the year. A simple desire to right the wrong that had been perpetrated on the stockholders and others by the false audited financial statement should have dictated that course. The failure to make open disclosure could hardly have been inadvertent, or a jury at least could so find, for appellants were themselves involved in determining the write-offs and their accounting treatment. The concealment of the retroactive adjustments to Marketing's 1968 year revenues and earnings could properly have been found to have been intentional for the very purpose of hiding earlier errors. There was evidence that Natelli himself changed the footnote to its final form.

The Eastern contract was a matter for deep suspicion because it was substituted so rapidly for the Pontiac contract to which Natelli had objected, and which had, itself, been produced after the end of the fiscal period, though dated earlier. It was still another unbilled commitment produced by Marketing long after the close of the fiscal period. Its spectacular appearance, as Natelli himself noted at the time, made its replacement of the Pontiac contract "weird." The Eastern "commitment" was not only in substitution for the challenged Pontiac "commitment" but strangely close enough in amount to leave the projected earnings figures for the proxy statement relatively intact. . . . Nevertheless, it was booked as if more than $500,000 of it had already been earned.

Natelli contends that he had no duty to verify the Eastern "commitment" because the earnings statement within which it was included was "unaudited."

This raises the issue of the duty of the CPA in relation to an unaudited financial statement contained within a proxy statement where the figures are reviewed and to some extent supplied by the auditors. It is common ground that the auditors were "associated" with the statement and were required to object to anything they actually "knew" to be materially false.

We reject the argument of insufficiency [of evidence] as to Natelli, who could have pointed out the error of his previous certification and deliberately failed to do so, . . .

SCANSAROLI—SUFFICIENCY OF EVIDENCE

There is some merit to Scansaroli's point that he was simply carrying out the judgments of his superior Natelli. The defense of obedience to higher authority has always been troublesome. There is no sure yardstick to measure criminal responsibility except by measurement of the degree of awareness on the part of a defendant that he is participating in a criminal act, in the absence of physical coercion such as a soldier might face. Here the motivation to conceal undermines Scansaroli's argument that he was merely implementing Natelli's instructions, at least with respect to concealment of matters that were within his own ken.

We think the jury could properly have found him guilty on the specification relating to the footnote.

With respect to the major item, the Eastern commitment, we think Scansaroli stands in a position different from that of Natelli. . . . Since in the hierarchy of the accounting firm it was not his responsibility to decide whether to book the Eastern contract, his mere adjustment of the figures to reflect it under orders was not a matter for his discretion. . . . [H]e cannot be held to have acted in reckless disregard of the facts.

We have considered the other arguments raised by appellants and find them without merit.

CASE QUESTIONS

1. What type of contracts were entered into between Marketing and its clients? How did Peat, Marwick, Mitchell & Co. (Peat) report these commitments in the 1968 annual report? Explain.
2. What portion, in dollars, of the oral commitments had to be written off? How was the write-off reported by Peat in the proxy statement? Was this proper under accounting principles?

3. Was the Pontiac commitment included in the 1969 earnings statement which was included in the proxy statement? If not, what was substituted? Was this proper?
4. In order to find a defendant criminally liable, must the court find actual intent of the defendant? Or can criminal intent be *inferred* from the circumstances of the case? If actual intent had to be shown, would there be any criminal convictions?
5. Did the court accept Scansaroli's defense that he was merely "carrying out the judgments of his superiors"? Why or why not?

Policy Issue. Should an accountant be held criminally liable under the securities laws? What are the pro and con arguments?

Economics Issue. Do you think the *U.S. v. Natelli* case had any impact on how accounting firms selected clients?

Ethics Issue. Were the activities of Natelli and Scansaroli ethical in this case? Why do you think Natelli and Scansaroli acted as they did in this case?

Social Responsibility. Does an accountant owe a duty of loyalty to his employer? Does an accountant owe a duty of social responsibility to divulge information of criminal activities he discovers during his work? Do these duties ever conflict?

NOTE: Natelli was later pardoned by President Nixon.

LIABILITY OF SECURITIES PROFESSIONALS

Securities brokers, dealers, underwriters and others may be held liable to shareholders under the securities laws for a number of activities, including:

1. "scalping" securities
2. "churning" securities
3. failure to "know the securities" traded
4. failure to "know the customer" to whom securities are sold.

"Scalping." A person may be held liable for fraud for "scalping" a security. In scalping, a person purchases a security and then recommends the security to investors in order to raise the price of the security. Securities brokers, dealers, and underwriters may be held liable for "scalping," as well as financial consultants, finance writers, and editors for newspapers and magazines.

"Churning." A securities broker may be held liable for "churning" a customer's account. Churning occurs where it is shown that there have been "excessive" trades instituted by a securities broker on behalf of a customer in order to obtain a commission on each transaction.

"Know the Security." A securities broker may be held liable for the unsubstantiated recommendation of securities. A securities broker is under a duty to "know the security" prior to making recommendations to clients to trade in the security. The test is whether the securities broker has conducted a sufficient investigation prior to recommending a transaction in the security.

"Know the Customer." A securities broker is under a duty to "know the customer" prior to recommending that a customer trade in securities. The

customer's age, education, financial status, and business experience are relevant factors that the securities broker should know before recommending that the customer trade in a certain security. The information that a broker is required to know prior to recommending a "blue chip" stock may differ from the information he should know before recommending trading in a high-risk security, such as a new issue.

Trend of the Law

Insider trading is presently one of the most important issues facing the SEC. The SEC has recently adopted a policy of increasing its enforcement efforts against unlawful insider trading. The volume of insider trading cases brought by the SEC has been increasing yearly, and is predicted to increase even more in the future.

Once these cases reach trial, the courts must apply the narrow standards of liability adopted by the U.S. Supreme Court in the *Chiarella* and *Dirks* cases. In order to meet the tests announced in these two cases, the SEC must allege and prove that the insider breached a fiduciary duty to the shareholders of the corporation, and that the insider-tipper received some personal gain from disclosing the material nonpublic information. Friendship, sexual favors, and prestige have each been alleged by the SEC and private plaintiffs to constitute the requisite "personal gain" received by the insider-tipper in support of a Section 10(b) insider-trading action.

A few federal District Courts have applied a "subjective" standard to Section 16(b) actions, holding that if no "abuse" of the insider's position is shown, Section 16(b) liability will not be imposed. This softening trend in applying Section 16(b) should continue in the future.

REVIEW QUESTIONS

1. Under an antitrust consent decree, Blue Chip Stamps ("New Blue Chip") was required to offer a large number of common stock shares in its new business to retailers who had previously used the stamp service of its corporate predecessor, Blue Chip Stamp Co. ("Old Blue Chip"). Ninety percent of Old Blue Chip's stock had been owned by nine retailers. Old Blue Chip was sued for antitrust violations and, as part of the settlement, it was required to sell a large portion of shares at a fixed price to other retailers who had used the old service and suffered damages leading to the antitrust action.

   New Blue Chip felt that the price of the shares was artificially low. Therefore, the corporate officers devised a scheme to dissuade potential retail investors from purchasing the stock by making materially misleading statements in the prospectus. The statements contained an overly pessimistic appraisal of the new business which discouraged roughly 50 percent of the potential investors from acquiring any New Blue Chip stock. New Blue Chip was able to sell the remaining stock to the public at a substantially higher price. A group of investors who did not purchase any stock filed a class action suit, charging a violation of Section 10(b) and Rule 10b-5. The group alleged that as a result of the misleading statements, they suffered $21,400,000 in damages, representing the lost opportunity to purchase the stock. Will the potential investors be successful? In an ethical sense, should the company be liable?

2. Taylor was president, general manager and director of Boston Electro Steel Casting Inc. (BESCO). During 1954 and 1955, the company faced severe financial difficulties due to a declining market, so the board of directors called a meeting to decide if the company should be sold or liquidated. At the meeting, the other directors asked Taylor if he "knew of any material change in the affairs of the company in the past months which would cause us to have any different opinion about the company" He replied that, "there was none, it was about the same." In fact, since the other directors left the company's affairs almost exclusively to Taylor, only he knew that the company had received an influx of new orders which would make it more profitable the following year. He also did not disclose that the company had changed its method of inventory accounting, which substantially depressed profits for 1955. In early 1956, following the directors' meeting, Taylor purchased virtually all of the company's stock from the other directors for $40,000. In December 1957, he sold it for $700,000. The other directors filed suit and alleged that Taylor had committed fraud as prohibited by Section 10(b) and Rule 10b-5. Will the plaintiffs be successful? If successful, what damages may they recover?

3. Santa Fe Industries acquired 95 percent of Kirby Lumber Company. Under Delaware state law, a parent company that owns at least 90 percent of the stock of a subsidiary may merge with the subsidiary without the approval of the minority shareholders. The parent is required to pay the fair value of the shares outstanding; should the minority shareholders dispute that amount, they may petition the Delaware courts to appraise the fair value. Santa Fe decided to buy out the minority shareholders for $150 per share without their approval. These shareholders were given a statement with the relevant financial data about Kirby, the appraisals of its assets and an investment banking firm's stock appraisal. In this statement, Santa Fe disclosed that Kirby's physical assets had been independently appraised at $640 per share. Morgan Stanley, the investment banking firm that was hired to value the stock, used these appraisals to value Kirby's stock at $125 per share. Rather than contesting the valuation, the minority stockholders sued, alleging violations of Section 10(b) ("using a deceptive or manipulative device") and Rule 10b-5 (any act "which operated or would operate as a fraud or deceit"). The complaint alleged that Santa Fe had breached its fiduciary duties to the shareholders since the shares had been undervalued and the merger served no justifiable business purpose. Will the shareholders be successful in stopping this corporate "freeze-

out"? State policy reasons arguing whether or not this type of freeze-out is unfair and should be protected by the Securities Acts.

4. Relying on the advice of their friend, Myzel, in 1946 four investors—Field, King, Verteney, and Cohen—all purchased various numbers of shares of Lakeside Plastics and Engraving (LPE), a close corporation, for $10 a share. Myzel was a director of the company, which made advertising signs. From 1946 to 1952, the company struggled, never paying any dividends. In 1953, the company secured a large contract with Blatz Brewery that guaranteed to increase sales dramatically and, as a result, the company made a large profit in the first four months of the year. The interim financial statements reflecting these increases were not disclosed at the June shareholders' meeting. Shortly thereafter, Myzel, acting as an undisclosed agent for Levine, the majority owner, purchased all the shares back from the investors for prices ranging from $6.67 to $45.00 a share. In each instance, Myzel stated that the stock was virtually worthless, that the company was not making money, that he was going to end his affiliation with the firm and that the company might go bankrupt. Myzel then later sold these shares to Levine for a substantial profit. Myzel was also paid for his services in buying the stock. Beginning in 1954, LPE's sales and profits increased rapidly. Fields, King, Verteney, and Cohen decided to sue Myzel and Levine under Section 10(b) and Rule 10b-5, alleging fraud. Were they successful? Why?

5. In 1960, Channing Corporation and its individual directors decided to acquire a majority interest in Agricultural Insurance Company (Agricultural). In order to facilitate the acquisition, Channing instituted a purchase program in which the firm was able to obtain about 35 percent of Agricultural's outstanding common stock through purchases on the over-the-counter market. Under the security registration laws in effect in 1960, Channing was not required to register this interest in Agricultural with the SEC. In fact, Channing did not disclose the existence of its buying program to the public. Once Channing obtained a 35 percent share, the firm placed new directors on Agricultural's board. This new board then decided to substantially reduce Agricultural's quarterly dividend. The board intended to artificially depress the price of Agricultural's stock. As a result of this dividend reduction, the value of Agricultural's stock did, in fact, drop sharply. This reduction enabled Channing to purchase the remaining 15 percent share that it required to gain complete control over Agricultural.

Cochran was a former stockholder who sold his stock during the price depression. He received $16 less per share than he would have received if he had sold the stock the day before Agricultural's dividend announcement. Cochran sued Channing and its individual directors, alleging that the firm committed fraud in violation of Section 10(b) and Rule 10b-5. Does Cochran have a valid claim?

6. On May 8, 1967, after unsuccessfully trying to merge with Kern County Land Co., Occidental Petroleum offered to purchase 500,000 shares of Kern Stock for $85 per share. By May 10 Occidental had purchased 500,000 shares, more than 10 percent of Kern's outstanding shares. On May 11, Occidental reopened its offer and acquired 337,549 additional shares.

Immediately after Occidental's announcement, Kern's directors tried to stop the takeover attempt by defensively merging with another firm. On May 19, Kern directors announced that they had approved a merger proposal by Tenneco. Tenneco would supply one share of preferred Tenneco stock for each share of Kern common stock. Occidental saw that its takeover attempt was being blocked and entered into negotiations directly with Tenneco, which was worried about having a large, potentially dissident minority shareholder. On June 2, Occidental and Tenneco agreed to an option contract that allowed Tenneco to purchase all of its preferred stock back from Occidental at $105 per share should the merger go through.

On August 30, the merger closed between Kern and Tenneco. Occidental abstained from voting any of its shares either way at the shareholder's meeting. Tenneco then exercised its option with Occidental and reacquired all of Tenneco's preferred stock. Occidental realized $19 million in profits on the exchange. Tenneco then filed suit, claiming that under Section 10(b) Occidental was a 10 percent beneficial owner and that since both Occidental's "purchase" and "sale" of the equities occurred within a six-month period, Occidental was required to reimburse Tenneco $19 million. Did Occidental have to disgorge the profits that it made on these transactions?

7. Provident Security Company was a personal holding company that sold some of its assets to Foremost-McKesson, Inc. Part of the purchase price paid by Foremost was in the form of immediately convertible debentures which, if converted, would comprise more than 10 percent of Foremost's outstanding common stock. A few days later, Provident sold some of the debentures to an underwriting group for a cash amount that exceeded the face value of the debentures. After making cash and debenture distributions to its stockholders, Provident Securities dissolved. Prior to dissolution, Provident, realizing that the sale of the securities came within a six-month period after purchase, went to federal District Court seeking a declaratory judgment that it was not liable to Foremost under Section 10(b) for the profits made. Should the court have issued the declaratory judgment? Given the purpose of Section 10(b), should Provident have been liable for the profits?

8. Belock Instrument Corporation derived a large portion of income from contracts it held with the Federal Government. In connection with these contracts, the company systematically and illegally overcharged the government. The Board of Directors knew of these hidden charges. The company's financial statements were not adjusted to reflect this illegal income; as a result, both net assets and net income were considerably understated. Belock filed these financial statements with both the American Stock Exchange and the SEC. Relying on Belock's financial statements filed with the SEC, Heit purchased $5,000 in face-amount convertible debentures. Also relying upon Belock's financial statements, Volk purchased 200 shares of Belock's common stock. Subsequent to these purchases, the Government discovered the overcharges and ordered repayment. Both Heit and Volk sued, alleging that Belock committed fraud in violation of Section 10(b) and Rule 10b-5. Will they be successful?

9. Douglas Aircraft Company planned to offer $75,000,000 in convertible subordinated debentures. The firm hired Merrill Lynch, Pierce, Fenner and Smith to be the chief managing underwriter on the issue. A registration statement was filed on June 7, which became effective on July 12. In the registration statement, Douglas disclosed its earnings for the first five months of the fiscal year, showing a profit of 85¢ per share. Soon thereafter, it became clear to Douglas' management that earnings for the entire six-month period as well as for the remainder of that year and the following year would be substantially lower. Douglas disclosed this material information to Merrill Lynch solely as a result of its connection with the debenture offering. During the period immediately after the disclosure, Merrill Lynch disclosed this confidential information to 13 institutional clients. Merrill Lynch and the clients knew that the information had not been disclosed publicly. During the period before disclosure by Douglas to the public, these investors sold from their existing positions or made short sales of more than 165,000 shares, over 50 percent of the issues traded during the period. The price of Douglas common stock on the New York Stock Exchange fell from 86¼ to 76 during this period. Plaintiffs, who purchased shares during this period, formed a class action and sued both Merrill Lynch and their institutional clients under Section 10(b) and Rule 10b-5, alleging fraud. Will the suit be successful? If so, who is liable and what damages may be recovered?

10. Weis, a securities brokerage firm, hired Touche Ross & Co., a public accounting firm, to audit the company's books in compliance with SEC reporting requirements. Section 17(a) of the Securities Act of 1934 requires all brokerage firms to file annual financial reports to the SEC. Subsequent to the audit, in which Touche Ross gave an unqualified opinion, Weis encountered severe financial problems and was taken over by a trustee in accordance with Federal law. There was no evidence to indicate that Touche Ross knew that Weis was in a precarious financial situation. Weis was liquidated but the firm's assets and insurance were not sufficient to cover all investor losses. A group of investors decided to sue Touche Ross, alleging that the firm should have known about the financial difficulties and therefore had misled potential investors into depositing money with Weis. Will the investors be successful?

11. Campbell, a financial columnist for the Los Angeles *Herald-Examiner*, wrote a column that very favorably described the financial condition of American Systems, Inc. American stock was traded on the over-the-counter market. Campbell obtained the information used in the column directly from an interview with American's directors. These directors intentionally made material misrepresentations and omissions, hoping that this false information would be printed and that this would inflate the price of American's stock. Campbell had no reason to believe that the information was incorrect; however, he did not independently verify any of the facts. Just before the column was published, Campbell bought 5,000 shares of stock directly from American at a 42 percent discount. Immediately after the column was published, the price rose rapidly and Campbell sold 2,000 shares, enabling him to recover his entire investment. On 22 previous occasions, Campbell had bought stock in a small company just prior to

publishing a favorable article and in all but one case he was able to sell the stock a short time later for a profit.

Before the article was published, Zweig and Bruno had entered into an agreement to merge their company with American. As a result of this contractual obligation, Zweig and Bruno were forced to buy the shares of American at an inflated price. Zweig and Bruno discovered Campbell's dealing and sued under Rule 10b-5, alleging fraud. They claimed that Campbell should have fully disclosed to his readers that he bought American stock at a discount and intended to sell it at a profit after the column was published and the price rose. Will Zweig and Bruno be successful?

15 PROXY CONTESTS AND TENDER OFFERS

INTRODUCTION

In the world of corporate finance, management and shareholders often find themselves embroiled in battles for control of their corporation against outside or competing parties. "Friendly" takeovers occur usually through the merger of two corporations where the incumbent (sitting) management of the target corporation has knowledge of the transaction and, as required by law, formally approves the transaction by resolution of the board of directors. In a *merger,* shareholders of the target corporation also have to formally approve the merger, in that they are receiving securities and/or cash from the dominant corporation in exchange for their present stock in the target corporation.

Hostile takeover attempts occur when incumbent management opposes a takeover of the corporation, usually for the stated reason of protecting the interests of shareholders, but often prompted by the unstated desire to protect their own jobs. Hostile struggles for control of a corporation can occur by two methods: proxy contest and tender offer. Proxy contests and tender offers are both regulated by federal securities laws.

The Proxy Contest.   In a proxy contest, a struggle for control of the corporation is waged by two groups, the *incumbent* management and an *insurgent* group, who try to win sufficient shareholder support to be elected to the board of directors of the corporation at the annual or special shareholders' meeting. The struggle is called a "proxy contest" because shareholder voting in most large corporations is conducted almost entirely by *proxy*, rather than personal attendance by shareholders at the meetings. The group that controls the board of directors thereby controls the management and policies of the corporation.

The Tender Offer.   The second method for waging a struggle for control of a corporation is through a tender offer. In a tender offer, the tendering corporation or group makes an offer to the shareholders of the target corporation to *purchase* all or a portion of their stock. In essence, the tendering company, if it can purchase enough stock in the target company to gain shareholder control, can then vote out the incumbent directors and install its own management and policies to operate the target corporation. In a tender offer the tendering group or company actually purchases *shares* of *stock* in the target corporation, whereas in a proxy contest the insurgent group attempts to elicit shareholder *votes* without purchasing stock from the shareholders. Even in a proxy contest, however, the insurgent group generally owns a substantial block of stock in the targeted corporation.

Proxy contests and tender offers are both regulated by federal securities laws. State law also regulates certain aspects of proxy solicitation and tender offers.

SOLICITATION OF PROXIES

Because of the tremendous number of shares that large corporations have outstanding, and the fact that the ownership of such stock is usually spread among thousands of shareholders, control of modern corporations is usually maintained *not* by ownership of the majority of the shares of the corporation, but by controlling shareholder *voting* of the corporation. In order to gain voting control of a corporation, proxies must be solicited from individual shareholders. A "proxy" is a written document from the owner of the securities authorizing some other party known as the "proxy holder" to *vote* the shares of the stock as directed by the owner of the shares. In the solicitation of proxies, contests between opposing groups often occur.

Management has the right, and duty, to solicit votes and proxies from shareholders for a number of corporate transactions. Proxies are generally solicited for voting for the board of directors, approval of mergers, approval of auditors, and other major business decisions of the corporation. Shareholder vote is not required for the day-to-day decisions required to operate the corporation.

Federal Proxy Rules.   Although proxies were once illegal under common law, they are permitted by most state statutes and the Securities Exchange Act of 1934. Section 14(a) of the 1934 Act gives the SEC authority to regulate the solicitation of proxies. Federal proxy rules apply to all companies registered under Section 12 of the 1934 Act ("registered companies"), and "over-the-counter" companies registered under Section 12(g) of the Act.

In this excerpt from *TSC Industries, Inc. v. Northway, Inc.*, 426 U.S. 438 (1976), Justice Thurgood Marshall of the U.S. Supreme Court discusses the purposes of federal proxy rules.

The proxy rules promulgated by the Securities and Exchange Commission under the Securities Exchange Act of 1934 bar the use of proxy statements that are false or misleading with respect to the presentation or omission of material facts. . . .

As we have noted on more than one occasion, Section 14(a) of the Securities Exchange Act "was intended to promote 'the free exercise of the voting rights of stockholders' by ensuring that proxies would be solicited with 'explanation to the stockholder of the real nature of the questions for which authority to cast his vote is sought.'" *Mills v. Electric Auto-Lite Co.*

The Proxy Statement.   Under Section 14(a) of the 1934 Act, a company planning to solicit proxies from its shareholders must file a "preliminary" copy of the proposed proxy statement, the proxy, and any additional solicitation materials with the SEC at least ten days before the materials are sent to the shareholders. A copy of the actual proxy materials sent to the shareholders must also be filed with the SEC. Under the federal rules, the *proxy statement* must contain:

1. a statement identifying for whom the solicitation is made
2. the means (e.g., mails) to be used for the solicitation
3. which party bears the cost of the solicitation
4. the amount already spent on the solicitation
5. an estimate of the monies to be spent on the proxy solicitation.

Detailed information must be disclosed as to the specific matter for which the proxy is being solicited (e.g., election of directors, merger).

Where directors are to be elected, a proxy statement must identify and give detailed information about the nominees of the soliciting party, the other directors whose terms of office continue beyond the meeting, and the officers of the issuer. Where a merger or authorization to issue new securities is proposed, financial statements of the company must be included in the proxy statement.

Shareholder Proposals.   The Securities Exchange Act of 1934 provides that under certain conditions a *dissident* shareholder who disagrees with specific policies of management may submit a proposal to be considered by the other shareholders. If management does not oppose the proposal, it may be included in the proxy statement issued by the company to its shareholders. If management opposes the proposal, the Act provides that the shareholder has the right to place a statement of up to 200 words regarding the proposal in the proxy statement issued by the company *if* the following conditions are met:

1. The proposal does not violate any state or federal law, including federal securities laws.

2. The proposal relates to the issuer's *business,* and does not merely advocate a personal position or political or social issue.
3. The proposal relates to a business *policy* issue, and does not merely concern the ordinary day-to-day operation of the company.
4. The proposal does not relate to the payment of a specific amount in dividends, which is a matter within the sole discretion of management.
5. No similar proposal has been presented to shareholders within the past five years that has been defeated within the past three years.

For example, in *Medical Committee for Human Rights v. SEC,* 432 F.2d 659 (1970), a dissident shareholder submitted for inclusion in the proxy statement of Dow Chemical Company a proposal to have the shareholders vote on whether the company should or should not continue to make napalm, which was used as a weapon by the U.S. military in Vietnam. The management of Dow Chemical Company opposed the proposal, and the courts upheld the management's decision, finding that the proposal was a political and social issue that did not qualify for inclusion in the proxy statement under federal securities laws. (In retrospect, based on the Agent Orange settlement, was this a wise decision?)

PROXY CONTESTS

Proxy contests usually result when an "insurgent" group of shareholders, who often have acquired a substantial ownership position in the company, challenge the incumbent management of the corporation for control of the company through the election of the board of directors. Under most state laws, the board of directors of a corporation must be elected by the shareholders each year. Some state corporation laws allow a board of directors to be *staggered.* For example, if there are nine members of a board of directors, under a staggered election three directors would be elected each year to serve three-year terms. State laws generally limit the number of years that a director can be elected to serve for a staggered term (e.g., to three years).

In addition to the election of a board of directors, proxy contests also arise with regard to proposals for mergers, sale of assets, recapitalization, liquidation and dissolution, increase the number of authorized shares of the corporation, and other matters.

When directors are to be elected to the board, management usually submits a "management's slate" of directors for shareholder approval. Insurgents usually submit a competing proposed slate of directors for shareholder approval.

Anyone other than management may solicit proxies from ten or fewer persons without having to comply with the federal proxy rules. "Beneficial" owners of securities (e.g., brokerage firms holding customers' securities in their own "street name") may also solicit proxies from registered owners without having to comply with the federal proxy rules.

Shareholder List. Although federal proxy rules do not require that management provide the list of shareholders of the corporation to the challenging group in all cases, when management itself is soliciting proxies it must either provide the shareholder list to the insurgent group or mail the proxy solicitation materials of the challenging group to the shareholders of the company.

Misrepresentations in Proxy Materials.   The object of the federal proxy rules is to encourage full disclosure and to prevent fraud in the solicitation of proxies. Soliciting proxies without proper disclosures, or making misrepresentations or omissions of material facts in proxy materials, is a violation of Section 14(a) of the Securities Exchange Act of 1934.

Private causes of action have been *implied* by the courts under Section 14(a). A shareholder may bring a direct action or may bring a derivative suit on behalf of the corporation. A Section 14(a) cause of action requires a misrepresentation or omission of a *material* fact that caused the shareholder injury. Justice Marshall describes the test of materiality in this excerpt from *TSC Industries, Inc. v. Northway, Inc.:*

The general standard of materiality that we think best . . . is as follows: An omitted fact is material if there is a substantial likelihood that a reasonable shareholder would consider it important in deciding how to vote. This standard is fully consistent with *Mills'* general description of materiality as a requirement that "the defect have a significant *propensity* to affect the voting process." It does not require proof of a substantial likelihood that disclosure of the omitted fact would have caused the reasonable investor to change his vote. What the standard does contemplate is a showing of a substantial likelihood that, under all the circumstances, the omitted fact would have assumed actual significance in the deliberations of the reasonable shareholder. Put another way, there must be a substantial likelihood that the disclosure of the omitted fact would have been viewed by the reasonable investor as having significantly altered the "total mix" of information made available.

Courts do not require an exhaustive disclosure, or even a "perfectly balanced" presentation of the facts by the competing parties. Instead, the courts assess the "fairness" of the transaction and of the information provided to the shareholders. If the information is not "fair," the proxy materials are considered deficient by reason of the misrepresentation or omission of the material fact.

Any affirmative *misrepresentation* or *omission* of a "material fact" in a proxy statement, proxy, notice of meeting, or any other communication to shareholders, whether oral or written, is also prohibited and is actionable under Section 10(b) and Rule 10b-5. Defendants have even been held liable where material facts, although disclosed, are not highlighted sufficiently in a proxy statement so that their significance can be understood (e.g., "fine print," footnotes).

Where there has been a misrepresentation or omission of a material fact in proxy materials, the courts have substantial discretion in fashioning whatever relief is proper in the circumstances, including awarding damages, rescinding transactions, unwinding mergers, and other remedies. The SEC may bring an action for an injunction to prevent the solicitation of proxies, to prevent the voting of proxies, or to require the solicitation of proxies.

In *Gladwin v. Medfield Corporation* the Court of Appeals affirmed a decision of the District Court that found numerous misrepresentations in a proxy statement sent to shareholders by management during a proxy fight with an insurgent group.

MISREPRESENTATIONS IN PROXY MATERIALS

GLADWIN v. MEDFIELD CORPORATION

540 F.2d 1266 (1976)
UNITED STATES COURT OF APPEALS, FIFTH CIRCUIT

Godbold, Circuit Judge.

The Gladwins own voting stock in Medfield, a publicly-held corporation engaged in operating hospitals and other health facilities. On February 6, 1974, in preparation for its March 1 annual shareholder meeting at which directors would be elected, Medfield sent to shareholders a 1973 annual report, a notice of annual meeting, and a proxy statement. Medfield sent additional proxy solicitation material on February 20 and 23. A group known as the Medfield Shareholders Committee nominated a rival slate of candidates and also solicited proxies.

At the annual meeting the slate nominated by the existing directors received 56 percent of the votes cast, against 44 percent for the candidates nominated by the rival group.

The Gladwins sued, alleging multiple instances of misstatements or material omissions in Medfield's proxy material in violation of Section 14(a) of the Securities and Exchange Act of 1934, and the applicable proxy rules adopted pursuant to the Act. The district court, sitting without a jury, found six violations of Section 14(a) in that Medfield's proxy materials:

1. failed to disclose the nature and extent of Medfield's Medicare liabilities;
2. failed to disclose and misrepresented a significant turnover in Medfield management and other related personnel problems;
3. failed to disclose substantial purchases of Medfield stock by directors;
4. failed to adequately disclose the true nature and extent of self-dealing by one of the directors with Medfield;
5. failed to disclose that attempts were being made to sell two major assets of Medfield; and
6. unlawfully impugned the character, integrity and personal reputation of one of the candidates opposed to management.

The court ordered a new election. It directed that proxy solicitation material for such election must include corrections of all illegal misstatements and omissions, a statement that the prior solicitations were in violation of the 1934 Act and the proxy rules, and an explanation that the resolicitation was the result of this suit. By a stipulation, approved by the trial court, the order was stayed pending appeal. We affirm the decision of the district court. . . .

DISCLOSURE OF MEDICARE LIABILITIES

During December 1973 Blue Cross informed Medfield of its determinations that it had been overpaid for the years 1970, 1971, and 1972 in the amounts of $367,243, $327,609, and $419,097, respectively.

On January 15, 1974, the fiscal intermediary told Medfield that the total amount "due and owing" from it was $1,836,272, consisting of the above amounts for 1969 through 1972, plus $163,783 for 1973 and current amounts of $304,987. Blue Cross also told Medfield that current Medicare funds were being withheld because of Medfield's nonpayment.

In the proxy solicitation the only information provided by Medfield to its stockholders concerning this controversy was in the form of a footnote to the consolidated financial statement in the 1973 annual report, . . .

We agree with the District Court that this footnote did not sufficiently describe the overpayment controversy as it then existed. It did not reveal the amount of the claim as asserted on January 15, the cessation of HEW payments, or the subsequent arrangements agreed to between Blue Cross and Medfield.

MANAGEMENT TURNOVER

Medfield did not reveal in its proxy material that between January 23, 1973, and February 4, 1974, a number of high-level management changes occurred in the company, that its president intended to resign, and that it had been seeking for six months to employ someone to operate the company on a day-to-day basis. The District Court found that the failure to disclose these matters violated Section 14(a).

DISCLOSURE OF STOCK PURCHASES

During 1973 Medfield's nominees purchased an aggregate of 34,972 shares of Medfield common stock. Proxy Rule 14a.3(a) requires, in an election contest subject to Rule 14a-11, that certain information from Schedule 14B be included in the solicitation. Schedule 14B requires a list of the purchases and sales of Medfield stock made within the past two years, the dates on which they were purchased or sold and the amount. The purchases were not disclosed in Medfield's proxy material.

Although the total number of shares purchased by the nominees in 1973 represented only 4.9% of the voting stock, the great majority of those shares were purchased by a single nominee, the president of Medfield. A shareholder, being advised of this fact, might believe that this officer-nominee was attempting to acquire a degree of influence or control.

DISCLOSURE OF SELF-DEALING

The District Court found a material omission in Medfield's failure to disclose full details of an arrangement whereby a professional corporation, partially owned by a Medfield director and nominee, provided all laboratory, pathology and diagnostic services for Medfield.

We agree with the District Court that neither the true extent of the economic benefit conferred on Dr. Willey nor its concomitant cost to the corporation was fully disclosed.

DISCLOSURE OF THE SALE OF MAJOR ASSETS

Medfield did not reveal in its proxy materials that it had been attempting to sell two nursing homes. In fact the materials stated that Medfield was hopeful that the profitability of these two major facilities would increase.

Medfield urges that these attempts to sell need not be disclosed because neither the proxy rules nor Florida law requires shareholder approval of the sale of these facilities. This misses the issue, which is not stockholder consent to a sale but disclosure of matters important to stockholders in voting at the annual meeting.

IMPUGNING THE CHARACTER OF A COMMITTEE NOMINEE

Medfield disseminated a letter pointing out the involvement of a Committee nominee in an unrelated patent infringement suit. The letter quoted from a lower court opinion that described the person as having infringed upon the patent of another. The case had been reversed on appeal and eventually settled. The settlement expressly avoided an admission of liability.

The District Court found that the reference in the letter implied that the nominee was of bad moral character because he was a patent infringer. We affirm this point on reasoning contained in the opinion of the district court.

[W]e *affirm.*

CASE QUESTIONS

1. Who were the "Medfield Shareholders Committee"? Did they support the management slate or insurgent slate of directors?
2. What law did the plaintiffs assert that the defendants had violated? What does this law provide?
3. Which of the following nondisclosures did the court find were *material?*
   a. Blue Cross overpayments and withheld Medicare payments
   b. management turnover
   c. stock purchases by nominees of directors
   d. self-dealing by directors
   e. sale of major assets
   f. impugning the character of an insurgent nominee
4. Do you agree that a "reasonable shareholder" would have considered these nondisclosures *material* in his decision to elect directors?

Policy Issue. Do proxy contests benefit or harm shareholders?

Economics Issue. Would an incumbent management benefit economically by defending against a proxy contest? Explain.

Ethics Issue. Did the incumbent management of the Medfield Corporation act ethically in this case? Why do you think they did not make the proper disclosure?

Social Responsibility. Does an incumbent management owe a duty of responsibility to shareholders to defend against a proxy contest? Do proxy contests benefit or harm society? Employees?

Reimbursement for Expenses in Proxy Contests.   Where the expenses incurred by management in waging a proxy fight are "reasonable," and a matter of corporate *policy* has been disputed in the proxy contest, management may be reimbursed by the corporation for all expenses incurred in fighting the contest, whether they *win or lose.* Questions often arise as to the reasonableness of expenditures by management in fighting a proxy contest. However, management wins most challenges to the reasonableness of its expenditures in fighting proxy contests. It is also often difficult for a challenger to prove that a proxy defense by management was for other purposes (e.g., personal reasons, such as to save their jobs).

Unsuccessful insurgents normally receive no reimbursement from the corporation for expenses incurred in soliciting proxies. If the insurgents in a proxy contest are successful, they may be reimbursed by the corporation for reasonable expenses incurred in soliciting proxies if the contest "benefited" the corporation, and if the shareholders ratify such reimbursement.

In *Rosenfeld v. Fairchild Engine and Airplane Corporation* the court addressed the question of the reimbursement by the corporation of expenses incurred by both sides during a proxy fight where the insurgent group won.

PROXY CONTEST, REIMBURSEMENT OF EXPENSES

ROSENFELD v. FAIRCHILD ENGINE AND AIRPLANE CORPORATION

128 N.E.2d 291 (1955)
COURT OF APPEALS OF NEW YORK

Froessel, Judge.

In a stockholder's derivative action brought by plaintiff, an attorney, who owns 25 out of the company's over 2,300,000 shares, he seeks to compel the return of $261,522, paid out of the corporate treasury to reimburse both sides in a proxy contest for their expenses. The Appellate Division has unanimously affirmed a judgment of an Official Referee, dismissing plaintiff's complaint on the merits, and we agree.

Of the amount in controversy $106,000 was spent out of corporate funds by the old board of directors while still in office in defense of their position in said contest; $28,000 were paid to the old board by the new board after the change of management following the proxy contest, to compensate the former directors for such of the remaining expenses of their unsuccessful defense as the new board found was fair and reasonable; payment of $127,000, representing reimbursement of expenses to members of the prevailing group, was expressly ratified by a 16 to 1 majority vote of the stockholders.

Other jurisdictions and our own lower courts have

held that management may look to the corporate treasury for the reasonable expenses of soliciting proxies to defend its position in a bona fide policy contest.

If directors of a corporation may not in good faith incur reasonable and proper expenses in soliciting proxies in these days of giant corporations with vast numbers of stockholders, the corporate business might be seriously interfered with because of stockholder indifference and the difficulty of procuring a quorum, where there is no contest. In the event of a proxy contest, if the directors may not freely answer the challenges of outside groups and in good faith defend their actions with respect to corporate policy for the information of the stockholders, they and the corporation may be at the mercy of persons seeking to wrest control for their own purposes, so long as such persons have ample funds to conduct a proxy contest. The test is clear. When the directors act in good faith in a contest over policy, they have the right to incur reasonable and proper expenses for solicitation of proxies and in defense of their corporate policies, and are not obliged to sit idly by.

It is also our view that the members of the so-called new group could be reimbursed by the corporation for their expenditures in this contest by affirmative vote of the stockholders.

The rule then which we adopt is simply this: In a contest over policy, as compared to a purely personal power contest, corporate directors have the right to make reasonable and proper expenditures, subject to the scrutiny of the courts when duly challenged, from the corporate treasury for the purpose of persuading the stockholders of the correctness of their position and soliciting their support for policies which the directors believe, in all good faith, are in the best interests of the corporation. The stockholders, moreover, have the right to reimburse successful contestants for the reasonable and bona fide expenses incurred by them in any such policy contest, subject to like court scrutiny. That is not to say, however, that corporate directors can, under any circumstances, disport themselves in a proxy contest with the corporation's moneys to an unlimited extent. Where it is established that such moneys have been spent for personal power, individual gain or private advantage, and not in the belief that

such expenditures are in the best interests of the stockholders and the corporation, or where the fairness and reasonableness of the amounts allegedly expended are duly and successfully challenged, the courts will not hesitate to disallow them.

The judgment of the Appellate Division should be *affirmed,* without costs.

CASE QUESTIONS

1. Who was the plaintiff? How many shares and what percent of Fairchild Engine stock did he own?
2. What is a "derivative" shareholder action? Who receives the award if a derivative action is successful?
3. In which of the following situations can an *incumbent* management be reimbursed by the corporation for expenses incurred in defending against a proxy contest?
   a. management wins over a policy issue
   b. management loses over a policy issue
   c. management wins over a personal issue
   d. management loses over a personal issue
4. In which of the following situations can an *insurgent* group be reimbursed by the corporation for expenses incurred in waging a proxy contest?
   a. insurgent group wins over a policy issue
   b. insurgent group loses over a policy issue
   c. insurgent group wins over a personal issue
   d. insurgent group loses over a personal issue
5. Does management lose many proxy contests? Why or why not?

Policy Issue. Should a corporation (and thus its shareholders) have to pay for the defense of a proxy contest? Should a shareholder vote be required before an incumbent management may spend money to fight a proxy contest?

Economics Issue. Why do you think the plaintiff brought the lawsuit in this case?

Ethics Issue. Is it ethical for the incumbent management of a poorly performing corporation to use corporate funds to defeat a proposed insurgent group of directors?

Social Responsibility. Does the rule that allows the reimbursement of expenses to successful insurgent groups in a proxy contest serve any social purpose? Explain.

REPORTING REQUIREMENTS

Section 13(d) of the Securities Exchange Act of 1934 requires that any party who acquires 5 percent or more of an equity security must report that acquisition to the SEC and disclose his *intention* with respect to the acquisition. The reporting requirement applies only to *equity* securities (e.g., common and preferred stock). The 5 percent test applies separately to each class of equity security. The SEC provides an information statement, Schedule 13D, on which must be disclosed:

1. the identity and background of the persons involved in the purchase of the securities
2. the number of shares owned beneficially and any rights to purchase additional shares
3. the sources and amounts of consideration paid for the securities
4. the existence of any contract, arrangement or understanding relating to the issuer or its securities
5. whether or not the purpose of the purchase is to acquire control of the issuer
6. if it is, any "present plans" the purchaser has regarding the liquidation, merger, sale of assets, or major change in the business or structure of the issuer.

Any person who acquires, within a twelve-month period, the beneficial ownership in excess of 2 percent of a class of equity securities registered under the 1934 Act, and who thereby or otherwise owns more than 5 percent of that class of security, must, within ten days after such acquisition, file a 13D information statement with the SEC, and send copies to the issuer of the securities and to each stock exchange on which the securities are traded.

TENDER OFFERS

In a conventional *tender offer,* one party or corporation (the tendering party) offers to purchase the securities of another corporation (the tendered corporation or "target" corporation). Unlike a merger, a tender offer does not require the approval of the target corporation's officers or board of directors since the tender offer is made directly to the shareholders of the target corporation. The majority of tender offers are made without the cooperation of the incumbent management of the target corporation. The tender offer may be made in cash, in securities of the tendering corporation or other corporation, or in a combination of cash and securities.

Prior to 1968, there was no federal law directed specifically toward regulating tender offers. If the bidder offered to exchange *securities* with the target corporation, the offer was subject to the usual registration and prospectus requirements. If the bidder used *cash* to acquire the shares of the target corporation, it was subject to no disclosure rules. In all cases the bidder was subject to Section 10(b) and Rule 10b-5 if it traded on inside information.

The Williams Act. In 1968, Congress enacted Sections 14(d), (e) and (f) of the Securities Exchange Act of 1934 (the "Williams Act") to specifically regulate tender offers. It is unlawful for any person to make use of interstate commerce to make a tender offer for any class of *equity* security registered under Section 12 of the 1934 Act unless the conditions of Section 14(d) of the Williams Act are met.

The purpose of the Williams Act is to protect investors from the confusion and complexities of a tender offer by requiring certain disclosures by the parties and providing recourse to shareholders for fraudulent and manipulative practices in tender offers. In this excerpt from *Piper v. Chris-Craft Industries, Inc.*, 430 U.S. 1 (1977), Chief Justice Burger describes a further purpose for the enactment of the Williams Act:

[T]he Williams Act . . . was adopted in 1968 in response to the growing use of cash tender offers as a means for achieving corporate takeovers. Prior to the 1960s, corporate takeover attempts had typically involved either proxy solicitations, regulated under Section 14 of the Securities Exchange Act, or exchange offers of securities, subject to the registration requirements of the 1933 Act. The proliferation of cash tender offers, in which publicized requests are made and intensive campaigns conducted for tenders of shares of stock at a fixed price, removed a substantial number of corporate control contests from the reach of existing disclosure requirements of the federal securities laws.

Definition of **Tender Offer.** The SEC has refused to provide a definition of what constitutes a tender offer, reasoning that the "dynamic nature of tender offers requires administrative and judicial flexibility in determining what types of transactions should be subject" to the Williams Act and its regulations. Privately negotiated purchases and sales of equity securities have generally been held not to be tender offers, because such transactions are usually between knowledgeable investors who are unlikely to make hasty, uninformed decisions. This exception is lost if the search for private investors is conducted by advertising or through the publicity usually used in conventional tender offers, or where the offer to purchase is made to a shareholder or related group (e.g., a family) who control a substantial block of the shares of the corporation. If the offer is to be considered a "tender offer," than it must be open equally to all shareholders and the rules of the Williams Act must be followed.

Upon *commencement* of a tender offer, Section 14(d) requires that the offeror furnish the SEC with the information required under Section 13(d), and any other information required by the SEC by rule or regulation.

In *Lewis v. McGraw* the court found that the shareholders of a target corporation could not maintain a lawsuit under the Williams Act because a formal tender offer had not been made by the interested company.

DEFINITION OF TENDER OFFER
LEWIS v. McGRAW

619 F.2d 192 (1980)
UNITED STATES COURT OF APPEALS, SECOND CIRCUIT

Per Curiam:

The instant action is a consolidation of five similar lawsuits brought on behalf of McGraw-Hill, Inc. stockholders, alleging that McGraw-Hill and its directors made false statements of material facts in response to two proposals of the American Express Company for the acquisition of substantial amounts of McGraw-Hill stock.

On January 8, 1979, American Express proposed to McGraw-Hill what plaintiff describes as a "friendly business combination" of the two companies through payment by American Express of $34 in cash for each McGraw-Hill share. Alternatively, American Express indicated its willingness to acquire 49 percent of McGraw-Hill's shares for cash or a combination of cash and securities. McGraw-Hill common stock was trading at $26 per share immediately prior to the announcement. On January 15, 1979, McGraw-Hill announced that its Board of Directors had rejected the proposal and made public a letter to American Express characterizing the offer as "reckless," "illegal," and "improper." The following day, American Express filed Schedule 14D-1 with the Securities and Exchange Commission concerning its intention to make a cash tender offer for any and all of McGraw-Hill's stock.

The proposed offer was never made, however, for on January 29, American Express retracted its earlier announcement, and in its place submitted a new proposal to the McGraw-Hill board. This offer, at a price of $40 per share, would not become effective unless McGraw-Hill's incumbent management agreed not to oppose it by "propaganda, lobbying, or litigation." The offer was rejected by the McGraw-Hill board two days later, and expired, by its own terms, on March 1.

Plaintiffs . . . each seek damages from the company and its directors for the difference between the $40 proposed tender price, and the $25 price to which the stock returned after the expiration of the American Express proposal.

[W]here the offer ultimately becomes effective . . . statements may well be made "in connection with a tender offer" as required by . . . [the Williams Act]. In this case, however, since American Express never made its proposed offer to the shareholders of McGraw-Hill, plaintiffs *cannot* state a cause of action for alleged misstatements under the Williams Act.

CASE QUESTIONS

1. What is a tender offer? Explain.
2. Does the management of a target corporation usually have to approve a tender offer? If not, why was the approval of the McGraw-Hill board of directors required in this case?
3. Was a tender offer subject to the provisions of the Williams Act made in this case?

Policy Issue. Should tender offers be regulated by the government? Why or why not?

Economics Issue. Were the plaintiff-shareholders damaged by the actions of the McGraw-Hill directors in this case?

Ethics Issue. Did the management of McGraw-Hill act ethically in this case? Why do you think they rejected the American Express offer?

Social Responsibility. Were the actions of American Express "reckless," "illegal," and "improper" as the directors of McGraw-Hill asserted? Do corporations owe a duty of social responsibility not to purchase other corporations?

Tender Offer Rules. The Williams Act does not require a tendering company to notify the management or shareholders of the target company, or even the SEC, in *advance* of the tender offer. However, upon the *commencement* of the tender offer, the tendering party must notify the management and shareholders of the target company, and the SEC, of the tender offer, and provide detailed information to these parties regarding the terms of the tender offer.

A tendering company may offer to purchase all or any percentage (e.g., 35 percent) of the stock of the target company. The offer may be for only one class or for several classes of stock of the target corporation.

A tender offer is subject to the following rules of the Williams Act:

Seven-Day Rule.   The Williams Act provides that a shareholder of the target corporation who tenders his shares has an *absolute* right to withdraw his shares during the first seven days of the tender offer. This rule is based on the rationale that a shareholder should be protected from making hasty and uninformed decisions, and to prevent quick "take-it-or-leave-it" offers by tendering companies.

Fifteen-Day Rule.   The tender offer must remain open for at least 15 business days from the date of commencement of the offer. The tendering company can set a date beyond this 15-day period for the consummation of the tender offer, subject to the following rule.

Sixty-Day Rule.   If an offeror has not purchased the tendered shares within 60 days of the commencement of the tender offer, the Williams Act provides that all shareholders may withdraw their shares from the tender offer. The reasoning behind this rule is that to require shareholders to tie up their shares for any longer period of time would be a *restraint on alienation* of their shares.

Pro-Rata Rule.   A shareholder may tender his shares at any time prior to the termination or consummation of the tender offer. If a greater number of shares have been tendered than the offeror has offered to purchase under the tender offer, the Williams Act requires that the tendered shares be purchased on a *pro rata* basis. For example, if the tendering company has offered to purchase 1,000,000 shares of the stock of the target corporation, but 2,000,000 shares have been tendered, the offeror must purchase no more than 50 percent of the stock tendered by each shareholder.

Changes in the Terms of a Tender Offer.   Based on the dynamic nature of a tender offer, and the usual resistance to a tender offer by the management of the target corporation, the terms of most tender offers change during the course of the tender offer. Various types of changes in tender offer terms are treated differently under the Williams Act.

Increase in the Number of Shares.   The tendering company can at any time during a tender offer increase the number of shares that it will purchase pursuant to the other terms of its tender offer. Under the Williams Act, an announcement by a tendering company that it will accept a greater number of shares pursuant to its tender offer has no effect on the timing or other terms of the tender offer. However, a tendering company may not *decrease* the number of shares that it will take pursuant to its tender offer.

Increase in Price. A tender offeror may increase the price it will pay for the tendered stock at any time during the tender offer. However, under the "best-price rule" of the Williams Act, the increased price must be made available to all shares equally, even those shares already tendered. The reasoning behind this rule is that it prevents a tendering company from purchasing the shares of the target corporation in pre-arranged steps at different prices. An increase in price does not start a new tender offer. However, after an offeror increases the price for tendered shares, the tender offer must be kept open for at least ten days from the date of the increase. A tender offeror may not *decrease* the price it will pay under a tender offer.

Substantial Change in the Tender Offer. If there is a *substantial* change in the terms of the tender offer, a new tender offer is deemed to have begun. The timing rules of the Williams Act begin to run anew. For example, if the original tender offer called for the purchase of tendered shares for cash, but the tender offeror subsequently announces that it will follow the cash tender offer with a merger of the two firms, there has been a substantial change in the terms of the tender offer. Since the original tender offer is terminated, the shareholders who tendered their shares may now withdraw those shares and decide whether or not to tender them under the new tender offer.

Antifraud Provisions of the Williams Act. Section 14(e) of the Williams Act prohibits fraudulent, deceptive, and manipulative practices in connection with tender offers. Section 14(e) is patterned after Section 10(b). The courts often refer to decisions made under Section 10(b) in interpreting Section 14(e). Section 14(e) provides:

It shall be unlawful for any person to make any untrue statement of a material fact or omit to state any material fact necessary in order to make the statements made, in the light of the circumstances under which they are made, not misleading, or to engage in any fraudulent, deceptive, or manipulative acts or practices, in connection with any tender offer or request or invitation for tenders, or any solicitation of security holders in opposition to or in favor of any such offer, request, or invitation.

Courts have *implied* a private cause of action under Section 14(e). In order to be successful in a civil action under Section 14(e), a plaintiff must prove that the defendant made a misrepresentation or omission of a material fact which was relied on by the plaintiff and by which the plaintiff has been injured. Reliance is usually implied from a showing of the misrepresentation. Section 14(e) generally prohibits *intentional* conduct. It has also been held to apply to "gross negligence." *Negligence* alone is not sufficient to support an action under Section 14(e).

The SEC may enforce the provisions of the Williams Act, including violations of Section 14(e), by seeking injunctions, by issuing orders for compliance, or by bringing criminal actions.

In *Piper v. Chris-Craft Industries, Inc.* the Supreme Court cited legislative history and the purposes of the Williams Act in holding that a rival tender offeror did not have an implied cause of action for damages under 14(e).

THE WILLIAMS ACT

PIPER v. CHRIS-CRAFT INDUSTRIES, INC.

430 U.S. 1 (1977)
UNITED STATES SUPREME COURT

Mr. Chief Justice Burger delivered the opinion of the Court.

Chris-Craft Industries, Inc., a diversified manufacturer of recreational products, attempted to secure voting control of Piper through cash and exchange tender offers for Piper common stock. Chris-Craft's takeover attempt failed, and Bangor Punta Corp. (Bangor or Bangor Punta), with the support of the Piper family, obtained control of Piper in September 1969. Chris-Craft brought suit under Section 14(e) of the Securities Exchange Act of 1934 . . . alleging that Bangor Punta achieved control of the target corporation as a result of violations of the federal securities laws by the Piper family, Bangor Punta, and Bangor Punta's underwriter, First Boston Corp., who together had successfully repelled Chris-Craft's takeover attempt.

Before either side had achieved control, the contest moved from the marketplace to the courts. Then began more than seven years of complex litigation growing out of the contest for control of Piper Aircraft.

THE WILLIAMS ACT

Besides requiring disclosure and providing specific benefits for tendering shareholders, the Williams Act also contains a broad antifraud prohibition, [Section 14(e)], which is the basis of Chris-Craft's claim. This provision was expressly directed at the conduct of a broad range of persons, including those engaged in making or opposing tender offers or otherwise seeking to influence the decision of investors or the outcome of the tender offer.

The threshold issue in these cases is whether tender offerors such as Chris-Craft, whose activities are regulated by the Williams Act, have a cause of action for damages against other regulated parties under the statute on a claim that antifraud violations by other parties have frustrated the bidder's efforts to obtain control of the target corporation.

The legislative history thus shows that Congress was intent upon regulating takeover bidders, theretofore operating covertly, in order to protect the shareholders of target companies. That tender offerors were not the intended beneficiaries of the bill was graphically illustrated by the statements of Senator Kuchel, cosponsor of the legislation, in support of requiring takeover bidders, whom he described as "corporate raiders" and "takeover pirates," to disclose their activities.

> Today there are those individuals in our financial community who seek to reduce our proudest businesses into nothing but corporate shells. They seize control of the corporation with unknown sources, sell or trade away the best assets, and later split up the remains among themselves. The tragedy of such collusion is that the corporation can be financially raped without management *or shareholders* having any knowledge of the acquisitions. . . . The corporate raider may thus act under a cloak of secrecy while obtaining the shares needed to put him on the road to a successful capture of the company. 113 Cong. Rec. 857–858 (1967) (*Emphasis supplied.*)

The legislative history thus shows that the sole purpose of the Williams Act was the protection of investors who are confronted with a tender offer. As we stated in *Rondeau v. Mosinee Paper Corp.,* "The purpose of the Williams Act is to insure that public shareholders who are confronted by a cash tender offer for their stock will not be required to respond without adequate information. . . ." We find no hint in the legislative history, on which respondent so heavily relies, that Congress contemplated a private cause of action for damages by one of several contending offerors against a successful bidder or by a losing contender against the target corporation.

[A]s Judge Friendly observed in *Electronic Specialty Co. v. International Controls Corp.,* in corporate control contests the stage of preliminary injunctive relief, rather than post-contest lawsuits, "is the time when relief can best be given." Furthermore, awarding damages to parties other than the protected class of shareholders has only a remote, if any, bearing upon implementing the congressional policy of protecting shareholders who must decide whether to tender or retain their stock. Indeed, as we suggested earlier, a damages award of this nature may well be inconsistent with the interests of many members of the protected class and of only indirect value to shareholders who accepted the exchange offer of the defeated takeover contestant.

We therefore conclude that Chris-Craft, as a defeated tender offeror, has *no implied cause of action* for damages under Section 14(e).

CASE QUESTIONS

1. Who made the first tender offer on Piper Corp.? Was it successful? Explain.

2. Who made the second tender offer on Piper Corp.? Was it successful? If so, why?
3. Prior to 1968 did the federal securities laws regulate any of the following? If so, cite the law.
   a. proxy contests
   b. tender offers made by the tendering corporation issuing securities
   c. cash tender offers
4. Does Section 14(e) expressly provide for *civil* causes of action by private parties? Are private causes of action usually allowed under Section 14(e)?
5. Are rival tendering companies given an implied right of action under Section 14(e)? Would this further or hinder the purposes of the Williams Act?

Policy Issue. Do you agree with Senator Kuchel's remarks that tendering companies are "corporate raiders" and "takeover pirates" who "financially rape" target companies?

Economics Issue. Who benefits economically from tender offers? Explain.

Ethics Issue. Does the management of a target company have a "conflict of interest" with shareholders when fighting a tender offer?

Social Responsibility. Do tender offers increase the productivity of society? Do tender offers serve any useful social purpose?

FIGHTING TENDER OFFERS

No later than ten business days after the date that a tender offer has commenced, the Williams Act requires that the management of the *target* corporation disseminate to its shareholders a written statement taking one of three positions:

1. recommending acceptance or rejection of the tender offer
2. expressing no opinion and remaining neutral regarding the tender offer
3. stating that management is unable to take a position with regard to the tender offer

No matter which position the management of the target corporation takes, it must include the reasons that support its position in the written statement provided to the shareholders.

The incumbent management of most target corporations attempt to fight a tender offer. This is usually prompted by a fear of management losing their jobs if the tendering party is successful in its tender offer. The strategies used to fight a tender offer are only limited by the ingenuity of the incumbent management and their lawyers. Some of the strategies and tactics used by incumbent managements to defend against tender offers are described below.

Persuasion of Shareholders.   The target company management may engage in a campaign to persuade the shareholders of the corporation that the tender offer is not in their best interests, usually alleging that the tender offeror will "rape" the corporation if it gains control. Target company managements usually hire lawyers, investment banking firms, appraisers, public relations firms, and other professionals to assist in the preparation and dissemination of information to shareholders.

Staggering the Board.   The target corporation can modify the structure of the corporation to provide for a staggered board of directors, thereby assuring that the tendering company, even if successful in its tender offer, cannot gain control of the board of directors for a couple of years to come. Shareholder vote may be required to change the provisions for the election of directors.

Filing Delaying Lawsuits.   The target company management can file legal actions against the tender offeror, alleging violations of antitrust or securities laws or other laws. Such lawsuits are generally filed to hinder and delay the tender offer, with the hope that the delay will chase away the tender offeror. The most successful type of lawsuit is one where the target company management persuades a court to issue an *injunction* against the tender offer until the merits of the lawsuit can be decided, which may be years in the future. Injunctions are rarely granted in these situations.

Issuing Additional Stock.   The management of the target company may issue additional stock of the corporation and put it into friendly hands. If the *authorized* shares are greater than the *issued* shares, management may issue the additional stock without shareholder approval. If all the authorized stock has previously been issued, shareholder approval must be obtained to increase the authorized stock of the corporation so that it may issue the shares into friendly hands. Issuing additional stock *dilutes* the ownership interest of the tender offeror and makes it harder and more expensive for the tender offeror to purchase enough stock to gain control of the target corporation.

Repurchasing Stock.   The target company may make a tender offer on its own stock. In this way the corporation repurchases its own stock and keeps it out of the hands of the tender offeror.

Purchasing a Regulated Company.   The target company's management may acquire a regulated firm, the subsequent purchase of which requires a regulatory agency's approval. The obtaining of such approval by a tender offeror takes time, and often requires the merits approval of the administrative agency. For example, if the target company now owns a financial institution, the tendering company would have to obtain the approval of the Comptroller of the Currency, the Federal Reserve Board, or the Federal Home Loan Bank Board.

Asserting Antitakeover Statutes. An antitakeover statute may be asserted if the state has enacted one. Where there is an antitakeover statute, the target company management usually files a state court action to prevent the acquisition of the company by the tender offeror.

"Poison Pill." The management of the target company may include in its contracts and leases a provision that a major change in ownership of the corporation causes these contracts and leases (e.g., bank loans) to terminate or become due. These provisions are commonly referred to as "poison pills" because if the tender offeror acquires the target company it destroys itself.

Selling a "Crown Jewel." A tendering firm usually has a specific reason for purchasing the shares of another corporation. This is often to gain control of a valuable asset of the target corporation, which may be the ownership of a natural resource, a well-established chain of retail outlets, a patent, etc. In order to defeat a tender offer the management of the target corporation often makes arrangements to sell the "crown jewel" that the tender offeror wants. Once the crown jewel has been sold, the tendering company may no longer wish to buy the target corporation.

The sale of a crown jewel or the activation of poison-pill provisions are often referred to as "scorched earth" tactics when they destroy the successful operation of the target company in the future.

"White Knight" Merger. Where there has been a tender offer by a hostile party, and the management of the target company are fearful of losing their jobs yet probably cannot defeat the tender offer, they often attempt to find a "white knight" merger partner who will be more sympathetic to retaining the incumbent management.

Payment of "Greenmail." Where a tender offeror has purchased a block of stock in the target corporation prior to making the tender offer, which is often the case, the management of the target corporation may enter into an agreement with the tender offeror to purchase back all the stock of the target corporation from the tender offeror, at a profit, in order to have the offeror terminate its tender offer. Such payment to a tender offeror by the target corporation is commonly referred to as "greenmail."

The most famous payment of greenmail occurred in June, 1984, when the management of Walt Disney Productions paid financier Saul Steinberg $325 million, a $32 million profit for the 12.2 percent of Disney stock he previously purchased, and $28 million, labeled "out-of-pocket" expenses, in return for Steinberg dropping his proposed tender offer for Disney shares and an agreement that Steinberg would not purchase any Disney stock for ten years.

"Pac-Man" Tender Offer. Where there has been a tender offer, the management of the target corporation may make a *reverse* tender offer on the tender-

ing company. This strategy has been referred to as the "Pac-Man" defense to tender offers.

Bendix–Martin Marietta–United Technologies–Allied Tender Offers.   The first major tender offer to use the "Pac-Man" defense occurred in the summer of 1982 when Bendix Corporation, under the leadership of its president, William Agee, made a tender offer on the stock of the Martin Marietta Corporation. In defense to the Bendix tender offer, Martin Marietta made a reverse "Pac-Man" tender offer on the stock of Bendix Corporation. Both corporations arranged for lines of credit at major banks to provide the necessary cash to complete their tender offers. Martin Marietta also obtained the assistance of United Technologies Corporation in making the tender offer on Bendix. Eventually, to save itself from the Martin Marietta tender offer, Bendix sought the assistance of Allied Corporation. The end result was that Allied purchased Bendix, who in turn owned the majority of the stock of Martin Marietta.

Golden Parachutes.   Frequently, the management of a potential target corporation will enter into long-term contracts with their corporation (e.g., five-year employment contracts, stock option contracts), which become due if the corporation is acquired by another party. The corporation enters into these contracts usually because the management controls or has substantial influence on the board of directors. These contracts are referred to as "golden parachutes." For example, in the Bendix-Martin Marietta-United Technologies-Allied tender offer situation, the top 15 executives of Bendix received benefits totalling over $15 million under their golden-parachute contracts, with the majority of this money going to the top executives.

Mobil Corporation v. Marathon Oil Company is one of the numerous lawsuits brought in connection with the acquisition of the Marathon Oil Company. The following case shows actions by an incumbent management of a target company in fighting a tender offer.

FIGHTING A TENDER OFFER

MOBIL CORPORATION v. MARATHON OIL COMPANY

669 F.2d 366 (1981)
UNITED STATES COURT OF APPEALS, SIXTH CIRCUIT

Engel, Circuit Judge.

On October 30, 1981, Mobil Corporation ("Mobil") announced its intention to purchase up to 40 million outstanding common shares of stock in Marathon Oil Company ("Marathon") for $85 per share in cash. Mobil conditioned that purchase upon receipt of at least 30 million shares, just over one-half of the outstanding shares. It further stated its intention to acquire the balance of Marathon by merger following its purchase of those shares.

Marathon directors were concerned about the effects of a merger with Mobil, and they immediately held a board meeting. The directors determined that, together with consideration of other alternatives, they would seek a "white knight"—a more attractive candidate for merger.

On November 1, 1981, Marathon filed an antitrust suit against Mobil in the United States District Court for the Northern District of Ohio, claiming that a merger between Marathon and Mobil would violate Section 7 of the Clayton Act.

Negotiations developed between Marathon and several companies. . . . United States Steel Corporation ("U.S. Steel") indicated its interest, and on November 18, 1981, offered what it termed a "final proposal" to be acted upon that day. By that proposal U.S. Steel offered $125 per share for 30 million shares of Marathon stock, with a plan for a follow-up merger with its subsidiary, U.S.S. Corporation ("USS").

The Marathon directors voted to recommend the U.S. Steel offer to the shareholders on November 18, 1981. Marathon, U.S. Steel and USS executed a formal merger agreement on that day. USS made its tender offer on November 19, 1981. Both USS and Marathon filed the appropriate documents with the Securities [and] Exchange Commission.

The USS offer, and subsequently the merger agreement, had two significant conditions. First, they required a present, irrevocable option to purchase 10 million authorized but unissued shares of Marathon common stock for $90 per share ("stock option"). These shares equalled approximately 17 percent of Marathon's outstanding shares. Next, they required an option to purchase Marathon's 48 percent interest in oil and mineral rights in the Yates Field for $2.8 billion ("Yates Field option"). The latter option could be exercised only if USS's offer did not succeed and if a third party gained control of Marathon. Thus, in effect, a potential competing tender offeror could not acquire Yates Field upon a merger with Marathon.

The value of Yates Field to Marathon and to potential buyers is significant; Marathon has referred to the field as its "crown jewel." As Judge Kinneary has indicated, it is viewed as an enormous resource:

> One of the world's most remarkable oil fields is the Yates field in Pecos County (of the Permian basin province of West Texas).

Following this agreement, Mobil filed suit in the United States District Court for the Southern District of Ohio, seeking to enjoin the exercise of the options and any purchase of shares in accordance with the [USS] tender offer. Named as defendants were Marathon, its directors, and USS. Mobil alleged that the options granted to USS served as a "lock-up" arrangement to defeat any competitive offers of Mobil or third parties, thereby constituting a "manipulative" practice "in connection with a tender offer," in violation of Section 14(e) of the Williams Act. It claimed further that Marathon failed to disclose material information regarding the purpose of the options to its shareholders, also in violation of Section 14(e).

The term "manipulative" is not defined in either the Securities Exchange Act or the Williams Act. "Manipulation" in securities markets can take many forms but the Supreme Court has recently indicated that manipulation is an affecting of the market for, or price of, securities by *artificial* means, i.e., means unrelated to the natural forces of supply and demand.

The District Court found that the $2.8 billion which Marathon would receive from USS in exchange for the Yates Field oil reserves is a fair price, but there was evidence that the field might be worth as much as $3.639 billion. . . . As a result, we cannot say that Mobil and other potential bidders for control of Marathon would not be willing to make tender offers reflecting a Yates Field valuation far greater than $2.8 billion, were it not for the Yates Field option which USS possesses. Only the open market contemplated by the [Williams] Act provides a means to measure its value.

The Yates Field option is exercisable if, and only if, control of Marathon is obtained by a third party. The only effect of this option can be to deter Mobil and any other potential tender offerors from competing with USS in an auction for control of Marathon. Others cannot compete on a par with USS; its bid of $125 per share thus amounts to an artificial ceiling on the value Marathon shareholders can receive for their shares. Therefore, there is a substantial likelihood that the option is manipulative under Section 14(e) of the Williams Act.

The stock option gave USS the right to purchase 10 million authorized but unissued shares of Marathon for $90 per share. USS could exercise its option at any time during the takeover contest and acquire 10 million newly issued shares; presently there are 58,685,906 Marathon common shares outstanding. The original Mobil tender offer was for 40 million shares at a price of $85 per share. The

USS tender offer was for 30 million shares at $125 per share. An estimate prepared by the First Boston Corporation, Marathon's investment banker, calculated that because of the stock option, it would cost Mobil (or any other outside bidder seeking 40 million shares of Marathon) 1.1 to 1.2 billion additional dollars to match the USS tender offer. A chart contained in page six of the first Boston report discloses that every dollar raise in the bid by USS would cost USS $30 million, while each such dollar raise would cost Mobil $47 million.

The size and price of the stock option, together with the fact that it was granted to USS, a tender offeror, prevented all others from competing on a par with USS for a controlling block of Marathon shares, and tipped the scales decidedly in favor of USS. In our opinion, the stock option artificially and significantly discouraged competitive bidding for the Marathon stock.

The Yates Field option and the stock option, both individually and in combination, have the effect of circumventing the natural forces of market demand in this tender offer contest. . . . The purpose of the Williams Act, protection of the target shareholders, requires that Mobil and any other interested bidder be permitted an equal opportunity to compete in the marketplace and persuade the Marathon shareholders to sell their shares to them.

The defendants argue that Section 14(e) requires full disclosure and nothing more. . . . In short, to find compliance with Section 14(e) solely by the full disclosure of a manipulative device as a *fait accompli* would be to read the "manipulative acts and practices" language completely out of the Williams Act.

RELIEF

In this respect, the fashioning of appropriate equitable relief requires, and we so order, that the tender offer of USS of $125 per share be kept open for a reasonable time but free of the inhibiting and unlawful impact of the two options which it extracted from the Marathon board as a condition of its agreement. . . . The period of time likewise should be sufficient to permit the acceptance of any competing tender offers by Marathon from others who may now have an interest in bidding, uninhibited by the coercive impact of the two options which have been declared violative of Section 14(e).

Reversed and *remanded* to the District Court for further proceedings consistent with this option. The mandate shall issue forthwith.

CASE QUESTIONS

1. What actions did the Marathon directors take to defeat the Mobil tender offer? Explain.
2. Do you think that the Marathon directors were actually concerned with the possible antitrust violations of the Mobil tender offer when they filed their lawsuit against Mobil?
3. What did the *stock option* that the Marathon directors granted to U.S. Steel provide? Was Mobile granted a similar option? Did the stock option subsidize the U.S. Steel tender offer? Explain.
4. What did the *Yates Field option* that the Marathon directors granted to U.S. Steel provide? Was Mobil granted a similar option? What was the purpose of this option? Explain.
5. How did the court in this case define the term "manipulation" as contained in Section 14(e)?
6. Is "full disclosure" all that is required under Section 14(e)? If it were, as Marathon asserted, could a target company's management engage in manipulative practices but not be liable for violating Section 14(e)? Did the court accept Marathon's assertion?
7. In *Piper v. Chris-Craft* the court refused to find that a rival tender offeror had a private cause of action for *damages* against another tender offeror under Section 14(e). In *Mobil v. Marathon* the court held that a rival tender offeror could seek an injunction against a rival tender offeror. How can these two decisions be reconciled?

Policy Issue. Should the management of a target company be allowed to spend corporation funds to fight a tender offer? Why or why not?

Economics Issue. Who benefited economically from the actions of the Marathon directors in this case?

Ethics Issue. Did the directors of Marathon act ethically in this case?

Social Responsibility. Did the Mobil-U.S. Steel tender offers serve any social purpose?

NOTE: U.S. Steel eventually was successful in its tender offer for Marathon Oil Company.

STATE ANTITAKEOVER STATUTES

Many states have enacted statutes with the purpose of preventing or forestalling the takeover of corporations domiciled or doing business within the state by the use of tender offers. Many of these statutes attempt to give an appropriate state regulatory agency authority to approve or deny a proposed takeover. The purpose usually cited for the passage of state antitakeover laws is to protect local businesses and jobs. Numerous state antitakeover statutes have been challenged in courts as being unconstitutional, with varying results. The usual challenge is that state antitakeover statutes conflict with the federal Williams Act in violation of the Commerce and Supremacy Clauses of the U.S. Constitution.

In *Edgar v. MITE Corporation* the U.S. Supreme Court held that a state antitakeover statute was unconstitutional as an undue burden on interstate commerce.

STATE ANTITAKEOVER STATUTE

EDGAR, SECRETARY OF STATE OF ILLINOIS, v. MITE CORPORATION

457 U.S. 624 (1982)
UNITED STATES SUPREME COURT

Justice White delivered an opinion, Parts I, II, and V-B of which are the opinion of the Court. [Parts II, III and V-A are not presented in this edited version of this case.]

The issue in this case is whether the Illinois Business Take-Over Act is unconstitutional under the Supremacy and Commerce Clauses of the federal Constitution.

I

Appellee MITE Corporation and its wholly-owned subsidiary, MITE Holdings, Inc., are corporations organized under the laws of Delaware with their principal executive offices in Connecticut. Appellant James Edgar is the Secretary of State of Illinois and is charged with the administration and enforcement of the Illinois Act. Under the Illinois Act any takeover offer for the shares of a target company

must be registered with the Secretary of State. A target company is defined as a corporation or other issuer of securities of which shareholders located in Illinois own 10 percent of the class of equity securities subject to the offer, or for which any two of the following three conditions are met: the corporation has its principal executive office in Illinois, is organized under the laws of Illinois, or has at least 10 percent of its stated capital and paid-in surplus represented within the state. An offer becomes registered 20 days after a registration statement is filed with the Secretary unless the Secretary calls a hearing. The Secretary may call a hearing at any time during the 20-day waiting period to adjudicate the substantive fairness of the offer if he believes it is necessary to protect the shareholders of the target company, and a hearing must be held if requested by a majority of a target company's outside directors or by Illinois shareholders who own 10 percent of the class of securities subject to the offer. If the Secretary does hold a hearing, he is directed by the statute to deny registration to a tender offer if he finds that it "fails to provide full and fair disclosure to the offerees of all material information concerning the takeover offer, or that the take-over offer is inequitable or would work or tend to work a fraud or deceit upon the offerees. . . ."

On January 19, 1979, MITE initiated a cash tender offer for all outstanding shares of Chicago Rivet and Machine Co., a publicly held Illinois corporation, by filing a Schedule 14D-1 with the Securities and Exchange Commission in order to comply with the Williams Act. The Schedule 14D-1 indicated that MITE was willing to pay $28.00 per share for any and all outstanding shares of Chicago Rivet, a premium of approximately $4.00 over the then-prevailing market price. MITE did not comply with the Illinois Act, however, and commenced this litigation on the same day by filing an action in the United States District Court for the Northern District of Illinois. The complaint asked for a declaratory judgment that the Illinois Act was preempted by the Williams Act and violated the Commerce Clause.

IV

The Court of Appeals identified three provisions of the Illinois Act that upset the careful balance struck by Congress and which therefore stand as obstacles to the accomplishment and execution of the full purposes and objectives of Congress. We agree with the Court of Appeals in all essential respects.

The Illinois Act requires a tender offeror to notify the Secretary of State and the target company of its intent to make a tender offer and the material terms of the offer 20 business days before the offer becomes effective. During that time, the offeror may not communicate its offer to the shareholders. Meanwhile, the target company is free to disseminate information to its shareholders concerning the impending offer. The contrast with the Williams Act is apparent. Under that Act, there is no precommencement notification requirement; the critical date is the date a tender offer is "first published or sent or given to security holders."

We agree with the Court of Appeals that by providing the target company with additional time within which to take steps to combat the offer, the precommencement notification provisions furnish incumbent management with a powerful tool to combat tender offers, perhaps to the detriment of the stockholders who will not have an offer before them during this period. These consequences are precisely what Congress determined should be avoided, and for this reason, the precommencement notification provision frustrates the objectives of the Williams Act.

For similar reasons, we agree with the Court of Appeals that the hearing provisions of the Illinois Act frustrate the congressional purpose by introducing extended delay into the tender offer process. The Illinois Act allows the Secretary of State to call a hearing with respect to any tender offer subject to the Act, and the offer may not proceed until the hearing is completed. The Secretary may call a hearing at any time prior to the commencement of the offer, and there is no deadline for the completion of the hearing. Although the Secretary is to render a decision within 15 days after the conclusion of the hearing, that period may be extended without limitation. Not only does the Secretary of State have the power to delay a tender offer indefinitely, but incumbent management may also use the hearing provisions of the Illinois Act to delay a tender offer. . . . As the Court of Appeals observed, these provisions potentially afford management a "powerful weapon to stymie indefinitely a takeover." In enacting the Williams Act, Congress itself "recognized that delay can seriously impede a tender offer" and sought to avoid it.

As we have said, Congress anticipated investors and the takeover offeror be free to go forward without unreasonable delay. The potential for delay provided by the hearing provisions upset the balance struck by Congress by favoring management at the expense of stockholders. We therefore agree with the Court of Appeals that these hearing provisions conflict with the Williams Act.

The Court of Appeals also concluded that the Illinois Act is pre-empted by the Williams Act insofar as it allows the Secretary of State of Illinois to pass on the substantive fairness of a tender offer. Under paragraph 137.57.E of the Illinois law, the Secretary is required to deny registration of a takeover offer if he finds that the offer "fails to provide full and fair disclosure to the offerees . . . *or that the take-*

over offer is inequitable. . . ." (Emphasis added). The Court of Appeals understood the Williams Act and its legislative history to indicate that Congress intended for investors to be free to make their own decisions. We agree. Both the House and Senate Reports observed that the Act was "designed to make the relevant facts known so that shareholders have a fair opportunity to make their decision." H. R. Rep. No. 1711, 90th Cong., 2d Sess. 3 (1968); Senate Report at 3.

V-B

We conclude with the Court of Appeals that the Illinois Act imposes a substantial burden on interstate commerce which outweighs its putative local benefits. It is accordingly invalid under the Commerce Clause.

The judgment of the Court of Appeals is *affirmed.*

CASE QUESTIONS

1. Was the tender offer in this case subject to the provisions of the Williams Act? If so, did MITE Corporation comply with the Williams Act?
2. Did the Illinois antitakeover statute require *advance* notice of a proposed tender offer? Does the Williams Act contain a *precommencement* notice requirement?

3. Did the Illinois statute provide for a *hearing* before the Illinois Secretary of State? Does the Williams Act provide for such hearing before the SEC?
4. Did the Illinois Secretary of State have the authority to *deny* the tender offer? Does the Williams Act provide the SEC with authority to deny a tender offer?
5. What was the *decision* of the Supreme Court in this case? Is Part IV of Justice White's *opinion* precedent?

Policy Issue. Should states be able to enact antitakeover statutes?

Economics Issue. Who benefits from state antitakeover statutes? Shareholders? Employees? Consumers? Incumbent management?

Ethics Issue. Is it ethical for local corporations to lobby their state legislatures to enact state antitakeover statutes?

Social Responsibility. Do state legislatures owe a duty of social responsibility to residents of the state to enact antitakeover statutes to protect local businesses from out-of-state takeovers?

Trend of the Law

Struggles for control of corporations have become intense during the 1980s. With regard to tender offers, this is particularly because of the low stock prices of many corporations relative to the value of their underlying assets. During the 1980s tender offers have affected some of America's largest corporations. In 1984 the largest tender offer in history took place when Standard Oil of California (Chevron) paid $11 *billion* for Gulf Oil Corporation, snatching Gulf from the jaws of the proposed tender offer of Exxon Corporation.

Tender offers will continue in the future as long as tendering companies find it less expensive to wage a tender offer on an existing target corporation than to expand their business *de novo.* Congress is attempting however, to enact legislation to further regulate tender offers, particularly the ability of the incumbent managements of target corporations to enter into golden parachute arrangements with their companies.

Incumbent managements have been much more successful in defeating proxy contestants than in defeating tender offers. Although proxy contests may remain a problem for many corporations, they will be used less frequently than tender offers to gain corporate control. Many proxy contests are waged between long-established stockholders of corporations, and then often between family members.

REVIEW QUESTIONS

1. Plaintiff Borak owned 2,000 shares of common stock of J. I. Case Co. prior to Case's merger with American Tractor Corporation. The merger was approved by Case stockholders by a small margin. Borak later discovered what he believed to be false and misleading statements in the proxy materials issued by J. I. Case. Borak sued in Federal District Court seeking to rescind the merger, collect damages, and recover "any other equitable relief available." Borak's complaint had two counts: one based on a corporate derivative suit, claiming that the directors had breached their fiduciary duty to the shareholders; and the other claiming that Case had violated Section 14(a) of the Securities Exchange Act of 1934. Assume that Case did in fact include material misrepresentations in the proxy statements. Can Borak recover on both counts of his complaint? What type of relief can the court award?

2. National Industries acquired the 34 percent interest held by Schmidt, the founder and principal shareholder of TSC Industries. Schmidt and his son resigned from TSC's board of directors and five National nominees were placed on the board. Eight months later the TSC board, with the National nominees abstaining, approved a proposal to liquidate and sell all of TSC's assets to National. TSC and National issued a joint proxy statement to their shareholders, recommending approval. The proxy statement did not disclose that Schmidt had transferred his 34 percent interest to National although it did state that National owned a 34 percent share and that no other person owned more than 10 percent of TSC. It also stated that five of the ten directors were National nominees. The proxy statement included a favorable opinion from an investment banking firm stating that the terms of exchange were fair, since National was offering a "substantial premium over current market values." The proxy did not include a letter sent by the same investment banker a week later explaining that the valuation was in part based on certain warrants being valued at $15.25 per warrant. The letter stated that the firm now believed that this was an incorrect assumption and that the market price on the day of exchange should be near $3.50 per share. With the first assumption, National would be offering a 27 percent premium over correct market values whereas with the later assumption the premium

would drop to 22 percent. The proxy solicitation was successful and TSC was dissolved. Northway, a former TSC shareholder, sued for damages, alleging that TSC and National presented a misleading proxy in violation of Section 14(a) because they omitted material facts. Was Northway successful?

3. General Outdoor Advertising Co. (GOA) was the largest company in the outdoor advertising business in the United States. GOA operated 36 plants in 23 states as well as the largest outdoor advertising companies in Canada and Mexico. In April 1961, Gamble-Skogmo (Skogmo) acquired a 50.12 percent interest in GOA, and shortly thereafter gained a majority on the board of directors. Unfortunately, outdoor advertising sales dropped rapidly in many areas in late 1961 and early 1962. In May 1962, GOA, under the direction of the Skogmo directors, began selling a number of its plants, both profitable and unprofitable units. Sales were temporarily stopped by an SEC investigation in December 1962 but resumed again in March, 1963 (the SEC was concerned that GOA should have been classified as an investment company because the firm had accepted a large number of notes from the buyers of the GOA plants). In June 1963, the Skogmo directors decided that GOA should merge with Skogmo. Up until that time, GOA had actively tried to sell its remaining advertising plants. In the proxy statement issued to GOA's shareholders, GOA stated that it had sold 23 of the 36 plants for a net after-tax profit of $14,184,368. The firm did not state that considerable additional profits could be realized from the sale of the remaining plants. Had these potential profits been included or the plants been valued at their market rather than historical value, the value of GOA's stock for merger purposes would have been considerably higher. The Company stated that while there may have been outside interests that had discussed acquiring the remaining plants, "at the present time, there are no such agreements, arrangements or other understandings . . . and no negotiations are presently being conducted." Two days prior to the proxy meeting, GOA concluded discussions with Metromedia, Inc., which ultimately led to Metromedia's purchase of two additional plants shortly after the merger was approved by a majority of GOA's shareholders. Between the time of the merger, October 17, 1963 and May, 1964, GOA successfully liquidated the remainder of its outdoor sign business for an additional after-tax profit of $11,740,875. GOA's net worth increased 26 percent as a result of these sales. In July, 1964 a group of former minority shareholders sued GOA, alleging that it issued a false and misleading proxy statement in violation of Section 14(a). After the suit was filed but before the trial began, GOA acquired Stedman Clothiers and Claude Neon Clothiers with the proceeds from the plant sales. Were the minority shareholders successful? Assuming that they were successful, what was the proper remedy for the Court to award in this case?

4. The Medical Committee for Human Rights was a nonprofit organization composed of medical professionals. In 1968, the Committee received a gift of several shares of Dow Chemical stock. Shortly thereafter, the Committee sent a letter to Dow's board of directors requesting that the following resolution be included in that year's proxy statement to be voted upon at the annual stockholder's meeting:

RESOLVED, that the shareholders of Dow Chemical Company request the Board of Directors, in accordance with the laws [sic] of the Dow Chemical Company, consider the advisability of adopting a resolution setting forth an amendment to the composition certificate of incorporation that the company shall not make napalm."

Dow was the world's largest maker of napalm and the major supplier of the substance to the U.S. Army, which was using it extensively in the Vietnam War. After consideration, Dow decided not to include the resolution in the annual proxy materials. The Committee sued in District Court, attempting to force Dow to include the resolution. Was the Committee successful? Ethically, should Dow be forced to accept these types of resolutions or should they be able to choose not to include them?

5. Curtiss-Wright Corporation wanted to obtain an interest in Kennecott Copper Corporation. Curtiss-Wright viewed Kennecott as a good investment and as a possible merger candidate. By March 17, Curtiss-Wright acquired 9.9 percent of Kennecott's common stock for $77 million. On that date, which was less than ten days after Curtiss-Wright reached a 5 percent ownership level, the firm filed a Schedule 13D with the SEC. Curtiss-Wright purchased nearly all of the stock on the national exchanges. In one instance, a Curtiss-Wright broker solicited 50 Kennecott shareholders off the exchange floor but the sales were consummated on the floor. Another broker solicited about a dozen institutional holders of Kennecott, closing a few sales off the floor. In all cases, potential Kennecott sellers were merely asked if they wanted to sell. Curtiss-Wright did not offer any premium nor did it give any deadline within which to respond. The majority of Curtiss-Wright's purchases were made from sophisticated institutional shareholders. Kennecott sued Curtiss-Wright claiming that the firm had made a tender offer for Kennecott common stock without first filing a Schedule 13D. Under the Williams Act, will Kennecott be successful in its claim?

6. Triumph American, Inc. was a Delaware corporation whose sole major asset was a 95 percent interest in Resolute Insurance Company. Triumph made a tender offer to acquire 51 percent of the common stock of General Host Corp. (Host). Triumph's tender offer, proposed to purchase 1,075,000 shares of Host's common stock for $18.50 per share. In both its tender offer and filed Schedule 13D, Triumph stated that to finance the entire purchase it had borrowed $20,000,000 in a high-interest two-year term note from Lloyds-Bolsa International Bank and that it intended to gain control of Host. A number of internal memoranda that circulated between Triumph and its holding company, Triumph International, indicated that the firm was seriously considering liquidating Host's assets for cash, which could then be invested elsewhere. Triumph's only other previous investment (Resolute) was acquired in much the same manner. Thirty-four days after Resolute was purchased, Triumph installed a new board of directors who immediately declared a $3,000,000 dividend (over 20 percent of Resolute's net equity) to pay back part of the loan used to finance Triumph's stock purchase. Triumph's tender offer for Host did not discuss any plans to possibly liquidate Host and it did not disclose the nature of Triumph's acquisition of Resolute. Triumph's only mention of a possible liquidation was that "it may also evaluate General Host's operation to determine whether there should be any

disposition of assets." At the time of the tender offer, Triumph had net assets slightly in excess of $15,000,000. Host sued Triumph in Federal Court, alleging that Triumph's tender offer was false and misleading. Was Triumph's tender offer valid and complete?

7. In an apparent effort to gain substantial influence, Gulf and Western Industries made a tender offer for 3,750,000 shares (15 percent) of Great Atlantic & Pacific Tea Co. common stock. Gulf & Western, which already owned over 4 percent of A&P, offered $20 for each additional share. Gulf & Western was a major conglomerate with significant investments in food processing and distribution. Since A&P was the largest retail grocer in the United States, any substantial combination between the two firms was very likely to violate antitrust laws. In Gulf and Western's tender offer the firm did not mention the possible antitrust violations. Furthermore, there was strong evidence to indicate that Gulf and Western intended to either acquire a controlling interest in A&P or at least try to exercise significant control over management; however, the tender offer was silent concerning these plans. A&P brought suit in District Court, claiming that Gulf and Western violated Section 4(e). In order to be successful, what must A&P prove? Will the court rule in favor of A&P?

8. Corenco Corporation, a diversified raw products processor, was seeking to acquire small businesses in related industries. The firm held preliminary discussions with Michael Schiavone and Sons, Inc. (Michael Schiavone) to acquire its subsidiary, Schiavone & Sons, Inc. (Schiavone), a scrap metal dealer. Both Michael Schiavone and Schiavone were small close corporations that did not release any financial information to the public. The discussions were terminated before any tender offer was made.

Shortly before the discussions were terminated, Michael Schiavone acquired 4.8 percent of the outstanding shares of Corenco, without Corenco's knowledge. Three months later, Schiavone filed a Schedule 13D and made a public tender offer to purchase as little as 29 percent or as much as 39 percent of Corenco's outstanding common stock for $33 per share. The stock was trading for $28 on the over-the-counter market. In the tender offer, Schiavone disclosed that the purpose in making the offer was to gain control of Corenco with a view to a possible merger or other combination. The offer included financial information about Corenco, the market value of its stock, information about the officers and directors of Schiavone and the source of the loan which was being used to finance the entire tender offer. The offer did not contain any financial information about either Schiavone or Michael Schiavone. Within two days Corenco management unanimously decided to oppose the tender offer.

The firm sent letters and placed hundreds of phone calls to shareholders urging them to delay action because the offer was "inadequate." Management declared an extra cash dividend and a 10 percent stock dividend to shareholders of record the day after Schiavone's offer was due to expire. As another part of its effort to stop the hostile tender offer, the firm filed a lawsuit in United States District Court claiming that Schiavone's tender offer contained material omissions in violation of Section 14(e). Did Schiavone's tender offer contain any material omissions? Were Corenco's efforts to delay and oppose the merger fair and ethical?

9. Great Western United Corporation (Great Western) is a publicly-owned Delaware corporation. Sunshine Mining and Metal Co. (Sunshine) is a publicly-owned company incorporated in the State of Washington. Sunshine's principal operations are located in Idaho. The firm has a wholly owned subsidiary based in Maryland and it does significant business in New York. In March, Great Western decided to make a tender offer for 2,000,000 shares (35 percent) of Sunshine common stock at $15.75 per share. Great Western filed a Schedule 13D prior to making a public announcement. The information provided in both documents satisfied the requirements of the Williams Act.

Had only the Williams Act regulated Great Western's proposed tender offer, the offer would have commenced on March 21. Idaho, New York, and Maryland, however, all had antitakeover statutes that were arguably applicable. New York and Maryland decided not to challenge the tender offer. Great Western attempted to comply with Idaho's statute by filing documents intended to satisfy Idaho's requirements. This was the first filing ever made under the Idaho statute. Among other things, Idaho's takeover law required that: (1) Great Western submit a letter to the Idaho Department of Finance prior to filing Schedule 13D, stating Great Western's intentions; (2) that Great Western send a copy of this filing to Sunshine; (3) that Great Western participate in a hearing to determine the merits of the offer, which would be mandatory if Sunshine requested one; and (4) that Great Western delay its tender offer until final determination of any proceeding brought by Idaho for violation of its takeover law. There was no time limit on when the Idaho Director of Finance had to rule on the registration statement. The director could summarily delay the offer if he felt that the registration was insufficient. The law also allowed Sunshine to circumvent the entire process if it so chose by approving the offer outright.

On March 25, the Idaho Director of Finance, Thomas McEldouney, objected to the filing and ordered a delay in the tender offer. Great Western filed suit in United States District Court seeking an order declaring that the Idaho law was unconstitutional and that the tender offer should be reopened immediately. Will Great Western's suit be successful?

16

COMMODITIES REGULATION

INTRODUCTION

In recent years, the trading of *commodities* futures contracts has become an increasingly important investment market in this country. The major commodities market in America is the Chicago Board of Trade, located in Chicago, Illinois. Other commodities contract markets are located in different parts of the country. This section covers the history of commodities trading and the current federal regulation of commodities trading.

Before the development of "futures" trading, farmers would harvest their crops and haul them to the closest market for sale for cash. The most important cash commodities markets developed at major transportation centers such as Chicago and St. Louis. Gluts of crops occurred each fall as farmers thronged at the commodities markets. Crops were piled in the streets, prices fell, and considerable spoilage occurred.

"Forward" Contracts. In an attempt to avoid the chaos of fall cash crop sales, farmers and processors began to enter into "forward" contracts for the sale of commodities. In a *forward contract,* farmers and processors would negotiate the sale and delivery of crops to be planted and delivered at some time in the future. The agreed-upon price usually reflected the cost of the crop, storage costs, and transportation expenses.

A forward contract required individual negotiation between a farmer and processor. No formal market for buying and selling forward contracts existed. Because prices generally fluctuated between the time a forward contract was executed and the time the crop was delivered, there was a constant problem of parties breaching forward contracts to take advantage of price changes.

Eventually, a "futures" market in commodities developed. Similar to the stock market, *futures markets* and exchanges dealt in an impersonal manner, where standardized forward contracts on commodities were traded. Usually a farmer would *sell* a forward contract on a commodities exchange, and a food processor would *buy* a forward contract on a commodities exchange.

The two major purposes served by commodities futures contracts were: (1) to allow farmers and food processors to *hedge* their actions, and (2) to provide an opportunity for speculators to take *risks* in order to attempt to make profits on the trading of futures contracts.

THE COMMODITY EXCHANGE ACT

Congress first attempted to regulate the trading in commodities in the early 1920s. The Futures Trading Act was enacted by Congress in 1922 as part of the Grain Futures Act. Congress changed the name of the statute in 1936 to the Commodity Exchange Act (CEA) and enlarged its coverage. The Commodity Exchange Act was again amended in 1968, 1974, and 1978. All references in this chapter are to sections of the Commodity Exchange Act, as amended.

The Commodity Futures Trading Commission. The 1974 amendments to the Commodity Exchange Act created the Commodity Futures Trading Commission ("Commission"). The Commission is a regulatory body consisting of five members appointed by the President and confirmed by the Senate. One member is appointed Chairman of the Commission.

The Commission has *exclusive* jurisdiction in regulating commodities futures transactions. The Commission's jurisdiction, where applicable, supersedes that of other federal agencies. The Commission is responsible for administering and enforcing the Commodity Exchange Act, and for issuing rules thereunder. The Commission has the power to institute administrative proceedings against anyone who violates the Act or the regulations issued by the Commission.

The Commodity Futures Trading Commission has very broad emergency powers. Congress has given the Commission extensive powers to deal with emergency situations because of the unique nature of the products the Commission is charged to regulate (i.e., perishable crops), and the speculative nature of the marketplace. Orders issued by the Commission under its emergency powers are *not* reviewable by the courts.

Designation of Contract Markets. The Commission has authority to designate "contract markets." A *contract market* is a commodity exchange that is designated by the Commission to trade in a particular commodities futures contract. An exchange may be designated a "contract market" for a number of different commodities. Only formally designated contract markets may legally trade commodities futures contracts (e.g., soybeans). Persons who trade commodities futures contracts other than on a contract market are liable for violating the Commodity Exchange Act.

In order to qualify to be designated as a "contract market," an exchange must agree to adhere to the Commodity Exchange Act and regulations issued by the Commission, and to engage in a considerable amount of self-regulation.

The designation of a contract market may be revoked or suspended by the Commission where an exchange has been found to have violated the Commodity Exchange Act or regulations of the Commission. Decisions regarding revocation or suspension of a contract market designation is reviewable by the Court of Appeals.

Commodity Futures Contracts. The Commodity Futures Trading Commission sets standards for the operation of contract markets. For example, the terms (e.g., type, quantity, and quality of the commodity, time and place of delivery) of contracts or "intruments" have been standarized by the Commission. Commodities futures contracts are thereby *fungible* and interchangeable with all other contracts for delivery at a specified time in the future (e.g., in a designated month).

Over 90 percent of current commodities futures contracts are purchased for speculation. The majority of futures contracts never require delivery. Section 4(a) of the Commodity Exchange Act authorizes the Commission to set limits on the amount of speculative trading in a futures contract. Cash contracts for commodities are *not* covered by the Commodities Exchange Act or regulated by the Commodities Futures Trading Commission.

In *Merrill Lynch, Pierce, Fenner & Smith, Inc. v. Curran,* Justice Stevens of the Supreme Court comprehensively reviewed the history of commodities trading and described the current regulation of commodities markets.

COMMODITIES REGULATION

MERRILL LYNCH, PIERCE, FENNER & SMITH, INC. v. CURRAN

456 U.S. 353 (1982)
UNITED STATES SUPREME COURT

Justice Stevens delivered the opinion of the Court.

The Commodity Exchange Act (CEA), has been aptly characterized as "a comprehensive regulatory structure to oversee the volatile and esoteric futures trading complex."

Prior to the advent of futures trading, agricultural products generally were sold at central markets. When an entire crop was harvested and marketed within a short time span, dramatic price fluctuations sometimes created severe hardship for farmers or for processors. Some of these risks were alleviated by the adoption of quality standards, improvements in storage and transportation facilities, and the practice of "forward contracting"—the use of executory contracts fixing the terms of sale in advance of the time of delivery.

When buyers and sellers entered into contracts for the future delivery of an agricultural product, they arrived at an agreed price on the basis of their judgment about expected market conditions at the time of delivery. Because the weather and other imponderables affected supply and demand, normally the market price would fluctuate before the contract was performed. A declining market meant that the executory agreement was more valuable to the seller than the commodity covered by the contract; conversely, in a rising market the executory contract had a special value for the buyer, who not only was assured of delivery of the commodity but also could derive a profit from the price increase.

The opportunity to make a profit as a result of fluctuations in the market price of commodities covered by contracts for future delivery motivated speculators to engage in the practice of buying and selling "futures contracts." A speculator who owned no present interest in a commodity but anticipated a price decline might agree to a future sale at the current market price, intending to purchase the commodity at a reduced price on or before the delivery date. A "short" sale of that kind would result in a loss if the price went up instead of down. On the other hand, a price increase would produce a gain for a "long" speculator who had acquired a contract to purchase the same commodity with no intent to take delivery but merely for the purpose of reselling the futures contract at an enhanced price.

In the 19th century the practice of trading in futures contracts led to the development of recognized exchanges or boards of trade. At such exchanges standardized agreements covering specific quantities of graded agricultural commodities to be delivered during specified months in the future were bought and sold pursuant to rules developed by the traders themselves. Necessarily the commodities subject to such contracts were fungible. For an active market in the contracts to develop, it also was essential that the contracts themselves be fungible. The exchanges therefore developed standard terms describing the quantity and quality of the commodity, the time and place of delivery, and the method of payment; the only variable was price. The purchase or sale of a futures contract on an exchange is therefore motivated by a single factor—the opportunity to make a profit (or to minimize the risk of loss) from a change in the market price.

The advent of speculation in futures markets produced well-recognized benefits for producers and processors of agricultural commodities. A farmer who takes a "short" position in the futures market is protected against a price decline; a processor who takes a "long" position is protected against a price increase. Such "hedging" is facilitated by the availability of speculators willing to assume the market risk that the hedging farmer or processor wants to avoid. The speculators' participation in the market substantially enlarges the number of potential buyers and sellers of executory contracts and therefore makes it easier for farmers and processors to make firm commitments for future delivery at a fixed price. The liquidity of a futures contract, upon which hedging depends, is directly related to the amount of speculation that takes place.

Because Congress has recognized the potential hazards as well as the benefits of futures trading, it has authorized the regulation of commodity futures exchanges for over 60 years. In 1921 it enacted the Future Trading Act, . . . The 1921 statute was held unconstitutional as an improper exercise of the taxing power in *Hill* v. *Wallace,* (1922), but its regulatory provisions were promptly reenacted in the Grain Futures Act, and upheld under the commerce power in *Chicago Board of Trade v. Olsen* (1923).

In 1936 Congress changed the name of the statute to the Commodity Exchange Act, enlarged its coverage to include other agricultural commodities, and added detailed provisions regulating trading in futures contracts. . . . In 1968 the CEA again was amended to enlarge its coverage and to give the Secretary additional enforcement authority. The Secretary was authorized to disapprove exchange rules that were inconsistent with the statute, and the contract markets were required to enforce their rules; the Secretary was authorized to suspend a contract market or to issue a cease and desist order upon a showing that the contract market's rules were not being enforced.

In 1974, after extensive hearings and deliberation, Congress enacted the Commodity Futures Trading Commission Act of 1974. Like the 1936 and the 1968 legislation, the 1974 enactment was an amendment to the existing statute that broadened its coverage and increased the penalties for violation of its provisions. . . . The 1974 amendments . . . did make substantial changes in the statutory scheme; Congress authorized a newly created Commodities Futures Trading Commission to assume the powers previously exercised by the Secretary of Agriculture, as well as certain additional powers.

The latest amendments to the CEA, the Futures Trading Act of 1978, 92 Stat. 865, again increased the penalties for violations of the statute.

ANTIFRAUD PROVISIONS

The Commodity Exchange Act contains Section 4b, which is an *antifraud* provision similar to Section 10(b) of the Securities Exchange Act of 1934. Generally, Section 4b prohibits any person dealing in commodities from:

1. manipulating or attempting to manipulate prices
2. willfully deceiving or attempting to deceive another person
3. willfully making false or misleading statements in any registration application or report filed with the Commission, or
4. violating any provision of the Commodity Exchange Act or any rules, regulations, or orders issued thereunder by the Commission.

Pursuant to its authority from Congress, the Commodity Futures Trading Commission has adopted Rule 32.9, which provides:

It shall be unlawful for any person directly or indirectly—

(a) To cheat or defraud or attempt to cheat or defraud any other person;
(b) To make or cause to be made to any other person any false report or statement thereof or cause to be entered for any person any false record thereof;
(c) To deceive or attempt to deceive any other person by any means whatsoever; in or in connection with an offer to enter into, the entry into, or the confirmation of the execution of, any commodity option transaction.

As adopted, Rule 32.9 is as broad as, if not broader than, Rule 10b-5 as adopted by the Securities and Exchange Commission. The legislative history of the Commodity Exchange Act and the Commodity Futures Trading Commission's express intent in adopting Rule 32.9 indicate that the rule, like Rule 10b-5, should be read so as to advance the purposes of the Act and the policies of the Commission in regulating commodities trading. The courts consider cases decided under the antifraud provisions of the Securities Act as guidelines for interpreting Rule 32.9.

Commodities exchanges are responsible for preventing the dissemination of false or misleading crop or market information, manipulation of prices, and "cornering" of commodities markets. The Commodity Exchange Act prohibits fraud by commodity trading advisors and pool operators.

Implied Civil Right of Action. The Commodities Exchange Act does not expressly provide a civil cause of action for anyone injured by another person who has violated the Act or regulations, rules, or orders issued thereunder. In 1967, a federal district court held that a *private civil action* for damages was *implied* under the Commodities Exchange Act. In 1982, the U.S. Supreme Court affirmed the implied right of action by a civil plaintiff under the Act.

In *Merrill Lynch, Pierce, Fenner & Smith, Inc. v. Curran*, which was previously excerpted to illustrate commodities regulation, the Supreme Court also found numerous violations of the Commodity Exchange Act where the defendants engaged in "manipulation" of commodities trading in Maine potatoes.

FRAUD IN COMMODITIES TRADING

MERRILL LYNCH, PIERCE, FENNER & SMITH, INC. v. CURRAN

456 U.S. 353 (1982)
UNITED STATES SUPREME COURT

Justice Stevens delivered the opinion of the Court.

In the . . . cases before us, the allegations in the complaints filed by respondents are assumed to be true. The first involves a complaint by customers against their broker. The other three arise out of a malfunction of the contract market for futures contracts covering the delivery of Maine potatoes in May 1976, "when the sellers of almost 1,000 contracts failed to deliver approximately 50,000,000 pounds of potatoes, resulting in the largest default in the history of commodities futures trading in this country."

NOS. 80–757, 80–895, AND 80–936

One of the futures contracts traded on the New York Mercantile Exchange provided for the delivery of a railroad car lot of 50,000 pounds of Maine potatoes at a designated place on the Bangor and Aroostook Railroad during the period between May 7, 1976, and May 25, 1976. Trading in this contract commenced early in 1975 and terminated on May 7, 1976. On two occasions during this trading period the Department of Agriculture issued reports containing estimates that total potato stocks, and particularly Maine potato stocks, were substantially down from the previous year. This information had the understandable consequences of inducing investors to purchase May Maine potato futures contracts (on the expectation that they would profit from a shortage of potatoes in May) and farmers to demand a higher price for their potatoes on the cash market.

To counteract the anticipated price increases, a group of entrepreneurs described in the complaints

as the "short sellers" formed a conspiracy to depress the price of the May Maine potato futures contract. The principal participants in this "short conspiracy" were large processors of potatoes who then were negotiating with a large potato growers association on the cash market. The conspirators agreed to accumulate an abnormally large short position in the May contract, to make no offsetting purchases of long contracts at a price in excess of a fixed maximum, and to default, if necessary, on their short commitments. They also agreed to flood the Maine cash markets with unsold potatoes. This multifaceted strategy was designed to give the growers association the impression that the supply of Maine potatoes would be plentiful. On the final trading day the short sellers had accumulated a net short position of almost 1900 contracts, notwithstanding a Commission regulation limiting their lawful net position to 150 contracts. They did, in fact, default.

The trading limit also was violated by a separate group described as the "long conspirators." Aware of the short conspiracy, they determined that they not only could counteract its effects but also could enhance the price the short conspirators would have to pay to liquidate their short positions by accumulating an abnormally large long position—at the close of trading they controlled 911 long contracts—and by creating an artificial shortage of railroad cars during the contract delivery period. Because the long conspirators were successful in tying up railroad cars, they prevented the owners of warehoused potatoes from making deliveries to persons desiring to perform short contracts.

Respondents are speculators who invested long

in Maine futures contracts. Allegedly, if there had been no price manipulation, they would have earned a significant profit by reason of the price increase that free market forces would have produced.

Petitioners in No. 80–757 are the New York Mercantile Exchange and its officials. Respondents' complaints alleged that the Exchange knew, or should have known, of both the short and the long conspiracies but failed to perform its statutory duties to report these violations to the Commission and to prevent manipulation of the contract market. The Exchange allegedly had the authority under its rules to declare an emergency, to require the shorts and the longs to participate in an orderly liquidation, and to authorize truck deliveries and other measures that would have prevented or mitigated the consequences of the massive defaults.

Petitioners in No. 80–895 and No. 80–936 are the firms of futures commission merchants that the short conspirators used to accumulate their net short position. The complaint alleged that petitioners knowingly participated in the conspiracy to accumulate the net short position, and in doing so violated position and trading limits imposed by the Commission and Exchange rules requiring liquidation of contracts that obviously could not be performed. Moreover, the complaint alleged that petitioners violated their statutory duty to report violations of the CEA to the Commission.

[I]t is abundantly clear that an implied cause of action under the CEA was a part of the "contemporary legal context" in which Congress legislated in 1974.

The antifraud provision, Section 4b, by its terms makes it unlawful for any person to deceive or defraud any other person in connection with any futures contract. This statutory language does not limit its protection to hedging transactions; rather, its protection encompasses every contract that "is or may be used for (a) hedging . . . or (b) determining the price basis of any transaction . . . in such commodity." . . . In other words, all purchasers or sellers of futures contracts—whether they be pure speculators or hedgers—necessarily are protected by Section 4b.

Although the speculator has never been the favorite of Congress, Congress recognized his crucial role in an effective and orderly futures market and intended him to be protected by the statute as much as the hedger.

Having concluded that exchanges can be held accountable for breaching their statutory duties to enforce their own rules prohibiting price manipulation, it necessarily follows that those persons who are participants in a conspiracy to manipulate the market in violation of those rules are also subject to suit by futures traders who can prove injury from these violations. . . . The elements of liability, of causation, and of damages are likely to raise difficult issues of law and proof in litigation arising from the massive price manipulation that is alleged to have occurred in the May 1976 futures contract in Maine potatoes. We express no opinion about any such question. We hold only that a cause of action exists on behalf of respondents against petitioners.

The judgments of the Courts of Appeals are *affirmed*.

CASE QUESTIONS

1. What is a commodity futures contract? How does it differ from a typical contract to purchase a security (e.g., common stock)?
2. When are the commodities to be delivered under a commodity futures contract? Most commodity futures contracts are not delivered. Why?
3. What does Section 4(b) of the Commodities Exchange Act provide?
4. Who were the plaintiff-respondents?
5. Who were the "short sellers"? What is a "short sale"? What would have been the effect of their abnormally large *short* position on:
   a. the current prices of potatoes?
   b. the prices of potato futures contracts?
6. Who were the "long conspirators"? What was their plan? What would have been the effect of their abnormally large *long* positions on:
   a. current prices of potatoes?
   b. prices of potato futures contracts?
7. Do private plaintiffs have an *implied* cause of action under Section 4(b) of the Commodities Exchange Act?

Policy Issue. Is investing in commodities futures contracts "gambling"? Or investing?

Should speculation in commodity futures contracts be prohibited? Why or why not?

Economics Issue. Is there an opportunity to make greater profits in the trading of commodity futures contracts than in trading in normal securities (e.g., common stock)? For greater losses? Why?

Ethics Issue. Was the short sellers' conspiracy ethical? Were the activities of the long conspirators ethical?

Social Responsibility. Did the short conspirators breach their duty of social responsibility in this case? Did the long conspirators breach their duty of social responsibility?

REGISTRATION OF COMMODITIES PROFESSIONALS

Under the Commodity Exchange Act and the regulations issued thereunder, almost anyone dealing with the public in connection with the sale of commodities must be registered with the Commodity Futures Trading Commission. Persons who must be registered include:

1. floor brokers on an Exchange ("floor traders")
2. salespersons who solicit or accept orders for futures contracts ("futures commission merchants")
3. persons who operate syndicates or trusts for investments in commodities futures ("commodity pool operators")
4. any advisor ("commodity trading advisor") or other person associated with commodities trading.

Commission Remedies. The Commodities Futures Trading Commission may institute an administrative proceeding against any person for violating the Commodities Exchange Act, or regulations, rules, or orders issued by the Commission. A *complaint* must be served on the person being charged, with notice of the hearing date. After the appropriate hearing, the Commission may order any of a number of remedies, including:

1. issuing an order revoking, or suspending for up to six months, the registration of any person registered with the Commission
2. issuing a "cease and desist" order
3. ordering that reparation be made to the injured party
4. assessing a civil penalty of up to $100,000 for each violation
5. issuing an injunction.

The Commodity Exchange Act requires that every contract market provide an arbitration procedure to settle claims of traders that do not exceed $15,000. The Act authorizes the Commission to order the payment of reparation to traders by commodities professionals where there has been a violation of the Act or regulations issued thereunder. The Act authorizes the Commission to investigate all complaints and to hold hearings on such matters before an Administrative Law Judge.

Criminal Penalties. The Commission may also access *criminal* penalties for violations of the Act or regulations, rules, or orders of the Commission. Where a person is found guilty of a *felony*, the Commission can impose a fine of up to $500,000 for any firm, and a fine of $100,000 and/or imprisonment for up to five years for any individual. *Felonies* in this area include:

1. embezzlement of customer funds
2. manipulation or attempting to manipulate commodity prices
3. cornering or attempting to corner a commodity
4. knowingly delivering false market information
5. failing to comply with a cease-and-desist order involving any one of these four offenses.

Misdemeanors may be punished by the Commission by a fine of up to $100,000 and/or imprisonment for up to one year. The following are considered *misdemeanors:*

1. failing to register with the Commission
2. failing to file required reports with the Commission
3. speculators exceeding dollar limits for trading in commodities as set by the Commission
4. violating the antifraud provisions of Sections 4b and 4o
5. engaging in prohibited transactions such as wash sales, cross trades, or accommodation trades
6. trading off of a designated contract market
7. violating a Commission order
8. violating a cease-and-desist order issued by the Commission.

Any Commission order, except those issued pursuant to emergency authority, may be reviewed by the Court of Appeals upon proper petition. Any person subject to a Commission order has 15 days from the date of the order to petition the federal Court of Appeals for review. The Court of Appeals may affirm, reverse, or remand the case.

In the following case, *Commodity Futures Trading Commission v. Crown Colony Commodity Options, Ltd.,* the court issued an injunction against commodities brokers for engaging in fraudulent conduct and deceiving customers in connection with purchases of commodities options.

FRAUD BY COMMODITIES BROKERS

COMMODITY FUTURES TRADING COMMISSION v. CROWN COLONY COMMODITY OPTIONS, LTD.

434 F.SUPP. 911 (1977)
UNITED STATES DISTRICT COURT, S.D. NEW YORK

Edward Weinfeld, District Judge.

Since February 1976, Crown Colony has been engaged primarily in the business of offering and selling London commodity options. . . . [T]he defendants purposefully engaged in the sort of contin-uous, concerted fraudulent practices that lie at the core of the prohibitions contained in Rule 32.9. The essence of the Commission's charges is that the defendants actively operated a high-powered "boiler room," principally from the Miami office, in attempting to sell, and selling, London commodity future options to persons throughout the United States, and in so doing engaged in various acts and conduct aimed to cheat, to defraud, or to deceive their customers.

The origin of the Miami branch office of Crown Colony suggests the nature of its operations. . . . The building housed numerous telephones tied into a long distance WATS facility and a central monitoring system that allowed salesmen's supervisors to listen in on conversations or to broadcast such conversations to other salesmen over a speaker system. Crown Colony established its offices in a section of the building not being used by the wig and chemical operations, and it made use of the WATS facilities during the evening hours when wigs and chemicals were not being sold.

The Miami sales room, out of which Crown Colony's telephone operators made their calls, was divided into two work areas, each of which contained approximately 25 telephone cubicles with directional microphones that allowed supervisors to address the salesmen without being overheard by customers on the line. Crown Colony made no attempt to hire salesmen with any knowledge of the commodity markets and only instructed salesmen in the rudimentary terms applicable to options trading. The training given salesmen was geared to produce sales and overcome customer resistance, and salesmen were told that the less they knew about commodities the better salesmen they would be. The salesmen worked in two three-hour evening shifts of approximately 50 persons each; each supervisor was responsible for the activities of approximately twelve salesmen. The salesmen received a commission of 10 percent of the purchase price paid by a customer for an option, and supervisors received a commission of 10 percent on their own sales and of .5 percent on the sales of their salesmen. The evidence establishes that intense pressure was brought to bear on salesmen to produce sales; those who could not generate approximately $500 in commissions each week were often dismissed from their jobs.

The names and telephone numbers of potential investors were apparently purchased in bulk from third parties specializing in the generation and distribution of "mailing lists." The initial contact with a customer consisted of the presentation of a script or canned sales pitch called a "front." These fronts, irrespective of the commodity options to which they related, were calculated to do two things only: first, "to stimulate the greed" of potential customers by emphasizing the opportunity for unlimited profits in commodity options, and second, to screen out those who simply did not have funds available or obtainable to invest in options. . . . The fronts were . . . misleading and inaccurate, and the predictions contained therein were made without a reasonable belief of their accuracy. Moreover, Crown Colony frequently informed investors that a commodity was trading at less than its actual market price in order to be able to report a sharp price "rise" at a later date and thus pressure customers to "get in while the getting was good."

After being qualified during the front, an investor was ordinarily "papered," or sent various brochures purporting to describe the mechanics of option trading, the nature of Crown Colony's business and the advantages of investing in whatever option was being promoted at the time. This literature abounds in misleading, incomplete and deceptive statements.

After being papered an investor was again telephoned by a Crown Colony salesman, who presented a second canned sales pitch called a "drive." Like the fronts used by Crown Colony, the drives contained many misleading and deceptive statements intended to pressure customers into investing in options.

When Crown Colony salesmen encountered resistance on the part of customers, they often departed from the prepared scripts and made misrepresentations even more egregious than those contained in the canned pitches. The tape recording made by the Texas securities commissioner, for example, contained statements by a salesman in the New York office that both assured profits and represented that no Crown Colony customer ever lost money on his investment.

It was also the regular practice of Crown Colony to "load" and "roll" customers who made an initial option purchase. "Loading" refers to the policy of attempting to sell additional options to a customer who has once purchased, without respect to the investor's realistic ability to afford further investment and without regard to the soundness of the investments themselves at the time of the loading.

"Rolling" consists of exercising a customer's option that has turned out to be profitable and reinvesting all or a portion of the proceeds in another option on a different commodity for the purpose of generating extra commissions. Crown Colony regularly appropriated large portions of investors' profits by rolling them without regard to whether the new investment was more advantageous than the old, if advantageous at all. Indeed, old customers were at times urged to sell coffee and buy sugar options with the proceeds while Crown Colony was extolling the virtues of coffee options to new customers.

Finally, Crown Colony effected purchases and sales of options that were unauthorized by customers and refused to comply with direct customer orders to exercise options.

The defendants, apparently recognizing the overwhelming proof of violations, nevertheless assert that they should not be preliminarily enjoined from further violating the Commodity Act because each of them has ceased all activity with respect to commodity options, and there is thus no likelihood of future violations. However, as the Court of Appeals for this circuit has recently noted, "the commission of past illegal conduct is highly suggestive of the likelihood of future violations."

Their past actions speak louder than their present words. Under these circumstances, the Court is fully persuaded that a *preliminary injunction* against further violations should issue forthwith.

Submit order in accordance with the foregoing.

CASE QUESTIONS

1. What law were the defendants alleged to have violated? What does this law provide?
2. What is a "boiler room"? Define the following terms as used in this case:
   a. front
   b. papered
   c. drive
   d. loading
   e. rolling
3. Which of the following types of contracts were the defendants selling in this case?
   a. commodities futures contract
   b. *options* on commodity futures contracts
   Explain the difference. Which is more speculative?

Policy Issue. What relief did the court grant in this case? Was the remedy adequate?

Economics Issue. Are there large commissions to be made by brokers in selling commodity futures contracts and options?

Ethics Issue. Did the defendants in this case act ethically? Should they be forgiven for their past transgressions and be allowed to conduct future trading?

Social Responsibility. Did the commodities brokers in this case breach their duty of social responsibility? Explain.

STOCK INDEX FUTURES

The most recent development in the futures markets has been the advent of trading in stock index futures. A *stock index future* is a futures contract where the underlying commodity is an *index number* that represents the value of a bundle of stocks. The function of stock index futures is purely speculative, with parties gambling that the index will go up or down in the future. The stock index future is traded like any other commodity, but delivery of the bundle of stocks indexed is never made. All stock index futures are settled in cash.

For example, if the Dow Jones Industrial Index is at 1,200, an investor can enter into an index contract where he estimates that the index will be at 1,300 within a specified period of time (e.g., one month). If the index is greater than 1,300 at the end of the contract period, the investor makes a profit in accordance with the terms of the contract. If the index is lower than 1,300, he loses his investment. There are numerous indexes upon which stock futures index contracts are based, with additional indexes being developed.

Trend of the Law

Trading in commodity futures contracts literally exploded during the 1980s in the United States. The number of commodities subject to futures contracts and the number of contract markets offering such contracts have been increasing steadily. Options contracts trading and the trading in stock index futures have also become extremely popular during the 1980s. Trading in these speculative forms of investment will continue to increase in the future. However, much of the trading will be done by specialists, because it is often difficult for a small investor to respond to the marketplace and make timely trades. The courts will be faced with an increasing volume of fraud actions brought under the provisions of the Commodity Exchange Act and the rules adopted by the Commodity Futures Trading Commission.

REVIEW QUESTIONS

1. In June 1975, Ruddy bought several call options on coffee through Badoian, a broker. A call option allows the purchaser to buy a commodity at a certain price for a specified period of time. In this case, Ruddy had the option to buy 15 tons of coffee at $1,080 per ton until the end of the year. In July and August the price of coffee started falling and Ruddy expressed concern to Badoian. Badoian told Ruddy that he should take advantage of the drop by hedging. Hedging would effectively cancel out any gain that Ruddy would make if the price of coffee rose, but could be very profitable if coffee prices dropped further. Hedging is a very complicated process and Ruddy did not understand it completely. Ruddy told Badoian to go ahead and hedge as long as it did not hurt his "up position," i.e., if coffee prices rose he would still make money. Badoian assured Ruddy that hedging would not hurt his "up position." On July 17, a "killer" frost hit Brazil and the price of coffee tripled over the next three months. However, since Badoian hedged against Ruddy's option contract, Ruddy did not make the money that he assumed he had made. Ruddy sued Badoian and Badoian's firm claiming that they had violated the Commodities Exchange Act. Was he successful? What type of damages could he sue for?

2. A group of Idaho and Washington potato farmers conspired to depress the value of Maine potato futures, which enabled them to supply their western potatoes at a higher price later in the year. The group pooled their resources and bought almost 2,000 short contracts in May potato futures. A short contract obligates the holder to deliver a specified quantity of potatoes in a future month (May) at a specified price. Usually the holder of the contract

does not actually own any potatoes; rather, he is hoping that the price will go down before delivery is required. By maintaining short positions, the growers felt that they could control the majority of the Maine potato market, thereby lowering prices. At the same time, a group of Eastern potato farmers discovered the attempt and decided to beat the Western farmers at their own game. The Eastern farmers bought about 1000 long contracts in May Maine potato futures. The Eastern group then decided to hold out for a high price for the potatoes. In order for the Western group to actually deliver the potatoes that they were required to deliver by their short positions, the Western group would have to buy potatoes from the Eastern group holding the long positions. As May rapidly approached, neither side budged; the Eastern farmers demanded an unreasonably high price and the western farmers offered an unreasonably low price. Each side held to its position throughout May and as a result, the sellers of almost 1000 contracts (the Western group) failed to deliver approximately 50,000,000 pounds of potatoes, resulting in one of the largest defaults in the history of commodities futures trading in the United States. As a result of this default, a large number of buyers, brokers and traders were substantially injured. Each group formed a class action, suing separately the Western farmers and their brokers and the Eastern farmers and their brokers for violations of the Commodities Exchange Act. Have these farmers violated the Act? Can the different groups of plaintiffs recover for their damages? Can the Commodities Futures Trading Commission sue the farmers? What type of damages can be recovered?

IV

THE SOCIAL RESPONSIBILITY OF BUSINESS

17 ENVIRONMENTAL PROTECTION

INTRODUCTION

Federal concern for protecting the environment from pollution is of recent origin. Before the 1970s, most cases of pollution were dealt with under the common-law doctrine of private or public *nuisance*. The common-law liability rules of the doctrine of nuisance were inadequate to advance a broad legal attack on modern-day pollution problems.

As concern for the environment and for the health of human beings increased, many state and local governments passed laws during the 1950s and 1960s in an attempt to deal with pollution problems. It was not, however, until about 1970 that the federal government began enacting comprehensive legislation to protect the environment from pollution from all sources. Since 1970, both state and federal environmental laws have burgeoned. The development of this vast body of law in such a short period of time is unique in the history of the United States.

Pollution is not of a recent origin. Only the magnitude is. This excerpt from *Ethyl Corporation v. EPA*, 541 F.2d 1 (1976), highlights the pollution problem presently facing America.

Never before have massive quantities of asbestiform tailings been spewed into the water we drink. Never before have our industrial workers been occupationally exposed to vinyl chloride or to asbestos dust. Never before has the food we eat been permeated with DDT or the pesticides aldrin and dieldrin. And never before have hundreds of thousands of tons of lead emissions been disgorged annually into the air we breathe.

Business is responsible for a substantial amount of the pollution in this country. Air pollutants spew forth from the smokestacks of the industrial east and midwest. Toxic substances are deposited at dump sites with little concern for the dangers they pose to the health of human beings and other animals living near the sites. Business is not responsible for all of the pollution in the United States. For example, a substantial amount of the air pollution in urban areas is caused by automobile emissions. However, even in this instance business is indirectly the cause of the pollution in that it produces and sells the product that emits the pollutants.

Corporations and other businesses have made major strides in recent years to limit pollution in this country. However, instead of being voluntary, most of the efforts of business to control pollution have been in response to the passage of strict federal and state environmental protection laws. The cost of complying with environmental standards can be substantial. Some businesses that cannot afford compliance are driven out of business. Other businesses suffer a decrease in earnings, or must limit their expansion plans, in order to comply with environmental laws.

Environmental protection is one of the most important, and controversial, topics facing business and society today. In most environmental protection issues the opposing parties tend to take polar "all-or-nothing" positions, leaving little room for compromise as in most other issues faced by business. In recent years, a substantial "backlash" has developed against the stringent enforcement of environmental laws. Thus, the study of environmental law is as much a study of public policy and economics as it is a study of law. These issues, as well as the social responsibility of business in complying with environmental laws, are covered in this chapter.

DO TREES HAVE STANDING?

In order to bring and maintain any type of lawsuit, the plaintiff must have *standing* to sue. The doctrine of standing requires that the plaintiff allege and prove that he has been injured by the defendant in order to sue the defendant for damages. If the plaintiff can prove that he *will be* injured by the defendant's actions, he can bring an action for an injunction to prohibit the defendant from causing such injury.

In a typical civil lawsuit for breach of contract or negligence, the party in privity of contract with the defendant, or the party who was negligently harmed by the defendant (e.g., in an automobile accident) has *standing* to sue the defendant. A third party has no legal right to bring a lawsuit against a defendant for causing injury to someone else, except under a few special legal doctrines, such as that of the third-party beneficiary to a contract.

However, in environmental matters, where the injury may be to the general public, or possibly not to a human being at all but to an animal, bird, reptile, or tree, it is much more difficult for a plaintiff to prove that he has standing to bring and maintain an action against the defendant.

In *Sierra Club v. Morton, 405 U.S.* 727 (1972), the United States Forest Service, which is entrusted with the administration of the national forests, invited bids from private developers to construct and operate a ski resort and summer recreation area in the Mineral King Valley in the Sierra Mountains of Northern California. A proposal by Walt Disney Enterprises, Inc. was chosen. The Sierra Club, an environmental protection organization, filed suit in U.S. District Court under certain federal and state environmental laws to prevent the construction of the resort. On appeal, the Court of Appeals held that the Sierra Club lacked "standing" to sue because the Club failed to allege that it or its members would be personally affected in any of their activities or pastimes by the Disney development. The United States Supreme Court affirmed the decision of the Court of Appeals.

After the *Sierra Club v. Morton* decision, if an environmental group wishes to bring an action under environmental protection laws, it must allege and prove that individual members of the group have been, or will be, injured by the actions of the defendant. For example, a resident of New York who has never used the beaches in California cannot fly to California and bring an action to prevent the development of the California coastline. Further, injury to an animal or natural object itself is not sufficient for a person to bring a lawsuit on behalf of the animal or natural object. The injury that the defendant has or will cause to the animal or natural object must cause injury to the plaintiff (e.g., the plaintiff takes walks in the woods to watch the animals that are threatened) before the plaintiff can bring an action against the defendant under most environmental laws.

The famous dissenting opinion of Justice Douglas in *Sierra Club v. Morton* is set forth following.

DO TREES HAVE STANDING?

SIERRA CLUB v. MORTON

405 U.S. 727, 741 (1972)
UNITED STATES SUPREME COURT

Mr. Justice Douglas, dissenting.

The critical question of "standing" would be simplified and also put neatly in focus if we fashioned a federal rule that allowed environmental issues to be litigated before federal agencies or federal courts in the name of the inanimate object about to be despoiled, defaced, or invaded by roads and bulldozers and where injury is the subject of public outrage. Contemporary public concern for protect-

ing nature's ecological equilibrium should lead to the conferral of standing upon environmental objects to sue for their own preservation.

Inanimate objects are sometimes parties in litigation. A ship has a legal personality, a fiction found useful for maritime purposes. The corporation sole—a creature of ecclesiastical law—is an acceptable adversary and large fortunes ride on its cases. The ordinary corporation is a "person" for purposes of the adjudicatory processes, whether it represents proprietary, spiritual, aesthetic, or charitable causes.

So it should be as respects valleys, alpine meadows, rivers, lakes, estuaries, beaches, ridges, groves of trees, swampland, or even air that feels the destructive pressures of modern technology and modern life. The river, for example, is the living symbol of all the life it sustains or nourishes—fish, aquatic insects, water ouzels, otter, fishes, deer, elk, bear, and all other animals, including man, who are dependent on it or who enjoy it for its sight, its sound, or its life. The river as plaintiff speaks for the ecological unit of life that is part of it. Those people who have a meaningful relation to that body of water—whether it be a fisherman, a canoeist, a zoologist, or a logger—must be able to speak for the values which the river represents and which are threatened with destruction.

The voice of the inanimate object, therefore, should not be stilled. That does not mean that the judiciary takes over the managerial functions from the federal agency. It merely means that before these priceless bits of Americana (such as a valley, an alpine meadow, a river, or a lake) are forever lost or are so transformed as to be reduced to the eventual rubble of our urban environment, the voice of the existing beneficiaries of these environmental wonders should be heard.

Perhaps they will not win. Perhaps the bulldozers of "progress" will plow under all the aesthetic wonders of this beautiful land. That is not the present question. The sole question is, who has standing to be heard?

Those who hike the Appalachian Trail into Sunfish Pond, New Jersey, and camp or sleep there, or run the Allagash in Maine, or climb the Guadalupes in West Texas, or who canoe and portage the Quetico Superior in Minnesota, certainly should have standing to defend those natural wonders before courts or agencies, though they live 3,000 miles away. Those who merely are caught up in environmental news or propaganda and flock to defend these waters or areas may be treated differently. That is why these environmental issues should be tendered by the inanimate object itself. Then there will be assurances that all of the forms of life which it represents will stand before the court—the pileated woodpecker as well as the coyote and bear, the lemmings as well as the trout in the streams. Those inarticulate members of the ecological group cannot speak. But those people who have so frequented the place as to know its values and wonders will be able to speak for the entire ecological community.

CASE QUESTIONS

1. What does the doctrine of "standing" require?
2. Do environmental groups such as the Sierra Club serve a useful purpose in protecting the environment? Do such groups help or harm business? Explain.

Policy Issue. Should injury to an alpine forest, animal, reptile, bird, or inanimate object alone be a sufficient basis to support a lawsuit under environmental protection laws? Should otters have standing? Should grass have standing?

Economics Issue. If all animals, birds, reptiles, and inanimate objects were absolutely protected from destruction and harm, what would happen to our economy?

Ethics Issue. Is it ethical for business to propose projects that it knows will cause harm to the environment?

Social Responsibility. Do corporations owe a duty of social responsibility not to harm the environment? To provide jobs and produce products and services? Do these duties often conflict? Can they be reconciled?

THE NATIONAL ENVIRONMENTAL POLICY ACT

The federal government first seriously began regulating the environment when it enacted the National Environmental Policy Act (NEPA), which became effective on January 1, 1970. The NEPA requires all *federal* agencies to consider any "adverse impact" that their actions, proposals, legislation, or regulations would have on the environment, and to prepare an Environmental Impact Statement. The NEPA is only applicable to *federal* action.

The Environmental Protection Agency.　In 1970 Congress created the Environmental Protection Agency (EPA). The EPA is responsible for the administration and enforcement of almost all of the federal environmental laws discussed in this chapter, including the NEPA. The EPA shares the enforcement responsibility of several environmental laws with other federal governmental agencies. The EPA has taken its charge seriously, having instituted thousands of cases and proceedings to enforce the environmental laws under its jurisdiction. Congress has delegated to the EPA broad powers to adopt rules and regulations in order to advance the policies of the environmental laws that it is responsible for enforcing. The EPA also has been delegated broad adjudicative powers to hold hearing and make decisions in cases involving environmental law. This excerpt from *Ethyl Corporation v. EPA* describes the task that faces the EPA and other agencies charged with enforcing environmental laws:

Man's ability to alter his environment developed far more rapidly than his ability to foresee with certainty the effects of his alterations. It is only recently that we have begun to appreciate the danger posed by unregulated modification of the world around us, and have created watchdog agencies whose task it is to warn us, and protect us, when technological "advances" present dangers unappreciated—or unrevealed—by their supporters. Such agencies, unequipped with crystal balls and unable to read the future, are nonetheless charged with evaluating the effects of unprecedented environmental modifications, often made on a massive scale. Necessarily, they must deal with predictions and uncertainty, with developing evidence, with conflicting evidence, and, sometimes, with little or no evidence at all.

Environmental Impact Statements.　An *Environmental Impact Statement* (EIS) is a written document that is prepared by the federal government, often with the assistance of certain professionals such as engineers, geologists, and accountants. The purpose of an EIS is to provide a full and fair discussion of the significant environmental impacts of proposed federal projects. An EIS must disclose the following information:

1. a summary of the EIS
2. a statement of the purposes of the EIS
3. a description of the affected environment
4. a description of the environmental impact of the proposed federal action
5. an identification and discussion of the alternatives to the proposed action
6. a list of the resources that will be committed to the action
7. a cost-benefit analysis of the proposed action and alternative actions.

An EIS need only be prepared whenever the federal action is "major" and will "significantly" affect the quality of the *human* environment. In many projects, such as the construction of a federal highway, development of federal lands for public use, and licensing nuclear power plants, these standards are met and the preparation of an EIS is obviously required. However, where the federal action is only managerial (e.g., a park ranger leases campsites in an approved federal campground), or is only minimally a "federal" action (e.g., federal roads are used to reach a proposed construction site), an EIS does not have to be prepared by the federal government. Federal projects that fall between these extremes must be reviewed on a case-by-case basis to determine whether an EIS must be prepared.

The EIS provides the federal agency with information for making a decision to go forward with the proposed project, or to abandon or alter the plan to avoid adversely affecting the environment. An EIS also provides the courts with sufficient information for review whenever the government agency's action or the contents or adequacy of an EIS are challenged.

Whenever a federal agency makes a *negative* declaration in the EIS that its proposed action will have *no* significant impact on the quality of the human environment, the declaration must be open for public review for 30 days before the proposed action is to be taken or begun. Comments from the public are solicited. Federal agencies must respond to public comments either individually or collectively. The EPA will then issue an order as to whether or not the proposed action or project may proceed. Decisions and rules of the EPA are appealable to the appropriate federal Court of Appeals.

State Environmental Protection Laws.   Most states have enacted detailed legislation to protect the environment of the state. Most states also require the preparation of a state environmental impact statement where state or local government action will affect the quality of the environment. Pursuant to their police power to protect the "health, safety and welfare" of their residents, most states also require private industry to prepare environmental impact studies prior to taking certain actions. Environmental standards are quite strict in special environmental zones. For example, California has created the California Coastal Commission to review and approve developments planned along or within a certain distance of the California coastline. Although one case in this chapter illustrates the application of state environmental law to the protection of wildlife, a detailed coverage of state environmental laws is beyond the scope of this book.

AIR POLLUTION

Prior to the advent of the internal combustion engine, most air pollution was visible, usually consisting of smoke from factories. In the late 1800s and early 1900s, many cities adopted ordinances regulating smoke emissions from factories. However, today, the majority of the air pollution comes from *mobile* sources in the transportation sector, and almost all of that is caused by the internal combustion engine. Pollution from internal combustion engines mostly consists of carbon monoxide, hydrocarbons, and oxides of nitrogen. *Stationary* sources of pollution, such as factories, households, and public utilities, usually emit sulfur oxides, particles, and oxides of nitrogen. The combining of hydrocarbons and oxides of nitrogen in sunlight produces photochemical oxidants, commonly known as "smog."

Many of today's harmful air pollutants are invisible, and often odorless. The effects of any single dose of air pollution may be immeasurably small. However, the aggregation of air pollution over the lifespan of a human being, animal, or plant may be severe and ultimately fatal.

The Clean Air Act of 1970.　　Congress passed the Clean Air Act in 1963, and amended it in 1965 and 1967, to control pollution from automobiles. In 1970, Congress enacted a new Clean Air Act, a comprehensive federal law to regulate air pollution. The primary purpose of the 1970 Clean Air Act was to set pollution controls on both stationary and mobile sources of pollution. The Clean Air Act authorizes the Environmental Protection Agency (EPA) to conduct testing and certification programs to increase compliance with the Act and regulations adopted thereunder. Pursuant to a 1977 amendment to the Clean Air Act, the EPA has begun to regulate many sources of pollutants that were previously unregulated, including ozone levels in the stratosphere.

The Clean Air Act of 1970 sets certain standards for reducing dangerous carbon monoxide and hydrocarbons from automobile emissions. The standards, which were originally to be implemented by 1975, have received several extensions. Emission standards have also been set by the EPA for other mobile sources of pollution, including trucks, buses, motorcycles, and airplanes. The Clean Air Act also attempts to stimulate technological development by setting fuel economy standards, and by providing special treatment for the development of low-emission vehicles.

The Clean Air Act of 1970 also authorizes the EPA to regulate fuel and fuel additives. The EPA has issued regulations that prohibit the sale of leaded gasoline for use in automobiles with catalytic converters. Only unleaded gasoline may be used in such engines. The Act also provides civil penalties for tampering with pollution-control devices on vehicles.

The Clean Air Act expressly provides for lawsuits by private citizens to enforce emission standards, limitations contained in the Act, orders of the EPA, and "nondiscriminatory" duties of the EPA.

National Ambient Air Quality Standards.　　Under the Clean Air Act, the EPA is directed to determine "national ambient air quality standards" (NAAQS) for particular pollutants. The original six "criteria" pollutants are:

1. nitrogen dioxide
2. carbon monoxide
3. sulfur dioxide
4. ozone
5. total suspended particulates
6. hydrocarbons.

States are required to attain the NAAQS for each pollutant within specified time periods. Additional ambient air quality standards for other pollutants such as lead may be set by the EPA.

Ambient air quality standards are set at two different levels by the EPA. "Primary" ambient standards are those set to protect human beings from harm. "Secondary" ambient standards are adopted to protect plants, climate, visibility, materials, and "economic values" from harm.

The first step in trying to meet the ambient air quality standards set by the EPA is for a state to prepare a "State Implementation Plan" (SIP). The plan must provide for the attainment of the EPA's ambient standards no later than three years from the date of the approval of the plan. Detailed federal regulation covers the preparation of the state plan. Setting and attaining ambient air quality standards on *stationary* sources of pollution, e.g., factories, is the primary emphasis of state plans. The EPA has divided each state into Air Quality Control Regions (AQCR). The EPA then monitors each region to assure that the national ambient air standards for each designated pollutant is met.

If an Air Quality Control Region does not meet the ambient air quality standards set by the EPA, the EPA can designate the area as a "nonattainment area." The state must develop a revised State Implementation Plan to bring the designated area into attainment within a certain period of time. In order to provide an incentive for state compliance, the EPA may prohibit any further development in the nonattainment area until the area meets compliance levels.

Current environmental law provides that pollution *offsets* can be used to further the economic development of an area. For example, if a proposed new factory would cause an increase in a type of pollution in an air-quality control region that does not meet the current ambient-air-quality standards for that pollutant set by the EPA, a reduction of that type of pollution from another source, or even a reduction of a different type of pollution, can be used to "*offset*" the increase in pollution from the new factory, enabling the new factory to be built. The purpose of the offset rule is to allow local areas to meet federal ambient-air-quality standards without curtailing the economic development of the area (e.g., the creation of new jobs).

Although the EPA sets ambient-air standards for certain geographical areas, the source of the pollution may actually be located outside the boundary of the Air Quality Control Region or the state. Problems of compliance often occur where there is "transboundary" or interstate air pollution. "Acid rain," rain that brings air pollutants to the ground, enhances the problems of transboundary air pollution because the pollutants commonly drift on the wind from one state to fall in rain in another.

In *Ethyl Corporation v. EPA* the court upheld an EPA regulation requiring the reduction of lead additives in gasoline.

AIR POLLUTION

ETHYL CORPORATION, PPG INDUSTRIES, INC., E. I. Du PONT de NEMOURS & COMPANY, NALCO CHEMICAL COMPANY, NATIONAL PETROLEUM REFINERS ASSOCIATION v. ENVIRONMENTAL PROTECTION AGENCY

541 F.2D 1 (1976)
UNITED STATES COURT OF APPEALS, D.C. CIRCUIT

J. Skelly Wright, Circuit Judge.
Hard on the introduction of the first gasoline-powered automobiles came the discovery that lead "an-

tiknock" compounds, when added to gasoline, dramatically increase the fuel's octane rating. Increased octane allows for higher compression engines, which operate with greater efficiency. Since 1923 antiknocks have been regularly added to gasoline, and a large industry has developed to supply those compounds. Today, approximately 90 percent of motor gasoline manufactured in the United States contains lead additives, even though most 1975 and 1976 model automobiles are equipped with catalytic converters, which require lead-free gasoline. From the beginning, however, scientists have questioned whether the addition of lead to gasoline, and its consequent diffusion into the atmosphere from the automobile emission, poses a danger to the public health.

Lead is an ubiquitous element. It is found in the land, in the sea, in plants, in animals, and, ultimately, in humans. Traces of lead ranging from 10 to 40 micrograms per 100 grams of blood (10–40 mg/100g) are found in everyone, including those living in environments with almost no atmospheric lead. Despite its universal presence however, lead serves no known purpose in the human body, and at higher concentrations is toxic, causing anemia, severe intestinal cramps, paralysis of nerves, fatigue, and even death.

Human body lead comes from three major sources. In most people, the largest source is the diet.

A second major source of the body's lead burden, at least among urban children, is regarded as controllable, although effective control may be both difficult and expensive to achieve. Ingestion of lead paint by children with pica (the abnormal ingestion of non-food substances, a relatively common trait in pre-school children, particular ages 1–3) is generally regarded as "the principal environmental source in cases of severe acute lead poisoning in young children."

The last remaining major source of lead exposure for humans is the ambient air. This source is easily the most controllable, since approximately 90 percent of lead in the air comes from automobile emissions, and can be simply eliminated by removing lead from gasoline.

In the Clean Air Act Amendments of 1970, . . . [Congress] . . . gave the newly-created EPA authority to control or prohibit the sale or manufacture of any fuel additive whose emission products "will endanger the public health or welfare."

Given this mandate, EPA published on January 31, 1971 advance notice of proposed rule-making. . . . Under the final regulations, lead in all gasoline would be reduced over a five-year period to an average of 0.5 grams per gallon.

Petitioners, various manufacturers of lead additives and refiners of gasoline, appealed the promulgation of low-lead regulations to this court. . . .

Petitioners argue that the "will endanger" standard requires a high quantum of factual proof, proof of actual harm rather than of a "significant risk of harm."

The Precautionary Nature of "Will Endanger"

Simply as a matter of plain meaning, we have difficulty crediting petitioners' reading of the "will endanger" standard. The meaning of "endanger" is not disputed. Case law and dictionary definition agree that *endanger* means something less than actual harm. When one is endangered, harm is *threatened;* no actual injury need ever occur. Thus, for example, a town may be "endangered" by a threatening plague or hurricane and yet emerge from the danger completely unscathed. A statute allowing for regulation in the face of danger is, necessarily, a precautionary statute. Regulatory action may be taken before the threatened harm occurs; . . .

[W]e conclude that the "will endanger" standard is precautionary in nature and does not require proof of actual harm before regulation is appropriate.

The Administrator's Power to Assess Risks

. . . Questions involving the environment are particularly prone to uncertainty. Technological man has altered his world in ways never before experienced or anticipated. The health effects of such alterations are often unknown, sometimes unknowable. . . . Yet the statutes—and common sense—demand regulatory action to prevent harm, even if the regulator is less than certain that harm is otherwise inevitable.

The problems faced by EPA in deciding whether lead automotive emissions pose a threat to the public health highlight the limitations of awaiting certainty. First, lead concentrations are, even to date, essentially low-level, so that the feared adverse effects would not materialize until after a lifetime of exposure. Contrary to petitioners' suggestion, however, we have not yet suffered a lifetime of exposure to lead emissions. At best, emissions at present levels have been with us for no more than 15–20 years. Second, lead exposure from the ambient air is pervasive, so that valid control groups cannot be found against which the effects of lead on our population can be measured. Third, the sources of human exposure to lead are multiple, so that it is difficult to isolate the effect of automobile emissions. Lastly, significant exposure to lead is toxic, so that considerations of decency and morality limit the flexibility of experiments on humans that would otherwise accelerate lead exposure from years to months, and measure those results.

That petitioners, and their scientists, find a basis to disagree is hardly surprising, since the results are still uncertain, and will be for some time. But if the statute accords the regulator flexibility to assess risks and make essentially legislative policy judgments, as we believe it does, preventive regulation based on conflicting and inconclusive evidence may be sustained.

Propriety of the Cumulative Impact Approach

In addition to demanding that the Administrator act solely on facts, petitioner Ethyl insists that those facts convince him that the emission product of the additive to be regulated "in and of itself," i.e., considered in isolation, endangers health. The Administrator contends that the impact of lead emissions is properly considered together with all other human exposure to lead.

[U]nder Ethyl's approach, EPA regulation of lead on health grounds would be impossible and that Congress could not possibly have intended the restrictive "by itself" reading. . . . [L]ead enters the human body from multiple sources, so that the effect of any one source is meaningful only in cumulative terms. If, for example, airborne lead were the only source of the lead body burden, and it caused, by itself, a blood lead level of 30 ug, there would be no danger to the public health. But if that hypothetical 30 ug is added to a possible 30 ug attributable to dietary ingestion, the blood lead level would be 60 ug, a definite threat to health. Under Ethyl's approach, despite obvious endangerment such a cumulative finding is insufficient to justify regulation. Airborne lead, in and of itself, may not be a threat. But the realities of human lead exposure show that

no one source in and of itself (except possibly leaded paint) is a threat. Thus, under Ethyl's tunnel-like reasoning, even if parallel legislation permitted regulation of other sources of lead exposure, which it does not, no regulation could ever be justified.

Such cannot be the case. Congress understood that the body lead burden is caused by multiple sources. It understood that determining the effect of lead automobile emissions, by themselves, on human health is of no more practical value than finding the incremental effect on health of the fifteenth sleeping pill swallowed by a would-be suicide. It did not mean for "endanger" to be measured only in incremental terms. . . . We find no error in the Administrator's use of the cumulative impact approach.

CONCLUSION

The complex scientific questions presented by this rule-making proceeding were "resolved in the crucible of debate through the clash of informed but opposing scientific and technological viewpoints."

Because of the importance of the issues raised, we have accorded this case the most careful and exhaustive consideration. We find that in this rule-making proceeding the EPA has complied with all the statutory procedural requirements and that its reasons as stated in its opinion provide a rational basis for its action. Since we reject all of petitioners' claims of error the Agency may enforce its low-lead regulations.

Affirmed.

CASE QUESTIONS

1. What are the three sources of lead in the human body? What are the harmful effects of lead?
2. What law was involved in this case? Where did the EPA get its rule-making authority?
3. What does the "will endanger" standard provide? Does it require a showing of actual harm? Explain.
4. Can the EPA use "speculation," "theoretical extrapolation," and "conflicting evidence" in making its decisions?
5. What did the EPS's *cumulative impact approach* standard provide? Did the court accept the plain-

tiff's "tunnel-like reasoning" or the EPA's approach?

6. Was the "crucible of debate" successful in deciding this case? Can there be opposing "scientific and technological" viewpoints? Is science an art?

Policy Issue. Should government agencies such as the EPA be authorized to engage in *preventative* regulation? Or only in *reactive* regulation based on actual evidence of harm?

Economics Issue. Why did the manufacturers of lead additives and refiners of gasoline challenge the EPA ruling? What economic effects will this ruling have on these parties? Explain.

Ethics Issue. Was it ethical for Ethyl Corp. to argue that the lead emitted by automobiles should be measured separately from lead from other sources? What would be the result if the court had accepted this argument? Explain.

Social Responsibility. Did the manufacturers of lead additives and refiners of gasoline breach their duty of social responsibility when they produced products that introduced dangerous lead into the air? When they fought the EPA ruling?

WATER POLLUTION

Natural water is not pure. Water quality is affected by minerals, biological factors, sediments, decaying vegetation and animal wastes. However, it has only been since man started causing substantial additional pollution that water resources have required legal protection from pollution. Unnatural, man-made water pollution occurs from the discharge of industrial water, municipal sewage systems, wastes from commercial feedlots, agricultural chemicals, oil spills, and toxic substances.

The River and Harbor Act of 1886 was the first of a series of federal legislation enacted to regulate water resources and pollution. The River and Harbor Act of 1899 established a permit system for the discharge of "refuse" (litter, rubbish, sewage, etc.) into navigable waterways. In 1948, the Federal Water Pollution Control Act (FWPCA) was enacted by Congress with a goal of eliminating all discharges of pollutants into the nation's waterways. The EPA was authorized to, and has, prepared industry-wide *effluent standards* for water pollution. Water effluent limitations are established for all existing "point sources" such as factories.

The Clean Water Act. Congress amended the FWPCA by enacting the Clean Water Act of 1972. The Clean Water Act of 1972 requires a *permit* for all discharges into navigable streams from any "point source." States may choose to administer the permit program, or allow the EPA to administer it. The 1972 amendments also provide for the federal government to share the cost of constructing municipal sewage treatment plants. Originally set at 75 percent, the federal government's share of the cost of planning and constructing approved municipal treatment works was reduced to 55 percent as of October 1, 1984.

Congress again amended the FWPCA by enacting the Clean Water Act of 1977. The amended act is now simply known as the "Clean Water Act." The Act establishes two different *standards* for requiring industrial point sources to install equipment to control the discharge of pollutants into the country's waterways. These are the "best practical technology" (BPT) standard and the "best available technology" (BAT) standard.

BPT Standard.   This standard requires *existing* industrial sources of water pollution to immediately install pollution-control equipment of the "best practical" technology. The *BPT* standard requires industrial point sources (e.g., factories) to install water pollution controls that are the most *practical* for the point source under the circumstances. Such factors as cost of the pollution-control equipment, severity of the pollution, and the amount of time required to install such equipment may be considered in determining the most practical solution for a point source to use in controlling water pollution. Thus, under the BPT standard, a point source does *not* have to immediately install the most effective pollution control equipment if the cost of such equipment would be prohibitive.

BAT Standard.   The EPA has established certain time periods within which *existing* point sources *must* install the *most effective*, "best available" technology for controlling water pollution. The *BAT* standard requires that, *not* immediately but within those time periods, the most effective water-pollution control equipment be installed by industrial point sources without regard to the cost of this equipment. No less effective alternatives than the BAT technology will then be permitted, even if they are less expensive. The EPA has repeatedly extended the time periods within which such BAT technology must be installed by industrial point sources. BAT equipment will eventually replace BPT equipment at most industrial point sources.

Any *new* industrial point source of water pollution (such as a factory) must install the *most effective* water pollution control equipment under the *BAT* standard. The most practical pollution control equipment under a BPT standard is *not* acceptable for new industrial point sources of water pollution.

The Clean Water Act provides for *criminal* penalties of $2,500 to $25,000 per day for the first violation, and up to $50,000 per day for each violation thereafter, for "willful" or "negligent" violations of the Act. A citizen may bring a *civil* action against anyone who violates the effluent standards of the Clean Water Act, the limitations of the Act, or orders issued by the EPA or a state pursuant to the Act. A citizen may also bring an action for *mandamus* to force the EPA to enforce the law.

The following decision, *U.S. v. Reserve Mining Company,* is one of many lawsuits brought against the defendant, Reserve Mining Company, for pollution problems caused by the defendant's discharge of taconite tailings (a toxic metal waste product) into the waters of Lake Superior.

WATER POLLUTION

UNITED STATES v. RESERVE MINING COMPANY

8 ENVIR. REP. CASES 1978 (1976)
UNITED STATES DISTRICT COURT, MINNESOTA

Devitt, J.

It has been established that Reserve [Mining Company] has violated Minnesota's pollution control laws and regulations. *Reserve Mining Co. v. Environmental Protection Agency, United States v. Reserve Mining Co.* Minn. Stat. Section 115.071 subd. 3 (1974) authorizes a court to impose a fine of up to $10,000 per day for each violation of, *inter alia,* the laws and regulations violated by Reserve. Minnesota contends that defendants should be fined for daily violations of these laws and regulations for almost a full year.

[T]he daily dumping of approximately 67,000 tons of carcinogenic waste into Lake Superior polluting public water supplies in violation of its state discharge permits is, by far, Reserve's most serious offense.

In 1947 Reserve obtained from two state agencies, identical permits authorizing it to discharge tailings into Lake Superior. Subsection (d) of those permits prohibits discharges which

> result in any material clouding or discoloration of the water at the surface outside of [the specified discharge] zone . . . nor shall such tailings be discharged so as to result in any material adverse effects on . . . public water supplies. . . .

The District Court concluded that "the terms of the permits are being violated" because

> [t]he discharge causes discoloration of the surface waters outside of the zone of discharge, causes an increase in turbidity, and adversely affects the public water supplies of several communities resulting in unlawful pollution of the lake.

The Court of Appeals agreed, stating that:

> The record shows that Reserve is discharging a substance into Lake Superior waters which under an acceptable but unproved medical theory may be considered as carcinogenic. [T]his discharge gives rise to reasonable medical concern over the public health.

Clearly, these findings justify the conclusion that Reserve violated its discharge permits. The trial court has determined that Reserve was in violation of its state discharge permits every day during the May 20, 1973 to April 20, 1974 period.

[T]he only remaining issue is the amount of the penalty. In making this determination, the court is aware that, as a result of these discharges, defendants are liable for the costs, expected to be approximately six million dollars, of supplying clean water to the affected communities. In addition, the injunction resulting from this litigation will compel Reserve to either cease operations or expend substantial sums, estimated at over three hundred million dollars, to develop an alternative means of disposing of production wastes.

It is not disputed that Reserve, by supplying needed jobs and services, has revitalized the economy of Northeastern Minnesota and, by adding to the supply of domestically produced raw iron, has contributed to the economy of the entire country. But similar contributions have been made by other corporations while complying with applicable pollution control laws and regulations.

It should be appreciated that Reserve did not set out to spoil the air and water or cause inconvenience to or apprehension among residents of the area. It launched its business venture with the encouragement, even the importuning, of all segments of government and society. But in this business venture, the record shows it returned very substantial profits to its corporate owner-parents, Republic and Armco. It is reasonable to conclude that some of those profits are attributable to operations made less costly by discharging tailings in Lake Superior rather than on land, as is done by its competitors.

[T]he record shows that Reserve, particularly through its Vice President Haley, frustrated the court in prompt resolution of the controversy by violation of court rules and orders and thus prolonged the status quo.

While the daily discharge of 67,000 tons of tailings into Lake Superior is shocking in these days of improved environmental awareness, those discharges were expressly authorized in 1947 by the State of Minnesota. Hindsight tells us that was a mistake, but the gravity of it has not yet been determined. The court of appeals held that Reserve's discharges have not yet been found to be harmful to the public health and that the danger is potential, not imminent. The Court of Appeals found that Reserve need not terminate its operations but directed that preventive and precautionary steps be taken. They have been taken. So while the record shows violations of the permits, it has not been shown, and in the view of the Court of Appeals it is not likely it can be shown, that the past violations have caused actual harm to the public health.

Upon consideration of all the factors and pursuant to authority of Minn. Stat. Section 115.071 subd. 3 (1974), the court imposes on defendants a penalty of $2,500.00 per day for violations of the terms of Reserve's state discharge permits. The penalty must be limited to the period between enactment of the penalty statute, May 20, 1973, and the date the trial concluded and the injunction issued, April 20, 1974—a period of 335 days.

SUMMARY

We determine that:

1. Defendants violated the terms of the state granted water discharge permits daily between May 20, 1973 and April 20, 1974—a period of 335 days—and are assessed penalties of $2,500.00 per day for a total of $837,500.00.
2. Reserve violated court rules and orders as to discovery and is assessed sanctions of $200,000.00.

CASE QUESTIONS

1. Who was the plaintiff? What was the plaintiff suing for in this case?
2. Was the pollution discharged into Lake Superior with the government's permission? Did Reserve Mining violate the permits?
3. Had Reserve Mining been found previously liable for polluting Lake Superior? If so, what penalty had been previously assessed against Reserve Mining?
4. How much money would it have cost Reserve Mining to develop lawful nonpolluting means for discharging industrial wastes into Lake Superior?
5. What penalty did the court in this case assess against Reserve Mining? Was this the largest penalty allowed by law? Do you think it was an adequate penalty in the circumstances? Explain.

Policy Issue. If human beings were harmed by the carcinogenic wastes dumped into Lake Superior by Reserve Mining, should Reserve Mining be held *civilly* liable to these people? Even if Reserve Mining didn't know the wastes were dangerous?

Economics Issue. If Reserve Mining had to go out of business because of the pollution problem, would it have any significant impact on the economy of northern Minnesota?

Ethics Issue. Do you think Reserve Mining intended to harm the environment when it began operations in 1947? In 1973? Were the actions of Reserve Mining's vice president ethical?

Social Responsibility. Did Reserve Mining owe a duty of social responsibility to discontinue discharging wastes into Lake Superior once it found out that these wastes may be dangerous to human beings? Even if it meant discontinuing business and firing all its employees?

Oil Spills. Oil spills from ocean tankers have caused some of the most tragic water pollution accidents in recent history. The Clean Water Act authorizes the United States government to clean up oil spills and other hazardous substances in ocean waters that occur within 12 miles of the ocean shore, and on the continental shelf. The owners and operators of vessels and other sources of oil spills such as oil platforms, oil rigs, etc., are strictly liable for up to a maximum of $150 per gross ton of oil spilled, or $250,000, whichever is greater.

The liability for spills by inland barges is $125 per gross ton of oil spilled, or $125,000, whichever is greater.

In 1972, Congress enacted the Marine Protection, Research, and Sanctuaries Act. The Act extended environmental regulation to the oceans, and provides for a system of permits for dumping waste and other materials into ocean waters. The Act also provides for the establishment of marine sanctuaries in ocean waters as far seaward as the seaward edge of the continental shelf, and in the Great Lakes and their connecting waters.

The Safe Drinking Water Act was enacted by Congress in 1974. The Act established national quality standards for drinking water. States are responsible for establishing an underground drinking water inspection and control program. If a state fails to do so, the EPA can establish and enforce such an inspection and control program.

Thermal Pollution.   The Clean Water Act specifically defines *heat* as a "pollutant." Discharge of heated waters and materials into the nation's waterways may upset the ecological balance of the waterways, decrease the oxygen content of waters, and harm fish, birds, and animals who use the waterways. The electrical utility industry has been the major source of thermal pollution in this country. Sources of thermal pollution are subject to the standards of the Clean Water Act and regulations adopted thereunder by the EPA. Heated waters at times, however, may be a beneficial resource to the environment— they may stimulate growth of vegetation, etc.

HAZARDOUS SUBSTANCES

Pollution may occur from *hazardous* substances. Hazardous substances that are regulated by the state and federal governments include (1) solid wastes, (2) toxic substances, and (3) the use of pesticides.

Solid Wastes.   Prior to the mid-1970s, the disposal of *solid waste* (garbage, sewage, etc.) was generally regarded as a problem for local governments. Solid waste disposal, however, is closely related to water and air pollution, in that solid wastes often are discharged into waterways and the toxic fumes from solid wastes enter the air. Solid waste management, therefore, in addition to being a local problem, is also a state and federal problem. State and federal laws have been enacted to supplement local laws to regulate the management, transportation, and disposal of solid wastes. *Solid waste* includes not only solid materials, but also liquid and gaseous wastes.

Federal Legislation on Hazardous Wastes.   In 1976 Congress passed the *Resource Conservation and Recovery Act* (RCRA). The Act authorizes the federal government to provide financial and technical assistance to state and local governments to help them develop and implement solid waste plans. An Office of Solid Waste has been established within the Environmental Protection Agency.

Certain solid wastes are considered to be "hazardous wastes." RCRA Section 1004(5) defines "hazardous waste" as:

(A) Solid waste . . . which because of its quantity, or concentration, of physical, chemical, or infectuous characteristics may cause or significantly contribute to an increase in mortality or an increase in . . . serious illness; or pose a substantial present or potential hazard to human health or the environment when improperly [managed].

The EPA has specifically designated certain substances as "hazardous." To determine if nondesignated substances are to be considered "hazardous," the EPA applies four specific tests:

1. reactivity
2. ignitability
3. corrosivity
4. toxicity.

The majority of "new" hazardous materials are chemicals that are classified as toxic. Nuclear wastes are classified as hazardous because they are radioactive. In 1980, in an attempt to prevent past mistakes in the handling of hazardous wastes, the EPA began implementing a "cradle to grave" regulation of hazardous wastes. The specific regulations adopted by the EPA:

1. provide for the identification of hazardous wastes
2. set standards for transporting solid wastes
3. define standards for the adequate treatment, storage, and disposal of hazardous wastes
4. set procedures for obtaining permits to handle hazardous wastes.

Sanitary Landfills. In 1980, the EPA issued regulations establishing federal standards for sanitary landfills. The EPA reviewed all existing landfill facilities and issued a list of sites that did not meet federal standards. States are required to bring the designated sites up to federal compliance standards, or to close such sites, within five years. States that do not comply will not qualify for federal financial assistance.

"Bottle" Laws. Many states have recently enacted so-called "bottle laws." Under these laws, a cash deposit must be paid by the purchaser on all glass containers that he buys, particularly glass containers of liquid beverages— soft drinks, beer, etc. The deposit is refunded upon returning the glass container to a center, usually a grocery store, authorized to accept the containers and refund the deposit. Some states have extended the coverage of their bottle laws to include other types of containers. The objective of bottle laws is to help prevent pollution in the form of bottles and other debris thrown alongside the highways and roads of the state. The rationale behind the passage of bottle laws is that persons will be less apt to discard their containers if they are also throwing away the available deposit. Bottle laws have been held to be constitutional.

Toxic Substances.   Toxic substances are poisonous substances, usually in the form of chemicals. Toxic substances were first regulated by the Food and Drug Administration when they were found in food and drug products. Toxic substances have now been discovered in many other products besides foods and drugs. The most notable current toxic substance litigations revolve around: (1) Vietnam veterans exposed to "Agent Orange," a defoliant used in the Vietnam War, (2) persons exposed to asbestos, generally at work, who have contracted asbestosis, and (3) persons exposed to the chemical dioxin, e.g., by its use in the paving of streets in Times Beach, Missouri, and elsewhere in the country. Injuries caused by toxic substances loom as one of the greatest liability exposures for many of the major industries and companies in the United States.

Toxic Substance Control Act.   On January 1, 1977, the *Toxic Substances Control Act* (TSCA) became effective. The Act is the most comprehensive federal regulation of toxic substances, and provides for the testing and control of chemicals that are believed to provide "risk of harm to health or the environment." Under the Act, the EPA can prohibit or limit the manufacture and use of toxic substances. In addition to the TSCA as administered by the EPA, numerous other federal laws and agencies are involved in the regulation of toxic substances, including the following.

1. The Occupational Safety and Health Administration (OSHA) regulates toxic hazards in the workplace.
2. The Department of Transportation regulates the transportation of toxic substances.
3. The Federal Railroad Administration regulates the transportation of toxic substances on railroads.
4. The Coast Guard administers the shipment of toxic substances on waterways.
5. The Mine Safety Administration controls toxic substances in mines.
6. The Consumer Product Safety Commission controls the use of toxic substances in consumer products under several federal acts.
7. The Food and Drug Administration controls the use of toxic chemicals and substances in food, drug, and cosmetic products.

The transportation of dangerous toxic substances through areas of the country has caused considerable concern to citizens located along the transportation routes. In the mid-1980s "death trains" carrying toxic substances through the West to reach certain approved dump sites have been met with substantial protests along their routes.

Private citizens who are injured or are victims of pollution from toxic substances may sue the manufacturer or supplier of the toxic chemical for damages. Recovery is usually obtained in a civil lawsuit based on a theory of negligence, but may also be brought under the doctrine of "strict liability" where applicable. However, proving causation and damages is often difficult because cancer and other injuries may not become acute for many years.

The author's description of the settlement of the Agent Orange toxic chemical class action lawsuit follows.

TOXIC SUBSTANCES
AGENT ORANGE SETTLEMENT

MAY, 1984
UNITED STATES DISTRICT COURT, E.D. NEW YORK

Judge Weinstein presided over the settlement conference.

During America's involvement in the Vietnam conflict the United States military used a herbicide called "Agent Orange." Agent Orange was sprayed by airplanes to defoliate the jungles of Vietnam during the 1960s. People on the ground, including United States military personnel, were exposed to the spray. Agent Orange contained *dioxin,* a poison thought to cause cancer and other health problems. After returning home from Vietnam, often years later, veterans who had been exposed to Agent Orange began contracting cancer, suffering skin problems, and also finding birth defects in their children.

The veterans brought a *class action* lawsuit against the seven chemical companies that manufactured Agent Orange. In a class action, plaintiffs who share an interest in a single fact situation join together as a "class" and bring one lawsuit against the defendant. The courts allow class actions in order to save the cost of several hundreds or thousands of individual lawsuits. A person who has an individual claim against the defendant can reject the offer to join the class and reserve the right to sue the defendant individually. However, the courts can order the *consolidation* of individual lawsuits involving shared fact situations.

The notice of the Agent Orange class action, which appeared in many of the national magazines and newspapers in the country, is set forth following. This notice appeared in *Time* magazine.

Legal Notice

TO ALL PERSONS WHO SERVED IN OR NEAR VIETNAM AS MEMBERS OF THE ARMED FORCES OF THE UNITED STATES, AUSTRALIA AND NEW ZEALAND FROM 1961–1972

If you or anyone in your family can claim injury, illness, disease, death or birth defect as a result of exposure to "Agent Orange" or any other herbicide while as-

signed in or near Vietnam at any time from 1961 to 1972, you are a member of a class in an action brought on your behalf in the United States District Court for the Eastern District of New York unless you take steps to exclude yourself from the class. The class is limited to those who were injured by exposure to "Agent Orange" or any other herbicide while serving in the armed forces in or near Vietnam at any time during 1961–1972. The class also includes members of families who claim derivative injuries such as those to spouses and children.

The court expresses no opinion as to the merit or lack of merit of the lawsuit.

For details about your rights in this "Agent Orange" class action lawsuit, call 1–800–645–1355 if you are *outside* of New York State, or call 1–800–832–1303 if you are *within* New York State, or write Clerk of the Court, P.O. Box 887, Smithtown, New York 11787.

Robert C. Heinemann
Clerk, United States District Court for the Eastern District of New York

DATED Brooklyn, New York
          January 12, 1984

The Agent Orange class action, which would have been the largest, and probably the longest private toxic-injury action in history, was set to go to trial in May, 1984, in the U.S. District Court in Brooklyn, New York. At the last minute (3:00 A.M. on the day the case was set to go to trial) the parties reached a settlement of the case.

Pursuant to the settlement, the seven manufacturers agreed to establish a $180 million trust fund, which will be administered to help pay for the medical costs and other expenses of veterans who were subject to Agent Orange spraying in Vietnam. Monsanto paid approximately half of the settlement, Dow Chemical about twenty percent, and the other five defendants the remainder. In the settlement agreement the chemical companies did *not* admit that Agent Orange caused cancer or other health problems.

The lawyers for the veterans claimed that the settlement was reasonable because, as in all toxic chemical lawsuits, it is often difficult for the plaintiffs to prove a causal relation between their injury and the chemical. Moreover, there were procedural problems with the lawsuit. (E.g., what state law would apply? Judge Weinstein proposed to apply "national consensus" law.) Even if the veterans won at trial, they added, the chemical companies were sure to appeal the decision, which would have delayed any payments for years.

Many veterans criticized the settlement as being too small for the amount of injury that they have suffered and will suffer. With over 100,000 veterans having been subjected to Agent Orange, the settlement agreement will provide each veteran with less than $2,000 in damages.

SETTLEMENT QUESTIONS

Policy Issue. Should soldiers be permitted to sue for injuries incurred during a war? (Vietnam was never declared as a "war," but was instead referred to as a "military conflict.") Should the Vietnamese people who suffered the same consequences from Agent Orange spraying be allowed to sue the chemical companies?

Economics Issue. Was the settlement sufficient? Who really benefited from the settlement of this case? If you were the president of Monsanto or Dow Chemical, what would you have done? If you were a veteran, what would you have done?

Ethics Issue. Was it ethical for the manufacturers of Agent Orange to fight this lawsuit? Should lawyers provide their services free of charge to help plaintiffs fight these kind of lawsuits?

Social Responsibility. Do corporations, such as the defendants in this case, owe a duty of social responsibility to provide medical care and support for life for persons injured by their products? If so, what should have been the dollar amount of the settlement in this case? Does the United States government owe a duty of social responsibility to pay for all the injury caused by Agent Orange?

Pesticides.   The danger of pesticides was recognized early by federal and state governments. In 1972, amendments to the Federal Insecticide, Fungicide and Rodenticide Act (FIFRA) established comprehensive federal pesticide regulation. States may still concurrently regulate pesticides where such regulation does not conflict with federal law.

The FIFRA requires that all pesticides be registered with the Environmental Protection Agency prior to distribution in commerce. The EPA has substantial discretion in denying registration. Exemptions from registration are provided for certain experimental or emergency uses of pesticides. Pesticides registered under the FIFRA are classified for either "general use" or "restricted use," or both, and must be marked accordingly.

The EPA may cancel or suspend the registration of a pesticide upon proper notice and hearing. Under this authority, the EPA has banned the use of the pesticide DDT and other chlorinated hydrocarbon compounds.

The Opinion and Order of the Administrator of the Environmental Protection Agency in *Consolidated DDT Hearings,* which ordered the removal of the use of the pesticide DDT on food products, follows.

PESTICIDES

CONSOLIDATED DDT HEARINGS
OPINION AND ORDER OF THE ADMINISTRATOR

37 FED. REG. 13,369 (1972)
BEFORE THE ENVIRONMENTAL PROTECTION AGENCY

William D. Ruckelshaus, *Administrator.*

DDT is the familiar abbreviation for the chemical (1,1,1, trichlorophenyl ethane), which was for many years the most widely used chemical pesticide in this country. DDT's insecticidal properties were originally discovered, apparently by accident, in 1939, and during World War II it was used extensively for typhus control. Since 1945, DDT has been used for general control of mosquitoes, boll weevil infestation in cotton-growing areas, and a variety of other uses. Peak use of DDT occurred at the end of the 1950s and present domestic use of DDT in various formulations has been estimated at 6,000 tons per year. According to Admission 7 of the record, approximately 86 percent or 10,277,258 pounds of domestically used DDT is applied to cotton crops. The same admission indicates that 603,053 pounds and 937,901 pounds, or approximately 5 percent and 9 percent of the total formulated by 27 of the petitioners in these hearings are used respectively on soybean and peanut crops. All other uses of the 11,966,196 pounds amount to 158,833 of the total, or little over 1 percent.

Public concern over the widespread use of pesticides was stirred by Rachel Carson's book, *Silent Spring,* and a natural outgrowth was the investigation of this popular and widely sprayed chemical. DDT, which for many years had been used with apparent safety, was, the critics alleged, a highly dangerous substance which killed beneficial insects, upset the natural ecological balance, and collected in the food chain, thus posing a hazard to man and other forms of advanced aquatic and avian life. In 1969, the U.S. Department of Agriculture commenced a review of the health and environmental hazards attendant to the use of DDT.

Certain uses of DDT were canceled by the Department of Agriculture in 1969 and informal review of remaining uses continued through 1970. In early 1971, this Agency commenced formal administra-tive review of DDT registrations by the cancellation of all registrations for DDT products and uses pursuant to Section 4(c) of the Federal Insecticide, Fungicide, and Rodenticide Act (FIFRA).

Thirty-one registrants have challenged 15 of the canceled uses of DDT and its metabolite, TDE. These uses of DDT include applications to cotton fields to control the boll weevil and bollworm applications to various vegetable crops, and a variety of lesser uses in public programs.

ANALYSIS OF EVIDENCE

I am convinced by a preponderance of the evidence that, once dispersed, DDT is an uncontrollable, durable chemical that persists in the aquatic and terrestrial environments. Given its insolubility in water and its propensity to be stored in tissues, it collects in the food chain and is passed up to higher forms of aquatic and terrestrial life. There is ample evidence to show that under certain conditions DDT or its metabolites can persist in soil for many years, that it will volatilize or move along with eroding soil. While the degree of transportability is unknown, evidence of record shows that it is occasionally found in remote areas or in ocean species, such as whales, far from any known area of application.

The case against DDT involves more, however, than a long-range hazard to man's health. The evidence presented by the Agency's Pesticides Office and the intervenors, EDF, compellingly demonstrates the adverse impact of DDT on fish and birdlife. Several witnesses testified to first-hand observed effects of DDT on fish and birdlife, reporting lethal or subacute effects on aquatic and avian life exposed in DDT-treated areas. Laboratory evidence is also impressively abundant to show the acute and chronic effects of DDT on avian animal species and suggest that DDT impairs their reproductive capabilities.

The petitioner-registrants' assertion that there is

no evidence of declining aquatic or avian populations, even if actually true, is an attempt at confession and avoidance. It does not refute the basic proposition that DDT causes damage to wildlife species. Group petitioners' argument that DDT is only one toxic substance in a polluted environment, and thus, whatever its laboratory effects, it cannot be shown to be the causative agent of damage in nature, does not redeem DDT, but only underscores the magnitude of effort that will be necessary for cleaning up the environment.

Finally, I am persuaded that a preponderance of the evidence shows that DDE causes thinning of eggshells in certain bird species.

I am convinced by the evidence that continued use of DDT is not necessary to insure an adequate supply of cotton at a reasonable cost. Only 38 percent of cotton-producing acreage is treated with DDT, although the approximately 10,277,258 pounds used in cotton production is a substantial volume of DDT and accounts for most of its use.

APPLICATION OF RISK-BENEFIT TO CROP USES OF DDT

The evidence of record showing storage in man and magnification in the food chain is a warning to the prudent that man may be exposing himself to a substance that may ultimately have a serious effect on his health.

As Judge Leventhal recently pointed out, cancer is a "sensitive and fright-laden" matter and noted earlier in his opinion that carcinogenic effects are "generally cumulative and irreversible when discovered." The possibility that DDT is a carcinogen is at present remote and unquantifiable; but if it is not a siren to panic, it is a semaphore which suggests that an identifiable public benefit is required to justify continued use of DDT.

The risks to the environment from continued use of DDT are more clearly established. . . . The Agency staff established, as well, the existence of acceptable substitutes for all crop uses of DDT except on onions and sweet potatoes in storage and green peppers.

Accordingly, all crop uses of DDT are hereby *canceled* except for application to onions for control of cutworm, weevils on stored sweet potatoes, and sweet peppers.

CASE QUESTIONS

1. What federal statute was involved in this case? Why was it being asserted? Explain.
2. Was DDT found to be *toxic?* Did DDT have any harmful effects on:
   a. animals?
   b. birds?
   c. nontarget insects?
   d. human beings?
3. What was the "risk–benefit" test referred to in this case? What decision did the court reach in applying this test to this case?
4. Was there an alternative to using DDT as a pesticide? Explain.

Policy Issue. Was there actual evidence that DDT caused cancer in human beings? Should actual evidence be required before environmental laws can be invoked to prevent the use of pesticides?

Economics Issue. If there were no alternatives to DDT as a pesticide to be used on cotton, and all cotton crops in the United States would be destroyed if DDT were taken off the market, do you think the court would have reached the same decision? Explain.

Ethics Issue. Was it ethical for the registrant companies to argue that aquatic and avian populations were not declining, so therefore they could kill more members of these groups? Was this an attempt at "confession and avoidance" by the companies as stated by the court?

Social Responsibility. Did the producers and users of DDT breach their duty of social responsibility by not voluntarily discontinuing the use of DDT? Was there sufficient evidence of danger to society to raise this duty?

NOISE POLLUTION

Unwanted sound, "noise pollution," affects almost every member of the U. S. population daily. The sources of noise pollution include airplanes, manufacturing plants, construction equipment, garbage trucks, alarm systems, radios, toys, and other sources. Noise pollution causes hearing loss, difficulty in hearing and speaking, loss of sleep, depression, and other emotional and psychological symptoms and injuries. Noise pollution is dealt with by a myriad of local, state, and federal laws.

State and local governments were the first to recognize the dangers of excessive noise to human beings. Most state and local governments have enacted specific statutes and ordinances that regulate noise from certain loud sources, such as motorcycles and snowmobiles. Local ordinances generally establish maximum noise levels within city boundaries, and specific levels for certain special zones such as hospital zones.

The federal Quiet Communities Act of 1978, which is administered by the Environmental Protection Agency, was passed to encourage development of noise-control programs by state and local government. Under the Act, the federal government provides financial and technical assistance to state and local governments in controlling noise pollution.

The Noise Control Act of 1972.   At the federal level, the major piece of legislation dealing with noise pollution is the Noise Control Act of 1972. Under this Act, the EPA is given extensive control in setting noise standards for new manufactured products. Also under the Act, the EPA and the Federal Aviation Administration (FAA) are authorized to issue noise limitations for new types of aircraft, and the EPA and the Department of Transportation are empowered to regulate noise emissions from trucks, railroads, and other interstate carriers.

In addition to the powers granted to the EPA under the Noise Control Act, other federal agencies also share the responsibility for controlling noise pollution. The Occupational Safety and Health Administration (OSHA) sets and enforces noise level standards in the workplace. The Housing and Urban Development Administration (HUD) includes noise planning in its planning for new residential construction and in the substantial rehabilitation of existing housing under its jurisdiction.

Doctrine of "Nuisance."   The common law doctrine of "nuisance" provides a *private* cause of action to plaintiffs to recover damages for invasion of their right to the "quiet use and enjoyment" of their property caused by noise pollution. The doctrine of "nuisance" must be distinguished from the doctrine of "trespass." In order for there to be a "trespass," there must be an interference with the plaintiff's physical *possession* of the property. This generally does not occur when there is noise pollution. Nuisance, on the other hand, requires only an interference with the "use and enjoyment," rather than the physical possession, of the plaintiff's property. For example, the emission of low-density sound waves from a power generating plant, which causes mental distress to adjoining property owners, is actionable as a nuisance and not as a trespass.

NUCLEAR POWER

One of the most recently developed and most controversial sources of energy is nuclear power. Nuclear power has the potential for replacing or supplementing many of the traditional sources of energy, such as coal, oil, etc. In 1985, nuclear power generated less than 5 percent of the total energy used in the United States. This compares with over 30 percent in France, approximately 15 percent for both Japan and Great Britain, and close to 10 percent for the Soviet Union.

Nuclear power has generated substantial interest in the United States. Supporters of nuclear energy cite a safety record surpassing that of the coal industry, environmental advantages over fossil fuels, and the abundance of energy that can be provided by nuclear power. Opponents of nuclear energy cite the dangers of radiation, the substantial damage that could be caused by a single nuclear accident, and the possibility of terrorist action against nuclear power plants. The future development of nuclear power in the United States will depend on whether the laws enacted promote or constrain the use of nuclear energy.

Federal Regulation of Nuclear Power. From the beginning of the Atomic Age during World War II (1941–1945), the federal government has exercised strong control over the development and use of atomic energy. Congress enacted the Atomic Energy Act of 1946 to place the development of nuclear energy under federal *civilian* control. The 1946 Act created the Atomic Energy Commission (AEC) and the Congressional Joint Committee on Atomic Energy to provide administrative and legislative control over the development of nuclear power. The Joint Commission was abolished in 1977, and its responsibilities were allocated to other Congressional committees. The Atomic Energy Commission was also abolished in 1977; its responsibilities are now shared by the Nuclear Regulatory Commission (NRC) and the Department of Energy.

Licensing Nuclear Power Plants. In 1954, the Atomic Energy Act was amended to stimulate the commercial use of nuclear power. The 1954 amendments authorized the AEC to license a variety of peaceful commercial uses of nuclear technologies. The primary commercial use of nuclear power is for generating electricity. There are approximately 80 licensed operating nuclear power plants in the United States, and over 200 nuclear power plants in the rest of the world. With regard to the issuance of licenses to construct and operate nuclear power plants, the 1946 Atomic Energy Act provides:

[N]o license may be issued . . . if, in the opinion of the Commission, the issuance of a license . . . would be inimical to the common defense and security or to the health and safety of the public.

The Nuclear Regulatory Commission sets standards for the design and construction of nuclear power plants. After holding public hearings, reviewing the applicant utility's need for power, and considering the environmental impact of the proposed nuclear power plant, the NRC may issue a permit to the utility to begin construction of the nuclear power reactor. The NRC oversees the actual construction of the nuclear power plant, and will issue an operating license only if the plant meets certain specifications of construction, and passes a final safety analysis.

The NRC is empowered to inspect all nuclear power plants, and may halt construction of such plants or close plants temporarily or permanently for violations of the required safety standards.

State Regulation of Nuclear Power.　In 1959, Congress enacted Public Law 86–373, Atomic Energy Cooperation With States, which created the "agreement state" concept. Under this concept, the AEC (now the NRC) and the governor of a state can reach an agreement whereby the Commission would turn over some of its licensing responsibility to that state. Under this program, Congress permits the states to regulate nuclear power "for purposes other than protection against radiation hazards." The federal government retains the right to regulate nuclear energy in its military applications. Over half the states have entered into an agreement with the Commission to share the regulation of nuclear power development.

Under an appropriate agreement with the Commission, states are permitted to set restrictions and requirements for the location of nuclear power plants within its boundaries, set standards and locations for the disposal of nuclear wastes, and adopt plans for nuclear emergencies. Under the Clean Air Act Amendments of 1977, states are given authority to regulate radioactive air emissions from nuclear plants, and can adopt standards that are even more stringent than those enforced by the federal government. By setting sufficiently restrictive standards, a state may effectively prohibit the construction of nuclear power plants within its boundaries.

Nuclear Accidents.　Nuclear energy is a high-risk energy source. A nuclear accident could cause substantial damage and injury to the population located near the nuclear power plant at which an accident occurred. The Three Mile Island crisis of 1979 caused substantial concern over the safety of nuclear power in this country. In regulating nuclear energy, the government must weigh the probability of a nuclear accident, the energy needs of the community and nation, and the economic gains and losses that could result from the development or nondevelopment of nuclear power.

Under the federal Price-Anderson Act, initially enacted in 1957 and extended and amended since, licensees of larger commercial nuclear power plants must demonstrate that they have obtained financial protection, in the form of private nuclear-liability insurance or in some other form, against the economic consequences of a nuclear accident.

A secondary layer of financial protection was established by the 1975 amendments to the Price-Anderson Act, which provide that where a nuclear accident causes damages that exceed $160 million, every commercial nuclear power plant licensee in the country will be assessed a prorated share of damages in excess of the primary insurance coverage of the accident, up to $5 million per reactor per incident.

In the following case, *Metropolitan Edison Co. v. People Against Nuclear Energy,* the U.S. Supreme Court held that the Nuclear Regulatory Commission did *not* have to evaluate the potential "psychological" harm to nearby residents in approving a nuclear power reactor for operation.

NUCLEAR POWER

METROPOLITAN EDISON CO. v. PEOPLE AGAINST NUCLEAR ENERGY

103 S.CT 356 (1983)
UNITED STATES SUPREME COURT

Justice Rehnquist delivered the opinion of the Court.

The issue in these cases is whether petitioner Nuclear Regulatory Commission (NRC) complied with the National Environmental Policy Act, (NEPA), when it decided to permit petitioner Metropolitan Edison Co. to resume operation of the Three Mile Island Unit 1 nuclear power plant (TMI-1).

Metropolitan owns two nuclear power plants at Three Mile Island near Harrisburg, Pennsylvania. Both of these plants were licensed by the NRC after extensive proceedings, which included preparation of Environmental Impact Statements (EIS). On March 28, 1979, TMI-1 was not operating; it had been shut down for refueling. TMI-2 was operating, and it suffered a serious accident that damaged the reactor. Although, as it turned out, no dangerous radiation was released, the accident caused widespread concern. The Governor of Pennsylvania recommended an evacuation of all pregnant women and small children, and many area residents did leave their homes for several days.

PANE [People Against Nuclear Energy] is an association of residents of the Harrisburg area who are opposed to further operation of either TMI reactor. PANE contended that restarting TMI-1 would cause both severe psychological health damage to persons living in the vicinity, and serious damage to the stability, cohesiveness, and well-being of the neighboring communities.

The Court of Appeals concluded that . . . NEPA requires the NRC to evaluate "the potential psychological health effects of operating" TMI-1 which have arisen since the original EIS was prepared.

Section 102(C) of NEPA, directs all federal agencies to

include in every recommendation or report on proposals for legislation and other major Federal actions significantly affecting the quality of the human environment, a detailed statement by the responsible official on—

(i) the environmental impact of the proposed action, [and]

(ii) any adverse environmental effects which cannot be avoided should the proposal be implemented. . . .

The theme of Section 102 is sounded by the adjective "environmental": NEPA does not require the agency to assess *every* impact or effect of its proposed action, but only the impact or effect on the environment. . . . [w]e think the context of the statute shows that Congress was talking about the physical environment—the world around us, so to speak. NEPA was designed to promote human welfare by alerting governmental actors to the effect of their proposed actions on the physical environment.

Some effects that are "caused by" a change in the physical environment in the sense of "but for" causation, will nonetheless not fall within Section 102 because the causal chain is too attenuated. For example, residents of the Harrisburg area have relatives in other parts of the country. Renewed operation of TMI-1 may well cause psychological health problems for these people. They may suffer "anxiety, tension and fear, a sense of helplessness," and accompanying physical disorders, because of the risk that their relatives may be harmed in a nuclear accident. However, this harm is simply too remote from the physical environment to justify requiring the NRC to evaluate the psychological health damage to these people that may be caused by renewed operation of TMI-1.

The federal action that affects the environment in this case is permitting renewed operation of TMI-1. The direct effects on the environment of this action include release of low-level radiation, increased fog in the Harrisburg area (caused by operation of the plant's cooling towers), and the release of warm water into the Susquehanna River. The NRC has considered each of these effects in its EIS, and again in the EIA. Another effect of renewed operation is a risk of a nuclear accident. The NRC has also considered this effect.

PANE argues that the psychological health damage it alleges "will flow directly from the risk of [a nuclear] accident." But a *risk* of an accident is not an effect on the physical environment. A risk is, by definition, unrealized in the physical world.

If contentions of psychological health damage caused by risk were cognizable under NEPA, agencies would, at the very least, be obliged to expend considerable resources developing psychiatric expertise that is not otherwise relevant to their congressionally assigned functions. The available resources may be spread so thin that agencies are unable adequately to pursue protection of the physical environment and natural resources.

It would be extraordinarily difficult for agencies to differentiate between "genuine" claims of psychological health damage and claims that are grounded solely in disagreement with a democratically adopted policy. Until Congress provides a more explicit statutory instruction than NEPA now contains, we do not think agencies are obliged to undertake the inquiry.

NEPA addresses environmental effects of federal actions. . . . If a harm does not have a sufficiently close connection to the physical environment, NEPA does not apply.

[T]he Court of Appeals noted that PANE's claim was made "in the wake of a unique and traumatic nuclear accident." We do not understand how the accident at TMI-2 transforms PANE's contentions into "environmental effects." The Court of Appeals "cannot believe that the psychological aftermath of the March 1979 accident falls outside" NEPA. On the contrary, NEPA is not directed at the effects of past accidents and does not create a remedial scheme for past federal actions. It was enacted to require agencies to assess the future effects of future actions. There is nothing in the language or the history of NEPA to suggest that its scope should be expanded "in the wake of" any kind of accident.

For these reasons, we hold that the NRC need not consider PANE's contentions. NEPA does not require agencies to evaluate the effects of risk, *qua* risk. The judgment of the Court of Appeals is *reversed*, and the case is *remanded* with instructions to *dismiss* the petition for review.

CASE QUESTIONS

1. What happened at Three Mile Island that closed one of the nuclear power plants? Was this the same one that was proposed to be opened?
2. Was an Environmental Impact Statement (EIS) prepared regarding the opening of the nuclear power plant? What did the plaintiff allege should have been considered in the EIS? Explain.
3. What physical effects did the NRC find that the opening of TMI-1 would have on the environment? Were these effects sufficient to halt the reopening of TMI-1?
4. Does the NEPA cover *physical* effects of an activity on the environment? Does it also cover *psychological* effects? Explain what the court decided.
5. Did the court find that the *risk* of a future nuclear accident was an effect on the physical environment and as such was required to be considered under the NEPA? Explain.
6. Did it matter to the decision of this case that Three Mile Island had witnessed one of the most publicized nuclear accidents in history?

Policy Issue. Should "psychological effects" on human beings be considered in an EIS? Can as much harm be caused to human beings from psychological effects as from the physical effects of dangerous conditions?

Economics Issue. What would have been the economic effects if Three Mile Island had not been allowed to open?

Ethics Issue. Is it ethical for business and government to subject people to a known but highly improbable danger, such as a nuclear accident?

Social Responsibility. Should nuclear power plants be banned in the United States? Why or why not?

PRESERVATION OF WILDLIFE

An old legal doctrine held that each state "owned" the wildlife located within its borders. Current law, as interpreted by the U.S. Supreme Court, holds that wildlife regulation by the states is subject to federal power under the Commerce Clause of the U.S. Constitution. Federal law preempts state law with regard to the regulation and protection of wildlife when state and federal law conflict.

A substantial volume of state wildlife law is concerned with issuing hunting and fishing licenses. Although a state may legitimately charge different hunting and fishing license fees to residents and nonresidents for *recreational* purposes, the U.S. Supreme Court has held that it is generally a violation of the Privileges and Immunities Clause of the U.S. Constitution to charge substantially different fees to residents and nonresidents for *commercial* hunting or fishing licenses.

The Federal Endangered Species Act.   The most comprehensive federal law protecting wildlife is the Endangered Species Act. The Act protects both "endangered" and "threatened" species of animals, and empowers the EPA to enforce many of its provisions. The Act also authorizes the Secretary of Commerce to enforce the provisions of the Act with regard to marine species. The EPA and Department of Commerce must designate the "critical habitat" of each endangered and threatened species, which is defined as the area "essential to the conservation of the species."

The Endangered Species Act applies both to government and private persons, and prohibits the "taking" of any listed endangered species. The definition of *taking* includes "harass, harm, pursue, hunt, shoot, wound, kill, trap, capture, or collect." The Act covers both personal and commercial "taking." Amendments to the Endangered Species Act in 1978 and 1979 provide methods for seeking exemptions from the provisions of the Act. Exemptions to the coverage of the Act are narrowly construed by the courts.

There are numerous other federal laws to protect wildlife. These laws include:

1. the Migratory Bird Treaty Act: prohibits the "taking" of any species of migratory bird except pursuant to federal permit
2. the Bald Eagle Protection Act
3. the Wild Free-Roaming Horses and Burros Act: prevents killing of and commerce in wild horses and burros
4. the Marine Mammal Protection Act: places a total moratorium on the "taking" of whales, porpoises, seals, polar bears, and other marine mammals, and includes an area of protection extending 200 miles offshore
5. the Migratory Bird Conservation Act of 1929: authorizes the Secretary of the Interior to acquire land for bird sanctuaries
6. the Fishery Conservation and Management Act
7. the Fish and Wildlife Coordination Act
8. the National Wildlife Refuge System: provides a habitat for wildlife on public lands.

Many states have also adopted laws that protect certain endangered species located within their boundaries.

In *West Michigan Environment Action Council, Inc. v. Natural Resources Commission of the State of Michigan* the Michigan Supreme Court reversed a decision of the Michigan Department of Natural Resources and prevented a proposed oil drilling program that would have "adversely affected" an elk herd.

PROTECTION OF WILDLIFE

WEST MICHIGAN ENVIRONMENTAL ACTION COUNCIL, INC. v. NATURAL RESOURCES COMMISSION OF THE STATE OF MICHIGAN

275 N.W.2D 538 (1979)
SUPREME COURT OF MICHIGAN

Moody, Justice.

In 1968 the Department of Natural Resources (DNR) sold oil and gas leases covering 546,196.89 acres of state-owned land, including 57,669 acres in what is now known as the Pigeon River Country State Forest (Pigeon River Forest or Forest).

Over a period of years, various plans to provide for controlled oil and gas development in the Forest were considered by the DNR. A management plan (the "limited development plan"), allowing oil and gas development in the southern one-third of the Forest while prohibiting development in the northern two-thirds, was submitted by the Director of the DNR, Howard Tanner, to the Natural Resources Commission (NRC). The DNR was asked to prepare an Environmental Impact Statement with respect to this management plan. In December, 1975, the Environmental Impact Statement (EIS) was completed.

On June 12, 1977 Shell Oil Company applied for permits to drill ten exploratory wells in the limited development region. On August 24, 1977 the Supervisor of Wells granted these permits.

On September 17, 1976 plaintiffs [The West Michigan Environmental Action Council (WMEAC) and the Pigeon River Country Association (PRCA)] filed the complaint in this action under the Michigan environmental protection act claiming that the consent order was entered into unlawfully and was likely to lead to the impairment of wildlife in the Forest. Plaintiffs sought an order restraining the

state from issuing any permits to drill for oil and/ or gas in the Forest or from implementing the June 11, 1976 consent order.

On December 5, 1977 the court rendered its final decision against plaintiffs and denied a motion for a stay and/or injunctive order pending appeal.

Plaintiffs allege that the trial court deferred to the DNR's conclusion that no pollution, impairment or destruction of the air, water or other natural resources or the public trust therein was likely to result from the contemplated drilling. Plaintiffs claim that such deference constituted error by the trial court and that the court had a responsibility to independently determine whether such pollution, impairment or destruction would occur. We agree that the trial court so erred.

Therefore, we conclude that the trial judge erred in failing to exercise his own totally independent judgment. We find, however, no need to order remand because we conclude that a judgment in favor of plaintiffs is required on the record presented.

Defendants in this case have not sought to raise any affirmative defenses, but, rather, have rested their case on a denial that plaintiffs have made a *prima facie* showing that the conduct of defendants has, or is likely to pollute, impair, or destroy the air, water, or other natural resources or the public trust therein. We find that plaintiffs have demonstrated a likelihood of impairment or destruction of natural resources, specifically of elk, as a result of the proposed drilling of ten exploratory wells.

Testimony before the trial court indicated that six of the ten proposed sites were not adjacent to any road, requiring that roads be built to such sites. The EIS cites studies in Montana, by the Intermountain Forestry and Range Experiment Station, 1973, which concluded that "[e]lk avoid roads even when there is no traffic." The EIS also observed that "[w]hether the elk will return to their former range following completion of the last seismic survey work is unknown."

Dr. Inman, who participated in the development of the EIS, testified that a slow recovery time is considered to be 40 to 50 years or more, a short recovery time less than 20 years, and a great recovery time is about 100 years or more.

The Environmental Impact Matrix predicts that elk will be adversely affected by the development of roads and pads. . . . Applying Dr. Inman's definitions of what constitutes a slow recovery time to the matrix predictions, it would appear that elk would avoid the impacted areas for 40 to 50 years.

If oil or gas development does not take place, the oil and gas will not be adversely impacted. On the other hand, if such development does take place, wildlife is adversely affected. Thus, the choice is whether or not *any* adverse impact on natural resources will be allowed.

We recognize that virtually all human activities can be found to adversely impact natural resources in some way or other. The real question before us is when does such impact rise to the level of impairment or destruction?

The DNR's environmental impact statement recognizes that "[e]lk are *unique* to this area of Michigan" and that the herd is "the *only* sizable wild herd east of the Mississippi River. Several attempts to introduce elk elsewhere in Michigan have been unsuccessful."

It is estimated that the herd's population, which numbered in excess of 1500 in 1963, now probably lies between 170 and 180. Expert testimony has established that the Pigeon River Country State Forest, particularly unit 1 in which the exploratory drilling is to take place, provides excellent habitat for elk and that the elk frequent this area. Furthermore, it is clear from the record that available habitat is shrinking. The result of a further shrinkage of this habitat by the intrusion of exploratory drilling

and its concomitant developments is that "an unknown number [of elk] will not survive."

In light of the limited number of the elk, the unique nature and location of this herd, and the apparently serious and lasting, though unquantifiable, damage that will result to the herd from the drilling of the ten exploratory wells, we conclude that defendants' conduct constitutes an impairment or destruction of a natural resource.

Accordingly, we *reverse* and *remand* to the trial court for entry of a permanent injunction prohibiting the drilling of the ten exploratory wells pursuant to permits issued on August 24, 1977.

CASE QUESTIONS

1. What law did the plaintiff assert was violated in this case? What did this law provide?
2. Can a trial court *defer* to the findings of an administrative agency? Or must the court make its own independent findings?
3. What animals were alleged to be at risk in this case? Was it an endangered or threatened species? If thousands of worms would have been destroyed by the digging of the wells, would the decision have been the same?
4. If human activity adversely impacts natural resources, is the activity *absolutely* prohibited under the Michigan law? Explain.
5. Do you agree with the decision in this case? Why or why not?

Policy Issue. Should a building project always be prohibited where an animal population will be adversely affected?

Economics Issue. If a decision were made on economic principles only, would the elk have been spared?

Ethics Issue. Is it ethical for human beings to place their interests above the interests of other animals in this world? Do the other animals act unethically toward human beings?

Social Responsibility. Did Shell owe a duty of social responsibility not to dig the wells because the elk would be endangered? Can a balance be struck between economic growth and the protection of wildlife?

LAND USE CONTROL

The United States has the most advanced *private* property system in the world. Except for the property owned by federal, state, and local governments, *private* individuals and business entities (corporations, partnerships) may purchase, own, and use property in this country. Persons may also devise property by will at their death.

However, the ownership and use of property in the United States is not totally without government control. Traditional forms of regulation of land use consist of zoning laws, building codes, and the taking of private property by the government under the power of eminent domain. Additional modern methods of "land use control" consist of preservation of historic buildings, application of antidiscrimination laws to the sale and lease of real property, limitations on growth through restrictions on building, and requirements for esthetic approval prior to the construction of a building. This chapter examines the major laws that regulate the use of land in the United States.

"Police power," which is neither expressly provided nor prohibited by the U.S. Constitution, has been held by the Supreme Court to have been "reserved to the states" under Article X of the U.S. Constitution. "Police power" allows states to enact laws to protect the public "health, safety, and general welfare." The police power accorded to the states under the constitution may be delegated by the states to local government bodies, which may then adopt zoning ordinances that apply to real property located within their jurisdiction.

Zoning Ordinances.   Under a typical zoning ordinance, a municipal government usually divides the city into zoning districts, which are then generally classified as residential, commercial, and industrial areas. Subclassification within these general categories is usually also provided. For example, the "residential" category may be further divided into single-family dwelling areas and multiple-family dwelling areas (i.e., allowing condominiums or apartment buildings). Further classifications, such as by height and size of buildings, are also usually provided in city zoning ordinances. A zoning map is commonly prepared, which identifies zoned areas and their classification. Most cities provide for the appointment or election of a special zoning commission to enforce the zoning ordinances of the municipality.

The most common rationale given for adoption and enforcement of zoning laws is that such laws provide for the orderly expansion and development of the city. Zoning laws are also justified on grounds of promoting safety (as by keeping dangerous industries from locating in residential areas), enhancing the values of real property (as by restricting garbage dumps to nonresidential areas), and promoting economy and efficiency in providing government services (e.g., the water and sewage resources required by industrial users are different from those required by residential users). Many other countries of the world (for example, Mexico) have selected a different policy and have developed without substantial zoning laws.

Building Codes.   In addition to general zoning laws, most municipalities have also adopted "building codes" pursuant to the delegation of police power from the state. Building codes traditionally are quite complex, providing for such details as the number and type of rest-room facilities per square foot of building space, the number and location of electrical outlets, location of plumbing and quality of pipes, strength of installation, and a myriad of other details for the safe construction of buildings in the community.

Most municipalities appoint building inspectors who inspect buildings during different phases of construction to see if the building is being constructed "to code."

Any person desiring to construct a building or other structure on his personal property, or desiring to initiate, or sometimes continue, a specific use of his property (such as raising pigs), must apply for and obtain appropriate government approval to do so. Where new construction or the substantial remodeling of an existing building is contemplated, plans showing the proposed construction, and data showing compliance with local zoning laws and building codes, must be prepared and submitted to the proper government authority for approval and issuance of a *building permit*. After appropriate review, the municipality or agency will either grant or deny the permit. If the permit is denied, changes are generally made to the original plans to comply with local government requirements.

Esthetic Control.   In order to promote the esthetics of their communities, many states and local governments have enacted laws that either prevent or severely restrict the use of signs and billboards along certain highways and in certain areas (often residential areas). Most city ordinances generally restrict the size of signs, types of signs, and locations of signs and billboards. The courts have held such limited regulation of signs to be a valid exercise of a state's police power. However, the restrictions and regulation of *existing* signs and billboards may constitute a "taking," for which the government must pay "just compensation" to the injured party. An absolute prohibition barring all signs and billboards may unconstitutionally interfere with protected "commercial free speech."

Many cities have adopted zoning ordinances that give authority to zoning boards or special zoning committees to control the "esthetics" of the design and construction of houses and other structures in the municipality. Generally, the application of esthetic-control ordinances prevents the construction of specific buildings that deviate substantially from the design of existing structures in a neighborhood. Courts have held that the application of esthetic controls must not be "unreasonable," and must advance the "general welfare" in order to be sustained under a state's police power.

Zoning laws and zoning commission decisions are subject to judicial review. The most common grounds upon which the courts invalidate zoning laws or overturn decisions of zoning commissions are:

1. The zoning ordinance is found to be invalid because it is not related to the "health, safety, or welfare" of the public, and is therefore an improper exercise of the state's police power.
2. The zoning ordinance exceeds the authority granted to the city zoning authorities by the state's enabling act.

3. The classification of the plaintiff's property is "unreasonable" when compared to contiguous properties.
4. The classification of the plaintiff's property constitutes a "taking" under due process for which just compensation must be paid.

In *State of Missouri ex rel. Stoyanoff v. Robert Berkeley, Building Commissioner, City of Ladue, Missouri* which follows, the court upheld a city's refusal to issue a building permit where a proposed residence was considered a "grotesque" design in violation of an esthetic standard contained in a local zoning ordinance.

LAND USE CONTROL

STATE OF MISSOURI, EX REL. DIMITER STOYANOFF v. ROBERT BERKELEY, BUILDING COMMISSIONER, CITY OF LADUE, MISSOURI

458 S.W.2D 305 (1970)
SUPREME COURT OF MISSOURI

Pritchard, Commissioner.

Upon summary judgment the trial court issued a peremptory *writ of mandamus* to compel appellant to issue a residential building permit to respondents. . . . Relators' petition pleads that they applied to appellant Building Commissioner for a building permit to allow them to construct a single family residence in the City of Ladue, and that plans and specifications were submitted for the proposed residence, . . .

It is further pleaded that relators were refused a building permit for the construction of their proposed residence upon the ground that the permit was not approved by the Architectural Board of the City of Ladue. Ordinance 131, as amended by Ordinance 281 of that city, purports to set up an Architectural Board to approve plans and specifications for buildings and structures erected within the city and in a preamble to

> conform to certain minimum architectural standards of appearance and conformity with surrounding structures, and that unsightly, grotesque and unsuitable structures, detrimental to the stability of value and the welfare of surrounding property, structures and residents, and to the general welfare and happiness of the community, be avoided, and that appropriate standards of beauty and conformity be fostered and encouraged.

Richard D. Shelton, Mayor of the City of Ladue, deponed that the facts in appellant's answer were true and correct, as here pertinent: that the City of Ladue constitutes one of the finer suburban residential areas of Metropolitan St. Louis, the homes therein are considerably more expensive than in cities of comparable size, being homes on lots from three fourths of an acre to three or more acres each; that a zoning ordinance was enacted by the city regulating the height, number of stories, size of buildings, percentage of lot occupancy, yard sizes, and the location and use of buildings and land. . . . It is then pleaded that relators' description of their proposed residence as

> 'unusual in design' is the understatement of the year. It is in fact a monstrosity of grotesque design, which would seriously impair the value of property in the neighborhood.

To the south [of the site] is the conventional frame residence of Mrs. T. R. Collins. To the west is the Colonial two-story frame house of the Lewis family. To the northeast is the large brick English Tudor home of Mrs. Elmer Hubbs. Immediately to the north are the large Colonial homes of Mr. Alex Cornwall and Mr. L. Peter Wetzel.

Photographic exhibits of relators' proposed residence were also attached to Mr. Riley's affidavit.

They show the residence to be of a pyramid shape, with a flat top, and with triangular shaped windows or doors at one or more corners.

The preamble to Ordinance 131, quoted above in part, demonstrates that its purpose is to conform to the dictates of [the law], with reference to preserving values of property by zoning procedure and restrictions on the use of property. This is an illustration of what was referred to in *Deimeke v. State Highway Commission, Mo.,* as a growing number of cases recognizing a change in the scope of the term "general welfare." In the *Deimeke* case . . . it is said,

> Property use which offends sensibilities and debases property values affects not only the adjoining property owners in that vicinity but the general public as well because when such property values are destroyed or seriously impaired, the tax base of the community is affected and the public suffers economically as a result.

Relators say . . . that Ordinances 131 and 281 are invalid and unconstitutional as being an unreasonable and arbitrary exercise of the police power. . . . The argument ignores the further provisos in the ordinance:

> . . . and that unsightly, grotesque and unsuitable structures, *detrimental to the stability of value and the welfare of surrounding property, structures, and residents,* and *to the general welfare and happiness of the community,* be avoided, and that appropriate standards of beauty and conformity be fostered and encouraged." (Italics added.)

Relators' proposed residence does not descend to the "patently offensive character of vehicle graveyards . . ." referred to in the *Deimeke* case. Nevertheless, the esthetic factor to be taken into account by the Architectural Board is not to be considered alone. Along with that inherent factor is the effect that the proposed residence would have upon the property values in the area. In this time of burgeoning urban areas, congested with people and structures, it is certainly in keeping with the ultimate ideal of general welfare that the Architectural Board, in its function, preserve and protect existing areas in which structures of a general conformity of architecture have been erected. The area under consideration is clearly, from the record, a fashionable one. In *Stove ex rel. Civello v. City of New Orleans,* the court said,

> If by the term 'aesthetic considerations' is meant a regard merely for outward appearances, for good taste in the matter of the beauty of the neighborhood itself, we do not observe any substantial reason for saying that such a consideration is not a matter of general welfare. The beauty of a fashionable residence neighborhood in a city is for the comfort and happiness of the residents, and it sustains in a general way the value of property in the neighborhood.

In the matter of enacting zoning ordinances and the procedures for determining whether any certain proposed structure or use is in compliance with or offends the basic ordinance, it is well settled that courts will not substitute their judgments for the city's legislative body, if the result is not oppressive, arbitrary or unreasonable and does not infringe upon a valid preexisting nonconforming use.

The denial by appellant of a building permit for relators' highly modernistic residence in this area where traditional Colonial, French Provincial and English Tudor styles of architecture are erected does not appear to be arbitrary and unreasonable when the basic purpose to be served is that of the general welfare of persons in the entire community.

The judgment is *reversed.*

CASE QUESTIONS

1. What is a *writ of mandamus?* Explain.
2. What type of home did the plaintiffs propose to build? What type of homes were already built in the neighborhood?
3. What did Ordinances 131 and 281 of the City of Ladue provide? Who was in charge of enforcing these ordinances?
4. What does state *police power* provide? Were the ordinances found to be constitutional? Would an ordinance that gave the city the right to approve or disapprove *interior* colors and decorations in a home be constitutional? Explain.

Policy Issue. Should the esthetics of a community be considered part of the "general welfare" that deserves protection under the police power of local government?

Economics Issue. If the plaintiffs had been allowed to build their proposed home, do you think it would have had any economic effect on the value of the homes in the neighborhood? Explain.

Ethics Issue. Is it ethical for city officials to prevent the construction of buildings that do not meet their tastes?

Social Responsibility. Do communities owe a duty to protect their citizens from unsightly projects such as the "vehicle graveyards" referred to in the *Deimeke* case? What about from eccentric neighbors (e.g., a neighbor who paints his house black with orange trim)?

Trend of the Law

Environmental protection will be one of the most important areas of the law in the future. Past indiscretions of business in dumping solid and toxic wastes into the water sources and landfills in this country can cause *latent* diseases in human beings and other animals. Businesses will be faced with an increasing number of civil damage lawsuits as these injuries and diseases surface. The magnitude of this liability exposure to business cannot be estimated with certainty. Many successor corporations (e.g., through merger) will find themselves liable for past pollution perpetrated by their predecessors.

Little can be done to rectify the damage already inflicted on the environment by past pollution. However, thousands of laws and regulations have been enacted over the past 20 years to establish standards that must be met by business in protecting the environment and the health of human beings. The legal framework for addressing environmental issues is in place. Courts are just beginning to have sufficient experience to properly address environmental issues, particularly in interpreting the broad-based statutes enacted by Congress. Legal precedents are beginning to be established, which will provide benchmarks against which business executives can compare their conduct to make better decisions as to whether or not their actions will violate environmental law.

Environmentalists think that not enough is being done to protect the environment. Many business executives believe that environmental laws are unnecessarily stringent, too costly to comply with, and place American business at a disadvantage in competing in world markets. Lobbying efforts of both sides will intensify in addressing this volatile issue. Since judgments from most civil lawsuits can be discharged in bankruptcy, courts will also be faced with an increasing number of bankruptcies that will be filed by companies facing substantial losses from civil liability lawsuits under environmental laws.

REVIEW QUESTIONS

1. In 1971, the Department of the Interior announced that it was planning to sell oil and natural gas leases covering tracts on the outer continental shelf near Louisiana. The Department filed an Environmental Impact Statement on the project. This statement recognized the environmental danger to wildlife, to the marine biological community, and to human recreation posed by the project's oil spill threat but stated that there was no feasible alternative available to the Department. Stating that energy needs were important, the Department expressly rejected the alternatives of modifying the scope of the sale or delaying it until new technology was developed to increase environmental protections. The Department refused to consider other proposed alternatives (e.g., elimination of import quotas, development of onshore reserves, oil shale, nuclear energy, coal, etc.) on the ground that the exploitation of such alternatives required a broad federal effort—beyond the scope of the powers of the Department alone to undertake. May a federal agency properly limit the scope of an Environmental Impact Statement to alternatives that the agency itself has power to implement?

2. The Atomic Energy Commission (AEC) issued a construction license to build two nuclear reactors approximately 17 miles from Charlotte, North Carolina. In judging the environmental impact of the project, the AEC classified hypothetical reactor accidents from Class 1 (trivial, with high occurrence probability) to Class 9 (ultimate severity breach-of-reactor containment accidents, with occurrence highly unlikely). Experts estimated that a Class 9 accident, which would necessarily involve a simultaneous malfunction of all safety systems, would produce most severe consequences, but had such a small probability of occurrence as to make the environmental risk extremely low. The Carolina Environmental Study Group challenged this type of evaluation, alleging that the AEC improperly equated probability with risk when it assessed the environmental impact of possible Class 9 accidents. Should the AEC consider both the probability and the consequences of certain occurrences when it estimates their environmental impact?

3. The General Services Administration authorized the construction of a nine-story federal jail adjacent to the United States Court House in New York, New York. The GSA did not file an Environmental Impact Statement because it concluded that the project would not have a "substantial environmental impact." A group of landlords who owned property adjacent to the proposed jail site sued the GSA, arguing that the Agency should have considered what effect the project would have on the quality of life of the city residents near it. (The GSA had ignored these considerations.) Did the landlords' suit have any merit?

4. In 1977 the Environmental Protection Agency enacted a regulation that set industry-wide effluent limitations on the organic chemicals industry. E. I. du Pont challenged the regulation, claiming that the Federal Water Pollution Control Act only permitted the EPA to set individual limitations on each plant during the permit-issuing process. Does the Federal Water Pollution Control Act allow the EPA to set industry-wide standards?

5. A group of environmentalists sued the Tennessee Valley Authority to stop the construction of the Telleco Dam. After the litigation had been started, it was discovered that the construction would endanger the survival of a previously unknown species of small fish, the snail darter. Despite this finding, Congress continued to fund the construction of the dam. As the dam neared completion, the environmentalists' case was heard by the District Court. The court stopped construction of the dam because it violated the Endangered Species Act of 1973. Should the judiciary enforce the law in light of the fact that Congress continued funding the project and it was so near completion?

6. Weyerhaeuser Co. and others in the pulp and papermaking industry challenged the validity of Environmental Protection Agency (EPA) regulations limiting the effluent discharges of many pulp, paper, and paperboard mills. They contended that the EPA had acted improperly in not taking into consideration the "receiving water capacity" in setting effluent limitations. Their main argument was that the EPA should have taken into account the capacity of large bodies of water, such as the Pacific Ocean or Puget Sound, to dilute, naturally treat, or otherwise absorb waste dumped into them. Under the Federal Water Pollution Control Act, was the EPA required to consider receiving water capacity when setting effluent limitations?

7. The National Crushed Stone Association challenged certain provisions of a 1977 EPA regulation that limited the pollutants dumped into the water by the crushed stone industry. Specifically, National claimed that the best practicable technology (BPT) variance provision should have allowed consideration of the economic capability of an individual discharger to afford the costs of the BPT limitation. Is the EPA required to consider the economic capability of an individual firm when it considers a best practicable technology exception?

8. The EPA sued Vertac Chemical Corporation to enjoin its continued discharge of toxic waste from its Arkansas plant. The EPA introduced evidence showing that certain chemicals present in the waste had killed all of the bottom life and even the vegetation along the banks of the waterways into which the discharged wastewater flowed after being dumped directly onto the ground at the west end of the plant. Other evidence showed that one particular chemical, which was present only during a manufacturing process particular to Vertac, had been buried in steel drums in a public landfill near Vertac's plant. Should the court issue an injunction requiring Vertac to abate this health hazard? If so, what type of abatement should be required?

9. The Environmental Defense Fund petitioned the EPA to cancel pesticide registrations for Heptachlor and Chlordane. The Fund also asked for an interim suspension of the registrations pending the final decision in the cancellation hearing. The Defense Fund presented evidence from mouse studies that showed carcinogenic effects after the mice ingested the pesticides. The Fund also presented evidence that the pesticides were present in human tissues. The EPA granted the request for an interim suspension based on this evidence. A number of manufacturers intervened. They argued that although the mouse studies were valid, they did not warrant

an inference that the pesticides had a carcinogenic effect when they were inhaled or absorbed through the skin. The manufacturers, however, did not present any evidence directly refuting the inference. Under these circumstances, should the EPA lift its temporary suspension order?

10. Spur Industries had been operating a feedlot in an area just west of Phoenix, Arizona for many years. Del Webb Development Co. decided to build a retirement community, known as Sun City, near the feedlot. Prior to the development, the feedlot had few neighbors. Once the development was completed, however, there were many developed areas near the lot including Sun City itself. Once Sun City was completed, Del Webb sued Spur seeking a permanent injunction against the feedlot's operation. Although it was well managed and kept in a clean condition for that type of business, the feedlot was a nuisance under Arizona state law. The law declared any condition or place in a populous area to be a nuisance if it was a breeding place for flies or other pests that were capable of carrying or transmitting disease-causing organisms to people. Should Del Webb be required to pay Spur for the cost of shutting down or moving its business?

11. The Port Authority of New York and New Jersey banned the landing of supersonic transports (SST's) at Kennedy Airport. The Port Authority enacted the ban because it was concerned that there was not sufficient information to determine the effects of low-frequency sound, which was unique to SST operations. British Airways challenged the constitutionality of the ban claiming that the federal government had preempted the states' ability to impose reasonable noise limitations on aircraft takeoffs and landings. Was there any merit to British Airways' argument?

12. When dealing with a proposal to build a nuclear power plant at Seabrook, New Hampshire, the Nuclear Regulatory Commission (NRC) decided that "alternatives" to the proposed action had not been adequately reviewed and it remanded the proposal to its Licensing Board to conduct the required studies. The NRC declared that "the test to be employed in assessing whether a proposed site is to be rejected in favor of any of the alternative sites considered . . . (is) where an alternate site is obviously superior to the site the applicant had proposed." The NRC further stated that "in comparing construction costs of the proposed site and alternate sites, actual completion costs should be used." The New England Coalition challenged these standards under the National Environmental Policy Act, arguing that they skewed the mandated comparison in favor of the proposed site by insisting on clear superiority and by giving effect to money already spent on the proposed site. Does the use of these standards violate the National Environment Protection Act?

13. Congress passed a federal statute, the Wild Free-Roaming Horses and Burros Act, which protected all unbranded horses and burros on public lands from being captured. It provided that the owners of private land onto which such animals strayed could require the government to retrieve them. The wild horse population rapidly grew in New Mexico, causing many problems for local ranchers. As a result, New Mexico's state game officers went onto federal public land and removed some of the wild horses. Subsequently, New Mexico challenged the constitutionality of the Act, arguing that it was not supported by the Property Clause of the Constitu-

tion. The Property Clause provides that "Congress shall have power to dispose of and make all needful Rules and Regulations respecting the Territory or other property belonging to the United States." Does the federal government have the right to completely regulate wildlife on public lands?

18 PRODUCT SAFETY

INTRODUCTION

In recent years there has been an increased focus on the safety of products purchased by consumers. Under the common law, the doctrine of *caveat emptor* ("let the buyer beware") generally applied to the purchase of products. Slowly the courts held that certain implied warranties applied to products purchased by consumers. In addition, specific agencies, the most important of which is the Federal Food and Drug Administration, were created to regulate the manufacture and distribution of consumer products. And recently, the courts have developed and expanded the tort doctrine of "strict liability" to apply to products.

This chapter on product safety is divided into three major sections: (1) federal legislation and regulation of products by the Food and Drug Administration, (2) judicially developed contract theories of implied warranties, and (3) the doctrine of strict liability in tort.

THE FOOD, DRUG, AND COSMETIC ACT

The Federal Government has been involved with the regulation of the safety of food and drugs since around the turn of the century. In the late 1800s, after a proliferation of the distribution and sale of adulterated foods by merchants, most states adopted legislation regulating the sanitation of food sold to consumers.

In 1902, Dr. Harvey W. Wiley, Chief Chemist of the Bureau of Chemistry in the Federal Department of Agriculture, organized "Doctor Wiley's poison squad" consisting of personnel of the Department of Agriculture who were tested for the harmful effects of preservatives used in food. Based on Dr. Wiley's research and the effectiveness of state laws, and at the urging of farmers, Congress adopted the Food and Drug Act of 1906. The Act prohibited interstate commerce in adulterated and misbranded food and drugs.

The 1906 Act had many shortcomings. First, the Act did not cover cosmetics, which was becoming a booming business, and inadequately covered the distribution and sale of patent medicines. Second, the statutory language regarding adulterated foods was vague and ambiguous, and did not provide the FDA with the authority to set quality and identification standards. Third, the government had to prove "fraudulent intent" of the defendant in all misbranding cases. And fourth, the FDA was almost powerless to move against the danger presented by the addition of dangerous preservatives to food. Based on these reasons, and spurred by the scandal of Elixir Sulfanilamide, a drug from which approximately a hundred persons died, Congress enacted the Food, Drug, and Cosmetic Act (FD&C Act) in 1938.

The 1938 Act was much more comprehensive than the 1906 Act, and to this day this Act, as amended, provides the basis for regulating the testing, manufacture, distribution, and sale of foods, drugs, cosmetics, and medicinal devices in the United States. The FD&C Act is, as compared to modern regulatory acts, old-fashioned. Its most important provisions are couched in broad, general language, accompanied by few procedural instructions, providing substantial discretion to the FDA in the administration of the Act. The Act does provide expanded and comprehensive definition of the terms "adulterated" and "misbranding" as compared to the 1906 Act. In structure, the 1938 Act follows the 1906 Act, emphasizing two basic concepts: "adulteration" and "misbranding."

Over the years there have been several major amendments to the Food, Drug, and Cosmetic Act of 1938, the most notable of which include:

1. the Pesticides Amendment of 1954, which gave the FDA the power to establish tolerances for pesticides used on agricultural commodities
2. the Food Additives Amendment of 1958, which requires premarket approval of the FDA for new food ingredients and articles that come in contact with food (e.g., food wrappings and packaging materials)
3. the Color Additives Amendment of 1960, which requires premarket approval of the FDA for color to be used in foods, drugs, and cosmetics,
4. the Animal Drugs Amendment of 1968, which requires approval of the FDA for use of new animal drugs and food additives. Under the 1938 Act, the FDA has authority to regulate and prosecute offenders for manufactur-

ing, distributing, or selling adulterated animal feed, or misbranding animal feed or animal drugs.

5. the Medical Devices Amendment of 1976, which gave the FDA broad powers to seize and remove "quack" medical devices from the marketplace and to require proper labeling of such devices. Medical devices include heart pacemakers, kidney dialysis machines, defibrillators, surgical units, and numerous other diagnostic and therapeutic devices.

The Food and Drug Administration.   The United States Food and Drug Administration (FDA) is presently a component of the Department of Health and Human Services (HHS), formerly known as the Department of Health, Education and Welfare (HEW). Prior to the creation of HEW over three decades ago, the FDA was a branch of the Federal Security Administration, and prior to that, a division of the U.S. Department of Agriculture. Although the FDA is one of the oldest administrative agencies, legal responsibility for administering the Food, Drug, and Cosmetics Act lies with the Secretary of the HHS, who in turn appoints the Commissioner of the FDA. The FDA is given authority under several statutes discussed in this chapter, and is generally responsible for the safety and labeling of foods, food additives, drugs, cosmetics, medicinal devices, animal drugs and feeds, and a variety of other products. Approximately 25 cents of every consumer retail dollar, over $300 billion a year, is spent on products subject to FDA jurisdiction.

Congress, in the FD&C Act of 1938, mandated the regulation of foods, drugs, and cosmetics in very broad terms. Congress actually set forth the fundamental objectives of providing safe, wholesome, effective, and truthfully-labeled products, leaving substantial discretion in the FDA to administer the Act. To bring suit under the FD&C Act, and other acts authorized to be administered by the FDA, the FDA must rely on the Department of Justice and local U.S. Attorneys to initiate suits to enforce the acts. In *United States v. 3 Unlabeled 25-Pound Bags Dried Mushrooms,* 157 F.2d 722 (1946), the court stated:

The continued existence of the mushrooms is essential to our right to proceed against the things themselves. The action is an action *in rem.* In such a proceeding, there is no party defendant. The goods stand to answer. They are the offenders . . .

In addition to the Food, Drug, and Cosmetic Act, the FDA administers several other statutes, including:

1. the Biologics Act, originally enacted in 1902 and since amended, which gives the FDA power to regulate biological products, such as vaccines, blood, blood components and derivatives, and allergenic products

2. Section 361 of the Public Health Service Act, which gives the FDA power to control sanitation in food service establishments and in interstate carriers

3. the Radiation for Health and Safety Act of 1968 and Section 354 of the Public Health Service Act, under which the FDA regulates the use of X-ray machines, microwave ovens, ultrasound equipment, and other products capable of emitting radiation.

Subject to obtaining an appropriate search warrant, or without one in emergency situations, the FDA may inspect the products or premises of any party manufacturing or dealing in foods, drugs, cosmetics, or medical devices or other items subject to its jurisdiction. The FDA is empowered to seize, recall, or condemn products under its jurisdiction. The FDA also may seek injunctions against manufacturers and distributors of foods, drugs, cosmetics, and medical devices and other products that it is authorized to regulate. Under certain circumstances, violators of the FD&C Act and other acts under the jurisdiction of the FDA may be held criminally liable. A person who in good faith merely receives and later delivers an illegal article is exempt from criminal liability.

Adulterated Food. The FD&C Act does not specifically forbid the marketing of decomposed or filthy food, but it provides standards for determining when such foods shall be "deemed adulterated." Section 301 of the Act then enumerates a number of prohibited acts, including the shipment, distribution, and sale of "adulterated" food. Section 342 (a) (3) of the 1938 Act provides that a food is deemed *adulterated* "if it consists in whole or in part of any filthy, putrid, or decomposed substance, or if it is otherwise unfit for food."

Courts have held that the two clauses of Section 342 (a) (3) are independent and complementary, so that a food substance may be condemned as "filthy, putrid, or decomposed" even though it is fit as food, and condemned as "unfit for food" even though it is not filthy, putrid, or decomposed. One court has stated that in order for a food to be considered unfit, it "must be proved to be so tough and rubbery that the average, normal person, under ordinary conditions, could not chew and swallow it."

Mislabelling. Section 403(a) of the 1938 Act prohibits statements in labels or labeling that are "false or misleading in any particular." For example, in *Federation of Homemakers v. Earl Butz, Secretary of Agriculture* 466 F.2d 462 (1972), the Court of Appeals upheld a lower court ruling that invalidated a regulation issued by the Secretary of Agriculture which allowed frankfurters containing up to 15 percent water, filler, and spices to be labeled "All Meat." The court reasoned that the term "All Meat" would be taken at its literal meaning by consumers, and would therefore be misleading.

In addition to prohibiting certain types of misrepresentations in labeling, Section 403 mandates affirmative disclosure of four types of information on every food label:

1. the name of the food
2. the name and place of business of the manufacturer
3. a statement of ingredients
4. the net quantity of contents.

In 1973, the FDA promulgated general regulations that standardized the format of food labels and required large type size for the mandatory information on food labels.

Deceptive Packaging. A manufacturer may be held liable under the Food, Drug, and Cosmetic Act of 1938 for "deceptive packaging." Deceptive packaging usually arises when a manufacturer "slack-fills" a box or container to deceive a consumer into believing he is purchasing a larger portion of the product.

Deceptive packaging violates Section 403 (d) of the Act. A defendant manufacturer may raise the defense to a charge of deceptive packaging that the large box or container was required for safety reasons.

In *U.S. v. Capital City Foods, Inc.* the court applied Section 342 (a) (3) of the Food, Drug, and Cosmetic Act of 1938 and found the contamination to be a trifle and not in violation of the Act.

ADULTERATED FOOD

UNITED STATES v. CAPITAL CITY FOODS, INC.

345 F.SUPP. 277 (1972)
UNITED STATES DISTRICT COURT, D. NORTH DAKOTA

Van Sickle, J.

This is a criminal prosecution by information, based on a claimed violation of . . . [The Federal Food, Drug, and Cosmetic Act].

Specifically, the defendants are charged with having introduced, or delivered for introduction, into interstate commerce, food that was adulterated. The food is claimed to be adulterated because it consisted in part of a filthy substance, i.e., insect fragments.

Section 342 (a) (3) provides that the food is adulterated if it consists in whole or in part of any filthy, . . . substance, or if it is otherwise unfit for food. Insect fragments in other than infinitesimal quantity are filth.

The facts show that miniscule insect fragments were discovered in the butter, and these fragments were identifiable under a 470 power microscope. Some of the fragments were discernable, although none were identifiable with the naked eye. The manufacturing process, while not condemned by the government, did not assure a filter between the raw milk and the pasteurization or cooking process (although there were two in-line filters between the pasteurization and churning units). Thus, we can assume any fatty substance reasonably related to the miniscule insect fragments was cooked and distributed into the finished butter. The defendant manager was shown to be responsible for the conduct of the dairy.

But, in its "Notice of Proposed Rule Making On Natural or Unavoidable Defects in Food for Human Use that Present No Health Hazard," of the Food and Drug Administration, published in the Federal Register, Volume 37, No. 62, March 30, 1972, the introduction language includes this:

> Few foods contain no natural or unavoidable defects. Even with modern technology, all defects in foods cannot be eliminated. Foreign material cannot be wholly processed out of foods, and many containments introduced into foods through the environment can be reduced only by reducing their occurrence in the environment.

I accept as a rational, workable approach, the reasoning of the writer in 67 Harv.L.Rev.,

> Indeed, if the section were interpreted literally, almost every food manufacturer in the country could be prosecuted since the statute bans products contaminated "in whole or in part." This undesirable result indicates that the section should not receive so expansive a reading. In fact, in several cases judicial common sense has led to recognition that the presence of a minimal amount of filth may be insufficient for condemnation.

The foreign matter found was mainly miniscule fragments of insect parts. They consisted of 12 particles of fly hair (seta), 11 unidentified insect fragments, 2 moth scales, 2 feather barbules, and 1 particle of rabbit hair. The evidence showed that some of these particles were visible to the naked eye, and some, the fly hair, would require a 30x microscope to see. They were identifiable with the aid of a 470x microscope. The only evidence as to size showed that there was one hair, 1½ millimeters long, and one unidentified insect fragment 0.02 millimeters 0.2 millimeters.

In all, 4125 grams (9.1 lbs.) of butter were checked and 28 miniscule particles were found. This is an overall ratio of 3 miniscule particles of insect fragments per pound of butter.

Thus, there having been no standard established, and no showing that this number of miniscule fragments is excludable in the manufacturing process, I find that this contamination is a trifle, not a matter of concern to the law.

The defendants are found *not guilty*. Judgment will be entered accordingly.

CASE QUESTIONS

1. What does Section 342 (a) (3) of the Food, Drug, and Cosmetic Act provide? Explain.
2. Was this a civil or criminal action? Do you think it made a difference to the court's decision?
3. What kind of foreign matter was found in the butter?
4. Did the court find that the butter was "adulterated" in violation of the Act? Did it apply a *literal* interpretation of Section 341 (a) (3)?

Policy Issue. Does the presence of foreign matter in food make it "adulterated" under the Food, Drug, and Cosmetic Act? Should it? Would you have purchased the butter if you knew it contained insect fragments, fly hair, rabbit hair, and moth scales?

Economics Issue. If Section 342 (a) (3) had been read literally, would food prices increase or decrease?

Ethics Issue. Is it ethical for food processors and manufacturers to distribute food which, although meeting Section 342 (a) (3), contains foreign matter?

Social Responsibility. Do food processors owe a duty of social responsibility to keep food *pure?* Or only not adulterated?

Regulation of Cosmetics. The FDA acquired responsibility to regulate cosmetics with the enactment of the 1938 Act. The definition of "cosmetic" is broad, and includes all substances and preparations intended for cleansing, or altering the appearance of, or promoting the attractiveness of the person. Cosmetics may be used externally or internally. Ordinary toilet and household soaps are specifically exempted from the definitions of "cosmetics" under 1938 Act. Soaps sold as pharmaceutical articles or with medicinal claims are considered "drugs" under the 1938 Act.

The FDA has issued regulations requiring labeling of ingredients in cosmetics, and the placing of certain warnings on cosmetics that may be dangerous to health. The FDA has issued special regulations for warnings regarding cosmetics that use coal-tar hair dyes and cancer-causing chemicals and products.

In 1976, the Cosmetic, Toiletry, and Fragrance Association, a voluntary association of cosmetic manufacturers and dealers, created the "Cosmetic Ingredient Review Program" to provide comprehensive review of ingredients used in cosmetics by a panel of experts.

Manufacturers and sellers of cosmetics may be held liable for misbranding cosmetics, or for manufacturing, distributing, or selling adulterated cosmetics.

Regulation of Drugs and Devices. The Food, Drug, and Cosmetic Act of 1938 gives the FDA broad powers to regulate the testing, manufacture, and distribution of drugs. *Drugs,* for the purposes of the Act, include:

1. "articles" recognized in the Official United States Pharmacopeia, and other identified compendia

2. "articles" intended for use in the diagnosis, cure, mitigation, treatment, or prevention of disease in man or other animals
3. "articles" intended to affect the structure or any function of the body of man or other animals.

The FDA has refused to include cigarettes in the definition of *drugs* under the 1938 Act.

The Drug Amendments of 1962.   In 1962, the Drug Amendments were added to the Food, Drug, and Cosmetic Act of 1938. With the passage of this legislation, the regulation of drugs became the single most important, and most controversial, activity of the FDA. Although the 1938 Act provided a premarketing review scheme for "new drugs," the 1962 Drug Amendments substantially broadened the FDA's authority regarding the licensing of "new drugs." In order for a new drug to be marketed, a new drug application has to be filed with the FDA. The application becomes effective if the FDA does not disapprove the application.

Under Section 505 of the 1938 Act as amended, the Secretary is required to refuse approval of any new drug application if, after notice and opportunity for hearing, the Secretary determines that "there is a lack of substantial evidence that the new drug will have the effects it purports or is represented to have." Further, Section 505 of the 1938 Act has been amended to require the Secretary to withdraw approval of any drug after notice and opportunity for hearing if the Secretary finds that "on the basis of new information before him" substantial evidence of its efficacy is lacking. Where there is an imminent hazard to health, the Secretary is empowered to withdraw FDA approval of a drug before holding a hearing on the matter.

The FDA's performance of its licensure of new drugs has been the target of severe criticism both by proponents who want stricter licensing standards and by proponents of reduced regulations, who counter that the FDA's review is too time-consuming, thus preventing needed drugs from being marketed and raising the cost of drugs once they are approved (not disapproved) by the FDA.

Over-the-Counter Drugs.   In 1972, the FDA adopted rules regarding the review of the estimated 100,000 to one-half million "over-the-counter" drugs that had not previously been subject to FDA licensing procedures. Generally, most over-the-counter drugs are compounded from an estimated 200 active ingredients. The FDA, therefore, established procedures for classifying certain over-the-counter drugs into categories generally considered safe and effective if properly labelled. Any over-the-counter drug not meeting these requirements must file a "new drug" application with the FDA.

The Food, Drug, and Cosmetic Act of 1938, as amended, requires that prescription drugs bear proper directions for use and adequate warnings of dangers to health if used, information regarding unsafe dosages, and methods and duration of administration or application. A drug manufacturer or seller may be held liable for *misbranding* drugs, or for manufacturing, distributing, or selling *adulterated* drugs.

In *U.S. v. 43½ Gross Rubber Prophylactics Labeled in Part "Xcello's Prophy-*

lactics" which follows, the court sustained the government's inspection and condemnation of a defective product.

ADULTERATED DEVICE, MISLABELED DEVICE

UNITED STATES v. 43½ GROSS RUBBER PROPHYLACTICS LABELED IN PART "XCELLO'S PROPHYLACTICS"

65 F.SUPP. 534 (1946)
UNITED STATES DISTRICT COURT, D. MINNESOTA

Nordbye, District Judge.

A libel of information was filed against the goods described in the caption on the theory that they were adulterated within the meaning of Section 351 (c) and that they were misbranded within the meaning of Section 352 (a). The goods were labeled "Prophylactics" on the carton in which they were contained, and the Government contends that such labeling constitutes misbranding within the meaning of the Act. The articles consist of certain rubber devices sold ostensibly for the purpose of preventing transmission of venereal disease. The government witnesses testified that, of the Xcello brand, 180 were tested and 14 contained holes; that 228 of the Silver-Tex brand were tested and 16 contained holes. Medical witnesses testified that the defective devices would not serve as a means for the successful prevention of the transmission of venereal disease.

Section 351 provides:

A drug or device shall be deemed to be adulterated . . . (c) If . . . its strength differs from, or its purity or quality falls below, that which it purports or is represented to possess.

Section 352 provides:

A drug or device shall be deemed to be misbranded . . . (a) If its labeling is false or misleading in any particular.

The government inspection has established that the devices tested were defective in the number indicated, and there can be no serious doubt that the strength and quality of these particular defective articles fell below that which they purported or were represented to possess. Furthermore, it seems clear that, being labeled "Prophylactics," there was misbranding within the meaning of the statute. These defective devices are not efficacious in furnishing protection from disease.

Suffice it to say that, on the state of the facts herein, and assuming that the same ratio of defectives would be found in the entire shipment, it would follow that over 1,500 defective articles would be found in this shipment. Such a number, if sold on the market, would constitute a potential menace to public health, and, in view of the claimed purpose and object of the devices, that is, the prevention of disease, are sufficient to sustain the libel proceedings herein.

The purpose of the Federal Food, Drug, and Cosmetic Act requires that the Act be interpreted liberally. "One of the declared purposes of the Federal Food, Drug, and Cosmetic Act is to prohibit the movement in interstate commerce of adulterated and misbranded foods, drugs, devices and cosmetics. Thereby Congress hoped to "prevent injury to the public health" by prohibiting "the sale of inferior for superior articles" and protecting the uninformed from buying an article which was different from what it purported to be.

If claimant's contention were adopted here, this purpose could not be carried out, for the practical difficulties involved would permit defective articles to move in commerce and to be sold to uninformed persons without affording the protection represented.

It follows from the foregoing that the Government is entitled to findings of fact and conclusions of law in harmony with the foregoing, as prayed for in its libel of information, . . .

CASE QUESTIONS

1. Who was the named *defendant* in this case? Was it the company that made the product? Explain.
2. What do the following sections of the Food, Drug, and Cosmetic Act provide?
   a. Section 351
   b. Section 352
3. What product was involved in this case? What evidence did the court cite to prove that the device was adulterated and mislabeled? Was it sufficient to support the condemnation and seizure of the product?
4. Was this product, in its present condition, a "menace to public health" as the court asserted?

Policy Issue. Should the government regulate drugs, cosmetics, and devices such as the one in this case? Why or why not?

Economics Issue. Why do you think manufacturers would ship a defective product? Should the product in this case have been allowed to be shipped to the public, and then only the individual defective products be *recalled* (like automobiles)?

Ethics Issue. Was it ethical for the manufacturer of the product to allow a defective product of this kind to be shipped for use by the public?

Social Responsibility. One of the purposes of the FD&C Act is to protect the "uninformed from buying an article which was different from what it purported to be." What *surprises* might be in store for the uninformed users of the product in this case?

WARRANTIES

When a consumer purchases a product, often the seller or seller's agent (e.g., salesman) will make an express statement regarding the quality, condition, performability or quantity of the product being sold. Such a statement becomes an *express warranty.* Express warranties become part of the contract between the buyer and seller, and if the warranties are not met, the buyer can sue the seller for breach of warranty. Because of its concern for the safety of consumers, and to protect consumers from fraud, the legislatures and the courts have developed certain warranties which the law implies attach to the sale of products. If these *implied warranties* are not met, the buyer can also sue the seller for breach of warranty. Generally, the legislatures and courts of most jurisdictions have developed three implied warranties:

1. implied warranty of merchantability
2. implied warranty of fitness for a particular purpose
3. implied warranty of fitness for human consumption.

It is important to note that the warranty theory of product liability is based on *contract* law. By contrast, product liability based on the strict liability theory is a *tort* action.

Express Warranties. A seller may *expressly* state that certain warranties apply to a product. A manufacturer's statement that a tire "is guaranteed safe for 40,000 miles" is an example of an express warranty. If the warranty is not met (i.e., the tire blows out and causes injury before it has traveled 40,000 miles), an injured party may sue for breach of warranty. The plaintiff does not have to prove that the defendent was negligent, only that the warranty was breached, which caused injury. Manufacturers and sellers may provide for only "limited warranties" (e.g., replacement of product only).

A manufacturer or retailer does not have to provide express warranties for products, and many do not. Many express warranties are also so strictly limited that they provide little protection for consumers injured by unsafe products. Injured consumers can always sue under the theory of negligence; however, this tort doctrine places the burden of proof on the plaintiff to show that the defendant was negligent in the manufacture of the product.

Implied Warranty of Merchantability.

In every mercantile contract of sale the law implies a warranty that the goods are of "merchantable" quality. This "implied warranty of merchantability" generally holds that a product is fit for the *ordinary purposes* for which the goods are to be used. For example, the implied warranty of merchantability implies that a chair may safely be used as, and will perform the function of, a chair. If a normal-sized person sits in a chair that has not been tampered with, and the chair collapses and the person is injured, there has been a breach of the implied warranty of merchantability.

The *implied warranty of merchantability* also requires products be properly and safely packaged (that is, it applies to the milk bottle as well as to the milk), and that the goods may be safely used in accordance with the labeling and packaging instructions on the products or containers. If goods are fungible (e.g., grains, ores) the implied warranty of merchantability requires that the goods meet some average or middle range of quality.

An implied warranty of merchantability only applies to products (not to services), only to sales (not to leases or consignments), and only to sales by merchants who normally sell the product in the usual course of business (not to "casual" sales).

In *Maybank v. S. S. Kresge Company* the court held that there was a breach of the implied warranty of merchantability when a flashcube exploded in the plaintiff's face, causing injury to the plaintiff.

IMPLIED WARRANTY OF MERCHANTABILITY

MAYBANK v. S. S. KRESGE COMPANY

266 S.E.2D 409 (1980)
COURT OF APPEALS OF NORTH CAROLINA

Vaughn, Judge.

Plaintiff, a Greensboro, North Carolina resident, made a trip to New York City in July, 1972 to visit her son and her two-year-old grandson. For the trip, she borrowed her daughter's Argus camera, which was about three years old. Two days before she left for New York, defendant, trading under the name of K-Mart, sold her a package of G. T. E. Sylvania flashcubes for $.88. The package contained three flashcubes with four flashes on each.

Plaintiff carried the flashcubes to New York in her pocketbook. The package remained sealed from time of purchase until she first began to take pictures of her son's home and her grandson about a week after she arrived in New York. On 21 July 1972, she opened the carton and used one of the flashcubes to take four pictures without any problems. She removed the second cube from the package and placed it on the camera. The flashcube in no way appeared abnormal. When she pushed down the camera lever to take a picture of her grandson, the flashcube exploded. The explosion, which sounded like the blast of a gun, knocked her glasses off and caused cuts in her left eye.

Only her two-year-old grandson was with her at the time of the injury. At first, she could not see at all. When her son returned home, about an hour later, he took her immediately to the hospital. She was hospitalized for eight days and was out of work for three weeks because of the injury. Her vision, which is still not as good as before the accident, improved some. She continued to see doctors after her release from the hospital. The camera has been used since without incident.

At the close of plaintiff's evidence on motion of defendant, the court directed a verdict for defendant. Plaintiff appeals. . . . The sole question of this appeal is whether a directed verdict was erroneously entered for defendant.

[A]n action for breach of implied warranty of merchantability . . . entitles a plaintiff to recover without any proof of negligence on a defendant's part where it is shown that "(1) a merchant sold goods, (2) the goods were not "merchantable" at the time of sale, (3) the plaintiff (or his property) was injured by such goods, (4) the defect or other condition amounting to a breach of an implied warranty of merchantability proximately caused the injury, and (5) the plaintiff so injured gave timely notice to the seller."

Defendant sold the flashcube to plaintiff and "is a merchant with respect to goods of that kind." A flashcube which does not work properly and which causes the unexpected harm this flashcube caused is not merchantable. . . . A flashcube which shatters might be merchantable. An exploding flashcube is not, however, merchantable.

It is not sufficient that plaintiff prove the flashcube was not merchantable. The evidence must establish that the flashcube was not merchantable at the time of sale. The evidence presented by plaintiff was to the effect that she purchased the flashcube in a sealed package, placed it in her purse where

it remained for about nine days before use. . . . The flashcube did not appear defective or abnormal at any time from when purchased to when used. . . . In this case where the defective product was enclosed in its original container until use and nothing occurred between the purchase and use of the product which would indicate that plaintiff mishandled, damaged or altered the product, the evidence does not compel a finding that the product was not merchantable at the time of sale but the evidence is sufficient to permit a reasonable inference to the effect that the flashcube was not merchantable at the time of sale. It is, therefore, a matter of fact for the jury to decide and not a matter of law for the trial court.

There is no question that plaintiff has proved injury to her person which is a compensable consequential damage for breach of an implied warranty of merchantability.

This brings us to the fourth element of plaintiff's claim for breach of an implied warranty. . . . In a light most favorable to the plaintiff, the defective flashcube proximately caused plaintiff's injury.

Finally, an injured buyer must give notice to the seller of the breach of the warranty. Plaintiff testified that she did not inform defendant on her return from New York of the injury. The suit itself appears to be the first notice of the breach to defendant. Defendant, however, has not asserted failure to give notice as an affirmative defense and it is, therefore, deemed waived.

It was error to direct a verdict for defendant at the close of plaintiff's evidence. Plaintiff made out a *prima facie* case of breach of an implied warranty of merchantability.

Reversed and *remanded*.

CASE QUESTIONS

1. What injury did the plaintiff suffer? How did the injury occur?
2. What does the doctrine of *implied warranty of merchantability* provide? Explain.
3. Which of the following is it easier for an injured plaintiff to sue under? Why? Explain the difference in the two doctrines.
   a. the *tort* doctrine of negligence
   b. the *contract* doctrine of warranty

4. Were the following elements of the implied warranty of merchantability met in this case?
   a. Defendant was a merchant who normally sold such goods.
   b. The goods were not merchantable.
   c. The plaintiff was injured.
   d. The defective good was the *proximate cause* of the plaintiff's injury.
   e. The plaintiff gave timely notice to the seller.

Policy Issue. Should implied warranties attach to the sale of products? Or should a seller only be liable for breach of express warranties?

Economics Issue. Do implied warranties increase or decrease the cost of products? Is it really an indirect insurance program? Explain.

Ethics Issue. Did the plaintiff properly notify the defendants in this case? Was it ethical for the plaintiff to accept the court's finding that the defendant had *waived* the right to receive such notice?

Social Responsibility. Do manufacturers of products owe a duty of social responsibility to produce products that will perform the purpose for which they are sold? Does the implied warranty of merchantability require anything more than this?

Implied Warranty of Fitness for a Particular Purpose. Where a seller uses his skill and expertise in selecting a product to be used by a consumer who has stated the *particular purpose* to be served by the product, an "implied warranty of fitness for a particular purpose" may attach to the product. For example, where a seller warrants that a certain type of cement is appropriate for buyer's stated purpose of providing a foundation for a building, and buyer actually relies on the seller's statement, and buys and uses the product, but the cement is not strong enough to support the building, then the seller is liable for breach of the *implied warranty of fitness for a particular purpose.* By contrast, the implied warranty of *merchantability* is not breached if the cement is appropriate for the lighter jobs it was meant to be used for. The "implied warranty of fitness for a particular purpose" is breached if the following elements are shown:

1. The buyer, either expressly or by implication, makes his particular purpose for buying a good known to the seller.
2. The seller makes a statement regarding the fitness of the good for the particular purpose of the buyer
3. The buyer purchases and uses the good in reliance on the seller's representations regarding the good.
4. The good does not perform as represented by the seller.
5. The buyer suffers injury from using the good for the purpose and in the manner which the seller represented as appropriate.

In certain cases the courts have held that the implied warranty of fitness for a particular purpose is not breached unless the plaintiff-buyer proves that not only did he incur injury, but also that "an appreciable number" of users would have suffered a similar result. For example, if a hair lotion caused the buyer's hair to fall out, the buyer must prove it was not a personal, unique, or abnormal reaction by showing that an "appreciable number" of other persons *could* have been similarly affected. The plaintiff does not have to show that these other persons actually suffered an injury.

Many states have integrated the implied warranty of merchantability and implied warranty of fitness for a particular purpose under the general title "implied warranty."

Implied Warranty of Fitness for Human Consumption. When the goods sold are either foods or beverages, courts have generally held that a special implied warranty of wholesomeness arises. This warranty is commonly referred to as the "implied warranty of fitness for human consumption." The *implied warranty of fitness for human consumption* is technically not a separate warranty, but is based on the imposition of the doctrine of the implied warranty of merchantability.

The implied warranty of fitness for human consumption extends to both restaurants and grocery stores. The liability of restaurants applies whether the food is sold for consumption on the premises, or is taken out. The liability of a grocery store applies whether foods are selected by the consumer or the grocer, but the implied warranty only guarantees fitness for "normal" use (e.g., there is a warranty that meat is wholesome when cooked, but not if it is eaten raw). The implied warranty of fitness for human consumption covers products purchased from self-service vending machines and in prepackaged sealed containers.

Two different tests are applied by the courts in determining whether there has been a breach of the implied warranty of fitness for human consumption. Some states have adopted one test, while other states have adopted the second test. The two tests are (1) the foreign substance test and (2) the reasonable expectations test.

"Foreign Substance" Test. Until recently, courts usually applied a "foreign substance" test in determining if there was a breach of the implied warranty of fitness for human consumption. Under this test, the plaintiff had to prove that a *foreign substance* (e.g., a piece of glass, a stone, a tack) was in the food and caused him injury. If the substance that caused the injury was natural to the food consumed (e.g., a bone), the plaintiff could not recover under the foreign substance test.

"Reasonable Expectations" Test. The modern rule and trend of the law is for the courts to use a "reasonable expectations" test in determining whether there has been a breach of the implied warranty of fitness for human consumption. The reasonable expectations test requires that the court determine what a normal consumer would expect when he ate the food. The reasonable expectations test changes with time and as the quality of food-processing methods and preparation improves.

In *Hunt v. Ferguson-Paulus Enterprises* the court discussed both the "foreign substance" test and the "reasonable expectations" test in a case involving an alleged breach of the implied warranty of fitness for human consumption.

IMPLIED WARRANTY OF FITNESS FOR HUMAN CONSUMPTION

HUNT v. FERGUSON-PAULUS ENTERPRISES

415 P.2D 13 (1966)
SUPREME COURT OF OREGON

Lusk, Justice.

The plaintiff bought a cherry pie from the defendant through a vending machine owned and maintained by the defendant. On biting into the pie one of plaintiff's teeth was broken when it encountered a cherry pit. He brought this action to recover damages for the injury, alleging breach of warranty of fitness of the pie for human consumption. In a trial to the court without a jury the court found for the defendant and plaintiff has appealed.

FOREIGN SUBSTANCE TEST

In the consideration of similar cases some of the courts have drawn a distinction between injury caused by spoiled, impure, or contaminated food or food containing a foreign substance, and injury caused by a substance natural to the product sold. In the latter class of cases, these courts hold there is no liability on the part of the dispenser of the food. Thus in the leading case of *Mix v. Ingersoll Candy Co.,* the court held that a patron of a restaurant who ordered and paid for chicken pie, which contained a sharp sliver or fragment of chicken bone, and was injured as a result of swallowing the bone, had no cause of action against the restaurateur either for breach of warranty or negligence. Referring to cases in which recovery had been allowed the court said:

> All of the cases are instances in which the food was found not to be reasonably fit for human consumption, either by reason of the presence of a foreign substance, or an impure and noxious condition of the food itself, such as for example, glass, stones, wires or nails in the food served, or tainted, decayed, diseased, or infected meats or vegetables.
>
> [D]espite the fact that a chicken bone may occasionally be encountered in a chicken pie, such chicken pie, in the absence of some further defect, is reasonably fit for human consumption. Bones which are natural to the type of meat served cannot legitimately be called a foreign substance, and a consumer who eats meat dishes ought to anticipate and be

on his guard against the presence of such bones.

Certainly no liability would attach to a restaurant keeper for the serving of a T-bone steak, or a beef stew, which contained a bone natural to the type of meat served, or if a fish dish should contain a fish bone, or if a cherry pie should contain a cherry stone—although it be admitted that an ideal cherry pie would be stoneless.

REASONABLE EXPECTATIONS TEST

Other courts have rejected the so-called foreign-natural test in favor of what is known as the "reasonable expectation" test, among them the Supreme Court of Wisconsin, which, in *Betehia v. Cape Cod Corp.,* held that a person who was injured by a chicken bone in a chicken sandwich served to him in a restaurant, could recover for his injury either for breach of an implied warranty or for negligence. "There is a distinction," the court said, "between what a consumer expects to find in a fish stick and in a baked or fried fish, or in a chicken sandwich made from sliced white meat and in roast chicken. The test should be what is reasonably expected by the consumer in the food as served, not what might be natural to the ingredients of that food prior to preparation. What is to be reasonably expected by the consumer is a jury question in most cases; . . .

CONCLUSION

[W]e are not required in this case to make a choice between the two rules. Under the foreign-natural test the plaintiff would be barred from recovery as a matter of law. The reasonable expectation test calls for determination of a question of fact: . . . The [trial] court has found the fact in favor of the defendant and this court has no power to disturb the finding.

There are no other assignments of error and the judgment is *affirmed.*

CASE QUESTIONS

1. What injury did the plaintiff suffer? How did the injury occur?
2. What does the doctrine of the *implied warranty of fitness for human consumption* provide? Explain.
3. What do each of the following two tests of the implied warranty of fitness for human consumption require? Explain the differences between the two tests. Which one would a plaintiff want the court to adopt?
   a. the foreign substance test
   b. the reasonable expectations test
4. What does the doctrine of the *implied warranty of fitness for a particular purpose* provide? Why wasn't this doctrine applicable to this case? Explain.
5. Did the court decide between the two tests in this case? Do you agree with the court's decision in favor of the defendant in this case? Explain.

Policy Issue. Which test, the foreign substance test or the reasonable expectations test, best serves the purpose of protecting consumers from injury caused by products?

Economics Issue. Does the implied warranty of fitness for human consumption increase the cost of food products? If so, is this cost worth it?

Ethics Issue. Is it ethical for a food manufacturer to argue for the foreign substance test? Why or why not?

Social Responsibility. Do food processors and distributors owe a greater duty of social responsibility to distribute safe products than the manufacturers of other products?

Disclaimer of Warranties. Once a manufacturer or seller has made an *express* warranty (e.g., this automobile will go 80 miles per hour), it cannot thereafter in another part of the contract *disclaim* that warranty. Otherwise, the original warranty would be found to be meaningless. *Implied* warranties may be disclaimed as follows:

1. The implied warranty of merchantability, which includes the implied warranty of fitness for human consumption, may be specifically disclaimed as long as the disclaimer includes the term "merchantability." The disclaimer may be either written or oral.
2. The implied warranty of fitness for a particular purpose can be disclaimed by general language, and does *not* have to include the term "particular purpose." However, this disclaimer must be in writing.
3. All implied warranties are generally considered to be disclaimed by the legal term "as is"—e.g., "this product is sold 'as is.'"

In order to be valid, all disclaimers must be *conspicuously* displayed in the contract. For example, most states require that disclaimers of warranties be presented in larger letters than the rest of the contract, or in color, in order to draw attention to the disclaimer. This is to prevent a seller from burying the disclaimer in a footnote to the contract where the consumer is likely not to see it.

The Magnuson-Moss Warranty Act. Prior to 1975, warranties were regulated by state laws. However, because of the complexities of these laws, the incomprehensible and often deceptive nature of many warranties, and the fact that warrantors often breached their warranties with little recourse for consumers, Congress enacted the Magnuson-Moss Warranty Federal Trade

Commission Improvement Act of 1975. The Act requires that if a written warranty is made, it must be printed in understandable language, be printed in a conspicuous style, and disclose the terms and conditions of the warranty; and it may provide for the voluntary establishment of an informal dispute resolution procedure.

The Magnuson-Moss Warranty Act only applies to a *consumer* product, defined by the Act as "any tangible personal property which is distributed in commerce and which is normally used for personal, family, or household purposes." The Act is administered by the Federal Trade Commission, which is authorized to promulgate rules to enforce the Act.

Warranty Disclosure.   The Magnuson-Moss Warranty Act does *not* require a manufacturer or seller to provide a warranty with the sale or distribution of a product. However, if a manufacturer or seller does give a *written* warranty in connection with the sale of a product, then the provisions of the Act apply. If a written warranty is given where the product costs over $15, the Act requires that the warrantor "fully and conspicuously disclose in simple and readily understandable language the terms and conditions of the warranty." The warranty must include:

1. the name and address of the warrantor
2. a description of the product or parts covered by the warranty
3. any exceptions or exclusions from the terms of the warranty
4. the time period and terms for enforcing the warranty
5. the purchaser's remedies under the warranty.

Where a manufacturer or seller makes a written warranty, it cannot disclaim *implied* warranties that attach to the sale by operation of law. The provisions of the Magnuson-Moss Warranty Act do not apply to *oral* warranties. Oral warranties may be enforced pursuant to state law.

Full and Limited Warranties.   Where a written warranty is given involving the sale or distribution of a consumer product that costs more than $10, the Magnuson-Moss Warranty Act requires that the warranty distinguish whether it is a "full" or "limited" warranty. A warranty is considered a *full* warranty, and may be so labeled, if it provides the following:

1. that there is no *duration* limitation on the warranty
2. that where the product is found to be defective, the warrantor will *remedy* (cure) the product within a "reasonable" time without charge to the consumer
3. that, if after a "reasonable" number of attempts to cure the defect the defect is not remedied, the consumer may elect to obtain a *refund* or *replacement* of the product without charge to the consumer
4. that any exclusions or limitations on *consequential* damages (e.g., liability for personal injuries) be conspicuously displayed in the warranty. It is questionable whether most state laws permit the exclusion of consequential damages from warranties. Such exclusionary language is often considered *unconscionable* and *void* under most state laws.

If a written warranty does not meet the above disclosure standards, the warranty must be conspicuously designated as a "limited" warranty.

Remedies Under the Magnuson-Moss Warranty Act. The Magnuson-Moss Warranty Act provides that a consumer may bring a *civil* action against a defendant manufacturer or seller for violating the provisions of the Act. A plaintiff may recover damages, attorney's fees, and other costs and expenses incurred in bringing the action. A warrantor may choose to voluntarily establish an informal dispute resolution procedure pursuant to rules adopted by the FTC. If this procedure is conspicuously described in the written warranty, a consumer must proceed to press his claim through this procedure. If the consumer is not satisfied with the outcome of this informal procedure, he may then bring a legal action under the Act.

The FTC may bring an action in federal court to obtain a cease-and-desist order against a deceptive warranty that violates the provisions of the Act. A violation of the Magnuson-Moss Warranty Act is also a violation of the Federal Trade Commission Act.

STRICT LIABILITY IN TORT

After the doctrines of negligence and implied warranties proved to be of little value to consumers injured by defective products, the judiciary developed the theory of "strict liability in tort." The two landmark cases that ushered in the new era of consumer safety were *Henningsen v. Bloomfield Motors,* 161 A.2d 69 (New Jersey, 1960) and *Greenman v. Yuba Power Products, Inc.,* 377 P.2d 897 (California, 1963).

The *Hennsingsen* case eliminated the requirement of *privity* for a plaintiff to sue a defendant where a defective product causes the plaintiff injury. In *Hennsingsen* a wife was permitted to sue the manufacturer of an automobile for injuries she suffered in an automobile accident even though it was her husband who actually purchased the automobile and was in *privity of contract* with the manufacturer and dealer.

In *Greenman* a man was injured when a piece of wood flew out of a lathe he was working on and hit him in the forehead. The language of *Greenman,* which ushered in the era of *strict liability* for products, is:

[I]t was not necessary for [the] plaintiff to es' ablish [a] . . . warranty. . . . A manufacturer is strictly liable in tort when an article he places on the market, knowing that it is to be used without inspection for defects, proves to have a defect that causes injury to a human being.

The majority of states have since adopted, either by judicial decision or legislative enactment of a statute, the doctrine of *strict liability in tort.* Product liability based on the doctrine of strict liability has become one of the most important and expansive areas of the law. Currently, the costs of product liability (e.g., jury awards, settlements with plaintiffs, and insurance) to manufacturers, wholesalers, retailers, and other businesses approaches over $100 *billion* each year. This figure is approximately 4 percent of the gross national product. Considering the fact that over half the GNP is composed of services, to which the doctrine of strict liability does not apply, the cost of product liability lawsuits, settlements, and insurance coverage amounts to approximately 8 percent of the cost of all products purchased in America.

This section traces the doctrine of strict liability as it has been developed and expanded by the judiciary in one jurisdiction, California. California has been one of the leading jurisdictions in advancing the doctrine of strict liability.

Restatement of Torts.   The *Greenman* rule of strict liability in tort is embodied in the *Restatement of Torts,* Section 402A, which provides:

Special Liability of Seller of Product for Physical Harm to User or Consumer

1. One who sells any product in a defective condition unreasonably dangerous to the user or consumer or to his property is subject to liability for physical harm thereby caused to the ultimate user or consumer, or to his property, if
   a. the Seller is engaged in the business of selling such a product, and
   b. it is expected to and does reach the user or consumer without substantial change in the condition in which it is sold.
2. The rule stated in Subsection (1) applies although
   a. the seller has exercised all possible care in the preparation of the sale of his product, and
   b. the user or consumer has not bought the product from or entered into any contractual relation with the seller.

Strict liability in tort is not concerned with the conduct of the defendant. It is an expression of policy that once a business entity is instrumental in placing a defective product into the stream of commerce, liability may attach *without regard to fault.* Under the doctrine of strict liability in tort, a plaintiff can prevail in a product liability action *without* having to establish the elements of negligence against the defendant, or having to prove that an express or implied warranty attached to the product and was breached.

A trend of the law, as adopted by California and a minority of jurisdictions, is that the plaintiff does not have to prove that the defect was "unreasonably dangerous" as set forth in the Restatement of Torts, Section 402A(1). The argument behind such a ruling is that the "unreasonably dangerous" element rings of being a negligence standard, which the doctrine of strict liability in tort was developed to avoid.

All in "Chain of Distribution" Liable.   The doctrine of strict liability has been broadly defined to be applicable to all persons in the production and marketing "chain of distribution," including manufacturers, distributors, wholesalers, retailers, manufacturers of component parts, assemblers, and others who help to place a defective product in the stream of commerce. For example, if a manufacturer produces a defective product that is passed along by a wholesaler to a retailer, and ultimately to a consumer who is injured by the defective product, the manufacturer, wholesaler, and retailer are *all* liable to the injured consumer under the doctrine of strict liability in tort. A manufacturer may be strictly liable even though the defective part was supplied by someone else, or if the manufacturer delegated assembling, adjustment, or inspection to dealers.

The doctrine of strict liability has been expanded to include lessors, licensors, and bailors. Successor corporations (through merger, purchase, or other form of acquisition), assume the strict liability exposure of their predecessor corporations. Although an ordinary builder of a dwelling or other structure has not been held to be strictly liable, a trend in the law is to hold the builder-seller of mass-produced tract houses strictly liable in tort.

Strict liability has its underpinnings in public policy. The purpose of imposing strict liability is to ensure that the costs of injuries resulting from defective *products* are borne by the manufacturers and others who put such products on the market, rather than by injured persons who are powerless to protect themselves. By placing the product on the market, the maker impliedly represents that the product is safe for use. The imposition of strict liability on business assumes that business will obtain insurance against the risk of loss and distribute the cost among consumers through higher prices. Further, placing the risk of loss on manufacturers and distributors provides an incentive for these businesses to use their research capabilities to design and produce fail-safe products that exceed reasonable standards of safety.

If one of the parties in the chain of distribution has been sued as a defendant by an injured plaintiff and has paid a judgment or settlement to the plaintiff, that defendant may sue the party responsible for causing the defect (usually the manufacturer) under the theory of negligence. A defendant who has paid an award or settlement may also seek a contribution from all other parties in the chain of distribution for their *pro rata* share of the amount of the judgment or settlement.

Transactions to Which the Doctrine Applies. The doctrine of strict liability in tort has been held applicable to sale transactions, lease transactions, licensing transactions, and to a manufacturer for failure to repair a product properly. The doctrine does *not* apply to the provision of services (e.g., the professional services of lawyers, architects, engineers), or where a product is supplied only as an "incidental" part of a service. For example, where defective blood is provided during the course of an operation, the "dominant part" of the transaction is the provision of a service—surgery—and the provision of the blood is an "incidental" part of the transaction to which the doctrine of strict liability in tort does not apply.

The occasional seller (in a "casual sale") is exempted from the doctrine of strict liability in tort based on the argument that a casual seller is not engaged in the activity as part of his normal business. For example, a person who sells a defective product to his neighbor in a casual sale is not held strictly liable for damage caused by the defect. The doctrine of strict liability in tort has generally been held not to apply to financial institutions who merely finance a borrower's purchases or lease of real and personal property.

Persons Who May Recover. Strict liability has been held to extend to "any human being to whom an injury from the defect is reasonably foreseeable." The right to recover in an action for strict liability in tort does not depend on "privity of contract" between the parties. The benefits of the doctrine of strict liability extend not only to the purchaser of the product, but also to the ultimate *user* or consumer of the product, including his or her spouse, family, relatives, employees, customers of the buyer, etc. *Users* include those passively enjoying the benefits of a product, such as passengers in automobiles or airplanes. Strict liability also extends to protect lessor (tenants) and licensees.

The trend of the law is to allow "bystanders" to bring an action for product liability based on the doctrine of strict liability. For example, a pedestrian who is injured by a defective automobile may bring an action based on strict liability in tort against the manufacturer and others in the chain of distribution of the defective automobile. In *Elmore v. American Motors Corporation,* C.2d (1969), Justice Peters of the California Supreme Court stated:

If anything, bystanders should be entitled to greater protection than the consumer or user where injury to bystanders from the defect is reasonably foreseeable. Consumers and users, at least, have the opportunity to inspect for defects and to limit their purchases to articles manufactured by reputable manufacturers and sold by reputable retailers, whereas the bystander ordinarily has no such opportunity. In short, the bystander is in greater need of protection from defective products which are dangerous, and if any distinction should be made between bystanders and users, it should be made, contrary to the position of defendants, to extend greater liability in favor of the bystanders.

The plaintiff in a product liability suit based on strict liability may include all parties in the chain of distribution as defendants in the lawsuit, or may sue any one or any number of the parties without suing all. The policy underlying this rule is that the injured plaintiff should have the ability to sue the party or parties who can financially respond to the lawsuit. (This is known as the "deep pocket theory.")

To establish liability of a defendant under the doctrine of strict liability in tort, it is not enough that an accident happened and the plaintiff was injured. The plaintiff must be able to prove by competent evidence that the product was "defective." The requisite defect may be in: (1) manufacture, (2) design, (3) failure to warn, or (4) failure to give proper instructions.

Defect in Manufacture.   The most obvious "defect" on which to base an action for strict liability in tort is a defect in the *manufacture* of the product, such as a chair with a defective leg, a ladder with a defective rung, a spring mattress with a defective spring, or a food product containing harmful ingredients.

The doctrine of strict liability in tort has always been held to apply to concealed product defects (*latent* defects) that have caused injury to users. However, early court decisions did not extend the doctrine to cases where the defect was open and obvious (*patent* defect), even though the defect could have been eliminated by proper design. The courts argued that the user should have been aware of the defect. The minority view, and the trend in the law, is to hold the doctrine of strict liability in tort applicable to *all* defects, whether latent, patent, or otherwise.

In *Luque v. McLean,* which follows, the California Supreme Court held that the doctrine of strict liability applied to a *patent* defect in a power lawn-mower that caused injury to a user.

PATENT DEFECT

LUQUE v. McLEAN

8 C.3D 136 (1972)
SUPREME COURT OF CALIFORNIA

Sullivan, Justice.

Plaintiff Celestino Luque lived in Millbrae with his cousins, Harry and Laura Dunn, who purchased from defendant Rhoads Hardware (Rhoads) a rotary power lawn mower manufactured by defendant Air Capital Manufacturing Company (Air Capital). The record discloses that the basic principle of a rotary mower is the rotation at extreme speed of a single blade which cuts the grass like a machete and ejects it through an unguarded hole in the front of the mower. In the machine used by plaintiff, the blade revolved at a speed of 175 miles per hour, passing the unguarded hole 100 times a second. Adjacent to this hole, the word "caution" was printed on the appliance.

On December 4, 1965, a friend of the Dunns asked plaintiff to cut her lawn. With the help of Mr. Dunn, plaintiff took the Dunns' mower to the friend's residence a few blocks away. Plaintiff testified that as he was cutting the grass, which was wet, he noticed a small carton in the path of the mower. He left the mower in a stationary position with its motor running and walked over to remove the carton. As he did so, he suddenly slipped on the grass and fell backward. His left hand went into the unguarded hole of the mower, was caught in the revolving rotary blade and was severely mangled and lacerated.

Plaintiff brought this action against Air Capital, Rhoads, and the distributor Garehime Corporation. . . . A verdict was returned in favor of defendants. Judgment was entered accordingly. This appeal followed.

In *Greenman,* the plaintiff was struck and injured by a piece of wood which flew out of a lathe he was using. Inadequate set screws were used to hold together the parts of the machine, thereby allowing vibration to cause the tailstock of the lathe to release the piece of wood. This defect was latent and not one of which the plaintiff was aware.

Defendants take the position that under California law a manufacturer is strictly liable in tort only for products which have latent defects. However, they have not called to our attention, nor has our independent research disclosed, any reported decisions in this state which have made a distinction between latent and patent defects in applying the doctrine of strict liability.

[T]he policy underlying the doctrine of strict liability compels the conclusion that recovery should not be limited to cases involving latent defects. . . . Requiring the defect to be latent would severely limit the cases in which the financial burden would be shifted to the manufacturer. . . . The result would be to immunize from strict liability manufacturers who callously ignore patent dangers in their products while subjecting to such liability those who innocently market products with latent defects.

The judgment is *reversed.*

CASE QUESTIONS

1. Who was injured? What injuries did the plaintiff suffer?
2. How did the injury occur? Was it caused by a *latent* or *patent* defect? What is the difference between these two types of defects?
3. What does the doctrine of *strict liability* provide? Who can be held liable under this doctrine? Explain.
4. What did the trial court hold? What did the Supreme Court of California hold in this case?

Policy Issue. Should the doctrine of strict liability have been adopted by the courts to apply to products? Or is the doctrine of negligence sufficient to protect injured consumers? Explain.

Economics Issue. Does the doctrine of strict liability have any economic implications? If so, explain what these are.

Ethics Issue. Is it ethical for a manufacturer or distributor to defend against a lawsuit when a product it has manufactured or sold causes injury?

Social Responsibility. Do manufacturers owe a duty of social responsibility to protect consumers from *patent* defects as well as from *latent* defects? Why or why not?

Defect in Design. A product may be defective under the strict liability doctrine because of a defect in *design* as well as a defect in manufacture. A product may be found to be defective in design if the product failed to perform as safely as "an ordinary consumer would expect when the product is used in an intended or reasonably foreseeable manner." In evaluating the adequacy of a product's design under this test, the jury may consider, along with other relevant factors, the gravity of the danger posed by the challenged design, the likelihood that such danger would occur, the mechanical feasibility of a safer alternative design, and the adverse consequences to the product and to the consumer that would result from an alternative design.

Noncompliance with federal or state safety standards furnishes probative evidence of a defective design of a product. However, compliance with such safety standards does not necessarily absolve a defendant of product liability under the doctrine of strict liability in tort.

In *Self v. General Motors Corporation* the court examined the alleged defect in *design* of an automobile the gas tank of which exploded in an accident and caused injury to the plaintiff.

DEFECT IN DESIGN

SELF v. GENERAL MOTORS CORPORATION

42 C.A.3D 1 (1974)
COURT OF APPEALS OF CALIFORNIA

Fleming, Associate Justice.

At 11 P.M. on 10 April 1968, Verne Prior, driving on U.S. 101 under the influence of alcohol and drugs at a speed of 65 to 85 miles an hour, crashed his 1963 Chrysler into the left rear of a 1962 Chevrolet station wagon stopped on the shoulder of the freeway for a flat tire. In the crash the Chevrolet station wagon was knocked into a gully, its fuel tank ruptured, and the vehicle caught fire. Two of its occupants were killed, and two others, one of

whom was plaintiff Christine Smith, a passenger in the front seat, sustained severe burn injuries.

Smith and others brought an action for personal injuries against Prior for negligent driving and against General Motors in . . . strict liability for defective manufacture and defective design of the station wagon, in particular the welding of the fuel tank and its placement in the left rear fender section . . . [The] jury's verdict . . . included damages of $350,000 for Smith against both defendants, . . .

General Motors appeals the denial of judgment notwithstanding the verdict, . . . In brief, General Motors contends its station wagon contained no defects in design, but if it did, defective design did not cause or contribute to Smith's injuries.

DEFECT IN DESIGN

Plaintiff's experts testified that the station wagon's fuel tank was located in a vulnerable position, that this location made the vehicle unreasonably dangerous to use, that earlier-model station wagons and passenger automobiles had their fuel tanks located underneath the body inside the crossbars of the frame, that if the station wagon's fuel tank had been similarly located it would have been well-protected in the collision.

The foregoing testimony was sufficient to make a *prima facie* case in support of plaintiff's claim that the station wagon had been defectively designed. While the word "defect" is not capable of precise definition in all cases and while defective design is an amorphous and elusive concept once we have progressed beyond the idea of fitness for intended use, its contours certainly include the notion of excessive preventable danger.

General Motors, however, contends that defective design was not properly an issue in the case, for a design is defective only if it results in a product which is unsafe for its intended use. Here, no evidence was produced to show the station wagon was unsafe for its intended use of operation on the highway. Since the station wagon was obviously not intended to be used as a stationary target for another vehicle traveling at 65 to 85 miles an hour, the injuries that resulted from the collision were not attributable to the design of the station wagon, and therefore judgment notwithstanding the verdict should have been entered in General Motors' favor. This argument of General Motors follows a logical course, but its premise has been repudiated by the Supreme Court in *Cronin v. J. B. E. Olson Corp.*

[The] argument that the van was built only for "normal" driving is unavailing. We agree that strict liability should not be imposed upon a manufacturer when injury results from a use of its product that is not reasonably foreseeable. Although a collision may not be the 'normal' or intended use of a motor vehicle, vehicle manufacturers must take accidents into consideration as reasonably foreseeable occurrences involving their products. The design and manufacture of products should not be carried out in an industrial vacuum but with recognition of the realities of their everyday use.

A motor vehicle manufacturer is required to foresee that as an incident of normal operation in the environment in which his product will be used accidents will occur, including high-speed collisions between vehicles. Because of this possibility he is required to design his vehicle to minimize unreasonable risks of injury and death. From this duty it follows that a motor vehicle manufacturer must take into account the possibility of high-speed collision when it selects a location for the fuel tank in the vehicle.

The manufacturer must evaluate the crashworthiness of his product and take such steps as may be reasonable and practicable to forestall particular crash injuries and mitigate the seriousness of others. . . .

SUPERSEDING CAUSE

However, our discussion on causation and superseding cause is not yet finished. The theory of General Motors' defense was that no matter where the fuel tank might have been located the station wagon would have caught fire in a vehicular impact of the magnitude of the one that took place and plaintiff's injuries would have been the same. It is a commonplace to observe that a litigant is entitled to have the jury properly instructed on its theory of the case. This, we believe, did not happen. We think the trial court prejudicially erred in refusing to give the following specific instruction on superseding cause requested by General Motors:

If you find that the gasoline tank in the 1962 Chevrolet station wagon was improperly located, but that the fire would have occurred even if the tank had been properly located, its location was not a substantial factor in bringing about the fire and was, therefore, not a contributing cause thereof.

This instruction is a correct statement of law, and its use would have brought into focus for the jury the critical issue of superseding cause raised by this defendant.

[General Motors is granted a *new trial*].

CASE QUESTIONS

1. How did the accident in this case occur? Who was injured?
2. What was the alleged *defect* in this case? Explain the plaintiff's argument regarding this alleged defect.
3. Did the court find the requisite defect for a strict liability action in this case? Did the court rule in favor of the plaintiff? Why or why not?
4. What is a "superseding cause"? Does it absolve a defendant from liability under the strict liability theory? How do you think the court will rule on this issue on remand?

Policy Issue. In order to avoid liability for strict liability based on a defect in *design,* where would you have placed the gas tank? In the front? On the left side? The right side? Under the back seat? The front seat? Where?

Economics Issue. Does the requirement that automobile manufacturers design their automobiles to withstand collisions increase the cost of automobiles? By how much money do you think? Is the price worth it?

Ethics Issue. Why didn't the court *only* hold the drunk driver who caused the accident liable? What is a "deep pocket"? Are some defendants only named because of their financial position? Is this ethical?

Social Responsibility. Does a manufacturer of a product owe a duty of social responsibility to design a product that can withstand accidents when the product is not being used for what it was primarily designed to be used for? Is the "foreseeability" test a good test? Is there any better test?

Failure to Warn.   Even if a product is faultlessly made, it may still be deemed "defective" if it is placed in the hands of a user *without* suitable *warnings* of its dangerous propensities. For example, where a chemical is harmful if swallowed, the manufacturer is under a duty to place an adequate and conspicuous warning on the product of this danger and will be held strictly liable in tort for failure to do so.

Generally, a manufacturer of a dangerous product that *cannot* be manufactured or designed to eliminate or reduce the dangerous condition or dangerous propensity may insulate himself from strict liability by adding a warning of the danger or giving directions on the container for counteracting it. This warning generally keeps the product from being deemed dangerous. Where a proper warning has been given, a seller may reasonably assume that it will be read and heeded by the user. A product bearing a proper warning, which would be safe if the warning is heeded, is not considered to be defective.

A manufacturer or seller does not have to add a warning to a product when the danger, or the potential danger, is generally known or is recognized. For example, where a minor buys a slingshot and injures another minor with a projectile shot from the slingshot, the manufacturer is not held liable in strict liability for failure to warn because the potential danger is "generally known and recognized."

A manufacturer of a product does not have a duty to warn a user of the dangers of a product caused by the user's unknown or unknowable allergies, sensitivities, or idiosyncrasies. The argument for this rule is that such a duty would recast the manufacturer in the role of an insurer.

Where a manufacturer overpromotes the use of a product (e.g., by saturation advertising of a prescription medicine), and thus waters down its own warnings of a known harmful effect of the product, the courts have deemed the warnings to be insufficient and have held the manufacturer strictly liable in tort for injuries caused by the product.

Manufacturers cannot avoid designing their product safely, or avoid adding safety devices to them, simply by warning or providing instructions on how to protect against the dangers. Such warnings and instructions are of no avail to one who does not see them, who does not know of them, who does not realize their importance, or who is a bystander. The courts have generally held, at least with regard to a defective product, that such warnings do not absolve a manufacturer of liability.

In *Burke v. Almaden Vineyards, Inc.* the court addressed the issue of whether the defendant was liable for failure to warn about the danger of a cork popping out of a champagne bottle.

DEFECT: FAILURE TO WARN

BURKE v. ALMADEN VINEYARDS, INC.

86 C.A.3D 768 (1978)
COURT OF APPEALS OF CALIFORNIA

Good, Associate Justice.

A jury returned a verdict against appellant Virginia Burke and in favor of Almaden Vineyards, Inc. and Automatic Plastic Molding Corporation, the respective manufacturers of Le Domaine champagne and the plastic cork used by Almaden in packaging its product. She had sought recovery of damages for injuries sustained in a household accident when a cork struck and shattered the left lens of her eyeglasses, driving pieces of glass into her eye. She . . . proceeded to trial solely on the theory of a manufacturer's strict liability in tort. . . . She appealed from the judgment entered on the verdict. . . .

The determinative issues arise out of the following occurrence at trial: *In camera,* before the jury was seated, appellant's counsel informed the court that she would produce evidence that four years after the accident Almaden had placed the following warning on its bottles:

> Use care. Sparkling wines contain natural high pressure. Point bottle away from people when removing wire stopper.

Almaden objected that the evidence was more prejudicial than probative. . . . [I]n view of Almaden's proffered stipulation the probative value of

the evidence of subsequent warning was outweighed by the risk of undue prejudice and . . . he would sustain the objection.

Where a manufacturer or supplier of a product is or should have been aware that a product is unreasonably dangerous absent a warning and such warning is feasible, strict liability in tort will attach if appropriate and conspicuous warning is not given. Liability does not attach if the dangerous propensity is either obvious or known to the injured person at the time he uses the product.

We do not believe that the consuming public is chargeable with knowledge that the pressure of carbonation in a sparkling wine is such that a plastic cork will eject itself when the wire seal is removed within 3 to 60 seconds at speeds between 37 and 49 miles per hour, depending upon bottle temperatures between 39° and 70.7° F., with no pressure on or twisting of the cork and no agitation of the bottle's contents. At such speeds an early ricochet of the missile could produce harm to someone not within its direct trajectory.

The fact of the subsequent warning would have directly supported an inference that a hazard existed which was not obvious and which created an unreasonable risk of harm in the absence of warning. A manufacturer does not ordinarily red-flag a product unless there is a potential danger which requires a warning. The proffered evidence afforded a reasonable, logical and natural inference thereof.

If the hazard was within common knowledge and in the same category as knowledge that knives cut and unstable ladders will cause a user to fall then no warning was required.

[Plaintiff] testified . . . she had never seen a cork spontaneously eject and thought that some finger pressure had to be exercised after the wire seal was removed in order to extrude the cork.

The exclusionary order constituted an abuse of discretion which deprived appellant of a fair trial. The judgment is *reversed.*

CASE QUESTIONS

1. How was the plaintiff injured in this case? Explain.
2. What was the alleged *defect* in this case? Explain.
3. Did Almaden subsequently place a warning on its champagne bottles? Was this important to the decision of the court? Explain.
4. Did the court find that the fact that a champagne cork explodes was a matter of "common knowl-

edge"? If it had, could the plaintiff have won her case? Was it part of *your* "common knowledge" prior to this case?

Policy Issue. Should a product be considered defective if it fails to contain a warning about its dangerous propensities?

Economics Issue. Did the decision of this case substantially increase the cost of making champagne? If used as precedent, does it substantially increase the cost of making other products? Why or why not?

Ethics Issue. Do you think consumers read many of the warnings on the products they use? Do you? Is it ethical for plaintiffs to sue manufacturers for failing to put warnings on products when the consumer probably wouldn't have read them anyway?

Social Responsibility. Should manufacturers and distributors be absolved from strict liability if they place notices on products warning consumers of the dangerous conditions of the product? If they warn of correctable latent defects? Correctable patent defects?

Failure to Provide Proper Instructions. A manufacturer is strictly liable in tort for failing to provide adequate instructions for assembling a product that, if improperly assembled, causes injury. The failure to provide proper instructions is considered the requisite *defect* for a strict liability action.

In *Midgley v. S. S. Kresge Company* the court held the defendant liable to a plaintiff who suffered severe eye injury, finding that the defendant failed to provide adequate instructions for the assembly of a telescope to be used to view the sun.

DEFECT: FAILURE TO PROVIDE PROPER INSTRUCTIONS

MIDGLEY v. S. S. KRESGE COMPANY

55 C.A.3D 67 (1976)
COURT OF APPEAL OF CALIFORNIA

Puglia, Presiding Justice.

This appeal presents the perplexing question whether liability for failure to warn of dangerous properties of a product is measured by the doctrine of strict liability. . . . [T]he trial court . . . refused plaintiff's proffered instruction that failure to warn of dangerous propensities likewise rendered a product defective.

Plaintiff, Thomas Midgley, was 13 years old when he purchased from defendant Kresge a refracting telescope manufactured in Japan. When purchased the telescope was dismantled, its components in a cardboard box accompanied by a booklet of instructions on assembly, use and maintenance. The box bore the legend "Manufactured in Japan for S. S. Kresge Company. . . ." The telescope itself bore a label "K-Mart" accompanied by the phrase "Quality Guaranteed." Kresge, owner of K-Mart Discount Stores, the retailer, was the only named defendant. The Japanese manufacturer was not a party.

Among the components of the telescope, is a sun filter consisting of a dark lens labeled "Sun." The only instructions or warnings received by plaintiff relative to use of the telescope to view the sun are contained in the instruction booklet which provides:

> Sun and moon glasses are deposited in the eyepieces cases; screwed into the eyepiece bottom. Be sure to use sun glass for solar observation and moon glass for moon observation. CAUTION: Please refrain from looking up the sun [sic] without attaching the sun glass. Also the sun should not be seen through the finderscope.

The instruction book contains no diagramatic or pictorial illustrations of the proper installation of the sun filter. Upon reading the warning, plaintiff knew he should view the sun only through the sun filter. He also knew before purchasing the telescope that it was dangerous to look at the sun with the naked eye.

In the first two months that he had the telescope, plaintiff used it to view the sun 15 to 20 times, always through the sun filter. In preparing to do so, plaintiff would remove the eyepiece lens and replace it with the sun filter. Properly assembled for sun viewing, the eyepiece lens should remain in place and the sun filter be screwed into the opposite or bottom end of the cylinder. When properly assembled the system is safe for sun viewing. As assembled by plaintiff, however, harmful sunlight could leak around the sun filter into the eye of the viewer. Plaintiff's evidence, including expert testimony, tended to show that in so using the telescope

he sustained a solar burn on the retina of his eye, irreparably impairing his vision.

A retailer engaged in the business of distributing goods to the public is strictly liable in tort for personal injuries caused by defects in the products it sells. The retailer's liability is coextensive with that of the manufacturer of the product.

[T]he defendant herein marketed a technically complex product intended for use by technically unsophisticated consumers, to be assembled and used by them in accordance with instructions prepared and supplied by the technically knowledgeable supplier. Failure to assemble or use the product in accordance with these directions may well cause physical injury and thus constitutes a potential danger. . . . Therefore, the supplier is strictly liable for injury proximately resulting from composing and furnishing a set of instructions for assembly and use which does not adequately avoid the danger of injury.

The judgment is *reversed*.

CASE QUESTIONS

1. How was the plaintiff injured in this case? Explain.
2. What was the alleged *defect* in this case? Explain.
3. Read the instructions provided for placing the "Sun" lens on the telescope. Do you understand them? Do you think a thirteen-year-old would understand them?
4. If you were the plaintiff's lawyer, how would you convince the jury of the defect?
5. Which party was held liable in this case, the manufacturer who wrote the instructions? Or the retailer who sold the product and instructions?

Policy Issue. Should failure to provide proper instructions be a *defect* for which a manufacturer and distributor should be held liable? Why or why not? Are most instructions well written?

Economics Issue. Under the doctrine of strict liability, should all in the "chain of distribution" be held liable? Does this increase the cost to retailers? How do they *cover* this cost?

Ethics Issue. Is it ethical for a manufacturer, as in this case, to allow a retailer to be held liable for its negligence? Can a retailer sue the manufacturer to recover what it had to pay?

Social Responsibility. Was Kresge Co. under a special duty to review the instructions for the telescope since the product was made and the instructions written overseas?

Defenses to Strict Liability.   In the majority of jurisdictions, the fact that a plaintiff has contributed to the happening of the accident and the injuries that he suffers does *not* relieve the defendant manufacturer and distributor of a defective product from liability under the doctrine of strict liability. There are, however, several *defenses* that a defendant can raise to a strict liability action, including:

1. assumption of the risk
2. supervening event
3. known and avoidable danger
4. correction of a defect
5. statute of limitation
6. abnormal misuse.

These defenses are usually narrowly interpreted by the courts.

Assumption of the Risk.   Under current law, traditional assumption of the risk by the user is still a valid defense in a product liability case based on strict liability in tort. However, in order for this defense to apply, the user or consumer must become aware of the defect and danger, and still proceed "voluntarily" and "unreasonably" to encounter the known danger by making use of the product. The defense of assumption of the risk is restrictively applied by the courts in actions based on strict liability in tort. The defense of assumption of risk is merged with contributory negligence in those jurisdictions that apply the doctrine of comparative fault, and in those cases is only meaningful in determining damages.

Supervening Event.   Where a product is sufficiently *altered* or *modified* between the time it left the hands of the manufacturer and the time it causes injury, such alteration or modification is deemed an "intervening" or "supervening" cause, which absolves the original manufacturer from strict liability. The parties who altered the product and who later distributed the product are strictly liable to anyone who suffers injury from the defectively altered product. Time alone is not sufficient to absolve a manufacturer of strict liability. A defective ladder remains a defective ladder until such time as it causes injury.

Known and Avoidable Dangers.   Many products that are not defective in the ordinary sense of the term, such as alcohol and tobacco, involve common dangers known and contemplated by the user. As a matter of public policy, the doctrine of strict liability has not been held applicable to such products. Many drugs and vaccines are *unavoidably unsafe* in that they are either experimental or involve elements of danger that cannot be wholly eliminated. Because the social value of such products outweighs the risks, and with a public policy of promoting their development, the courts will *not* hold a seller who prepares unavoidably unsafe products carefully and markets them with appropriate restrictions or warnings strictly liable for their injurious consequences.

Correction of a Defect. A manufacturer who has taken all reasonable steps to *correct* a defect in manufacture or design may succeed in absolving itself from future liability. For example, when a manufacturer discovers a defect in a hood latch of an automobile, distributes a corrected auxiliary latch to its dealers with instructions to install the corrected latch, and notifies the purchasers of the automobile of the availability of the replacement latch, the manufacturer's liability for the defective design terminates, even as to those purchasers who do not have the replacement latch installed.

Statute of Limitations. A statute of limitations requires that a plaintiff bring an action within a certain period of time (e.g., three years) after he suffers injury from a defective product, or he loses the right to bring such actions. The majority of states have not enacted statutes of limitations regarding bringing of actions under strict liability in tort. Where an appropriate statute of limitations does exist, it may be raised as a defense to an action based on strict liability in tort. That is, if a plaintiff brings such an action too long after the alleged injury, the court will refuse to hear the case.

Abnormal Misuse. A manufacturer or seller of a product is entitled to assume that the product will be put to its intended use, and is not liable in strict liability for an unintended, unexpected, or "abnormal" misuse. For example, where a fencing mask is designed to withstand a blow from a sanctioned round-pointed fencing blade, but the plaintiff was injured while sparring with someone who used an illegal sharp-pointed sabre that pierces the mask, the manufacturer of the mask is not strictly liable.

In *Dosier v. Wilcox-Crittendon Co.* the court held that the plaintiff's abnormal misuse of the defendant's product was an absolute defense to plaintiff's strict liability suit.

ABNORMAL MISUSE

DOSIER v. WILCOX-CRITTENDON CO.

45 C.A.3D 74 (1975)
COURT OF APPEALS OF CALIFORNIA

Arata, Associate Justice.

Plaintiff-appellant Edward Dosier takes this appeal from a judgment for defendants Wilcox-Crittendon Company and North and Judd Manufacturing Company in a personal injury action based on strict liability.

The evidence reveals that North and Judd are engaged principally in the manufacture of harness and saddlery hardware, belt buckles, shoe buckles, dog leads, handbag hardware, hooks and eyes for men's trousers, and a line of plastics used for electrical fittings. Wilcox-Crittendon is a wholly-owned subsidiary of North and Judd. The "hook" involved in this case was manufactured by North and Judd, and bears the company's trademark. It is described in its catalog as a No. 333 snap. The snap, hereinafter referred to as "hook," is made of cast malleable iron having the following dimensions:

> overall length of four and three-quarters inches, a seven-eighths of an inch swivel eye with a ring size opening of one-half inch; it has a tongue that opens outward. It is manufactured principally to be used as a bull tie, stallion chain or cattle tie; it is distributed or marketed through wholesale hardware houses, and houses that sell harness and saddlery wares.

The particular "hook" at issue in this case was purchased by a buyer for United Air Lines for its plant maintenance shop at San Francisco Airport for use in connection with a "safety rope around a workstand." It was bought from Keystone Brothers, a harness and saddlery wares outlet in San Francisco in 1964. At the time of the purchase the "hook" was selected by the buyer from a display board featuring harness equipment such as bridles, spurs and bits; there was no discussion as to intended use when the purchase was made. The buyer was familiar with this type of "hook" as a result of his earlier experience on a farm.

On March 28, 1968, the plaintiff, as an employee of United Air Lines, was working with a crew installing a grinding machine at its maintenance plant. As part of the rigging process, he attached the "hook" to a 1,700-pound counterweight and lifted it to a point where it was suspended in the air. At this point plaintiff reached under the suspended counterweight in search of a missing bolt when suddenly the "hook" gave way and the counterweight fell on his arm causing the injuries for which he seeks damages.

In order to invoke the doctrine of strict liability, the plaintiff must prove that the product was being used, at the time of injury, in a way the manufacturer intended it to be used. In applying this rule our courts have held that it should not be narrowly applied and that even an "unusual use" which the manufacturer *is required to anticipate* should not relieve the manufacturer of liability in the absence of warnings against such use. Just what a manufacturer is "required to anticipate" in connection with

the use of a product is a question of reasonable foreseeability. It has been repeatedly held that the foreseeability of the misuse of a product is a question for the trier of fact.

One of plaintiff-appellant's main complaints on appeal is that the trial judge committed prejudicial error by receiving evidence concerning the circumstances surrounding the purchase of the "hook" and its use by United. We cannot agree. In deciding whether or not a product is being used in a way the manufacturer intended it to be used, the market for which it is produced is a most important consideration. This bears directly upon the issue of foreseeability.

For the foregoing reasons the judgment is *affirmed*.

CASE QUESTIONS

1. How was the plaintiff injured in this case? Explain.
2. What purpose was the "hook" designed for? What was it used for in this case? Explain.
3. Explain the difference between the following. Do both absolve a defendant from liability under the doctrine of strict liability? If not, which one does? Why?
   a. *foreseeable* misuse
   b. *abnormal* misuse
4. Which of the preceding misuses did the court find in this case? Do you agree? Why?
5. What is the difference between the following two doctrines?
   a. doctrine of *strict* liability
   b. doctrine of *absolute* liability

Policy Issue. Should the doctrine of strict liability be extended to cover the provision of *services* (e.g., legal services, medical services, accounting services)?

Economics Issue. Has the doctrine of strict liability caused any major changes in the way American companies do business? If so, how?

Ethics Issue. Was it ethical for the plaintiff to sue the defendant in this case? Was it ethical for the defendant to try to keep out the evidence as to where the "hook" was purchased?

Social Responsibility. Should manufacturers and distributors of products be held *absolutely* liable for all injuries caused by the products they manufacture and sell?

Foreseeable Misuse. If a consumer misuses a product, but the misuse was *foreseeable,* the manufacturer and distributor of the product may still be held liable under the doctrine of strict liability for injuries suffered by the consumer. For example, when the plaintiff was injured when she leaned against the top of a washing machine in a laundromat and the glass gave way, such misuse is considered foreseeable. If the top of the washing machine could have been designed to prevent such an occurrence, the manufacturer is held strictly liable in tort for injuries sustained by the plaintiff.

In *Horn v. General Motors Corporation* the California Supreme Court held that a plaintiff's nonuse of a seat belt was a "foreseeable misuse," and held the manufacturer and automobile dealer liable to the plaintiff under the doctrine of strict liability.

ASSUMPTION OF THE RISK: FORESEEABLE MISUSE

HORN v. GENERAL MOTORS CORPORATION

17 C.3D 359 (1976)
SUPREME COURT OF CALIFORNIA

By the Court

About 9 P.M. on the evening of September 23, 1966, plaintiff Lillian Y. Horn was driving her 1965 Chevrolet station wagon down Laurel Canyon Boulevard, a curving Los Angeles street. She was accompanied by her two sons; her six-year-old son was in the front seat and her nine-year-old son in the rear. As she wound downhill, at approximately 25 miles per hour, a car rounding a curve suddenly swung into her lane, its headlights temporarily blinding her. She swerved to her right to avoid the car, bounced off the right curb across the street to the left and into a concrete reinforced abutment.

As she steered to the right, plaintiff brought her left hand across the horn cap in the center of the steering wheel; at the same time, with her right hand, she tried to hold her son on the front seat. She felt and saw something fly between herself and her son; it was later established that this was the horn cap. When the car hit the abutment, plaintiff felt a burning sensation as her face hit the "cen-

ter part" of the steering wheel. The "center part," following removal of the horn cap, contained three sharp prongs that held the horn cap in place. Plaintiff sustained a laceration of the chin, a displaced fracture of her jaw, a fracture of her left ear canal, and the loss of two teeth.

Plaintiff brought this action against defendant General Motors Corporation, the manufacturer of the station wagon, and defendant Fletcher Chevrolet, Inc., the dealer from whom she purchased it. The case was tried on the single theory of strict liability in tort based on a defective product. . . . The jury returned a verdict against both defendants for damages in the sum of $45,000.

Plaintiff's expert testified that the horn cap was defective in that it could be easily knocked off in the course of normal use of the car, thereby exposing the sharp prongs underneath and that there were several alternative ways of designing the horn cap to prevent its being knocked off. . . . This evidence is clearly supportive of the jury's implied finding that the fastening of the horn cap by three sharp prongs in such a way that it could be easily displaced and the prongs thereby exposed to possible contact by the driver during a collision or sudden stop, constituted a defect in design or manufacture.

ASSUMPTION OF THE RISK

Plaintiff's station wagon was equipped with seat belts admittedly in good working order. She admitted that she was not using them at the time of the collision. At a hearing outside the jury's presence, defendants offered to prove by the testimony of an expert that failure to use seat belts was a misuse of the automobile and that if plaintiff had been using the seat belts at the time of the accident, her injuries would have been substantially reduced.

Defendants . . . argue that plaintiff consciously chose not to use her seat belt with the knowledge that such conduct would increase the risk of injury in the event of a collision, since she would probably be thrown about the interior of the car. In sum, defendants argue, plaintiff voluntarily and unreasonably proceeded to encounter a known danger. . . . In *Luque* we said:

> The only form of plaintiff's negligence that is a defense to strict liability is that which consists in *voluntarily and unreasonably proceeding to encounter a known danger,* more commonly referred to as assumption of risk. For such a defense to arise, the user or consumer must become aware of the defect and danger and still proceed unreasonably to make use of the product.

There is no evidence in the present record showing, or from which it can be reasonably inferred, that plaintiff was aware of the defect in this case, namely the easily removable horn cap exposing sharp prongs, or that she was aware of any danger caused by such defect. The evidence offered by defendants as to plaintiff's failure to use her seat belt did not purport to show that plaintiff knew that the horn cap was defective and that her failure to use her seat belt would expose her to the risk of injury from the prongs beneath the horn cap in the event the cap itself came off. The offered evidence did not establish the defense of assumption of the risk, . . . We conclude that the trial court properly excluded the evidence in question.

FORESEEABLE MISUSE

Defendant's final claim as to the admissibility of this evidence is to the effect that it would tend to prove that the product—the station wagon—was misused. It is true as indicated earlier in this opinion that if the product is put to a use by the consumer that is not reasonably foreseeable, then strict liability should not be imposed. The simple answer to defendants' argument is that the driving of an automobile without using a seat belt is an entirely foreseeable use of the vehicle.

The judgment is *affirmed.*

CASE QUESTIONS

1. How did the accident happen in this case? What injuries did the plaintiff suffer?
2. Was there a *defect* in the product? If so, what type of defect was it? Explain.
3. What does the doctrine of *assumption of the risk* provide? What are the necessary elements to prove this?
4. Is assumption of the risk a *defense* to a strict liability action? Did the defendant prove this defense in this case? Explain.
5. Did the plaintiff *misuse* the product in this case? If so, how? Was it sufficient to absolve the defendant from strict liability? Explain.

Policy Issue. How do manufacturers and distributors of products protect themselves against the possibility of huge damage awards under the doctrine of strict liability? Is the doctrine of strict liability really a massive insurance program mandated by the courts? Explain.

Economics Issue. What does the doctrine of *contributory negligence* provide? Does it apply to strict liability actions? What does the doctrine of *comparative negligence* provide? Does it help or hurt defendants in strict liability actions? Explain.

Ethics Issue. Is it ethical for a consumer to sue a defendant manufacturer or dealer when he has failed to use the safety devices provided by the manufacturer? Do you wear your seat belt?

Social Responsibility. Does the doctrine of strict liability in tort serve any useful social purposes? If so, what? Are these social benefits worth the cost?

Damages Recoverable.   Recovery of damages in an action based on strict liability in tort generally extends to both *personal* injuries and *property* damage caused by the defect. For example, if a defect in an automobile causes both the automobile to burn and the occupants to suffer personal injuries, damages may be awarded, both for the property damage to the automobile and for the personal injuries suffered by the occupants. Under the theory of strict liability, a plaintiff may recover not only for physical injuries directly inflicted as a result of the accident, but also for emotional shock.

Punitive damages may be recovered in a lawsuit predicated on strict liability in tort in the following circumstances:

1. where the defendant has been guilty of concealing material facts concerning the safety of the product
2. where there has been an intentional misrepresentation of the product
3. where it is shown that the manufacturer has deliberately neglected to repair a known defect (e.g., where there is proof that defendant conducted a cost-benefit analysis which showed it was less expensive to pay actual damages to injured plaintiffs than to recall the product and repair the defect).

In many jurisdictions, judges dislike awarding punitive damages in actions based on the doctrine of strict liability. The most celebrated example of an award of punitive damages was a jury award of $125 million in punitive damages against Ford Motor Company in a case where a Ford Pinto in which the plaintiff was riding was hit from the rear and the gas tank (located in the rear) exploded, causing serious personal injuries to the plaintiff. The damages in this case were later commuted to $3.5 million by the court.

A plaintiff *cannot* recover for purely *economic* or commercial loss under the theory of strict liability in tort. For example, if the automobile referred to in the above example was used in the course of plaintiff's business, the plaintiff cannot recover under strict liability for the economic injury (i.e., loss of sales) caused by the loss of his automobile. The plaintiff may, however, recover for economic loss under the warranty theory of product liability if applicable.

Comparative Negligence.   The minority rule, and the trend in the law, is to apply the doctrine of *comparative fault* to strict liability actions. Under this doctrine, the plaintiff may still maintain an action for strict liability against a manufacturer if he has contributed to his own injuries, but the award of damages is reduced in proportion to plaintiff's own fault. For example, in a product liability case where the defendant is found to be 80 percent responsible and plaintiff is found to be 20 percent responsible for the injuries suffered by the plaintiff, and the plaintiff has incurred expenses and injuries of $100,000, the defendant is liable for $80,000 of damages.

Trend of the Law

Recently, in a specialized area of product safety, the power of the Federal Food and Drug Administration has been somewhat curtailed by Congress. In 1976, Congress enacted the Vitamin-Mineral Amendments to the Food, Drug, and Cosmetic Act, which severely limited the FDA's authority to regulate the composition and promotion of dietary supplements, nutritional products, and health foods. In 1977, Congress passed legislation that postponed FDA action to ban the use of saccharin in food. In that same year Congress also passed legislation that directed the FDA to refrain from implementing a system for controlling the limitation of shellfish harvested in U.S. waters. The trend of the law in curtailing, or at least limiting, the authority of the FDA is expected to continue into the near future.

As can be seen by the cases in this chapter, the courts have been instrumental in developing and expanding the general doctrine of strict liability in tort. The present trend is for the judiciary to continue to expand the applicability of the doctrine to injuries caused by defective products. In *Sindell v. Abbott Laboratories*, 26 C.3d 588 (1980), the California Supreme Court decided one of the most controversial cases yet in the strict liability area. In that case the court assessed liability on *all* companies that manufactured DES for damages suffered by a daughter of a woman who took DES where the manufacturer of the DES taken by the mother could not be identified. Few states have yet adopted this "market share liability" doctrine. The *Sindell* case is presented in Chapter 2 of this book.

In an attempt to protect themselves and curtail the expansion of the doctrine of strict liability by the judiciary, businesses have begun to petition legislators for statutory limitations on the doctrine. Currently, legislatures of many jurisdictions have enacted statutes that limit the scope of the coverage of the doctrine of strict liability, establish exceptions to coverage of the doctrine, set dollar limits on awards, and establish a statute of limitations for bringing actions based on strict liability in tort.

REVIEW QUESTIONS

1. Fautis, an importer, paid $9,000 for 449 cases of tomato paste that he imported from Portugal. After the paste arrived in New York, U.S. Government inspectors took samples for inspection. The government testing re-

vealed that the tomato paste had a higher than allowable mold content as allowed by government standard. Apparently all tomato paste has some mold; government regulations allow a mold count of 40 percent. Fautis' tomato paste had 42 percent mold count. Although mold in tomato products indicates decomposition, a consumer who looked at, smelled, or tasted a tomato paste containing a 42 percent mold content would not be able to tell that the paste had mold in it. Only an expert using a microscope could detect the high mold count. The government seized Fautis' shipment and ordered it to be destroyed under the Federal Food, Drug and Cosmetic Act. Should the shipment be destroyed?

2. Sicard purchased a hair preparation, Roux Shampoo Tint, to tint her hair color. The label on the Roux container stated that if it was used according to directions, Roux Shampoo Tint was safe and proper in every respect. The package stated "Roux Shampoo Tint washes out 'Creeping Grey'; shampoos life and color into the hair; penetrates the hair; and does not wash out, streak or run; imparts a natural life-like tone; does not create a glossy superficial appearance. If you use the proper color of Roux Shampoo Tint for the application, and allow the color to develop throughly, human eyes should not be able to detect anything unnatural in the appearance of the hair. Eliminates the need for softening. Also you will find preliminary shampooing absolutely unnecessary unless the hair is particularly oily or greasy. It is very desirable for toning down overbleached hair." After Sicard applied the tint according to the directions, she suffered a severe case of dermatitis, which affected her hands, face and arms. Her skin became dry and swollen. Her condition did not result from hypersensitive skin, rather the tint contained certain poisonous chemicals which reacted with her natural skin acid balance to cause the dermatitis. Given this experience, can the FDA remove the product under the Food, Drug, and Cosmetic Act?

3. Parrillo, a bartender, was injured when he tried to open a bottle of grenadine syrup and it exploded. Parrillo sued Giroux Company, the firm that made the syrup. Giroux purchased the bottles from a bottle manufacturer and then packaged the grenadine. Giroux's employees visually inspected the bottles before shipment and usually discarded about one out of every 500 bottles because of a defect. Since Parrillo did not mishandle the bottle in any way, at trial Parrillo showed evidence of his injury and then asked the court to infer Giroux's negligence under the doctrine of *res ipsa loquitur*. Can *res ipsa loquitur* be successfully used by Parrillo in this case?

4. Martinez, a relatively ignorant buyer, purchased a used Volkswagen camper from Valley Datsun after a salesman told him that it was in "excellent condition." Two days after Martinez bought the camper, its clutch burned out and it suffered a thrown rod. Martinez sued Valley Datsun and at trial the jury found that the salesman's representation was not true. Could Martinez recover for a breach of an express warranty?

5. Vlases purchased 2,000 day-old chicks from Montgomery Ward Company's catalogue. The birds had leukosis (avian cancer) when they were delivered to him and most died shortly thereafter. Medically, there is no known way to determine whether newly hatched chicks have leukosis and there is no medication available to prevent an outbreak of this highly contagious

disease. Can Vlases recover for a breach of the implied warranty of merchantability?

6. Shortly after he purchased a Gallen houseboat, Miller began experiencing trouble with the boat's power systems. Repairs made by authorized Chrysler representatives did not help, so Miller sought the advice of the president of the Chrysler Marine Division regarding which power system would best suit the houseboat; he then installed the recommended system. It proved inadequate, and Miller's problems did not cease until he installed a different Chrysler system. Miller sued Chrysler to recover the cost of the first power plant that he installed, under the theory of an implied warranty of fitness for a particular purpose. Could he recover?

7. Nash's home was damaged by a fire that started near a toaster-oven manufactured by General Electric. The toaster had been purchased in an unopened manufacturer's box, there was no evidence of damage in shipment, it had not been repaired in the five years that Nash owned it, and it had worked perfectly up to the time of the fire. There was evidence to indicate that an electrical failure had occurred in the oven. A normal toaster-oven should last at least ten years with no electrical defects. Can Nash recover under strict liability? What type of defect should he try to show?

8. Buccery was injured when his Chevrolet LUV pickup truck was struck from the rear by a Chevrolet El Camino pickup. The driver of the El Camino testified that his vehicle was not traveling more than five miles per hour faster than Buccery's vehicle; and expert testimony showed that the El Camino struck Buccery's vehicle with a relatively minor impact. The impact was, however, sufficient to cause the rear of Buccery's head to strike the window at the back of the cab of his vehicle. There was no padded head restraint in the LUV and the top of the seat was well below head level. The lack of a head restraint was a contributing cause to Buccery's injuries. Federal safety standards required head restraints on automobiles but had exempted trucks from this requirement. Despite this exemption, truck head restraints could have been easily installed at a relatively low cost by all truck makers. Buccery sued General Motors and contended that GM should be held liable under a strict liability theory because compliance with federal standards did not release it from any common-law liability. Could Buccery recover?

9. Huff was killed when the truck in which he was driving was involved in a collision and the fuel tank ruptured, causing a fire. There was evidence to indicate that the fuel tank had been defectively designed and that a properly designed tank would not have erupted as the result of Huff's collision. Can Huff's wife recover in a strict liability suit?

10. Frey purchased a gas space heater sold by Montgomery Ward under its own label, but manufactured by McGraw-Edison. Frey told the Montgomery Ward clerk that he intended to use the space heater in a house trailer where he planned to raise chinchillas for profit. For almost a year the heater operated satisfactorily; then one morning Frey found the temperature inside the trailer to be over 110 degrees and, as a result of exposure to the excessive heat, most of the chinchillas died. The instructions furnished by McGraw-Edison did not state that the heaters should not be

used in house trailers; however, the product was not designed for use in a house trailer. There was no evidence to indicate that the heater had been defectively manufactured. Frey sued McGraw-Edison and Montgomery Ward under a strict liability theory but the court dismissed the case before submitting it to the jury for final determination. Frey appealed. Did Frey present a valid strict liability claim, one which should have been submitted to the jury for a determination?

11. Hanlon, a new employee at Wayne Iron Works, was severely injured while operating a piece of machinery manufactured by Cyril Bath Company. Hanlon severed the fingers on his left hand when he activated the machine by pressing his foot upon an electrical foot switch while attempting to remove a piece of metal with his hand. The electrical starting device had been substituted by Wayne for a mechanical treadle, which had been a component of the machine when Cyril Bath sold it. The old mechanical treadle required the operator to lift his foot a considerable distance and exert some 65 pounds of downward pressure to activate the machine, whereas the new electrical starting device required about 15 pounds of pressure. Hanlon sued Cyril Bath under a strict liability theory. Can he recover?

12. Eshbach, a minor, was injured when she jumped on the back of a riding lawnmower behind her young brother, who was operating it, and her foot slipped and was caught in the unguarded chain and sprocket of the machine. Since the lawnmower did not have either brakes or an ignition switch, Eshbach's injuries were further enhanced during the time it took her brother to stop the machine. Eshbach sued W. T. Grant's, the seller, under a strict liability theory. What doctrine will the court use to decide the case?

13. White, a healthy nine-year-old girl, drank a bottle of Coca-Cola on July 30, 1974. The beverage "tasted terrible" to her, and she asked an adult friend nearby to look at it. It was discovered that the drink contained discernible parts of the head, front legs, body, and tail of a mouse. White became upset and began crying and refused supper that evening. She was ill all that night with spells of stomach cramps, vomiting, and nightmares. The next day and three times thereafter, White was taken to a doctor as a result of the illness. From then until March 1975, she suffered stomach aches, nervousness, weight loss, and listlessness as a result of this experience. On one occasion at school, when the children were singing a song about a mouse, she became ill and fainted. Many times during the next six months White's parents were required to take her home from school because she was ill with stomach cramps. White's parents sued Coca-Cola on her behalf and sought actual damages as well as damages for her pain and suffering. What could they recover?

19 DEBTOR-CREDITOR RELATION

INTRODUCTION

The American economy has become a *credit* economy. Consumers borrow money for major purchases and to expand their businesses, and use credit cards to pay for dinners at restaurants, gasoline, and retail sales. Currently, U.S. consumers owe nearly $2 *trillion* in debts, with over 750,000 credit cards issued and outstanding. The "credit explosion" in the United States has not been without problems, particularly for consumer-debtors. The most blatant abuses have occurred in debt collection practices and in discrimination in granting credit.

In order to correct abuses in the extension and collection of credit, both federal and state governments have enacted comprehensive legislation to regulate the debtor-creditor relation. In particular, the Congress enacted the Consumer Credit Protection Act, which is a series of titles that cover the disclosure of credit terms, prohibit discrimination in extending credit, protect consumers from discrimination resulting from incorrect or misleading reports by credit reporting agencies, and regulate the collection of debts by collection agencies.

USURY LAWS

In most credit transactions the debtor is obligated to repay the principal amount borrowed *and* an *interest* charge on the amount borrowed. The rate of interest is usually agreed upon by the parties to a credit transaction and specified in the credit contract. Even in the current economy, loan sharks are willing to lend money to poor or destitute consumers, usually at exorbitant interest rates, e.g., "two-for-one dollars in one week".

In order to discourage loan-sharking and to protect debtors against high interest rates, most states have passed *usury* laws. State usury laws set a specific upper limit on the interest rate that may be charged by a creditor-lender on covered transactions. Any interest rate charged that exceeds the rate of interest set by the state usury law is illegal as a "usurious" rate of interest. The majority of states do not require that the debtor prove that the creditor *intended* to charge a usurious interest rate. The essential elements of proving a usurious credit transaction are:

1. the existence of a state usury law
2. a loan of money where there is an absolute obligation to repay the principal
3. a credit transaction covered by the state usury law
4. a rate of interest charged by the creditor that exceeds the state usury law.

Transactions Covered by Usury Laws.   The issue of usury is usually raised by a *debtor* as a defense to an action by a *creditor* to collect on the debt. Although usury laws differ from state to state, the highest usual rate of interest that may legally be charged on a debt is 18 percent to 20 percent. Often, creditors attempt to avoid usury laws by imposing certain charges for the extension of credit and calling such charges "fees" instead of a payment of interest. Most state laws provide that certain fees charged in association with the extension of credit must be included with the interest charged in determining whether the state usury law has been violated.

State usury laws are generally very broad in their coverage, and usually cover almost all loans made to consumers. Many states have established exemptions from usury laws for (1) loans on real estate; (2) loans to corporations and businesses; and (3) loans above a certain dollar amount (e.g., above $25,000).

States differ considerably as to the remedies available to a consumer-debtor who has been charged a usurious rate of interest. The most prevalent rule is that where a usurious interest rate has been charged, the debtor does not have to pay *any* interest on the debt, but must repay the principal amount borrowed according to the terms of the loan agreement. Other states allow the debtor to rescind the loan contract upon return of the principal to the creditor. A rule adopted by a few states provides that a debtor can collect *treble* the amount of interest charged on a usurious loan. Very few states provide for forfeiture by the creditor of both interest *and* principal where a loan is found to be usurious. Almost all states provide for the payment of attorneys' fees and costs of litigation where a loan is found to have been usurious. A creditor may also be held criminally liable for charging a usurious rate of interest. Courts may permit a creditor to raise the equitable doctrine of estoppel against a charge of usury where facts and circumstances warrant, e.g., when the debtor is an experienced borrower of substantial means.

In *Aclin Ford Co. v. Cordell* the court held that the interest rate charged on an extension of credit violated state usury laws where the commission earned by the creditor-seller on the sale of required credit life insurance was added to the interest charge on the debt.

USURY LAW

ACLIN FORD CO. v. CORDELL

625 S.W. 2D 459 (1982)
SUPREME COURT OF ARKANSAS

George Rose Smith, Justice.

In February, 1980, the appellees, Mr. and Mrs. Cordell, bought a new car from Aclin Ford Company, the unpaid balance of the purchase price being payable in 48 monthly installments of $175 each. Aclin assigned the purchase contract to Ford Motor Credit Company. The Cordells brought this suit five months later to cancel the sale for usury. The chancellor canceled the contract, finding that the Cordells had been compelled to purchase credit life insurance in the transaction, that the $252 premium was part of the total amount to be financed, and that the inclusion of Aclin's 35 percent commission for selling the insurance pushed the interest rate past 10 percent per annum.

Despite the many cases cited by both sides in their briefs, the controlling principles of law are settled. If a buyer or borrower is compelled as a condition to the extension of credit to buy insurance on which the seller or lender receives a commission, the commission may be treated as interest in the determination of usury. On the other hand, if the buyer or borrower voluntarily agrees to the purchase of the insurance and the premium is not excessive, the commission is not to be considered as interest.

Mrs. Cordell testified that she told the Aclin salesman she did not want credit life insurance, but the salesman went into the office (presumably to check with Horton, the manager) and came back saying, "You have to have the credit life insurance." Cordell

testified that he commented that the insurance was not worth having, but the salesman said, "You've got to have it."

After the couple bought the car they became dissatisfied with its performance and with what they regarded as Aclin's unwillingness or inability to repair it. Finally the Cordells resorted to picketing Aclin by displaying signs at a point near the company's place of business. One of the signs, for example, read: "Want a junk or a lemon, buy a car from Aclin Ford."

In the circumstances the chancellor may well have viewed the case as a whole and concluded that justice would be achieved by relieving the Cordells of the greater part of their debt on the contract. . . . If that was in fact the chancellor's conclusion, we do not think he was wrong.

Affirmed.

CASE QUESTIONS

1. What does a *usury* law provide?
2. Why was the loan in this case considered usurious? Explain.
3. If the Cordells had *voluntarily* purchased the credit life insurance, would the loan have been usurious?

Policy Issue. Should there be usury laws? Or should lenders be allowed to charge whatever "the market will bear" for extending credit?

Economics Issue. Do usury laws allow lenders to balance interest rates with credit risk? Do usury laws help or hurt people who have poor credit histories obtain credit from legal sources? Do "loan sharks" like or dislike usury laws?

Ethics Issue. Was it ethical for Aclin Ford Co. to require the Cordells to purchase credit life insurance? For the Cordells to picket Aclin Ford?

Social Responsibility. Does a lender owe a duty of social responsibility to help people with *poor credit ratings* to obtain credit? To help *poor* people obtain credit?

THE TRUTH-IN-LENDING ACT

Prior to 1968, in many credit transactions consumers were charged excessively high interest rates or were subject to harsh credit terms not readily understood in the credit contract. In 1968, Congress enacted the Truth-in-Lending Act (TILA) as Title I of the Consumer Credit Protection Act. The TILA was amended in 1982 by the Truth-in-Lending Simplification and Reform Act. All references in this section are to the TILA as currently amended.

The TILA was passed with the stated purpose of requiring sellers to make meaningful disclosure of credit terms so that consumers could understand all the charges associated with credit, could easily compare credit charges, and thereby be able to shop for the best credit terms among merchants. The TILA also prohibits discrimination between consumers in extending credit. The TILA is not a usury statute, and does not set a limit on the interest rates that may be charged for consumer credit. Instead the TILA sets standards for the *disclosure* of the terms and interest rates charged for consumer credit. The primary purpose of the Truth-in-Lending Act is expressed in Section 102 of the Act.

The Congress finds that economic stabilization would be enhanced and the competition among the various financial institutions and other firms engaged in the extension of consumer credit would be strengthened by the informed use of credit. The informed use of credit results from an awareness of the cost thereof by consumers. It is the purpose of this subchapter to assure a meaningful disclosure of credit terms so that the consumer will be able to compare more readily the various credit terms available to him and avoid the uninformed use of credit.

Transactions Covered. The TILA requires disclosure of credit terms only when *consumer credit* is extended by a statutorily defined creditor. Under the Act, a *creditor* is any party who regularly extends credit in the normal course of business where the credit extended is payable in at least four monthly installments *or* a finance charge is required for the extension of the credit. Parties who *arrange* for the extension of credit to consumers from other parties who do not normally extend credit are also covered by the TILA. However, "casual sales" that involve the extension of credit (e.g., a neighbor sells another neighbor a car on credit) are not covered by the provisions of the TILA.

The TILA only covers the extension of consumer credit. *Consumer credit* is credit extended to *natural* persons for "personal, family, or household" purposes. Credit extended to corporations, partnerships, limited partnerships, or other nonnatural legal entities is not covered by the TILA. Further, credit extended to natural persons for commercial, business, or agricultural purposes is not "consumer credit" and is not covered by the TILA. For example, if Sally Smith borrows money to open a bookstore, the transaction is not covered by the TILA. If instead Sally Smith, as a housewife, borrows money to purchase a set of encyclopedias, it is this extension of *consumer* credit to a natural person that is covered by the provisions of the TILA.

Most purchases where the amount *financed* exceeds $25,000.00 are exempt from coverage by the TILA. The rationale for this rule is that generally persons who qualify to borrow at least $25,000.00 are more sophisticated than normal consumers and are thought not to need the protection of the TILA. Also, transactions in securities and commodities by a broker-dealer registered with the Securities and Exchange Commission (SEC) are exempt from the TILA. The rationale for this rule is that the SEC and other government authorities are already charged with the responsibility of regulating broker-dealers.

Required Disclosures. Generally, where a consumer credit *installment* sale is made, the TILA requires that the following information be disclosed to the consumer-debtor:

1. cash price
2. down payment or trade-in allowance
3. unpaid cash price
4. the finance charge, including interest, points, and other fees required for the extension of the credit
5. charges not included in the finance charge
6. the total dollar amount to be financed
7. the annual percentage rate (APR) of the finance charge as calculated or provided in the TILA
8. the date the finance charge begins to accrue
9. the number, amounts and due dates of payments
10. a description of the security interest, if any
11. penalties in case of delinquent payments and other late charges
12. prepayment penalties
13. comparative costs of credit (optional).

The two most important disclosures required by the TILA are the finance charge and the APR (items 4 and 7 above).

Finance Charge. The term *finance charge* includes all "charges . . . imposed directly or indirectly" by the creditor that are "incidental" to the extension of credit to the consumer-debtor. The finance charge includes the stated rate of interest, service charges, loan fees, "points," finders' fees, fees for credit reports, charges for required life, health, accident, or credit insurance, appraisal fees, and other fees required for the extension of the credit to the consumer.

Fees and costs that are *not* considered part of the finance charge are recording fees, taxes, fees for title insurance, abstract fees, notary fees, and attorney fees for preparing deeds. These charges are not considered part of the finance charge because they do not inure to the benefit of the party extending the credit.

APR. The TILA requires that the finance charge be disclosed as a single "annual percentage rate" of interest (APR). The disclosure of a *single-figure* APR allows consumer-debtors to compare complex credit arrangements in order to determine the lowest-cost credit purchase. The TILA specifies the exact method for computing the interest paid on the amount of borrowed money used by the consumer during a given credit period.

For example, if a consumer borrows $5,000.00 for one year, the finance charge is $1,000.00 and the principal and interest are payable in full at the end of the year, and the consumer-debtor has the use of the borrowed $5,000.00 for the entire year, then the APR is 20 percent: $5,000.00 principal, $1,000.00 finance charge. However, if the consumer borrows $5,000.00, where the "finance charge" is $1,000.00 and the principal and interest are to be repaid in twelve equal monthly installments during the year, the consumer-debtor only has the use of an *average* of one-half of the principal during the year; in this case the APR is 40 percent: $2,500.00 average principal, $1,000.00 finance charge. Although the consumer-debtor may not understand the actual calculation, the required disclosure of the APR summarizes in one figure the previously "hidden" finance charges in consumer credit transactions.

The finance charge, APR and other required information must be disclosed to a consumer *prior* to the extension of credit. This disclosure is made by the use of a *financing statement.* The Board of Governors of the Federal Reserve Board provides model financing statements that contain nontechnical disclosure language which consumer-debtors can understand. Use of these forms, with truthful disclosures, insures compliance with the TILA. Creditors may use their own forms as long as the required disclosures are properly made. In this excerpt from *Mourning v. Family Publications Services, Inc.,* 411 U.S. 356 (1972), the U.S. Supreme Court announced its policy for requiring the disclosure of finance charges.

The Truth in Lending Act reflects a transition in congressional policy from a philosophy of "Let the buyer beware" to one of "Let the seller disclose." By erecting a barrier between the seller and the prospective purchaser in the form of hard facts, Congress expressly sought "to . . . avoid the uninformed use of credit."

Some may claim that it is a relatively easy matter to calculate . . . . total [credit] payments . . . , but at the time of sale, such computations are often not encouraged by the solicitor or performed by the purchaser. Congress had determined that such purchasers are in need of protection; . . .

Remedies. Where a creditor does not accurately disclose information to a consumer-debtor as required by the TILA and Regulation Z, or otherwise fails to meet the requirements of the TILA or Regulation Z, the creditor may be held *civilly* liable to the consumer-debtor. The civil-liability provision of the TILA provides that a creditor is liable to the debtor for an amount *twice* the finance charge, which amount cannot be less than $100.00 or more than $1,000.00, plus costs and attorneys' fees incurred in bringing the action against the creditor. If a creditor *willfully* gives false or inaccurate information regarding credit terms, or otherwise willfully fails to comply with the provisions of the TILA, the creditor is subject to *criminal* liability, which includes a fine of up to $5,000.00 or imprisonment of up to one year, or both.

Where a creditor has made an error in disclosing credit terms, the creditor may escape civil liability under the TILA by notifying the consumer-debtor of the error within 60 days of the discovery of the error. The TILA, however, only allows corrections to be in favor of the debtor. Thus, a creditor cannot correct an error in its form and collect a finance charge from the consumer-debtor which is greater than the originally disclosed finance charge. A creditor can generally escape civil liability by showing that it employed "reasonable procedures" to assure compliance with the TILA but an error occurred because of a *bona fide* unintentional mistake (e.g., a computer error).

Regulation Z.   Congress placed responsibility for interpreting the TILA with the Board of Governors of the Federal Reserve Board. Under this authority, the Board of Governors adopted Regulation Z, which sets forth detailed rules for compliance with the TILA. The Board of Governors also issues official and unofficial announcements regarding the interpretation of the TILA and Regulation Z. The actual enforcement of the TILA depends on the parties involved in the credit transaction. For example, the Civil Aeronautics Board (CAB) is charged with the responsibility for enforcing the TILA with regard to air carriers under CAB jurisdiction. Where no other federal agency is responsible for the enforcement of the TILA, the Federal Trade Commission is charged with that responsibility. In *Ford Motor Credit Co. v. Milhollin*, 444 U.S. 555 (1980), the Supreme Court described its policy of generally deferring to the Federal Reserve Board in the adoption of regulations under the Truth-in-Lending Act.

Finally, wholly apart from jurisprudential considerations or congressional intent, deference to the Federal Reserve is compelled by necessity; a court that tries to chart a true course to the Act's purpose embarks upon a voyage without a compass when it disregards the agency's views. The concept of "meaningful disclosure" that animates TILA . . . cannot be applied in the abstract. Meaningful disclosure does not mean more disclosure. Rather, it describes a balance between "competing considerations of complete disclosure . . . and the need to avoid . . . 'informational overload.' " And striking the appropriate balance is an empirical process that entails investigation into consumer psychology and that presupposes broad experience with credit practices. Administrative agencies are simply better suited than courts to engage in such a process.

In *Mourning v. Family Publications Service, Inc.* the U.S. Supreme Court upheld a regulation adopted by the Federal Reserve Board that required all sellers who sold goods in more than *four installment sales* to meet the disclosure requirements of the TILA and Regulation Z even where a finance charge was *not* expressly assessed in the transaction.

REGULATION Z

MOURNING v. FAMILY PUBLICATIONS SERVICE, INC.

411 U.S. 356 (1972)
UNITED STATES SUPREME COURT

Mr. Chief Justice Burger delivered the opinion of the Court.

We granted the writ of *certiorari* in this case to resolve whether the Federal Reserve Board exceeded its authority under . . . the Truth in Lending Act in promulgating that portion of Regulation Z commonly referred to as the "Four Installment Rule."

Respondent is a Delaware corporation which solicits subscriptions to several well-known periodicals. In 1969, one of respondent's door-to-door salesmen called on the petitioner, a 73-year-old widow residing in Florida, and sold her a five-year subscription to four magazines. Petitioner agreed to pay $3.95 immediately and to remit a similar amount monthly for 30 months. The contract form she signed contained a clause stating that the subscriptions could not be canceled and an acceleration provision similar to that found in many installment undertakings, providing that any default in installment payments would render the entire balance due. The contract did not recite the total purchase price of the subscriptions or the amount which remained unpaid after the initial remittance, and made no reference to service or finance charges. The total debt assumed by the petitioner was $122.45; the balance due after the initial payment was $118.50.

Petitioner made the initial payment, began to receive the magazines for which she had contracted, and then defaulted. Respondent declared the entire balance of $118.50 due and threatened legal action. Petitioner brought this suit in United States District Court, alleging that respondent had failed to comply with the disclosure provisions of the Truth in Lending Act. She sought recovery of the statutory penalty and reimbursement for the costs of the litigation, including reasonable attorney's fees.

Accordingly, the Board has promulgated Regulation Z, which defines the circumstances in which a seller who regularly extends credit must make the disclosures outlined in [the Truth in Lending Act]. The regulation provides that disclosure is necessary whenever credit is offered to a consumer

> for which either a finance charge is or may be imposed or which pursuant to an agreement, is or may be payable in more than four installments.

Relying on the rule governing credit transactions of more than four installments, the District Court granted summary judgment for petitioner. The court found that respondent had extended credit to petitioner, which by agreement was payable in more than four installments, but had failed to comply with the disclosure provisions of the Act. . . . The Court of Appeals reversed, holding that the Board had exceeded its statutory authority in promulgating the regulation upon which the District Court relied.

[The Truth in Lending Act] delegated to the Federal Reserve Board broad authority to promulgate regulations necessary to render the Act effective. The language employed evinces the awareness of Congress that some creditors would attempt to characterize their transactions so as to fall one step outside whatever boundary Congress attempted to establish. It indicates as well the clear desire of Congress to insure that the Board had adequate power to deal with such attempted evasion.

One means of circumventing the objectives of the Truth in Lending Act, as passed by Congress, was that of "burying" the cost of credit in the price of goods sold. Thus in many credit transactions in which creditors claimed that no finance charge had been imposed, the creditor merely assumed the cost of extending credit as an expense of doing business, to be recouped as part of the price charged in the transaction. . . . Congress was clearly aware that merchants could evade the reporting requirements of the Act by concealing credit charges. In delegating rulemaking authority to the

Board, Congress emphasized the Board's authority to prevent such evasion. . . . [T]he Four Installment Rule serves to insure that the protective disclosure mechanism chosen by Congress will not be circumvented.

That the approach taken may reflect what respondent views as an undue paternalistic concern for the consumer is beside the point. The statutory scheme is within the power granted to Congress under the Commerce Clause. It is not a function of the courts to speculate as to whether the statute is unwise or whether the evils sought to be remedied could better have been regulated in some other manner.

Reversed and remanded.

CASE QUESTIONS

1. What does the Truth in Lending Act require? What is a finance charge? The APR? Explain.
2. Did the defendant charge a finance charge to Mrs. Mourning? How were the magazines to be paid for?
3. What does the "four-installment" rule of Regulation Z provide? Was this transaction covered by the rule?
4. Why did Congress adopt the four-installment rule? Explain.

Policy Issue. Are the Truth-in-Lending Act and Regulation Z too "paternalistic"? Should consumers be required to calculate finance charges themselves? Why or why not?

Economics Issue. Is there much profit to be made by lenders through not disclosing the true cost of credit? Explain.

Ethics Issue. Is it unethical for lenders to fail to fully disclose "buried" credit terms?

Social Responsibility. Do lenders owe a duty of social responsibility to fully disclose credit terms to consumers? Was this duty abused prior to the enactment of the Truth-in-Lending Act?

Advertising of Credit. The advertising of the availability of credit also falls within the provisions of the TILA. If an advertisement contains *any* term regarding the extension of credit, then the TILA requires that the advertisement contain other statutory terms of credit. The disclosure of credit terms in advertisements depends on whether the credit plan is "open-ended" (like credit cards, revolving charge accounts), or "closed-ended" (such as the extension of credit of a fixed amount for the purchase of an automobile). Where the advertisement concerns the credit terms of an "open-ended" credit plan, the TILA requires that the advertisement conspicuously disclose:

1. the annual percentage rate of interest (APR)
2. the minimum or fixed dollar amount that could be imposed under the plan
3. any other term required to be disclosed by regulations adopted by the Federal Reserve Board.

Where the advertisement concerns the extension of credit under a "closed-ended" credit plan, the TILA, in addition to the previous disclosures, also requires that the advertisement of the availability of credit conspicuously discloses:

4. the cash price of the item or the amount of the loan
5. the down payment required

6. the number, amount, and due dates of the payments required to repay the loan.

Home Security Credit Transactions. The TILA provides that a consumer-debtor has the right to *rescind* (cancel) consumer credit transactions within a specified time period where the consumer has used his *principal dwelling* as *security* for the extension of credit. The purpose of this rule is to protect debtor-homeowners from entering into unwise and hasty credit transactions where their homes may be foreclosed upon by the creditor for the nonpayment or late payment of the credit. The recission rule was enacted particularly to correct abuses in home-repair credit contracts. Under the TILA, the creditor must give the consumer-homeowner a written *notice* of the latter's right to rescind the home-security credit transaction.

The recission of a home-security credit transaction must be made by the debtor-homeowner within three business days from the *later* of two dates: (1) the date the credit transaction was entered into, or (2) the date the consumer was given the required notice of his or her right to rescind. Thus, the time period for recission is *extended* by the failure of the creditor to give the debtor-homeowner the proper required notice. If the cancellation has been properly made, the debtor-homeowner is relieved of *all* obligations under the credit transaction, is not held liable for any finance charge, and the security interest of the creditor in the consumer's home is *void*. After cancellation, the creditor has 20 days to refund any monies paid by the consumer-homeowner to the creditor under the contract.

Generally, a creditor-contractor may not begin work on a home-security credit contract during the three-day recission period. However, where the debtor-homeowner states in writing that an emergency exists which will cause substantial damage to the home unless quickly remedied (e.g., a plumbing fixture has broken, causing severe water damage), *and* where the debtor-homeowner waives in writing his TILA right of recission, the creditor-contractor may begin the contracted-for work immediately.

POST-JUDGMENT REMEDIES

In addition to a creditor's attempts to collect a debt from a debtor either through its own actions or by means of a collection agency, a creditor may bring a lawsuit against the debtor to collect the debt. While the action is pending, or even after the court has issued a judgment in favor of the plaintiff-creditor, the creditor may try to obtain a *lien* on property of the debtor that is either in the possession of the debtor or in the possession of some third party. The two most common types of post-judgment remedies are garnishment and attachment.

Attachment. Once a creditor seeking payment of a debt has filed a lawsuit against a debtor, the creditor may be concerned that the debtor will transfer property to others prior to the completion of the lawsuit. In such circumstances where a creditor can demonstrate the danger of the debtor transferring or wasting assets prior to the completion of a lawsuit, most states provide that the creditor can seek a *writ of attachment* against the debtor's property in the possession of the *debtor* pending the outcome of the lawsuit. An action for attachment is not a distinct legal proceeding, but is ancillary to an action for breach of contract to pay the debt. By contrast, property of the debtor in the hands of a third party is not subject to attachment, but may be subject to *garnishment,* which is covered in the following section.

Because of the important effect that attachment has on a debtor and his property, the courts generally interpret attachment statutes narrowly, often finding that the notice and hearing provisions of attachment statutes are inadequate and therefore violate the Due Process Clauses of the Fifth and Fourteenth Amendments to the U.S. Constitution and state constitutions.

Writ of Attachment.   Generally, all debtors, whether individuals, partnerships, or corporations, are subject to attachment. However, only their *unsecured* property is subject to attachment. Most states provide that certain types of property of the debtor are *exempt* from attachment by a creditor, e.g., clothes, personal items, tools of a trade. In order for a creditor to be issued a writ of attachment against a debtor, most states' laws require that the plaintiff-creditor file an affidavit with the court setting forth:

1. that the debtor is in default on the payment of a debt owed to the creditor
2. the statutory grounds under which the attachment is sought
3. evidence that the defendant-debtor is attempting to transfer property from his possession prior to trial.

The plaintiff-creditor who seeks a writ of attachment must usually post a *bond* in an amount to cover court costs, loss of value of the property attached because of the attachment, and the loss of use of the attached property in case the creditor loses on the merits of the underlying lawsuit for the payment of the alleged debt.

After proper notice and hearing, and if the court grants the plaintiff-creditor's motion for a attachment against the debtor, the court will issue a *writ of attachment* that directs the sheriff or some other officer of the law to seize nonexempt property of the debtor in the possession of the *debtor.* Where a debtor perfects an attachment on property subject to the court's order, a *lien* attaches to the property in favor of the plaintiff-creditor. The lien remains on the property even where the debtor sells or otherwise transfers the property subject to the levy of attachment. The priority of attachment liens is determined by the time sequence in which they are granted.

Where a writ of attachment has been issued, the property may be gathered and held by the court, or the court may appoint a trustee to take possession of the attached property for safekeeping during the pending lawsuit for collection of the debt. If the plaintiff-creditor is successful in the lawsuit to collect the debt from the defendant-debtor and a judgment is issued in favor of the creditor, the property subject to the writ of attachment can be sold to satisfy the judgment against the debtor.

A creditor may be held liable for "wrongful attachment" if the creditor loses the underlying lawsuit and the debtor can show that the creditor sought the attachment with "malice."

Garnishment. An action for *garnishment* against a debtor is an ancillary proceeding to a legal action by a creditor to collect a debt from a debtor. Under garnishment, the creditor attempts to place a lien against property of the debtor that is in the possession of a *third party*. The creditor must make application to the court and obtain an order of the court to properly perfect a garnishment. In the most usual form of garnishment, a creditor seeks to garnishee the *wages* of a debtor. In this case, the creditor is the *garnishor* and the debtor-wage earner is the *garnishee*. The court order is directed at the employer of the debtor to withhold a specified portion of the debtor-employee's wages.

Only legal debts may be garnisheed. For example, any money, personal property, bank accounts, or rights to collect under insurance policies may be garnisheed. In addition to wages, most debts or credits of a debtor may be garnisheed. A *debt* is money that is owed to a debtor by a third party, such as an "I.O.U." A *credit* is something owned by the debtor that is in the possession of a third party, such as an automobile. Uncertain, contingent, equitable, or unliquidated debts or interests, funds held in trust, and funds held by the court or in the possession of a court-appointed receiver cannot be garnisheed.

Federal Regulation of Garnishment. Congress sought to remedy many of the abuses caused by an overextension of credit by creditors and to protect debtors from excessive garnishment by adopting Title III of the Consumer Credit Protection Act. The Secretary of Labor, acting through the Wage and Hour Division of the Department of Labor, is entrusted with the enforcement of Title III of the Consumer Credit Protection Act.

The main protection offered debtors by Title III is the limitations on the *percentage* of a debtor-employee's *wages* that may be garnisheed by creditors. Specifically, the Act provides that not more than 65 percent of a person's wages can be garnisheed to pay support payments (e.g., child support, alimony), and that not more than 25 percent of a person's wages can be garnisheed to pay nonsupport debts (e.g., credit extended to purchase a stereo, automobile).

Many states also provide either percent or dollar limitations on the garnishment of a debtor-employee's wages by creditors. If state law is more stringent than the federal limitations, state law controls. The Secretary of Labor may by regulation exempt debtor-creditor relations from the provisions of Title III in states where state law provides restrictions on garnishment similar to those provided by federal law.

In *Long Island Trust Company v. United States* the court held that an attempted garnishment of a debtor-employee's wages by a creditor was void because it exceeded the statutory money limitations for the garnishment of wages of a debtor specified in Title III of the Consumer Credit Protection Act.

GARNISHMENT

LONG ISLAND TRUST COMPANY v. UNITED STATES POSTAL SERVICE

647 F.2D 336 (1981)
UNITED STATES COURT OF APPEALS, SECOND CIRCUIT

Kearse, Circuit Judge

The facts are not in dispute. On August 15, 1978, Long Island Trust recovered a judgment in the amount of $914.38 against one Donald Cheshire, Jr. On October 20, the judgment remained unsatisfied to the extent of $607.50, and Long Island Trust caused an income execution to be served on United States Postal Service [USPS], Cheshire's employer, directing that 10 percent of Cheshire's bi-weekly wages be paid to the county sheriff for the benefit of Long Island Trust. USPS refused to comply with the income execution, claiming that more than 25 percent of Cheshire's disposable income was already being withheld for court ordered support payments under New York Pers. Prop. Law, and that any further deductions from Cheshire's wages were barred under the Consumer Credit Protection Act [Act].

Long Island Trust commenced the present proceeding . . . to recover the accrued installments from USPS. USPS moved for summary judgment on the basis of the fact that $214 of Cheshire's bi-weekly disposable income of $508, or 42 percent, was already being garnisheed pursuant to orders of support issued by the Nassau County Family Court.

Preliminarily we note that the Act does not seek to establish any order of priority among garnishments. There being no other federal statutory provision setting priorities as between support order garnishments and creditor garnishments, the matter of priority is thus to be determined by state law. New York law provides that as between garnishments of the same type, the prior in time is to be satisfied first. As between creditor garnishments and support order garnishments, New York gives priority to those for support, regardless of the timing of those garnishments. On either basis in the present case, the support order garnishments of Cheshire's wages have priority over Long Island Trust's income execution.

Turning to the language of the Act, we read Section 1673 as placing a ceiling of 25 percent on the amount of an employee's disposable earnings that is subject to garnishment, with the exception that the ceiling may be raised as high as 65 percent if the garnishment is to enforce family support orders. Thus, when garnishments are sought only by creditors, no more than 25 percent of disposable earnings may be withheld for that purpose; when the garnishments are sought only to enforce support orders, as much as 65 percent of disposable earnings may be withheld for that purpose. . . . [Long Island Trust] argues, from this premise, that support garnishments should be considered entirely independently of creditor garnishments, and that the Act should be construed as reserving 25 percent of the employee's earnings for attachment by creditors and leaving 75 percent for personal and family expenses, including the satisfaction of family support orders.

In passing the Consumer Credit Protection Act, Congress acted principally not to protect the rights of creditors, but to limit the ills that flowed from the unrestricted garnishment of wages. . . . The Act was thus designed . . . in the context of the following overview which reveals Congress's principal concern with the welfare of the debtor:

> The limitations on the garnishment of wages adopted by your committee, while permitting the continued orderly payment of consumer debts, will relieve countless honest debtors driven by economic desperation from plunging into bankruptcy in order to preserve their employment and insure a continued means of support for themselves and their families.

Indeed, as originally introduced, the House bill contained a blanket prohibition against all garnishment of wages. Later, yielding to the argument that a complete ban on garnishment "would unduly restrict honest and ethical creditors, while permitting those fully capable of paying just debts to escape such responsibilities," the bill was amended, initially to allow garnishment of wages to the extent of approximately 10 percent, and eventually, as enacted in 1968, to allow garnishment to the extent of 25 percent.

Given the overall purpose of the Act and the priority accorded in New York to garnishments for support, we find no merit in Long Island Trust's argument, that 25 percent of an employee's disposable earnings are reserved for creditors and that up to 65 percent *more* may be garnished to enforce a support order.

The judgment dismissing the complaint is *affirmed.*

CASE QUESTIONS

1. What does *garnishment* mean? Explain.
2. Prior to October 20, 1978, had Cheshire's wages been garnisheed? If so, by whom? For what purpose? What percent of Cheshire's wages had been garnisheed?
3. What percentage limits did the Consumer Credit Protection Act place on the following types of garnishment?

a. for support payments
b. for nonsupport payments
   Would dollar limits work better than percentage limits? Why or why not?
4. Did the court find that these two percentage limitations were *cumulative* as argued by Long Island Trust Company? Explain the court's decision.

Policy Issue. Should there be a total ban on the garnishment of wages? Why or why not?

Economics Issue. Do the limitations on garnishment of the Consumer Credit Protection Act help or hurt wage earners obtain credit? Explain.

Ethics Issue. Did Long Island Trust Company act unethically in this case? Was there a legitimate legal question as to whether or not Long Island's garnishment of Cheshire's wages was lawful?

Social Responsibility. Do lenders owe a duty of social responsibility not to garnishee debtor's wages?

THE EQUAL CREDIT OPPORTUNITY ACT

In 1975, Congress enacted the Equal Credit Opportunity Act (ECOA) as Title VII of the Consumer Credit Protection Act. Originally, the ECOA prohibited *discrimination* in the extension of credit based on (1) sex or (2) marital status. In 1977, Congress amended the ECOA to also prohibit discrimination in the extension of credit because of (3) race, (4) color, (5) religion, (6) national origin, (7) age, (8) the applicant's income derived from any public assistance program; or (9) because the applicant has exercised a right under the Consumer Credit Protection Act. The ECOA does not guarantee credit to members of these protected classes, but does prohibit discrimination against *members* of such classes. Section 1691 of the ECOA, as amended, provide that:

(a) It shall be unlawful for any creditor to discriminate against any applicant, with respect to any aspect of a credit transaction—

(1) on the basis of race, color, religion, national origin, sex or marital status, or age (provided that applicant has the capacity to contract); . . .

The ECOA applies to all creditors who extends credit in the *normal course of business,* including financial institutions, retail stores, credit card issuers, and any other party who regularly makes decisions regarding the extension of credit. The Federal Reserve Board, which is charged with interpreting the ECOA, has announced that automobile dealers, real estate brokers, and others who customarily direct consumers to third parties who extend credit are also covered by the provision of the ECOA.

The enforcement of the ECOA depends on the parties involved in the credit transaction. For example, the Securities and Exchange Commission is responsible for enforcing the ECOA with respect to extensions of credit by securities brokers and dealers, and the Federal Home Loan Bank Board (FHLBB) is responsible for enforcing the ECOA with respect to the extension of credit by savings and loan associations within its jurisdiction. Where no other federal government authority regulates the parties to a credit transaction, the Federal Trade Commission is charged with the responsibility of enforcing the ECOA therein.

Credit Discrimination and Females. Although the ECOA prohibits discrimination in the extension of credit on many grounds, its primary purpose is to prevent discrimination in credit extension on *sex* or *marital status*, with the particular goal of promoting equality in credit extension to females. As the number of females in the labor force increases, divorce rates climb, women marry later in life, and married women seek credit separately from their husbands, the ECOA will take on added importance in guaranteeing equality in credit extension to females in the future. The protection of the ECOA particularly applies to widows, divorced women, housewives, and single working women.

For example, a creditor may not discourage a female or other consumer from filing an application for credit. In promoting the purpose of the ECOA of protecting female credit applicants, a creditor must consider alimony, child support, and other disclosed maintenance payments when making a credit decision. The creditor must inform the applicant that she does not have to disclose income from these sources unless she wants the income to be considered in making the credit decision. A potential creditor may consider the probability of continued receipt of such payments based on the past history of the applicant's receipt of alimony, child support, and other maintenance payments. A potential creditor must also consider income from part-time employment and public assistance programs when making a credit decision.

Under the ECOA, a creditor cannot ask a credit applicant her race, color, religion, national origin, or age unless required to do so by the government for statistical monitoring purposes. It is illegal under the ECOA for a creditor to ask a female credit applicant about her marital status, plans for childbearing, or birth control practices. A creditor may never consider the childbearing age of a credit applicant as a negative factor in making a credit decision. A creditor *may* ask an applicant about her marital status if:

1. she is opening a joint account with her husband
2. she is relying on her husband's income to establish her credit
3. security is required for the opening of the account
4. state property laws require such disclosure, as in community property law states.

A married woman may seek to establish credit independently from her husband. The creditor cannot require the husband to cosign for the account except under the situations of items 1–4 above. Where a husband and wife have established credit accounts in the names of both, the wife is entitled under the ECOA to direct that the credit-reporting agency report the credit history in both the husband's and wife's name. Each creditor in which joint credit accounts are held must report the credit experience of the account in both the husband's and wife's name. Where the joint account shows an unfavorable past credit experience, the ECOA prohibits a creditor from using the unfavorable information if the wife or ex-wife can show that the past history does not reflect her current ability and willingness to pay.

If a widow attempts to establish credit, and her credit history was previously reported in her deceased husband's name, under the ECOA creditors must treat the reported credit history as hers as well as his if she can show that the credit history reflects her willingness and ability to pay.

Notification of Adverse Action. When a consumer makes an application for credit, the creditor must notify the applicant within 30 days regarding the action taken on the application. If the creditor takes any "adverse action," defined as a denial of credit, revocation of credit, or change in the terms of an existing credit arrangement, the creditor must provide a statement to the consumer of the *specific reasons* for the adverse action, or inform the consumer that he has a *right to request* the specific reason for the adverse action. General statements that an applicant has failed to meet the "credit standards" of the creditor are not sufficient to meet the specific-disclosure requirements of the ECOA. The following legislative history of the 1976 amendments to the ECOA emphasized the congressional intent behind the passage of the Act:

The requirement that creditors give reasons for adverse action is, in the Committee's view, a strong and necessary adjunct to the antidiscrimination purpose of the legislation, for only if creditors know they must explain their decisions will they effectively be discouraged from discriminatory practices. Yet this requirement fulfills a broader need: rejected credit applicants will now be able to learn where and how their credit status is deficient and this information should have a pervasive and valuable educational benefit. Instead of being told only that they do not meet a particular creditor's standards, consumers particularly should benefit from knowing, for example, that the reason for the denial is their short residence in the area, or their recent change of employment, or their already over-extended financial situation. In those cases where the creditor may have acted on misinformation or inadequate information, the statement of reasons gives the applicant a chance to rectify the mistake.

Remedies. Under the ECOA, an injured plaintiff-applicant may bring a *civil* lawsuit against a violating defendant-creditor and recover actual damages, including mental distress and embarrassment, and punitive damages up to $10,000.00. Punitive damages can be recovered even though actual damages have not been incurred. In a class action lawsuit alleging a violation of the ECOA, the total award of punitive damages cannot exceed the lesser of $500,000 or 1 percent of the net worth of the creditor-defendant. Punitive damages cannot be recovered from a governmental unit under the ECOA.

A plaintiff may also seek an injunction against a creditor to prevent the creditor from discriminating against an ECOA protected class in the future. A plaintiff in an ECOA action can also recover the costs of bringing the lawsuit and reasonable attorney's fees. The government may also bring action for injunctions and to assess civil penalties under the ECOA.

In *Carroll v. Exxon Company, U.S.A.* the court found that a creditor had violated the user requirements of the Fair Credit Reporting Act and also violated the ECOA by failing to provide specific reasons to the consumer-plaintiff regarding the adverse action taken by the creditor-defendant on an application of credit.

EQUAL CREDIT OPPORTUNITY

CARROLL v. EXXON COMPANY, U.S.A.

434 F.Supp 557 (1977)
UNITED STATES DISTRICT COURT, E. D. LOUISIANA

Mitchell, District Judge.

In August of 1976, Kathleen Carroll, a single working woman, applied for an Exxon credit card. In response to her application, the plaintiff received correspondence from defendant, dated September 14, 1976, whereby she was informed that her application for credit was denied; but no specific reason for the denial was provided. Thereafter, by her letter of September 28, 1976, Ms. Carroll requested Exxon to furnish her with the specific reasons for the credit denial. An undated response to this request revealed that the credit bureau which was contacted in regard to plaintiff's application did not respond adversely, but was unable to furnish sufficient information regarding her established credit. However, this undated letter, like that of September 14, 1976, did not contain the name of the credit bureau used by Exxon to investigate certain aspects of plaintiff's credit application. . . .

The instant lawsuit was filed on October 26, 1976. The plaintiff . . . contends that Exxon violated the terms of the Equal Credit Opportunity Act (ECOA) by failing to provide her with the specific reasons for the credit denial, and by discriminating against her on the basis of marital status in evaluating her credit application.

The ECOA also provides for the promulgation of regulations by the Federal Reserve Board to carry out the purposes of the Act. One such regulation, 12 CFR 202.5(m)(2), provides that

> [a] creditor shall provide each applicant who is denied credit or whose account is terminated the reasons for such action, if the applicant so requests.

Ms. Carroll takes the position that Exxon's undated letter, which was sent to her as a result of her request for specific reasons for the credit denial, violated the plain terms of 12 CFR 202.5(m)(2) in failing to provide the reasons for the negative action. . . . The ECOA . . . provides that

> [a] statement of reasons meets the requirements of this section *only if it contains the specific reasons for the adverse action taken* (Emphasis added).

Our independent examination of the record of this case reveals that a number of factors contributed to the denial of Ms. Carroll's credit card application. For example, the plaintiff did not have a major credit card, she did not list a savings account on her application, she had been employed for only one year, and she had no dependents. However, for some reason, Exxon chose only to list, as its reasons for the denial of credit, that the Credit Bureau which had been contacted could furnish little or no definitive information regarding plaintiff's established credit. . . . Exxon's responses to plaintiff's request for specific reasons for the credit denial fail to achieve the informative purposes legislated in the ECOA.

Finally, Ms. Carroll contends that, in evaluating her credit application, Exxon considered the number of her dependents, which evinces a bias on the basis of marital status in violation of 12 CFR 202.5(f) and 202.5(h). Plaintiff argues that, since it is unusual for an unmarried person to have any dependents, the fact that Exxon considers the number of the applicant's dependents in its scoring system constitutes discrimination on the basis of marital status, which the ECOA condemns. We disagree. We cannot conclude that, as a matter of law, Exxon's interrogatory regarding dependency violates Regulation B or the ECOA. The regulations cited by plaintiff in this regard do not prohibit the credit grantor's investigation into this area. Dependency is not limited to one's biological descendants, and is not necessarily included in "assumptions relating to the likelihood of any group of persons bearing or rearing children" within the ambit of 12 CFR 202.5(h). . . . The plaintiff in this case has not made out a *prima facie* case of discrimination under the ECOA.

Therefore, for these reasons, *it is ordered, adjudged, and decreed* that the motion of plaintiff, Kathleen Carroll, for summary judgment on the issue of liability under 12 CFR 202.5(m)(2) of the ECOA, be and the same is hereby *Granted,* and that plaintiff's motion for summary judgment under 12 CFR 202.5(f) and 202.5(h) is hereby *Denied;*

It is further ordered that this matter be referred to a Magistrate for a determination of the amount of damages, both actual and punitive, and attorney's fees. . . .

CASE QUESTIONS

1. What does the Equal Credit Opportunity Act prohibit? Explain.
2. Was the plaintiff in a protected class covered by the ECOA?
3. Did the court accept the plaintiff's argument that she was discriminated against because of her *marital status* because Exxon required the disclosure of the number of dependents of a credit applicant? Explain.
4. What disclosure does the ECOA require when a person is given a negative credit decision? Did the defendant meet this disclosure requirement in this case? If it had, would it have been held liable for anything in this case?

Policy Issue. Should lenders be permitted to discriminate against a *class* of persons in extending credit? Even if it can be shown that the class as a whole is a poor credit risk? Why or why not?

Economics Issue. Are nonworking married women a good credit risk? Why or why not? Working women?

Ethics Issue. Do you think Exxon intended to discriminate against Ms. Carroll because she was a female? Or was Exxon merely negligent in its actions?

Social Responsibility. Do lenders owe a duty of social responsibility to favor female credit applicants over male applicants for credit in order to make up for past discrimination against females?

CREDIT CARDS

The use of credit cards to make consumer purchases burgeoned in the American economy during the 1970s and 1980s. Companies that extend credit through credit cards, known as "issuers," range from national companies whose cards are accepted at thousands of business establishments (such as MasterCard, Visa, American Express) to local businesses whose cards are only accepted by the issuer, such as department stores. A consumer who accepts a credit card is known as a *cardholder.* A cardholder is liable for actual authorized purchases made with a credit card, even if the authorized purchases exceed the established dollar limitation of the credit card.

The Truth in Lending Act (TILA) regulates the issuance and use of credit cards, and particularly addresses problems regarding (1) liability for unsolicited credit cards, (2) lost and stolen credit cards.

Unsolicited Credit Cards.   The TILA does not prohibit an issuer from sending an unsolicited credit card to a consumer. The TILA does provide, however, that if an issuer sends an unsolicited credit card to a consumer, and the card is either lost or stolen and used by another person prior to its acceptance by the addressee, the addressee is not held liable for *any* charges made against the credit card. If an addressee accepts an unsolicited credit card, the provisions of the TILA apply to the addressee as if that person had solicited the card.

Lost or Stolen Credit Cards.   Before the enactment of the credit card provisions of the TILA, a credit-card holder was subject to substantial risk that if his credit card was lost or stolen he would be held liable for payments for unauthorized use of his credit card. This liability exposure caused considerable concern to credit-card holders.

With the enactment of the TILA, Congress limited the liability of credit cardholders to a *maximum* of $50.00 for the "unauthorized" use of a credit card, usually of a lost or stolen credit card. In order for the creditor to even collect the $50.00 from the card holder for unauthorized use of a credit card, the creditor must show that:

1. the card holder accepted the credit card
2. the issuer notified the card holder of his potential liability for accepting a credit card
3. the issuer told the card holder how to notify the issuer if his credit card was lost or stolen
4. the issuer provided a method for identifying the credit card user as the authorized card holder, e.g., a signature block for the card holder on the credit card that can be matched to the user's signature.

If the card holder notifies the issuer that his credit card has been lost or stolen *prior* to any unauthorized use of the card, the card holder will not be held liable for the $50.00 maximum amount as otherwise provided.

Under Federal law, any party who uses a stolen, lost, forged, counterfeit, altered, or fraudulently obtained credit card is subject to criminal penalties under the TILA if (1) the retail value of the unauthorized credit purchases is $5,000.00 or more and (2) the credit card was used in a credit transaction affecting interstate or foreign commerce. Criminal penalties include a fine of up to $10,000.00, imprisonment for up to five years, or both. Most states have adopted criminal statutes that prohibit the unauthorized use of credit cards. State criminal laws usually cover a greater number of unauthorized uses of credit cards than the TILA.

In *Martin v. American Express, Inc.* the court held that a cardholder had given "apparent authority" to a business associate to use his credit card and was therefore liable for approximately $5,300.00 of purchases by that associate.

CREDIT CARDS

MARTIN v. AMERICAN EXPRESS, INC.

361 So.2D 597 (1978)
COURT OF CIVIL APPEALS OF ALABAMA

Bradley, Judge.

This appeal is the result of an order by the Circuit Court of Montgomery County granting appellee's (American Express, Inc.) motion for summary judgment.

In the summer of 1972 appellant (Robert A. Martin) applied for and was issued an American Express credit card. Approximately three years later, in April of 1975, Martin gave his credit card to a business associate named E. L. McBride. The reason for this action by Martin was apparently to enable McBride to use the card for the purpose of a joint business venture into which the two men had entered. Martin claimed that he orally authorized McBride to charge up to $500 on the credit card. However, in June of 1975 Martin received a statement from American Express which indicated that the amount owed on his credit card account was approximately $5,300. Martin denied that he had signed the credit card invoices which demonstrate that an amount has been charged to the cardholder's account. Upon learning of Martin's refusal to pay the charges incurred through the use of his credit card, American Express filed suit against Martin to obtain the money which it claimed Martin owed.

Section 1643(a) [of the Consumer Credit Protection Act], which is of principal concern in this case, limits a cardholder's liability to $50 for the "unauthorized use of a credit card." However, the statutory limitation on liability comes into play only where there is an "unauthorized use" of a credit card.

Martin says he gave no authority for McBride to charge the large sum which eventually resulted in this suit. Furthermore, Martin asserts that prior to giving the card to McBride, he (Martin) wrote American Express and requested that its employees not allow the amounts charged to his credit card account to exceed $1,000. And since no such action was taken, Martin argues that any sum charged in excess of $1,000 constituted an "unauthorized" charge on his credit card.

We cannot accept either of the above contentions. McBride was actually authorized by Martin to use the latter's card. Martin admitted this fact. And the authority to use it, if not actual, remained apparent even after McBride ignored Martin's directions by charging over $500 to Martin's credit card account.

Nor are we aware of any requirement, either by statute, contract or trade usage, which would compel a credit card issuer to undertake a policy whereby the issuer would see to it that charges on a cardholder's account do not exceed a specified amount. Such a policy would place a difficult and potentially disastrous burden on the issuer.

We believe that Section 1643(a) clearly indicates that . . . protection is warranted where the card is obtained from the cardholder as a result of loss, theft or wrongdoing. However, we are not persuaded that Section 1643(a) is applicable where a cardholder voluntarily and knowingly allows another to use his card and that person subsequently misuses the card.

Were we to adopt any other view, we would provide the unscrupulous and dishonest cardholder with the means to defraud the card issuer by allowing his or her friends to use the card, run up hundreds of dollars in charges and then limit his or her liability to $50 by notifying the card issuer. We do not believe such a result was either intended or sanctioned by Congress when it enacted Section 1643(a).

Accordingly, the judgment of the trial court granting American Express's motion for summary judgment is affirmed.

Affirmed.

CASE QUESTIONS

1. Did McBride steal Martin's credit card? If not, how did McBride come to possess Martin's credit card?

2. What does Section 1643(a) of the Consumer Credit Protection Act provide regarding the "unauthorized" use of credit cards? Explain.
3. Did the court find an authorized or unauthorized use of the credit card in this case? Explain.

Policy Issue. Should a credit card issuer be responsible for the unauthorized use of a credit card that exceeds $50? Or should card holders be responsible for lost and stolen credit cards?

Economics Issue. Does the $50 legal limit on the liability of card holders for unauthorized use of credit cards help or harm credit card issuers?

Ethics Issue. If this case had been decided in Martin's favor, would that have been a boon to "unscrupulous and dishonest" card holders as asserted by the court? Explain.

Social Responsibility. Should credit card issuers be held responsible to obey the individual instructions of card holders? Or would it place a "disastrous burden" on the issuer as asserted by the court?

THE FAIR CREDIT BILLING ACT

In 1974, Congress enacted the Fair Credit Billing Act (FCBA) as an amendment to the Truth-in-Lending Act with the stated purposes of protecting consumers against inaccurate and unfair billing practices by creditors and to limit the liability of consumers for unauthorized use of their credit cards. The provisions of the FCBA cover (1) issuers of credit cards and (2) creditors who extend credit in the normal course of business where (a) more than four installment payments are required *or* (b) a finance charge is imposed.

When a consumer opens a credit account that is subject to the FCBA, the creditor must advise the consumer as to his or her rights and responsibilities under the FCBA at the time the account is opened and semi-annually thereafter. The creditor must disclose on each of these notices and on each billing statement where the consumer can address inquiries regarding the billing of the credit account.

Billing Errors. The FCBA protects consumers from billing errors. When a consumer receives a billing statement that he believes contains an error he must within 60 days thereafter notify the creditor in writing of the alleged billing error. In the notice, the consumer must identify himself by name and account number, if any, identify the item in dispute and the amount of the alleged error, state the reasons why he believes the billing to be in error, and include any other information or documentation pertinent to resolving the dispute. The consumer may also request further documentation from the creditor regarding the disputed item.

The creditor must notify the consumer-debtor within 30 days that it has received the consumer's notice of the billing dispute. Upon receipt of a consumer's notice of a dispute in a billing statement, the creditor must investigate the disputed item, and within the shorter of 90 days or two billing cycles thereafter notify the consumer of the result of the investigation.

During the period after the creditor receives the consumer's notice of a billing error but before sending a response to the consumer regarding the outcome of its investigation, the creditor cannot take any action to collect the disputed debt from the consumer-debtor. The creditor may, however, send billing statements to the consumer that include the disputed item, but must indicate on the billing statement that payment of the disputed item is not required pending the creditor's investigation. The FCBA also prohibits the creditor from closing or otherwise restricting the consumer's account during this period. The creditor may, however, include the amount of the disputed item in calculating whether the consumer has reached his or her credit limit as previously established.

If after its investigation the creditor finds that the billing error did exist, it must correct the error on the consumer's account and notify the consumer of the correction. If the creditor concludes that the billing statement is correct, it must notify the consumer of the reasons for its conclusion, and include documentation to substantiate its findings. A creditor must wait ten days after sending its response to the consumer before making any adverse credit report regarding the consumer or taking any action to collect the disputed item. The ten-day period provides time for the consumer to pay the disputed item or to take other action before the creditor institutes collection procedures.

After receiving a negative response from a creditor regarding an alleged billing error, the consumer may continue to dispute the amount in question. The resolution of the dispute may require legal action. During the period prior to the resolution of the billing dispute, a creditor making a credit report to a third party regarding its credit experience with the consumer must note on the credit report the item disputed by the consumer. If the consumer is found to have been incorrect regarding the billing dispute, the creditor may recover the amount originally billed and an appropriate finance charge for the time it took to resolve the dispute.

Faulty Product. Where a consumer purchases a product in a credit transaction subject to FCBA and the product proves to be faulty, the purchaser can withhold payment on the credit extended until the dispute regarding the faulty product is resolved. A credit purchaser may wait until receipt of a billing statement before notifying the creditor of the dispute regarding a faulty product. A better practice is to notify the creditor immediately upon discovering the defect in the product. The FCBA places a duty upon the creditor to intervene and attempt to resolve the dispute regarding the faulty product. If the dispute is not settled, a legal action may be necessary to resolve the dispute. In order to be protected by the provisions of the FCBA, the consumer-debtor must have acted in good faith in raising the issue of a defective product.

If a creditor violates any of the requirements of the FCBA regarding the resolution of a billing dispute or faulty product problem, the creditor forfeits the right to collect up to $50.00 per disputed item. The $50.00 may be credited to either principal or interest or both.

THE FAIR CREDIT REPORTING ACT

Often when a consumer purchases an item of significant value on credit such as an automobile or appliance, purchases life or credit insurance, or is seeking employment, the seller or employer will obtain a *credit report* on the consumer-applicant. Credit reports are generally prepared by privately-owned credit reporting agencies, commonly referred to as *credit bureaus.* The requester of the credit report usually pays a fee to the reporting agency for the credit report. The use of computer-based information systems, combined with the desire of creditors for information on potential debtors, has caused a substantial increase in the number of credit reports sought by debtors and employers during the 1980s. Prior to 1970, substantial abuses of credit reporting occurred, leading Congress to enact the Fair Credit Reporting Act (FCRA) in 1970 as Title VI of the Consumer Credit Protection Act.

The purposes of the Fair Credit Reporting Act are to protect consumers from (1) damages caused from inaccurate or arbitrary information contained in credit reports and (2) undue invasion into their privacy by the collection and dissemination of confidential credit information. The FCRA applies to any party who prepares a credit report *or* uses a credit report with regard to:

1. the extension of consumer credit
2. the sale of insurance
3. the employment or discharge of an employee.

The FCRA does not apply when a person applies for credit or insurance for *commercial* purposes, for example, when purchasing a business.

Consumer Reporting Agencies. The FRCA covers "consumer reporting agencies," which compile and evaluate credit information on individuals and sell credit reports to certain third parties such as creditors and employers, who use the information to assess the risk of applicants for credit or employment.

If an entity compiles credit information on an individual for its own use, it is not a "consumer reporting agency" subject to the Act. Further, the Act does *not* cover transactions where an entity reports to a third party its *own* credit experience with the subject. For example, if a third party requests credit information regarding an individual's payment history with a bank, and the bank reports this information to the third party, there is no "consumer report" subject to the FRCA. If the bank, however, reported any information from *another* source, or gave its own opinion as to the general credit-worthiness of the individual being reported on, it would be a "consumer reporting agency" subject to the provisions of the FRCA.

The FRCA specifically provides that the consumer reporting agency may only furnish credit reports on an individual for the following purposes:

1. to a party that the consumer reporting agency has reason to believe will use the information in determining the eligibility of the consumer for the extension of credit or insurance for:
   a. personal reasons
   b. employment purposes
   c. other legitimate business purposes
   d. the granting of a government license

2. in response to a valid court order for the credit information
3. upon the written request of the consumer to whom the credit information pertains.

A consumer can have a credit report *withheld* from any party who does not have a legitimate need for the report as specified in the FRCA.

The FRCA attempted to correct many abuses of consumer reporting agencies in the gathering and discrimination of information by (1) providing for *disclosure* to consumers of information contained in credit reports; (2) giving the consumer the right to *correct errors* in credit reports; and (3) providing for the *removal of obsolete information* from a consumer's credit report.

Disclosure of Information.   Under the FRCA, the consumer is entitled, upon request, to a disclosure of the information contained in the credit files of a reporting agency. Except for medical information, the consumer is entitled to a disclosure of all the information contained in the file and where it was obtained. Consumers are also entitled, upon request, to a disclosure from the consumer reporting agency of the *names* of all parties who requested information on the consumer for *employment* purposes during the preceding six months, and who requested information on the consumer for *all other* purposes during the preceding two years.

Removal of Obsolete Information.   Consumer reporting agencies are under a duty to keep consumer credit reports up to date, and to not report certain obsolete data. The FRCA expressly provides that the following data *not* be reported in a consumer credit report:

1. bankruptcies of the consumer more than 14 years prior to the date of the report
2. lawsuits, judgments, tax liens, accounts placed for collection, and accounts written off as bad debts more than seven years prior to the date of the report
3. records of arrests, indictments, or convictions of a crime where the disposition, release, or parole occurred more than seven years prior to the date of the report
4. any other unfavorable information that is over seven years old.

These limitations do not apply where the credit report is sought in conjunction with an application for credit or life insurance of $50,000.00 or more or employment at an annual salary of at least $20,000.00.

Correction of Errors.   Where a consumer challenges the accuracy of information contained in his credit files, the FRCA requires the consumer reporting agency to *reinvestigate* the accuracy of the information unless the agency has "reasonable grounds" to believe that the consumer's request is frivolous. If the reinvestigation does not confirm the information, the consumer reporting agency must delete the unverified information from the consumer's file. If the consumer still disputes the accuracy of the information, the FRCA provides that the consumer may file a written statement of his version of the dispute, not to exceed 100 words, with the consumer reporting agency. The agency must then inform any party who requests a credit report on the consumer that the consumer disputes the information in the file, and provide either the consumer's statement or an accurate abstract of the statement to the requester.

Where inaccurate or unverified information is deleted from a consumer's credit file, the consumer may request that the consumer reporting agency notify of the correction any party who received the inaccurate information in a credit report on the consumer (1) for employment purposes during the preceding two years or (2) for any other purpose during the preceding six months.

Investigative Consumer Reports.   Often, an employer or insurance company will request a consumer reporting agency not only to provide credit information on an individual, but also to conduct an *investigation* as to an individual's character, reputation, morals, and mode of living. Such an investigation generally consists of conducting personal or telephone interviews with neighbors, friends, associates, professors, and anyone else who is familiar with the subject of the investigation. Such a report on the general character of an individual is called an *investigative consumer report.*

The FRCA permits the compilation of investigative consumer reports, and does not limit the type of information that may be gathered on the subject of the investigation. Any party desiring an investigative consumer report on an individual must give that individual three days' advance notice that the investigative report will be sought. The FRCA regulates the *use* of the information contained in an investigative consumer report. For example, any adverse nonpublic information that is over three months old (e.g., a neighbor discloses information regarding a Christmas party two years ago) may not be included in an investigative consumer report *unless* it is reverified, for example by another neighbor.

Where a written investigative consumer report has been requested by a third party of a consumer reporting agency, the consumer-subject has a right under FRCA to receive a complete and accurate disclosure of the nature and scope of the investigation. However, the subject of the report is entitled neither to a copy of the report nor to a disclosure of the sources of information contained in the report. Nor is the subject entitled to a disclosure of the nature and degree of the investigation if the report is being compiled to determine the subject's suitability for a job for which the subject has not applied.

User Requirements.   The party who orders a credit report from a consumer reporting agency—the *user*—may deny a consumer credit, insurance, or employment because of information contained in the credit report. The FRCA requires that the user of the credit report advise the consumer:

1. that the denial of credit is being made because of an adverse credit report
2. of the name and address of the consumer reporting agency that provided the credit report

3. that the consumer has 60 days to file a written request for the information contained in the credit report.

Upon request of the consumer, the user must provide to the consumer free of charge the information contained in the credit report: It is often upon this disclosure that the consumer requests a reinvestigation of the information contained in the credit report.

Where the user denies credit, or increases the charge for credit, based on information received from a source other than the consumer reporting agency, the FRCA requires the user to disclose to the consumer the nature of that information.

Remedies. The FRCA does not make a consumer reporting agency strictly liable for inaccuracies contained in the credit reports it issues. However, the FRCA requires that a consumer reporting agency institute and maintain "reasonable procedures":

1. to make prospective users of the report identify themselves and prove that their purpose for requesting a credit report on a consumer falls within the permissible purposes specified by the FRCA
2. to remove obsolete information from credit reports
3. to assure the accuracy of information contained in credit reports
4. to verify information contained in public records that would adversely affect the consumer, such as a criminal conviction or bankruptcy.

A violation of the FRCA may lead to several types of legal action, including (1) a *civil* action by an injured plaintiff, (2) a *criminal* action, and (3) an *administrative* proceeding. A party who had been injured by a violation of the FRCA may bring a civil action for damages against the reporting agency or report user. Where the defendant has *willfully* violated the FRCA, the plaintiff may recover actual damages, punitive damages, costs of the lawsuit, and reasonable attorneys' fees. If a defendant reporting agency or user has only acted *negligently* and not willfully in violating the provisions of the FRCA, the plaintiff may recover actual damages, costs of the lawsuit, and reasonable attorney's fees, but not punitive damages, from the defendant.

The FRCA expressly provides *criminal* penalties of fines up to $5,000.00 or imprisonment up to one year, or both, where (1) an officer or employee of a consumer reporting agency *knowingly* provides credit information about an individual to a party who is not authorized to receive the information or (2) a user obtains credit information on an individual from a consumer reporting agency under false pretenses.

A violation of the FRCA is an "unfair and deceptive practice" that violates Section 5 of the Federal Trade Commission Act. The Federal Trade Commission may seek a cease-and-desist order against a violator of the FRCA, and may also seek criminal and civil penalties available under the FTC Act.

In *Millstone v. O'Hanlon Reports, Inc.* the court found that the defendant consumer reporting agency had willfully violated the Fair Credit Reporting Act and awarded actual and punitive damages to the plaintiff-consumer.

CREDIT REPORT

MILLSTONE v. O'HANLON REPORTS, INC.

383 F.Supp 269 (1974)
UNITED STATES DISTRICT COURT, E. D. MISSOURI

Wangelin, District Judge.

Plaintiff, James C. Millstone (herein Millstone) brought this action alleging violation of 15 U.S.C. Section 1681 *et seq.,* commonly known as the "Fair Credit Reporting Act", against the defendant O'Hanlon Reports, Inc. (herein O'Hanlon).

FINDINGS OF FACT

In August of 1971, Millstone and his family moved to St. Louis, Missouri, so that he might take up his duties as news editor for the St. Louis Post-Dispatch. He thereafter contacted his insurance agent, Norman Kastner, and asked Kastner to place auto insurance for him. Kastner placed the policy with Firemen's Fund Insurance Company. The policy took effect on November 15, 1971, and several days later Millstone, in accordance with 15 U.S.C. Section 1681d received a notice that a personal investigation would be made in connection with the new policy.

On December 20, 1971, Walter McPherson from the Firemen's Fund Insurance Company informed Kastner (and Kastner informed Millstone) that the policy would be cancelled. . . . Millstone discovered from McPherson that the cancellation had been brought about because of a consumer credit report which had been made by the defendant, O'Hanlon Reports, Inc.

On December 22, 1971, Millstone went to the office of O'Hanlon Reports where he spoke to William O'Connell, the Office Manager. Millstone was told that he was entitled to know what was in his report but that O'Hanlon was entitled to reasonable notice of ten (10) days before giving the information. When Millstone protested, O'Connell called the New York home office of O'Hanlon and allowed Millstone to speak to a Kenneth Mitchell. Mitchell told Millstone that the information would be available as soon as possible but that he could not give disclosure immediately because the Millstone file was en route from St. Louis to New York through

the mails. After Millstone left the office, O'Connell then mailed the file to New York.

On December 28, 1971, Millstone received the disclosure of the information in its file from O'Connell at the O'Hanlon offices. O'Connell read the disclosure from a single sheet of paper which had been prepared by David Slayback, the Vice President of O'Hanlon. The disclosure sheet stated in part that:

> The file shows that you are very much disliked by your neighbors at that location [Millstone's Washington residence], and were considered to be a 'hippy type.' The file indicates that you participated in many demonstrations in Washington, D.C., and that you also housed out-of-town demonstrators during demonstrations. The file indicates that these demonstrators slept on floors, in the basement and wherever else there was room on your property. The file shows that you were strongly suspected of being a drug user by neighbors but they could not positively substantiate these suspicions. You are shown to have had shoulder length hair and a beard on one occasion while living in Washington, D.C. The file indicates that there were rumors in the neighborhood that you had been evicted by neighbors from these previous residences in Washington, D.C. prior to living at the 48th Street, N.W. location.

After protesting virtually all the information contained in the disclosure, Millstone asked O'Connell to explain certain facts contained therein. O'Connell told Millstone that he had no further information and could not answer the questions. He told Millstone that his instructions from the home office were only to read the disclosure sheet prepared in New York and to take careful note of any dispute from the customer. At no time was Millstone allowed to look at the actual consumer report file maintained by O'Hanlon upon him, nor were any actual portions of that file read to Millstone at any time by Mr. O'Connell.

[O'Hanlon] ordered the Manager of [the] Silver . . . Springs office, the office which had conducted the original investigation of Millstone, to re-investigate the information. Raymond T. Jonas, the Branch Manager, took approximately three days to complete the re-investigation and then sent his report to the New York office. This re-investigation report contained statements that the Millstone children had "torn up" part of a neighbor's garden and that Mrs. Millstone had used terms such as "pig", and "old hag" to a neighbor and his wife and that she was considered by the neighbors to be a "paranoid," and that Mr. Millstone was considered to be a "hippy type" because he allowed peace demonstrators to stay in his house. Mrs. Millstone was also alleged to have stated that she would allow her children to use drugs.

The original report on Millstone was prepared by Alexander Mayes, an employee of defendant in defendant's Silver Springs office. Mayes contacted four neighbors of the Millstones on the block where they last lived while residing in Washington, D.C.

Of the four persons contacted, one refused to speak to Mayes, two others told him that they knew of trouble in the neighborhood but knew nothing first hand and wished not to become involved. All the data recovered in Mayes' report was gleaned from a discussion with one neighbor identified as one McMillan, now deceased. Mayes gathered the data in a period of less than one-half hour. Mayes worked on a commission basis and received approximately one-third of the fee charged by the defendant, which amounted approximately to $1.85 in the Millstone investigation.

CONCLUSIONS OF LAW

[T]his action revolves around the questions of whether or not defendant O'Hanlon is liable under Section 1681n and Section 1681o of this aforecited title. Section 1681n shows the recovery of actual damages, costs and reasonable attorneys' fees along with punitive damages for willed non-compliance with the Act in question, and Section 1681o allows actual damages along with costs and attorneys' fees for negligent non-compliance with this Act. The standard of care imposed by the aforecited statutory sections is that:

> Whenever a consumer reporting agency prepares a consumer report it shall follow reasonable procedures to assure maximum possible accuracy of the informa-

tion concerning the individual about whom the report relates. 15 U.S.C. Section 1681e(b).

It is clear to this Court as the trier of fact that the defendant was in violation of Section 1681e(b), in that its procedures of gathering personal information about consumers, such as Millstone, was only from neighbors from the consumer's residence and that these items were not verified. The evidence also shows that defendant's agent Mayes knowingly included false information in the report which defendant compiled concerning Millstone. In his report agent Mayes refers to a poll of four neighbors, with full knowledge that he spoke only to three neighbors. Also, the report repeatedly asserts that all of the sources were in agreement when Mayes in fact received information from only one source, Mr. McMillan. Considering the prior unblemished record of Millstone and the fact that defendant's own operations manual concerning such derogatory information states:

> When adverse information is developed, it should be verified by at least one other source to avoid the reporting of any prejudicial or inaccurate information

[T]he actions of O'Hanlon's agent Mayes are so wanton as to be certainly a willful non-compliance with the standard of care imposed by the Act. These actions by defendant's agent Mayes are so heinous and reprehensible as to justify the harsh damages imposed by Section 1681n. Defendant's methods of reporting on consumer's credit backgrounds as shown at trial were so slip-shod and slovenly as to not even approach the realm of reasonable standards of care as imposed by the statute. Defendant's reporting methods were so wanton as to be clearly willful non-compliance with the Fair Credit Reporting Act in the eyes of this Court.

The actions of O'Hanlon in having the file mailed to its New York office, and instructing its employee in St. Louis to tell Millstone that the file was en route to New York and that he could not tell Millstone what was in it when the file was actually in St. Louis are further indications of the willful non-compliance of defendant with this Act. . . . The evidence in the case at bar as a whole is so overwhelming and persuasive as to leave no other conclusion [than] that O'Hanlon was in willful violation of various previously discussed portions of the Fair

Credit Reporting Act and should therefore be subject to the liabilities enumerated in Section 1681n.

DAMAGES

In regards to damages, the Court further finds that although plaintiff suffered no lost wages nor incurred medical expenses on the account of the injuries therein, he suffered by reason of his mental anguish and had symptoms of sleeplessness and nervousness which were amply testified to, and because of the repeated and numerous times in which plaintiff had to contact O'Hanlon, in many cases having to leave his employment for meetings on account of the defendant's actions as stated above, the plaintiff is entitled to actual damages in the amount of $2,500.00.

Considering the willful noncompliance of O'Hanlon with the requirements of the statute, this Court will assume the sum of $25,000 against defendant O'Hanlon as punitive damages in this action. This Court also finds that the sum of $12,500 will be awarded to plaintiff from defendant for attorneys' fees and the Court will further order that defendant pay costs in this matter. In consequence, *judgment for the plaintiff* as stated above will be entered.

CASE QUESTIONS

1. Who issued the credit report on Millstone? Who requested the report?
2. What did the credit report on Millstone state? Was it prepared from reliable sources?
3. What does Section 1681e(b) of the Fair Credit Reporting Act provide? Explain.
4. Did O'Hanlon Reports meet its duty under this section? What evidence did the court cite in supporting its decision on this issue? Describe in detail.

Policy Issue. Should "opinions" of neighbors and others be allowed to be included in credit reports? Or should only past *credit* history be permitted to be used in making a credit decision?

Economics Issue. What are *punitive* damages? Were they an important item in this case?

Ethics Issue. Did O'Hanlon Reports, and its agents, act ethically in this case?

Social Responsibility. Do credit reporting agencies owe a duty of social responsibility in preparing accurate credit reports?

THE FAIR DEBT COLLECTION PRACTICES ACT

In order to correct abuses and harassment caused to consumer-debtors by collection agencies, in 1977 Congress enacted the Fair Debt Collection Practices Act (FDCPA). The Act covers debt collectors who collect bills for creditors. A *debt collector* is defined by the Act as (1) a collection agent who is engaged in the business of collecting debts for third parties and (2) a creditor who collects its own debts under a name different from the name under which it sold the product or service to the consumer. The FDCPA does not cover department stores, retail stores, financial institutions, or other businesses that collect their own debts under their own names. The Federal Trade Commission (FTC) is charged with the responsibility of administering and enforcing the FDCPA.

About two thirds of the states of the union have enacted statutes to regulate debt collection practices. Federal law provides exemptions from the FDCPA where state law provides either equal or greater protection than the FDCPA, and where the state effectively enforces its debt collection practices act. If the state law provides insufficient coverage, debt collectors in that state are subject to both state and federal law. If a state has not adopted a debt collection practices act, the debt collectors of that state are subject to the provisions of the FDCPA. The FTC has the authority to determine whether a state's debt collection practices act provides the same protection to consumer-debtors as the FDCPA, and to issue the proper exemption based on its finding.

Debt Collectors. The FDCPA sets forth in detail the activities of debt collectors that violate the Act. Its prohibitions for debt collectors generally fall into three categories: (1) prohibited contact with third parties, (2) prohibited contact with the debtor; and (3) general prohibitions against harassing, unfair, or misleading practices.

Prohibited Contact with Third Parties. The FDCPA particularly limits the contact that a debt collector may have with *third parties* regarding the collection of a debt owed by a consumer. The reason for limiting contact with third parties is to protect the privacy of the debtor and to protect innocent third parties from overzealous debt collectors. The main prohibitions of the FDCPA regarding contact by the debt collector with third parties are described below.

1. Unless authorized to do so by the courts, a debt collector may not contact any person other than the debtor, the debtor's spouse, or the debtor's parents if the debtor is a minor, except to find out "locational information" on the debtor. "Locational information" is narrowly construed as ascertaining the debtor's residence address, place of employment, and telephone number. If a debt collector knows the locations of the debtor, he may not contact such third parties regarding the collection of the debtor's bill.
2. When a debt collector contacts a third party (for example, to find out locational information on the debtor), the debt collector may not inform the third party as to the nature of his business unless the third party specifically asks the nature of the inquiry. At no time may a debt collector inform a third party that the consumer owes a debt that is in the process of collection.
3. A debt collector may not contact a third party more than once to request locational information on the debtor unless the debt collector has a "reasonable belief" that the third party gave the debt collector incorrect information, or if the third party voluntarily contacts the debt collector.

Prohibited Contact with the Debtor. The FDCPA also severely limits the contact that a debt collector may have with the debtor. The reason for these rules is to protect the debtor from constant contact and communications from debt collectors and to protect the private life of the debtor. The primary prohibition of the FDCPA regarding contact by a debt collector with the debtor are the following.

1. The FDCPA prohibits a debt collector from contacting a consumer-debtor at any *time* or *place* that "should be known to be inconvenient." The Act expressly provides that only the hours between 8:00 A.M. and 9:00 P.M. are considered "convenient." For persons who work normal hours, all other hours are thereby considered "inconvenient" under the Act. For example, a debt collector may not call a debtor in the middle of the night. If a debtor works unusual hours (such as a night shift), the debt collector may not contact the debtor during hours "inconvenient" to the specific debtor (such as daylight hours when the debtor may be sleeping).

2. A debt collector may also not contact a debtor at inconvenient places, such as a bowling league or Bible class.

3. If a debtor is represented by an attorney, the debt collector must deal with the attorney and may not contact the debtor directly unless the attorney permits it, or the attorney fails to reasonably and timely respond to the inquiries of the debt collector.

4. Under the provisions of the FDCPA, a debtor may give notice to a debt collector in writing that he refuses to pay the debt or that he does not wish the debt collector to contact him again. If a debt collector receives such a notice, it must terminate all contact with the debtor. At this point the creditor often institutes a legal action against the debtor. The creditor must inform the debtor of the legal actions that are being taken to collect the debt.

5. The FDCPA does not prohibit a debt collector from contacting a debtor at his place of employment. However, if the *employer* objects to the debt collector contacting the debtor-employee at work, the Act provides that the debt collector must cease contacting the debtor at his place of employment.

General Prohibitions.   The FDCPA contains several general limitations on the activities in which debt collectors may engage in attempting to collect a debt. The following rules generally prohibit debt collectors from engaging in harassing, oppressive, unfair, or misleading activities in trying to collect a debt.

1. The FDCPA provides that a debt collector may not engage in any conduct in connection with the collection of a debt the natural consequence of which is to "harass, oppress, or abuse" *any persons.* For example, a debt collector may not use abusive language as an intimidating tactic against any third party or the debtor.

2. The FDCPA prohibits a debt collector from using "false or misleading" tactics in the process of collecting a debt. For example, a debt collector may not falsely pass as an attorney, police officer, or other government official in attempting to collect a debt.

3. The FDCPA prohibits a debt collector from engaging in "unfair or unconscionable" practices in the process of collecting a debt. Unfair or unconscionable practices would include telling a debtor that a legal action will be taken against the debtor that would actually be illegal (e.g., "100 percent of your wages will be garnisheed"), or threatening to physically take a debtor's property, which would first require a proper legal proceeding.

4. If a debtor tenders a post-dated check to a debt collector, and the debt collector accepts the check, the FDCPA prohibits the deposit of the check before the date on the check.

Remedies.   The FTC may issue cease-and-desist orders and order civil penalties against debt collectors who violate the FDCPA. A plaintiff-debtor may bring a *civil* action against a defendant-debt collector to recover actual injuries, including mental distress and embarrassment, incurred in violation of the FDCPA. Under the Act, a defendant may also be assessed additional civil damages of up to $1,000.00 per violation where the defendant's actions have been malicious, extreme, outrageous, or repeated. A plaintiff-debtor may recover attorney's fees if he wins a lawsuit against a defendant-debt collector. A defendant-debtor may recover attorney's fees if he wins the lawsuit brought by a plaintiff-debt collector and the court finds that the debt collector brought the lawsuit to "harass" the debtor.

In the following case, *Rutyna v. Collection Accounts Terminal, Inc.* the court found that a debt collector had harassed a debtor and engaged in "unfair" practices in violation of the Fair Debt Collection Practices Act.

COLLECTION AGENCY

RUTYNA v. COLLECTION ACCOUNTS TERMINAL, INC.

478 F.Supp. 980 (1979)
UNITED STATES DISTRICT COURT, N.D. ILLINOIS

McMillen, District Judge.

This is an action for violations of the Fair Debt Collection Practices Act, (the F.D.C.P.A.). The F.D.C.P.A. was enacted by Congress to eliminate abusive, deceptive, and unfair debt collection practices and became effective on March 20, 1978.

The facts of this case are undisputed, except where noted herein. Plaintiff is a 60-year-old widow and Social Security retiree. She suffers from high blood pressure and epilepsy. In December 1976 and January 1977, she incurred a debt for medical services performed by a doctor with Cabrini Hospital Medical Group. Her belief was that Medicare or other, private, medical insurance had paid in full this debt for medical treatment. She contends that in July 1978, an agent of defendant telephoned her and informed her of an alleged outstanding debt for $56.00 to Cabrini Hospital Medical Group. When she denied the existence of this debt, the voice on the telephone responded, "you owe it, you don't want to pay, so we're going to have to do something about it." . . . On or about August 10, 1978, plaintiff received a letter from defendant which supplies the basis for her complaint. It stated:

> You have shown that you are unwilling to work out a friendly settlement with us to clear the above debt.
> Our field investigator has now been instructed to make an investigation in your neighborhood and to personally call on your employer.
> The immediate payment of the full amount, or a

personal visit to this office, will spare you this embarrassment.

The top of the letter notes the creditor's name and the amount of the alleged debt. The letter was signed by a "collection agent." The envelope containing that letter presented a return address that included defendant's full name: Collection Accounts Terminal, Inc.

Upon receiving this letter from defendant, plaintiff alleges that she became very nervous, upset, and worried, specifically that defendant would cause her embarrassment by informing her neighbors of the debt and about her medical problems.

HARASSMENT OR ABUSE (1692d)

The first sentence of Section 1692d provides:

> A debt collector may not engage in any conduct the natural consequence of which is to harass, oppress, or abuse any person in connection with the collection of a debt.

This section then lists six specifically prohibited types of conduct, without limiting the general application of the foregoing sentence. The legislative history makes clear that this generality was intended:

> In addition to these specific prohibitions, this bill prohibits in general terms any harassing, unfair or deceptive collection practice. This will enable the courts,

where appropriate, to proscribe other improper conduct which is not specifically addressed.

Plaintiff does not allege conduct which falls within one of the specific prohibitions contained in Section 1692d, but we find that defendant's letter to plaintiff does violate this general standard.

Without doubt defendant's letter has the natural (and intended) consequence of harassing, oppressing, and abusing the recipient. The tone of the letter is one of intimidation, and was intended as such in order to effect a collection. The threat of an investigation and resulting embarrassment to the alleged debtor is clear and the actual effect on the recipient is irrelevant.

DECEPTION AND IMPROPER THREATS (1692e)

Section 1692e bars a debt collector from using any "false, deceptive, or misleading representation or means in connection with the collection of any debt." Sixteen specific practices are listed in this provision, without limiting the application of this general standard. Section 1692e(5) bars a threat "to take any action that cannot legally be taken or that is not intended to be taken." Defendant also violated this provision.

Defendant's letter threatened embarrassing contacts with plaintiff's employer and neighbors. This constitutes a false representation of the actions that defendant could legally take. Section 1692c(b) prohibits communication by the debt collector with third parties (with certain limited exceptions not here relevant). Plaintiff's neighbors and employer could not legally be contacted by defendant in connection with this debt. The letter falsely represents, or deceives the recipient, to the contrary. This is a deceptive means employed by defendant in connection with its debt collection. Defendant violated Section 1692e(5) in its threat to take such illegal action.

UNFAIR PRACTICE/RETURN ADDRESS (1692f)

The envelope received by plaintiff bore a return address, which began "COLLECTION ACCOUNTS TERMINAL, INC." Section 1692f bars unfair or unconscionable means to collect or attempt to collect any debt. Section 1692f specifically bars:

> Using any language or symbol, other than the debt collector's address, on any envelope when communicating with a consumer by use of the mails or by telegram, except that a debt collector may use his business name if such name does not indicate that he is in the debt collection business.

Defendant's return address violated this provision, because its business name does indicate that it is in the debt collection business. The purpose of this specific provision is apparently to prevent embarrassment resulting from a conspicuous name on the envelope, indicating that the contents pertain to debt collection.

It is therefore ordered, adjudged and decreed that judgment is *entered in favor of plaintiff* on the issue of liability.

CASE QUESTIONS

1. What was the amount of the debt that the plaintiff owed? Who did she owe it to? Who was the defendant?
2. What actions did the defendant take to collect the debt? Explain.
3. Did the actions of the defendant violate any of the following provisions of the Fair Debt Collection Practices Act?
   a. harrassment or abuse (Section 1692d)
   b. deception and improper threats (Section 1692e)
   c. unfair practice regarding the return address (Section 1692f)

Policy Issue. Should debtors be protected from certain collection practices by collection agencies? Or should creditors be allowed to take whatever action is necessary to collect the debts owed them?

Economics Issue. What economic effects will this decision have on creditors? On debtors? On collection agencies?

Ethics Issue. Was it ethical for the collection agency to take the actions it did to collect the debt from Mrs. Rutyna in this case?

Social Responsibility. Do collection agencies owe a duty of social responsibility not to engage in harsh tactics to collect debts? If certain collection tactics cannot be used, is there much incentive for some debtors to pay their debts?

THE CONSUMER LEASING ACT

In 1976, Congress enacted the Consumer Leasing Act (CLA) as part of the Truth-in-Lending Act. The major impetus for enacting the CLA was the substantial increase in the *leasing* of consumer goods, particularly automobiles, and the confusion caused by the complexity of the financing arrangements for the leases. The CLA was enacted with the stated purpose of providing meaningful *disclosure* of lease terms for consumer goods and to protect consumers from *misleading* lease information. The CLA only applies to leases of "consumer goods," which is defined as a lease of *personal property* by a party (lessor) to a consumer (lessee) for "personal, family, or household" purposes where: (1) the lease period is over four months; *and* (2) the total lease obligation does not exceed $25,000.00.

A *lessor* is any natural person or legal entity who engages in leasing, or arranging leases, as a normal course of business. "Casual leases" (such as those between neighbors) or leases of real property (such as the lease on an apartment) are not covered by the CLA. For example, a lease of an automobile for personal, family, or household use is subject to the provisions of the CLA, whereas a lease of an automobile for business purposes is *not* subject to the disclosure requirements of the Act. Where a consumer lease is subject to the provisions of the CLA, the lessor must provide the consumer-lessee with a written lease agreement that includes:

1. the date of the lease
2. the identity of the lessor
3. the identity of the lessee
4. a clear description of the personal property subject to the lease
5. an itemization of all lease and financing charges
6. information as to the date and amount of periodic lease payments
7. information as to the insurance to be carried on the personal property
8. the lessor's and lessee's financial responsibility regarding payment of insurance costs
9. any express warranties made regarding the leased property
10. information regarding the consumer-lessee's liability at the end of the lease
11. notice that the creditor must pay any legal fees incurred by the consumer-lessee in a suit involving the creditor's claims for excess payments at the end of the lease agreement
12. the method, terms and conditions for terminating the lease agreement prior to the expiration of the lease period.

Any creditor who violates the provisions of the Consumer Leasing Act is subject to the same civil liability and criminal penalties as provided in the Truth-in-Lending Act.

THE UNIFORM CONSUMER CREDIT CODE

With the aid of practitioners and academics, a Uniform Consumer Credit Code (UCCC) was proposed in 1961 for adoption by states. The UCCC is a comprehensive uniform act that applies to almost every transaction involving the extension of credit. The salient features of the proposed Act are that it:

1. places strict limitations on a creditor's ability to garnishee wages of a debtor
2. provides for civil penalties of up to 10 times a finance charge that exceeds the limit allowed by the UCCC
3. eliminates payment for consumer debts by the use of promissory notes or other negotiable instruments (only payment by check or cash allowed)
4. eliminates the holder-in-due-course status according to the Uniform Commercial Code where a credit sale or lease is involved
5. provides criminal penalties for violations of the UCCC.

Only a few states have adopted the UCCC.

Trend of the Law

The number and complexity of the federal and state statutes that regulate the debtor-creditor relation ensures that a substantial number of lawsuits will be brought in this area in the future. The majority of these lawsuits will be brought under the array of federal credit statutes enacted by Congress to protect consumer-debtors. The detail of some of these statutes means that many businesses will be sued for unintentional violations of federal statutes in the future. The courts will also be faced in the future with continuing to interpret and define the law in this relatively new area of consumer protection.

Consumer-debtors will continue to be protected in the future by state and federal law from excessive attachment and garnishment of their property and wages by creditors. Although millions of dollars are loaned at usurious rates of interest each year, often to poor and less educated persons, only a few of the many potential cases will actually be brought in this area. (Why?)

As consumers become aware of their rights regarding the correction of mistaken information contained in credit reports and the protection from overzealous debt collectors that is provided in federal credit statutes, the number of lawsuits in these areas will continue to increase substantially in the future.

REVIEW QUESTIONS

1. Ives, a Connecticut resident, filed a class action suit against W. T. Grant Company alleging that the company's coupon book credit plan violated Connecticut's usury laws. Customers were sold books of coupons that could be redeemed for merchandise at a Grant's store or returned for a cash

refund. In exchange for the use of the coupons, customers were obliged to execute retail installment contracts which required them to make monthly payments. Interest on the coupon principal amounted to more than 19 percent, even though Connecticut state law set a maximum interest rate of 12 percent. Did W. T. Grant's coupon plan violate Connecticut usury laws?

2. LaLanne, Inc. and Universal, Inc. were interlocking corporations with common ownership and control. When members purchased seven-year memberships in LaLanne's Health Spa, they were charged $408, regardless of whether they paid in cash or in monthly installments over a two-year period. Most people elected to pay for their membership in installments and so they signed a firm contract which declared that there was no service charge attached for the extension of credit and that default on any payment would render the entire balance due. LaLanne then would sell all the installment contracts to Universal at a 37.5 percent discount and receive $255 in cash. Installment contract holders were then obligated to pay their monthly installments to Universal. Did LaLanne's and Universal's practices violate the Truth-in-Lending Act?

3. The Brown family borrowed $648.30 from Commercial Credit Plan, Inc. at a disclosed interest rate of 27.25 percent. The Browns' total indebtedness was $802, which was payable in monthly installments. Included in this total amount was: household goods insurance, required by the lender, $11.25; an accident and health insurance policy, not required, $26.46; and a finance charge of $165.12, of which $105.84 was interest and $59.28 a service charge. The Browns did not sign any disclosure forms concerning the insurance. The Browns sued Commercial for alleged violations of the Truth-in-Lending Act (TILA) and Regulation Z. They argued that the service charge of $59.28 was actually a prepaid finance charge and should have been separately disclosed, and that the cost of the personal insurance should have been disclosed as part of the finance charge in the absence of an affirmative indication, dated and signed, that the borrower voluntarily wished such insurance. Did Continental's contract violate the Truth-in-Lending Act and Regulation Z?

4. Sampson was transferred by his company from Washington, D.C., to Los Angeles. Rather than driving there in his old car, Sampson decided to sell it and to lease a new car when he reached Los Angeles. Shortly after his arrival, Sampson contacted Thrifty Car Leasing and arranged to lease a $15,000 late model sports car for 36 months. Thrifty prepared the leasing documents. Under the Consumer Leasing Act, what terms were required to be disclosed by Thrifty?

5. Carroll, a single working woman, applied for an Exxon credit card, but was advised by a letter that her application for credit had been denied; no reason was given. On Carroll's application, she did not list any major credit cards, she did not list any savings account, she stated that she had only been employed for one year and she stated that she had no dependents. After her denial, she wrote to Exxon and asked for specific reasons why she was denied credit. Exxon sent a letter in response advising Carroll that the credit bureau contacted by Exxon had not responded adversely but had been unable to supply sufficient information concerning her credit.

The letter did not name the credit bureau used by Exxon and it provided no other reasons for her credit denial. Carroll sued Exxon, alleging violations of both the Fair Credit Reporting Act and the Equal Credit Opportunity Act. Did Exxon violate either Act?

6. Sniadach, a Wisconsin resident, signed a promissory note with Family Finance Corp. When Sniadach fell behind on her payments, Family Finance instituted a garnishment action. Under Wisconsin's garnishment statute, when wages were the subject of garnishment, the employer (garnishor) could withhold up to 50 percent of their employee's (garnishee's) wages once a complaint was filed against the employee. After Family Finance filed a complaint and served a summons on both Sniadach and Sniadach's employer, Sniadach's employer immediately began to withhold 50 percent of her wages, even though a hearing had not been held to determine the validity of the garnishment action. Sniadach challenged the constitutionality of the Wisconsin statute, arguing that a prejudgment garnishment of wages was unconstitutional. Did her argument have merit?

7. The Credit Bureau of Santa Clara Valley began garnisheeing Czap's wages in an effort to collect a $250 debt that Czap had incurred for legal fees in connection with her divorce. Czap, who had two dependent children, had offered to pay back $20 per month, but the Credit Bureau had rejected her proposal. According to Czap, the Credit Bureau knew that virtually all her wages were exempt from execution, but it had proceeded with garnishment so that she would satisfy the entire debt rather than risk jeopardizing her employment. Czap sued the Credit Bureau, charging that the Bureau violated the California garnishment statute. The basis of her suit was that the Bureau had an impermissible motive and therefore improperly used the garnishment procedure. Does her claim have merit?

8. Carrigan was a legal services clinic attorney in Gainesville, Florida. He owed a debt for his schooling to the University of Florida. He fell behind in his payments and the University turned over his account to the Central Adjustment Bureau (CAB), a collection agency. When Carrigan received a letter from the University informing him of this action, he immediately contacted the school. He was able to reach an agreement with officials at the University establishing a satisfactory repayment schedule. Shortly thereafter, he received a number of phone calls from CAB making demands for payment. Carrigan did not pay and then sent a letter to the firm directing it to cease further telephone communications with him. The letter stated that he had reached a new repayment plan so there was no further need to contact him. No contacts were made for nine months and Carrigan made the required monthly payments under his new schedule; then CAB called again on three different occasions asking for payment. Did CAB's actions violate the Fair Debt Collection Practices Act?

20 BANKRUPTCY

INTRODUCTION

The extension of credit by lenders (creditors) to borrowers (debtors) in commercial and personal transactions is of substantial importance to the viability of the American economy. On occasion, however, some borrowers overextend themselves and are unable to meet all of their debt obligations.

In former times in Europe, persons who could not meet their debts were often sentenced to debtors' prisons, or made the ward of their creditor until the debt was "worked off." In order to avoid the harsh results of these situations, many European countries adopted bankruptcy laws to achieve a better balance between the rights of debtors and creditors. In 1542, England adopted a bankruptcy law that applied to commercial debtors, and by 1801 had expanded bankruptcy law to cover almost all individual debtors as well.

The founders of our country thought the plight of debtors important enough to include a provision in the U.S. Constitution providing for bankruptcy. Article I, Section 8, clause 4 of the Constitution provides that

the Congress shall have the power . . . to establish . . . uniform Laws on the subject of Bankruptcies throughout the United States.

THE BANKRUPTCY REFORM ACT OF 1978

Under authority granted in the Constitution, Congress in 1878 enacted the original Bankruptcy Act, which was amended by the Chandler Act in 1938. It was not until 1978, when Congress enacted the Bankruptcy Reform Act, that the bankruptcy laws were substantially changed. All section references in this Chapter are to sections of the Bankruptcy Reform Act of 1978.

The 1978 Bankruptcy Reform Act created a federal bankruptcy court system: a U.S. Bankruptcy Court is located in each federal judicial district. The federal bankruptcy courts were authorized by the Act to exercise judicial power over all controversies affecting bankruptcies. Each bankruptcy court is presided over by a bankruptcy judge, who is appointed by the President and confirmed by the Senate. The appointment of a bankruptcy judge is for a term of 14 years. Decisions of the Bankruptcy Courts can be appealed to the federal District Court in the district in which the Bankruptcy Court is located.

In enacting a federal bankruptcy law, Congress did not choose to *wholly* preempt the area of debtor-creditor relations, and left it to the states to develop insolvency laws where federal bankruptcy law did not apply (e.g., garnishment of wages, collection practices). When state law and federal bankruptcy law conflicts, federal bankruptcy law controls. The administration of federal bankruptcy law relies heavily on state law, particularly state contract law, property ownership rules, partnership law, and corporation law.

Types of Bankrupties.   The Bankruptcy Reform Act provides for three major types of bankruptcies:

1. liquidations
2. reorganizations
3. consumer debt adjustments.

Liquidations.   A business may seek or be placed into liquidation proceedings under Chapter 7 of the Bankruptcy Reform Act. In a *liquidation* proceeding, the assets of a business are reduced to cash, the creditors are paid the cash pursuant to statutory priority, and the unpaid debts of the debtor are discharged. Both businesses and natural persons may file for bankruptcy liquidation under Chapter 7.

Reorganization.   A business may also seek or be placed into reorganization proceedings under Chapter 11 of the Bankruptcy Reform Act. Under a *reorganization* proceeding, a business is reorganized under the protection of the bankruptcy court; the creditors, and often the equity holders, generally receive a reduced interest in the business; and the business debtor is released from bankruptcy to continue in business. Natural persons who are not operating as a business cannot file for bankruptcy under Chapter 11.

Consumer Debt Adjustment.   A *natural* person who is not operating as a business may file for a *consumer debt adjustment* proceeding under Chapter 13 of the Bankruptcy Reform Act. In a consumer debt adjustment, the debtor petitions for a new payment plan for his debts, which, if granted, usually consists of extending the time period for paying his debts, or even a reduction in the amount of debts he owes. Chapter 13 is considered to be the reorganization bankruptcy provision for *consumers.*

"Fresh Start."   The primary purpose of federal bankruptcy law is to discharge the debtor from burdensome debts in order to give the debtor an opportunity for a "fresh start" free of oppressive financial burdens. In this excerpt from *Local Loan Co. v. Hunt,* 292 U.S. 234 (1934), Justice Sutherland of the U.S. Supreme Court discussed this purpose of the bankruptcy laws.

One of the primary purposes of the bankruptcy act is to "relieve the honest debtor from the weight of oppressive indebtedness and permit him to start afresh free from the obligations and responsibilities consequent upon business misfortunes." *Williams v. U.S. Fidelity & G. Co.* This purpose of the act has been again and again emphasized by the courts as being of public as well as private interest, in that it gives to the honest but unfortunate debtor who surrenders for distribution the property which he owns *at the time of bankruptcy,* a new opportunity in life and a clear field for future effort, unhampered by the pressure and discouragement of pre-existing debt.

Additional purposes of the federal bankruptcy laws are:

1. to provide for an equitable distribution of the debtor's nonexempt property to the creditors and other interest holders
2. to protect creditors from actions by the debtor that would diminish the value of the debtor's assets
3. to prevent certain creditors from obtaining an unfair advantage over other creditors
4. to preserve existing business relations of the debtor
5. to provide the means for a speedy and efficient distribution of the debtor's assets.

In *In Re Graham* the court held that a debtor who earned over $200,000 per year was entitled to a discharge of his debts and a "fresh start" under Chapter 7 liquidation.

"FRESH START"

IN RE GRAHAM

21 B.R. 235 (1982)
UNITED STATES BANKRUPTCY COURT, N.D. IOWA

William W. Thinnes, Bankruptcy Judge.

Charles W. Graham, debtor/respondent, is a 59-year-old radiologist. He works at three hospitals, earning approximately $200,500 per year.

On June 5, 1980, the Cherokee County District Court granted Dr. Graham and Mrs. Graham, creditor/movant, (herein referred to as Ms. Smith) a dissolution of marriage. In the dissolution, Ms. Smith received the couple's 360-acre farm. The Steele State Bank held two mortgages on this farm; Steele

Farms, Inc., also held two mortgages on it, ...[D]r. Graham assumed the obligations on the mortgages.

On April 24, 1981, Dr. Graham filed a Petition under Chapter 7 of the Bankruptcy Code. Dr. Graham listed the Internal Revenue Service as the holder of $124,884.46 in disputed priority claims. After amending his Petition on May 14, 1981, Dr. Graham listed four relevant unsecured creditors:

1. the Steele State Bank with an estimated $252,145.00 claim;
2. Steele Farms, Inc., with an estimated $98,600.00 claim;
3. the Doupe Estate with an estimated $182,000.00 claim;
4. Ms. Smith with an estimated $475,000.00 claim.

Dr. Graham claimed that his nonexempt property was worth only $97,338.96.

Subsequently, Ms. Smith moved to convert Dr. Graham's case from a Chapter 7 [liquidation] proceeding to a Chapter 11 [reorganization] proceeding.

The best interests of the debtor's creditors, especially the interest of his nonpriority, unsecured creditors, would be served by granting Ms. Smith's motion. The debtor is a highly skilled professional who earns over $200,000 a year in gross income. He suffers no known physical or mental impairment, and, although he is certainly not a young man, he has several years of peak earning power left before retirement. The Debtor, however, discounts such consideration entirely. He argues that his debts to the Internal Revenue Service, his normal business expenses, and his ordinary living expenses are such that very little of his gross income would remain after the payment of those debts to fund a reorganization plan that would provide any type of meaningful dividend to nonpriority unsecured creditors and that, consequently, a workable plan that would provide a significant repayment of creditors' claims could not be formulated.

The Debtor further argues that, even if a workable plan could be confirmed, he is considering cutting down the extent of his practice over the next several years, and, thus, there would be even less money to fund a plan.

The best interest of the Debtor, however, would be served by denying Ms. Smith's motion. By receiving a bankruptcy discharge immediately, Dr. Graham would be free from the burden of substantial debt and would be able to obtain a fresh start immediately. He does not want to spend the last years before his retirement working to pay back his pre-petition creditors, especially Ms. Smith, who is his ex-spouse. Rather, he prefers to be free from such pre-petition financial burdens, obligated only upon the unpaid balance of the claim of the IRS, and that portion of his debt to Ms. Smith that is nondischargeable [child support payments].

An order converting Dr. Graham's bankruptcy proceedings from Chapter 7 to Chapter 11 would have the effect, assuming a reorganization plan were subsequently confirmed and complied with, of diverting some of the fruits of Dr. Graham's future labors from himself to his pre-petition creditors.

In the view of Congress, it is more important to encourage a debtor to retain his or her employment, instead of running the risk of a debtor's walking away from his or her job in order to avoid working to fund a repayment plan that primarily benefits someone else. Applying this policy to the facts of the instant case, it is better, for Dr. Graham, and presumably, for society, that Dr. Graham continue to service three hospitals instead of cutting back on his services because of an unwillingness to fund a Chapter 11 reorganization plan.

[T]he Court is forced to *deny* the Movant's motion.

CASE QUESTIONS

1. Who filed the petition for bankruptcy? What type of bankruptcy was filed for?
2. How large were the debts that Dr. Graham was attempting to have discharged in bankruptcy? What were Dr. Graham's assets? Income?
3. Why did Ms. Smith (the former Mrs. Graham) file her motion to have the type of bankruptcy changed? Explain.

Policy Issue. Should a debtor be given a "fresh start" through bankruptcy? Should a person of Dr. Graham's income be allowed to declare bankruptcy? Are the bankruptcy laws being abused? Did the Framers anticipate the current uses of the bankruptcy laws?

Economics Issue. What are the economic

consequences of bankruptcy for the debtor? For creditors? For society?

Ethics Issue. Was Dr. Graham's actions in this case ethical?

Social Responsibility. Do debtors in society owe a duty of social responsibility to repay their debts? Do debtors breach their duty to society by declaring bankruptcy?

BANKRUPTCY PROCEDURE

Bankruptcy is governed by a very procedurally oriented law. It consists of filing a *petition* for bankruptcy with the appropriate Bankruptcy Court in order to initiate the action, and thereafter following prescribed procedures to maintain and complete the proceeding.

Voluntary and Involuntary Petitions. All bankruptcy proceedings are initiated by the filing of a *petition* for bankruptcy with the appropriate Bankruptcy Court. Depending on the type of bankruptcy, the petition may be either (1) a *voluntary* petition filed by the *debtor* or (2) an *involuntary* petition filed by *creditors* of the debtor.

Voluntary Petition. Generally, any sole proprietorship, partnership, corporation, or other business debtor may file a *voluntary petition* for bankruptcy under Chapter 7 (liquidation) or Chapter 11 (reorganization) of the Bankruptcy Reform Act. The petition must allege that the debtor has debts. A natural person may file a voluntary petition for bankruptcy under Chapter 7 (liquidation) or Chapter 13 (consumer debt adjustment). Approximately 90 percent of all petitions for bankruptcy are voluntary petitions filed by the debtor.

Involuntary Petitions. The creditors of a business debtor may file a petition to place the debtor into bankruptcy under Chapter 7 (liquidation) or Chapter 11 (reorganization). The creditors of a natural person not operating a business (consumer) may file a petition to place that consumer into bankruptcy under Chapter 7 (liquidation). Creditors *cannot,* however, file an involuntary petition to place a consumer into bankruptcy under Chapter 13 (consumer debt adjustment).

In order to file an *involuntary petition* against a debtor, the creditor or creditors who file the petition must have valid claims against the debtor that either exceed $5,000 in amount or exceed the security interest in property held by the debtor by that amount. The petition must allege that the debtor is not paying his debts as they become due. Where a debtor has less than 12 creditors, any single creditor who meets the dollar amount requirement may file an involuntary petition for bankruptcy against the debtor. Where a debtor has twelve or more creditors, an involuntary petition for bankruptcy against a debtor must be signed by at least three creditors who in aggregate meet the dollar amount total. An involuntary petition for bankruptcy may also be filed against any debtor where a state court receiver has been appointed.

Order for Relief.   Where a debtor has filed a voluntary petition, or where a debtor does not contest an involuntary petition, the Bankruptcy Court will enter an *order for relief* against the debtor. If a debtor contests an involuntary petition, the Bankruptcy Court will hold a trial to determine whether an order for relief should be granted against the debtor. In most proceedings, the Bankruptcy Court will issue an order for relief and accept the case for further bankruptcy proceedings. If the Bankruptcy Court refuses to issue an order for relief, the bankruptcy proceeding is terminated. A denial of an order for relief can be appealed to the appropriate federal District Court.

Once a bankruptcy petition is filed, the debtor must file a list of creditors, a schedule of assets and liabilities, and a statement of financial affairs with the Bankruptcy Court. Creditors and other interested parties may obtain a copy of the information filed with the court by the debtor. The debtor must also turn over his records to the bankruptcy trustee, if the court has named a trustee, and cooperate with the court and trustee in all respects regarding surrendering the debtor's property to the trustee.

First Meeting of the Creditors.   Within a reasonable time after the Bankruptcy Court grants an order for relief against a debtor, the court will set a date and time for the first meeting of the creditors. At this meeting, which is held at the Bankruptcy Court, or at the office of the debtor's attorney, or at some other convenient location, the debtor must appear and submit to questioning by the creditors under oath. Questions usually concern the debtor's assets, liabilities, and financial condition, and are aimed at trying to discern if the debtor has concealed any property, or has fraudulently disposed of property prior to the filing of the petition for bankruptcy.

The Creditors' Committee.   In a Chapter 7 liquidation proceeding, the creditors generally elect a *creditors' committee* at the first meeting of creditors, and may also elect a trustee to replace the court-appointed trustee. The responsibility of the creditor's committee is to represent the interests of the creditors in the bankruptcy proceeding. In a Chapter 11 reorganization proceeding, the bankruptcy court usually appoints a committee of unsecured creditors, which generally is composed of the creditors who hold the seven largest claims against the debtor. In addition, the court usually appoints other committees of creditors and equity holders in order to assure adequate representation of all interests in the bankrupt debtor's estate.

With the court's approval, committees may employ attorneys, accountants, and other representatives or agents to assist and perform services to aid the committee. Committees may investigate the debtor's affairs, participate in the formulation of a plan of reorganization, and consult and participate in the administration of the case and the debtor's estate.

Appointment of a Trustee.   Where an order for relief is issued, the court may either (1) permit the debtor to control his own assets and operate any businesses involved in the bankruptcy or (2) appoint a *trustee* to take over the property of the debtor and to operate any businesses of the debtor. In order to appoint a trustee, the Bankruptcy Court must find "cause," such as a showing of fraud, dishonesty, gross mismanagement, or incompetence of the debtor, or that it would be in the "best interests" of the creditors or equity holders.

A bankruptcy trustee is generally a private party, often an attorney, whom the Bankruptcy Court finds suitable for the position. The parties often recommend a person to serve as the bankruptcy trustee. The trustee receives payment for his or her services from the bankruptcy estate. The trustee must generally file, within five days of his appointment, a *bond* in an amount determined by the Bankruptcy Court, which assures the careful and faithful performance of the official duties required of a bankruptcy trustee.

Once appointed by the court, a bankruptcy trustee becomes the legal representative of the bankrupt party's estate. Generally, the duties of a bankruptcy trustee are:

1. to take immediate possession of the property and businesses of the debtor
2. to employ disinterested professionals (attorneys, accountants, auctioneers, appraisers)
3. to arrange for appraisals of the debtor's estate
4. to separate secured and unsecured property
5. to set aside items of property that the debtor is permitted to keep under applicable state or federal law
6. to investigate the financial condition of the debtor
7. to provide reports to the bankruptcy court and other parties of interest
8. to examine proof of claims filed against the debtor
9. to initiate and maintain lawsuits on behalf of the debtor
10. to defend lawsuits filed against the debtor or the debtor's estate
11. to deposit or invest the assets of the estate in bankruptcy prudently so as to yield the maximum reasonable net return.

Further duties of a bankruptcy trustee in a Chapter 11 reorganization proceeding are:

12. to use, sell, and lease property of the estate in bankruptcy
13. operate any businesses of the estate in bankruptcy
14. to assume or reject any executory contracts or unexpired leases of the debtor
15. to determine the desirability of continuing the debtor's businesses
16. to prepare and file a plan of reorganization, or file a report as to why no plan of reorganization is being filed.

If the Bankruptcy Court does not appoint a trustee, and the debtor remains in possession of the estate in bankruptcy, the debtor possesses the same rights, duties, and powers as would be accorded a bankruptcy trustee. If the Bankruptcy Court does appoint a trustee, it may terminate such appointment at any time during the bankruptcy proceeding and restore the possession and management of the estate to the debtor.

The bankruptcy trustee must keep accurate records of all money and property he receives or expends during the administration of the estate in bankruptcy. The trustee must prepare a final report and accounting of his administration of the estate in bankruptcy when the final meeting of creditors is held.

Automatic Stay.   The filing of bankruptcy brings all the affairs of the debtor under the authority of the Bankruptcy Court. An order for relief acts as an automatic *stay* on all other legal actions against the debtor, that is, these actions cannot be further pursued against the debtor except as permitted by the Bankruptcy Court pursuant to bankruptcy law. In this exerpt from *In Re Alyucian Interstate Corp.*, 12 B.R. 803 (1981) the court discusses the purpose of the automatic stay provision in bankruptcy proceedings.

The automatic stay . . . is designed "to prevent a chaotic and uncontrolled scramble for the debtor's assets in a variety of uncoordinated proceedings in different courts." It grants a "breathing spell" for debtors to regroup. It shields creditors from one another by replacing "race" and other preferential systems of debt collection with a more equitable and orderly distribution of assets. It encourages rehabilitation: debtors may seek its asylum while recovery is possible rather than coasting to the point of no return; creditors, realizing that foreclosure is useless, may rechannel energies toward more therapeutic ends.

The following actions are generally *stayed* by bankruptcy:

1. continuing or beginning other judicial actions against the debtor
2. attempts to enforce legal judgments previously obtained against the debtor
3. legal actions to enforce, perfect, or create liens against the debtor's property
4. legal actions to obtain possession of the debtor's property (The automatic stay of legal actions applies to both secured and unsecured creditor actions.)
5. attempts to "set off" debts owed by the creditor to the debtor against the claims of the creditor in bankruptcy.

Often, bankruptcy proceedings may take a long time, up to several years for larger debtors. A secured creditor may wish to have the collateral for a secured interest released from the automatic stay of bankruptcy. A secured creditor may petition the Bankruptcy Court to release the secured property from the bankruptcy. Such petitions are often granted where the release of the property will not jeopardize the claims of other creditors. Also, if a secured creditor proves that his secured property is not afforded adequate protection under bankruptcy (e.g., the property will decrease in value during bankruptcy), the court can also order the release of the secured property. In the alternative, the Bankruptcy Court can order that periodic payments be made to the secured creditor, or grant a replacement lien or increase the lien of the secured creditor.

Proof of Claims.   The Bankruptcy Reform Act defines a "creditor" as any entity or individual that has a *claim* against the debtor that was incurred prior to the granting of an order for relief by the Bankruptcy Court. A *claim* is defined as a "right to payment, whether or not such right is reduced to judgment, liquidated or unliquidated, fixed, contingent, matured, unmatured, disputed, undisputed, legal, equitable, secured, or unsecured."

Generally, if a creditor wishes to participate in the bankruptcy proceedings, and ultimately in the bankruptcy estate, he must file a *proof of claim* with the Bankruptcy Court. The proof of claim is usually filed on a form provided by the Bankruptcy Court, and states the amount of the creditor's claim against the debtor. The proof of claim must be filed within six months of the first meeting of the creditors. If a creditor fails to file a proof of claim, the debtor or bankruptcy trustee may file a proof of claim on behalf of the creditor. If a proof of claim is filed late, the claim is not accorded the same priority as timely filed claims.

All *unsecured* creditors must file a proof of claim with the Bankruptcy Court. A *secured* creditor is not required to file a proof of claim. The security interest in the collateral property protects the interest of a secured creditor without a proof of claim. However, if a secured claim *exceeds* the value of the collateral, the secured creditor must file a proof of claim for the difference if it wants to become an unsecured creditor for the amount by which the claim exceeds the value of the collateral.

Once a proof of claim has been filed, the claim must be "allowed" by the Bankruptcy Court before the creditor is permitted to participate in the bankruptcy proceeding. A creditor claim that is properly filed is allowed if no "party in interest" (such as a bankruptcy trustee or other creditor) objects. If an objection to a claim is raised, the bankruptcy court holds a hearing on the objection to determine the validity and amount of the claim. If the bankruptcy trustee objects, it is usually in order to:

1. assert a defense that the debtor had against the creditor (e.g., fraud, duress, breach of warranty)
2. assert that monies owed by the creditor to the debtor be "offset" against the creditor's claim
3. assert that the bill for services of the bankruptcy trustee, attorneys, or insiders is in excess of the "reasonable value" of such services.

THE BANKRUPTCY ESTATE

The *bankruptcy estate* subject to creditors' claims is composed of all nonexempt legal and equitable interests of the debtor in tangible, real, and intangible property at the time that the bankruptcy petition is filed. The bankruptcy estate also includes any rent, dividends, interest, or other income generated during the bankruptcy proceeding from the property contained in the bankruptcy estate.

The Bankruptcy Reform Act of 1978 also provides that the bankruptcy estate includes any property that the debtor acquires by devise, bequest, inheritance, or as the beneficiary of a life insurance policy within 180 days from the date of the filing of the petition for bankruptcy.

In *U.S. v. Whiting Pools, Inc.*, 103 S.Ct. 2309 (1983), the Supreme Court held that the bankruptcy estate of a debtor in a reorganization proceeding included property which had been previously seized pursuant to a tax lien. This excerpt from that case explained the purpose for including such property within an estate in bankruptcy:

In proceedings under the reorganization provisions of the Bankruptcy Code, a troubled enterprise may be restructured to enable it to operate successfully in the future.

Until the business can be reorganized pursuant to a plan under 11, the trustee or debtor-in-possession is authorized to manage the property of the estate and to continue the operation of the business. By permitting reorganization, Congress anticipated that the business would continue to provide jobs, to satisfy creditors' claims, and to produce a return for its owners. Congress presumed that the assets of the debtor would be more valuable if used in a rehabilitated business than if "sold for scrap." The reorganization effort would have small chance of success, however, if property essential to running the business were excluded from the estate. Thus, to facilitate the rehabilitation of the debtor's business, all the debtor's property must be included in the reorganization estate.

This authorization extends even to property of the estate in which a creditor has a secured interest. Although Congress might have safeguarded the interests of secured creditors outright by excluding from the estate any property subject to a secured interest, it chose instead to include such property in the estate and to provide secured creditors with "adequate protection" for their interests. At the secured creditor's insistence, the bankruptcy court must place such limits or conditions on the trustee's power to sell, use, or lease property as are necessary to protect the creditor. The creditor with a secured interest in property included in the estate must look to this provision for protection, rather than to the nonbankruptcy remedy of possession.

Both the congressional goal of encouraging reorganizations and Congress' choice of methods to protect secured creditors suggest that Congress intended a broad range of property to be included in the estate. . . . We see no reason why a different result should obtain when the IRS is the creditor.

Exempt Property.   Based on the concept of providing a debtor with a "fresh start," and on the belief that a debtor should not be left destitute after a bankruptcy proceeding, federal bankruptcy law provides that certain property of the debtor should be *exempt* from the bankruptcy estate and not be subject to satisfying the claims of creditors. The Bankruptcy Reform Act gives the debtor the option of choosing between two alternative exemption provisions: (1) the federal exemptions as specified in Section 522 of the Act or (2) the exemptions provided by state law, if any.

The exemptions permitted under state law vary from state to state. Most states provide somewhat greater exemptions than federal law permits; e.g., California law allows a married couple to exempt up to $45,000 equity in a primary residence. States with extremely liberal bankruptcy exemptions are known as "debtor's havens." The 1978 Bankruptcy Reform Act provides that states may enact statutes which require bankrupt debtors to take state law exemptions rather than federal bankruptcy exemptions.

The following property is exempt from the bankruptcy estate under *federal* bankruptcy law:

1. up to $7,500 of equity in real and personal property used by the debtor or dependents of the debtor as a primary residence
2. up to $1,200 of equity in one motor vehicle
3. the debtor's interest in household furnishings, goods, wearing apparel, appliances, books, animals, crops, or musical instruments that are held primarily for personal, family, or household use of the debtor or the dependents of the debtor, not to exceed $200 in value as to any one item
4. up to $500 in jewelry held primarily for personal use

5. up to $400 in value of any item or items of property that the debtor chooses
6. up to $750 in implements, professional books, or tools of the debtor's trade
7. life insurance contracts, other than credit life insurance
8. professionally prescribed health aids
9. social security, veterans' benefits, disability benefits, alimony, and unemployment compensation
10. payments from pension, profit sharing, and annuity plans
11. wrongful death awards, personal injury awards, and payments from victim compensation funds.

The Bankruptcy Reform Act further provides that a debtor may *void* certain liens which are attached to exempt property. For example, a bankrupt debtor may void security interests and judicial liens that apply or have been levied against:

1. implements, professional books, and tools of trade
2. professionally prescribed health aids
3. household furnishings, goods, wearing apparel, appliances, books, animals, crops, musical instruments, or jewelry that are held primarily for the personal, family, or household use of the debtor or the dependents of the debtor.

The Bankruptcy Reform Act also permits a bankrupt debtor to *redeem* from the estate in bankruptcy other exempt property by paying any secured creditor a dollar amount equal to the value of his collateral in the property.

ILLEGAL TRANSFERS AND PAYMENTS

A debtor usually has substantial notice that he is headed toward bankruptcy. Often, a debtor attempts to transfer some of his property into "friendly" hands or to pay "preferred" creditors prior to declaring bankruptcy. By this means, the bankruptcy estate, which will be used to partially pay off the claims of creditors, is reduced. The Bankruptcy Reform Act of 1978 makes four types of payments and transfers of property *prior* to declaring bankruptcy *voidable* by the bankruptcy trustee:

1. payments or transfers of property to "insiders"
2. transfers of property to *defraud* creditors
3. *preferential* payments to some creditors
4. grants of *preferential* liens to some creditors.

Preferential Transfers to "Insiders."   Often, prior to filing for bankruptcy, a debtor may try to transfer property to "insiders" for safekeeping, out of the reach of the bankruptcy court. Under the Bankruptcy Reform Act, an "insider" is considered to be any relative, partner, officer of a related corporation, or any other related party of the debtor. Where it is shown that the insider had knowledge of the debtor's insolvency at the time of the payment or transfer, or that the insider had reasonable grounds to believe the debtor was insolvent, the bankruptcy trustee can void any such transfer or payment made between *90 days* and *one year* of the filing of a petition in bankruptcy. In this exerpt from *Matter of Montanino*, 15 B.R. 307 (1981), the court stated the necessary elements for a trustee to *void* a transfer made by a debtor to an "insider" prior to filing for bankruptcy.

Section 547(b) of the Bankruptcy Code enumerates the five necessary elements of an action to void a transfer made to an "insider." The transfer is made (1) to or for the benefit of a creditor, (2) on account of an antecedent debt owed by the debtor before the transfer was made, (3) the transfer was made between ninety (90) days and one (1) year before the date of the filing of the petition in bankruptcy, (4) was made while the debtor was insolvent and the creditor had reasonable cause to believe that the debtor was insolvent at the time of the transfer, and (5) the transfer enabled the creditor to receive payment of a greater percentage of his claim than he would have under the distributive provisions of Chapter 7 if the transfer had not been made.

Transfers of Property to Defraud Creditors.   Any *transfer* of property (i.e., deeding of property) by a debtor to another between *90 days* and *one year* of the filing of a petition for bankruptcy that is made with the intent to "hinder, delay, or defraud" creditors is voidable by the bankruptcy trustee. It is the *debtor's* intent, not the intent or knowledge of the recipient of the transfer, that is crucial in applying this rule. This intent may be inferred from the facts and circumstances surrounding the transfer of the property (e.g., transfer of property for substantially less than fair market value).

Where an unlawful transfer to an insider or a transfer by the debtor to delay, hinder, or defraud creditors is found, the Bankruptcy Court can refuse to discharge the unpaid debts of the debtor, and the debtor is subject to criminal prosecution.

Preferential Payments.   The Bankruptcy Reform Act *presumes* that all debtors have been insolvent during the *90 days* immediately preceding the filing of a petition for bankruptcy. Any "preferential" payments made to favorable creditors during this 90-day period are *voidable* by the bankruptcy trustee. A "preferential payment" is *any* payment by the debtor to a creditor within the 90-day period that pays that creditor a greater percentage of a pre-existing debt than the percentage that other creditors would receive on their debts from the bankruptcy estate.

For example, if a debtor owed three creditors each $10,000, and the debtor paid Creditor A $5,000 seventy days prior to declaring bankruptcy, and Creditors B and C would only receive $1,000 from the bankruptcy estate, Creditor A has received a "preferential payment" that may be voided by the bankruptcy trustee. The 90-day "preferential payment" rule is an *objective* test, that is, it is immaterial whether or not Creditor A had knowledge of the debtor's insolvency at the time he received the preferential payment.

Preferential Liens.   When a debtor is going bankrupt, he may try to place certain creditors in positions of *priority* prior to the bankruptcy proceeding so that these preferential creditors will receive more from the bankruptcy estate than they would receive without the preferred status. An unsecured creditor is placed in a preferred status in bankruptcy when the debtor grants the unsecured creditor a *secured* position in some property owned by the debtor. Under bankruptcy law, secured creditors have an exclusive claim to the collateral property up to the amount of the secured interest.

The Bankruptcy Reform Act provides that any lien or security interest placed on property to secure a *pre-existing* debt of the debtor within 90 days immediately preceding the filing of a petition for bankruptcy is a "preferential lien" that is *voidable* by the bankruptcy trustee. The preferential lien rule is also an objective test, and does not require that the preferred creditor have knowledge of the insolvency of the debtor at the time that the preferential lien is given. The preferential lien rule applies to both unsecured creditors whose pre-existing unsecured debt has been converted to a secured interest, and to secured creditors whose interest has been enlarged prior to bankruptcy.

Current Business Transactions.   Where a debtor is permitted to operate a business during the bankruptcy proceeding, the debtor may enter into new contracts, usually with the permission of the bankruptcy court, without being subject to the "preferential treatment" rule with regard to them. For example, if a debtor needed a new delivery truck during the bankruptcy proceeding, he could purchase the truck, either for cash or on credit, and the transaction would not be voidable as either a preferential payment or a preferential lien. A debtor who is operating a business that is subject to a bankruptcy proceeding can also make regular payments on account in the "ordinary course of business" if the accounts payable are paid within 45 days after they are incurred.

In *Barash v. Public Finance Corporation* the court held that certain payments made by the debtor on installment sales within 90 days of filing a petition for bankruptcy were "preferential" payments that were validly *voided* by the bankruptcy trustee.

VOIDABLE PREFERENCES

BARRY M. BARASH, CHAPTER 7 TRUSTEE FOR TIM R. DENNIS AND DAWN M. DENNIS v. PUBLIC FINANCE CORPORATION

658 F.2d 504 (1981)
UNITED STATES COURT OF APPEALS, SEVENTH CIRCUIT

Jameson, District Judge.

This consolidated appeal involves eight bankruptcy cases in which Barry M. Barash, Chapter 7 Trustee for the debtors, sought recovery of alleged preferential transfers. In each case the Bankruptcy Court found in favor of the defendant creditor. The cases were consolidated on appeal to the District Court, which affirmed the decision of the Bankruptcy Court in all cases.

ELEMENTS OF A PREFERENCE

The Bankruptcy Code prescribes five requirements for a preference, all of which must be met for the Trustee to avoid a transfer. A transfer is preferential if it is (1) to a creditor, (2) on account of a pre-existing debt, (3) made while the debtor is insolvent, (4) made on or within 90 days before the date of filing the petition, . . . and which (5) enables the creditor to receive more than he would receive if the estate were liquidated under Chapter 7. 11 U.S.C. Section 547(b).

There is no dispute that the first four elements of a preference are established in each case. The installment payments were all made by a debtor to a creditor, on a pre-existing debt, within 90 days of the bankruptcy filing. The debtors are presumed insolvent during the 90-day period, and no evidence was presented to rebut the presumption. Appellees argue, however, that they have not improved their position vis-a-vis other creditors, as required by Section 547(b). The Trustee, on the other hand, contends that the payments received within the 90-day period enabled the creditors to receive a greater proportion of their respective debts than they would if the estate were liquidated under Chapter 7.

A principal goal of the preference provisions is the assurance of equal distribution among creditors.

Section 547(b) is directed at transfers which *enable* creditors to receive more than they would have received had the estate been liquidated and the disputed transfer not been made. As long as the transfers diminish the bankrupt's estate available for distribution, creditors who are allowed to keep transfers would be enabled to receive more than their share. The creditors in the instant case must account for the payments they received during the 90 days preceding the bankruptcy filing, or they will ultimately receive a larger share of their *unsecured* claims than other unsecured creditors. Of course, they will still receive the full benefit of their collateral as to their secured claims.

NORMAL COURSE OF BUSINESS EXCEPTIONS

Because all five elements of Section 547(b) have been satisfied in each of the cases here on appeal, we must determine whether the exception urged by appellees and amicus defeats the Trustee's attempt to avoid the transfers. 11 U.S.C. Section 547(c) sets out specific exceptions to the preference rules discussed above, including the following:

> The Trustee may not avoid under this section a transfer . . . (2) to the extent that such transfer was: (A) in payment of a debt incurred in the ordinary course of business or financial affairs of the debtor and the transferee; (B) made not later than 45 days after such debt was incurred; (C) made in the ordinary course

of business or financial affairs of the debtor and the transferee; and (D) made according to ordinary business terms.

Again, without dispute, all but one of the criteria are met—the payments were made in the ordinary course of financial affairs of the debtors and the normal course of business of the creditors, on debts incurred in the normal course, and according to normal business terms. The only question concerns the second requirement—whether the payments were made within 45 days after the debts were "incurred."

Appellees and *amicus* argue that for consumer installment transactions, a new debt should be deemed incurred as each monthly payment falls due. . . . We agree with the reasoning in 4 *Collier* paragraph 547.38 that

> [t]he probably better view is that the debt is incurred whenever the debtor obtains a property interest in the consideration exchanged giving rise to the debt.

[T]he creditor's knowledge or state of mind is no longer relevant. . . . Congress eliminated this requirement in favor of the objective criteria under the new Code.

CONCLUSION

We hold that regular installment payments on consumer debts, made within 90 days preceding the filing of a bankruptcy petition, may be avoided as preferential transfers to the extent the payments are credited to unsecured claims. . . . The exception for normal transactions in 11 U.S.C. Section 547(c)(2) extends only to situations where payment is made within 45 days after the debtor first becomes legally bound to pay.

Reversed and *remanded.*

CASE QUESTIONS

1. What is an "installment sale"? In an installment sale, is the full price of the goods paid upon purchase?
2. What is a "preferential payment" under Bankruptcy law? What are the five elements required to find a preferential payment? Which element was in dispute in this case?
3. What exception to the preferential payment rule was argued by the creditors in this case? Explain.

4. When did the court find that an installment payment is "incurred"? Did the exception to the preferential payment rule apply in this case?

Policy Issue. Should all payments made by a debtor 90 days prior to filing bankruptcy be considered voidable preferential payments even though the creditors who received the payments did not have knowledge of the debtor's insolvency?

Economics Issue. What economic effect does this decision have on trade creditors?

Ethics Issue. Did the trade creditors who received payments from the debtor within 90 days of the debtor's bankruptcy act unethically in this case? Did the debtor act unethically? Does a debtor who transfers property to an "insider" within one year of declaring bankruptcy act unethically?

Social Responsibility. Does a bankruptcy trustee owe a duty of social responsibility to take *every* action possible to protect and enhance the bankruptcy estate?

LIQUIDATION (CHAPTER 7)

Chapter 7 of the Bankruptcy Reform Act of 1978 provides for the termination and *liquidation* of a business through bankruptcy. Liquidation, which is commonly referred to as "straight bankruptcy," consists of:

1. filing a petition for bankruptcy under the provisions of Chapter 7 of the Bankruptcy Reform Act
2. converting the debtor's assets to cash
3. distributing the bankruptcy cash estate to the creditors based on statutory priority of claims
4. discharging the remaining unpaid debts against the creditor.

The liquidation of a debtor under Chapter 7 can occur pursuant to a petition for either a voluntary or an involuntary bankruptcy. A petition for involuntary bankruptcy for liquidation under Chapter 7 of the Bankruptcy Reform Act *cannot* be filed against: (1) farmers, (2) ranchers, (3) municipal corporations, (4) insurance companies, (5) nonprofit organizations, (6) banking corporations, (7) savings and loan associations, or (8) credit unions.

Priority of Distribution. In a Chapter 7 liquidation proceeding, the bankruptcy estate is distributed according to the statutory priority as set forth in Section 507 of the Bankruptcy Reform Act. Generally, there are three broad classes of claims and interests that may participate in the distribution of the bankruptcy estate:

1. secured claims
2. unsecured claims
3. equity interests.

Secured Claims. Where certain properties of the debtor are subject to *secured claims,* the secured creditor has the right to receive the value of his secured interest in the collateral. If the value of the secured property is *less* than the secured interest, the secured creditor is paid an amount equal to the value of the collateral, and becomes an unsecured creditor for the difference, assuming the proper proof of claim was filed. If the value of the secured property *exceeds* the secured interest, the secured creditor is paid an amount equal to the secured interest, and the excess above that amount is available to satisfy other claims against the bankruptcy estate.

Often, bankruptcy proceedings may take a long time, up to several years for larger debtors. A secured creditor may wish to have the collateral for a secured interest released from the bankruptcy. A secured creditor may petition the bankruptcy court to release the secured property from the bankruptcy. Such petitions are often granted where the release of the property will not jeopardize the claims of other creditors. If the value of the collateral exceeds the value of the secured claim, the secured creditor will have to pay the difference to the bankruptcy court in order to have the secured property released from the bankruptcy proceeding. In the alternative, if a secured creditor proves that his secured property is not afforded adequate protection under bankruptcy (i.e., the property will decrease in value during the bankruptcy), the court can also order the release of the secured property, order that periodic payments be made to the secured creditor, grant a replacement lien, or increase the lien of the secured creditor.

Unsecured Claims.   Once the secured claims are satisfied, the Bankruptcy Reform Act provides that the *unsecured* claims against the bankruptcy estate will be satisfied based on a statutory priority of claims. The classes of unsecured claims and the priority of payment under bankruptcy law are:

1. fees and expenses of administering the bankruptcy estate, e.g., bankruptcy trustee's fees, attorney's fees
2. unsecured claims of "gap" creditors who sold goods on credit to the debtor in the "ordinary course of business" between the date of the filing of the petition for bankruptcy and the date of the appointment of a trustee or issuance of the order for relief by the Bankruptcy Court, whichever occurred first
3. unsecured claims up to $2,000 per individual for "wages, salaries, or commissions" earned within 90 days immediately preceding the filing of the petition for bankruptcy
4. claims for contributions to employee benefit plans based on services performed within 180 days immediately preceding the filing of the petition for bankruptcy
5. taxes of all types
6. other unsecured claims, such as trade creditors.

Every claim of each preceding class of claims must be paid *in full* before any claim of the next succeeding class may be paid. If a class cannot be paid in full, the claims within the class are paid *pro rata*. In practice, the unsecured creditors generally receive little, if anything, against their claims in a "straight bankruptcy" proceeding under Chapter 7.

Equity Interests.   If there is any money left over after all classes of claims have been satisfied, the excess is distributed to the debtor, if the debtor was an individual, or to the owners of the debtor (e.g., to the shareholders of a debtor corporation). *Equity* interests are paid in order of priority; for example, preferred shareholders first and common shareholders last. Liquidation *preferences* of equity issues must be honored before payments are made to equity issues that did not carry a liquidation preference.

The following outline summarizes the *priority of distribution* of the estate in bankruptcy on liquidation.

Priority of Distribution of Estate in Bankruptcy

A. Secured Claims:
   1. If the value of the secured property equals or exceeds the amount of the security interest, the claim must be paid, namely:
      a. The value of the security interest; any excess is part of the bankruptcy estate
   2. If the value of the secured property is less than the amount of the security interest, the claim must be paid, namely:
      a. the value of the secured property; the unsatisfied portion of security interest is an *unsecured* claim in the bankruptcy estate
B. Unsecured Claims:
   1. Each of the following unsecured claims must be paid in full before any succeeding claim receives anything; if a class cannot be paid in full, the claims of the members of the class must be paid *pro rata:*
      a. administrative fees and expenses (e.g., trustee's fees)
      b. "gap" creditors
      c. claims of up to $2,000 for wages, salaries, and commissions earned within 90 days of the filing of the petition for bankruptcy
      d. contributions to employee benefit plans earned within 180 days of the filing of the petition for bankruptcy
      e. taxes of all types
      f. other unsecured claims
C. Equity interests:
   1. Liquidation preferences must be honored; each of the following interests must be paid in full before any succeeding interest receives anything; if a class cannot be paid in full, the interests of the members of that class must be paid *pro rata:*
      a. preferred stock
      b. common stock

Discharge of Unpaid Debts. When the assets of the bankruptcy estate have been exhausted in meeting creditor claims, but all creditor claims have not been satisfied, the remaining claims are discharged by the Bankruptcy Court. *Discharge* means that the debtor is no longer legally responsible for the unsatisfied debts which the Bankruptcy Court has discharged. This is consistent with the goal of bankruptcy in providing debtors with a financial "fresh start." A discharge in bankruptcy also voids any outstanding judgments against the debtor, and acts as an injunction against the continuation or commencement of lawsuits to recover debts that have been discharged.

If a corporation is the debtor in a Chapter 7 liquidation proceeding, the corporation must be terminated and dissolved after the bankruptcy proceeding is completed. If the corporation wants to continue in business after bankruptcy, it should seek protection under the reorganization provisions of Chapter 11 of the Bankruptcy Reform Act.

A debtor cannot be granted a discharge in bankruptcy if it was granted such a discharge within the previous six years. The policy behind this rule is to prevent debtors from taking excessive risks on a continual basis with the hope of hitting it "big," and planning to declare bankruptcy each time they lose out.

Waiver of Discharge.   A debtor may waive his right to have a debt discharged in bankruptcy. A *waiver agreement,* which is also known as a *reaffirmation agreement,* is valid where it is entered into with a creditor prior to the Bankruptcy Court granting a discharge of the debt. A creditor may pursue payment of the debt under the terms of the waiver agreement immediately after the Bankruptcy Court enters a final order in the bankruptcy proceeding. If the debtor is an individual, the Bankruptcy Court must instruct the debtor of the consequences of entering into a waiver agreement. An individual debtor also has 30 days after the date of the waiver agreement to rescind the agreement.

Nondischargeable Debts.   Certain debts cannot be discharged in bankruptcy. The Bankruptcy Reform Act provides that the following debts are *not* dischargeable in bankruptcy:

1. taxes and fines owed to the United States or any state or local government unit
2. liability for obtaining money or property through fraud or false pretenses
3. liability for causing willful or malicious injury to a person or his property, such as by battery or trespass
4. monies due for alimony and child support
5. debts created by fraud or embezzlement by the debtor while acting in a fiduciary capacity
6. debts that the debtor did not place on the schedule of creditors which was submitted to the bankruptcy court, provided the creditor was not otherwise notified or had knowledge of the bankruptcy proceeding
7. debts that were or could have been listed in a previous bankruptcy, where the debtor was denied or waived discharge of the debt.

Before 1978, a substantial number of students declared straight bankruptcy immediately upon graduation in order to have their student loans discharged in bankruptcy. Under the Bankruptcy Reform Act of 1978, a student loan cannot be discharged in bankruptcy earlier than five years after it is "due," and then only if nondischarge would cause "undue hardship" on the debtor.

If a debt is *not* discharged in bankruptcy, the creditor may participate in the distribution of the bankruptcy estate, *and* retains the right to recover the unpaid balance at a later date from the debtor.

Acts of the Debtor that Bar Discharge. The Bankruptcy Court will *refuse* to grant a discharge of unsatisfied debts where the debtor has engaged in certain actions, including:

1. a false representation about his financial position when he obtained credit (e.g., he filed a false financial statement with the lender)
2. transfer, concealment, or removal of property from his estate with the intent to "hinder, delay, or defraud" creditors
3. falsification, destruction, or concealment of records
4. failure to obey court orders
5. failure to account for any assets
6. failure to appear at a hearing on an objection to discharge
7. failure to submit to questioning by the creditors
8. failure to answer any questions approved to be asked of the debtor by the court.

The Bankruptcy Court may revoke a discharge within one year of the granting of the discharge where it is shown that the discharge was obtained through fraud by the debtor. A request for revocation of the discharge must be made by the bankruptcy trustee or a creditor, and will be granted by the Bankruptcy Court only after proper notice and hearing.

In the following case, *In the Matter of Sam Ramos,* the Bankruptcy Court denied discharge to a debtor in a Section 7 liquidation proceeding where the debtor had made transfers of property to an "insider" within one year of the filing for bankruptcy with the intent to "hinder, delay, and defraud" creditors.

DENIAL OF DISCHARGE

IN THE MATTER OF SAM RAMOS. SEMMERLING FENCE & SUPPLY, INC. V. SAM RAMOS, D/B/A AMERICAN FENCE CO.

8 B.R. 490 (1981)
UNITED STATES BANKRUPTCY COURT, W. D. WISCONSIN

Robert D. Martin, Bankruptcy Judge.

Until he filed in bankruptcy on April 11, 1980, Ramos had since 1965 operated a fencing company as a sole proprietor. The fencing business is seasonal and involves virtually no work in December, January, February and March of each year. Although aware of his insolvency since December of 1978, Ramos operated the business through 1979. In late February, 1980, he closed all accounts of the business transferring remaining funds to his personal account. Accounts receivable of the business when it stopped active operation in December

of 1979 were collected by Ramos and applied to personal expenses rather than the payment of business obligations.

During January, 1980, Ramos drew from his business by means of checks payable to his wife an amount of $1,500. In addition, during that month he took cash from the business in the amount of $520. In February, 1980, the last month in which business accounts were maintained, he drew $2,800 from the business by checks payable to his wife and drew an additional $3,000 in checks payable to cash.

Section 727(a)(2)(A) states:

> The court shall grant the debtor a discharge, unless . . . the debtor, with intent to hinder, delay, or defraud a creditor or an officer of the estate charged with custody of property under this title, has transferred, removed, destroyed, mutilated, or concealed, or has permitted to be transferred, removed, destroyed, mutilated, or concealed . . . property of the debtor, within one year before the date of the filing of the petition.

As part of Ramos' voluntary Chapter 7 petition, filed April 11, 1980, he filed a "Statement of Financial Affairs for Debtor Engaged in Business." That statement inquires:

> Have you made any other transfer, absolute or for the purpose of security, or any other disposition which was not in the ordinary course of business during the year immediately preceding the filing of the original petition herein? (Give a description of the property, the date of the transfer or disposition, to whom transferred or how disposed of, and state whether the transferee is a relative, partner, shareholder, officer, director or insider, the consideration, if any, received for the property, and the disposition of such consideration.)

Ramos' response was "No." . . . Ramos signed the schedules next to the declaration, "I Sam Ramos certify under penalty of perjury that I (we) have read the foregoing schedules, consisting of 15 sheets, and that they are true and correct to the best of my (our) knowledge, information and belief."

Transfers of defendant's property have also been questioned. The check records clearly show transfers from his business funds to his wife within one year of the filing of the petition.

[I]n *In Re Gurney* a debtor transferred $3,800 to his wife for "household expenses" shortly before filing his petition in bankruptcy. The debtor explained that his wife was a "better person" to have the money. The court denied debtor a discharge. Included in the court's finding was

> the only apparent reason why his wife was a 'better person' to have the money than himself would seem

to be the probability that his creditors would try to reach whatever assets he had.

The inference that Ramos had actual intent to hinder, delay or defraud his creditors by the transfers of business funds to his wife, may be drawn in the instant case.

Upon the foregoing which constitutes my findings of fact and conclusions of law in this case, it is hereby *ordered* that the *discharge* of the debts of Sam Ramos be and hereby is *denied*.

CASE QUESTIONS

1. Who was the debtor?
   a. Mr. Ramos, personally
   b. Mr. Ramos, d/b/a
2. What type of *petition* for bankruptcy was filed in this case? By whom? What does Chapter 7 *liquidation* provide? Explain.
3. What does *discharge* in bankruptcy mean? Is the debtor still obligated to pay his discharged debts after bankruptcy?
4. What does Section 727(a)(2)(A) of the Bankruptcy Code provide? Explain.
5. Did the court find that Ramos intended to "hinder, delay, or defraud" his creditors? What remedy did the court order? Explain.

Policy Issue. Should unpaid debts be totally discharged in bankruptcy? Or should a debtor only be granted an extension of time to meet his obligations?

Economics Issue. Why was Mrs. Ramos a "better person" to have Mr. Ramos's property (at least in Mr. Ramos's eyes)?

Ethics Issue. Did Mr. Ramos act ethically in this case?

Social Responsibility. When filing for bankruptcy, does a debtor owe a duty of social responsibility to disclose all of his assets to the Bankruptcy Court and to his creditors?

REORGANIZATION (CHAPTER 11)

In many situations, it may be in the best interests of the creditors and the debtor to have the debtor *reorganized* as a going concern, rather than liquidated. Chapter 11 of the Bankruptcy Reform Act of 1978 provides the authority and procedures for reorganizing the financial affairs of the debtor under the supervision of the Bankruptcy Court. The primary goal of Chapter 11 is to reorganize the debtor so that it may continue in business without the crushing debt that caused the debtor to go into bankruptcy, while also considering the rights of the creditors and equity holders of the debtor. Creditors have "claims" and equity holders have "interests" in a debtor who is in bankruptcy reorganization.

A petition for reorganization of a debtor under Chapter 11 may be filed either voluntarily by the debtor or involuntarily by its creditors. Chapter 11 reorganization is only available to *businesses,* which may include sole proprietorships, partnerships, limited partnerships, corporations and other business entities. Individuals not operating as a business cannot file for reorganization under Chapter 11. Banks, savings and loan associations, stockbrokers, and commodities brokers cannot be reorganized under Chapter 11.

Plan of Reorganization.   In order to eventually reach a reorganization solution of the debtor under Chapter 11, a *plan of reorganization* must be approved by the bankruptcy court. A plan of reorganization under Chapter 11 contemplates a compromise solution whereby each creditor and equity holder class gives up some rights in order to effectuate the reorganization of the debtor. Generally, creditors receive either a reduced creditor claim or an equity ownership interest in the reorganized debtor. Common and preferred shareholders' interests are often eliminated in reorganization; if they are allowed to participate in the reorganization, shareholders' interests in the reorganized debtor are usually substantially reduced. A plan of reorganization sets forth:

1. the proposal of how the debtor will be reorganized
2. the new capital and debt structure of the debtor
3. the rights that each class of claims or class of equity holders will receive in the reorganized debtor and
4. other pertinent information regarding the proposed reorganization.

The debtor has an *exclusive* right to file a plan of reorganization during the 120 days immediately following the issuance of an order for relief by the Bankruptcy Court. The debtor also has a right to file a plan of reorganization at any time during the bankruptcy proceeding. Any "party in interest," which includes the bankruptcy trustee, a creditor's committee, indenture trustee, or equity holder's committee, may file a plan of reorganization if:

1. the debtor has not filed a plan within the 120-day exclusive period
2. the debtor has filed a plan during the 120-day exclusive period, but the plan has not been accepted by the required creditors within a 180-day period from the date of the issuance of the order for relief
3. at any time after the Bankruptcy Court has appointed a bankruptcy trustee, even if this is during the 120-day exclusive period.
4. Where a trustee has not been appointed, a creditor or shareholder can seek approval of the Bankruptcy Court to file a plan of reorganization if

it can be shown that the debtor is acting fraudulently, is unduly resisting reorganization, or for any other "cause."

Each class of creditors (secured creditors, bondholders, trade creditors) and each class of equity holders (preferred stockholders, common stockholders) may submit a *separate* plan of reorganization of the debtor for consideration by the Bankruptcy Court.

Disclosure Statements.   Any party in interest who wishes to submit a plan of reorganization to the creditors and equity holders of the debtor must first submit a written *disclosure statement* to the Bankruptcy Court for approval. A disclosure statement generally contains information about the financial position of the debtor, a summary of the proposed plan of reorganization, and whatever other information the court deems relevant for an "investor typical of the holders of claims or interests" of each class to make an informed judgment about the proposed plan of reorganization.

After appropriate notice and hearing, the court will approve a disclosure statement that contains "adequate information." "Adequacy of information" in a disclosure statement is determined on a case-by-case basis. In approving a disclosure statement, the Bankruptcy Court considers the need for investor protection, the speed required for the reorganization of the debtor, and the cost of preparation of the materials. The Bankruptcy Court may approve a disclosure statement without a formal valuation of the debtor or an appraisal of the debtor's assets. The approved disclosure statement, and either the plan of reorganization or a summary of the plan, must be transmitted to creditors and equity holders before or at the time that a party in interest seeks approval of the plan.

The Securities and Exchange Commission.   Originally, the Securities and Exchange Commission (SEC) was empowered to propose its own plans of reorganization for debtors in Chapter 11 proceedings. The SEC took an active role in many early reorganization proceedings under the guise of protecting creditors' and equity holders' interests. The SEC position often, however, was opposed to the plan that the creditors and equity holders had approved.

Under the Bankruptcy Reform Act of 1978, the powers of the SEC in the bankruptcy area has been curtailed. The SEC may appear in a reorganization proceeding under Chapter 11 and be heard on any issue. However, the SEC can no longer take an appeal from any judgment, order, or decree entered by the court in a reorganization case. The current policy of the SEC, which was announced in 1983, is not to become involved in a reorganization bankruptcy proceeding except in extreme cases. State Corporation Commissioners have the same rights as the SEC in reorganization proceedings.

Confirmation of a Plan of Reorganization.   The bankruptcy court is *required* to confirm a plan of reorganization that meets all of the requirements of Section 1129(a) of the Bankruptcy Reform Act. In order to comply with Section 1129(a), the following four tests must be met:

1. the "best interests" test
2. the nonimpairment test

3. the "acceptance by at least one class of claims" test
4. the "feasibility" test

Test 1: The Best Interests Test.   The bankruptcy court cannot confirm a plan of reorganization *unless* it is in the "best interests" of *each* class of claims (creditors) and *each* class of interests (equity holders). A plan of reorganization is considered in the "best interests" of a class of claims or interests if *all* (100 percent) of the members of the class accept it.

In the alternative, if some members of a class of claims or interest reject a plan of reorganization, the plan is still considered to be in the "best interests" of the class if each holder of that class receives under the plan property of greater value than the property which he would have received had the debtor been *liquidated*. Thus, whenever a claim holder or equity holder would receive *as much* in reorganization under Chapter 11 as he would under Chapter 7 liquidation, the "best interests" test for reorganization has been met, because financially the holder would be no worse off under reorganization than he would be under liquidation. A class that receives less in reorganization than it would in liquidation can still meet the "best interests" test if it votes unanimously for the plan of reorganization.

Test 2: The Nonimpairment Test.   The bankruptcy court cannot confirm a plan of reorganization unless *each* class of claims (creditors) and *each* class of interests (equity holders) either "accepts" the plan as specified in the Act, *or* is "nonimpaired" by the plan.

A class of *claims* is considered to have accepted a plan of reorganization where at least one half of the number of claims within the class *and* at least two thirds of the dollar amount of the class accept the plan. The calculation of the number of claims is determined as half the number of claims that actually vote. The calculation of the dollar amount is determined as a percentage of the total dollar amount of all outstanding claims in the relevant class.

A class of *interests* is considered to have accepted a plan of reorganization where the holders of at least two thirds of the dollar amount of the interests within the class accept the plan. The calculation of the dollar amount is determined as a percentage of the total dollar amount of all outstanding interests in the relevant class.

In the alternative, if the requisite vote of class of claims or interests is not received, the plan of reorganization is considered to still meet the "nonimpairment" test as to this class if the class is not *impaired* by the plan of reorganization. "Impairment" generally means that the members of a class would receive something less than they otherwise would be entitled to receive if the debtor were not reorganized. Section 1124 of the Bankruptcy Reform Act of 1978 provides that a class of claims or interests is "nonimpaired":

1. where the plan of reorganization does *not* alter the legal, equitable, or contractual rights of the holders of the claim or interest (for example, a secured creditor's security interest in a piece of property of the debtor is allowed to remain in place on reorganization)
2. where the plan or reorganization reinstates a claim or interest (that is, where the debtor is in default in payments to a creditor, or the debtor is

in arrears on interest payments to preferred shareholders, the Bankruptcy Court orders that the payments be brought current and the claim or interest reinstated)
3. where the debtor *pays off* the claim or interest, which then does not become part of the reorganized estate, by paying the greater of:
   a. the fixed *liquidation* preference, if any is provided
   b. the fixed *redemption* price, if any is provided
   c. the *discounted present* value of the holder's claim or interest in the debtor as of the effective date of the plan of reorganization.

If the "pay-off" method is selected to meet the nonimpairment test, the pay-off may be substantially less than the original amount of the claim or interest. In order to meet the "best interests" test, however, this amount cannot be less than the amount the creditor or interest holder would have received in liquidation. The payment may be made in cash or property, but *not* in the securities of the debtor or in the securities of an affiliate or successor in interest of the debtor.

Test 3: Acceptance by at Least One Class of Claims.   In order for the Bankruptcy Court to confirm a plan of reorganization, at least *one* class of *claims* (creditors) must accept the plan. That is, at least half the number of claim holders of one voting class, which represents at least two thirds of the dollar amount of the outstanding claim, vote to accept the plan of reorganization. This test is not met if only a class of equity interests votes to accept the plan.

Test 4: The Feasibility Test.   The preceding tests have focused on the rights of claim holders and interest holders in a plan of reorganization. However, in order for a Bankruptcy Court to approve a plan of reorganization, the plan must make economic and financial sense for the successful operation of the reorganized debtor in the *future.* Thus, the plan of reorganization must be found to be "feasible" in order to be approved by the bankruptcy court.

In order to determine the "feasibility" of a plan of reorganization, the Bankruptcy Court must estimate the future earnings of the reorganized debtor and determine if interest expenses, administrative expenses, operating costs, and other expenses of the reorganized debtor can be met. The Bankruptcy Court must also consider whether or not the reorganized debtor is likely to file for bankruptcy protection again in the near future, or whether it can be a viable "going concern" with a good probability of surviving under its proposed reorganized capital and debt structure. There are no set objective tests for determining whether a plan of reorganization is feasible. The Bankruptcy Court must consider all relevant factors on a case-by-case basis.

The following outline summarizes the tests necessary to be met in order for a plan of reorganization to be confirmed by the Bankruptcy Court under Section 1129(a) of the Bankruptcy Reform Act of 1978.

Confirmation of a Plan of Reorganization [Section 1129(a)]

I. "Best Interests" Test:
   A. For *each* class of *claims;* for *each* class of *interests:*

1. all of the members of that class (100 percent) vote to accept the plan, *or*
2. the members of that class would receive property under the plan which exceeds what they would receive if the debtor were *liquidated.*

II. *Nonimpairment* Test:
  A. For *each* class of *claims:*
    1. half the *number* of claims that vote and two thirds the dollar amount of the claim outstanding vote to accept the plan, *or*
    2. (see 2 below)
  B. For *each* class of *interests:*
    1. two thirds of the dollar amount of the interest vote to accept the plan, *or*
    2. the class is *nonimpaired,* where:
      a. its legal, equitable or contractual rights are *not* altered, *or*
      b. the plan reinstates the claim or interest, *or*
      c. the debtor *pays off* the claim or interest by paying the *greater* of:
        i. its fixed *liquidation* preference
        ii. its fixed *redemption* preference
        iii. the *discounted present value* of the claim or interest

III. Acceptance by at Least One Class of Claims Test:
  A. At least one class of *claims* accepts the plan by meeting the prior test; if only an equity class meets the prior test, than *this* test is not met.

IV. Feasibility Test:
  A. The debtor will have a good probability of surviving and operating successfully in the future under the proposed plan.

If all of the above four tests are met, the Bankruptcy Court *must* confirm the plan of reorganization under Section 1129(a) of the Bankruptcy Reform Act. The court, however, can only confirm one plan. If more than one plan of reorganization meets the appropriate requirements of Section 1129(a), the court may consider the preferences of the creditors and equity holders in determining which plan of reorganization to confirm. The court may also consider the interests of employees, suppliers, and others in choosing between qualifying plans.

The Bankruptcy Reform Act of 1978 contains a "safe harbor" rule which provides that where a reorganized debtor issues securities in "good faith" pursuant to a plan of reorganization, the issuance is exempt from the antifraud provisions of federal and state securities laws. However, the Bankruptcy Court can deny the confirmation of an otherwise qualified plan of reorganization where it is shown that the primary purpose of the plan is to avoid registration of securities under securities laws—for example, where a debtor files for bankruptcy reorganization in an attempt to effectuate an unregistered recapitalization issuance of securities.

In this case, *In re Weathersfield Farms, Inc.,* the Bankruptcy Court refused to confirm a plan of reorganization, finding that the plan was not "feasible."

"FEASIBILITY" TEST

IN RE WEATHERSFIELD FARMS, INC.

14 B.R. 572 (1981)
UNITED STATES BANKRUPTCY COURT, D. VERMONT

Charles J. Marro, Bankruptcy Judge.

The hearing on confirmation of the plan of the Debtor, filed December 20, 1980 with the addition filed February 14, 1981, and the objection of First Inter-State Bank to confirmation came on for hearing on March 4, 1981.

From the testimony adduced at said hearing it appears that the Debtor's long-range plan is the construction and operation of one or all self-contained communities for emotionally and socially maladjusted persons, modelled after the Spring Farm Ranch at Cuttingsville, Vermont, an apparently successful operation. The proposed plan is supposed to operate in two stages, the first of which would be the generation of necessary cash from the cutting of timber from approximately 30 acres of land out of a total of approximately 250 owned by the Debtor. The testimony of Raymond Phelan, President of the Debtor, indicates that a minimum of $5,000.00 and a maximum of $10,800.00 would result from this operation.

The plan contemplates the execution and delivery by the Debtor to the First Inter-State Bank of a first mortgage in the amount of $54,718.80 on all of the Debtor's property in Thetford, Vermont with interest at 9½ percent amortized over 25 years with the Debtor to pay interest only for the first 7 years. . . . The Bank, in this proceeding, has vigorously opposed the plan submitted by the Debtor.

The Debtor has no cash and its only asset is the 250 acres of land in Thetford, Vermont.

The Debtor faces additional and very serious problems if it should reach the second phase of the plan. It would have to comply with the requirements of Act 250, which relates to conditions for the protection of the environment which must be satisfied before the project is approved. Roads would have to be built as an access to the property and this would be very expensive since the terrain is very steep and ledgy. All and all, the cost of satisfying the requirements of Act 250 and constructing the necessary facility would be almost prohibitive in comparison with the amount of cash that the Debtor could raise from any project in its initial stage.

This Court feels that the purpose of the Debtor, as exhibited through its president, is praiseworthy and noble. However, from the testimony presented the conclusion is inevitable that the plan is visionary, impractical, and speculative. It is not feasible.

In accordance with the foregoing, *it is ordered* that confirmation of the plan is *denied*.

CASE QUESTION

1. Who owned the real estate in this case? Was it subject to a mortgage?
2. What does Chapter 11 of the Bankruptcy Reform Act provide? Explain.
3. Did the creditor accept or reject the plan of reorganization?

Policy Issue. Should a debtor be allowed to reorganize its affairs under bankruptcy law?

Economics Issue. Do you think the debtor's plan of reorganization in this case was "feasible"? Why or why not?

Ethics Issue. Did the debtor act ethically in this case? Did it matter to the court that the debtor's plan was "praiseworthy and noble"?

Social Responsibility. Does a creditor owe a duty of social responsibility to extend further loans to overextended debtors? Or should it foreclose and take the property?

"Cram-down." Where any one class does not accept a proposed plan of reorganization and that class would be *impaired* by the plan, the Bankruptcy Court cannot confirm the plan under Section 1129(a) of the Bankruptcy Court. However, the Bankruptcy Reform Act provides that the plan may be *"crammed down the throats"* of the dissenting class if the provisions of Section 1129(b) of the Act are met. The purpose of the "cram-down" provision of Section 1129(b) is to take away the leverage of any individual class being in a position to prevent an otherwise economically fair and sound plan of reorganization.

In order for the bankruptcy court to "cram down" a plan of reorganization on a dissenting-impaired class of claims or interests, the court must find that the plan: (1) is "fair and equitable" to the class; *and also* (2) "does not discriminate unfairly" among members of the class.

"Fair and Equitable." A plan of reorganization can be "crammed down" if it is "fair and equitable" to the dissenting-impaired class. The determination of "fair and equitable" depends on whether the dissenting-impaired class is a class of (1) secured claims, (2) unsecured claims, or (3) equity interests.

Secured Class of Creditors. A plan of reorganization is "fair and equitable" to a dissenting-impaired class of *secured* creditors if:

1. that class will retain its lien on the collateral after the reorganization, whether the collateral is kept by the reorganized debtor or transferred to another party
2. the collateral for the secured claim is sold free and clear of the lien and the lien attaches to the proceeds of the sale
3. the secured class of claims is given an "indubitable equivalent" in exchange for their secured claim (i.e., given a lien on a similar piece of collateral).

The policy behind this rule is to prevent the members of any secured class from hindering a reorganization of a debtor that is in the best interests of all parties. Under the "cram-down," the secured creditors receive substantial protection of their interests.

Unsecured Class of Creditors. A plan of reorganization is "fair and equitable" to a dissenting-impaired class of *unsecured* creditors where the plan of reorganization provides that the class will receive cash or property, including securities of the reorganized debtor, which has a *discounted present value* equal to the amount of the claim. Under this rule, the dissenting-impaired class of unsecured creditors may be forced to take securities in the reorganized debtor as long as they receive an amount of new securities estimated to be equal in value to their claim. Further, under this "cram-down" rule unsecured creditors may be converted from *creditors* of the old debtor to *equity holders* in the new reorganized debtor.

As an alternative, a plan of reorganization is deemed to be "fair and equitable" to a class of dissenting-impaired *unsecured* creditors if *no* class of claim or interest *junior* to the dissenting-impaired class receives anything of value under the plan of reorganization *unless* the dissenting-impaired class of unsecured creditors is paid in full. This rule, commonly referred to as the "absolute priority rule," is a statutory codification of a rule previously applied to bankruptcy reorganizations by the courts. For example, where a class of impaired-unsecured creditors rejects a plan of reorganization, the Bankruptcy court can "cram down" the plan on the dissenting-impaired class if—and only if—the plan of reorganization gives nothing to the preferred or common equity holders who are junior to them. In this instance, the Bankruptcy Court may force the dissenting-impaired class to take a claim, or even an equity interest in the new reorganized debtor that is substantially below the value of their previous claim on the debtor.

Class of Equity Holders.   A plan of reorganization is considered "fair and equitable" to a dissenting-impaired class of *equity* holders (i.e., preferred or common stockholders) if the members of that equity class are paid either their *liquidation* preference or *redemption* preference, if either is provided for.

In the alternative, a plan of reorganization may be crammed down on an equity class under the absolute priority rule as provided in Section 1129(b). Often where the *absolute priority rule* is used to cram a plan of reorganization down on an equity class, that class is totally eliminated from participating in the reorganization as long as no class junior to them receives anything under the plan. There is often no class junior to the class of holders of common stocks.

"Does Not Discriminate Unfairly."   The bankruptcy court may "cram down" a plan of reorganization on a dissenting-impaired class of claims or interests only if the plan "does not discriminate unfairly" against members within the class, or against members of *equal* classes. This test requires that no member of any class of claims or interests receive more than any other member of *that* class in the plan of reorganization.

A proponent of a plan of reorganization must request confirmation of a plan of reorganization under the "cram-down" provisions of Section 1129(b) of the Bankruptcy Reform Act. The Bankruptcy Court cannot order a "cram-down" on its own motion. Further, in order for a plan of reorganization to be crammed down under Section 1129(b), the tests of Section 1129(a) other than the nonimpairment test must be met. No class of claims or interests may be paid more than in full under a Section 1129(b) cram-down.

The following outline summarizes the two special tests that must be met in order for a plan of reorganization to meet the cram-down provisions of Section 1129(b).

Cram-Down [Section 1129(b)]

I. Fair and Equitable Test:
   A. Secured class of creditors:
      1. will retain lien on property in reorganization, *or*
      2. collateral is sold and lien follows the property, *or*
      3. are given an "indubitable equivalent" (e.g., original lien replaced by lien on similar property)

B. Unsecured class of creditors:
1. receives cash, property, or securities in reorganization that equals the discounted present value of their claim, *or*
2. the absolute priority rule is met (no junior class receives anything in reorganization)

C. Class of equity interests:
1. are paid liquidation or redemption preference, *or*
2. the absolute priority rule is met (no junior class receives anything in reorganization)

II. Does Not Discriminate Unfairly Test:
All members of each class of claims and interests are treated equally within that class

In *In re W. E. Parks Lumber Co., Inc.* the Bankruptcy Court held that a plan of reorganization was "fair and equitable" to a dissenting-impaired class, and confirmed the plan of reorganization under the "cram-down" provisions of Section 1129(b) of the Bankruptcy Reform Act of 1978.

"CRAMDOWN"

IN RE W. E. PARKS LUMBER CO., INC.

19 B.R. 285 (1982)
UNITED STATES BANKRUPTCY COURT, W. D. LOUISIANA

LeRoy Smallenberger, Bankruptcy Judge.

The trustee herein, through counsel, moved to confirm his First Amended Plan of Reorganization; this matter was brought on for hearing on December 29, 1981, at 10:00 o'clock A.M. The plan was confirmed on January 27, 1982.

HISTORY AND POSTURE OF REORGANIZATION PROCEEDING

The debtor began operations in 1953 and was operated by William E. Parks, its sole shareholder, until his death in 1978. The company's operations initially centered upon a sawmill in Newellton, Louisiana. The Newellton mill produced hardwood timber and was apparently operated very profitably for many years. . . . However, in 1972, the company determined to construct a new sawmill in Port Gibson, Louisiana. The new mill cost an extremely large amount of money and never was sufficiently productive to be successful.

In 1978, Mr. Parks died, and the company was left without any effective management for the most part. At this point in time, approximately

$15,000,000.00 appeared to be owed by the company.

The company's problems were further exacerbated in the spring of 1979 when the underlying stockholders of the debtor sold all of the stock of the company to Mr. Ernesto Ancira of San Antonio, Texas. Ancira looted the company over the next two years, literally stripping it of all current assets and working capital. When Ancira began negotiations toward buying the company in late 1978, the financial statements indicated that the company had approximately $8,000,000.00 in "current assets." By the time the trustee took over control of the company in the spring of 1981, it had been looted and "current assets" were arguably less than $500,000.00.

Historically, the debtor corporation is the largest employer in Tensas Parish, Louisiana. This company's demise has a greater significance and aura than the normal company, since its cessation disrupts the lives and finances of this relatively small parish in northeast Louisiana.

At filing [of bankruptcy] the debt structure of the

company (as classified under the trustee's plan) was as follows:

Classes 1 and 2 (priority debts)	$ 340,322.00
Class 3 (FmHA)	18,257,871.00
Class 4 (other creditors)	274,519.00
TOTAL	$18,872,712.00

ANALYSIS OF THE PLAN

Classes 1 and 2 are unimpaired; they will be paid in cash and in full at confirmation, or shortly thereafter; *except,* tax debts will be paid over six years as allowed under Section 1129(a). Therefore, Classes 1 and 2 are not impaired . . .; and because of this, they are deemed to have accepted the plan . . .

Hence, as required by Section 1129(a), at least one class of claims is deemed to have accepted the trustee's plan.

As to Class 5, stockholders' rights are totally eradicated under the plan. . . . [T]he corporation has been deemed to be insolvent; and therefore, the exclusion of this class' participation in the plan is permitted by law, since their claims are valueless. Under Section 1129(b) of the Act, the plan can be confirmed over the dissent of stockholders [under the absolute priority rule]. As was stated in the legislative history:

> If the interests are "under water" then they will be valueless and the plan may be confirmed notwithstanding the dissent of that class of interests even if the plan provides that the holders of such interests will not receive any property . . .

As to Class 3, the FmHA, they are to retain (or receive new) mortgages on all of their collateral after confirmation to secure repayment of their claim to the extent of their value of collateral. The company will be reorganized and stock will be issued to the unsecured creditors, including the unsecured portion of the FmHA claim. The "Reorganized Corporation" will issue a form of debt instrument (hereinafter termed "income bonds") to the FmHA which will be secured by collateral mortgages on the property of the Reorganized Corporation.

The Court feels that the adjustments and modifications in the plan made by the trustee at confirmation insure that the FmHA is receiving "fair and equitable" treatment in accordance with Section 1129(b). Since the FmHA is retaining its lien on its present collateral and receiving deferred cash payments satisfying the entire allowed amount of its secured claim, it is receiving "fair and equitable" treatment under Section 1129(b); and the trustee's plan was confirmed over the dissent of the FmHA for these reasons.

As to Class 4, this is comprised of the unsecured claims of the debtor, including the undersecured portion of the FmHA claim. All of these unsecured claims will receive the stock of the reorganized corporation on a *pro-rata* basis; and the Reorganized Corporation will amend the charter of the debtor to authorize and provide for consummation of the plan. Because this class of creditors is receiving the residual value of the corporation, which is more than the liquidation value of the debtor, and since *no junior* claim or interest is receiving and retaining any property under the plan, this class is receiving fair and equitable treatment under . . . [the absolute priority rule]. Therefore, the Court *confirmed* this plan without the vote of this class of creditors.

CASE QUESTIONS

1. What do the following tests require?
   a. best interests test
   b. nonimpairment test
   c. acceptance by at least one class of claims test
   d. feasibility test
2. Which one of the previous tests was not met, thus making it impossible for the judge to confirm the plan under Section 1129(a)? As to what class was the test not met?
3. What does the "cram-down" provision provide? What purpose does it serve? What do the following tests of Section 1129(b) require?
   a. fair and equitable test
   b. does not discriminate unfairly test
4. What is the "absolute priority rule"? Explain.
5. Under the plan of reorganization in this case, was the "fair and equitable" test met regarding the following classes?
   a. unsecured creditors (Class 4)
   b. equity holders (Class 5)

Policy Issue. Should the Bankruptcy Court be authorized to "cram down" a plan of reorganization on a creditor who does not approve of the plan? Why or why not?

Economics Issue. What happened to the equity holders in this reorganization? Do you think this was fair? Why or why not? If there was no absolute priority rule, what would the equity holders be able to do in a proposed reorganization?

Ethics Issue. Did Mr. Ancira act ethically in this case? Should the bankruptcy trustee bring a legal action against Mr. Ancira?

Social Responsibility. Do you think that the fact that the debtor was the largest employer in Tensas Parish influenced the court's decision in this case?

Valuation of Debtor. In order to determine the amount that creditors should receive on the liquidation of a debtor, or the amount that creditor claims and equity interests should receive in a reorganization of a debtor, the *value* of the debtor and its assets must usually be calculated in a bankruptcy proceeding. There are generally two broad valuations that can be made of a debtor: (1) a *liquidation* value if the company is to be dissolved and its assets sold, and (2) a "going concern" value if the company is to continue in business.

Liquidation Value. A "liquidation value" of a debtor in bankruptcy is required to be determined under many provisions of the Bankruptcy Reform Act (e.g., under the "best interest" test of Section 1129(a)). In order to determine the liquidation value of a debtor, the bankruptcy court may consider many factors. Usually, the parties will call "expert witnesses" such as appraisers or professors to calculate liquidation values. Under the Bankruptcy Reform Act, there is some confusion as to what *liquidation value* actually means. Courts have held that liquidation value in bankruptcy can mean:

1. the value produced by selling all of the assets of the debtor on a piece-by-piece basis
2. the value produced by selling the entire firm as a "going concern"
3. the value produced by selling some assets on a piece-by-piece basis and other portions of the debtor's estate as a "going concern."

The majority rule considers the "asset value" of a sale on a piece-by-piece basis as the proper means of determining the liquidation value of a debtor in bankruptcy. The determination of liquidation value may also be affected by whether or not there is sufficient time for an orderly distribution of assets, or whether the assets must be sold at an immediate distress sale to avoid further losses. Other factors that also may affect the determination of liquidation value are the number and credit-worthiness of buyers, expenses of conducting the sale of assets, and the time necessary to complete the liquidation of the bankruptcy assets.

"Going Concern" Value. Although the reorganization provisions of Chapter 11 of the Bankruptcy Reform Act do not require that a formal valuation of the debtor corporation be made, in most circumstances the bankruptcy court

will demand that some form of valuation of the bankrupt firm and its assets be made prior to confirming a plan of reorganization. Such a valuation would be necessary to determine how much each class of claims and interests will receive in the reorganized debtor.

The most commonly applied rule for determining a "going concern" value of a debtor in bankruptcy is an "earnings" test, whereby an estimate of the future earnings of the reorganized debtor is made for a relevant time period (e.g., three years), a rate of capitalization is selected based on current interest rates and industry and firm risks, and that rate of capitalization is applied to the estimated earnings to reach an estimate of the "going concern" value of the reorganized debtor.

In this excerpt from *Citibank, N.A., as Indenture Trustee v. Charles Baer, Trustee for King Resources Company*, 651 F.2d 1341 (1980), the Court of Appeals quoted the record of the trial court to show the trial court's frustration in attempting to determine the "going concern" value of a debtor in a reorganization proceeding.

With all of these things, to say that you can forecast—that you can appraise the values in the Canadian Arctic is to say that you can attend the County Fair with your crystal ball, because that is absolutely the only possible way you can come up with a result. And I question that any result that I come up with in the Canadian Arctic is but little more than what I hope is an informed guess.

However, the burden imposed on me by the United States Supreme Court in *Consolidated Rock Products v. DuBois* is, I quote, "An estimate as distinguished from mathematical certainty [*sic*] is all that can be made."

My final conclusion as to the value of the company is that it is worth somewhere between $90 million and $100 million as a going concern, and to satisfy the people who want precision on the value, I fix the exact value of the company at the average of those, $96,856,850, which of course is a total absurdity that anybody could fix a value with that degree of precision, but for the lawyers who want me to make that fool estimate, I have just made it.

Rejection of Union Contracts in Bankruptcy. Under the Bankruptcy Reform Act of 1978, the bankruptcy trustee is given the authority to *assume* or *reject* executory contracts of the debtor. An *executory* contract is one that has not yet been fully performed. A collective bargaining agreement between a company and a union may fall in this category. After the employees of a company have selected a union to represent them, the management and the union engage in negotiations to arrive at an agreement regarding wages, fringe benefits, and other terms and conditions of employment. These terms are then contained in the collective bargaining agreement signed by the management and the union.

If the company files for bankruptcy under Chapter 7 for *liquidation*, the collective bargaining contract is obviously terminated. If a company files for *reorganization* under Chapter 11, the bankruptcy trustee then has authority to assume or reject the collective bargaining agreement. If the trustee rejects the agreement, the company in reorganization is free to hire both the former union employees and new employees at whatever wages and other terms of employment they will accept. The collective bargaining agreement is thereafter null and void.

In *NLRB v. Bildisco and Bildisco* the U.S. Supreme Court affirmed the right of companies in reorganization to reject union collective bargaining agreements as executory contracts.

REJECTION OF UNION CONTRACTS
NATIONAL LABOR RELATIONS BOARD V. BILDISCO AND BILDISCO

104 S.CT. 1188 (1984)
UNITED STATES SUPREME COURT

Justice Rehnquist delivered the opinion of the Court.

On April 14, 1980, respondent Bildisco and Bildisco ("Bildisco"), a New Jersey general partnership in the business of distributing building supplies, filed a voluntary petition in bankruptcy for reorganization under Chapter 11 of the Bankruptcy Code. Bildisco was subsequently authorized by the Bankruptcy Court to operate the business as debtor-in-possession. . . .

At the time of the filing of the petition in bankruptcy, approximately 40 to 45 percent of Bildisco's labor force was represented by Local 408 of the International Brotherhood of Teamsters, Chauffeurs, Warehousemen and Helpers of America ("Union"). Bildisco had negotiated a three-year collective-bargaining agreement with the Union that was to expire on April 30, 1982, and which expressly provided that it was binding on the parties and their successors even though bankruptcy should supervene.

In December, 1980, Bildisco requested permission from the Bankruptcy Court . . . to reject the collective-bargaining agreement. At the hearing on Bildisco's request the sole witness was one of Bildisco's general partners, who testified that rejection would save his company approximately $100,000 in 1981. The Union offered no witnesses of its own, but cross-examined the witness for Bildisco. On January 15, 1981, the Bankruptcy Court granted Bildisco permission to reject the collective-bargaining agreement. . . .

The Court of Appeals . . . held that a collective-bargaining agreement is an executory contract sub-

ject to rejection by a debtor-in-possession under Section 365(a) of the Bankruptcy Code. Section 365(a) . . . provides:

> the trustee, subject to the court's approval, may assume or reject any executory contract or unexpired lease of the debtor.

Obviously, Congress knew how to draft an exclusion for collective-bargaining agreements when it wanted to; its failure to do so [for collective-bargaining agreements] in this instance indicates that Congress intended that Section 365(a) apply to all collective-bargaining agreements covered by the NLRA.

We agree with the Court of Appeals below, and with the Court of Appeals for the Eleventh Circuit in a related case, *In re Brada-Miller Freight System, Inc.,* that the Bankruptcy Court should permit rejection of a collective-bargaining agreement under Section 365(a) of the Bankruptcy Code if the debtor can show that the collective-bargaining agreement burdens the estate, and that after careful scrutiny, the equities balance in favor of rejecting the labor contract.

The fundamental purpose of reorganization is to prevent a debtor from going into liquidation, with an attendant loss of jobs and possible misuse of economic resources. In some cases reorganization may succeed only if new creditors infuse the ailing firm with additional capital. . . . [A] beneficial recapitalization could be jeopardized if the debtor-in-possession were saddled automatically with the debtor's prior collective-bargaining agreement. Thus, the authority to reject an executory contract is vital to the basic purpose to a Chapter 11 reorganization, because rejection can release the debtor's estate from burdensome obligations that can impede a successful reorganization.

Accordingly, the judgment of the Court of Appeals is *affirmed*.

CASE QUESTIONS

1. What type of bankruptcy did Bildisco file for?
2. Were the employees of Bildisco represented by a union? Did the union have a collective-bargaining agreement (contract) with the company?
3. What is an *executory contract?* What power is given to a bankruptcy trustee (or debtor-in-possession if there is no trustee) regarding executory contracts?

4. What did Bildisco request permission from the Bankruptcy Court to do with the collective-bargaining agreement?

Policy Issue. Should a debtor in bankruptcy be given the option to either affirm or reject executory contracts? If so, should union contracts be exempted from this power?

Economics Issue. Was this case an important case to unions and their members? Why or why not?

Ethics Issue. Was the action taken by Bildisco in this case ethical?

Social Responsibility. Does business owe a duty of social responsibility to honor its union contracts? Did Bildisco breach its duty of social responsibility in this case?

CORPORATE BAILOUTS

Often when an industry or company has fallen on hard times and is heading for insolvency, it will seek the assistance of government to prevent bankruptcy. This assistance often takes the form of subsidy payments, tariffs to protect the industry from foreign corporations, the granting of government contracts, and other forms of assistance or protection.

One of the largest corporate bailouts in history occurred in 1980 when Chrysler Corporation, then the sixth largest company in America, was on the brink of declaring bankruptcy. Chrysler had made major research, design, and marketing mistakes, committing itself to the production of large automobiles when the consumer market, heavily influenced by the OPEC oil embargo of the early 1970s, opted for smaller automobiles.

Chrysler, under the leadership of Chairman Lee Iacocca, sought the help of Congress to save the company. After much lobbying and debate, Congress enacted the Chrysler Corporation Loan Guarantee statute in 1980. The statute provided that the United States government, under the auspices of a newly created Chrysler Corporation Loan Guarantee Board, would guarantee new loans made to Chrysler, up to $1.5 *billion*. The statute required certain wage concessions from the employees of Chrysler and prohibited the payment of dividends to shareholders while the loan guarantees were outstanding. The agreement also gave the government certain stock options to purchase stock in the Chrysler Corporation.

The Chrysler Corporation, under the name "The New Chrysler Corporation," proceeded to change its design and product mix to include smaller and sportier automobile models and embarked on a substantial marketing campaign consisting of television advertising and cash rebates on car purchases.

By 1983 the Chrysler Corporation was in the black, and proceeded to repay the loans guaranteed by the government.

Pertinent parts of the Chrysler Corporation Loan Guarantee legislation are presented following.

CORPORATE BAILOUTS

CHRYSLER CORPORATION LOAN GUARANTEE

15 U.S.C. SECTIONS 1861–1875

SECTION 1861. DEFINITIONS

For purposes of this chapter—

(1) the term "Board" means the Chrysler Corporation Loan Guarantee Board established by Section 1862 of this title;

(2) the term "borrower" means the Chrysler Corporation, any of its subsidiaries or affiliates, or any other entity the Board may designate from time to time which borrows funds for the benefit or use of the Corporation; . . .

SECTION 1862. CHRYSLER CORPORATION LOAN GUARANTEE BOARD

There is established a Chrysler Corporation Loan Guarantee Board which shall consist of the Secretary of the Treasury who shall be the Chairperson of the Board, the Chairman of the Board of Governors of the Federal Reserve System, and the Comptroller General of the United States. The Secretary of Labor and the Secretary of Transportation shall be *ex officio* nonvoting members of the Board.

SECTION 1863. COMMITMENTS FOR LOAN GUARANTEES

(a) Subject to the provisions of this chapter, the Board, on such terms and conditions as it deems appropriate, may make commitments to guarantee the payment of principal and interest on loans to a borrower only if at the time the commitment is issued, the Board determines that

(1) there exists an energy-savings plan which—

  (A) is satisfactory to the Board;

  (B) is developed in consultation with other appropriate Federal agencies;

  (C) focuses on the national need to lessen United States dependence on petroleum; and

  (D) can be carried out by the borrowers;

(2) the commitment is needed to enable the Corporation to continue to furnish goods or services, and failure to meet such need would adversely and seriously affect the economy of, or employment in, the United States or any region thereof;

(3)(A) the Corporation has submitted to the Board a satisfactory operating plan (including budget and cash flow projections) for the 1980 fiscal year and the next succeeding three fiscal years demonstrating the ability of the Corporation to continue operations as a going concern in the automobile business, and after December 31, 1983, to continue such operations as a going concern without additional guarantees or other Federal financing; . . .

(6) the Corporation's existing creditors have certified to the Board that they will waive their rights to recover under any prior credit commitment which may be in default unless the Board determines that the exercise of those rights would not adversely affect the operating plan . . . or the financing plan [of the Corporation]

(7) no credit extended or committed on a nonguaranteed basis prior to October 17, 1979, is being converted to a guaranteed basis pursuant to this chapter; and

(8) the financing plan . . . provides that expenditures under such financing plan will contribute to the domestic economic viability of the Corporation.

SECTION 1865. REQUIREMENTS APPLICABLE TO EMPLOYEES

(a) No loan guarantee may be issued under this chapter if at the time of issuance or the proposed issuance the Board determines that—

(1) collective bargaining agreements entered into by the Corporation after September 14, 1979, with labor organizations representing employees of the Corporation which govern the payment of wages and benefits to such employees from September 14, 1979, to September 14, 1982, have not been modified so that the cost to the Corporation of such wages and benefits, as determined by the Board, shall be reduced by a total amount of at least $462,500,000 for the three-year period ending on September 14, 1982, below the cost of such wages and benefits which the Corporation would otherwise have been obligated to incur during such period, . . .

SECTION 1867. LIMITATIONS ON GUARANTEE AUTHORITY

(a) The authority of the Board to extend loan guarantees under this chapter shall not at any time exceed $1,500,000,000 in the aggregate principal amount outstanding.

SECTION 1868. TERMS AND CONDITIONS OF LOAN GUARANTEES

(a) Loans guaranteed under this chapter shall be payable in full not later than December 31, 1990, and the terms and conditions of such loans shall provide that they cannot be amended, or any provision waived, without the Board's consent.

SECTION 1870. PROTECTION OF GOVERNMENT'S INTEREST

(i)(1) Notwithstanding any other provision of law whenever any person is indebted to the United States as a result of any loan guarantee issued under this chapter and such person is insolvent or is a debtor in a case under Title 11, the debts due to the United States shall be satisfied first. . . . .

(j) The Corporation may not pay any dividend on its common or preferred stock during the period beginning January 7, 1980, and ending on the date on which loan guarantees issued under this chapter are no longer outstanding.

SECTION 1874. AUTHORIZATION OF APPROPRIATIONS

(a) There are authorized to be appropriated beginning October 1, 1979, and to remain available without fiscal year limitation, such sums as may be necessary to carry out the provisions of this chapter.

(b) Notwithstanding any other provision of this chapter, the authority of the Board to make any loan guarantee under this chapter shall be limited to the extent such amounts are provided in advance in appropriation Acts.

SECTION 1875. TERMINATION

The authority of the Board to make commitments to guarantee or to issue guarantees under this chapter expires on December 31, 1983.

STATUTE QUESTIONS

Policy Issue. Does the government bailout of a bankrupt company violate the free enterprise economic system of this country? Does the Chrysler bailout establish a dangerous precedent?

Economics Issue. Who benefited by this bailout? Who suffered? Was this a fair exchange?

Ethics Issue. When Chrysler paid back the guaranteed loans, it quietly lobbied to have the government relinquish its stock options in Chrysler stock. Was this activity by the management of Chrysler ethical?

Social Responsibility. Should the government be responsible for bailing out large corporations that get into financial trouble? What about small entrepreneurs? Would you like to have the government *guarantee* your debts?

CONSUMER CREDIT ADJUSTMENT (CHAPTER 13)

An individual may file for straight bankruptcy liquidation under Chapter 7 *or* for a consumer debt adjustment under Chapter 13 of the Bankruptcy Act. Generally, Chapter 13 allows a debtor to arrange, under court supervision, for the payment of his unpaid debts by installment. Prior to the 1978 Bankruptcy Act, consumer debt adjustments were known as "wage earner plans." The 1978 Bankruptcy Act substantially expanded the proceedings covered under consumer debt adjustments. A *consumer debt adjustment* under Chapter 13 may only be filed:

1. by *individuals*
2. with a regular income
3. who owe individually or with their spouse liquidated or unsecured debts of less than $100,000
4. secured debts of less than $350,000.

A sole proprietorship that meets the preceding tests may also file under Chapter 13. A Chapter 13 consumer debt adjustment can only be filed *voluntarily* by the debtor. An involuntary petition cannot be filed by creditors of a debtor under Chapter 13. During an active Chapter 13 proceeding, all straight bankruptcy proceedings and actions by creditors to perfect judgments or collect consumer debts against the debtor are *stayed*. If qualified to do so, a debtor can petition the bankruptcy court to convert a Chapter 7 or Chapter 11 proceeding to a Chapter 13 proceeding.

When the debtor files a petition under Chapter 13, he must state that he is insolvent or is unable to pay his debts when they become due. The petitioner-debtor usually files a list of his creditors and his assets and liabilities at the same time, and asks that he be accorded an extension or a composition of his debts, or both, so that the debts can be paid out of future earnings or income. In an *extension* of debts, the petitioner is given additional time to pay his debts. In a *composition* of debts, the amount of the debts owed by a petitioner is reduced.

Plan of Payment.   Following a debtor's filing of a petition with the Bankruptcy Court under Chapter 13, the court will set a meeting of his creditors. At this meeting the debtor will submit himself to questioning by his creditors, and will propose a *plan of repayment*. The debtor may modify his prepared plan at any time prior to confirmation by the court. A creditor may not submit a plan of payment, but may object to the plan as submitted by the debtor. The payment plan as submitted by the debtor must meet three requirements:

1. It must provide for the submission of all the debtor's future earnings and income to the trustee as is necessary to effectuate the proposed plan.
2. It must provide that all priority claims will be paid in full on a deferred basis unless the preferred claim holder agrees otherwise.
3. Each claim of the same class must be treated equally.

Generally, the debtor's proposed plan may modify rights of unsecured creditors (e.g., Sears) and secured creditors (e.g., mortgage holders such as banks), except that a security interest in the debtor's principal residence *cannot* be modified under a Chapter 13 proceeding. The debtor's plan of adjustment of his debts cannot provide for an extension of payments for a period that exceeds three years. The bankruptcy court may approve a longer period, up to five years.

Confirmation of Plan.   The debtor's plan will be *confirmed* by the bankruptcy court if certain requirements are met:

1. The plan is proposed in "good faith."
2. The plan complies with applicable state and federal law.
3. The debtor must be able to make all payments and comply with the plan.
4. Unsecured creditors will receive property as of the effective date of the plan that is not less in value than what they would receive under a Chapter 7 liquidation proceeding.
5. The secured creditors either
   a. accept the plan
   b. receive the collateral for their security from the debt
   c. retain their security interest and the value of the property to be distributed to them is not less than the amount of their claim.

Discharge.   Once the debtor completes the payments required under the plan, the Bankruptcy Court will grant an order that discharges the debtor from all debts covered by the plan, except long-term debts whose maturity extends beyond the expiration date of the plan and nondischargeable debts for alimony, support, and maintenance.

If a debtor fails to complete the payments under a Chapter 13 plan, but such failure is due to circumstances for which the debtor cannot justly be held accountable, the court may still grant a discharge of the debtor's debt if (1) the value of the property actually distributed to the creditors is not less than what they would have received under a Chapter 7 liquidation proceeding, *and* (2) modification of the plan is not practicable.

In the following case, *In the Matter of Bellgraph,* the Bankruptcy Court held that a debtor's proposed payment plan under Chapter 13 was made in "good faith," and confirmed the plan even though it provided for no payment to unsecured creditors.

CONSUMER CREDIT ADJUSTMENT

IN THE MATTER OF EVELYN DOLORES BELLGRAPH, DEBTOR

4 B.R. 421 (1980)
UNITED STATES BANKRUPTCY COURT, W. D. NEW YORK

Edward D. Hayes, Bankruptcy Judge

The facts of this matter are as follows. The debtor, a 56-year-old mother of seven children, owns a home at 516 Luce Street in the city of Elmira, New York and has resided there for 48 years. The home has an assessed value of $17,500 and in that particular community assessments approximate the value of the house. Mrs. Bellgraph has one minor child living at home. The child is seventeen. Mrs. Bellgraph was divorced in 1970 and receives $50.00 per month for support of her daughter from her exhusband. Her other income comes from Social Security Disability, SSI, and Public Assistance and amounts to $390.74 per month. She is totally disabled under the Social Security definition and is currently receiving treatment for emphysema, a back problem, and a nervous condition.

She has had a great deal of problems in recent years in managing her money. In late November, 1979, a tax foreclosure proceeding was brought against her for back taxes owed to the City of Elmira. On February 28, 1980, a Chapter 13 plan was filed in the Western District of New York on behalf of Mrs. Bellgraph by Chemung County Neighborhood Legal Services, Inc. No charges were assessed for legal fees. The plan proposed offers a 100 percent payment to a class of secured creditors that included the City of Elmira, the Elmira School District, Chemung County and Chemung County Sewer District. All of these debts were for taxes and fees. . . . To make these payments, Mrs. Bellgraph is going to take approximately five years and hence no payments are offered to any unsecured creditors. She claimed as exempt under the plan $7,287.61 on the home under the Federal Exemption, $940.00 in total of household goods and personal effects, and $764.00 in a checking account.

At the meeting of creditors held on April 28, 1980, acceptances of the plan were filed by the Small Business Administration, the City of Elmira, who filed on behalf of itself and the County of Chemung, the Elmira City School District, the Chemung County Sewer District and the Arnot-Ogden Hospital. No objections were filed by any creditor.

"Good faith" has been the stumbling block for the confirmations of a number of Chapter 13 plans. . . . It is one thing to deny confirmation of a plan for lack of "good faith" when the debtor is making no effort to pay his unsecured creditors and proposes to pay only those secured creditors who have liens upon the luxuries the debtors wish to keep, but debtors like the one in the case at bar are a different matter. Attempts to prevent the abuse of creditors' interest by defining "good faith" are laudable until a case such as this case founders upon the rocks of a too restrictive definition of "good faith." Congress' failure to define "good faith" is

a mandate to the bankruptcy judges to review each case on its merits and to confirm only those cases which . . . measure up to the Courts' sense of what is equitable in a given case. The approach must and should be a flexible one. There should be no exact percentage payment that will insure confirmation. Each case must be decided on its own merits.

The case at bar involves "exceptional circumstances." . . . It is an exceptional case that requires confirmation because the debtor, to save her home from foreclosure, is proposing to pay off the taxes, pay off her secured creditors, or allow them to maintain their security. The secured creditors have consented. No money is being spent to give her this relief. Her plan runs nearly five years. Chapter 7 relief would result in the loss of the home and probably less than full payment to even the secured creditors. No creditors will receive less than they would have in a liquidation. This plan, because of the debtor's limited income, is not only her "best effort," a test considered too strict under the Code, but it is a super effort by the debtor to pay her debts and maintain her home.

Under these circumstances, to deny the debtor confirmation of her plan because of a restrictive definition of "good faith," would work an injustice. The plan is *confirmed.* It is so *ordered.*

CASE QUESTIONS

1. What does Chapter 13 of the Bankruptcy Reform Act of 1978 provide? Who can qualify to file for bankruptcy under this Chapter?
2. What did the debtor's Chapter 13 plan provide in this case? How were the following creditors treated under the plan?
   a. secured creditors
   b. unsecured creditors
3. What does the "good faith" test of Chapter 13 provide? Define this test. Can you? Would an *objective* percentage test be better?
4. Would the secured creditors have been any better off if the debtor had filed for liquidation under Chapter 7? What about the unsecured creditors?

Policy Issue. Should consumers be allowed to file for bankruptcy just because they overextend themselves? Why or why not? Should consumers be treated differently from businesses under federal bankruptcy law?

Economics Issue. Who bears the cost of bankruptcies? Explain.

Ethics Issue. Did the debtor in this case only attempt to pay the creditors who held liens on her "luxuries"? Was the Chapter 13 payment plan in this case a "super effort"? Why?

Social Responsibility. Do courts owe a duty of social responsibility to interpret the law to help poor people?

Trend of the Law

The Bankruptcy Reform Act of 1978 made it much easier for debtors to file for and receive discharge of unpaid debts in bankruptcy. Bankruptcy filings are at an all-time high, with about 90 percent of those being voluntary petitions for bankruptcy. The number of bankruptcies is somewhat correlated with the performance of the economy, but is predicted to remain high throughout the remainder of the 1980s. Further, it is not expected that Congress will narrow the scope of the bankruptcy laws in the near future.

One of the most important policy issues that will be facing the courts in the future is the use of bankruptcy laws by firms that are not actually failing businesses in the traditional sense. For example, in 1983, the Johns-Manville Corporation filed for bankruptcy protection under the reorganization provisions of Chapter 11 in order to limit its liability exposure from the thousands of actual and potential lawsuits alleging injuries suffered by asbestosis victims. When Continental Airlines filed for Chapter 11 bankruptcy protection in 1983, it was alleged that the bankruptcy action was filed principally with the intent of breaking the unions at Continental.

Bankruptcies and controversies of this nature will continue to increase in the future. The bankruptcy courts will have to address more complex policy issues involving not only debtors and creditors but also employees, unions, and consumers. The courts will have to decide on a case-by-case basis whether the bankruptcy action was filed in "good faith" and will be allowed, or whether it was filed in "bad faith" and the protection of the bankruptcy laws should be denied the petitioner.

REVIEW QUESTIONS

1. Heath and his wife filed a Chapter 13 plan to enable them to discharge his unpaid student loan from the University of Illinois. Heath requested the University to provide him with a transcript of his academic record so that he could obtain employment and thus provide the money necessary to complete his proposed plan. The University, however, refused to issue

the transcript until Heath paid his pre-petition student loan debt in full. Heath sued the University, arguing that federal bankruptcy law overrules any state law or action which conflicts with bankruptcy policy. Is Heath correct?

2. Davis, an automobile dealer, frequently borrowed money from Aetna Acceptance Company, which enabled him to purchase his automobile inventory used for retail sale. After borrowing money to finance several cars, Davis sold them without tendering a check for the outstanding loan amount on them to Aetna. He then promised to promptly tender a check to Aetna, his usual practice, but, instead, he filed a petition for bankruptcy. There was no evidence to indicate that he willfully attempted to defraud Aetna; his business simply collapsed before he was able to pay the firm. Davis was eventually discharged from his debts in a bankruptcy proceeding. Aetna later brought an action to recover the unpaid debt, charging Davis with conversion of property. Could Aetna sue for the unpaid debt?

3. Cargill Corp. filed an involuntary bankruptcy petition against the Hills, claiming that they owed it $1,250,000 plus interest on a debt they had personally guaranteed on behalf of the Warren Grain and Seed Company. In contesting the petition, the Hills stated that Warren Grain had initiated an as-yet-uncompleted state proceeding against Cargill for antitrust violations that sought damages in excess of the amount of the alleged debt. Furthermore, they showed that an appeal in state court was still pending regarding the defenses and counterclaims that they had raised in response to Cargill's action against them in state court. They contended, therefore, that the statutory prerequisites for obtaining relief in the form of involuntary bankruptcy were not met, including the requirement that the debtor is generally not paying his debts as they became due. The Hills maintained that the pending state litigation rendered the Cargill claim a yet-to-be-established debt. Did the Hills' claim have merit or should the court grant the petition placing the Hills in involuntary bankruptcy?

4. Terra Del Mar Development (TMD) held a mortgage covering the purchase price of a marina. Due to nonpayment on the mortgage, TMD obtained a court order granting a foreclosure sale to enable TMD to recover most of the outstanding mortgage. The court delayed the sale for one year to permit the debtors, Terra Mar Associates (TMA), to extensively advertise the sale of the marina. Since they were unable to find any buyers during this period, one day before the sale was due to take place, TMA filed a Chapter 11 petition in Bankruptcy Court. TMD petitioned the Bankruptcy Court, asking the court to modify its automatic stay to permit bidding. Under what circumstances will the Bankruptcy Court modify its automatic stay? Should a modification be granted in this case?

5. Kokoszka filed for bankruptcy. His sole asset was a tax refund check for $250.90. The Bankruptcy Court ordered Kokoszka to turn over the check to the trustee once he received it. Kokoszka appealed this decision, arguing that the tax refund was not property so it should not have been included in his bankruptcy estate. Was the tax refund part of his bankruptcy estate?

6. McKloskey owned an automobile dealership. The business had been moderately successful in the past. However, a new freeway was constructed nearby that effectively isolated the dealership from passersby; as a result,

business declined dramatically. McKloskey tried to sell the business for $45,000 but was unable to. He then tried to find refinancing but was unable to obtain any. Eventually his mortgage was foreclosed. During foreclosure, McKloskey contacted Johnson, who refused to refinance the business but agreed to purchase it outright for $25,000. McKloskey, in order to get some cash out of the business, agreed. The first mortgage of $18,800 was paid; $1,234 in back taxes were paid; McKloskey was given three months' free rent; and they agreed that if McKloskey could sell the business for a higher price within those three months, Johnson would retransfer the business back to him for a nominal profit. Approximately five months later McKloskey went bankrupt. Kielb, the bankruptcy trustee, instituted a suit to declare that the transaction was fraudulent. At trial, the evidence indicated the property was worth approximately $28,000. McKloskey was rendered insolvent by the transfer, but the court found that Johnson did not know and had no reason to suspect that the transfer could cause McKloskey's insolvency. The court also found that the transfer was not intended to actually defraud creditors. Should the court have found that the transfer was fraudulent?

7. Metropolitan Life held a $400,500 first mortgage on an apartment building owned by Muriel Holding Corporation. Muriel filed a petition in Bankruptcy Court and submitted a proposed reorganization plan in which the firm was to provide $11,000 to be used to alter certain apartments to make them more leasable. Under the plan, this advance was to have priority over all other liens except tax arrears. Metropolitan objected to the plan since the tax liens and the first mortgage totaled $500,000, whereas the property was only assessed for $450,000. Additionally, under the plan, Metropolitan would be forced to forego all amortization payments on its mortgage for ten years. When can a dissenting creditor be compelled to accept a reorganization plan? Should Metropolitan be compelled to accept this plan?

8. While driving under the influence of alcohol, Bryson collided with a car carrying the Williams family, who suffered a number of injuries. Before the claim was settled, Bryson declared bankruptcy. Was the debt that Bryson owed to the Williams family dischargeable under the Bankruptcy Code?

9. The Mazzolas conceded that there were inaccuracies in the schedules and statement of affairs they had filed in connection with their Chapter 7 petition. However, they contended that there had been no fraudulent intent, that the inaccuracies were the result of innocent misunderstandings and mistakes, and that Mrs. Mazzola had signed the documents without reading them. The evidence, however, indicated that all of the "misunderstandings" and "mistakes" were in the Mazzolas' favor. At the very least, the evidence indicated a reckless disregard for the truth; at the most, it indicated that the Mazzolas had been intentionally fraudulent. Under these circumstances, should the Mazzolas' debts be discharged?

10. Seman proposed the confirmation of a Chapter 13 plan to which both the trustee and one unsecured creditor objected. Under the plan, Seman planned to repay a secured automobile loan but she did not plan to pay any of her unsecured creditors. Since all of Seman's assets were exempt,

the unsecured creditors would have received nothing had she undergone straight liquidation under Chapter 7. Therefore, she argued that the creditors would receive "not less than" the amount that would have been paid if the estate had been liquidated under Chapter 7. In response, the creditors argued that a zero plan designed to discharge an otherwise nondischargeable debt must be regarded as lacking the necessary "good faith." Should this Chapter 13 zero payment plan be rejected?

11. The Federal Deposit Insurance Corporation, as Bonder's sole creditor, moved to have Bonder's Chapter 13 case dismissed. Bonder had received a discharge in a Chapter 14 proceeding which had commenced within six years of the filing of his Chapter 13 case. The FDIC contended that this was grounds for dismissal of his current Chapter 13 case. Was the FDIC's argument valid?

V ETHICAL CONSIDERATIONS AND BUSINESS

21 ADVERTISING

INTRODUCTION

As the American economy expanded in the 1900's, and a proliferation of products and services became available to consumers, a large and prominent advertising industry developed to promote these goods and services. The traditionally stated function of advertising is to provide information to consumers as to the availability and quality of products and services offered by the advertisers. In the past 25 years, advertising in the United States has been transformed from relatively simple factual information or "puffing" of a product or service, to a sophisticated marketing tool that often relies on complex marketing research and subtle psychological messages.

Critics often argue that the money spent on advertising is wasted, and advertising only increases the cost of products and services to consumers. Critics also argue that advertising "creates" demand for products and services that would not otherwise be produced. Other critics argue that the "demand" economy that is created in the United States through the pressure of advertising is immoral. Whatever the criticisms, the reality is that advertising has become an important and influential form of marketing in the American and world economies. Over $75 *billion* is spent annually in the United States for advertising. A 60-second advertisement during the Super Bowl costs $500,000. The importance of advertising cannot be underestimated, both in the United States and in other countries around the world.

THE CONSTITUTION AND ADVERTISING

Advertising by most media (radio, television, magazines, newspapers) is a form of speech. Although prior to the 1970s it was unclear whether commercial speech was constitutionally protected, in *Virginia State Board of Pharmacy v. Virginia Citizens Consumer Council, Inc.* and a number of cases since, the United States Supreme Court has held that "commercial speech" is "free speech" protected under the First Amendment to the Constitution. "Commercial speech" is not currently accorded equal protection with noncommercial speech, and is also subject to proper "time, manner, or place" restrictions under state "police power" without violation of the First Amendment. The Supreme Court has yet to announce a precise rule regarding the boundaries of the protection accorded to commercial free speech, and may choose instead to review commerical speech issues on a case-by-case basis only.

In *Bates v. State Bar of Arizona* the United States Supreme Court found that a State Bar Association rule prohibiting price advertising by attorneys was unconstitutional under the First Amendment to the Constitution.

CONSTITUTIONAL PROTECTION OF ADVERTISING

BATES v. STATE BAR OF ARIZONA

433 U.S. 350 (1977)
UNITED STATES SUPREME COURT

Mr. Justice Blackmun delivered the opinion of the Court.

Appellants John R. Bates and Van O'Steen are attorneys licensed to practice law in the State of Arizona. As such, they are members of the appellee, the State Bar of Arizona. After admission to the bar in 1972, appellants worked as attorneys with the Maricopa County Legal Aid Society.

In March 1974, appellants left the Society and opened a law office, which they call a "legal clinic," in Phoenix. Their aim was to provide legal services at modest fees to persons of moderate income who did not qualify for governmental legal aid. In order to achieve this end, they would accept only routine matters, such as uncontested divorces, uncon-

tested adoptions, simple personal bankruptcies, and changes of name, for which costs could be kept down by extensive use of paralegals, automatic typewriting equipment, and standardized forms and office procedures. More complicated cases, such as contested divorces, would not be accepted. Because appellants set their prices so as to have a relatively low return on each case they handled, they depended on substantial volume.

After conducting their practice in this manner for two years, appellants concluded that their practice and clinical concept could not survive unless the availability of legal services at low cost was advertised and, in particular, fees were advertised. Con-

DO YOU NEED A LAWYER?

LEGAL SERVICES
AT VERY REASONABLE FEES

- Divorce or legal separation—uncontested (both spouses sign papers)
  $175.00 plus $20.00 court filing fee

- Preparation of all court papers and instructions on how to do your own simple uncontested divorce
  $100.00

- Adoption—uncontested severance proceeding
  $225.00 plus approximately $10.00 publication cost

- Bankruptcy—non-business, no contested proceedings
  Individual
  $250.00 plus $55.00 court filing fee
  Wife and Husband
  $300.00 plus $110.00 court filing fee

- Change of Name
  $95.00 plus $20.00 court filing fee

Information regarding other types of cases furnished on request

Legal Clinic of Bates & O'Steen
617 North 3rd Street
Phoenix, Arizona 85004
Telephone (602) 252-8888

Exhibit 21–1. Today, legal services may be advertised.

sequently, in order to generate the necessary flow of business, that is, "to attract clients," appellants on February 22, 1976, placed an advertisement [reproduced above] in the Arizona Republic, a daily newspaper of general circulation in the Phoenix metropolitan area.

Appellants concede that the advertisement constituted a clear violation of Disciplinary Rule 2–101

(B), incorporated in Rule 29 (a) of the Supreme Court of Arizona. The disciplinary rule provides in part:

> (B) A lawyer shall not publicize himself, or his partner, or associate, or any other lawyer affiliated with him or his firm, as a lawyer through newspaper or magazine advertisments, radio or television announcements, display advertisements in the city or telephone directories or other means of commercial publicity, nor shall he authorize or permit others to do so in his behalf."

Upon the filing of a complaint initiated by the president of the State Bar a hearing was held before a three-member Special Local Administrative Committee. . . . The committee recommended that each of the appellants be suspended from the practice of law for not less than six months.

THE FIRST AMENDMENT

The heart of the dispute before us today is whether lawyers also may constitutionally advertise the *prices* at which certain routine services will be performed. Numerous justifications are proffered for the restriction of such price advertising. We consider each in turn:

1. The Adverse Effect on Professionalism

Appellee places particular emphasis on the adverse effects that it feels price advertising will have on the legal profession. The key to professionalism, it is argued, is the sense of pride that involvement in the discipline generates. It is claimed that price advertising will bring about commercialization, which will undermine the attorney's sense of dignity and self-worth. The hustle of the marketplace will adversely affect the profession's service orientation, and irreparably damage the delicate balance between the lawyer's need to earn and his obligation selflessly to serve. Advertising is also said to erode the client's trust in his attorney: Once the client perceives that the lawyer is motivated by profit, his confidence that the attorney is acting out of a commitment to the client's welfare is jeopardized. And advertising is said to tarnish the dignified public image of the profession.

We recognize, of course, and commend the spirit of public service with which the profession of law is practiced and to which it is dedicated. The pres-

ent Members of this Court, licensed attorneys all, could not feel otherwise. And we would have reason to pause if we felt that our decision today would undercut that spirit. But we find the postulated connection between advertising and the erosion of true professionalism to be severely strained. At its core, the argument presumes that attorneys must conceal from themselves and from their clients the real-life fact that lawyers earn their livelihood at the bar. We suspect that few attorneys engage in such self-deception. And rare is the client, moreover, even one of modest means, who enlists the aid of an attorney with the expectation that his services will be rendered free of charge. . . . If the commercial basis of the relationship is to be promptly disclosed on ethical grounds, once the client is in the office, it seems inconsistent to condemn the candid revelation of the same information before he arrives at that office.

Moreover, the assertion that advertising will diminish the attorney's reputation in the community is open to question. Bankers and engineers advertise, and yet these professions are not regarded as undignified. In fact, it has been suggested that the failure of lawyers to advertise creates public disillusionment with the profession. The absence of advertising may be seen to reflect the profession's failure to reach out and serve the community: Studies reveal that many persons do not obtain counsel even when they perceive a need because of the feared price of services or because of an inability to locate a competent attorney. Indeed, cynicism with regard to the profession may be created by the fact that it long has publicly eschewed advertising, while condoning the actions of the attorney who structures his social or civic associations so as to provide contacts with potential clients.

2. The Inherently Misleading Nature of Attorney Advertising

It is argued that advertising of legal services inevitably will be misleading. . . . The argument that legal services are so unique that fixed rates cannot meaningfully be established is refuted by the record in this case: The appellee State Bar itself sponsors a Legal Services Program in which the participating attorneys agree to perform services like those advertised by the appellants at standardized rates.

3. The Adverse Effect on the Administration of Justice

Advertising is said to have the undesirable effect of stirring up litigation. . . . But advertising by attorneys is not an unmitigated source of harm to the administration of justice. It may offer great benefits. Although advertising might increase the use of the judicial machinery, we cannot accept the notion that it is always better for a person to suffer a wrong silently than to redress it by legal action.

4. The Undesirable Economic Effects of Advertising

It is claimed that advertising will increase the overhead costs of the profession, and that these costs then will be passed along to consumers in the form of increased fees. Moreover, it is claimed that the additional cost of practice will create a substantial entry barrier, deterring or preventing young attorneys from penetrating the market and entrenching the position of the bar's established members.

These two arguments seem dubious at best. Neither distinguishes lawyers from others, see *Virginia Pharmacy Board v. Virginia Consumer Council,* and neither appears relevant to the First Amendment. The ban on advertising serves to increase the difficulty of discovering the lowest cost seller of acceptable ability. As a result, to this extent attorneys are isolated from competition, and the incentive to price competitively is reduced. Although it is true that the effect of advertising on the price of services has not been demonstrated, there is revealing evidence with regard to products; where consumers have the benefit of price advertising, retail prices often are dramatically lower than they would be without advertising. It is entirely possible that advertising will serve to reduce, not advance, the cost of legal services to the consumer.

The entry-barrier argument is equally unpersuasive. In the absence of advertising, an attorney must rely on his contacts with the community to generate a flow of business. In view of the time necessary to develop such contacts, the ban in fact serves to perpetuate the market position of established attorneys. Consideration of entry-barrier problems would urge that advertising be allowed so as to aid the new competitor in penetrating the market.

5. The Adverse Effect of Advertising on the Quality of Service

It is argued that the attorney may advertise a given "package" of service at a set price, and will be inclined to provide, by indiscriminate use, the standard package regardless of whether it fits the client's needs. . . . Even if advertising leads to the creation of "legal clinics" like that of appellants—clinics that emphasize standardized procedures for routine problems—it is possible that such clinics will improve service by reducing the likelihood of error.

6. The Difficulties of Enforcement

Finally, it is argued that the wholesale restriction is justified by the problems of enforcement if any other course is taken. Because the public lacks sophistication in legal matters, it may be particularly susceptible to misleading or deceptive advertising by lawyers.

It is at least somewhat incongruous for the opponents of advertising to extol the virtues and altruism of the legal profession at one point, and, at another, to assert that its members will seize the opportunity to mislead and distort. We suspect that, with advertising, most lawyers will behave as they always have: They will abide by their solemn oaths to uphold the integrity and honor of their profession and of the legal system.

In sum, we are not persuaded that any of the proffered justifications rise to the level of an acceptable reason for the suppression of all advertising by attorneys. . . . As with other varieties of speech, it follows as well that there may be reasonable restrictions on the time, place, and manner of advertising. See *Virginia Pharmacy Board v. Virginia Consumer Council.*

The constitutional issue in this case is only whether the State may prevent the publication in a newspaper of appellants' truthful advertisement concerning the availability and terms of routine legal services. We rule simply that the flow of such information may not be restrained, and we therefore hold the present application of the disciplinary rule against appellants to be *violative* of the First Amendment.

Mr. Justice Rehnquist, dissenting in part.

I continue to believe that the First Amendment

speech provision, long regarded by this Court as a sanctuary for expressions of public importance or intellectual interest, is demeaned by invocation to protect advertisements of goods and services. I would hold quite simply that the appellants' advertisement, however truthful or reasonable it may be, is not the sort of expression that the Amendment was adopted to protect.

CASE QUESTIONS

1. What is the State Bar of Arizona? Were the appellants subject to the regulations and rule of the Bar?
2. What did the appellants advertise? Did their advertisement violate any rule? Explain.
3. Is advertising protected by the freedom of speech clause of the First Amendment of the U.S. Constitution? Explain.
4. How did the U.S. Supreme Court answer the arguments asserted by the Bar to prevent advertising by lawyers that advertising will:
   a. cause adverse effects on the profession
   b. diminish the reputation of lawyers
   c. cause inherently misleading advertising
   d. create an adverse effect on the administration of justice
   e. increase the costs of legal services
   f. create barriers of entry for young lawyers
   g. decrease the quality of legal services
   h. create a difficulty in enforcing advertising rules
5. Under this decision, can lawyer advertising ever be regulated (e.g., sky-writing, handing out advertisments at emergency rooms of hospitals)? Explain.

Policy Issue. Do you think a lawyer's primary goal is to "selflessly serve"? Or to make a living? (Ask your professor!) Do most lawyers make more or less than the average American income?

Economics Issue. Why do you think that the Bar fought so vigorously against lawyer advertising? Who controls the Bar, old or young lawyers? Did this make a difference? Will lawyers' fees be higher or lower with advertising being allowed?

Ethics Issue. Was it ethical for the Bar to permit lawyers to seek clients by "gladhanding" at social and civic functions but not by advertising: Is there any correlation between lawyer competency and social skills? Explain.

Social Responsibility. Do lawyers, and the Bar, owe a duty of social responsibility to make the public aware of the services they offer and the price? Do lawyers owe a duty of social responsibility to engage in *pro bono* work? Any greater duty than, say, plumbers?

CONSUMER ACTIONS FOR FALSE ADVERTISING

Often, in order to entice consumers to purchase products or services, advertisers include false or unsubstantiated claims in their advertisments. Consumers who are defrauded and injured by misrepresentations contained in advertisments may bring a *tort* action for common law *deceit* against the false advertiser. In order to establish a *prima facie* case of common law deceit, the plaintiff must prove:

1. that the defendant advertiser made a material misrepresentation of fact
2. that the defendant knew that the statement was false
3. that the defendant intended to defraud the plaintiff
4. that the plaintiff justifiably relied on the misrepresentation
5. that the plaintiff suffered damage from relying on the misrepresentation.

It is often difficult for a consumer to prove all the necessary elements of common-law deceit against an advertiser for false advertising. For example, it is often difficult for the consumer to prove that the advertiser had knowledge of the falsity of its statements, that the misrepresentation was a statement of "fact" and not merely a salesperson's "puffing" or opinion, or that the plaintiff actually relied on the misrepresentation in making the purchase. Where an advertiser has engaged in false advertising, the government may bring a criminal action against the advertiser for *fraud.*

Government Regulation of Advertising.   Often, consumers are dissuaded from bringing civil actions against false advertisers based on deceit or breach of warranty because of the high costs of litigation, the small amount involved in many purchases, or the difficulty in proving the necessary elements of these tort and contract actions. In order to help protect consumers from the abuses of deceptive and false advertising, the government, particularly at the federal level, has chosen to regulate advertising. The remainder of this chapter focuses on the two main federal statutes that regulate advertising: the Federal Trade Commission Act and the Lanham Act.

THE FEDERAL TRADE COMMISSION ACT

In 1914, Congress enacted the Federal Trade Commission Act and created the Federal Trade Commission (FTC). The FTC staff is divided into three bureaus (see Exhibit 21–2):

1. the Bureau of Competition, which shares jurisdiction with the Justice Department in enforcing the Clayton Antitrust Act
2. the Bureau of Economics, which is responsible for gathering data, conducting research, and supporting the work of the other two bureaus of the FTC
3. the Bureau of Consumer Protection, which is responsible for enforcing the FTC Act, particularly Section 5, which prohibits "unfair methods of competition" and "unfair or deceptive acts or practices in commerce."

The FTC also has two main offices within the organization, namely the Office of General Counsel, which represents the FTC in litigation, works with Congress in drafting proposed legislation, and acts as legal advisor to the commission and staff of the FTC; and the Office of Administration Law Judges, which is composed of staff FTC lawyers who conduct administrative hearings on behalf of the FTC.

The organizational chart of the Federal Trade Commission on the following page is taken from the *United States Government Manual.*

The FTC has exclusive jurisdiction in administering Section 5 of the FTC Act. The Justice Department cannot bring actions to enforce the Act, and consumers are *not* provided a civil cause of action under Section 5.

Unfair and Deceptive Advertising.   Section 5 of the Federal Trade Commission Act of 1914, as amended by the Wheeler-Lea Act of 1938, prohibits "unfair and deceptive trade practices." An unfair and deceptive trade practice

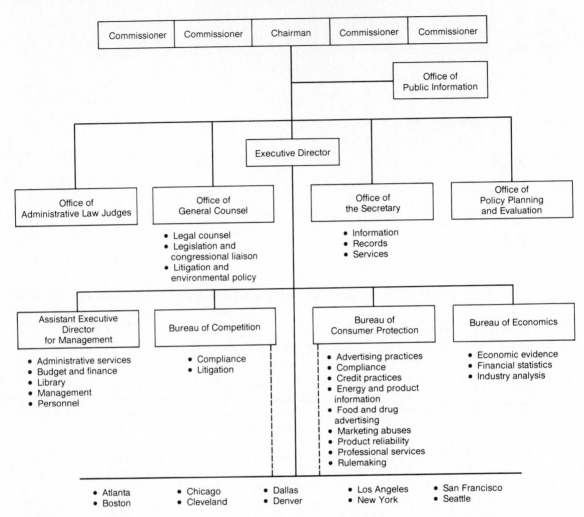

Exhibit 21-2. Organizational chart of the Federal Trade Commission.

commonly attacked by the FTC under FTC Act Section 5 is false and misleading advertising. The FTC is restricted in taking action under Section 5 to only those cases where the proceeding is in the "public interest." Most cases of false and deceptive advertising easily fall within the "public interest" proviso. The FTC generally seeks cease-and-desist orders against companies found liable for false and deceptive advertising.

One of the earliest cases brought by the FTC for false advertising is *Charles of the Ritz Distributors Corporation v. FTC,* where the court found Charles of the Ritz liable for false advertising for having engaged in unsupported advertising of a product as a "rejuvenescence" cream.

THE FEDERAL TRADE COMMISSION ACT

CHARLES OF THE RITZ DISTRIBUTORS CORPORATION v. FEDERAL TRADE COMMISSION

143 F.2d 676 (1944)
UNITED STATES COURT OF APPEALS, SECOND CIRCUIT

Clark, Circuit Judge.

This is a petition to review and set aside a cease and desist order issued by the Federal Trade Commission, pursuant to a complaint charging petitioner with having violated the Federal Trade Commission Act, by falsely advertising its cosmetic preparation "Charles of the Ritz Rejuvenescence Cream."

Petitioner is a New York corporation engaged in the sale and distribution in interstate commerce of various cosmetics, one of which is the cream in issue. This is a preparation of the type commonly known to the trade as a powder base or foundation cream for make-up. During the years from 1934 until December, 1939, when sales were "temporarily discontinued" because of the issuance of the present complaint, petitioner's Rejuvenescence Cream enjoyed a vast popularity, with total sales amounting to approximately $1,000,000.

The extensive advertising campaign which accompanied this business placed emphasis upon the rejuvenating proclivities of the product. The advertisements typically referred to "a vital organic ingredient" and certain "essences and compounds" which Rejuvenescence Cream allegedly contained, and stated that the preparation brings to the user's "skin quickly the clear radiance . . . the petal-like quality and texture of youth," that it *"restores natural moisture* necessary for a live, healthy skin," with the result that "Your face need know no *drought years,"* and that it gives to the skin "a bloom which is wonderfully rejuvenating," and is "constantly active in keeping your skin clear, radiant, and young looking." (Emphasis as in the original.)

After a hearing, the Commission found that such advertising falsely represented that Rejuvenescence Cream will rejuvenate and restore youth or the appearance of youth to the skin, regardless of the condition of the skin or the age of the user, since external applications of cosmetics cannot overcome skin conditions which result from sys-

temic causes or from physiological changes occurring with the passage of time and since there is no treatment known to medical science by which changes in the condition of the skin of an individual can be prevented or by which an aged skin can be rejuvenated or restored to a youthful condition. It, therefore, ordered petitioner to cease and desist disseminating in commerce any advertisement of Charles of the Ritz Rejuvenescence Cream: "(a) In which the word 'Rejuvenescence,' or any other word or term of similar import or meaning, is used to designate, describe, or refer to respondent's [petitioner's] said cosmetic preparation; or (b) which represents, directly or by inference, that respondent's said cosmetic preparation will rejuvenate the skin of the user thereof or restore youth or the appearance of youth to the skin of the user."

On the merits, petitioner first attacks the finding of fact that its preparation does not act as a rejuvenating agent and preserve or restore the youthful appearance of the skin. Two medical experts, one a leading dermatologist, testified for the Commission; and both affirmatively stated that there was nothing known to medical science which could bring about such results. There was no testimony to the contrary; . . .

Next, and as the crux of its appeal, petitioner attacks the propriety of the finding that by use of the trade-mark "Rejuvenescence" it has represented that its preparation will rejuvenate and restore the appearance of youth to the skin. In view of the finding which we have just held supported on the evidence, that in fact there are no rejuvenating qualities in petitioner's cream, the question is then simply whether or not the trade-mark is deceptive and misleading within the meaning of the Federal Trade Commission Act.

[T]he dictionaries treat "rejuvenescence" as a common word with a plain meaning of "a renewing of youth" or the perhaps more usual "rejuvenation";

cf. Webster's New International Dictionary, 2d Ed., Unabridged, 1939. Nor does the record show any other special meaning to have developed in the trade. On the contrary, the Commission's expert and practicing dermatologist testified directly that rejuvenescence still meant not only to him, but also, as far as he knew, to his female patients, the restoration of youth. In the light of this plain meaning, petitioner's contention can hardly be sustained that "rejuvenescence" is a nondeceptive "boastful and fanciful word," utilized solely for its attractiveness as a trade-mark. That the Patent Office has registered "Rejuvenescence" as a trade-mark is not controlling.

There is no merit to petitioner's argument that, since no straight-thinking person could believe that its cream would actually rejuvenate, there could be no deception. Such a view results from a grave misconception of the purposes of the Federal Trade Commission Act. That law was not

> made for the protection of experts, but for the public— that vast multitude which includes the ignorant, the unthinking and the credulous. [The] fact that a false statement may be obviously false to those who are trained and experienced does not change its character, nor take away its power to deceive others less experienced.

[W]hile the wise and the worldly may well realize the falsity of any representations that the present product can roll back the years, there remains "that vast multitude" of others who, like Ponce de Leon, still seek a perpetual fountain of youth. As the Commission's expert further testified, the average woman, conditioned by talk in magazines and over the radio of "vitamins, hormones, and God knows what," might take "rejuvenescence" to mean that this "is one of the modern miracles" and is "something which would actually cause her youth to be restored." It is for this reason that the Commission may "insist upon the most literal truthfulness" in advertisements, and should have the discretion, undisturbed by the courts, to insist if it chooses "upon a form of advertising clear enough so that, in the words of the prophet Isaiah, 'wayfaring men, though fools, shall not err therein.' "

Petitioner contends finally that, even if the Commission's findings of fact be upheld, that part of the order is inappropriate which bars use of the word "rejuvenescence." To delete this part of the order, however, would be not merely to create a patent ambiguity as to the meaning and effect of the board prohibition of the remaining part of the order, but also to a large extent to frustrate the purposes of the whole proceeding to insure truth telling in the cosmetic trade.

The order is *affirmed* and an enforcement decree will be entered.

CASE QUESTIONS

1. Who was the plaintiff? The defendant? Why did the plaintiff bring an action against the defendant?
2. What remedy was ordered by the FTC and affirmed by the court? Explain.
3. Did the fact that the term "Charles of the Ritz Rejuvenescence Cream" had been granted a trademark affect the decision of the court in this case?
4. Would you have been fooled by the name of the cream in this case? Do you use any creams now? Lipstick that "moisturizes"? After-bath lotion for "smooth skin"? Etc.? Are you a modern-day Ponce de Leon?

Policy Issue. Are the vast multitude of consumers "ignorant, unthinking, and credulous?" What test did the court adopt in determining whether or not an advertisement is deceptive?
a. the average *smart* person test
b. the average *average* person test
c. the average *dumb* person test
Do you agree? Which test do you think should have been used?

Economics Issue. Do you think that the cease-and-desist order had any adverse economic effects on Charles of the Ritz? Explain.

Ethics Issue. Did Charles of the Ritz act unethically in this case by naming its cream as it did?

Social Responsibility. Do manufacturers owe a duty of social responsibility not to deceive the public with their advertisements? Even though the deception increases sales? Should cosmetics advertisers be required to use "average" women and men when advertising their products? Is the use of only "10's" deceptive?

Deceptive Advertising on Television.   Television, with its ability to reach and convince millions of viewers, has become the most important advertising medium in the country. Along with its persuasive power and wide audience, it also affords a greater opportunity to engage in deceptive and false advertising. The FTC is empowered under the broad reach of Section 5 to bring actions against false advertising that appears on television. In *FTC v. Colgate-Palmolive Co.*, 380 U.S. 374 (1965), in which an advertiser was found to have violated Section 5 of the FTC Act where it had used undisclosed props to demonstrate the alleged qualities of one of its products, the U.S. Supreme Court stated:

In reviewing the substantive issues in the case, it is well to remember the respective roles of the Commission and the courts in the administration of the Federal Trade Commission Act. When the Commission was created by Congress in 1914, it was directed by Section 5 to prevent "[u]fair methods of competition in commerce." Congress amended the Act in 1938 to extend the Commission's jurisdiction to include "unfair or deceptive acts or practices in commerce"—a significant amendment showing Congress' concern for consumers as well as for competitors. It is important to note the generality of these standards of illegality; the proscriptions in Section 5 are flexible, "to be defined with particularity by the myriad of cases from the field of business."

This Court has frequently stated that the Commission's judgment is to be given great weight by reviewing courts. This admonition is especially true with respect to allegedly deceptive advertising since the finding of a Section 5 violation in this field rests so heavily on inference and pragmatic judgment.

The *FTC v. Colgate-Palmolive Co.* case follows.

DECEPTIVE ADVERTISING ON TELEVISION

FEDERAL TRADE COMMISSION v. COLGATE-PALMOLIVE CO.

380 U.S. 374 (1965)
UNITED STATES SUPREME COURT

Mr. Chief Justice Warren delivered the opinion of the Court.

The case arises out of an attempt by respondent Colgate-Palmolive Company to prove to the television public that its shaving cream, "Rapid Shave," outshaves them all. Respondent Ted Bates & Company, Inc., an advertising agency, prepared for Colgate three one-minute commercials designed to show that Rapid Shave could soften even the toughness of sandpaper. Each of the commercials contained the same "sandpaper test." The announcer informed the audience that,

To prove Rapid Shave's super-moisturizing power,

we put it right from the can onto this tough, dry sandpaper. It was apply . . . soak . . . and off in a stroke.

While the announcer was speaking, Rapid Shave was applied to a substance that appeared to be sandpaper, and immediately thereafter a razor was shown shaving the substance clean.

The Federal Trade Commission issued a complaint against respondents Colgate and Bates charging that the commercials were false and deceptive. The evidence before the hearing examiner disclosed that sandpaper of the type depicted in the commercials could not be shaved immediately following the application of Rapid Shave, but required a substantial soaking period of approximately 80 minutes. The evidence also showed that the substance resembling sandpaper was in fact a simulated prop, or "mock-up," made of plexiglass to which sand had been applied.

The [hearing] examiner dismissed the complaint because neither misrepresentation—concerning the actual moistening time or the identify of the shaved substance—was in his opinion a material one that would mislead the public. . . . The Commission, in an opinion dated December 29, 1961, reversed the hearing examiner.

An appeal was taken to the Court of Appeals for the First Circuit, which rendered an opinion on November 20, 1962. That court sustained the Commission's conclusion that respondents had misrepresented the qualities of Rapid Shave, . . . We granted *certiorari*, . . .

We agree with the Commission . . . that the undisclosed use of plexiglass in the present commercials was a material deceptive practice, independent and separate from the other misrepresentation found. We find unpersuasive respondents' other objections to this conclusion. Respondents claim that it will be impractical to inform the viewing public that it is not seeing an actual test, experiment or demonstration, but we think it inconceivable that the ingenious advertising world will be unable, if it so desires, to conform to the Commission's insistence that the public be not misinformed. If, however, it becomes impossible or impractical to show simulated demonstrations on television in a truthful manner, this indicates that television is not a medium that lends itself to this type of commercial, not that the commercial must survive at all costs. Similarly unpersuasive is respondent's objection that the Commission's decision discriminates against sellers whose product claims cannot be "verified" on television without the use of simulations. All methods of advertising do not equally favor every seller. If the inherent limitations of a method do not permit its use in the way a seller desires, the seller cannot by material misrepresentation compensate for those limitations.

The Court of Appeals . . . could find no difference between the Rapid Shave commercial and a commercial which extolled the goodness of ice cream while giving viewers a picture of a scoop of mashed potatoes appearing to be ice cream.

We do not understand this difficulty. In the ice cream case the mashed potato prop is not being used for additional proof of the product claim, while the purpose of the Rapid Shave commercial is to give the viewer objective proof of the claims made. If in the ice cream hypothetical the focus of the commercial becomes the undisclosed potato prop and the viewer is invited, explicitly or by implication, to see for himself the truth of the claims about the ice cream's rich texture and full color, and perhaps compare it to a "rival product," then the commercial has become similar to the one now before us. Clearly, however, a commercial which depicts happy actors delightedly eating ice cream that is in fact mashed potatoes or drinking a product appearing to be coffee but which is in fact some other substance is not covered by the present order.

Finally, we find no defect in the provision of the order which prohibits respondents from engaging in similar practices with respect to "any product" they advertise. . . . In this case the respondents produced three different commercials which employed the same deceptive practice. This we believe gave the Commission a sufficient basis for believing that the respondents would be inclined to use similar commercials with respect to the other products they advertise. We think it reasonable for the Commission to frame its order broadly enough to prevent respondents from engaging in similarly illegal practices in future advertisements. As was said in *Federal Trade Comm'n v Ruberoid Co.*, "[T]he Commission is not limited to prohibiting the illegal practice in the precise form in which it is found to have existed in the past." Having been caught violating the Act, respondents "must expect some fencing in."

The judgment of the Court of Appeals is *reversed* and the case *remanded* for the entry of a judgment *enforcing* the Commission's order.

Mr. Justice Harlan, whom **Mr. Justice Stewart** joins, dissenting in part.

It is commonly known that television presents certain distortions in transmission for which the broadcasting industry must compensate. Thus, a white towel will look a dingy gray over television, but a blue towel will look a sparkling white. . . . A perhaps more commonplace example suggests itself: Would it be proper for respondent Colgate.

in advertising a laundry detergent, . . . to wash a white (not a blue) sheet with the competitor's detergent?

CASE QUESTIONS

1. What commercial was involved in this case? How was the commercial prepared? Explain.
2. What does Section 5 of the Federal Trade Commission Act provide? Does it apply to deceptive advertising?
3. What was the decision of:
   a. the hearing examiner?
   b. the Federal Trade Commission?
   c. the Court of Appeals?
   d. the U.S. Supreme Court?
4. How did the Supreme Court distinguish the ice-cream/mashed-potatoes commercial from the Rapid Shave commercial in this case? Do you agree with the distinction?

5. Would there be a violation of Section 5 of the FTC Act if a white towel were used on television to show the effect of a competitor's detergent as Justice Harlan asserts in his dissent? Would the commercial be *literally* true?

Policy Issue. Is this the type of case that should be heard by the U.S. Supreme Court?

Economics Issue. Should props such as "sandpaper on plexiglass" be allowed where no other means of demonstrating the attributes of a product would be effective?

Ethics Issue. Did Colgate need the "fencing in" that the FTC order provided? Or was the order too broad?

Social Responsibility. Do TV advertisers owe a special duty of social responsibility because of the persuasive impact of this medium?

Deceptive Price Advertising. In addition to false advertisements about the quality of a good or service, advertisements that deceptively advertise the price of a product or service violate FTC Act Section 5. Deceptive price advertising often occurs where companies advertise "two-for-the-price-of-one" sales, "one-half off" sales, and "buy two, get one free" type of sales. These and similar statements are only relevant when they are compared to the usual and customary price of the good or service. If there is no history of prior sales at higher prices, or if the prior sales were not at a level that would make the new advertised price a bargain, these are unfair and deceptive trade practices in violation of FTC Act Section 5.

In *FTC v. Mary Carter Paint Co.* the U.S. Supreme Court held that a defendant's "two-for-the-price-of-one" advertisement was an unfair and deceptive practice in violation of FTC Act Section 5, because the defendant had no previous history of sales at a higher price.

DECEPTIVE PRICE ADVERTISING

FEDERAL TRADE COMMISSION v. MARY CARTER PAINT CO.

382 U.S. 46 (1965)
UNITED STATES SUPREME COURT

Mr. Justice Brennan delivered the opinion of the Court.

Respondent Mary Carter Paint Company manu-

factures and sells paint and related products. The Federal Trade Commission ordered respondent to cease and desist from the use of certain representations found by the Commission to be deceptive and in violation of Section 5 of the Federal Trade Commission Act.

The representations appeared in advertisements which stated in various ways that for every can of respondent's paint purchased by a buyer, the respondent would give the buyer a "free" can of equal quality and quantity. The Court of Appeals for the Fifth Circuit set aside the Commission's order. We granted *certiorari.*

Although there is some ambiguity in the Commission's opinion, we cannot say that its holding constituted a departure from Commission policy regarding the use of the commercially exploitable word "free." Initial efforts to define the term in decisions were followed by "Guides Against Deceptive Pricing." These informed businessmen that they might advertise an article as "free," even though purchase of another article required, so long as the terms of the offer were clearly stated, the price of the article required to be purchased was not increased, and its quality and quantity were not diminished. With specific reference to two-for-the-price-of-one offers, the Guides required that either the sales price for the two be "the advertiser's usual and customary retail price for the single article in the recent, regular course of his business," or where the advertiser has not previously sold the article, the price for two be the "usual and customary" price for one in the relevant trade areas.

The gist of the Commission's reasoning is in the hearing examiner's finding, which it adopted, that

> the usual and customary retail price of each can of Mary Carter paint was not, and is not now, the price designated in the advertisement [$6.98] but was, and is now, substantially less than such price. The second can of paint was not, and is not now, 'free,' that is, was not, and is not now, given as a gift or gratuity. The offer is, on the contrary, an offer of two cans of paint for the price advertised as or purporting to be the list price or customary and usual price of one can.

In sum, the Commission found that Mary Carter had no history of selling single cans of paint; it was marketing twins, and in allocating what is in fact the price of two cans to one can, yet calling one "free," Mary Carter misrepresented. . . . There was substantial evidence in the record to support the Commission's finding; its determination that the practice here was deceptive was neither arbitrary nor clearly wrong. The Court of Appeals should have sustained it.

The judgment of the Court of Appeals is therefore *reversed* and the case is *remanded* to that court with directions to remand to the Commission for clarification of its order.

Mr. Justice Harlan, dissenting.

In administering Section 5 in the context of the many elusive questions raised by modern advertising, it is the duty of the Commission to speak and rule clearly so that law-abiding businessmen may know where they stand. In proscribing a practice uncomplained of by the public, effectively harmless to the consumer, allowed by the Commission's long-established policy statement, and only a hairbreadth away from advertising practices that the Commission will continue to permit, I think that the Commission in this instance has fallen far short of what is necessary to entitle its order to enforcement.

CASE QUESTIONS

1. What did the Mary Carter Paint Company advertisement promise? Explain.
2. Had Mary Carter Paint previously sold one can of paint for the price of $6.98? Was the second can really "free"?
3. Does Section 5 of the Federal Trade Commission Act prohibit deceptive *price* advertising?

Policy Issue. Should the FTC concern itself with the type of advertising used in this case? Or do you agree with Justice Harlan's dissent that this advertisement was "effectively harmless to the consumer"?

Economics Issue. Do you think this decision hampered the sale of paint by Mary Carter Paint Company? Was this the usual method used by the company to sell paint?

Ethics Issue. Did Mary Carter Paint Company act ethically in using the "two-for-one" advertisement?

Social Responsibility. Do companies owe a duty of social responsibility to only show advertisements that are technically correct? Or should some "puffing" be allowed (e.g., buy one, get one "free")? Are consumers actually fooled that they are getting one of the items "free"?

"Bait and Switch." In another often-used deceptive advertising practice, a company advertises the availability of a discounted sale item (the "bait") in order to attract customers to its store. However, once the customers are in the store, defendant's sales representatives put undue pressure on customers to purchase other more expensive and profitable merchandise (the "switch"). The courts have held that bait-and-switch operations are unfair and deceptive trade practices, which are unlawful under FTC Act Section 5. The line between merchandising by using lawful "loss leaders" and engaging in unlawful "bait-and-switch" tactics is often unclear.

In *Tashof v. FTC* the court found that the defendant had engaged in an unlawful "bait-and-switch" operation in the sale of eyeglasses, which violated FTC Act Section 5.

"BAIT AND SWITCH"

TASHOF v. FEDERAL TRADE COMMISSION

437 F.2d 707 (1970)
UNITED STATES COURT OF APPEALS, DISTRICT OF COLUMBIA

Bazelon, Chief Judge:

Appellant Leon A. Tashof is engaged in the retail trade as New York Jewelry Co. (NYJC). His store is located in an area that serves low-income consumers, many of whom hold low-paying jobs, and have no bank or charge accounts. About 85 percent of NYJC's sales are made on credit. The Commission found, after a Hearing Examiner had dismissed the charges as unsubstantiated, that NYJC falsely advertised the availability of discount eyeglasses, and misrepresented its prices and credit practices.

The Commission first found that NYJC employed a "bait and switch" maneuver with respect to sales of eyeglasses. The evidence showed that NYJC advertised eyeglasses "from $7.50 complete," including "lenses, frames and case." The newspaper advertisements, but not the radio advertisements, mentioned a "moderate examining fee." During this period, NYJC offered free eye examinations by a sign posted in its store, and through cards it mailed out and distributed on the street. NYJC claimed that it offered $7.50 eyeglasses only to persons with their own prescriptions. But we have no doubt that the record amply supports the Commission's finding that the advertising campaign taken as a whole offered complete eyeglass service for $7.50.

That much shows "bait." There was no direct evidence of "switch"—no direct evidence, that is, that NYJC disparaged or discouraged the purchase of the $7.50 eyeglasses, or that the glasses were unavailable on demand, or unsuited for their purpose. The evidence on which the Commission rested its finding was a stipulation that out of 1,400 pairs of eyeglasses sold each year by NYJC, less than 10 were sold for $7.50 with or without a prescription. NYJC claims that this evidence does not support the finding. We disagree.

It seems plain to us that the Commission drew a permissible inference of "switch" from the evidence of bait advertising and minimal sales of the advertised product. At best only nine sales—64/100 of one percent of NYJC's eyeglass sales—were made at $7.50. The record leaves unexplained why NYJC's customers, presumably anxious to purchase at as low a price as possible, would so consistently have bought more expensive glasses if suitable glasses at $7.50 were available. Further, NYJC continued to advertise the $7.50 glasses for a year and a half despite the scarcity of sales, a fact which tends to support a finding of a purpose to bring customers into the store for other reasons. This evidence, we think, was sufficient to shift the burden of coming forward to the respondent. But NYJC offered no evidence to negate the inference of "switch." The relevant facts are in NYJC's possession, and it was in the best position to show, if it could be shown at all that the $7.50 glasses were actually available in the store. Yet the most NYJC could produce was its sales manager's denial that the $7.50 glasses were disparaged. NYJC never did point to even a single sale of the advertised product.

It is worth noting that even if the prevailing prices were computed as NYJC has urged, NYJC's customers still paid a higher than prevailing price more often than not.

Thus the order must be *enforced.*

CASE QUESTIONS

1. What is a "bait-and-switch" tactic? Explain.
2. What were the following in this case?

a. the "bait"
b. the "switch"

3. Was there any direct evidence of the switch in this case? If not, from what evidence did the court *infer* the switch? Why do you think the defendant failed to introduce any evidence to refute this inference?
4. Did the fact that the defendant continued to advertise the $7.50 glasses when it hardly sold any at that price support the inference of the switch?

Policy Issue.   Are bait-and-switch tactics really deceptive? Don't consumers buy what they want?

Economics Issue.   Are bait-and-switch tactics profitable? Do they bring more people into the store than would otherwise come?

Ethics Issue.   Was it ethical for the defendant to engage in the bait-and-switch tactic in this case? To charge the customers more than they would have to pay elsewhere? Were the customers in this case more susceptible to these tactics than most? Explain.

Social Responsibility.   Does a seller owe a duty of social responsibility not to engage in bait-and-switch tactics? Not to use "loss leaders"?

Other Consumer Laws Administered by the FTC.   In addition to the Federal Trade Commission Act, the FTC is also responsible for administering the following consumer laws:

1. the Wool Products Labeling Act, which protects consumers from manufacturers who substitute other materials for wool without revealing this fact on the label
2. The Fur Products Labeling Act, which protects consumers from false advertising and misbranding of furs and fur products
3. the Fair Packing and Labeling Act, which protects consumers from "unfair and deceptive" methods of packing and labeling of consumer products
4. the Textile Fiber Products Identification Act, which protects consumers against false advertising and misbranding of the fiber content of textile fiber products
5. the Export-Import Act, which protects consumers and others from unfair and deceptive practices involving imports
6. the Consumer Credit Protection Act ("Truth in Lending" Act), which re-

quires full disclosure of finance charges and other credit terms and limits the ability of debtors to garnishee the wages of consumer-creditors

7. the Lanham Trademark Act, which protects consumers and others from false and deceptive advertising.

THE LANHAM ACT

In 1946, Congress enacted the Lanham Trademark Act to provide *competitors* with a statutory remedy with which to attack false advertising by competitors. Section 43(a) of the Lanham Act prohibits the use of any false description or representation that tends to describe a product. Section 43(a) of the Lanham Act provides in relevant part:

Any person who shall . . . use in connection with any goods or services . . . any false designation of origin . . . or any false description or representation, including words or symbols tending falsely to describe or represent the same . . . shall be liable to a civil action by any person . . . who believes that he is or is likely to be damaged by the use of any such false description or representation.

The Lanham Act provides a federal statutory cause of action that is often easier to prove than a common law action for palming off or disparagement. Unlike most common-law business torts, a Lanham Act cause of action does *not* require a showing of either the defendant's intent to deceive or the plaintiff having suffered actual injury. Thus, a *non*intentional deceptive practice *is* actionable under the Lanham Act, and a plaintiff-competitor need only show that there is a "likelihood" that he will suffer a loss from the false or deceptive acts of the defendant.

False Designation or Representation. The majority of the cases brought under the Lanham Act are for false or deceptive advertising. Although the Lanham Act was originally considered to provide a new federal tort of "false advertising," the courts have been reluctant to expand the application of the statute beyond cases where the *defendant* has made a false or deceptive representation about the *plaintiff's* goods or services. Where a business overstates or misrepresents the quality of *its own* products or services, the courts generally refuse to allow a competitor to bring an action based on the Lanham Act. At least one federal circuit still requires a showing of an actual misuse of a trademark (e.g., palming off an inferior product as if produced by a famous company) before a violation of the Lanham Act will be found. The current trend in the law, however, is for the courts to expand the applicability of the Lanham Act to more situations involving false and deceptive advertising.

In *Johnson & Johnson v. Carter-Wallace, Inc.* the court found that advertisements by the defendant stating that its products contained "baby oil," a product made by the plaintiff, contained an implicit false representation that the defendant's product was made by the plaintiff, in violation of Section 43(a) of the Lanham Act.

THE LANHAM ACT

JOHNSON & JOHNSON v. CARTER-WALLACE, INC.

631 F.2d 186 (1980)
UNITED STATES COURT OF APPEALS, SECOND CIRCUIT

Mansfield, Circuit Judge:

Johnson & Johnson ("Johnson"), manufacturer of Johnson's Baby Oil and Johnson's Baby Lotion, appeals from a judgment of the United States District Court for the Southern District of New York, entered by Judge Constance Baker Motley, dismissing at the end of the plaintiff's case during a nonjury trial its suit for injunctive relief brought under Section 43(a) of the Lanham Act, against Carter-Wallace ("Carter"), the manufacturer of NAIR, a leading depilatory product.

Johnson's claim arises out of Carter's use of baby oil in NAIR and its advertising campaign regarding that inclusion. In 1977, Carter added baby oil to its NAIR lotion and initiated a successful advertising campaign emphasizing this fact. NAIR is sold in a pink plastic bottle with the word "NAIR" written in large, pink letters. A bright turquoise-blue banner, open at both ends, contains the words "with baby oil." In addition to its packaging of NAIR, Carter's television advertisements emphasize that NAIR contains baby oil.

Alleging (1) that Carter is making false claims for NAIR with baby oil and (2) that it is packaging and advertising NAIR so as to give consumers the false impression that NAIR is a Johnson & Johnson product, plaintiff filed the instant suit for injunctive relief under Section 43(a) of the Lanham Act, . . .

Section 43(a) of the Lanham Act provides for two separate causes of action: one is for "false designation of origin," the other for a "false description or representation, including words or symbols tending falsely to describe or represent" the product. Johnson's false representation claim alleges that Carter's "NAIR with baby oil" campaign falsely represents to consumers that the baby oil in NAIR has moisturizing and softening effect on the skin of the user.

Prior to the enactment of Section 43(a) of the Lanham Act, false advertising claims were governed by the common law of trade disparagement.

. . . [Many] instances of false advertising were safe from actions by competitors due to the difficulty of satisfying the requirement of proof of actual damage caused by the false claims. In an open market it is normally impossible to prove that a customer, who was induced by the defendant through the use of false claims to purchase the product, would have bought from the plaintiff if the defendant had been truthful.

The passage of Section 43(a) represented a departure from the common law action for trade disparagement and from the need to prove actual damages as a prerequisite for injunctive relief. This departure marked the creation of a "new statutory tort" intended to secure a market-place free from deceitful marketing practices. The new tort, as subsequently interpreted by the courts, differs from the common law action for trade disparagement in two important respects: (1) it does not require proof of intent to deceive, and (2) it entitles a broad range of commercial parties to relief.

The broadening of the scope of liability results from a provision in Section 43(a) allowing suit to be brought "by any person who believes that he is or is likely to be damaged by the use of any false description or representation."

The statute demands only proof providing a reasonable basis for the belief that the plaintiff is likely to be damaged as a result of the false advertising. The correct standard is whether it is *likely* that Carter's advertising has caused or will cause a loss of Johnson sales, not whether Johnson has come forward with specific evidence that Carter's ads actually resulted in some definite loss of sales. . . . We believe that the evidence offered by Johnson, though not overwhelming, is sufficient to prove a likelihood of damage from loss of sales.

Initially, we find that Johnson has shown that it and Carter are competitors in a relevant market. Although Johnson's Baby Oil and Lotion do not compete with NAIR in the narrower depilatory market, they do compete in the broader hair removal market. NAIR is used for hair removal by depilation. Johnson's Baby Lotion has been promoted as a substitute for shaving cream and is used for removal of hair by shaving. Also, both of Johnson's products are used as skin moisturizers after shaving or after the use of depilatories. Such indirect competitors may avail themselves of the protection of Section 43(a); the competition need not be direct.

Finally, Johnson's inability to point to a definite amount of sales lost *to Carter* (a failure which would bar monetary relief) does not preclude injunctive relief. Likelihood of competitive injury sufficient to warrant a Section 43(a) injunction has been found in the absence of proof of actual sales diversion in numerous cases.

Accordingly, this cause is *reversed* and *remanded* for further proceedings in conformity with this opinion. We retain jurisdiction.

CASE QUESTIONS

1. What does Section 43(a) of the Lanham Act provide? Which of the following does it protect?
   a. consumers
   b. competitors
2. What product did the following parties make? Were they "competitors" within the meaning of the Lanham Act?

   a. plaintiff Johnson and Johnson (J&J)
   b. defendant Carter-Wallace (Carter)
3. Which of the following violations of the Lanham Act did J&J charge Carter was responsible for in this case? What is the difference?
   a. false designation of origin
   b. false description or representation
4. Does an action by a competitor under the Lanham Act require a showing of actual damages? Or only that such injury is *likely?* Is this a radical shift from the common law? Explain.
5. Did J&J sue for *damages?* Or *injunctive* relief? What is the difference? Explain.

Policy Issue. Should Congress statutorily protect competitors from the actions of other competitors? Or are common-law damage actions sufficient protection?

Economics Issue. Did Carter "piggy-back" on J&J's reputation in this case? Did the allegation that NAIR contained "baby oil" help or hurt sales of NAIR? Of J&J skin moisturizers?

Ethics Issue. Was what Carter did in this case ethical?

Social Responsibility. Do companies owe a duty of social responsibility not to use the reputation of other companies in selling their products? Why or why not?

Comparative Advertising. On many occasions, a business will produce an advertisement in which it compares its products to the products of other competitors. The "Pepsi challenge" is the most recent notable example of *comparative advertising.* Comparative advertising is presently being encouraged by the Federal Trade Commission, as long as the comparison is truthful and is supported by adequate testing and research. Where comparative advertising is false or deceptive, a plaintiff may bring an action for damages or injunctive relief against the defendant-advertiser under the Lanham Act. Section 43(a) of the Lanham Act has been held to apply to literal misrepresentations of fact, as well as to innuendo, indirect intimations, and ambiguous suggestions by an advertiser that would likely cause the public to be misled.

In *American Home Products Corp. v. Johnson & Johnson* the court enjoined, pursuant to the Lanham Act, comparative advertising by the maker of Anacin that contained deliberate ambiguities and unsubstantiated claims about a competitor's product, Tylenol.

COMPARATIVE ADVERTISING

AMERICAN HOME PRODUCTS CORP. v. JOHNSON & JOHNSON

577 F.2d 160 (1978)
UNITED STATES COURT OF APPEALS, SECOND CIRCUIT

Oakes, Circuit Judge:

Comparative advertising in which the competing product is explicitly named is a relatively new weapon in the Madison Avenue arsenal. These cross-appeals by two of the leading manufacturers of analgesics—pain relief tablets—raised questions regarding the permissible boundaries of this novel approach to consumer persuasion.

The parties appeal from an order of the United States District Court for the Southern District of New York . . . enjoining the use in television and printed advertising of certain product superiority claims of "Anacin" over "Tylenol." The order was issued in an action for a declaratory judgment initiated by appellant American Home Products Corp. (AHP), the manufacturer of Anacin, against McNeil Laboratories, Inc., the manufacturer of Tylenol, and its parent corporation, Johnson & Johnson (collectively McNeil), seeking a ruling that the advertising is not false. McNeil counterclaimed, alleging, *inter alia,* that the advertisements were false and misleading under Section 43(a) of the Lanham Act.

The District Court found that the advertising violated Section 43(a), and accordingly the judgment enjoined AHP from representing that Anacin provides superior analgesia to Tylenol "in the context of a representation as to any anti-inflammatory property of Anacin. . . ."

AHP's product, Anacin, is a compound of aspirin (ASA), its analgesic component, and caffeine. McNeil's product, Tylenol, affords analgesia through the ingredient acetaminophen (APAP). Anacin advertises more heavily than the other leading aspirin brands. It took over the Number One pain reliever spot from another aspirin-based product, Bayer Aspirin, a few years ago. Since the summer of 1976, however, Tylenol has replaced Anacin as the largest selling over-the-counter (OTC) internal analgesic product. Anacin remains the largest selling aspirin-based analgesic.

The lawsuit arose out of two Anacin advertisements initiated shortly after Tylenol became market leader. The first is a thirty-second television commercial initially aired by CBS in late November, 1976, and by NBC in early December, 1976. It commences with the phrase: "Your body knows the difference between these pain relievers . . . and Adult Strength Anacin," and asserts its superiority to Datril, Tylenol and Extra-Strength Tylenol. The second advertisement was introduced in national magazines in late January, 1977. It carries a similar theme, stating that "Anacin can reduce inflammation that comes with most pain," "Tylenol cannot."

The controversy began when McNeil protested the television commercial to the networks and the magazine advertisement to the print media on the ground that they were deceptive and misleading. McNeil also complained to the National Advertising Division of the Better Business Bureau. These protests were, for the most part, unsuccessful. CBS, NBC and the print media continued to carry the two advertisements without alteration.

After denying McNeil's motion for a preliminary injunction, Judge Stewart held an expedited trial on the merits. . . . The district court . . . concluded that the preponderance of the evidence indicated that [the claims] . . . that Anacin is a superior analgesic in general to Tylenol and a superior analgesic for conditions which have an inflammatory component were false.

That Section 43(a) of the Lanham Act encompasses more than literal falsehoods cannot be questioned. Were it otherwise, clever use of innuendo, indirect intimations, and ambiguous suggestions could shield the advertisement from scrutiny precisely when protection against such sophisticated deception is most needed. It is equally well established that the truth or falsity of the advertisement usually should be tested by the reactions of the public.

Applying these principles to the facts of this case, we are convinced that the District Court's use of consumer response data was proper. We believe that the claims of both the television commercial and the print advertisement are ambiguous.

We conclude, therefore, that the judge correctly held, principally on the basis of consumer reaction tests, that both advertisements claim greater pain relief. On the assumption that this claim is false, as the District Court held, it was perfectly proper for the trial court to enjoin future advertisements containing superior analgesic claims.

The judgment is *affirmed*.

CASE QUESTIONS

1. What products did the following parties make in this case? Were they "competitors" within the definition of the Lanham Act?
   a. American Home Products Corp. (AHP)
   b. McNeil Laboratories, a subsidiary of Johnson & Johnson (McNeil)
2. What is a *declaratory relief* action? Why did AHP products bring a declaratory relief action in this case?
3. What did McNeil's *counterclaim* assert? Explain.
4. Did the court find that the Anacin advertisement violated Section 43(a) of the Lanham Act? What evidence did it cite?

Policy Issue. Should comparative advertising be allowed? If so, under what conditions, if any?

Economics Issue. Why do smaller companies with lesser-known products often engage in comparative advertising with well-known products of larger companies? Does the reverse often occur? Why or why not?

Ethics Issue. Was it ethical for AHP to advertise that Anacin was superior to Tylenol in this case? Why or why not?

Social Responsibility. Do companies owe a duty of social responsibility to conduct sufficient tests to support their comparative advertising claims? Should companies who conduct taste tests (e.g., the "Pepsi Challenge") be required to put people who didn't like their product in their TV commercials along with the people who did like their product? Should these be in the same proportion as the final results of the test indicate? If a company runs a taste test and the results come out negative, should it be forced to announce the results in advertisements?

CORRECTIVE ADVERTISING

Where the FTC finds false advertising in violation of Section 5 of the FTC Act, it may generally issue a cease-and-desist order against the defendant to prevent the defendant from engaging in similar practices in the future. A violation of a valid cease-and-desist order carries criminal penalties.

In an extreme cases of false advertising the FTC may order the defendant to engage in *corrective advertising*. The purpose of corrective advertising is to counter a false belief about a product that may have been raised in the minds of consumers by previous false advertising by the defendant. In such circumstances, a cease-and-desist order against future violations would be ineffective in correcting the false belief already held by the public. In order to warrant the imposition of an order for corrective advertising, the FTC must find (1) that the defendant's previously deceptive advertising created a false belief about the product in the public's mind, and (2) that the belief would linger on after the false advertising ceased. In *Warner-Lambert Company v. FTC*, 562 F.2d 749 (1977) the court cited the following instances where corrective advertising has been ordered:

For example, the Commission has ordered the sellers of treatments for baldness to disclose that the vast majority of cases of thinning hair and baldness are attributable to heredity, age, and endocrine balance (so-called "male pattern baldness") and that their treatment would have no effect whatever on this type of baldness. It has ordered the promoters of a device for stopping bedwetting to disclose that the device would not be of value in cases caused by organic defects or diseases. And it has ordered the makers of Geritol, an iron supplement, to disclose that Geritol will relieve symptoms of tiredness only in persons who suffer from iron deficiency anemia, and that the vast majority of people who experience such symptoms do not have such a deficiency.

In the *Warner-Lambert Company v. FTC* case, which follows, the court ordered the defendant to engage in corrective advertising to help correct the false impression made by years of advertising Listerine as a cold and sore-throat remedy.

CORRECTIVE ADVERTISING

WARNER-LAMBERT COMPANY v. FEDERAL TRADE COMMISSION

562 F.2d 749 (1977)
UNITED STATES COURT OF APPEALS, DISTRICT OF COLUMBIA

J. Skelly Wright, Circuit Judge:

The Warner-Lambert Company petitions for review of an order of the Federal Trade Commission requiring it to cease and desist from advertising that its product, Listerine Antiseptic mouthwash, prevents, cures, or alleviates the common cold. The FTC order further requires Warner-Lambert to disclose in future Listerine advertisements that: "Contrary to prior advertising, Listerine will not help prevent colds or sore throats or lessen their severity."

BACKGROUND

Listerine has been on the market since 1879. Its formula has never changed. Ever since its introduction it has been represented as being beneficial in certain respects for colds, cold symptoms, and sore throats. Direct advertising to the consumer, including the cold claims as well as others, began in 1921.

Following the 1972 complaint, hearings were held before an administrative law judge (ALJ). The hearings consumed over four months and produced an evidentiary record consisting of approximately 4,000 pages of documentary exhibits and the testimony of 46 witnesses. In 1974 the ALJ issued an initial decision sustaining the allegations of the complaint. Petitioner appealed this decision to the Commission. On December 9, 1975 the Commission issued its decision essentially affirming the ALJ's findings. It concluded that petitioner had made the challenged representations that Listerine will ameliorate, prevent, and cure colds and sore throats, and that these representations were false.

SUBSTANTIAL EVIDENCE

The first issue on appeal is whether the Commission's conclusion that Listerine is not beneficial for colds or sore throats is supported by the evidence. The Commission's findings must be sustained if they are supported by substantial evidence on the record viewed as a whole. We conclude that they are.

Both the ALJ and the Commission carefully analyzed the evidence. They gave full consideration to the studies submitted by petitioner. The ultimate conclusion that Listerine is not an effective cold remedy was based on six specific findings of fact.

First, the Commission found that the ingredients of Listerine are not present in sufficient quantities to have any therapeutic effect.

Second, the Commission found that in the process of gargling it is impossible for Listerine to reach the critical areas of the body in medically significant concentrations.

Third, the Commission found that even if significant quantities of the active ingredients of Listerine were to reach the critical sites where cold viruses enter and infect the body, they could not interfere with the activities of the virus because they could not penetrate the tissue cells.

Fourth, the Commission discounted the results of a clinical study conducted by petitioner on which petitioner heavily relies.

Fifth, the Commission found that the ability of Listerine to kill germs by millions on contact is of no medical significance in the treatment of colds or sore throats. Expert testimony showed that bacteria in the oral cavity, the "germs" which Listerine purports to kill, do not cause colds and play no role in cold symptoms. Colds are caused by viruses.

Sixth, the Commission found that Listerine has no significant beneficial effect on the symptoms of sore throat.

THE COMMISSION'S POWER

Petitioner contends that even if its advertising claims in the past were false, the portion of the Commission's order requiring "corrective advertising" exceeds the Commission's statutory power.

According to petitioner, "The first reference to corrective advertising in Commission decisions occurred in 1970, nearly fifty years and untold numbers of false advertising cases after passage of the Act." In petitioner's view, the late emergence of this "newly discovered" remedy is itself evidence that it is beyond the Commission's authority. This argument fails on two counts. First, the fact that an agency has not asserted a power over a period of years is not proof that the agency lacks such power. Second, and more importantly, we are not convinced that the corrective advertising remedy is really such an innovation. The label may be newly coined, but the concept is well established. It is simply that under certain circumstances an advertiser may be required to make affirmative disclosure of unfavorable facts.

Listerine has built up over a period of many years a widespread reputation. When it was ascertained that reputation no longer applied to the product, it was necessary to take action to correct it. Here, . . . it is the accumulated impact of *past* advertising that necessitates disclosure in *future* advertising.

To allow consumers to continue to buy the product on the strength of the impression built up by prior advertising—an impression which is now known to be false—would be unfair and deceptive.

THE REMEDY

The Commission has adopted the following standard for the imposition of corrective advertising:

> [I]f a deceptive advertisement has played a substantial role in creating or reinforcing in the public's mind a false and material belief which lives on after the false advertising ceases, there is clear and continuing injury to competition and to the consuming public as consumers continue to make purchasing decisions based on the false belief. Since this injury cannot be averted by merely requiring respondent to cease disseminating the advertisement, we may appropriately order respondent to take affirmative action designed to terminate the otherwise continuing ill effects of the advertisement.

We think this standard is entirely reasonable. It dictates two factual inquiries: (1) did Listerine's advertisements play a substantial role in creating or reinforcing in the public's mind a false belief about the product? and (2) would this belief linger on after the false advertising ceases? It strikes us that if the answer to both questions is not yes, companies everywhere may be wasting their massive advertising budgets. Indeed, it is more than a little peculiar to hear petitioner assert that its commercials really have no effect on consumer belief.

We turn next to the specific disclosure required: "Contrary to prior advertising, Listerine will not help prevent colds or sore throats or lessen their severity." Petitioner is ordered to include this statement in every future advertisement for Listerine for a defined period. In printed advertisements it must be displayed in type size at least as large as that in which the principal portion of the text of the advertisement appears and it must be separated from the text so that it can be readily noticed. In television commercials the disclosure must be presented simultaneously in both audio and visual portions. During the audio portion of the disclosure in television and radio advertisements, no other sounds, including music, may occur.

These specifications are well calculated to assure that the disclosure will reach the public. It will necessarily attract the notice of readers, viewers, and listeners, and be plainly conveyed. Given these safeguards, we believe the preamble "Contrary to prior advertising" is not necessary. It can serve only two purposes: either to attract attention that a correction follows or to humiliate the advertiser. The Commission claims only the first purpose for it, and this we think is obviated by the other terms of the order.

[P]etitioner challenges the duration of the disclosure requirement. By its terms it continues until respondent has expended on Listerine advertising a sum equal to the average annual Listerine advertising budget for the period April 1962 to March 1972. That is approximately ten million dollars. Thus if petitioner continues to advertise normally the corrective advertising will be required for about one year. We cannot say that is an unreasonably long time in which to correct a hundred years of cold claims. But, to petitioner's distress, the requirement will not expire by mere passage of time. If petitioner cuts back its Listerine advertising, or ceases it altogether, it can only postpone the duty to disclose. The Commission concluded that correction was required and that a duration of a fixed period of time might not accomplish that task, since petitioner could evade the order by choosing not to advertise at all. The formula settled upon by the Commission is reasonably related to the violation it found.

Accordingly, the order, as modified, is *affirmed*.

CASE QUESTIONS

1. What claims did defendant Warner-Lambert Co. make regarding the attributes of Listerine? Were these claims false? Explain.

2. Is the issuance of an order for corrective advertising within the statutory power delegated to the Federal Trade Commission by Congress?
3. Why was the FTC concerned about the *future* effects of Warner-Lambert's *past* advertising? Explain.
4. Would a *cease-and-desist* order that would have prevented Warner-Lambert from engaging in any false advertising in the future have been effective in this case? Why or why not?
5. What remedy did the FTC order in this case? Explain. Was the dollar requirement of the corrective advertising order necessary? Why or why not?

Policy Issue. Is corrective advertising an effective way to combat false advertising claims? If corrective advertising were not allowed, would there be any incentive for companies not to engage in massive false advertising campaigns?

Economics Issue. What are the economic consequences of corrective advertising?

Ethics Issue. Was it ethical for Warner-Lambert to engage in the Listerine advertising in this case? Was it ethical for it to argue that its past advertising was not effective? Do you think company management believed this argument? Why or why not?

Social Responsibility. Did Warner-Lambert breach its duty of social responsibility when it advertised Listerine as preventing colds and sore throats when it actually did not do so? Why do you think it engaged in this advertising?

CORPORATE ADVERTISING OF POLICY ISSUES

Corporations have in recent years expanded their advertising to advance their positions on *policy issues* that affect society. Current campaigns concern environmental issues, particularly nuclear power, alcohol and drug abuse, the need for trade barriers to protect American business from foreign competition, and other such issues. Some of these advertising campaigns are obviously self-serving, extolling the virtues of the company's product but couched in social terms, while others are noncompany- and nonproduct-oriented advertisements.

The U.S. Supreme Court has held that corporate advertising on social issues is protected by the Free Speech Clause of the First Amendment. However, such advertisements are subject to review under Section 5 of the Federal Trade Commission Act as a "deceptive" or "unfair" method of competition, or as a violation of relevant state law prohibiting false advertising.

Trend of the Law

With the increased sophistication and persuasive force of advertising on consumers, the FTC and other government agencies (e.g., the Federal Drug Administration) will continue and probably increase their efforts in the future to prevent unfair and deceptive advertising. As the advertising executives and advertisers become more aware of the psychological nature of advertising and develop more subtle methods of delivering advertising messages to consumers, new laws may have to be enacted, and the coverage of existing laws expanded, to curtail future advertising abuses. In this vein, subliminal advertising on television is presently prohibited.

Several examples of comprehensive self-regulation of advertising presently exist in this country. For example, each of the major television networks has a department that reviews all television advertisements to see if they meet legal standards, meet the ethical standards set by the network, are truthful, and if their claims are supported by sufficient evidence. By agreement among the major television networks, several forms of commercials are presently either highly restricted or forbidden to be shown on network television. For example, persons in beer commercials are not permitted to be shown actually drinking the beer advertised. Advertisements for alcohol other than beer and wine and advertising for cigarettes are no longer permitted on network television. The Better Business Bureaus around the country also have adopted rules against deceptive or unfair advertising by members. Self-regulation will continue to expand in the future, both by the media and by organizations representing advertisers.

REVIEW QUESTIONS

1. Chrestensen owned an old Navy submarine that he wished to exhibit for profit in New York City. He prepared a handbill that advertised the boat and solicited customers at a stated admission fee but Police Comissioner Valentine refused to allow the handbills to be passed out. Valentine cited Section 318 of the Sanitary Code, which made it illegal to distribute advertising matter in the streets. Chrestensen was told, however, that dissemination of information leaflets or material registering a public protest could not be restrained. Accordingly, Chrestensen prepared a two-sided handbill.

On one side he advertised the ship, although the admission price no longer appeared. On the reverse side of the new handbill Chrestensen protested the City Dock Department's refusal to grant him wharfing privileges at a city pier. Chrestensen was told that distribution of the advertising portion of the message was illegal, and police eventually restrained him from passing out the handbill. Does a law that prohibits handbill advertising violate the Free Speech clause of the First Amendment?

2. Bigelow was the director and managing editor of the *Virginia Weekly*, a newspaper that was circulated in Albemarle County, Virginia and on the University of Virginia campus. Bigelow published an advertisement by the Women's Pavilion, a New York City abortion referral service. Among other things, the advertisement stated that abortions were legal in New York state and that there were no residency requirements. Bigelow was charged with violating Virginia Code Section 18.1–63 which made it a crime for ". . . any person, by publication . . . sale or circulation of any publication, or in any other manner, (to) encourage or prompt the procuring of abortion or miscarriage. . . ." Bigelow was convicted and he appealed, claiming that the First Amendment protections of free speech allowed him to publish the advertisement. May a First Amendment right be asserted to protect this type of commercial advertisement?

3. In their advertising campaign promoting the value of eggs in the diet, the National Commission on Egg Nutrition (NCEN) made the following claims: (1) there is no competent and reliable scientific evidence that eating eggs increases the risk of heart attacks or heart disease; (2) there is overwhelming scientific evidence that eating eggs does not increase such risk; (3) there is competent scientific evidence that dietary cholesterol decreases the risk of heart disease; (4) eating eggs does not increase a normal person's blood cholesterol level; (5) the human body increases or decreases the manufacture of cholesterol in relation to the amount of dietary cholesterol intake; (6) dietary cholesterol is necessary for the production of sex hormones, transmitting nerve impulses, and maintaining cell life; and (7) avoiding dietary cholesterol increases the risk of heart disease. NCEN also claimed that cholesterol did not increase the risk of heart attacks and that dietary cholesterol decreases the risk of heart attacks, and that avoiding cholesterol increases the risk of heart disease.

The FTC sought a temporary injunction against some of the claims, arguing that they were deceptive and misleading. The principal representation challenged by the FTC was that there is no scientific evidence that eating eggs, even in quantity, increases the risk of heart attacks or heart disease. The evidence introduced by the FTC indicated that many well-qualified medical science experts subscribed, with varying degrees of intensity, to the opinion that the ingestion of cholesterol and saturated fats is positively related to the incidence of coronary heart disease and that decreased consumption will reduce that risk. This diet/heart disease hypothesis is based upon the propositions that dietary cholesterol affects the level of cholesterol in the blood, that higher rates of blood cholesterol are associated with higher levels of risk of coronary heart disease, and that the level of blood cholesterol is "causally implicated" in the formation of artery-clogging lesions, which precipitate heart disease.

NCEN introduced evidence indicating that some experts have stated that eating eggs will not cause or increase the risk of heart disease. NCEN then argued that the phrase "no evidence" would be regarded by consumers as a statement of opinion that existing scientific studies lend no support to the hypothesis that eating eggs increased the risk of heart disease. NCEN's literature also claimed that cholesterol is the building block of sex hormones, that cholesterol is needed to transmit nerve impulses, and that cholesterol is essential for the life of body cells in an ad explaining what consumers would give up if they avoided eggs. However, at the FTC hearing, NCEN acknowledged that the body does not need to get cholesterol from eggs because the body itself manufactures cholesterol for these functions. Should NCEN's advertisements have been protected by the First Amendment against any sanctions that the FTC might have imposed?

4. Pfizer manufactured a sunburn lotion called *Un-burn*. In its television and radio announcements describing the product, Pfizer claimed that the product anesthetized nerves and relieved sunburn pain of sensitive skin. Prior to its ad campaign the firm conducted two scientific tests that tended to support the claims but, standing alone, did not adequately support the representations. The firm uncovered substantial medical writings, however, which concluded that the active ingredients in Un-burn did provide sunburn relief. Pfizer also found a clinical study which seemed to show that doctors had had some success treating sunburn with the active ingredients in Un-burn. Did Pfizer engage in deceptive advertising in violation of the Federal Trade Commission Act since the firm made claims that had not been verified by controlled scientific studies or tests?

5. ITT Continental Baking Co. manufactured and sold Wonder Enriched Bread and Hostess Snack Cakes. In 1964, ITT's national advertising campaign began emphasizing the nutritional benefits of Wonder Bread. The advertisements stated that the bread contained vitamins, minerals, proteins, carbohydrates and other nutrients, and would help "build strong bodies 12 ways." One scene in a television commercial showed a child actually growing from infancy to the size of a 12-year-old in a matter of moments after consuming Wonder Bread. Another campaign featured commercials asking children, "How big do you want to be?" These advertisements, which also featured the instant growth sequence, stated that Wonder Bread contained "All vital elements for growing minds and bodies," including the nutrients needed to develop muscle, strong bones and teeth, energy, and nerves. Medical evidence, however, established that Wonder Bread was not unusually effective as a growth-inducing agent. In 1970, ITT commenced a campaign heralding "a major nutritional advance" which enabled ITT to enrich and fortify its Hostess Snack Cakes. Vitamins and minerals, the advertisements stated, had been added to the cakes. Even though these ingredients had been added, the cakes still contained a very high percentage of processed sugar. Did ITT engage in unfair advertising in respect to either its Wonder Bread or Hostess Snack Cake campaigns? If so, what aspect(s) was (were) unfair?

6. For more than a year and a half, Firestone Tire & Rubber Company published an advertisement which compared its Super Sports Wide Oval

Tire to regular tires and stated that the tire would "stop 25% quicker." The Federal Trade Commission filed a complaint against Firestone claiming that the advertisements were unfair and deceptive within the meaning of the Federal Trade Commission Act. The FTC argued that the claim that the tire would stop 25 percent quicker had not been sufficiently substantiated through rigorous scientific testing. At a hearing before the FTC, Firestone presented evidence that it had tested its wide oval against one of its own tires by subjecting each to ten sample runs on a wet surface at 15 miles per hour under identical conditions. The results showed an average stopping distance of 53.2 feet for the wide oval and 75.8 feet for the regular tire. Dr. Brenner, an expert witness for the FTC, acknowledged that a tire which stopped more quickly on a wet surface would be expected to enjoy an even greater comparative advantage on a dry surface, but implied that any test conducted on only one surface was unlikely to provide an adequate basis for the forming of opinions concerning performance in general. Was Firestone's advertising campaign unfair and deceptive?

7. Bristol-Myers ran an advertising campaign on television for Dry Ban, an antiperspirant manufactured by the firm. Dry Ban was a roll-on product with a clear alcohol base rather than an oil base. After being applied, the alcohol dried on the user's skin much faster than oil did. Bristol-Myers' advertising compared Dry Ban to an unidentified leading spray. The advertisments claimed that Dry Ban was drier than the leading spray. In the commercials, Dry Ban looked somewhat moist when applied to the actor's skin. The commercials also described Dry Ban as being "clean" and "clear." The FTC issued a complaint against Bristol-Myers, charging that the commercials falsely represented that Dry Ban was not wet when applied to the body and that it left no visible residue. Did Bristol-Myers engage in unfair advertising as alleged by the FTC?

8. Minjac Corporation owned a toy store that had three signs in the window which offered toys, including standard brands, at "20% to 40% off." When Minjac received new inventory, it routinely marked up the price of the toys to a level higher than the prevailing price in the community. When the firm then placed the toys on the store's shelves, a second tag was added, which cut the inflated price by 20–40 percent. A competing toy dealer entered Minjac's store and bought three standard board games, two for a price higher than that prevailing in the community and the third at a price which was no lower than the prevailing price. The toy dealer then complained to local authorities, who charged Minjac with engaging in deceptive advertising. Was Minjac guilty of deceptive advertising?

9. Ford Motor Company advertised a 6 percent financing plan. The plan required new car buyers to pay 6 percent interest per year on the purchase of their automobiles. Total charges were calculated by determining the cash price of the car, then adding .5 percent interest for each month of the installment contract. The amount computed was then divided evenly over the life of the contract. As a result, monthly interest payments remained the same even though the balance due on the principal declined each month. The buyer therefore paid much more interest than he would

have if the 6 percent had been payable as simple interest on the declining balance of the principal. In fact, the 6 percent plan resulted in an annual charge equivalent to more than 11 percent at simple interest. The Federal Trade Commission issued a complaint against Ford, charging that the 6 percent plan constituted an unfair method of competition. Ford argued that no one would be misled by the advertisements. Did Ford deceive the public and therefore violate that Federal Trade Commission Act?

10. All-State Industries of North Carolina, Inc. sold and installed aluminum siding, storm windows, doors, and related fixtures. All-State sold two grades of product: "ADV" was the cheaper and less expensive grade, "PRO" was the higher quality, more expensive, product. All-State actively promoted "ADV" through both media advertising and direct mail contacts. All-State's sales pitch claimed to extend a "special offer" at prices which would be available for only a "limited time." In fact, "ADV" could always be purchased at the supposedly "special" price. Leads generated by All-State's promotion of "ADV" were pursued by an agent who attempted to induce customers to sign contracts, notes, and deeds even before the final sale price had been filled in. When signatures were secured, All-State's agents began trying to persuade customers to substitute "PRO" for the less expensive "ADV." Agents obtained commissions only if they succeeded in selling "PRO," and therefore they made persuasive representations concerning its superiority over "ADV." Prices of "PRO" varied; reluctant customers were offered various discounts. For example, reduced prices were offered if customers would agree to let their homes be used for demonstration purposes. What type of practice was All-State engaging in and does it violate the Federal Trade Commission Act?

11. During the energy crisis in early 1974, Chrysler tried to promote its line of Dodge and Plymouth compact cars with an ad campaign emphasizing their gas economy. The ads referred to a report that had appeared in Popular Science in October 1973. The ad stated that consumers could buy a Dodge Dart or Plymouth Valiant that would beat the Chevrolet Nova on gas mileage. Another ad asked, "Which small cars can go farther on a gallon of gas than Nova?" Small cars from Chrysler were the answer. The ad invited the reader to find out "why the small cars from Chrysler Corporation are outselling all other compact cars." The Popular Science report that Chrysler relied upon showed that Chrysler's six-cylinder Dodge Darts and Plymouth Valiants did have a gasoline economy edge over six- and eight-cylinder Novas. But the report also found that six- or eight-cylinder Novas were superior in gas mileage to Chrysler vehicles equipped with optional eight-cylinder engines. Did Chrysler engage in deceptive or misleading advertising when it cited only the favorable portion of the comparative study?

12. Atlantic Ocean Products, Inc. canned a flatfish known as *Reinhardtius hippoglossoides* and sold it in Oregon as "Greenland halibut." Since 1882, the scientific community had frequently referred to *Reinhardtius hippoglossoides* as "Greenland halibut," and Webster's New International Dictionary had regarded the two terms as synonymous in editions since 1912. Nevertheless, *Reinhardtius hippoglossoides* was known to the general public by other names, and the designation "Greenland halibut" had been

used in the United States only since 1963. True Greenland halibut is a much less desirable fish than other types of halibut. An Oregon statute provided that no fish sold in the state could be labeled "halibut," with or without additional language, other than *Hippoglossus hippoglossus* (Atlantic halibut) or *Hippoglossus stenolepis* (Pacific halibut). Once Oregon enforced this statute, Atlantic's sales of Greenland halibut dropped appreciably. The U.S. Government did not have any laws regulating which species could be labeled as *halibut*. Atlantic sued, claiming that Oregon did not have the proper authority to regulate commerical advertising in this manner. Was Oregon's statute valid?

13. The California Attorney General, acting for the people of the state, sued a number of encyclopedia sellers and other door-to-door salesmen, alleging that they had made false and misleading statements which violated the state's Business and Professions Code. The Attorney General sought to recover $2,500 for each act of false advertising as well as punitive damages for each act of unfair competition. In a consumer fraud case, does the court have the power to order that restitution be made to consumers who were defrauded?

22 TRADEMARKS, COPYRIGHTS AND PATENTS

INTRODUCTION

The United States in this century has been a world leader in developing technology and inventions. This is partially due to a comprehensive federal statutory scheme that provides protection for "intellectual" property. For example, if a person invents a new machine or process, he may *patent* it under our federal patent laws. By being granted a valid patent, the inventor is assured that he may reap the financial gain from his work and may be able to prevent the unauthorized use of his invention. In the area of marketing, a company may promote the name of the company on its products or in its advertising slogans and protect this name and these slogans under federal *trademark law*. Authors can protect their rights in their works under federal *copyright law*.

Competitors and others often attempt to misappropriate another party's intellectual property for their own use. Federal law specifically provides a civil cause of action to the holder of a patent, trademark, or copyright, who may then bring a lawsuit against the defendant for patent infringement, trademark infringement, or copyright infringement. The federal statutes regarding the protection of intellectual property are covered in the following order in this chapter: (1) trademarks, (2) copyright, and (3) patents.

TRADEMARKS

Trademark laws are designed to protect symbols, names, words, and devices adopted and used by businesses to identify their particular goods and services and distinguish them from the goods and services of other businesses. The purposes of trademarks laws are (1) to protect the trademark owner's good will and investment in a mark and (2) to protect the public from becoming confused regarding the source of goods or services.

Trademarks were originally afforded very limited protection by state common law. Congress, pursuant to the Commerce Clause of the U.S. Constitution, enacted the Lanham Act in 1946 to provide federal protection for trademarks and tradenames. Federal trademark law does not wholly preempt the area, and states may also enact trademark laws to apply to *intra*state commerce. State trademark laws that affect interstate commerce but do not conflict with federal trademark law are also valid. If a state trademark law directly conflicts with federal trademark law, the federal law prevails.

Types of Marks   Although many people refer to all marks as "trademarks," there are generally four types of marks that are accorded legal protection under the Lanham Act: (1) trademarks, (2) service marks, (3) certification marks, and (4) collective marks.

Trademark.   A *trademark* is any symbol, name, word, or device used by a manufacturer or retailer that identifies his *goods* and distinguishes those goods from those of any other manufacturer or retailer. For example, the words *Xerox, Coca-Cola* and *IBM* are valid trademarks.

Service Mark.   A service mark is a mark used by a company in the sale or advertising of *services.* The service mark identifies that user's services and distinguishes them from the services provided by others. For example, *Marriott Hotels, McDonalds,* and *Roto-Rooter* are valid service marks.

Certification Mark.   A "certification mark" is a mark that is used by a person other than the owner of the mark to certify: (1) that goods originate from a certain region (e.g., wines from the Napa Valley in California), (2) that certain standards are maintained (e.g., Grade A meats), or (3) that the manufacturer of the goods or provider of the services is a member of a certain organization (e.g., a member of the Florida Citrus Growers Association).

A certification mark can be only used to *certify.* The party who registers a certification mark must exercise control over the mark and not permit unauthorized use of the mark. If a manufacturer or retailer meets and maintains the conditions or standards that the mark certifies, the registrant of the mark must allow that manufacturer or retailer to use the certification mark.

Collective Mark. A *collective mark* is a mark used by an association, cooperative, or other type of collective organizations to identify its goods or services and distinguish its goods or services from those of nonmembers. Many collective marks are used by organizations that do not actually produce or sell goods or services. A collective mark is often registered to prevent others from using it for commercial purposes (e.g., "Boy Scouts of America").

Unless otherwise indicated, the terms *mark* and *trademark* will be used interchangeably in this section to refer to any of the four types of marks.

Federal Registration of Marks. A trademark may be registered with the Federal Patent and Trademark Office. If the mark meets the "use in commerce" and "distinctiveness" tests, it is protected whether or not it is registered on the federal Register of Trademarks. Federal registration does not create the mark, but provides jurisdiction of federal courts for lawsuits regarding the misuse of the mark (e.g., trademark infringement cases).

A mark may be registered on either (1) the "principal register" or (2) the "secondary register."

Principal Register. If a mark is *distinctive,* it should be registered on the federal Principal Register. Registration on the principal register provides *prima facie* evidence that the mark:

1. has been used in interstate commerce
2. is not "confusingly similar" to any other registered mark
3. has not acquired a "secondary" meaning
4. provides the registrant with the exclusive right to use the mark.

A "secondary meaning" is important for a trademark holder to prove if the term is *descriptive.* For example, in *Armstrong Paint v. Nu-Enamel Corp.,* 305 U.S. 315 (1938), the Supreme Court found the term "Nu-Enamel" to be descriptive of paint (i.e., "new enamel") and generally not subject to trademark protection. However, because the descriptive term had acquired a "secondary meaning" indicating the quality of paint produced by the Nu-Enamel Corporation, it enjoined Armstrong Paint from using this otherwise descriptive term. Terms that are not descriptive (e.g., *Dr. Pepper, 7-Up*) are easier to trademark than terms that are descriptive in that these terms are distinctive; they are not required to obtain a secondary meaning as are descriptive terms.

Secondary Register. A mark that is *not* "distinctive" may be registered on the Secondary Register. Registration on the Secondary Register merely means that the mark is capable of distinguishing the goods or services of the user, and provides for federal court jurisdiction for suits regarding the mark. For example, where a mark has not yet attained such distinctiveness that it would be recognized by the average purchaser, but the mark is *capable* of becoming so with proper use and advertising by the company, then it is registerable on the secondary register.

Prior to the Lanham Act, common law provided that if a person who was located in a different geographical area innocently and without prior knowledge used another's trademark, the prior user of the mark could *not* prevent the *innocent* second party from using the mark. The Lanham Act changed the common law and provided that after July 5, 1947, if a mark has been properly *registered,* "constructive notice" is thereby given to all persons that the mark is the personal property of the registrant. The Lanham Act gives *nationwide* effect to registered trademarks. Thus, a registrant can *enjoin* (block) the use of his mark by all other parties, whether such use is innocently or knowingly used by the third party.

A trademark registration is valid for 20 years under the Lanham Act. A trademark is renewable for additional periods of 20 years upon the filing of a verified application showing that the good or service to which the mark applies is still in "use in commerce."

Marks That Cannot Be Registered.   Marks that consist of or comprise "immoral, deceptive, or scandalous matter" may not be registered. For example, the use of the word *Madonna* for wine was refused registration as being scandalous, and the use of the words *Booby Trap* for brassieres was rejected as being immoral. Any mark that includes the flag or coat of arms of the United States, or any state of municipality, or of any foreign nation, cannot be registered. The name, portrait, or signature of a living person cannot be registered as a mark without his or her consent.

Generally, words that describe qualities, ingredients, or characteristics of a product (e.g., *smoothest, sugar-free*), geographical names (e.g., *Los Angeles, Northwest*), or surnames (e.g., *Cheeseman*) cannot be registered as trademarks unless a "secondary meaning" is shown. Even then, exclusive use of these types of words is prevented because they belong in the public domain. A mark cannot be registered if the mark has previously been used in the United States and has not been abandoned, or if it resembles a mark registered in the Patent Office.

A trademark that is *abandoned* falls into the public domain and is available to be trademarked by a subsequent user. A trademark is considered abandoned if the registrant discontinues use of the mark without any intent to reserve its use. Intent not to reuse a mark may be inferred from the circumstances. Nonuse of a mark for two consecutive years is *prima facie* evidence that a trademark has been abandoned. Failure of the registrant to control the use of its trademark may be considered abandonment of the mark. Nonuse caused by strikes, bankruptcy, war, or other such adverse circumstances is not evidence of intent to abandon the trademark.

Abandonment may also occur if the product to which the trademark applies is completely changed. However, merely introducing new models of old products (e.g., "new and improved Brand Z"), or introducing new product lines (e.g., of automobiles), is not considered abandonment. The rationale for this rule is that the public generally expects new lines or models of products to be marketed.

Any party other than the registrant may submit an *opposition* to the registration of a trademark. The opposition may be based on any one of several grounds, including the assertion that the word or symbol is descriptive and is:

1. not distinctive
2. a generic term
3. a mark of another party.

A party other than the registrant may seek the *cancellation* of a registered trademark. A grant of cancellation may be based on several grounds, including that the mark:

1. was invalid at the time of registration
2. was obtained through fraud
3. has subsequently become a generic term.

"Distinctiveness" of Mark.   In order to qualify for trademark protection, a mark must be "distinctive" and have been used in commerce. A common descriptive name that is not distinctive of the registrant's products or services is not a registrable mark under federal trademark law. The question whether a name is "distinctive," and therefore registrable, or whether the name is common, and therefore not registrable, is central to a large percentage of trademark cases.

"Use in Commerce."   In order for a trademark to receive legal protection under the Lanham Act, the mark must be perfected by "prior appropriation and use" in commerce. "Use in commerce" requires that a mark associated with goods be placed on:

1. the goods
2. the container of the goods
3. the display of the goods
4. the label or tag affixed to the goods.

Where services are involved, "use in commerce" requires that a mark be used or displayed in the advertising or sale of the services. A trademark that has not been used in commerce is *not* protected by federal trademark law. The term *use in commerce* requires a finding that the goods have been used in commerce regulated by the Congress, that is, in interstate commerce. This "interstate commerce" requirement is extremely broad, and applies to all goods or services that *affect* interstate commerce.

In *Roux Laboratories, Inc. v. Clairol Incorporated* the court found that the slogan, "Hair Color So Natural Only Her Hairdresser Knows For Sure," was "distinctive" and therefore was a valid trademark of Clairol.

TRADEMARK: DISTINCTIVENESS

ROUX LABORATORIES, INC. v. CLAIROL INCORPORATED

427 F.2d 823 (1970)
UNITED STATES COURT OF CUSTOMS AND PATENT APPEALS

McManus, Judge.
Roux Laboratories, Inc., [a manufacturer and seller of hair tinting, dyeing, and coloring prepara-tions] appeals from the decision of the Trademark Trial and Appeal Board dismissing its opposition to registration on the Principal Register by Clairol

Incorporated of the slogan "Hair Color So Natural Only Her Hairdresser Knows For Sure" for a "hair tinting, dyeing, and coloring preparation."

In 1956, Clairol's predecessor-in-title embarked on an extensive advertising campaign to promote the sale of its "Miss Clairol" hair color preparations, which included advertisements in national magazines, on outdoor billboards, and on car cards for bus and subway transit systems; mailing pieces; radio and television; and point-of-sale display material designed to be used by beauty salons and retailers as window or counter displays in association with the "Miss Clairol" product. The illustrative exhibits of record reflect a now familiar format for much of that advertising—a large, color photograph of an attractive woman, often accompanied by a young child; the question "Does she . . . or doesn't she?" prominently imprinted on or above the photograph; the slogan "Hair Color So Natural Only Her Hairdresser Knows For Sure" also conspicuously imprinted on or below the photograph, and set apart from the other portions of the advertisement; . . .

Though not free of controversy, we will assume for purposes of discussion that the words "hair color" and "natural"—indeed, the words of the slogan in its entirety—were, at inception of their use, apt descriptive words used in an informative, story-telling manner to describe the goods, their function, use and characteristics. The question is still presented, however, whether the slogan remains *merely* or only descriptive, or whether it now serves an origin-indicating function *in addition to* suitably describing attributes of the goods. That question leads naturally to a discussion of the second, broader issue posed earlier—whether the slogan is a trademark within the purview of the preamble to Section 2 and of Section 45 of the Act, and, in particular, whether it has "become distinctive" of the goods within the meaning of Section 2(f) so as to no longer be *merely* descriptive of them. In other words—is it . . . or isn't it?

The amount and character of the evidence, if any, required to establish that a given word or phrase is a trademark or "has become distinctive" of the goods necessarily depends on the facts of each case and particularly on the nature of the alleged mark.

[W]e . . . disagree with Roux's position, as did the board, that the slogan is so highly descriptive

or generic that it is utterly incapable of functioning as a trademark or acquiring distinctiveness, no matter what quantity of evidence of alleged distinctiveness or secondary meaning is submitted. It is true, of course, that mere advertising or other evidence of supposed secondary meaning cannot convert something unregistrable by reason of its being the common descriptive name or generic name for the goods—the antithesis of a trademark—into a registrable mark.

Considering all the factors here—exclusive, prominent and repeated use of the slogan by Clairol for at least ten years in association with the goods, expenditures in that period of over 22 million dollars for point-of-sale displays and other advertising material resulting in over a billion separate audio and visual impressions of the slogan, and substantial sales of the product with which the slogan has been associated—we do not think the board erred in concluding that Clairol's slogan has made an impact upon the purchasing public as an indication of origin, separate from and in addition to the impact of its "Miss Clairol" mark.

In conclusion, . . . we think [Clairol's slogan] has come, by virtue of its use in extensive advertising together with its use in commerce on displays associated with the goods, to serve as a means by which the public can identify the goods as those from a particular source and can distinguish those goods from those of others. It has "become distinctive" of those goods. That being the case, it performs the basic function of a trademark as set forth in the Trademark Act and as commonly understood.

The decision of the board is *affirmed*.

CASE QUESTIONS

1. What slogan did Clairol attempt to register? Had it been used before by other manufacturers of hair products?
2. What was Roux Laboratories' legal theory as to why Clairol's slogan should not be allowed federal registration? Explain.
3. Were the words of Clairol's slogan originally "descriptive"? At that time could Roux Laboratories have used the same slogan?
4. Did the slogan ever become "distinctive"? If so, when?
5. Do you think the slogan used by Clairol indicated

that the origin of the hair coloring products was Clairol? Would the use of the same slogan by other manufacturers have caused confusion in the minds of consumers?

Policy Issue. Should distinctive words and phrases be accorded federal trademark protection?

Ethics Issue. Was it ethical for Roux Laboratories to attempt to appropriate for its use a slogan that had been used by Clairol for over ten years? Why or why not?

Economics Issue. Do intangible marks or slogans (e.g., "McDonalds") have economic value? What would have been the economic implications for Clairol and Roux Laboratories if the court had held in favor of Roux Laboratories?

Social Responsibility. Does Roux Laboratories owe a duty of social responsibility to consumers not to cause confusion as to who manufactures products that bear certain slogans?

Trademark Infringement. An act of *infringement* of a trademark occurs where a defendant makes unauthorized "use" of the plaintiff's trademark "in connection with the sale, offering for sale, distribution, or advertising of any goods or service." The legal test of trademark infringement is whether the unauthorized use is likely to cause confusion or mistake or to deceive the public. The unauthorized use may be by the defendant placing plaintiff's trademark on the defendant's products, labels, packages, wrappers, or in the defendant's advertisements. Factors to be considered by the courts in determining whether unauthorized use of a trademark is "likely to cause confusion" are:

1. similarity of the marks
2. the fame of plaintiff's trademark
3. the "strength" and distinctiveness of the mark
4. the sophistication of the buyers of the products
5. whether the plaintiff's and defendant's goods are the type to emanate from the same source
6. whether the plaintiff's and defendant's products are usually sold through the same distributors
7. whether actual confusion was caused by defendant's unauthorized use of the plaintiff's trademark.

Proof of actual confusion is not essential to the plaintiff's case, but is generally determinative. In order to find trademark infringement, the goods of the plaintiff and defendant do not have to be interchangeable, nor do the plaintiff and defendant have to be in actual competition with one another.

Noninfringing Uses of Trademark. A person *may* use a trademark of another if:

1. the defendant is using his personal name or a name of one in privity with him in a nontrademark sense
2. the defendant uses a trademark that is a descriptive term qualifying for protection on the basis of having acquired a "secondary meaning" (e.g., "North American," etc.)
3. the defendant has used the trademark in a "permissible business use" (e.g., mentioned the trademark in comparative advertising).

Noninfringing use of a trademark is generally raised by defendants as a defense in trademark infringement cases.

Generic Name. Most companies promote their trademarks and other marks in order to increase the public's awareness of their products, the availability of their services, and the quality and other features of their products. However, at some point the public may begin to regard a trademark name as a common name which denotes the *type* of product being sold, and not merely the tradename of the manufacturer. Tradenames that are accorded such a common meaning are called *generic names*.

Once a trademark becomes a generic name, it is no longer "distinctive" and loses its trademark protection. For example, the words *Kleenex* and *Refrigerator* were once tradenames, but have been held by the courts to have become generic names. Companies such as Xerox and Coca-Cola are on constant alert, attempting to protect their trademarks from becoming generic names.

Under the Lanham Act, a successful plaintiff in a trademark infringement case may recover: (1) the profits the defendant made from the enjoined use of the trademark, (2) any damages incurred by the plaintiff, (3) the costs of bringing the action, except attorney's fees. Under Section 1117 of the Lanham Act, the court has the discretion to *treble* the damages if the circumstances warrant (e.g., it finds intentional trademark infringement). The court may also order the cancellation, impounding, and destruction of the mark in the possession of the defendant.

In *Miller Brewing Company v. Falstaff Brewing Corporation* the court found that the term *Lite*, as applied to beer, was a generic name, and that the Miller Brewing Company had therefore lost its trademark to the term *Miller Lite*.

TRADEMARK: GENERIC NAME

MILLER BREWING COMPANY v. FALSTAFF BREWING CORPORATION (1981)

655 F.2d 5
UNITED STATES COURT OF APPEALS, FIRST CIRCUIT

Wyzanski, Senior District Judge.

The plaintiff, Miller Brewing Co., brought against Falstaff Brewing Corporation, a Rhode Island corporation, and Falstaff Brewing Corporation, a Delaware corporation, (collectively referred to as "Falstaff") an action for preliminary and permanent injunctions. The complaint alleged that "LITE" was the recognized brand name under which Miller marketed its reduced calorie beer and that Falstaff's use of the word "LITE" in "FALSTAFF LITE BEER" constituted a false designation of origin in the violation of Section 43(a) of the Lanham Act, . . .

After a hearing upon the prayer for a preliminary injunction, the District Court, in its October 29, 1980 opinion, found *inter alia* that (1) Miller since 1972 had sold millions of barrels of a reduced calorie beer under the name "LITE," (2) Miller had spent millions of dollars in advertising its beer under that name, (3) Miller is likely to succeed in proving (a) that the consuming public has come to associate the symbol LITE with the Miller brand of reduced calorie beer, and (b) that "LITE" presently signifies to the public Miller's and no one else's product, and (4) Falstaff since July 11, 1980 has been brewing reduced calorie beer, and has been bottling and shipping it in containers bearing the label "Falstaff Lite."

[T]he District Court on October 30, 1980 enjoined Falstaff preliminarily, pending trial of the action upon the merits, from selling or marketing a reduced calorie beer using the symbol or bearing the word "LITE."

In the law governing trademarks and unfair competition, "a generic or common descriptive term is one which is commonly used as the name or description of a kind of goods." . . . Under no circumstances is a generic term susceptible of *de jure* protection under Section 43(a) of the Lanham Act, . . . In two leading cases Judge Friendly gave the following rationale for the rule: "No matter how much money and effort the user of a generic term has poured into promoting the sale of its merchandise and what success it has achieved in securing public identification, it cannot deprive competing manufacturers of the product of the right to call an article by its name." "The reason is plain enough. To allow trademark protection for generic terms, i.e., terms which describe the genus of goods being sold, even when these have identified with a first user, would grant the owner of the mark a monopoly since a competitor could not describe his goods as what they are."

Miller as the holder of the purported trademark "LITE" [previously] brought against Heileman an action to restrain it from using in connection with its beer the word "LIGHT," and an earlier action against Schlitz to restrain it from using in connection with its beer the same word "LIGHT." In *Heileman* and likewise in *Schlitz* among the issues raised were whether "LITE" was a generic name, . . . In both *Heileman* and *Schlitz* the . . . question was answered affirmatively.

The determinations in both *Heileman* and *Schlitz*, having been based on a full and fair consideration of the issues, bind Miller in the subsequent litigation not only against the defendants in those cases but also against Falstaff as an alleged infringer of Miller's putative trademark "LITE."

Collateral estoppel bars patentee from relitigating issue of validity of patent where issue has been decided adversely to him in a prior case in which patentee had a full and fair chance to litigate issue of validity.

We disagree with the District Court's view that Miller is not collaterally estopped because of a supposedly dramatic alteration between the 1970s and the 1980s in the low calorie beer market and in public understanding of the term "LITE." For present purposes, we assume that a judgment determining a state of facts existing in the 1970s may not preclude a fresh determination of a state of facts existing in the 1980s. But in the instant case the evidence before the District Court showed, at best, merely that in the last half decade the public perception of Miller as the source of "LITE" has increased and become *dominant* in the public mind. However, evidence to that effect is irrelevant. . . . There was no evidence that as of today "LITE" has *ceased* to have in current usage among consumers of beer the generic meaning, "beer of low caloric content."

Reversed. Preliminary injunction vacated.

CASE QUESTIONS

1. What is a "generic name"? Does a generic name lose its federal trademark protection? If so, why?
2. Had Miller previously sued any other brewers for using the term "Lite"? If so, what was the outcome of these prior cases?
3. What does the doctrine of "collateral estoppel" provide?
4. Had the public's perception of the term "Lite" as being associated with Miller beer increased in the 1970s and early 1980s? If so, had the term "Lite" become a protectable trademark of Miller?

Policy Issue. Should a name or slogan lose its trademark protection because a manufacturer or seller does such a good job of promotion that the name becomes a generic name?

Ethics Issue. Was it ethical for Falstaff, Heileman, and Schlitz to have used the word *Lite* which Miller had made famous in their advertising? Why or why not?

Economics Issue. What are the economic consequences to a trademark holder if its trademark is found to be an unprotectable generic name? What is the optimal amount of money a company should spend on promoting the name of a product?

Social Responsibility. Did Miller owe a duty of social responsibility to allow the name "Lite" to be used by other brewers since the public was using the name generically anyway? Why or why not?

COPYRIGHT

The common law provided limited copyright protection to authors. *Copyright protection* the United States today is generally provided by the Federal Copyright Statute, which was adopted by Congress pursuant to Article I, Section 8, Clause 8 of the U.S. Constitution:

The Congress shall have Power . . . To promote the Progress of Science and useful Arts, by securing for limited Times to Authors and Inventors the exclusive Right to their respective Writings and Discoveries.

In 1976, Congress enacted a new Copyright Act that substantially changed the law of copyright. Generally, the Copyright Act of 1976 abolished common-law protection of copyrights, changed the time periods for the length of copyrights, and clarified the procedures for registering a copyright.

The purpose of the federal copyright law is to provide an incentive for writers to profit from their work by protecting copyrighted works from misappropriation. Only writings in tangible form that are capable of visual perception are statutorily copyrightable. For example, the courts have held that the written script of a play may be copyrighted, but the actual live performance of the play cannot be copyrighted. The term "writing" has been broadly defined by the courts, and includes motion picture prints, three-dimensional effects and other forms of communication. Written works that may be copyrighted are divided into the following fourteen classes by the Federal Copyright Statute:

1. books, including encyclopedias, directories, etc.
2. periodicals, including newspapers
3. lectures, sermons, and addresses
4. dramatic and dramatic-musical compositions (operas, operettas, plays, motion pictures, radio, television, etc.)
5. musical compositions
6. maps
7. works of art (paintings, drawings, sculpture, jewelry, glassware, tapestries, etc.)
8. reproductions of works of art (e.g., lithographs, posters, etc.)
9. drawings or plastic works of a scientific or technical character (graphs, models, etc.)
10. photographs, including prints, filmstrips, and slides

11. prints, pictorial illustrations, and commercial prints and labels (greeting cards, picture postcards, etc.)
12. motion pictures and photoplays, including feature films, cartoons, etc.
13. motion pictures other than photoplays (newsreels, travelogues, training films, etc.)
14. sound recordings (music, narration, drama, etc.) as published in the form of tapes, cartridges, disks, or phonorecords.

The following classes of material are generally *not* subject to copyright: (1) titles of books or other works (*but note:* these may be subject to *trademark* protection), (2) ideas, (3) news, and (4) certain fictional characters that were not substantially developed in the original copyrighted material (i.e., courts have held that "Sam Spade" and "Paladin" are not protected, but that "Superman" *is* protected).

A copyright may be taken in a work by:

1. the author
2. an employer of the author where the work has been produced "for hire"
3. an executor, administrator, or heirs of a deceased author
4. an assignee of the work
5. either of two or more authors where a work has joint authorship.

Where there is joint authorship, if either author has copyrighted the work, he must account to the other author for royalties obtained from the use of the work.

Copyright Notice. Where a work is *published,* copyright is obtained by placing the proper copyright "notice" *on* the published materials. The "notice of copyright" on the published materials must contain three items:

1. the word "Copyright," or the abbreviation "Copr.," or the symbol ©
2. the name of the copyright owner
3. the year in which the copyright was secured by publication.

In all cases the notice must be of a size that is legible to the naked eye. The notice must be applied to *all* publications of the work. However, the negligent omission of the notice on a few copies of the work is generally excused by the courts. The copyright notice must be appropriately placed on the copyright material as follows:

1. for books and other printed material, on the title page or the page immediately thereafter
2. for periodicals (magazines, newspapers), on the title page, under the title heading, on the "masthead" page, or on the first page of text
3. for musical works, on the title page or the first page of music
4. for sound recordings, on the surface of the reproduction or on the label or the container of the recording (e.g., on the label of a phonograph record);
5. for all other works, on any portion of the work that will apprise others of the copyright.

Registration of a Copyright. Once the materials have been published with the notice of copyright on them, the copyright may be *registered* by filing two copies of the materials together with a claim of copyright with the Copyright Office. The name of the copyright holder must appear precisely the same on the application for registration as on the copyright notice affixed to the published work, or the application for registration will not be accepted. The Copyright Office returns one copy of the registered work to the publisher with the registration number.

Where works are *not* published, statutory copyright may also be obtained by depositing one copy of the complete work and filing a claim of copyright with the Copyright Office.

Exclusive Rights of the Copyright Holder. Once a copyright has been secured, the copyright holder has certain *exclusive* rights in the copyrighted work, including:

1. the right to make and publish tangible copies of the work
2. the right to translate the work
3. the right to make other versions of the work (i.e., to convert a novel to dramatic form, etc.)
4. the right to print, reprint, and use the work
5. the right to complete or finish a model or design
6. the right to arrange, adapt, and make records of copyrighted musical compositions
7. the right to transcribe and record copyrighted dramatic or nondramatic works
8. the right to perform musical compositions, dramatic works, or nondramatic literary works, including both film and live performances.

Where an individual registers a copyright, it is protected under federal law for the life of the creator plus 50 years. If a business registers a copyright, it may be copyrighted for a maximum of 100 years from the date of its creation *or* 75 years from the date of its publication.

Originality. In order for a work to qualify to be copyrighted, it must be an "original" work of the author. The test made by the courts is whether the work is from the "independent labor" of the author. Thus, if two authors write the same work independently, they may each copyright their own work. The work, however, does not have to be wholly original to be copyrighted. For example, adaptations, abridgements, new arrangements, and translations of works qualify for copyright.

In *Hoehling v. Universal City Studios, Inc.* the court held that the defendant was not liable for copyright infringement where it produced a motion picture regarding an historical event about which another author had previously written a book.

COPYRIGHT: ORIGINALITY

HOEHLING v. UNIVERSAL CITY STUDIOS, INC.

618 F.2d 972 (1980)
UNITED STATES COURT OF APPEALS, SECOND CIRCUIT

Irving R. Kaufman, Chief Judge:

A grant of copyright in a published work secures for its author a limited monopoly over the expression it contains. The copyright provides a financial incentive to those who would add to the corpus of existing knowledge by creating original works. Nevertheless, the protection afforded the copyright holder has never extended to history, be it documented fact or explanatory hypothesis. The rationale for this doctrine is that the cause of knowledge is best served when history is the common property of all, and each generation remains free to draw upon the discoveries and insights of the past. Accordingly, the scope of copyright in historical accounts is narrow indeed, embracing no more than the author's original expression of particular facts and theories already in the public domain.

This litigation arises from three separate accounts of the triumphant introduction, last voyage, and tragic destruction of the Hindenburg, the colossal dirigible constructed in Germany during Hitler's reign. The zeppelin, the last and most sophisticated in a fleet of luxury airships, which punctually floated its wealthy passengers from the Third Reich to the United States, exploded into flames and disintegrated in 35 seconds as it hovered above the Lakehurst, New Jersey Naval Air Station at 7:25 P.M. on May 6, 1937. Thirty-six passengers and crew were killed but, fortunately, 52 persons survived. Official investigations conducted by both American and German authorities could ascertain no definitive cause of the disaster, but both suggested the plausibility of static electricity or St. Elmo's Fire, which could have ignited the highly explosive hydrogen that filled the airship. Throughout, the investigators refused to rule out the possibility of sabotage.

The final pages of the airship's story marked the beginning of a series of journalistic, historical, and literary accounts devoted to the Hindenburg and its fate. . . . In 1957, Nelson Gidding . . . wrote an unpublished "treatment" for a motion picture based on the deliberate destruction of the airship. . . . In 1962, Dale Titler released *Wings of Mystery,* in which he too devoted a chapter to the Hindenburg.

Appellant A. A. Hoehling published *Who Destroyed the Hindenburg?,* a full-length book based on his exhaustive research, in 1962. Mr. Hoehling studied the investigative reports, consulted previously published articles and books, and conducted interviews with survivors of the crash as well as others who possessed information about the Hindenburg. His book is presented as a factual account, written in an objective, reportorial style. . . . In the final chapter, spanning eleven pages, Hoehling suggests that all proffered explanations of the explosion, save deliberate destruction, are unconvincing. He concludes that the most likely saboteur is one Eric Spehl, a "rigger" on the Hindenburg crew who was killed at Lakehurst.

Ten years later appellee Michael MacDonald Mooney published his book, *The Hindenburg.* Mooney's endeavor might be characterized as more literary than historical in its attempt to weave a number of symbolic themes through the actual events surrounding the tragedy.

Mooney acknowledges, in this case, that he consulted Hoehling's book, and that he relied on it for some details. He asserts that he first discovered the "Spehl-as-saboteur" theory when he read Titler's *Wings of Mystery.* Indeed, Titler concludes that Spehl was the saboteur, for essentially the reasons stated by Hoehling. Mooney also claims to have studied the complete National Archives and New York Times files concerning the Hindenburg as well as all previously published material. Moreover, he traveled to Germany, visited Spehl's birthplace, and conducted a number of interviews with survivors.

After Mooney prepared an outline of his anticipated book, his publisher succeeded in negotiations to sell the motion picture rights to appellee Universal City Studios. Universal then commissioned a screen story by writers Levinson and Link, best known for their television series, *Columbo,* in which a somewhat disheveled but wise detective unravels artfully conceived murder mysteries. In their screen story, Levinson and Link created a Columbo-like character who endeavored to identify the saboteur on board the Hindenburg.

Upon learning of Universal's plans to release the film, Hoehling instituted this action against Universal for copyright infringement and common law unfair competition in the District Court for the District of Columbia in October 1975. Judge Smith declined to issue an order restraining release of the film in December, and it was distributed throughout the nation.

It is undisputed that Hoehling has a valid copyright in his book. To prove infringement, however, he must demonstrate that defendants "copied" his work and that they "improperly appropriated" his "expression." Ordinarily, wrongful appropriation is shown by proving a "substantial similarity" of *copyrightable* expression.

Hoehling's principal claim is that both Mooney and Universal copied the essential plot of his book—i.e., Eric Spehl, influenced by his girlfriend, sabotaged the Hindenburg by placing a crude bomb in Gas Cell 4.

[A]ppellees . . . argue that Hoehling's plot is an "idea," and ideas are not copyrightable as a matter of law.

Hoehling, however, correctly rejoins that while ideas themselves are not subject to copyright, his "expression" of *his* idea is copyrightable. He relies on . . . Augustus Hand's analysis in *Detective Comics. Inc. v. Bruns Publications, Inc.,* concluding that the exploits of "Wonderman" infringed the copyright held by the creators of "Superman," the original indestructible man.

[D]etective Comics, however, dealt with works of fiction, where the distinction between an idea and its expression is especially elusive. But, where, as here, the idea at issue is an interpretation of an historical event, our cases hold that such interpretations are not copyrightable as a matter of law. In *Rosemont Enterprises, Inc. v. Random House, Inc.,* we held that the defendant's biography of Howard Hughes did not infringe an earlier biography of the reclusive alleged billionaire. Although the plots of the two works were necessarily similar,

there could be no infringement because of the "public benefit in encouraging the development of historical and biographical works and their public distribution." To avoid a chilling effect on authors who contemplate tackling an historical issue or event, broad latitude must be granted to subsequent authors who make use of historical subject matter, including theories or plots.

In the instant case, the hypothesis that Eric Spehl destroyed the Hindenburg is based entirely on the interpretation of historical facts, including Spehl's life, his girlfriend's anti-Nazi connections, the explosion's origin in Gas Cell 4, Spehl's duty station, discovery of a dry-cell battery among the wreckage, and rumors about Spehl's involvement dating from a 1938 Gestapo investigation. Such an historical interpretation, whether or not it originated with Mr. Hoehling, is not protected by his copyright and can be freely used by subsequent authors.

In works devoted to historical subjects, it is our view that a second author may make significant use of prior work, so long as he does not bodily appropriate the expression of another. This principle is justified by the fundamental policy undergirding the copyright laws—the encouragement of contributions to recorded knowledge. The "financial reward guaranteed to the copyright holder is but an incident of this general objective, rather than an end in itself." Knowledge is expanded as well by granting new authors of historical works a relatively free hand to build upon the work of their predecessors.

The judgment of the District Court is *affirmed.*

CASE QUESTIONS

1. Who wrote the following books:
   a. *Wings of Mystery?*
   b. *Who Destroyed the Hindenburg?*
   c. *The Hindenburg?*
2. When Mooney wrote his book, did he consult Hoehling's book?
3. How did Universal City Studios become the defendant? On which of the preceding books did Universal City Studios base its movie?
4. Who was the saboteur in the movie? In Hoehling's book? Was there any similarity? Explain.
5. Are works of *fiction* easier to copyright than historical works? What is the extent of the copyright protection accorded historical works? Explain.

6. Can an *idea* be copyrighted? Can the *expression* of an idea be copyrighted?

Policy Issue. Should intangible intellectual property rights be accorded copyright protection? Is intellectual property any less valuable than tangible property?

What are the policies underlying copyright law?

Ethics Issue. Was it ethical for Mooney to use Hoehling's book as a reference for his own book?

Economics Issue. What would have been the economic conseqences for Hoehling and Universal City Studios if Hoehling had won his lawsuit?

Social Responsibility. Do authors owe a duty of social responsibility to make their works available to the public free of charge? Should authors be treated any differently from landlords?

Copyright Infringement.   Where a defendant has violated one of the exclusive rights of the copyright holder, there is copyright *infringement*. Proving copyright infringement is usually an evidentiary problem. Copyright infringement may be proved by either direct evidence or circumstantial evidence. For example, a showing that the defendant had access to the copyrighted work is often important circumstantial evidence in a copyright infringement case.

Evidence of copyright infringement may consist of showing passages or errors common to the original and the copy. The test is whether a "substantial and material" part of the copyrighted work has been copied. The copying does not have to be literally word for word, but may consist of close paraphrasing of the copyrighted work. The defendant's *intent* to infringe is immaterial.

A copyright holder may seek a number of remedies against a defendant copyright infringer, including:

1. an injunction to prevent future infringement
2. impoundment and destruction of infringed works
3. recovery of damages suffered by the copyright holder because of the infringement and
4. recovery of profits made by the defendant infringer from the infringed work.

Most courts restrict the plaintiff-copyright holder to choosing between seeking damages and recovering the infringer's profits. In order to obtain an award of damages or attorney's fees from a copyright infringer, the copyright holder must have registered the copyright with the Copyright Office within three months of publication. Where no injury is shown, or where computation of damages is difficult, the court has the discretion, "in lieu" of damages, to award from a statutory minimum of $250.00 up to a statutory maximum of $5,000.00 to the plaintiff copyright holder for copyright infringement by the defendant.

"Fair Use" Doctrine.   The judicial doctrine of "fair use" may be raised by a defendant as a defense to a charge of copyright infringement. Noninfringing *fair use* of copyrighted materials has generally been held to consist of:

1. quotation of the copyrighted work for review or criticism, or in a scholarly or technical work
2. use in a parody
3. brief quotation in a news report
4. reproduction by a teacher or student of a small part of a work to illustrate a lesson
5. incidental reproduction of a work in a newsreel or broadcast of an event being reported
6. reproduction of a work in a legislative or judicial proceeding.

The doctrine of "fair use" has not been specifically defined by the courts. Each case is decided by the courts based on a "rule of reason," taking into consideration such factors as the extent of the copying, the purpose of the copying, whether the copying is related to learning or for commercial purposes, and whether the copied materials served a different function from the copyrighted materials.

In *Elsmere Music, Inc. v. National Broadcasting Company, Inc.* the court held that a "Saturday Night Live" skit which was a parody on the song "I Love New York," was "fair use" of copyrighted materials and not copyright infringement.

COPYRIGHT: "FAIR USE"

ELSMERE MUSIC, INC. v. NATIONAL BROADCASTING COMPANY, INC.

482 F.SUPP 741 (1980)
UNITED STATES DISTRICT COURT, S.D. NEW YORK

Goettel, District Judge:

In the dark days of 1977, when the City of New York teetered on the brink of bankruptcy and its name had become synonymous with sin, there came forth upon the land a message of hope. On the television screens of America there appeared the image of a top-hatted Broadway showgirl, backed by an advancing phalanx of dancers, chanting:

"I-I-I-I-I-I Love New Yo-o-o-o-o-o-rk!"

As an ad campaign for an ailing city, it was an unparalleled success. Crucial to the campaign was the brief but exhilarating musical theme written by Steve Karmen, who had previously authored a number of highly successful commercial jingles, including "You Can Take Salem Out of the Country" and "Weekends Were Made for Michelob." While the

"I Love New York" song was written for the New York State Department of Commerce, its initial use and identity focused on New York City.

The success of this campaign did not go unnoticed in the entertainment world. On May 20, 1978, the popular weekly variety program "Saturday Night Live" ("SNL") performed a comedy sketch over defendant National Broadcasting Company's network. In this sketch the cast of SNL, portraying the mayor and the members of the Chamber of Commerce of the Biblical city of Sodom, are seen discussing Sodom's poor public image with out-of-towners, and the effect this was having on the tourist trade. In an attempt to recast the City's image in a more positive light, a new advertising campaign emphasizing the less sensational aspects of Sodom nightlife is unveiled. As the highlight of this campaign the song "I Love Sodom" is sung *a cappella* by a chorus line of three SNL regulars to the tune of "I Love New York," with the words "I Love Sodom" repeated three times.

The plaintiff, Elsmere Music, Inc., the copyright proprietor of "I Love New York," did not see the humor of the sketch. It sued for copyright infringement.

[T]he Court must . . . address the question of whether the defendant's copying of the plaintiff's jingle constituted a fair use which would exempt it from liability under the Copyright Act. Fair use has been defined as "a privilege in others than the owner of the copyright to use the copyrighted material in a reasonable manner without his consent, notwithstanding the monopoly granted to the owner of the copyright." . . . The determination of whether a use constitutes a fair use or is a copyright infringement requires an examination of the facts in each case.

The defendant asserts that the purpose and nature of its copying of "I Love New York" was parody, and that its copying was thus a fair use of the song. It has been held that an author is entitled to more extensive use of another's copyrighted work in creating a parody than in creating other fictional or dramatic works, since "short of . . . [a] complete identity of content, the disparity of functions between a serious work, and a satire based upon it, may justify the defense of fair use even where substantial similarity exists." *Nimmer on Copyright*.

The song "I Love Sodom," as well as the sketch of which it was a part, was clearly an attempt by the writers and cast of SNL to satirize the way in which New York City has attempted to improve its somewhat tarnished image through the use of a slick advertising campaign. As such, the defendant's copying of the song "I Love New York" seems to come within the definition of parody.

In *MCA, Inc. v. Wilson,* the court was presented with the question of whether the song "Cunnilingus Champion of Company C" as used in the play "Let My People Come—A Sexual Musical" infringed upon the copyright of the song "Boogie Woogie Bugle Boy of Company B." Finding that the defendant's song, although it "may have sought to parody life,

or more particularly sexual mores and taboos," did not attempt to parody or "comment ludicrously upon 'Bugle Boy' " itself, the court held that there had been no fair use and that as a result the plaintiff's copyright had been infringed.

The plaintiff asserts that, as the defendants did not attempt to parody the song "I Love New York" itself, the singing of "I Love Sodom" did not, under *MCA,* . . . constitute a fair use. We cannot agree. The song "I Love Sodom" in the sketch was intended to symbolize a catchy, upbeat tune that would divert a potential tourist's attention from the town's reputation for gambling, gluttony, idol worshipping, and, of course, sodomy. The song was as much a parody of the song "I Love New York,"— a catchy, upbeat tune intended to alter a potential tourist's perceptions of New York—as it was of the overall "I Love New York" advertising campaign.

Having found that the SNL sketch and song validly parodied the plaintiff's jingle and the "I Love New York" advertising campaign in general, the Court next turns to the important question of whether such use has tended to interfere with the marketability of the copyrighted work. In this regard, it is clear to the court that the defendant's playing of the song "I Love Sodom" has not so interfered. The song has not affected the value of the copyrighted work. Neither has it had—nor could it have— the "effect of fulfilling the demand for the original." Just as imitation may be the sincerest form of flattery, parody is an acknowledgment of the importance of the thing parodied. In short, the defendant's version of the jingle has not in the least competed with or detracted from plaintiff's work.

Basing its decision on undisputed facts presented by the parties, as well as on a videotaped viewing of the television sketch containing the alleged infringement, the Court finds that the defendant's use of the plaintiff's jingle in the SNL sketch was a fair use, and that as a result no copyright violation occurred. Accordingly, the plaintiff's motion for summary judgment is denied, and the defendant's motion for summary judgment is granted. This action is hereby *dismissed*.

COPYRIGHT: "FAIR USE" AFFIRMED

ELSMERE MUSIC, INC. V. NATIONAL BROADCASTING COMPANY

623 F.2d 252 (1980)
UNITED STATES COURT OF APPEALS, SECOND CIRCUIT

Per Curiam:

This copyright infringement suit concerns a skit, shown on the television program "Saturday Night Live," poking fun at New York City's public relations campaign and its theme song. In the four-minute skit the town fathers of Sodom discuss a plan to improve their city's image. The satire ends with the singing of "I Love Sodom" to the tune of "I Love New York." The District Court for the Southern District of New York (Gerard L. Goettel, Judge) rejected appellant's claim of copyright infringement, concluding that the parody was protected fair use. Believing that, in today's world of often unrelieved solemnity, copyright law should be hospitable to the humor of parody, and that the District Court correctly applied the doctrine of fair use, we *affirm* on Judge Goettel's thorough opinion.

CASE QUESTIONS

1. What type of TV show was "Saturday Night Live"? How did "Saturday Night Live" use Elsmere's copyrighted song?

2. What is copyright infringement? What does the doctrine of "fair use" provide?

3. Are parodies on copyrighted material accorded greater leeway that other unauthorized uses of copyrighted materials? If so, why?

4. How did "Saturday Night Live's" use of the "I Love New York" song differ from the use of the "Boogie Woogie Bugle Boy of Company B" song in *MCA, Inc. v. Wilson?* Explain.

Policy Issue. Should there be any exceptions to the unauthorized use of copyrighted materials?

Ethics Issue. Was it ethical for "Saturday Night Live" and NBC to perform a satire on the song "I Love New York"?

Economics Issue. Why do you think Elsmere Music brought the lawsuit? What would have been the economic consequences for the parties if Elsmere had won the lawsuit?

Social Responsibility. Do satirical shows like "Saturday Night Live" serve any useful social purpose?

PATENTS

The patent law of the United States was enacted pursuant to Article I, Section 8, Clause 8 of the U.S. Constitution, quoted previously in the copyright section. Congress enacted patent laws to provide an incentive to inventors to invent and to make their inventions public, and to protect patented inventions from unauthorized use. Federal patent law wholly preempts the area. States cannot enact legislation to regulate patents. A major revision of the Federal Patent Statute was enacted by Congress in 1952. There has not been a major change in federal patent laws since that time.

Congress established the Patent and Trademark Office in Washington, D.C. to enforce the provisions of the Federal Patent Statute. The Patent and Trademark Office receives and grants applications for patents. Congress also established the Court of Customs and Patent Appeals to hear appeals from decisions of the Patent and Trademark Office.

Application for a Patent. In order to perfect a patent, four procedural requirements must be met.

1. The inventor or his representative must file an *application* for a patent with the Patent and Trademark Office.
2. The application must be filed within *one year* of the "public use" or "publication" of the invention.
3. The application must contain "a written description of the invention, and of the manner and process of making and using it, in such full, clear, concise, and exact terms as to enable any person skilled in the art to which it pertains to make and use the same."
4. The application must conclude with one or more *claims* "pointing out and distinctly claiming the subject matter" that constitutes the invention, and no more.

In order to meet the statutory requirements of "particularity" and "distinctiveness," the *claims* must distinguish that which is claimed from that which went before in the art, and clearly describe what is foreclosed from future use by the claim. Claims often fail as being too broad, vague, or ambiguous. Any fraudulent statement made to the Patent Office with regard to an application for a patent results in the invalidation of the patent.

Problems may arise if there are multiple inventors of the same invention. Generally, a second inventor's patent or right to a patent fails if another inventor has previously conceptualized the invention *and* reduced it to practice in the United States. The first inventor's patent or right to patent is primary. However, if the prior inventor has not used "diligence," from the date of conception, to reduce his invention to practice, and the second inventor reduces the invention to practice first, the second inventor has the valid patent on or the right to patent the invention.

Once a patent is issued, generally the patentee does *not* have to "work" or license his patent. Statutes provide certain exceptions where the withholding of a patent would be detrimental to "public health." In such areas as these the government, under the doctrine of *eminent domain*, may *require* the practice or use of a patent.

An inventor may abandon his invention. Abandonment requires a showing of the *intent* of the inventor to withdraw his or her patent application.

Assignment of a Patent. A patent holder may assign all his interests in a patent. A patent can only be assigned by a written document. The assignee obtains all the rights to make, use, and sell the patented invention, and may maintain a patent infringement suit against a third party.

A patent holder can transfer to another party an "exclusive license," usually by geographical region, to make, use, and sell the patented invention. The exclusive licensee may transfer all or part of the rights acquired by an assignment. An exclusive licensee may maintain an action for patent infringement against a third party. A grant of a "nonexclusive" license usually means that the patent holder-licensor only transfers certain limited rights to the licensee (for example, the licensor retains rights to sell the patented invention in competition with the licensee, or the licensee is granted the right to sell, but not to make, the patented invention). A nonexclusive licensee may not maintain an action for patent infringement.

A licensee who has paid royalties to a licensor may not recover the royalties from the licensor even where the patent is found to be invalid. The argument for this rule is that if the licensee could recover the royalties, patent licensing would be discouraged.

Patentable Subject Matter.   Not all new inventions are entitled to patent protection. The invention must fall within one of the statutory clauses of invention, which are:

1. a process (e.g., a method of hatching eggs)
2. machine
3. a manufacture (i.e., not a process, machine, or composition or matter; for example, a drive-in movie theater)
4. a composition of matter (i.e., a mixture of two or more ingredients)
5. an improvement (i.e., an addition, simplification, or variance) to an existing machine, process, manufacture, or composition of matter)
6. an asexually reproduced plant (i.e., mutant, hybrid, variety, etc.)
7. a design for an article of manufacture (i.e., a design by means of lines, images, and configuration that makes an impression on the mind of the observer through the eye).

A mere idea, abstraction, scientific principle, or natural process cannot be patented unless it is part of a *tangible* environment. A physical law or law of nature is not patentable.

In *Diamond, Commissioner of Patents and Trademarks v. Chakrabarty,* 447 U.S. 303 (1980), the Supreme Court held that *living* material invented by man was patentable under the Federal Patent Statute. This excerpt is taken from the majority opinion written by Chief Justice Burger.

In 1972, respondent Chakrabarty, a microbiologist, filed a patent application, assigned to the General Electric Co. The application asserted 36 claims related to Chakrabarty's invention of "a bacterium from the genus *Pseudomonas* containing therein at least two stable energy-generating plasmids, each of said plasmids providing a separate hydrocarbon degradative pathway." This human-made, genetically engineered bacterium is capable of breaking down multiple components of crude oil. Because of this property, which is possessed by no naturally occurring bacteria, Chakrabarty's invention is believed to have significant value for the treatment of oil spills.

The patent examiner . . . rejected claims for the bacteria. His decision rested on two grounds: (1) that micro-organisms are "products of nature," and (2) that as living things they are not patentable subject matter under 35 U.S.C. Section 101.

The Court of Customs and Patent Appeals, by a divided vote, reversed on the authority of its prior decision in *In re Bergy,* which held that "the fact that microorganisms . . . are alive . . . [is] without legal significance" for purposes of the patent law.

In choosing such expansive terms as "manufacture" and "composition of matter," modified by the comprehensive "any," Congress plainly contemplated that the patent laws would be given wide scope.

The laws of nature, physical phenomena, and abstract ideas have been held not patentable. Thus, a new mineral discovered in the earth or a new plant found in the wild is not patentable subject matter. Likewise, Einstein could not patent his celebrated law that $E = mc^2$; nor could Newton have patented the law of gravity. Such discoveries are "manifestations of . . . nature, free to all men and reserved exclusively to none."

Judged in this light, respondent's micro-organism plainly qualifies as patentable subject matter. His claim is not to a hitherto unknown natural phenomenon, but to a nonnaturally occurring manufacture or composition of matter—a product of human ingenuity. . . .

Here . . . the patentee has produced a new bacterium with markedly different characteristics from any found in nature and one having the potential for significant utility. His discovery is not nature's handiwork, but his own; accordingly it is patentable subject matter under Section 101.

The Federal Patent Statute expressly exempts from patent protection inventions "useful solely in the utilization of special nuclear material or atomic energy in an atomic weapon." In *Gottschalk v. Benson,* 409 U.S. 63 (1972), the U.S. Supreme Court held that computer programs were not patentable because they generally involve ideas and mathematical formulas, which are not patentable subject matter.

Requirements for a Patent. In addition to the requirement of a patentable subject matter, there are four other statutory requirements that must be met before an invention can be granted a patent. The invention must: (1) be original, (2) be novel, (3) serve a practical purpose (utility), and (4) be nonobvious.

Originality. An invention or discovery must be "original" to be patentable. It is generally held that it is *not* a patentable invention to:

1. substitute new material for old material
2. change the size or dimensions of article or machine
3. make an article portable
4. multiply or combine parts
5. reverse the position of parts
6. convert a batch method to a continuous method.

A combination of old elements can be patented only if a *synergy* results, that is, if the value of the new whole exceeds the value of the sum of its old parts.

Novelty. In order to be patentable, the invention or discovery must be "novel." Thus, if the invention or discovery was actually known in the *prior art,* it is not "novel" and is not patentable. It is immaterial that the inventor had no knowledge of the prior invention, or whether or not the prior invention was patentable. In order for a foreign invention to preclude the patentability of an invention in the United States under the "novelty" test, the foreign invention must have been granted a patent in the country of origin.

Utility. In order to be patentable, the invention must be able to accomplish some beneficial purpose in a *practical manner* (e.g., the new machine will produce a good). Any degree of "practical use" will qualify the invention under the "utility" test of patentability. Where an invention has as its purpose only an unlawful purpose (such as a gambling device), it is not "useful" in the patent sense. Further, an invention must provide a *current* practical use or benefit. A claim of potential use in the future is not patentable.

Nonobviousness.   In order to be patentable, the invention or discovery must be "nonobvious." For example, the U.S. Supreme Court has held that frosting a light bulb on the inside instead of the outside to solve the problem of an outside surface that collected dirt was "obvious," and therefore the patent was not valid.

Parties may challenge the validity of a patent during the pendency of a patent application *or* after a patent has been issued by the Patent and Trademark Office. A patent may be challenged on several grounds, including (1) that the patent *claim* filed with the Patent and Trademark Office is not specific, or (2) that the subject matter is not patentable, or (3) that one of the substantive requirements (e.g., originality, novelty, utility, or nonobviousness) has not been met.

During the period from 1930 to the mid-1970s, patent applicants and holders were generally on the defensive; over half of the patents challenged were found to be invalid during this period. Since about 1978, there has been a philosophical shift in federal court decisions to favor the upholding of the validity of federal patents. To summarize, the following are the tests that must be met in order to patent a process, invention, or composition:

1. patentable subject matter
2. originality
3. novelty
4. utility
5. nonobviousness.

In *U.S. v. Adams* the Supreme Court upheld a patent for a "wet" battery as being both "novel" and "nonobvious" as required by the patent laws.

PATENTS: NOVELTY AND NONOBVIOUSNESS

UNITED STATES v. ADAMS

383 U.S. 39 (1966)
UNITED STATES SUPREME COURT

Mr. Justice Clark delivered the opinion of the Court.

The United States seeks review of a judgment of the Court of Claims, holding valid and infringed a patent on a wet battery issued to Adams.

THE PATENT IN ISSUE AND ITS BACKGROUND

The patent under consideration, U.S. No. 2,322,210, was issued in 1943 upon an application filed in December 1941 by Adams. It relates to a nonrechargeable, as opposed to a storage, electrical battery. Stated simply, the battery comprises two electrodes—one made of magnesium, the other of cuprous chloride—which are placed in a container. The electrolyte, or battery fluid, used may be either plain or salt water.

For several years prior to filing his application for the patent, Adams had worked in his home experimenting on the development of a wet battery. He found that when cuprous chloride and magnesium were used as electrodes in an electrolyte of either plain water or salt water an improved battery resulted.

The Adams invention was the first practical, water-activated, constant potential battery which could be fabricated and stored indefinitely without any fluid in its cells. It was activated within 30 minutes merely by adding water. Once activated, the battery continued to deliver electricity at a voltage which remained essentially constant regardless of the rate at which current was withdrawn. Furthermore, its capacity for generating current was exceptionally large in comparison to its size and weight. The battery was also quite efficient in that substantially its full capacity could be obtained over a wide range of currents.

Less than a month after filing for his patent, Adams brought his discovery to the attention of the Army and Navy. Arrangements were quickly made for demonstrations before the experts of the United States Army Signal Corps. The Signal Corps scientists who observed the demonstrations and who conducted further tests themselves did not believe the battery was workable.

However, in November 1943, at the height of World War II, the Signal Corps concluded that the battery was feasible. The Government thereafter entered into contracts with various battery companies for its procurement. The battery was found adaptable to many uses.

Surprisingly, the Government did not notify Adams of its changed views nor of the use to which it was putting his device, despite his repeated requests. In 1955, upon examination of a battery produced for the Government by the Burgess Company, he first learned of the Government's action. His request for compensation was denied in 1960, resulting in this suit.

THE PRIOR ACT

The basic idea of chemical generation of electricity is, of course, quite old. Batteries trace back to the epic discovery by the Italian scientist Volta in 1795, who found that when two dissimilar metals are placed in an electrically conductive fluid an electromotive force is set up and electricity generated. . . . At trial, the Government introduced in evidence 24 patents and treatises as representing the art as it stood in 1938, the time of the Adams invention.

THE VALIDITY OF THE PATENT

The Government challenges the validity of the Adams patent on grounds of lack of novelty . . . as well as obviousness. . . . As we have seen in *Graham v. John Deere Co.,* novelty and nonobviousness—as well as utility—are separate tests of patentability and all must be satisfied in a valid patent.

There are several basic errors in the Government's position. First, the fact that the Adams battery is water-activated sets his device apart from the prior art. It is true that Claims 1 and 10, *supra,* do not mention a water electrolyte, but, as we have noted, a stated object of the invention was to provide a battery rendered serviceable by the mere addition of water. . . . We believe that the Court of Claims was correct in concluding that the Adams battery is novel.

The court below found, and the Government apparently admits, that the Adams battery "wholly unexpectedly" has shown "certain valuable operating advantages over other batteries" while those from which it is claimed to have been copied were long ago discarded. Moreover, most of the batteries relied upon by the Government were of a completely different type designed to give intermittent power and characterized by an absence of internal action when not in use.

We conclude the Adams battery was also nonobvious. As we have seen, the operating characteristics of the Adams battery have been shown to have been unexpected and to have far surpassed then-existing wet batteries.

Nor are these the only factors bearing on the question of obviousness. We have seen that at the time Adams perfected his invention noted experts expressed disbelief in it. Several of the same experts subsequently recognized the significance of the Adams invention, some even patenting improvements on the same system. Furthermore, in a crowded art replete with a century and a half of advancement, the Patent Office found not one reference to cite against the Adams application.

We conclude that the Adams patent is valid. The judgment of the Court of Claims is *affirmed.*

CASE QUESTIONS

1. What was the plaintiff's invention? How did the plaintiff's invention differ from previous products in the field? Explain.

2. Did the plaintiff offer his invention to the U.S. government? Did the government use the invention? Did it pay the plaintiff for the use of the invention?
3. Was plaintiff Adams's invention "novel"? Explain.
4. Was plaintiff Adam's invention "nonobvious"? Explain.

   Policy Issue. Should a private party be granted a *monopoly* patent on an invention? Does this help or harm society?

Ethics Issue. Did the United States government act ethically in this case? Why or why not?

Economics Issue. Did Adams have much to gain financially from the outcome of this case? Explain.

Social Responsibility. Does a patent holder owe a duty of social responsibility to allow the government to use a patented invention without the payment of compensation? Why or why not?

Patent Infringement.   A person commits direct patent *infringement* when, without the authorization of the patent holder, he:

1. uses a complete patented process
2. makes, uses, or sells a complete patented machine, article of manufacture, or composition of matter
3. makes, uses or sells an article of manufacture that incorporates a patented design
4. asexually reproduces a patented plant or sells or uses the plant as reproduced.

Courts generally excuse *experimental* use of patented items, or where the infringement was *de minimis.* The "making," "using," and "selling" of a patented invention are separate and independent acts of infringement. Thus, a patent holder can sue a manufacturer for the unauthorized *making* of the patented item, and also sue the purchaser for *using* the item. The mere purchase of the item, without use, is not an act of infringement.

Any person who advises, persuades, encourages, or prevails upon another to directly infringe upon a patent may be held liable for "inducing infringement." A seller of an infringed patented item may be held liable for "contributory infringement if he knowingly assists or aids in patent infringement.

Remedies for Patent Infringement.   A patent holder may seek a number of remedies against a defendant for patent infringement, including:

1. an injunction precluding use of the patent
2. damages measured as the "reasonable royalty" that the patent holder should have received for the use of the patent by the defendant, together with interest and costs of the suit
3. any other monies that the patent holder would have made had there been no patent infringement (e.g., profits from "lost sales" that the plaintiff patent holder was able and willing to make but that defendant infringer made)
4. *treble* damages if the court finds "deliberate" infringement and in its discretion believes the circumstances warrant the award of treble damages
5. reasonable attorney's fees in exceptional patent cases.

"Public Use" Doctrine. A defendant in a patent infringement case may raise the defense that the patented item was used by the public more than one year prior to the grant of the patent. The day one year prior to the *application* for a patent is called the "critical date." The defendant must prove either (1) that some person other than the inventor made a nonsecret, nonexperimental use of the invention prior to the critical date, or (2) that the inventor used the patent for trade and profit prior to the critical date. A single sale of an invention or discovery more than one year prior to the filing of the patent application has been held to bar the issuance of a valid patent under the public use doctrine.

Employer–Employee Relation. Generally, where an employee is hired by an employer *to invent*, the employer may enforce employment agreements assigning all inventions by the employee to the employer, whether made on company time or not and whether made on company property or not. However, where an employee has been hired in a *noninventive* position, the employer has *no* right of assignment to any invention of the employee made by the employee on his or her own time and not using the employer's place of business or equipment. This rule applies whether the invention applies to the employer's business or not. Nevertheless, where the invention occurs during hours of employment, or using the employer's materials and equipment, the employer is given a common-law "shop right" license to the invention even absent an employment agreement.

In *Cali v. Eastern Airlines, Inc.,* where an employee sued his employer for patent infringement, the court held that the "public use" doctrine which was raised as a defense by the employer did not apply to the facts of the case.

PATENTS: "PUBLIC USE" DOCTRINE

CALI v. EASTERN AIRLINES, INC.

442 F.2d 65 (1971)
UNITED STATES COURT OF APPEALS, SECOND CIRCUIT

Irving R. Kaufman, Circuit Judge:

Cali, plaintiff and appellant in this patent infringement action, is a mechanic employed by one of the pioneers in the airlines industry, Pan American World Airways (Pan Am). The kernel of the patented invention which is the subject of this suit was contained in an idea which Cali submitted to Pan Am on a standard form soliciting employees' suggestions in December 1962. Although of course Eastern Airlines, Inc., the appellee and alleged infringer, seeks to minimize its value, Cali's proposal apparently resulted in the correction of a persistent defect in the design of the JT-4 jet engine, then used in Pan Am's Boeing 707 and Douglas DC-8 aircraft before the introduction of the fan jet. Cali's "suggestion-box" solution had eluded the industry's professional engineers.

Judge Dooling, whose opinion is reported at 318 F.Supp. 474, decided that Cali's "invention was . . . in public use" and not used primarily for experimental purposes "more than one year prior to the date" Cali filed his application for a patent and hence the patent was invalid. Accordingly, the action was dismissed.

Cali applied for his patent on September 1, 1964. The key date for purposes of the "public use" bar of Section 102(b) is thus September 1, 1963.

[B]y a telegram dated January 4, 1963, Pratt & Whitney authorized use of the tie rod on a "trial basis." Similarly, on February 8, 1963, Pratt & Whitney wired Pan Am that it had "no objection" to use of the weld "on token number of engines based on your assertion that no assembly difficulty will be encountered." Pursuant to this authorization, Pan Am subsequently installed and used engines incorporating the tie rod technique on one engine and incorporating the weld approach on at least three other engines. In each instance, the engines were installed and used on commercial aircraft in the normal course of Pan Am's business.

We turn to the issue principally briefed and argued, *viz.,* whether Pan Am's public use of Cali's invention prior to September 1, 1963 falls within the judicially created exception to the "public use" bar for uses which are shown by "full, unequivocal, and convincing" proof, to have been primarily intended as experimental rather than commercial.

At the threshold, we differ with the District Court's interpretation of the scope of the "experimental use" exception. Judge Dooling appears to have believed that even Pan Am's "first use" of the tie rod and weld was not predominantly experimental even assuming that the primary purpose of the use was to determine whether Cali's idea should be adopted or rejected. Apparently the District Court assumed that a use may not be "experimental" if the purpose is to see if the idea in question has any value at all, rather than to explore ways of improving the invention or "to determine or guide the direction of *modification* of an *emergent* inventive concept." . . . We find it unduly restrictive.

The leading case defining the reach of the experimental use exception, *Elizabeth v. Pavement Co.,* involved experimentation to test the *durability* of the inventor's new kind of pavement. There was no indication that the inventor put the pavement to the test of six years' public wear to determine what improvements he might make, rather than simply to discover whether the idea was worth pursuing. Indeed, the Court's decision in favor of the patentee was premised on the assumption that the aim of the test might be "to bring his invention to

perfection, *or* to ascertain whether it [would] answer the purpose intended."

The crucial date therefore becomes that when Pan Am first publicly used Cali's concept with a predominantly commercial intent, rather than with the primary purpose of determining whether or in what form the idea should be put into general use.

Applying these familiar standards to this record, we conclude that the motion for summary judgment should have been denied. . . . In sum, we find that the record discloses a genuine issue of fact as to whether Pan Am publicly used Cali's invention prior to September 1, 1963, for predominantly nonexperimental purposes.

Reversed.

CASE QUESTIONS

1. Who was the plaintiff-inventor? Why did he develop his invention?
2. What does the doctrine of "public use" provide? What is the "critical date"? What happens if the inventor or a third party commercially uses the invention prior to the critical date?
3. When did the plaintiff apply for a patent? What was the "critical date"? Did Pan Am use the invention prior to the critical date?
4. What does the "experimental use" exception to the public use doctrine provide?
5. How would you decide this case on remand?

Policy Issue. Should a person be given more than one year from the date of the commercial use of an invention to patent the invention? Why or why not?

Ethics Issue. Was what Pan Am and Eastern did in this case in attempting to defeat Cali's patent ethical? Why or why not?

Economics Issue. What are the economic implications if a patent is found to be invalid? Should patents be allowed to be found to be invalid after the Patent Office has granted a patent? Why or why not?

Social Responsibility. Did Pan Am owe a duty of social responsibility to assist its employee Cali to file for a proper patent on his invention? Explain.

Patents and Antitrust Law. In several situations, the use or accumulation of patents may violate the antitrust laws. Antitrust violations may include:

1. tie-in arrangements with other products or services
2. fixing a resale price of a patented item (resale price maintenance)
3. accumulation of a web of patents ("act of monopolization")
4. territorial restrictions on a licensee regarding the resale of a patent (restraint of trade)
5. price-fixing or territorial restrictions (restraints of trade)
6. attempts by a patent holder to require distributors to confine their activities to the products of the patent holder (exclusive dealing).

Several courts have held that the accumulation of an impenetrable "web" of otherwise valid patents may violate the antitrust laws if the acquisition or maintenance of such patents is an "act of monopolization." If a patent holder is found guilty of violating antitrust laws with regard to the acquisition and use of its patents, the holder may be forced by the court to divest itself of a patent, or be required to license other parties to produce and sell the patented item. In addition, an award of *treble* damages may be made to the plaintiff in a monopolization action.

Trend of the Law

The protection of intellectual property will become an even more important area of the law in the future in the United States. This is particularly so because the country has entered an age often characterized as the "Information Revolution." As the country moves even further towards a service-based economy (over one-half of the U.S. gross national product is represented by the service sector), the protection of information and intellectual property will become of paramount importance.

In the area of trademark protection, certain companies with well-established products must be careful not to overpromote their products to the point where the trademarked names of the products become unprotected generic names. A substantial amount of the cases in the trademark area in the future will consist of trademark holders protecting their trademarked names and slogans from misappropriation.

Critical problems of protecting intellectual property are developing in the high-technology and computer industries. In the computer software industry it is presently estimated that for every single authorized copy of many well-known copyrighted software packages there are over *eight* unauthorized copies in use by owners and users of personal and business computers. The courts in the future will be faced with difficult problems in applying well-established statutory schemes to an ever-changing business environment.

One of the most controversial cases in the area of the protection of intellectual property was decided by the U.S. Supreme Court in *Sony Corporation v. Universal City Studios* (1984). In that case the court held in a 5–4 decision that Sony Corporation and other manufacturers of video tape recorders were not "contributory infringers" of copyrighted materials produced by Universal City Studios, Walt Disney Productions, and other plaintiffs when these copyrighted materials were recorded by consumers on equipment manufactured by the defendants. This case is presented as the first case in this book on page 4.

REVIEW QUESTIONS

1. Coca-Cola Co. challenged 7-Up Company's attempted registration of "The Uncola" as a trademark. The Patent Office dismissed the complaint, finding that the term had acquired a secondary meaning. Coca-Cola appealed, claiming that the term had not acquired a secondary meaning, since the public infrequently uses the term when ordering 7-Up. Should the mark be registrable?

2. Springfield Fire & Marine Insurance Co. used a depiction of a "covered wagon" drawn by oxen on its policies, stationery, and advertising media, which is registered as a "service mark" under the provisions of the Lanham Act. Founders' Fire & Marine Insurance Co. used a fairly similar logo. Springfield sued Founders to try to prevent the firm from using the similar "service mark" even though it did not have any evidence to show that the use of Founders' mark was likely to cause any confusion about the origin of the firm's services. Can a firm prevent another from using a service mark if such use is not likely to cause confusion about the origin of the services it identifies?

3. The "Pump Room" was a dining room in a Chicago hotel owned by Ambassador East, Inc. The restaurant had been in operation since 1938 and during that time the name "Pump Room" had acquired a very distinctive and far-reaching reputation. The name "Orsatti's Pump Room" had been used by Orsatti, Inc. since 1951. On Orsatti's restaurant marquee, however, the name "Pump Room" was much more prominent than "Orsatti's." Ambassador East sued Orsatti in 1958 seeking to prohibit the use of the name "Pump Room." Should Ambassador East have been allowed to protect its name?

4. Sears, Roebuck & Co. used the trade name "Allstate" for a line of automobile accessories, and a wholly Sears-owned subsidiary sold insurance under the same name. The insurance company organized the Allstate Foundation for Driving Education, which made grants to colleges and universities to help improve driver training, and provided discounts in insurance rates for high school students who took courses in driver training. Johnson started a driving school near a Sears location and named it "All-State." Did Johnson's use of "All-State" infringe upon Sears use of "Allstate"?

5. Several well-known Disney comic book characters were featured in a coun-

terculture comic book published by Air Pirates, which covered their exploits as members of a free-thinking, promiscuous, drug-ingesting counterculture. Disney sued for copyright infringement, claiming that these characters were protected as component parts of the copyrighted works in which they appeared. Disney sought injunctive relief, destruction of the infringing materials, damages, costs, and attorney's fees. Were the Disney characters protected by the copyright laws?

6. Zapruder had been near the scene of President Kennedy's assassination and managed to get photographs of it, which were purchased by *Time*, Inc. and used in its copyrighted magazines. Thompson wrote a book that was a study of the assassination and that set forth his theory as to how it had occurred. To illustrate some of his points, Thompson and his publisher asked *Time*, Inc. for permission to use some of the photos; however, they could not reach an agreement. Consequently, they hired an artist who made sketches of several Zapruder frames and these sketches were published in the book; they also fully reproduced certain parts of each frame. Can a photograph be given copyright protection? Did the sketch of the photograph constitute fair use?

7. In a speech delivered before thousands of onlookers during a civil rights march at the Lincoln Memorial, Dr. Martin Luther King, Jr., discussed some of the thoughts and ideas he had expressed in an earlier speech in Detroit. In both speeches he used the same catch phrase, "I have a dream." The speech was widely covered by the media, and the press was given an advance text. Impressed with the way the speech stirred the crowd, the *New York Post*, without King's consent, published the complete text under the title "I Have a Dream." Thereafter, 20th-Century-Fox and Mister Maestro produced recordings that included the Washington speech, again without King's consent. King had already consented to a recording of his Detroit speech produced by Motown. Claiming infringement of his common-law copyright, King sought an injunction and damages. The defendants argued in response that both the delivery of the speech and the advanced distribution of its text to the press constituted a general publication of its contents, thereby divesting it of any common-law copyright protections. Was King's speech protected?

8. "H. R. Pufnstuf" was a popular children's television show that had been developed by Sid & Marty Krofft Television Productions, Inc. The show featured a fantasyland populated by several costumed characters, moving trees, talking books, a boy named Jimmy, and a yellow-and-orange-costumed dragon named Pufnstuf. A commercial agency contacted Krofft and attempted to negotiate a deal in which Krofft would license the use of the characters to McDonalds for use in an advertising campaign. The negotiations fell through and McDonalds began a series of McDonaldland commercials featuring the fantasyland theme and characters, such as Ronald McDonald, that were substantially similar to Krofft's. Krofft sued for copyright infringement and the District Court held that McDonalds had infringed upon Krofft's copyright since a reasonable person would have found that the works contained substantially similiar expressions of the same idea. Was this the proper test to apply? Did McDonalds have any valid First Amendment defenses?

9. Aiken owned a fast food business. He decided to provide music for his customers and his employees, so he installed four speakers in the ceiling of the dining area and then played normal public-radio broadcasts. Since many of the musical compositions that were broadcast were copyrighted, a group of music companies sued Aiken for copyright infringement. Was Aiken "performing" the copyrighted material in violation of copyright law?

10. Park-In applied for and was issued a patent for a drive-in theater which placed patrons' cars on planes of differing inclines so that all patrons would be able to view the theater screen from their cars without being obstructed. Other drive-in theaters adopted the same design, and Park-In sued claiming patent infringement. The defendants argued that the patent was void since it lacked patentable subject matter. Was this architectural design patentable?

11. Hotchkiss received a patent on doorknobs that were made of clay or porcelain connected to a metal shank. This type of connection was commonly used in other standard doorknobs; the only difference with Hotchkiss' design was that he used a different type of material for the knob. In fact, any ordinary mechanic acquainted with the business could have easily substituted the materials. Was Hotchkiss' device patentable?

12. Murphy developed a new type of slot machine. He applied for a patent but his application was denied because the Patent Office determined that all slot machines lack patentable utility. Was his device useful within the meaning of patent law?

13. Pillsbury held the patent on angel food cake mix. Although General Mills did not sell angel food cake mix in violation of the patent, it did manufacture and sell an angel food cake base, which was used by bakers who illegally infringed upon Pillsbury's patent. General Mills also included directions on its bags of base, which explained how to turn it into angel food cake. Did General Mills' actions infringe Pillsbury's patent?

23 BUSINESS TORTS

INTRODUCTION

The American economy is based on the principle of "freedom of competition," whereby persons and businesses compete freely with each other in producing and distributing goods and services. Freedom of competition generally guarantees the opportunity to every person to become an entrepreneur and open a business, and guarantees that consumers will receive the greatest selection of goods and services at the best price and highest quality. In this excerpt from *Katz v. Kapper*, 7 C.A.2d 1 (1935), the court described the doctrine of free competition.

Plaintiff and defendants were rival wholesale fish dealers in the city of Los Angeles. . . . The complaint alleges that plaintiff had a well-established wholesale fish business, the good will of which was valuable; . . . It was further alleged that the defendants did open . . . a store, did widely advertise and sell fish at lower prices than plaintiff . . . ; that all of said acts were done for the purpose of driving plaintiff out of business; and that as a result thereof "a considerable number of said retailers and peddlers and customers ceased from doing business with plaintiff and made their purchases from these defendants to plaintiff's damages."

In deciding whether the conduct of defendants alleged in the complaint is actionable, it is necessary to apply certain well-settled rules relating to competition in business. These may be generally stated as follows: "Competition in business, though carried to the extent of ruining a rival, is not ordinarily actionable, but every trader if left to conduct his business in his own way, so long as the methods he employs do not involve wrongful conduct such as fraud, misrepresentation, intimidation, coercion, obstruction, or molestation of the rival or his servants or workmen or the procurement of the violation of contractual relations. If disturbance or loss comes as the result of competition, or the exercise of like rights by others, as where a merchant undersells or oversells his neighbor, it is *damnum absque injuria.*"

The fact that the methods used were ruthless, or unfair, in a moral sense, does not stamp them as illegal. It has never been regarded as the duty or province of the courts to regulate practices in the business world beyond the point of applying legal or equitable remedies in cases involving acts of oppression or deceit which are unlawful. Any extension of this jurisdiction must come through legislative action. In this case no questions of statutory law are involved. The alleged acts of defendants do not fall within the category of business methods recognized as unlawful, and hence they are not actionable. The demurrer to the complaint was properly sustained.

Freedom of competition is not wholly without restrictions, as the antitrust laws against collusion and monopoly, securities laws requiring full disclosure, and the statutory prohibitions against trademark, copyright, and patent infringement attest.

UNFAIR COMPETITION

In many circumstances, the ideas, processes, customer lists, and other elements that commonly make a business successful do not qualify for statutory protection as a trademark, copyright, or patent. However, many state legislatures have enacted statutes to supplement federal trademark, copyright, and patent laws, and the courts have developed special common-law doctrines in the law of *torts*, which give businesses a civil right of action against others for unfair competition.

The term *unfair competition* is a broad generic term that describes an array of business torts. The most common forms of unfair competition are (1) palming off a product as that of another company, (2) product disparagement, and (3) misappropriation of trade secrets.

Palming Off. One of the oldest forms of unfair competition is the business tort of "palming off." The tort of *palming off* consists of one party selling or distributing a product under the guise that it is really another party's product. For example, if Infrastructure Business Machines, Inc., a small manufacturer of computers, places a blue "IBM" logo on its computers for sale, it most likely would be held liable for the tort of "palming off."

In *Compco Corporation v. Day-Brite Lighting, Inc.,* 376 U.S. 235 (1964), the U.S. Supreme Court stated:

A State . . . has power to impose liability upon those who, knowing that the public is relying upon an original manufacturer's reputation for quality and integrity, deceive the public by palming off their copies as the original.

In order to prove the tort of palming off, the plaintiff must show that there is a *"likelihood* of confusion as to the source of the product." Actual consumer confusion need not be shown. Other relevant factors in determining whether there has been a "palming off" of goods are (1) whether the article could have been made in some way other than as an identical duplicate of the original, (2) whether a "secondary meaning" has attached to the original maker's product, and (3) whether members of the public have actually been confused as to the origin of the copied product.

In *Sears, Roebuck & Co. v. Stiffel Company* the Supreme Court found that Sears' copying and sale of a *non*patented product of a smaller competitor did not constitute "palming off."

patent was invalid ∴ can't use palming off as a substitute for patent protection.

"PALMING OFF"

SEARS, ROEBUCK & CO. v. STIFFEL COMPANY

376 U.S. 225 (1964)
UNITED STATES SUPREME COURT

Mr. Justice Black delivered the opinion of the Court.

The respondent, Stiffel Company, secured design and mechanical patents on a "pole lamp"—a vertical tube having lamp fixtures along the outside, the tube being made so that it will stand upright between the floor and ceiling of a room. Pole lamps proved a decided commercial success, and soon after Stiffel brought them on the market Sears, Roebuck & Company put on the market a substantially identical lamp, which it sold more cheaply, Sears' retail price being about the same as Stiffel's wholesale price. Stiffel then brought this action against Sears in the United States District Court for the Northern District of Illinois, claiming in its first count that by copying its design Sears had infringed Stiffel's patents and in its second count that by selling copies of Stiffel's lamp Sears had caused confusion in the trade as to the source of the lamps and had thereby engaged in unfair competition under Illinois law.

The Court of Appeals . . . court held that, to make out a case of unfair competition under Illinois law, there was no need to show that Sears had been "palming off" its lamps as Stiffel lamps; Stiffel

had only to prove that there was a "likelihood of confusion as to the source of the products"—that the two articles were sufficiently identical that customers could not tell who had made a particular one. Impressed by the "remarkable sameness of appearance" of the lamps, the Court of Appeals upheld the trial court's findings of likelihood of confusion and some actual confusion, findings which the appellate court construed to mean confusion "as to the source of the lamps." The Court of Appeals thought this enough under Illinois law to sustain the trial court's holding of unfair competition, and thus held Sears liable under Illinois law for doing no more than copying and marketing an unpatented article.

In the present case the "pole lamp" sold by Stiffel has been held not to be entitled to the protection of either a mechanical or a design patent. An unpatentable article, like an article on which the patent has expired, is in the public domain and may be made and sold by whoever chooses to do so. What Sears did was to copy Stiffel's design and to sell lamps almost identical to those sold by Stiffel. This it had every right to do. . . . That Stiffel originated the pole lamp and made it popular is immaterial.

Sharing in the goodwill of an article unprotected by patent or trade-mark is the exercise of a right possessed by all—and in the free exercise of which the consuming public is deeply interested."

To allow a State by use of its law of unfair competition to prevent the copying of an article which represents too slight an advance to be patented would be to permit the State to block off from the public something which federal law has said belongs to the public. The result would be that while federal law grants only 14 or 17 years' protection to genuine inventions, States could allow perpetual protection to articles too lacking in novelty to merit any patent at all under federal constitutional standards. This would be too great an encroachment on the federal patent system to be tolerated.

The judgment below . . . gave Stiffel the equivalent of a patent monopoly on its unpatented lamp. That was error, and Sears is entitled to a judgment in its favor.

Reversed.

CASE QUESTIONS

1. What is "unfair competition"? Is it actionable at law? Is all competition that drives competitors out of business considered unfair competition?
2. Is the mere copying and sale of an article similar to an unpatented product of a competitor unfair competition? Why or why not?
3. What is "palming off"? Is it unfair competition? Did Sears palm off its lamp as a Stiffel lamp in this case?
4. Did the Stiffel Company have a *valid* patent on its lamp? If it had, would the decision of this case have been different?
5. Did the State of Illinois try to enact a law of unfair competition that was broader than the tort of palming off? Broader than the federal patent laws? Did the Supreme Court find this state law to be invalid? Explain.

Policy Issue. Which lawsuit alleging palming off is more likely to occur? Why?
a. a small company suing a large well-known company
b. a large well-known company suing a small company

Economics Issue. Is palming off economically advantageous to a firm? Is copying another firm's product without engaging in palming off economically advantageous? Explain.

Ethics Issue. Was it ethical for Sears to copy the Stiffel lamp design in this case?

Social Responsibility. Do manufacturers and retailers owe a duty of social responsibility to copy expensive well-known designs and sell them to the public at cheaper prices?

Product Disparagement. The tort of *defamation of character* is a well-developed doctrine in the American legal system. Defamation, which is known as *libel* if written and *slander* if oral, requires the plaintiff to show that the defendant published an untrue statement about the plaintiff to a third party that caused injury to the personal reputation of the plaintiff. An *untrue* statement about another's property or product (e.g., about the quality of a competitor's product) has been generally held by the courts *not* to cause the damage to the personal reputation of the owner required for an action for defamation of character. Instead, the courts have developed the separate business tort of *product disparagement,* also known as *trade libel* and *slander of title,* to apply to situations where an untrue statement is made about a plaintiff's property, business, or products. Although the elements of the tort of disparagement have not been fully developed by the courts, and are not uniform among the states, the majority rule requires the plaintiff to show:

1. that the defendant published to a third person, either orally or in written form, an untrue statement about the plaintiff's property or products

2. that the defendant knew that the statement was untrue
3. that the defendant made the statement with malice and with the intent to injure the plaintiff
4. that the plaintiff was caused *special* damages, e.g., loss of a specific customer.

A mere showing of general damages is not sufficient in an action for product disparagement. By comparison, a showing of general damages is sufficient in a normal libel action, but in a normal slander action a showing of special damages is required. A few states have extended the tort of product disparagement to include cases of *negligent* misrepresentation, thereby eliminating the knowledge, intent, and malice elements of the tort.

In *Bose Corporation v. Consumers Union, Inc.* the U.S. Supreme Court announced that an appellate court must apply the *independent review* standard in product disparagement cases and held that the defendant was not liable for trade disparagement because it did not have the requisite actual malice when it published an untrue statement about one of the plaintiff's products.

only public figures have to prove malice
(most lg. company's are public figures) *couldn't prove malice*

PRODUCT DISPARAGEMENT

BOSE CORPORATION v. CONSUMERS UNION OF UNITED STATES, INC.

104 S. CT. 1949 (1984)
UNITED STATES SUPREME COURT

Justice Stevens delivered the opinion of the Court.

An unusual metaphor in a critical review of an unusual loudspeaker system gave rise to product disparagement litigation. . . . In the May 1970 issue of its magazine, *Consumer Reports,* respondent published a seven-page article evaluating the quality of numerous brands of medium priced loudspeakers. In a boxed-off section occupying most of two pages, respondent commented on "some loudspeakers of special interest," one of which was the Bose 901—an admittedly "unique and unconventional" system that had recently been placed on the market by petitioner. After describing the system and some of its virtues, and after noting that a listener "could pinpoint the location of various instruments much more easily with a standard speaker than with the *Bose* system," respondent's article made the following statements:

Worse, individual instruments heard through the Bose system seemed to grow to gigantic proportions and tended to wander about the room. For instance, a violin appeared to be 10 feet wide and a piano stretched from wall to wall. With orchestral music, such effects seemed inconsequential. But we think they might become annoying when listening to soloists. . . .

We think the *Bose* system is so unusual that a prospective buyer must listen to it and judge it for himself. We would suggest delaying so big an investment until you were sure the system would please you after the novelty value had worn off.

Petitioner took exception to numerous statements made in the article, and when respondent refused to publish a retraction, petitioner commenced this product disparagement action in the United States District Court for the District of Massachusetts. After a protracted period of pretrial discovery, the District Court denied respondent's motion for summary judgment and conducted a 19-day bench trial on the issue of liability. In its lengthy, detailed opinion on the merits of the case the District Court ruled in respondent's favor on most issues. Most significantly, the District Court ruled that the petitioner is a "public figure" as that term is defined in *Gertz v. Robert Welsh, Inc.* for purposes of this case and therefore the First Amendment, as interpreted in *New York v. Sullivan,* precludes recovery in this product disparagement action unless the petitioner proved by clear and convincing evidence that respondent made a false disparaging statement with "actual malice."

On three critical points, however, the District Court agreed with petitioner. First, it found that one sentence in the article contained a "false" statement of "fact" concerning the tendency of the instruments to wander. Based primarily on testimony by the author of the article, the District Court found that instruments heard through the speakers tended to wander "along the wall," rather than "about the room" as reported by respondent. Second, it found that the statement was disparaging. Third, it concluded

> on the basis of proof which it considers clear and convincing, that the plaintiff has sustained its burden of proving that the defendant published a false statement of material fact with knowledge that it was false or with reckless disregard of its truth or falsity."

Judgment was entered for petitioner on the product disparagement claim. . . . The United States Court of Appeals for the First Circuit reversed. . . . Based on its own review of the record, the Court of Appeals concluded:

> [W]e are unable to find clear and convincing evidence that CU published the statement that individual instruments tended to wander about the room with knowledge that it was false or with reckless disregard of whether it was false or not. The evidence presented merely shows that the words in the article may not have described precisely what the two panelists heard during the listening test. CU was guilty of using imprecise language in the article—perhaps resulting from an attempt to produce a readable article for its mass audience. Certainly this does not support an inference of actual malice.

Petitioner correctly reminds us that Rule 52(a) provides:

> Findings of fact shall not be set aside unless clearly erroneous, and due regard shall be given to the opportunity of the trial court to judge of the credibility of the witnesses.

On the other hand, respondent correctly reminds us that in cases raising First Amendment issues we have repeatedly held that an appellate court has an obligation to "make an independent examination of the whole record" in order to make sure "that the judgment does not constitute a forbidden intrusion on the field of free expression." *New York Times v. Sullivan.*

The First Amendment presupposes that the freedom to speak one's mind is not only an aspect of individual liberty—and thus a good unto itself—but also is essential to the common quest for truth and the vitality of society as a whole. Under our Constitution "there is no such thing as a false idea. However pernicious an opinion may seem, we depend for its correction not on the conscience of judges and juries but on the competition of other ideas." *Gertz v. Robert Welch, Inc.* Nevertheless, there are categories of communication and certain special utterances to which the majestic protection of the First Amendment does not extend because they "are no essential part of any exposition of ideas, and are of such slight social value as a step to truth that any benefit that may be derived from them is clearly outweighed by the social interest in order and morality."

Libelous speech has been held to constitute one such category, *Beauharnais v. Illinois;* others that have been held to be outside the scope of the freedom of speech are fighting words, *Chaplinsky v. New Hampshire,* incitement to riot, *Brandenburg v. Ohio,* obscenity, *Roth v. United States,* and child pornography, *New York v. Ferber.* . . . In such cases, the Court has regularly conducted an independent review of the record both to be sure that the speech in question actually falls within the unprotected category and to confine the perimeters of any unprotected category within acceptably narrow limits in an effort to ensure that protected expression will not be inhibited.

Similarly, although under *Miller v. California,* the questions of what appeals to "prurient interest" and what is "patently offensive" under the community standard obscenity test are "essentially questions of fact," we expressly recognized the "ultimate power of appellate courts to conduct an independent review of constitutional claims when necessary."

Hence, in *New York Times v. Sullivan,* after announcing the constitutional requirement for a finding of "actual malice" in certain types of defamation actions, it was only natural that we should conduct an independent review of the evidence on the dispositive constitutional issue. We explained our action as follows:

> This Court's duty is not limited to the elaboration of constitutional principles; we must also in proper cases review the evidence to make certain that those principles have been constitutionally applied. . . . We must 'make an independent examination of the whole record.

[W]e agree with the Court of Appeals that the difference between hearing violin sounds move around the room and hearing them wander back and forth fits easily within the breathing space that gives life to the First Amendment. We may accept all of the purely factual findings of the District Court and nevertheless hold as a matter of law that the record does not contain clear and convincing evidence that . . . [Consumers Union] prepared the loudspeaker article with knowledge that it contained a false statement, or with reckless disregard of the truth.

Appellate judges in such a case must exercise independent judgment and determine whether the record establishes actual malice with convincing clarity.

The judgment of the Court of Appeals is *affirmed.*

Justice Rehnquist, with whom **Justice O'Connor** joins, dissenting.

There is more than one irony in this "Case of the Wandering Instruments," which subject matter makes it sound more like a candidate for inclusion in the "Adventures of Sherlock Holmes" than in a casebook on constitutional law. It is ironic in the first place that a constitutional principle which originated in *New York Times v. Sullivan,* because of the need for freedom to criticize the conduct of public officials is applied here to a magazine's false statements about a commercial loudspeaker system.

CASE QUESTIONS

1. What is *product disparagement?* How does it differ from *defamation?* Explain.
2. What did the defendant write about the plaintiff's product? Was it false?
3. Was the plaintiff in this case a "public figure"? Where a plaintiff is a public figure, what does the *New York Times v. Sullivan* case require the plaintiff to prove?
4. Did the Supreme Court extend the *New York Times v. Sullivan* rule to product disparagement cases? Was this an important decision? Why or why not?
5. Describe the following tests for review of a trial court decision by an appellate court. What is the difference between the two tests? When is each used?
   a. clearly erroneous test
   b. independent judgment test
6. Which of those two tests did the Supreme Court apply in this case? Why does the Supreme Court distrust jury decisions in First Amendment cases? Explain.

Policy Issue. If the Supreme Court had found in favor of the plaintiff, would critics in this country (e.g., movie and restaurant critics) have been hindered in their work?

Economics Issue. If a critic mistakenly makes a false representation about a company's product, would it cause the same economic damage to the company as if the critic had made the same statement with actual malice?

Ethics Issue. Did Consumers Union act unethically in this case? Did the Bose Corporation? Explain.

Social Responsibility. Should a party be given the right to voice his *opinions* about the quality of a product without the fear of being sued for disparagement? Why or why not?

Misappropriation of Trade Secrets. Many businesses are successful because of certain "trade secrets" that set them apart from the rest of their competitors. *Trade secrets* may consist of a product formula, pattern, customer list, or other device or compilation of information. Access to many trade secrets may develop through an employer-employee relation, client-professional relation, or through clandestine activities by a defendant.

Trade secrets that do not qualify for patent, copyright, or trademark protection are accorded limited protection by state unfair competition laws, and then generally only from *misappropriation*. Thus, if a competitor can determine the formula, configuration, or design of a trade-secret product through an examination of the product itself, and produces a similar product that does not cause a "likelihood of confusion" as to the source of the product (palming off), there has been no unlawful misappropriation of a trade secret. Actionable misappropriation of a trade secret usually requires that the competitor discover the trade secret through espionage, bribery, theft, or some other form of unlawful activity. Further, the plaintiff in a misappropriation-of-a-trade-secret case must have taken all reasonable precautions to protect its trade secret from discovery (e.g., have placed fences around its buildings, hired guards, used locks).

The plaintiff in a misappropriation-of-a-trade-secret case can recover all damages caused by the use and disclosure of the trade secret by the defendant and any profits obtained by the defendant in using the trade secret. A plaintiff may also obtain an injunction against any further use or disclosure of the trade secret by the defendant.

In *E. I. Du Pont De Nemours & Company v. Christopher* the court found that the defendant's aerial photography of the plaintiff's construction of a methanol plant was an unlawful misappropriation of a trade secret.

TRADE SECRETS

E. I. Du PONT De NEMOURS & COMPANY, INC. v. CHRISTOPHER

431 F.2d 1012 (1970)
UNITED STATES COURT OF APPEALS, FIFTH CIRCUIT

Goldberg, Circuit Judge:

This is a case of industrial espionage in which an airplane is the cloak and a camera the dagger. The defendants-appellants, Rolfe and Gary Christopher, are photographers in Beaumont, Texas. The Christophers were hired by an unknown third party to take aerial photographs of new construction at the Beaumont plant of E. I. duPont deNemours & Company, Inc. Sixteen photographs of the DuPont facility were taken from the air on March 19, 1969, and these photographs were later developed and delivered to the third party.

DuPont employees apparently noticed the airplane on March 19 and immediately began an investigation to determine why the craft was circling over the plant. By that afternoon the investigation had disclosed that the craft was involved in a photographic expedition and that the Christophers were the photographers. DuPont contacted the Christophers that same afternoon and asked them to reveal the name of the person or corporation requesting the photographs. The Christophers refused to disclose this information, giving as their reason the client's desire to remain anonymous.

Having reached a dead end in the investigation, DuPont subsequently filed suit against the Christophers, alleging that the Christophers had wrongfully obtained photographs revealing DuPont's trade secrets, which they then sold to the undisclosed third party.

DuPont contended that it had developed a highly secret but unpatented process for producing methanol, a process which gave DuPont a competitive advantage over other producers. This process, Du-Pont alleged, was a trade secret developed after much expensive and time-consuming research, and a secret which the company had taken special precautions to safeguard. The area photographed by the Christophers was the plant designed to produce methanol by this secret process, and because the plant was still under construction parts of the process were exposed to view from directly above the construction area. Photographs of that area, Du-Pont alleged, would enable a skilled person to deduce the secret process for making methanol.

The question remaining, therefore, is whether aerial photography of plant construction is an improper means of obtaining another's trade secret.

We think, . . . , that the Texas rule is clear. One may use his competitor's secret process if he discovers the process by reverse engineering applied to the finished product; one may use a competitor's process if he discovers it by his own independent research; but one may not avoid these labors by taking the process from the discoverer without his permission at a time when he is taking reasonable precautions to maintain its secrecy. To obtain knowledge of a process without spending the time and money to discover it independently is *improper* unless the holder voluntarily discloses it or fails to take reasonable precautions to ensure its secrecy.

[W]e realize that industrial espionage of the sort here perpetrated has become a popular sport in some segments of our industrial community. However, our devotion to freewheeling industrial competition must not force us into accepting the law of the jungle as the standard of morality expected in our commercial relations. Our tolerance of the espionage game must cease when the protections required to prevent another's spying cost so much that the spirit of inventiveness is dampened. Commercial privacy must be protected from espionage which could not have been reasonably anticipated or prevented.

We do not mean to imply, however, that everything not in plain view is within the protected vale, nor that all information obtained through every extra optical extension is forbidden. Indeed, for our industrial competition to remain healthy there must be breathing room for observing a competing industrialist. A competitor can and must shop his competi-

tion for pricing and examine his products for quality, components, and methods of manufacture. Perhaps ordinary fences and roofs must be built to shut out incursive eyes, but we need not require the discoverer of a trade secret to guard against the unanticipated, the undetectable, or the unpreventable methods of espionage now available.

In the instant case DuPont was in the midst of constructing a plant. Although after construction the finished plant would have protected much of the process from view, during the period of construction the trade secret was exposed to view from the air. To require DuPont to put a roof over the unfinished plant to guard its secret would impose an enormous expense to prevent nothing more than a school boy's trick. We introduce here no new or radical ethic since our ethos has never given moral sanction to piracy. The market place must not deviate far from our mores. We should not require a person or corporation to take unreasonable precautions to prevent another from doing that which he ought not do in the first place. Reasonable precautions against predatory eyes we may require, but an impenetrable fortress is an unreasonable requirement, and we are not disposed to burden industrial inventors with such a duty in order to protect the fruits of their efforts.

"Improper" will always be a word of many nuances, determined by time, place, and circumstances. We therefore need not proclaim a catalogue of commercial improprieties. Clearly, however, one of its commandments does say

> thou shall not appropriate a trade secret through deviousness under circumstances in which countervailing defenses are not reasonably available.

The decision of the trial court is *affirmed* and the case *remanded* to that court for proceedings on the merits.

CASE QUESTIONS

1. What is a *trade secret?* Is it protected by law from misappropriation? Explain.
2. What type of plant was DuPont constructing in this case? Was it a trade secret?
3. What action did the Christophers take in this case? Was it *espionage?* Or a "school boy's trick"?

4. Must a party take precautionary steps to protect its trade secrets? Did DuPont take appropriate steps to protect its trade secret in this case? Could it have done more? Was it required to do so?

5. What is *reverse engineering?* Can a trade secret be legally discovered if a competitor examines another competitor's product? Explain.

6. Why do you think that the third party that hired the Christophers wanted to remain anonymous? Why do you think the Christophers didn't disclose the identity of this third party?

Policy Issue. Should trade secrets be protected by law? Or should only ideas, inventions, and works that can be trademarked, copyrighted or patented be protected from misappropriation?

Economics Issue. What are the economic consequences of the following?

a. a competitor keeps a *trade secret* secret from its competitors

b. a competitor discovers the trade secret of a competitor through *lawful* means

c. a competitor discovers the trade secret of a competitor through *unlawful* means

Ethics Issue. Were the actions by the Christophers, and the party that hired them, ethical in this case? Why or why not?

Social Responsibility. Do competitors owe a duty of social responsibility to not copy another competitor's products and trade secrets? Or to try to lawfully discover others' trade secrets and duplicate them? Why or why not?

INVASION OF PERSONAL RIGHTS

Businesses at times may invade certain rights of parties with whom they deal. The courts have developed a body of law to protect individuals and businesses from the invasion of certain personal rights. Generally, businesses are subject to civil liability for (1) intentional invasion of the right to privacy, (2) intentional infliction of emotional distress, and (3) misappropriation of the right to publicity.

Invasion of the Right to Privacy. Generally, a person has the right to be left alone, to live his life in privacy without being subjected to unwarranted and undesired publicity. The violation of this right to privacy constitutes an intentional tort for which the plaintiff is entitled to recover damages. For example, defendants who engage in clandestine photography of the plaintiff in the privacy of his home, unauthorized publication of private facts, unauthorized commercial use of the plaintiff's picture, wiretapping, eavesdropping, or electronic spying have been held *civilly* liable for damages for the intentional tort of invasion of privacy.

The necessary element for an action for the *invasion of the right to privacy* is the *public disclosure* by a defendant of a *private fact* of the plaintiff. The tort is determined by the test as to what would appear offensive to the "ordinary man of ordinary sensitivities." The publication of a private *truthful* fact about the plaintiff may be the basis for a lawsuit for the intentional invasion of privacy. (By contrast, in order to bring a lawsuit for defamation of character or disparagement, the plaintiff must prove that the defendant published an *untrue* fact about the plaintiff or its product).

The information disclosed must be a *private* fact. Disclosure of what is public information (e.g., police reports) generally cannot be the basis of a lawsuit for invasion of privacy. The intentional tort of invasion of the right to privacy also requires the written *publication* by the defendant of the private fact about the plaintiff to a third person. If there is no publication to a third person there is no basis for an action for invasion of privacy. However, an action for the intentional infliction of emotional distress may arise, and the defendant may be liable for violating local laws prohibiting "peeping Toms," etc.

The courts have generally held that the right to privacy cannot be violated by word of mouth alone. Thus, if the defendant only verbally tells someone a private fact about the plaintiff, there is usually no basis for a lawsuit for invasion of the right to privacy. The majority of the states require some form of written publication, such as a picture, tape recording, etc., in order for there to be an invasion of privacy. A minority of states have extended the tort of invasion of privacy to include oral communications, particularly if publicized over the radio.

Where a person by his own activities, or by force of circumstances, becomes a *public figure,* he relinquishes his right to privacy to the extent that the public has a legitimate interest in his affairs or activities. For example, the love affairs of show business celebrities may be reported without constituting an invasion of privacy, whereas the reporting of the same type of love affair of a nonpublic figure would form the basis for a lawsuit for the intentional invasion of the right to privacy. Even public figures are protected from the publication of certain private facts, which would constitute an invasion of their privacy (e.g., telephoto pictures of bedroom activities).

In *Briscoe v. Reader's Digest Association, Inc.* the court held that the publication by the defendant of information about the prior criminal activities of the plaintiff formed the basis for an action for the intentional invasion of the right to privacy.

INVASION OF THE RIGHT TO PRIVACY
BRISCOE v. READER'S DIGEST ASSOCIATION, INC.

4 C.3d 529 (1971)
SUPREME COURT OF CALIFORNIA

Peters, J.

Plaintiff Marvin Briscoe filed suit against defendant Reader's Digest Association, alleging that defendant had willfully and maliciously invaded his privacy by publishing an article which disclosed truthful but embarrasing private facts about plaintiff's past life. . . . The allegations of the complaint may be summarized as follows: On December 15, 1956, plaintiff and another man hijacked a truck in Danville, Kentucky.

[I]mmediately subsequent to said incident, plaintiff abandoned his life of shame and became entirely rehabilitated and has thereafter at all times lived an exemplary, virtuous and honorable life . . . he has assumed a place in respectable society and made many friends who were not aware of the incident in his earlier life.

"The Big Business of Hijacking," published by defendant 11 years after the hijacking incident, commences with a picture whose caption reads, "Today's highwaymen are looting trucks at a rate of more than $100 million a year. But the truckers have now declared all-out war." The article describes various truck thefts and the efforts being made to stop such thefts. Dates ranging from 1965 to the time of publication are mentioned throughout the article, but none of the described thefts is itself dated. One sentence in the article refers to plaintiff:

> Typical of many beginners, Marvin Briscoe and [another man] stole a 'valuable-looking' truck in Danville, Ky., and then fought a gun battle with the local police, only to learn that they had hijacked four bowling-pin spotters.

There is nothing in the article to indicate that the hijacking occurred in 1956. . . . As the result of defendant's publication, plaintiff's 11-year-old daughter, as well as his friends, for the first time learned of this incident. They thereafter scorned and abandoned him.

Conceding the truth of the facts published in defendant's article, plaintiff claims that the public disclosure of these private facts has humiliated him and exposed him to contempt and ridicule. Conceding that the *subject* of the article may have been "newsworthy," he contends that the use of his *name* was not, and that the defendant has thus invaded his right to privacy.

Acceptance of the right to privacy has grown with the increasing capability of the mass media and electronic devices with their capacity to destroy an individual's anonymity, intrude upon his most intimate activities, and expose his most personal characteristics to public gaze. . . . A common law right to privacy . . . is now recognized in at least 36 states. California has recognized the right to privacy for 40 years. *Melvin* v. *Reid* (1931).

The right to keep information private was bound to clash with the right to disseminate information to the public. . . . Particularly deserving of First Amendment protection are reports of "hot news," items of possible immediate public concern or interest. . . . There can be no doubt that reports of current criminal activities are the legitimate province of a free press. The circumstances under which crimes occur, the techniques used by those outside the law, the tragedy that may befall the victims— these are vital bits of information for people coping with the exigencies of modern life.

It is also generally in the social interest to identify

adults currently charged with the commission of a crime. While such an identification may not presume guilt, it may legitimately put others on notice that the named individual is suspected of having committed a crime. Naming the suspect may also persuade eyewitnesses and character witnesses to testify. For these reasons, while the suspect or offender obviously does not consent to public exposure, his right to privacy must give way to the overriding social interest.

In general, therefore, truthful reports of *recent* crimes and the names of suspects or offenders will be deemed protected by the First Amendment. . . . The instant case, however, compels us to consider whether reports of the facts of *past* crimes and the identification of *past* offenders serve these same public-interest functions.

We have no doubt that reports of the facts of past crimes are newsworthy. Media publication of the circumstances under which crimes were committed in the past may prove educational in the same way that reports of current crimes do. The public has a strong interest in enforcing the law, and this interest is served by accumulating and disseminating data cataloguing the reasons men commit crimes, the methods they use, and the ways in which they are apprehended. Thus in an article on truck hijackings, *Reader's Digest* certainly had the right to report the *facts* of plaintiff's criminal act.

However, identification of the *actor* in reports of long past crimes usually serves little independent public purpose. Once legal proceedings have terminated, and a suspect or offender has been released, identification of the individual will not usually aid the administration of justice. Identification will no longer serve to bring forth witnesses or obtain succor for victims. Unless the individual has reattracted the public eye to himself in some independent fashion, the only public "interest" that would usually be served is that of curiosity.

There may be times, of course, when an event involving private citizens may be so unique as to capture the imagination of all. In such cases—e.g., the behavior of the passengers on the sinking *Titanic,* the heroism of Nathan Hale, the horror of the Saint Valentine's Day Massacre—purely private individuals may by an accident of history lose their privacy regarding that incident for all time. . . . An individual whose name is fixed in the public's memory, such as that of the political assassin, never becomes an anonymous member of the community again. But in each case it is for the trier of fact to determine whether the individual's infamy is such that he has never left the public arena; we cannot do so as a matter of law.

It would be a crass legal fiction to assert that a matter once public never becomes private again. Human forgetfulness over time puts today's "hot" news in tomorrow's dusty archives. In a nation of 200 million people there is ample opportunity for all but the most infamous to begin a new life.

Plaintiff is a man whose last offense took place 11 years before, who has paid his debt to society, who has friends and an 11-year-old daughter who were unaware of his early life—a man who has assumed a position in "respectable" society. Ideally, his neighbors should recognize his present worth and forget his past life of shame. But men are not so divine as to forgive the past trespasses of others, and plaintiff therefore endeavored to reveal as little as possible of his past life. Yet, as if in some bizarre canyon of echoes, petitioner's past life pursues him through the pages of *Reader's Digest,* now published in 13 languages and distributed in 100 nations, with a circulation in California alone of almost 2,000,000 copies.

On the assumed set of facts before us we are convinced that a jury could reasonably find that plaintiff's identity as a former hijacker was not newsworthy. . . . [W]e find it reasonable to require a plaintiff to prove, in each case, that the publisher invaded his privacy with reckless disregard for the fact that reasonable men would find the invasion highly offensive. . . . We do not hold today that plaintiff must prevail in his action. It is for the trier of fact to determine:

1. whether plaintiff had become a rehabilitated member of society
2. whether identifying him as a former criminal would be highly offensive and injurious to the reasonable man
3. whether defendant published this information with a reckless disregard for its offensiveness
4. whether any independent justification for printing plaintiff's identity existed.

We hold today only that, as pleaded, plaintiff has stated a valid cause of action, sustaining the demurrer to plaintiff's complaint was improper, and that the ensuing judgment must therefore be *reversed. . . . [R]emanded to the trial court.*

CASE QUESTIONS

1. What does the intentional tort of the invasion of the right to privacy provide? What elements are necessary? Explain.
2. What activity had Briscoe participated in that *Reader's Digest* had reported? Was he successful? Do you think this had something to do with why *Reader's Digest* reported it?
3. Was it "hot news"? When did it happen? When did *Reader's Digest* report it?
4. Was it a private fact? Had it ever been *public* knowledge? Why did the court find it to be a private fact in this case? Explain.
5. Was Briscoe's activity newsworthy enough to have retained its public status? Do you think the following news items will ever revert to private facts?
   a. the sinking of the *Titanic*
   b. the Saint Valentine's Day Massacre
   c. Senator Kennedy's episode at Chappaquiddick
   d. the Charles Manson murders
   e. the assassination attempt on President Reagan by John W. Hinckley, Jr.

Policy Issue. Should the right to privacy be protected by law? Should *oral* disclosure of private facts receive the same protection as written disclosure of the same private facts would? Why or why not?

Economics Issue. Is the publication of private facts about public figures and celebrities a big business? Explain.

Ethics Issue. Is it unethical for a person to disclose a private fact about another person? If so, have you ever been unethical?

Social Responsibility. Do newspapers and magazines owe a duty of social responsibility not to publish private facts when they are doing an article on a person? Or do they owe a greater social responsibility under the First Amendment to dissiminate such information?

Intentional Infliction of Emotional Distress.   A person is protected by law from harassing tactics of businesses to collect debts and other monies due them. For example, a collection agency cannot continually call a debtor during the middle of the night trying to collect a debt. If a party does so, it may be liable to the plaintiff in a civil lawsuit for the *intentional infliction of emotional distress.* The elements of the tort of intentional infliction of emotional distress are: (1) outrageous and extreme conduct by the defendant, (2) which causes severe emotional distress to the plaintiff, (3) which is manifested by some form of physical injury to the plaintiff.

Mere rough language or inconsiderate or unkind activity by the defendant is usually not sufficient to constitute intentional infliction of emotional distress. The conduct, in order to reach the level protected by the tort, must be *extreme* and *outrageous.* Further, the emotional distress suffered by the plaintiff must be *severe.* Such mental reactions as fright, grief, shame, humiliation, embarrassment, anger, chagrin, and worry have been held to constitute severe emotional distress for which damages can be awarded.

This tort does not require a publication of information to a third party as the basis for a lawsuit for intentional infliction of emotional distress. It may be caused by the direct contact of the defendant with the plaintiff without any third-party witnesses. Nor does the tort require a touching of the plaintiff by the defendant—a telephone call by the defendant to the plaintiff may be the basis of a lawsuit for the intentional infliction of emotional distress.

Generally, the plaintiff must manifest the severe emotional distress through some physical injury. However, the trend of the law is for the courts to not require an outward manifestation of the severe emotional distress. This, of course, makes it more difficult for the courts to appraise the merits of a claim for intentional infliction of emotional distress.

Misappropriation of the Right to Publicity.   During a given person's lifetime, that person has the exclusive legal right to control and profit from commercial use of his or her name and personality. This is a particularly valuable right to such persons as sports figures, movie stars, and other famous people. Any attempt by another party to appropriate a living person's name or identity for commercial purposes (e.g., television commercials, billboards) is actionable. The plaintiff may obtain an injunction against further unauthorized use of his name or identity, and recover damages for past unauthorized use of his name or identity by the defendant.

The courts have held, however, that a person's "right to publicity" does not survive that person's death. Thus, after a celebrity's death, the right to publicize that person's name is open to all, and does not vest in the heirs of the deceased celebrity. This rule is patterned after the rule in defamation cases, where a person's right to sue for defamation does not survive his death.

In *Memphis Development Foundation v. Factors Etc., Inc.* which involved the defendant's commercial use of the name and image of Elvis Presley after Elvis's death, the court held that the exclusive "right to publicity" does not survive a celebrity's death.

RIGHT TO PUBLICITY

MEMPHIS DEVELOPMENT FOUNDATION v. FACTORS ETC., INC.

616 F.2d 956 (1980)
UNITED STATES COURT OF APPEALS, SIXTH CIRCUIT

Merritt, Circuit Judge.

Elvis Presley died in Memphis on August 16, 1977. To honor him, the Memphis Development Foundation, a Tennessee nonprofit corporation, laid plans to erect a large bronze statue of Presley in downtown Memphis. The Foundation solicited public contributions to pay for the sculpture. Donors of $25 or more received an eight-inch pewter replica of the proposed statue from the Foundation.

The District Court held that the heirs and assigns of Presley retained his exclusive right of publicity after his death. It held that the exclusive right to exploit Elvis Presley's name and likeness currently belongs to Factors Etc., Inc., the assignee of Elvis Presley's "right of publicity." The District Court thus enjoined further distribution of the replicas by the Foundation.

Prior to his death, Presley had conveyed the exclusive right to exploit the commercial value of his name and likeness. . . .

The Foundation instituted this action seeking a declaratory judgment that Factors' license does not preclude distribution by the Foundation of the pewter replicas and that the foundation has the right to erect the Presley statue.

At common law, there is a right of action for the appropriation or unauthorized commercial use of the name or likeness of another. An individual is entitled to control the commercial use of these personal attributes during life. But the common law has not heretofore widely recognized this right to control commercial publicity as a property right which may be inherited.

Recognition of a post-mortem right of publicity would vindicate two possible interests: the encouragement of effort and creativity, and the hopes and expectations of the decedent and those with whom he contracts that they are creating a valuable capital asset. Although fame and stardom may be ends in themselves, they are normally by-products of one's activities and personal attributes, as well as

luck and promotion. The basic motivations are the desire to achieve success or excellence in a chosen field, the desire to contribute to the happiness or improvement of one's fellows and the desire to receive the psychic and financial rewards of achievement.

The desire to exploit fame for the commercial advantage of one's heirs is by contrast a weak principle of motivation. It seems apparent that making the right of publicity inheritable would not significantly inspire the creative endeavors of individuals in our society.

On the other hand, there are strong reasons for declining to recognize the inheritability of the right. A whole set of practical problems of judicial line-drawing would arise should the courts recognize such an inheritable right. How long would the "property" interest last? In perpetuity? For a term of years? Is the right of publicity taxable? At what point does the right collide with the right of free expression guaranteed by the First Amendment? Does the right apply to elected officials and military heroes whose fame was gained on the public payroll, as well as to movie stars, singers and athletes? Does the right cover posters or engraved likenesses of, for example, Farrah Fawcett Majors or Mahatma Gandhi, kitchen utensils ("Revere Ware"), insurance ("John Hancock"), electric utilities ("Edison"), a football stadium ("RFK"), a pastry ("Napoleon"), or the innumerable urban subdivisions and apartment complexes named after famous people?

Our legal system normally does not pass on to heirs other similar personal attributes even though the attributes may be shared during life by others or have some commercial value. Titles, offices and reputation are not inheritable. Neither are trust or distrust and friendship or enmity descendible. An employment contract during life does not create the right for heirs to take over the job. Fame falls in the same category as reputation; it is an attribute from which others may benefit but may not own.

Heretofore, the law has always thought that leaving a good name to one's children is sufficient reward in itself for the individual, whether famous or not. Commercialization of this virtue after death in the hands of heirs is contrary to our legal tradition and somehow seems contrary to the moral presuppositions of our culture.

There is no indication that changing the traditional common law rule against allowing heirs the exclusive control of the commercial use of their ancestor's name will increase the efficiency or productivity of our economic system. It does not seem reasonable to expect that such a change would enlarge the stock or quality of the goods, services, artistic creativity, information, invention or entertainment available. Nor will it enhance the fairness of our political and economic system. It seems fairer and more efficient for the commercial, esthetic, and political use of the name, memory and image of the famous to be open to all rather than to be monopolized by a few. An equal distribution of the opportunity to use the name of the dead seems preferable. The memory, name and pictures of famous individuals should be regarded as a common asset to be shared, an economic opportunity available in the free market system.

We do not think that whatever minimal benefit to society may result from the added motivation and extra creativity supposedly encouraged by allowing a person to pass on his fame for the commercial use of his heirs or assigns outweighs the considerations discussed above.

Accordingly, the judgment of the District Court is *reversed* and the case is *remanded* for further proceedings consistent with the principles announced above.

CASE QUESTIONS

1. What does the *right to publicity* provide? Explain.
2. State the legal issue of this case. Read what you have written. Restate the issue more succinctly.
3. How did the Foundation propose to honor Elvis after his death? Was it going to commercially exploit Elvis's name?
4. Would the Foundation have been allowed to do the same thing while Elvis was alive?
5. Were the line-drawing problems (how long would the right to publicity survive a deceased celebrity?) and analogies (since friendships are not inheritable neither should the right to publicity be) used by the court in this case persuasive? Explain.

Policy Issue. Should the "right to publicity" be considered an inheritable property right? Should it be treated differently from personal and real property for inheritance purposes?

Economics Issue. Do you think the children of Elvis Presley and other famous people agree with the following statement of the court: "Leaving a good name to one's children is sufficient reward in itself"?

Ethics Issue. Is it ethical for someone who has not been connected with a celebrity during the celebrity's life to make money off the name and reputation of the celebrity after the celebrity is dead?

Social Responsibility. Should there be any inheritance? Or should all property rights in a person's death escheat (pass by default) to the public?

BUSINESS TORTS ASSOCIATED WITH CONTRACTS

Generally, a party cannot sue another for breach of contract unless an express or implied contract is shown, and then he can only recover the *benefit of the bargain* as damages. The courts have developed several *torts* associated with contracts. Where a plaintiff proves one of these contract-related torts, he may recover general tort damages, which may include pain and suffering, emotional distress, and possibly punitive damages, all of which are otherwise not recoverable in a straight breach-of-contract action. The major torts associated with contracts are (1) breach of the implied covenant of good faith and fair dealing by one of the contracting parties, and (2) intentional interference with a contract or prospective economic advantage by a third person not a party to the contract.

Implied Covenant of Good Faith and Fair Dealing. The minority rule and modern trend is to hold that an *implied* covenant of "good faith and fair dealing" attaches to certain contracts. A breach of this implied covenant is a tort, for which there are tort remedies. The doctrine is based on the argument that the parties to a contract should not only be held to the literal terms of the contract, but should also be required to act in "good faith" and deal fairly with the other party in attaining the objectives of the contract. Only *parties to* a contract, and not third parties, may be held liable for the breach of this implied covenant. The majority view is that there does not have to be a breach of the underlying contract for there to be a cause of action for the breach of the implied covenant of good faith and fair dealing.

The majority of the cases in which the tort of a breach of the implied covenant of good faith and fair dealing has been applied have been in the insurance field. For example, where an insurance company refuses to settle an insurance claim with an insured to take advantage of the insured's perilous position (for example, a business has been destroyed by fire, and the insured is relying on insurance proceeds to rebuild), the courts have found a breach of this implied covenant and awarded tort damages to the plaintiff.

In *Crisci v. The Security Insurance Company of New Haven, Connecticut*, the California Supreme Court held that the defendant insurance company had breached the implied covenant of good faith and fair dealing when it refused to settle a lawsuit brought by an injured plaintiff against one of its insureds, causing the case to go to trial, where a large jury award against the insured defendant caused her to lose almost all of her possessions.

IMPLIED COVENANT OF GOOD FAITH AND FAIR DEALING

CRISCI v. THE SECURITY INSURANCE COMPANY OF NEW HAVEN, CONNECTICUT

66 C.2d 425 (1967)
SUPREME COURT OF CALIFORNIA

Peters, J.

In an action against The Security Insurance Company of New Haven, Connecticut, the trial court awarded Rosina Crisci $91,000 (plus interest) because she suffered a judgment in a personal injury action after Security, her insurer, refused to settle the claim. Mrs. Crisci was also awarded $25,000 for mental suffering. Security has appealed.

June DiMare and her husband were tenants in an apartment building owned by Rosina Crisci. Mrs. DiMare was descending the apartment's outside wooden staircase when a tread gave way. She fell through the resulting opening up to her waist and was left hanging 15 feet above the ground. Mrs. DiMare suffered physical injuries and developed a very severe psychosis. In a suit brought against

Mrs. Crisci the DiMares alleged that the step broke because Mrs. Crisci was negligent in inspecting and maintaining the stairs. They contended that Mrs. DiMare's mental condition was caused by the accident, and they asked for $400,000 as compensation for physical and mental injuries and medical expenses.

Mrs. Crisci had $10,000 of insurance coverage under a general liability policy issued by Security. The policy obligated Security to defend the suit against Mrs. Crisci and authorized the company to make any settlement it deemed expedient. Security hired an experienced lawyer, Mr. Healy, to handle the case.

The exact chronology of settlement offers is not established by the record. However, by the time the DiMares' attorney reduced his settlement demands to $10,000, Security had doctors prepared to support its position and was only willing to pay $3,000 for Mrs. DiMare's physical injuries. Security was unwilling to pay one cent for the possibility of a plaintiff's verdict on the mental illness issue. This conclusion was based on the assumption that the jury would believe all of the defendant's psychiatric evidence and none of the plaintiff's. Security also rejected a $9,000 settlement demand at a time when Mrs. Crisci offered to pay $2,500 of the settlement.

A jury awarded Mrs. DiMare $100,000 and her husband $1,000. . . . [T]he insurance company paid $10,000 of this amount, the amount of its policy. The DiMares then sought to collect the balance from Mrs. Crisci. A settlement was arranged by which the DiMares received $22,000, [and] a 40 percent interest in Mrs. Crisci's claim to a particular piece of property. . . . Mrs. Crisci, an immigrant widow of 70, became indigent. She worked as a babysitter, and her grandchildren paid her rent. The change in her financial condition was accompanied by a decline in physical health, hysteria, and suicide attempts. Mrs. Crisci then brought this action.

The liability of an insurer in excess of its policy limits for failure to accept a settlement offer within those limits was considered by this court in *Comunale v. Traders & General Ins. Co.* It was there reasoned that in every contract, including policies of insurance, there is an implied covenant of good faith and fair dealing that neither party will do anything which will injure the right of the other to receive

the benefits of the agreement; that it is common knowledge that one of the usual methods by which an insured receives protection under a liability insurance policy is by settlement of claims without litigation; that the implied obligation of good faith and fair dealing requires the insurer to settle in an appropriate case although the express terms of the policy do not impose the duty; that in determining whether to settle the insurer must give the interests of the insured at least as much consideration as it gives to its own interests; and that when

> there is great risk of a recovery beyond the policy limits so that the most reasonable manner of disposing of the claim is a settlement which can be made within those limits, a consideration in good faith of the insured's interest requires the insurer to settle the claim.

In determining whether an insurer has given consideration to the interests of the insured, the test is whether a prudent insurer without policy limits would have accepted the settlement offer. . . . Liability is imposed not for a bad faith breach of the contract but for failure to meet the duty to accept reasonable settlements, a duty included within the implied covenant of good faith and fair dealing. Moreover, examination of the balance of [California cases] makes it abundantly clear that recovery may be based on unwarranted rejection of a reasonable settlement offer and that the absence of evidence, circumstantial or direct, showing actual dishonesty, fraud, or concealment is not fatal to the cause of action.

Obviously, it will always be in the insured's interest to settle within the policy limits when there is any danger, however slight, of a judgment in excess of those limits. Accordingly the rejection of a settlement within the limits where there is any danger of a judgment in excess of the limits can be justified, if at all, only on the basis of interests of the insurer, and, in light of the common knowledge that settlement is one of the usual methods by which an insured receives protection under a liability policy, it may not be unreasonable for an insured who purchases a policy with limits to believe that a sum of money equal to the limits is available and will be used so as to avoid liability on his part with regard to any covered accident. In view of such expectation an insurer should not be permitted to further its own interests by rejecting opportunities to settle within the policy limits unless it is also willing to absorb losses which may result from its failure to settle.

Finally, and most importantly, there is more than a small amount of elementary justice in a rule that would require that, in this situation where the insurer's and insured's interests necessarily conflict, the insurer, which may reap the benefits of its determination not to settle, should also suffer the detriments of its decision.

[T]he evidence is clearly sufficient to support the determination that Security breached its duty to consider the interests of Mrs. Crisci in proposed settlements.

The general rule of damages in tort is that the injured party may recover for all detriment caused whether it could have been anticipated or not. In accordance with the general rule, it is settled in this state that mental suffering constitutes an aggravation of damages when it naturally ensues from the act complained of, and in this connection mental suffering includes nervousness, grief, anxiety, worry, shock, humiliation and indignity as well as physical pain. . . . We are satisfied that a plaintiff who as a result of a defendant's tortious conduct loses his property and suffers mental distress may recover not only for the pecuniary loss but also for his mental distress.

Recovery of damages for mental suffering in the instant case does not mean that in every case of breach of contract the injured party may recover such damages. Here the breach also constitutes a tort.

The judgment is *affirmed*.

CASE QUESTIONS

1. What accident and injuries did the tenant, Mrs. DiMare, suffer? Whom did she sue? For how much money?

2. Did the landlord, Mrs. Crisci, carry any insurance? If so, how much? With whom? Was the insurance company obligated to defend Mrs. Crisci at trial?

3. Prior to the *DiMares v. Crisci* trial, how much money was Mrs. DiMare willing to settle for? Was the settlement offer accepted by Mrs. Crisci? By the Security Insurance Co.?

4. Did the *DiMare v. Crisci* case go to trial? Who won? How much money? Who paid? Explain.

5. What does the *implied covenant of good faith and fair dealing* provide? Is it a contract or tort action? What is the difference in the damages that can be awarded under contract and tort actions? Explain.

6. What damages were awarded Mrs. Crisci in this case?

Policy Issue. Should a covenant of good faith and fair dealing be *implied* in all contracts? Or should the parties to a contract only be held to its literal terms?

Economics Issue. Do you think this decision had a major impact on the insurance industry? Do you think this decision increased or decreased the cost of insurance?

Ethics Issue. Did the Security Insurance Co. of New Haven act ethically in this case? Why do you think the company went to trial in this case rather than settling the DiMares' claim?

Social Responsibility. When an insurance company sells you insurance, should it be obligated to pay the amount of the coverage whenever you are sued? Would you expect it to? Would this help or hurt plaintiffs? And plaintiff's attorneys?

Interference with Contracts. A party to a valid contract may sue a *third party* not a party to the contract for intentional interference with the contract. This business tort was established in the famous English case of *Lumley v. Gye,* 119 Eng. Rep. 749 (Q.B. 1853), where the defendant was held liable for inducing an opera singer to breach her contract with the plaintiff. The argument for the tort of intentional interference with contracts is that contracts are voluntary arrangements of rights and duties among members of society, and deserve protection from interference by third parties. In order to establish a cause of action for the *tort of intentional interference with contracts,* a plaintiff must show that:

1. he has a valid contract with another party
2. the defendant third party interfered with that contract by either preventing the performance of the contract *or* making the performance of the contract difficult or onerous (e.g., defendant induced one of the parties to breach the contract; defendant destroyed the subject matter of the contract)
3. the defendant was aware of the plaintiff's contract at the time the defendant committed the act that interfered with it
4. the defendant acted with *intent* to cause interference with that contract
5. the plaintiff suffered injury because of the defendant's interference with the contract.

A very small minority of states allow recovery for *negligent* interference with contracts.

The tort of intentional interference with contracts applies to all contracts except contracts to marry, illegal contracts, and contracts against public policy. The tort applies even where the original contract is unenforceable (because of, for example, lack of consideration, violation of the Statute of Frauds). Where a party to a contract is already in breach of contract (e.g., an employee who breaches his contract with his employer and looks for a new job), a third party may contract with that person without becoming liable for the tort of interference with contracts. The rationale for this rule is that because one of the contracting parties has previously breached the contract, the third party who deals with the breaching party is not interfering with the prior contract. Because the intentional interference with a contract is a *tort,* all normal tort damages are available to the plaintiff.

Interference with Prospective Economic Advantage. The business tort of intentional interference with contracts has been expanded by a minority of jurisdictions to a general theory of "interference with prospective economic advantage." This broader tort includes interference by *third parties* with *non-*contractual economic expectancies. Examples of this tort are when a defendant steals a plaintiff's prospective client or interferes with a gift expected by the plaintiff.

Although presently a minority rule, the modern trend is for jurisdictions to adopt and expand the business tort of *intentional interference with prospective economic advantage.* The argument for the tort is that there are many situations where parties have invested considerable time and expense in negotiating a transaction, and are so close to making a deal that the right to proceed should be protected from interference by meddling third parties. Very few states have expanded the doctrine to include *negligent* interference with prospective economic advantage. Where a defendant is held liable for interfering with the plaintiff's prospective economic advantage, traditional tort remedies are available.

In *Buckaloo v. Johnson* the court found that the plaintiff's complaint stated a cause of action for liability under the tort of intentional interference with prospective economic advantage.

INTENTIONAL INTERFERENCE WITH A PROSPECTIVE ECONOMIC ADVANTAGE
BUCKALOO v. JOHNSON

recovers $ = to the commission he would have made

14 C.3d 122 (1975)
SUPREME COURT OF CALIFORNIA

Mosk, J.

The facts alleged in the complaint are as follows: Plaintiff Buckaloo is a licensed real estate broker doing business in Little River, California. Defendant Mildred Benioff was the owner of certain undeveloped beach property in Mendocino County, known as Dark Gulch. In 1967 and 1968 plaintiff had an exclusive right to sell the Dark Gulch parcel. No sale was consummated during this period and the exclusive listing expired in 1968. . . . In 1972, Benioff erected a sign on the property which read: "For Sale—Contact Your Local Broker."

On May 3, 1972, plaintiff was approached at his place of business by defendants Virginia Arness, her daughter, and Cecil Johnson, the latter a real estate salesman in the employ of defendant Ferne Goodwin. The potential buyers indicated an interest in coastal investment property and a general discussion followed. . . . Plaintiff was well aware of the merits of the [Dark Gulch] property from his prior association with Benioff and was able to inform the Arness group of its assets and liabilities. Plaintiff advised that the asking price was high for investment purposes but the parcel might be attractive to an owner-user. The conversation then progressed to a discussion of other properties but eventually returned to the Dark Gulch parcel when Arness showed continuing interest. At the end of the day plaintiff found accommodations for the group and they left, promising to return the next day.

The group never returned. Plaintiff sent Benioff a note informing her that he was the "procuring cause" of the Arness group and asking her to refer them to him should the group contact Benioff directly. Some weeks later plaintiff learned that a sale had been made to the Arness group without his participation. He contacted Benioff requesting a commission but was informed by her attorney that he would not share in any commissions paid.

Plaintiff sued Arness (buyer), Benioff (seller),

Johnson (salesman), Goodwin (Johnson's superior), and six unnamed defendants as members of the Arness group.

Civil Code Section 1624, subdivision 5, requires a writing subscribed by the party to be charged for

> An agreement authorizing or employing an agent, broker, or any other person to purchase or sell real estate, . . . or to procure, introduce, or find a purchaser or seller of real estate . . . for compensation or a commission.

However, plaintiff included in his complaint a cause of action not dependent on compliance with the Statute of Frauds: intentional interference with prospective economic advantage. This is a tort theory of recovery rather than contract, and is based on interference with a "relationship" between parties irrespective of the enforceability of the underlying agreement. As stated in the leading California case of *Zimmerman v. Bank of America:*

> The tort of interference with an advantageous relationship, or with a contract, does not, however, disintegrate because it relates to a contract not written *or an advantageous relation not articulated into a contract.* The nature of the tort does not vary with the legal strength, or enforceability, of the relation disrupted. The actionable wrong lies in the inducement to break the contract or to sever the relationship, not in the kind of contract or relationship so disrupted, whether it is written or oral, enforceable or not enforceable. (Italics added.)

This tort, although infrequently invoked, is not new to the law. Interference with contractual relations was recognized as an actionable wrong over a century ago in the celebrated English case of *Lumley v. Gye* (Q. B. 1853) 118 Eng. Rep. 749. . . . The great weight of authority is that the tort of interference with contract is merely a species of the broader tort of interference with prospective economic advantage. . . . [W]e note the elements of the tort itself. In the real estate brokerage context these are: (1) an economic relationship between broker and vendor or broker and vendee containing the probability of future economic benefit to the broker, (2) knowledge by the defendant of the existence of the relationship, (3) intentional acts on the part of the defendant designed to disrupt the relationship, (4) actual disruption of the relationship, (5) damages to the plaintiff proximately caused by the acts of the defendant.

[An intentional interference with prospective economic advantage occurs] where the buyer, after taking advantage of the broker's efforts and stock in trade, induces the seller to accept the "low net price" through the expedient of excluding the broker's commission. There is no public policy to be served by encouraging such devious dealings; on the contrary, such an intrusion into a protected economic relationship is precisely the conduct condemned by the traditional tort of interference with contract.

[P]laintiff alleges . . . (1) that Benioff *intended* her sign to constitute an open listing with all area brokers, (2) that Benioff *intended* that brokers induced by the sign to cooperate with buyers would be paid a commission for procuring a buyer on terms Benioff would accept, and (3) that plaintiff understood this to constitute an invitation to himself and other area brokers to attempt to find a buyer for the Benioff property. These facts, plus any evidence that may establish the real estate custom and practice in the community, establish a colorable economic relationship between Benioff and plaintiff with the potential to develop into a full contractual relationship.

We therefore conclude that viewing the allegations in the complaint in a manner most favorable to the pleader, a cause of action of intentional interference with prospective advantage was stated against the demurring parties. Whether plaintiff will ultimately establish the elements of the tort is a factual matter and as such properly in the domain of the trier of fact.

CASE QUESTIONS

1. Who was the plaintiff? The defendants? Who were the following parties?
   a. Buckaloo
   b. Benioff
   c. Johnson
   d. Goodwin
   e. The Arness Group
2. What did the California *Statute of Frauds* require regarding real estate agents' contracts? Did the plaintiff have a contract with the defendant to sell the Dark Gulch property in this case?
3. What do the following doctrines provide? Are they *tort* or *contract* doctrines? Which one did the plaintiff raise in this case?
   a. intentional interference with contract
   b. intentional interference with prospective economic advantage
4. Must there be an enforceable legal contract in order for the doctrine of interference with prospective economic advantage to be raised?
5. On remand, who would you decide for? Why?

Policy Issue. Should the law protect *prospective* economic advantage? Or should only binding contracts be protected from interference from third parties?

Economics Issue. Do you think that attempts to cut real estate agents out of their commissions occur often in real estate transactions? Why or why not?

Ethics Issue. Were the actions of the Arness Group in this case ethical? Were the actions by Benioff, the seller, ethical?

Social Responsibility. Does the protection of prospective economic advantage harm or promote free competition? Is this good or bad for society?

MISAPPROPRIATION OF IDEAS

Often, a person may have an idea, plan, or composition that he desires to sell, license, or otherwise commercially promote. In seeking the assistance of others, (e.g., financiers, agents, movie producers, book publishers) for the promotion of his idea, a conflict commonly develops between the creator or inventor's refusal to disclose the idea unless he is compensated, and the other party's refusal to pay for an undisclosed idea. Therefore, the creator often discloses all or a major portion of his idea to the other party prior to the formation of an express contract between them in order to give the other party enough information to make a decision as to the value of the idea.

If the party to whom the disclosure is made misappropriates and uses the idea, and does not compensate the creator, the creator cannot sue for breach of an express contract because no express contract has been formed between the parties. However, the courts have adopted the doctrine of *implied-in-fact* contract to apply to such situations. The implied-in-fact contract is a legal fiction which holds that the parties entered into an *implied* contract, the breach of which is actionable, where it is shown that (1) the creator or inventor disclosed the idea in a setting where the disclosure was made in contemplation of payment to the creator if the idea was used and (2) the other party knew or should have known from the facts and circumstances that the disclosure was made in expectation of such payment for use. A plaintiff may sue a defendant for contract damages for the breach of an implied-in-fact contract. However, tort damages are not available for a breach of an implied-in-fact contract unless the plaintiff can, in addition, establish one of the business torts discussed in this and other chapters.

In *Minniear v. Tors* the court held that the defendant breached an implied-in-fact contract when the defendant took an idea for a television program from the plaintiff.

MISAPPROPRIATION OF AN IDEA

MINNIEAR v. TORS

266 C.A.2d 495 (1968)

COURT OF APPEAL OF CALIFORNIA

Nutter, J. *pro tem.*

In mid-1955, plaintiff Minniear, a teacher for RKO Radio Pictures, who had been connected with motion picture studios for 22 years, conceived the idea of making an underwater adventure series for sale to TV. Up to that time such a series had never been attempted on TV. Minniear sought the assistance of an underwater photographer, defendant Boren, and the two agreed to pool their efforts and money in making a pilot film for the adventure series for the purpose of showing it to prospective purchasers, sponsors and TV stations. While no agreement was ever reduced to writing, appellant agreed to furnish the ideas, talent, cast, writers, directors,

script, film editor and artistic requirements while defendant Boren was to photograph the pilot and the series and furnish technical skills and laboratory work. Thereafter, Minniear completed a script and engaged a director and cast for the pilot film.

Appellant [Minniear] engaged Thomas Scott, a film editor of defendant Ziv, to edit and cut the film. Scott had worked for defendants Tors and Ziv previously. During the cutting and editing, Scott used the facilities of Ziv and retained possession of the footage on the Ziv lot. Scott worked on his own time; his work for appellant and his use of Ziv facilities were with knowledge of his superiors. Other Ziv employees were aware of the film cutting on the Ziv lot. A format and the film *Sea Divers* was completed as a pilot for a series involving underwater adventure and intrigue. The director of the film was Leslie Goodwins, who had directed a science fiction episode for Tors and Ziv.

On April 11, 1956, appellant arranged for a private showing of the pilot film to members of the cast, crew and a few interested friends in the Ziv projection room. In response to a request by Director Goodwins to appellant, appellant granted defendant Tors permission to see the film at this showing.

Tors watched the film and a prologue, accompanied by his assistant and a Ziv writer. Following the showing, Tors stated to appellant that he found the pilot interesting; that he had been *contemplating making a series on underwater skindivers* but had not found a satisfactory format; that he felt *Sea Divers contained an excellent idea.* Tors then asked appellant's director Goodwins "Where do you go from here?" Goodwins replied that appellant had several follow-up ideas sufficient for an entire season and referred to one involving a jet pilot trapped underwater. Appellant offered defendant Tors a booklet containing the outline of future series which Tors retained. Included was a story about a jet pilot who was trapped under the sea. About a month subsequent to this date, Tors commenced production of *Sea Hunt* for Ziv. He employed defendant Boren as underwater photographer and attempted to hire appellant's leading man as actor.

Sea Hunt like *Sea Divers* was based on an underwater adventure format involving an ex-Navy frogman named Mike, using scuba and special underwater equipment. In each series the hero or heroes operated their own boat on a commission for dangerous underwater work. Attractive young girls were featured.

Generally, appellant contends that *Sea Hunt* was basically *Sea Divers* and defendants employed the same format, stories, character, development and plot plays. In particular, appellant contends the show "The Gold Below" was a substantial copy of the *Sea Divers* pilot; the *Sea Hunt* jet plane story was taken from the prologue and written synopsis obtained by Tors.

Appellant contends in the contract case that while there was no express contract between Ziv and appellant to pay for the *Sea Divers,* there was an implied contract, and it is understood in the industry that when a showing is made, the offeror shall be paid for any ideas or material used therein.

Generally, ideas are not the property of anyone and may be used by all absent a contract to pay for them. . . . The leading California case which discusses the law pertaining to literary property is *Desny v. Wilder,* . . . [where] the court stated:

> 'Literary property' is a general term which is used either to describe the interest of an author (or those who claim under him) in his works (whether before or after publication or before or after copyright has been secured) or to denote the corporeal property in which an intellectual production is embodied.
>
> A so-called 'implied-in-fact' contract, however, as the term is used by some writers, may be found although there has been no meeting of the minds.
>
> [T]he assent of the writer is found in his submission of the idea or material to the producer, with the *reasonable expectation of payment which can be inferred from the facts and circumstances.* The assent of the producer is manifested by his acceptance of the idea or material submitted under the circumstances, a part of which is that it is reasonably understood that a professional author expects payment of the reasonable value of the *idea* or the *material, if used,* so that the conduct of the producer in accepting it implies a promise to fulfill those reasonable expectations. . . .
>
> There is nothing unreasonable in the assumption that a producer would obligate himself to pay for the disclosure of an idea which he would otherwise be legally free to use, but which in fact, he would be unable to use but for the disclosure.
>
> [T]he fact that the producer may later determine, with a little thinking, that he could have had the same ideas and could thereby have saved considerable money for himself, is no defense against the claim of the writer. *This is so even though the material to be purchased is abstract and unprotected material.*"

Mr. Justice Carter in his concurring opinion in the *Desny* case declared:

> It seems to me that in the ordinary situation, when the so-called 'idea man' has an opportunity to see, or talk with, the *prospective* purchaser, or someone in his employ, it is at that time, without anything being said, known to both parties that the one is there to sell, and the other to buy." (Italics added.)

Here there is substantial evidence in the record for the jury to infer a reasonable expectation by appellant that the defendant Ziv might buy the idea for a TV underwater series in the spring of 1956. It is not necessary that the seller should definitely state that he is selling his merchandise to the prospective buyer. The agreement of sale may be inferred by the circumstances.

There is substantial evidence to support an inference that appellant submitted his idea to Tors with the reasonable expectation he would be paid by Ziv if his idea was used. There is also sufficient evidence to support the further inference that Tors acting for Ziv accepted the submission of the idea with full awareness of appellant's expectation of payment in the event of use.

An underwater sea adventure series, like a cowboy adventure series, has certain basic similarities which cannot be avoided. However, there are enough similarities in the basic plot ideas, themes, sequences and dramatic "gimmicks" between *Sea Divers* and *Sea Hunt* for a jury to infer that appellant's ideas and format were the inspiration for *Sea Hunt* and respondent Ziv, in fact, *used* appellant's ideas and format.

The judgment is *reversed* in the contract action. . . . Appellant is to recover his costs on appeal.

CASE QUESTIONS

1. What idea did Minniear have for a TV series? Whom did he disclose it to? Under what circumstances?
2. What is an *implied-in-fact* contract? What is an *express* contract? How do they differ? Explain.
3. What TV series did Tors and Ziv make? Was it similar to Minniear's idea? If so, how close?

Policy Issue. Should the law recognize implied-in-fact contracts? Or should only express contracts be recognized? Or only written contracts?

Economics Issue. Should "idea men" be paid for their ideas? Or is this too easy money to make? What would be the consequences if idea men did not get paid for their ideas?

Ethics Issue. Was what Tors and Ziv did in this case ethical? What about what Borens did?

Social Responsibility. Is society benefited by the doctrine of implied-in-fact contracts? If so, how?

Trend of the Law

Unethical conduct by business persons in the form of business torts will continue in the future. The only difference from the past may be that future unfair competition will be aided by new technology (e.g., computers, electronics), which may make the scale and scope of future unfair activity even greater. Businesses will have to spend substantial sums of money to defend against espionage and the misappropriation of trade secrets. Future cases of trade disparagement will be analyzed by appellate courts under the independent review standard announced by the U.S. Supreme Court in *Bose Corporation v. Consumers Union, Inc.,* discussed in this chapter. The number of palming-off cases is increasing as style pirates copy the designs and logos of designer clothes and unknown companies manufacture and sell computer equipment under well-known names. For example, after the Apple company introduced its original and later models of the personal computer, a substantial number of fake Apple computers came on the market.

The courts and business will be faced with a growing number

of cases alleging violations of personal rights. Many businesses, particularly newspapers, magazines, and other media that report the news, will have to be concerned with invasion-of-the-right-to-privacy lawsuits when they report private facts about news subjects. The trend of the law is for the courts to expand the tort of intentional invasion of the right to privacy. Creditors and collection agencies will face an increase in the number of lawsuits alleging intentional infliction of emotional distress. These cases will pose considerable problems for both businesses and the courts because of the difficulty in defending against a claim of emotional distress, particularly with the trend being toward states recognizing the tort without requiring any showing of physical injury. There is also a minor trend for the courts to recognize a cause of action for the *negligent* infliction of emotional distress.

Contracts have long been protected by the common law from interference from third parties. However, the tort of intentional interference with *prospective* economic advantage is presently being expanded by the courts. As this doctrine is adopted by more states, business will have to be more careful where they know that the party with whom they are dealing has an implied arrangement with someone else. The most important development in the area of contracts in the future will be the expansion of the doctrine of the implied covenant of good faith and fair dealing. Although this tort has not been adopted by many states, and is currently particularly applied to insurance contracts, if it is adopted by many courts and is applied to *all* contracts, it will open up a new era of contract law. Also, the courts in the future will be more apt to find an implied-in-fact contract where no express contract between parties exists.

In all, the expansion of the tort doctrines discussed in this chapter will increase the liability exposure and legal costs of business to defend against such lawsuits in the future.

REVIEW QUESTIONS

1. Both Compco Corporation and Day-Brite Lighting, Inc. manufactured fluorescent lighting fixtures that were widely used in offices and stores. In 1955, Day-Brite secured a design patent on a reflector having cross-ribs, which it claimed gave both strength and attractiveness to the fixture. Day-Brite also sought, but was refused, a mechanical patent on the same device. After Day-Brite began selling its fixture, Compco began making and selling fixtures which were very similar to Day-Brite's even though several other choices of ribbing functionally equivalent to Day-Brite's were available. Evidence showed that as a result of these similiar designs, in some instances, consumers believed that Compco's product was actually a Day-Brite fixture. Day-Brite sued Compco, alleging that Compco violated its design patent

and that Compco unfairly competed with Day-Brite since, by copying Day-Brite's distinctive design, the firm confused and deceived its customers into thinking that Compco's fixtures were actually Day-Brite's. The District Court, however, ruled that Day-Brite's patent was invalid. Under those circumstances, did Compco's actions amount to unfair competition?

2. On December 5, 1970, Howard Hughes discharged Robert A. Maheu, effectively ending a 14-year relationship between Maheu, Hughes, and the Summa Corp. In a widely publicized action, Maheu sued to retain his position, claiming that either Hughes had been coerced into firing him or someone other than Hughes had ordered the firing. Finally, in a telephone news conference, Hughes told newsmen assembled in Los Angeles, California, that Maheu had been fired "because he is a no-good, dishonest son of a bitch, and he stole me blind." Hughes had no factual basis for his statement. Can Maheu recover for defamation? What type of damages?

3. Smith developed a unique unpatentable cargo container system. He designed uniformly sized freight containers that greatly increased the capacity of ship-to-shore cargo handling. Dravo Corporation, a large competitor, engaged Smith's eastern representative in negotiations for the purported purpose of purchasing containers and possibly the entire container-producing business. Based on this display of interest, Smith's representative sent Dravo detailed information concerning the design of the containers and then allowed Dravo representatives to view the plant producing the containers as well as the actual container units. After rejecting an offer to purchase the plant, Dravo began manufacturing its own containers and Smith sued. Dravo contended that it could not be held liable since the containers were in public use and the publicity material sent out in connection with them would have, on inspection, allowed anyone to discover their design. Did Dravo misappropriate a protectable trade secret?

4. Avery, a former employee of American Chain & Cable Company, formed a new company to manufacture and sell abrasive cutting wheels. American manufactured the same type of wheels and decided to sue Avery, charging him with illegally using trade secrets that he had acquired while working for the firm. Avery argued in response that he was not using any information that qualified as a trade secret and that he and the other former employees of American involved in his new business only used information that was common knowledge in the industry. The information allegedly appropriated included the ingredients used in making abrasive cutting wheels and the companies supplying them; formulas, processes, and techniques for manufacturing such wheels; and information remembered about the identities and needs of American's customers. Does an employee have the right to use everything he has learned at his place of employment except trade secrets?

5. Continental Casualty Company issued two insurance policies to A. W. Huss Company, which protected Huss for up to $1,100,000 in the event that a Huss employee was involved in an automobile accident. On May 20, 1977, a Huss employee, while within the period of insurance coverage, collided with Magnin. The accident was caused by the Huss employee's negligence and Magnin suffered severe injuries as a result. Initially it was unclear whether the Huss employee was at fault, so Continental's settlement offer

of $75,000 was rejected by Magnin's attorney. In October 1979, new evidence was uncovered which made it clear that Huss was liable. Continental, however, refused to settle the claim until May 1981, when it settled for $1,100,000. During the intervening period, Huss was forced to retain an attorney to protect its interests. After the case was settled Huss sued Continental, alleging that the insurance company breached its implied covenant of good faith and fair dealing since, in bad faith, it had refused to immediately settle the claim. Huss sought $1,000,000 for "anxiety" and business loss, $13,207 for attorney's fees and $2,000,000 in punitive damages. Did Continental act not in "good faith" and can Huss recover?

6. *Takuwan* is a pickled turnip or radish that is a common item of Japanese food. Prior to 1952 it was imported into California from Japan packed in wooden tubs and small cans; there was no market in the United States for *takuwan* of Hawaiian origin. In February 1952, Waimanalo Ko-Ko Company, of Hawaii, signed an exclusive distribution agreement with the Star Rice Company to distribute Ko-Ko brand *takuwan*, which was made in Hawaii and packed in glass jars. From 1952 to 1958 Star Rice Co. signed a consecutive series of one-year licensing agreements and the firm successfully marketed the product. Early in 1958, the Japan Food Corporation became interested in marketing Hawaiian *takuwan* and was able to convince Waimanalo Ko-Ko to refuse to renew its license agreement with Star Rice and to sign a new agreement with Japan Food instead. There was no evidence to indicate that Japan Food used any improper means to persuade Waimanalo, or that any illegal restraint of competition was created, or that the firm had any purpose beyond the obvious objective of advancing its own interest as a competitor. Did Japan Food commit the tort of interference with contractual relations?

7. Krigbaum was a real estate broker located in Napa Valley, California. Napa Valley was a prime area for the cultivation of wine grapes and consequently many large vineyards were located in the area. Italian Swiss Colony either directly owned or had contracts to purchase most of the wine grapes grown in the region. One of the few independent growers wanted to sell his vineyard and he asked Krigbaum to help to arrange a sale. Krigbaum entered into negotiations with the California Wine Association (CWA), which was interested in purchasing the vineyards. After a long negotiation period, CWA decided to purchase the property and with the exception of a few undisclosed minor details, the group was ready to enter into a purchase agreement. At that point, Swiss Colony threatened, intimidated, and coerced CWA into reversing their earlier decision and the deal fell through. Krigbaum, therefore, lost his commission and he later sued Swiss Colony. Did Swiss Colony commit the tort of interference with prospective economic relations?

8. Blaustein decided to produce Shakespeare's play, *The Taming of the Shrew.* He wanted to have Richard Burton and Elizabeth Taylor play the lead roles. Blaustein approached the Burtons' agent about their availability and suggested he had something in mind for them. The agent said he would like to hear what Blaustein had in mind, and Blaustein told him. His response was favorable. Eventually, Blaustein met with the Burtons, and they said they would like to do the movie and gave every indication that the project

would go forward from there. When the Burtons did subsequently make the movie, but without Blaustein's participation or any payment to him, he sued for damages for breach of express and implied-in-fact contracts. He alleged that the circumstances surrounding the disclosure of his idea would imply a contract for the Burtons to do the picture with him if they liked it and that, therefore, he should be compensated. Does Blaustein have at least a claim that an implied-in-fact contract existed?

24 BUSINESS CRIMES

INTRODUCTION

In order for society to peacefully exist, persons and their property must be protected from injury from other members of society. The state, therefore, has developed a substantial body of law known as *criminal law.* In criminal law it is the *state,* not an individual, who prosecutes the accused for violating his duty to society. The state is seeking some form of *punishment,* either a fine or imprisonment or both, against the accused for the commission of the crime. A "crime" is defined as any act done by an individual in violation of those duties that he owes to society and for the breach of which the law provides that the wrongdoer shall make amends to the public.

The United States has one of the most advanced and humane criminal law systems in the world. It differs from many other criminal law systems in several respects. A person charged with a crime in the United States is presumed innocent until proven guilty. The "burden of proof" is on the state to prove that the accused is guilty of the crime charged. Further, the accused must be found guilty "beyond a reasonable doubt." Under many other legal systems, the person accused of a crime is presumed guilty *unless* he can prove he is not. A person charged with a crime in the United States is also provided with substantial constitutional safeguards (e.g., search and seizure laws, right to a lawyer) during the criminal justice process.

Society defines the conduct which it considers to be "crime" through its legislatures and governing bodies. Thus, the primary source of criminal law is *statutory*. Most states have adopted comprehensive *penal codes* that define in detail the activities considered to be crimes within their jurisdiction and the penalties that will be imposed for their commission. Federal statutes define many additional crimes and penalties. Many activities have been considered crimes through the ages (e.g., murder, rape, treason), while other crimes (e.g., computer crime) are of recent origin.

Elements of a Crime.   Liability for a crime usually requires the proof of two elements. The first element is external, consisting of an act or failure to act that is prohibited by criminal law. This is known as the *actus reus*. The second element is internal, and is generally referred to as *criminal intent*. This element is known as *mens rea*. For example, for the crime of murder, the *actus reus* is the taking of another's life, while the *mens rea* is the intent to take another's life. The requirement of *mens rea* generally means that a person can never be found criminally liable for his or her negligence alone. In some circumstances, "gross negligence" or "reckless disregard for the safety of others" may be sufficient to establish criminal liability (e.g., for manslaughter). The legislature may also define certain acts as being criminal without requiring proof of any culpable mental state.

WHITE-COLLAR CRIME

Murder, burglary, robbery, and other crimes involving violence are generally considered to be crimes most often committed by the lower classes of society. The term *white-collar crime*, on the other hand, has been applied to many nonviolent crimes traditionally committed by businessmen, businesses, and their agents and employees. White-collar crime is generally linked to the occupation of the wrongdoer, and ranges from petty "kickbacks" to multimillion-dollar "organized crime." White-collar crime is currently estimated to cost over $50 *billion* per year in the United States.

White-collar crime has been defined as "a crime committed by a person of respectability and high social status in the course of his occupation." It has also been defined as "illegal acts characterized by a guile, deceit, and concealment." White-collar crime is distinguished from other crime in that it is usually not dependent upon the use or the threat of physical force. Much of the white-collar crime committed in America has unfair competition with competitors as its main objective.

The law regulating white-collar crime is based upon both state and federal law. Many white-collar crimes had their basis in common law, while others are of recent origin. A substantial body of law defining and regulating white-collar crime is found in the *penal codes* of each of the 50 states. The federal government has also recently been instrumental in enacting many statutes to help regulate criminal activity. Many of the federal statutes are oriented to specific industries, such as energy and banking, while other federal statutes provide criminal liability without regard to industry, such as those forbidding mail and wire fraud.

Embezzlement.   Unknown at common law, the crime of embezzlement is now a statutory criminal offense in almost all jurisdictions. *Embezzlement* is defined generally as the "fraudulent appropriation of property by a person to whom it has been entrusted." The essence of the crime embezzlement is that the property has been *entrusted* with the accused. Employees, accountants, lawyers, trust officers, administrators, partners, and others in trust or fiduciary positions who occupy the proper status and who are entrusted with control over other persons' property can be found liable for the crime of embezzlement.

The elements of a *prima facie* case of embezzlement are:

1. that property belonging to a person
2. is lawfully *entrusted* in the possession of the accused
3. who is an agent, trustee, bailee, servant, employee or other fiduciary of that person
4. that the fiduciary converts or appropriates the property
5. which deprives the lawful owner of his property.

Embezzlement requires a *fraudulent intent.* Courts have generally held that an intent by the defendant to restore or return the property is not sufficient to defend against a charge of embezzlement. The minority rule allows an intent to return the property as a defense to the crime of embezzlement. Embezzlement differs from larceny in that embezzlement is a crime against *ownership* (entrusted property is taken and converted to that of the embezzler), whereas common larceny is a crime against *possession* (a thief takes property from the owner, who has *not* entrusted the thief with dominion over the property).

Extortion.   The crime of extortion, which had its roots in common law, has since been codified as a crime in most jurisdictions. *Extortion* is defined generally in penal codes as the "obtaining of property from another with his consent, or the obtaining of an official act of public officers, by the wrongful use of force or fear or under color of official right." Extortion may be committed against either public officials (extortion "under color of official right") or private individuals (blackmail). Because of its possible evil effects on otherwise honest victims and the damage it can do to society, extortion is considered a vicious crime and is treated as a felony in most jurisdictions.

The basis of the crime of extortion is the use of force or a threat of force made to the victim in order to obtain property or an act from the victim. Some element of coercion is necessary. The extortion can be either blatant (e.g., a threat to cause physical injury) or subtle (e.g., a threat to cause economic injury or to expose a secret). It does not change the crime if what is threatened to be exposed is *true*. It is the fear of exposure that creates the leverage for the crime of extortion. The threat need not be stated, but may be inferred from the circumstances. It is the fear of exposure or fear of physical injury caused by the *threat,* coupled with the accused's *demand* for property or demand for a certain action from the victim, that is the genesis of the crime of extortion.

For example, if the defendant knows that someone had cheated on his taxes and threatens to expose this person to the Internal Revenue Service unless the victim paid the defendant $1,000, the defendant has committed the crime of extortion. The crime of extortion has been committed by the defendant even though the defendant could have legally reported the victim to the IRS and obtained a statutory reward from the IRS (10 percent of the additional taxes collected). The crime of extortion, where *consent* to transfer property or to perform a requested act is given by the victim, *albeit coerced and unwilling,* can be distinguished from larceny, where property is taken without the consent of the victim.

Many states have enacted "public extortion statutes" that make it a crime for any public official to solicit a political contribution from a public employee where there is a "connection" between the contribution and the security or value of the public employee's work.

Bribery. At common law, the crime of *bribery* was defined generally as the voluntary giving or receiving of anything of value in corrupt payment for an "official act" done or to be done. The common-law crime of bribery was concerned with preventing unlawful payments to judicial officials, but was later expanded to include unlawful payments to jurors, witnesses, legislators, executives, and other government officials. *Intent* to affect the recipient's action is the essential element of the crime of bribery.

Most jurisdictions have codified the crime of bribery to include the giving or promising to give anything of value or advantage, either present or prospective, with the corrupt intent to influence, unlawfully, the person to whom it is given in his action, vote, or opinion. The crime of bribery currently applies to both public officials and private persons. Both the party giving and the party receiving the item of value or promise of advantage are guilty of the crime of bribery in most jurisdictions. For example, a payment to a purchasing agent of a corporation to influence the purchasing agent's decision to purchase products or services from the defendant is bribery. If the official does not accept the bribe, only the person offering the bribe is guilty of bribery.

The crime of bribery is distinguishable from the crime of extortion in that in extortion the accused makes a demand accompanied by coercion to obtain a fee or gift, whereas in bribery the accused offers a fee or gift or receives one, without any use of coercion. Bribery is considered one of the most dangerous of crimes because it undermines the impartiality of official decisions in society. Many federal statutes contain a prohibition against bribery.

In *Dixon and Hinton v. U.S.,* the U.S. Supreme Court upheld the criminal convictions of two defendants who sought a series of bribes in awarding contracts in connection with building HUD housing tracts.

Justice Marshall delivered the opinion of the Court.

In 1979, the City of Peoria received two federal block grants from the Department of Housing and Urban Development (HUD). The first was a $400,000 Community Development Block Grant; the second a $636,000 Metro Reallocation Grant. Both grants were funded through the Housing and Community Development Act of 1974 (HCDA).

The City of Peoria subsequently designated United Neighborhoods, Inc. (UNI), a community-based, social-service organization, to be the City's subgrantee in charge of the administration of the federal block grant funds. UNI in turn hired petitioner Dixon to serve as the corporation's Executive director and petitioner Hinton as its Housing Rehabilitation Coordinator. Petitioner Dixon was responsible for the general supervision of UNI's programs, including fiscal control and execution of contracts. Petitioner Hinton's duties included contracting with persons applying for housing rehabilitation assistance, and contracting with demolition firms.

A federal grand jury named petitioners in an 11-count indictment filed on March 12, 1981. The indictment charged that petitioners, as "public officials" had sought a series of bribes in return for "being influenced in their performance of an official act in respect to the awarding of housing rehabilitation contracts" in violation of 18 U.S.C. Section 201(c)(1), (2).

According to the Government's evidence at trial, petitioners used their positions to extract $42,604 in kick-backs from contractors seeking to work on UNI's housing rehabilitation projects. One contractor testified how he was approached by petitioner Hinton and persuaded to pay petitioners 10 percent of each housing rehabilitation contract that petitioners awarded him. The contractor explained that on ten occasions, he received his first checks from UNI for 20 percent of the contract price, deposited the checks at his bank, and paid half the amount of each check in cash to petitioners. A second contractor testified as to substantially the same arrangement.

Before trial, petitioners moved to dismiss the indictment on the grounds that they were not "public officials" within the meaning of the federal statute. Their motions were denied, and following a jury trial in the United States District Court for the Central District of Illinois, petitioners were convicted as charged. The District Court sentenced each to 7½ years imprisonment, to be followed by 3 years' probation. Petitioners appealed to the United States Court of Appeals for the Seventh Circuit, which affirmed. Both petitioners filed petitions for writs of *certiorari,* and we granted the writs.

Congress passed the HCDA to meet the social, economic, and environmental problems facing cities. The primary objective of the Act is "the development of viable urban communities." While the HCDA addressed a national problem, Congress enacted the legislation as a federal block grant statute, under which the day-to-day administration of the federal program, including the actual expenditure of federal funds, is delegated to State and local authorities. . . . By administering HCDA funds, private nonprofit organizations subject themselves to numerous federal restrictions beyond those imposed directly by HUD.

[T]here is no suggestion in the record that petitioners and other UNI executives failed to understand that they were involved in a federal program.

Petitioners contend now, as they have throughout this litigation, that, as executives of a private nonprofit corporation unaffiliated with the federal government, they were never "public officials" as Congress defined that term. . . . Under Section 201(a), the term "public official" includes

an officer or employee or person acting for or on behalf of the United States, or any department, agency or branch of Government thereof, . . . in any official function, under or by authority of any such department, agency or branch of Government.

There being no basis for claiming that petitioners were officers or employees of the United States, the Government's sole contention is that petitioners acted "for or on behalf of" the United States "in an official function" under the authority of HUD.

Because we agree with the Seventh Circuit that petitioners were public officials under Section 201(a), the judgment of the Court of Appeals is *affirmed*.

CASE QUESTIONS

1. What is the crime of *bribery?* Explain.
2. What positions did the defendants hold? How did the bribery scheme in which they engaged operate? Explain.
3. What criminal statute was involved in this case? Was it a state or federal statute?

4. On appeal to the Supreme Court, did the defendants deny that they had participated in the bribery scheme? What was their argument on appeal? Did the Supreme court accept this argument?

Policy Issue. Should bribery be outlawed? Or is it merely a price for doing business? Do you think bribery is very prevalent in business?

Economics Issue. Does bribery make economic sense? For whom? Who gets hurt?

Ethics Issue. Is it ethical to demand bribes? To receive bribes? To pay bribes?

Social Responsibility. Do businesses owe a duty of social responsibility not to pay bribes? To report persons that request bribes to their employers and to the criminal authorities?

Receiving Stolen Property.   Under the common law, one who received stolen property was not held liable for a crime because he did not actually assist the criminal. However, in order to protect public safety and control the commission of crime, most states have enacted statutes that make it a crime to "receive stolen goods."

The crime of *receiving stolen property* usually requires proof of the following elements:

1. the property was received by the accused
2. at the time of its receipt the property was stolen
3. the defendant who received the property had knowledge that it was stolen
4. the defendant had a fraudulent intent in receiving the property and depriving the owner thereof.

The stolen property may be tangible property, money, negotiable instruments, stock certificates, etc.

The mere presence of stolen property at a location or in the possession of a person is not sufficient to support a conviction for the crime of receiving stolen property. The required "knowledge" and "intent" of the accused must be shown. "Intent" may be inferred from the circumstances. Receipt of *non*stolen property, where the accused *believed* it to have been stolen, has been held by many courts to constitute the crime of receiving stolen property. The majority rule is that the person who actually stole the property cannot also be convicted of the crime of receiving stolen property. The minority rule allows the actual thief to be convicted of either the crime of larceny or the crime of receiving stolen property, but not both.

With the recent substantial increase in the use of stolen credit cards, many states have enacted specific statutes making it a crime to receive a stolen credit card with the intent to use it.

FALSE PRETENSES (DECEIT)

Under common law, obtaining title to property through deception or trick, rather than obtaining possession through physical taking, was not considered larceny. Most jurisdictions have closed this loophole by the enactment of the statutory crime of "false pretenses" or "deceit." Commonly referred to as "swindling," the crime of *false pretenses* consists of the following five elements:

1. that the defendant made a false representation of a material existing or past fact to the victim
2. with knowledge of its falsity
3. with the intent to defraud the victim
4. the victim relied on the false representation and
5. and surrendered money or property to the accused because of the false representation.

A misrepresentation of a "past or existing fact" is generally required to commit the crime of false pretenses. A misrepresentation of a future fact or promise is usually not sufficient. The misrepresentation must be of a "material" fact and must have been the "controlling inducement" and cause for the victim to have parted with his money or property. The accused must also have had knowledge of the falsity and an intent to defraud the victim. A minority of jurisdictions hold that a mere "false promise" (e.g., a promise made with no intent to perform it) is sufficient to constitute the crime of false pretenses.

Examples of the crime of false pretenses are: (1) where a person makes a false representation of an existing fact to obtain an investment of money (e.g., "This well produces oil," when the person knows that it does not); (2) where a person makes a false representation of what an investment of money will be used for (e.g., the accused promises to construct a building, but instead intended to, and does, use the money for personal expenses); and (3) where a person assumes a false identity to obtain money or property from another person.

The crime of false pretenses differs from the crime of embezzlement in that in false pretenses the property has been wrongfully acquired from the victim by a false representation, whereas in embezzlement the property was entrusted to the defendant, who then took it from the victim. The crime of false pretenses differs from the crime of larceny in that in false pretenses the defendant obtains title to the property with the consent of the victim, whereas in larceny the defendant obtains possession of the victim's property by physically taking the property without the consent of the victim. In false pretenses the defendant, through deceit, obtains *title* to the victim's property. In both embezzlement and larceny, the defendant obtains only possession, but not title, to the victim's property. Criminal deceit is also actionable in a civil lawsuit for *fraud*. As Judge Holmes stated in *Weiss v. United States*, 122 F.2d 675 (1941):

The law does not define fraud; it needs no definition; it is as old as falsehood and as versatile as human ingenuity.

Pyramid ("Ponzi") Schemes.   One of the oldest types of *criminal deceit* is the "pyramid" scheme. It consists of a promise by the defendant to a person that if that person places a certain amount of money or property with the accused, the accused will return the original investment plus a substantial profit within a short period of time. The accused then approaches others with the same story, obtains their money or property, and pays off the principal and interest to the first investor when due. The first investor is usually so impressed that he reinvests his money. The defendant continues to "pyramid" the scheme, paying off the promised return to the second layer of investors with the money from the third layer of investors, etc. The defendant usually does not invest the money in the promised investment (e.g., real estate), but pockets a portion of each investor's money and uses the remainder to keep the pyramid functioning. The problem with this scheme is that when new investors can no longer be found, the pyramid must eventually "collapse."

Pyramid schemes, also known as "Ponzi" schemes (a name derived from one of its most famous users), continue in many forms today, particularly in real estate partnerships, investments, and other such schemes involving numerous investors. The most notable example of a pyramid scheme was the collapse of Equity Funding, a New York Stock Exchange-listed insurance company, which sold bogus life insurance policies to reinsurers.

The fact situation of the most famous pyramid scheme of all time is described in the following excerpt from the Supreme Court's decision in *Cunningham, Trustee of Ponzi v. Brown*, 265 U.S. 1 (1924).

PYRAMID SCHEME

CUNNINGHAM, TRUSTEE OF PONZI v. BROWN

265 U.S. 1 (1924)
UNITED STATES SUPREME COURT

Mr. Chief Justice Taft delivered the opinion of the Court.

The litigation grows out of the remarkable criminal financial career of Charles Ponzi. In December, 1919, with a capital of $150, he began the business of borrowing money on his promissory notes. He did not profess to receive money for investment for account of the lender. He borrowed the money on his credit only. He spread the false tale that on his own account he was engaged in buying international postal coupons in foreign countries and selling them in other countries at 100 percent profit, and that this was made possible by the excessive differences in the rates of exchange following the war. He was willing, he said, to give others the opportunity to share with him this profit. By a written promise in 90 days to pay them $150 for every $100 loaned, he induced thousands to lend him.

He stimulated their avidity by paying his 90-day notes in full at the end of 45 days, and by circulating the notice that he would pay any unmatured note presented in less than forty-five days at 100% of the loan. Within eight months he took in $9,582,000 for which he issued his notes for $14,374,000. He paid his agents a commission of 10 percent. With the 50 percent promised to lenders, every loan paid in full with the profit would cost him 60 percent. He was always insolvent and became daily more so, the more his business succeeded. He made no investments of any kind, so that all the money he had at any time was solely the result of loans by his dupes.

By July 1st, Ponzi was taking in about one million dollars a week. Because of an investigation by public authority, Ponzi ceased selling notes on July 26th, but offered and continued to pay all unmatured notes for the amount originally paid in, and all matured notes which had run 45 days, in full. The report of the investigation caused a run on Ponzi's Boston office by investors seeking payment and this developed into a wild scramble when, on August 2nd, a Boston newspaper, most widely circulated, declared Ponzi to be hopelessly insolvent, with a full description of the situation written by one of his recent employees. To meet this emergency, Ponzi concentrated all his available money from other banks in Boston and New England in the Hanover Trust Company, a banking concern in Boston, which had been his chief depository.

At the opening of business July 19th, the balance of Ponzi's deposit accounts at the Hanover Trust Company was $334,000. At the close of business July 24th it was $871,000. This sum was exhausted by withdrawals of July 26th of $572,000, of July 27th of $288,000, and of July 28th of $905,000, or a total of more than $1,765,000. In spite of this, the account continued to show a credit balance because new deposits from other banks were made by Ponzi. It was finally ended by an overdraft on August 9th of $331,000. The petition in bankruptcy was then filed. The total withdrawals from July 19th to August 10th were $6,692,000.

CASE QUESTIONS

1. What is a "Ponzi" (pyramid) scheme? Can a "Ponzi" scheme be used to defraud investors in the modern world? Explain.
2. Can a "Ponzi" scheme go on indefinitely? Why or why not?
3. What are the elements of criminal *fraud?* Does a "Ponzi" scheme qualify as a criminal fraud?

Policy Issue. Should there be any laws against fraud? Or should we return to an absolute rule of *caveat emptor* (let the buyer beware)?

Economics Issue. Why do you think people invested their money with Ponzi? Why do you think people invest their money in "Ponzi" schemes today?

Ethics Issue. Do you think Mr. Ponzi acted ethically in this case?

Social Responsibility. Do criminals who steal money from investors through white-collar "Ponzi" schemes and other frauds cause more or less harm to society than common burglars?

Forgery.   Originally a part of the common-law crime called "cheats," the crime of forgery eventually was distinguished by its own particular name. The elements necessary to constitute the crime of *forgery* are:

1. the defendant falsely made or altered a written instrument
2. with fraudulent intent and
3. the instrument must be apparently capable of effectuating the fraud.

Forgery cannot be committed by an oral statement. (By contrast, oral misrepresentation *can* constitute the crime of false pretenses).

The most common form of forgery consists of signing another person's signature to a written instrument. Signing another's signature without forming an "intent" to defraud does not constitute forgery (e.g., husband gives wife permission to sign his name to checks). However, forgery may also occur by materially adding, altering, or erasing written words from a properly executed document (e.g., changing the amount of $10.00 on a check to $10,000,000). In order to constitute forgery, the instrument must have "apparent legal significance" (e.g., a check, stock certificate, or bond). Therefore, signing a painting with the name of another does not constitute the crime of forgery. However, falsely signing a painting does constitute the crime of false pretenses.

At common law, the "passing" or "uttering" of an instrument (a writing) known to have been forged and with the intent to defraud was a crime separate from the crime of forgery. Most states have absorbed the crime of "uttering" into their forgery statutes.

Bad Check Legislation.   Most states have enacted specific "bad-check" legislation that makes it a crime for a person to make, draw, or deliver a check at a time when there are insufficient funds in the account to cover the amount of the check, and the accused has knowledge of such insufficiency of funds. A minority of states requires a showing of "intent to defraud" in order to prove a violation of a bad-check statute.

INCHOATE CRIMES

Often business persons will begin the commission of a crime, but the actual crime will not be committed for one reason or another. However, the persons involved with the planning or attempt to commit a crime are often liable for committing one of several *inchoate* crimes, such as (1) conspiracy to commit a crime; (2) attempt to commit a crime; and (3) aiding and abetting the commission of a crime.

Conspiracy.   Often people agree to commit a crime, but may not actually do so because they eventually decide not to or are somehow thwarted in their efforts to carry out the crime (as when the victim of a planned murder dies before the murder can be carried out). The majority of jurisdictions define the *agreement* to commit a crime as itself a crime, which is independent of the planned substantive crime. Most state and federal statutes broadly define *criminal conspiracy* as "a combination between two or more persons by concerted action to accomplish some criminal or unlawful purpose or to accomplish a lawful purpose by an unlawful means."

The elements necessary to establish a "criminal conspiracy" are:

1. two or more persons have entered into an agreement
2. to commit a crime and
3. one or more of the conspirators took some overt act in the furtherance of the conspiracy.

Words are *not* required to form a conspiracy. In addition to oral and written agreements to commit a crime, a wink of the eye, a nod of the head, or a handshake have been held to form the basis of a conspiratorial agreement.

Conspiracy by implication may be inferred from the facts and circumstances of the case.

By itself, an agreement to commit a crime is not sufficient to constitute the crime of conspiracy. Some *overt act* to further the unlawful objective is required. For example, if two persons agree on the telephone to kill a third person, the crime of conspiracy does not occur until one of the coconspirators takes some action in furtherance of the conspiracy (e.g., purchases the murder weapon or stakes out the area where the crime is to occur).

The government frequently brings an action for criminal conspiracy against defendants when it lacks evidence to prove the substantive criminal offense that was the object of the conspiracy or where the substantive offense was not committed. The charge of criminal conspiracy may be brought in addition to the charge of the substantive crime, and a person can be convicted and sentenced on both charges. The old common-law doctrine that the crime of conspiracy "merged" with the substantive crime which was the object of the conspiracy has been abandoned in most jurisdictions.

Attempt to Commit a Crime.   Often a person may attempt to commit a crime, but fails to actually complete it. Under modern statutes, the *attempt* to commit a crime is considered a crime itself. For example, if a person intends to kill someone, aims the pistol at the victim, pulls the trigger, and the bullet misses the victim, the defendant is not liable for the crime of murder but will be liable for the crime of "attempt to commit murder." Most states hold an accused guilty of the crime of attempt even if it would have been impossible for the accused to have completed the substantive crime (e.g., if the pistol fired was not loaded).

In order to be held liable for the crime of attempt, the defendant must have intended to commit the crime and must have taken some action in furtherance of the crime (e.g., broke into a house with the intent to commit a burglary). The mere formation of an intent to commit a crime is not sufficient to constitute the crime of attempt. For example, if you hate your neighbor and think about killing him as he walks across the street in front of your car, but you stop and let him proceed unharmed, you are not liable for the crime of attempt to commit murder. But if you intentionally step on the gas, but the neighbor jumps out of the way, you are liable for the crime of attempt to commit murder.

The crime of attempt differs from the crime of conspiracy in that the crime of attempt may be committed by one person whereas the crime of conspiracy requires an agreement between at least two persons. Where a defendant attempts to commit a crime and succeeds, the crime of attempt "merges" with the substantive crime when the defendant is tried on the substantive crime.

Aiding and Abetting.   It is a distinct and separate crime for a person to "aid and abet" another in the commission of a crime. *Aiding and abetting* includes all assistance rendered by acts or words of encouragement, support, or presence to render assistance in the commission of a crime. For example, harboring a criminal after he has committed a crime, or purchasing a gun for a person with knowledge that it will be used to commit a crime, has been held to constitute the crime of aiding and abetting. However, the mere presence at the scene of a crime, without holding out some assistance to the criminal, is not sufficient to constitute the crime of aiding and abetting.

In *Standefer v. U.S.* a businessman was found guilty of the crime of aiding and abetting an Internal Revenue Service employee to accept unauthorized payments, even though the IRS agent was acquitted of the charge of accepting the unauthorized payments.

AIDING AND ABETTING

STANDEFER v. UNITED STATES

447 U.S. 10 (1980)
UNITED STATES SUPREME COURT

Mr. Chief Justice Burger delivered the opinion of the Court.

In June 1977, petitioner Standefer was indicted [for] aiding and abetting a revenue official in accepting compensation in addition to that authorized by [federal] law. . . . The indictment charged that petitioner, as head of Gulf Oil Corp.'s tax department, had authorized payments for five vacation trips to Cyril Niederberger, who then was the Internal Revenue Service agent in charge of the audits of Gulf's federal income tax returns. Specifically, the indictment alleged that Gulf, on petitioner's authorization, had paid for vacations for Niederberger in Pompano Beach (July 1971), Miami (January 1973), Absecon (August–September 1973), Pebble Beach (April 1974), and Las Vegas (June 1974).

In July 1977, following Niederberger's trial and before the trial in his own case commenced, petitioner moved to dismiss the counts which charged him with aiding and abetting Niederberger in connection with the Pompano Beach, Miami, and Absecon vacations. Petitioner argued that because Niederberger, the only named principal, had been acquitted of accepting unlawful compensation as to those vacations, he could not be convicted of aiding and abetting in the commission of those offenses. The District Court denied the motion.

Petitioner's case then proceeded to trial on all counts. At trial, petitioner admitted authorizing payment for all five vacation trips, but testified that the trips were purely social and not designed to influence Niederberger in the performance of his official duties. The jury returned guilty verdicts on all nine counts. Petitioner was sentenced to concurrent terms of six months' imprisonment followed by two years' probation; he was fined a total of $18,000—$2,000 on each count.

Petitioner appealed his convictions to the Court of Appeals for the Third Circuit claiming, *inter alia,* that he could not be convicted of aiding and abetting a principal, Niederberger, when that principal had been acquitted on the charged offense. By a divided vote, the Court of Appeals, sitting en banc, rejected that contention. It concluded that "the outcome of Niederberger's prosecution has no effect on [petitioner's] conviction." . . . Because the question presented is one of importance to the administration of criminal justice on which the Courts of Appeals are in conflict, we granted *certiorari.*

Petitioner . . . [argues] that Congress . . . did not intend to authorize prosecution of an aider and abettor after the principal has been acquitted of the offense charged. . . . 18 U.S.C. Section 2 [provides]:

> Whoever directly commits any act constituting an offense defined in any law of the United States, or aids, abets, counsels, commands, induces, or procures its commission, *is a principal.* (emphasis added).

The statute "abolishe[d] the distinction between principals and accessories and [made] them all principals." *Hammer v. United States.* Read against its common-law background, the provision evinces a clear intent to permit the conviction of accessories to federal criminal offenses despite the prior acquittal of the actual perpetrator of the offense.

[W]e do not deviate from the sound teaching that "justice must satisfy the appearance of justice." This case does no more than manifest the simple, if discomforting, reality that "different juries may reach different results under any criminal statute. That is one of the consequences we accept under our jury system." *Roth v. United States.* While symmetry of results may be intellectually satisfying, it is not required.

The judgment of the Court of Appeals is *affirmed.*

CASE QUESTIONS

1. What are the following *inchoate* crimes?
   a. conspiracy
   b. attempt
   c. aiding and abetting
   Which one was alleged in this case?
2. Who was the defendant? Who did he work for? What was his position?
3. Who was Niederberger? Whom did he work for? Did he receive any compensation from Gulf Oil Corp.? Explain.

4. Was Niederberger found guilty of accepting unlawful compensation? Was Standefer found criminally liable for *aiding and abetting* Niederberger in accepting unlawful compensation? Can these two decisions be reconciled?
5. If Niederberger had worked for a purchaser or supplier to Gulf, would the case have had the same importance? Why or why not?

Policy Issue. Should the law punish inchoate activities as crimes? Why or why not?

Economics Issue. Do you think Gulf's payments for Niederberger's vacations "were purely social and not designed to influence Niederberger in the performance of his official duties"?

Ethics Issue. Do you think Standefer acted ethically in this case? Did Niederberger?

Social Responsibility. Do the courts owe a duty of social responsibility to reach the same result regarding the same fact situation? Are the implications of the following statement by the court acceptable? "This case does no more than manifest the simple, if discomforting, reality that different juries may reach different results under any criminal statute. That is one of the consequences we accept under our jury system."

CORPORATE CRIMINAL LIABILITY

A corporation is a *fictitious* legal person granted life by the state upon the filing of articles of incorporation. A corporation can sue and be sued, own and transfer property, enter into contracts, and generally take most other actions allowed by law to individuals. A corporation, however, cannot act on its own accord, but must rely on *agents* to take action on its behalf. The agents of a corporation are its officers, directors, and employees.

The question of whether or not a corporation can be held criminally liable itself, since it cannot form the requisite intent (*mens rea*), has intrigued legal scholars for some time. The courts, however, have taken a pragmatic view and have generally held that under certain criminal statutes, particularly those of a regulatory nature (e.g., antitrust laws, securities laws), a corporation can be held criminally liable for the acts of its agents.

A corporation cannot, of course, be put in prison. Therefore, the usual criminal penalty of a corporation is the assessment of a fine or the loss of some right, such as its license to operate a certain type of business.

In *U.S. v. Hilton Hotels Corporation* the court upheld the criminal conviction and assessment of a fine against a corporation where its executives had participated in an illegal restraint of trade in violation of federal antitrust law.

CRIMINAL LIABILITY OF THE CORPORATION FOR ACTS OF ITS AGENTS

UNITED STATES v. HILTON HOTELS CORPORATION, WESTERN INTERNATIONAL HOTELS COMPANY, *ET AL.*

---

467 F.2d 1000 (1973)
UNITED STATES COURT OF APPEALS, NINTH CIRCUIT

Browning, Circuit Judge:

This is an appeal from a conviction under an indictment charging a violation of Section 1 of the Sherman Act [illegal restraint of trade].

Operators of hotels, restaurants, hotel and restaurant supply companies, and other businesses in Portland, Oregon, organized an association to attract conventions to their city. To finance the association, members were asked to make contributions in predetermined amounts. Companies selling supplies to hotels were asked to contribute an amount equal to one per cent of their sales to hotel members. To aid collections, hotel members, including appellant, agreed to give preferential treatment to suppliers who paid their assessments, and to curtail purchases from those who did not.

The court instructed the jury that a corporation is liable for the acts and statements of its agents "within the scope of their employment," defined to mean "in the corporation's behalf in performance of the agent's general line of work," including "not only that which has been authorized by the corporation, but also that which outsiders could reasonably assume the agent would have authority to do."

With such important public interests at stake, it is reasonable to assume that Congress intended to impose liability upon business entities for the acts of those to whom they choose to delegate the conduct of their affairs, thus stimulating a maximum effort by owners and managers to assure adherence by such agents to the requirements of the Act.

Sherman Act violations are commercial offenses. They are usually motivated by a desire to enhance profits. They commonly involve large, complex, and highly decentralized corporate business enterprises, and intricate business processes, practices, and arrangements. More often than not they also involve basic policy decisions, and must be implemented over an extended period of time.

Complex business structures, characterized by decentralization and delegation of authority, commonly adopted by corporations for business purposes, make it difficult to identify the particular corporate agents responsible for Sherman Act violations. At the same time, it is generally true that high management officials, for whose conduct the corporate directors and stockholders are the most clearly responsible, are likely to have participated in the policy decisions underlying Sherman Act violations, or at least to have become aware of them.

Violations of the Sherman Act are a likely consequence of the pressure to maximize profits that is commonly imposed by corporate owners upon managing agents and, in turn, upon lesser employees. In the face of that pressure, generalized directions to obey the Sherman Act, with the probable effect of forgoing profits, are the least likely to be taken seriously. And if a violation of the Sherman Act occurs, the corporation, and not the individual agents, will have realized the profits from the illegal activity.

In sum, identification of the particular agents responsible for a Sherman Act violation is especially difficult, and their conviction and punishment is peculiarly ineffective as a deterrent. At the same time, conviction and punishment of the business entity itself is likely to be both appropriate and effective.

For these reasons we conclude that as a general rule a corporation is liable under the Sherman Act for the acts of its agents in the scope of their employment, even though contrary to general corporate policy and express instructions to the agent. *Affirmed.*

CASE QUESTIONS

1. Can a corporation take any action on its own behalf? Or must it operate through *agents?*
2. Who were the agents of the corporation in this case? What illegal activity did the agents participate in? Explain.
3. Was the corporation held *criminally* liable for the acts of its agents in this case?

   Policy Issue. Should the corporation be held liable for the acts of its executives? Or should only the individual executives be held criminally liable for their own actions? Why or why not?

   Economics Issue. Does the profit motive often conflict with obeying the law? Explain.

   Ethics Issue. Did the corporate executives of the hotels and other companies act unethically in this case? Did the *corporations* act unethically? Can they?

   Social Responsibility. Does a corporation owe a duty of social responsibility to inform its executives and employees of what the law is? To hire business law professors to give seminars?

Criminal Liability for Product Defects. Since the adoption of the doctrine of strict liability in tort, corporations are often sued and held *civilly* liable for injuries caused by defective products that they produce and distribute (see Chapter 18, "Product Safety"). However, it is now feasible that under certain circumstances a corporation and its officers may be sued and held *criminally* liable for knowingly distributing defective products that cause injury.

The most celebrated case in this area was *State v. Ford Motor Company*, Elkhart County, No. 5324 (1980), which was brought in 1979 by the State of Indiana against the Ford Motor Company. In that case, the state charged that Ford had commited *reckless homicide* by recklessly designing, manufacturing, and distributing a 1973 Pinto, the gas tank of which exploded in an automobile accident causing the deaths of three persons. The criminal statutes that Ford was accused of violating provided:

A person who recklessly kills another human being commits reckless homicide, a Class C felony. However, if the killing results from the operation of a vehicle, the offense is a Class D felony. [Indiana Code, Section 35-42-1-5]

(a) A person who recklessly, knowingly, or intentionally performs an act that creates a substantial risk of bodily injury to another person commits criminal recklessness, a Class B misdemeanor. However, the offense is a Class A misdemeanor if the conduct includes the use of a vehicle or deadly weapon. (b) A person who recklessly, knowingly, or intentionally inflicts serious bodily injury on another person commits criminal recklessness, a Class D felony. [Indiana Code, Section 35-42-2-2]

A person engages in conduct 'recklessly' if he engages in the conduct in plain, conscious, and unjustifiable disregard of harm that might result and the disregard involves a substantial deviation from acceptable standards of conduct. [Indiana Code, Section 35-40-2-2(c)]

After a ten-week trial, and after being deadlocked for four days of deliberations, the seven-man five-woman jury returned a consensus verdict of *not guilty* on the three charges of *criminal* homicide. Ford Motor Company spent approximately $1 million defending the lawsuit. The state spent approximately $20,000, and elicited the assistance of volunteer lawyers and law students to prosecute the case.

Although the case only involved a demand for an assessment of monetary damages for the alleged criminal violation, the case was watched closely by other businesses and covered extensively by the press, because a jury verdict of guilty would have constituted the first time that an American company had been found criminally liable for a product defect.

The *indictment* issued by the Elkhart County Grand Jury against Ford Motor Company is set forth following.

CRIMINAL LIABILITY FOR A PRODUCT DEFECT

STATE v. FORD MOTOR CO.
INDICTMENT IN FOUR COUNTS CHARGING THREE COUNTS OF RECKLESS HOMICIDE, A CLASS D FELONY AND ONE COUNT OF CRIMINAL RECKLESSNESS, A CLASS A MISDEMEANOR

NO. 5324 (1979)
INDIANA SUPERIOR COURT, ELKHART COUNTY, INDIANA

The grand Jurors of Elkhart County, State of Indiana, being first duly sworn upon their oaths do present and say:

COUNT I

That Ford Motor Company, a corporation, on or about the 10th day of August, 1978, in the County of Elkhart, State of Indiana, did then and there through the acts and omissions of its agents and employees acting within the scope of their authority with said corporation recklessly cause the death of Judy Ann Ulrich, a human being, to-wit: that the Ford Motor Company, a corporation, did recklessly authorize and approve the design, and did recklessly design and manufacture a certain 1973 Pinto automobile, Serial Number F3T10X298722F, in such a manner as would likely cause said automobile to flame and burn upon rear-end impact; and the said Ford Motor Company permitted said Pinto automobile to remain upon the highways and roadways of Elkhart County, State of Indiana, to-wit: U.S. Highway Number 33, in said County and State; and the said Ford Motor Company did fail to repair and modify said Pinto automobile; and thereafter on said date as a proximate contributing cause of said reckless disregard for the safety of other per-

sons within said automobile, including, the said Judy Ann Ulrich, a rear-end impact involving said Pinto automobile did occur creating fire and flame which did then and there and thereby inflict mortal injuries upon the said Judy Ann Ulrich, and the said Judy Ann Ulrich did then languish and die by incineration in Allen County, State of Indiana, on or about the 11th day of August, 1978.

And so the Grand Jurors aforesaid, upon their oaths aforesaid, do say and charge that the said Ford Motor Company, a corporation, did recklessly cause the death of the said Judy Ann Ulrich, a human being, in the manner and form aforesaid, and contrary to the form of the statutes in such cases made and provided, to-wit: Burns Indiana Statutes, Indiana Code Section 35-42-1-5; and against the peace and dignity of the State of Indiana.

COUNTS II AND III

[Counts II and III repeat the allegations of Count I as to the deaths of Donna M. Ulrich and Lynn M. Ulrich, respectively.]

COUNT IV

That Ford Motor Company, a corporation, on or about the 10th day of August, 1978, and diverse days prior thereto, in the County of Elkhart, State of Indiana, did through the acts and omissions of its agents and employees acting within the scope of their authority with said corporation, recklessly create a substantial risk of bodily injury to the persons of Judy Ann Ulrich, Donna M. Ulrich and Lynn M. Ulrich, human beings, and each of them, to-wit: that the Ford Motor Company, a corporation, did recklessly permit a certain 1973 Pinto automobile, Serial Number F3T10X298722F, designed and manufactured by the said Ford Motor Company to remain upon the highways and roadways of Elkhart County, State of Indiana, to-wit: U.S. Highway Number 33 in said County and State; and said Pinto automobile being recklessly designed and manufactured in such a manner as would likely cause said automobile to flame and burn upon rear-end impact; and that the said Ford Motor Company had a legal duty to warn the general public and certain occupants of said Pinto automobile, namely: Judy Ann Ulrich, Donna M. Ulrich and Lynn M. Ulrich of the dangerous tendency of said Pinto automobile to flame and burn upon rear-end impact; and the said Ford Motor Company did fail to repair and modify said Pinto automobile; and that as a proximate contributing cause of said Ford Motor Company's acts, omissions and reckless disregard for the safety of other persons within said Pinto automobile, including the said Judy Ann Ulrich, Donna M. Ulrich and Lynn M. Ulrich, a rear-end impact involving said Pinto automobile did occur on or about August 10, 1978, in Elkhart County, Indiana, creating fire and flame which did then and there and thereby inflict bodily injury upon the persons of the said Judy Ann Ulrich, Donna M. Ulrich and Lynn M. Ulrich, human beings, and each of them.

And so the Grand Jurors aforesaid, upon their oaths aforesaid, do say and charge that the said Ford Motor Company, a corporation, did recklessly create a substantial risk of bodily injury to the persons of Judy Ann Ulrich, Donna M. Ulrich and Lynn M. Ulrich, human beings, and each of them, in the manner and form aforesaid, and contrary to the form of the Statutes in such cases made and provided, to-wit: Burns Indiana Statutes, Indiana Code Section 35-42-2-2, and against the peace and dignity of the State of Indiana.

A true bill

CASE QUESTIONS

1. Who was the plaintiff in this case? Was it one of the persons who died when the Pinto gas tank exploded?
2. Who was the defendant in this case? Was it Ford Motor Company? Or individual executives of Ford?
3. What was the defendant accused of in this case? Was it a *civil* or *criminal* lawsuit?
4. Why was this case important to business? Explain.

   Policy Issue. Should a corporation or its officers be held *criminally* liable for injury caused by defective products that they knowingly allow to be distributed and sold to consumers? Why or why not?

   Economics Issue. Would the fine sought in this case have caused any grave economic consequences for the defendant? Any symbolic consequences? Explain.

   Ethics Issue. Do you think the executives of Ford Motor Co. acted ethically in this case? In producing the Pinto automobile with the gas tank in the rear?

   Social Responsibility. Does a corporation owe a duty of social responsibility to recall a product which it discovers is defective? Even if it would be cheaper to pay for the damage done by the defective product? What if a recall would bankrupt the company?

CRIMINAL LIABILITY OF MANAGERS

An executive of a corporation is always individually liable for the crimes that he or she commits for personal benefit or on behalf of the corporation. However, in certain circumstances an executive may also be held *criminally* liable for illegal activities of his or her subordinates. Generally, in order for such liability to attach, it must be established that the manager was responsible for the subordinate and failed to exercise his authority and supervision over the subordinate. Most criminal convictions under this doctrine have occurred where there has been a violation of a regulatory statute. This is one area of the law where actual intent (*mens rea*) is not required to convict a defendant of a crime.

In *U.S. v. Park* the Supreme Court held a manager criminally liable for failing to properly exercise supervisory responsibility over the actions of subordinates, which failure caused a violation of the Federal Food, Drug, and Cosmetic Act.

LIABILITY OF MANAGERS FOR CRIMES OF SUBORDINATES

UNITED STATES v. PARK

421 U.S. 658 (1974)
UNITED STATES SUPREME COURT

Mr. Chief Justice Burger delivered the opinion of the Court.

Acme Markets, Inc., is a national retail food chain with approximately 36,000 employees, 874 retail outlets, 12 general warehouses, and four special warehouses. Its headquarters, including the office of the president, respondent Park, who is chief executive officer of the corporation, are located in Philadelphia, Pa. In a five-count information filed in the United States District Court for the District of Maryland, the Government charged Acme and respondent with violations of the Federal Food, Drug, and Cosmetic Act. Each count of the information alleged that the defendants had received food that had been shipped in interstate commerce and that, while the food was being held for sale in Acme's Baltimore warehouse following shipment in interstate commerce, they caused it to be held in a building accessible to rodents and to be exposed to contamination by rodents. These acts were alleged to have resulted in the food's being adulterated. . . .

Acme pleaded guilty to each count of the information. Respondent pleaded not guilty. The evidence at trial demonstrated that in April 1970 the Food and Drug Administration (FDA) advised respondent by letter of insanitary conditions in Acme's Philadelphia warehouse. In 1971 the FDA found that similar conditions existed in the firm's Baltimore warehouse. An FDA consumer safety officer testified concerning evidence of rodent infestation and other insanitary conditions discovered during a 12-day inspection of the Baltimore warehouse in November and December 1971. He also related that a second inspection of the warehouse had been conducted in March 1972. On that occasion the inspectors found that there had been improvement in the sanitary conditions, but that "there was still evidence of rodent activity in the building and in the warehouses and we found some rodent-contaminated lots of food items."

Respondent was the only defense witness. He testified that, although all of Acme's employees were in a sense under his general direction, the company had an "organizational structure for responsibilities for certain functions" according to which different phases of its operation were "assigned to individuals who, in turn, have staff and departments under them.". . . The relevant portion of the trial judge's instructions to the jury challenged by respondent is set out . . . [following].

> The statute makes individuals, as well as corporations, liable for violations. An individual is liable if it is clear, beyond a reasonable doubt, that the elements of the adulteration of the food as to travel in interstate commerce are present. As I have instructed

you in this case, they are, and that the individual had a responsible relation to the situation, even though he may not have participated personally.

The individual is or could be liable under the statute, even if he did not consciously do wrong. However, the fact that the Defendant is pres[id]ent and is a chief executive officer of the Acme Markets does not require a finding of guilt. Though, he need not have personally participated in the situation, he must have had a responsible relationship to the issue. The issue is, in this case, whether the Defendant, John R. Park, by virtue of his position in the company, has a position of authority and responsibility in the situation out of which these charges arose.

The jury found respondent guilty on all counts of the information, and he was subsequently sentenced to pay a fine of $50 on each count. . . . The Court of Appeals reversed the conviction and remanded for a new trial. . . . The Court of Appeals concluded that the trial judge's instructions "might well have left the jury with the erroneous impression that Park could be found guilty in the absence of 'wrongful action' on his part.". . . We granted *certiorari* because of an apparent conflict among the Courts of Appeals with respect to the standard of liability of corporate officers under the Federal Food, Drug, and Cosmetic Act. . . .

[I]n *United States v. Dotterweich* . . . this Court looked to the purposes of the Act and noted that they "touch phases of the lives and health of people which, in the circumstances of modern industrialism, are largely beyond self-protection." It observed that the Act is of "a now familiar type" which

> dispenses with the conventional requirement for criminal conduct—awareness of some wrongdoing. In the interest of the larger good it puts the burden of acting at hazard upon a person otherwise innocent but standing in responsible relation to a public danger.

The rationale of the interpretation given the Act in *Dotterweich,* as holding criminally accountable the persons whose failure to exercise the authority and supervisory responsibility reposed in them by the business organization resulted in the violation complained of, has been confirmed in our subsequent cases.

Thus *Dotterweich* and the cases which have followed reveal that in providing sanctions which reach and touch the individuals who execute the corporate mission—and this is by no means necessarily

confined to a single corporate agent or employee—the Act imposes not only a positive duty to seek out and remedy violations when they occur but also, and primarily, a duty to implement measures that will insure that violations will not occur. The requirements of foresight and vigilance imposed on responsible corporate agents are beyond question demanding, and perhaps onerous, but they are no more stringent than the public has a right to expect of those who voluntarily assume positions of authority in business enterprises whose services and products affect the health and well-being of the public that supports them.

The theory upon which responsible corporate agents are held criminally accountable for "causing" violations of the Act permits a claim that a defendant was "powerless" to prevent or correct the violation to "be raised defensively at a trial on the merits." *United States v. Wiesenfeld Warehouse Co.*

Reading the entire charge satisfies us that the jury's attention was adequately focused on the issue of respondent's authority with respect to the conditions that formed the basis of the alleged violations. Viewed as a whole, the charge did not permit the jury to find guilt solely on the basis of respondent's position in the corporation; rather, it fairly advised the jury that to find guilt it must find respondent "had a responsible relation to the situation," and "by virtue of his position . . . had . . . authority and responsibility" to deal with the situation.

Reversed.

CASE QUESTIONS

1. How big was Acme Markets? What position did respondent Park hold with the corporation?
2. What *crime* was respondent convicted of committing? Did he have the actual intent (*mens rea*) to commit the crime? Explain.
3. Does the Food, Drug, and Cosmetic Act impose the following duties on a corporate manager? Was Park found to have breached these duties?
   a. to seek out and remedy existing violations of the Act
   b. to implement measures to ensure that violations of the Act will not occur in the future
4. Do you understand the jury charge given in this

case? Do you think an average juror would have understood the jury instruction?

5. What does the defense announced in *U.S. v. Wiesenfeld Warehouse Co.* provide? Do you think Park qualified for this defense?

Policy Issue. Should a corporate manager be held *criminally* liable for acts of his subordinates? Why or why not?

Economics Issue. Should executive salaries increase because of this case? Explain.

Ethics Issue. Do you think Park acted unethically in this case?

Social Responsibility. Do managers who "execute the corporate mission" owe a duty of social responsibility to prohibit dangerous activities of their subordinates?

ORGANIZED CRIME

Multimillion-dollar "organized crime" operates many illegal activities in the United States in the areas of prostitution, gambling, and narcotics. These activities are extremely lucrative. State laws, however, have been and are quite impotent to deal with many of the activities of organized crime. In order to assist in the apprehension and prosecution of organized crime, Congress enacted a web of legislation with the goal of curtailing much of the activity of organized crime. Some of these statutes are broad in scope and include other than "organized crime" within their ambit (e.g., mail fraud, wire fraud). The violation of a *federal* criminal statute is an offense separate from the violation of any *state* criminal law statute that occurs because of the same activity (e.g., extortion).

Fed. act aimed at Racketeering

RICO. In order to find investment opportunities for the substantial amount of profits being generated by the illegal operations, organized crime invests substantial proceeds in legitimate businesses. In 1970, Congress enacted the Racketeer Influenced and Corrupt Organizations Act ("RICO") as a chapter of the Organized Crime Control Act of 1970 to address many of the problems concerning organized crime in the United States. In addition to making it a federal crime to participate in "racketeering" activities, RICO provides for the forfeiture of profits and proceeds made illegally by racketeering activities. In addition to confiscating the actual illegal goods or monies, under RICO the federal government can also "trace" illegally made profits and proceeds and confiscate legitimate businesses purchased by organized crime with proceeds from illegal activities.

The courts have generally given a broad reading of the activities that violate RICO, which include illegal gambling, narcotics, extortion, bribery, etc. The courts will be faced with further defining the activities that fall within the definition of "racketeering" and are then subject to the provisions of RICO. Although the courts have stated that RICO's main purpose is to "keep racketeers out of business, not to make racketeers out of businessmen," the civil suit provisions of RICO have recently been criticized for being applied to activities of defendants unconnected to organized crime.

In *Russello v. U.S.* the Supreme Court affirmed a lower court judgment ordering a criminal defendant to forfeit $340,048 in profits made from arson and racketeering activities in violation of the federal RICO statute.

RICO

RUSSELLO v. UNITED STATES

104 S.CT. 296 (1983)
UNITED STATES SUPREME COURT

Justice Blackmun delivered the opinion of the Court.

This is yet another case concerning the Racketeer Influenced and Corrupt Organizations (RICO) chapter of the Organized Crime Control Act of 1970.

On June 8, 1977, petitioner Joseph C. Russello and others were indicted for racketeering, conspiracy, and mail fraud. . . . After a jury trial in the United States District Court for the Middle District of Florida, petitioner was convicted as charged in four counts of the indictment. The jury then returned special verdicts for the forfeiture to the United States of four payments aggregating $340,048.09, made to petitioner by a fire insurance company. These verdicts related to the racketeering activities charged in the second count of the indictment under which petitioner had been convicted. The District Court, accordingly, entered a judgment of forfeiture against petitioner in that amount.

Petitioner took an appeal to the former United States Court of Appeals for the Fifth Circuit. . . . The full court . . . affirmed the forfeiture judgment entered by the District Court. . . . Because of this significant division among the judges of the Court of Appeals . . . we granted *certiorari.*

So far as the case in its present posture is concerned, the basic facts are not in dispute. The majority opinion of the [District Court] described them succinctly:

> Briefly, the evidence showed that a group of individuals associated for the purposes of committing arson with the intent to defraud insurance companies. This association in fact enterprise, composed of an insurance adjuster, homeowners, promoters, investors, and arsonists, operated to destroy properties in Tampa and Miami, Florida between July 1973 and April 1976.

The [District Court] summarized the ring's operations as follows:

> At first the arsonists only burned buildings already owned by those associated with the ring. Following a burning, the building owner filed an inflated proof of loss statement and collected the insurance proceeds from which his co-conspirators were paid. Later, ring members bought buildings suitable for burning, secured insurance in excess of value and, after a burning, made claims for the loss and divided the proceeds.

Specifically, petitioner was the owner of the Central Professional Building in Tampa. This structure had two parts, an original smaller section in front and a newer addition at the rear. The latter contained apartments, offices, and parking facilities. Petitioner arranged for arsonists to set fire to the front portion. He intended to use the insurance proceeds to rebuild that section. The fire, however, spread to the rear. Joseph Carter, another member of the arson ring, was the adjuster for petitioner's insurance claim and helped him to obtain the highest payments possible. The resulting payments made up the aggregate sum of $340,043.09 mentioned above. From those proceeds, petitioner paid Carter $30,000 for his assistance.

Title 18 U.S.C. Section 1962(c) [RICO] states that it shall be unlawful

> for any person employed by or associated with any enterprise engaged in, or the activities of which affect, interstate . . . commerce, to conduct or participate, directly or indirectly, in the conduct of such enterprise's affairs through a pattern of racketeering activity or collection of unlawful debt.

Section 1962(d) makes it unlawful to conspire to violate Section 1962(c). Section 1963(a)(1) provides that a person convicted under Section 1962 shall forfeit to the United States "any interest he has acquired or maintained in violation of Section 1962."

The term "interest" is not specifically defined in the RICO statute. . . . The ordinary meaning of "interest" surely encompasses a right to profits or proceeds. See Webster's Third New International Dictionary 1178 (1976).

Before profits of an illegal enterprise are divided, each participant may be said to own an "interest" in the ill-gotten gains. After distribution, each will have a possessory interest in currency or other items so distributed. We therefore conclude that the language of the statute plainly covers the insurance proceeds petitioner received as a result of his arson activities.

We note that the RICO statute's definition of the term "enterprise" in Section 1961(4) encompasses both legal entities and illegitimate associations-in-fact. Forfeiture of an interest in an illegitimate association-in-fact ordinarily would be of little use because an association of that kind rarely has identifiable assets; instead, proceeds or profits usually are distributed immediately. Thus, construing Section 1963(a)(1) to reach only interests in an enterprise would blunt the effectiveness of the provision in combatting illegitimate enterprises, and would mean that "[w]hole areas of organized criminal activities would be placed beyond" the reach of the statute. (*United States v. Turkette*)

Congress emphasized the need to fashion new remedies in order to achieve its far-reaching objectives. . . . From all this, the intent to authorize forfeiture of racketeering profits seem obvious.

[W]e *affirm* the judgment of the United States Court of Appeals for the Fifth Circuit.

CASE QUESTIONS

1. What crime does the federal RICO statute prohibit? Is it a narrow or broad statute? Explain.
2. What does the forfeiture provision of the RICO statute provide? Does it only apply to money in an illegal enterprise? Or may it trace the investment of illegally obtained money into investments in legitimate enterprises? Explain.
3. What activities did the petitioner engage in? Did they constitute "racketeering" under RICO?
4. How much money was the petitioner order to forfeit? Did the Supreme Court agree with the order of the District Court?

Policy Issue. Is RICO needed to help attack the criminal activities of organized crime in this country? Or are existing laws sufficient?

Economics Issue. Do you think the economic consequences of the forfeiture provisions of RICO will have much impact on organized crime? Why or why not?

Ethics Issue. Did the petitioners and others involved in this case act ethically?

Social Responsibility. Does the government owe a duty of social responsibility to eliminate organized crime in this country? Do any of the government's policies promote organized crime in this country? Explain.

FOREIGN CORRUPT PRACTICES ACT

The Foreign Corrupt Practices Act (FCPA) was enacted by Congress in 1977 in response to the widespread bribery of foreign government officials by American companies. The Act makes it a criminal offense for SEC reporting companies and "domestic concerns" (e.g., individuals, partnerships, corporations), through their employees or agents, to make payments to a "foreign official" to influence any act or decision of the recipient in his official capacity.

The definition of a "foreign official" under the FCPA includes most foreign government workers above clerical positions. For example, "grease" payments made to customs officials would not be covered. Political candidates are included within the definition of "foreign official" as used in the Act. Payments made by U.S. businesses to foreign officials under extortion are not covered. The maximum fine for violation of the Act by a reporting company is quite substantial ($1 million).

The Foreign Corrupt Practices Act requires covered companies and concerns to implement certain internal accounting controls so that violations of the Act may be more easily uncovered. The enforcement of the Act is quite difficult because most transactions that constitute violations of the Act occur overseas, and may be "buried" in incorrect accounts. The Foreign Corrupt Practices Act has been criticized for placing U.S. companies at a disadvantage in dealing in international transactions. The present administration has adopted a policy of not strictly enforcing the FCPA.

SENTENCING OF WHITE-COLLAR CRIMINALS

Generally, the courts have been criticized for failing to sentence white-collar criminals to long prison terms or assessing sufficient fines in relation to the crimes they have committed.

In *Browder v. U.S.*, the federal judge discussed the sentencing of white-collar criminals in holding that a 25-year sentence of a white-collar criminal did not violate the Cruel and Unusual Punishment Clause of the U.S. Constitution.

PUNISHMENT FOR WHITE COLLAR CRIME

BROWDER v. UNITED STATES

398 F.SUPP. 1042 (1975)
UNITED STATES DISTRICT COURT, D. OREGON

Skopil, District Judge:

Petitioner seeks *habeas corpus* relief. . . . Petitioner, Edward Browder, alias James Chisum-Burns, was charged by federal indictments in Oregon, Florida, and California and by federal information in Georgia with pledging stolen securities transported in interstate commerce.

His pleas of guilty to all charges were accepted by the Court. On January 6, 1971, he was sentenced by The Honorable Gus J. Solomon, who imposed four ten-year terms and one five-year term, 25 years of which were to run consecutively. . . . He is presently incarcerated at the U.S. Penitentiary at McNeil Island in Washington.

Petitioner challenges the validity of his conviction and sentence on the following grounds: The sentence imposed constituted cruel and unusual pun-

ishment and denied petitioner equal protection of the law.

Edward Browder is a 53-year-old-man with extensive business experience in promotion and sales. He has a college background in aeronautical engineering. His testimony on the witness stand revealed a degree of intelligence and a facility with the English language that would be the pride of most attorneys. The quality of his *in forma pauperis* brief enhances that observation.

In 1958 Mr. Browder somehow became involved with organized crime. A crime syndicate apparently stole the bonds which he was indicted for transporting and pledging. . . . He moved to Ashland, Oregon, from Florida and assumed the name of James Chisum-Burns.

Petitioner . . . claims that the sentencing judge

relied upon erroneous information in petitioner's criminal record. This claim is based upon the sentencing judge's remark that petitioner was

> the worst crook that has ever come before this Court. . . . [His] record is one of the most abominable records I have ever seen.

These expressions of opinion may have been exaggerated but are not clearly refuted by petitioner's record.

Petitioner's final argument is that imposition of a twenty-five year sentence for his "white collar" property crimes constituted cruel and unusual punishment and violated equal protection of the law.

The basis for petitioner's claim is a study he conducted of 100 cases involving similar white-collar crimes. If accurate, his study contains startling statistics. Of the 100 defendants studied, 20% received fines, probation, or suspended sentences only for acts involving $350,000,000 or more. The others studied received light sentences for a variety of swindles in which the public became victim to members of the Mafia, labor union officials, mayors, attorneys, stockbrokers, business executives, bankers, a former state Attorney General, a governor, a federal judge, and others. As Mr. Browder observes,

> wherein the greater the offense against capital, the lesser the punishment imposed by the sentencing court.

If Mr. Browder's study is accurate, the pattern of sentencing revealed is deplorable. . . . If there is a logic to this parodox, it eludes me. I cannot reconcile a policy of sending poorly educated burglars from the ghetto to jail when men in the highest positions of public trust and authority receive judicial coddling when they are caught fleecing their constituencies. Penology's recent enchantment with rehabilitation as a wholesale justification for imprisonment has dissolved in the face of numerous studies proving that rehabilitation rarely occurs. A minority of the prison population are rightfully locked up because they are too dangerous to release. If we are to justify imprisonment for the rest, it must be on the grounds of punishment or deterrence. And if this is our premise, the white collar criminal must come to expect equal or greater treatment than the common, nonviolent thief. The consequences

of a white-collar property crime tend to reach a higher magnitude in direct proportion to the level of status and power held by the criminal involved. The men Browder studied abused their influence to defraud thousands of people throughout the country out of millions of dollars. Apparently this has been tolerated through light sentencing because of the staggering proportions of the crime.

The defect in Browder's reasoning is his conclusion that because other white-collar criminals have been receiving disparate treatment, he should too. As a matter of law, I cannot review the propriety of the sentence he received. The sentence was within statutory limits. Therefore it was a constitutional product of the trial court's discretion. (*United States v. Floyd*)

As a matter of jurisprudence, I will comment on his sentence in the context of his study. The sentencing judge may have shared my dismay, and Browder's, at the pattern of white collar crime sentences. White collar crime pays. It will continue to do so as long as judges endorse it through their sentencing policy. . . . I doubt that deterrence will be very effective until the "executive" becomes convinced that if he embarks on a criminal adventure, he will be severely—though proportionately—punished. Certainty is the key.

Edward Browder was convicted of pledging over $500,000 worth of stolen securities. He concedes his guilt for those crimes. The fact that they were accomplished by means of wit and charm rather than a burglar's tool does not minimize the damage done to the public. The judge who sentenced Browder obviously shared that view. It is a tragedy, if Browder's study is accurate, that fewer judges—and not more of them—subscribe to it also.

Petitioner's petition is *denied*.

CASE QUESTIONS

1. What crime had the petitioner Browder been convicted of committing? Was he the "worst crook" you've ever heard of?
2. What sentence did Browder receive from the court?
3. How did Browder argue that the sentence was "cruel and unusual" punishment? What was the *usual* sentence in a case like this?
4. Which of the following criminal defendants

should receive the greater punishment? Why?

a. "men in the highest positions of public trust and authority" who commit white-collar crimes

b. "poorly educated burglars from the ghetto"

Policy Issue. Should the punishment for white-collar crime be increased? Why or why not?

Economics Issue. If it is true that "the greater the offense against capital, the lesser the punish-

ment," if you are going to be a crook, how much should you steal?

Ethics Issue. Was it ethical for Browder to argue that he should receive a light sentence because other criminal defendants had previously received light sentences?

Social Responsibility. Do judges owe a duty of social responsibility to mete out harsher sentences? Or lighter sentences? Should judges have any discretion in passing out sentences?

Trend of the Law

With a larger percentage of the population working in white-collar positions, advances in technology, increased sophistication in the perpetration of crime, greater rewards for participating in criminal activity, and light sentences if a person is apprehended and convicted, white-collar crime has been on the increase in America. This trend is expected to continue in the future. Computer-assisted crimes in particular will increase as an area of white-collar crime in the future.

Crimes such as embezzlement, extortion, and bribery will exist as long as business exists. The dishonest business executive who participates in these criminal activities should expect to receive a severer sentence than those issued by the courts in the past. Moreover, even otherwise honest business managers are subject to criminal liability for failing to properly exercise their supervisory responsibilities over subordinates. This area of the law is presently in a state of development. Further, more cases such as *State v. Ford Motor Co.* are expected to be brought in the future to force business executives to correct defects in the products that they manufacture and distribute to consumers.

REVIEW QUESTIONS

1. Nolan was the office manager of the Federal Discount Corporation, a finance company that made loans and collections. As payments were received by the company they would be placed in the cash drawer. At the end of the day an accomplice would prepare a report showing the daily cash receipts. Nolan would then appropriate some of the cash from the drawer and split it with the accomplice. The accomplice would then recom-

pute the daily adding tapes to equal the remaining sum of cash. Nolan was charged with embezzlement and larceny. Which crime(s), if any, did Nolan commit?

2. Taylor drove a truck for the Utah By-Products Company. He would pick up scraps of meat from various places. He gave each customer a receipt that showed the weight of the items. The company would then issue a check to those customers. One of the customers, Hill Field Air Force Base, required payment in cash rather than by check. The company issued a check payable to Taylor, who would cash it and pay Hill Field. Taylor issued short-weighted slips to the customers other than Hill Field and he was therefore able to accumulate $84.25 worth of scraps. He then made out a slip for that amount showing a pickup at Hill Field. The scraps were delivered to the company and he was given a check payable to himself for that amount. He cashed the check and kept the money for himself. Taylor was charged with two counts of embezzlement, one for his activities in connection with Utah By-Products and one in connection with his activities with Hill Field. Was he guilty of embezzlement on either or both counts?

3. Jaffe purchased, from a police undercover officer, 20 yards of cloth that he believed was stolen. However, before Jaffe made the purchase, the police had actually arrested the real thief and had returned the cloth to the true owner. The true owner then consented to a police request that he allow them to offer to sell the cloth to Jaffe. Therefore, when Jaffe actually purchased the cloth from the undercover officer it was not stolen. Was Jaffe guilty of the crime of attempting to receive stolen property?

4. Ashley obtained a $7,200 loan from an elderly woman by promising her that the loan would be secured by a first mortgage on certain improved property owned by his corporation. Ashley, in fact, gave her no more than a note for that amount and when she later questioned him about it, he threatened to kill himself so that she could be repaid out of the proceeds on his life insurance. Ashley did not repay the loan. Could Ashley be convicted of the crime of obtaining property by false pretenses?

5. Brown knowingly drew up a number of fraudulent applications for third parties for loans that were available through the National Housing Act. Brown as well as all the individual applicants were convicted of conspiracy. Kotteakos, one applicant, appealed his conviction contending that, since there was no connection between himself and the other applicants shown at trial other than the fact that Brown had acted as a broker for each person, there was no evidence to show that he had participated in a conspiracy. Where one person deals with two or more persons who have no connection with each other, are they all necessarily guilty of a single conspiracy?

6. New York Central & Hudson River Railroad Company and one of its traffic managers were convicted of giving rebates to customers who made certain shipments. Under federal law at the time, all railroads were required to charge a set fee structured by the federal government. New York Central was found guilty of violating the Elkins Act, which provided that anything done or committed to be done by a corporation common carrier that would constitute a misdemeanor if done by one of its officers, agents,

etc., would be held to be a misdemeanor if committed by the corporation. Can a corporation commit a crime?

7. Beneficial Finance Company, two unrelated corporations, and two Beneficial employees, Farrell and Glynn, conspired to bribe and then actually bribed two officials of the Small Loans Regulatory Board. The conspiracy's purpose was to influence the Board to set a high maximum interest rate on certain loans within its jurisdiction. Glynn was the direct contact with the bribed officials, while Farrell supervised Glynn's conspiratorial activities and chaired the intercorporate meeting during which the bribery plan was eventually adopted. Can Beneficial be held liable for the criminal acts which were committed?

8. Several defendants were tried en masse and convicted of violating the Racketeer Influenced and Corrupt Organizations Act (RICO). They had essentially agreed to participate in a criminal enterprise to produce a profit; however, they had individually committed crimes in furtherance of the enterprise of which the other defendants were not aware. All the defendants appealed, arguing that it was improper to try them together and to present evidence of multiple conspiracies when they were only being charged with collectively entering into one single overall conspiracy. If defendants are charged with conspiracy to engage in criminal enterprise under RICO rather than conspiracy to commit a crime, is it proper to try them jointly and to introduce evidence of the specific crimes that each participated in to further the conspiracy despite the fact that some of the defendants might not have had knowledge of or participated in those particular crimes?

9. Davis, the elected Sheriff of Mahoning County, Ohio, through threats and extortion forced a number of his deputies to make monthly "contributions" to a special "flower fund," a war chest used by Davis in his political campaigns. Davis threatened the deputies with possible loss of job assignments or dismissal from employment if they did not contribute. Wallace, a local businessman, conducted a program that provided escorts for trucks and other vehicles which failed to comply with state vehicle weight and size limitations. Escorts were provided by Sheriff's department vehicles. On several occasions Wallace received bribes from the truckers who were escorted. Could Davis and Wallace be prosecuted together under the Racketeer Influenced and Corrupt Organizations Act?

10. Tri-No Enterprises was faced with a severe financial crisis. In an attempt to rectify the situation, Starnes, the firm's president, entered into a conspiracy with Roland to set fire to the building housing the firm. Shortly before the building was destroyed, Starnes increased his insurance coverage on the building, and immediately after the fire occurred he mailed a fraudulent claim to the insurer. The federal prosecutor investigated the suspicious circumstances surrounding the fire and eventually discovered the conspiracy. Could he prosecute Roland and Starnes for any violation of the Racketeer Influenced and Corrupt Organizations Act?

11. Decker, a shareholder, bought a new issue of stock from an American-based corporation, Massey-Ferguson, and later sued the company, contending that the corporation had made false and misleading statements as well as material omissions on its registration statement. One accusation

alleged that the document did not disclose that some of Massey's foreign subsidiaries had made illegal bribes to foreign officials. Specifically, Decker alleged that Massey made payments, as a matter of course, to stimulate new business deals. These "facilitating" payments were made in the form of nonrecorded consulting contracts with high-level foreign government officials who had discretion in carrying out government functions. If these allegations were true, did Massey violate the Foreign Corrupt Practices Act? If so, what provisions were violated?

VI

THE EMPLOYER-EMPLOYEE RELATION

25 Labor Unions

INTRODUCTION

One of the most important factors in conducting business in the United States, as well as in many other countries, is the constant conflict between management and workers over compensation, fringe benefits, and other aspects of the employment relation. In America, workers often join together to form a labor union to represent them in negotiations with management. In order to protect and regulate dealings between large companies and equally powerful labor unions, the federal government has enacted and enforces an integrated statutory scheme of labor laws. This chapter covers the laws regarding the organization of labor unions in the United States, collective bargaining between unions and management over salary and other benefits, strikes and picketing by union members, and other aspects of the labor-management relation in this country. Chapter 26 discusses discrimination in employment, and Chapter 27 covers occupational safety laws.

The American economy became highly industrialized during the period 1865–1914. Craft societies, to which most skilled workers belonged during this period, promoted individual negotiation between employees and employers. The Knights of Labor, one of the first attempts at organizing labor in the United States, was formed in 1880. The Knights of Labor not only included workingmen, but also allowed farmers and capitalists to be members. The Knights of Labor advocated moral and reformist goals. The organization disappeared around 1900.

The American Federation of Labor.   In 1886, under the leadership of Samuel Gompers, the American Federation of Labor (AFL) was formed. The AFL was originally composed mostly of craft workers. Semiskilled and unskilled workers were not permitted membership in the AFL. In contrast to many unions in European countries, the AFL rejected the idea of becoming a separate political party, and accepted capitalism as an economic system, rather than advocating communism or socialism.

The Congress of Industrial Organizations.   In 1935, after an attempt to take over the AFL, John L. Lewis formed the Congress of Industrial Organizations (CIO). The CIO allowed semiskilled and unskilled workers to become members. It originally had considerable Communist influence within its leadership.

AFL-CIO.   In 1955, after competing for members for approximately 20 years, the AFL and the CIO combined to form a new federation known as the AFL-CIO. Unions that had a substantial Communist influence were suspended from the AFL-CIO. The AFL-CIO remains one of the largest and most powerful union organizations in the United States. Most of the largest unions in America (e.g., Teamsters, United Auto Workers, United Steel Workers) are presently composed of manufacturing and blue collar workers.

FEDERAL LABOR LAW

Labor law in the United States is currently based on four major pieces of federal legislation:

1. the Norris-LaGuardia Act (1932)
2. the National Labor Relations Act (1935)
3. the Taft-Hartley Act (1947)
4. the Landrum-Griffin Act (1959).

In the interests of promoting a uniform national labor policy, federal labor law supersedes state labor law in most circumstances. States, however, have jurisdiction in enacting and administering other laws that affect workers, including workers' compensation laws, unemployment laws, and employment safety laws.

The Norris-LaGuardia Act.   With the advent of the Depression, and the government's New Deal programs of the 1930s, sympathy for industrial unionism increased. In 1932, Congress passed the Norris-LaGuardia Act. The major feature of the Act was that it removed the power of federal courts to enjoin union activity unless such activity involved "fraud or violence." The federal courts often ignored the Act, or found union violence in order to escape the provisions of the Act.

The National Labor Relations Act. In 1935, Congress enacted the National Labor Relations Act (NLRA). The NLRA established the right of employees to form, join, or assist labor organizations, to bargain collectively with their employers, and to engage in concerted activity for the purpose of collective bargaining or mutual aid and protection. The NLRA also places an affirmative duty upon employers to bargain and deal in "good faith" with unions. The NLRA is the heart of labor law in America.

The Taft-Hartley Act. During the period 1945–1947, industry-wide strikes in the rail, maritime, coal, lumber, oil, and textile industries, multifirm strikes in the automobile industry, and numerous community-oriented strikes devastated the country. Public sympathy for unions waned. In 1947, Congress passed the *Labor Management Relations Act* (the "Taft-Hartley Act") to curtail abuses by "labor bosses" and to curb unfair labor practices.

The Landrum-Griffin Act. After the discovery of substantial corruption in labor unions, in 1959 Congress enacted the *Labor Management Reporting and Disclosure Act* (the "Landrum-Griffin Act"). The Act imposes regulation on the internal affairs of labor unions and the election of union leaders, and establishes a bill of rights for union members.

The Sherman Antitrust Act of 1890, which prohibited any "combination or conspiracy in restraint of trade," was used to combat early union attempts to organize. In 1917, Congress enacted the Clayton Antitrust Act, which generally *exempted* labor unions from antitrust laws and expressly barred the use of injunctions against labor union organizing. The courts, however, ignored the literal reading of the Clayton Act and continued to apply antitrust prohibitions to thwart union organization until the Norris-LaGuardia Act was passed in 1932.

The National Labor Relations Board. The NLRA is administered by the National Labor Relations Board (NLRB). The NLRB is composed of five members, appointed by the President with Senate approval. The Board is supported by an Office of General Counsel, field agents, and other staff personnel. The main functions of the NLRB are (1) to conduct elections for unions for designated bargaining units and (2) to decide by the administrative hearing process whether a challenged management or union activity constitutes an "unfair labor practice" under the NLRA.

Compulsory Union Membership. In many instances, unions attempt to negotiate some form of *compulsory* union membership as a provision of a collective bargaining agreement (union "security clause"). Union security clauses include: (1) a "closed shop," (2) a "union shop," and (3) an "agency shop."

Closed Shop. In a "closed shop," membership in a union is required *before* hiring, and is made a condition of employment. A closed shop is illegal under Sections 8(a)(3) and 8(f) of the NLRA. Closed shops were made unlawful on the rationale that if union membership were required prior to employment, nonunion employees would be discriminated against in hiring decisions.

Union Shop. In "union shop," membership in a union is compulsory only *after* an employee is hired. The argument for a union shop is that once a union is recognized, the union should be entitled to protection from "free rider" nonunion employees who would take advantage of the union's negotiations with management without having to pay union fees. By requiring all employees of the covered employment group to join the union, the union can avoid the free rider problem. Where there is a "union shop," new employees generally have a 30-day grace period after being hired in which to join the union. Union shops are legal in the United States.

Agency Shop. In an "agency shop," union membership is *not* required even after employment, but all employees are required to pay union dues and initiation fees. The reason for having an "agency shop" is to avoid the "free rider" problem while allowing employees to choose not to join the union if they so desire. An "agency shop" is a legal union security agreement in the United States. In *Oil, Chemical & Atomic Workers International Union, AFL-CIO v. Mobil Oil Corp.*, 426 U.S. 407 (1976), the U.S. Supreme Court stated:

Under Section 8(3) of the Wagner Act, enacted in 1935, closed shops, union shops, and agency shops were all permitted. But in 1947, in Section (a)(3), as added by the Taft-Hartley Act, Congress reacted to widespread abuses of closed-shop agreements by banning such arrangements. Union and agency shops were still permitted, however, by Section 8(a)(3).

[C]ongress' decision to allow union-security agreements at all reflects its concern that, at least as a matter of federal law, the parties to a collective-bargaining agreement be allowed to provide that there be no employees who are getting the benefits of union representation without paying for them.

Where a valid union shop or agency shop agreement exists, an employer is required by law, if properly notified by the union, to deduct union dues from employees' wages ("checkoff" provision) and forward the dues to the union. Further, where a valid union shop agreement exists and a new employee's 30-day grace period for joining the union has passed, on notification by the union the employer is required by law to discharge the employee for not joining the union within the allotted period.

State "Right-to-Work" Laws. Section 14(b) of the NLRA provides that states may enact "right-to-work" laws that make all forms of union security agreements illegal. Where a "right-to-work" law has been properly enacted by a state's legislature, employees in the state cannot be required to join a union even where a union has been properly elected by the bargaining unit to which the employees belong. By making "union shops" and "agency shops" illegal, right-to-work laws substantially erode the power of unions. Approximately half the states have enacted "right-to-work" laws. The passage of "right-to-work" laws is generally encouraged by management and fought bitterly by unions.

In *Oil, Chemical & Atomic Workers International Union, AFL-CIO v. Mobil Oil Corp.* the U.S. Supreme Court held that a state's "right-to-work" law did not void an agency shop agreement that covered maritime employees who performed most of their work on the high seas.

"RIGHT TO WORK" LAW

OIL, CHEMICAL & ATOMIC WORKERS INTERNATIONAL UNION, AFL-CIO v. MOBIL OIL CORP.

426 U.S. 407 (1976)
UNITED STATES SUPREME COURT

Mr. Justice Marshall delivered the opinion of the Court.

Section 8(a)(3) of the National Labor Relations Act, permits employers as a matter of federal law to enter into agreements with unions to establish union or agency shops. Section 14(b) of the Act, however, allows individual States and Territories to exempt themselves from Section 8(a)(3) and to enact so-called "right-to-work" laws prohibiting union or agency shops.

Petitioners (hereinafter Union) represent the unlicensed seamen who work on respondent employer's oil tankers. In November 1969 the Union and respondent entered into a collective-bargaining agreement which provided for an agency shop:

> For the duration of the Agreement all employees hired shall, as a condition of employment, become members of the Union and/or in the alternative pay the regular union dues and initiation fees within 31 days from the employment date.

Almost two years after entering into the agreement, respondent filed suit in the United States District Court for the Eastern District of Texas . . . , claiming that the agency-shop provision was invalid and unenforceable because it violated Texas' right-to-work laws.

Respondent is a division of Mobil Oil Corp., a New York corporation, and operates a fleet of eight oceangoing tankers which transport respondent's petroleum products from Texas to Atlantic coast

ports. Respondent is headquartered in Beaumont, Tex., and maintains its personnel records there. Sixty percent of the applications to be unlicensed seamen on respondent's ships are made in Beaumont and 40 percent in New York. The final hiring decisions are made in Beaumont. Of the 289 unlicensed seamen who are employed to man the tankers, 123 maintain residence in Texas, and 60 in New York.

A typical trip by one of respondent's tankers from Beaumont, the Texas port, to Providence or New York, the Atlantic ports, takes from 4½ to 5 days. Loading and unloading in port takes from 18 to 30 hours. No more than 10 percent to 20 percent of the seamen's work time is spent within the territorial bounds of Texas. . . . Based on the above evidence, fully reflected in its findings of fact, the District Court concluded that

> [t]he acts performed in the State of Texas in the administration and performance of the collective bargaining agreement are such that the State of Texas is intimately concerned with the collective bargaining agreement and with the employees working thereunder.

Relying on this "intimate concern," the court held that the Texas right-to-work laws were applicable under Section 14(b) and that the agency-shop provision was therefore void and unenforceable. . . . A three-member division of the United States Court of Appeals for the Fifth Circuit, one judge dissenting, reversed.

Having concluded that predominant *job situs* is the controlling factor in determining whether, under Section 14(b), a State can apply its right-to-work laws to a given employment relationship, the disposition of this case is clear. Because most of the employees' work is done on the high seas, outside the territorial bounds of the State of Texas, Texas' right-to-work laws cannot govern the validity of the agency-shop provision at issue here. It is immaterial that Texas may have more contacts than any other State with the employment relationship in this case, since there is no reason to conclude under Section 14(b) that in every employment situation *some* State or Territory's law with respect to union-security agreements must be applicable. Federal policy favors permitting such agreements unless a State or Territory with a sufficient interest in the relationship expresses a contrary policy via right-to-work laws. It is therefore fully consistent with national labor policy to conclude, if the predominant job situs is outside the boundary of any State, that no State has a sufficient interest in the employment relationship and that no State's right-to-work laws can apply.

Accordingly, the judgment of the Court of Appeals is *reversed*.

Mr. Justice Stewart, with whom **Mr. Justice Rehnquist** joins, dissenting.

In conclusion, I believe that the place of hiring is the critical factor in determining the choice of law for union-security agreements. But even if the place where the work is to be performed is the criterion, Texas law should still be applied, since under this collective-bargaining agreement more work is performed in that State than in any other, and Congress has refrained from either establishing or indicating a need for a uniform rule to the contrary in maritime employment. I would, therefore, affirm the judgment before us.

CASE QUESTIONS

1. What do the following types of union security agreements provide? Which are legal?
   a. closed shop
   b. agency shop
   c. union shop
2. Why do unions want security agreements? What is the "free rider" problem? Explain.
3. What is a "right-to-work" law? Who enacts such a law? What effect does it have on union security agreements?
4. In this case, where did the Supreme Court determine the *job situs* of the workers to be? Did the Texas right-to-work law apply? Explain.

Policy Issue. Should a worker be forced to join or pay for a union under an agency shop or union shop agreement when he does not want to join or support the union? Why or why not?

Economics Issue. What are the economic consequences when a state enacts a right-to-work law? Explain.

Ethics Issue. Did either party, company or union, act unethically in this case? Why or why not?

Social Responsibility. Does a state legislature owe a duty of social responsibility to enact a "right-to-work" law? Or to allow union security agreements?

ORGANIZING A UNION

The most important provision of the labor laws is Section 7 of the NLRA, which gives employees the right to band together to form unions. This right is protected by Section 8(a) of the NLRA, which makes it an "unfair labor practice" for an employer to interfere with, coerce, or restrain employees from exercising their rights to form and join unions under Section 7.

Under Section 8(a)(2) of the NLRA, an employer may not form a "company union," nor dominate or assist (e.g., solicit membership, provide financial assistance) in the formation of a union. The rationale for this rule is that a company-dominated union would not truly represent the interests of the employees. Where two rival unions are competing to organize the employees of an employer, the employer must remain neutral with regard to the contests and election. For example, if an employer makes company facilities available to one union, it must do so for all competing unions.

Employees' rights to organize a union under Section 7 of the NLRA often conflict with the employer's free speech and property rights. The courts have tried to fashion rules to balance these competing interests.

Right of Free Speech. An employer is guaranteed the right to free speech by the Constitution. An employer may give *non*coercive antiunion speeches to its employees on company time and property without giving the union the right to plead its own cause similarly. However, because of the economic power wielded by an employer, certain statements by an employer to its employees may be construed as an "unfair labor practice." For example, a threat of force or reprisal by an employer to its employees (e.g., "I'll close this plant if the union comes in here") is an unfair labor practice in violation of Section 8(a) of the NLRA. However, statements by an employer based on objective facts, such as "You may be replaced if you strike," or "The union will make costly demands that will reduce the number of employees" are constitutionally protected.

A union is guaranteed the right to free speech by the Constitution. However, if a union's statement to an employee is coercive, e.g., "join the union or you'll lose your job," it is an unfair labor practice that violates Section 8(b) of the NLRA. Section 8(b) applies to both physical coercion—threats of violence against employees—and to economic coercion—threat of loss of benefits. Under agency law, a union is held responsible for the coercive acts of union subordinates. Expressions of opinions by a union, no matter how insulting (e.g., "You rotten scab!"), are absolutely protected by the Constitution. Unions are provided greater latitude of free speech under Section 8(b) than employers are allowed under Section 8(a).

Organizing Activities on Company-Owned Property.

The legality of union organizing activities on company-owned property depends on the extent to which these activities are carried on by employees or nonemployees, and whether union solicitation and organizing activities by employees are carried on during work time or during off-hours.

Generally, where the union solicitation is conducted by *employees,* their employer may restrict such prounion activities to the employee's free time, such as coffee breaks, lunch, before and after work. Further, an employer may restrict employee union activities to *nonworking areas*—parking lots, cafeteria, restrooms, exits, etc. An employer may generally bar off-duty employees from union solicitation on company premises. If an employee violates any of these rules (e.g., participates in union solicitation during work hours), the employer may "discipline" the employee, which includes the right to fire him or her.

An employer may generally prohibit *nonemployee* union organizers from union solicitation anywhere on company property. The Supreme Court has held that there is an exception to this rule where the union has no other "alternative" means of communicating with the employees and the property has taken on some of the attributes of "public" property, as in the case of a company town.

In *Whitcraft Houseboat Division,* the National Labor Relations Board upheld a corporation's dismissal of two employees for engaging in union solicitation during work hours.

union meetings during work hours is grounds for firing

UNION SOLICITATION

WHITCRAFT HOUSEBOAT DIVISION, NORTH AMERICAN ROCKWELL CORPORATION v. INTERNATIONAL ASSOCIATION OF MACHINISTS AND AEROSPACE WORKERS, AFL-CIO

195 NLRB 1046 (1972)
NATIONAL LABOR RELATIONS BOARD

By **Chairman Miller** and members **Fanning** and **Jenkins**

By registered letter dated April 23, 1971, which was received by the Company on Monday, April 26, the Union notified the Company that it was seeking to organize its employees. According to uncontradicted testimony, on the morning of April 26, Assistant Plant Manager Leo Carty began his regular morning tour through the plant at about 7:15 A.M. When Carty walked into Plant No. 2, where assembly work is performed, he found a group of employees conversing with a fellow employee. This was about 15 minutes after starting time and Carty observed that none of the people had started to work. As Carty approached, some of the employees dispersed, and he told the others to go to work. Carty encountered similar situations in two other areas of the plant. In each instance, it was necessary for him to instruct the employees to go back to work. When he completed his tour of the plant, he reported the problem he had encountered to General Manager Fritz Weiss.

It is undisputed that the employees continued to congregate in groups during working hours for the remainder of April 26, all day on April 27, and throughout the morning of April 28. As a result, there was a substantial adverse effect on production. During these 3 days, production in three departments was down by almost 50 percent.

[T]he plant no-solicitation rule . . . was posted on the bulletin boards by Carty at about 11 A.M. on April 28:

> As you well know working time is for work. No one will be allowed to solicit or distribute literature during our working time, that is, when he or she should be working. Anyone doing so and neglecting his work or interfering (*sic*) with the work of another employee will be subject to discharge. Any other rule concerning solicitation is no longer effective.

The Company also mailed to each of its employees a "Dear Whitcraft Employee" letter which contained the revised no-solicitation rule.

Although Daniel and Wolfram engaged in oral union solicitation during working time with two other employees for a period of about 20 minutes on April 30, the Trial Examiner nevertheless found that the men were in fact discharged because of their union activities and not for violating the revised no-solicitation rule, because he reasoned in this connection that the conversation was a single isolated instance and was "intermittent" and "rather brief"; Respondent's firing of the men was precipitate; the discharge was contemporaneous with the beginning of the union campaign; . . . .

[T]he Company had the right to enforce the rule against Daniel and Wolfram according to its terms. The conduct of these two men plainly violated the rule, which specified that anyone engaged in such prohibited activity "will be subject to discharge."

Finally, the timing of the discharge must be viewed realistically. True, it occurred shortly after the Respondent became aware of the union campaign. But any discipline for violating a valid no-solicitation rule which is caused by an employee's prohibited solicitation of union support or membership is bound to occur during a union campaign. In this context, therefore, our usual presumptions about timing have little applicability.

Upon review of the record as a whole, we are persuaded that Daniel and Wolfram were discharged for their misconduct in violating a valid rule.

Accordingly, we shall *dismiss* this allegation of the complaint.

CASE QUESTIONS

1. Was there a union which represented the employees at Whitcraft? Or was a union *attempting* to organize the employees?
2. What did the "no-solicitation" rule of Whitcraft provide? Was it lawful under federal labor law?
3. What did Leo Carty find the employees doing on his rounds? Was it during company time? Did production suffer because of the activities of the employees? Explain.

4. What did the company do to Daniel and Wolfson? Was this legal?
5. Would the decision of this case have been different if the union solicitation of Daniel and Wolfson had taken place during any of the following?
   a. before work in the company parking lot
   b. during a coffee break on company property
   c. during lunch in the company cafeteria
   d. after work in the company parking lot
   e. at a bowling alley during off hours
   f. at the opera during off hours

Policy Issue. Should employees be fired for participating in union solicitation activities during work time? Why or why not?

Economics Issue. Does the "no solicitation on company time" rule have any economic consequences? If it is violated?

Ethics Issue. Is it ethical for an employee to use company work time to discuss forming a union?

Social Responsibility. Do companies owe a duty of social responsibility to allow their employees to discuss the formation of a union and to solicit union members during working hours? Why or why not?

"Appropriate Bargaining Unit." The employees of an entire corporation do not usually belong to the same union. Often several unions are represented among a corporations' employees. Before a union may be recognized through an election as the bargaining agent of employees, the "appropriate bargaining unit" must be determined. There are no objective standards as to which employees constitute an "appropriate bargaining unit." The courts have held that any group of employees who share a "mutuality of interest" (e.g., similar skills, hours, wages) may be designated as the *appropriate bargaining unit* for organization by a union. Appropriate bargaining units often are defined by a common employer, craft unit, plant, or any subdivision thereof.

Professional employees (e.g., managers, engineers) and security guards may not be included in the "bargaining unit." Managers and other professionals within a corporation may not generally belong to unions because they are part of "management." Security guards may not join unions that represent other types of employees, but may form their own unions.

Petition for Election. At some point after initial organizational activities, the union attempting to organize the employees will call for an election of the employees of the "appropriate bargaining unit" to determine whether the employees want the union to represent them. An election is usually initiated by filing a *petition* with the National Labor Relations Board (NLRB). The NLRB is responsible for supervising the conduct of the election. Although usually a petition for an election is filed by the union, an employer may file the petition when it is presented with a union demand for recognition.

The NLRB will not investigate a petition for an election unless the petitioner produces evidence which shows that at least 30 percent of the employees of the "appropriate bargaining unit" favor the certification of a particular union. The evidence of support may be shown by producing union membership cards, dues receipts, authorization cards, or petitions signed by employees constituting at least 30 percent of the appropriate bargaining unit. After such a showing of support is made, the NLRB will hold a hearing and proceed with its investigation of the matter. If its findings are favorable, the NLRB will set a date in the future for the holding of the election to determine if the employees want the union to represent them.

Once a petition for an election has been filed with the NLRB, the employer must give the petitioners a list of all of its employees. This list is commonly referred to as the "*Excelsior* list," after the case in which it was held that such a list is mandatory. A petition for election may be withdrawn at any time. However, a new petition may not be filed for six months after a petition has been withdrawn. Unions often file an initial petition for an election only to obtain the *Excelsior* list, then withdraw the petition to spend the next six months organizing the employees for a later election. The NLRB will refuse to proceed with an election, even if the petitioner has supplied evidence of sufficient support, in three situations:

1. if a valid election by the members of the appropriate bargaining unit for any union, even where the union lost, has been held within the past 12 months
2. if there is a unremedied union "unfair labor practice"
3. if the employees of the appropriate bargaining unit are presently represented by a union under an existing collective bargaining agreement.

In the latter situation, which is commonly referred to as the *contract bar rule,* a new election may not be held for the duration of the collective bargaining agreement, or three years, whichever is shorter. The "contract bar" rule does not apply to collective bargaining agreements without a fixed term, where the former union has died out, or where a "change in circumstances" (e.g., the employer merges with another company, or materially expands operations) justifies disregarding the prior collective bargaining agreement.

Cooling-Off Period.   Generally, neither a union nor an employer may require employees to attend *speeches* during the 24-hour period preceding a representative election. This 24-hour period is commonly referred to as the *cooling-off period*. Dissemination of campaign literature by both sides, the use of the media (e.g., radio advertisements), and voluntary attendance by employees at meetings held by either management or a union are generally allowed during the cooling-off period.

"Eleventh-Hour" Statements. The courts have held that neither the union nor the employer may make statements in any form so near the election that the other party "does not have sufficient time to respond" to the statement. Any statement that falls within this rule is commonly referred to as an "eleventh-hour" statement. The "eleventh-hour" statement rule applies to the dissemination of information even before the "cooling-off" period. The purpose of the eleventh-hour rule is to prevent either side from making a false representation so near the election that the other side will not have time to reply to the statement. If an "eleventh-hour" statement contains a factual misrepresentation, the NLRB may set the election aside. The NLRB reaffirmed this view in this matter in *General Knit of California, Inc.*, 239 NLRB 619 (1972), where it stated:

[A]n election should be set aside only where there has been a misrepresentation or other similar campaign trickery, which involves a substantial departure from the truth, at a time which prevents the other party or parties from making an effective reply, so that the misrepresentation, whether deliberate or not, may reasonably be expected to have a significant impact on the election.

Types of Elections. Once evidence of union support has been shown, and the NLRB completes its investigation of the *petition*, the election for the union is held. In a union election, each union that is trying to organize the employees of the appropriate bargaining unit, and the alternative of "no union," must be on the ballot. There are several types of elections that may be held in selecting a union as a bargaining representative, including:

1. a contested election
2. a run-off election
3. a consent election
4. a certification election.

Contested Election. Where the employees and employer cannot agree on the bargaining unit, on the employees eligible to vote, or when or where an election is to be held, the election is called a *contested election.* Where there is a contested election, the NLRB must investigate the petition for election and monitor the election. The majority of union elections are contested elections. A simple majority vote for any union, or for the choice of "no union," wins. If a union obtains the necessary vote, the NLRB will *certify* the union as the official representative of the bargaining unit. If no union is selected, the employer is free from another union election for at least 12 months.

Run-Off Election Where two or more unions are trying to organize the same employees and are on the ballot and no single union or the alternative of "no union" receives a simple *majority* of the votes, a run-off election must be held between the top two vote-receiving alternatives, whether these are two unions or one union and the alternative of "no union." The NLRB must supervise the run-off election.

Consent Election. Where the employees and employer agree as to (1) the employees who make up the appropriate bargaining unit, (2) that the union has shown sufficient evidence of support to hold an election, and (3) when and where an election is to be held, the union and management may agree to hold a "consent election." A consent election may be held without either a hearing or supervision by the NLRB, because all the parties have consented to the holding of the election and to the result of a valid election.

Certification Election. Where a union provides the employer with the necessary evidence of support, and the employer recognizes and bargains with the union, the union may still wish to petition the NLRB to hold a certification election. A certification election requires an NLRB hearing and supervision of the election, and formally recognizes the union as the bargaining agent of the employees.

Employer Interference With an Election. The U.S. Supreme Court has held that an election for a union should ideally take place under "laboratory conditions" without *undue influence* by the employer. An election will be set aside where an employer "unduly influences" the vote of its employees. For example, an employer showing a motion picture on the eve of an election that falsely implied violence by union strikers and an employer injecting racial prejudice into an election have both been held to constitute undue influence by an employer on a union election.

An employer may not withhold *or* increase economic benefits of employees (e.g., increase wages, institute overtime pay, provide additional vacation time or holidays) to influence a union election. The denial or confirmation of benefits by an employer on the eve of an election is considered an "unfair labor practice" for which an election may be set aside by the NLRB. This rule applies even if the increased benefits are permanent and unconditional. The rationale behind this rule is that the employer may be reminding the employees of its power over them.

Where either management or a union has violated the employees' right to organize under Section 7 of the NLRA, the courts may grant any one of a number of remedies, including:

1. issuing a cease-and-desist order, which is usually directed against specific conduct
2. issuing a temporary injunction in an "emergency" situation to restrain employer or union conduct
3. issuing an order for affirmative action, such as reinstatement of an employee, posting of notices
4. setting an election aside and ordering a new election.

Where a union has been found guilty of coercive statement or act in violation of Section 8(b), the NLRB may set the election aside.

In *NLBR v. Exchange Parts Co.* (1964), the Supreme Court held that a company which had conferred additional benefits on its employees on the eve of a union election unlawfully interfered with the election in violation of the National Labor Relations Act.

[handwritten: anything to interfere w/ employee — is an unfair labor practice]

[handwritten: can't promise employees things to interfer w/ union elections]

EMPLOYER INTERFERENCE WITH UNION ELECTION

NATIONAL LABOR RELATIONS BOARD v. EXCHANGE PARTS CO.

375 U.S. 405 (1964)
UNITED STATES SUPREME COURT

Mr. Justice Harlan delivered the opinion of the Court.

The respondent, Exchange Parts Company, is engaged in the business of rebuilding automobile parts in Fort Worth, Texas. Prior to November 1959 its employees were not represented by a union. On November 9, 1959, the International Brotherhood of Boilermakers, Iron Shipbuilders, Blacksmiths, Forgers and Helpers, AFL-CIO, advised Exchange Parts that the union was conducting an organizational campaign at the plant and that a majority of the employees had designated the union as their bargaining representative. On November 16 the union petitioned the Labor Board for a representation election. The Board conducted a hearing on December 29, and on February 19, 1960, issued an order directing that an election be held. The election was held on March 18, 1960.

At two meetings on November 4 and 5, 1959, C. V. McDonald, the Vice-President and General Manager of Exchange Parts, announced to the employees that their "floating holiday" in 1959 would fall on December 26 and that there would be an additional "floating holiday" in 1960. On February 25, six days after the Board issued its election order, Exchange Parts held a dinner for employees at which Vice President McDonald told the employees that they could decide whether the extra day of vacation in 1960 would be a "floating holiday" or would be taken on their birthdays. The employees voted for the latter. McDonald also referred to the forthcoming representation election as one in which, in the words of the trial examiner, the employees would "determine whether . . . [they] wished to hand over their right to speak and act for themselves." He stated that the union had distorted some of the facts and pointed out the benefits obtained by the employees without a union. He urged all the employees to vote in the election.

On March 4 Exchange Parts sent its employees a letter which spoke of "the *Empty Promises* of

the Union" and "the *fact* that *it is the Company that puts things in your envelope.. . .*" After mentioning a number of benefits, the letter said:

> The Union can't put any of those things in your envelope—*only the Company can do that.* . . . [I]t didn't take a Union to get any of those things and . . . it won't take a Union to get additional improvements in the future.

Accompanying the letter was a detailed statement of the benefits granted by the company since 1949 and an estimate of the monetary value of such benefits to the employees. Included in the statement of benefits for 1960 were the birthday holiday, a new system for computing overtime during holiday weeks which had the effect of increasing wages for those weeks, and a new vacation schedule which enabled employees to extend their vacations by sandwiching them between two weekends. Although Exchange Parts asserts that the policy behind the latter two benefits was established earlier, it is clear that the letter of March 4 was the first general announcement of the changes to the employees. In the ensuing election the union lost.

The Board, affirming the findings of the trial examiner, found that the announcement of the birthday holiday and the grant and announcement of overtime and vacation benefits were arranged by Exchange Parts with the intention of inducing the employees to vote against the union. It found that this conduct violated Section 8(a)(1) of the National Labor Relations Act and issued an appropriate order. . . . [T]he Court of Appeals . . . denied enforcement of the Board's order. It believed that it was not an unfair labor practice under Section 8(a)(1) for an employer to grant benefits to its employees in these circumstances.

Section 8(a)(1) makes it an unfair labor practice for an employer

> to interfere with, restrain, or coerce employees in the exercise of the rights guaranteed in Section 7.

The broad purpose of Section 8(a)(1) is to establish "the right of employees to organize for mutual aid without employer interference." *Republic Aviation Corp. v. Labor Board.* We have no doubt that it prohibits not only intrusive threats and promises but also conduct immediately favorable to employees which is undertaken with the express purpose of impinging upon their freedom of choice for or against unionization and is reasonably calculated to have that effect. In *Medo Photo Supply Corp. v. Labor Board,* this Court said:

> The action of employees with respect to the choice of their bargaining agents may be induced by favors bestowed by the employer as well as by his threats of domination.

The danger inherent in well-timed increases in benefits is the suggestion of a fist inside the velvet glove. Employees are not likely to miss the inference that the source of benefits now conferred is also the source from which future benefits must flow and which may dry up if it is not obliged.

The beneficence of an employer is likely to be *ephemeral* if prompted by a threat of unionization which is subsequently removed. Insulating the right of collective organization from calculated good will of this sort deprives employees of little that has lasting value.

Reversed.

CASE QUESTIONS

1. What union attempted to organize the employees of Exchange Parts Co.?

2. On what dates did the following activities take place?
   a. organizational campaign began
   b. petition for election filed
   c. order for election issued by the NLRB
   d. employee dinner (what was announced?)
   e. letter to employees (what did it say?)
   g. election
3. Did the union win or lose the election? What did the union then do?
4. What does NLRA Section 8(a)(1) provide? Was this section found to have been violated by the company in this case?

Policy Issue. Should a company be prohibited from either giving or taking away benefits of employees in its fight with a union? Why or why not?

Economics Issue. Do you think the granting of a floating holiday, increased overtime pay, and a more flexible vacation schedule affected the outcome of the election in this case? Can employees be "bought"?

Ethics Issue. Were the activities of the Exchange Parts Co. ethical? Did these activities constitute a "fist in a velvet glove"? Why or why not?

Social Responsibility. Do companies owe a duty of social responsibility not to attempt to influence union elections? Why or why not?

COLLECTIVE BARGAINING

Once an election has been held, and a union has been chosen by the employees and certified as the bargaining agent for the appropriate bargaining unit, the process of bargaining between the union and employer over employment benefits begins. This process is commonly referred to as *collective bargaining,* and has as its goal the negotiation and execution of a collective bargaining agreement between the union and management that contains the terms and conditions of employment of union members.

Under Section 9(a) of the NLRA, the union has exclusive authority to represent *all* employees of the bargaining unit. An employer and union members may not negotiate and enter into individual contracts unless the contracts do not conflict with the collective bargaining agreement. The collective bargaining agreement is paramount over all other labor contracts, because courts have held that the employer should not be subjected to individual employee demands as well as union demands, and an officially elected union's right to bargain on behalf of all employees should not be undermined by its own members.

Subjects of Collective Bargaining.   The matters that can be the subjects of collective bargaining have been classified into three categories by the NLRA and the courts: (1) compulsory subjects, (2) illegal subjects, and (3) permissive subjects.

Compulsory Subjects.   Section 8(d) of the NLRA classifies "wages, hours, and other terms and conditions of employment" as *compulsory* subjects of collective bargaining. Compulsory subjects *must* be bargained for in good faith by both the union and management. In addition to "wages, salaries, and hours," the courts have held that items such as retirement plans, fringe benefits, health benefits, work assignments, and safety rules are "terms and conditions of employment" that are compulsory subjects of collective bargaining. The statutory language, "other terms and conditions of employment," has been given a broad definition by the NLRB and the courts.

Illegal Subjects.   Certain subjects have been held by the courts to be "illegal" subjects of collective bargaining that cannot be bargained for between the union and employer. Examples of illegal subjects that cannot be bargained for between management and the union are requests for "closed shops" and demands for preferential or discriminatory hiring of union members.

Permissive Subjects.   All subjects of employment that are not required to be bargained for as "compulsory" subjects, or prohibited from negotiation as "illegal" subjects, fall into a third residual category called *permissive* subjects of collective bargaining. Permissive subjects of collective bargaining include the size and composition of a supervisory force, corporate organization, location of plants, and other general business practices that affect the employment relation.

Generally, the union tries to force management into bargaining over permissive subjects, whereas management tends to refuse to expand the issues that it considers proper for collective bargaining. Where management and the union do bargain and agree to terms regarding a permissive subject of collective bargaining, the terms agreed to become part of the collective bargaining agreement.

Duty to Bargain in Good Faith.   Under Section 8(d) of the NLRA, both the employer and the union are under a statutory duty to bargain in good faith to reach a collective bargaining agreement. The test of good faith is based on the subjective intent of the parties as it can be inferred from their external actions. Making "unreasonable" proposals (i.e., proposals which a reasonable employee representative would not accept), or engaging in dilatory tactics, such as continual shifting of positions, are proof of bad faith. Making "take-it-or-leave-it" proposals has been held by the courts to be a breach of the duty to bargain in good faith.

Where a union or employer has failed to bargain in good faith, the NLRB may take "such action as will effectuate the policies of the Act," including: (1) issuing a "bargaining order" that directs a party to bargain in good faith, (2) making an award of compensatory damages, or (3) issuing an order that *forces* an employer or union to accept a particular agreement or provision.

Arbitration of Grievances. Once a collective bargaining agreement has been entered into by a union and an employer, disputes may arise as to the enforcement or interpretation of the agreement. Most collective bargaining agreements contain provisions for "arbitration" of labor disputes. The selection of an arbitrator is usually provided for in the agreement, and may be on an *ad hoc* case-by-case basis or by permanent appointment. Once a hearing is held before the arbitrator, the arbitrator usually issues a decision in the matter.

Where a grievance is *both* a breach of the collective bargaining agreement subject to arbitration *and* an unfair labor practice subject to resolution by the NLRB, the NLRB follows a general policy of *deferral* to the arbitrator's decision. The courts likewise usually decline jurisdiction and defer to the arbitrator's decisions as to disputes over the interpretation or enforcement of the terms of a collective bargaining agreement. Only in exceptional circumstances will the NLRB or courts overturn an arbitrator's decision.

Under the NLRA, it is an unfair labor practice for an *employer* to discriminate in hiring, in firing, or in any other term or condition of employment so as to discourage the organization of the union, or to affect its collective bargaining with a union. Under the NLRA, it is an unfair labor practice for a *union* to discriminate, or to cause or attempt to cause an employer to discriminate, against an employee in hiring, in promotion, or in granting any other employment benefit.

In *First National Maintenance Corp. v. NLRB* the Supreme Court held that a decision of a corporation to close part of its operation was not a mandatory subject of collective bargaining.

COLLECTIVE BARGAINING

FIRST NATIONAL MAINTENANCE CORP. v. NATIONAL LABOR RELATIONS BOARD

452 U.S. 666 (1981)
UNITED STATES SUPREME COURT

Justice Blackmun delivered the opinion of the Court.

Petitioner, First National Maintenance Corporation (FNM), is a New York corporation engaged in the business of providing housekeeping, cleaning, maintenance, and related services for commercial customers in the New York City area. It supplies each of its customers, at the customer's premises, contracted-for labor force and supervision in return for reimbursement of its labor costs (gross salaries, FICA and FUTA taxes, and insurance) and payment of a set fee. It contracts for and hires personnel separately for each customer, and it does not transfer employees between locations.

During the spring of 1977, petitioner was performing maintenance work for the Greenpark Care Center, a nursing home in Brooklyn. Its written agreement dated April 28, 1976, with Greenpark specified that Greenpark "shall furnish all tools, equiptment [*sic*], materials, and supplies," and would pay petitioner weekly "the sum of five hundred dollars plus the gross weekly payroll and fringe benefits." . . . Petitioner employed approximately 35 workers in its Greenpark operation.

Petitioner, however, became aware that it was losing money at Greenpark. . . . [O]n July 6, it informed Greenpark in writing that it would discontinue its operations there on August 1. . . . By telegram on July 25, petitioner gave final notice of termination.

While FNM was experiencing these difficulties, District 1199, National Union of Hospital and Health Care Employees, Retail, Wholesale and Department Store Union, AFL-CIO (union), was conducting an organization campaign among petitioner's Greenpark employees. On March 31, 1977, at a Board-conducted election, a majority of the employees selected the union as their bargaining agent.

The union filed an unfair labor practice charge against petitioner, ... The Administrative Law Judge recommended an order requiring petitioner to bargain in good faith with the union about its decision to terminate its Greenpark service operation and its consequent discharge of the employees, as well as the effects of the termination. . . . The National Labor Relations Board adopted the Administrative Law Judge's findings. . . . The United States Court of Appeals for the Second Circuit, with one judge dissenting in part, enforced the Board's order. . . .

Although parties are free to bargain about any legal subject, Congress has limited the mandate or duty to bargain to matters of "wages, hours, and other terms and conditions of employment." . . . Congress deliberately left the words "wages, hours, and other terms and conditions of employment" without further definition, for it did not intend to de-

prive the Board of the power further to define those terms in light of specific industrial practices.

Nonetheless, in establishing what issues must be submitted to the process of bargaining, Congress had no expectation that the elected union representative would become an equal partner in the running of the business enterprise in which the union's members are employed.

Some management decisions, such as choice of advertising and promotion, product type and design, and financing arrangements, have only an indirect and attenuated impact on the employment relationship. Other management decisions, such as the order of succession of layoffs and recalls, production quotas, and work rules, are almost exclusively "an aspect of the relationship" between employer and employee. The present case concerns a third type of management decision, one that had a direct impact on employment, since jobs were inexorably eliminated by the termination, but had as its focus only the economic profitability of the contract with Greenpark, a concern under these facts wholly apart from the employment relationship. This decision, involving a change in the scope and direction of the enterprise, is akin to the decision whether to be in business at all, ... Cf. *Textile Workers v. Darlington Co.* ("an employer has the absolute right to terminate his entire business for any reason he pleases").

If labor costs are an important factor in a failing operation and the decision to close, management will have an incentive to confer voluntarily with the union to seek concessions that may make continuing the business profitable. At other times, management may have great need for speed, flexibility, and secrecy in meeting business opportunities and exigencies. It may face significant tax or securities consequences that hinge on confidentiality, the timing of a plant closing, or a reorganization of the corporate structure. The publicity incident to the normal process of bargaining may injure the possibility of a successful transition or increase the economic damage to the business. The employer also may have no feasible alternative to the closing, and even good-faith bargaining over it may both be futile and cause the employer additional loss.

There is an important difference, also, between permitted bargaining and mandated bargaining. Labeling this type of decision mandatory could afford a union a powerful tool for achieving delay, a power that might be used to thwart management's intentions in a manner unrelated to any feasible solution the union might propose.

We conclude that the harm likely to be done to an employer's need to operate freely in deciding whether to shut down part of its business purely for economic reasons outweighs the incremental benefit that might be gained through the union's participation in making the decision, and we hold that the decision itself is *not* part of [the] "terms and conditions," over which Congress has mandated bargaining.

The decision to halt work at this specific location represented a significant change in petitioner's operations, a change not unlike opening a new line of business or going out of business entirely.

The judgment of the Court of Appeals, accordingly, is *reversed,* and the case is *remanded* to that court for further proceedings consistent with this opinion.

CASE QUESTIONS

1. Once a union has been elected, is that the end of the bargaining process? What is *collective bargaining?*
2. What do the following subjects of collective bargaining include? Explain.

   a. compulsory subjects
   b. illegal subjects
   c. permissive subjects

3. What did the company do with its Greenpark Care Center operation in this case? Which of the preceding three types of subjects did the union want this activity classified as? Why?
4. Is the closing of a *company* a compulsory subject matter for collective bargaining? What did *Textile Workers v. Darlington Co.* hold?
5. Did the Supreme Court hold that the closing of the *plant* in this case was a compulsory subject matter of collective bargaining? What reasoning did the Court cite for its decision? Explain.

Policy Issue. Should a union be given a voice in whether or not a company will close? Whether a company will close a plant (e.g., an automobile plant in Detroit)?

Economics Issue. Does a decision by a company to close a plant have any economic effect on union members working at the plant? More so than a change in wages or other terms and conditions of employment? Explain.

Ethics Issue. Is it ethical for a company to close a plant or business when this will put employees out of work? Even when the company is losing money?

Social Responsibility. Do companies owe a duty of social responsibility to train displaced workers for other job positions? To support them while they look for other work? To pay moving expenses if they find jobs in other places?

STRIKES

In order to help persuade an employer to recognize a union or to bargain collectively, employees often go on strike against their employer. *Going on strike* usually means walking off the job, often accompanied by the picketing of the employer's premises. Although several provisions of the Constitution have been asserted as possibly providing a constitutional right to strike (First Amendment right of free speech, press and assembly, Fifth and Fourteenth Amendment prohibitions against the deprivation of life, liberty, and property without due process of law, and the Thirteenth Amendment prohibition against slavery and involuntary servitude), the Supreme Court has never held that employees have an absolute constitutional right to strike. The right of employees to strike is *statutory,* as expressly provided in Section 13 of the NLRA, and implied in Section 7 of the NLRA (the right of employees to engage in "concerted activity").

Work Preservation.

Work Preservation. The U.S. Supreme Court has recognized the right of unions to strike in order to try to *preserve* the work normally done by members of the union even where more economical and efficient technology is available to do the work.

In *NLRB v. International Longshoremen's Assn.* the Supreme Court affirmed the work preservation rule.

WORK PRESERVATION

NATIONAL LABOR RELATIONS BOARD v. INTERNATIONAL LONGSHOREMEN'S ASSN., AFL-CIO

447 U.S. 490 (1980)
UNITED STATES SUPREME COURT

Mr. Justice Marshall delivered the opinion of the Court.

This controversy arises out of the collective-bargaining response of the ILA [International Longshoremen's Association] and the east coast shipping industry to containerization, a technological innovation which has had such a profound effect on that industry that it has frequently been termed "the container revolution." In the words of one observer, "containerization may be said to constitute the single most important innovation in ocean transport since the steamship displaced the schooner."

Containers are large, reusable metal receptacles, ranging in length from 20 to 40 feet and capable of carrying upwards of 30,000 pounds of freight, which can be moved on and off an ocean vessel unopened. Container ships are specially designed and constructed to carry the containers, which are affixed to the hold. A container can also be attached to a truck chassis and transported intact to and from the pier like a conventional trailer.

Before the introduction of container ships, and as is still the case with conventional vessels, trucks delivered loose, or break-bulk, cargo to the head of the pier. The cargo was then transferred piece by piece from the truck's tailgate to the ship by longshoremen employed by steamship or stevedoring companies. The longshoremen checked the cargo, sorted it, placed it on pallets and moved it by forklift to the side of the ship, and lifted it by means of a sling or hook into the ship's hold. The process was reversed for cargo taken off incoming ships. With the advent of containers, the amount of on-pier work involved in cargo handling has been drastically reduced, since the cargo need not be loaded and unloaded piece by piece. The amount of work available for longshoremen has been further reduced by the shipping companies' practice of making their containers available to shippers and consolidators for loading and unloading away from the pier.

In 1967, ILA demanded in collective-bargaining negotiations that longshoremen stuff and strip all containers crossing the piers. Following a lengthy strike, ILA and NYSA in 1969 adopted, as part of their 1968–1971 collective-bargaining agreement, the Rules on Containers (Rules). . . . The practical effect of the Rules is that some 80 percent of containers pass over the piers intact. The remaining 20 percent are stuffed and stripped by longshoremen, regardless of whether that work duplicates work done by non-ILA employees off-pier.

Among the primary purposes protected by the [National Labor Relations] Act is

the purpose of preserving for the contracting employees themselves work traditionally done by them.

In many instances, technological innovation may change the method of doing the work, instead of merely shifting the same work to a different location. One way to preserve the work of the employees represented by the union in the face of such a change is simply to insist that the innovation not be adopted and that the work continue to be done in the traditional way.

In *National Woodwork* we held that carpenters could seek to preserve their traditional work of finishing blank doors at the construction jobsite by prohibiting the employer, a general contractor, from purchasing prefinished doors from the factory.

Similarly, *Pipefitters* involved an agreement between a subcontractor and a pipefitters' union that pipe threading and cutting were to be performed on the jobsite. Relying on the agreement, the union refused to install climate-control units whose internal piping had been cut, threaded, and installed at the factory. The Board held that the provision was a lawful work preservation agreement, ... This case presents a much more difficult problem than either *National Woodwork* or *Pipefitters*. . . .

Respondents assert that the stuffing and stripping reserved for the ILA by the Rules is functionally equivalent to their former work of handling break-bulk cargo at the pier. Petitioners-intervenors, on the other hand, argue that containerization has worked such fundamental changes in the industry that the work formerly done at the pier by both longshoremen and employees of motor carriers has been completely eliminated [and therefore does not qualify as work preservation].

These questions are not appropriate for initial consideration by reviewing courts. They are properly raised before the Board, whose determinations are, of course, entitled to deference. Since the Board has not had an opportunity to consider these questions in relation to a proper understanding of the work at issue, we will not address them here. . . . [W]e therefore [*remand* this case] to the Board for further proceedings.

Mr. Chief Justice Burger, with whom **Mr. Justice Stewart, Mr. Justice Rehnquist,** and **Mr. Justice Stevens** join, dissenting.

When a prepacked container which "violates" the Rules is taken off its trailer at the pier, the ILA demands that its members be paid for the utterly useless task of removing the contents and then repacking them, or alternatively that a fine be imposed on the shipping company which owns or leased the container. This is nothing less than an invidious form of "featherbedding" to block full implementation of modern technological progress.

CASE QUESTIONS

1. What was the "container revolution"? How did it affect the work of the members of the International Longshoreman's Association?
2. What does the "work preservation" rule provide? Is *work preservation* recognized by the U.S. Supreme Court as a lawful union activity? Can a union strike to force work preservation?
3. What work was allowed to be preserved in the following cases?

   a. *National Woodwork*
   b. *Pipefitters*

4. How did the respondent companies try to avoid the work preservation rule in this case? Explain. Were they successful?
5. Why do you think the U.S. Supreme Court avoided making a final decision in this case? How would you decide this case on remand?

Policy Issue. Should a union be allowed to inhibit the adoption of cost-saving technological advancements under the work preservation rule? Should this rule be eliminated? Why or why not?

Economics Issue. Does the work preservation rule increase or decrease the cost of products made in America? Explain.

Ethics Issue. Is it ethical for a union and its members to invoke the work preservation rule to save otherwise worthless job positions? Why or why not?

Social Responsibility. Do unions owe a duty of social responsibility to preserve jobs that could be done more economically by other means? Does society owe a duty to support these workers?

Illegal Strikes.   Although employees have the statutory right to strike in support of their demands, several types of strikes have been held to be illegal and not protected by law. The major types of *illegal* strikes are:

1. violent strikes
2. "sit-down" strikes
3. "wildcat" strikes
4. partial or intermittment strikes
5. strikes during a cooling-off period
6. strikes to enforce a "hot cargo" provision
7. strikes to obtain work assignments from nonunion workers
8. strikes in violation of a "no strike" clause contained in a collective bargaining agreement.

Violent Strikes.   Violent strikes are not protected under the National Labor Relations Act. A *violent strike* is one where striking employees cause substantial damage to the property of the employer or of a third party. A "violent strike" may occur when the employees first walk off the job, or may result when striking employees turn an otherwise lawful strike into an illegal strike by engaging in violent activity. The courts usually tolerate a certain amount of isolated violence before holding that the strikers have engaged in substantial violence sufficient to make the strike illegal.

"Sitdown" Strike.   In a "sitdown" strike, employees go on strike but stay at the work premises and continue to occupy the employer's buildings and property, refusing to work or leave. *Sitdown strikes* have been held to be illegal and outside the protection of the NLRA. The argument for this rule is that if employees strike, they should leave the employer's premises so that the employer may continue operations, if it chooses to do so, by using management personnel or hiring replacements for the striking employees.

"Wildcat Strikes."   A "wildcat" strike is one where employees go on strike without official union sanction or authorization. The term *wildcat* describes the suddenness with which this type of strike generally occurs. Wildcat strikes are usually caused by small dissident subgroups within a union. Generally, wildcat strikes are not protected by the NLRA. The rationale for this rule is that the purpose of labor law, which is to promote peaceful labor-management relations through formal negotiation between employers and elected unions, would be substantially undermined if workers could go out on strike whenever they wished without union–management negotiations or proper union authorization.

Courts have recognized two limited exceptions where wildcat strikes are considered legal: (1) where the wildcat strike is quickly ratified by a majority of the union members; and (2) where the wildcat strike is directed to support a "specific, previously considered and articulated union objective."

Partial or Intermittent Strikes.   Workers generally have two choices, to work or to engage in a lawful strike. Therefore, workers cannot engage in a "partial" or "intermittent" strike against their employer. In a *partial* or *intermittent* strike, employees do not walk completely off the job, but instead engage in a limited strike, e.g., work every morning and strike every afternoon. A partial or intermittent strike differs from a "sitdown" strike in that the workers actually leave the company premises during the strike portion of the partial strike. A partial or intermittent strike is an illegal strike not protected by the NLRA. The argument for this rule is that it is unfair for employees to sporadically disrupt or shut down an employer's business.

Strikes During 60-Day Cooling-Off Period.   In order to legally strike an employer, a union must first give the employer 60 days notice of the proposed strike. This 60-day notice period is commonly referred to as the *cooling-off period.* Where a union and management have entered into a collective bargaining agreement with a fixed term (e.g., a two-year agreement), the union must give 60 days' notice prior to the termination date of the contract if it wishes to strike when the contract is over. If a union wishes to terminate or seek changes in a fixed-term collective bargaining agreement, it must give 60 days' notice of its intended strike. Where the collective bargaining agreement is for an indefinite term, a strike may be called on 60 days' notice at any time.

Strikes during the 60-day cooling-off period are illegal and not protected under the NLRA. The rationale behind this rule is that often the parties can work out a settlement of their differences during the cooling-off period without having to resort to a strike. A 60-day notice of a strike is not required if the strike is held to protest an employer's unfair labor practice.

Strikes to Enforce "Hot Cargo" Provisions.   A union may not go on strike against an employer in order to prevent the employer from doing business with another person. For example, the Teamsters Union has traditionally required clauses in its union contracts which provide that if non-Teamsters-Union employees of any employer went on strike, the Teamsters would honor the strike and refuse to handle and transport that employer's goods. The product of the originally struck employer is called *hot cargo,* and the supporting-strike provision prohibiting the second union from carrying the struck product is commonly referred to as a *hot cargo* provision. Hot cargo provisions violate NLRA Section 8(b) as illegal "secondary strikes aimed at neutral parties."

Strikes to Obtain Work Assignments from Nonunion Members.   If a union institutes a strike against an employer in an attempt to force the employer to assign certain work to union employees that is presently performed by nonunion employees, that strike is illegal and constitutes an "unfair labor practice" that violates Section 8(b) of the NLRA. However, where rival unions are seeking the same work assignment, a strike to force an employer to assign work to one union over another union is considered a "jurisdictional dispute." NLRA Section 10(b) provides for a special preliminary hearing to settle jurisdictional disputes without requiring recourse to an unfair labor practice procedure.

"No Strike" Clause.   In consideration of other terms in a collective bargaining agreement, a union may enter into a "no strike" agreement with management whereby the union agrees not to strike during the term of the collective bargaining contract. If the union or any of its members breach the "no strike" clause and go on strike, that strike is illegal and is not accorded protection under the NLRB.

Other strikes that are illegal and considered "unfair labor practices" are:

1. strikes to force the employer to compel nonunion employees to join the union
2. strikes to force the employer to pay for services not performed or not to be performed ("featherbedding" agreements)
3. strikes to coerce the employer to recognize or bargain with an uncertified union where another union is already lawfully recognized
4. strikes against a "neutral" employer in order to pressure a "primary" employer to recognize or bargain with an uncertified union where another union is already lawfully recognized.

Discharge and Reinstatement of Strikers. Section 2(3) of the NLRB generally provides that strikers retain their status as "employees" while on strike. However, whether or not striking employees are entitled to *reinstatement* after engaging in a strike depends on whether the strikers are classified as (1) "illegal strikers," (2) "economic strikers," or (3) "unfair labor practice strikers."

Illegal Strikers. Employees who have engaged in any type of illegal strike (e.g., a violent strike, a wildcat strike, a partial strike) are considered *illegal strikers.* An illegal striker may be discharged by an employer while on strike without any right to reinstatement.

Economic Strikers. An *economic striker* is one who strikes for increased economic benefits, such as increased pay or improved fringe benefits. "Economic strikers" receive little protection as to reinstatement under the NLRA. During a strike, an employer may hire replacements to take the positions of economic strikers; the employer is not required to discharge the replacements to make room for the economic strikers once the strike is over. An employer may find it difficult and costly to replace striking workers during a strike.

Economic strikers may apply for reinstatement after a strike is over. Economic strikers are entitled to the nondiscriminatory review and disposition of their job applications for rehiring. However, an economic striker is not entitled to reinstatement if his job has been abolished by the employer during the strike due to changed economic or business conditions.

Unfair Labor Practice Strikers. Where employees have engaged in a lawful strike and the strike was caused by an employer's unfair labor practice, they are considered *unfair labor practice strikers.* Unfair labor practice strikers are entitled to reinstatement during or after a strike, even if this makes it necessary to discharge replacements hired during the strike. Owing to this reinstatement rule, a substantial amount of litigation arises over whether or not striking employees were "unfair labor practice strikers."

Employer "Lockout." In a *lockout,* an employer refuses to allow employees to return to work at the employer's premises. Under proper circumstances, lockouts are permitted by federal labor law. For example, if an employer reasonably anticipates a strike by its employees, the employer may close its plant and lock out the employees. Further, an employer may lock out its employees where collective bargaining negotiations with a union have hit an impasse, or under other "special circumstances," such as threat of damage to plant or equipment. However, it is an unfair labor practice for an employer to lock out employees to avoid his duty to negotiate a collective bargaining agreement with a union in good faith. The legality of lockouts is decided on a case-by-case basis.

In *NLRB v. Shop Rite Foods, Inc.* the court held that an employer had not violated labor law when it discharged and refused to reinstate employees who had engaged in an illegal "wildcat" strike.

employers didn't have to hold their jobs open for them because

ILLEGAL STRIKE

NATIONAL LABOR RELATIONS BOARD v. SHOP RITE FOODS, INC.

430 F.2d 786 (1970)
UNITED STATES COURT OF APPEALS, FIFTH CIRCUIT

Godbold, Circuit Judge:

In September, 1966, after a Board election, the United Packinghouse, Food and Allied Workers was certified as the exclusive bargaining representative for an appropriate unit of employees at Shop Rite's warehouse in Lubbock, Texas. There were approximately 130 employees in the unit at the time of the events in question. The union set up a local, and officers were chosen. . . . In late November negotiations for a collective bargaining agreement began.

Beginning in late February and continuing into March, Warehouse Superintendent Belcher and Warehouse Manager Probasco noted a significant increase in the amount of damaged merchandise in the warehouse. They concluded that the damage was being intentionally caused by dissident employees as a pressure tactic to secure concessions from the company in the collective bargaining negotiations. Probasco told employee Hawkland, president of the local, that he regarded the increase in damage as deliberate. He requested Hawkland use his influence to control the damage, and told him damage tactics would not affect the bargaining negotiations. Hawkland, while denying knowledge of unusual damage, agreed to convey the request to union members.

The damage, according to management, continued to be excessive. For three days off-duty policemen were hired to stand guard in the warehouse. They were dismissed at Hawkland's request. Excess damage stopped for ten days until March 30, when 29 sacks of dog food were found cut. Wenk, a vice-president of the company, conferred with President Hawkland, Chief Union Steward Lee, and Committeeman Ivey and asked their help so that it would not be necessary to recall the guards.

On the morning of March 31, a Friday, Superintendent Belcher observed employee Bownds in the flour section, where he had no business to be, making quick motions with his hands. He went to the place at once and found several bags of flour had been cut, apparently with a sharp instrument. Superintendent Belcher reported to Manager Probasco and Vice-President Wenk that he had seen Bownds cut sacks of flour. Wenk instructed that Bownds be discharged. Bownds was called to the office and told he was being fired for intentionally cutting sacks of flour.

Approximately half an hour later, during their coffee break, Hawkland, Lee and Ivey, accompanied by about 10 other employees, came into Probasco's office where Wenk was also. One or more of the officers demanded proof of why Bownds was fired.

Wenk told them that this was not the time or place to discuss it, that he was not obligated to prove it, and that unless they left the office at once and returned to work he would fire them for insubordination. They threatened to walk out, and Wenk told them if they did so they were quitting.

Hawkland and Ivey solicited and led an immediate walkout of about 30 employees. Eight more joined it later that day or the next morning.

Immediately after the walkout began the participants went to the union hall and told Ramon, the field representative of the international union, what had transpired. . . . [Ramon] telephoned Hawkland that the union would not authorize the strike and wired Hawkland that the strike was unauthorized and members were to return to work. He wired the company attorney that the "wildcat strike" had been terminated and the participants ordered back to work.

[M]ost of the strikers applied for reinstatement, but none was rehired. . . . [They then filed a petition with the NLRB].

[T]he [National Labor Relations] Act indicates a preference for collective as opposed to individual action in negotiating with the employer. . . . A major reason for this preference is to protect the ultimate goal of labor adjustment:

> Since the employer is required to bargain with the representatives of the worker, it must have some assurance, first, as to the identity of that agent. More important, however, it must be able to deal with that agent as the responsible spokesman for the employees of the unit. There cannot be bargaining in any real sense if the employer has to deal with individuals or splinter groups.

The failure of the group which entered Probasco's office to notify their bargaining representative that they desired to contest Bownds' discharge could only undermine the goals of democracy in the unions and effective labor adjustment through the bargaining process.

Enforcement [of the order discharging Bownds] is *granted*. . . .

CASE QUESTIONS

1. Who were the following persons involved in this case? What were their positions?
   a. Belcher
   b. Probasco
   c. Wenk
   d. Hawkland
   e. Lee
   f. Ivy
   g. Bownds
2. Describe the following types of strikes. Which ones are illegal?
   a. violent strikes
   b. sit-down strikes
   c. wildcat strikes
   d. partial or intermittent strikes
   e. strikes during a cooling-off period
   f. strikes to enforce "hot cargo" provisions
   g. strikes to obtain work from nonunion employees
   h. strikes in violation of no-strike clauses
3. Why was Bownds fired? What did his fellow union members do in protest? What type of strike was this?
4. What is the difference between the following type of strikers and their right to reinstatement? Which type were the strikers in this case?
   a. economic strikers
   b. illegal strikers
   c. unfair labor practice strikers

Policy Issue. If union members were allowed to go on strike without union authorization, would it hinder the goals of federal labor law? Explain.

Economics Issue. What are the economic consequences of being found to be an *illegal* striker?

Ethics Issue. Is it ethical for a company not to rehire illegal strikers? What about not rehiring the strikers in this case?

Social Responsibility. Do union members owe a duty of social responsibility to obey union orders not to strike even if they personally disagree with the union? Why or why not?

PICKETING

Often when employees go on strike they will commence picketing in order to try to bring pressure on the employer to settle the strike. "Informational picketing" is usually conducted by a union to try to induce consumers to be sympathetic to the union's cause and refrain from dealing with the struck employer. Picketing usually takes the form of employees and union representatives walking in front of the employer's premises carrying signs announcing the strike. The right of striking employees to picket has been *implied* under Sections 7 and 13 of the NLRA. Even "mass picketing," when it does not prevent other employees from entering or leaving the employer's plant, has been held to be lawful. Picketing is generally held to be lawful *unless*

1. it obstructs other nonstriking employees from entering the employer's premises
2. it prevents consumers from entering the employer's place of business
3. it is accompanied by violence.

Mass picketing often is held unlawful where it prevents other employees from crossing the picket line to enter the employer's premises. Picketing also loses its protection when it interferes with pick-ups and deliveries at the employer's plant or place of business. Courts generally tolerate isolated and minor violence that occurs along picket lines. However, substantial violence or threats of violence are prohibited as a *union* unfair labor practice under Section 8(b) of the NLRA. Most courts have generally held that picketing , to be unlawful, requires some form of confrontation between the picketers and the employees of an employer.

Under NLRA Section 8(b)(7), it is unlawful for an *uncertified* union to picket, cause to be picketed, or threaten to picket an employer where:

1. the employer currently recognizes another union,
2. the employer does not currently recognize another union, and an uncertified union pickets the employer with the objective of forcing it to recognize or bargain with the uncertified union, or to force its employees to accept the uncertified union as their bargaining agent, *and* the picketing union has failed to file an election petition within a "reasonable time" not exceeding 30 days after the commencement of picketing,
3. a valid union election has been held within the preceding 12 months.

Secondary Boycott. A union may attempt to bring pressure against the *primary* struck employer by picketing *another* party, such as a supplier or customer of the primary employer. It is lawful for a striking union to engage in "product picketing" at the premises of such a secondary employer to try to induce people who deal with the secondary employer not to purchase the product of the primary employer. However, where the picketing is aimed at the *neutral secondary employer* in order to try to force *that neutral employer* not to deal with the primary struck employer, rather than aimed at the product, it is an illegal secondary boycott in violation of Section 8(b) of the NLRA. Courts are often faced with the difficult situation of determining whether the picketing at the site of a secondary employer is lawful "product picketing" or is an illegal "secondary boycott."

Where more than one employer occupies the same premises (e.g., on a construction site), a problem often develops in determining whether there has even been a secondary boycott. The NLRB has developed the *Moore Dry-dock* rules, named after the case in which they were announced, to deal with competing interests in a *common-situs* situation. Generally, the *Moore Drydock* rules provide that if there are separate gates or entrances of different employers at a common site, picketing may only be conducted at the entrance of the targeted employer; any picketing at the entrances of neutral secondary employers is prohibited. If there is only one common entrance at a common site where many employers are working, a striking union can picket that entrance but may not block or otherwise obstruct employees of any employer from using that entrance. Management and unions have fought bitterly in the courts and in lobbying the legislature regarding the issue of common-situs picketing.

A striking union is always allowed to *request* the employees of a neutral employer to honor the strike and not cross the picket lines set by the striking employees. If the employees of the neutral employer voluntarily honor another union's picket line, there is no illegal secondary boycott.

Where an employer is faced with an illegal strike, picketing, or boycott, the employer may file an unfair labor practice charge against the union with the NLRB. If, after reasonable investigation, the NLRB determines that "reasonable cause" for the charge exists, it *must* seek an immediate federal court injunction against the illegal activity. An employer or any other party who suffers economic loss because of an illegal strike, picketing, or boycott may file a civil action for damages against the union.

In *NLRB v. Retail Store Employees Union* the U.S. Supreme Court held that employees who were on strike against their employer engaged in an illegal secondary boycott when they picketed neutral third parties who purchased services from the primary employer.

employees of 1 co. picketing another co.

SECONDARY BOYCOTT

NLRB v. RETAIL STORE EMPLOYEES UNION, LOCAL 1001, RETAIL CLERKS INTERNATIONAL ASSN., AFL-CIO

447 U.S. 607 (1980)
UNITED STATES SUPREME COURT

Mr. Justice Powell delivered the opinion of the Court.

Safeco Title Insurance Co. underwrites real estate title insurance in the State of Washington. It maintains close business relationships with five local title companies. The companies search land titles, perform escrow services, and sell title insurance. Over 90 percent of their gross incomes derives from the sale of Safeco insurance. Safeco has substantial stockholdings in each title company, and at least one Safeco officer serves on each company's board of directors. Safeco, however,

difference between 1st limit & this

has no control over the companies' daily operations. It does not direct their personnel policies, and it never exchanges employees with them.

Local 1001 of the Retail Store Employees Union became the certified bargaining representative for certain Safeco employees in 1974. When contract negotiations between Safeco and the Union reached an impasse, the employees went on strike. The Union did not confine picketing to Safeco's office in Seattle. The Union also picketed each of the five local title companies. The pickets carried signs declaring that Safeco had no contract with the Union, and they distributed handbills asking consumers to support the strike by canceling their Safeco policies.

Safeco and one of the title companies filed complaints with the National Labor Relations Board. They charged that the Union had engaged in an unfair labor practice by picketing in order to promote a secondary boycott against the title companies. The Board agreed. . . . The Board therefore rejected the Union's reliance upon *NLRB v. Fruit Packers* (*Tree Fruits*), which held that Section 8(b)(4)(ii)(B) allows secondary picketing against a struck product. It ordered the Union to cease picketing and to take limited corrective action.

The United States Court of Appeals for the District of Columbia Circuit set aside the Board's order. The court agreed that the title companies were neutral parties entitled to the benefit of Section 8(b)(4)(ii)(B). It held, however, that *Tree Fruits* leaves neutrals susceptible to whatever consequences may flow from secondary picketing against the consumption of products produced by an employer involved in a labor dispute.

Section 8(b)(4)(ii)(B) of the National Labor Relations Act makes it "an unfair labor practice for a labor organization . . . to threaten, coerce, or restrain" a person not party to a labor dispute

> where . . . an object thereof is . . . forcing or requiring [him] to cease using, selling, handling, transporting, or otherwise dealing in the products of any other producer . . . or to cease doing business with any other person. . . .

In *Tree Fruits,* the Court held that Section 8(b)(4)(ii)(B) does not prohibit all peaceful picketing at secondary sites. There, a union striking certain Washington fruit packers picketed large supermarkets in order to persuade consumers not to buy Washington apples. . . . Congress intended to protect secondary parties from pressures that might embroil them in the labor disputes of others, but not to shield them from business losses caused by a campaign that successfully persuades consumers "to boycott the primary employer's goods." Thus, the Court drew a distinction between picketing "to shut off all trade with the secondary employer unless he aids the union in its dispute with the primary employer" and picketing that "only persuades his customers not to buy the struck product." The picketing in that case, which "merely follow[ed] the struck product," did not "'threaten, coerce, or restrain'" the secondary party within the meaning of Section 8(b)(4)(ii)(B).

The product picketed in *Tree Fruits* was but one item among the many that made up the retailer's trade. If the appeal against such a product succeeds, the Court observed, it simply induces the neutral retailer to reduce his orders for the product or "to drop the item as a poor seller." The decline in sales attributable to consumer rejection of the struck product puts pressure upon the primary employer, and the marginal injury to the neutral retailer is purely incidental to the product boycott. The neutral therefore has little reason to become involved in the labor dispute.

In this case, on the other hand, the title companies sell only the primary employer's product and perform the services associated with it. Secondary picketing against consumption of the primary product leaves responsive consumers no realistic option other than to boycott the title companies altogether. If the appeal succeeds, each company "stops buying the struck product, not because of a falling demand, but in response to pressure designed to inflict injury on [its] business generally." Thus, "the union does more than merely follow the struck product; it creates a separate dispute with the secondary employer." Such an expansion of labor discord was one of the evils that Congress intended Section 8(b)(4)(ii)(B) to prevent.

As long as secondary picketing only discourages consumption of a struck product, incidental injury to the neutral is a natural consequence of an effective primary boycott. But the Union's secondary appeal against the central product sold by the title companies in this case is "reasonably calculated to induce customers not to patronize the neutral parties at all." . . . Product picketing that reasonably can be expected to threaten neutral parties with ruin or substantial loss simply does not square with the language or the purpose of Section 8(b)(4)(ii)(B).

Since successful secondary picketing would put the title companies to a choice between their survival and the severance of their ties with Safeco, the picketing plainly violates the statutory ban on the coercion of neutrals with the object of "forcing or requiring [them] to cease . . . dealing in the [primary] produc[t] . . . or to cease doing business with" the primary employer.

Accordingly, the judgment of the Court of Appeals is *reversed,* and the case is *remanded* with directions to enforce the National Labor Relations Board's order.

Mr. Justice Brennan, with whom **Mr. Justice White** and **Mr. Justice Marshall** join, dissenting.

[T]he single product secondary firm is likely to be the primary employer's strongest ally because of the alignment of their respective economic interests. [It is not] . . . especially unfair to subject the single product retailer to a primary product boycott. Whatever the percentage of a retailer's business that is constituted by a given item, the retailer necessarily assumes the risks of interrupted supply or declining sales that follow when labor conflict embroils the manufacturer of the item. . . . I would adhere to the primary product test. Accordingly, I dissent.

CASE QUESTIONS

1. What is *picketing?* What is a *secondary boycott?* Explain.
2. Describe the secondary boycott in the *Tree Fruits* case. What did the "primary product" test adopted by the Supreme Court in that case provide?
3. What company was struck in the present case? What companies were picketed? Was this a *secondary boycott?*
4. Under the *Tree Fruits* primary product test, would the boycott in this case have been lawful? Explain.
5. What does the "economic loss" test adopted by the Supreme Court in this case provide? Will some secondary boycotts which would have previously been lawful under the *Tree Fruits* doctrine now be unlawful? Explain.

Policy Issue. Should *all* secondary boycotts be prohibited? Should *all* secondary boycotts be allowed? Does the middle ground taken by the Supreme Court make sense? Why or why not?

Economics Issue. Why would a union engage in a secondary boycott against a neutral employer? Does the economic loss test adopted by the Supreme Court eliminate the desirability of this kind of boycott by the union?

Ethics Issue. Is it ethical for a union to picket a neutral employer? Were the title companies in this case really neutral employers? Explain.

Social Responsibility. Do unions owe a duty of social responsibility not to involve neutral parties in their strikes with an employer? Why or why not?

INTERNAL UNION RULES

Under the NLRA, a union has the right to adopt *internal rules* with regard to acquiring or retaining membership in the union. In order to be valid, internal rules must serve the "legitimate interests" of the union, and not impair the overriding policy of federal labor law. Where a union rule is held to be valid, the union may not use illegal means, such as violence, to enforce it.

A union may discipline and punish members for participating in certain activities, including (1) walking off the job in a nonsanctioned wildcat strike, (2) working for wages below scale, (3) spying for an employer, (4) any other activity that has an economic impact adverse to the union. The union may impose certain sanctions on union members who violate valid internal union rules, including fines, deprivation of voting rights, and removal from union office.

A union may not punish a union member for participating in a civic duty, such as testifying in court against the union or reporting law violations of fellow union members. To protect a worker's constitutional right of "free speech," courts have held that a union cannot generally discipline a member for participating in "political" activities unless the union member's political activity is in "patent" conflict with the union's "best interests." Internal union rules that impinge on constitutional rights are carefully examined by the courts on a case-by-case basis.

Labor's "Bill of Rights."   In 1959, prompted by the undemocratic manner in which many unions were operated, Congress enacted Title I of the Landrum-Griffin Act, commonly referred to as "labor's bill of rights." Labor's bill of rights gives each union member "equal rights and privileges" to nominate candidates for union office, vote on internal matters, and participate in membership meetings. The "bill of rights" further guarantees union members the right of free speech and assembly, provides for "due process" (i.e., notice and hearing) before a union member is disciplined by a union, and permits a union member to initiate an administrative or judicial action.

Election of Union Officials.   Section 401 of the Landrum-Griffin Act provides minimum requirements for conducting democratic elections of union officials. Section 401 provides:

1. that every member in good standing is eligible to be a candidate for election, subject to "reasonable qualifications"
2. that reasonable opportunity for the nomination of candidates must be given
3. that local officers must be elected at least every three years, and international officers every five years
4. that all members in good standing be allowed to vote in a union election, and each union member is allowed one vote.

For example, in *Steelworkers v. Usery,* 429 U.S. 305 (1977), the U.S. Supreme Court held that an internal union rule which restricted candidates for union office to members who had attended at least half of the union's meetings over the previous three years was an invalid internal union rule which violated the Landrum-Griffin Act, where 96.5 percent of the 660 union members would be ineligible to hold office and of the 23 eligible candidates 9 were incumbent union officials.

In *Ellis v. Brotherhood of Railway, Airline and Steamship Clerks, Freight Handlers, Express and Station Employees* the U.S Supreme Court delineated the activities on which a union may expend union membership dues.

USE OF MEMBERSHIP DUES

ELLIS, ET AL. v. BROTHERHOOD OF RAILWAY, AIRLINE AND STEAMSHIP CLERKS, FREIGHT HANDLERS, EXPRESS AND STATION EMPLOYEES

104 U.S. 1883 (1984)
UNITED STATES SUPREME COURT

Justice White delivered the opinion of the Court.

In 1951, Congress amended the Railway Labor Act (the Act or RLA) to permit what it had previously prohibited—the union shop. Section 2, Eleventh of the Act permits a union and an employer to require all employees in the relevant bargaining unit to join the union as a condition of continued employment. In *Machinists v. Street,* the Court held that the Act does not authorize a union to spend an objecting employee's money to support political causes. The use of employee funds for such ends is unrelated to Congress' desire to eliminate "free riders" and the resentment they provoked. The Court did not express a view as to "expenditures for activities in the area between the costs which led directly to the complaint as to 'free riders,' and the expenditures to support union political activities." Petitioners challenge just such expenditures.

In 1971, respondent Brotherhood of Railway, Airline and Steamship Clerks (the union or BRAC) and Western Airlines implemented a previously negotiated agreement requiring that all Western's clerical employees join the union within 60 days of commencing employment. As the agreement has been interpreted, employees need not become formal members of the union, but must pay agency fees equal to members' dues. Petitioners are present or former clerical employees of Western who objected to the use of their compelled dues for specified union activities.

1. Conventions

Every four years, BRAC holds a national convention at which the members elect officers, establish bargaining goals and priorities, and formulate overall union policy. We have very little trouble in holding that petitioners must help defray the costs of these conventions. Surely if a union is to perform its statutory functions, it must maintain its corporate or associational existence, must elect officers to manage and carry on its affairs, and may consult its members about overall bargaining goals and policy. Conventions such as those at issue here are normal events about which Congress was thoroughly informed and seem to us to be essential to the union's discharge of its duties as bargaining agent.

2. Social Activities

Approximately .7 percent of Grand Lodge expenditures go toward purchasing refreshments for union business meetings and occasional social activities. . . . While these affairs are not central to collective bargaining, they are sufficiently related to it to be charged to all employees. As the Court of Appeals noted, "[t]hese small expenditures are important to the union's members because they bring about harmonious working relationships, promote closer ties among employees, and create a more pleasant environment for union meetings."

3. Publications

The Grand Lodge puts out a monthly magazine, the *Railway Clerk/Interchange,* paid for out of the union treasury. The magazine's contents are varied and include articles about negotiations, contract demands, strikes, unemployment and health benefits, proposed or recently enacted legislation, general news, products the union is boycotting, and recreational and social activities. . . . The union must have a channel for communicating with the employees, including the objecting ones, about its activities. . . . By the same token, the Act surely allows it to charge objecting employees for reporting to them about those activities it can charge them for doing.

4. Organizing

The Court of Appeals found that organizing expenses could be charged to objecting employees because organizing efforts are aimed toward a stronger union, which in turn would be more successful at the bargaining table. Despite this attenuated connection with collective bargaining, we think such expenditures are outside Congress' authorization.

[W]here a union shop provision is in place and enforced, all employees in the relevant unit are already organized. By definition, therefore, organizing expenses are spent on employees outside the collective-bargaining unit already represented.[13] Using dues exacted from an objecting employee to recruit members among workers outside the bargaining unit can afford only the most attenuated benefits to collective bargaining on behalf of the dues payer.

[T]he free-rider rationale does not extend this far. The image of the smug, self-satisfied nonmember, stirring up resentment by enjoying benefits earned through other employees' time and money, is completely out of place when it comes to the union's overall organizing efforts. . . .

[T]he free rider Congress had in mind was the employee the union was required to represent and from whom it could not withhold benefits obtained for its members. Non-bargaining unit organizing is not directed at that employee. Organizing money is spent on people who are not union members, and only in the most distant way works to the benefit of those already paying dues.

5. Litigation

The expenses of litigation incident to negotiating and administering the contract or to settling grievances and disputes arising in the bargaining unit are clearly chargeable to petitioners as a normal incident of the duties of the exclusive representative. The same is true of fair representation litigation arising within the unit, of jurisdictional disputes with other unions, and of any other litigation before agencies or in the courts that concerns bargaining unit employees and is normally conducted by the exclusive representative. The expenses of litigation not having such a connection with the bargaining unit are not to be charged to objecting employees.

6. Death benefits

BRAC pays from its general funds a $300 death benefit to the designated beneficiary of any member or nonmember required to pay dues to the union. . . . Although [the petitioners] objected to the use of their funds to support the benefits plan, they remained entitled to the benefits of the plan as long as they paid their dues; they thus enjoyed a form of insurance for which the union collected a premium. We doubt that the equities call for a refund of those payments.

It is so ordered.

CASE QUESTIONS

1. Can unions spend members' dues on *political* activities? Should unions in this country be allowed to form a separate political party, as is done in many European countries? Why or why not?
2. Can unions spend members' dues on the following activities? Explain.
   a. conventions
   b. social activities
   c. publications
   d. litigation
   e. death benefits
3. Can unions spend members' dues on *organizing* activities? Why or why not? Did the "free rider" argument used by the Supreme Court make sense?

Policy Issue. Should union leaders have unlimited discretion how to spend the dues collected from union members? Why or why not? Should the money be used to finance casinos in Las Vegas?

Economics Issue. Do you think the total union dues paid in this country are very substantial? How about union pension funds?

Ethics Issue. Where is Jimmy Hoffa?

Social Responsibility. Do unions owe a duty of social responsibility to their members regarding how their union dues are spent and invested?

Trend of the Law

During the late 1970s and 1980s labor unions in the manufacturing industries lost substantial membership and power as the economy weathered a recession-depression, and the "information revolution" began to take hold in the United States. In many instances, unions representing manufacturing employees were forced to give up benefits obtained over the years. Once-powerful "blue-collar" manufacturing unions will continue to lose membership in the future, and will provide the courts with complex issues regarding the lawfulness of "work preservation" as they attempt to hold onto jobs which would otherwise be eliminated by advanced technology such as robotics and computers.

The present trend in unionization in America is toward the organization of workers in the service industries and government employees. White-collar workers at middle-management levels and certain professional employees (e.g., professors) will also be the subject of union organization in the future. Unions will attempt in the future to force employers to negotiate over a greater number of "permissive" subjects of collective bargaining.

Attempts by states to enact "right-to-work" laws will continue in the future to be one of the most important legal battles in labor–management relations.

REVIEW QUESTIONS

1. As a result of multiemployer, multistate collective bargaining with the Central States Drivers Council, comprising local unions of truck drivers affiliated with the Teamsters, a collective bargaining agreement, the "Central States Area Over-the-Road Motor Freight Agreement," was signed by the local transport operators who operated in twelve midwestern states, including Ohio. Article XXXII regulated the minimum rental rates for trucks leased to a carrier by an owner-driver. Owner-drivers were not allowed to rent their trucks for a rate which would result in net profits to the driver falling below the union wage scale for the equivalent time worked. Oliver, a member of the union who worked as the driver of his own truck, secured employment under terms which would have resulted in a net profit that was lower than the union wage scale. The union attempted to force Oliver not to accept this employment. Oliver sued in Ohio state court and was able to obtain a permanent injunction from the state court against the enforcement of Article XXXII on the grounds that it violated Ohio antitrust law as a price-fixing agreement. The provisions did not violate federal law. The union appealed to the federal court

system. Should the federal courts uphold or overturn the state court ruling?

2. The Amalgamated Meat Cutters attempted to organize the employees in Golub Corporation's retail food store. Prior to the election, Golub's president sent three letters and made one speech to the employees warning them of the possible consequences of unionization. Among the consequences he discussed were a possible reduction of staff in order to remain competitive with other markets and a possible elimination of special privileges given to employees, such as time off for personal needs and emergencies. At no time did he specifically threaten that these actions would be inflicted in return for unionization; however, the intent of his actions was clear to the employees. Did his prediction of adverse consequences resulting from unionization violate Section 8(c) of the National Labor Relations Act?

3. Local 404 of the Teamsters attempted to unionize all 13 of Gissel Packing Company's wire weavers at the firm's Holyoke, Virginia facility. Gissel's president refused to bargain with the union. Instead, he met with all his employees and attempted to persuade them not to join the union. He emphasized the results of a strike 13 years earlier that had caused the plant to shut down for three months. He warned that the company was financially insecure, that a strike could lead to the plant's closing since the parent company had excess manufacturing capacity elsewhere, and that because of the employees' age and limited skills they might not be able to obtain other employment. The president also sent out a pamphlet that called the union a "happy strike outfit" controlled by hoodlums and that listed those local businesses which had gone out of business due to union demands, eliminating approximately 3,500 jobs. He had no factual basis for attributing these other plant closings to unionization efforts. The union lost the election 7–6 and then petitioned the NLRB, claiming that Gissel had violated Section 8(c). Did the employer's speech activities violate the National Labor Relations Act?

4. Prior to a representation election held to decide whether to unionize Savair Manufacturing's employees, the Union issued "recognition slips." These slips allowed any employee who signed them before the election to become a member of the Union and to waive any initiation fees should the union win the election. The Union officials did not actually solicit signatures for the slips; however, they explained to the employees what their signature entitled them to and then hand-picked five employees to do the soliciting. Under the Union by-laws, the initiation fee could not be higher than $10, but the employees were not told how large the fee would be. Does this pre-election solicitation of union memberships, which allows the employee to avoid the union initiation fee, violate the National Labor Relations Act?

5. The steelworkers' union and the steamfitters' union both were actively seeking to organize the workers at Midwest Piping and Supply Company's main plant. For various reasons, Midwest preferred the steamfitters. Both unions obtained authorization cards and presented them to the company. The steamfitters had a majority of the authorization cards. Midwest immediately entered into a contract with the steamfitters even though it knew

that a genuine question concerning who represented the employees still existed. Did Midwest violate the National Labor Relations Act?

6. Mallinckrodt Chemical Works was the sole company that mined and completely processed uranium ore for the Atomic Energy Commission. Twelve specialized instruments mechanics at the Weldon Spring, Missouri location were employed to keep the process functioning. The employees were skilled workmen, similiar to journeymen or craft instrument mechanics. A small local of the International Brotherhood of Electrical Workers Union sought to organize these employees as a separate bargaining unit. The union was not a traditional representative of the instrument mechanics. Further, the workers had fared well in past negotiations with Mallinckrodt and had shown little interest in maintaining a separate identity. What factors should the NRLB consider when determining if the employees should be a separate bargaining unit? Should the employees constitute a separate unit apart from the several hundred other employees who worked at the facility?

7. White, a large manufacturing concern, bargained with its relatively small union for a new wage agreement for its hourly employees. The negotiations centered around nine points of contention and White insisted on provisions favorable to the company in all nine cases. As part of those provisions, White demanded that the union surrender its right to strike; however, the firm was unwilling to accept the union's request for an arbitration clause. The company also demanded that it be given unilateral control of virtually all aspects of its business, including wages, hiring, discharging, and promotion. Despite these demands, there was no other evidence to indicate that White was attempting to disrupt serious negotiations. The union filed a complaint with the NRLB, alleging that White was not bargaining in good faith. Did White fail to bargain in good faith?

8. The Insurance Agents' International Union was negotiating a contract between its members and their employer, Prudential Insurance. During the contract negotiations, the Union announced that if an agreement was not reached by a certain deadline, it would authorize its members to begin using tactics to place economic pressure on Prudential. When an agreement was not achieved by the deadline and while negotiations continued, union members stopped soliciting insurance policies, failed to follow company procedures, refused to participate in special promotional campaigns, reported late to work, engaged in "sit-in mornings," picketed and distributed leaflets to policyholders, and solicited policyholders' signatures on various petitions. Prudential filed a complaint with the NRLB charging that the union had failed to bargain in good faith. There was no question that, if it stood alone, the record of negotiations at the bargaining table itself would show that the union bargained in good faith. Did the union fail to bargain in good faith?

9. After rejecting Laidlaw Corporation's wage offer, the union announced that it was going on strike. The day before the strike began, Laidlaw announced that all striking employees would forever lose their right to work for the company. Two days after the strike began, Massey, one of the striking employees, applied for reinstatement. Laidlaw told him that

his job was filled and that even if it was available he would be paid the lower wage of a new employee. Massey continued to strike but when his job later became vacant, Laidlaw asked him to return at the lower wage. Massey refused. When the union voted to return to work, most of the jobs had been filled and the strikers' reinstatement applications were only considered as of the day on which they were made. Therefore, when several jobs became available after the strike ended, they were filled by new employees who had applied for the positions before the striking employees had applied for reinstatement. These new employees were hired solely because of the timeliness of their applications, not because of any other legitimate or substantial business reason. A group of former employees, including Massey, petitioned the NRLB seeking immediate reinstatement at their former wage level. When, if at any time, was Laidlaw required to rehire former striking employees? At what wage rate?

10. Doose & Lintner, the general contractor for the construction of a commercial building in Denver, Colorado, awarded a subcontract for electrical work to Gould & Preisner. Doose & Lintner as well as all the other subcontractors were unionized; Gould & Priesner was nonunion and had been engaged in a long dispute with the Denver Building and Construction Trades Council, the local construction industry union. The Council told Doose that if Gould performed any work, the Council would picket the site. Doose refused to release Gould from the work and the union picketed. During the time of the picketing, only Gould's men reported to work. As a result, Doose finally ordered Gould off the project so it could continue the work. Gould filed a petition with the NRLB claiming that the Council had engaged in an illegal secondary boycott. Did the union conduct an illegal secondary boycott?

11. Local 761 of the International Union of Electrical Workers struck their employer, General Electric Corp. The local picketed every gate to the G.E. plant with signs reading "Local 761 on strike, G.E. unfair!!," including one gate which was specifically used only for independent contractors who were doing work at the site. These contractors were employed to construct new buildings, install and repair heating and ventilation equipment, retooling, and general maintenance. This work was generally unrelated to the normal operations of the plant. General Electric petitioned the NRLB, claiming that the union had engaged in a secondary boycott. Does the claim have merit?

12. American Ship Building, which operated shipyards on the Great Lakes, was negotiating for a new contract with eight unions. Previous contracts with the unions had all been preceded by strikes. The bargaining reached an impasse during the summer, so what little work the company obtained was performed quickly to prevent immobilization of the ships. Fearing that a strike would threaten its ability to finish ship repairs before the lakes froze over, American gradually laid off almost all of its employees. The layoff was also motivated by American's desire to bring economic pressure against the Union and to secure settlement of the dispute on favorable grounds. Shortly thereafter, negotiations resumed and an agreement was reached. Did this temporary layoff of employees violate the National Labor Relations Act?

13. During a lawful strike against Allis-Chalmers Manufacturing Co. by the United Auto Workers, certain union members crossed the picket lines and continued to work. After the strike was over, the union brought disciplinary hearings against these members and fined them from $20 to $100 apiece. Do these union sanctions violate the National Labor Relations Act?

26

DISCRIMINATION IN EMPLOYMENT

INTRODUCTION

One of the most rapidly expanding areas of liability exposure for employers is *discrimination* in employment. Discrimination based on race, sex, age or other classifications was not unlawful or actionable at common law. It was not until Congress and state legislatures enacted *statutes* prohibiting certain types of discrimination that employers became subject to liability for discriminatory practices in employment. The majority of lawsuits alleging discrimination in employment are based on several broad federal statutes, including:

1. Title VII of the Civil Rights Act of 1964, which generally prohibits discrimination in employment based on race, color, religion, national origin, or sex

2. the Equal Pay Act of 1963, which prohibits differentials in pay in employment based on *sex*

3. the Age Discrimination in Employment Act of 1967, which makes employ-

ment discrimination against individuals between the ages of 40 and 70 unlawful

4. Sections 503 and 504 of the Rehabilitation Act of 1973, which prohibit employment discrimination against handicapped persons by federal contractors

5. Section 1981 of the Civil Rights Act of 1866, which prohibits employment discrimination on *race*.

Most states have enacted antidiscrimination laws to prevent discrimination in employment based on race, sex, age, and other classifications. Several state statutes prohibit discrimination based on "sexual preference," discrimination against veterans, and discrimination based on other classifications generally not covered by federal statutes. The coverage of the numerous state antidiscrimination statutes is beyond the scope of this book.

Although Congress and the state legislatures have enacted statutes that prohibit certain types of employment discrimination, it is the courts that are charged with the application of these laws to specific fact situations. Most antidiscrimination statutes are broadly drafted, leaving substantial discretion to the courts in interpreting and applying the statutes. Therefore, much of the current law regarding discrimination in the employment relation is the result of major court decisions.

DISCRIMINATION IN EMPLOYMENT

In order for a plaintiff to successfully bring an action charging discrimination, the plaintiff must prove that the employment action taken against him (e.g., discharge, demotion) was caused because of *discrimination* and not solely because of the employer's "business judgment." Merely because a person in a protected class is affected by a business's action does not make that action discriminatory. In order to prove alleged unlawful discrimination, the plaintiff must show both that he or she is a member of a class protected by an antidiscrimination law *and* that the employer's action was unlawfully discriminatory.

In *Ackerman v. Diamond Shamrock Corporation*, 670 F.2d 66 (1982), the court held that a 59-year-old man was discharged based on a valid business decision by the company and not because of unlawful age discrimination. In that case Judge Phillips wrote:

Edward Ackerman appeals from a summary judgment in favor of his defendant employer in an action under the Age Discrimination in Employment Act (ADEA).

Appellant was an employee of the appellee Diamond Shamrock Corporation (Diamond) and predecessor corporations for 23 years. In 1978, he held the title of Director of Corporate Communications. On August 31, 1978, at a meeting with his superior, he was informed that his job was to be eliminated in the corporate reorganization, and that his duties were to be divided between two employees who had been reporting to him.

There is evidence in the record . . . that the quality of Ackerman's work, in addition to the corporate decision to reorganize, influenced Diamond's decision to request him to take early retirement. His job performance had been the subject of an in-house investigation. The result of the investigation was a recommendation that Ackerman should not remain in charge of Corporate Communications. The report of the investigation indicated that Ackerman was a good individual performer, but he had a distaste for "people problems," and was unable to delegate responsibility effectively. In addition, the problems with his job performance were exacerbated by the use of alcohol. In his own deposition Ackerman admitted that he sometimes indulged in the proverbial "three-martini lunch." On at least two occasions, his overindulgence in alcohol was the catalyst in embarrassing incidents during corporate dinner meetings.

The only evidence in the record concerning the basis for Diamond's suggestion that Ackerman select early retirement indicates that Diamond made a legitimate business decision to eliminate Ackerman's job and divide his duties between two other employees. The only motivation for that decision, from the evidence in the record, was the desire to increase corporate efficiency. Nothing in the record, other than personal conclusions by Ackerman, suggests that Ackerman's age in any way was a factor in the decision.

TITLE VII OF THE CIVIL RIGHTS ACT OF 1964

After substantial public debate, Congress passed the Civil Rights Act of 1964. This Act provides a comprehensive statutory scheme for attacking discrimination in this country. Title VII of the 1964 Act, the Fair Employment Practices Act, prohibits certain discriminations in employment. Title VII was amended by the Equal Employment Opportunity Act in 1972. Section 703(a)(2) of Title VII provides in pertinent part:

It shall be an unlawful employment practice for an employer—

(1) to fail or refuse to hire or to discharge any individual, or otherwise to discriminate against any individual with respect to his compensation, terms, conditions, or privileges of employment, because of such individual's race, color, religion, sex or national origin; or

(2) to limit, segregate, or classify his employees or applicants for employment in any way which would deprive or tend to deprive any individual of employment opportunities or otherwise adversely affect his status as an employee, because of such individual's race, color, religion, sex, or national origin.

Title VII of the Civil Rights Act prohibits employment discrimination based on five criteria: (1) race, (2) color, (3) religion, (4) national origin, and (5) sex. "Sex" as a covered criterion was added to the language of the Act only the day before the Act was passed by the House. Age is *not* a protected criterion under Title VII. The purpose of Title VII is to create equality of *employment opportunities* by requiring covered employers to make employment decisions based on a candidate's ability to perform, and not on some non-job-related criterion.

The scope of the employment practices covered by Title VII is broad; Title VII prohibits discrimination in job hiring, in payment of compensation or fringe benefits, in availability of training programs and apprenticeship opportunities, in decisions regarding promotion or demotion, in decisions regarding dismissal, in referral systems for employment, in work rules, and in any other "term, condition, or privilege of employment."

Title VII only covers certain employers. The Act defines an *employer* as one who is "engaged in an industry affecting commerce who has 15 or more employees for each working day in each of 20 or more calendar weeks in the current or preceding calendar year, and any agent of such person." Generally, any business, company, or state or local government meeting this definition is subject to the provisions of Title VII. Employment agencies and unions are also prohibited from engaging in employment discrimination in their referral or membership practices. Expressly *excluded* from Title VII coverage are the United States government, corporations wholly owned by the United States, Indian tribes, agencies of the District of Columbia, and tax-exempt private clubs.

Hishen v. King & Spaulding.   The Supreme Court is currently expanding the employment relations that are covered by Title VII. In *Elizabeth Anderson Hishen v. King & Spaulding,* 104 U.S. 2229 (1984), the U.S. Supreme Court held that Title VII was applicable to a decision for selecting a partner for a law firm. In that case, the plaintiff, who was an associate lawyer with a prestigious Southern law firm, sued the firm under Title VII alleging sex discrimination when she was rejected twice for partnership status in the firm.

The law firm asserted that Hishen did not have a right to sue, arguing that Title VII did not apply to decisions to promote persons to partnership status, and that lawyers made such a "distinctive contribution" to society that their partnership decisions were constitutionally protected by the First Amendment right of freedom of association. The Supreme Court rejected the defendant's arguments and held that a decision whether to advance someone to partnership status was a "benefit" of employment to which Title VII applied, and remanded the case for trial. All partnerships with 15 or more employees (e.g., law firms, accounting firms, architectural and engineering firms) are now subject to Title VII review whenever they make a decision whether to promote an employee to partnership status.

Records and Reporting Requirements.   Title VII requires all covered employers, unions, and employment agencies to keep records regarding the employment of protected classes. All records regarding employment "opportunities," such as job applications, hiring decisions, promotions and demotions, pay increases and decreases, and layoffs, must be kept for six months, and may not be destroyed while a discrimination charge is pending before the EEOC or in federal court. Employers, unions, and employment agencies covered by Title VII must file annual reports with the EEOC regarding their minority-group employment.

Each covered employer, union, and employment agency must conspicuously display in the workplace a notice summarizing the relevant provisions of Title VII. The notice must be posted in either English or Spanish, whichever is better understood by the work force. A willful violation of the notice requirement is punishable by a fine of $100 per violation.

Filing a Title VII Charge. The Equal Employment Opportunity Commission (EEOC) is charged with administering Title VII. A person alleging a discriminatory act by an employer, union, or employment agency in violation of Title VII must file a *complaint* with the state or local agency assigned the responsibility to hear discrimination claims. Sixty days thereafter the charging party (employee) may file a complaint with the EEOC, generally at a regional office, whether or not the state or local body has made a determination in the matter. The accused employer, union, or employment agency is the "responding party" in an EEOC procedure.

The EEOC then notifies the respondent of the charge, and proceeds to investigate the matter. The investigation may consist of sending interrogatories to the respondent, making visits to the work site, review of employment records, questioning employees, etc. The EEOC may issue subpoenas to obtain relevant documents and information. If, after its investigation, the EEOC finds "reasonable cause" to believe that a Title VII violation occurred, it will issue a "determination letter" notifying the respondent-employer of its finding. The EEOC usually attempts to resolve discrimination charges through informal conciliation with the employer. A conciliation conference is held, at which the employer is usually represented by an attorney and the charging party by the EEOC. If a conciliation agreement is reached, it must be signed by all parties and approved by the EEOC regional director. A conciliation agreement is binding on all parties.

If a conciliation agreement is not reached, the EEOC regional office may refer the case to its litigation department for further action. In the alternative, the EEOC may notify the charging party that a conciliation agreement has not been reached and that the charging party has the right to file a *civil* action within 90 days against the respondent. If the EEOC at any time dismisses the charge against the respondent, the charging party has the same right to file a civil lawsuit against the respondent. A Title VII discrimination action must be brought in the proper federal court. Title VII actions are mandatorily expedited in the federal courts. The suit may be brought on behalf of the individual claimant or as a "class action" on behalf of all similarly situated employees or prospective employees.

Discrimination in Employment Defined.

Employment discrimination in violation of Title VII may result in three ways: (1) from the "disparate treatment" of a specific individual, (2) from a "pattern or practice" of discrimination, (3) from the "disparate impact" of an employment rule or practice.

"Disparate Treatment" of an Individual. Unlawful discrimination often occurs where an employer treats a specific individual less favorably than other employees because of race, color, religion, national origin, or sex. In *McDonnell Douglas Corp. v. Green*, 411 U.S. 792 (1973), the U.S. Supreme Court set forth the elements that a claimant must show in order to establish a "disparate treatment" based on racial discrimination in violation of Title VII:

The complainant in a Title VII trial must carry the initial burden under the statute of establishing a *prima facie* case of racial discrimination. This may be done by showing:

(i) that he belongs to a racial minority;

(ii) that he applied and was qualified for a job for which the employer was seeking applicants;

(iii) that, despite his qualifications, he was rejected; and

(iv) that, after his rejection, the position remained open and the employer continued to seek applicants from persons of complainant's qualifications.

The *McDonnell Douglas* test may also be applied to determine disparate-treatment violations of Title VII based on sex, color, national origin, and religion. Where a claimant proves a *prima facie* case of disparate treatment, the employer must prove that he had a job-related nondiscriminatory reason for denying the claimant an employment opportunity.

"Pattern or Practice" of Discrimination.   A violation of Title VII occurs when an employer engages in a general *pattern or practice* of discrimination based on race, color, religion, national origin, or sex. This violation differs from the disparate-treatment violation in that a whole *class* of persons (e.g., a racial group) is discriminated against by the employer, rather than a specific individual.

A pattern or practice of discrimination is usually proved through circumstantial evidence, generally consisting of statistical comparisons. For example, where it is shown that the percentage of minorities in an employer's work force is substantially lower than in the general population or some other relevant population, the court may conclude that the employer has engaged in an unlawful "pattern or practice" of discrimination. The legislature has not established objective criteria in Title VII for determining whether an unlawful pattern or practice of discrimination has occurred (e.g., the percentage of minority workers compared to the percentage of minorities in the relevant population), but has left it to the courts to draw conclusions on a case-by-case basis.

Once a pattern or practice of discrimination has been shown, a presumption of discrimination against *all* applicants of the protected class arises. Thereafter, each minority applicant does not have to individually prove his discrimination case against the employer. Even persons who did not actually apply for a job may be entitled to relief from a discriminating employer where it can be shown that the employer's discriminating practices *deterred* members of the protected class from seeking employment or employment benefits.

An employer may defend against a charge of a pattern or practice of discrimination on numerous grounds, including:

1. that the statistical comparison used is invalid because an inappropriate population was chosen (for example, the position requires highly skilled candidates, therefore defeating the use of general population statistics)

2. there are not enough trained minority applicants for the position

3. living and commuting patterns significantly affect the availability of labor (for example, there is no public transportation to bring minority workers to the job site)

4. other business and job-related factors show a nondiscriminatory explanation of the inference of the statistical evidence.

"Disparate Impact" Discrimination. Employers often adopt work rules or requirements that appear neutral or objective on their face, but that in reality discriminate against a protected class. Where a seemingly neutral or objective work requirement has a *disparate impact* on a class protected by Title VII, it is unlawful. For example, in *Dothard v. Rawlinson,* 433 U.S. 321 (1977), the U.S. Supreme Court held that a minimum height requirement of 5′2″ and a minimum weight requirement of 120 pounds for a job as a correctional counselor in Alabama prisons had a disparate impact on female applicants in violation of Title VII. Employment tests for hiring and promotion have often been found to have an unlawful disparate impact on employment opportunities for minorities and females. In *Griggs v. Duke Power Co.,* 401 U.S. 425 (1971), Chief Justice Burger wrote for the Court:

Congress did not intend by Title VII, however, to guarantee a job to every person regardless of qualifications. In short, the Act does not command that any person be hired simply because he was formerly the subject of discrimination, or because he is a member of a minority group. Discriminatory preference for any group, minority or majority, is precisely and only what Congress has proscribed. What is required by Congress is the removal of artificial, arbitrary, and unnecessary barriers to employment when the barriers operate invidiously to discriminate on the basis of racial or other impermissible classification.

Congress has now provided that tests or criteria for employment or promotion may not provide equality of opportunity merely in the sense of the fabled offer of milk to the stork and the fox. On the contrary, Congress has now required that the posture and condition of the job-seeker be taken into account. It has—to resort again to the fable—provided that the vessel in which the milk is proffered be one all seekers can use. The Act proscribes not only overt discrimination but also practices that are fair in form, but discriminatory in operation.

In a disparate-impact discrimination case, the claimant must show that the apparently neutral employment practice had a significantly discriminatory impact. The burden of proof then shifts to the employer to show that the work rule is "job-related." However, even where an employer shoulders this burden, the claimant may still prove his disparate-impact case if he can then show that the employer was using the work rule or practice as a "mere pretext for discrimination."

Discrimination by Labor Unions. A *labor union* is broadly defined in Title VII as including any labor organization, agency, or committee that represents employees in their grievances or disputes with employers and that either has 15 or more members or operates a hiring hall or hiring office. Title VII makes it an unlawful employment practice for a *labor organization:*

1. to exclude or expel from its membership, or otherwise discriminate against an individual
2. to limit, segregate, or classify its membership or applicants for membership or fail or refuse to refer such individuals for employment
3. to cause or attempt to cause an employer to discriminate against an individual because of "race, color, religion, sex, or national origin"
4. to discriminate in its apprenticeship or training programs.

Section 704(a) of Title VII makes it an unlawful employment practice for an employer, labor union, or employment agency to discriminate against an employee or applicant who has participated in any Title VII proceeding or opposed any unlawful employment practice. A similar prohibition against retaliation is also contained in the Age Discrimination in Employment Act.

Remedies Under Title VII.   Where a court finds a violation of Title VII, it may issue an injunction to prohibit such action in the future or grant such affirmative action as may be appropriate in the circumstances. Courts may award the payment of back pay, which is limited to two years under Title VII. The court may also grant *fictional* seniority to a discriminated-against class to make up for past discrimination against an individual. Section 706(b) specifically authorizes an award of "reasonable attorneys' fees" to the prevailing party in a Title VII action. Under appropriate circumstances (e.g., intentional discrimination), punitive damages may also be awarded in Title VII proceedings.

Many collective bargaining agreements contain "nondiscrimination" clauses. Where a nondiscrimination clause is provided in a collective bargaining agreement, if an employee feels he has been discriminated against, he may file a lawsuit against the employer for breach of contract. Actions for discrimination under Title VII are independent of any valid contract action, and may be maintained in lieu of the contract action or in addition to it.

SEX DISCRIMINATION

Employment discrimination based on sex has been a substantial problem for women in the United States. Although the prohibition against sex discrimination in Title VII applies equally to men and women, the majority of sex discrimination cases are brought by women. Employment discrimination against women was the result of social mores, stereotypes of the roles of men and women, and a traditional view that a woman's place is in the home.

As educational opportunities increase, as our country changes from a manufacturing to a service economy, and as birth control methods and advanced technology free women's time from household chores, a new awareness of women's freedom to select and pursue careers has arisen. At present, women comprise approximately 40 percent of the work force. Over 65 percent of women are presently in the job force. In many of the better business schools, women comprise 40 percent to 50 percent of entering classes. Today, employment opportunities for women are the greatest of any time in the history of this country. Women often are the highest earners in today's families. Title VII actions are available to extinguish the vestiges of sex discrimination that still remain in the employment relation.

Sex-Plus Discrimination.   Direct "disparate treatment" of an individual female employee often occurs in the employment relation. Direct discrimination against individual female employees or job applicants is a violation of Title VII. More often, however, employment discrimination based on sex is aimed at females as a *class.* Sex discrimination is often in the form of "sex-plus discrimination," where an additional qualification is required or is considered a negative factor for one sex and not the other. For example, an old policy of the airline industry, which has since been held unlawful, was to allow both single and married male flight attendants but only single female flight attendants. In *Philips v. Martin Marietta Corporation,* 400 U.S. 542 (1971), the U.S. Supreme Court held that a corporate employer's policy of refusing to hire women with preschool-age children, where the corporation would hire fathers in the same category, was *sex-plus* discrimination in violation of Title VII.

Sexual Harassment. Sexual harassment has been a continual problem in the work environment. The difficulty of the issue is determining whether the statement or advance is a nonoffensive social gesture or unlawful sexual harassment. Any requirement by a supervisor of sexual relations or favors from employees or job applicants to obtain an employment "opportunity" is a violation of Title VII. Any employee who is promoted based on having sexual relations with his or her supervisor has been given an employment benefit not available to qualified candidates who did not succumb to the sexual harassment. Even employees who quit their job because of sexual harassment may file a suit under Title VII based on a claim of being "constructively [in effect] discharged."

In *Dothard, Director, Department of Public Safety of Alabama v. Rawlinson* the Supreme Court held that Alabama's rule prohibiting female "correctional counselors" at male maximum-security prisons was not sex discrimination under Title VII.

2 basis for challenging

SEX DISCRIMINATION

DOTHARD, DIRECTOR, DEPARTMENT OF PUBLIC SAFETY OF ALABAMA v. RAWLINSON

433 U.S. 321 (1977)
UNITED STATES SUPREME COURT

Mr. Justice Stewart delivered the opinion of the Court.

Appellee Dianne Rawlinson sought employment with the Alabama Board of Corrections as a prison guard, called in Alabama a "correctional counselor." After her application was rejected, she brought this class suit under Title VII of the Civil Rights Act of 1964. . . .

FACTS

At the time she applied for a position as correctional counselor trainee, Rawlinson was a 22-year-old college graduate whose major course of study had been correctional psychology. She was refused employment because she failed to meet the minimum 120-pound weight requirement established by an Alabama statute. The statute also establishes a height minimum of 5 feet 2 inches.

After her application was rejected because of her weight, Rawlinson filed a charge with the Equal Employment Opportunity Commission, and ultimately received a right-to-sue letter. She then filed a complaint in the District Court on behalf of herself and other similarly situated women, challenging the statutory height and weight minima as violative of Title VII. . . . A three-judge court was convened. While the suit was pending, the Alabama Board of Corrections adopted Administrative Regulation 204, establishing gender criteria for assigning correctional counselors to maximum-security institutions for "contact positions," that is, positions requiring continual close physical proximity to inmates of the institution. Rawlinson amended her class-action complaint by adding a challenge to Regulation 204 as also violative of Title VII.

Like most correctional facilities in the United States, Alabama's prisons are segregated on the basis of sex. . . . The Julia Tutwiler Prison for Women and the four male penitentiaries are maximum-security institutions. Their inmate living quarters are for the most part large dormitories, with communal showers and toilets that are open to the dormitories and hallways. The Draper and Fountain penitentiaries carry on extensive farming operations, making necessary a large number of strip searches for contraband when prisoners re-enter the prison buildings. . . . A correctional counselor's primary duty within these institutions is to maintain security and control of the inmates by continually supervising and observing their activities.

Because most of Alabama's prisoners are held at the four maximum-security male penitentiaries, 336 of the 435 correctional counselor jobs were in those institutions, a majority of them concededly in the "contact" classification. Thus, even though meeting the statutory height and weight requirements, women applicants could under Regulation 204 compete equally with men for only about 25 percent of the correctional counselor jobs available in the Alabama prison system.

HEIGHT AND WEIGHT REQUIREMENT

The District Court found that the minimum statutory height and weight requirements that applicants for employment as correctional counselors must meet constitute the sort of arbitrary barrier to equal employment opportunity that Title VII forbids. . . . [T]he District Court found that the 5′2″ requirement would operate to exclude 33.29 percent of the women in the United States between the ages of 18–79, while excluding only 1.28 percent of men between the same ages. The 120-pound weight restriction would exclude 22.29 percent of the women and 2.35 percent of the men in this age group. When the height and weight restrictions are combined, Alabama's statutory standards would exclude 41.13 percent of the female population while

excluding less than 1 percent of the male population.

We turn, therefore, to the appellants' argument that they have rebutted the *prima facie* case of discrimination by showing that the height and weight requirements are job related. These requirements, they say, have a relationship to strength, a sufficient but unspecified amount of which is essential to effective job performance as a correctional counselor. In the District Court, however, the appellants produced no evidence correlating the height and weight requirements with the requisite amount of strength thought essential to good job performance. Indeed, they failed to offer evidence of any kind in specific justification of the statutory standards.

If the job-related quality that the appellants identify is *bona fide,* their purpose could be achieved by adopting and validating a test for applicants that measures strength directly. Such a test, fairly administered, would fully satisfy the standards of Title VII because it would be one that "measure[s] the person for the job and not the person in the abstract." (*Griggs v. Duke Power Co.*) But nothing in the present record even approaches such a measurement.

For the reasons we have discussed, the District Court was not in error in holding that Title VII of the Civil Rights Act of 1964, as amended, prohibits application of the statutory height and weight requirements to Rawlinson and the class she represents.

REGULATION 204

The environment in Alabama's penitentiaries is a peculiarly inhospitable one for human beings of whatever sex. Indeed, a Federal District Court has held that the conditions of confinement in the prisons of the State, characterized by "rampant violence" and a "jungle atmosphere," are constitutionally intolerable. The record in the present case shows that because of inadequate staff and facilities, no attempt is made in the four maximum-security male penitentiaries to classify or segregate inmates according to their offense or level of dangerousness—a procedure that, according to expert testimony, is essential to effective penological administration. Consequently, the estimated 20 percent of the male prisoners who are sex offenders are scattered throughout the penitentiaries' dormitory facilities.

In this environment of violence and disorganization, it would be an oversimplification to characterize Regulation 204 as an exercise in "romantic paternalism." In the usual case, the argument that a particular job is too dangerous for women may appropriately be met by the rejoinder that it is the purpose of Title VII to allow the individual woman to make that choice for herself. More is at stake in this case, however, than an individual woman's decision to weigh and accept the risks of employment in a "contact" position in a maximum-security male prison.

The essence of a correctional counselor's job is to maintain prison security. A woman's relative ability to maintain order in a male, maximum-security, unclassified penitentiary of the type Alabama now runs could be directly reduced by her womanhood. There is a basis in fact for expecting that sex offenders who have criminally assaulted women in the past would be moved to do so again if access to women were established within the prison. There would also be a real risk that other inmates, deprived of a normal heterosexual environment, would assault women guards because they were women. In a prison system where violence is the order of the day, where inmate access to guards is facilitated by dormitory living arrangements, where every institution is understaffed, and where a substantial portion of the inmate population is composed of sex offenders mixed at random with other prisoners, there are few visible deterrents to inmate assaults on women custodians.

The likelihood that inmates would assault a woman because she was a woman would pose a real threat not only to the victim of the assault but also to the basic control of the penitentiary and protection of its inmates and the other security personnel. The employee's very womanhood would thus directly undermine her capacity to provide the security that is the essence of a correctional counselor's responsibility.

[W]e conclude that the District Court was in error in ruling that being male is not a bona fide occupational qualification for the job of correctional counselor in a "contact" position in an Alabama male maximum-security penitentiary.

The judgment is accordingly *affirmed in part* and *reversed in part,* and the case is *remanded* to the District Court for further proceedings consistent with this opinion.

CASE QUESTIONS

1. What does Title VII provide? Is it only applicable to the *employment* situation? Is sex discrimination prohibited by Title VII?
2. What did Regulation 204 of the Alabama Board of Corrections provide? Explain.
3. What position did the plaintiff apply for? Was she rejected for the job? Why?
4. Which of the following forms of discrimination was the height and weight requirement? What form of discrimination was Regulation 204?
   a. disparate treatment
   b. pattern or practice
   c. disparate impact
5. How did the Supreme Court decide each of the following alleged violations of Title VII? What reasoning did the Court use in reaching its decision?
   a. height and weight requirement
   b. Regulation 204

Policy Issue. Do you agree with the following statement of the Supreme Court, "The employee's very *womanhood* would thus directly undermine her capacity to provide the security that is the essence of a correctional counselor's responsibility." Why or why not?

Economics Issue. Should a woman be allowed to make a decision herself as to whether a job is too dangerous?

Ethics Issue. Do you think Regulation 204 was adopted to discriminate against females and keep the jobs of correctional counselors for males?

Social Responsibility. Does society owe a duty of social responsibility to protect women from dangerous job positions? Or is this "romantic paternalism"? Explain.

The Pregnancy Discrimination Act. In 1978, Congress enacted the Pregnancy Discrimination Act as an amendment to Title VII. The Act amended the definitional section of Title VII by adding the language "because of or on the basis of pregnancy, childbirth, or related medical conditions" to the terms "because of sex" and "on the basis of sex" contained in Title VII. Section 701 of the Act further provides:

[W]omen affected by pregnancy, childbirth, or related medical conditions shall be treated the same for all employment-related purposes, including the receipt of benefits under fringe benefit programs, as other persons not so affected but similar in their ability or inability to work.

Thus, work rules prohibiting the hiring of pregnant women, or dismissing or requiring women to leave work during their pregnancy, violate Title VII. However, in *General Electric Co. v. Gilbert*, 429 U.S. 125 (1976), the U.S. Supreme Court held that the exclusion of pregnancy from an employer's disability benefit plan did *not* constitute sex discrimination within the meaning of Title VII.

Sexual Preference. Title VII does not prohibit discrimination in employment based on *sexual preference* (e.g., homosexuality). The courts have tended to construe Title VII narrowly when defining the sex discrimination that it prohibits. This excerpt is from *Somers v. Budget Marketing, Inc.* 667 F.2d 748 (1982), where the court granted a summary judgment in favor of the employer when a transsexual employee sued the employer for sex discrimination under Title VII.

Appellant Audra Sommers, plaintiff below, also known as Timothy Cornish, appeals from an order of the district court entering summary judgment in favor of the defendant below, Budget Marketing, Incorporated. . . . Sommers claims to be a "female with the anatomical body of a male."

Although this circuit has not previously considered the issue raised on this appeal, we are in agreement with the district court that for the purposes of Title VII the plain meaning must be ascribed to the term "sex" in absence of clear congressional intent to do otherwise. Furthermore, the legislative history does not show any intention to include transsexualism in Title VII. The amendment adding the word "sex" to the Civil Rights Act was adopted one day before the House passed the Act without prior legislative hearings and little debate. It is, however, generally recognized that the major thrust of the "sex" amendment was towards providing equal opportunities for women.

Also, proposals to amend the Civil Rights Act to prohibit discrimination on the basis of "sexual preference" have been defeated. Three such bills were presented to the 94th Congress and seven were presented to the 95th Congress. Sommers's claim is not one dealing with discrimination on the basis of sexual preference. Nevertheless, the fact that the proposals were defeated indicates that the word "sex" in Title VII is to be given its traditional definition, rather than an expansive interpretation. Because Congress has not shown an intention to protect transsexuals, we hold that discrimination based on one's transsexualism does not fall within the protective purview of the Act.

The appropriate remedy is not immediately apparent to this court. Should Budget allow Sommers to use the female restroom, the male restroom, or one for Sommers's own use? Perhaps some reasonable accommodation could be worked out between the parties.

The decision of the district court granting summary judgment in favor of the employer is *affirmed*.

Some states and local governments have passed laws to protect persons from discrimination based on sexual preference.

RACIAL DISCRIMINATION

The Civil Rights Act of 1964 was primarily passed to address the problem of racial discrimination in the United States. Title VII was primarily enacted to address the problem of racial discrimination in the employment relation. Racial discrimination lawsuits make up a substantial portion of Title VII cases.

Racial discrimination may occur prior to a person being hired for a job (e.g., in a job interview), or after the person is hired (e.g., in a discriminatory employment test for advancement). Like other forms of discrimination, racial discrimination may be in the form of disparate treatment of an individual member of a race, a pattern or practice of discrimination against all members of a race, or an otherwise neutral employment practice that causes a disparate impact on a particular race.

Job Interviews.   Title VII and other antidiscrimination laws regulate what questions may be asked of a job applicant in a job interview. Generally, only job-related questions are lawful. For example, asking a job applicant if he or she is married or has children, what religion he or she practices, where he or she lives, what means of transportation will be taken to work, and other non-job-related questions may constitute discrimination in violation of Title VII. A job applicant may *volunteer* such information without liability to the employer.

Professionally Developed Ability Tests.   To assess candidates for employment opportunities an employer may use any "professionally developed ability test" that is job-related and does not discriminate in violation of Title VII. Questions often arise as to whether a particular test is "job-related" and may validly be used to screen job applicants and employees seeking an employment "opportunity," e.g., promotion, or whether the test is merely a disguised form of discrimination. An employer bears the burden of justifying the job-relatedness of an employment test by any one of three methods: (1) criteria validity, (2) content validity, or (3) construct validity.

1. Criteria validity is established where a statistical relationship between performance on the test and performance on the job can be shown.
2. Content validity is proven where a test representatively samples a function to be performed on the job (e.g., a typing test for applicants for a typing position).

3. Construct validity is proven where a test of a psychological trait is shown to be required for the job (e.g., a leadership test for a police commander).

In *Connecticut v. Winnie Teal* the Supreme Court held that an employment test used by an employer caused a *disparate impact* and was racial discrimination that violated Title VII.

If exam is discriminatory

RACIAL DISCRIMINATION

CONNECTICUT v. WINNIE TEAL

457 U.S. 440 (1982)
UNITED STATES SUPREME COURT

Justice Brennan delivered the opinion of the Court.

Four of the respondents, Winnie Teal, Rose Walker, Edith Latney, and Grace Clark, are black employees of the Department of Income Maintenance of the State of Connecticut. Each was promoted provisionally to the position of Welfare Eligibility Supervisor and served in that capacity for almost two years. To attain permanent status as supervisors, however, respondents had to participate in a selection process that required, as the first step, a passing score on a written examination. This written test was administered on December 2, 1978, to 329 candidates. Of these candidates, 48 identified themselves as black and 259 identified themselves as white. The results of the examination were announced in March 1979. With the passing score set at 65, 54.17 of the identified black candidates passed. This was approximately 68 percent of the passing rate for the identified white candidates. The four respondents were among the blacks who failed the examination, and they were thus excluded from further consideration for permanent supervisory positions.

In April 1979, respondents instituted this action in the United States District Court for the District of Connecticut against petitioners, the State of Connecticut, two state agencies, and two state officials. Respondents alleged, *inter alia,* that petitioners violated Title VII by imposing, as an absolute condition for consideration for promotion, that applicants pass a written test that excluded blacks in dispro-

portionate numbers and that was not job related.

More than a year after this action was instituted, and approximately one month before trial, petitioners made promotions from the eligibility list generated by the written examination. In choosing persons from that list, petitioners considered past work performance, recommendations of the candidates' supervisors and, to a lesser extent, seniority. Petitioners then applied what the Court of Appeals characterized as an affirmative action program in order to ensure a significant number of minority supervisors. Forty-six persons were promoted to permanent supervisory positions, 11 of whom were black and 35 of whom were white. The overall result of the selection process was that, of the 48 identified black candidates who participated in the selection process, 22.9 percent were promoted and of the 259 identified white candidates, 13.5 percent were promoted. It is this "bottom-line" result, more favorable to blacks than to whites, that petitioners urge should be adjudged to be a complete defense to respondents' suit.

[In *Griggs v. Duke Power Co.* this Court stated:]

> [Title VII] proscribes not only overt discrimination but also practices that are fair in form, but discriminatory in operation. The touchstone is business necessity. If an employment practice which operates to exclude Negroes cannot be shown to be related to job performance, the practice is prohibited.

In suggesting that the "bottom line" may be a defense to a claim of discrimination against an individual employee, petitioners and *amici* appear to confuse unlawful discrimination with discriminatory intent. The Court has stated that a nondiscriminatory "bottom line" and an employer's good faith efforts to achieve a nondiscriminatory work force, might in some cases assist an employer in rebutting the inference that a particular action had been intentionally discriminatory.

It is clear that Congress never intended to give an employer license to discriminate against some employees on the basis of race or sex merely because he favorably treats other members of the employees' group. . . . Title VII does not permit the victim of a facially discriminatory policy to be told that he has not been wronged because other persons of his or her race or sex were hired.

In sum, petitioners' nondiscriminatory "bottom line" is no answer, under the terms of Title VII, to respondents' *prima facie* claim of employment discrimination. Accordingly, the judgment of the Court of Appeals for the Second Circuit is *affirmed,* and this case is *remanded* to the District Court for further proceedings consistent with this opinion.

Justice Powell, with whom **The Chief Justice, Justice Rehnquist,** and **Justice O'Connor** join, dissenting.

Today's decision takes a long and unhappy step in the direction of confusion. Title VII does not require that employers adopt merit hiring or the procedures most likely to permit the greatest number of minority members to be considered for or to qualify for jobs and promotions. Employers need not develop tests that accurately reflect the skills of every individual candidate; there are few if any tests that do so. Yet the Court seems unaware of this practical reality, and perhaps oblivious to the likely consequences of its decision. By its holding today, the Court may force employers either to eliminate tests or rely on expensive, job-related testing procedures, the validity of which may or may not be sustained if challenged. For state and local governmental employers with limited funds, the practical effect of today's decision may well be the adoption of simple quota hiring. This arbitrary method of employment is itself unfair to individual applicants, whether or not they are members of minority groups. And it is not likely to produce a competent workforce.

CASE QUESTIONS

1. Does Title VII prohibit *race* discrimination in employment?
2. What position did the plaintiffs apply for in this case? Why were they originally rejected for the position?
3. What do the following types of discrimination prohibit? Which type was alleged in this case?
   a. disparate treatment
   b. pattern or practice
   c. disparate impact
4. What did the "bottom line" theory that was asserted by the defendant provide? Did the Supreme Court accept this defense?
5. You have to promote someone to the supervisor position involved in this case; rank and weigh the following criteria in importance in making your decision regarding job applicants. Add whatever other criteria you think should be considered.
   a. intelligence test
   b. past work experience
   c. recommendations of supervisors
   d. seniority

Policy Issue. Is intelligence a proper job-related requirement for a supervisor's position such as the one involved in this case? How can intelligence be tested?

Economics Issue. Is a college degree a surrogate measure of intelligence? If a company only hired recruits for management positions from the top ten business schools, would this violate Title VII? Why or why not?

Ethics Issue. Do you think the employer in this case acted unethically?

Social Responsibility. Will this decision force *quota* hiring as asserted by Justice Powell in his dissenting opinion? Will this decision help produce an *incompetent* work force?

Appearance Standards. Many claims of racial and sexual discrimination are based on *work rules,* particularly appearance standards. Generally, an employer may validly set *appearance standards* such as dress codes and hair standards. An employer does not have to justify the imposition of nondiscriminatory appearance standards. An employer has the right to enforce nondiscriminatory standards, even by dismissing nonconforming employees.

The right to dress or to groom in a certain manner is not itself protected under Title VII. However, if it can be shown that an appearance standard affects "unchangeable characteristics" peculiar to a certain race, sex, or national origin, the rule may cause a disparate impact and violate Title VII. For example, a rule that all employees must wear full beards would cause a disparate impact in the form of sex discrimination and possibly racial discrimination. A work rule requiring all employees to wear dresses would be sex discrimination.

In *Rogers v. American Airlines, Inc.* the court upheld an employer's appearance rule that prohibited the wearing of the "corn row" style of hair as not constituting sex or racial discrimination.

APPEARANCE STANDARDS

ROGERS v. AMERICAN AIRLINES, INC.

527 F.SUPP 229 (1981)
UNITED STATES DISTRICT COURT, S.D. NEW YORK

Sofaer, District Judge.

Plaintiff is a black woman who seeks $10,000 damages, injunctive, and declaratory relief against enforcement of a grooming policy of the defendant American Airlines that prohibits employees in certain employment categories from wearing an all-braided hairstyle. Plaintiff has been an American Airlines employee for approximately 11 years, and has been an airport operations agent for over one year. Her duties involve extensive passenger contact, including greeting passengers, issuing boarding passes, and checking luggage. She alleges that the policy violates her rights . . . under Title VII of the Civil Rights Act. . . . She claims that denial of the right to wear her hair in the "corn row" style intrudes upon her rights and discriminates against her.

SEX DISCRIMINATION

The policy is addressed to both men and women, black and white. Plaintiff's assertion that the policy has practical effect only with respect to women is not supported by any factual allegations. Many men have hair longer than many women. Some men have hair long enough to wear in braids if they choose to do so. Even if the grooming policy imposed different standards for men and women, however, it would not violate Title VII. It follows, therefore, that an even-handed policy that prohibits to both sexes a style more often adopted by members of one sex does not constitute prohibited sex discrimination. This is because this type of regulation has at most a negligible effect on employment opportunity. It does not regulate on the basis of any immutable characteristic of the employees involved. It concerns a matter of relatively low importance in terms of the constitutional interests protected by the Fourteenth Amendment and Title VII, rather than involving fundamental rights such as the right to have children or to marry. The complaint does not state a claim for sex discrimination.

RACIAL DISCRIMINATION

The considerations with respect to plaintiff's race discrimination claim would clearly be the same, except for plaintiff's assertion that the "corn row" style has a special significance for black women. She contends that it

> has been, historically, a fashion and style adopted by Black American women, reflective of cultural, historical essence of the Black women in American society. . . . The style was 'popularized' so to speak, within the larger society, when Cicely Tyson adopted the same for an appearance on nationally viewed Academy Awards presentation several years ago. . . . It was and is analogous to the public statement by the late Malcolm X regarding the Afro hair style. . . . At the bottom line, the completely braided hair style, sometimes referred to as corn rows, has been and continues to be part of the cultural and historical essence of Black American women.

Plaintiff is entitled to a presumption that her arguments, largely repeated in her affidavit, are true. But the grooming policy applies equally to members of all races, and plaintiff does not allege that an all-braided hair style is worn exclusively or even predominantly by black people. Moreover, it is proper to note that defendants have alleged without contravention that plaintiff first appeared at work in the all-braided hairstyle on or about September 25, 1980, soon after the style had been popularized by a white actress in the film "10."

Plaintiff may be correct that an employer's policy prohibiting the "Afro/bush" style might offend Title VII and Section 1981. But if so, this chiefly would be because banning a natural hairstyle would implicate the policies underlying the prohibition of discrimination on the basis of immutable characteristics. . . . In any event, an all-braided hairstyle is a different matter. It is not the product of natural hair growth but of artifice. An all-braided hair style is an "easily changed characteristic," and, even if socioculturally associated with a particular race or nationality, is not an impermissible basis for distinctions in the application of employment practices by an employer. . . .

Moreover, the airline did not require plaintiff to restyle her hair. It suggested that she could wear her hair as she liked while off duty, and permitted her to pull her hair into a bun and wrap a hairpiece around the bun during working hours. . . . Plaintiff has done this, but alleges that the hairpiece has caused her severe headaches. A larger hairpiece would seem in order. But even if any hairpiece would cause such discomfort, the policy does not offend a substantial interest.

This action is *dismissed,* . . .

CASE QUESTIONS

1. What rule of the employer did the plaintiff challenge? Explain.
2. How did the court answer the following alleged violations of Title VII?
   a. sex discrimination
   b. race discrimination
3. Why was the movie "10" cited by the court?
4. If the grooming standard in this case had prohibited the "Afro-bush" style of hair rather than the "corn row" style of hair, would the case have been decided differently? Why or why not?

Policy Issue. Should an employer be allowed to set grooming standards for its employees? Or should an employee be free to set whatever grooming standard he or she personally chooses?

Economics Issue. Are employee grooming standards important economically to employers? Explain.

Ethics Issue. Did the employer in this case act unethically when it set the grooming standard it did in this case? Do you think it intended to discriminate when it adopted this standard?

Social Responsibility. Does a company owe a duty of social responsibility to provide cleanly groomed personnel to serve the public?

NATIONAL ORIGIN AND DISCRIMINATION

Title VII prohibits employment discrimination based on national origin. *Race* refers to broad categories such as blacks, caucasians, Orientals, and Indians.

National origin, on the other hand, refers to the national heritage of a person. For example, Title VII would prohibit employment discrimination against Italians, Irish, Koreans, etc. Often, no Title VII violation is shown unless an employer discriminates against persons with surnames indicative of a certain national origin. Courts have held that an English language requirement is discriminatory where English language skills are not required for the work to be performed.

The U.S. Supreme Court has held that Title VII does *not* prohibit employment discrimination against *aliens,* whether illegal or not. Therefore, an employer *may* validly require United States citizenship as an employment qualification. However, aliens are protected from employment discrimination based on national origin.

RELIGIOUS DISCRIMINATION

Title VII prohibits discrimination in employment based on religion. Section 701(j), contained in a 1972 amendment to Title VII, provides:

The term "religion" includes all aspects of religious observance and practice, as well as belief, unless an employer demonstrates that he is unable to reasonably accommodate to an employee's or prospective employee's religious observance or practice without undue hardship on the conduct of the employer's business.

Charges of discrimination based on religion have not been frequent. Therefore a body of judicial law has not developed to interpret the broad language of Section 701(j). Most cases alleging religious discrimination are brought when a work rule and a religious practice conflict (for example, when work is required on a religious holiday). The right of an employee to practice his religion in conflict with a business practice is not absolute. An employer is only under a duty to "reasonably accommodate" the religious observance, practice, or belief. Where an employer shows that the religious observance, practice, or belief cannot be "reasonably accommodated" without "undue hardship" on business, the employer is not liable for religious discrimination.

Most current religious discrimination cases are concerned with applying the broad standards "reasonably accommodate" and "undue hardship" to specific fact situations. Factors such as size of the company, importance of the employee's position, availability of alternative workers, etc., are considered by the courts when applying these standards. The definition of "religion" is also commonly at issue in religious discrimination cases.

In *Trans World Airlines, Inc. v. Hardison,* which follows, the U.S. Supreme Court applied the "reasonably accommodate" and "undue hardship" standards of Title VII and found that an employer's work rule requiring employees to work on Saturday did not constitute employment discrimination based on religion.

RELIGIOUS DISCRIMINATION

TRANS WORLD AIRLINES, INC. v. HARDISON

432 U.S. 63 (1977)
UNITED STATES SUPREME COURT

Mr. Justice White delivered the opinion of the Court.

Section 703 (a)(1) of the Civil Rights Act of 1964, Title VII, makes it an unlawful employment practice for an employer to discriminate against an employee or a prospective employee on the basis of his or her religion. At the time of the events involved here, a guideline of the Equal Employment Opportunity Commission (EEOC), required, as the Act itself now does, that an employer, short of "undue hardship," make "reasonable accommodations" to the religious needs of its employees.

Petitioner Trans World Airlines (TWA) operates a large maintenance and overhaul base in Kansas City, Mo. On June 5, 1967, respondent Larry G. Hardison was hired by TWA to work as a clerk in the Stores Department at its Kansas City base. Because of its essential role in the Kansas City operation, the Stores Department must operate 24 hours per day, 365 days per year, and whenever an employee's job in that department is not filled, an employee must be shifted from another department, or a supervisor must cover the job, even if the work in other areas may suffer.

Hardison, like other employees at the Kansas City base, was subject to a seniority system contained in a collective-bargaining agreement that TWA maintains with petitioner International Association of Machinists and Aerospace Workers (IAM). The seniority system is implemented by the union steward through a system of bidding by employees for particular shift assignments as they become available. The most senior employees have first choice for job and shift assignments, and the most junior employees are required to work when the union steward is unable to find enough people willing to work at a particular time or in a particular job to fill TWA's needs.

In the spring of 1968 Hardison began to study the religion known as the Worldwide Church of God. One of the tenets of that religion is that one must observe the Sabbath by refraining from performing any work from sunset on Friday until sunset on Saturday. The religion also proscribes work on certain specified religious holidays.

The problem soon . . . [appeared] when Hardison bid for and received a transfer from Building 1, where he had been employed, to Building 2, where he would work the day shift. The two buildings had entirely separate seniority lists; and while in Building 1 Hardison had sufficient seniority to observe the Sabbath regularly, he was second from the bottom on the Building 2 seniority list. . . . In Building 2 Hardison was asked to work Saturdays when a fellow employee went on vacation.

TWA agreed to permit the union to seek a change of work assignments for Hardison, but the union was not willing to violate the seniority provisions set out in the collective-bargaining contract, and Hardison had insufficient seniority to bid for a shift having Saturdays off. . . . When an accommodation was not reached, Hardison refused to report for work on Saturdays. A transfer to the twilight shift proved unavailing since that schedule still required Hardison to work past sundown on Fridays. After a hearing, Hardison was discharged on grounds of insubordination for refusing to work during his designated shift.

Hardison, having first invoked the administrative remedy provided by Title VII, brought this action for injunctive relief in the United States District Court against TWA and IAM, claiming that his discharge by TWA constituted religious discrimination in violation of Title VII. . . . After a bench trial, the District Court ruled in favor of the defendants. . . . As the District Court construed the Act, TWA had satisfied its "reasonable accommodations" obligation, and any further accommodation would have worked an undue hardship on the company. . . . The Court of Appeals for the Eighth Circuit reversed the judgment for TWA. It agreed with the District Court's constitutional ruling, but held that TWA had not satisfied its duty to accommodate.

Hardison and the EEOC insist that the statutory

obligation to accommodate religious needs takes precedence over both the collective-bargaining contract and the seniority rights of TWA's other employees. . . . [W]e do not believe that the duty to accommodate requires TWA to take steps inconsistent with the otherwise valid agreement. Collective bargaining, aimed at effecting workable and enforceable agreements between management and labor, lies at the core of our national labor policy, and seniority provisions are universally included in these contracts. Without a clear and express indication from Congress, we cannot agree with Hardison and the EEOC that an agreed-upon seniority system must give way when necessary to accommodate religious observances.

It was essential to TWA's business to require Saturday and Sunday work from at least a few employees even though most employees preferred those days off. Allocating the burdens of weekend work was a matter for collective bargaining. In considering criteria to govern this allocation, TWA and the union had two alternatives: adopt a neutral system, such as seniority, a lottery, or rotating shifts; or allocate days off in accordance with the religious needs of its employees. TWA would have had to adopt the latter in order to assure Hardison and others like him of getting the days off necessary for strict observance of their religion, but it could have done so only at the expense of others who had strong, but perhaps nonreligious, reasons for not working on weekends. There were no volunteers to relieve Hardison on Saturdays, and to give Hardison Saturdays off, TWA would have had to deprive another employee of his shift preference at least in part because he did not adhere to a religion that observed the Saturday Sabbath.

Title VII does not contemplate such unequal treatment. . . . It would be anomalous to conclude that by "reasonable accommodation" Congress meant that an employer must deny the shift and job preference of some employees, as well as deprive them of their contractual rights, in order to accommodate or prefer the religious needs of others, and we conclude that Title VII does not require an employer to go that far. . . . TWA was not required by Title VII to carve out a special exception to its seniority system in order to help Hardison to meet his religious obligations.

The Court of Appeals also suggested that TWA could have permitted Hardison to work a four-day week if necessary in order to avoid working on his Sabbath. . . . To require TWA to bear more than a *de minimis* cost in order to give Hardison Saturdays off is an undue hardship. . . . While incurring extra costs to secure a replacement for Hardison might remove the necessity of compelling another employee to work involuntarily in Hardison's place, it would not change the fact that the privilege of having Saturdays off would be allocated according to religious beliefs. . . . [W]e will not readily construe the statute to require an employer to discriminate against some employees in order to enable others to observe their Sabbath.

Reversed.

Mr. Justice Marshall, with whom **Mr. Justice Brennan** joins, dissenting.

Particularly troublesome has been the plight of adherents to minority faiths who do not observe the holy days on which most businesses are closed—Sundays, Christmas, and Easter—but who need time off for their own days of religious observance. . . . An employer, the Court concludes, need not grant even the most minor special privilege to religious observers to enable them to follow their faith. As a question of social policy, this result is deeply troubling, for a society that truly values religious pluralism cannot compel adherents of minority religions to make the cruel choice of surrendering their religion or their job.

CASE QUESTIONS

1. Does Title VII prohibit discrimination based on *religion?*
2. What religion did the plaintiff practice? Was it a major religion? What conflict developed between the plaintiff's religion and his job? Explain.
3. Why did Hardison not have preference in choosing work times? How was *seniority* arrived at for the choice of work times?
4. Is an employer under a legal duty to try to *accommodate* the religious preferences of its employees? If so, are there any limits on this duty? Explain.
5. What reasoning did the Supreme Court use in holding that TWA was *not* required to do the following?

a. give Hardison preference over all other employees for choice of work times
b. require other workers to work overtime and pay them higher overtime pay to take Hardison's shifts
c. let Hardison only work four days each week

Policy Issue. Should an employer be free to assign work without having to consider all of its employees' religious preferences? Why or why not?

Economics Issue. What would be the economic consequences if an employer had to ac-commodate *all* religious preferences of its employees? Would employees become more religious?

Ethics Issue. Do you think the employer in this case intended to discriminate against Hardison because of his religious beliefs? Why or why not?

Social Responsibility. Do employers owe a duty of social responsibility to accommodate the religious preferences of their employees? Do employees owe a duty of responsibility to not apply for jobs that will conflict with their religious beliefs?

THE AGE DISCRIMINATION IN EMPLOYMENT ACT

Employers have often in the past implemented a policy of not employing persons over a certain age. Under such an employment practice, younger candidates were often hired over similarly qualified older workers. Title VII of the Civil Rights Act of 1964 did not, and does not, prohibit age discrimination. In 1967, Congress enacted the Age Discrimination in Employment Act (ADEA) to address the problem of age discrimination in employment. The Act is presently administered by the EEOC. The Act parallels the provision of Title VII by prohibiting covered employers from discriminating against persons in covered age categories in hiring, compensation, and other conditions of employment in the "segregation or classification" of employers.

When the Age Discrimination in Employment Act of 1967 was first enacted, Congress prohibited employment discrimination by employers against persons between the ages of 40 and 65. In 1978, Congress amended the Act by extending coverage to nonfederal employees up to age 70. An employer would violate the Age Discrimination in Employment Act of 1967 if he refused to hire, or discriminated against, job applicants or employees falling within the 40–70 age category.

Persons *under* 40 or *over* 70 in nonfederal jobs are *not* protected by the Act. An employer may maintain an *age preference* to hire only workers in the 40–70 age category, and discriminate against younger (below 40) or older (above 70) job applicants or employees, without violating the Act. If an employer discriminates against some members of the protected age group (e.g., by setting an age preference for persons between ages 40–50) to the exclusion of other members of the protected class (e.g., by refusing to hire or promote persons between ages 50–70), the employer is liable for violating the Act.

The Age Discrimination in Employment Act covers all nonseasonal employers with 20 or more employees whose business affects interstate commerce. The "interstate commerce" requirement is extremely broad, with few nonseasonal employers with 20 or more employees escaping coverage of the Act. Domestic contractors working abroad and United States subsidiaries of foreign firms are subject to the Act if they meet the other qualifications of the Act.

Employment agencies who locate employees are subject to the provisions of the Act with regard to *all* their clients. Thus, the Act covers an employment agency even though the employer for whom it is finding an employee is not so covered.

All covered employers must post in the workplaces, in a conspicuous place and manner, a notice setting forth the provision of the Act. Certain record-keeping requirements are also imposed on covered employers by the Act. Covered employers and employment agencies may not indicate an illegal age preference on any advertisement or notice of a job opening. Where an employer has been found liable for age discrimination in paying covered employees less than noncovered employees, the employer may not lower the wages of the noncovered employees, but instead must raise the wages of the discriminated-against employees.

BONA FIDE OCCUPATIONAL QUALIFICATION (BFOQ)

Section 703(e) of Title VII statutorily provides that an employer may discriminate in employment opportunities if such discrimination can be shown to be a "bona fide occupational qualification" (BFOQ). A Title VII BFOQ allows an employer to discriminate based on *sex, religion,* or *national origin* where the employer can show that the discrimination is essential for the operation of his business. The Age Discrimination in Employment Act also provides a BFOQ exception for *age* discrimination. *Race* discrimination can never be justified as a BFOQ. The BFOQ exceptions are narrowly interpreted by the courts.

For example, merely showing that men are better accepted as waiters by patrons of gourmet restaurants is not a BFOQ sufficient to deny employment to females as waitresses. However, a rule prohibiting the hiring of men as locker room attendants in the women's shower room of a hotel's recreation facilities would be a valid BFOQ. Controversy reigns over the admission of reporters into the dressing rooms of athletes of the opposite sex for pre- or post-game interviews.

In *Murnane v. American Airlines, Inc.* the court held that an employer's age discrimination in hiring flight officers was a lawful bona fide occupational qualification (BFOQ) and therefore did not violate the Age Discrimination in Employment Act of 1967.

AGE DISCRIMINATION, BFOQ

MURNANE v. AMERICAN AIRLINES, INC.

667 F.2D 98 (1981)
UNITED STATES COURT OF APPEALS, D.C. CIRCUIT

James F. Gordon, Senior United States District Judge:

This appeal follows the District Court's entry of judgment, following trial, dismissing the complaint of plaintiff-appellant Edward L. Murnane and intervenor Equal Employment Opportunity Commission (EEOC). Appellant alleges that appellee American Airlines (American) discriminated against him on account of age. He initiated this cause under the Age Discrimination in Employment Act of 1967 (ADEA), as amended, which declares in relevant part that it shall be unlawful for an employer

> to fail or refuse to hire or to discharge any individual or otherwise discriminate against any individual with respect to his compensation, terms, conditions, or privileges of employment, because of such individual's age. . . .

On April 1, 1976, appellant applied for employment as a Flight Officer with American, stating in his application that he was 43 years of age. The position of Flight Officer is the first of three employment levels, i.e., Flight Officer, Co-pilot and Captain, which ultimately leads to a captaincy in an American cockpit. However, consideration of appellant for employment never advanced beyond the application phase, nor was he ever accorded an interview with American Airlines.

The gravemen of appellant's claim arises out of appellee's established employment hiring practices. American maintains three cockpit positions, Flight Officer, Co-pilot and Captain. It is American's fixed policy to require all Flight Officers to advance to the position of Captain. No one is hired by American without this goal in mind. This is referred to as American's "up-or-out" policy. More specifically, if a Flight Officer or Co-pilot has received the maximum amount of training required for such position and is not qualified at that juncture to advance to the next post, then it is American's policy to terminate such person's employment. American's procedures do not allow for a career as a Flight Officer or Co-pilot. Finally, *American has a general guideline against hiring persons over the age of 30 for the beginning position of Flight Officer.*

The District Court correctly found that appellant is a member of that class of persons intended to be protected under the ADEA, and that appellant established a *prima facie* case of discrimination. However, the District Court dismissed appellant's complaint because it went on to find: That American's age . . . guideline was a bona fide occupational qualification. . . . The ADEA provides . . . that:

> It shall not be unlawful for an employer . . . to take any action . . . where age is a bona fide occupational

qualification reasonably necessary to the normal operation of the particular business, or where the differentiation is based on reasonable factors other than age. . . .

The issue before this court, then, is whether age is a "bona fide occupational qualification" (BFOQ) which is "reasonably necessary to the normal operation" of the airline business. We conclude that it is.

The evidence entered at trial indicates that "pilot error" accounts for 90 percent of all aviation accidents, but that the incidence of aviation accidents decreases as the pilot gains experience. Moreover, the District Court found "credible and persuasive" evidence that "the *best* experience an American Captain can have is acquired by flying American aircraft in American's three cockpit positions." Thus, the safest Captain will be experienced, and as much of that experience as possible will have been with American.

But since it takes at least ten to fifteen years to progress from Flight Officer to Co-pilot to Captain, if appellant were hired as Flight Officer in his forties he would probably not become Captain until his late fifties. The Federal Aviation Administration itself requires retirement at age 60, so that he would be able to serve only briefly as an American Captain before he had to retire. Appellant would then be replaced by another pilot, also new to captaincy in an American cockpit. On the other hand, by limiting its new hiring to relatively young pilots, American thereby ensures that the experience with American of its active Captains will be maximized. This, as we pointed out earlier, maximizes safety.

Appellant contends that the District Court's findings indicate only a marginal increase in the safety of the passengers on an American aircraft, and that such marginal safety is insufficient to support a blanket age rule. . . . We disagree. . . . We believe that the District Court's findings of fact, many of which were agreed to by the parties, support the conclusion that American's hiring policies, including the age 40 guideline, might result in the death of one less person than were American required to abandon or modify these policies.

We conclude that American's age 40 guideline was a bona fide occupational qualification "reasonably necessary to the normal operation" of American Airlines.

The decision of the District Court is therefore *affirmed*.

CASE QUESTIONS

1. What does the Age Discrimination in Employment Act of 1967 (ADEA) provide? What ages are protected from employment discrimination under the Act?
2. What position did the plaintiff apply for at American Airlines? Was he covered by the provisions of ADEA?
3. What was American Airlines "up-or-out" policy? How did this policy effect the plaintiff? Explain.
4. What is a *bona fide occupational qualification* (BFOQ)? Under a BFOQ, can an otherwise protected class be legally discriminated against? Can BFOQs be applied to defeat actions under the following statutes?
   a. Title VII
   b. ADEA
5. Was there a valid BFOQ in this case? What evidence did the court cite to support its finding regarding the BFOQ in this case?

Policy Issue. Should *age* be allowed to be a factor in hiring decisions? Why or why not? Should BFOQs be allowed?

Economics Issue. Did the "up-or-out" policy of American Airlines make economic sense? Why or why not?

Ethics Issue. Do you think American Airlines acted unethically in this case? Do you think it intended to discriminate against the plaintiff and persons his age?

Social Responsibility. Should persons under 40 and over 70 be protected from age discrimination in employment? Can you think of any legally sanctioned age discrimination in society? Explain.

THE EQUAL PAY ACT OF 1963

A substantial amount of sexual discrimination in employment has resulted not from an employer's refusal to hire or promote females, but by employers providing *disparate pay* to members of the two sexes for the same or similar work. A traditional reason given for such disparities was that the man was the breadwinner of the family and the female's income was merely supplemental. This rationale is not now viable (if it ever was) with over 40 percent of the work force being female, and over half the households in the United States consisting of unmarried persons, many of whom are female. In 1963, Congress enacted the Equal Pay Act as an amendment to the Fair Labor Standards Act (FELA) to specifically address the problem of disparity of wages based on sex. The Equal Pay Act is currently administered by the EEOC. The Equal Pay Act of 1963 provides:

No employer . . . shall discriminate . . . between employees on the basis of sex by paying wages . . . at a rate less than the rate at which he pays wages to employees of the opposite sex . . . for equal work on jobs, the performance of which requires equal skill, effort, and responsibility, and which are performed under similar working conditions . . .

The Equal Pay Act applies not only to a disparity in actual wages, but also to disparities in fringe benefits, insurance programs, and pension programs. Many fact situations where a disparity of wages exists between the sexes are hard to prove as violations of the Equal Pay Act. This is because the terms *"equal* skill, effort, and responsibility" and "performed under *similar* working conditions" are so broad that an employer may attempt to avoid their application by differentiating positions through job descriptions. However, slight differences in job descriptions will not justify a disparity in wages under the Equal Pay Act. Courts must decide claims of violations of the Equal Pay Act on a case-by-case basis.

Exceptions to the Equal Pay Act.   The Equal Pay Act does not apply to employment arrangements specifically excepted from coverage by the Act. These exceptions are where wages are paid pursuant to:

1. a seniority system
2. a merit system
3. a system that measures earnings by quantity or quality of production
4. a differential based on any factor *other than sex.*

Under the first express exception, an employer can justify paying *different* wages for the *same* work where the differential is based on *how long* an employee has worked for the employer (seniority). However, within each seniority class the employer cannot discriminate in the payment of wages. The *merit* system exception allows an employer to compensate employees on the basis of their proven ability on the job. Although such assessments must be based on objective criteria, subjectivity and the danger of sex discrimination may enter into any merit decision.

The third exception, which allows wage systems based on the "quantity or quality" or work, permits employers to lawfully institute commission, piecemeal, and quality-control payment structures. Courts have not been prone to accept justifications of payment differentials between sexes that employers claim fit into the fourth exception of a "factor other than sex."

Where an employer is found to have violated the Equal Pay Act, the Act prohibits the employer from complying with the Act by reducing the wage rate of any employee. Thus, to be in compliance, the employer must *increase* the wage of the discriminated-against employee to eliminate the disparity of wages. Back pay awards and injunctive relief are also available to address violations of the Equal Pay Act.

 In *City of Los Angeles Department of Water and Power v. Manhart* the U.S. Supreme Court held that an employer's requirement that female employees make larger money contributions to a pension fund than male employees, as sought to be justified by the use of actuarial tables, violated the Equal Pay Act of 1963.

no $ back, but employer was intact

EQUAL PAY ACT

CITY OF LOS ANGELES DEPARTMENT OF WATER AND POWER v. MANHART

435 U.S. 702 (1978)
UNITED STATES SUPREME COURT

Mr. Justice Stevens delivered the opinion of the Court.

As a class, women live longer than men. For this reason, the Los Angeles Department of Water and Power required its female employees to make larger contributions to its pension fund than its male employees.

For many years the Department has administered retirement, disability, and death-benefit programs for its employees. Upon retirement each employee is eligible for a monthly retirement benefit computed as a fraction of his or her salary multiplied by years of service. The monthly benefits for men and women of the same age, seniority, and salary are equal. Benefits are funded entirely by contributions from the employees and the Depatment, augmented by the income earned on those contributions. No private insurance company is involved in the administration or payment of benefits.

Based on a study of mortality tables and its own experience, the Department determined that its 2,000 female employees, on the average, will live a few years longer than its 10,000 male employees. The cost of a pension for the average retired female is greater than for the average male retiree because more monthly payments must be made to the average woman. The Department therefore required female employees to make monthly contributions to the fund which were 14.84 percent higher than the contributions required of comparable male employees. Because employee contributions were withheld from paychecks, a female employee took home less pay than a male employee earning the same salary.

There are both real and fictional differences between women and men. It is true that the average man is taller than the average woman; it is not true that the average woman driver is more accident prone than the average man. Before the Civil Rights Act of 1964 was enacted, an employer could fashion his personnel policies on the basis of assumptions about the differences between men and women, whether or not the assumptions were valid.

It is now well recognized that employment decisions cannot be predicted on mere "stereotyped" impressions about the characteristics of males or females. Myths and purely habitual assumptions about a woman's inability to perform certain kinds of work are no longer acceptable reasons for refusing to employ qualified individuals, or for paying them less. This case does not, however, involve a fictional difference between men and women. It involves a generalization that the parties accept as unquestionably true: Women, as a class, do live longer than men. The Department treated its women employees differently from its men employees because the two classes are in fact different. It is equally true, however, that all individuals in the respective classes do not share the characteristic that differentiates the average class representatives. Many women do not live as long as the average man and many men outlive the average woman. The question, therefore, is whether the existence or nonexistence of "discrimination" is to be determined by comparison of class characteristics or individual characteristics. A "stereotyped" answer to that question may not be the same as the answer that the language and purpose of the statute command.

The Equal Pay Act requires employers to pay members of both sexes the same wages for equivalent work, except when the differential is pursuant to one of four specified exceptions. The Department contends that the fourth exception applies here. That exception authorizes a "differential based on any other factor other than sex."

The Department argues that the different contributions exacted from men and women were based on the factor of longevity rather than sex. It is plain, however, that any individual's life expectancy is based on a number of factors, of which sex is only one. The record contains no evidence that any factor other than the employee's sex was taken into account in calculating the 14.84 percent differential between the respective contributions by men and women. We agree with Judge Duniway's observation that one cannot "say that an actuarial distinction based entirely on sex is 'based on any other factor other than sex.' Sex is exactly what it is based on."

The Department challenges the District Court's award of retroactive relief to the entire class of female employees and retirees. Title VII does not require a district court to grant any retroactive relief. A court that finds unlawful discrimination

> may enjoin [the discrimination] . . . and order such affirmative action as may be appropriate, which may include, but is not limited to, reinstatement . . . with or without back pay . . . or any other equitable relief as the court deems appropriate.

To the point of redundancy, the statute stresses that retroactive relief "may" be awarded if it is "appropriate." . . . Although we now have no doubt about the application of the statute in this case, we must recognize that conscientious and intelligent administrators of pension funds, who did not have the benefit of the extensive briefs and arguments presented to us, may well have assumed that a program like the Department's was entirely lawful. The courts had been silent on the question, and the administrative agencies had conflicting views. . . . As commentators have noted, pension administrators could reasonably have thought it unfair—or even illegal—to make male employees shoulder more than their "actuarial share" of the pension burden. There is no reason to believe that the threat of a backpay award is needed to cause other administrators to amend their practices to conform to this decision.

Nor can we ignore the potential impact which changes in rules affecting insurance and pension plans may have on the economy. Fifty million Americans participate in retirement plans other than Social Security. The assets held in trust for these employees are vast and growing—more than $400 billion was reserved for retirement benefits at the end of 1976 and reserves are increasing by almost $50 billion a year. These plans, like other forms of insurance, depend on the accumulation of large sums to cover contingencies. The amounts set

aside are determined by a painstaking assessment of the insurer's likely liability. Risks that the insurer foresees will be included in the calculation of liability, and the rates or contributions charged will reflect that calculation. The occurrence of major unforeseen contingencies, however, jeopardizes the insurer's solvency and, ultimately, the insureds' benefits. Drastic changes in the legal rules governing pension and insurance funds, like other unforeseen events, can have this effect. Consequently, the rules that apply to these funds should not be applied retroactively unless the legislature has plainly commanded that result. The EEOC itself has recognized that the administrators of retirement plans must be given time to adjust gradually to Title VII's demands. Courts have also shown sensitivity to the special dangers of retroactive Title VII awards in this field.

There can be no doubt that the prohibition against sex-differentiated employee contributions represents a marked departure from past practice. Although Title VII was enacted in 1964, this is apparently the first litigation challenging contribution differences based on valid actuarial tables. Retroactive liability could be devastating for a pension fund.

Accordingly, although we agree with the Court of Appeals' analysis of the statute, we *vacate* its judgment and *remand* the case for further proceedings consistent with this opinion.

CASE QUESTIONS

1. What does the Equal Pay Act provide? Does it cover any discrimination other than *sex* discrimination?
2. How did the City of Los Angeles classify its employees for pension purposes? Explain.
3. Was the difference between men and women in this case "real" or "fictional"? Did it qualify for one of the exceptions to the Equal Pay Act? Why or why not?
4. Why did the Supreme Court vacate the District Court's award of retroactive pension benefits to women? Explain.
5. Why do women on average live longer than men? George Carlin calls them the "survivors." Why? Will this continue in the future?

Policy Issue. Should the law force equal pay for women? Should an employer be able to pay what the market will bear? Is the Equal Pay Act really a form of union? Is discrimination on the basis of sex more justifiable than discrimination for other reasons? Why or why not?

Economics Issue. What would have been the economic consequences if the Supreme Court had affirmed the District Court's award of retro-active pension benefits to women? What part of the judgment did the Supreme Court affirm?

Ethics Issue. Is it ethical for an employer to pay a woman less than a man for the same job?

Social Responsibility. Do men owe a duty of social responsibility to subsidize the pensions of women?

DISCRIMINATION AGAINST THE HANDICAPPED

In 1973, Congress enacted the Rehabilitation Act, which prohibits discrimination in employment against handicapped persons by persons and organizations who receive federal contracts or assistance. The objective of the Act is to require covered employers to consider handicapped job applicants based on their ability to perform the tasks of a job, and not discriminate against them because of their handicaps. Section 504 of the Act provides:

No otherwise qualified handicapped individual in the United States, . . . shall, solely by reason of his handicap, be excluded from the participation in, be denied the benefits of, or be subject to discrimination under any program or activity receiving Federal financial assistance.

The Labor Department is authorized to enforce the Rehabilitation Act of 1973. The provisions of the Act are particularly applicable to contractors doing work under federal contracts. States and municipalities are also covered by the 1973 Act. The Rehabilitation Act does not require employers to hire unqualified applicants for job positions. The Act does require a covered employer to hire the handicapped person who can perform the job after "reasonable accommodation" for his or her handicap at the "minimum level of productivity" expected of a normal person performing the job. Contractors with federal contracts in excess of $2,500.00 are required to take "affirmative action" to hire handicapped employees.

Handicapped Individuals. The Rehabilitation Act defines a "handicapped individual" as any person who has a physical or mental impairment that "substantially limits one or more of such person's major life activities." Persons who suffer from diabetes, epilepsy, heart disease, cancer, retardation, blindness, or hearing impairment have been held to be covered by the Act. Persons with a history of alcoholism and drug abuse are also considered "handicapped" under the Act. A 1978 amendment to the Rehabilitation Act provides that an employer does not have to give an "employment opportunity" to job applicants with a history of alcohol or drug abuse where it can be shown that the prior addiction or abuse would prevent successful performance of the job applied for.

In *Davis v. Butcher*, the court found that former drug users qualified as "handicapped persons" and had been discriminated against in violation of the Rehabilitation Act of 1973.

presently drug addictions not handicap protective included under handicap protection

DISCRIMINATION AGAINST HANDICAPPED PERSONS
DAVIS, ET AL. v. BUTCHER, COMMISSIONER, CIVIL SERVICE COMMISSION OF THE CITY OF PHILADELPHIA

451 F.SUPP. 791 (1978)
UNITED STATES DISTRICT COURT, E. D. PENNSYLVANIA

Cahn, District Judge.

At various times, plaintiffs filed job applications with the City of Philadelphia. Plaintiff Davis reported for a medical examination on January 27, 1977, at the Municipal Medical Dispensary after having been notified by the City that he had been selected for the next class of firemen. During the examination the physician noticed a scar. Davis explained that during a four-month period in 1972 he had used nonnarcotic amphetamines injected intravenously, but that he had not engaged in drug use since that time. The doctor agreed that the scar was old. Nevertheless, plaintiff was told that he could not be employed in any city job because the City would not hire anyone with a past drug history.

Salvatore D'Elia is a former narcotics addict. . . . D'Elia applied for a position with the City of Philadelphia under Title II of the Comprehensive Employment and Training Act (CETA). . . . [H]e was denied employment because of his history of drug use.

Plaintiff Herbert Sims is a former user of morphine and heroin. . . . [H]e was rejected for employment [by the Department of Streets] because of his admitted former drug abuse.

The facts, as demonstrated by the undisputed affidavits, show that Davis, D'Elia, and Sims are rehabilitated. They were all fully qualified for the positions for which they applied.

Plaintiffs claim that former drug addicts fall within the protection of the Rehabilitation Act of 1973 (hereinafter "Act"), and that the Act provides them with a remedy for the discrimination alleged here.

The City contends that Congress did not intend drug addicts to be included within the definition of *handicapped* for purposes of Section 504. However, although there are no cases on point, I am persuaded that the clear words of the statute do encompass drug addiction. . . . Section 706(6) defines a handicapped individual as:

[A]ny person . . . who (a) has a physical or mental impairment which substantially limits one or more of such person's major life activities, (b) has a record of such impairment, or (c) is regarded as having such an impairment.

It is undisputed that drug addiction substantially affects an addict's ability to perform major life activities, defined by Department of Health, Education and Welfare regulations supplementing the Act (hereinafter "the Regulations") as

caring for one's self, performing manual tasks, walking, seeing, speaking, breathing, learning, and working.

[P]rior addiction and drug use clearly fall within the definition of having a "record of such impairment," as defined in . . . the Regulations. . . . I therefore conclude that persons with histories of drug use . . . are "handicapped individuals" within the meaning of the statutory and regulatory language.

[P]laintiffs Davis, D'Elia, and Sims will be permitted to prove their damages at a hearing to be held before me on Thursday, June 8, 1978, at 1:30 P.M.

CASE QUESTIONS

1. What does the Rehabilitation Act of 1973 provide? Explain.
2. Why were the plaintiffs rejected as job applicants by the City of Philadelphia?
3. Does drug abuse qualify as a *handicap* under the Rehabilitation Act? Does it substantially limit a person's major life activities?
4. What damages would you award on remand?

Policy Issue. Should an employer be allowed to *not* hire a job applicant because of prior drug abuse? Present drug abuse? Why or why not?

Economics Issue. Do you think that prior drug abusers will be more expensive to keep as employees than nondrug abusers? Why or why not?

Ethics Issue. Is it unethical to discriminate against prior drug or alcohol abusers?

Social Responsibility. Do employers owe a duty of social responsibility to hire handicapped workers? Should handicapped workers be given a preference in employment decisions?

THE CIVIL RIGHTS ACT OF 1866

The issue of slavery precipitated the Civil War. After the war, the Thirteenth Amendment to the U.S. Constitution was ratified, which eliminated "slavery" and "involuntary servitude" in the United States. Pursuant to power given Congress by the Thirteenth Amendment, Congress enacted the Civil Rights Act of 1866. Section 1981 of the Act provides that all persons in the United States:

shall have the same right in every State and Territory to make and enforce contracts, to sue, to be parties, to give evidence, and to the full and equal benefit of all laws and proceedings for the security of persons and property as is enjoyed by white citizens.

Section 1981 of the Civil Rights Act of 1866 was originally applied to enslavement cases. During most of the twentieth century the Act lay dormant. However, with the advent of the civil rights movement in the 1960s, Section 1981 was accorded new meaning. The courts held employment to be a "contract" and a "property" right protected under the language of Section 1981. Therefore, discrimination in employment has been held to be prohibited under Section 1981.

Section 1981 only expressly prohibits *racial* discrimination. Courts have generally held that Section 1981 applies to discrimination against aliens. A few federal courts have expanded Section 1981 to cover discrimination based on national origin. By contrast, Title VII of the 1964 Act prohibits discrimination based on race, color, *religion*, national origin, or *sex*.

In the following excerpt from *McDonald v. Santa Fe Trail Transportation Co.*, 427 U.S. 274 (1976), the Supreme Court held that Section 1981 of the Civil Rights Act of 1866 prohibited employment discrimination against whites.

On September 26, 1970, petitioners, both white, and Charles Jackson, a Negro employee of Santa Fe, were jointly and severally charged with misappropriating 60 one-gallon cans of antifreeze, which was part of a shipment Santa Fe was carrying for one of its customers. Six days later, petitioners were fired by Santa Fe, while Jackson was retained. A grievance was promptly filed with Local 988, . . .

The 1866 statute, [respondents] assert, was concerned predominantly with assuring specified civil rights to the former Negro slaves freed by virtue of the Thirteenth Amendment, and not at all with protecting the corresponding civil rights of white persons.

[T]he Act was meant, by its broad terms, to proscribe discrimination in the making or enforcement of contracts against, or in favor of, any *race*. Unlikely as it might have appeared in 1866 that white citizens would encounter substantial racial discrimination of the sort proscribed under the Act, the statutory structure and legislative history persuade us that the 39th Congress was intent upon establishing in the federal law a broader principle than would have been necessary simply to meet the particular and immediate plight of the newly freed Negro slaves. . . . Thus, we conclude that the District Court erred in dismissing petitioners' claims under Section 1981 on the ground that the protections of that provision are unavailable to white persons.

Under Section 1981, courts are implicitly allowed to fashion legal and equitable relief broader than that allowed under Title VII of the 1968 Act. For example, Title VII limits an award of unpaid back pay to two years, while Section 1981 contains no such limitation. The relevant state Statute of Limitation applies to actions brought under Section 1981. Courts have also held that the BFOQ defense available to defendants in Title VII actions is not available to a Section 1981 action for discrimination based on national origin. Title VII provides for assistance from the Labor Department in the investigation and defense of a discrimination case. Such assistance is not available in an action brought under Section 1981. Except in cases where a plaintiff seeks back pay damages for more than a two-year period, the majority of racial discrimination cases will be brought under Title VII of the 1968 Act instead of Section 1981 of the 1866 Act.

THE EXECUTIVE ORDER PROGRAM

The executive branch of government issues Executive Orders that prohibit discrimination by many types of employers dealing with the federal government. The most important is Executive Order 11246, which requires that all federal government contracts contain a provision stating that the contractor agrees not to discriminate on the basis of "race, color, creed, or national origin." A separate Executive Order requires the same statement to be included in government contracts prohibiting age discrimination.

Executive Order 11246 requires federal government contractors to establish programs and take affirmative action to employ persons from minority groups. Revised Order No. 4 requires federal government contractors, even those not within the construction industry, to establish affirmative action programs. The Order requires any federal government contractor with 50 or more employees or federal contracts of $50,000 or more to take the following steps in developing an affirmative action program:

1. analyze the employment of minority and female employees
2. identify deficiencies
3. establish affirmative action employment goals
4. develop methods for meeting such goals.

If an employer attempts in good faith to meet its affirmative action goals established pursuant to Revised Order No. 4, it will not be held in violation of the affirmative action plan if it does not achieve these goals. Where a violation of antidiscrimination Executive Orders is found, the federal government may cancel or suspend the contract in question, or declare the violating contractor ineligible for further federal government contracts.

AFFIRMATIVE ACTION PROGRAMS

Not only are employers prohibited from discriminating against job applicants and employees based on race and sex, they are also under a duty to develop *affirmative action* programs to further the goal of minority employment. Affirmative action programs require an employer to develop methods for seeking out minority applicants (e.g., by advertising job openings in minority newspapers), providing job training programs for minorities, and providing other assistance to minority applicants and employees.

REVERSE DISCRIMINATION *— relies on equal protection laws*

In many instances, employers set *quotas* by requiring that a specific number or percentage of job openings be set aside for minority applicants. Many *reverse discrimination* lawsuits have been brought by white job applicants who argue that such quotas constitute *racial* discrimination in violation of Title VII. In *University of California Regents v. Bakke*, 438 U.S. 265 (1978), a white applicant who was denied admission by the Medical School of the University of California at Davis sued, alleging that the quota system of the University, which set aside a specific number of entering spots for minority applicants, and accepted minority applicants who were less qualified than the plaintiff, violated Title VII. The U.S. Supreme Court in that case held that specific *quotas* were illegal, but further announced that *race* can still be a factor to consider when making a decision on an applicant. At present, employers face the delicate task of promoting affirmative action without being liable for reverse discrimination.

Seniority Systems. Most employers institute and maintain seniority systems whereby employees who have been with the company for a designated number of years receive higher wages or fringe benefits, choice of the best jobs and work shifts, protection against layoff, more vacation days, and other employment benefits that workers with less time with the company may not be entitled to receive. The purposes of *seniority systems* are to reward loyal employees and to provide an incentive for trained employees to stay with the company. Many seniority systems are expressly set forth in collective bargaining agreements between unions and employers. Congress has legislated those seniority systems are legal that are not the result of "intentional" discrimination. Section 703(h) of Title VII provides:

Notwithstanding any other provision of this subchapter, it shall not be an unlawful employment practice for an employer to apply different standards of compensation, or different terms, conditions, or privileges of employment pursuant to a bona fide seniority . . . system, . . . provided that such differences are not the result of an intention to discriminate because of race . . . or national origin . . .

In *Firefighters Local Union No. 1784 and Memphis Fire Department v. Stutts,* the most important discrimination case to be decided by the Supreme Court in a decade, the Court held that a lower court order which prevented the laying off of employees on a "last hired, first fired" basis constituted *reverse discrimination* against more senior white workers who were laid off while less senior black workers were not.

REVERSE DISCRIMINATION

FIREFIGHTERS LOCAL UNION NO. 1784 and MEMPHIS FIRE DEPARTMENT v. CARL W. STOTTS, ET AL.

104 U.S. 2576 (1984)
UNITED STATES SUPREME COURT

Justice White delivered the opinion of the Court.

In 1977 respondent Carl Stotts, a black holding the position of fire-fighting captain in the Memphis, Tennessee, Fire Department, filed a class action complaint in the United States District Court for the Western District of Tennessee. The complaint charged that the Memphis Fire Department and other city officials were engaged in a pattern or practice of making hiring and promotion decisions on the basis of race in violation of Title VII of the Civil Rights Act of 1964. . . . Discovery proceeded, settlement negotiations ensued, and in due course, a consent decree was approved and entered by the District Court on April 25, 1980.

[T]he 1980 decree established an interim hiring goal of filling on an annual basis 50 percent of the job vacancies in the Department with qualified black applicants. The 1980 decree contained an additional goal with respect to promotions: the Department was to attempt to ensure that 20 percent of the promotions in each job classification be given to blacks.

In early May, 1981, the City announced that projected budget deficits required a reduction of non-essential personnel throughout the City Government. Layoffs were to be based on the "last hired, first fired" rule under which city-wide seniority, determined by each employee's length of continuous service from the latest date of permanent employment, was the basis for deciding who would be laid off. If a senior employee's position were abolished or eliminated, the employee could "bump down" to a lower ranking position rather than be laid off.

On May 4, at respondents' request, the District Court entered a temporary restraining order forbidding the layoff of any black employee. The Union, which previously had not been a party . . . , was permitted to intervene. At the preliminary injunction hearing, it appeared that 55 then-filled positions in the Department were to be eliminated and that 39 of these positions were filled with employees having "bumping" rights. It was estimated that 40 least-senior employees in the fire-fighting bureau of the Department would be laid off and that of these 25 were white and 15 black. It also appeared that 56 percent of the employees hired in the Department since 1974 had been black and that the percentage of black employees had increased from approximately 3 or 4 percent in 1974 to 11½ percent in 1980.

On May 18, the District Court entered an order granting an injunction. . . . [C]oncluding that the proposed layoffs would have a racially discriminatory effect and that the seniority system was not a bona fide one, the District Court ordered that the

City "not apply the seniority policy insofar as it will decrease the percentage of black lieutenants, drivers, inspectors and privates that are presently employed. . . ." On June 23, the District Court broadened its order to include three additional classifications. A modified layoff plan, aimed at protecting black employees in the seven classifications so as to comply with the court's order, was presented and approved. Layoffs pursuant to the modified plan were then carried out. In certain instances, to comply with the injunction, non-minority employees with more seniority than minority employees were laid off or demoted in rank.

On appeal, the Court of Appeals for the Sixth Circuit affirmed. . . . The City and the Union filed separate petitions for *certiorari.* The two petitions were granted. . . .

The issue at the heart of this case is whether the District Court exceeded its powers in entering an injunction requiring white employees to be laid off, when the otherwise applicable seniority system would have called for the layoff of black employees with less seniority. We are convinced that the Court of Appeals erred in resolving this issue and in affirming the District Court.

Section 703(h) of Title VII provides that it is not an unlawful employment practice to apply different standards of compensation, or different terms, conditions, or privileges of employment pursuant to a bona fide seniority system, provided that such differences are not the result of an intention to discriminate because of race. It is clear that the City had a seniority system, that its proposed layoff plan conformed to that system. . . .

[W]hen an individual shows that the discriminatory practice has had an impact on him, he is not automatically entitled to have a non-minority employee laid off to make room for him. He may have to wait until a vacancy occurs, . . . *Teamsters v. United States.* Here, there was no finding that any of the blacks protected from layoff had been a victim of discrimination. . . .

Our ruling in *Teamsters* that a court can award competitive seniority only when the beneficiary of the award has actually been a victim of illegal discrimination is consistent with the policy behind Section 706(g) of Title VII, which affects the remedies available in Title VII litigation. That policy, which is to provide make-whole relief only to those who

have been actual victims of illegal discrimination, was repeatedly expressed by the sponsors of the Act during the congressional debates. Opponents of the legislation that became Title VII charged that if the bill were enacted, employers could be ordered to hire and promote persons in order to achieve a racially-balanced work force even though those persons had not been victims of illegal discrimination. Responding to these charges, Senator Humphrey explained the limits on a court's remedial powers as follows:

> Contrary to the allegations of some opponents of this title, there is nothing in it that will give any power to the Commission or to any court to require . . . firing . . . of employees in order to meet a racial 'quota' or to achieve a certain racial balance. That bugaboo has been brought up a dozen times; but is nonexistent. 110 Cong. Rec. 6549

An interpretative memorandum of the bill entered into the Congressional Record by Senators Clark and Case likewise made clear that a court was not authorized to give preferential treatment to non-victims.

> No court order can require hiring, reinstatement, admission to membership, or payment of back pay for anyone who was not discriminated against in violation of [Title VII]. This is stated expressly in the last sentence of Section [706(g)]. . . .

The Court of Appeals holding that the District Court's order was permissible as a valid Title VII remedial order ignores not only our ruling in *Teamsters* but the policy behind Section 706(g) as well. . . . Accordingly, the judgment of the Court of Appeals is *reversed.*

Justice O'Connor, concurring.

I join the opinion and judgment rendered by the Court today.

Justice Stevens, concurring in the judgment.

In my judgment, the Court's discussion of Title VII is wholly advisory. This case involves no issue under Title VII; it only involves the administration of a consent decree. . . . Accordingly, because I conclude that the District Court abused its discretion in entering the preliminary injunction at issue here, I concur in the judgment.

Justice Blackmun, with whom **Justice Brennan** and **Justice Marshall** join, dissenting.

Today's opinion is troubling less for the law it creates than for the law it ignores. The issues in these cases arose out of a preliminary injunction that prevented the city of Memphis from conducting a particular layoff in a particular manner. Because that layoff has ended, the preliminary injunction no longer restrains any action that the city wishes to take. . . . The Court appears oblivious . . . to the fact that any continuing legal consequences of the preliminary injunction would be erased by simply vacating the Court of Appeals' judgment, which is this Court's longstanding practice with cases that become moot. . . . I regret the Court's insistence upon unnecessarily reviving a past controversy.

CASE QUESTIONS

1. What is *affirmative action?* Are *quotas* legal under affirmative action?
2. What did the affirmative action program (decree) of the Memphis Fire Department provide? Was it successful?
3. What did the "last hired, first fired" rule of the Fire Department provide? What was the consequences of this rule? Who sought the injunction against the application of this rule?
4. What is *reverse discrimination?* Was there reverse discrimination in this case? Explain.

5. Which, if either, of the following can be granted *fictitious* seniority?
    a. a *class* of minority members who have been discriminated against
    b. an *individual* minority member who has been discriminated against

Policy Issue. Why is seniority protected from the effects of affirmative action more than any other employment benefit (e.g., hiring, promotion)? Explain.

Economics Issue. What are the economic effects of affirmative action on the following parties?
    a. minorities
    b. nonminorities
    c. employers

Ethics Issue. Is it ethical for whites to argue reverse discrimination? Is it ethical for young whites today to suffer the effects of affirmative action to counteract discrimination caused by others in the past?

Social Responsibility. Do employers owe a duty of social responsibility to take race into consideration as a factor in making employment decisions? Why or why not?

Trend of the Law

The courts and employers will be faced with an increasing number of discrimination lawsuits in the future. This is particularly true because most employees are now aware of their rights under federal antidiscrimination laws, and because of the past successes of fellow employees. Cases based on racial and sex discrimination will constitute the majority of such lawsuits, particularly those based on the alleged disparate impact of seemingly neutral employment practices.

The courts will be faced with a greater number of sexual harassment cases in the future as female employees decide to bring Title VII charges rather than merely switching jobs to avoid the problem. A number of sexual harassment cases have recently been brought by male employees alleging sexual harassment by female supervisors. In addition, the courts will be faced with the issue of whether sexual harassment by supervisors who are members of the same sex as the harassed employee are actionable under Title VII.

As Hispanics and other persons of diverse national heritages immigrate to this country and compose a greater portion of our working population, Title VII cases based on charges of national-origin discrimination will increase in the future.

Unless a specific statute, either federal or state, expressly prohibits a specific type of discrimination, the discrimination is not unlawful. The Congress and state legislatures will continue to be lobbied by special groups (e.g., sexual preference groups) to enact statutes to protect members of their classes from employment and other discrimination. Further, the courts are being requested, through individual lawsuits, to interpret existing antidiscrimination statutes to include certain classes of persons. For example, should the definition of "handicapped individual" in the Rehabilitation Act of 1973 protect fat people or short people from discrimination?

The courts will also be faced with deciding a greater number of "reverse discrimination" cases in the future. For example, see *Steelworkers v. Weber* in Chapter 3 of this book.

REVIEW QUESTIONS

1. Jones was a line worker at an Acme aircraft manufacturing facility. He was well qualified for his job and had an excellent work record. Jones was heavily involved in union activities and participated in a long and somewhat violent strike against the firm. During the strike he helped illegally block one entrance gate to the aircraft facility. After the strike had concluded, Acme had to reduce its work force and Jones was not reinstated. At the time, the company told Jones that he was not being rehired because he had participated in illegal activities during the strike. Jones, who was black, sued the firm under Title VII claiming that he was not rehired because he was black. What must Jones prove in order to substantiate his claim under Title VII? Can Acme raise any defenses?

2. T.I.M.E.-D.C. Inc. was a national trucking company. It was sued in 1974 by a number of former employees who alleged that the company had engaged in racial discrimination in violation of Title VII. The company had a number of different job classifications, which it had refused to fill with minority candidates until 1969. By the time the suit was filed, only .4 percent of the company's drivers were black and only .3 percent were Hispanic. Of the company's 6,472 employees, only 5 percent were black and 4 percent were Hispanic. Of these employees, 83 percent occupied lower-paying jobs whereas only 39 percent of the nonminority employees filled lower-paying positions. In addition, the plaintiffs were able to present voluminous personal testimony indicating that T.I.M.E. discriminated

against minorities due to thinking in terms of racial stereotypes. Was the evidence sufficient to show that T.I.M.E. had engaged in a pattern or practice of discriminating against minorities?

3. Donnell, a black General Motors employee in St. Louis, applied for admission into a GM skilled trade apprenticeship program established by the company and the UAW. Donnell was rejected for failure to meet the requirement that applicants be high school graduates. Statistical evidence showed that only 27.9 percent of black males over age 14 in the St. Louis area had completed four years of high school in the 1970 census while 49.1 percent of white males over 14 had done so. The median number of school years completed by black males 25 years and older in St. Louis was 9.6 years, while the median school years completed for all males in the area was 10.8 years. Further, only 3.3 percent of the St. Louis General Motors employees in the skilled trades and skilled trades' programs at the time were black. Only .3 percent of the black employees were in skilled trades, whereas 3.2 percent of the white employees were in skilled-trades positions. On the other hand, program applicant statistics indicated that 12.4 percent of the black applicants to the apprenticeship program were rejected for failure to meet the educational requirements and 12.7 percent of the white applicants were rejected for the same reason. Given this data, can Donnell establish a *prima facie* case of disparate impact?

4. Wells was employed by Murphy Motor Freight Lines, Inc. as a dockman at its Roseville, Minnesota, terminal from May 1967 until his discharge in July 1974. Wells sued Murphy, claiming that the firm had violated Title VII because it failed to provide him with a work environment free of racial hostility, intimidation, and harassment. Wells introduced a substantial amount of evidence at trial to show that he had been subjected to vicious, frequent, and reprehensible instances of racial harassment, which occurred in several guises. He further showed that management made no effort to prevent the harassment. Can an employee recover for racial discrimination under Title VII when he can show that he was continually harassed by his fellow workers?

5. Espinoza sought employment as a seamstress at a division of Farah Manufacturing Company in San Antonio, Texas. Her application was denied based on a longstanding company policy against employment of aliens. Espinoza was a lawful resident of the United States but not a U.S. citizen. Espinoza brought suit against Farah alleging that the company policy violated Title VII of the Civil Rights Act. Section 703 makes it "an unlawful employment practice for an employer . . . to fail or refuse to hire . . . any individual because of such individual's race, color, religion, sex or national origin." Espinoza argued that the national-origin provision prevented Farah from denying her a position based on her lack of citizenship. Did Farah violate Title VII?

6. Bundy was a Vocational Rehabilitation Specialist with the District of Columbia Department of Corrections (the Agency). In 1972 she received and rejected sexual propositions from Jackson, a fellow employee and later the Director of the Agency. Burton, her second-line supervisor, began harassing Bundy in June 1974, continually calling her into his office to request that she spend the workday afternoon with him at his apartment

and to question her about her sexual proclivities. Shortly thereafter, Gainey, her first-line supervisor, also began making advances, asking her to join him at a motel and on a trip to the Bahamas. Bundy complained about these advances to Swain, who supervised both Burton and Gainey. Swain casually dismissed Bundy's complaints, telling her that "any man in his right mind would want to rape you." Swain then proceeded to request that she begin a sexual relationship with him in his apartment. Bundy rejected his request. Does Bundy have any claim for relief under Title VII?

7. Ninety percent of Eastern Air Lines flight attendants were female. The airline enacted five policies for dealing with attendants who became pregnant: (1) a requirement that flight attendants must commence maternity leave immediately upon knowledge of pregnancy; (2) a policy that pregnant flight attendants lose all accumulated seniority if they transfer to ground positions rather than taking maternity leave, whereas flight attendants temporarily transferring to ground positions because of disabilities other than pregnancy continued to accumulate seniority; (3) a policy fixing time limits on guaranteed rights to reinstatement of flight attendants taking maternity leave; (4) the separate treatment of pregnancy under Eastern's Group Comprehensive Medical Insurance; and (5) the exclusion of pregnancy from Eastern's paid sick leave policy. Federal Aviation Administration regulations prohibited any flight attendant from flying after the thirteenth week of maternity. Which, if any, of Eastern's provisions violated the Pregnancy Discrimination Act?

8. Cummins was hired in 1958 as a production scheduler in the Banbury Department of Parker Seal Company's Berea, Kentucky plant. In May 1965, Cummins was promoted to supervisor of the first (7:00 A.M. to 3:00 P.M.) Banbury shift. As a supervisor, he was salaried and was obligated to work whatever hours were scheduled, including Saturdays. In 1970, Cummins joined the World Wide Church of God, which forbids work on the Sabbath (Friday sundown to Saturday sundown) and on certain holy days. From that time he refused to work on Saturdays. After complaints arose from fellow supervisors who were forced to substitute for Cummins on Saturdays, Parker Seal Company discharged him despite the fact that it could accommodate him without any undue hardship. Did this dismissal violate any provision of Title VII?

9. Pan American World Airways refused to hire male flight attendants. The firm based its hiring policy on these considerations: (1) its experience showed that female flight attendants "were superior in such nonmechanical aspects of the job as providing reassurance to anxious passengers, giving courteous personalized service and, in general, making flights as pleasurable as possible within the limitations imposed by aircraft operations;" and (2) passenger surveys overwhelmingly showed that Pan Am's customers preferred females over males. Pan Am argued that the exclusion of males was the best way for the firm to select the type of personnel needed. Do these special customers' psychological needs justify the occupational qualification established by Pan Am?

10. Prior to 1925, Corning Glass Works operated its plants in Wellsboro and Corning, New York only during the day, and all inspection work was per-

formed by women. Between 1925 and 1930, the company began to introduce automatic production equipment, which made it desirable to institute a night shift. During this period, however, state laws prohibited women from working at night. As a result, in order to fill inspector positions on the new night shift, the company had to recruit male employees from among its male day workers. The male employees so transferred demanded and received wages substantially higher than those paid to women inspectors working on the two day shifts. During this same period, however, no plant-wide shift differential existed and male employees working at night, other than inspectors, received the same wages as their day shift counterparts. Thus a situation developed where the night inspectors were all male, the day inspectors all female, and the male inspectors received significantly higher wages. In 1944, the company established a plant-wide shift differential, but this change did not eliminate the higher base wage paid to male night inspectors. Rather, the shift differential was superimposed on the existing difference in base wages between male night inspectors and female day inspectors. Following a change in the applicable state law, beginning in June 1966, Corning started to open up jobs on the night shift to women. Previously separate male and female seniority lists were consolidated and women became eligible to exercise their seniority, on the same basis as men, to bid for the higher-paid night inspection jobs as vacancies occurred. On January 20, 1969 a new system went into effect, which abolished for the future the separate base wages for day and night shift inspectors and imposed a uniform base wage for inspectors exceeding the wage rate for the night shift previously in effect. All inspectors hired after January 20, 1969, were to receive the same base wage, whatever their sex or shift. The agreement further provided, however, for a higher "red circle" rate for employees hired prior to January 20, 1969, when working as inspectors on the night shift. This "red circle" rate served essentially to perpetuate the differential in base wages between day and night inspectors. Did Corning's actions violate the Equal Pay Act of 1963?

11. T.I.M.E.-D.C., the company discussed in question 2, was also sued by the government, which alleged that the company's seniority system was discriminatory. The seniority system established seniority for bidding for particular jobs and for layoff purposes on the basis of length of service in the bargaining unit. As a result, if a city driver applied for and obtained a transfer to line driver, he went to the bottom of the seniority roster of the line driver unit. Since the firm had engaged in and still was engaging in racial discrimination, the seniority system tended to perpetuate the effects of this discrimination. Does a bona fide seniority system that has the effect of perpetuating past discrimination violate Title VII?

27 OCCUPATIONAL SAFETY AND SECURITY

INTRODUCTION

Generally, the common law of torts and contracts provided little protection or rights to employees regarding working hours and conditions, job safety, loss of employment, or retirement. As the American economy became highly industrialized and profitable, the government, particularly the federal government, enacted a substantial number of laws and programs to provide job safety and security for workers both during and after employment.

This chapter addresses issues concerning worker safety and security, and includes coverage of (1) child labor laws, (2) hour and wage legislation, (3) state workers' compensation benefits, (4) the federal Occupational Safety and Health Act, (5) unemployment compensation benefits, and (6) social security benefits.

CHILD LABOR LAWS

One of the worst abuses of the early Industrial Revolution was the extensive use of children as laborers in heavy industry, particularly in the steel mills, mines, and textile industries. The widespread use of children occurred because of the cheapness of their labor and the fact that children were less likely to rise against the system than adults. Further, many poor families saw their children as an additional source of income for an otherwise destitute family. The following exchange, which occurred in 1911 between Pennsylvania Judge Gray and Helen Suschak, an 8-year-old textile mill employee, shows the plight of child workers in that era:

Judge: Helen, what time do you go to work?
Helen: Half after 6 evenin's.
Judge: When do you come home from the mill?
Helen: Half after 6 mornin's.
Judge: How far do you live from the mill?
Helen: I don't know. I guess it mostly takes an hour to git there.
Judge: And the inspector tells me it's across lonely fields exposed to storms that sweep the valley. What's your pay, Helen?
Helen: I get 3 cents an hour, sir.
Judge: If my arithmetic is good that is almost 36 cents for a night's work. Well, now, we do indeed find the flesh and blood of little children coined into money.

The Child Labor Act of 1916.   In 1916, Congress passed the Child Labor Act with the stated purpose of regulating child labor by prohibiting the movement of products in interstate commerce that were made by child labor. In a famous case *Hammer v. Dagenhart*, 247 U.S. 251 (1918), the U.S. Supreme Court held that the Child Labor Act was an invalid exercise of Congressional authority. In 1929, in another attempt to regulate the use of child labor, Congress imposed an excise tax on certain businesses that employed children. The Supreme Court, instead of holding that the legislation was valid as a proper revenue-raising statute within the power of Congress, found the statute to be an unconstitutional exercise of Congressional authority.

Current Child Labor Laws.   In 1938, Congress enacted the Fair Labor Standards Act. Section 16 of the Act specifically addressed the child labor question. Generally, the Act and regulations adopted thereunder by the Department of Labor prohibit the employment of children under 13 as laborers, make it unlawful to ship goods in interstate commerce that have been produced in an establishment where "oppressive child labor" has been employed, and authorize the Secretary of Labor to conduct investigations of child labor practices. The burden is on an employer to prove the age of all of its employees.

The provisions of the Fair Labor Standards Act and regulations adopted thereunder attempt to strike a balance by prohibiting child labor abuses without foreclosing the job market to all minors. Thus, the child labor provisions of the Act do not apply to employees who are over 17 years of age, while employment of children age 13 and younger is generally prohibited by the Act. The employment of children between the ages of 13 and 17 is restricted and regulated by the provisions of the Act.

Under current child labor laws, children 16 and 17 years of age may generally be employed in industries that are not declared "hazardous" by the Secretary of Labor. Hazardous industries include coal mining, working with explosives, roofing, logging, and excavation work, among others. Children 14 and 15 years of age may be employed in certain approved jobs, such as in gasoline stations, restaurants, and fast food outlets. Children who are 14 years of age may lawfully be employed in administrative or school-related jobs, and in career programs.

Exemptions from the child labor restrictions of the Fair Labor Standards Act exist for agricultural employees and child performers. Generally, children engaged in agricultural employment are exempt from the child labor restrictions of the Fair Labor Standards Act even if they are under the age of 13. However, regulations regarding hours of employment, type of job, and school attendance must be met. Parental consent is usually required to employ a child under the age of 12 in agriculture.

Child actors and actresses and other child performers are also generally exempt from child labor laws. However, most states require parental consent, and often judicial approval, for the employment of child performers. Many states further require that a certain portion of the wages earned by child actors or performers (e.g., 50 percent) be placed in a trust fund that cannot be used by the parents and that will become the property of the child when he or she reaches a certain age (e.g., 21 years of age).

WAGE AND HOUR LAWS

At the start of the Industrial Revolution in the early 1800s, when the United States changed from a simple agrarian society to a complex urban-commercial economy, there were no federal or state laws that regulated the terms or conditions of employment of workers. Many industrial companies took advantage of immigrant and poor workers, extracting long hours of work for subsistence wages.

In the mid-1800s, a movement began at the state level to enact "Legal Day's Work" laws, which attempted to set limits on the maximum number of hours a worker could be required to work in a day or a week. It was not until 1912, however, that Massachusetts enacted the first minimum wage law. Early attempts by the government to regulate wages and hours of work met with strong resistance from the courts, who generally held that the right to contract regarding wages and hours was a "property right" protected by the Due Process Clause of the U.S. Constitution. Employers and employees were allowed to negotiate terms of employment without government protection notwithstanding the unequal bargaining power of the parties.

The Fair Labor Standards Act. In the 1930s, this country and the rest of the world suffered an economic crisis known as the Great Depression. One of the consequences of the Great Depression was that over 30 percent of the workers in the United States were unemployed. President Franklin D. Roosevelt spearheaded the enactment of innovative social legislation through a liberal Congress. In 1937, Roosevelt appointed Hugo L. Black to the U.S. Supreme Court. In 1938, the Fair Labor Standards Act (FLSA), originally introduced by Mr. Black when he was a U.S. Senator from Alabama, emerged from Congress. The FLSA is currently administered by the Secretary of Labor through the Wage and Hour Division of the Department of Labor.

The FLSA of 1938 had two major economic objectives: (1) to increase the wages of workers by placing a *floor* under wages paid to employees covered by the Act (*minimum wage*); and (2) to encourage employment of more people by requiring employers to pay higher *overtime* wages to employees for hours worked in excess of a "standard work week" (*maximum hours*). The FLSA originally accomplished these goals by guaranteeing a minimum wage of 25 cents per hour for a maximum standard workweek of 44 hours, and a wage of not less than 1.5 times the worker's regular wage for every hour worked beyond the standard 44-hour workweek. Currently, the standard workweek has been lowered to 40 hours, and the minimum hourly wage is set at $3.75 by Congress under the FLSA. FLSA minimum wage and maximum hours standards may not be waived by employees.

In *U.S. v. Darby*, 312 U.S. 100 (1941), from which this excerpt is taken, the Supreme Court unanimously upheld the validity of the minimum wage and maximum hour provisions of the Fair Labor Standards Act.

The Fair Labor Standards Act set up a comprehensive legislative scheme for preventing the shipment in interstate commerce of certain products and commodities produced in the United States under labor conditions as respects wages and hours which fail to conform to standards set up by the Act. Its purpose . . . is to exclude from interstate commerce goods produced for the commerce and to prevent their production for interstate commerce, under conditions detrimental to the maintenance of the minimum standards of living necessary for health and general well-being, . . . and as the means of spreading and perpetuating such substandard labor conditions among the workers of the several states.

The Act is sufficiently definite to meet constitutional demands. One who employs persons, without conforming to the prescribed wage and hour conditions, to work on goods which he ships or expects to ship across state lines, is warned that he may be subject to the criminal penalties of the Act. No more is required.

Employees Covered by the FLSA.   As originally drafted, and as retained in current statutory language, the FLSA applies to employees who are either engaged "in commerce" or in the "production of goods for commerce." The FLSA does not specifically define the word *employee,* leaving the definition for the courts to develop on a case-by-case basis. Questions often arise as to whether an individual worker is an "employee" and thus covered by the FLSA, or is an "independent contractor" and thus not covered by the Act. Many companies try to avoid the provisions of the FLSA by calling certain employees "independent contractors" and entering into contracts with such workers on this basis. However, the courts will ignore the designation of "independent contractor" if, considering all of the circumstances surrounding the employment relation, the worker is actually an "employee."

Under the traditional "interstate commerce" requirement necessary for the FLSA to apply, often *local* activity of an employee would not be covered by the Act. For example, an employer could have two employees doing the exact same job, where one would be covered by the FLSA (e.g., a delivery man who makes deliveries to a retailer who sells goods in interstate commerce), and the other would not be so covered (e.g., a deliveryman who makes deliveries only to a local warehouse).

The FLSA specifically exempts certain workers from the scope of its coverage. Most important, Section 13(a)(1) exempts *bona fide* "executive, administrative, and professional" employees. This exemption includes most "white-collar" administrative positions, including salespersons. The "professional" exemption includes traditional professions such as law and medicine, and other "artistic" professions requiring prolonged study that leads to positions requiring the exercise of discretion and judgment. Workers who are employed in certain facets of agriculture and commercial fishing operations, in casual domestic service, and in certain retail and service establishments are specifically exempted from much of the coverage of the FLSA. The tendency has been for the courts to construe the exemptions from FLSA coverage narrowly.

"Enterprise" Coverage. Under the traditional coverage of the FLSA, most of the employees of manufacturing, transportation, and communication sectors of the economy were covered by the Act, whereas employees of retail, service and "Mom-and-Pop" establishments were not covered by the Act. For example, less than 3 percent of the retail employees were covered under the traditional definition of "employee" of the FLSA.

As small general stores and corner grocery stores gave way to major department stores and supermarket chains, and the service and retail sectors of the economy became larger (currently estimated at 55–60 percent of the labor force), Congress decided to include many of the employees in these sectors within the minimum wage and maximum hour provisions of the FLSA. In 1961, Congress modified the FLSA by adding the "enterprise" definition to the Act. Any business "enterprise" with gross annual sales of $250,000 or more is subject to the minimum wage and maximum hour coverage of the FLSA as amended in 1969. Under the "enterprise" definition, few business establishments escape the coverage of the Act. The question of whether two or more closely related small businesses aggregate to form one "enterprise" subject to FLSA coverage has been the source of substantial litigation.

Since the adoption of the "enterprise" definition for coverage under the FLSA, the traditional problems of defining an "employee" under the Act have all but disappeared.

Federal Employees. The FLSA does not cover federal government employees. In 1962, Congress enacted the Federal Salary Reform Act, as amended in 1970 by the Federal Pay Comparability Act, which regulates the payment of wages and fringe benefits to federal employees based on the following principles:

1. Federal pay rates should be comparable with private enterprise pay rates for the same level of work.
2. Equal pay should be paid for equal work.
3. Differences in federal pay should be maintained in keeping with work and performance distinctions.
4. Pay levels for different federal statutory pay systems should be interrelated.

In 1972, Congress enacted the Government Employees Prevailing Rate Systems Law to apply policies similar to those outlined above to blue-collar workers in the federal government.

Government Contracts.   The Walsh-Healy Act sets minimum wage and overtime standards for employees who work on government contracts exceeding $10,000. Instead of setting a single minimum wage for all work as does the FLSA, the Walsh-Healy Act sets a series of minimum wages for many different occupations. These minimum wages are based on "comparable wages" paid by private industry in the area for similar occupations.

Unlike the FLSA, where overtime pay is determined on a weekly basis, the Walsh-Healy Act requires overtime pay of 1.5 times the regular wage of an employee to be paid for every hour worked by an employee over 8 hours *per day.* For example, if an employee covered by the Walsh-Healy Act worked at an occupation paying a prevailing wage of $5.00 per hour, and worked 12 hours on Monday, 4 hours on Tuesday, and 8 hours each on Wednesday, Thursday and Friday, for a total of 40 hours for the week, the employee must be paid for the 4 overtime hours worked on Monday.

Where an employer has employees who work on both private and government contracts, the employer must keep adequate records regarding the time each employee spends on the private and government contracts in order to properly determine minimum wages and overtime pay due under the FLSA and the Walsh-Healy Act. If separate and accurate time records are not kept, the courts have held that there is a presumption that every employee has been working on the government contracts. Other federal statutes which regulate employee wages and hours include:

1. the Davis-Bacon Act of 1921, as amended, which guarantees minimum wages and fringe benefits, based on prevailing standards, for laborers and mechanics employed by contractors and subcontractors engaged in federal public works projects
2. the Motor Carrier Act of 1935, which delegates authority to the Interstate Commerce Commission to set maximum hours, based on safety, for employees of employers who operate motor vehicles in interstate or foreign commerce
3. the Service Contract Act of 1935, which provides for the payment of minimum wages, based on prevailing wages, to employees of contractors furnishing services to the federal government.

Many states have also enacted legislation that regulates minimum wages and maximum hours of employment. The coverage of such state laws is beyond the scope of this book.

Wages, Hours and Compensable Time.   The FLSA provides methods for computing wages and hours of employees covered by the Act. Specifically, it provides for the computation of (1) minimum wages, (2) overtime pay, and (3) the determination of "compensable time."

Computing the Minimum Wage. Section 6(2) of the FLSA sets the minimum wage for covered employees. In calculating the minimum wage that must be paid under the FLSA, an employer may reduce the minimum wage by an amount equal to the "reasonable" cost of food, lodging, and other facilities furnished to employees. For example, a restaurant that provides meals to employees may deduct the "reasonable cost" of such meals from an employee's minimum wages. Further, under the FLSA, an employer is permitted to pay only half the current minimum wage to employees who regularly earn more than $20.00 a month in tips. This provision usually covers waitresses and waiters, parking lot attendants, bellhops and other tipped employees. An employer must notify its employees of the FLSA credit provision regarding tips.

Computing Overtime Pay. Section 7(a) of the FLSA provides that a covered employee is to be paid at least 1.5 times his "regular rate" of pay for each hour worked in excess of the standard 40-hour work week. Usually, where employees are working under a contract that provides for a set *hourly* rate of pay, the computation of the total weekly wage, and thus overtime pay, is a relatively simple calculation: for example, an hourly rate of $5.00 would require overtime pay of $7.50 per hour.

Where an employee receives a fixed *weekly* or *monthly* salary, the U.S. Supreme Court has held that the "regular hourly rate" is computed by dividing the compensation attributed to the week or month by the number of hours usually worked during that period. For example, if an employee's monthly salary is $1,600.00 and 160 hours of work are required of the employee each month, the hourly wage rate would be $10.00, and the statutory overtime rate would be $15.00 per hour.

The determination of an employee's regular wage is often a problem where the employee regularly receives nonstandard compensation *in addition* to an hourly wage. For example, if an employee receives a regular incentive bonus (such as payment for piecemeal work), or regularly participates in a profit-sharing plan, such regular nonstandard compensation must be included in the employee's regular wage for the purpose of determining overtime pay. However, the FLSA statutorily excludes such incidental payments as Christmas bonuses, reimbursements for expenses, and completely "discretionary" bonuses from an employee's regular wage when computing overtime pay.

Each *week* is treated separately when determining an employee's overtime pay under the FLSA. For example, if in one week an employee works 50 hours, and in the second week the employee only works 30 hours, the employee must be paid for the 10 "overtime" hours worked during the first week. Only in rare specified employment situations is "averaging" of weeks allowed under the FLSA in determining overtime pay.

"Compensable Time." Before the minimum wage or overtime pay provisions of the FLSA can be applied, the "compensable time" of the covered employee must be determined. Generally, time spent traveling between work and home is not considered compensable time under the FLSA. However, courts have held that compensable time for specific employees includes certain "preliminary" and "postliminary" activities. For example, courts have held

that where miners are required to gather on company property to be driven to work at a mine, the transportation time to the mine is compensable time in determining wages. Also, courts have held that the time required by butchers to sharpen knives is a "preliminary" activity that must be included in the calculation of compensable time under the FLSA.

Remedies Under the FLSA.   Where there has been a violation of the provisions of the FLSA, the Secretary of Labor may:

1. seek an injunction to enjoin future violations
2. file a lawsuit on behalf of individual claimants to collect damages, consisting of reimbursement of past-due wages, and in the discretion of the court an award of interest on the amount of damages
3. seek administrative penalties for violation of the child labor provisions of the Act
4. seek criminal sanctions for certain "willful" violations of the Act.

Aggrieved employees may also bring injunctive and damage actions against employers under the FLSA.

In *Steiner v. Mitchell,* which follows, the U.S. Supreme Court held that certain preliminary and postliminary activities by employees constituted "compensable time" under the FLSA.

COMPENSABLE TIME

STEINER v. MITCHELL, SECRETARY OF LABOR

350 U.S. 247 (1956)
UNITED STATES SUPREME COURT

Mr. Chief Justice Warren delivered the opinion of the Court.

The Secretary of Labor . . . brought this action in the United States District Court for the Middle District of Tennessee to enjoin petitioners from violating the overtime and record-keeping requirements of . . . the Fair Labor Standards Act of 1938, as amended. . . . The District Court gave judgment for the plaintiff, and the Court of Appeals for the Sixth Circuit affirmed.

The petitioners own and operate a plant where they are engaged in manufacturing automotive-type wet storage batteries which they sell in interstate commerce. All of the production employees, such as those with whom we are here concerned, customarily work with or near the various chemicals used in the plant. These include lead metal, lead oxide, and lead sulphate, lead peroxide, and sul-

phuric acid. Some of these are in liquid form; some are in powder form, and some are solid. In the manufacturing process, some of the materials go through various changes and give off dangerous fumes. Some are spilled or dropped, and thus become a part of the dust in the air. In general, the chemicals permeate the entire plant and everything and everyone in it. Lead and its compounds are toxic to human beings. . . .

The primary ways in which lead poisoning is contracted are by inhalation and ingestion; i.e., by taking in particles through the nose or mouth, an open cut or sore, or any other body cavity. The risk is "very great" and even exists outside the plant because the lead dust and lead fumes which are prevalent in the plant attach themselves to the skin, clothing, and hair of the employees. Even the families of battery workers may be placed in some danger if lead particles are brought home in the workers' clothing or shoes. Sulphuric acid in the plant is also a hazard. It is irritating to the skin and can cause severe burns. When the acid contacts clothing, it causes disintegration or rapid deterioration. Moreover, the effects of sulphuric acid make the employee more susceptible than he would otherwise be to contamination by particles of lead and lead compounds.

Accordingly, in order to make their plant as safe a place as is possible under the circumstances and thereby increase the efficiency of its operation, petitioners have equipped it with shower facilities and a locker room with separate lockers for work and street clothing. Also, they furnish without charge old but clean work clothes which the employees wear. The cost of providing their own work clothing would be prohibitive for the employees, since the acid causes such rapid deterioration that the clothes sometimes last only a few days. Employees regularly change into work clothes before the beginning of the productive work period, and shower and change back at the end of that period.

Petitioners do not record or pay for the time which their employees spend in these activities, which was found to amount to thirty minutes a day, ten minutes in the morning and twenty minutes in the afternoon, for each employee. . . . They do contend that these activities fall without the concept of "principal activity" and that, being performed off the production line and before or after regular shift hours, they are beyond the protection of the Fair Labor Standards Act.

We . . . conclude that activities performed either before or after the regular work shift, on or off the production line, are compensable under the portal-to-portal provisions of the Fair Labor Standards Act if those activities are an integral and indispensable part of the principal activities for which covered workmen are employed. . . .

We find no difficulty in fitting the facts of this case to that conclusion because it would be difficult to conjure up an instance where changing clothes and showering are more clearly an integral and indispensable part of the principal activity of the employment than in the case of these employees.

The judgment is *affirmed.*

CASE QUESTIONS

1. What does the FLSA provide regarding the payment of the following?
   a. minimum wages
   b. overtime pay
2. Who was the plaintiff in this case? What remedy was the plaintiff seeking?
3. What activity did the employees engage in that the plaintiff asserted constituted "compensable time" under the FLSA? Explain.
4. Did the court find that the activity was part of the "primary activity" of the employees, and therefore compensable under the FLSA?

Policy Issue. Should employers be forced by law to pay overtime pay that is greater than regular pay rates? Or should employers and employees be able to privately contract regarding wages?

Economics Issue. Do the FLSA provisions regarding minimum wages and overtime pay increase or decrease the cost of products and services?

Ethics Issue. Was it ethical for the employer to argue that the time spent by the employees changing their clothes in this case was not compensable time under the FLSA?

Social Responsibility. Do employers owe a duty of social responsibility to workers for the time they spend traveling between work and home?

WORKER'S COMPENSATION

Prior to the enactment of Worker's Compensation statutes, *employees* who were injured on the job were treated no differently from other parties who were injured in society. Employees were left with the ability to bring an action at law against their employer for "negligence." A typical negligence lawsuit required the employee to hire an attorney, and to incur the costs and time, often years, of waging a lawsuit against his employer. The legislatures of many countries realized that traditional negligence actions against employers provided little protection for employees injured on the job. In 1884, Germany enacted the first comprehensive worker's compensation statute. Great Britain followed with the passage of worker's compensation statute in 1897, and by 1908 almost all countries on the European continent had enacted comprehensive worker's compensation statutes.

In 1903, Congress enacted the Federal Employer's Liability Act (FELA). The Act provided worker's compensation benefits for employees of common carriers (such as railroads, barges) engaged in interstate or foreign commerce. A 1939 amendment of the FELA totally abolished the defense of assumption of the risk. Federal statutes provided worker's compensation benefits to two other specific classes of workers: The Longshoremen's and Harbor Workers' Compensation Act for waterfront workers and the Merchant Marine Act (the "Jones Act") for seamen.

States began enacting worker's compensation statutes in 1902; these originally applied to specific industries, usually railroading, mining, and manufacturing. Gradually states began enacting general Worker's Compensation laws, and just after World War II every state in the Union had some form of Worker's Compensation law.

Worker's Compensation statutes as enacted by state legislatures provide for the payment of damages to injured workers through an administrative procedure without the need for an employee to sue his employer. The injured employee is guaranteed at least a minimum amount, providing immediate cash to meet his emergency. Worker's Compensation differs from a conventional negligence lawsuit in two major aspects: (1) fault on the part of either the employer or employee is eliminated from consideration; and (2) damages are paid according to statutorily set amounts—actual damages suffered by the injured worker are irrelevant.

The compensation principle underlying Worker's Compensation statutes is based on the economic theory that the persons who enjoy the products of businesses, both businesses and the consumers, should bear the cost of the industrial injuries and death incidental to the manufacture, production, and distribution of such goods and services. The personal-fault principle on which the law of negligence was based could not meet this goal. In *Whetro v. Awkerman,* 174 N.W.2d 783 (Michigan, 1970), the court stated:

The purpose of the compensation act . . . is to promote the welfare of the people of Michigan relating to the liability of employers for injuries or death sustained by their employees. . . . The act allocates the burden of such payments to the most appropriate source of payment, the consumer of the product.

Funding Worker's Compensation Programs. Worker's Compensation can be viewed as a form of compulsory social insurance. Worker's Compensation statutes mandate by law that covered employers must pay statutorily set damages to injured employees. Generally, funding for Worker's Compensation is accomplished by one of three methods:

1. company self-insurance,
2. purchase of private insurance
3. where applicable, payments made to a state fund.

About one third of the states require payments into a state insurance fund. The other states generally permit employers to provide for adequate self-insurance or to purchase insurance from private insurance companies. Currently, insurance protection by any one of the three methods (self-insurance, private insurance, or state fund) is *compulsory* in all states except Louisiana.

The amount required to be paid by an employer into a state insurance fund, or the amount of Worker's Compensation insurance to be provided, is determined by each state. The amount is based on a number of factors, including the type of industry, special risk hazards, and prior accident experience. Rates are usually set by state administrative agencies, and are generally appealable. Most states provide for a "merit" rating program for employers with few injuries, thus providing an incentive for employers to increase safety in the workplace. Many European countries have made worker's compensation part of their social security legislation, paying claims out of tax revenues.

The success of Worker's Compensation laws depends on their effective administration. Most states have created a special administrative agency to hear and decide workers' compensation claims. A few states provide that such claims are heard by an established court system. Initial decisions regarding workers' compensation claims are appealable. A claimant must file a claim, supported by appropriate evidence (e.g., medical reports) to the proper agency or court. All Worker's Compensation statutes provide a Statute of Limitation within which period the claim must be filed (e.g., within two years from time of injury). All states provide that a specific period of time must elapse after an injury (e.g., one or two weeks) before disability benefits are available. Medical benefits are available immediately.

Approximately 80 percent of our Worker's Compensation cases are uncontested. Where a claim is contested, a hearing will be held. Although the administrative hearing is judicial in nature, the process is usually simple and informal in nature. Testimony may be received and evidence introduced. The decision of the administrative agency or court in a contested case is appealable.

Coverage of Worker's Compensation Statutes. The coverage of state Worker's Compensation statutes is broad. Under most statutes, all employers are subject to coverage except those who employ fewer than a minimum number of employees. The most common minimum number is from three to five employees. Further, only "regular" and "continuous" employees are counted. Nonprofit and charitable organizations are excluded from coverage under most workers' compensation statutes.

The majority of statutes exclude household employees and domestic servants (i.e., cleaners, maids, etc.) who are hired for nonbusiness purposes, agricultural and farm laborers, casual workers, and public employees and officers. Illegally employed minors have generally been held to be covered by workers' compensation statutes. It is generally immaterial whether the injured worker is a minimum wage earner or a high-salaried administrative employee. Several states have special Worker's Compensation statutes that cover public employees. Coverage is generally determined by reference to the nature of the employee's work, rather than the business of the employer.

A question is often posed as to whether an injured worker was an "employee" covered by a Worker's Compensation statute or an "independent contractor," who is generally *not* covered by such a statute. For example, a lawyer who has his own law firm and who is hired to represent a corporation is an independent contractor. On the other hand, if a lawyer is hired to be "in-house" counsel for a corporation, he is an employee. Often, the distinction between an employee and an independent contractor is based on a determination of how much *control* the employer had over the work of the person. Where an employer controls the details of the work (the time when it is performed, the specific way it is performed, the amount of time the worker spends on it, etc.), the worker is generally considered an employee covered by Worker's Compensation statutes.

Worker's Compensation Benefits.   The *purpose* of Worker's Compensation statutes is to provide payments of money to an injured employee or to relatives of a deceased employee. These payments are commonly referred to as "benefits." Benefit payments fall into three categories: (1) medical benefits, (2) disability benefits, and (3) death benefits.

Medical Benefits.   Ordinarily, *medical* benefits under Worker's Compensation statutes include the cost of the services of physicians and nurses, hospitalization expenses, and the cost of recuperation equipment (e.g., crutches, prosthetic devices). Many modern Worker's Compensation statutes include the cost of psychiatric treatment. A minority of jurisdictions allow payment for practical nursing care at home, even if provided by a spouse or relative. The majority of states allow an injured worker to select his or her own physician.

Disability Benefits.   Disability benefits are money payments made to an employee to indemnify him for wages lost by injury. Usually, disability benefits for wage loss range between one half and two thirds of the normal wage of the injured employee. Overtime wages are generally excluded from the computation. Statutes generally set minimum and maximum amounts that may be paid per week to an employee, and also limit the number of weeks that disability payments can be paid.

Most Worker's Compensation statutes provide a table of specific benefits for the loss of specific members of the body (e.g., an arm, a leg, a finger). These benefits are commonly referred to as "schedule benefits." Schedule benefits differ substantially from state to state. For example, at the time of writing this book, the loss of an arm entitled the injured employee to the following schedule benefits: in Michigan, 269 weeks; in Rhode Island, 312 weeks; and in Wisconsin, 500 weeks. Many states have enacted special provisions to their Worker's Compensation statutes to pay compensation for disfigurement. There is widespread criticism that the amount and duration of Worker's Compensation benefits are inadequate.

Payments of disability benefits commonly depend on the degree of disability and whether the disability is temporary or permanent. The majority of work injuries involve "temporary total" disability, where an employee is unable to work for a specified period of time, i.e., while in the hospital and recuperating from surgery. In this situation, the worker usually returns to work after he has recovered.

The second major type of disability benefit is paid for "permanent total" disability. Under this concept, it is recognized that the injury is of a permanent nature and is of such a degree that the employee cannot do any substantial work at all after suffering the compensable injury. The majority of jurisdictions apply an "ability to earn" test in determining compensation for wage loss. For example, if a disabled manual laborer qualifies as a teacher, Worker's Compensation will be paid based on his "ability to earn" a living if he can obtain a teaching position, and not on the actual lost wages from his previous manual labor job. Most Worker's Compensation statutes specifically define certain injuries as constituting "permanent total" disability. The following list sets forth the California statute that defines permanent total disability.

Permanent Total Disability, Section 4662, California Labor Code

Any of the following permanent disabilities shall be conclusively presumed to be total in character:

    (a) Loss of both eyes or the sight thereof.
    (b) Loss of both hands or the use thereof.
    (c) An injury resulting in a practically total paralysis.
    (d) An injury to the brain resulting in incurable imbecility or insanity.

In all other cases, permanent total disability shall be determined in accordance with fact.

Death Benefits.   Most Worker's Compensation statutes provide for certain "death benefits" if a worker has died from a compensable injury. Death benefits usually consist of paying an amount to cover burial expenses (usually $2,000–$4,000), and payments to members of the deceased's immediate family (i.e., spouse and children) and other persons who were economically dependent on the deceased employee. *Children* as defined in most statutes includes step-children, adopted children, posthumous children, and out-of-wedlock children. Death benefits are also paid pursuant to specific schedules contained in Worker's Compensation laws.

Exclusive Remedy.   Most Worker's Compensation statutes expressly provide that the benefits as provided in the act are the employee's *exclusive* remedy against his employer, thus precluding a lawsuit against the employer for negligence. The argument for this rule is that there is a proper trade-off in that injured employees are provided with immediate benefits under Worker's Compensation laws in exchange for giving up the right to sue employers. Generally, the injured employee does not have the right to choose between claiming Worker's Compensation benefits and suing his employer for negligence. In over half the states, the statute expressly confers the employer's "tort immunity" (immunity to a charge of negligence) upon co-employees. In many states the injured employee can sue negligent co-employees for tort damages if they contributed to causing the injury.

Some states have held that this exclusive remedy does not prevent other members of the employee's family from suing the employer for direct injuries to themselves; for example, a spouse may sue for loss of consortium—that is, loss of marital relations. An employee who collects benefits under Worker's Compensation statutes can still sue the manufacturer and distributor of the product that injured him or her (e.g., a machine) for product liability.

Accidents "in the Course of Employment."   In order to be covered under Worker's Compensation statutes, the accident must occur "in the course of employment." Where an accident occurs while an employee is actively at work, it is clearly within the course of his employment. Questions often arise as to whether injuries that occur during employer-sponsored outings, dinners, and other social events, or while an employee is participating in a civic or patriotic act requested by his employer, are within the "course of employment." Although state decisions have differed, the trend of the law is to include such functions within the injured employee's "course of employment."

For example, in *Charley v. Koerner Ford, Inc.,* 249 N.Y.S.2d 4 (New York, 1967), an employee who, at a company-sponsored function, attempted to follow up strenuous dancing with intercourse was held to be covered by Worker's Compensation upon suffering a heart attack. In *Carson v. Industrial Comm.,* 539 P.2d 189 (Arizona, 1975) an employee who suffered injuries while serving as a member of a volunteer fire department at the request of his employer was held to be covered under his employer's Worker's Compensation.

Where an employee renders personal assistance to a third person at the request of his employer, the injuries suffered by the employee are generally held to be incurred in the "course of employment." However, where an employee renders such assistance without orders from his employer, the assistance has generally been held to be a personal act not rendered in the course of employment.

Acts by an employee for his own personal benefit that are performed on work premises during idle or spare time have received divergent treatment by state courts. In *Chrisman v. Farmers Cooperative Association* 140 N.W.2d 809 (Nebraska, 1966), a service station attendant who was injured while working on his own car on work premises was held to be covered by Worker's Compensation. In *Minor v. U.S. Fidelity & Insurance Company,* 356 So.2d 1049 (Louisiana, 1977), a policeman who was "on call" was found to be covered by Worker's Compensation when he discharged his revolver and injured his hand while at home.

Employees often engage in horseplay on the job from which injuries result. Where the claimant is the "aggressor" or "prankster," the tendency is for the courts to deny Worker's Compensation. However, where the claimant is an innocent victim of the horseplay who did not participate in the prank, injuries are usually held to be covered by Worker's Compensation. For example, in *Birns v. Merritt Engineering Co.,* 96 N.E.2d 739 (New York, 1951), a co-employee offered the claimant a bottle that purported to contain gin. Although there was a rule against drinking on the job, the claimant drank the contents, which was later shown to be a poisonous liquid, and suffered severe damage to internal organs. The court held that the claimant's injury was covered by the state's Worker's Compensation statute.

Lunch-Hour Injuries.   Most courts hold that where an employee takes his meals off the work premises on his own time he is outside the "course of his employment" as to injuries suffered when proceeding to or from, or while at, the eating place. A few jurisdictions have ruled otherwise. If a lunch-hour accident happens on the work premises, in designated eating areas, or in company cafeterias, and is attributable to a hazard in the employment environment, the accident is generally held to occur within the course of employment. Injuries that occur during "break" periods are usually analyzed under the same rules as lunch-hour injuries. For example, in *Puffin v. General Electric Company,* 43 A.2d 746 (Connecticut, 1945), where during a "break" a co-employee who was smoking ignited the angora sweater of the injured employee, Worker's Compensation was awarded.

Coming and Going Rule.   The general rule is that while an employee is en route between home and work, he is outside the "course of employment" and therefore not covered by Worker's Compensation for injuries suffered during this time. This judicial rule is commonly known as the *coming and going rule.*

There are, of course, many exceptions to the coming and going rule. For example, employees who are regularly engaged in traveling (e.g., salesmen) or who have no fixed place for the performance of their duties (e.g., copying machine repairmen) are usually considered within the course of their employment while leaving or returning home. Where an employer undertakes to transport employees to and from work (e.g., on company buses or trains), the journey is considered to be within the course of employment. Employees who are required to live away from home (e.g., who are sent to another city for training programs) are covered by Worker's Compensation while at work and during off hours, i.e., while eating, sleeping, or participating in recreation.

Where an employee is called in by an employer to work at irregular hours (e.g., on Saturdays or holidays), the worker is generally covered by Worker's Compensation for injuries suffered going to or from work and home. Where an employer pays an employee for the time spent in traveling between work and home, or pays the travel expenses of the employee (e.g., at 15 cents per mile), accidents that occur on the journey between work and home are considered to be within the course of employment. For example, in *Reading & Bates, Inc. v. Whittington,* 208 So.2d 437 (Mississippi, 1968), an employee who was drinking while driving home from work and was injured when he parked, went behind his car to relieve himself, and stepped in a hole, was held to be covered by Worker's Compensation.

The courts have developed many ill-defined exceptions to the coming and going rule. For example, courts have held that accidents in parking lots while employees are coming and going from work, or at bus stops, or in any places "close" to work, are covered by Worker's Compensation. This rule has gone under numerous labels, including the "so-close" rule, the "proximity" rule, and the "threshold" doctrine.

Dual-Purpose Missions.   Among the most difficult questions that must be decided by state Worker's Compensation agencies and the courts are situations in which an accident occurs where the injured employee is on a "dual-purpose" mission, partially running an errand for his employer and partially on a mission for his own personal benefit. The majority of jurisdictions have adopted the "dominant purpose" rule in deciding dual-purpose cases. This rule was stated by the court in *Marks v. Gray*, 167 N.E. 181 (New York, 1929) at pp. 182–183, as follows:

> The test in brief is this: If the work of the employee creates a necessity for travel, he is in the course of his employment, though he is serving at the same time some purpose of his own [covered by worker's compensation during mission]. . . . If, however, the work has had no part in creating the necessity for travel, if the business errand had been dropped, and would have been cancelled upon failure of the private purpose, though the business errand was undone, the travel is then personal, and personal the risk [not covered by worker's compensation during mission].

Many jurisdictions (and this is the trend of the law) apply a "deviations" test rather than a pure "dominant purpose" test to dual-purpose missions. Under the *deviations test*, the court must first determine if the overall trip was for business or personal reasons (the "dominant" purpose). The court must then apply a two-pronged "deviations" test: (1) If the overall trip is determined to be for a "business purpose," yet the accident occurs on a part of the journey that can clearly be separated and attributed to a deviation for personal reasons (e.g., the employee departs from the direct route to visit a friend), the accident is not compensable under Worker's Compensation laws; and (2) if the overall trip is determined to be for personal reasons, but the accident occurs on a part of the journey that is clearly separated and attributed to a deviation for business purposes (e.g., to run an errand for the employer), the accident is compensable under the Worker's Compensation law.

In *Shunk v. Gulf American Land Corp.* the court, facing a difficult fact situation, held that the claimant's injury occurred "in the course" of her employment and was therefore covered by the state Worker's Compensation statute.

ACCIDENT "IN THE COURSE OF EMPLOYMENT"

JOCQUELYN H. SHUNK v. GULF AMERICAN LAND CORP., MARYLAND CASUALTY CO. and THE FLORIDA INDUSTRIAL COMMISSION

224 SO.2D 269 (1969)
SUPREME COURT OF FLORIDA

Ervin, Chief Justice.

Claimant, Mrs. Jocquelyn H. Shunk, testified she has a real estate license; that her employment with Gulf American Land Corporation was to find prospective lot purchasers and to solicit them to travel in a plane provided by employer from the points where the prospects were assembled and em-planed to her employer's real estate development near Naples, Florida.

In Daytona Beach, Florida, claimant solicited one Luther Carrol Tanly, with the knowledge of her immediate supervisor, Howard Keller, to make the plane trip. In the course of persuading Tanly to make the trip, Mrs. Shunk had dinner with Tanly and Keller and a Mrs. Catherine W. Morris, her fellow employee. After a late dinner (completed about 12:30 A.M.) the night of the claimant's accident, according to claimant's version of the affair, she accompanied Tanly to the Ritz Apartments in Daytona Beach where he was stopping. She said she went to his apartment for the purpose of ascertaining where he stayed so that she could awaken him in time the next morning to see that he got on board the plane along with other prospective customers for the trip to Naples.

Claimant testified that upon arriving at the Ritz Apartments she had an altercation with Tanly; that he made improper advances toward her; that in attempting to elude him, she fell 25 feet from a window of the apartment building, injuring herself. The injury occurred at about 2:30 A.M.

Mrs. Shunk testified she had only had two cocktails, one before dinner and one afterwards; that she became nauseated after eating shrimp at the dinner, and that upon arriving at Tanly's apartment she asked him if she could use his bathroom to relieve her nausea. She testified that upon leaving the bathroom and attempting to leave the apartment Tanly's advances and the altercation ensued.

Officer Browne testified Tanly had told him that he and Mrs. Shunk had been drinking at a list of bars. Tanly was booked for vagrancy, but not actually charged with anything and was released the same day of his arrest.

In a statement made at the hospital just after the accident (but later contradicted at the hearing on the claim) claimant said she was accosted in a telephone booth by a short white male with a gun who took her to his apartment from which she jumped.

Mr. Howard Keller, the immediate supervisor of the claimant, testified by deposition that the duties of the solicitors employed by Gulf American Land Corporation included the following: Finding prospects anywhere, any time, any place they could do so (including restaurants, beaches, motels); obtaining from the prospects their hotel or motel room numbers, telephone numbers, and the responsibility for getting the prospects up early in the mornings to catch the 7:00 A.M. plane for the real estate development located near Naples.

The Judge of Industrial Claims accepted the testimony of the claimant as corroborated by Mr. Keller and other witnesses for the claimant, including Mrs. Catherine Morris, and found that the accident and injury arose out of and in the course of her employment and are compensable. . . . However, the Full Commission reversed, holding:

> Whatever motivation the claimant may have had for jumping from the window, we feel that the injury cannot be considered to have arisen out of and in the course of her employment.

It is quite true that the particular circumstances related above present a suspicious inference that claimant was not acting in the course of her employment at the time of her injury; that there may have been a deviation by claimant from her employment, and that her presence in the apartment at the late hour may have been a social engagement of her own, rather than one required for the discharge of her employment duties. However, a suspicious inference in these particular circumstances is not necessarily conclusive. The nature of claimant's employment, according to the testimony, involved solicitation, salesmanship and persuasion, and follow-up action to see that prospective customers were on scheduled flights to the development site, not dischargeable only during working hours normal to most employees. Consequently, it seems fairly well established that promotion of real estate sales to prospective customers of the kind here considered involves techniques and methods in a special class that have been found to be necessary in persuading prospective customers to agree to make the related plane trips.

In a debatable situation, such as this one, we conclude we should rest our judgment with the trier of the facts and lay aside our skepticism and natural inclination to be cynically suspicious.

The writ is *granted;* the Commission's order of reversal is quashed with direction that the order of the Judge of Industrial Claims be *reinstated.*

CASE QUESTIONS

1. What does the "in the course of employment" test of the Worker's Compensation laws require? Explain.
2. What was Mrs. Shunk's occupation? What were her employment duties? Did they involve solicitation, salesmanship, persuasion, and follow-up? Explain.

3. How did the accident occur in this case? Explain.
4. Did the court find that the "in the course of employment" test was met in this case? Do you agree? Did you lay aside your skepticism and natural inclination to be cynically suspicious?

Policy Issue. Is the "in the course of employment" test an important limitation on the payment of Worker's Compensation benefits? Why or why not? Explain.

Economics Issue. Why did Mrs. Shunk seek Worker's Compensation benefits? Why didn't she sue Mr. Tanly?

Ethics Issue. Was Mrs. Shunk justified in jumping?

Social Responsibility. Do employers owe a duty of social responsibility to compensate employees for injuries suffered during personal time?

Accidents "Arising Out of Employment." In order for an accident to be compensable under Worker's Compensation, the accident must "arise out of" the employment. If an employee, while at work, is injured by a bolt of lightning, stabbed by an insane stranger, or injured by some other force not associated with his work, did the accident "arise out of" the employee's employment? The original cases held that in such circumstances, the accident did not "arise out of" the employment and was therefore not compensable under Worker's Compensation.

The modern trend is to extend the "arise out of" requirement to include dangers not connected with the injured employee's employment. The courts do so by applying either of two theories: (1) the argument that such occurrences as lightning bolts, injury caused by third parties, etc., are "foreseeable" damages and therefore arise out of the employment, or (2) the "positional risk" doctrine, which holds that "but for the employment, the appellant [claimant] would not have been in the . . . path" of the danger. The "positional" theory was applied to award Worker's Compensation benefits in *Gargiulo v. Gargiulo*, 93 A.2d 598 (New Jersey, 1952), where a butcher's helper was accidentally struck and injured, while working, by an arrow shot by a small boy next door.

In *Whetro v. Awkerman* the court held that where employees were injured and killed by a tornado, the injury "arose out of" their employment and they were covered by a state Worker's Compensation statute.

ACCIDENT "ARISING OUT OF" EMPLOYMENT

WHETRO v. AWKERMAN and MICHIGAN STATE ACCIDENT FUND
and
EMERY, WIDOW v. THE HUGE COMPANY and INSURANCE COMPANY OF NORTH AMERICA

174 N.W.2D 783 (1970)
SUPREME COURT OF MICHIGAN

T. G. Kavanagh, Justice.
These cases were consolidated. . . . They turn on the same question, for the damages for which workmen's compensation was awarded in each case were caused by the Palm Sunday 1965 tornadoes which devastated parts of Southern Michigan.

Carl Whetro was injured when the tornado destroyed the residence wherein he was working for his employer and seeks reimbursement for his medical expenses. Henry E. Emery was killed when the motel in which he was staying while on a business trip for his employer was destroyed by the tornado, and his widow seeks compensation for his death.

In each case the hearing referee found that the employee's injury arose out of and in the course of his employment. The award was affirmed by the appeal board in each case and by the Court of Appeals in the Whetro case.

The defendant-appellants in both cases base their defense on the assertion that tornadoes are "acts of God" or acts of nature and injuries which are caused by them do not arise "out of" the employment and hence are not compensable under the Workmen's Compensation Act.

[W]e no longer regard an "act of God" whether it be a tornado, lightning, earthquake, or flood as a defense to a claim for a work-connected injury. Such a defense retains too much of the idea that an employer should not pay compensation unless he is somehow at fault. This concept from the law of tort is inconsistent with the law of workmen's compensation. . . . Fault has nothing to do with whether or not compensation is payable. The economic impact on an injured workman and his family is the same whether the injury was caused by the employer's fault or otherwise.

Accordingly, we hold that the employment of Carl Whetro and Henry E. Emery in each case was the occasion of the injury which they suffered and therefore the injuries arose "out of" and in the course of their employment.

The award in each case is *affirmed*.

Brennan, Chief Justice.

The terms "arising out of" and "in the course of" are not redundant. They mean two different things. An adulterous cobbler shot at his last by his jealous wife may be "in the course of" his employment. But the injury does not "arise out of" his job. On what basis of moral responsibility should his injuries be paid for by his employer? By what logic would society decree that his disability should add a farthing to the price of shoes?

The workmen's compensation law is not a utopian attempt to put a price tag on all human suffering and incorporate it into the cost of living.

Lightning, flood, tornadoes and estranged wives will always be with us, in this vale of tears. They were the occasion of human injury when our forebears were tilling the soil with sharp sticks. They are not a byproduct of the Industrial Revolution, nor are they in any sense the moral responsibility of those who profit by or enjoy the fruits of our modern industrialized society.

I would reverse without apology for the precedents.

CASE QUESTIONS

1. What caused the injuries to the employees in this case? Explain.
2. What does the "arose out of" test of Worker's Compensation statutes require? Explain.
3. Under this decision, are injuries caused by circumstances other than the results of the Industrial Revolution covered by Worker's Compensation statutes? Should they be?
4. Do you think workmen's compensation a "utopian attempt to put a price tag on all human suffering and incorporate it into the cost of living?"

Policy Issue. Must an employer be at fault before an employee's injuries are covered by Worker's Compensation statutes? Should employer fault be required?

Economics Issue. Do Worker's Compensation programs have any effect on the price of goods produced in America? Does it put American business at a disadvantage in international markets?

Ethics Issue. Are injuries caused by "lightning, tornadoes, and estranged wives" the "moral responsibility of those who "profit by or enjoy the fruits of our modern industrialized society"?

Social Responsibility. Do you think *employees* should support Worker's Compensation laws? Employers? Consumers?

The Concept of "Accident."   The usual form of accident, in which an external object (e.g., an automobile) hits a human being and causes injury, such as a broken leg, has always been covered by Worker's Compensation. However, the concept of "accident" compensable by Worker's Compensation has been interpreted more broadly. Although traditionally accidents have been viewed as occurring unexpectedly from a definite act, courts today recognize that many injuries occur from a series of acts and incidents, no one of which is identifiable as the sole cause of the injury.

Courts have applied a "repeated trauma" doctrine in holding that injuries that result from repeated events (e.g., constant jolting of the spine from riding a bulldozer) constitute an accident compensable by Worker's Compensation. Suicide is generally not covered by Worker's Compensation statutes. A minority of jurisdictions hold that suicide is compensable under Worker's Compensation if the cause of the suicide is traceable to a work-connected incident.

In this excerpt from *Matteus v. R. T. Allen & Sons, Inc.*, 266 A.2d 240 (Maine, 1970), Justice Weatherbee explained the modern concept of "accident" under Worker's Compensation laws:

> The Workmen's Compensation Law represents a relatively recent concept of responsibility without negligence. While the early cases usually concerned accidental injuries where an external force was applied to an external portion of the body, our own Court decided early in the development of our law that the term *injury by accident* includes incidents where internal parts of the physical structure break down under external force, including the stress of labor. While this may more dramatically occur as a result of a slip, a fall, or a single unusual strained effort, we have found other such internal breakdowns to have resulted from the usual work which the workman was performing in his usual, normal way. In short, we have construed the term "accident" to include not only injuries which are the results of accidents but also injuries which are themselves accidents.

> In *Brown's Case*, [where] a fatal heart dilation resulted from the exertion of shovelling snow, [the court stated]: "If a laborer performing his usual task, in his wonted way, by reason of strain, breaks his wrist, nobody would question the accidental nature of the injury. If instead of the wrist, it is an artery that breaks, the occurrence is just as clearly an accident."

Occupational Diseases.   Originally, occupational diseases were not considered accidents compensable under Worker's Compensation statutes. In *Connelly v. Hunt Furniture Company*, 147 N.E. 366 (New York, 1925), where an embalmer's helper cut his hand, allowing germs from a gangrenous corpse to enter his body, causing blood poisoning and ultimately death, Judge Cardozo wrote an opinion which held that the disease was an "accident" covered by the state's Worker's Compensation law. Most jurisdictions quickly adopted the reasoning of the *Connelly* case.

Most modern Worker's Compensation statutes expressly include as compensable certain occupational diseases that are closely related to the claimant's employment. Questions often arise, however, as to whether a disease is an "occupational disease," which is compensable, or an "ordinary disease of life" contracted through nonoccupational means. A minority of statutes specifically list a schedule of diseases considered to be occupational diseases. Most statutes, however, merely include the term *occupational disease,* leaving for the administrative agencies and courts to determine on a case-by-case basis whether a specific disease is covered. Factors to be considered are length of employment, possibility of contracting the disease while at work, employees' prior history with the disease, etc. For example, in *The State ex rel. Ohio Bell Telephone Company v. Krise,* 327 N.E.2d 756 (Ohio, 1975) a Worker's Compensation award was made when an outdoor telephone installer and repairman showed that the histoplasmosis (damage to the lymph nodes) that he contracted had been caused by constant contact with pigeon droppings during his work.

Although the etiological "cause" of cancer is unknown, and the link of cancer to the work environment is not certain, the trend is for administrative agencies and courts to cover cancer under Worker's Compensation laws. Most jurisdictions include allergies as occupational diseases covered by Worker's Compensation statutes.

Mental Injury. The most recent major problem faced by administrative agencies and courts is the thousands of claims for Worker's Compensation that have been filed alleging mental injury. Generally, the courts have distinguished three types of mental injury cases:

1. In the first type of claim, the worker suffers mental injury as a result of suffering a work-connected physical blow or trauma. Most courts have held that mental injury caused by physical injury is compensable under workers' compensation laws. For example, in *Employers Insurance Company v. Wright,* 150 S.E.2d 257 (Georgia, 1966), where an employee was raped at work and suffered a disabling emotional trauma, the court awarded Worker's Compensation for the mental injury.
2. The second type of mental injury claim arises where a worker is exposed to a mental stimulus that *causes* a physical injury (by contrast, in (1) the physical injury *caused* the mental injury). The majority of jurisdictions hold that this type of injury is also compensable under worker's compensation. For example, in *Wolfe v. Sibley, Lindsay & Curr Company,* 330 N.E.2d 603 (New York, 1975), Worker's Compensation was awarded where the claimant discovered the body of her superior at work after he had committed suicide, and she thereafter suffered acute depressive reactions.
3. The third type of mental injury occurs where there is no physical contact that causes the injury and no one mental stimulus that causes physical injury. Jurisdictions are split on whether worker's compensation awards should be paid where an emotional disorder is brought about by the stress of a protracted series of anxiety-producing work situations. Most states that include such mental injury within their Worker's Compensation statutes require a showing that the injury was caused by "unusual strain." A minority of states have abandoned the "unusual strain" doctrine and cover mental injuries caused by the "ordinary strain of work."

In *Albanese's Case,* which follows, the court held that a series of work-related stressful incidents that caused emotional stress to an employee were compensable under a Worker's Compensation statute.

MENTAL STRESS

JOSEPH ALBANESE'S CASE

389 N.E.2d 83 (1979)
SUPREME JUDICIAL COURT OF MASSACHUSETTS

Abrams, Justice.

The question presented is whether a mental or emotional disorder causally related to stressful incidents at work is a "personal injury arising out of and in the course of . . . employment" under the Workmen's Compensation Act. . . . The reviewing board found that Joseph Albanese was totally disabled as a result of his mental illness, and that his illness was related to a series of emotionally stressful work-related incidents. However, the board concluded

> that as a matter of law the illness set forth above in these circumstances do not constitute a "personal injury" under the Massachusetts Workmen's Compensation Act.

Albanese appealed to the Superior Court, where the judge ruled that he was entitled to compensation. . . . The insurer appealed from the judgement entered in the Superior Court.

We summarize the facts as found by the board. The claimant, Joseph Albanese, was employed as a "working foreman" by Atlantic Steel Co., Inc., for approximately twenty years prior to 1970. His duties included the supervision of shipping as well as the supervision of certain activities of the plant's employees. In 1967 the business was sold to a new owner and thereafter attempts to unionize the employees were commenced.

In 1969, the employees voted to unionize, and friction developed between Albanese as working foreman and the workers. Part of the friction was caused by the management's decision to eliminate overtime work, which frequently "required [Albanese] to go out into the shop and prod the men to expedite the work."

Additional friction between Albanese and the men resulted from the activities of Albanese's direct supervisor, the plant manager. On one occasion in 1968, the manager informed Albanese that the company practice of distributing Thanksgiving turkeys was to be discontinued. On a second occasion, the manager told Albanese that the company did not intend to give the workers a Christmas bonus in 1969. On each occasion, after Albanese relayed this information to the workers, the plant manager reversed his own decision. Albanese viewed these incidents as humiliating, and felt that the manager was intentionally attempting to undermine Albanese's relationship with the workers.

On April 17, 1970, Albanese became involved in a "heated argument" with one of the workers over the question whether the worker was entitled to overtime pay. The plant manager informed Albanese that the company did not intend to pay any overtime wages to the worker involved. . . . Five days later, a meeting was held to discuss the worker's overtime pay. Albanese, the plant manager, the worker, and the union agent attended the meeting. After another "heated discussion," the manager ordered Albanese to give the overtime pay to the worker. When this occurred, Albanese

> became distressed, developed chest pains, nausea, and went into the conference room where he laid down for ten minutes. When the chest pains got sharper he went home to bed. . . . [Albanese] has not worked since and has experienced continuing complaints of pains, sweatiness, shortness of breath, headaches, and depression.

Albanese filed a claim under the Workmen's Compensation Act on July 28, 1970.

On appeal, the insurer . . . argues that Albanese's condition is the result of gradual "wear and tear" and thus is not a compensable personal injury under the statute as interpreted by this court.

Based on the board's findings, we conclude that Albanese's injury was not the result of everyday stress or "[b]odily wear and tear resulting from a long period of hard work." Rather, it resulted from a series of identifiable stressful work-related incidents occurring over a relatively brief period of time, compared with his 20-year employment. . . . Therefore, Albanese is entitled to workmen's compensation for his disability.

The judgment of the Superior Court is *affirmed*.

CASE QUESTIONS

1. What do Worker's Compensation laws provide? Explain.
2. Could Albanese have sued his employer for damages in a civil lawsuit for the mental stress he suffered? Why or why not?
3. If Alabanese's mental stress had been caused by "wear and tear" over a long period of time, would the decision have been the same? Should it have been?
4. How many jobs do you think are as stressful as Mr. Albanese's job? Should teacher "burn-out" be compensated under Worker's Compensation laws?

Policy Issue. Should "mental stress" be covered under Worker's Compensation statutes? Why or why not? Can mental stress be as debilitating as a physical injury?

Economics Issue. What is the potential liability exposure to Worker's Compensation programs (in dollars) if all states include mental stress as a compensable injury?

Ethics Issue. Does the inclusion of mental stress as a compensable injury under Worker's Compensation statutes leave room for many fraudulent claims? How would this differ from fraudulent claims for physical injuries?

Social Responsibility. Do employers owe a duty of social responsibility to compensate employees for mental stress suffered on the job?

OCCUPATIONAL SAFETY AND HEALTH ACT (OSHA)

One of the primary concerns of a working person is the safety of the job. In the average year, over 15,000 workers die from occupational accidents, over 2 million workers are injured in occupational accidents, and a substantial number of workers contract occupational diseases. Nonserious injuries suffered by workers from job-related accidents bring the total of industrial injuries to a staggering level.

Before 1970, the federal government left the regulation of industrial safety to the states. The myriad of state laws did not provide sufficient incentives for business to increase the safety of the workplace. In 1970, Congress enacted the Occupational Safety and Health Act (OSHA), a comprehensive piece of legislation that regulates the safety of the work environment. The purpose of OSHA is to reduce industrial fatalities and accidents by setting specific safety standards for the workplace that business must meet. The preamble of OSHA declares that its policy is:

to assure so far as possible every working man and woman in the Nation safe and healthful working conditions and to preserve our human resources. . . .

The Secretary of Labor is charged with the duty of administering OSHA. The Act establishes three federal administrative agencies:

1. the Occupational Safety and Health Administration
2. the National Institute of Occupational Safety and Health
3. the Occupational Safety and Health Review Commission.

The Occupational Safety and Health Administration (the Administration) is a federal agency located within the Department of Labor. The Administration's main functions are to formulate and enact safety and health standards, conduct investigations, and enforce compliance with OSHA.

The National Institute of Occupational Safety and Health (the Institute) is a federal agency located within the Department of Health and Human Services. The Institute makes recommendations to the Secretary of Labor regarding safety standards, conducts research regarding occupational diseases and health problems, and develops training programs designed to educate workers regarding safety at work.

The Occupational Safety and Health Review Commission (the Commission) is an independent agency created by OSHA. The Commission is composed of three members who are appointed by the President for staggered six-year terms. The duties of the Commission consist of hearing appeals from OSHA citations, assessing penalties, and setting abatement periods for the correction of safety and health standard violations.

A National Advisory Committee on Occupational Safety and Health, which is composed of representatives of management, labor, the health professions, and the public, advises the Secretary of Labor regarding occupational safety and health issues.

Coverage of OSHA. OSHA applies to all employers "engaged in a business affecting commerce." The coverage of OSHA is the broadest coverage of any regulatory scheme enacted by Congress under the Commerce Clause of the U.S. Constitution. There are literally few employers who are not subject to coverage by OSHA. For example, the courts have held that OSHA covered workers who were clearing land for the planting of bushes to grow grapes, based on the rationale that the grapes would eventually be grown, picked, and used to make wine that would be sold in interstate commerce.

OSHA and rules adopted thereunder provides particular problems for general contractors. Under the sweeping definition of "employer" in the Act, as interpreted, the courts have held that a general contractor is liable for a violation of an OSHA safety standard on equipment owned by a subcontractor where the general contractor had sufficient "control" over the job site to have forced the subcontractor to comply with the OSHA standard. Multiemployer construction sites also create special problems of conflicting OSHA responsibilities among the several general contractors and subcontractors. The Commission has announced a position whereby a *general contractor* is liable for OSHA violations for *all* employers at a multiemployer worksite where the general contractor possesses sufficient control over the other contractors to force them to comply with OSHA standards.

In addition to OSHA, several other federal statutes contain provisions for the setting and enforcement of safety and health regulations, including:

1. the Railway Safety Act
2. the Coal Mine Safety Act
3. the National Environment Protection Act.

OSHA Rules and Standards. The Secretary of Labor is directed by OSHA to promulgate occupational safety and health *standards*. Under this authority, the Secretary of Labor has set specific safety and health standards for most dangerous chemicals and toxins, including asbestos, vinyl chloride, and carcinogens. The Secretary of Labor is constantly adopting new standards for specific hazardous chemicals, toxins, and other harmful materials and physical agents.

OSHA standards are set through the adoption of legal *rules* by the Secretary of Labor. Rulemaking procedures are prescribed by OSHA, which requires the publication of each proposed OSHA rule in the *Federal Register,* sufficient time for public comment, and the holding of public hearings if requested by the public. Each rule adopted by the Secretary of Labor must contain a general statement of its basis and purpose. Any person "adversely affected" by a proposed OSHA standard may seek judicial review in the appropriate Court of Appeals at any time within 60 days from the date that the proposed rule is published in the *Federal Register.* The courts generally uphold any OSHA administrative rule if the rule is supported by "substantial evidence" considering the record as a whole.

Once an OSHA standard has been properly adopted, an employer may seek a temporary variance from the standard for a certain time period, during which the company can institute procedures to comply with the standard. A permanent variance from an OSHA standard may be issued where an employer demonstrates that the "variant condition" would be as safe and healthful as if the OSHA standard had been fully complied with. Permanent variances from OSHA standards adopted by the Secretary of Labor are seldom granted.

In the following excerpt from *AFL–CIO v. Brennan, Secretary of Labor,* 530 F.2d 109 (1975), the court held that both *technological feasibility* and *economic feasibility* should be considered by OSHA in adopting safety standards which apply to business.

Technological Infeasibility

Acknowledging that for many applications the "no hands in dies" standard is technologically infeasible, and that the result of its universal application will be the elimination of some businesses and some jobs, petitioner urges that this is exactly the result the Congress sought to accomplish. Neither this court nor, so far as our research discloses any other court, has construed OSHA in so Procrustean a fashion. Undoubtedly the most certain way to eliminate industrial hazards is to eliminate industry. But the congressional statement of findings and declaration of purpose and policy in . . . the Act shows that the upgrading of working conditions, not the complete elimination of hazardous occupations, was the dominant intention.

[W]e agree with the Second Circuit in *Society of Plastics Industry, Inc. v. OSHA,* that, at least to a limited extent, OSHA is to be viewed as a technology-forcing piece of legislation. Thus the Secretary would not be justified in dismissing an alternative to a proposed health and safety standard as infeasible when the necessary technology looms on today's horizon.

Nevertheless, we are satisfied that the Secretary in this case has placed this factor in its proper perspective. The Secretary found, and we believe there is substantial evidence to support such a finding, that compliance with no hands in dies is not technologically feasible in the "near future." This finding necessarily implies consideration both of existing technological capabilities and imminent advances in the art. We do not believe that the Act imposes any heavier obligation.

Economic Infeasibility

Congress does not appear to have intended to protect employees by putting their employers out of business—either by requiring protective devices unavailable under existing technology or by making financial viability generally impossible.

This qualification is not intended to provide a route by which recalcitrant employers or industries may avoid the reforms contemplated by the Act. Standards may be economically feasible even though, from the standpoint of employers, they are financially burdensome and affect profit margins adversely. Nor does the concept of economic feasibility necessarily guarantee the continued existence of individual employers. It would appear to be consistent with the purposes of the Act to envisage the economic demise of an employer who has lagged behind the rest of the industry in protecting the health and safety of employees and is consequently financially unable to comply with new standards as quickly as other employers.

As the effect becomes more widespread within an industry, the problem of economic feasibility becomes more pressing. For example, if the standard requires changes that only a few leading firms could quickly achieve, delay might be necessary to avoid increasing the concentration of that industry. Similarly, if the competitive structure or posture of the industry would be otherwise adversely affected—perhaps rendered unable to compete with imports or with substitute products—the Secretary could properly consider that factor.

We therefore conclude that the Secretary may in the weighing process consider the economic consequences of his quasi-legislative standard-setting. We reject the petitioner's contrary contention.

Correlative Duties of Employees. Employees of covered employers have a correlative duty under OSHA to "comply with Occupational Safety and Health Standards and all rules, regulations, and orders . . . which are applicable to their own actions and conduct" [Section 5(b)1]. Although the Secretary of Labor can seek an injunction against an employee who is creating a safety hazard, OSHA does not provide for penalties to be imposed on employees who violate provision of the Act. OSHA provides, however, that *employers* may take disciplinary action against recalcitrant employees who refuse to abide by OSHA rules.

Where an employer is charged with a violation of OSHA, the employer may generally raise an employee's refusal to comply with OSHA as a defense to the charge. The defense is lost, however, if the employer merely "made available" safety regulations and safety equipment, and failed to instruct the employees as to the OSHA regulations, or to require them to wear proper safety equipment. For example, courts have consistently refused to accept an employer's defense that an employee did not wear a hard hat as required by OSHA to be worn at certain job sites. The argument for this rule is that the denial of the defense will force employers themselves to enforce OSHA regulations.

OSHA Inspections. Under OSHA, the Secretary of Labor is empowered to enter workplaces, inspect working conditions, inspect records, and question employees and employers concerning occupational safety and health, injuries, deaths, and related questions. Section 8(2) of OSHA provides that the Secretary of Labor (in the person of OSHA inspectors), upon presenting "appropriate credentials," may enter a workplace "without delay and at reasonable times . . . to inspect and investigate . . . within reasonable limits and in a reasonable manner" working conditions, machinery, and related matters. There are approximately 1,000 OSHA inspectors to inspect over 5 million business establishments, which employ over 70 million workers who are subject to OSHA coverage.

Advance notification of the inspection of a workplace by OSHA inspectors is generally prohibited. In a few situations advance notice is permitted, but the notice even in these cases may not exceed 24 hours prior to the proposed inspection. With the limited resources of the OSH Administration, inspections are generally conducted according to the following priorities:

1. investigations where a worker may be killed or seriously injured by a safety hazard if immediate corrective action is not taken
2. investigations of a catastrophe or fatality
3. investigation of a complaint
4. investigation of "target" high-hazard industries
5. general "random" inspections of businesses.

Most businesses voluntarily allow OSHA inspectors to investigate their work premises. However, in *Marshall v. Barlows, Inc.,* 436 U.S. 307 (1978), the U.S. Supreme Court held that the Secretary of Labor must obtain a *search warrant* where an employer refuses an inspector's request for permission to inspect business premises pursuant to OSHA. The criterion for obtaining an OSHA search warrant is less stringent than the showing of "probable cause" needed for the issuance of most search warrants. The Secretary of Labor, through his inspectors, needs only to show that there is a "neutral" criterion (such as a random inspection) for requesting the search warrant. Further, OSHA search warrants may be issued in an *ex parte* proceeding. A court has also held that a warrantless OSHA inspection is permitted where there is reasonable cause to believe that an "imminent danger" to worker safety exists.

Once within the workplace, an OSHA inspector has authority to make a "walk-around" inspection of the premises. The employer has a mandatory right to accompany the OSHA inspector on the walk-around inspection. If the walk-around right is denied to the employer for no valid reason, any safety citations that are issued because of what is found during the inspection are *void.*

As provided in OSHA, an employee may file a written request for an OSHA inspection of his employer where a violation of an OSHA standard "threatens physical harm" or an "imminent danger exists." An employee can also refuse to work where there is an OSHA violation if he "with no reasonable alternative, refuses in good faith to expose himself to the dangerous condition." The U.S. Supreme Court has held, however, that OSHA does not require employers to pay employees who refuse to work because of a safety hazard. Section 11(c) of OSHA makes it unlawful for an employer to discharge or in any manner discriminate against an employee for filing a complaint, instituting a proceeding, or testifying against an employer for an OSHA violation.

OSHA Enforcement Procedures. Once an OSHA violation has been found, the enforcement procedures of OSHA proceed in three stages: (1) citation; (2) administrative hearing; and (3) judicial review. Each stage is distinct. Unless a cited employer initiates the next level of review, the assessed penalty becomes final and is not subject to further review. Courts have held that a party to an OSHA proceeding is *not* entitled to a jury trial as generally provided in the Seventh Amendment to the U.S. Constitution. The streamlined enforcement procedure of OSHA has been recommended as a blueprint for a major revision of the enforcement systems of all other federal agencies.

Step 1: Citation. If, after acting pursuant to a complaint or other valid investigation an OSHA inspector finds a violation of OSHA, which may be either a violation of a specific standard or the "general duty" standard, the inspector can issue a *citation* which: (a) describes the violation in detail; (b) states the OSHA standard that has been violated; and (c) sets forth a reasonable time in which the employer is to "abate" (correct) the violation. Within a reasonable time thereafter, the Secretary of Labor will notify the employer of the penalty, if any, that is being levied on the employer for the violation. If within 15 days of the receipt of the citation the employer does not notify the Secretary of Labor that it intends to challenge the penalty, the penalty becomes final and unreviewable.

Step 2: Administrative Hearing. If an employer challenges the citation within the allotted 15-day period, the Secretary of Labor is required to initiate an administrative hearing. An Administrative Law Judge (ALJ) conducts the hearing. After the hearing, the ALJ makes a report to the OSH Review Commission, with a recommended decision. The ALJ's "decision" becomes final if the Commission chooses not to review the matter. If the Commission reviews the matter, it may review the entire record of the administrative hearing. The parties usually may not present additional evidence to the Commission. The Commission will issue a decision, which becomes final 30 days after it is issued.

Step 3: Judicial Review. Any person who is "adversely affected or aggrieved" by the OSH Review Commission's decision may, within 60 days of the issuance of the decision, petition the appropriate federal Court of Appeals for review of the Commission's decision. The Court of Appeals will apply the "substantial evidence on the record considered as a whole" standard in reviewing the OSH Review Commission's decision. Thereafter, discretionary review of the Court of Appeals's decision may be undertaken by the U.S. Supreme Court. Review by the Supreme Court is highly unlikely unless an issue of constitutional importance is involved in the case.

"General Duty" Clause. In addition to the standards set by the Secretary of Labor for specific chemicals and toxins, the Act also contains a "general duty" clause that requires employers to provide a safe working environment for its employees. The general duty clause is the subject of substantial OSHA litigation. The general duty clause (OSHA Section 572) requires all covered employers at all times to:

furnish to each of his employees employment and a place of employment which are free from recognized hazards that are causing or likely to cause death or serious physical harm to his employees.

Although all of the provisions of OSHA and the rules adopted thereunder are supposed to be prospective in nature, so as to provide an incentive for employers to provide a safe working environment, often the Secretary of Labor and the OSHA Administration end up in an adversary position, with both employers who do not wish to bear the cost of OSHA compliance and employees who are fearful of losing their jobs if OSHA is stringently enforced.

OSHA Penalties. The Occupational Safety and Health Act of 1970 expressly provides for the assessment of penalties against employers who violate OSHA and rules and orders issued thereunder. Penalties are set forth in the Act with the goal of providing an incentive for employers to create and maintain a safe working environment.

Where a "serious" *or* "willful" violation of OSHA is found, an employer is subject to a *civil* fine of up to $10,000 for each violation. Additional civil fines may be assessed for repeated violations. Where both a "serious" and a "willful" violation are found, the Secretary of Labor may seek *criminal* penalties against the employer, which, upon conviction, subject the employer to a fine up to $10,000 and a sentence of up to six months in jail. The Secretary of Labor can also seek an injunction against an employer to prevent future violations of OSHA.

Courts have unanimously held that the Occupational Safety and Health Act of 1970 does *not* create a private cause of action for injured workers, either against their employer or against the federal government for failure to enforce OSHA. OSHA does not affect an employee's right to seek reparation for injuries under state Worker's Compensation laws. However, state courts often consider violations of OSHA standards in analyzing employee workers' compensation or negligence actions against employers.

In *Getty Oil Company v. OSH Review Commission,* which follows, the court affirmed an assessment of a penalty against an employer for violating the "general duty" clause of OSHA.

GENERAL DUTY CLAUSE

GETTY OIL COMPANY v. OCCUPATIONAL SAFETY AND HEALTH REVIEW COMMISSION

530 F.2d 1143 (1976)
UNITED STATES COURT OF APPEALS, FIFTH CIRCUIT

Tuttle, Circuit Judge:

The facts surrounding the alleged violation are undisputed. Among its many interests, Getty owns and operates a gas and oil lease in Matagorda County, Texas. Located on this lease is a separation facility which gathers gas and oil from wells on the lease and transmits them to an outgoing pipeline at higher pressures. In late 1972 it became apparent to the company that the separation facility lacked the capacity to handle the level of fluids passing through the system. After studying the problem, Getty engineers decided to remedy it by installing a type of pressure vessel known as a fluid booster tank to step up the pressure in the lines. Getty's Area Engineer, Joseph King, designed the vessel and instructed one of the company's field mechanics, Robison, to have the vessel fabricated and pressure tested at a local welding shop. Throughout the course of discussing possible structural designs, King emphasized to Robison the necessity of pressure testing the vessel before placing it into operation.

On the morning of February 20, 1973 Robison went to the welding shop to pick up the vessel. The shop owner told Robison that the vessel had not yet been pressure tested but Robison simply shrugged his shoulders and left taking the vessel with him.

By late that afternoon installation of the untested vessel had been completed. After a brief conversation with the lease operator and the production foreman, both Getty's employees and both of whom were present at the installation site, but neither of whom inquired of Robison as to whether the vessel had been tested, Robison proceeded to put the pressure vessel into operation by activating a valve. The pressure in the vessel increased from 300 to 930 pounds per square inch, and an explosion occurred, ripping the vessel loose and hurling it some 45 feet. Gas and oil erupted from the vessel and ignited, fatally injuring Robison and severely burning the production foreman. The ensuing fire consumed one of the company's pickup trucks and was not extinguished until half an hour later.

Based on the above facts, the Administrative Law Judge conducting the hearing found Getty guilty of a "serious violation" of Section 5(a)(1) of the Act, issued the company a citation for the violation, and assessed a fine of $550. Getty unsuccessfully appealed the decision to the Occupational Safety and Health Review Commission, and now brings this action. . . .

The section of the Act which Getty is charged with violating is the "general duty" clause requiring every employer to

> furnish to each of his employees employment and a place of employment which are free from recog-

nized hazards that are causing or likely to cause death or serious physical harm to his employees.

To establish a violation of the general duty section, the Secretary must prove

> (1) that the employer failed to render its workplace 'free' of a hazard which was (2) 'recognized' and (3) 'causing or likely to cause death or serious physical harm.'

The uncontroverted evidence in the record shows that failure to pressure test a pressure vessel before activation is a universally-recognized hazard in the oil industry and that omitting such tests was likely to cause serious injury and created an extremely high probability of rupture and ensuing harm in the instant case. Thus, it is clear that the hazard at issue here was both "recognized" and likely to cause serious harm, as well as preventable by the simple expedient of pressure testing.

For the reasons stated above, the Commission's Decision and Order are *affirmed*.

CASE QUESTIONS

1. What does the "general duty" clause of OSHA provide? Explain.
2. How did the accident happen in this case? Was the vessel pressure tested before it was activated in this case? What injuries did Robison suffer?
3. Who was the plaintiff in this case? Who was the defendant?

Policy Issue. Should an employer be held liable under OSHA where an employee ignores the employer's instructions?

Economics Issue. Why did Getty Oil fight this case rather than pay the $550 fine? Weren't the lawyer's fees and court costs much more expensive?

Ethics Issue. Would it be ethical for some companies to promote the establishment of OSHA rules that would eliminate small firms in the industry?

Social Responsibility. Does the government owe a duty of social responsibility to make the work environment perfectly safe for workers? What would be the consequences?

UNEMPLOYMENT COMPENSATION

One of the most feared possibilities for an employee in the work force is that of being unemployed. At one time during the Great Depression of the 1930s, 14 million workers—almost 30 percent of the work force—were unemployed. The resulting hardship was immeasurable as workers lost their homes and the means of supporting their families. As employment rose during the World War II years and thereafter, unemployment decreased. Unemployment ranged from 4 to 8 percent through most of the 1950s. Unemployment again began to increase in the 1970s, and reached almost 12 percent nationally during the recession of the early 1980s. The first programs designed to pay unemployed workers money during their period of unemployment were voluntary programs instituted by trade unions in Europe. Although American trade unions tried to emulate European unions, such attempts were weak and they failed.

During the midst of the Great Depression, the U.S. Congress decided to establish a government *unemployment compensation program* whereby unemployed workers would be guaranteed certain monetary support during their unemployment. Congress could not force the states to adopt unemployment compensation programs. However, Congress accomplished its goal by giving states an incentive to adopt unemployment compensation programs, using its taxing power as provided in the U.S. Constitution. When Congress enacted the Social Security Act of 1935 it included Title IX, which imposed a 3 percent *excise* tax on the payroll of certain designated employers. The Act also provided that if a state itself were to impose an unemployment compensation tax on the payrolls of employers, the state could take a *credit* of up to 90 percent of the federal 3 percent excise tax (2.7 percent of the gross amount taxed). Thus, either the state (through its unemployment tax) or the federal government (through its excise tax) would collect a substantial payroll tax from employers.

The federal Social Security Act did *not* provide for the payment of unemployment compensation benefits by the federal government, leaving this aspect of the program to the states. Thus, if a state chose not to enact an unemployment tax and program, the employers of the state would be charged a 3 percent federal excise tax with no benefits being distributed to unemployed workers in the state. Within two years of the passage of the federal Act, every state in the Union had enacted an unemployment compensation tax and program for the payment of benefits.

In *Chase C. Steward Machine Co. v. David,* 301 U.S. 548 (1937), against a multi-issue challenge, the United States Supreme Court held that the 3 percent unemployment excise tax as imposed by the Social Security Act was valid. Title IX, which imposes the federal excise tax and permits a state to take the allowed *credit* if it imposes an unemployment compensation tax, is now Section 160c of the Internal Revenue Code. The federal "unemployment" excise tax is currently set at 3.4 percent of the first $6,000 of each covered employee's annual wage. Each state may adopt a higher unemployment tax. However, the *credit* that a state can take for imposing its own unemployment compensation tax remains at 79.4 percent credit against the federal excise tax of 3.4 percent.

Coverage and Benefits.   As originally enacted in 1935, the federal excise tax was imposed on employers with over eight employees who worked 28 or more weeks in "industrial and commercial" establishments. Agricultural, domestic, government and nonprofit institution employers were excluded from coverage. In 1970, Congress extended the 3.4 percent federal excise tax to include all employers who employ at least *one* employee for a minimum period of 28 weeks a year, and employers who have a quarterly payroll of at least $1,500. Congress has also eliminated many of the original exclusions, extending coverage to federal government employees (1955), employees of nonprofit organizations engaged in commercial and industrial activities (1950), ex-servicemen (1958), and employees of nonprofit organizations engaged in scientific, charitable, and educational activities (1970).

Under the Federal Social Security Act, an "employee" is defined generally as "any individual who, under the usual common-law rules applicable in determining the employer–employee relationship, has the status of an employee." Questions often arise as to whether a person whose wages have been paid is an "employee" or an "independent contractor." An employer–independent contractor relationship is not covered by the Act. "Domestic" service in a private home, college fraternity or sorority, or local college club is excluded from unemployment coverage. There are many other narrow exceptions to unemployment coverage. Agricultural employers are covered only if (1) the employer has paid $20,000 or more in a calendar quarter in the present or previous year to agricultural laborers, or (2) on each of some 20 days during the present or previous calendar year the employer employed 10 or more individual agricultural workers.

State unemployment compensation laws set specific dollar amounts in weekly or semiweekly payments as unemployment compensation. The amount is usually dependent upon average wages earned during a specified base period (e.g., four of the last five calendar pay periods). Most state statutes also set a minimum amount (e.g., $50) and sustaining amount (e.g., $150) that may be paid weekly as unemployment compensation. The majority of states limit the duration of unemployment compensation benefits to 26 weeks. In 1970, Congress enacted the *Federal-State Extended Unemployment Act,* which was incorporated into state laws, which extended unemployment compensation benefits an additional 13 weeks during times of "chronic unemployment" (defined as 4.5 percent of the work force unemployed). Congress enacted temporary extensions beyond even this period of time during the high unemployment periods of the 1970s and early 1980s.

Eligibility for Unemployment Benefits.   In order to receive unemployment compensation benefits, a person must qualify under his or her state's unemployment compensation law. Each state sets separate eligibility standards to qualify for unemployment compensation benefits. For example, Texas law provides in pertinent part:

An unemployed individual shall be eligible to receive benefits with respect to any benefit period only if the [Employment] Commission finds that:

a. He has registered for work at, and thereafter has continued to report at, an unemployment office in accordance with such regulations as the Commission may prescribe;

b. He has made a claim for benefits in accordance with the provisions of [State law];

c. He is able to work;

d. He is available for work.

The "able to work" requirement means that a claimant will be denied unemployment compensation benefits if he or she is ill, incapacitated, or otherwise unable to accept employment. Worker's Compensation benefits may, however, be available to the claimant. The "available for work" standard, along with the requirement that a claimant report periodically to the unemployment agency (every week or every two weeks), prevents people from collecting unemployment benefits while taking long vacations, i.e., going to Florida for the winter. Most state laws provide for transferability of valid unemployment compensation claims where the claimant has validly moved to another state to seek employment.

Many states have also adopted a separate standard that the claimant be "actively seeking work." Courts have held that this requirement measures the claimant's mental attitude, whether he "wants to go to work or is content to remain idle." The unemployment agency may consider the number of contacts a claimant makes with prospective employers in determining whether this standard has been met.

"Suitable Work." An unemployed person who is receiving state unemployment compensation benefits must accept "suitable work" that is offered to him. All qualifying state unemployment compensation statutes include the following required provision of the Federal Unemployment Tax Act:

No work shall be deemed suitable and benefits shall not be denied under this chapter o any otherwise eligible individual for refusing to accept new work under any of he following circumstances:

1. If the position offered is vacant due directly to a strike, lockout, or other dispute;

2. If the wages, hours, or other conditions of the work offered are substantially less favorable to the individual than those prevailing for similar work in the locality;

3. If as a condition of being employed, the individual would be required to join a company union or to resign from or refrain from joining any bona fide labor organization.

The application of the preceding standards to individual fact situations has been the subject of a substantial percentage of the lawsuits in the unemployment compensation area.

In *New York Telephone Company v. New York State Department of Labor* the U.S. Supreme Court held that a state was free, by law, to authorize the payment of unemployment compensation benefits to union strikers even though the employer who was being struck would have to bear much of the cost of the payment of such benefits.

UNEMPLOYMENT COMPENSATION

NEW YORK TELEPHONE CO. v. NEW YORK STATE DEPARTMENT OF LABOR

440 U.S. 519 (1979)
UNITED STATES SUPREME COURT

Mr. Justice Stevens announced the judgment of the Court and delivered an opinion, in which **Mr. Justice White** and **Mr. Justice Rehnquist** joined.

The question presented is whether the National Labor Relations Act, as amended, implicitly prohibits the State of New York from paying unemployment compensation to strikers.

Communication Workers of America, AFL–CIO (CWA), represents about 70 percent of the nonmanagement employees of companies affiliated with the Bell Telephone Co. In June 1971, when contract negotiations had reached an impasse, CWA recommended a nationwide strike. The strike commenced on July 14, 1971, and, for most workers, lasted only a week. In New York, however, the 38,000 CWA members employed by petitioners remained on strike for seven months.

New York's unemployment insurance law normally authorizes the payment of benefits after approximately one week of unemployment. If a claimant's loss of employment is caused by "a strike, lockout, or other industrial controversy in the establishment in which he was employed," Section 592 (1) of the law suspends the payment of benefits for an additional 7-week period. In 1971, the maximum weekly benefit of $75 was payable to an employee whose base salary was at least $149 per week.

After the 8-week waiting period, petitioners' striking employees began to collect unemployment compensation. During the ensuing five months more than $49 million in benefits were paid to about 33,000 striking employees at an average rate of somewhat less than $75 per week. Because New York's unemployment insurance system is financed primarily by employer contributions based on the benefits paid to former employees of each employer in past years, a substantial part of the cost of these benefits was ultimately imposed on petitioners.

Petitioners brought suit in the United States District Court for the Southern District of New York against the state officials responsible for the administration of the unemployment compensation fund. They sought a declaration that the New York statute authorizing the payment of benefits to strikers conflicts with federal law and is therefore invalid, an injunction against the enforcement of Section 592 (1), and an award recouping the increased taxes paid in consequence of the disbursement of funds to their striking employees. After an 8-day trial, the District Court granted the requested relief.

The District Court concluded that the availability of unemployment compensation is a substantial factor in the worker's decision to remain on strike, and that in this case, as in others, it had a measurable impact on the progress of the strike. The court held that the payment of such compensation by the State conflicted

> with the policy of free collective bargaining established in the federal labor laws and is therefore invalid under the Supremacy Clause of the United States Constitution.

The Court of Appeals for the Second Circuit reversed.

Because New York's program, like those in other States, is financed in part by taxes assessed against employers, it is not strictly speaking a public welfare program. It nevertheless remains true that the payments to the strikers implement a broad state policy that does not primarily concern labor-management relations, but is implicated whenever members of the labor force become unemployed. Unlike most States, New York has concluded that the community interest in the security of persons directly affected by a strike outweighs the interest in avoiding any impact on a particular labor dispute.

As this Court has held in a related context, such unemployment benefits are not a form of direct compensation paid to strikers by their employer; they are disbursed from public funds to effectuate a public purpose. This conclusion is no less true because New York has found it most efficient to base employer contributions to the insurance program on "experience ratings." Although this method makes the struck, rather than all, employers primarily responsible for financing striker benefits, the employer-provided moneys are nonetheless funneled through a public agency, mingled with other—and clearly public—funds, and imbued with a public purpose.

In an area in which Congress has decided to tolerate a substantial measure of diversity, the fact that the implementation of this general state policy affects the relative strength of the antagonists in a bargaining dispute is not a sufficient reason for concluding that Congress intended to pre-empt that exercise of state power.

The judgment of the Court of Appeals is *affirmed.*

Mr. Justice Brennan, concurring in the result.

Mr. Justice Blackmun, with whom **Mr. Justice Marshall** joins, concurring in the judgment.

CASE QUESTIONS

1. What strike occurred in this case? How much did the individual strikers receive in unemployment compensation? Collectively?
2. Who pays for unemployment compensation insurance? How? What does "experience rating" provide?

3. What was the telephone company's *legal* argument in this case? Explain. What remedy did it seek in this case?
4. How can the following two positions of the Supreme Court be reconciled?
   a. "Unemployment programs are not 'public welfare' programs."
   b. "The taxes paid by employers are clearly 'public funds.' "
5. Was this a *majority* opinion? A *plurality* opinion? What is the difference?

Policy Issue. Are strikers given an advantage in a labor dispute if they can collect unemployment compensation benefits during a strike? Will this lead to fewer or more strikes?

Economics Issue. Who pays for unemployment compensation insurance? Who *really* pays? Is American business at a disadvantage in relation to foreign business because of the cost of our unemployment insurance?

Ethics Issue. Is it ethical for union members to go on strike for personal reasons (e.g., to obtain higher wages) and expect that unemployment compensation benefits, "public funds," will support them?

Social Responsibility. Do corporations owe a duty of social responsibility not only to pay their employees but also to pay for the unemployed?

SOCIAL SECURITY

In 1935, Congress created the federal social security insurance program. The original purpose of the social security system was to provide *minimum* payments to elderly retired persons to help *supplement* their income during their retirement years. The American social security system in general covers the working population, while most European social security systems cover the entire population. Almost all workers in the United States are covered by social security, or by similar programs such as the Railroad Retirement Act and the Civil Service Retirement Act. Since its narrow beginnings, social security coverage and benefits have burgeoned.

Social Security is *not* like a savings account in that social security payments by a worker are not set aside for that worker's retirement. Instead, the social security system is funded on a "pay-as-you-go" basis, with the contributions of *current* employees and employers going to pay the cost of social security benefits of *current* retirees and other beneficiaries. The social security system is at present in a state of financial crisis. The elderly and other recipients of social security benefits claim that benefits should be increased. Members of the work force often argue that social security taxes, along with other taxes, take such a large portion of their earnings as to leave them little left over to save for their own future, and that if present projections are correct the social security system will be bankrupt by the time they retire. The solution of the social security system financial crisis is one of the most important economic and political issues facing Congress.

The term *social security* commonly refers to benefits received pursuant to the Old Age, Survivors, and Disability Insurance (OASDI) provisions of the Social Security Act. In *Helvering v. Davis*, 301 U.S. 619 (1937), from which this excerpt from Justice Cardozo's opinion is taken, the U.S. Supreme Court held that the Social Security Act was constitutional.

This suit is brought by a shareholder of the Edison Electric Illuminating Company of Boston, a Massachusetts corporation, to restrain the corporation from making the payments and deductions called for by the act, which is stated to be void under the Constitution of the United States.

The hope behind this statute is to save men and women from the rigors of the poor house as well as from the haunting fear that such a lot awaits them when journey's end is near.

Congress did not improvise a judgment when it found that the award of old age benefits would be conducive to the general welfare. . . . Among the relevant facts are these: The number of persons in the United States 65 years of age or over is increasing proportionately as well as absolutely. What is even more important the number of such persons unable to take care of themselves is growing at a threatening pace. More and more our population is becoming urban and industrial instead of rural and agricultural. . . . Approximately three out of four persons 65 or over were probably dependent wholly or partially on others for support.

The problem is plainly national in area and dimensions. Moreover, laws of the separate states cannot deal with it effectively. Congress, at least, had a basis for that belief. States and local governments are often lacking in the resources that are necessary to finance an adequate program of security for the aged. . . . A system of old age pensions has special dangers of its own, if put in force in one state and rejected in another. The existence of such a system is a bait to the needy and dependent elsewhere, encouraging them to migrate and seek a haven of repose. Only a power that is national can serve the interests of all.

Whether wisdom or unwisdom resides in the scheme of benefits set forth in Title II, it is not for us to say. The answer to such inquiries must come from Congress, not the courts. Our concern here, as often, is with power, not with wisdom. Counsel for respondent has recalled to us the virtues of self-reliance and frugality. There is a possibility, he says, that aid from a paternal government may sap those sturdy virtues and breed a race of weaklings. . . . The issue is a closed one. It was fought out long ago. When money is spent to promote the general welfare, the concept of welfare or the opposite is shaped by Congress, not the states. So the concept be not arbitrary, the locality must yield. Constitution, Art. VI. Par. 2.

Social Security Taxes.   Participation by workers and employers in the old age, survivors, and disability insurance program is *compulsory* in the United States.

Funding for the social security system is obtained through levying of social security taxes on workers and employers, which are collected by the Internal Revenue Service pursuant to the provisions of the Federal Insurance Contribution Act. Social security taxes are required by law to be deducted from employee paychecks. The employer must remit this amount, and a matching amount, to the Internal Revenue Service.

The payment of social security taxes is based on two factors: the *wage base* and the *tax rate*. Social security taxes do not apply to all income, but only to income under a certain set wage base. Although originally set very low, the wage base has been continuously adjusted upward by Congress. In 1978 the wage base was only $17,700, but was increased over 100 percent in five years until it reached $35,700 in 1983. The wage base is increased automatically each year with the national average wage.

The second factor in determining the social security taxes paid by workers is the *tax rate* (percentage) by which the wage base is multiplied. Also originally set low, the tax rate has been continuously increased by Congress. In 1984, the tax rate was 7 percent. Therefore, each employee who earns income equal to or greater than the wage base currently pays social security taxes of approximately $2,500 per year. The employer pays a matching amount.

The self-employed must also participate in the social security system. Social security taxes are collected from the self-employed by the filing of quarterly estimated returns and in annual tax returns. The self-employed are taxed on the same wage base as employees. Under 1983 amendments to the Social Security Act, the rate of tax on self-employed individuals increased to 14 percent in 1984. Self-employed workers are allowed a credit of 2.7 percent in 1984, 2.3 percent in 1985 and 2.0 percent from 1986 to 1989, which will reduce the effective social security tax rate from 14 to approximately 11.3 percent to 12.0 percent during this period. In 1990, the contributions of the self-employed will be placed on a parity with the employee-employer contributions into the social security system.

Eligibility to Receive Social Security Benefits. Social security benefits are generally paid to retired workers, disabled workers, and dependents of such workers. Eligibility for social security benefits is based on the number of quarters of work for which persons receive credit. A quarter of credit is granted for each calendar quarter in which an employee earns at least $50 of income or a self-employed worker earns at least $100. These are three categories of insured status for social security benefits: (1) fully insured status, (2) currently insured status, and (3) disability status.

Fully Insured Status. Fully insured status entitles a person to receive all old age and survivors' benefits. To qualify for fully insured status, a worker must receive credit for a number of calendar *quarters* that equals or exceeds the number of *years* since the attainment of age 21 *or* the number of years that have elapsed since 1950, whichever is *less*. For example, if a person is age 35, he must have earned at least 14 calendar quarters of credit to receive full social security benefits.

Currently Insured Status. A person qualifies for currently insured status by having received credit for at least six calendar quarters in the 13-quarter period ending with the death, disability, or retirement of the worker. A person who qualifies for currently insured status receives only a portion of the benefits allowed under fully insured status.

Disability Status. A person qualifies for disability status by having received credit for at least 20 quarters in the 40 quarters preceding disablement. A worker who has been in the work force for less than 20 quarters qualifies for partial disability benefits only.

Social Security Benefits. Social security benefits are paid monthly. Monthly retirement benefits for retired persons 65 years of age and older range from $243 to $827 per month (in 1983). Spouses and children of retired workers generally receive an amount equal to 50 percent of the retired worker's social security benefits. Family benefits of disabled workers range from $255 to $1,240 per month (in 1983).

Since 1975, social security benefits have been increased by an annual cost-of-living adjustment based on increases in the consumer price index (CPI). The 1983 amendments to the Social Security Act continued these cost-of-living adjustments for social security benefits, based on the annual increase in the CPI calculated for the period from 18 months to six months prior to the adjustment.

The social security benefit formulas provide greater benefits to low-income contributors than to upper-income contributors per dollar contributed to the social security system during a worker's employment period. Social security benefits are adjusted downward for income earned by retirees over a certain amount. In 1983, social security benefits were reduced by $1 for every $2 earned over $6,600 if the retiree was 65 years or older, and for every $2 earned over $4,920 if the retiree was under 65.

Up until 1984, old age and survivors' benefits were tax free to the recipient. In 1983, Congress enacted an amendment to the Social Security Act, which became effective in 1984 and which required certain affluent retirees to pay income tax on a portion of their social security benefits if their income exceeded a certain dollar amount. Taxpayers whose total adjusted gross income, tax-exempt income, and social security benefits exceed a base amount of $25,000 for a single person and $32,000 for a joint return will be taxed on one half of the social security benefits received in excess of the base amount. For example, if a single retiree received income from qualifying sources of $30,000, and his social security benefits totaled $8,000, he would be taxed on $2,500 ($30,000 income − $25,000 base × 1/2).

Medicare. In 1965, Congress enacted a program officially entitled "Health Insurance for the Aged and Disabled." Commonly referred to as "medicare," this program provides extensive medical and health care insurance for elderly and disabled persons. Since its beginning approximately 20 years ago, medicare has burgeoned.

The Hospital Insurance portion of medicare pays for hospital and related benefits for all persons who are 65 years old or older and who qualify for OASDI benefits. Hospital benefits are available to qualified persons as a matter of entitlement. Persons who are eligible for Railroad Retirement benefits also qualify for Hospital Insurance under OASDI. The costs of physician and related medical services are covered by the Supplementary Medical Insurance portion of OASDI. The Supplemental Medical Insurance program is voluntary, and must be elected by its beneficiaries, who pay an additional premium for the coverage. Supplemental Medical Insurance coverage is similar to a private health insurance plan that is subsidized by the government.

Recent amendments have reduced the amount of benefits available under medicare. Hospitals must enter into contracts with the government whereby they agree to provide certain services to persons covered by medicare at a certain set price per medical treatment.

Private Pension Plans.   Large corporations and unions have long provided pension plans for their employees and members. In 1974, Congress enacted the Employee Retirement Income Security Act (ERISA). ERISA is a complex law that authorizes small corporations and individuals to also establish certain pension plans. Generally, small corporations and individuals can establish Defined Benefit Plans, whereby a certain percentage of a corporation's income can be set aside tax free in a pension account for its officers and employees. The money is not taxed until it is withdrawn during retirement. Under a Defined Benefit Plan, the corporation can also establish medical and health plans. An individual operating as a business (e.g., a sole proprietorship, a general partner in a partnership) can establish a *Keogh plan,* where he can set aside $15,000 or 15 percent of his net income, whichever is less, tax free. This money also is not taxed until it is withdrawn during retirement. There are considerable restrictions on the investment of monies set aside in Defined Benefit and Keogh Plans. A discussion of the detailed restrictions and procedures of these pension plans is beyond the scope of this book.

Any individual who makes an income, whether an employee or self-employed, may establish an Individual Retirement Account (IRA) where he can set aside up to $3,000 per year tax free. This is in addition to other pension plans. Money set aside in IRA accounts is not taxed until withdrawn during retirement. Nonworking spouses may also establish IRAs, with their income being calculated according to the value of their unpaid domestic services.

STATE OCCUPATIONAL SAFETY LAWS

Federal law does not preempt the regulation of safety in the employment environment. Many states have enacted detailed legislation to regulate safety in the work environment. Further, courts have generally tended to broadly interpret such legislation in order to protect workers.

In *Shimp v. New Jersey Bell Telephone Company* the court held that an employee had the right to work in an environment free from the noxious second-hand cigarette smoke of co-employees, and ordered the employer to prohibit cigarette smoking except in designated nonworking areas.

RIGHT TO A SMOKE-FREE WORK ENVIRONMENT?

SHIMP v. NEW JERSEY BELL TELEPHONE COMPANY

368 A.2d 408 (1976)
SUPERIOR COURT OF NEW JERSEY

Gruccio, Judge of the Superior Court

This case involves a matter of first impression in this State: whether a nonsmoking employee is denied a safe working environment and entitled to injunctive relief when forced by proximity to smoking employees to involuntarily inhale "second hand" cigarette smoke.

Plaintiff seeks to have cigarette smoking enjoined in the area where she works. She alleges that her employer, defendant N.J. Bell Telephone Co., is causing her to work in an unsafe environment by refusing to enact a ban against smoking in the office where she works. The company allows other employees to smoke while on the job at desks situated in the same work area as that of plaintiff. . . . The pleadings indicate plaintiff has tried every avenue open to her to get relief prior to instituting this action for injunctive relief.

It is clearly the law in this State that an employee has a right to work in a safe environment. An employer is under an affirmative duty to provide a work area that is free from unsafe conditions.

This right to safe and healthful working conditions is protected not only by the duty imposed by common law upon employers, but has also been the subject of federal legislation. In 1970 Congress enacted the Occupational Safety and Health Act (OSHA) which . . . imposed upon the employer a duty to eliminate all foreseeable and preventable hazards. OSHA in no way preempted the field of occupational safety. . . . [It] recognizes concurrent state power to act either legislatively or judicially under the common law with regard to occupational safety.

The authority of this court has not been affected by the Workmen's Compensation Act. . . . This provision bars only the common law action in tort for damages resulting from work-related injury and make the workmen's compensation system the exclusive method of securing *money recoveries*. The

act is silent with respect to the question of injunctive relief against occupational hazards.

In 1965 Congress officially recognized the dangerous nature of cigarette smoke and declared a national policy to warn the public of the danger and to discourage cigarette smoking. . . . In furtherance of this policy 15 U.S.C.A. Section 1333 makes it unlawful to sell cigarettes in the United States unless they bear the statement,

> Warning: The Surgeon General Has Determined That Cigarette Smoking Is Dangerous To Your Health

conspicuously imprinted on the side of every package. . . . Consequently, Congress took remedial action in the public interest and banned cigarette promotion on the airwaves.

The HEW report for 1975, *The Health Consequences of Smoking,* and the Surgeon General's report by the same title for 1972 reveal distressing new evidence in the continuing investigation of the toxic nature of cigarette smoke. The reports indicate that the mere presence of cigarette smoke in the air pollutes it, changing carbon monoxide levels and effectively making involuntary smokers of all who breathe the air.

The 1972 report of the Surgeon General . . . indicates that a burning cigarette contaminates the air with "sidestream" smoke which comes from the burning cone and mouthpiece of the cigarette between puffs as well as with the smoke exhaled by the smoker. The presence of this smoke in the air not only contributes to the discomfort of nonsmokers, but also increases the carbon monoxide level and adds tar, nicotine and the oxides of nitrogen to the available air supply. These substances are harmful to the health of an exposed person, particularly those who have chronic coronary heart or bronchopulmonary disease.

[A] large proportion of the nonsmoking population finds it unpleasant and uncomfortable to be exposed to significant amounts of tobacco smoke. Having reviewed the scientific data and medical evidence available, Dr. Terry, who served as Surgeon General of the United States from 1961 to 1965, concludes that passive smoking in the workplace can be injurious to the health of a significant percentage of the working population.

The right of an individual to risk his or her own health does not include the right to jeopardize the health of those who must remain around him or her in order to properly perform the duties of their jobs. The portion of the population which is especially sensitive to cigarette smoke is so significant that it is reasonable to expect an employer to foresee health consequences and to impose upon him a duty to abate the hazard which causes the discomfort. I order New Jersey Bell Telephone Company to do so.

The company already has in effect a rule that cigarettes may not be smoked around the telephone equipment. The rationale behind the rule is that the machines are extremely sensitive and can be damaged by the smoke. Human beings are also very sensitive and can be damaged by cigarette smoke. Unlike a piece of machinery, the damage to a human is all too often irreparable. If a circuit or wiring goes bad, the company can install a replacement part. It is not so simple in the case of a human lung, eye or heart.

A company which has demonstrated such concern for its mechanical components should have at least as much concern for its human beings. Plaintiff asks nothing more than to be able to breathe the air in its clear and natural state.

Accordingly, I *order* defendant New Jersey Bell Telephone Company to provide safe working conditions for plaintiff by restricting the smoking of employees to the nonwork area presently used as a lunchroom. No smoking shall be permitted in the offices or adjacent customer service area.

CASE QUESTIONS

1. What remedy was the plaintiff seeking in this case? Explain.
2. Why wasn't this action precluded by the state Worker's Compensation statute? Did OSHA preempt state regulation of the field of occupational safety? Explain.
3. What did the 1972 report of the Surgeon General disclose about the dangers of cigarette smoking? What did the 1975 report say about it? Has further evidence been produced since then regarding the dangers of smoking *and* smoke?
4. Was the machine–human being comparison used by the court persuasive? Why or why not?

Policy Issue. Is there a *right* to breathe clean air? Does a smoker have the *right* to smoke? To jeopardize the health of others? How can these positions be reconciled? Is a total ban on smoking in public places the only solution to this argument?

Economics Issue. Should cigarette manufacturers be liable for all diseases, emphysema, and other respiratory problems caused to *smokers* by the use of their products? To *nonsmokers* for the same injuries caused by "second-hand" smoke? For all ruined meals? For cleaning of smoke-drenched clothing?

Ethics Issue. Is it *ethical* for smokers to smoke in public knowing they are polluting the air and causing discomfort to others?

Social Responsibility. Do cigarette manufacturers owe a duty of social responsibility to discontinue making their product because of the dangerous health hazards it poses? Do employers owe a duty of social responsibility to provide a smoke-free environment for their workers? What about restaurants? Department stores?

Trend of the Law

Certain issues of occupational safety and security will continue to be expanding areas of the law. However, violations of child labor laws and wage and hour laws will comprise a small part of future litigation regarding the employment relation.

The trend of the law is to expand the coverage of Worker's Compensations statutes to cover most accidents suffered by workers while somehow, even incidentally, connected with work or the workplace. The "arising out of" and in the "course of employment" tests are being expanded to cover a myriad of situations that would not previously have been covered by Worker's Compensation statutes. Exceptions to coverage, such as the "coming and going" rule, are being minimized by the courts, and a further degeneration of the exceptions to Worker's Compensation statutes is predicted for the future. Courts will continue to expand the definitions of "accident" and "disease" as covered by Worker's Compensation laws. Claims for Worker's Compensation benefits based on "stress" related disabilities will also increase substantially in the future.

Compliance with the detailed provisions of OSHA and the rules adopted thereunder will continue to pose a significant problem for business in the future. The majority of OSHA cases will be concerned with testing the validity of rules and standards adopted by the Occupational Safety and Health Administration, as well as applying these standards to individual fact situations.

Technological changes, demographic shifts in population and economic considerations will force federal and state governments to reappraise and modify the social welfare programs they now administer. For example, the Information Revolution has eliminated many white- and blue-collar jobs, particularly those requiring mechanical or clerical tasks. Unemployment benefits provide only a short-term solution to a long-range problem. Further, demographic shifts in the population and improved medical care will increase the number of persons eligible for retirement and health care benefits under social security programs. Unless additional funding is found, the social security system is presently heading for bankruptcy. The development of future law will have an enormous impact on addressing these problems.

REVIEW QUESTIONS

1. Taylor owned an automobile dealership in Beaver, Pennsylvania. Ewing was a general utility man employed by Taylor whose main duties consisted

of cleaning the dealership offices, showroom, and garage as well as servicing cars. One morning, Ewing had finished all his normal tasks and Taylor told him to go to Taylor's personal residence and mow his lawn. While attempting to adjust the belt on Taylor's power mower, Ewing accidentally caught his finger in the mechanism. As a result, a portion of his finger had to be amputated. At the time, Taylor had a standard workman's compensation and employer's liability policy. What is the major issue in this case? Can Ewing recover for the injury he sustained from Taylor's Worker's Compensation insurance carrier?

2. Meo was employed for several years by Commercial Can Corp. as its plant superintendent in charge of production. He had multiple duties and was "on call" at all hours of the day and night when the occasion required, in order to maintain the plant's uninterrupted operation. Commercial Can's plant was struck by the local Teamster's Union. Meo was ordered to keep the plant in operation despite the strike, and among his other duties he interviewed and hired various persons to replace those who were out on strike. One morning during the strike Meo was attacked by union members as he prepared to leave his personal residence for work. Before Meo could leave his home he was hit over the back of the head and he sustained serious injuries. Under Worker's Compensation laws, can Meo recover from Commercial Can for the injuries that he sustained?

3. Hornyak was a shipper who was employed at Great Atlantic and Pacific Tea Company's Florence, New Jersey warehouse. Hornyak's working hours were from 9:30 P.M. until 6:00 A.M. He had two 15-minute coffee breaks and a half-hour lunch period from 1:30 to 2:00 A.M. Hornyak was required to check in and out of the facility at the beginning and end of his shift but not if he left the premises to go to lunch. Although there was a lunch room on the premises, only about 25 of the 85 night shift employees ate lunch at the facility. Since the lunchroom did not provide food, those employees who did eat there brought their own lunch. Most of the other employees customarily left the warehouse and ate at nearby dining places. A&P's supervisory personnel knew of this practice and never suggested that it was not permissible. One night on the way back from a nearby diner, Hornyak was involved in a serious vehicular accident. As a result, he was hospitalized for two weeks and remained off the job for several months. Hornyak filed a claim for Worker's Compensation with the New Jersey Workmen's Compensation Division. What rule is applicable in this case? Under that rule, should Hornyak be compensated for his injuries?

4. Kaplan was a housemother for the Alpha Epsilon Phi Sorority. She lived in the sorority house located near the University of Minnesota campus in Minneapolis. As housemother, Kaplan performed duties akin to those of a mother who looks after her home and family. Kaplan ordered food, supervised meal preparation and house cleaning, acted as a chairperson, hostess, confidante, and adviser for the sorority members and was responsible for making sure that reasonable hours were observed. One Halloween evening, Kaplan left the house to go to a local drugstore to obtain first aid replacement supplies and then to continue on to her temple for a religious service. Before she reached the drugstore, however, she slipped, fell, and broke her hip when she stepped on a curb that had been greased as a prank by

a neighboring fraternity. To recover for her injuries under Worker's Compensation laws, what, if anything, does Kaplan need to prove in her subsequent request for compensation?

5. Holberg retired as a machinist from the American Bridge Company at age 69. A few days after he retired, he filed a claim for unemployment benefits with the Texas Employment Commission. He reported to their office every week for five months. During that period he also applied to three of nearly twenty machine shops which were located in his local area. The commission rejected Holberg's application for unemployment benefits, holding that he was not available for work as required by the Texas Unemployment Act. Holberg sued in state court to reverse the decision. Should the state count grant Holberg's request for compensation?

6. The contract for the employees of National Gypsum Company's Louisiana facility expired on February 1st, but the employees continued to report to work while negotiations on their new contract continued. On February 3rd, National Gypsum told union negotiators that the employees would be locked out by the firm on February 5th if they did not sign the new contract offered by management. The union refused to sign and the firm locked the gates to its facility. The union members continued to report to work but no work was available since they were denied access to the plant. During the collective bargaining sessions, the union had informed management that the employees would continue to work without a contract and would not strike until management had received sufficient notice to assure orderly closure of the plant. Under these circumstances, were the union members eligible for unemployment benefits?

7. Mohs owns and operates the Ivy Inn and Motor Hotel in Madison, Wisconsin. The Ivy Inn is a two-story building containing motel rooms, a restaurant, a cocktail lounge, and banquet rooms. For a period of time, Mohs operated the entire motor hotel facility. In 1972, however, Mohs leased the restaurant, cocktail lounge, and banquet facilities and equipment (including the stove, refrigerator, dishwashers, furnishings, fixtures, utensils, barware, chinaware, glassware, silverware, and other items) to GNH. GNH does business as the "Ivy Supper Club and Lounge." The lease contains numerous terms designed to ensure that the GNH restaurant will be operated to complement the Mohs motel. Mohs and GNH are completely separate organizations with no common owners. The motel maintains separate telephone listings apart from the restaurant although motel patrons may order room service through the motel switchboard. Neither Mohs nor GNH pays the minimum wage required under the Fair Labor Standards Act. Individually, their sales volumes are low enough to allow them to legally refuse to pay the minimum wage; however, if their sales volumes were aggregated they would be required to pay minimum wage. Should each firm be required to pay the minimum wage?

APPENDICES

A *The Constitution of the United States*

B *The Administrative Procedure Act (excepts)*

C *The Sherman Act (excerpts)*

D *The Clayton Act (excerpts)*

E *The Robinson-Patman Act (excerpts)*

F *The Federal Trade Commission Act (excerpts)*

G *The Securities Act of 1933 (excerpts)*

H *The Securities Exchange Act of 1934 (excerpts)*

I *The Federal Food, Drug and Cosmetic Act (excerpts)*

J *The Consumer Protection Credit Act (excerpts)*

K *The Bankruptcy Reform Act of 1978 (excerpts)*

L *The Lanham Act (excerpts)*

M *The Trademark Act of 1946 (excerpts)*

N *The Copyright Act of 1976 (excerpts)*

A THE CONSTITUTION OF THE UNITED STATES OF AMERICA

PREAMBLE

We the People of the United States, in Order to form a more perfect Union, establish Justice, insure domestic Tranquility, provide for the common defence, promote the general Welfare, and secure the Blessings of Liberty to ourselves and our Posterity, do ordain and establish this Constitution for the United States of America.

ARTICLE I

SECTION 1. All legislative Powers herein granted shall be vested in a Congress of the United States, which shall consist of a Senate and House of Representatives.

SECTION 2. (1) The House of Representatives shall be composed of Members chosen every second Year by the People of the several States, and the Electors in each State shall have the Qualifications requisite for Electors of the most numerous Branch of the State Legislature.

(2) No Person shall be a Representative who shall not have attained to the Age of twenty five Years, and been seven Years a Citizen of the United States, and who shall not, when elected, be an Inhabitant of that State in which he shall be chosen.

(3) Representatives and direct Taxes shall be apportioned among the several States which may be included within this Union, according to their respective Numbers, which shall be determined by adding to the whole Number of free Persons, including those bound to Service for a Term of Years, and excluding Indians not taxed, three fifths of all other Persons. The actual Enumeration shall be made within three Years after the first Meeting of the Congress of the United States, and within every subsequent Term of ten Years, in such Manner as they shall by Law direct. The Number of Representatives shall not exceed one for every thirty Thousand, but each State shall have at Least one Representative; and until such enumeration shall be made, the State of New Hampshire shall be entitled to chuse three, Massachusetts eight, Rhode Island and Providence Plantations one, Connecticut five, New York six, New Jersey four, Pennsylvania eight, Delaware one, Maryland six, Virginia ten, North Carolina five, South Carolina five, and Georgia three.

(4) When vacancies happen in the Representation from any State, the Executive Authority thereof shall issue Writs of Election to fill such Vacancies.

(5) The House of Representation shall chuse their Speaker and other Officers; and shall have the sole Power of Impeachment.

SECTION 3. (1) The Senate of the United States shall be composed of two Senators from each State, chosen by the Legislature thereof, for six Years; and each Senator shall have one Vote.

(2) Immediately after they shall be assembled in Consequence of the first Election, they shall be divided as equally as may be into three Classes. The Seats of the Senators of the first Class shall be vacated at the Expiration of the Second Year, of the second Class at the Expiration of the fourth Year, and of the third Class at the Expiration of the sixth Year, so that one third may be chosen every second Year; and if Vacancies happen by Resignation, or otherwise, during the Recess of the Legislature of any State, the Executive thereof may make temporary Appointments until the next Meeting of the Legislature, which shall then fill such Vacancies.

(3) No Person shall be a Senator who shall not have attained to the Age of thirty Years, and been nine Years a Citizen of the United States, and who shall not, when elected, be an Inhabitant of that State for which he shall be chosen.

(4) The Vice President of the United States shall be President of the Senate, but shall have no Vote, unless they be equally divided.

(5) The Senate shall chuse their other Officers, and also a President pro tempore, in the Absence of the Vice President, or when he shall exercise the Office of President of the United States.

(6) The Senate shall have the sole Power to try all Impeachments. When sitting for that Purpose, they shall be on Oath or Affirmation. When the President of the United States is tried, the Chief Justice shall preside: And no Person shall be convicted without the Concurrence of two thirds of the Members present.

(7) Judgment in Cases of Impeachment shall not extend further than to removal from Office, and disqualification to hold and enjoy any Office of honor, Trust, or Profit under the United States: but the Party convicted shall nevertheless be liable and subject to Indictment, Trial, Judgment, and Punishment, according to Law.

SECTION 4. (1) The Times, Places and Manner of holding Elections for Senators and Representatives, shall be prescribed in each State by the Legislature thereof; but the Congress may at any time by Law make or alter such Regulations, except as to the Places of chusing Senators.

(2) The Congress shall assemble at least once in every Year, and such Meeting shall be on the first Monday in December, unless they shall by Law appoint a different Day.

SECTION 5. (1) Each House shall be the Judge of the Elections, Returns, and Qualifications of its own Members, and a Majority of each shall constitute a Quorum to do Business; but a smaller Number may adjourn from day to day, and may be authorized to compel the Attendance of absent Members, in such Manner, and under such Penalties as each House may provide.

(2) Each House may determine the Rules of its Proceedings, punish its Members for disorderly Behavior, and, with the Concurrence of two thirds, expel a Member.

(3) Each House shall keep a Journal of its Proceedings, and from time to time publish the same, excepting such Parts as may in their Judgment require Secrecy; and the Yeas and Nays of the Members of either House on any question shall, at the Desire of one fifth of those Present, be entered on the Journal.

(4) Neither House, during the Session of Congress, shall, without the Consent of the other, adjourn for more than three days, nor to any other Place than that in which the two Houses shall be sitting.

SECTION 6. (1) The Senators and Representatives shall receive a Compensation for their Services, to be ascertained by Law, and paid out of the Treasury of the United States. They shall in all Cases, except Treason, Felony and Breach of the Peace, be privileged from Arrest during their Attendance at the Session of their respective Houses, and in going to and returning from the same; and for any Speech or Debate in either House, they shall not be questioned in any other Place.

(2) No Senator or Representative shall, during the Time for which he was elected, be appointed to any civil Office under the Authority of the United States, which shall have been created, or the Emoluments whereof shall have been encreased during such time; and no Person holding any Office under the United States, shall be a Member of either House during his Continuance in Office.

SECTION 7. (1) All Bills for raising Revenue shall originate in the House of Representatives; but the Senate may propose or concur with Amendments as on other Bills.

(2) Every Bill which shall have passed the House of Representatives and the Senate, shall, before it becomes a Law, be presented to the President of the United States; If he approve he shall sign it, but if not he shall return it, with his Objections to the House in which it shall have originated, who shall enter the Objections at large on their Journal, and proceed to reconsider it. If after such Reconsideration two thirds of that House shall agree to pass the Bill, it shall be sent together with the Objections, to the other House, by which it shall likewise be reconsidered, and if approved by two thirds of that House, it shall become a Law. But in all such Cases the Votes of both Houses shall be determined by yeas and Nays, and the Names of the Persons voting for and against the Bill shall be entered on the Journal of each House respectively. If any Bill shall not be returned by the President within ten Days (Sundays excepted) after it shall have been presented to him, the Same shall be a Law, in like Manner as if he had signed it, unless the Congress by their Adjournment prevent its Return in which Case it shall not be a Law.

(3) Every Order, Resolution, or Vote, to Which the Concurrence of the Senate and House of Representatives may be necessary (except on a question of Adjournment) shall be presented to the President of the United States; and before the Same shall take Effect, shall be approved by him, or being disapproved by him, shall be repassed by two thirds of the Senate and House of Representatives, according to the Rules and Limitations prescribed in the Case of a Bill.

SECTION 8. (1) The Congress shall have Power To lay and collect Taxes, Duties, Imposts and Excises, to pay the Debts and provide for the common Defence and general Welfare of the United States; but all Duties, Imposts and Excises shall be uniform throughout the United States;

[handwritten margin note: people were concerned about paying Creditors]

(2) To borrow money on the credit of the United States;

(3) To regulate Commerce with foreign Nations, and among the several States, and with the Indian Tribes;

[handwritten margin note: Laws for Business "Commerce Clause"]

(4) To establish an uniform Rule of Naturalization, and uniform Laws on the subject of Bankruptcies throughout the United States;

(5) To coin Money, regulate the Value thereof, and of foreign Coin, and fix the Standard of Weights and Measures;

(6) To provide for the Punishment of counterfeiting the Securities and current Coin of the United States;

(7) To Establish Post Offices and Post Roads;

(8) To promote the Progress of Science and useful Arts, by securing for limited Times to Authors and Inventors the exclusive Right to their respective Writings and Discoveries;

(9) To constitute Tribunals inferior to the supreme Court;

(10) To define and punish Piracies and Felonies committed on the high Seas, and Offenses against the Law of Nations:

(11) To declare War, grant Letters of Marque and Reprisal, and make Rules concerning Captures on Land and Water;

(12) To raise and support Armies, but no Appropriation of Money to that Use shall be for a longer Term than two Years;

(13) To provide and maintain a Navy;

(14) To make Rules for the Government and Regulation of the land and naval Forces;

(15) To provide for calling forth the Militia to execute the Laws of the Union, suppress Insurrections and repel Invasions;

(16) To provide for organizing, arming, and disciplining, the Militia, and for governing such Part of them as may be employed in the Service of the United States, reserving to the States respectively, the Appointment of the Officers, and the Authority of training the Militia according to the discipline prescribed by Congress;

(17) To exercise exclusive Legislation in all Cases whatsoever, over such District (not exceeding ten Miles square) as may, by Cession of particular States, and the Acceptance of Congress, become the Seat of the Government of the United States, and to exercise like Authority over all Places purchased by the Consent of the Legislature of the State in which the Same shall be, for the Election of Forts, Magazines, Arsenals, dock-Yards, and other needful Buildings;—And

(18) To make all Laws which shall be necessary and proper for carrying into Execution for the foregoing Powers, and all other Powers vested by this Constitution in the Government of the United States, or in any Department or Officer thereof.

SECTION 9. (1) The Migration or Importation of Such Persons as any of the States now existing shall think proper to admit, shall not be prohibited by the Congress prior to the Year one thousand eight hundred and eight, but a Tax or duty may be imposed on such Importation, not exceeding ten dollars for each Person.

(2) The privilege of the Writ of Habeas Corpus shall not be suspended, unless when in Cases of Rebellion or Invasion the public Safety may require it.

(3) No Bill of Attainder or ex post facto Law shall be passed.

(4) No Capitation, or other direct, Tax shall be laid, unless in proportion to the Census or Enumeration herein before directed to be taken.

(5) No Tax or Duty shall be laid on Articles exported from any State.

(6) No Preference shall be given by any Regulation of Commerce or Revenue to the Ports of one State over those of another: nor shall Vessels bound to, or from, one State be obliged to enter, clear, or pay Duties in another.

(7) No money shall be drawn from the Treasury, but in Consequence of Appropriations made by Law; and a regular Statement and Account of the Receipts and Expenditures of all public Money shall be published from time to time.

(8) No Title of Nobility shall be granted by the United States: And no Person holding any Office of Profit or Trust under them, shall, without the Consent of the Congress, accept of any present, Emolument, Office or Title, of any kind whatever, from any King, Prince, or foreign State.

SECTION 10. (1) No State shall enter into any Treaty, Alliance, or Confederation; grant Letters of Marque and Reprisal; coin Money; emit Bills of Credit; make any Thing but gold and silver Coin a Tender in Payment of Debts; pass any Bill of Attainder, ex post facto Law, or Law impairing the Obligation of Contracts, or grant any Title of Nobility.

(2) No State shall, without the Consent of the Congress, lay any Imposts or Duties on Imports or Exports, except what may be absolutely necessary for executing its inspection Laws: and the net Produce of all Duties and Imposts, laid by any State on Imports or Exports, shall be for the Use of the Treasury of the United States; and all such Laws shall be subject to the Revision and Controul of the Congress.

(3) No State shall, without the Consent of Congress, lay any Duty of Tonnage, keep Troops, or Ships of War in time of Peace, enter into any Agreement or Compact with another State, or with a foreign Power, or engage in War, unless actually invaded, or in such imminent Danger as will not admit of delay.

ARTICLE II

SECTION 1. (1) The executive Power shall be vested in a President of the United States of America. He shall hold his Office during the Term of four Years, and, together with the Vice President, chosen for the same Term, be elected, as follows:

(2) Each State shall appoint, in such Manner as the Legislature thereof may direct, a Number of Electors, equal to the whole Number of Senators and Representatives to which the State may be entitled in the Congress; but no Senator or Representative, or Person holding an Office of Trust or Profit under the United States, shall be appointed an Elector.

(3) The Electors shall meet in their respective States, and vote by Ballot for two Persons, of whom one at least shall not be an Inhabitant of the same State with themselves. And they shall make a List of all the Persons voted for, and of the Number of Votes for each; which List they shall sign and certify, and transmit sealed to the Seat of the Government of the United States, directed to the President of the Senate. The President of the Senate shall, in the Presence of the Senate and House of Representatives, open all the Certificates, and the Votes shall then be counted. The Person having the greatest Number of Votes shall be the President, if such Number be a Majority of the whole Number of Electors appointed; and if there be more than one who have such Majority, and have an equal Number of Votes, then the House of Representatives shall immediately chuse by Ballot one of them for President; and if no Person have a Majority, then from the five highest on the List the said House shall in like Manner chuse the President. But in chusing the President, the Votes shall be taken by States, the Representation from each State having one Vote; A quorum for this Purpose shall consist of a Member or Members from two thirds of the States, and a Majority of all the States shall be necessary to a Choice. In every Case, after the Choice of the President, the Person having the greater Number of Votes of the Electors shall be the Vice President. But if there should remain two or more who have equal Votes, the Senate shall chuse from them by Ballot the Vice President.

(4) The Congress may determine the Time of chusing the Electors, and the Day on which they shall give their Votes; which Day shall be the same throughout the United States.

(5) No person except a natural born Citizen, or a Citizen of the United States, at the time of the Adoption of this Constitution, shall be eligible to the Office of President; neither shall any Person be eligible to that Office who shall not have attained to the Age of thirty five Years, and been fourteen Years a Resident within the United States.

(6) In case of the removal of the President from Office, or of his Death, Resignation or Inability to discharge the Powers and Duties of the said Office, the Same shall devolve on the Vice President, and the Congress may by Law provide for the Case of Removal, Death, Resignation or Inability, both of the President and Vice President, declaring what Officer shall then act as President, and such Officer shall act accordingly, until the Disability be removed, or a President shall be elected.

(7) The President shall, at stated Times, receive for his Services, a Compensation, which shall neither be increased nor diminished during the Period for which he shall have been elected, and he shall not receive within that Period any other Emolument from the United States, or any of them.

(8) Before he enter on the Execution of his Office, he shall take the following Oath or Affirmation: "I do solemnly swear (or affirm) that I will faithfully execute the Office of President of the United States, and will to the best of my Ability, preserve, protect and defend the Constitution of the United States."

SECTION 2. (1) The President shall be Commander in Chief of the Army and Navy of the United States, and of the militia of the several States, when called into the actual Service of the United States; he may require the Opinion, in writing, of the principal Officer in each of the executive Departments, upon any Subject relating to the Duties of their respective Offices, and he shall have Power to grant Reprieves and Pardons for Offenses against the United States, except in Cases of Impeachment.

(2) He shall have Power, by and with the Advice and Consent of the Senate, to make Treaties, provided two thirds of the Senators present concur; and he shall nominate, and by and with the Advice and Consent of the Senate, shall appoint Ambassadors, other public Ministers and Consuls, Judges of the supreme Court, and all other Officers of the United States, whose Appointments are not herein otherwise provided for, and which shall be established by Law; but the Congress may by Law vest the Appointment of such inferior Officers, as they think proper, in the President alone, in the Courts of Law, or in the Heads of Departments.

(3) The President shall have Power to fill up all Vacancies that may happen during the Recess of the Senate, by granting Commissions which shall expire at the End of their next Session.

SECTION 3. He shall from time to time give to the Congress Information of the State of the Union, and recommend to their Consideration such Measures as he shall judge necessary and expedient; he may, on extraordinary Occasions, convene both Houses, or either of them, and in Case of Disagreement between them, with Respect to the Time of Adjournment, he may adjourn them to such Time as he shall think proper; he shall receive Ambassadors and other public Ministers; he shall take Care that the Laws be faithfully executed, and shall Commission all the Officers of the United States.

SECTION 4. The President, Vice President and all civil Officers of the United States, shall be removed from Office on Impeachment for, and Conviction of, Treason, Bribery, or other high Crimes and Misdemeanors.

ARTICLE III

SECTION 1. The judicial Power of the United States, shall be vested in one supreme Court, and in such inferior Courts as the Congress may from time to time ordain and establish. The Judges, both of the supreme and inferior Courts, shall hold their Offices during good Behaviour, and shall, at stated Times, receive for their Services a Compensation, which shall not be diminished during their Continuance in Office.

SECTION 2. (1) The judicial Power shall extend to all Cases, in Law and Equity, arising under this Constitution, the Laws of the United States, and Treaties made, or which shall be made, under their Authority;—to all Cases affecting Ambassadors, other public Ministers and Consuls;—to all Cases of admiralty and maritime Jurisdiction,—to Controversies to which the United States shall be a Party;—to Controversies between two or more States;—between a State and Citizens of another State;—between Citizens of different States;—between Citizens of the same State claiming Lands under the Grants of different States, and between a State, or the Citizens thereof, and foreign States, Citizens or Subjects.

(2) In all Cases affecting Ambassadors, other public Ministers and Consuls, and those in which a State shall be a Party, the supreme Court shall have original Jurisdiction. In all the other Cases before mentioned, the supreme Court shall have appellate Jurisdic-

tion, both as to Law and Fact, with such Exceptions, and under such Regulations as the Congress shall make.

(3) The trial of all Crimes, except in Cases of Impeachment, shall be by Jury; and such Trial shall be held in the State where the said Crimes shall have been committed; but when not committed within any State, the Trial shall be at such Place or Places as the Congress may by Law have directed.

SECTION 3. (1) Treason against the United States, shall consist only in levying War against them, or, in adhering to their enemies, giving them Aid and Comfort. No Person shall be convicted of Treason unless on the Testimony of two Witnesses to the same overt Act, or on Confession in open Court.

(2) The Congress shall have Power to declare the Punishment of Treason, but no Attainder of Treason shall work Corruption of Blood, or Forfeiture except during the Life of the Person attainted.

ARTICLE IV

SECTION 1. Full Faith and Credit shall be given in each State to the public Acts, Records, and judicial Proceedings of every other State. And the Congress may by general Laws prescribe the Manner in which such Acts, Records and Proceedings shall be proved, and the Effect thereof.

SECTION 2. (1) The Citizens of each State shall be entitled to all Privileges and Immunities of Citizens in the several States.

(2) A Person charged in any State with Treason, Felony, or other Crime, who shall flee from Justice, and be found in another State, shall on demand of the executive Authority of the State from which he fled, be delivered up, to be removed to the State having Jurisdiction of the Crime.

(3) No Person held to Service or Labour in one State, under the Laws thereof, escaping into another, shall, in Consequence of any Law or Regulation therein, be discharged from such Service or Labour, but shall be delivered up on Claim of the Party to whom such Service or Labour may be due.

SECTION 3. (1) New States may be admitted by the Congress into this Union; but no new State shall be formed or erected within the Jurisdiction of any other State; nor any State be formed by the Junction of two or more States, or Parts of States, without the Consent of the Legislatures of the States concerned as well as of the Congress.

(2) The Congress shall have Power to dispose of and make all needful Rules and Regulations respecting the Territory or other Property belonging to the United States; and nothing in this Constitution shall be so construed as to Prejudice any Claims of the United States, or of any particular State.

SECTION 4. The United States shall guarantee to every State in this Union a Republican Form of Government, and shall protect each of them against Invasion; and on Application of the Legislature, or of the Executive (when the Legislature cannot be convened) against domestic Violence.

ARTICLE V

The Congress, whenever two thirds of both Houses shall deem it necessary, shall propose Amendments to this Constitution, or, on the Application of the Legislatures of two thirds of the several States, shall call a Convention for proposing Amendments, which, in either Case, shall be valid to all Intents and Purposes, as part of this Constitution, when ratified by the Legislatures of three fourths of the several States, or by Conventions in three fourths thereof, as the one or the other Mode of Ratification may be proposed by the Congress; Provided that no Amendment which may be made prior to the Year One thousand eight hundred and eight shall in any Manner affect the first and fourth Clauses in the Ninth Section of the first Article; and that no State, without its Consent, shall be deprived of its equal Suffrage in the Senate.

ARTICLE VI

(1) All Debts contracted and Engagements entered into, before the Adoption of this Constitution shall be as valid against the United States under this Constitution, as under the Confederation.

(2) This Constitution, and the Laws of the United States which shall be made in Pursuance thereof; and all Treaties made, or which shall be made, under the Authority of the United States, shall be the supreme Law of the Land; and the Judges in every State shall be bound thereby, any Thing in the Constitution or Laws of any State to the Contrary notwithstanding.

(3) The Senators and Representatives before mentioned, and the Members of the several State Legislatures, and all executive and judicial Officers, both of the United States and of the several States, shall be bound by Oath or Affirmation, to support this Constitution; but no religious Test shall ever be required as a Qualification to any Office or public Trust under the United States.

ARTICLE VII

The Ratification of the Conventions of nine States shall be sufficient for the Establishment of this Constitution between the States so ratifying the Same.

Bill of Rights I - X

AMENDMENT I [1791]

Congress shall make no law respecting an establishment of religion, or prohibiting the free exercise thereof; of abridging the freedom of speech, or of the press; or the right of the people peaceably to assemble, and to petition the Government for a redress of grievances.

AMENDMENT II [1791]

A well regulated Militia, being necessary to the security of a free State, the right of the people to keep and bear Arms, shall not be infringed.

AMENDMENT III [1791]

No Soldier shall, in time of peace be quartered in any house, without the consent of the Owner, nor in time of war, but in a manner to be prescribed by law.

AMENDMENT IV [1791]

The right of the people to be secure in their persons, houses, papers, and effects, against unreasonable searches and seizures, shall not be violated, and no Warrants shall issue, but upon probable cause, supported by Oath or affirmation, and particularly describing the place to be searched, and the persons or things to be seized.

AMENDMENT V [1791]

No person shall be held to answer for a capital, or otherwise infamous crime, unless on a presentment or indictment of a Grand Jury, except in cases arising in the land or naval forces, or in the Militia, when in actual service in time of War or public danger; nor shall any person be subject for the same offence to be twice put in jeopardy of life or limb; nor shall be compelled in any criminal case to be a witness against himself, nor be deprived of life, liberty, or property, without due process of law; nor shall private property be taken for public use, without just compensation.

Rights of Criminals

AMENDMENT VI [1791]

In all criminal prosecutions, the accused shall enjoy the right to a speedy and public trial, by an impartial jury of the State and district wherein the crime shall have been committed, which district shall have been previously ascertained by law, and to be informed of the nature and cause of the accusation; to be confronted with the witnesses against him; to have compulsory process for obtaining witnesses in his favor, and to have the Assistance of Counsel for his defence.

AMENDMENT VII [1791]

In Suits at common law, where the value in controversy shall exceed twenty dollars, the right of trial by jury shall be preserved, and no fact tried by jury, shall be otherwise re-examined in any Court of the United States, than according to the rules of the common law.

AMENDMENT VIII [1791]

Excessive bail shall not be required, nor excessive fines imposed, nor cruel and unusual punishments inflicted.

AMENDMENT IX [1791]

The enumeration in the Constitution, of certain rights, shall not be construed to deny or disparage others retained by the people.

AMENDMENT X [1791]

The powers not delegated to the United States by the Constitution, nor prohibited by it to the States, are reserved to the States respectively, or to the people.

AMENDMENT XI [1798]

The Judicial power of the United States shall not be construed to extend to any suit in law or equity, commenced or prosecuted against one of the United States by Citizens of another State, or by Citizens or Subjects of any Foreign State.

AMENDMENT XII [1804]

The Electors shall meet in their respective states and vote by ballot for President and Vice-President, one of whom, at least, shall not be an inhabitant of the same state with themselves; they shall name in their ballots the person voted for as President, and in distinct ballots the person voted for as Vice-President, and they shall make distinct lists of all persons voted for as President, and of all persons voted for as Vice-President, and of the number of votes for each, which lists they shall sign and certify, and transmit sealed to the seat of the government of the United States, directed to the President of the Senate;—The President of the Senate shall, in the presence of the Senate and House of Representatives, open all the certificates and the votes shall then be counted;—The person having the greatest number of votes for President, shall be the President, if such number be a majority of the whole number of Electors appointed; and if no person have such majority, then from the persons having the highest numbers not exceeding three on the list of those voted for as President, the House of Representatives shall choose immediately, by ballot, the President. But in choosing the President, the votes shall be taken by states, the representation from each state having one vote; a quorum for this purpose shall consist of a member or members from two-thirds of the states, and a majority of all the states shall be necessary to a choice. And if the House of Representatives shall not choose a President whenever the right of choice shall devolve upon them before the fourth day of March next following, then the Vice-President shall act as President, as in the case of the death or other constitutional disability of the President.—The person having the greatest number of votes as Vice-President, shall be the Vice-President, if such number be a majority of the whole number of Electors appointed, and if no person have a majority, then from the two highest numbers on the list, the Senate shall choose the Vice-President; a quorum for the purpose shall consist of two-thirds of the whole number of Senators, and a majority of the whole number shall be necessary to a choice. But no person constitutionally ineligible to the office of President shall be eligible to that of Vice-President of the United States.

AMENDMENT XIII [1865]

SECTION 1. Neither slavery nor involuntary servitude, except as a punishment for crime whereof the party shall have been duly convicted, shall exist within the United States, or any place subject to their jurisdiction.

SECTION 2. Congress shall have power to enforce this article by appropriate legislation.

AMENDMENT XIV [1868]

SECTION 1. All persons born or naturalized in the United States, and subject to the jurisdiction thereof, are citizens of the United States and of the State wherein they reside. No <u>State</u> shall make or enforce any law which shall abridge the privileges or immunities of citizens of the United States; nor shall any State deprive any person of life, liberty, or property, without due process of law; nor deny to any person within its jurisdiction the equal protection of the laws.

SECTION 2. Representatives shall be apportioned among the several States according to their respective numbers, counting the whole number of persons in each State, excluding Indians not taxed. But when the right to vote at any election for the choice of electors for President and Vice President of the United States, Representatives in Congress, the Executive and Judicial officers of a State, or the members of the Legislature thereof, is denied to any of the male inhabitants of such State, being twenty-one years of age, and citizens of the United States, or in any way abridged, except for participation in rebellion, or other crime, the basis of representation therein shall be reduced in the proportion which the number of such male citizens shall bear to the whole number of male citizens twenty-one years of age in such State.

SECTION 3. No person shall be a Senator or Representative in Congress, or elector of President and Vice President, or hold any office, civil or military, under the United States, or under any State, who having previously taken an oath, as a member of Congress, or as an officer of the United States, or as a member of any State legislature, or as an executive or judicial officer of any State, to support the Constitution of the United States, shall have engaged in insurrection or rebellion against the same, or given aid or comfort to the enemies thereof. But Congress may by a vote of two-thirds of each House, remove such disability.

SECTION 4. The validity of the public debt of the United States, authorized by law, including debts incurred for payment of pensions and bounties for services in suppressing insurrection or rebellion, shall not be questioned. But neither the United States nor any State shall assume or pay any debt or obligation incurred in aid of insurrection or rebellion against the United States, or any claim for the loss or emancipation of any slave; but all such debts, obligations and claims shall be held illegal and void.

SECTION 5. The Congress shall have power to enforce, by appropriate legislation, the provisions of this article.

AMENDMENT XV [1870]

SECTION 1. The right of citizens of the United States to vote shall not be denied or abridged by the United States or by any State on account of race, color, or previous condition of servitude.

SECTION 2. The Congress shall have power to enforce this article by appropriate legislation.

AMENDMENT XVI [1913]

The Congress shall have power to lay and collect taxes on incomes, from whatever source derived, without apportionment among the several States, and without regard to any census or enumeration.

AMENDMENT XVII [1913]

(1) The Senate of the United States shall be composed of two Senators from each State, elected by the people thereof, for six years; and each Senator shall have one

vote. The electors in each State shall have the qualifications requisite for electors of the most numerous branch of the State legislatures.

(2) When vacancies happen in the representation of any State in the Senate, the executive authority of such State shall issue writs of election to full such vacancies: *Provided,* That the legislature of any State may empower the executive thereof to make temporary appointments until the people fill the vacancies by election as the legislature may direct.

(3) This amendment shall not be so construed as to affect the election or term of any Senator chosen before it becomes valid as part of the Constitution.

AMENDMENT XVIII [1919]

SECTION 1. After one year from the ratification of this article the manufacture, sale, or transportation of intoxicating liquors within, the importation thereof into, or the exportation thereof from the United States and all territory subject to the jurisdiction thereof for beverage purposes is hereby prohibited.

SECTION 2. The Congress and the several States shall have concurrent power to enforce this article by appropriate legislation.

SECTION 3. This article shall be inoperative unless it shall have been ratified as an amendment to the Constitution by the legislatures of the several States, as provided in the Constitution, within seven years from the date of the submission hereof to the States by the Congress.

AMENDMENT XIX [1920]

(1) The right of citizens of the United States to vote shall not be denied or abridged by the United States or by any State on account of sex.

(2) Congress shall have power to enforce this article by appropriate legislation.

AMENDMENT XX [1933]

SECTION 1. The terms of the President and Vice President shall end at noon on the 20th day of January, and the terms of Senators and Representatives at noon on the 3d day of January, of the years in which such terms would have ended if this article had not been ratified; and the terms of their successors shall then begin.

SECTION 2. The Congress shall assemble at least once in every year, and such meeting shall begin at noon on the 3d day of January, unless they shall by law appoint a different day.

SECTION 3. If, at the time fixed for the beginning of the term of the President, the President elect shall have died, the Vice President elect shall become President. If the President shall not have been chosen before the time fixed for the beginning of his term or if the President elect shall have failed to qualify, then the Vice President elect shall act as President until a President shall have qualified; and the Congress may by law provide for the case wherein neither a President elect nor a Vice President elect shall have qualified, declaring who shall then act as President, or the manner in which one who is to act shall be selected, and such person shall act accordingly until a President or Vice President shall have qualified.

SECTION 4. The Congress may by law provide for the case of the death of any of the persons from whom the House of Representatives may choose a President whenever the right of choice shall have devolved upon them, and for the case of the death of any of the persons from whom the Senate may choose a Vice President whenever the right of choice shall have devolved upon them.

SECTION 5. Sections 1 and 2 shall take effect on the 15th day of October following the ratification of this article.

SECTION 6. This article shall be inoperative unless it shall have been ratified as an amendment to the Constitution by the legislatures of three-fourths of the several States within seven years from the date of its submission.

AMENDMENT XXI [1933]

SECTION 1. The eighteenth article of amendment to the Constitution of the United States is hereby repealed.

SECTION 2. The transportation or importation into any State, Territory, or possession of the United States for delivery or use therein of intoxicating liquors, in violation of the laws thereof, is hereby prohibited.

SECTION 3. This article shall be inoperative unless it shall have been ratified as an amendment to the Constitution by conventions in the several States, as provided in the Constitution, within seven years from the date of the submission hereof to the States by the Congress.

AMENDMENT XXII [1951]

SECTION 1. No person shall be elected to the office of the President more than twice, and no person who has held the office of President, or acted as President, for more than two years of a term to which some other person was elected President shall be elected to the office of President more than once. But this Article shall not apply to any person holding the office of President when this Article was proposed by the Congress, and shall not prevent any person who may be holding the office of President, or acting as President, during the term within which this Article becomes operative from holding the office of President or acting as president during the remainder of such term.

SECTION 2. This article shall be inoperative unless it shall have been ratified as an amendment to the Constitution by the legislatures of three-fourths of the several States within seven years from the date of its submission to the States by the Congress.

AMENDMENT XXIII [1961]

SECTION 1. The District constituting the seat of Government of the United States shall appoint in such manner as the Congress may direct:

A number of electors of President and Vice President equal to the whole number of Senators and Representatives in Congress to which the District would be entitled if it were a State, but in no event more than the least populous state; they shall be in addition to those appointed by the states, but they shall be considered, for the purposes of the election of President and Vice President, to be electors appointed by a state; and they shall meet in the District and perform such duties as provided by the twelfth article of amendment.

SECTION 2. The Congress shall have power to enforce this article by appropriate legislation.

AMENDMENT XXIV [1964]

SECTION 1. The right of citizens of the United States to vote in any primary or other election for President or Vice President, for electors for President or Vice President, or for Senator or Representative in Congress, shall not be denied or abridged by the United States or any State by reason of failure to pay any poll tax or other tax.

SECTION 2. The Congress shall have power to enforce this article by appropriate legislation.

AMENDMENT XXV [1967]

SECTION 1. In case of the removal of the President from office or of his death or resignation, the Vice President shall become President.

SECTION 2. Whenever there is a vacancy in the office of the Vice President, the President shall nominate a Vice President who shall take office upon confirmation by a majority vote of both Houses of Congress.

SECTION 3. Whenever the President transmits to the President pro tempore of the Senate and the Speaker of the House of Representatives his written declaration that he is unable to discharge the powers and duties of his office, and until he transmits to them a written declaration to the contrary, such powers and duties shall be discharged by the Vice President as Acting President.

SECTION 4. Whenever the Vice President and a majority of either the principal officers of the executive departments or of such other body as Congress may by law provide, transmit to the President pro tempore of the Senate and the Speaker of the House of Representatives their written declaration that the President is unable to discharge the powers and duties of his office, the Vice President shall immediately assume the powers and duties of the office as Acting President.

Thereafter, when the President transmits to the President pro tempore of the Senate and the Speaker of the House of Representatives his written declaration that no inability exists, he shall resume the powers and duties of his office unless the Vice President and a majority of either the principal officers of the executive departments or of such other body as Congress may by law provide, transmit within four days to the President pro tempore of the Senate and the Speaker of the House of Representatives their written declaration that the President is unable to discharge the powers and duties of his office. Thereupon Congress shall decide the issue, assembling within forty-eight hours for that purpose if not in session. If the Congress, within twenty-one days after receipt of the latter written declaration, or, if Congress is not in session, within twenty-one days after Congress is required to assemble, determines by two-thirds vote of both Houses that the President is unable to discharge the powers and duties of his office, the Vice President shall continue to discharge the same as Acting President; otherwise, the President shall resume the powers and duties of his office.

AMENDMENT XXVI [1971]

SECTION 1. The right of citizens of the United States, who are eighteen years of age or older, to vote shall not be denied or abridged by the United States or by any State on account of age.

SECTION 2. The Congress shall have power to enforce this article by appropriate legislation.

B THE ADMINISTRATIVE PROCEDURE ACT [EXCERPTS]

RIGHT OF REVIEW

SECTION 702. A person suffering legal wrong because of agency action, or adversely affected or aggrieved by agency action within the meaning of a relevant statute, is entitled to judicial review thereof.

ACTIONS REVIEWABLE

SECTION 704. Agency action made reviewable by statute and final agency action for which there is no other adequate remedy in a court are subject to judicial review. A preliminary, procedural, or intermediate agency action or ruling not directly reviewable is subject to review on the review of the final agency action. Except as otherwise expressly required by statute, agency action otherwise final is final for the purposes of this section whether or not there has been presented or determined an application for a declaratory order, for any form of reconsiderations, or, unless the agency otherwise requires by rule and provides that the action meanwhile is inoperative, for an appeal to superior agency authority.

SCOPE OF REVIEW

SECTION 706. To the extent necessary to decision and when presented, the reviewing court shall decide all relevant questions of law, interpret constitutional and statutory provisions, and determine the meaning or applicability of the terms of an agency action. The reviewing court shall—

(1) compel agency action unlawfully withheld or unreasonably delayed; and
(2) hold unlawful and set aside agency action, findings, and conclusions found to be—
(A) arbitrary, capricious, an abuse of discretion, or otherwise not in accordance with law;
(B) contrary to constitutional right, power, privilege, or immunity;
(C) in excess of statutory jurisdiction, authority, or limitations, or short of statutory right;
(D) without observance of procedure required by law;
(E) unsupported by substantial evidence in a case subject to sections 556 and 557 of this title or otherwise reviewed on the record of an agency hearing provided by statute; or
(F) unwarranted by the facts to the extent that the facts are subject to trial de novo by the reviewing court.

In making the foregoing determinations, the court shall review the whole record or those parts of it cited by a party, and due account shall be taken of the rule of prejudicial error.

C THE SHERMAN ACT [EXCERPTS]

TRUSTS, ETC., IN RESTRAINT OF TRADE ILLEGAL; PENALTY

SECTION 1. Every contract, combination in the form of trust or otherwise, or conspiracy, in restraint of trade or commerce among the several States, or with foreign nations, is declared to be illegal. Every person who shall make any contract or engage in any combination or conspiracy hereby declared to be illegal shall be deemed guilty of a felony, and, on conviction thereof, shall be punished by fine not exceeding one million dollars if a corporation, or, if any other person, one hundred thousand dollars, or by imprisonment not exceeding three years, or by both said punishments, in the discretion of the court.

MONOPOLIZING TRADE A FELONY; PENALTY

SECTION 2. Every person who shall monopolize, or attempt to monopolize, or combine or conspire with any other person or persons, to monopolize any part of the trade or commerce among the several States, or with foreign nations, shall be deemed guilty of a felony, and, on conviction thereof, shall be punished by fine not exceeding one million dollars if a corporation, or, if any other person, one hundred thousand dollars, or by imprisonment not exceeding three years, or by both said punishments, in the discretion of the court. . . .

"PERSON" DEFINED

SECTION 7. The word "person," or "persons," wherever used in sections 1 to 7 of this title shall be deemed to include corporations and associations existing under or authorized by the laws of either the United States, the laws of any of the Territories, the laws of any State, or the laws of any foreign country.

D THE CLAYTON ACT [EXCERPTS]

SALE, ETC., ON AGREEMENT NOT TO USE GOODS OF COMPETITOR

SECTION 3. It shall be unlawful for any person engaged in commerce, in the course of such commerce, to lease or make a sale or contract for sale of goods, wares, merchandise, machinery, supplies, or other commodities, whether patented or unpatented, for use, consumption, or resale within the United States or any Territory thereof or the District of Columbia or any insular possession or other place under the jurisdiction of the United States, or fix a price charged therefor, or discount from, or rebate upon, such price, on the condition, agreement, or understanding that the lessee or purchaser thereof shall not use or deal in the goods, wares, merchandise, machinery, supplies, or other commodities of a competitor or competitors of the lessor or seller, where the effect of such lease, sale, or contract for sale or such condition, agreement, or understanding may be to substantially lessen competition or tend to create a monopoly in any line of commerce.

SUITS BY PERSONS INJURED

SECTION 4. (a) . . . [a]ny person who shall be injured in his business or property by reason of anything forbidden in the antitrust laws may sue therefor in any district court of the United States in the district in which the defendant resides or is found or has an agent, without respect to the amount in controversy, and shall recover three-fold the damages by him sustained, and the cost of suit, including a reasonable attorney's fee. The court may award under this section, pursuant to a motion by such person promptly made, simple interest on actual damages for the period beginning on the date of service of such person's pleading setting forth a claim under the antitrust laws and ending on the date of judgment, or for any shorter period therein, if the court finds that the award of such interest for such period is just in the circumstances.

JUDGMENTS; PRIMA FACIE EVIDENCE

SECTION 5. (2) A final judgment or decree heretofore or hereafter rendered in any civil or criminal proceeding brought by or on behalf of the United States under the antitrust laws to the effect that a defendant has violated said laws shall be prima facie evidence against such defendant in any action or proceeding brought by any other party against such defendant under said laws as to all matters respecting which said judgment or decree would be an estoppel as between the parties thereto: *Provided,* That this section shall not apply to consent judgments or decrees entered before any testimony has been taken.

ANTITRUST LAWS NOT APPLICABLE TO LABOR ORGANIZATIONS

SECTION 6. The labor of a human being is not a commodity or article of commerce. Nothing contained in the antitrust laws shall be construed to forbid the existence and operation of labor, agricultural, or horticultural organizations, instituted for the purposes of mutual help, and not having capital stock or conducted for profit, or to forbid or restrain individual members of such organizations from lawfully carrying out the legitimate objects thereof; nor shall such organizations, or the members thereof, be held or construed to be illegal combinations or conspiracies in restraint of trade, under the antitrust laws.

ACQUISITION BY ONE CORPORATION OF STOCK OF ANOTHER

SECTION 7. No person engaged in commerce or in any activity affecting commerce shall acquire, directly or indirectly, the whole or any part of the stock or other share capital and no person subject to the jurisdiction of the Federal Trade Commission shall acquire the whole or any part of the assets of another person engaged also in commerce or in any activity affecting commerce, where in any line of commerce or in any activity affecting commerce in any section of the country, the effect of such acquisition may be substantially to lessen competition, or to tend to create a monopoly.

No person shall acquire, directly or indirectly, the whole or any part of the stock or other share capital and no person subject to the jurisdiction of the Federal Trade Commission shall acquire the whole or any part of the assets of one or more persons engaged in commerce or in any activity affecting commerce, where in any line of commerce or in any activity affecting commerce in any section of the country, the effect of such acquisition, of such stocks or assets, or of the use of such stock by the voting or granting of proxies or otherwise, may be substantially to lessen competition, or to tend to create a monopoly.

This section shall not apply to persons purchasing such stock solely for investment and not using the same by voting or otherwise to bring about, or in attempting to bring about, the substantial lessening of competition. Nor shall anything contained in this section prevent a corporation engaged in commerce or in any activity affecting commerce from causing the formation of subsidiary corporations for the actual carrying on of their immediate lawful business, or the natural and legitimate branches or extensions thereof, or from owning and holding all or a part of the stock of such subsidiary corporations, when the effect of such formation is not to substantially lessen competition.

Nor shall anything herein contained be construed to prohibit any common carrier subject to the laws to regulate commerce from aiding in the construction of branches or short lines so located as to become feeders to the main line of the company so aiding in such construction or from acquiring or owning all or any part of the stock of such branch lines, nor to prevent any such common carrier from acquiring and owning all or any part of the stock of a branch or short line constructed by an independent company where there is no substantial competition between the company owning the branch line so constructed and the company owning the main line acquiring the property or an interest therein, nor to prevent such common carrier from extending any of its lines through the medium of the acquisition of stock or otherwise of any other common carrier where there is no substantial competition between the company extending its lines and the company whose stock, property, or an interest therein is so acquired.

Nothing contained in this section shall be held to affect or impair any right heretofore legally acquired: *Provided*, That nothing in this section shall be held or construed to authorize or make lawful anything heretofore prohibited or made illegal by the antitrust laws, nor to exempt any person from the penal provisions thereof or the civil remedies therein provided.

Nothing contained in this section shall apply to transactions duly consummated pursuant to authority given by the Civil Aeronautics Board, Federal Communications Commission, Federal Power Commission, Interstate Commerce Commission, the Securities and Exchange Commission in the exercise of its jurisdiction under section 79j of this title, the United States Maritime Commission, or the Secretary of Agriculture under any statutory provision vesting such power in such Commission, Secretary, or Board.

INTERLOCKING DIRECTORATES AND OFFICERS

SECTION 8. No person at the same time shall be a director in any two or more corporations, any one of which has capital, surplus, and undivided profits aggregating more than $1,000,000, engaged in whole or in part in commerce, other than banks, banking associations, trust companies, and common carriers subject to subtitle IV of Title 49, if such corporations are or shall have been theretofore, by virtue of their business and location of operation, competitors, so that the elimination of competition by agreement between them would constitute a violation of any of the provisions of any of the antitrust laws. The eligibility of a director under the foregoing provision shall be determined by the aggregate amount of the capital, surplus, and undivided profits, exclusive of dividends declared but not paid to stockholders, at the end of the fiscal year of said corporation next preceding the election of directors, and when a director has been elected in accordance with the provisions of this Act it shall be lawful for him to continue as such for one year thereafter.

E THE ROBINSON-PATMAN ACT [EXCERPTS]

DISCRIMINATION IN PRICE, SERVICES, OR FACILITIES—PRICE; SELECTION OF CUSTOMERS

SECTION 2. (a) It shall be unlawful for any person engaged in commerce, in the course of such commerce, either directly or indirectly, to discriminate in price between different purchases of commodities of like grade and quality, where either or any of the purchases involved in such discrimination are in commerce, where such commodities are sold for use, consumption, or resale within the United States or any Territory thereof or the District of Columbia or any insular possession or other place under the jurisdiction of the United States, and where the effect of such discrimination may be substantially to lessen competition or tend to create a monopoly in any line of commerce, or to injure, destroy, or prevent competition with any person who either grants or knowingly receives the benefit of such discrimination, or with customers of either of them: *Provided,* That nothing herein contained shall prevent differentials which make only due allowance for differences in the cost of manufacture, sale, or delivery resulting from the differing methods or quantities in which such commodities are to such purchasers sold or delivered: *Provided, however,* That the Federal Trade Commission may, after due investigation and hearing to all interested parties, fix and establish quantity limits, and revise the same as it finds necessary, as to particular commodities or classes of commodities, where it finds that available purchasers in greater quantities are so few as to render differentials on account thereof unjustly discriminatory or promotive of monopoly in any line of commerce; and the foregoing shall then not be construed to permit differentials based on differences in quantities greater than those so fixed and established: *And provided further,* That nothing herein contained shall prevent persons engaged in selling goods, wares, or merchandise in commerce from selecting their own customers in bona fide transactions and not in restraint of trade: *And provided further,* That nothing herein contained shall prevent price changes from time to time where in response to changing conditions affecting the market for or the marketability of the goods concerned, such as but not limited to actual or imminent deterioration of perishable goods, obsolescence of seasonal goods, distress sales under court process, or sales in good faith in discontinuance of business in the goods concerned.

BURDEN OF REBUTTING PRIMA-FACIE CASE OF DISCRIMINATION

(b) Upon proof being made, at any hearing on a complaint under this section, that there has been discrimination in price or services or facilities furnished, the burden of rebutting the prima-facie case thus made by showing justification shall be upon the person charged with a violation of this section, and unless justification shall be affirmatively shown, the Commission is authorized to issue an order terminating the discrimination: *Provided, however,* That nothing herein contained shall prevent a seller rebutting the prima-facie case thus made by showing that his lower price or the furnishing of services or facilities to any purchaser or purchasers was made in good faith to meet an equally low price of a competitor, or the services or facilities furnished by a competitor.

PAYMENT OR ACCEPTANCE OF COMMISSION, BROKERAGE OR OTHER COMPENSATION

(c) It shall be unlawful for any person engaged in commerce, in the course of such commerce, to pay or grant, or to receive or accept, anything of value as a commission, brokerage, or other compensation, or any allowance or discount in lieu thereof, except for services rendered in connection with the sale or purchase of goods, wares, or merchandise, either to the other party to such transaction or to an agent, representative, or other intermediary therein where such intermediary is acting in fact for or in behalf, or is subject to the direct or indirect control, of any party to such transaction other than the person by whom such compensation is so granted or paid.

PAYMENT FOR SERVICES OR FACILITIES FOR PROCESSING OR SALE

(d) It shall be unlawful for any person engaged in commerce to pay or contract for the payment of anything of value to or for the benefit of a customer of such person in the course of such commerce as compensation or in consideration for any services or facilities furnished by or through such customer in connection with the processing, handling, sale, or offering for sale of any products or commodities manufactured, sold, or offered for sale by such person, unless such payment or consideration is available on proportionally equal terms to all other customers competing in the distribution of such products or commodities.

FURNISHING SERVICES OR FACILITIES FOR PROCESSING, HANDLING, ETC.

(e) It shall be unlawful for any person to discriminate in favor of one purchaser against another purchaser or purchasers of a commodity bought for resale, with or without processing, by contracting to furnish or furnishing, or by contributing to the furnishing of, any services or facilities connected with the processing, handling, sale, or offering for sale of such commodity so purchased upon terms not accorded to all purchasers on proportionally equal terms.

KNOWINGLY INDUCING OR RECEIVING DISCRIMINATORY PRICE

(f) It shall be unlawful for any person engaged in commerce, in the course of such commerce, knowingly to induce or receive a discrimination in price which is prohibited by this section.

DISCRIMINATION IN REBATES, DISCOUNTS, OR ADVERTISING SERVICE CHARGES; UNDERSELLING IN PARTICULAR LOCALITIES; PENALTIES

SECTION 3. It shall be unlawful for any person engaged in commerce, in the course of such commerce, to be a party to, or assist in, any transaction of sale, or contract to sell, which discriminates to his knowledge against competitors of the purchaser, in that, any discount, rebate, allowance, or advertising service charge is granted to the purchaser over and above any discount, rebate, allowance, or advertising service charge available at the time of such transaction to said competitors in respect of a sale of goods of like grade, quality, and quantity; to sell, or contract to sell, goods in any part of the United States at prices lower than those exacted by said person elsewhere in the United States for the purpose of destroying competition, or eliminating a competitor in such part of the United States; or, to sell, or contract to sell, goods at unreasonably low prices for the purpose of destroying competition or eliminating a competitor.

 THE FEDERAL TRADE COMMISSION ACT [EXCERPTS]

UNFAIR METHODS OF COMPETITION UNLAWFUL—DECLARATION OF UNLAWFULNESS

SECTION 5. (a)(1) Unfair methods of competition in or affecting commerce, and unfair or deceptive acts or practices in or affecting commerce, are declared unlawful.

PENALTY FOR VIOLATION OF ORDER: INJUNCTIONS AND OTHER APPROPRIATE EQUITABLE RELIEF

(b) Any person, partnership, or corporation who violates an order of the Commission after it has become final, and while such order is in effect, shall forfeit and pay to the United States a civil penalty of not more than $10,000 for each violation, which shall accrue to the United States and may be recovered in a civil action brought by the Attorney General of the United States. Each separate violation of such an order shall be a separate offense, except that in the case of a violation through continuing failure to obey or neglect to obey a final order of the Commission, each day of continuance of such failure or neglect shall be deemed a separate offense. In such actions, the United States district courts are empowered to grant mandatory injunctions and such other and further equitable relief as they deem appropriate in the enforcement of such final orders of the Commission.

PROCEDURES AND RULES OF PRACTICE FOR THE FEDERAL TRADE COMMISSION

POLICY

SECTION 1.1. (a) Any person, partnership, or corporation may request advice from the Commission with respect to a course of action which the requesting party proposes to pursue. The Commission will consider such requests for advice and inform the requesting party of the Commission's views, where practicable, under the following circumstances.

(1) The matter involves a substantial or novel question of fact or law and there is no clear Commission or court precedent;

(2) A proposed corporate merger or acquisition is involved; or

(3) The subject matter of the request and consequent publication of Commission advice is of significant public interest.

(b) The Commission has authorized its staff to consider all requests for advice and to render advice, where practicable, in those circumstances in which a Commission opinion would not be warranted. Hypothetical questions will not be answered, and a request for advice will ordinarily be considered inappropriate where (1) the same or substantially the same course of action is under investigation or is or has been the subject of a current proceeding involving the Commission or another governmental agency, or (2) an informed opinion cannot be made or could be made only after extensive investigation, clinical study, testing, or collateral injury.

RULEMAKING—NATURE AND AUTHORITY

SECTION 1.22. (a) For the purpose of carrying out the provisions of the statutes administered by it, the Commission is empowered to promulgate rules and regulations applicable to unlawful trade practices. Such rules and regulations express the experience and judgment of the Commission, based on facts of which it has knowledge derived from studies, reports, investigations, hearings, and other proceedings, or within official notice, concerning the substantive requirements of the statutes which it administers.

 THE SECURITIES ACT OF 1933 [EXCERPTS]

DEFINITIONS

SECTION 2. When used in this title, unless the context otherwise requires—(1) The term "security" means any note, stock, treasury stock, bond, debenture, evidence of indebtedness, certificate of interest or participation in any profit-sharing agreement, collateral-trust certificate, preorganization certificate or subscription, transferable share, investment contract, voting-trust certificate, certificate of deposit for a security, fractional undivided interest in oil, gas, or other mineral rights, any put, call, straddle, option, or privilege on any security, certificate of deposit, or group or index of securities (including any interest therein or based on the value thereof), or any put, call, straddle, option, or privilege entered into on a national securities exchange relating to foreign currency, or, in general, any interest or instrument commonly known as a "security," or any certificate of interest or participation in, temporary of interim certificate for, receipt for, guarantee of, or warrant or right to subscribe to or purchase, any of the foregoing.

(2) The term "person" means an individual, a corporation, a partnership, an association, a joint-stock company, a trust, any unincorporated organization, or a government or political subdivision thereof.

EXEMPTED SECURITIES

SECTION 3. (b) The Commission may from time to time by its rules and regulations, and subject to such terms and conditions as may be prescribed therein, add any class of securities to the securities exempted as provided in this section, if it finds that the enforcement of this title with respect to such securities is not necessary in the public interest and for the protection of investors by reason of the small amount involved or the limited character of the public offering; but no issue of securities shall be exempted under this subsection where the aggregate amount at which such issue is offered to the public exceeds $5,000,000.

EXEMPTED TRANSACTIONS

SECTION 4. The provisions of section 5 shall not apply to—

(1) transactions by any person other than an issue, underwriter, or dealer.

(2) transactions by an issuer not involving any public offering. . . .

(4) brokers' transactions executed upon customers' orders on any exchange or in the over-the-counter market but not the solicitation of such orders.

PROHIBITIONS RELATING TO INTERSTATE COMMERCE
AND THE MAILS

SECTION 5. (a) Unless a registration statement is in effect as to a security, it shall be unlawful for any person, directly or indirectly—

(1) to make use of any means or instruments of transportation or communications in interstate commerce or of the mails to sell such security through the use or medium of any prospectus or otherwise; or

(2) to carry or cause to be carried through the mails or in interstate commerce, by any means or instruments of transportation, any such security for the purpose of sale or for delivery after sale.

(b) It shall be unlawful for any person, directly or indirectly—

(1) to make use of any means or instruments of transportation or communication in interstate commerce or of the mails to carry or transmit any prospectus relating to any security with respect to which a registration statement has been filed under this title, unless such prospectus meets the requirements of section 10; or

(2) to carry or cause to be carried through the mails or in interstate commerce any such security for the purpose of sale or for delivery after sale, unless accompanied or preceded by a prospectus that meets the requirements of subsection (a) of section 10.

(c) It shall be unlawful for any person, directly or indirectly, to make use of any means or instruments of transportation or communication in interstate commerce or the mails to offer to sell or offer to buy through the use or medium of any prospectus or otherwise any security, unless a registration statement has been filed as to such security, or while the registration statement is the subject of the refusal order or stop order. . . .

REGISTRATION OF SECURITIES AND SIGNING
OF REGISTRATION STATEMENT

SECTION 6. (a) Any security may be registered with the Commission under the terms and conditions hereinafter provided, by filing a registration statement in triplicate, at least one of which shall be signed by each issuer, its principal executive officer or officers, its principal financial officer, its comptroller or principal accounting officer, and the majority of its board of directors or persons performing similar functions (or, if there is no board of directors or persons performing similar functions, by the majority of the persons or board having the power of management of the issuer), . . .

CIVIL LIABILITIES ON ACCOUNT OF FALSE
REGISTRATION STATEMENT

SECTION 11. (a) In case any part of the registration statement, when such part became effective, contained an untrue statement of a material fact or omitted to state a material fact required to be stated therein or necessary to make the statements therein not misleading, any person acquiring such security (unless it is proved that at the time of such acquisition he knew of such untruth or omission) may, either at law or in equity, in any court of competent jurisdiction, sue—

(1) every person who signed the registration statement;

(2) every person who was a director of (or person performing similar functions) or partner in, the issuer at the time of the filing of the part of the registration statement with respect to which his liability is asserted;

(3) every person who, with his consent, is named in the registration statement as being or about to become a director, person performing similar functions, or partner;

(4) every accountant, engineer, or appraiser, or any person whose profession gives authority to a statement made by him, who has with his consent been named as having prepared or certified any part of the registration statement, or as having prepared or certified any report or valuation which is used in connection with the registration statement, with respect to the statement in such registration statement, report, or valuation, which purports to have been prepared or certified by him;

(5) every underwriter with respect to such security.

If such person acquired the security after the issuer has made generally available to its security holders an earning statement covering a period of at least twelve months beginning after the effective date of the registration statement, then the right of recovery under this subsection shall be conditioned on proof that such person acquired the security relying upon such untrue statement in the registration statement or relying upon the registration statement and not knowing of such omission, but such reliance may be established without proof of the reading of the registration statement by such person.

(b) Notwithstanding the provisions of subsection (a) no person, other than the issuer, shall be liable as provided therein who shall sustain the burden of proof—

(1) that before the effective date of the part of the registration statement with respect to which his liability is asserted (A) he had resigned from or had taken such steps as are permitted by law to resign from, or ceased or refused to act in, every office, capacity, or relationship in which he was described in the registration statement as acting or agreeing to act, and (B) he had advised the Commission and the issuer in writing that he had taken such action and that he would not be responsible for such part of the registration statement; or

(2) that if such part of the registration statement became effective without his knowledge, upon becoming aware of such fact he forthwith acted and advised the Commission, in accordance with paragraph (1), and, in addition, gave reasonable public notice that such part of the registration statement had become effective without his knowledge; or

(3) that (A) as regards any part of the registration statement not purporting to be made on the authority of an expert, and not purporting to be a copy of or extract from a report or valuation of an expert, and not purporting to be made on the authority of a public official document or statement, he had, after reasonable investigation, reasonable ground to believe and did believe, at the time such part of the registration statement became effective, that the statements therein were true and that there was no omission to state a material fact required to be stated therein or necessary to make the statements therein not misleading; and (B) as regards any part of the registration statement purporting to be made upon his authority as an expert or purporting to be a copy of or extract from a report or valuation of himself as an expert, (i) he had, after reasonable investigation, reasonable ground to believe and did believe, at the time such part of the registration statement became effective, that the statements therein were true and that there was no omission to state a material fact required to be stated therein or necessary to make the statements therein not misleading, or (ii) such part of the registration statement did not fairly represent his statement as an expert or was not a fair copy of or extract from his report or valuation as an expert; and (C) as regards any part of the registration statement purporting to be made on the authority of an expert (other than himself) or purporting to be a copy of or extract from a report or valuation of an expert (other than himself), he had no reasonable ground to believe and did not believe, at the time such part of the registration statement became effective, that the statements therein were untrue or that there was an omission to state a material fact required to be stated therein or necessary to make the statements therein not misleading, or that such part of the registration statement did not fairly represent the statement of the expert or was not a fair copy of or extract from the report or valuation of the expert; and (D) as regards any part of the registration statement purporting to be a statement made by an official person or purporting to be a copy of or extract from a public official document, he had no reasonable ground to believe and did not believe, at the time such part of the registration statement became effective, that the statements therein were untrue, or that there was an omission to state a material fact required to be stated therein or necessary to make the statements therein not misleading, or that such part of the registration statement did not fairly represent the statement made by the official person or was not a fair copy of or extract from the public official document.

(c) In determining, for the purpose of paragraph (3) of subsection (b) of this section, what constitutes reasonable investigation and reasonable ground for belief, the standard of reasonableness shall be that required of a prudent man in the management of his own property.

(d) If any person becomes an underwriter with respect to the security after the part of the registration statement with respect to which his liability is asserted has become effective, then for the purposes of paragraph (3) of subsection (b) of this section such part of the registration statement shall be considered as having become effective with respect to such person as of the time when he became an underwriter.

(e) The suit authorized under subsection (a) may be to recover such damages as shall represent the difference between the amount paid for the security (not exceeding the price at which the security was offered to the public) and (1) the value thereof as of the time such suit was brought, or (2) the price at which such security shall have been disposed of in the market before suit, or (3) the price at which such security shall have been disposed of after suit but before judgment if such damages shall be less than the damages representing the difference between the amount paid for the security (not exceeding the price at which the security was offered to the public) and the value thereof as of the time such suit was brought: . . .

(f) All or any one or more of the persons specified in subsection (a) shall be jointly and severally liable, and every person who becomes liable to make any payment under this section may recover contribution as in cases of contract from any person who, if sued separately, would have been liable to make the same payment, unless the person who has become liable was, and the other was not, guilty of fraudulent misrepresentation.

(g) In no case shall the amount recoverable under this section exceed the price at which the security was offered to the public.

CIVIL LIABILITIES ARISING IN CONNECTION WITH PROSPECTUSES AND COMMUNICATIONS

SECTION 12. Any person who— (1) offers or sells a security in violation of section 5, or

(2) offers or sells a security (whether or not exempted by the provisions of section 3, other than paragraph (2) of subsection (a) thereof), by the use of any means or instruments of transportation or communication in interstate commerce or of the mails, by means of a prospectus or oral communication, which includes an untrue statement of a material fact or omits to state a material fact necessary in order to make the statements, in the light of the circumstances under which they were made, not misleading (the purchaser not knowing of such untruth or omission), and who shall not sustain the burden of proof that he did not know, and in the exercise of reasonable care could not have known, of such untruth or omission, shall be liable to the person purchasing such security from him, who may sue either at law or in equity in any court of competent jurisdiction, to recover the consideration paid for such security with interest thereon, less the amount of any income received thereon, upon the tender of such security, or for damages if he no longer owns the security.

LIMITATION OF ACTIONS

SECTION 13. No action shall be maintained to enforce any liability created under section 11 or section 12(2) unless brought within one year after the discovery of the untrue statement or the omission, or after such discovery should have been made by the exercise of reasonable diligence, or, if the action is to enforce a liability created under section 12(1), unless brought within one year after the violation upon which it is based. In no event shall any such action be brought to enforce a liability created under section 11 or section 12(1) more than three years after the security was bona fide offered to the public, or under section 12(2) more than three years after the sale.

FRAUDULENT INTERSTATE TRANSACTIONS

SECTION 17. (a) It shall be unlawful for any person in the offer or sale of any securities by the use of any means or instruments of transportation or communication in interstate commerce or by the use of the mails, directly or indirectly—

(1) to employ any device, scheme, or artifice to defraud, or

(2) to obtain money or property by means of any untrue statement of a material fact or any omission to state a material fact necessary in order to make the statements made, in the light of the circumstances under which they were made, not misleading, or

(3) to engage in any transaction, practice, or course of business which operates or would operate as a fraud or deceit upon the purchaser.

(b) It shall be unlawful for any person, by the use of any means or instruments of transportation or communication in interstate commerce or by the use of the mails, to publish, give publicity to, or circulate any notice, circular, advertisement, newspaper, article, letter, investment service, or communication which, though not purporting to offer a security for sale, describes such security for a consideration received or to be received, directly or indirectly, from an issuer, underwriter, or dealer, without fully disclosing the receipt, whether past or prospective, of such consideration and the amount thereof.

(c) The exemptions provided in section 3 shall not apply to the provisions of this section.

PENALTIES

SECTION 24. Any person who willfully violates any of the provisions of this title, or the rules and regulations promulgated by the Commission under authority thereof, or any person who willfully, in a registration statement filed under this title, makes any untrue statement of a material fact or omits to state any material fact required to be stated therein or necessary to make the statements therein not misleading, shall upon conviction be fined not more than $10,000 or imprisoned not more than five years, or both.

H THE SECURITIES EXCHANGE ACT OF 1934 [EXCERPTS]

SECURITIES AND EXCHANGE COMMISSION

SECTION 4. (a) There is hereby established a Securities and Exchange Commission (hereinafter referred to as the "Commission") to be composed of five commissioners to be appointed by the President by and with the advice and consent of the Senate. Not more than three of such commissioners shall be members of the same political party, and in making appointments members of different political parties shall be appointed alternately as nearly as may be practicable.

TRANSACTIONS ON UNREGISTERED EXCHANGES

SECTION 5. It shall be unlawful for any broker, dealer, or exchange, directly or indirectly, to make use of the mails or any means or instrumentality of interstate commerce for the purpose of using any facility of an exchange within or subject to the jurisdiction of the United States to effect any transaction in a security, or to report any such transaction, unless such exchange (1) is registered as a national securities exchange under . . . this title, or (2) is exempted from such registration upon application by the exchange because, in the opinion of the Commission, by reason of the limited volume of transactions effected on such exchange, it is not practicable and not necessary or appropriate in the public interest or for the protection of investors to require such registration.

REGULATION OF THE USE OF MANIPULATIVE AND DECEPTIVE DEVICES

SECTION 10. It shall be unlawful for any person, directly or indirectly, by the use of any means or instrumentality of interstate commerce or of the mails, or of any facility of any national securities exchange—

(a) To effect a short sale, or to use or employ any stop-loss order in connection with the purchase or sale, of any security registered on a national securities exchange, in contravention of such rules and regulations as the Commission may prescribe as necessary or appropriate in the public interest or for the protection of investors.

(b) To use or employ, in connection with the purchase or sale of any security registered on a national securities exchange or any security not so registered, any manipulative or deceptive device or contrivance in contravention of such rules and regulations as the Commission may prescribe as necessary or appropriate in the public interest or for the protection of investors.

REGISTRATION REQUIREMENTS FOR SECURITIES

SECTION 12. (a) It shall be unlawful for any member, broker, or dealer to effect any transaction in any security (other than an exempted security) on a national securities exchange unless a registration is effective as to such security for such exchange in accordance with the provisions of this title and the rules and regulations thereunder.

PERIODICAL AND OTHER REPORTS

SECTION 13. (d)(1) Any person who, after acquiring directly or indirectly the beneficial ownership of any equity security of a class which is registered pursuant to section 12 of this title, or any equity security of an insurance company which would have been required to be so registered except for the exemption contained in section 12(g)(2)(G) of this title, or any equity security issued by a closed-end investment company registered under the Investment Company Act of 1940, is directly or indirectly the beneficial owner of more than 5 per centum of such class shall, within ten days after such acquisition, send to the issuer of the security at its principal executive office, by registered or certified mail, send to each exchange where the security is traded, and file with the Commission, a statement containing such of the following information, and such additional information, as the Commission may by rules and regulations prescribe as necessary or appropriate in the public interest or for the protection of investors—

(A) the background, and identity, residence, and citizenship of, and the nature of such beneficial ownership by, such person and all other persons by whom or on whose behalf the purchases have been or are to be effected;

(B) the source and amount of the funds or other consideration used or to be used in making the purchases, and if any part of the purchase price is represented or is to be represented by funds or other consideration borrowed or otherwise obtained for the purpose of acquiring, holding, or trading such security, a description of the transaction and the names of the parties thereto, except that where a source of funds is a loan made in the ordinary course of business by a bank, as defined in section 3(a)(6) of this title, if the person filing such statement so requests, the name of the bank shall not be made available to the public;

(C) if the purpose of the purchases or prospective purchases is to acquire control of the business of the issuer of the securities, any plans or proposals which such persons may have to liquidate such issuer, to sell its assets to or merge it with any other persons, or to make any other major change in its business or corporate structure;

(D) the number of shares of such security which are beneficially owned, and the number of shares concerning which there is a right to acquire, directly or indirectly, by (i) such person, and (ii) by each associate of such person, giving the background, identity, residence, and citizenship of each such associate; and

(E) information as to any contracts, arrangements, or understandings with any person with respect to any securities of the issuer, including but not limited to transfer of any of the securities, joint ventures, loan or option arrangements, puts or calls, guaranties of loans, guaranties against loss or guaranties of profits, division of losses or profits, or the giving or withholding of proxies, naming the persons with whom such contracts, arrangements, or understandings have been entered into, and giving the details thereof.

(2) If any material change occurs in the facts set forth in the statements to the issuer and the exchange, and in the statement filed with the Commission, an amendment shall be transmitted to the issuer and the exchange and shall be filed with the Commission, in accordance with such rules and regulations as the Commission may prescribe as necessary or appropriate in the public interest or for the protection of investors.

(3) When two or more persons act as a partnership, limited partnership, syndicate, or other group for the purpose of acquiring, holding, or disposing of securities of an issuer, such syndicate or group shall be deemed a "person" for the purposes of this subsection.

PROXIES

SECTION 14. (a) It shall be unlawful for any person, by the use of the mails or by any means or instrumentality of interstate commerce or of any facility of a national securities exchange or otherwise, in contravention of such rules and regulations as the Commission may prescribe as necessary or appropriate in the public interest or for the protection of investors, to solicit or to permit the use of his name to solicit any proxy or consent or authorization in respect of any security (other than an exempted security) registered pursuant to section 12 of this title.

(b) It shall be unlawful for any member of a national securities exchange, or any broker or dealer registered under this title, in contravention of such rules and regulations as the Commission may prescribe as necessary or appropriate in the public interest or for the protection of investors, to give, or to refrain from giving a proxy, consent, or authorization in respect of any security registered pursuant to section 12 of this title and carried for the account of a customer.

(c) Unless proxies, consents, or authorizations in respect of a security registered pursuant to section 12 of this title are solicited by or on behalf of the management of the issuer from the holders of record of such security in accordance with the rules and regulations prescribed under subsection (a) of this section, prior to any annual or other meeting of the holders of such security, such issuer shall, in accordance with rules and regulations prescribed by the Commission, file with the Commission and transmit to all holders of record of such security information substantially equivalent to the information which would be required to be transmitted if a solicitation were made, but no information shall be required to be filed or transmitted pursuant to this subsection before July 1, 1964.

(d)(1) It shall be unlawful for any person, directly or indirectly, by use of the mails or by any means or instrumentality of interstate commerce or of any facility of a national securities exchange or otherwise, to make a tender offer for, or a request or invitation for tenders of, any class of any equity security which is registered pursuant to section 12 of this title, or any equity security of an insurance company which would have been required to be so registered except for the exemption contained in section 12(g)(2)(G) of this title, or any equity security issued by a closed-end investment company registered under the Investment Company Act of 1940, if, after consummation thereof, such person would, directly or indirectly, be the beneficial owner of more than 5 per centum of such class, unless at the time copies of the offer or request or invitation are first published or sent or given to security holders such person has filed with the Commission a statement containing such of the information specified in section 13(d) of this title, and such additional information as the Commission may by rules and regulations prescribed as necessary or appropriate in the public interest or for the protection of investors. All requests or invitations for tenders or advertisements making a tender offer or requesting or inviting tenders of such a security shall be filed as a part of such statement and shall contain such of the information contained in such statement as the Commission may by rules and regulations prescribe. Copies of any additional material soliciting or requesting such tender offers subsequent to the initial solicitation or request shall contain such information as the Commission may by rules and regulations prescribe as necessary or appropriate in the public interest or for the protection of investors, and shall be filed with the Commission not later than the time copies of such material are first published or sent or given to security holders. Copies of all statements, in the form in which such material is furnished to security holders and the Commission, shall be sent to the issuer not later than the date such material is first published or sent or given to any security holders.

(2) When two or more persons act as a partnership, limited partnership, syndicate, or other group for the purpose of acquiring, holding, or disposing of securities of an issuer, such syndicate or group shall be deemed a "person" for purposes of this subsection.

(3) In determining, for purposes of this subsection, any percentage of a class of any security, such class shall be deemed to consist of the amount of the outstanding securities

of such class, exclusive of any securities of such class held by or for the account of the issuer or a subsidiary of the issuer.

(4) Any solicitation or recommendation to the holders of such a security to accept or reject a tender offer or request or invitation for tenders shall be made in accordance with such rules and regulations as the Commission may prescribe as necessary or appropriate in the public interest or for the protection of investors.

(5) Securities deposited pursuant to a tender offer or request or invitation for tenders may be withdrawn by or on behalf of the depositor at any time until the expiration of seven days after the time definitive copies of the offer or request or invitation are first published or sent or given to security holders, and at any time after sixty days from the date of the original tender offer or request or invitation, except as the Commission may otherwise prescribe by rules, regulations, or order as necessary or appropriate in the public interest or for the protection of investors.

(6) Where any person makes a tender offer, or request or invitation for tenders, for less than all the outstanding equity securities of a class, and where a greater number of securities is deposited pursuant thereto within ten days after copies of the offer or request or invitation are first published or sent or given to security holders than such person is bound or willing to take up and pay for the securities taken up shall be taken up as nearly as may be *pro rata*, disregarding fractions, according to the number of securities deposited by each depositor. The provisions of this subsection shall also apply to securities deposited within ten days after notice of an increase in the consideration offered to security holders, as described in paragraph (7), is first published or sent or given to security holders.

(7) Where any person varies the terms of a tender offer or request or invitation for tenders before the expiration thereof by increasing the consideration offered to holders of such securities, such person shall pay the increased consideration to each security holder whose securities are taken up and paid for pursuant to the tender offer or request or invitation for tenders whether or not such securities have been taken up by such person before the variation of the tender offer or request or invitation.

(8) The provisions of this subsection shall not apply to any offer for, or request or invitation for tenders of, any security—

(A) if the acquisition of such security, together with all other acquisitions by the same person of securities of the same class during the preceding twelve months, would not exceed 2 per centum of that class;

(B) by the issuer of such security; or

(C) which the Commission, by rules or regulations or by order, shall exempt from the provisions of this subsection as not entered into for the purpose of, and not having the effect of, changing or influencing the control of the issuer or otherwise as not comprehended within the purposes of this subsection.

(e) It shall be unlawful for any person to make any untrue statement of a material fact or omit to state any material fact necessary in order to make the statements made, in the light of the circumstances under which they are made, not misleading, or to engage in any fraudulent, deceptive, or manipulative acts or practices, in connection with any tender offer or request or invitation for tenders, or any solicitation of security holders in opposition to or in favor of any such offer, request, or invitation. The Commission shall, for the purposes of this subsection, by rules and regulations define, and prescribe means reasonably designed to prevent, such acts and practices as are fraudulent, deceptive, or manipulative.

REGISTRATION AND REGULATION OF BROKERS AND DEALERS

SECTION 15. (a)(1) It shall be unlawful for any broker or dealer which is either a person other than a natural person or a natural person not associated with a broker or dealer which is a person other than a natural person (other than such a broker or dealer whose business is exclusively intrastate and who does not make use of any facility of a national securities exchange) to make use of the mails or any means of instrumentality of interstate commerce to effect any transactions in, or to induce or attempt to induce the purchase or sale of, any security (other than an exempted security or commercial paper, bankers' acceptances, or commercial bills) unless such broker or dealer is registered in accordance with . . . this section.

DIRECTORS, OFFICERS, AND PRINCIPAL STOCKHOLDERS

SECTION 16. (a) Every person who is directly or indirectly the beneficial owner of more than 10 per centum of any class of any equity security (other than an exempted security) which is registered pursuant to section 12 of this title, or who is a director or an officer of the issuer of such security, shall file, at the time of the registration of such security on a national securities exchange or by the effective date of a registration statement filed pursuant to section 12(g) of this title, or within ten days after he becomes such beneficial owner, director, or officer, a statement with the Commission (and, if such security is registered on a national securities exchange, also with the exchange) of the amount of all equity securities of such issuer of which he is the beneficial owner, and within ten days after the close of each calendar month thereafter, if there has been a change in such ownership during such month, shall file with the Commission (and if such security is registered on a national securities exchange, shall also file with the exchange) a statement indicating his ownership at the close of the calendar month and such changes in his ownership as have occurred during such calendar month.

(b) For the purpose of preventing the unfair use of information which may have been obtained by such beneficial owner, director, or officer by reason of his relationship to the issuer, any profit realized by him from any purchase and sale, or any sale and purchase, of any equity security of such issuer (other than an exempted security) within any period of less than six months, unless such security was acquired in good faith in connection with a debt previously contracted, shall inure to and be recoverable by the issuer, irrespective of any intention on the part of such beneficial owner, director, or officer in entering into such transaction of holding the security purchased or of not repurchasing the security sold for a period exceeding six months. Suit to recover such profit may be instituted at law or in equity in any court of competent jurisdiction by the issuer, or by the owner of any security of the issuer in the name and in behalf of the issuer if the issuer shall fail or refuse to bring such suit within sixty days after request or shall fail diligently to prosecute the same thereafter; but no such suit shall be brought more than two years after the date such profit was realized. This subsection shall not be construed to cover any transaction where such beneficial owner was not such both at the time of the purchase and sale, or the sale and purchase, of the security involved, or any transaction or transactions which the Commission by rules and regulations may exempt as not comprehended within the purpose of this subsection.

(c) It shall be unlawful for any such beneficial owner, director, or officer, directly or indirectly, to sell any equity security of such issuer (other than an exempted security), if the person selling the security or his principal (1) does not own the security sold, or (2) if owning the security, does not deliver it against such sale within twenty days thereafter, or does not within five days after such sale deposit it in the mails or other usual channels of transportation; but no person shall be deemed to have violated this subsection if he proves that notwithstanding the exercise of good faith he was unable to make such delivery or deposit within such time, or that to do so would cause undue inconvenience or expense.

LIABILITY FOR MISLEADING STATEMENTS

SECTION 18. (a) Any person who shall make or cause to be made any statement in any application, report, or document filed pursuant to this title or any rule or regulation thereunder or any undertaking contained in a registration statement as provided in subsection (d) of section 15 of this title, which statement was at the time and in the light of the circumstances under which it was made false or misleading with respect to any material fact, shall be liable to any person (not knowing that such statement was false or misleading) who, in reliance upon such statement, shall have purchased or sold a security at a price which was affected by such statement, for damages caused by such reliance, unless the person sued shall prove that he acted in good faith and had no knowledge that such statement was false or misleading. A person seeking to enforce such liability may sue at law or in equity in any court of competent jurisdiction. In any such suit the court may, in its discretion, require an undertaking for the payment of the costs of such suit, and assess reasonable costs, including reasonable attorneys' fees, against either party litigant.

(b) Every person who becomes liable to make payment under this section may recover contribution as in cases of contact from any person who, if joined in the original suit, would have been liable to make the same payment.

(c) No action shall be maintained to enforce any liability created under this section unless brought within one year after the discovery of the facts constituting the cause of action and within three years after such cause of action accrued.

LIABILITIES OF CONTROLLING PERSONS

SECTION 20. (a) Every person who, directly or indirectly, controls any person liable under any provision of this title or of any rule or regulation thereunder shall also be liable jointly and severally with and to the same extent as such controlled person to any person to whom such controlled person is liable, unless the controlling person acted in good faith and did not directly or indirectly induce the act or acts constituting the violation or cause of action.

(b) It shall be unlawful for any person, directly or indirectly, to do any act or thing which it would be unlawful for such person to do under the provisions of this title or any rule or regulation thereunder through or by means of any other person.

(c) It shall be unlawful for any director or officer of, or any owner of any securities issued by, any issuer required to file any document, report, or information under this title or any rule or regulation thereunder without just cause to hinder, delay, or obstruct the making or filing of any such document, report, or information.

RULES, REGULATIONS

SECTION 23. (a)(1) The Commission, the Board of Governors of the Federal Reserve System, and the other agencies enumerated in section 3(a)(34) of this title shall each have power to make such rules and regulations as may be necessary or appropriate to implement the provisions of this title for which they are responsible or for the execution of the functions vested in them by this title, . . .

PENALTIES

SECTION 32. (a) Any person who willfully violates any provision of this title . . . or any rule or regulation thereunder the violation of which is made unlawful or the observance of which is required under the terms of this title, or any person who willfully and knowingly makes, or causes to be made, any statement in any application, report, or document required to be filed under this title or any rule or regulation thereunder or any undertaking contained in a registration statement as provided in . . . this title or by any self-regulatory organization in connection with an application for membership or participation therein or to become associated with a member thereof, which statement was false or misleading with respect to any material fact, shall upon conviction be fined not more than $10,000, or imprisoned not more than five years, or both, except that when such person is an exchange, a fine not exceeding $500,000 may be imposed; but no person shall be subject to imprisonment under this section for the violation of any rule or regulation if he proves that he had no knowledge of such rule or regulation.

THE FEDERAL FOOD, DRUG AND COSMETIC ACT [EXCERPTS]

PROHIBITED ACTS

SECTION 301. The following acts and the causing thereof are hereby prohibited:

(a) The introduction or delivery for introduction into interstate commerce of any food, drug, device, or cosmetic that is adulterated or misbranded.

(b) The adulteration or misbranding of any food, drug, device, or cosmetic in interstate commerce.

(c) The receipt in interstate commerce of any food, drug, device, or cosmetic that is adulterated or misbranded, and the delivery or proffered delivery thereof for pay or otherwise.

PENALTIES

SECTION 303. (a) Any person who violates a provision of section 301 shall be imprisoned for not more than one year or fined not more than $1,000, or both.

(b) Notwithstanding the provisions of subsection (a) of this section, if any person commits such a violation after a conviction of him under this section has become final, or commits such a violation with the intent to defraud or mislead, such person shall be imprisoned for not more than three years or fined not more than $10,000, or both.

SEIZURE

SECTION 304. (a)(1) Any article of food, drug, or cosmetic that is adulterated or misbranded when introduced into or while in interstate commerce or while held for sale (whether or not the first sale) after shipment in interstate commerce, or which may not, under the provisions of section 404 or 505, be introduced into interstate commerce, shall be liable to be proceeded against while in interstate commerce, or at any time thereafter, on libel of information and condemned in any district court of the United States or United States court of a Territory within the jurisdiction of which the article is found: . . .

(b) The article, equipment, or other thing proceeded against shall be liable to seizure by process pursuant to the libel, and the procedure in cases under this section shall conform, as nearly as may be, to the procedure in admiralty; . . .

(d)(1) Any food, drug, device, or cosmetic condemned under this section shall, after entry of the decree, be disposed of by destruction or sale as the court may, in accordance with the provisions of this section, direct and the proceeds thereof, if sold, less the legal costs and charges, shall be paid into the Treasury of the United States; . . .

ADULTERATED FOOD

SECTION 402. A food shall be deemed to be adulterated—

(a)(1) If it bears or contains any poisonous or deleterious substance which may render it injurious to health; but in case the substance is not an added substance such food shall not be considered adulterated under this clause if the quantity of such substance in such food does not ordinarily render it injurious to health; or

(2)(A) if it bears or contains any added poisonous or added deleterious substance (other than one which is (i) a pesticide chemical in or on a raw agricultural commodity; (ii) a food additive; (iii) a color additive; or (iv) a new animal drug) which is unsafe . . . ;

(3) if it consists in whle or in part of any filthy, putrid, or decomposed substance, or if it is otherwise unfit for food; or (4) if it has been prepared, packed, or held under insanitary conditions whereby it may have become contaminated with filth, or whereby it may have been rendered injurious to health; or (5) if it is, in whole or in part, the product of a diseased animal or of an animal which had died otherwise than by slaughter; or (6) if its container is composed, in whole or in part, of any poisonous or deleterious substance which may render the contents injurious to health; or (7) if it has been intentionally subjected to radiation, unless the use of the radiation was in conformity with a regulation or exemption. . . .

ADULTERATED DRUGS AND DEVICES

SECTION 501. A drug or device shall be deemed to be adulterated—

(a)(1) If it consists in whole or in part of any filthy, putrid, or decomposed substance; or (2)(A) if it has been prepared, packed, or held under insanitary conditions whereby it may have been contaminated with filth, or whereby it may have been rendered injurious to health; or (B) if it is a drug and the methods used in, or the facilities or controls used for, its manufacture, processing, packing, or holding do not conform to or are not operated or administered in conformity with current good manufacturing practice to assure that such drug meets the requirements of this Act as to safety and has the identity and strength, and meets the quality and purity characteristics, which it purports or is represented to possess; or (3) if its container is composed, in whole or in part, of any poisonous or deleterious substance which may render the contents injurious to health; . . .

(b) If it purports to be or is represented as a drug the name of which is recognized in an official compendium, and its strength differs from, or its quality or purity falls below, the standards set forth in such compendium. . . .

(c) If it is not subject to the provisions of paragraph (b) of this section and its strength differs from, or its purity or quality falls below, that which it purports or is represented to possess.

(d) If it is a drug and any substance has been (1) mixed or packed therewith so as to reduce its quality or strength or (2) substituted wholly or in part therefor.

(e) If it is, or purports to be or is represented as, a device which is subject to a performance standard established under [the Act] unless such device is in all respects in conformity with such standard.

ADULTERATED COSMETICS

SECTION 601. A cosmetic shall be deemed to be adulterated—

(a) If it bears or contains any poisonous or deleterious substance which may render it injurious to users under the conditions of use prescribed in the labeling thereof, or, under such conditions of use as are customary or usual: *Provided,* That this provision shall not apply to coal-tar hair dye, the label of which bears the following legend conspicuously displayed thereon: "Caution—This product contains ingredients which may cause skin irritation on certain individuals and a preliminary test according to accompanying directions should first be made. This product must not be used for dyeing the eyelashes or eyebrows; to do so may cause blindness.", and the labeling of which bears adequate directions for such preliminary testing. For the purposes of this paragraph and paragraph (e) the term "hair dye" shall not include eyelash dyes or eyebrow dyes.

(b) If it consists in whole or in part of any filthy, putrid, or decomposed substance.

(c) If it has been prepared, packed, or held under insanitary conditions whereby it may have become contaminated with filth, or whereby it may have been rendered injurious to health.

(d) If its container is composed, in whole or in part, of any poisonous or deleterious substance which may render the contents injurious to health.

(e) If it is not a hair dye and it is, or it bears or contains, a color additive which is unsafe within the meaning of [the Act].

FACTORY INSPECTION

SECTION 504. (a) For purposes of enforcement of this Act, officers or employees duly designated by the Secretary, upon presenting appropriate credentials and a written notice to the owner, operator, or agent in charge, are authorized (1) to enter, at reasonable times, any factory, warehouse, or establishment in which food, drugs, devices, or cosmetics are manufactured, processed, packed, or held, for introduction into interstate commerce or after such introduction, or to enter any vehicle, being used to transport or hold such food, drugs, devices, or cosmetics in interstate commerce; and (2) to inspect, at reasonable times and within reasonable limits and in a reasonable manner, such factory, warehouse, establishment, or vehicle and all pertinent equipment, finished and unfinished materials, containers, and labeling therein. . . . A separate notice shall be given for each such inspection, but a notice shall not be required for each entry made during the period covered by the inspection. Each such inspection shall be commenced and completed with reasonable promptness.

J THE CONSUMER CREDIT PROTECTION ACT [EXCERPTS]

FINDINGS AND PURPOSE

SECTION 301. (a) The Congress finds:

(1) The unrestricted garnishment of compensation due for personal services encourages the making of predatory extensions of credit. Such extensions of credit divert money into excessive credit payments and thereby hinder the production and flow of goods in interstate commerce.

(2) The application of garnishment as a creditors' remedy frequently results in loss of employment by the debtor, and the resulting disruption of employment, production, and consumption constitutes a substantial burden on interstate commerce.

(3) The great disparities among the laws of the several States relating to garnishment have, in effect, destroyed the uniformity of the bankruptcy laws and frustrated the purposes thereof in many areas of the country.

(b) On the basis of the findings stated in subsection (a) of this section, the Congress determines that the provisions of this title are necessary and proper for the purpose of carrying into execution the powers of the Congress to regulate commerce and to establish uniform bankruptcy laws.

RESTRICTION ON GARNISHMENT

SECTION 303. (a) Except as [otherwise] provided . . . , the maximum part of the aggregate disposable earnings of an individual for any workweek which is subjected to garnishment may not exceed

(1) 25 per centum of his disposable earnings for that week, or

(2) the amount by which his disposable earnings for that week exceed thirty times the Federal minimum hourly wage prescribed by section 6(a)(1) of the Fair Labor Standards Act of 1938 in effect at the time the earnings are payable, whichever is less. In the case of earnings for any pay period other than a week, the Secretary of Labor shall by regulation prescribe a multiple of the Federal minimum hourly wage equivalent in effect to that set forth in paragraph (2).

(b)(1) The restrictions of subsection (a) do not apply in the case of

(A) any order for the support of any person issued by a court of competent jurisdiction or in accordance with an administrative procedure, which is established by State law, which affords substantial due process, and which is subject to judicial review.

(B) any order of any court of the United States having jurisdiction over cases under chapter 13 of title 11 of the United States Code.

(C) any debt due for any State or Federal tax.

(2) The maximum part of the aggregate disposable earnings of an individual for any workweek which is subject to garnishment to enforce any order for the support of any person shall not exceed

(A) where such individual is supporting his spouse or dependent child (other than a spouse or child with respect to whose support such order is issued), 50 per centum of such individual's disposable earnings for that week; and

(B) where such individual is not supporting such a spouse or dependent child described in clause (A), 60 per centum of such individual's disposable earnings for that week; except that, with respect to the disposable earnings of any individual for any workweek, the 50 per centum specified in clause (A) shall be deemed to be 55 per centum and the 60 per centum specified in clause (B) shall be deemed to be 65 per centum, if and to the extent that such earnings are subject to garnishment to enforce a support order with respect to a period which is prior to the twelve-week period which ends with the beginning of such workweek.

(c) No court of the United States or any State, and no State (or officer or agency thereof), may make, execute, or enforce any order or process in violation of this section.

RESTRICTION ON DISCHARGE FROM EMPLOYMENT
BY REASON OF GARNISHMENT

SECTION 304. (a) No employer may discharge any employee by reason of the fact that his earnings have been subjected to garnishment for any one indebtedness.

(b) Whoever willfully violates subsection (a) of this section shall be fined not more than $1,000, or imprisoned not more than one year, or both.

 THE BANKRUPTCY REFORM ACT OF 1978 [EXCERPTS]

GENERAL PROVISIONS

VOLUNTARY CASES

SECTION 301. A voluntary case under a chapter of this title is commenced by the filing with the bankruptcy court of a petition under such chapter by an entity that may be a debtor under such chapter. The commencement of a voluntary case under a chapter of this title constitutes an order for relief under such chapter.

INVOLUNTARY CASES

SECTION 303. (a) An involuntary case may be commenced only under chapter 7 or 11 of this title, and only against a person, except a farmer or a corporation that is not a moneyed, business, or commercial corporation, that may be a debtor under the chapter under which such case is commenced.

(b) An involuntary case is commenced by the filing with the bankruptcy court of a petition under chapter 7 or 11 of this title—

(1) by three or more entities, each of which is either a holder of a claim against such person that is not contingent as to liability or an indenture trustee representing such a holder, if such claims aggregate at least $5,000 more than the value of any lien on property of the debtor securing such claims held by the holders of such claims;

(2) if there are fewer than 12 such holders . . . by one or more of such holders that hold in the aggregate at least $5,000 of such claims; . . .

(f) . . . [E]xcept to the extent that the court orders otherwise, and until an order for relief in the case, any business of the debtor may continue to operate, and the debtor may continue to use, acquire, or dispose of property as if an involuntary case concerning the debtor had not been commenced. . . .

(h) If the petition is not timely controverted, the court shall order relief against the debtor in an involuntary case under the chapter under which the petition was filed. Otherwise, after trial, the court shall order relief against the debtor in an involuntary case under the chapter under which the petition was filed, only if—

(1) the debtor is generally not paying such debtor's debts as such debts become due; or

(2) within 120 days before the date of the filing of the petition, a custodian, other than a trustee, receiver, or agent appointed or authorized to take charge of less than substantially all of the property of the debtor for the purpose of enforcing a lien against such property, was appointed or took possession.

MEETINGS OF CREDITORS AND EQUITY SECURITY HOLDERS

SECTION 341. (a) Within a reasonable time after the order for relief in a case under this title, there shall be a meeting of creditors.

(b) The court may order a meeting of any equity security holders.

(c) The court may not preside at, and may not attend, any meeting under this section.

EXAMINATION OF THE DEBTOR

SECTION 343. The debtor shall appear and submit to examination under oath at the meeting of creditors under section 341(a) of this title. Creditors, any indenture trustee, or any trustee or examiner in the case may examiner the debtor.

AUTOMATIC STAY

SECTION 362. (a) Except as provided in subsection (b) of this section, a petition filed under . . . this title, operates as a stay, applicable to all entities, of—

(1) the commencement or continuation, including the issuance or employment of process, of a judicial, administrative, or other proceeding against the debtor that was or could have been commenced before the commencement of the case under this title, or to recover a claim against the debtor that arose before the commencement of the case under this title;

(2) the enforcement, against the debtor or against property of the estate, of a judgment obtained before the commencement of the case under this title;

(3) any act to obtain possession of property of the estate or of property from the estate;

(4) any act to create, perfect, or enforce any lien against property of the estate;

(5) any act to create, perfect, or enforce against property of the debtor any lien to the extent that such lien secures a claim that arose before the commencement of the case under this title;

(6) any act to collect, assess, or recover a claim against the debtor that arose before the commencement of the case under this title;

(7) the setoff of any debt owing to the debtor that arose before the commencement of the case under this title against any claim against the debtor; and

(8) the commencement or continuation of a proceeding before the United States Tax Court concerning the debtor.

EXECUTORY CONTRACTS AND UNEXPIRED LEASES

SECTION 365. (a) Except as provided in . . . this title . . . , the trustee, subject to the court's approval, may assume or reject any executory contract or unexpired lease of the debtor.

(b)(1) If there has been a default in an executory contract or unexpired lease of the debtor, the trustee may not assume such contract or lease unless, at the time of assumption of such contract or lease, the trustee—

(A) cures, or provides adequate assurance that the trustee will promptly cure, such default;

(B) compensates, or provides adequate assurance that the trustee will promptly compensate, a party other than the debtor to such contract or lease, for any actual pecuniary loss to such party resulting from such default; and

(C) provides adequate assurance of future performance under such contract or lease.

PRIORITIES

SECTION 507. (a) The following expenses and claims have priority in the following order:

(1) First, administrative expenses allowed under . . . this title, and any fees and charges assessed against the estate. . . .

(2) Second, unsecured claims allowed under . . . this title.

(3) Third, allowed unsecured claims for wages, salaries, or commissions, including vacation, severance and sick leave pay—

(A) earned by an individual within 90 days before the date of the filing of the petition or the date of the cessation of the debtor's business, whichever occurs first; but only

(B) to the extent of $2,000 for each such individual.

(4) Fourth, allowed unsecured claims for contributions to employee benefit plans—

(A) arising from services rendered within 180 days before the date of the filing of the petition or the date of the cessation of the debtor's business, whichever occurs first; but only

(B) for each such plan, to the extent of—

(i) the number of employees covered by such plan multiplied by $2,000; less

(ii) the aggregate amount paid to such employees under paragraph (3) of this subsection, plus the aggregate amount paid by the estate on behalf of such employees to any other employee benefit plan.

(5) Fifth, allowed unsecured claims of individuals, to the extent of $900 for each such individual, arising from the deposit, before the commencement of the case, of money in connection with the purchase, lease, or rental of property, or the purchase of services, for the personal, family, or household use of such individuals, that were not delivered or provided.

(6) Sixth, allowed unsecured claims of governmental units, to the extent that such claims are for—[taxes] . . .

(b) If the trustee, under this title, provides adequate protection of the interest of a holder of a claim secured by a lien on property of the debtor and if, notwithstanding such protection, such creditor has a claim allowable under subsection (a)(1) of this section . . .·, then such creditor's claim under such subsection shall have priority over every other claim allowable under such subsection.

EFFECT OF DISCHARGE

SECTION 524. (a) A discharge in a case under this title—

(1) voids any judgment at any time obtained, to the extent that such judgment is a determination of the personal liability of the debtor with respect to any debt discharged under . . . this title, whether or not discharge of such debt is waived;

(2) operates as an injunction against the commencement or continuation of an action, the employment of process, or any act, to collect, recover or offset any such debt as a personal liability of the debtor, or from property of the debtor, whether or not discharge of such debt is waived; and

(3) operates as an injunction against the commencement or continuation of an action, the employment of process, or any act, to collect or recover from, or offset against, property of the debtor . . . that is acquired after the commencement of the case, . . .

CHAPTER 7—LIQUIDATION

DISCHARGE

SECTION 727. (a) The court shall grant the debtor a discharge, unless—

(1) the debtor is not an individual;

(2) the debtor, with intent to hinder, delay, or defraud a creditor or an officer of the estate charged with custody of property under this title, has transferred, removed, destroyed, mutilated, or concealed, or has permitted to be transferred, removed, destroyed, mutilated, or concealed—

(A) property of the debtor, within one year before the date of the filing of the petition; or

(B) property of the estate, after the date of the filing of the petition;

(3) the debtor has concealed, destroyed, mutilated, falsified, or failed to keep or preserve any recorded information, including books, documents, records, and papers, from which the debtor's financial condition or business transactions might be ascertained, unless such act or failure to act was justified under all of the circumstances of the case;

(4) the debtor knowingly and fraudulently, in or in connection with the case—

(A) made a false oath or account;

(B) presented or used a false claim;

(C) gave, offered, received, or attempted to obtain money, property, or advantage, or a promise of money, property, or advantage, for acting or forbearing to act; or

(D) withheld from an officer of the estate entitled to possession under this title, any recorded information, including books, documents, records, and papers, relating to the debtor's property or financial affairs;

(5) the debtor has failed to explain satisfactorily, before determination of denial of discharge under this paragraph, any loss of assets or deficiency of assets to meet the debtor's liabilities;

(6) the debtor has refused, in the case—

(A) to obey any lawful order of the court, other than an order to respond to a material question or to testify;

(B) on the ground of privilege against self-incrimination, to respond to a material question approved by the court or to testify, after the debtor has been granted immunity with respect to the matter concerning which such privilege was invoked; or

(C) on a ground other than the properly invoked privilege against self-incrimination, to respond to a material question approved by the court or to testify;

(7) the debtor has committed any act specified in paragraph (2), (3), (4), (5), or (6) of this subsection, on or within one year before the date of the filing of the petition, or during the case, in connection with another case concerning an insider;

(8) the debtor has been granted a discharge under . . . the Bankruptcy Act, in a case commenced within six years before the date of the filing of the petition; . . .

(b) Except as provided in . . . this title, a discharge under subsection (a) of this section discharges the debtor from all debts that arose before the date of the order for relief under this chapter, . . .

CHAPTER 11—REORGANIZATION

WHO MAY FILE A PLAN

SECTION 1121. (a) The debtor may file a plan with a petition commencing a voluntary case, or at any time in a voluntary case or an involuntary case.

(b) Except as otherwise provided in this section, only the debtor may file a plan until after 120 days after the date of the order for relief under this chapter.

(c) Any party in interest, including the debtor, the trustee, a creditors' committee, an equity security holders' committee, a creditor, an equity security holder, or any indenture trustee, may file a plan if and only if—

(1) a trustee has been appointed under this chapter;

(2) the debtor has not filed a plan before 120 days after the date of the order for relief under this chapter; or

(3) the debtor has not filed a plan that has been accepted, before 180 days after the date of the order for relief under this chapter, by each class the claims or interests of which are impaired under the plan.

(d) On request of a party in interest and after notice and a hearing, the court may for cause reduce or increase the 120-day period or the 180-day period referred to in this section.

CONFIRMATION HEARING

SECTION 1128. (a) After notice, the court shall hold a hearing on confirmation of a plan.

(b) A party in interest may object to confirmation of a plan.

EFFECT OF CONFIRMATION

SECTION 1141. (a) Except as provided in subsections (d)(2) and (d)(3) of this section, the provisions of a confirmed plan bind the debtor, any entity issuing securities under the plan, any entity acquiring property under the plan, and any creditor or equity security holder of, or general partner in, the debtor, whether or not the claim or interest of such creditor, equity security holder, or general partner is impaired under the plan and whether or not such creditor, equity security holder, or general partner has accepted the plan.

(b) Except as otherwise provided in the plan or the order confirming the plan, the confirmation of a plan vests all of the property of the estate in the debtor.

(c) After confirmation of a plan, the property dealt with by the plan is free and clear of all claims and interests of creditors, of equity security holders, and of general partners in the debtor, except as otherwise provided in the plan or in the order confirming the plan.

(d)(1) Except as otherwise provided in this subsection, in the plan, or in the order confirming the plan, the confirmation of a plan—

(A) discharges the debtor from any debt that arose before the date of such confirmation, . . .

(B) terminates all rights and interests of equity security holders and general partners provided for by the plan.

(2) The confirmation of a plan does not discharge an individual debtor from any debt excepted from discharge under . . . this title.

(3) The confirmation of a plan does not discharge a debtor if—

(A) the plan provides for the liquidation of all or substantially all of the property of the estate;

(B) the debtor does not engage in business after consummation of the plan; and

(C) the debtor would be denied a discharge under . . . this title if the case were a case under chapter 7 of this title.

(4) The court may approve a written waiver of discharge executed by the debtor after the order for relief under this chapter.

DISTRIBUTION

SECTION 1143. If a plan requires presentment or surrender of a security or the performance of any other act as a condition to participation in distribution under the plan, such action shall be taken not later than five years after the date of the entry of the order of confirmation. Any entity that has not within such time presented or surrendered such entity's security or taken any such other action that the plan requires may not participate in distribution under the plan.

CHAPTER 13—ADJUSTMENT OF DEBTS OF AN INDIVIDUAL WITH REGULAR INCOME

FILING OF PLAN

SECTION 1321. The debtor shall file a plan.

CONTENTS OF PLAN

SECTION 1322. (a) The plan shall—

(1) provide for the submission of all or such portion of future earnings or other future income of the debtor to the supervision and control of the trustee as is necessary for the execution of the plan;

(2) provide for the full payment, in deferred cash payments of all claims entitled to priority under section 507 of this title, unless the holder of a particular claim agrees to a different treatment of such claim; and

(3) if the plan classifies claims, provide the same treatment for each claim within a particular class. . . .

(c) The plan may not provide for payments over a period that is longer than three years, unless the court, for cause, approves a longer period, but the court may not approve a period that is longer than five years.

CONFIRMATION HEARING

SECTION 1324. After notice, the court shall hold a hearing on the confirmation of the plan. A party in interest may object to the confirmation of the plan.

CONFIRMATION OF PLAN

SECTION 1325. (a) The court shall confirm a plan if—

(1) the plan complies with the provisions of this chapter and with other applicable provisions of this title;

(2) any fee, charge, or amount required . . . to be paid before confirmation, has been paid;

(3) the plan has been proposed in good faith and not by any means forbidden by law;

(4) the value, as of the effective date of the plan, of property to be distributed under the plan on account of each allowed unsecured claim is not less than the amount that would be paid on such claim if the estate of the debtor were liquidated under chapter 7 of this title on such date;

(5) with respect to each allowed secured claim provided for by the plan—

(A) the holder of such claim has accepted the plan;

(B)(i) the plan provides that the holder of such claim retain the lien securing such claim; and

(ii) the value, as of the effective date of the plan, of property to be distributed under the plan on account of such claim is not less than the allowed amount of such claim; or

(C) the debtor surrenders the property securing such claim to such holder; and

(6) the debtor will be able to make all payments under the plan and to comply with the plan.

(b) After confirmation of a plan, the court may order any entity from whom the debtor receives income to pay all or any part of such income to the trustee.

L THE LANHAM ACT [EXCERPTS]

FALSE DESIGNATIONS OF ORIGIN AND FALSE DESCRIPTIONS FORBIDDEN

SECTION 1125. (a) Any person who shall affix, apply, or annex, or use in connection with any goods or services, or any container or containers for goods, a false designation of origin, or any false description or representation, including words or other symbols tending falsely to describe or represent the same, and shall cause such goods or services to enter into commerce, and any person who shall with knowledge of the falsity of such designation of origin or description or representation cause or procure the same to be transported or used in commerce or deliver the same to any carrier to be transported or used, shall be liable to a civil action by any person doing business in the locality falsely indicated as that of origin or in the region in which said locality is situated, or by any person who believes that he is or is likely to be damaged by the use of any such false description or representation.

(b) Any goods marked or labeled in contravention of the provisions of this section shall not be imported into the United States or admitted to entry at any customhouse of the United States. The owner, importer, or consignee of goods refused entry at any customhouse under this section may have any recourse by protest or appeal that is given under the customs revenue laws or may have the remedy given by this chapter in cases involving goods refused entry or seized.

M THE TRADEMARK ACT OF 1946 AS AMENDED [EXCERPTS]

REGISTRATION

SECTION 1. The owner of a trademark used in commerce may register his trademark under this chapter on the principal register established:

(a) By filing in the Patent and Trademark Office—

(1) a written application, in such form as may be prescribed by the Commissioner, verified by the applicant, or by a member of the firm or an officer of the corporation or association applying, specifying applicant's domicile and citizenship, the date of applicant's first use of the mark, the date of applicant's first use of the mark in commerce,

the goods in connection with which the mark is used and the mode or manner in which the mark is used in connection with such goods, and including a statement to the effect that the person making the verification believes himself, or the firm, corporation, or association in whose behalf he makes the verification, to be the owner of the mark sought to be registered, that the mark is in use in commerce, and that no other person, firm, corporation, or association, to the best of his knowledge and belief, has the right to use such mark in commerce either in the identical form thereof or in such near resemblance thereto as to be likely, when applied to the goods of such other person, to cause confusion, or to cause mistake, or to deceive: *Provided,* That in the case of every application claiming concurrent use the applicant shall state exceptions to his claim of exclusive use, in which he shall specify, to the extent of his knowledge, any concurrent use by others, the goods in connection with which and the areas in which each concurrent use exists, the periods of each use, and the goods and area for which the applicant desires registration;

(2) a drawing of the mark; and

(3) such number of specimens or facsimiles of the mark as actually used as may be required by the Commissioner.

(b) By paying into the Patent and Trademark Office the filing fee.

(c) By complying with such rules or regulations, not inconsistent with law, as may be prescribed by the Commissioner.

SERVICE MARKS REGISTRABLE

SECTION 3. Subject to the provisions relating to the registration of trademarks, so far as they are applicable, service marks used in commerce shall be registrable, in the same manner and with the same effect as are trademarks, and when registered they shall be entitled to the protection provided in this chapter in the case of trademarks, except when used so as to represent falsely that the owner thereof makes or sells the goods on which such mark is used. The Commissioner may establish a separate register for such service marks. Applications and procedure under this section shall conform as nearly as practicable to those prescribed for the registration of trademarks.

COLLECTIVE MARKS AND CERTIFICATION MARKS REGISTRABLE

SECTION 4. Subject to the provisions relating to the registration of trademarks, so far as they are applicable, collective and certification marks, including indications of regional origin used in commerce, shall be registrable under this chapter, in the same manner and with the same effect as are trademarks, by persons, and nations, States, municipalities, and the like, exercising legitimate control over the use of the marks sought to be registered, even though not possessing an industrial or commercial establishment, and when registered they shall be entitled to the protection provided in this chapter in the case of trademarks, except when used so as to represent falsely that the owner or a user thereof makes or sells the goods or performs the services on or in connection with which such mark is used. The Commissioner may establish a separate register for such collective marks and certification marks. Applications and procedure under this section shall conform as nearly as practicable to those prescribed for the registration of trademarks.

CERTIFICATE AS PRIMA FACIE EVIDENCE

SECTION 7. (b) A certificate of registration of a mark upon the principal register provided by this chapter shall be *prima facie* evidence of the validity of the registration, registrant's ownership of the mark, and of registrant's exclusive right to use the mark in commerce in connection with the goods or services specified in the certificate, subject to any conditions and limitations stated therein.

REGISTRATION AS CONSTRUCTIVE NOTICE OF CLAIM OF OWNERSHIP

SECTION 22. Registration of a mark on the principal register provided by this chapter or under the Act of March 3, 1881, or the Act of February 20, 1905, shall be consecutive notice of the registrant's claim of ownership thereof.

NOTICE OF REGISTRATION; DISPLAY WITH MARK; RECOVERY OF PROFITS AND DAMAGES IN INFRINGEMENT SUIT

SECTION 29. Notwithstanding the provisions of section [22] of this title, a registrant of a mark registered in the Patent and Trademark Office, may give notice that his mark is registered by displaying with the mark as used the words "Registered in U.S. Patent and Trademark Office" of "Reg. U.S. Pat. & Tm. Off." or the letter R enclosed within a circle, thus ®; and in any suit for infringement under this chapter by such a registrant failing to give such notice of registration, no profits and no damages shall be recovered under the provisions of this chapter unless the defendant had actual notice of the registration.

REMEDIES: INFRINGEMENT

SECTION 32. (1) Any person who shall, without the consent of the registrant—

(a) use in commerce any reproduction, counterfeit, copy, or colorable imitation of a registered mark in connection with the sale, offering for sale, distribution, or advertising of any goods or services on or in connection with which such use is likely to cause confusion, or to cause mistake, or to deceive; or

(b) reproduce, counterfeit, copy, or colorably imitate a registered mark and apply such reproduction, counterfeit, copy, or colorable imitation to labels, signs, prints, packages, wrappers, receptacles or advertisements intended to be used in commerce upon or in connection with the sale, offering for sale, distribution, or advertising of goods or services on or in connection with which such use is likely to cause confusion, or to cause mistake, or to deceive.

[S]hall be liable in a civil action by the registrant for the remedies hereinafter provided. Under subsection (b) of this section, the registrant shall not be entitled to recover profits or damages unless the acts have been committed with knowledge that such imitation is intended to be used to cause confusion, or to cause mistake, or to deceive.

RECOVERY FOR VIOLATION OF RIGHTS; PROFITS, DAMAGES AND COSTS; ATTORNEY FEES

SECTION 35. When a violation of any right of the registrant of a mark registered in the Patent and Trademark Office shall have been established in any civil action arising under this chapter, the plaintiff shall be entitled, subject to the provisions of sections 1111 and 1114 of this title, and subject to the principles of equity, to recover (1) defendant's profits, (2) any damages sustained by the plaintiff, and (3) the costs of the action. The court shall assess such profits and damages or cause the same to be assessed under its direction. In assessing profits the plaintiff shall be required to prove defendant's sales only; defendant must prove all elements of cost or deduction claimed. In assessing damages the court may enter judgment, according to the circumstances of the case, for any sum above the amount found as actual damages, but not exceeding three times such amount. If the court shall find that the amount of the recovery based on profits is either inadequate or excessive the court may in its discretion enter judgment for such sum as the court shall find to be just, according to the circumstances of the case. Such sum in either of the above circumstances shall constitute compensation and not a penalty. The court in exceptional cases may award reasonable attorney fees to the prevailing party.

N THE COPYRIGHT ACT OF 1976 [EXCERPTS]

SUBJECT MATTER OF COPYRIGHT: IN GENERAL

SECTION 102. (a) Copyright protection subsists, in accordance with this title, in original works of authorship fixed in any tangible medium of expression, now known or later developed, from which they can be perceived, reproduced, or otherwise communicated, either directly or with the aid of a machine or device. Works of authorship include the following categories:

(1) literary works;
(2) musical works, including any accompanying words;
(3) dramatic works, including any accompanying music;
(4) pantomimes and choreographic works;
(5) pictorial, graphic, and sculptural works;
(6) motion pictures and other audiovisual works; and
(7) sound recordings.

(b) In no case does copyright protection for an original work of authorship extend to any idea, procedure, process, system, method of operation, concept, principle, or discovery, regardless of the form in which it is described, explained, illustrated, or embodied in such work.

SUBJECT MATTER OF COPYRIGHT: COMPILATIONS AND DERIVATIVE WORKS

SECTION 103. (a) The subject matter of copyright as specified by section 102 includes compilations and derivative works, but protection for a work employing preexisting material in which copyright subsists does not extend to any part of the work in which such material has been used unlawfully.

EXCLUSIVE RIGHTS IN COPYRIGHTED WORKS

SECTION 106. [T]he owner of copyright under this title has the exclusive rights to do and to authorize any of the following:

(1) to reproduce the copyrighted work in copies or phonorecords;

(2) to prepare derivative works based upon the copyrighted work;

(3) to distribute copies or phonorecords of the copyrighted work to the public by sale or other transfer of ownership, or by rental, lease, or lending;

(4) in the case of literary, musical, dramatic, and choreographic works, pantomimes, and motion pictures and other audiovisual works, to perform the copyrighted work publicly; and

(5) in the case of literary, musical, dramatic, and choreographic works, pantomimes, and pictorial, graphic, or sculptural works, including the individual images of a motion picture or other audiovisual work, to display the copyrighted work publicly.

LIMITATIONS ON EXCLUSIVE RIGHTS: FAIR USE

SECTION 107. Notwithstanding the provisions of section 106, the fair use of a copyrighted work, including such use by reproduction in copies or phonorecords or by any other means specified by that section, for purposes such as criticism, comment, news reporting, teaching (including multiple copies for classroom use), scholarship, or research, is not an infringement of copyright. In determining whether the use made of a work in any particular case is a fair use the factors to be considered shall include—

(1) the purpose and character of the use, including whether such use is of a commercial nature or is for nonprofit educational purposes;

(2) the nature of the copyrighted work;

(3) the amount and substantiality of the portion used in relation to the copyrighted work as a whole; and

(4) the effect of the use upon the potential market for or value of the copyrighted work.

COPYRIGHT REGISTRATION IN GENERAL

SECTION 408. (2) At any time during the subsistence of copyright in any published or unpublished work, the owner of copyright or of any exclusive right in the work may obtain registration of the copyright claim by delivering to the Copyright Office the deposit specified by this section, together with the application and fee specified by [this title]. . . . [s]uch registration is not a condition of copyright protection.

INFRINGEMENT OF COPYRIGHT

SECTION 501. (a) Anyone who violates any of the exclusive rights of the copyright owner . . . is an infringer of the copyright.

(b) The legal or beneficial owner of an exclusive right under a copyright is entitled . . . to institute an action for any infringement of that particular right committed while he or she is the owner of it.

REMEDIES FOR INFRINGEMENT: DAMAGES AND PROFITS

SECTION 504. (a) In General.   Except as otherwise provided by this title, an infringer of copyright is liable for either—

(1) the copyright owner's actual damages and any additional profits of the infringer, as provided by subsection (b); or

(2) statutory damages, as provided by subsection (c).

(b) Actual Damages and Profits.—The copyright owner is entitled to recover the actual damages suffered by him or her as a result of the infringement, and any profits of the infringer that are attributable to the infringement and are not taken into account in computing the actual damages. In establishing the infringer's profits, the copyright owner is required to present proof only of the infringer's gross revenue, and the infringer is required to prove his or her deductible expenses and the elements of profit attributable to factors other than the copyrighted work.

(c) Statutory Damages.—(1) Except as provided by clause (2) of this subsection, the copyright owner may elect, at any time before final judgment is rendered, to recover, instead of actual damages and profits, an award of statutory damages for all infringements involved in the action, with respect to any one work, for which any one infringer is liable individually, or for which any two or more infringers are liable jointly and severally, in a sum of not less than $250 or more than $10,000 as the court considers just. For the purposes of this subsection, all the parts of a compilation or derivative work constitute one work.

(2) In a case where the copyright owner sustains the burden of proving, and the court finds, that infringement was committed willfully, the court in its discretion may increase the award of statutory damages to a sum of not more than $50,000.

CRIMINAL OFFENSES

SECTION 506. (a) Criminal infringement.—Any person who infringes a copyright willfully and for purposes of commercial advantage or private financial gain shall be fined not more than $10,000 or imprisoned for not more than one year, or both: *Provided, however,* That any person who infringes willfully and for purposes of commercial advantage or private financial gain the copyright in a sound recording afforded by subsections (1), (2), or (3) of section 106 or the copyright in a motion picture afforded by subsections (1), (3), or (4) of section 106 shall be fined not more that $25,000 or imprisoned for not more than one year, or both, for the first such offense and shall be fined not more than $50,000 or imprisoned for not more than two years, or both, for any subsequent offense.

O THE PATENT ACT [EXCERPTS]

INVENTIONS PATENTABLE

SECTION 101. Whoever invents or discovers any new and useful process, machine, manufacture, or composition of matter, or any new and useful improvement thereof, may obtain a patent therefor, subject to the conditions and requirements of this title.

CONDITIONS FOR PATENTABILITY; NOVELTY AND LOSS
OF RIGHT TO PATENT

SECTION 102. A person shall be entitled to a patent unless—

(a) the invention was known or used by others in this country, or patented or described in a printed publication in this or a foreign country, before the invention thereof by the applicant for patent, or

(b) the invention was patented or described in a printed publication in this or a foreign country or in public use or on sale in this country, more than one year prior to the date of the application for patent in the United States, or

(c) he has abandoned the invention, or

(d) the invention was first patented or caused to be patented, or was the subject of an inventor's certificate, by the applicant or his legal representatives or assigns in a foreign country prior to the date of the application for patent in this country on an application for patent or inventor's certificate filed more than twelve months before the filing of the application in the United States, or

(e) the invention was described in a patent granted on an application for patent by another filed in the United States before the invention thereof by the applicant for patent, or on an international application by another who has fulfilled the requirements of paragraphs . . . of this title before the invention thereof by the applicant for patent, or

(f) he did not himself invent the subject matter sought to be patented, or

(g) before the applicant's invention thereof the invention was made in this country by another who had not abandoned, suppressed, or concealed it. In determining priority of invention there shall be considered not only the respective dates of conception and reduction to practice of the invention, but also the reasonable diligence of one who was first to conceive and last to reduce to practice, from a time prior to conception by the other.

CONDITIONS FOR PATENTABILITY; NON-OBVIOUS
SUBJECT MATTER

SECTION 103. A patent may not be obtained though the invention is not identically disclosed or described as set forth in section 102 of this title, if the differences between the subject matter sought to be patented and the prior art are such that the subject matter as a whole would have been obvious at the time the invention was made to a person having ordinary skill in the art to which said subject matter pertains. Patentability shall not be negatived by the manner in which the invention was made.

APPLICATION FOR PATENT

SECTION 111. Application for patent shall be made by the inventor, except as otherwise provided in this title, in writing to the Commissioner. Such application shall include: (1) a specification as prescribed by . . . this title; (2) a drawing as prescribed by . . . this title; and (3) an oath by the applicant as prescribed by . . . this title. The application must be signed by the applicant and accompanied by the fee required by law.

INFRINGEMENT OF PATENT

SECTION 271. (a) Except as otherwise provided in this title, whoever without authority makes, uses or sells any patented invention, within the United States during the term of the patent therefor, infringes the patent.

(b) Whoever actively induces infringement of a patent shall be liable as an infringer.

(c) Whoever sells a component of a patented machine, manufacture, combination or composition, or a material or apparatus for use in practicing a patented process, constituting a material part of the invention, knowing the same to be especially made or especially adapted for use in an infringement of such patent, and not a staple article or commodity of commerce suitable for substantial noninfringing use, shall be liable as a contributory infringer.

REMEDY FOR INFRINGEMENT OF PATENT

SECTION 281. A patentee shall have remedy by civil action for infringement of his patent.

DAMAGES

SECTION 284. Upon finding for the claimant the court shall award the claimant damages adequate to compensate for the infringement, but in no event less than a reasonable royalty for the use made of the invention by the infringer, together with interest and costs as fixed by the court.

When the damages are not found by a jury, the court shall assess them. In either event the court may increase the damages up to three times the amount found or assessed.

P THE FOREIGN CORRUPT PRACTICES ACT OF 1977 [EXCERPTS]

FOREIGN CORRUPT PRACTICES BY DOMESTIC CONCERNS

SECTION 104. (a) It shall be unlawful for any domestic concern, other than an issuer which is subject to section 30A of the Securities Exchange Act of 1934, or any officer, director, employee, or agent or such domestic concern or any stockholder thereof acting on behalf of such domestic concern, to make use of the mails or any means or instrumentality of interstate commerce corruptly in furtherance of an offer, payment, promise to pay, or authorization of the payment of any money, or offer, gift, promise to give, or authorization of the giving of anything of value to—

(1) any foreign official for purposes of—

(A) influencing any act or decision of such foreign official in his official capacity, including a decision to fail to perform his official functions; or

(B) inducing such foreign official to use his influence with a foreign government or instrumentality thereof to affect or influence any act or decision of such government or instrumentality, in order to assist such domestic concern in obtaining or retaining business for or with, or directing business to any person;

(2) any foreign political party or official thereof or any candidate for foreign political office for purposes of—

(A) influencing any act or decision of such party, official, or candidate in its or his official capacity, including a decision to fail to perform its or his official functions; or

(B) inducing such party, official, or candidate to use its or his influence with a foreign government or instrumentality thereof to affect or influence any act or decision of such government or instrumentality, in order to assist such domestic concern in obtaining or retaining business for or with, or directing business to, any person; or

(3) any person, while knowing or having reason to know that all or a portion of such money or thing of value will be offered, given, or promised, directly or indirectly, to any foreign official, to any foreign political party or official thereof, or to any candidate for foreign political office, for purposes of—

(A) influencing any act or decision of such foreign official, political party, party official, or candidate in his or its official capacity, including a decision to fail to perform his or its official functions; or

(B) inducing such foreign official, political party, party official, or candidate to use his or its influence with a foreign government or instrumentality thereof to affect or influence any act or decision of such government or instrumentality, in order to assist such domestic concern in obtaining or retaining business for or with, or directing business to, any person.

(b)(1)(A) Except as provided in subparagraph (B), any domestic concern which violates subsection (a) shall, upon conviction, be fined not more than $1,000,000.

(B) Any individual who is a domestic concern and who willfully violates subsection (a) shall, upon conviction, be fined not more than $10,000, or imprisoned not more than five years, or both.

(2) Any officer or director of a domestic concern, or stockholder acting on behalf of such domestic concern, who willfully violates subsection (a) shall, upon conviction, be fined not more than $10,000, or imprisoned not more than five years, or both.

(3) Whenever a domestic concern is found to have violated subsection (a) of this section, any employee or agent of such domestic concern who is a United States citizen, national, or resident or is otherwise subject to the jurisdiction of the United States (other than an officer, director, or stockholder acting on behalf of such domestic concern), and who willfully carried out the act or practice constituting such violation shall, upon conviction, be fined not more than $10,000, or imprisoned not more than five years, or both.

(4) Whenever a fine is imposed under paragraph (2) or (3) of this subsection upon any officer, director, stockholder, employee, or agent of a domestic concern, such fine shall not be paid, directly or indirectly, by such domestic concern.

(c) Whenever it appears to the Attorney General that any domestic concern, or officer, director, employee, agent, or stockholder thereof, is engaged, or is about to engage, in any act or practice constituting a violation of subsection (a) of this section, the Attorney General may, in his discretion, bring a civil action in an appropriate district court of the United States to enjoin such act or practice, and upon a proper showing a permanent or temporary injunction or a temporary restraining order shall be granted without bond.

(d) As used in this section:

(1) The term "domestic concern" means (A) any individual who is a citizen, national,

or resident of the United States; or (B) any corporation, partnership, association, joint-stock company, business trust, unincorporated organization, or sole proprietorship which has its principal place of business in the United States, or which is organized under the laws of a State of the United States or a territory, possession, or commonwealth of the United States.

(2) The term "foreign official" means any officer or employee of a foreign government or any department, agency, or instrumentality thereof, or any person acting in an official capacity for or on behalf of any such government or department, agency, or instrumentality. Such term does not include any employee of a foreign government or any department, agency, or instrumentality thereof whose duties are essentially ministerial or clerical.

 THE NATIONAL LABOR RELATIONS ACT [EXCERPTS]

RIGHTS OF EMPLOYEES

SECTION 7. Employees shall have the right to self-organization, to form, join, or assist labor organizations, to bargain collectively through representatives of their own choosing, and to engage in other concerted activities for the purpose of collective bargaining or other mutual aid or protection, and shall also have the right to refrain from any or all of such activities except to the extent that such right may be affected by an agreement requiring membership in a labor organization as a condition of employment as authorized in section 8(a)(3).

UNFAIR LABOR PRACTICES

SECTION 8. (a) It shall be an unfair practice for an employer—

(1) to interfere with, restrain, or coerce employees in the exercise of the rights guaranteed in section 7;

(2) to dominate or interfere with the formation or administration of any labor organization or contribute financial or other support to it: *Provided,* That subject to rules and regulations made and published by the Board pursuant to section 6, an employer shall not be prohibited from permitting employees to confer with him during working hours without loss of time or pay;

(3) by discriminating in regard to hire or tenure of employment or any term or condition of employment to encourage or discourage membership in any labor organization: *Provided,* That nothing in this Act, or in any other statute of the United States, shall preclude an employer from making an agreement with a labor organization (not established, maintained, or assisted by any action defined in section 8(a) of this Act as an unfair labor practice) to require as a condition of employment membership therein on or after the thirtieth day following the beginning of such employment or the effective date of such agreement, whichever is the later, (i) if such labor organization is the representative of the employees as provided in section 9(a), in the appropriate collec-

tive-bargaining unit covered by such agreement when made, and (ii) unless following an election held as provided in section 9(e) within one year preceding the effective date of such agreement, the Board shall have certified that at least a majority of the employees eligible to vote in such election have voted to rescind the authority of such labor organization to make such an agreement: *Provided further,* That no employer shall justify any discrimination against an employee for nonmembership in a labor organization (A) if he has reasonable grounds for believing that such membership was not available to the employee on the same terms and conditions generally applicable to other members, or (B) if he had reasonable grounds for believing that membership was denied or terminated for reasons other than the failure of the employee to tender the periodic dues and the initiation fees uniformly required as a condition of acquiring or retaining membership;

(4) to discharge or otherwise discriminate against an employee because he has filed charges or given testimony under this Act;

(5) to refuse to bargain collectively with the representatives of his employees, subject to the provisions of section 9(a).

(b) It shall be an unfair labor practice for a labor organization or its agents—

(1) to restrain or coerce (A) employees in the exercise of the rights guaranteed in section 7: *Provided,* That this paragraph shall not impair the right of a labor organization to prescribe its own rules with respect to the acquisition or retention of membership therein; or (B) an employer in the selection of his representatives for the purposes of collective bargaining or the adjustment of grievances;

(2) to cause or attempt to cause an employer to discriminate against an employee in violation of subsection (a)(3) or to discriminate against an employee with respect to whom membership in such organization has been denied or terminated on some ground other than his failure to tender the periodic dues and the initiation fees uniformly required as a condition of acquiring or retaining membership;

(3) to refuse to bargain collectively with an employer, provided it is the representative of his employees subject to the provisions of section 9(a);

(4) (i) to engage in, or to induce or encourage [the employees of any employer] an individual employed by any person engaged in commerce or in an industry affecting commerce to engage in, a strike or a refusal in the course of his employment to use, manufacture, process, transport, or otherwise handle or work on any goods, articles, materials, or commodities or to perform any services; or (ii) to threaten, coerce, or restrain any person engaged in commerce or in an industry affecting commerce, where in either case an object thereof is—

(A) forcing or requiring any employer of self-employed person to join any labor or employer organization or to enter into any agreement which is prohibited by section 8(e);

(B) forcing or requiring any person to cease using, selling, handling, transporting, or otherwise dealing in the products of any other producer, processor, or manufacturer, or to cease doing business with any other person, or forcing or requiring any other employer to recognize or bargain with a labor organization as the representative of his employees unless such labor organization has been certified as the representative of such employees under the provisions of section 9: *Provided,* That nothing contained in this clause (B) shall be construed to make unlawful, where not otherwise unlawful, any primary strike or primary picketing;

(C) forcing or requiring any employer to recognize or bargain with a particular labor organization as the representative of his employees if another labor organization has been certified as the representative of such employees under the provisions of section 9;

(D) forcing or requiring any employer to assign particular work to employees in a particular labor organization or in a particular trade, craft, or class rather than to employees in another labor organization or in another trade, craft, or class, unless such employer is failing to conform to an order or certification of the Board determining the bargaining representative for employees performing such work:

Provided, That nothing contained in this subsection (b) shall be construed to make unlawful a refusal by any person to enter upon the premises of any employer (other than his own employer), if the employees of such employer are engaged in a strike ratified or approved by a representative of such employees whom such employer is required to recognize under this Act: *Provided further,* That for the purposes of this paragraph (4) only, nothing contained in such paragraph shall be construed to prohibit publicity, other than picketing, for the purpose of truthfully advising the public, including consumers and members of a labor organization, that a product or products are produced by an employer with whom the labor organization has a primary dispute and are distributed by another employer, as long as such publicity does not have an effect of inducing any individual employed by any person other than the primary employer in the course of his employment to refuse to pick up, deliver, or transport any goods, or not to perform any services, at the establishment of the employer engaged in such distribution:

(5) to require of employees covered by an agreement authorized under subsection (a)(3) the payment, as a condition precedent to becoming a member of such organization, of a fee in an amount which the Board finds excessive or discriminatory under all the circumstances. In making such a finding, the Board shall consider, among other relevant factors, the practices and customs of labor organizations in the particular industry, and the wages currently paid to the employees affected;

(6) to cause or attempt to cause an employer to pay or deliver or agree to pay or deliver any money or other thing of value, in the nature of an exaction, for services which are not performed or not to be performed; and

(7) to picket or cause to be picketed, or threatened to picket or cause to be picketed, any employer where an object thereof is forcing or requiring an employer to recognize or bargain with a labor organization as the representative of his employees, or forcing or requiring the employees of an employer to accept or select such labor organization as their collective bargaining representative, unless such labor organization is currently certified as the representative of such employees:

(A) where the employer has lawfully recognized in accordance with this Act any other labor organization and a question concerning representation may not appropriately be raised under section 9(c) of this Act;

(B) where within the preceding twelve months a valid election under section 9(c) of this Act has been conducted, or

(C) where such picketing has been conducted without a petition under section 9(c) being filed within a reasonable period of time not to exceed thirty days from the commencement of such picketing: *Provided,* That when such a petition has been filed the Board shall forthwith, without regard to the provisions of section 9(c)(1) or the absence of a showing of a substantial interest on the part of the labor organization, direct an election in such unit as the Board finds to be appropriate and shall certify the results thereof: *Provided further,* That nothing in this subparagraph (C) shall be construed to prohibit any picketing or other publicity for the purpose of truthfully advising the public (including consumers) that an employer does not employ members of, or have a contract with, a labor organization, unless an effect of such picketing is to induce any individual employed by any other person in the course of his employment, not to pick up, deliver or transport any goods or not to perform any services.

Nothing in this paragraph (7) shall be construed to permit any act which would otherwise by an unfair labor practice under this section 8(b).

(c) The expressing of any views, argument, or opinion, or the dissemination thereof, whether in written, printed, graphic, or visual form, shall not constitute or be evidence of an unfair labor practice under any of the provisions of this Act, if such expression contains no threat of reprisal or force or promise of benefit.

(d) For the purpose of this section, to bargain collectively is the performance of the mutual obligation of the employer and the representative of the employees to meet at reasonable times and confer in good faith with respect to wages, hours, and other terms and conditions of employment, or the negotiation of an agreement, or any question arising thereunder, and the execution of a written contract incorporating any agreement reached if requested by either party, but such obligation does not compel either party to agree to a proposal or require the making of a concession: *Provided,* That where there is in effect a collective-bargaining contract covering employees in an industry affecting commerce, the duty to bargain collectively shall also mean that no party to such contract shall terminate or modify such contract, unless the party desiring such termination or modification—

(1) serves a written notice upon the other party to the contract of the proposed termination or modification sixty days prior to the expiration date thereof, or in the event such contract contains no expiration date, sixty days prior to the time it is proposed to make such termination or modification;

(2) offers to meet and confer with the other party for the purpose of negotiating a new contract or a contract containing the proposed modifications;

(3) notifies the Federal Mediation and Conciliation Service within thirty days after such notice of the existence of a dispute, and simultaneously therewith notifies any State or Territorial agency established to mediate and conciliate disputes within the State or Territory where the dispute occurred, provided no agreement has been reached by that time; and

(4) continues in full force and effect, without resorting to strike or lock-out, all the terms and conditions of the existing contract for a period of sixty days after such notice is given or until the expiration date of such contract, whichever occurs later:

The duties imposed upon employers, employees, and labor organizations by paragraphs (2), (3), and (4) shall become inapplicable upon an intervening certification of the Board, under which the labor organization or individual, which is a party to the contract, has been superseded as or ceased to be the representative of the employees subject to the provisions of section 9(a), and the duties so imposed shall not be construed as requiring either party to discuss or agree to any modification of the terms and conditions contained in a contract for a fixed period, if such modification is to become effective before such terms and conditions can be reopened under the provisions of the contract. Any employee who engages in a strike within [the sixty-day period specified in this subsection] shall lose his status as an employee of the employer engaged in the particular labor dispute, for the purposes of [section 8, 9, and 10 of this Act, as amended], but such loss of status for such employee shall terminate if and when he is reemployed by such employer.

(e) It shall be an unfair labor practice for any labor organization and any employer to enter into any contract or agreement, express or implied, whereby such employer ceases or refrains or agrees to cease or refrain from handling, using, selling, transporting, or otherwise dealing in any of the products of any other employer, or to cease doing business with any other person, and any contract or agreement entered into heretofore or hereafter containing such an agreement shall be to such extent unenforcable and void: *Provided,* That nothing in this subsection (e) shall apply to an agreement between a labor organization and an employer in the construction industry relating to the contracting or subcontracting of work to be done at the site of the construction, alteration, painting, or repair of a building, structure, or other work: *Provided further,* That for the purposes of this subsection (e) and section 8(b)(4)(B) the terms "any employer," "any person engaged in commerce or any industry affecting other producer, processor, or manufacturer," "any other employer," or "any other person" shall not include persons in the relation of a jobber, manufacturer, contractor, or subcontractor working on the goods or premises of the jobber or manufacturer or performing parts of an integrated process of production in the apparel and clothing industry: *Provided further,* That nothing in this Act shall prohibit the enforcement of any agreement which is within the foregoing exception.

(f) It shall not be an unfair labor practice under subsections (a) and (b) of this section for an employer engaged primarily in the building and construction industry to make an agreement covering employees engaged (or who, upon their employment, will be engaged) in the building and construction industry with a labor organization of which building and construction employees are members (not established, maintained, or assisted by any action defined in section 8(a) of this Act as an unfair labor practice) because (1) the majority status of such labor organizations has not been established under the provisions of section 9 of this Act prior to the making of such agreement, or (2) such agreement requires as a condition or employment, membership in such labor organization after the seventh day following the beginning of such employment or the effective date of the agreement, whichever is later, or (3) such agreement requires the employer to notify such labor organization of opportunities for employment with such employer, or gives such labor organization an opportunity to refer qualified applicants for such employment, or (4) such agreement specifies minimum training or experience qualifications for employment or provides for priority in opportunities for employment based upon length of service with such employer, in the industry or in the particular geographical area: *Provided,* That nothing in this subsection shall set aside the final proviso to section 8(a)(3) of this Act: *Provided further,* That any agreement which would be invalid, but for clause (1) of this subsection, shall not be a bar to a petition filed pursuant to section 9(c) or 9(e).

(g) A labor organization before engaging in any strike, picketing, or other concerted refusal to work at any health care institution shall, not less than ten days prior to such action, notify the institution in writing and the Federal Mediation and Conciliation Service of that intention, except that in the case of bargaining for an initial agreement following certification or recognition the notice required by this subsection shall not be given until the expiration of the period specified in clause (b) of the last sentence of section 8(d) of this Act. The notice shall state the date and time that such action will commence. The notice, once given, may be extended by the written agreement of both parties.

REPRESENTATIVES AND ELECTIONS

SECTION 9. (a) Representatives designated or selected for the purposes of collective bargaining by the majority of the employees in a unit appropriate for such purposes, shall be exclusive representatives of all the employees in such unit for the purposes of collective bargaining in respect to rates of pay, wages, hours of employment, or other conditions of employment: *Provided,* That any individual employee or a group of employees shall have the right at any time to present grievances to their employer and to have such grievances adjusted, without the intervention of the bargaining representative, as long as the adjustment is not inconsistent with the terms of a collective-bargaining contract or agreement then in effect: *Provided further,* That the bargaining representative has been given opportunity to be present at such adjustment.

(b) The Board shall decide in each case whether, in order to assure to employees the fullest freedom in exercising the rights guaranteed by this Act, the unit appropriate for the purposes of collective bargaining shall be the employer unit, craft unit, plant unit, or subdivision thereof: *Provided,* That the Board shall not (1) decide that any unit is appropriate for such purposes if such unit included both professional employees and employees who are not professional employees unless a majority of such professional employees vote for inclusion in such unit; or (2) decide that any craft unit is inappropriate for such purposes on the ground that a different unit has been established by a prior Board determination, unless a majority of the employees in the proposed craft unit vote against separate representation or (3) decide that any unit is appropriate for such purposes if it includes, together with other employees, any individual employed as a guard to enforce against employees and other persons rules to protect property of the employer or to protect the safety of persons on the employer's premises; but no later organization shall be certified as the representative of employees in a bargaining unit of guards if such organization admits to membership, or is affiliated directly or indirectly with an organization which admits to membership, employees other than guards.

(c)(1) Whenever a petition shall have been filed, in accordance with such regulations as may be prescribed by the Board—

(A) by an employee or group of employees or an individual or labor organization acting in their behalf alleging that a substantial number of employees (i) wish to be represented for collective bargaining and that their employer declines to recognize their representative as the representative defined in section 9(a), or (ii) assert that the individual or labor organization, which has been certified or is being currently recognized by their employer as the bargaining representative, is not longer a representative as defined in section 9(a); or

(B) by an employer, alleging that one or more individuals or labor organizations have presented to him a claim to be recognized as the representative defined in section 9(a); the Board shall investigate such petition and if it has reasonable cause to believe that a question of representation affecting commerce exists shall provide for an appropriate hearing upon due notice. Such hearing may be conducted by an officer or employee of the regional office, who shall not make any recommendations with respect thereto. If the Board finds upon the record of such hearing that such a question of representation exists, it shall direct an election by secret ballot and shall certify the results thereof.

(2) In determining whether or not a question of representation affecting commerce exists, the same regulations and rules of decision shall apply irrespective of the identity

of the persons filing the petition or the kind of relief sought and in no case shall the Board deny a labor organization a place on the ballot by reason of an order with respect to such labor organization or its predecessor not issued in conformity with section 10(c).

(3) No election shall be directed in any bargaining unit or any subdivision within which, in the preceding twelve-month period, a valid election shall have been held. Employees engaged in an economic strike who are not entitled to reinstatement shall be eligible to vote under such regulations as the Board shall find are consistent with the purposes and provisions of this Act in any election conducted within twelve months after the commencement of the strike. In any election where none of the choices on the ballot receives a majority, a run-off shall be conducted, the ballot providing for a selection between the two choices receiving the largest and second largest number of valid votes cast in the election.

(4) Nothing in this section shall be construed to prohibit the waiving of hearings by stipulation for the purpose of a consent election in conformity with regulations and rules of decision of the Board.

(5) In determining whether a unit is appropriate for the purposes specified in subsection (b) the extent to which the employees have organized shall not be controlling.

(d) Whenever an order of the Board made pursuant to section 10(c) is based in whole or in part upon facts certified following an investigation pursuant to subsection (c) of this section and there is a petition for the enforcement or review of such order, such certification and the record of such investigation shall be included in the transcript of the entire record required to be filed under section 10(e) or 10(f), and thereupon the decree of the court enforcing, modifying, or setting aside in whole or in part the order of the Board shall be made and entered upon the pleadings, testimony, and proceedings set forth in such transcript.

(e)(1) Upon the filing with the Board, by 30 per centum or more of the employees in a bargaining unit covered by an agreement between their employer and a labor organization made pursuant to section 8(a)(3), of a petition alleging they desire that such authority be rescinded, the Board shall take a secret ballot of the employees in such unit, and shall certify the results thereof to such labor organization and to the employer.

(2) No election shall be conducted pursuant to this subsection in any bargaining unit or any subdivision within which, in the preceding twelve-month period, a valid election shall have been held.

RIGHT TO STRIKE PRESERVED

SECTION 13. Nothing in this subchapter, except as specifically provided for herein, shall be construed so as either to interfere with or impede or diminish in any way the right to strike, or to affect the limitations or qualifications on that right.

CONSTRUCTION OF PROVISIONS

SECTION 14. . . . (b) Nothing in this subchapter shall be construed as authorizing the execution or application of agreement requiring membership in a labor organization as a condition of employment in any State or Territory in which such execution or application is prohibited by State or Territorial law.

R THE CIVIL RIGHTS ACT OF 1964, TITLE VII, AS AMENDED [EXCERPTS]

DEFINITIONS

SECTION 701. . . . (k) The terms "because of sex" or "on the basis of sex" include, but are not limited to, because of or on the basis of pregnancy, childbirth or related medical conditions; and women affected by pregnancy, childbirth, or related medical conditions shall be treated the same for all employment-related purposes, including receipt of benefits under fringe benefit programs, as other persons not so affected but similar in their ability or inability to work, and nothing in Section 703(h) of this title shall not be interpreted to permit otherwise. This subsection shall not require an employer to pay for health insurance benefits for abortion, except where the life of the mother would be endangered if the fetus were carried to term, or except where medical complications have arisen from an abortion: Provided, That nothing herein shall preclude an employer from providing abortion benefits or otherwise effect bargaining agreements in regard to abortion.

UNLAWFUL EMPLOYMENT PRACTICES

SECTION 703. (a) It shall be an unlawful employment practice for an employer—

(1) to fail or refuse to hire or to discharge any individual, or otherwise to discriminate against any individual with respect to his compensation, terms, conditions, or privileges of employment, because of such individual's race, color, religion, sex, or national origin; or

(2) limit, segregate, or classify his employees or applicants for employment in any way which would deprive or tend to deprive any individual of employment opportunities or otherwise adversely affect his status as an employee, because of such individual's race, color, religion, sex, or national origin.

(b) It shall be an unlawful employment practice for an employment agency to fail or refuse to refer for employment, or otherwise to discriminate against, an individual because of his race, color, religion, sex, or national origin, or to classify or refer for employment any individual on the basis of his race, color, religion, sex, or national origin.

(c) It shall be an unlawful employment practice for a labor organization—

(1) to exclude or to expel from its membership, or otherwise to discriminate against, any individual because of his race, color, religion, sex, or national origin;

(2) to limit, segregate, or classify its membership or applicants for membership or to classify or fail or refuse to refer for employment any individual, in any way which would deprive or tend to deprive any individual of employment opportunities, or would limit such employment opportunities or otherwise adversely affect his status as an employee or as an applicant for employment, because of such individual's race, color, religion, sex, or national origin; or

(3) to cause or attempt to cause an employer to discriminate against an individual in violation of this section.

(d) It shall be an unlawful employment practice for any employer, labor organization, or joint labor-management committee controlling apprenticeship or other training or retraining, including on-the-job training programs to discriminate against any individual because of his race, color, religion, sex, or national origin in admission to, or employment in, any program established to provide apprenticeship or other training.

(e) Notwithstanding any other provision of this title, (1) it shall not be an unlawful employment practice for an employer to hire and employ employees, for an employment agency to classify, or refer for employment any individual, for a labor organization to classify its membership or to classify or refer for employment any individual, or for any employer, labor organization, or joint labor-management committee controlling apprenticeship or other training or retraining programs to admit or employ any individual in any such program, on the basis of his religion, sex, or national origin in those certain instances where religion, sex, or national origin is a bona fide occupational qualification reasonably necessary to the normal operation of that particular business or enterprise, and (2) it shall not be an unlawful employment practice for a school, college, university, or other educational institution or institution of learning to hire and employ employees of a particular religion if such school, college, university, or other educational institution or institution of learning is, in whole or in substantial part, owned, supported, controlled, or managed by a particular religion or by a particular religious corporation, association, or society, or if the curriculum of such school, college, university, or other educational institution or institution of learning is directed toward the propagation of a particular religion.

(f) As used in this title, the phrase "unlawful employment practice" shall not be deemed to include any action or measure taken by an employer, labor organization, joint labor-management committee, or employment agency with respect to an individual who is a member of the Communist Party of the United States or of any other organization required to register as a Communist-action or Communist-front organization by final order of the Subversive Activities Control Act of 1950.

(g) Notwithstanding any other provision of this title, it shall not be an unlawful employment practice for an employer to fail or refuse to hire and employ any individual for any position, for an employer to discharge an individual from any position, or for an employment agency to fail or refuse to refer any individual for employment in any position, or for a labor organization to fail or refuse any individual for employment in any position, if—

(1) the occupancy of such position, or access to the premises in or upon which any part of the duties of such position is performed or is to be performed, is subject to any requirement imposed in the interest of the national security of the United States under any security program in effect pursuant to or administered under any statute of the United States or any Executive order of the President; and

(2) such individual has not fulfilled or has ceased to fulfill that requirement.

(h) Notwithstanding any other provision of this title, it shall not be an unlawful employment practice for an employer to apply different standards of compensation, or different terms, conditions, or privileges of employment pursuant to a bona fide seniority or merit system, or a system which measures earnings by quantity or quality of production or to employees who work in different locations, provided that such differences are not the result of an intention to discriminate because of race, color, religion, sex, or national origin; nor shall it be an unlawful employment practice for an employer to give and to act upon the results of any professionally developed ability test provided that such test, its administration or action upon the results is not designed, intended, or used to discriminate because of race, color, religion, sex, or national origin. It shall not be an unlawful employment practice under this title for any employer to differentiate upon the basis of sex in determining the amount of wages or compensation paid or to be paid to employees of such employer if such differentiation is authorized by the provision of Section 6(d) of the Fair Labor Standards Act of 1938 as amended (29 U.S.C. 206(d)).

(i) Nothing contained in this title shall apply to any business or enterprise on or near an Indian reservation with respect to any publicly announced employment practice of such business or enterprise under which a preferential treatment is given to any individual because he is an Indian living on or near a reservation.

(j) Nothing contained in this title shall be interpreted to require any employer, employment agency, labor organization, or joint labor-management committee subject to this title to grant preferential treatment to any individual or to any group because of the race, color, religion, sex, or national origin or such individual or group on account of an imbalance which may exist with respect to the total number or percentage of persons of any race, color, religion, sex, or national origin employed by any employer, referred or classified for employment by any employment agency or labor organization, admitted to membership or classified by any labor organization, or admitted to, or employed in, any apprenticeship or other training program, in comparison with the total number or percentage of persons of such race, color, religion, sex, or national origin in any community, State, section, or other area, or in the available work force in any community, State, section, or other area.

OTHER UNLAWFUL EMPLOYMENT PRACTICES

SECTION 704. (a) It shall be an unlawful employment practice for an employer to discriminate against any of his employees or applicants for employment, for an employment agency, or joint labor-management committee controlling apprenticeship or other training or retraining, including on-the-job training programs, to discriminate against any individual, or for a labor organization to discriminate against any member thereof or applicant for membership, because he has opposed any practice, made an unlawful employment practice by this title, or because he has made a charge, testified, assisted, or participated in any manner in an investigation, proceeding, or hearing under this title.

(b) It shall be an unlawful employment practice for an employer, labor organization, employment agency, or joint labor-management committee controlling apprenticeship or other training or retraining, including on-the-job training programs, to print or cause to be printed or published any notice or advertisement relating to employment by such an employer or membership in or any classification or referral for employment by such a labor organization, or relating to any classification or referral for employment by such an employment agency, or relating to admission to, or employment in, any program established to provide apprenticeship or other training by such a joint labor-management committee indicating any preference, limitation, specification, or discrimination, based on race, color, religion, sex or national origin, except that such a notice or advertisement may indicate a preference, limitation, specification, or discrimination based on religion, sex or national origin when religion, sex, or national origin is a bona fide occupational qualification for employment.

S THE EQUAL PAY ACT OF 1963 [EXCERPTS]

DISCRIMINATORY PAYMENT PRACTICES

SECTION 3. Section 6 of the Fair Labor Standards Act of 1938, as amended (29, U.S.C. et seq.), is amended by adding thereto a new subsection (d) as follows:

(d)(1) No employer having employees subject to any provisions of this section shall discriminate, within any establishment in which such employees are employed, between employees on the basis of sex by paying wages to employees in such establishment at a rate less than the rate at which he pays wages to employees of the opposite sex in such establishment for equal work on jobs the performance of which requires equal skill, effort, and responsibility, and which are performed under similar working conditions, except where such payment is made pursuant to (i) a seniority system; (ii) a merit system; (iii) a system which measures earnings by quantity or quality of production; or (iv) a differential based on any other factor other than sex: *Provided,* That an employer who is paying a wage rate differential in violation of this subsection shall not, in order to comply with the provisions of this subsection, reduce the wage rate of any employee. . . .

(3) For purposes of administration and enforcement, any amounts owing to any employee which have been withheld in violation of this subsection shall be deemed to be unpaid minimum wages or unpaid overtime compensation under this Act.

GLOSSARY

Abate to remove, eliminate, or greatly reduce; used of bequests and taxes
Absent without, lacking, in the absence of
Accord agreement; *see also* **Satisfaction**
Actus reus criminal act
Ad infinitum limitless, forever
Ad valorem related to or tied to the value of an item; for example, if the sales tax on a car increased as the value of the car increased then the tax would be considered *ad valorem*
Admission a statement made by a party-opponent that a fact is true
Aegis protection, shield
Agent person acting on behalf of another, the **principal**
Ambit boundary, limit; farthest extent
Amicus curiae (pl. amici) friend of the court; concept allows a nonparty to file a brief and even sometimes appear and argue for a position in a legal action in which the nonparty has an important interest
Ancillary aiding or auxiliary; usually refers to a separate action or proceeding outside the main action that aids and proceeds along with the main action
Ante before, prior to
Anti against, opposed to
Appellant the party that files an appeal of a judgment; the party may have been either a plaintiff or a defendant in the original action
Appellee the party against whom the appeal is made or taken
Arguendo assuming something to be true for the purposes of an argument
Argument the persuasive discussion of law and fact made by counsel to the trier of fact that attempts to make the judge or jury decide in favor of counsel's client
Art in patent law, that which is generally known about a process or technique
Attach fixed to; a court may issue a writ of attachment against the property or a bank account of a party to an action so as to ensure payment of a debt; *see also* **Writ**

Bailee the person or persons to whom property is entrusted or loaned
Bailor the person who entrusts or loans property to another
Bar (*noun*) the group of attorneys who are permitted to practice law before a particular court or in a particular state; (*verb*) to prevent or prohibit; if an action is barred by the statute of limitations then it is prevented from being brought
Beneficiary a person who benefits from the creation of something; the person who receives the income from a trust is considered the trust beneficiary
Bequest in a will, a gift of property, personal or otherwise
Bona fide in good faith, honestly, fairly; a *bona fide* purchaser is someone who buys something with no knowledge that anyone other than the seller has a claim to it

Bond a promise to pay money; a debt; usually means a promise to pay a specific amount of money over a period of time

Bond, negotiable a bond issued by a corporation the ownership of which can be transferred by signing it over to another

Breach the failure to perform a legal duty; the breaking of a law or of a promise to perform a contract

Brief the written argument made by one party or side in a lawsuit that attempts to summarize the facts of a case, then summarizes the law that applies to those facts to justify a conclusion

Capias ad respondendum a writ that forces a person to come to court to defend a charge or to answer a claim

Cause of action the legal basis for a lawsuit; the essential facts needed to assert a legal proceeding

Caveat emptor "let the buyer beware," a rule that imposes responsibility for discovering defects on the buyer, not the seller

Certiorari "to make sure" (Latin); a request by a party for a higher court to grant an appeal of the party's case. If the high court wishes to grant a "writ of *certiorari*" then the lower court must send a record of the case to the higher court and the high court can hear the appeal. If the high court denies the writ of *certiorari* then the party cannot make an appeal.

Chattel property other than land; must be **tangible**

Civil law the branch of law that deals with private or public rights but not with criminal actions

Codify classify, condense, reduce to a formula

Colorable seemingly valid or genuine

Common law law created by judicial decisions rather than by a legislature

Commute reduce, as a penalty

Composition usually refers to a formal agreement made by a creditor or several creditors and a debtor that the creditors will take less than the full amount owed them by the debtor

Consideration payment for value received

Construe to interpret; to analyze grammatically

Contingent debt a debt that depends on a future occurrence or action to be determined. If a parent signed an agreement stating that the parent would pay for an item if his or her child did not pay, then the debt of the parent would depend upon the future action of the child, who either would or would not pay the debt.

Continuance adjournment of court proceedings to a future day

Criminal a person who has committed a crime; having to do with crimes or illegal activity

Damages money penalties assessed by the court in a civil action, whereby the liable defendant recompenses the victim

Damnum absque injuria damages for which no legal action may be brought

d/b/a abbreviation for "doing business as," used mainly by sole proprietorships

Debenture note of a company promising to pay a specified amount

De facto in fact; something that exists in fact. *De facto* segregation is segregation that exists because of social and economic conditions, not because a law requires it to exist.

De jure by right; lawful regardless of whether true or not in fact. *De jure* segregation is segregation that is required by law.

De minimis small, trivial, not important

De minimis non curat lex   "The law does not bother with such trivial things."

De novo   anew, begun anew

Debt   money or property that is owed to another

Defendant   a person in either a civil or criminal matter against whom an action is brought

Defense   the law, fact, and argument made by the side against which an action has been brought to refute the claims made by the opposing party

Deponent   the person who gives testimony at a deposition, the person who is deposed

Deposition   an out-of-court proceeding that allows an attorney representing a party to an action to ask questions of a witness before trial. The entire proceeding is considered sworn testimony and can be utilized to discredit a witness if the witness should later attempt to change his/her testimony.

Devise   a gift of land by way of a will

Dicta   unessential parts of a judicial decision; the portion of a judicial opinion that is not necessary to the result; the portions of an opinion that are *dicta* are not binding upon later courts as precedent and do not have to be followed

Dictum   singular of *dicta*

Discovery   the pretrial process by which information relating to the facts of a case is obtained. Depositions, requests for admissions, and interrogatories are considered discovery techniques that allow the parties to determine the facts in a particular case before the trial.

Dissent   disagreement; in legal opinions, a minority opinion. Dissents carry some weight as references for future decisions.

Divest   take away, remove

Domicile   the place that a person considers to be his/her permanent home

Due process   a right guaranteed by the U.S. Constitution that ensures that all persons are given notice and an opportunity to be heard before they are deprived of life, liberty, or property

Easement   the right of a nonowner of a piece of real property to use another's land for a particular purpose

Eminent domain   the government's power to take private land for public use by condemning property and then paying the owner the fair value of the property

Enjoin   require, force or demand; If a factory is polluting with heavy smoke, a court can enjoin (i.e., stop) the factory from producing the smoke. If the order is permanent it is called a *permanent injunction.*

En masse   in the mass, all at once, all together

Equitable   fair and just. An equitable solution is one that looks to the fairness of a particular result.

Equitable debt   a debt enforced because fairness, not a specific law, requires it to be enforced

Equity   the power of a court to make a fair and just decision in a particular situation when the law does not require that such a decision be made

Estoppel   the inability of a party to an action to use a defense or state a cause of action when that party has done something inconsistent with the defense or cause of action: if *X* allowed *Y* to believe that *A* was acting as *X*'s agent, then *X* would be estopped from denying that *A* was his/her agent even if *A* had never been given any agency power by *X*.

Et seq.   abbreviation for *et sequuntur,* "and the following;" "p. 302 *et seq.*" means that the reference includes the page cited and the following pages.

Evidence   any type of event, material, or information that tends to prove that the act in question did or did not occur. Also refers to the rules of law that govern the types of evidence which can be admitted to a judge or jury.

Exculpatory clause   a clause that seeks to limit the potential for damages by one party in a contract; *see also* **Damages**

Ex parte   by one party acting alone; used regarding legal proceedings

Felony   a serious crime, usually one that can be punishable by death or imprisonment for over one year in a state prison

Fiduciary   someone who occupies a position of trust, responsibility, and confidence in relation to another person; *see also* **Trustee**

Foreclose   to keep out, to shut off; if you have been foreclosed from asserting a particular cause of action then you are prevented from claiming the cause of action

Forfeiture   the loss of money or property by an individual as a result of an offense or neglect of duty. A lender may forfeit the right to collect any interest from a debtor if the lender charges a higher rate of interest than the law allows.

Forum   a court or place to hold a proceeding

Forum non conveniens   an inconvenient court (too far away, etc.) for one or both parties

Fraud   trickery or deceit used by one person to deprive another of something; considered a crime

Freedom of speech   the right set forth in the First Amendment that allows a person to speak out on any subject with any opinion as long as that speech does not interfere with the rights of others

Fungible   interchangeable, replaceable with ease. A bushel of wheat is a fungible commodity because it can be easily replaced with another identical bushel of wheat.

Garnishment   a statutory proceeding that can take place after a judgment has been obtained against a party. Garnishment allows the intangible assets of the debtor (e.g., wages) to be attached and thereby go to a creditor instead of the debtor.

Good faith   honest intentions, honesty in fact, fairness in dealing

Gratuitous   given without consideration of payment; offered freely; *sometimes* superfluous, unwanted

Gravamen   the important part, main point, essential content

Guarantee *or* **guaranty**   a promise by a third party to pay the debt of someone if the debtor does not pay

Guardian   the person who has the legal right and duty to take care of another person (e.g., a child or incompetent) because the second person is presumed to be unable to take care of himself/herself

Hedge   an arrangement that reduces the risk to seller or investor. If a dealer sold the right to receive 100 bushels of wheat to an investor, the dealer might hedge his investment by purchasing the right to receive 75 bushels of wheat from another source. Now, if the price of wheat went up the dealer would still be covered for 75 bushels of wheat and would not stand to lose as much money.

Holder in due course   a person who holds a negotiable instrument and has taken that instrument in good faith for value and without notice that the instrument is defective, or who has a valid defense against the defect; *see also* **Negotiable Instrument**

Homicide   any killing of another person. If a person has killed someone in self-defense, that person has committed a homicide but has not committed a crime.

Impasse   standstill in negotiations, where no party is willing to make concessions

Impeachment   showing to be false or wrongful; removal from public office following a hearing by a legislative body

Impinge   to strike, to collide with, to have an impact upon

Impossibility something that cannot possibly be performed because of a legal or physical occurrence or condition

Impracticability something that is not impossible to perform but which has changed so much that it would be unfair or unjust to require the act to be done

Imputed assumed. Even if someone does not know a fact the fact can be imputed to the person if a reasonable person should have known of the fact; for example, an agent's knowledge can be imputed to a principal since a reasonable principal should know the facts that have been told to his/her agent.

In camera "in chambers," in the judge's chambers or otherwise away from public view

Inchoate shapeless, formless; incomplete, imperfectly formed; only partially in existence

Indicia clues, signs, circumstances that indicate that a certain fact is probable; indicia of probability are those factors that courts look at to see if a witness is likely to be telling the truth

Indictment a formal charge or written accusation against a person by a grand jury, usually at the request of a prosecutor

Infra below or under. If a textbook stated "See *Shelly v. McCormick* p. 507 *infra,*" it would mean that *Shelly v. McCormick* could be found later in that same book at page 507.

Injunction an order from a judge commanding a person or company to do something or refrain from doing something. An injunction can be either temporary or permanent.

Intangible "not touchable," i.e., not specific or concrete; intangible assets are money and goodwill as opposed to property.

In personam refers to "the person," usually to a suit against another person rather than against something such as property. If a court has *in personam* jurisdiction then it has jurisdiction over the person in question.

In rem in contrast to *in personam, in rem* refers to a suit against property. A court that has *in rem* jurisdiction in a matter has jurisdiction over the property that is the subject matter of the litigation.

Inter alia among other things. "Previously the court discussed, *inter alia,* the defendant's right to counsel" would mean that the court discussed other issues in addition to the defendant's right to counsel.

Inter alii among other persons

Interstate between two or more states

Intrastate within the borders of one state

Inure occur, take effect, accrue; if Hilary was the sole beneficiary of a trust, then the trust proceeds could be said to inure to Hilary.

Jurisdiction the court's power and authority to apply and interpret the law in a particular case; when a court has no jurisdiction over the subject matter of the case then it cannot hear the case.

Jurisprudence the study of the law, the general philosophy of the law

Levy to assess; to seize at law

Liability legal obligation or responsibility; exposure to legal damages

Lien an encumbrance on property created by a statute or judicial proceeding; a tax lien on your property would mean that the government has a right to sell your property if you do not pay your tax debt.

Liquidated damages damages agreed to in advance by the parties to a contract, deemed to be a fair estimate of the actual damages that would be sustained by a party in the event of a breach of contract, and substituted for actual damages if a breach does in fact occur

Litigate   to proceed with a lawsuit, to engage in the necessary steps that promote a lawsuit

Malfeasance   the performance of a morally wrongful or illegal act
Malice   ill will, harmful intent
Malum in se   an act that is evil in itself or morally wrongful
Malum prohibitum   conduct prohibited by statute but not necessarily morally wrongful
Mandamus   a command from a court to a party ordering the party to do something; e.g., in *Marbury v. Madison,* a judge issued a writ of *mandamus* ordering a governmental official to appoint a person as justice of the peace.
Material   essential, important
Mens rea   criminal intent, a guilty mind
Misdemeanor   a criminal offense that is considered less serious than a felony and is usually punishable by a prison sentence of less than one year
Monopoly   a market structure in which one seller or one group of sellers has such a high level of control over the market as to control price or access to the market
Mortgage   usually the act of putting up land itself or land with improvements to secure repayment of a loan. If the person who owes the mortgage (the mortgagor) does not repay, the lender (the mortgagee) can take the property and sell it.
Motion   an action by a party requesting that a judge make a decision or ruling on an issue
Motion for summary judgment   a request to a judge to make a decision before the case goes to trial. If it is granted the party bringing the motion wins the case.

Negligence   failure to exercise the care of a reasonable person in similar circumstances
Negotiable instrument   a document convertible into cash, e.g., a stock, a bond, a bank check
Nexus   connection, link
Notice   being made aware of particular facts, usually in writing. A party is on notice of a lawsuit if the party receives information regarding the existence of the lawsuit.
Novation   the substitution of one person for another in the performance of a contract; must be made by agreement between the parties.
Nuisance   an unreasonable interference with the use or enjoyment of one's property.

Offer   a proposal to another party that gives the receiving party the power to make a contract by acceptance
Offset   an item that counterbalances or compensates for another item; *see also* **Hedge**
Option   the payment of a fee to ensure that the right to contract on specific terms will remain open for a fixed period of time

Parol evidence rule   the rule that once a written agreement has been made up by the parties, prior oral or written statements that are inconsistent with the writing cannot be brought up to contradict or interpret the terms of the writing
Pendente lite   during the time a lawsuit is ongoing
Penology   the study of prisons
Per se   inherently, automatically; the mere fact that an act that is negligent *per se* was committed makes the actor negligent without the showing of any additional facts
Perfect   to make enforceable, to complete. A contract is perfected when it is agreed to and signed by both parties.
Petitioner   the party who is petitioning the court
Plaintiff   the party who initiates a lawsuit; the person who brings the action at law
Post-date   the act of putting a date on a document that is later than the actual date

Precedent an earlier judicial decision that serves as a guide to later courts when attempting to decide similar questions of law and fact

Preclude to prevent, make impossible

Preemption the right to do something first; the more powerful right. If Congress passes a law regulating banking, the federal banking law will preempt any state or local law to the contrary.

Prejudice bias, favoritism; loss of right to reargue: if the plaintiff's case is dismissed with prejudice than the plaintiff cannot later bring the case

Prejudicial tending to influence the listener or reader unduly, especially in a negative direction; tending to injure or impair

Preponderance more than half, more likely than not; a plaintiff who must only prove the case by a preponderance of evidence need only prove that her version of the case is slightly more likely to have occurred than the defendant's version.

Presumption a means to prove a fact or conclusion merely by proving the existence of another fact

Prima facie "on the face," enough evidence to support a judgment

Principal the one who employs or allows an agent to act on his or her behalf. If a principal gives authority to an agent then the authorized actions of the agent are binding upon the principal.

Privilege a legal right to preferred treatment

Privity a closely tied business relationship; when a buyer and seller sign a contractual agreement they are considered to be in privity of contract.

Probative constituting positive proof

Procrustean unduly rigid; from Procrustes, an innkeeper in Greek mythology who tortured his guests to make them fit his bed

Proceeds income, profit, net

Pro forma a formality, a matter of form

Pro rata proportionately. If the damages for a breach of contract were fixed at only $1,000 and A's losses were shown to be $1,000 and B's losses were shown to be $2,000 then a *pro rata* distribution of the damages would be $333 to A and $667 to B.

Pro tanto to the extent that

Promise a statement that creates a moral or legal obligation in a person to do or to forbear from doing a particular act or acts.

Promissory estoppel the legal principle that a promise is enforceable even without consideration if the promise was one that could reasonably be relied upon, the promise was in fact relied upon, and the reliance caused legal detriment to the promisee.

Promulgate to formally announce, to publish; it is the duty of the SEC to promulgate rules regarding security regulations.

Proscribe prohibit, forbid

Prosecution (*party*) the state or governmental agency that brings an action against a criminal defendant on behalf of the public; (*process*) the process of initiating and continuing to pursue either a civil or a criminal action

Proviso provided that; a condition or a clause that introduces a condition

Proximate cause substantial cause; the action that will foreseeably and normally result in causing the harm or damage to occur

Proxy authority for a designated deputy to act in one's place

Public policy desired social goals sought to be encouraged and advanced. Judges and lawmakers attempt to take public policy into consideration when making decisions and new laws.

Puffing sales talk or general inflated opinions about goods; not material facts or specific representations

Punitive "punishing"; as a penalty, deterrent, or punishment, punitive damages are assessed as a penalty for intentional or malicious actions and seek to discourage similar future conduct.

Qua   as

Quantum meruit   "as much as he deserves"; the theory that allows one to get the reasonable value of services performed or goods provided if, for some reason, a formal contract does not exist

Quash   annul, eliminate, remove

Quasi   similar to, as if; a quasi contract is considered by a court to be a contract even though it may not meet all the formalities of a contract

Quid pro quo   something of value is exchanged for something of value, a benefit is given and a benefit is received

Ratification   the affirmation of a commitment made by an individual or a third party at an earlier time

Rebut   refute by evidence, dispute with facts and argument

Rebuttable presumption   a presumption that will be assumed unless the opposing party counters or rebuts it with evidence

Rejection   action by an offeree indicating that goods are unacceptable and will not be taken in satisfaction of a contract

Relevant   having a relationship with or impact on an issue or questions; to be legally relevant, a fact need only tend to make a material fact slightly more or less probable

Remand   send back. When an appellate court remands a case to the trial court, it sends it back down to the lower court for further findings.

Remedy   the legal means to recover a right or redress a wrong

Remittitur   the power of a judge to order a plaintiff to take a lesser amount in damages than the jury has awarded. The plaintiff can appeal the judge's order.

Representation   statement, especially in a contract; act of one person standing for another

Res ipsa loquitur   "the thing speaks for itself," the legal theory that allows a rebuttable presumption of negligence against a defendant when an act occurs that does not usually occur in the absence of negligence, when the defendant was in control of the cause of the accident, and when no third parties intervened in the action.

Res judicata   a thing decided, something that has already been decided in a judicial proceeding; once a final judgment has been entered the judgment is binding upon the two parties in a lawsuit, the cause of action is considered to be *res judicata* and cannot be relitigated.

Rescind   to eliminate, annul, revoke

Rescission   cancellation, revocation, annulment

Respondeat superior   "let the master respond," the legal theory that holds the employer liable for some of the torts of his employees if done in the course of employment

Respondent   the person who has an appeal taken against him or her

Reverse   overturn, set aside the prior decision

Revoke   cancel, eliminate, take away

Satisfaction   the relief of an obligation by some form of performance; when Sally agreed to take Fred's car instead of the $1,000 he owed her and Fred gave her the car, their actions constituted an accord and satisfaction.

Scienter   knowledge of criminal intent. Larceny is a crime that requires scienter, for in order to be found guilty of larceny the defendant must have intended to permanently deprive the owner of possession of his or her goods.

Sine qua non   a necessary or indispensable condition. Consideration is a *sine qua non* of a legally binding contract.

Situs   site, location of the matter in dispute

Sovereign immunity   the doctrine that makes the government immune or free from any damage claims against it unless the government has passed a specific law allowing itself to be sued under particular circumstances

Specific performance   an action that allows a plaintiff in an action for breach of contract to seek to have the breaching party perform the contract instead of seeking damages when damages would be inadequate or inappropriate

Standing   a person's ability to bring suit in an action because the issues to be decided in the matter directly affect the person bringing the suit

Stare decisis   "let the decision stand," the legal principle that requires later judicial decision-makers in similar cases to follow the established precedent or rules that were made in earlier cases. However, courts can deviate from this principle if fairness in a particular case requires it.

Status quo   the position of the parties prior to any dealings or contracting

Statute of frauds   the statute that requires certain contracts or transactions to be in writing in order to be enforceable, so as to prevent fraud and misrepresentation; *see also* **Fraud**

Statute of limitations   the various state and federal laws that restrict the time period within which an action may be brought—if an action is not brought within the time limit of the statute it is barred.

Stay   prevention, delay, postponement

Stipulation   an agreement between both sides in a lawsuit; if the parties have stipulated as to the authenticity of a document then there is no need to prove its authenticity.

Sub nom.   abbreviation of *sub nomine*, "under the name of" or "under the title of"

Subpoena   an order from a court commanding a person to appear before the court and give evidence.

Subpoena duces tecum   a court order that commands a person to bring documents to the court and to testify

Substantial performance   the equitable theory that allows a person who substantially completes a contract to be able to recover the contract price minus any damages caused by minor breaches

Supra   above, previously, earlier in the same book; if a reference in a book read "see *Lundy v. Lenihan,* p. 386 *supra,*" then you would find support or more information in *Lundy v. Lenihan* earlier in the same book at page 386.

Supremacy Clause   the portion of the U.S. Constitution that provides that federal law, including the Constitution, shall take priority over any conflicting portions of state or local law.

Surety   guarantor, a person who agrees to pay a debt if another refuses or is unable to pay

Tangible   "touchable," i.e., concrete, specific; refers to property as opposed to money

Tariff   an import tax or duty, which works to increase the price of imported goods and benefit local producers

Tender   (*verb*) to offer

Tender offer   offer to purchase a voting majority of shares of a company at a specified price

Third party   a person or party affected by a transaction but not directly involved in the transaction; a third-party check is a check made out to a payee other than the account holder or the issuing bank.

Third-party beneficiary   a person or party to whom the intended benefits of a contract are assigned; a third-party beneficiary is allowed to sue for performance of the contract since the benefits belong to it.

Tort   a private or civil wrong arising from the actions or inactions of another, which give the victim a right to damages

Tortfeasor   one who commits or has committed a tort

Trespass   a wrongful invasion of another's property interest; at common law, any invasion of a personal or property right of another

Trier of fact   either a judge or a jury entitled to make the determination of fact in a matter before the court

Trust   transfer or arrangement where property is given to a trustee to manage and hold for the benefit of another

Trustee   the person who holds the legal title to property for the benefit of another. A trustee is a fiduciary in regard to the funds that he/she manages in the trust for the benefit of the beneficiaries. The trustee must not use any of the trust proceeds for his/her own benefit. *See also* **Fiduciary**

Ultra vires   outside of or beyond the scope of authority of a corporation as defined by the corporate charter or applicable state law

Unconscionable   grossly unfair or inequitable; usually characterized by great disparity in bargaining power

Undue influence   improper and excessive influence used against someone, which succeeds in depriving that person of his free will to make decisions

Unilateral   by one side or one party only

Union shop   a place of employment where all the workers, once hired, must join a particular union

Unsecured   unprotected by an existing security interest such as a mortgage or lien; used of loans

Usury   a rate of interest charged on a debt that exceeds the statutory maximum

Vel non   or not

Vested   fixed, settled, irrevocable; once rights are vested, they cannot be removed

Voidable   capable of being enforced or avoided by only one party to the contract; the other party must perform as agreed

Voir dire   the pretrial process of jury selection in which prospective jurors are asked questions by counsel to determine whether they are biased or prejudiced

Waiver   the voluntary relinquishment of an existing right

Warrant   in contract, a promise or guarantee of a fact or performance

Witness   usually a person present at an event or occurrence who can testify as to what happened

Writ   a judicial order that something be done

TABLE OF CASES

Excerpted cases are in capitalized italics; italicized page numbers indicate location of excerpts. Cases are alphabetized by surname of first party named.

GENERAL INDEX

(See also Glossary, p. 889, and Table of Cases, p. 899.)